FDR
The War President
1940–1943

FDR

The War President
1940–1943

A HISTORY

Kenneth S. Davis

Random House   New York

*Grateful acknowledgment is made to the following for permission
to reprint previously published material:*

Doubleday, a division of Random House, Inc.: Excerpt from *Crusade in Europe* by Dwight D. Eisenhower.
Copyright © 1948 by Doubleday, a division of Random House, Inc. Excerpt from *Diplomat
Among Warriors* by Robert Murphy. Copyright © 1964 by Robert Murphy.
Used by permission of Doubleday, a division of Random House, Inc.

HarperCollins Publishers, Inc.: Excerpts from *Roosevelt and Hopkins: An Intimate History,*
Revised Edition, by Robert E. Sherwood. Copyright © 1948, 1950 by Robert E. Sherwood.
Copyright renewed 1976 by Mrs. Madeline Sherwood. Excerpts from *Commander in Chief: Franklin
Delano Roosevelt, His Lieutenants and Their War* by Eric Larrabee. Copyright © 1987 by Eric Larrabee.
Excerpts from *On Active Service in Peace and War* by Henry L. Stimson and McGeorge Bundy.
Copyright © 1948 by Henry L. Stimson and McGeorge Bundy. Copyright renewed 1976 by
McGeorge Bundy. Reprinted by permission of HarperCollins Publishers, Inc.

Houghton Mifflin Company: Excerpt from *Churchill: The Struggle for Survival, 1940–1965: Taken from
the Diaries of Lord Moran.* Copyright © 1966 Trustees of Lord Moran. Excerpts from *The Grand Alliance*
by Winston S. Churchill. Copyright © 1950 by Winston S. Churchill. Copyright renewed 1977 by
Lady Spencer-Churchill, The Honourable Lady Sarah Audley, and The Honourable Lady Soames.
Excerpts from *The Hinge of Fate* by Winston S. Churchill. Copyright © 1950 by Winston S. Churchill.
Copyright renewed 1977 by Lady Spencer-Churchill, The Honourable Lady Sarah Audley,
and The Honourable Lady Soames. Reprinted by permission of Houghton Mifflin Company.

Little, Brown & Company (Inc.): Excerpts from *The War Years: 1939–1945* by I. F. Stone.
Copyright © 1988 by I. F. Stone. Reprinted by permission of Little, Brown & Company (Inc.).

Random House, Inc.: Excerpts from *Special Envoy to Churchill and Stalin* by
W. Averell Harriman and Elie Abel. Copyright © 1975 by W. Averell Harriman and
Elie Abel. Reprinted by permission of Random House, Inc.

Oxford University Press: Excerpts from *Atomic Quest* by Arthur Holly Compton.
Copyright © 1956 by Oxford University Press. Reprinted by permission.

Library of Congress Cataloging-in-Publication Data

Davis, Kenneth Sydney
FDR, the war president, 1940–1943 : a history / Kenneth S. Davis. — 1st ed.
p.   cm.
Includes index.
ISBN 0-679-41542-4
1. Roosevelt, Franklin D. (Franklin Delano), 1882–1945.   2. Presidents—United States—Biography.
3. United States—Politics and government—1933–1945.   4. World War, 1939–1945—United States.
I. Title.

E807 .D38 2000   973.917'081—dc21
[B]   00-028194

Random House website address: www.atrandom.com
Printed in the United States of America on acid-free paper
4 6 8 9 7 5 3

To Jean,
for the last time

Special thanks are extended by the publisher to Ralph and Mary Ellen Titus
for their extraordinary help in preparing *FDR: The War President*
for the printer after Kenneth Davis's untimely death.

Contents

BOOK ONE

→»×«←

A Guided Drift
Toward War

I

⇢⟩X⟨⟵

Overture: Themes, Issues,
Recapitulations

I

"WE are facing difficult days in this country, but I think you will find me in the future just the same Franklin Roosevelt you have known a great many years."[1]

Roosevelt had spoken these words at midnight of the night before (it was now Wednesday morning, November 6, 1940) to a jubilant crowd of Hyde Park neighbors gathered on the wide Big House lawn—a crowd that had come in torchlight parade to celebrate with him his election to an unprecedented third term as President of the United States, defeating Republican challenger Wendell Willkie—and the promise thus made, despite being rendered strangely tentative and even dubious by the prefatory "I think," was evidently intended by him to soothe, to reassure. It failed to do so, however, for everyone who listened to it or read it in the papers. There were critical and well-informed minds in which the promise raised questions of identity that, viewed in terms of the future now rising as black clouds out of Europe, out of Asia, to cast gloom over the Republic, were both difficult to answer and profoundly disturbing.

Was this "Franklin Roosevelt" whom his listeners had "known a great many years" actually and wholly the Roosevelt upon whom now depended so much of the fate of America and, indeed, the world? Or was the "real" Franklin Roosevelt a man different in important ways, and perhaps contradictory ways, from his Hyde Park friends' perception of him? In either case, but especially in the latter, to what extent and in what ways would his remaining "just the same" be a boon for mankind, to what extent and in what ways a misfortune, in the "difficult days" to come?

II

THE man popularly perceived, the man whose face at midnight had been cooled by a mild springlike breeze as it was imbued by ruddy torchlight, was a big, warm, friendly, compassionate man with an acute sense of justice and a strong commitment to it. Through all the fifty-seven years of his life (he would be fifty-eight this coming January 30) he had been a lover of simple country living. He disliked cities, though his most solid political support came from urban areas, and had in the past, in public speech, more than hinted a belief that virtue, discouraged by the frenetic artificiality of crowded streets, could come to its full flowering only amid green growing things in such landscapes as the one he saw this morning out his bedroom window. For though the green growth was now in autumn retreat at Hyde Park, the hardwoods leafless, the evergreens nearly black, the fields and meadows gray and brown and swept by chill winds under a darkly lowering sky (the weather, he noted, had greatly changed since midnight)—though this was so, and though the present melancholy of it was felt, the window-framed landscape of wide fields and wild-wooded hills was yet seen through memory's eyes as a greenly living one. Through it, nourishing and ordering it, flowed the great theme-river of his life, the mighty Hudson, upon whose wide bosom he had spent many of his happiest youthful hours in sailboat and iceboat and from whose bank he and his devoted friend Louis Howe had launched the model sailboats they designed and built together during his long convalescence, as a middle-aged man, from near fatal illness. It now presented itself to his vision, beyond a fringe of treetop, as more lake than stream. A small inland sea. And it was in fact both an active arm of the sea and an active contributor of water to the sea, for it was one of the longest estuaries on earth, as Roosevelt had learned as a boy. Already, as it made its slow curve around Crum Elbow, it sometimes tasted faintly of the salt of the sea that flowed into it, if meagerly, at high tide, and into which soon it must die. Such facts greatly interested, and were known to interest, the man whom his neighbors had long known. He collected them avidly and, his admiring neighbors would have said, they now richly furnished a mind remarkable for its capacity.

Many of these neighbors knew, as we know, that his collecting of facts, like his collecting of stamps, old books, naval prints, and the like, had been a major part of the psychological strategy he had employed, to sustain his morale, in the long hard war he had waged—much of it in this house, in this very room—against the crippling effects of the polio that had struck him down in 1921, when he was thirty-nine. It was a war he had declared in the innermost recesses of his being, and to everyone around him, while he was yet wholly bedridden, unable even to sit erect. With an iron determination whose grimness he masked with smiling outward confidence, even gaiety, he had set out to conquer and destroy his affliction. He would walk again! He would walk unaided, without leg braces or crutches or canes! Alas, he never did. He became more mobile, less helpless physically, than had seemed possible to his doctors at the outset of his war, but no amount of willpower or arduous physical effort (he expended prodigious quantities of both) could regrow destroyed nerve tissue. In 1928, when his return to active political life forced him to suspend his recovery regimen after seven years of harsh effort, his legs yet remained nearly fleshless, hardly more than sticks of bone draped in wrinkled skin, and were almost totally unresponsive to his will. His public "walking" and "standing," in 1928 as in 1940, were difficult and often painful balancing acts on what were in effect stilts (steel rods locked around hips, knees, ankles), possible only if he leaned heavily on canes or had beside him a strong man whose arm he could grip. Nevertheless, his struggle had been far from fruitless. During it, as his neighbors knew, he had manifest and further developed an almost incredible fortitude, patience, and emotional self-control—a self-mastery that was part and parcel of his mastery of other people.

Discerned by some of the more acute of those who observed him with close attention, though from a distance, was the fact that his very disability had become in his way of handling it a source, an instrument, a protector and preserver of personal power. As regards this last, it prevented risk-engendering importunities that he could not have avoided, save at the further and possibly greater political risk of giving offense, had he been able to move freely about and therefore compelled to mingle casually with other people on occasions and grounds not of his choosing. The compulsion was now all the other way: people must come to him, and they must come always, to some extent, at least, with formality—that is, in accordance with formal rules whereby they were placed at an initial disadvantage insofar as their dealings with him were of an adversarial nature. This was true even in situations where his actual need for their support was considerably greater than theirs for his. For since they came as invited guests into his house, or by his permission into his office or onto other ground ruled by him, they came perforce under felt obligations and must assume in some degree, willy-nilly, a supplicatory attitude. By the manner of his welcome or greeting he could and did set the tone of every personal encounter and, having done so, could and did dominate the discussion.

Similar in effect, but different psychologically, was the way in which his physical handicap became per se a source and instrument of governing power. Conjoined or (more precisely) fused with the self-mastery he had gained through his struggle to overcome it, his perceived handicap, in part by weakening in other people their inward resistance to his will, actually increased his persuasiveness and enhanced his ability to command through sheer force of personality. It commonly made these others *want* at the outset to please, emulate, and, if at all possible, agree with this man who demonstrated so much courage, strength of character, and optimistic confidence—so much liking and concern for them personally, such sweetness of disposition—under pressures that would have crushed an ordinary mortal into chronic depression and resentful dependency. Moreover there was a natural assumption on the part of people in general, an assumption abundantly encouraged by his careful management of his public image, that he had earned through his prolonged and terrible ordeal a compassionate living wisdom remarkable for its width and depth. He was there-fore commonly deemed more likely to be right than his opponents were on is-sues concerning which the common view was not well informed. He might be so even on issues of which his own factual knowledge was meager: his "intu-ition" was famous, was encouraged by him so to be—an ability, as it seemed, to dispense with logical process as he plunged with lightning swiftness into the heart of a difficult problem and discovered there its solution—and though it was presumed that he had been born with this uncanny ability, it was further pre-sumed that prolonged anguish and arduous struggle had sharpened and strength-ened it.

But if an awareness by other people of Roosevelt's crippled condition was thus necessary for his translation of physical liability into psychological asset—if such awareness was, in fact, the very substance that was so translated—it was equally necessary for such purpose that the awareness be carefully limited and controlled; and this, too, was accurately surmised by the more acute of those who, from a distance, watched him with close attention. He was known to be at great pains to prevent a display before crowds of the fact that from his hips downward he was totally crippled (witness, again, his "walking," his "stand-ing"). He was at equal pains to hide through various devices the full extent of his physical helplessness from those who were not intimate associates of his but were brought into face-to-face contact with him. And this concealment was greatly aided by the afore-indicated fact that he virtually never manifested in ei-ther his public or his private life the psychological traits generally characteristic of handicapped people—never, that is, save on those very rare occasions when his doing so might serve a perceived tactical purpose, in which case his mani-festation, being deliberate, was precisely focused upon and confined to its per-ceived immediate efficacy. The result was that, known to be crippled, he was not *felt* to be so—was not thought of or treated as a cripple even by intimates. He had become as President the focus of powerful emotions, was as worshipfully admired and profoundly loved by millions of common folk as he was virulently hated and damned to everlasting hellfire by a majority of the affluent, but he was most emphatically *not* an object of pity. Indeed, the overall impression he made both upon the general public, who never saw his withered legs, and upon his closest associates, who did see them, was that of a remarkably healthy man—and this despite his high susceptibility to sinus infections, his abnormally frequent bouts with incapacitating head colds and flu. Nor was this a merely passive impression. Drawing upon his seeming superabundance of good health and joie de vivre, he spread amazing amounts of these around him. His rich en-joyment of life became the cause of such enjoyment by others, his display of im-mense self-confidence bred morale-lifting self-confidence in others. Exciting, stimulating, revivifying, he exerted upon other people the attractive force, he bestowed upon other people the radiant energy, that a blazing star exerts and be-stows upon orbiting planets.

Of the essence of his legendary charm, and of the public's overall perception of him, was his manifest interest in and liking for people. All kinds of people. He who demanded and commanded attention from others also paid attention to these others; he dealt with them, in both his personal and public life, as unique individuals and equals (though managing to remain always the dominating personality), in utter disregard of those differences of race, religion, or economic and social class that commonly serve as barriers to mutual understandings. Thus the general perception of him as a strong man, a boldly decisive man, a natural leader of men who not only relished power but welcomed the responsibility that went with it ("If you run into troubles," he often said to subordinates, "bring them to me; my shoulders are broad")—this perception was joined with, and increased in its popular appeal, by the perception of him as a remarkably frank, simple, unassuming, and open man. David Lilienthal, board chairman of the Tennessee Valley Authority, was among those who spread abroad this view of him;[2] and the Lilienthal view supported the conclusion reached by other people who had experienced Roosevelt directly, personally, and then published (through press interviews, mostly) reports of their experience—the conclusion that Roosevelt's openness was not only to new experience, but also to inspection by others of his inner self. The sum of such testimony persuaded the multitude that their President was a talkative man whose talk, if sometimes maddeningly digressive, was always interesting and often self-revealing to an extent that amazed and even disconcerted his listeners. He did not merely permit others to know him well, he insisted upon it. . . .

But it was here that the questions about his actual identity—about its possibly being, in important ways, different from his persona—became most acute, and most productive of anxiety, in those who were more than normally well-informed concerning him and who pondered their information seriously. For it was here that the general popular perception of him diverged most widely from the known views of several highly intelligent and quickly sensitive people—people who were or had been much more closely, prolongedly, and intimately associated with him than had been those whose summary testimony is presented above. His wife, Eleanor; his longtime personal secretary, Marguerite "Missy" LeHand; his longtime personal friend Secretary of Labor Frances Perkins; his even closer friend Secretary of the Treasury Henry Morgenthau; his formerly close working associates brain trusters Rex Tugwell and Raymond Moley—these were among the considerable number, well positioned to know him well, whose published testimony was that Roosevelt's inner self, where dwelt his deepest feelings, his essential motivations, was to them a deep, dark mystery. (Robert E. Sherwood, the playwright who had in recent months become one of a newly formed three-man speechwriting team in the White House, had already confessed to intimates his inability to penetrate what he would describe in a later year as Roosevelt's "heavily-forested interior.")[3] Those who knew him best were, it seemed, precisely those the least certain that they really knew him at all. And this called into question major elements of the general public's perception of him, elements upon which rested much of the great trust his admiring public placed in him.

Far from being simple and direct, according to some of this intimate testimony, he was complicated and devious, much given to embellishing statements of doubtful truth with the assertion that what he had just said or was about to say was a "definite fact" or a "simple and sincere fact." His seemingly frank communicativeness was, again according to this testimony, the very opposite of self-revealing—was, indeed, as regards his deepest self, the outward form of a profound reticence—his volubility a means not of true communication, but of concealment, diversion, dissemblement. He raised up colorful beguiling walls of words behind which to hide from those he talked to his real thought, his actual feelings, his true intent, while simultaneously eliciting from them the information he needed, the personal responses he desired. Consistent with this was the endlessly repeated observation (it was said in the public prints whenever these reported a major public address) that Roosevelt was the "consummate actor." What could this mean save that he was a master of make-believe, a role-player, capable of becoming convincingly whatever "character" it suited his purpose or need to become in the perception of those who saw and heard him? And how, then, was one to discover which if any of these "characters" should have the quotation marks removed from it since it was purely, authentically Franklin Delano Roosevelt himself, the living reality of him, undisguised?

There was, for instance, the Roosevelt famed for his personal democracy, the man who established himself upon a warmly friendly first-name basis with virtually everyone he met at the very first moment of the first meeting. To what extent was this democracy genuine, to what extent mere "manner"? Significantly, it failed to remove from those who experienced it their sense that his was the superior position and role, theirs the inferior, in their every contact and relationship with him. What it did do was prevent most people from resenting this. And who could say that such was not Roosevelt's manipulative purpose? Certainly it was in the view of those few, the relatively very few, who, accustomed to regarding themselves as superior human beings, were very sure that his self-regard was at least as great as their own. These reacted angrily against what they felt to be an aristocratic disdain, an implicitly insulting condescension, the potency of which, as personal insult, was actually increased by the ostentatious "democracy" in which it was clothed. Thus the aristocratic Dean Acheson, who had been a high Treasury official early in the New Deal, was sure that Roosevelt's essential attitude, which Acheson personally resented, was that of the manor lord who, graciously patronizing his peasants, expects them to respond spiritually with a forelock-pulling obeisance.[4]

Similarly called into question, and even more so, was Roosevelt's celebrated decisiveness, of which he himself often boasted. The testimony of several people who were intimately involved with him, as well as of not a few who worked closely under him, was that he hated to make decisions and went to great lengths to avoid doing so, employing much ingenuity (he was fertile of gaudy dramatic devices) to hide from the public and perhaps from himself the fact that really, fundamentally, no decision at all was being made. Especially did he hate and avoid to the fullest possible extent decisions of a flat either/or variety, evidently, in part, because he felt each such decision to be the final closing out of an option previously open to him, hence a reduction of his freedom to act. And the accuracy of this intimate testimony might well seem indicated, even to distant observers, by the abundant confusions and ambiguities of the New Deal. Surely a failure to make basic decisions, if not a basic incapacity to decide, was manifest in Roosevelt's disorderly, even chaos-engendering, ways of administration. Notorious in his presidential operation was his disregard for organization charts, once they were drawn up (he seemed often to enjoy the making of them, especially complicated ones). Only sometimes, in his practice, did authority reside in the compartment that defined it on the chart; only sometimes did power flow along the lines traced for it on the chart. And his tendency, obviously, when challenged to choose among inconsistent policies, was to "weave them together" in omnibus legislative proposals or executive orders. By these, government agencies were established with mandates so broad, so inclusive, so vaguely defined, as to insure bloody civil war within each of them, and also bloody wars between them insofar as their terms of reference were generally very far from being mutually exclusive. Denied a clearly defined common ground on which they might stand as they engaged in rational argument toward logical conclusions, the exponents of opposing policies must fight for final decisions that meant for each of them, not the achievement or denial of a specific truth, or of a public good, but a victory or defeat in a raw, often very bitter struggle for personal power. Had not the legislation or executive orders creating the Agricultural Adjustment Administration (AAA), the National Recovery Administration (NRA), the Tennessee Valley Authority (TVA), and the Public Works Administration (PWA) been of this nature? Also the sweeping relief legislation and subsequent executive orders whereby the Works Progress Administration (WPA) and the Resettlement Administration (RA) were established in 1935? And had not the result been indeed an angry quarrelsomeness within each of the agencies and/or between them? Of these quarrels the President was, of course, the ultimate arbiter; but his "decision" of them seemed itself to have been determined generally by an assessment not of the relative intrinsic merits of the opposing arguments, but of the relative weights of the opposing pressures. It was thus the heaviest pressure, not the reasoned purpose and personal will of Franklin Roosevelt, that was decisive.

What seemed indicated by all this was a mind that, if richly furnished with factual information upon an amazingly wide range of subjects, as his admiring

Hyde Park neighbors remarked, was deficient in logical intelligence and organizing principle, if not also in infused moral concern. In the absence of these,
and in the presence of an immediate need for important decision, the avidity
with which Roosevelt collected specific items of information, and the capa-
ciousness of the memory in which he stored them, might prove no unmixed
blessing, if a blessing at all. They might result, as some said they had resulted,
in a mind as cluttered with brute fact and inert idea as Roosevelt's office desks
were of mementos; and such constantly increasing clutter, far from aiding the
processes of decision, could impede them—could even impose so heavy a
weight upon a mind lacking in discriminatory and organizational faculties,
while also presenting to such a mind so great a number of objects (a paralyzing
number) among which choices might be made, that any real mental movement
whatever was prevented. As for the indicated deficiency itself, that of logic and
selective principle, if not also of moral feeling, one's recognition of it suggested
a dismaying answer to the question of who, essentially, Roosevelt was—the
question, that is, of his true identity. It suggested that Roosevelt's complexities,
though puzzlingly abundant, might also be wholly superficial; that beneath his
smiling outward self, beneath the brightly colored multilayers of this outward
self, with its swiftly changing roles and role-appropriate disguises, there was
very little of substance. For was not the mental deficiency in itself a deficiency
of essential selfhood, a lack of identity? Some there were, though again a relatively very few (all of them "intellectuals" in common parlance, among them
Walter Lippmann, Marriner Eccles, John Maynard Keynes, George Kennan),[5]
who, having had meaningful encounters with him, had come away with precisely this conclusion—that Roosevelt was at heart not a serious man, but a trivial, hollow one.

It is significant, however, that the validity of this conclusion was never a pure
and solid certainty in the minds of any of these men.

Uncertainty characterizes all comprehensive judgments of Roosevelt the
man, those that approve no less than those that condemn; virtually every one of
them carries within it a modicum, at least, of its own contradiction. And to this
general rule the above-stated dismaying conclusion was no exception. It was
shot through with qualification in the very minds that had reached it. Thus,
though his expressed contempt for Roosevelt's mentality was profound, George
Kennan never went so far as to assert that the President's mental deficiencies
made him unfit "for the great responsibilities he bore." Indeed, Kennan hinted
in print in a later year his belief that Roosevelt's inferior "qualities of intellect"
were compensated for to some indeterminate degree by superior "qualities of
temperament," and this belief pointed toward a flat contradiction of Kennan's
conclusion, in this very same statement, that Roosevelt was not a serious man,
but a trivial, hollow one.[6] It pointed, in other words, toward a convergence and
fusion, on this central point, of the closely critical and the widely popular views
of Roosevelt the man and of Roosevelt as historical personage. For was not the

Roosevelt temperament "first class" in all respects, as Justice Holmes had famously said it was? Did not its manifest qualities include extraordinary self-control, fortitude, cold nerve, tenacity, an almost incredible patience, along with an unfailing optimism that, as he spread it around him in the heaviest and darkest of circumstances, lightened the burdens and lighted the way for others? And how could such "qualities of temperament" be distinguished from those of essential character? They couldn't be. Temperament and character are not the same thing, the latter having a moral dimension that the former lacks, but the two overlap to a significant degree, and the character that sustained such qualities of temperament as those listed above could not possibly be deemed other than formidable. Moreover, one knew that Roosevelt, throughout his adult life, whether in or out of important office, had been a center of attention: wherever he was he was *empnatically* there, a presence that insisted upon and energetically exerted itself.

Hence the uneasiness with which critical minds entertained the notion of Roosevelt's essential triviality. It was an uneasiness that, in the end, resulted in a repudiation of this notion by many of these minds. Roosevelt's essential identity was tremendously difficult to define, it might be impossible to define with clarity and precision, but the fact that he had one of solid substance and large dimension seemed undeniable.

Indeed, even the assertion that the Roosevelt intellect was inferior did not go wholly unquestioned, was not without important qualification, in many of the minds that made it. True, he was intellectually untidy, prone to slovenly ways of thought. This was only too frequently obvious in those portions of his public addresses, and of his published papers, that (on the stylistic evidence) he himself had penned. But was intelligence to be defined wholly as a capacity for logical analysis and synthesis? There was, for instance, the matter of Roosevelt's popularly celebrated "intuition," of which his self-celebrated sense of timing was very much a part. Were there not signs—dubious, perhaps, and only occasionally, but signs nonetheless—that he did actually possess in abnormal quantity this mysterious intuitive faculty, an ability to *feel* in a flashing instant truths toward which the normal mind could make its way, if at all, only through arduous study and thought? Specifically, might not Roosevelt have a sense of history as ongoing process, along with ways of knowing and deciding in terms of this process, that were beyond normal comprehension and that would prove in the long run, in some cases, at least, a more accurate guide toward beneficent ends and a better shaper of means toward these ends than logical intelligence would have been?

For instance, several of his public statements suggested an intuited conclusion on his part that science with its consequent technology is the driving force of history in our time and that this driving force, advancing at a continuously accelerating pace, creates an ever-closer interdependence of human individuals and societies, thus rendering increasingly obsolete long-established institutions of economic individualism and national sovereignty. Indeed, some of his public words indicated a belief that socioeconomic collectivism is necessarily implied by high technology and that the great democratic challenge of our time is to develop collectives expressive rather than destructive of the free individual human spirit, collectives through which scientific technology is brought under truly human control and directed toward truly humane goals. Addressing a huge Tammany Hall assemblage on July 4, 1929, Roosevelt emphatically asserted that the "vast economic changes" through which "the country is passing" had rendered the "independence" of small business "a thing of the past" (no "man today" could "run a drug store, a cigar store, a grocery store" as a truly "independent" enterprise); that there was an increasingly exclusive concentration of "industrial control" in a few and ever-fewer "private hands"; and that this posed a threat to personal freedoms. Americans, he had said, must "reconsider the whole problem of liberty." In public speech about the conservation of natural resources, and about river development, he had stressed his conviction that "liberty" must now be defined in terms different from those of "rugged individualism"—that it must be defined in terms of community and have at its heart a commitment to community—and had added that, though the "liberty of the community" must thus take precedence over the "liberty of the individual" in this modern age, it would actually, if properly practiced, increase or enhance the latter. In many a philosophical mind that heard or read him, the individual freedom he here called for was, by clear implication, the responsible freedom of a cooperative rather than competitive economy. And that Roosevelt was of the same mind seemed indicated by those parts of his second inaugural address wherein he spoke of the need to make government "the instrument of our united purpose" in order to solve for "the individual" the problems arising out of an increasingly "complex civilization." The "aid of government," he had gone on to say, was essential to the creation of "those moral controls over the services of science that are necessary to make science a useful servant instead of a ruthless master of mankind"; only through government could "practical controls over blind economic forces and blindly selfish men" be established. Which is to say that, in Roosevelt's belief, the problems of our "complex civilization" could most emphatically *not* be solved through the operations of private entrepreneurs as they sought to maximize their private profit, nor through the blind operations of an allegedly "free" market that was actually increasingly a managed one. As a matter of fact, the linkage of high technology to unregulated or insufficiently regulated private moneymaking was the root from which the great problems grew; it was the means by which a hugely powerful technology had gone out of human control, resulting in an increasing domination of Man by Machine, an increasing pollution and destruction of the natural environment.* What was

*See *FDR: The New York Years,* pp. 284–85; *FDR: The New Deal Years,* pp. 226–27.

needed was a linkage of disinterested intelligence with physical power through truly democratic government. The "essential democracy of our nation and the safety of our people depend not upon the absence of power," said Franklin Roosevelt, "but upon the lodging of it with those whom the people can change or continue at stated intervals through an honest and free system of elections." Which seemed to mean that power now irresponsibly exercised by big-business men must be transferred to government and exercised by responsible public servants.[7]

But though Roosevelt's public speech thus seemed to express, on occasion, a clear sense of a central dynamic of modern history, hence of a long-term direction in history's flow, this sense had evidently not become for him a guiding principle when decisions on fundamental matters were called for. Regarding matters less basic, matters of immediate tactical concern, he was sometimes remarkably boldly decisive. There was, for instance, his decision to adhere to the schedule for the registration for the draft and for the drawing of lots for the first batch of draftees, under the newly passed Selective Service Act, even though the registration was less than three weeks, and the drawing of lots less than one week, before election day. He had done so against the frantic advice of his political advisers, nearly all of whom urged a postponement of both events until the election was over. Brave and firm indeed were the words he spoke over the radio on both occasions. ("In my opinion he showed good statesmanship," wrote a normally highly critical Secretary of War Henry L. Stimson into his diary on October 29, 1940, ". . . and the character of the speech which he made . . . served to change the event of the draft into a great asset in his favor.")[8] Even as regards tactical matters, however, this particular decisiveness stood out in sharp contrast with the equivocations by which it was surrounded—and of Roosevelt's chronic and sometime disastrous indecisiveness with regard to matters of fundamental importance the historical evidence remained all too abundant.

At the very outset of his administration, a total collapse of America's privately managed (and grossly mismanaged) credit structure presented him with a choice between private and public banking. He seemed not to realize that the choice existed; certainly he made no decision between the two. He simply yielded to what he perceived as the strongest immediate pressure. Instead of consulting the sense of history that the above quotes seemed to describe, he consulted the very men whose inordinate greed had caused the crisis—and, by and large, as regards fundamentals, he followed their advice. Similarly with regard to the need for choice between economic internationalism and economic nationalism that was presented to him at the outset of his administration.* Had he consulted the philosophy of history that his above-quoted public speech seemed

*See *FDR: The New Deal Years*, pp. 104–10, 122–23, 129–31, 153–56, 183–85, 187–98.

to indicate—a philosophy wherein the human implication of advancing scientific technology was clearly seen as a flow of world away from limitless nationalism toward world government—he would have been at great pains to shape a New Deal that could cooperate with other governments in actions that would stem the then-rising tide of economic and militaristic nationalism all over the world and especially in Germany, Italy, and Japan. Instead he committed the New Deal irrevocably to economic nationalism in action while committing it verbally to full and enthusiastic participation in the World Monetary and Economic Conference that opened in London in June 1933, a conference committed to economic internationalism. Never did he make a clear rational choice between nationalism and internationalism; the decision to wreck the London Conference, which he announced in his notorious "bombshell" message to London at the end of June 1933, was not really made by him, but was forced upon him by the pressure of events, albeit events that were set in motion by himself (though without grasp of their longtime significance) or in which he, who might have opposed them, acquiesced. Thus Roosevelt's historic role in 1933 might be viewed, and *was* viewed by many a philosophic mind, as that of an obstructionist whose failure to decide at a crucial moment in world history diverted the flow of that history from its "natural" human channel, contributed greatly to the oncoming of a new world war, and assured the accelerating growth of a technological tyranny whose end might be the destruction of both Man and Earth.

The indecisiveness had continued. Twice in the last five years—in 1935, again in 1938—his unconscionably lengthy postponement of a final definite choice between two basic and contradictory lines of general policy had been nearly fatal to his administration, his personal power to govern. Such was the firm conclusion of a number of close analytical observers of him. And many of these same observers saw (it was in fear and trembling that they contemplated) the same "weave them together" indecisiveness operating in Roosevelt's current dealings, amid the raging fires of world war, with the issue of American isolationism-vs.-collective security, with a current disagreement between Treasury (Secretary Henry Morgenthau) and State (Secretary Cordell Hull) over the use of stringent international financial exchange controls to foil Axis designs, and with flatly opposed policies for industrial mobilization for national defense. The ultimate consequence, in the now prevailing circumstances, might be the extinction, not just of an American President's capacity to govern, but of the United States as a free and open society, if not of the whole of world civilization.

III

OF Roosevelt's sense of his own identity, of himself personally as distinct from, though vitally connected to, the public personage bearing his name, we may derive some inkling by observing his progress through this first day (November 6, 1940) following his election victory.

It is unwontedly late in the morning when he awakens in his Hyde Park bed—
it had been unwontedly late (actually nearly three in the morning) when he came
to this bed last night—and as he emerges instantaneously, as he always does, out
of sound sleep into wide wakefulness he yet feels very tired, a bone-deep weariness resulting from weeks of unremitting strain. Through his bedroom window
he notes, as we have said, how greatly the weather has changed while he slept—
notes that what had been at midnight a balmy breeze is now a blustery bitter
wind scattering dead leaves out of the apple orchard behind the mansion down
the long brown slope of dead grass toward the wildwood beside the river—
notes that the sky is a dull gray wintry sky out of which, conceivably, snow may
fall. The window-framed landscape is melancholy. Melancholy too is the sound
of wind sighing through naked boughs, sobbing around the mansion eaves. And
Roosevelt's mood as he sees and hears these things, as he then turns his attention to his ritualistic perusal of the morning papers while breakfasting in bed,
accords well (his major words and deeds that day will testify to his mood's accordance) with the weather of the day. It is a somber mood, nostalgic, elegiac in
its sorrowful sense of a past forever lost, yet informed also by a sense of this
same past as alive in the present, of *then* as an aspect of *now,* providing the permanence that is the substance of change. Overall, his moody passive backward-
looking awareness of flowing Time exerts upon him this morning a comforting
stabilizing influence; it braces him against the shock of the onrushing future's
attack upon him.

As for himself *now,* though he feels vast relief over catastrophe averted,
being convinced that the end result of his election defeat would have been a
Fascist America, he feels almost nothing of elation, of exultation, over triumph
achieved. "Naturally it is too serious a time for the President to feel anything
but a great sense of responsibility," Eleanor Roosevelt told a *New York Times*
reporter last night. "Anyone would be deeply gratified" by "a vote of confidence on the part of the people," she further said, but the dominant effect of
this upon her husband would be to "renew a determination to give the best that
one has to give in so grave a crisis."[9] Her husband, to whom she is a nagging
conscience, cannot but approve these words, wearily, reluctantly, as he reads
them. They are both politic and truthful. It is indeed the heavy burden of his
responsibility that he now chiefly feels. And there is no escaping (forgetting)
either the responsibility or himself as he reads on. He encounters on every page
of every paper bits and pieces of himself or, more precisely, fragments of the
shadow he casts, the image he impresses upon the public mind—these interspersed with reported events that become in his reading of them insistent
portions of his accountability, his liability before the bar of history. His reading
thus becomes for him a process of self-definition, a delimiting of self through a
rejection of not-self, insofar as he continually distinguishes true from false
statements in the press accounts of his acts and purposes; accurate from distorted images of his personal thoughts, attitudes, feelings; and, far less sharply,

developments for which he is responsible from developments for which he is not.

It is a process more grim than cheerful for him this morning.

He feels a sting, for instance, in the quoted words of Norman Thomas, the perennial Socialist Party candidate for the presidency who, like Eleanor, still often speaks to him with the voice of conscience, though Thomas has become a leading isolationist (he has been made one by his profound commitment to Christian pacifism, just as he was made a Socialist by his perception of democratic socialism as the socioeconomic order implied by Christ's ethical teachings). Thomas now says that the campaign just ended was one of "the most disgraceful and disappointing in my long experience"[10]—and Roosevelt feels forced to agree with this assessment. Moreover he cannot but feel, deep down, that he himself is responsible, in important part, for the assessment's truth. If not actually ashamed, he is far from proud of certain presidential actions that were dictated by his overall contribution to the election debate.

He can take no pride, certainly, in his betrayal during the campaign of principles that had guided the New Deal's efforts to define the proper relations (that is, the relations most conducive to democratic values) between government and business—a betrayal especially flagrant with regard to subsidies and taxation.

In his fireside chat of last May 26[11] he had said emphatically that the urgently needed swift and vast expansion of America's armaments and armed forces must not be achieved at the expense of "the great social gains we have made in these past years." On the contrary, there is every need to retain and even extend these gains (strengthened labor organizations, wage-and-hour guarantees, unemployment insurance, old age pensions) "to other groups who do not now enjoy them." To retreat from the positions gained by the New Deal's "broad front" attack upon "social and economic inequalities and abuses which had made our society weak" would be to restore those fundamental weaknesses to our free society at a time when democracy is under mortal threat, worldwide; it would be self-contradictory insofar as it reduced or destroyed, in the name of "national defense," the very freedoms we would defend. He had also stressed, in that fireside chat, the need to guard against the greatly increased "economic inequalities" that would certainly result from merely reactive responses to our present emergency. A "common sense of decency" made it "imperative that no new group of war millionaires come into being in America as a result of the struggles abroad," he said, adding that the "American people will not relish the idea of any American citizen growing rich and fat in an emergency of blood and slaughter and human suffering." But in that same address he had announced that he was summoning to Washington "men now engaged in private industry to help us in carrying out" the industrial mobilization and rearmament programs, and had thus aroused liberal fears that he might reestablish the system of industrial mobilization, with its "dollar-a-year men," that Woodrow Wilson had employed in 1916–1918—a system that had assured unprecedented big-business domination of the American economy while creating war-profiteering million-aires by the score. A couple of days later he fully justified these liberal fears. He announced that, under an unrepealed 1916 statute for whose adoption he as assistant secretary of the navy had been in part responsible,* he was reviving the Council of National Defense of six cabinet officers and the council's seven-member National Defense Advisory Commission (NDAC), the latter being, as it had been in 1916–18, the truly important body of the two. To it he appointed, as industry's representatives, U.S. Steel board chairman Edward R. Stettinius, Jr., General Motors president William R. Knudsen, and Burlington Railroad chairman Ralph Budd. The three were to handle, respectively, industrial material acquisition, industrial production, and transportation—the three major segments of America's industrial mobilization program. As in 1916, the commission's initial overall terms of reference were left vague, nor was any member of it named chairman; like Wilson in 1916, Roosevelt intended to be, in effect, the commission's head.

But the establishment and initial operations of the NDAC had not resulted in the swift vast expansion of defense production that the times urgently called for. If the big-business men in Washington believe Roosevelt's production goals possible of achievement—and, on the evidence, such belief as they have is shot through with doubt—they have failed to convert to their faith the business community at large. Nor were they themselves persuaded last spring that they and their fellow industrialists would not be cutting their own throats if, without more safeguards than were then in place, they committed themselves to the defense production that Roosevelt called for. They were eager to restore to production, as the war-stimulated American economy revived, that portion of their existing plant (it was a high proportion) that had been rendered "surplus" by the Great Depression's market contraction. But they were naturally chary of plant expansion to supply a civilian market that might shrink abruptly and drastically, or even utterly disappear, when government defense expenditures were reduced at war's end. They were and are even more chary of converting existing plant from civilian to military production—from automobile to war plane manufacture, for instance. They claim that a public unpersuaded of the necessity for a limitation of consumption, and having more money in its pocket than it has had for a decade, would not stand for any curtailment of its freedom to buy automobiles. (Simultaneously, of course, the automakers have done and are still doing all they can to stimulate the public demand for automobiles through relentless massive advertising.) As for plant expansion to supply an exclusively military market that seemed *bound* to collapse at war's end, it was not to be thought of.

These facts had been foreseen and warned against by people who vividly remembered, or had learned via such educative enterprises as the Nye Committee hearings of 1935, how British and American businessmen handled war produc-

*See *FDR: The Beckoning of Destiny,* pp. 415, 421–22.

tion for profit during the Great War. This time around, the British acted upon what they learned in 1914–1918: having formed in the spring of 1940 a strong coalition government in which Laborites and Tories were equal partners, a government having almost universal popular support, they virtually eliminated private profit as a policy-determining factor in the war effort. They substituted for market incentives the "common-good" and "common-necessity" goals of a planned economy in which businessmen shared equally with the rest of the population, or as equally as it is possible for the highly competent British civil service to assure, the risks and sacrifices of the war. For instance, a steeply graduated income tax, culminating in a 100 percent tax on excess profit, has been imposed, and "excess profit" has been given, by the government, a precise and rigorous definition. Under this dispensation, with far fewer hitches than the United States is experiencing, the whole of British industry has been or is being swiftly mobilized.

But the possibility that the Roosevelt administration would attempt to follow the British example provoked a rancorous protest and a determined counterattack by the big-business community last summer. To the New Dealers' assertion that private profit must be forfeit to patriotism in this emergency, the businessman replied in effect that profit and patriotism were with him identical and that therefore, in proportion to the increase in the seriousness of the national emergency, the government must pay more, not less, for business "cooperation." "Industry will demand many concessions in the way of tax exemptions, amortization policies, relaxation of labor laws, et cetera" as the price for expanding production, said *The Wall Street Journal* on May 20, 1940. The U.S. Chamber of Commerce voiced loud opposition to any excess profits tax whatever and also demanded a relaxation or repeal of New Deal legislation that, by encouraging allegedly outrageous wage demands by organized labor, along with demands for industry-recognized collective bargaining rights, were allegedly major hazards to the rearmament program. Echoed *Newsweek,* then an extremely conservative magazine: "For success of the [rearmament] program, labor must bow to the national common effort. . . . The Walsh-Healy and the Wage-Hour laws will have to be relaxed to allow the needed speedups."[12] And this counterattack, focusing upon Roosevelt in the midst of what promised to be an extremely close election race, the winning of which was in his view essential to the very survival of American democracy, had gained in every area save that of labor-management relations a virtually total victory.

In the late spring it had been obvious that, to forestall a further distortion of America's already unfair income-distribution pattern, swift passage of a second Revenue Act of 1940 was required. The first had been but a gesture toward what was needed to prevent excessive profits from defense contracts and to increase federal revenues. Accordingly Roosevelt, having assigned to Morgenthau and Treasury the task of preparing the needed bill, had addressed to Congress on

July 1 one of the shortest (a mere eighty-nine words) and most emphatic of all his messages, saying in part: "It is our duty to see that the burden [of national defense cost] is equitably distributed according to ability to pay so that a few do not gain from the sacrifices of the many. I, therefore, recommend to the Congress the enactment of a steeply graduated excess profits tax, to be applied to all individuals and all corporations without discrimination."[13] But the Treasury tax bill, modeled upon but considerably less stringent than England's excess profit legislation, at once encountered strong opposition from the business community, from congressional conservatives representing the business interest, and from both Secretary of War Stimson* and Undersecretary Robert P. Patterson—a portentous instance of alliance between the War Department and big business whereby the interests of labor and small business will be (are already) gravely threatened, along with what is left of that "free market" ("free competition") that is supposed by classical capitalist theory to increase economic efficiency and enhance the general good. For congressional conservatives in both houses promptly accepted as their own a bill drafted by corporation lawyers that—inadequate as a revenue raiser; filled with loopholes; harsh in its effect on small business—not only substituted a flat-percentage corporate income tax for a graduated one, but also gave corporations a choice between calculating the tax on the basis of invested capital or calculating it on the basis of previous average earnings. This option "permitted almost a total escape from the excess profits tax for corporations with high earnings in recent years (including several large airplane companies), and for corporations with huge capital structures (including several major steel companies)," as Morgenthau complained to Roosevelt and to his diary. The Treasury secretary foresaw some corporations making, out of defense contracts, under this bill, profits of 30 to 50 percent on their capital earnings without paying any excess profits tax whatever![15]

At that time (early August), however, big-business men were refusing to sign defense contracts pending enactment of the new tax legislation. A mere $900,000 in defense contracts had been negotiated. ("It's like the sit-down strike of [French] capital against [French Premier] Léon Blum [during the years of the French Popular Front government]!" cried Morgenthau's wife, Elinor, to Roosevelt's wife, Eleanor.)[16] And Roosevelt, with election campaign pressures increasing upon him, had soon caved in. Reading now in *The New York Times* a news item about the need for early congressional action to raise the legal federal

---

*On August 26, 1940, when Stimson and the War Department were exerting the maximum possible pressure upon Congress and public opinion to assure passage of the military conscription bill, Stimson wrote in his diary: "If you are going to try to go to war, or to prepare for war, in a capitalist country, you have got to let business make money out of the process, or businessmen won't work, and there are a great many people in Congress who think they can tax business out of all proportion and still have businessmen work diligently and quickly. That is not human nature."[14]

debt ceiling to $60 billion, he is painfully reminded of a Sunday afternoon three
months ago when, seated in a rocking chair on the back porch here at Hyde
Park, he had talked about the tax bill with Morgenthau, who nervously paced
the porch floor. If he were to defeat Willkie in November, he indicated, he had
to have *at once* a bill whose public description and profession of purpose would
quiet the popular demand for excess-profits legislation while its very different
substantial reality let loose that flood of big-business defense-contract signings
that, in his political view, was immediately necessary. "The Treasury bill is
out," he told the Treasury secretary coldly, bluntly. "Contracts are being held up
and I want a tax bill . . . damned quick. I don't care what's in it; I don't want to
know. . . ."[17] So on October 8 he signed into law a bill that suspended earlier tax
law provisions limiting to 8 percent the legal profits permitted on army, navy,
and air equipment contracts and, in general, outraged every principle of taxation
to which the New Deal was loudly committed. It violated the principle of ability
to pay in that it would tax most heavily those corporations with the poorest
earning records; it could mortally wound small growing businesses by giving
to huge corporations a near monopoly control of their industries. And these
same huge corporations would be encouraged by the act "to complicate their
corporate structures in order to secure [further] unfair tax advantages," as Morgenthau pointed out;[18] to this end they would employ, with the same patriotic
fervor they had manifested in 1916–18, their platoons of highly paid lawyers,
each highly skilled in the arts of lying, cheating, and stealing within the law.
Roosevelt seeks to soothe his conscience on this matter with a renewed promise
to himself of future remedial action. He tells himself that by keeping the reins
of governing power firmly in his hands, he can and will defend American freedoms successfully against their domestic as well as foreign foes. But he knows
full well that his present yielding is bound so greatly to strengthen conservative
business interests—interests adamantly hostile to economic democracy and disturbingly open to the appeals of corporate statism; the very interests of which,
in his view, Wendell Willkie is a puppet—that the self-promised remedial action
will be increasingly difficult to take.

Business's triumph over the New Deal has been similarly great and similarly
gained with regard to plant conversion. Businessmen are in general loath to
admit in that season the need to choose flatly between "guns" (the production of
war matériel) and "butter" (the production of civilian goods). They prefer to believe that "butter" can be maintained in normal supply by the facilities they already have in hand, while such "guns" as are needed are produced by new plants
paid for in toto with federal tax dollars. Of course, it is unthinkable that the government directly operate these government-bought plants, drafting into service
for this purpose, as boys are being drafted into the army, whatever skilled administrative and technical personnel are needed for the job; plant operation
must remain the exclusive prerogative of corporations who do so for private

profit and to whose capital the new plant will be added, a virtually free gift, when the war emergency has passed. And this strong preference, with its corollary, was emphatically impressed upon the Office of Production Management's William Knudsen, who may himself have shared it when he, the former "production genius" of General Motors, tried to persuade his Detroit friends to convert their automobile plants to the making of tanks and planes. His friends could (would) do so, they said, only if the federal government paid the conversion and expansion costs required, either by building the converted and expanded plant and leasing it to them at extremely cheap rates or by permitting private corporations to build them and write off the cost for tax purposes in a mere five years. These terms had been presented to Roosevelt by Knudsen in a White House conference on July 10, 1940, and Roosevelt, in his desperately felt need for an upsurge in the signing of defense contracts, agreed to them. He promised to support congressional legislation to this effect.[19] The immediate result was a welcome increase in contract signing, accompanied by an increase in the number of corporation executives brought into the government. But there has been so far no major shift from, say, automobile production to tank or airplane production. Instead, automobile production is increasing; if the present trend continues,* the automakers will produce more cars for the civilian market in the first eight months of 1941 than they did during the same period in 1940.

Only in the area of labor-management relations has business failed thus far to have virtually all its own way. Here, despite bitter jurisdictional quarrels between the industrial unions of the Congress of Industrial Organizations (CIO) and the craft unions of the American Federation of Labor (AFL), organized labor constitutes a force strong enough to resist with some success the businessman's use of the war emergency to nullify New Deal labor law and prevent a further advance of industrial unionism.

The resistance is being exerted in good part through fifty-three-year-old Sidney Hillman, president of the Amalgamated Clothing Workers of America, whom Roosevelt appointed labor employment commissioner ("personnel manager") on the seven-member NDAC last spring. He and Knudsen are both immigrants, Knudsen coming from Norway and Hillman from Russian Lithuania— a fact much commented upon in the press at the time their appointments were announced. Born of a Jewish family that had produced rabbis for generations, Hillman was himself studying to be a rabbi in the Jewish theological seminary at Kovno when he became passionately involved in the trade union movement. Because trade unionism was outlawed in czarist Russia, this meant involvement in the rebellious political movement that culminated in the failed Russian revolution of 1905, following which Hillman, who had twice been im-

---

*In the event, it did continue. In those eight 1941 months, civilian auto manufacture will use up 80 percent of America's dangerously *shrinking rubber* supply and 18 percent of the available steel.

prisoned for his political activity, fled his native land. He came, age twenty, to New York and has since made a brilliant career as one of the most effective and innovative labor leaders in all American history, notable for his ability to achieve mutually advantageous compromises with employers but also for his fighting courage, his devotion to human freedom, and the absolute loyalty he commands from those he leads. Like Roosevelt, he is an astute and adroit politician with a shrewd sense of the need for tactical flexibility in the pursuit of strategic goals; and from 1936 through 1940 he did much to unite in support of the administration the members of both the CIO and the AF of L. He has thus become the labor leader most influential of the administration—an influence augmented by the warm personal friendship that has developed between him and the President. His intelligence is high, his energy immense, his sense of justice acute; he has great self-control combined with a sweet and even temper.

Viewed exclusively as labor's champion on the NDAC, however, he has a grave disability: He is unable to convince himself that organized labor's special interest is always and everywhere identical with that national interest that he, as government official and bitter foe of Hitlerism, is bound to serve. This places him at a disadvantage in adversarial encounters with corporation executives on the NDAC: few of them manifest the slightest doubt that in serving their private interest, they serve the nation, profit making being in their view the principal freedom we arm ourselves to defend; which means that they are single-minded and unswerving in their pursuit of business aims, whereas Hillman pursues labor's special interest only to the extent of his conviction (he is, of course, very largely convinced) that its satisfaction is essential to high worker morale and the prevention of strikes and slowdowns in defense industries. Consequently, in his dealings with his business colleagues, and with the purchasing officers of the army and navy, he has made several compromises and concessions that, without earning him the gratitude of businessmen (though Secretary Stimson praises him as a great patriot), has exposed him to the wrath of labor leaders. He is under constant withering fire from both sides, his only protection a White House support he can never be sure of—a support actually withheld or withdrawn during a crucial period of the election campaign, as Roosevelt must admit to himself, regretfully and in strictest privacy, soothing his sore spirit with a self-promise to "make up for it" now that the election is won. He knows that Hillman is in poor shape physically to bear the incessant strain, having developed arthritis along with a serious heart condition, a combine of illnesses that will make the oncoming winter hard for him to bear. Already, Hillman has been forced to moderate his activities; during the coming months he may have to retire from the battlefield altogether for considerable periods of rest and recuperation in Florida's warm sunlight.

The net result has been that even in this area of labor-management relations, big business has thus far won more battles than it has lost. For instance, Hillman's influence was publicly evident in two crucial policy directives issued by the National Defense Advisory Commission on August 31 and September 6, 1940; but more strongly evident, considering the fact that Hillman took his stand upon the law of the land, whereas his opponents defied the law, was the influence of the commission's business representatives. Said the first directive: "All work carried on as part of the defense program should [not 'must'] comply with Federal statutory provisions affecting labor wherever [i.e., 'but *only* where'] such provisions are applicable ['applicable' remaining undefined]. . . . There should [not 'must'] be compliance with state and local statutes affecting labor relations, hours of work, wages, workmen's compensation, safety, sanitation, etc. . . . Workers should not [not 'must not'] be discriminated against because of age, sex, race, or color." Said the second directive, entitled "General Principles Governing the Letting of Defense Contracts": "Adequate [*sic*] consideration must be given to labor. This means compliance with the principles [*sic*] on this subject stated by the Commission in its release of August 31, which is attached hereto."[20] During the preparation of these directives, Hillman sought and received personal assurances from Roosevelt that the stand he was taking had presidential approval. Nevertheless, when the directives were sent to Hyde Park, where Roosevelt happened then to be, for the President's signature, they were accompanied by a Hillman reminder of promises flatly made and also of Roosevelt's need, in that election season, for defense against vehement attacks that CIO's John L. Lewis threatened to launch against the administration. Roosevelt signed the directives (Lewis, unpersuaded that the directives would be enforced, launched his furious attacks anyway). And with the signed directives in hand, Hillman managed with some difficulty to persuade War Undersecretary Robert Patterson and Navy Undersecretary James V. Forrestal, each of whom is strongly biased against labor unions, to write letters for publication expressing, if in language that allowed for "emergency" exceptions, the commitment of War and Navy to the President's policy. He also obtained from Attorney General Robert H. Jackson a published opinion that the NDAC directives were lawful and that defense contractors who disobeyed the Wagner and wage-and-hour acts risked having their contracts canceled. As for new contracts: "Army and Navy contracts will no longer be given companies violating the Federal labor laws," said Hillman, flatly, triumphantly, to a specially called press conference on October 1, 1940.[21]

There has followed, however, not a single contract cancellation for noncompliance with labor law, but, instead, a firestorm of attacks upon Sidney Hillman, through press and radio and on the floor of Congress, for allegedly plotting "to use the defense program to bring industry to heel at the Wagner Act" (the words are those of W. H. Prentis, head of the National Association of Manufacturers).[22] He has been charged with plotting to use the national emergency to further additional radical pro-labor reforms. The usually mild-mannered and cooperative Knudsen, egged on by his virulently anti-labor chief deputy, John D. Biggers of the Libby-Owens-Ford Glass company, found the morrow of Hillman's press conference an opportune moment for the delivery of an anti-union speech before a meeting of businessmen. "We don't want any part of the Russian system over here!" Knudsen cried. The notoriously anti-labor representative Howard Smith of Virginia, chairman of a special congressional committee established to investigate the National Labor Relations Board, promptly summoned Hillman, Undersecretary Patterson, Secretary Knox, and Attorney General Jackson to appear before his committee on October 8. And by all this, Harry Hopkins was greatly agitated; he viewed with horror the possibility that top industrial executives would close plants in the last weeks of the election campaign, throwing hundreds of thousands out of work, on the grounds that their companies were being denied government contracts, a move that would assure a Willkie victory at the polls. He urged his anxieties upon Roosevelt, who, already sharing them, withdrew his support of the stand Hillman had taken. Orders came down from the White House to "soft-pedal" this labor-law compliance issue till after election day. In obedience to them, Knox's and Patterson's testimony before Smith's committee was to the effect that their policy endorsements weren't really endorsements. A shamefaced Jackson virtually repudiated, at that same hearing, the legal opinion he had rendered a week before; he now described it as merely a "curbstone" opinion whose only significance was "legal-technical." Hillman was for the moment exposed naked and alone to a high cold wind of opprobrium, and when he followed Jackson to the witness table he spent a long and miserable hour "eating crow"—a very large, fully feathered, and sour-tasting crow—before a national public. Conservative commentators have chortled gleefully ever since.[23]

Hence, from all this, and for all his self-promises to rectify the situation, now that the election is won, Roosevelt's soreness of spirit remains.

And it remains not only with regard to these labor organization and economic concerns, but also and even more so with regard to the flat campaign promise he repeatedly made to American "mothers" that "your boys are not going to be sent into any foreign wars"—this during the campaign's last days when Willkie's attacks upon him as warmonger proved to be, according to public opinion polls, alarmingly effective.[24] Unmistakably described in this morning's news is a world in which the survival of American democracy will almost certainly require America's joining with the British empire, sooner or later, in "foreign war," and Roosevelt's own words will now stand as a hazard to his effective leadership in such a world. . . .

But the grimness of his reading experience this morning is not wholly unalleviated. There are wryly humorous moments. He reads, for instance, and finds mildly amusing, a report that, because of him, neither the conservative Democrat John Nance Garner, Vice President of the United States, nor the bigoted reactionary Democrat Ellison D. ("Cotton Ed") Smith, senior senator from South Carolina, had gone yesterday to a polling booth. Election officials of Garner's hometown of Uvalde, Texas, "said they couldn't remember a time before when he [Garner] hadn't voted," and Cotton Ed said in his hometown of Lynchburg, South Carolina, that it was "impossible for me to consider voting for anything but the [straight] Democratic ticket and there was no Democrat [for President] to vote for." In Englewood, New Jersey, a reporter yesterday reached isolationist spokesman and aviation hero Charles Lindbergh, a man whose coldly aloof personality is antipathetic to Roosevelt's, a man whom Roosevelt loathes as a Nazi threat to American freedoms. Though Lindbergh brusquely refused to say for whom he voted, he "was known" throughout the campaign "to be a Willkie supporter"—and Roosevelt tries now to dismiss him contemptuously (let him sweat! let him stew!) but cannot wholly do so since the hero's isolationist argument, through which sound muted notes of Nazi racism and Hitler propaganda, remains evidently persuasive of a disturbingly large minority of the general citizenry. Of yet wryer humor and much greater immediate concern is news from the headquarters of the Congress of Industrial Organizations (CIO), whose founder and head, the flamboyant power-lustful Roosevelt-hating John L. Lewis, had promised to resign his post if Roosevelt were reelected. Clearly Lewis had deemed his promise a potent threat, one that would coerce reluctant workers into voting for Willkie. The CIO rank and file having instead voted for Roosevelt in overwhelming majority, Lewis must surely now be forced to keep his promise. A spokesman for him has said he will indeed "step down" (Lewis himself remains in silent retreat), and Philip Murray of the steelworkers union is preparing to accept election to the thus vacated CIO chairmanship. But a "Draft Lewis" movement is being organized by "left-wingers" in the CIO, meaning in this case "Communists" (the Communist Party had weirdly allied itself with the professional Republican Party leadership, and with American Fascist organizations, in opposition to Roosevelt during the campaign)—and only time will tell how much disruptive strength, within the giant union, these "left-wingers" have.[25]

It is with mixed emotions that Roosevelt goes on to read the quoted remarks, made after midnight last night, of his eighty-five-year-old mother, to whom he remains strongly tied emotionally. Sara Delano Roosevelt is still emphatically what she was on her wedding day sixty years ago, a strong-willed family-prideful class-prideful Hudson River aristocrat who is unaware, or at any rate refuses to admit, that her social opinions and attitudes are exclusively those of special privilege. What she now says in print testifies to this fact. She hadn't wanted her son to run again, says she, who had never wanted him to enter politics in the first place, politicians being generally such vulgar people. But since he did run she is glad he won and is "sure he is perfectly capable of getting through another four years." She simply cannot understand why "friends and even relatives of ours . . . spent so much money helping the other man," she adds plaintively; or why, in general, "business hates Franklin so. . . . They say he has been stirring up class hatred, but there is nothing in his heart to justify that. We were not [he was not] brought up to consider whether people were rich or poor."[26]

Roosevelt reads also with mixed emotions a background story about his running mate, now the Vice President–elect. His emotions are mixed because, under the headline WALLACE OFTEN LABELLED "MYSTIC," the story describes a distinctly "different" personality whose difference, having caused mild presidential perturbations now and then over the last seven years, recently caused acute ones. Henry Agard Wallace, born in 1888 in Iowa's Adair County and raised in a Republican family, is reported to have blue eyes, to stand slightly under six feet tall, to weigh 175 pounds, and to have generally a disheveled appearance, thanks to his "shock of unruly brown hair" and "indifference to clothes." He is of genius mentality. A skilled mathematician, an agricultural economist, a geneticist who pioneered in the development of hybrid seed corn, the author of several sound technical treatises (*Agricultural Prices, Corn and Corn Breeding, Correlations and Machine Calculations*), he is also a student of history and world affairs and an eloquent writer and speaker in these areas. He was thus uniquely prepared mentally for the cabinet post to which Roosevelt appointed him in 1933, that of secretary of agriculture (his father had been agriculture secretary in Harding's cabinet), and has in fact been an outstanding secretary. He is certainly qualified intellectually to become, unprecedentedly for a Vice President, the assistant President that Roosevelt wishes him to be, helping the White House through the abundant complexities of economic mobilization, the harnessing of America's science for war purposes, the stockpiling of strategic materials, and other technical matters. But there remains that troublesomely different personality. It causes professional politicians to distrust Wallace profoundly; it once caused Roosevelt himself to say, according to this news story, that Wallace lacks "political oomph." For Wallace, who is almost puritanically abstemious and addicted to strange food fads and hobbies (he has recently "taken up the rare and difficult art of boomerang throwing"), has in him an inordinately broad and deep streak of religiosity that contradicts his scientific bent. Because of it, though he deems himself an orthodox Christian (an Episcopalian), he has been powerfully attracted to decidedly unorthodox forms of Eastern mysticism. And this, which Roosevelt had always before shrugged off as a puzzling but unimportant aberration, resulted in a potentially dangerous embarrassment to the Roosevelt-Wallace ticket a couple of months ago. In the mid-1930s Wallace had written letters in extremely flowery language to a White Russian mystic whom, overruling vehement protests by several colleagues, he had appointed to head a Department of Agriculture mission to China. This Russian is a very dubious character. Wallace ultimately fired him. But by then the

Russian had in hand many letters from Wallace of which the salutation was "Dear Guru." A cache of these came into the hands of the Republican campaign organization in August, when photostatic copies of them came also into Roosevelt's hands. They might have done much harm to the Democratic presidential ticket had they been published in the closing days of a close-run election campaign. Fortunately they had not been. But Roosevelt, reading now about his running mate, is reminded of his intention to show the photostats to Wallace at some appropriate time in the near future. He will do so with a shrug and a laugh, as if the matter were merely amusing, but he wants Wallace to know that the White House is fully informed—a fact bound to be personally embarrassing to Wallace and so an insurance against his repetition of this kind of behavior.[27]

IV

THE election news has driven most of the world war news off the papers' front pages, but the inside pages are full of it—and virtually every item of it defines a difficult problem or piece of a problem that is fraught with danger for the Republic, for the free world as a whole, and that the President of the United States must confront and try to solve.

He reads, for instance, that 430 British ships totaling 3,400,000 tons have been sunk by German U-boats and pocket battleships since the start of the war, 420 of them since last June 1. Good news is the fact that the first of the overage U.S. destroyers involved in the "destroyers for bases" agreement reached with Britain in early September have begun arriving in British ports; their stormy passage across the North Atlantic has proved their seaworthiness. Bad news is that a new German pocket battleship, the *Scheer,* has just made forceful appearance in the North Atlantic, where it threatens to rival the havoc-wreaking *Graf Spee,* now sunk, as a threat to Britain's lifeline to America. The *Scheer* has attacked a convoy of thirty-seven merchant vessels escorted not by British warships (these have been withdrawn from the Atlantic to reinforce the British navy in the Mediterranean, now that Mussolini has launched an attack on Greece), but by an armed merchant cruiser, the *Jervis Bay.* The *Jervis Bay,* with its six-inch guns, is no match for the eight-inch-gunned *Scheer* but nevertheless has rushed to engage her, giving the convoy time in which to scatter before its ships are attacked. Most of the merchantmen will thus be saved, at the cost of *Jervis Bay*'s life and the lives of over 200 officers and men of the Royal Navy, but even so, as Roosevelt will later learn, five of the merchantmen totaling 47,000 tons, and the lives of 206 merchant seamen, are lost. The British shipping loss since June 1 is only half the average rate of loss in 1917, he now reads, but in one recent week it was higher than during any week in 1917; and in that earlier year "Britain could get bauxite, iron ore, wood pulp and paper, nickel, copper ore, tin, flax, cheese, butter, eggs, milk, and other food products from parts of Europe now controlled by Germany and Italy." Now these things must come to Britain across the ocean in ships that sail by "the convoy system," and this system "slows deliveries" because several days are required to assemble a convoy, and once it is on the high sea its speed is limited to that of the slowest ship in it.[28]

Meanwhile England remains threatened with immediate Nazi invasion, though the chance of this has greatly reduced (Roosevelt reads that the Royal Air Force (RAF) has "again pounded at invasion ports" on the Continent, with Le Havre especially heavily hit), and is under continuous heavy Nazi air attack. In diminishing force by day but increasing force by night, waves of German bombers drop their loads on a London of which whole blocks are now reduced to heaps of rubble. They were doing so at the very moment of Roosevelt's speaking last midnight to the crowd gathered on the Hyde Park lawn, it then being near the end (dawn light was rising over the British metropolis) of the fiftieth consecutive night of London's bombing ordeal. Millions of Londoners spend their nights in air raid shelters or in the tubes of the Underground, emerging in the mornings imperfectly rested, if not actually bleary-eyed with sleeplessness, to do the work that must be done. Other British cities are also attacked, sporadically, with frightful effect. Many thousands of British civilians—men, women, children—have been slaughtered from the air; night after night, the slaughter continues; and it must be assumed, for precaution's sake, that this aerial assault is a prelude to the long-awaited invasion, which may very well come in the spring of 1941.

Roosevelt is reminded of the ringing declaration he made in an address on hemisphere defense at Dayton, Ohio, on October 12: "No combination of dictator countries of Europe or Asia will stop the help we are giving to almost the last free people now fighting to hold them at bay."[29] But clearly, if Britain is to continue to stand through the coming year, she must receive far more aid from the United States than she presently receives. She must draw more and more upon the industrial and agricultural productive capacity of the United States, a capacity that must be vastly and rapidly expanded in order to rearm this country while at the same supplying Britain's desperate needs. And not only must the United States produce the goods, it must help assure their safe delivery across an Atlantic infested with Nazi warships and U-boats. How can this be done without taking frankly belligerent action (U.S. participation in an Atlantic patrol and convoy system is indicated)—action that leads directly toward that "foreign war" into which, he has promised, no American mother's son will be sent?

The question nags at Roosevelt's uneasy conscience and weary mind as he reads on. . . .

The Italian attack upon Greece is for the moment stymied by ferocious Greek resistance: Italian troops have been driven ignominiously from Greek soil, back into Albania, whence the invasion attack was launched. Once again, Mussolini's grandiose imperial ambition is being frustrated by his armed forces' lack of strength, lack of competence, and (most humiliatingly) lack of a will to fight. But this latest Italian misadventure increases the Atlantic's dangers for Britain and hence the United States, as the *Scheer*'s depredations indicate. For in April 1939, Chamberlain's ministry had promised Greece that Britain would come to her assistance in case of attack. In fulfillment of this promise the Churchill government has just sent five squadrons of fighter and bomber planes from Egypt to Greece and, with Greek permission, is militarily occupying Crete and the island of Lemnos. British naval power desperately needed in northern waters, and also at Singapore to guard against a threatened forceful move by Japan into Southeast Asia and Indonesia, is perforce being concentrated in the Mediterranean. And this dangerous thinning of both Atlantic and Pacific defenses, unless the deficiency is supplied by the United States, may well become a chronic condition. For the Mediterranean crisis will not subside. It is bound to rise higher still. The Italians, having been reorganized and reinforced, are reported to be about to renew their southward drive in greater strength; and one knows that if this strength proves insufficient for success, if the Italians are again halted and driven back, Hitler will come to his ally's aid with whatever German armed force is required to conquer and occupy Greece. Roosevelt must regard the Greek invasion as but an initial element of a grand strategy whose aim is Nazi-Fascist empire over the oil-rich Middle East, over Egypt, over, eventually, the whole of North Africa. And this must in turn be regarded as but an element of a yet grander grand strategy whose ultimate aim is nothing less than world conquest—a strategy whose planning and execution now actively involve the empire of Japan and impose upon Roosevelt more urgently than before the need for thinking of the Atlantic in terms of the Pacific, of the Pacific in terms of the Atlantic, and for stressing global strategical planning as a major item of his heavy load of responsibility.

He reads now a headline saying JAPAN PERTURBED OVER U.S. BALLOT and, perusing the story beneath it, is reminded of preelection reports that Tokyo was as anxious for a Willkie victory in the American election as were Berlin and Rome. In Tokyo as in Berlin and Rome the happy expectation had been (evidently assurances had been given) that Willkie, become President, would name as his secretary of state William R. Castle.[30] This means that Japan's militarists, in common with the Nazis and Fascists, have measured Wendell Willkie the man, and viewed Willkie's historic role, in much the same way as Roosevelt has done. They have seen in the Republican candidate a man who, whatever his private personal convictions may be, has been overwhelmed by worldly ambition and bound by it to become, in the circumstances, a pliant tool of American reaction and fascism. Had not Willkie the private citizen publicly avowed principles and expressed opinions that differed greatly from those proclaimed by

Willkie the presidential candidate, especially in the last few weeks of the campaign? And were not these earlier avowed principles and convictions utterly at odds with those known to be held by William Castle? Castle is an extreme right-wing isolationist. As undersecretary of state in the Hoover administration, in 1931, he used his personal relationship with the President to undercut Secretary of State Stimson's efforts to shape (with Britain) a collective security policy of forceful opposition to Japan's conquest of Manchuria. In that same year he helped facilitate an immensely publicized flight to the Far East made, for purposes unspecified, by Charles and Anne Lindbergh. He remains a warm personal friend and great admirer of Lindbergh's—is a warm friend also of the notoriously mendacious and reactionary radio journalist Fulton Lewis, Jr., through whom he helped arrange Lindbergh's first network radio broadcast as spokesman for isolationism's cause in the fall of 1939. Assuredly, Castle's appointment to State would signify a radical change in U.S. foreign policy, tilting it drastically away from aid to Britain toward the appeasement and accommodation of Axis imperialism. Now this won't happen; there will be instead a strengthening and hardening of present U.S. policy.

No wonder Japan, by these election results, is "perturbed"!

For Japan has now actually become what it had formerly only seemed almost certain to become, namely, a full and publicly avowed partner of the Berlin-Rome Axis. Less than six weeks ago, on September 27, 1940, after lengthy negotiations of which Roosevelt was sketchily but accurately informed by his very able and long-experienced ambassador in Tokyo, Joseph C. Grew, there was signed in Berlin a so-called Tripartite Pact whose major substance, as published, is also tripartite. The pact's first article says that Japan "recognizes and respects the leadership of Germany and Italy in the establishment of a new order in Europe." The second article says that Germany and Italy "recognize and respect the leadership of Japan in the establishment of a new order in Greater East Asia." The third and most ominous says that the three powers "undertake to assist one another with all political, economic and military means when ['if' is the evident contextual meaning] one of the Contracting Parties is attacked by a power not at present involved in the European War or in the Sino-Japanese Conflict." This last article would be a double-edged sword, cutting toward both the Soviet Union and the United States, were it unqualified. But in fact it *is* qualified: another pact article (Article V) says that "the aforesaid terms do not in any way affect the political status which exists at present between each of the three Contracting Powers and Soviet Russia"—and Japan, one must assume, has received assurances from Moscow that it is safe from attack by its traditional enemy (though Moscow continues actively to side with China in the Sino-Japanese conflict).[31] Hence the third pact article is addressed directly and exclusively to the United States. And though Roosevelt deems it, in essential nature, a move more defensive than offensive on Tokyo's part, it is a warning and threat that he must heed.

American public opinion heeds it, certainly, and responds to it in a way opposite that intended, one is sure, by the pact signers in Berlin. Last July 20, Gallup pollsters asked a poorly framed question of a representative sample of Americans: "Do you think the United States should let Japan get control of China, or do you think the United States should risk war with Japan to prevent it from doing so?" Forty-seven percent of the sample then said they preferred Japanese control to any U.S. action that risked war; a mere 12 percent were willing to risk war in order to stop Japan (41 percent of the sample either had a different opinion or no opinion on this matter, a fact evincing the confused state of the American mind as well as the confused nature of the Gallup question). But when Gallup asked the same question on September 30, three days after the Tripartite Pact signing, the percentage preferring Japanese conquest to the risk of war had dropped to 32 percent while the percentage willing to risk war to stop Japan had more than tripled, rising to 39 percent. And when Gallup asked the more precise question "Should the United States take steps to keep Japan from becoming more powerful even if this means risking war?" 57 percent replied "Yes."[32]

These poll results were called to Roosevelt's attention by one of his secretaries in mid-October. He found and finds them a gratifying indication that isolationism is weakening its hold on American popular opinion. But his estimate of the extent of this weakening is greatly lowered, his gratification is severely limited, by his knowledge that isolationism, streaked as it is with racism, has always been more inclined to oppose Japanese aggressions in the East than Nazi-Fascist aggressions in the West. Lindbergh, for instance, has hinted repeatedly at a Yellow Peril rising against "our Western civilization" and that members of the "white race" should stop quarreling with one another in order to unite against the common enemy.[33] One must assume that the great aviation hero and those he speaks for are somewhat jarred by the alliance of white-championing Germany with yellow-menacing Japan; but one is also sure that such pause as the event gives them will be slight and brief. They will quickly conclude that this Tripartite Pact, like the non-aggression pact between Berlin and Moscow, is a mere tactical maneuver on Hitler's part, changing nothing of fundamental importance. And with this last, Roosevelt himself is inclined to agree. The new development does not loosen, instead it tightens, his grasp upon the major premise of his current foreign policy, which is that Nazi Germany, not imperial Japan, is the gravest of the threats now facing the American democracy. This means that the maintenance of the British empire as bulwark against Hitlerian aggression remains the prime necessity of American defense, which means in turn that aid to Britain must, in all American strategical planning, continue to take precedence over the frustration of Japan's grandiose ambitions. The latter must be resisted and ultimately frustrated, of course. But for the time being our dealings with the Far Eastern situation must be subordinated to, and conditioned by, our handling of the European situation. Hence, as regards the Tripartite Pact, Roosevelt's greatest anxiety is that it may so increase the American public's hostility to Japan *at the expense* of its hostility toward Hitler's Germany that the administration will be forced to divert to Asia energies that should be devoted to Europe. He said as much to Secretary of State Hull, who agreed with him, when the two conferred immediately after the pact's signing, whereupon Hull issued a public statement of the government's position saying that "the reported agreement . . . does not . . . substantially alter a situation which has existed for several years."[34]

All the same, Roosevelt is as convinced as Hull is, and as the British Foreign Office is, that the published Tripartite Pact is not the whole of it—that there is a secret clause specifically bestowing Germany's blessing, and Italy's, upon any aggressive move that Japan might make southward into French Indo-China, the Malay peninsula, and the Dutch East Indies in its quest for oil, rubber, and other needed natural resources. Even before the pact was signed—indeed, three months before—Japan established itself as a forceful presence in Southeast Asia. On June 20, three days after France asked Germany for an armistice, the weak amoral totalitarian-minded men who by then constituted the French government (Vichy is now their capital) gave in to Japan's threatful demand that all movement of munitions and war matériel through French Indo-China into China be halted. A Japanese military mission was permitted into Indo-China to ensure that the terms of this agreement were kept. Then, when the Vichy French governor of Indo-China proved "obstructive," as the Japanese put it, some thirty thousand Japanese troops invaded Tonkin (this on September 23, four days before the pact signing) and, after a brief skirmish with French troops, occupied this northernmost Indo-Chinese province. Simultaneously oil was and is being demanded in increasing amounts from the Dutch East Indies by the Japanese, who, though they have as yet served no ultimatum upon the Dutch colonial government, are more and more threatful as their negotiations with the oil companies, to whom the Dutch governor-general has blandly evasively referred them, drag on and on.

All this enormously complicates the kind of global strategical thinking that Roosevelt is called upon to do. It is impossible to neatly separate Atlantic from Pacific concerns, dividing them between mutually exclusive classifications. It might then have been possible to make calculations of the relative importance of each concern within each classification, and of the relative overall importance of each classification within any given situation. As it is, the concerns are so mixed up together, so intimately intermingled and even interpenetrative, that they cannot be sharply classified, cannot be mentally dealt with as distinct ideas or as terms of a logical equation. Britain, for instance, increasingly worried about shipping losses in the Atlantic and urgently calling for help from the United States in the reduction of these, worries also and only somewhat less seriously about the shifting balance of sea power in the far Pacific, a balance shift determined in good part by European events, and calls more and more urgently upon Washington to send to the British naval base at Singapore, for a "friendly visit," at least (so Churchill put it in an early October cable to Roosevelt),[35] a portion of the U.S. Fleet currently based in Pearl Harbor, Hawaii. To this latter call, Roosevelt has thus far turned a deaf ear, as he has also to London's plea for some kind of firm answer to the question of what the U.S. response will be to, say, a Japanese naval and military strike at the East Indies or down the Malay peninsula. He has done so despite advice to the contrary given him by Ambassador Grew in a lengthy September 12 cable dubbed the "green light" message by the State Department because in it Grew, formerly opposed to the imposition of sanctions upon Japan, now expressed himself as in favor of them. "Japan today is one of the predatory powers," said Grew; "she has submerged all moral and ethical sense and has become frankly and unashamedly opportunist, seeking at every turn to profit by the weakness of others. . . . Until such time as there is a complete regeneration of thought in this country, a show of force, together with a determination to use it if need be, can alone contribute effectively to the achievement of . . . our own future security." The advice was reiterated in an opinion solicited from Secretary Stimson, whose dealings as secretary of state with the Manchurian crisis a decade ago are believed to qualify him to speak with some authority about Japanese psychology. Citing "historical" evidence that Japan yields to American firmness (witness its withdrawal from Siberia in 1919, its acceptance of inferior naval strength in the Washington Treaty of 1921) but interprets "a pacifistic policy" as "weakness," Stimson in an October 2 memorandum argued that "clear language and bold actions" by the United States, definitive of a firm Far Eastern policy, will cause Japan to "yield to that policy even though it conflicts with her own Asiatic policy and conceived interests."[36] Roosevelt, at that moment, rather flatly disagrees. He deems it more likely that such "firmness," if he employs it, will drive a desperate Japan into immediate desperate actions that the United States can neither permit nor, in the present state of its preparedness, forcibly prevent.

V

Thus the swirl and tangle of events, problems, and challenges through which Roosevelt must pick his way and to which his responses are and will be shaped by his sense of himself, of his own innate and adherent capacities. On this morning of rare passivity his self-felt identity is in some respects no larger, no more formidable, than the one his intellectual critics ascribe to him in their moments of severest censure. He completes his breakfast. He puts aside the newspapers. He rises from his bed (he must have help to do so), dresses himself (he must have help to do so), then rides his wheelchair down into the library living room to begin the (for him) relatively meager activities of the day. And as he does this

his consciousness of self, within which his awareness of physical dependency upon the strong arms of other men may be somewhat sharper than usual, has nothing in it of the conqueror's egotistical willfulness. Indeed, against the massive challenges he faces, he measures exceeding small, far smaller than others do, the powers he can wield—the innate powers (of mind, of will) granted him by almighty God, plus the powers that are his by virtue of his high office—and is reaffirmed in his conviction that he cannot actually dominate even immediate events of major importance, much less change the direction or set the course of world history. He can only nudge here, tug there, prod at this point, brake at that one—he can only cautiously encourage the energies of change or, if the impendent change is of the foundations of the present American domestic order, discourage them—as he attempts to guide the turbulent torrent of event, upon which he is otherwise and in general borne irresistibly, toward what he perceives or conceives to be God's goals.

Such perceptions or conceptions are, for him, highly tentative. They derive from and depend upon information that is imperfect and uncertain—information he obtains, for the most part, not through a thoughtful study of subject matter, but through three kinds of prayer. Two of these are objective, impersonal, almost devoid of religious feeling. One of the two might even be deemed empirically "scientific" insofar as it consists of various kinds of poll taking, various ways of defining the nature and measuring the strength of public opinion on specific issues—this on the tacit assumption that the will of the majority is the will of God. The other of the two is a species of teleological gambling, essentially superstitious[37]—a kind of betting aimed at achieving not material prizes, but signs of divine approval or disapproval of something he contemplates doing. For instance, he may assign to this or that small happening a large significance, saying to himself that if the trivial event occurs within an immediate time span (the next minute, perhaps, or before he can count to ten), it means that God approves what he has considered doing; if it does not occur, God disapproves. Or he may see as a sign of divine approval or disapproval his luck at cards when he plays poker or, as he does far more frequently, Miss Millikin, a game of solitaire of which he is fond.

The third kind of prayer, however, is truly religious insofar as it is intensely subjective, profoundly emotional, imbued with a sense of awe and personal dependency; and it is this prayerfulness, which is in perfect accord with his somber nostalgic mood on this gray wintry morning, that he now employs, or by which he is now caught up. He looks backward into time. Seeking stability, permanence, eternality, amid or underlying the unceasing flow of eventful change, he contemplates or (more accurately) *feels* his way into the past—his own individual personal past as well as the historic past of this little Hudson River town in which he grew up. And he does find permanence there. The past presents itself to the remembering mind as a completed reality wherein one can see how events conform to one another, are fitted together through the operations of causal efficacy, this thing happening because that thing does and in turn causing something else, shaping a structure from whose order the contemplative observer may learn something of the workings of God's mind, something of the nature of God's will. The lessons thus learned are highly qualified, however. Roosevelt knows well that the past never exactly repeats itself, is therefore no mirror of the future into which he can look for precise instructions as to what he should now do. He realizes through his feeling self that the past as persistent memory is the very stuff or substance of the living flowing present through which it extends, as an ongoing but continuously changing pattern of event, into anticipated, apprehended future time. *This* is the mainstream flow of world, *this* the felt essence of his profound conservatism. And on this morning of gray melancholy, he in his contemplation of the past is acutely yet gently aware of continuity between his present self and the boy he remembers himself to have been here at Hyde Park—also between this Georgian mansion that is now his one true home and the smaller, more modest Victorian house in which he was born; and between the town of Hyde Park today and the Hyde Park of distant and receding yesterdays. By this awareness his sore and weary spirit is somehow soothed and refreshed, his optimistic faith restored.

And such soothing is continued, such faith is augmented, by the good cheer with which he is greeted by those who are gathered in the library living room when he enters it.

Among these is Harry Hopkins.

At that moment Hopkins has no office. Ill health forced his resignation in August from his post as secretary of commerce (extremely conservative Jesse H. Jones now holds the commerce post while continuing to head the Federal Loan Administration), and since then he has received no new appointment. But never before has his influence upon the general course of public affairs been as great as it now is. He lives in the White House; he is constantly at Roosevelt's side there, as he is almost everywhere else that Roosevelt happens to be. In several respects he has become for Franklin Roosevelt a living echo of the late Louis Howe, whose last home was also the White House. Increasingly he plays in Roosevelt's life a role akin to that Howe played for more than two decades and that Colonel House played in Woodrow Wilson's life during the First World War. He is more and more an extension of Roosevelt's mind and personality, a "second-self" (so Wilson described House), who yet retains an identity that is emphatically, uniquely his own—a temperament bittersweet, sharp edged, irritable (he wholly lacks Roosevelt's remarkable patience), sardonically witty, allergically reactive to all phoniness, joined with an unsentimental operator's mind that, if uncreative, is also tough, resilient, and eminently practical. He wants to get things done *now*. By all this he is enabled to become on occasion what Howe constantly was, namely, a critical check upon Rooseveltian words,

Rooseveltian deeds, as well as a resourceful adviser. He is chronically physically ill, as Howe had been. Cancer surgery has removed half his stomach, so gravely impairing his digestive system that he is never adequately nourished. He operates always now at the outermost limit of his physical strength, often driving himself recklessly beyond it into total collapse. Death is his constant companion, but one he refuses to admit to his dealings with the world or with himself. He rejects it from his consciousness with a contemptuous defiance cloaked in gaiety—the same attitude that Roosevelt took toward his polio and now takes toward his crippled condition and frequent bouts with flu or cold. Like Roosevelt, Hopkins insists upon life against death. And, indeed, if he is but slenderly alive, he is intensely so; his tall, thin rickety scarecrow of a body is upheld and animated by a feverish energy that shines with preternatural brilliance through his eyes.

And on this Wednesday morning he is perhaps more vividly alive than usual. Many of the hundreds who came in torchlight to this house last night saw him dance a little jig of joy on the Big House porch as Roosevelt came out to greet the visitors. He remains exuberant; he now exchanges with Roosevelt jocular comments upon aspects of the happy event.

Sweet, gentle, yet shrewdly realistic Missy LeHand, who for nearly two decades has been Roosevelt's phenomenally efficient personal secretary and whose whole life has been and is devoted to him, greets him with a smile that, lighting her lovely dark blue eyes and widening her lips, confers a radiant beauty upon a countenance that, in repose, is rather too long and narrow and strong of jaw to be beautiful. She has long since ceased to function as Roosevelt's stenographer save on rare occasions. The task of taking his dictation has devolved almost wholly upon her assistant, the "number two girl" who is also her loved and loving friend—a pretty, vivacious, quick-tempered, fiercely loyal Irish Catholic named Grace Tully who has been in Roosevelt's service for a dozen years and who now, too, greets him with happy smile and cheerful words. Missy's role in the Roosevelt entourage is much more comprehensive. She is for Roosevelt on the level of human relationships what Hopkins is on the level of policy making and execution (though she is by no means without influence on the policy level), namely, an extension of the Roosevelt mind, the Roosevelt personality. From her, often, many of the most powerful in the land, including high officials of the administration, seek advice as to how to proceed in matters with which the White House is concerned. Through her they commonly seek access to the President's person or to the presidential mind when a direct approach is deemed impossible or unwise—access that with great shrewdness and unfailing tact she sometimes grants, sometimes refuses. Of her daily work, much is determined by cryptic spoken words, cryptic scribbled chits attached to letters and memos, initialed FDR. Some say merely: "Missy, to ack." Others: "Missy, not now, maybe later. . . ." "Missy, tell him 10 o'clock tomorrow. . . ." "Missy,

NO! ...." "Missy, arrange tea, ask him to bring his wife. ...." "Missy, not till after election." Thus she, who in recent years has seldom recorded Roosevelt's spoken words on her shorthand pad, is the actual composer of a great deal of the mail that Roosevelt signs. She also serves as substitute wife to an extent that, being unknown to anyone save her and her boss, is the subject of some speculation among Roosevelt's friends and much malicious gossip among his enemies. She lives in the White House, and in the Big House at Hyde Park and the cottage at Warm Springs (which Eleanor almost never enters) when Roosevelt is there. She accompanies the President on virtually his every trip, whereas Eleanor does so infrequently. She presides as hostess over dinner tables from which Eleanor is absent—and Eleanor is often absent. ...

The Missy-Eleanor relationship, which many a close observer finds passing strange, is the fruit of Roosevelt's temperamental addiction to the blurred, the anomalous, the ambiguous—an addiction having as its obverse an aversion to sharp clear lines of demarcation, to definitions that are mutually exclusive. This characterizes his private life as fully as it does his public one. In the latter, as has been remarked, it has resulted in an administration that is *personal* to a degree unique in modern presidential history—an administration having the virtues of flexibility and openness to new ideas but, as has been indicated, having also the grave defect of a bitter personal and bureaucratic quarrelsomeness that wastes energies that could otherwise be useful and creative. His private world is similarly ruled by and through his force of personality—and with similar results. Here, as in his public administration, having spread around him as an emanation of his own spirit a warmly genial spiritual climate, he manages to "weave together" in a fabric of outwardly amicable relationships living entities that are widely disparate, personalities that are naturally incongruous and whose private interests in him are, often enough, antagonistic to one another. This fabric is strong enough to bear normal operational strains. But it is nonetheless fragile, for it is but a bright and smiling surface that depends upon his present influence for its continuance. Beneath it seethe dark hostilities. Thus Missy LeHand and Eleanor Roosevelt are to all appearances, and in reality also to a degree, the best of friends. No angry words have been known to pass between them. They embrace one another when they meet after long separations. They kiss one another good night when they go to their separate White House bedrooms. They exchange holiday gifts and, when they are apart, occasional letters replete with expressions of affection. All the same, the two are jealous of one another, resentful of one another, or, to put it more accurately, jealous and resentful of each other's special relationships with the man who dominates Missy's life absolutely and Eleanor's (despite herself) substantially.[38] This resentful jealousy feeds on the fact that the special relationships that are its object remain undefined. Roosevelt refuses such definition. He to whom others commit themselves totally makes few if any such commitments of his own; he has not done so in the present instance; and consequently he has never precisely distinguished in his own mind the loyalties he owes Missy from those he owes Eleanor, much less measured the two sets of loyalties against each other on a calibrated scale of values. So it was as regards his mother and his fiancée during the months of his courtship of and engagement to Anna Eleanor Roosevelt—nor has he since made a clear distinction between the loyalties he owes his wife and those he owes his mother.

The same confusion ("weaving together") of contradictory commitments was at the root of the great crisis of his marriage when, after Eleanor had given birth to the fifth and youngest of his living children (John was born in March 1916), he became involved in a love affair with his wife's social secretary, Lucy Page Mercer.* That crisis had culminated in a focus upon Roosevelt of overwhelming pressures. On the one hand was his love for Lucy (it was the one great romantic love of his life) and his fervent wish to join his life to hers forever; but arrayed against this were his ambition (Eleanor and Howe reminded him that a divorce would end his political career), his material prosperity (his outraged mother threatened to cut him off without a penny), Lucy's Catholicism (she could not marry a divorced man without special dispensation from Rome), his sense of guilt over his betrayal of vital obligations (Eleanor's life would be ruined, the lives of his five children gravely injured), and, most basic of all, his profound sense of his own destiny, which he identified with God's will with regard to him. He had flouted God's will! He must suffer for it! A family conclave, in which Lucy participated, was held, ending with the illicit lovers' renunciation of their love forever. They pledged themselves, on their honor, never to see or communicate with one another again. Which is to say there issued from this culmination what was, for Roosevelt, a uniquely sharp definition, a uniquely clear-cut decision.

But were these actually *final* on Roosevelt's part? In her deepest self, Eleanor had doubts. Viewing her husband through hurt eyes in a new and glaringly unflattering light, she could not but suspect him of secret reservations—though, struggling desperately to piece her shattered self together (this in 1919–1920), she told herself that she no longer really cared. She may also, deep down, have eased her pain, reduced her sense of utter futility, by holding herself in some part responsible for what had happened. For would her charming brilliant young husband have strayed so far from virtue's path if she had provided him with the lighthearted fun-loving companionship, the casual gaiety, that he so obviously craved and needed? Or if she had truly enjoyed the sexual act with him and thereby ministered adequately to *his* enjoyment of that act (she confessed to her daughter Anna in a later year that she did *not* enjoy it)?[39] Her overwhelming concern at the moment, however, must be to make a life of her own, independent of her husband (she abruptly ceased to have any sexual relations with him

---

*The story of the Lucy Mercer affair is told on pp. 483–95 of *FDR: The Beckoning of Destiny.*

whatever) and of her overbearing mother-in-law. She must do this if she were to live at all. In the autumn of 1917, driven by growing suspicions of her husband's infidelity, she had plunged into "a variety of war activities" with which she filled her time and from which she began to draw, as she later wrote, "a certain confidence in myself and in my ability to meet emergencies and deal with them."[40] After the autumn of 1918, when her worst suspicions were confirmed, she increased the number and intensity of her activities. Her confidence in her abilities grew.

Then, when her husband was struck down by polio three years later, there must have come into her mind—out of the residue of the gloomy Calvinism in which she had been raised, and from which she was now (she believed) wholly liberated—the words of the wrathful God of the Old Testament: "Vengeance is mine. . . . I will repay!" Certainly the gist of these awful words entered her husband's mind, they were a ghastly permeation of his feeling self, when, in the darkest hour of his polio crisis, "I felt that God had abandoned me," as he later confessed in a unique self-revelation to Frances Perkins.[41] *This* was his punishment for his sins! And the "vengeance" was visited not only upon him, but also upon Eleanor: she was condemned to suffer through the worst, the most arduous year of her life (1921–1922) as, with Louis Howe, she nursed her husband through the crisis of his illness, through the early months of his crippling (he was at first almost totally paralyzed; only gradually did strength return to his upper body), and then did what she could to help him piece together *his* shattered life—all this while managing a large household, waging continuous defense war against the aggressions of her mother-in-law (Sara Delano Roosevelt fought relentlessly to condemn her son to the passive life of a crippled country gentleman), and dealing with the special emotional problems of her teenage daughter.

It was not until the end of this ghastly year that she was enabled truly to declare her independence, in deeds if not in words; she then set out, quite deliberately, with the aid of two new close friends (Marion Dickerman, Nancy Cook), to become what by the end of the 1920s she had emphatically become—a forceful personality in her own right, with a career of her own. She managed to make of herself a separate power in her husband's life. She was aided in this by her husband's inescapable guilt feelings over the Lucy Mercer affair. For whether or not she consciously employed these as a weapon (almost certainly she did not), she was aware of their existence and that, to the extent of their existence (the extent remained doubtful), they worked in her favor as regards the balance of power between them. Her independence, however, was far from complete. She drew heavily upon her husband's growing power, after he returned to politics, for energies she could direct toward her own ends. Without her use of these she could not have accomplished half of what she did in fact accomplish. But she was again and again reminded, forcibly, and brought up short by the reminder, that the ends she pursued must not contradict those her husband pursued, that the energies she borrowed from him remained *his,* and that her access to them was limited, her freedom of choice as to her disposal of them even more so. If the two had become by 1934 what they yet remain in public life—a working partnership, a team, recognized as such by a national public—there has never been any doubt in her mind, and certainly none in his, that *he* is team captain. . . .

Eleanor is not among those who greet him this morning in the library living room. She is on her way back to Washington, where, working with her personal secretary and great good friend, Malvina (Tommy) Thompson, she will soon be addressing a huge backlog of correspondence. But among those who do greet him are three key members of his official family who are often uneasy with Eleanor over her forthright active stand for Negro rights. They are pale and sickly Marvin McIntyre, the presidential appointments secretary; General Edwin (Pa) Watson, a genial humorous Southerner, liked by everyone, who has succeeded Roosevelt's son James as presidential secretary; and florid robust Stephen (Steve) Early, the presidential press secretary. Early, a fiery-tempered Virginian with his full share of the white Southerner's racial bigotry, has sometimes actually clashed with Eleanor on "the Negro question," asserting, as is undoubtedly true, that her anti-racist activities are politically harmful to her husband in a South where only white votes count. On this particular morning, however, he is in no mood, and certainly in no position, to protest her stand. In New York City's Pennsylvania Station on the night of October 28, immediately following Roosevelt's "Martin, Barton, and Fish" campaign address in Madison Square Garden, Early lost his temper when a black patrolman, assigned to guard the President, failed to recognize him and blocked his attempt to cross a police line. Furious, Early "kneed" or kicked the patrolman, who, furious in his turn, forced a police commissioner's investigation of the incident. Republican propagandists gleefully seized upon the publicity of this. Roosevelt has just read in *The New York Times* a back-page item saying that a report of the police investigation will soon be in the hands of politically ambitious District Attorney Thomas E. Dewey, a principal rival of Willkie's at last summer's Republican National Convention who is certain to be a leading candidate for the presidential nomination in the Republican National Convention of 1944. Between the press secretary and the First Lady there is, therefore, a reversal of roles. It is now Early, not Eleanor, whose attitudes toward race cause immediate political damage; it is Eleanor, not Early, who must attempt to undo the damage. (She does so by attempting to deny that racial bias was involved in the "unfortunate" incident. "Mr. Early has a hot temper," she writes in a letter to a black leader, "and would have behaved in exactly the same way, no matter who the person was.")[42] It is a subdued if not abashed Early who now checks with Roosevelt upon press coverage of the one newsworthy act, a minor act, that the President will perform today.

This act, now imminent, is the dedication of a new post office building in Hyde Park village—and Roosevelt's mental preparation for it is part and parcel of the nostalgia, the stability-seeking gaze into his past, which dominates his mood on this wintry morning. The painfully shy, lonely, overmothered little boy he remembers himself to have been was greatly interested in history as a true story of dramatic personalities, dramatic events. The man in his forties, continuous with that little boy, having had a sedentary life forced upon him by polio, took a particular antiquarian interest in local history, of which his own family were a prominent part. In the 1920s he edited *Records of the Town of Hyde Park, Dutchess County,* published as a book through the Dutchess County Historical Society. As chairman of the publications committee of the Holland Society, he raised in those years and subscribed personally to a sum of several thousand dollars for the issuance of a book of photographs, with accompanying text, entitled *Dutch Houses of the Hudson River Valley before 1776.* And it was perhaps in the course of this enterprise that he first came across a pencil sketch made in the 1860s or early 1870s of a house, since torn down, that was built in 1760 or thereabouts by one John Bard, on the Albany post road near the St. James Church, of which Roosevelt, like his father before him, is vestryman. Certainly it is at Roosevelt's instigation that the architect of the new post office modeled his design upon the pencil sketch—and it is of this that he plans to speak in his dedicatory remarks. The remarks will be wholly informal, extemporaneous, he now tells Early; he doesn't even have notes of what he is going to say. Hence, if Early thinks it important to have a verbatim account, for the press, a stenographer will have to take down the words as they are spoken.

And now a living portion of Roosevelt's past enters the room.

His mother is the one person in the whole of his intimate private world whom he has never dominated but to whom he himself has had wholly to adjust his own behavior when dealing with her. She is an unalterable fact—a distinct entity of indubitably vital stuff, which, however, is remarkably lacking in that capacity for change, that adaptability to change, normally characteristic of living substance. Spiritually she is the past as completed process (the past as "all there"), a distinct reality to which nothing can be added and from which nothing can be taken away by the flow of time unless or until all is taken away. Roosevelt looks up at her now with welcoming smile. She bends over his wheelchair to bestow upon his cheek her morning kiss, he responding affectionately. And what he sees as he does so is a stout, erect woman of something above medium height whose physical vigor seems to have been but slightly diminished during the most recent of her eight and a half decades of privileged living. Her broad, sturdy figure bears no resemblance to the tall, slenderly graceful figure—her broad, fleshy face, whose strong-jawed profile is remarkably similar to her son's, retains but traces of the finely chiseled features—of the haughty, dark-haired, dark blue–eyed beauty who, when she was twenty-six, caught the eye of widowed fifty-two-year-old James Roosevelt and drew him into marriage with her. Spiritually, however, she remains precisely what a young Swiss governess of the boy Franklin found her to be half a century ago: A grande dame! A personage *très formidable*![43] She is chock-full of noblesse oblige, but it is a noblesse oblige notably deficient in generosity. Indeed, her essential selfishness is so pure and monumental that it commands a certain respect from almost everyone, and a species of sneaking admiration from some, especially if they have not to suffer it directly. Her only son, though he retains in full his filial affection for her, has suffered it directly, and if he no longer suffers from it, it is because he has (as a boy) developed strategies and stratagems with which to deal with it in self-protective ways. By the time he departed for Groton School at age fourteen—indeed, some years before that time—his father, increasingly invalided by the heart disease that killed him when Franklin was eighteen, had ceased to be the dominant figure in the Roosevelt household. Sara was the dominant one—and as she focused upon her young, vulnerable, remarkably sensitive son much of the forceful energy (she had a vast store of it) that would otherwise have gone into her marital relationship, this son had had to defend himself against it if he were to develop and maintain an identity of his own. He did not do so through open rebellion. Initially he was too childishly helpless, then and later he was too lovingly attached to her, to make flat total angry rejections. Instead he hid behind a smiling, pleasing facade his true feelings, also his determination to go his own way whether or not it was the way she willed for him. He learned to do this while yet very young—learned reticence, subsequently developing his peculiar brand of voluble reticence. He mastered the arts of indirection and dissimulation. He became "the consummate actor."

VI

HE was not long in the library living room on this Wednesday morning, for it was approaching noon when he entered it. Soon, bundled up against the cold, blustery wind, he was seated behind the wheel of his hand-controlled Ford touring car, with his mother, similarly bundled up, seated beside him and his son John with new daughter-in-law, Ann, in the seat behind. The politician's need to be seen by the public took precedence over the man's fear of another head cold; the car's top was down as he turned into the long private lane leading to the Albany post road and then northward on that road to the new post office building in Hyde Park village. There, despite the cold, some three hundred of his fellow townsmen awaited and cheered him as, grasping the arm of son John, he rose and stood before them.

He was introduced to them informally (not with the ritual "Ladies and gentlemen, the President of the United States") by Arthur Smith, son of the Moses Smith who for decades was the farmer of the Roosevelt estate and in whose home was organized, way back in 1910, the now famous Roosevelt Home Club.

And the little talk he then gave made no reference whatever to foreign war or national dangers. It was wholly lovingly concerned with local history, its every word and phrase soaked through with nostalgic feeling, though the words were commonplace, the phrases devoid of eloquence—and the correspondents present took note, as he spoke, of how tired he seemed, how lacking in his usual zestful buoyancy.

He began by saying that every new post office erected in Dutchess County during his administration was a copy, as exact as possible, of some locally historic building—a fact for which he himself was responsible, though he did not now say so. The John Bard house of which Hyde Park's post office was a copy once stood "as near as we can make out about halfway between [the present locations of] the St. James Church and the Vanderbilt barn"—and the only major difference between that house and this new building was in construction material: the post office's outer walls were of local fieldstone, whereas the Bard house had been a wooden structure. The ground upon which the new building stood was part of the original Bard estate, which, "as you know . . . is probably the oldest estate in the North," having been "kept as an estate for nearly two hundred years and under the most careful supervision." John Bard, he went on to say, "was the grandson of the original patentee of the land north of the creek," this patentee being the man who named Hyde Park "in honor of the Hyde family—Lord Clarendon in England at that time." Thus it was the founder and founding of today's Hyde Park that was being now and here commemorated, along with "the fact that John Bard was a great naturalist." He closed: "I don't think we need any more ceremony, except that I would like to thank the men and the contractor, the builders and the architect, who are responsible for this very lovely building."[44]

Some nine or ten hours later, in the darkness of the night that closed this first post-election day, Roosevelt and his party boarded at Hyde Park station the railway car that would carry them southward through the world city at the Hudson's mouth and thence to the nation's capital.

2

⇢⟩⟩✕⟨⟨⇠

Of Conflagration, Fire Hose, and Hydrant

I

IN Washington, at eight-thirty or so next morning, he met with a conquering hero's triumph in which more than two hundred thousand people participated, many of them government employees who, for this event, were granted leave from their jobs. Greeting him in the Union Station train shed, into which his private railway car was slowly backed, were all ten members of his cabinet with their wives, his own wife, Eleanor, and Vice President–elect and Mrs. Henry Wallace, the last three of whom entered the open car into which he himself was assisted and which at once moved slowly, preceded and followed by cars carrying Secret Service agents, into the station plaza. There a throng numbering tens of thousands awaited him, their wild cheers drowning out completely the spirited march being played in his honor by an army band; and there, at a central spot where microphones and loudspeakers had been placed, he ordered the car to stop so that he might address, with brief informality, his "old friends of Washington." This warm welcome meant a great deal to him and his wife, he said, because "it isn't as if we were new to Washington"; people's "turning out this way" must therefore mean "that we get along pretty well." All of them knew "how very much we [Eleanor and himself] like farm life, but of all the cities in the world we would rather live in Washington . . . [and we] are glad of the prospect of staying here just a little longer."

Only a mile of city streets then separated him from the White House, but the sidewalks of these were jam-packed with people who loudly cheered his appearance and whose cheers he was determined to acknowledge with waves, and wide smiles, and repeated doffings of his famous battered old fedora—the "good luck" hat he had worn in his every political campaign since 1920. It was therefore by his order that the open car, with Wallace beside him in the front seat, with Eleanor and Mrs. Wallace in the seat behind, was driven in low gear, at a pace no faster than that of a strolling man, for a full twenty minutes before it turned at last into the White House grounds. The gates to these had been thrown wide open to the public that morning for the first time since early summer (they had been closed "for technical reasons" when France fell; building repairs allegedly made the grounds "dangerous"), and through them some five thousand people had crowded and were packed together, now, before the north portico. They cheered lustily, and the President and his party acknowledged the cheers for several long minutes before disappearing through the White House door. The cheering multitude's appetite for celebration was not yet satisfied, however; the crowd did not begin to disperse until the Roosevelts and Wallaces had twice emerged from the mansion to present themselves upon the porch.[1]

Newspaper correspondents who reported all this reported also, as those covering Roosevelt at Hyde Park had reported, that the President appeared to be extremely tired; he admitted that he was.

And weariness, a need for rest that was little less than desperate, dictated his refusal that morning to pay serious heed to any of the abundant problems, all gravely important, of which paper evidences were piled high in the incoming tray on his desk. He confined himself to a cursory review of three rough drafts of speeches he was to deliver in the next few days—one "off the record" at the annual National Press Club dinner, two ceremonial addresses on Armistice Day—and to the signing of a few presumably routine letters that had been prepared by others.[2] He read, evidently with decidedly mixed feelings, a warm congratulatory message from Winston Churchill that began: "I did not think it right for me as a foreigner to express any opinion upon American policies while the election was on [actually the Prime Minister's long silence had evidently offended a President who, during the anxious closing days of a close-run campaign, would have welcomed encouraging words], but now I feel you will not mind my saying that I prayed for your success and am truly thankful for it." Roosevelt put this aside, presumably intending a later answer. (He never did answer it, to Churchill's considerable consternation.)[3]

But it was impossible for him wholly to ignore the fact that virtually every one of the problems that had piled up during the closing weeks of the campaign had a severe time limit stamped upon it. Immediate answers, immediate actions by the Executive were demanded; and Roosevelt knew that official Washington had been awaiting impatiently the campaign's end in the expectation that such answers and actions would now be at once forthcoming. One such problem awaited him in the person of Sidney Hillman. We have told how this National Defense Advisory Commission labor and employment commissioner was humiliated when, just a month ago, having attempted to make compliance with federal labor law a must for defense contractors, he was compelled by a White House order to defer all such effort until after the election. This humiliation, which some deemed already great enough to fatally injure effectiveness in his job, had just been immensely augmented. For only yesterday, within twenty-four hours after a reelection triumph widely deemed a popular endorsement of liberal policies, the War Department had announced the granting of a $122 million contract for airplane engines to the Ford Motor Company, whose defiance of the Labor Relations Act was adamant, even physically violent. This was a direct slap in the face for Hillman. Roosevelt knew that he risked a rash of crippling strikes in defense industries, risked also the loss of Hillman's services, which he greatly valued, unless he took within a few days, or weeks at most, firm steps toward a solution of the issue Hillman was now bound to press with vehement force.

More immediate still was the pressure that would be exerted upon him by Henry Morgenthau, to whom he had assigned crucial portions of the problem of facilitating immediate aid to warring Britain and whose longtime intimacy with him promoted the frankest talk. For Morgenthau was to lunch with him that very day in the Oval Office; he was bringing with him Arthur D. Purvis, chief of the British Purchasing Commission, who during the last year had worked closely enough with the administration (behind the scene) to become virtually a part of it, and who was about to board a clipper bound for England, there to confer with the highest officials of his government on problems of American aid. This clearly meant not only that Morgenthau would insist upon "talking business," but also that the business would be of utmost importance.

And indeed it was.

For, as it happened, Morgenthau had been conferring through most of that morning with Secretary of War Stimson, Secretary of the Navy Frank Knox, and Army Chief of Staff George C. Marshall upon an argument he had devised for providing the British with American planes that they had not even ordered but would significantly strengthen their defense of the Atlantic lifeline against currently devastating German submarine attacks. These planes were the new Liberator (B-24) bombers whose range of 3,100 miles was well over a thousand miles greater than that of the new American Flying Fortress (B-17) or any other American or British heavy bomber. Only a few of the B-24s had as yet been delivered to the U.S. Army. The great legal obstacle to the release of these and future Liberators to the British was an amendment attached to last summer's navy expansion bill at the behest of Senator David I. Walsh, a conservative isolationist Democrat, chairman of the Senate Naval Affairs Committee, who had a Boston Irish Catholic's hatred of Perfidious Albion. The Walsh Amendment forbade the sale of any army or navy matériel to a foreign power without prior certification by the chief of staff or the chief of naval operations that said matériel was "not essential to the defense of the United States."[4] Morgenthau's argument was that Marshall could legitimately certify the proposed sales on a quid pro quo basis since development of the Liberator had been greatly facilitated by a British engine design, a highly secret one, which the British had released to the Americans. As a matter of fact, said Morgenthau, the British had given us ten times as much "secret stuff " (including tremendously valuable radar developments) as we had given them—and Morgenthau's cabinet colleagues, with Marshall, not only agreed that what Morgenthau said was true but also indicated their own desire to do what Morgenthau wished to have done. They were compelled to hesitate, however, by the still distinct if shrinking possibility that Britain, despite all the material aid the United States could give her, might yet go down under Hitler's attack within the next few months, especially if his attack were coordinated with Japanese aggressions in the Far East. The Liberators now released to Britain would in that case be desperately needed by U.S. armed forces for defense of the Western Hemisphere. And in any case, thanks to the Walsh Amendment, the final decision would have to be Marshall's alone—a grave responsibility whose difficulty Marshall acknowledged by saying that, while he favored helping the British "as far as possible without injuring ourselves," the question of what in this instance would be injurious to ourselves was one he could not answer on the spot; he must first gather and study all the relevant facts. Morgenthau then revealed that he had already discussed his proposal with the President and the President had responded to it with the remark that it was "about time we got on that one-and-one basis" (a fifty-fifty division of American military plane production between Great Britain and the United States) that he had tentatively proposed some time before (at the moment the division was running approximately 55–45 in favor of the United States).5

During this Oval Office luncheon, responding to Morgenthau's reminder of the President's announcement in Boston on October 30 that the British were being permitted to order twelve thousand U.S. planes and that this would require a major expansion of U.S. plane-production facilities, Roosevelt reiterated his "rule of thumb" for the division of plane production and expressed a wish to extend it to the munitions supply in general. The adoption of such a "rule" would absolve General Marshall and Admiral Harold R. Stark, the naval operations chief, of their obligations, under the Walsh Amendment, to make multitudinous individual decisions as to what items in what quantities were or were not "essential" for U.S. defense. But would it do this, so long as the Walsh Amendment remained on the books? questioned Morgenthau. Had not the time come to request a congressional repeal of this restrictive legislation? Roosevelt brushed the questions aside wearily. At the very least the rule of thumb should make the required certifications easier for both the general and the admiral, said he, who then and there decided to make public announcement of the rule at his press conference next day.6

Such luncheon talk was hardly designed to lift the spirits of a bone-weary man who wished only that, for the time being, he could be let alone. But the talk that followed was positively depressing. Its topic was Arthur Purvis's gloomy report, based on the latest statistics, of British and Allied merchant shipping losses in the Atlantic. If the current rate of sinkings continued—or even if that rate were reduced by the maximum amount that American-supplied bombers could reduce it through attacks upon U-boats—the British could not maintain the present inadequate shipping tonnage, much less increase that tonnage to what was necessary for long-term British survival. Ships were currently being sunk faster than they could be replaced. Unmentioned that day was the increasing probability that to ensure the delivery of material aid to Britain, the United States would soon have to join in armed convoys across the Atlantic, for it was a probability Roosevelt strove to refuse to admit; but Purvis may well have mentioned an ominous fact that threatened *all* American aid to Britain and of which warnings from London had piled up during the election campaign, namely, that the British approached the limit of their ability to pay for the aid they needed, having liquidated nearly all that they could liquidate of their American holdings. They were running out of dollars. Certainly this fact was very much on the minds of all three men, and Roosevelt was at that moment "touchy" about it. It was full of political dynamite. Given the impossibility of letting Britain go down, it pointed toward alternative courses of action that were fraught with grave political hazard. One was a repetition of money loans to the British, as in World War I. This would require repeal of the Johnson Act, which forbade U.S. loans to nations that had defaulted, as Britain had, on their World War I debts to this country. The alternative was an outright gift of matériel, a choice Morgenthau believed infinitely preferable to massive credit extensions (the Treasury secretary had told his staff in early October that he "would never be part . . . of lending them money again, and if we got to the place where they couldn't pay, I would recommend that we give it to them").7 But this, too, would require congressional action. It could not be done within existing neutrality law; it would require a specific grant of authority to the Executive by Congress. And Roosevelt, vividly imagining the violent reaction that an attempted adoption of either alternative would provoke from the all-too-sizable isolationist minority, and of the persuasive power such reaction might have over public opinion in general, interrupted Purvis at this point to muse aloud. He voiced a question he had been pondering for some time. "Might it not be possible," he wondered, "for the United States to build cargo vessels and lease them to Great Britain?"8

No answer to this was forthcoming during the luncheon, of course. Nor was it when he broached the matter at his cabinet meeting next day. Knox and Stimson were quick to point out the difficulties. How could this be done without a drastic revision of current neutrality law? And since the leased vessels would remain U.S. property, what flag would they sail under? The United States? The British? Roosevelt's attempt to dismiss such questions as "mere details" failed against his own recognition, and his auditors', that these "details" added up to a formidable if not insurmountable obstacle to what he suggested doing. Similarly with regard to Britain's dwindling dollar reserves, a crisis problem whose solution he sought to postpone with the wishful assertion that "England still has sufficient credits and property in this country to finance additional war supplies" for some time to come.⁹ Similarly, again, with the rule of thumb as applied to American plane deliveries to the British.

Stimson stressed this last in an hour-and-a-half session with the President on Tuesday, November 12. It was the first meeting the war secretary had had alone with Roosevelt in many weeks, and he, who had been repeatedly irritated and frustrated by the President's habit of dominating every interview with random digressive talk of his own upon almost any subject save the one at hand, was pleasantly surprised by the close and silent attention paid him on this occasion (was Roosevelt too tired this day to indulge his usual volubility?). The war secretary was glad to report that Marshall had indeed found it possible to certify the transfer of a number of B-24s to the British, this on the quid pro quo basis Morgenthau had proposed. Unhappily no such basis existed for the transfer of the B-17s (Flying Fortresses) that the British wanted and needed desperately; and since no B-17s were on British order, Marshall found it impossible to certify them for immediate delivery with the stipulation that they be later replaced, in the U.S. Army Air Corps, by those ordered by the British for future delivery. Marshall was stymied by the Walsh Amendment, said Stimson; that amendment and other restrictive legislation simply must be removed from the statute books as quickly as possible; congressional action could be no longer postponed. But Roosevelt was not ready for this; indeed, he was at that time publicly disavowing any intention even to revise either the Johnson Act or the Neutrality Act, much less repeal them. Nor, for all his weariness, was he yet barren of ingenious devices for circumventing rather than removing obstacles. He penciled onto a notepad, while Stimson talked, his notion of sending the Flying Fortresses to England with U.S. Air Corps personnel, allegedly for the purpose of observing the planes (testing them) in combat. This seemed "the only peg on which we could hang the proposition legally," said the President, adding that Stimson should clear the scheme with the State Department before submitting it to the attorney general for a legal opinion. Stimson did so at once. He went from the Oval Office to the office of the secretary of state, thence to the office of newly appointed Attorney General Robert H. Jackson, who, he found, was out of town. But Assistant Attorney General Newman A. Townsend, a former judge, promptly (that is, on the following day) opined that what the President had proposed could *not* be done legally: Congress had "entire dominion" over the property of the United States, which meant that no B-17s could be given the British, not even for alleged "testing" observations by Americans, without explicit congressional approval. Possibly, however, said Townsend, B-17s might go to England now as offsets for other types of bombers that the British had actually on order for future delivery—and it was this devious method that Marshall now employed. The general was a man of unusually forthright and straightforward disposition who was also profoundly committed to that subordination of the military to civilian authority that is prescribed by the U.S. Constitution. He therefore acted as he did with extreme reluctance, and only because it was the single conceivable means by which he could carry out within the bounds of even a dubious legality what he deemed to be virtual orders from his commander in chief. On December 5 and 6 *The New York Times* would carry stories announcing that twenty B-17s, relinquished by the air corps, were going to England, one of which was already delivered.[10]

And while a weary Roosevelt dealt thus fumblingly and by indirection with aid-to-Britain problems, he dealt only somewhat more forcefully with the issue between business and organized labor as regards the mandating of federal labor law compliance in government defense contracts. In the first NDAC meeting following the granting of the $123 million contract to Ford, Sidney Hillman vehemently protested the army's repeated ignorings of "labor standards established by law and adopted by this commission." He reminded his fellow commissioners of a letter he had received from Philip Murray, now the head of the CIO, last August, a copy of which had come into each commissioner's hand. Murray had fumed that the Bethlehem Steel Corporation was defying the government and flouting all labor laws as blatantly as it had done in 1917–1918; it flatly refused to pay the 62.3 cents minimum hourly wage established under the Fair Labor Standards Act or to obey the collective bargaining provisions of the Wagner Act, though the company was making huge profits out of defense contracts. Yet Bethlehem, whose head, Eugene Grace, was notorious even among his fellow business executives for the immense salary he managed to garner for himself, continued to receive huge army contracts. So did the International Shoe Company and the Brown Shoe Company, said Hillman, both of whom were as contemptuous of labor law as were Ford and Bethlehem. But in that NDAC meeting, Hillman's only firm support came from the toughly combative and loud-voiced price stabilization commissioner, Leon Henderson. When Hillman then went to Assistant Secretary of War Patterson, he was told that labor organization was no "paramount" concern of the War Department's, an attitude bound to encourage "more strikes and delays" in defense industries, as Hillman forcefully said. He knew, however, that strikes in defense industries, given the kind of "patriotism" encouraged among the general citizenry by mass media controlled by big business, were likely to lead to stringent anti-labor legislation in a Congress in which a coalition of Republicans and conservative Democrats yet held the balance of power. He perforce came finally to Roosevelt, perhaps on the very day of Roosevelt's interview with Stimson, perhaps on the day before or after, to appeal for desperately needed help. He obtained it in the form of a presidential letter addressed to the NDAC saying: ". . . I have had a great many complaints about the War Department contracts to the Ford Motor Company, to the International Shoe Company and to the Brown Shoe Company. I have been told that these companies have had definite trouble with labor and have been judicially held to be in the wrong. I am wondering what has been done to assure full compliance with Federal laws before these contracts were awarded."[11]

The letter, as we may anticipate, caused during the next weeks a flurry of activity by the businessmen commissioners of the NDAC and their assistants, most of it concerned with ways to answer the President's questions convincingly while continuing to circumvent labor laws on the grounds that doing so was essential to national defense. A proposed insert in the standard lump-sum supply contracts being issued by army procurement officers was drafted by one of Patterson's assistants, who did so, one suspects, with tongue in cheek, since the extreme severity of its terms seemed designed to arouse the sternest opposition, and the most plausibly argued, from army procurement officers. With no qualifying loopholes for "exceptional" cases, it required absolute obedience of all federal, state, and local labor laws by all prime contractors and subcontractors. It proposed to modify the standard termination clause "to give the Government the acknowledged right to terminate contracts without compensation on the part of the Government and, on the other hand, the right to levy a heavy penalty for any breach of these labor laws and to withhold payment without a judicial determination of the infraction, alleged or real." When it was sent by Patterson to the quartermaster general (he was Major General E. B. Gregory) for comment, the latter gave it as the "considered opinion" of his office that the insert (it appeared to untrained eyes notably explicit) would impose "indefinite and ambiguous requirements" that would "result in a substantial number of prospective bidders refusing to submit bids or in submitting unjustifiably high bids," thus "clearly" violating "the paramount aim, namely an expeditious accomplishment of the defense program."[12] And in undeviating support of this "paramount aim," so profitable to the big-business community, the War Department issued to Ford in mid-December another defense contract, this one for a mere $1,387,000 worth of midget scout cars for the army—a transaction so small that it could easily have been handled by any of a number of auto manufacturers (Chrysler, for instance) that complied with labor law. The latter fact added to the sting of what was plainly another slap in the face for Hillman, and this time his normally mild and conciliatory disposition was overcome by flaming anger. He raised a storm of protest in the next NDAC meeting. Receiving no satisfaction there, he went again to the White House.[13] And Roosevelt, as we shall soon see, prodded by this newest addition to the pile of troubles that rose up to him out of the industrial mobilization effort, in good part because he had established no adequate administrative machinery for this effort—was at last moved to take remedial action. . . .

Through all the first weeks immediately following his return to Washington, Roosevelt's mind was evidently so befogged with weariness that his ability to recognize causal connections between one of his acts and another, one decision and others, was severely limited. There was, for instance, the fumbling manner in which he initiated diplomatic relations between Washington and Vichy, where the aged Marshal Henri Pétain now headed the government of unoccupied France.

The decision had been made to recognize this authoritarian, collaborationist Vichy regime as the continuing legitimate government of France, ignoring the claims of exiled General Charles de Gaulle, now operating in London, that *he* headed the *real* France (Free France, the Fighting French). This decision had been made on purely pragmatic grounds: of crucial importance was the denial to Hitler of the formidable French fleet, a fleet that was under the command of British-hating Admiral Jean-François Darlan; and an effective American ambassador in Vichy might exert a considerable influence upon the event. Accordingly, William Bullitt, who had returned to the United States soon after the French surrender yet remained officially the American ambassador to France. He had submitted his written resignation to the President on November 7—this "in accordance with an excellent custom," as he had said—but Roosevelt had promptly replied in a written note (November 9): "Dear Bill: 1. Resignation not accepted. 2. We will talk about that and the future later. 3. Hope to see you very soon." A week later he did have a personal interview with Bullitt in the Oval Room of the White House ("Whatever time you may fix, please, for many reasons, make the place the White House and not the [Executive] office," Bullitt had written him).[14]

On that Saturday, November 16, Roosevelt had returned, almost two days early, from what had been planned as a restful four-day cruise, Thursday through Sunday, on the presidential yacht *Potomac*. Late on Wednesday, November 12, the day of his long talk with Stimson, he had boarded the yacht in company with Harry Hopkins, Attorney General Jackson, and Frank Walker, who had replaced Jim Farley as postmaster general—men chosen to accompany him not for consultation on governmental matters, but solely and strictly for restful companionship. The yacht then cruised leisurely down the Potomac and out onto Chesapeake Bay. Alas, the weather had turned abominable by Thursday morning; it remained so the next three days. Even on the relatively smooth-watered bay the shallow-drafted *Potomac* pitched and rolled a good deal; and it was no doubt for this reason that—though he spent much of his time alone in his large and comfortable cabin, presumably catching up on his sleep—Roosevelt was little if at all rested when he returned to the White House.

There, as his first business, he addressed himself to the Vichy diplomatic problem.

Just before boarding his yacht he had dictated a letter (it was dated November 13, 1940) to General John J. Pershing, who had commanded the American Expeditionary Force during World War I, asking him if he would accept appointment as ambassador to France. "Your personal prestige with the French people," Roosevelt had said, "would prove of the greatest value in this endeavor, and your close relationship with Marshal Pétain would undoubtedly make it easier for the views of this Government to be expressed through you in a friendly way but without reserve. I feel your acceptance of this mission would be of the greatest benefit to this country." The aged and ailing Pershing was not physically able, however, to accept the appointment, as Pa Watson had quickly concluded during a personal visit to the general, a visit made as the President's emissary. Roosevelt, learning of this, and that Pershing was writing him a letter saying so, now at once turned to his second choice, Admiral William D. Leahy, whose long, distinguished, and remarkably varied naval career had been crowned by his appointment as chief of naval operations in 1937, a post he had relinquished upon reaching the mandatory retirement age of sixty-four in 1939. Leahy was now serving in San Juan as governor of Puerto Rico. To him there went a Roosevelt radiogram (November 16, 1940) saying: "I feel you are the best man available for this mission. You can talk to General Pétain in language which he would understand and the position you have held in our own Navy would undoubtedly give you great influence with the higher officers of the French Navy who are now openly hostile to Great Britain." Simultaneously, Undersecretary of State Sumner Welles was instructed to ask the Vichy French ambassador in Washington, Gaston Henry-Haye, to inquire whether Leahy was acceptable to the Vichy government.[15]

Nevertheless, in conversation with Bullitt in the afternoon of this same Saturday, Roosevelt reiterated that Bullitt, though he was to go on holiday until mid-December, yet remained the ambassador to France and would so continue, news that Bullitt promptly released to reporters who were besieging him for news. This fact became a huge personal embarrassment to him a few hours later when he learned, accidentally, that Leahy was slated to replace him. In high dudgeon he phoned the President to protest. Roosevelt was all apologies; the mix-up was all his fault. He had, during their conversation of a few hours ago ("believe it or not, Bill"), simply forgotten that he had initiated the move toward Leahy ("I forgot about the whole business completely!"). In any case Bullitt was still the ambassador and would remain so until after "we hear from France," and why couldn't he just say that to the press, if the reporters came back to him? Something of Roosevelt's weariness, his sense of being lost in a fog of weariness while events overwhelmed him, must have crept into his voice, for when he asked "Bill" in a pleading tone to "let it go . . . for the time being," *please,* Bullitt relented.

"Well, my dear fellow, I don't hold anything against you for it," he said. "I never held anything against you in my life. . . . I understand how it happened. Good-bye and God bless you."[16]

II

HE was still too tired a man, evidently, to make fresh starts or any bold decisive
attack upon the other problems that grew daily more numerous, grave, and urgent.

There was, for instance (a most important instance) the problem of industrial
mobilization and the obvious failure of the National Defense Advisory Commission to deal adequately with it. Not only did the NDAC have no administrative head, it also lacked a clearly defined administrative authority or precisely
defined goals. Almost everything about it was vague and ambiguous save the
fact that it operated wholly as an agency of the White House and could do nothing in the way of final policy making or execution save in consultation with the
President. And the President, with the multitude of other vital concerns pressing
constantly, increasingly, upon him, was lacking, especially at that time, in the
energy and time needed to exercise effectively this particular authority. The immediate need for drastic changes in the defense-production setup was clear to all
the knowledgeable, and more and more voices called more and more loudly for
the establishment of a single agency on the order of the War Industries Board
that Bernard Baruch had headed during World War I—an agency having authority over government purchases as well as authority to establish price guidelines and enforce priorities of industrial production and distribution. The nearest
approach to this that had been thus far made was Roosevelt's establishment
within the NDAC, on October 21, 1940, of a Priorities Board headed by Donald M. Nelson, a former executive vice president of Sears, Roebuck & Co. who
since May had served Morgenthau as Treasury's director of procurement. This
was a short step indeed toward what needed doing; the demand for a wide and
final step was increasingly insistent. In popular parlance, the call was for a "production czar" to whom would be delegated the bulk of the ultimate administrative power now exercised in this field, to the extent that it was exercised at all,
by the President.

To this call, Roosevelt had turned and continued to turn an ear deafened, said
his enemies, by his clamorous lust for personal power, his loud insistence upon
being himself the "czar" of everything. Actually, the root of his inaction was
simple indecision. And at the root of his indecision was a deeper, wider, more
selfless concern than animated most of his severest critics. He would have done
at that moment what he himself felt he would probably have to do (substantially) in the end, if only he could have figured out how to do it without placing
at fatal risk those social gains of the New Deal that, in last May's national defense fireside chat, he had described as part and parcel of the human freedoms
we sought to defend. The term *czar* was, in this connection, anathema to him: it
smacked of the very totalitarianism against which we armed ourselves; and
he was acutely aware that those who called most loudly for such "czardom"

counted upon its being, or were not averse to its becoming, a big-business domination of America.

Equally indecisive or procrastinative, for reasons less clear but certainly causally linked to the reiterated campaign promise that America would become involved in no "foreign war," was Roosevelt's dealing with fundamental questions of grand military strategy. These questions were, of course, intimately intertwined with the problems of industrial mobilization insofar as military strategy dictated the kinds and amounts of war goods that must be produced— and they were questions to which only the President as commander in chief could provide ultimate definite answers. . . .

On the morning of June 17, 1940, the day France fell, General Marshall had assembled the key members of his staff to discuss the following (his phrasing): "Are we not forced into a question of reframing our naval policy, that is, purely defensive action in the Pacific, with the main effort on the Atlantic side? [At that moment, as we know, America's naval power was concentrated in the Pacific.] We have to be prepared for the worst situation that may develop, that is, if we do not have the Allied fleet in the Atlantic."[17]

The military strategy thus indicated had evolved through a long series of contingency plans developed during the 1920s and 1930s by a Joint Planning Committee of army and navy officers operating under a Joint Board of the Army and Navy, which was then, and in 1940 yet remained, the agency of cooperation between the army and the navy "at the highest level" (it was much too loose and incoherent a cooperation, as tragic events would soon prove). First had come a series of so-called Color Plans of which ORANGE received the greatest attention, being based on the assumption that Japan would be the U.S. enemy and that the war would be fought without allies on either side. But one of the plans, RED-ORANGE, had dealt with the highly unlikely possibility of an alliance of Great Britain (RED) and Japan (ORANGE) against the United States, forcing upon the latter a two-ocean naval war. In that case, said the RED-ORANGE planners, the United States should assume a defensive posture in the Pacific and "concentrate on obtaining a favorable decision in the Atlantic"—this because Great Britain was the stronger power of the two and the American Northeast, where was concentrated a major portion of American industrial might, was of all American areas the most vulnerable to British invasion. Moreover, it was "not unreasonable to hope" that the defeat of RED would "induce ORANGE to yield rather than face a war carried to the Western Pacific," the planners concluded. Which is to say that RED-ORANGE provided the model for the thinking about two-ocean defensive-offensive warfare that the Joint Planning Committee had to do when, in 1938, it was moved to consider what United States strategy should be if this country's interests were threatened simultaneously by Japanese aggressions in Southeast Asia and German and Italian aggressions in Europe. From this thinking issued five so-called Rainbow plans (actually recommended plans; none was formally adopted), of which Rainbow-5 had to do with a war alliance of the United States, Britain, and France against an alliance of Germany, Italy, and Japan. Rainbow-5 proposed a defensive stance by the United States in the Pacific while American troops were sent across the Atlantic to Africa or Europe or both "to effect the decisive defeat of Germany, Italy, or both," this to be followed, if Japan did not then yield, by a major offensive across the Pacific. But when France fell, American strategic planning emphasis shifted from Rainbow-5 to Rainbow-4, a recommended plan based on the assumption that the United States stood alone against Japan, Germany, and Italy and must therefore defend the whole of the Western Hemisphere against possibly simultaneous attacks across both the Pacific and the Atlantic.

It was this shift in strategic thinking that Marshall was voicing in his staff meeting of June 17.

To Brigadier General George V. Strong, chief of the War Plans Division (WPD) of the general staff, was assigned the task of estimating the relative probabilities of various moves the Axis powers might now make. The result was a lengthy memorandum, dated September 25, 1940. In it, the possibility that Hitler would directly attack the United States while Britain remained unconquered was deemed remote, and the likelihood of a Nazi invasion of Britain was deemed less with every day of its postponement; but in proportion to the latter's reduction was an increase in the danger to the Strait of Gibraltar from a Nazi move through a cooperative Spain, this in conjunction with Nazi occupation of French North Africa—also in the danger to the Suez Canal from Italian attacks eastward and northward from her North African possessions. If Spain and Portugal became effectively a part of the Axis coalition, the Atlantic islands of these two countries would become bases from which Anglo-American command of the Atlantic could be seriously challenged (the Canaries, owned by Spain, and especially the Azores, owned by Portugal, assumed great strategic importance) and a way opened for aerial attack upon, followed by Axis penetration of, northeast Brazil. This last was (to repeat) highly improbable unless or until the British fleet was withdrawn from the Atlantic in consequence of a British surrender, and it was believed that as much as a year might intervene between the British fleet's withdrawal and a serious Axis drive upon South America. But the latter event could occur much sooner than that if Britain's collapse coincided with, or was immediately followed by, a Japanese attack upon the United States.

This Strong memorandum, as it was promptly dubbed, was intended for the guidance of the President and his chief advisers. There is, however, considerable doubt that Roosevelt, then entering the closing weeks of a close-fought election campaign, even read it. Certainly he made no active response to it.

Nor did he react to the memorandum that was drafted by navy planners working with and under the orders of Admiral Stark. Signed by Stark and addressed to Secretary of the Navy Knox on November 12, 1940, the memo, with concurring commentary by Stimson and Marshall, was in Roosevelt's hands a few days later. It was an analysis of the war situation as it affected American security following the Royal Air Force's success in the Battle of Britain. It stressed at the outset that "if Britain wins decisively against Germany we could win everywhere; but . . . if she loses the problem confronting us would be very great; and while we might not *lose everywhere,* we might, possibly, not *win* anywhere." The memo then stated in question-and-answer form four alternative courses of action, listed alphabetically A to D, which might be pursued by the United States if forced into the war. The last of these (paragraph "Dog" in naval parlance) was phrased: "Shall we direct our efforts toward an eventual strong offensive in the Atlantic as an ally of the British, and a defensive in the Pacific?" To this, the memo's answer was an emphatic "yes"; and it went on to urge that Plan Dog, as this strategy was at once named, be worked out jointly by the army and navy on the basis of a "clear understanding between the nations involved as to the strength and extent of the participation which may be expected in any particular theater." This last required for its achievement the initiation as soon as possible of staff talks with the British to "reach agreements and lay down plans for promoting unity of Allied effort should the United States find it necessary to enter the war"—staff talks that, for domestic political as well as for military security reasons, must be highly secret. Precisely such secret formal talks had been urged upon the President by British ambassador Lord Lothian, with no perceptible effect, for weeks before Lothian left for England in late October (the ambassador thus tactfully absented himself from the American scene during the closing days of the election campaign). Also, almost simultaneously with his receipt of the memorandum, Roosevelt was informed that Churchill and the British chiefs of staff were in general agreement with it, they having learned of it through Rear Admiral Robert L. Ghormley, who was at the time stationed in London as U.S. liaison officer with the British.[18] Time was of the essence. Yet as November waned, Roosevelt refused to approve in any unequivocal way either Plan Dog or the international staff talks it implied, evidently out of fear that despite all precautions, news of his doing so might leak to the isolationist press and cause a political uproar.

III

ON the weekend before Thanksgiving, trouble of a peculiarly vexatious kind pursued Roosevelt from Washington to Hyde Park, where he went in quest of peace and quiet.

It pursued him in the person of Joseph P. Kennedy.

Indeed, the highly conservative and power-lustful Kennedy had been troublesome if often also importantly useful to Roosevelt almost from the moment he declared his support of Roosevelt for President prior to the Democratic National Convention in 1932. A wealthy man who had become so largely through stock market speculations in the unregulated markets of the 1920s, he had contributed generously to Democratic presidential campaign coffers in 1932 and 1936. An Irish Catholic (from Boston), he had a considerable influence with the Church hierarchy in the United States. His preconvention support of Roosevelt in 1932 had done much to blunt conservative businessmen's attacks upon the candidate as a "dangerous radical." He was a personal friend of chain newspaper publisher William Randolph Hearst's. And it is possible that without his exercise on Roosevelt's behalf of his political potency, a deadlock between the candidacies of Roosevelt and Catholic Al Smith would have resulted in the 1932 presidential nomination of Newton D. Baker. Thus Roosevelt owed Kennedy a sizable political debt, and Kennedy proved a stubbornly insistent creditor. He had been appointed ambassador to Britain partly in payment of this debt, partly because the idea of sending an Irish Catholic (a notably undiplomatic one, at that) to the Court of St. James tickled Roosevelt's fancy, and partly (perhaps mostly) because Roosevelt wanted him out of Washington, where, so Morgenthau was told, he was "too dangerous."[19]

But not long after his arrival in London in late February 1938, Kennedy had proved a greater menace to Roosevelt's foreign policy, insofar as this was a policy of collective security, than he would have been to Roosevelt's domestic policy had he remained in America. He was soon on such intimate terms with the "Cliveden set" of upper-class British appeasers as to be virtually a member of it. He became as warm a personal friend of Neville Chamberlain's as the coldness of the Chamberlain personality permitted. He made speeches and gave press interviews in which advocacy of American isolationism was coupled with pleas for peacemaking "cooperation" between the democracies and dictatorships (he publicly championed the Chamberlain "accommodations" that culminated in the Munich "settlement"). And in private but reported conversations he manifested a disturbingly sympathetic "understanding" of Hitler's approach to the "Jewish problem." Small wonder that he was soon in bad odor with the State Department and uncertain of his standing with the White House. By the late summer of 1940, repeatedly hurt and angered by what he interpreted as snubs and put-downs from Washington, he contemplated resigning his post and permitted the fact to be widely known. Simultaneously, public opinion polls revealed that Willkie was gaining ground upon Roosevelt in the presidential race and that part of the gain was the defection of Catholic votes by the million from the Democrats to the Republicans. Clearly, had Kennedy resigned and then come out for Willkie in these circumstances, as it was rumored he might do (this on the ground that Roosevelt was more likely than Willkie to lead the country into war), Roosevelt's reelection chances would have been greatly diminished, if not wholly eliminated.

It hadn't happened, however.

Instead, in perhaps the most amazing of all of Roosevelt's exercises of personal charm conjoined with political deal making (according to Kennedy's later account, Roosevelt promised to support Joe Kennedy, Jr.'s candidacy for governor of Massachusetts in 1942),[20] the disgruntled ambassador, having returned to this country a week before election day, was persuaded not only to retain his post for the time being, but also to endorse the Roosevelt candidacy in a nationally broadcast radio speech, delivered with great effectiveness on October 29.

The event was not wholly happy for Roosevelt, however, since it placed him again in political debt to Kennedy and so enhanced the latter's capacity to make trouble for him.

The capacity was promptly exercised.

On the morrow of election day, in an interview with Assistant Secretary of State Breckinridge Long, Kennedy exposed the nature of the influence he would exert upon American policy. The British empire was doomed, he said; Hitler was and would remain the master of Europe as Japan was becoming master of the Far East. The U.S. government should therefore "take some steps to implement a realistic policy and make some approach to Germany and Japan which would result in economic collaboration," to quote Long's phrasing of Kennedy's views in the Long diary that evening. Kennedy "thinks that we will have to assume a Fascist form of government here or something similar if we are to survive in a world of concentrated and centralized power," added Long, who was personally more sympathetic to the opinions he now listened to than most other high government officials would have been (as Roosevelt's first ambassador to Italy, Long had been much taken with Mussolini and some aspects of the Fascist regime; his anti-Semitism was more than a match for Kennedy's). Three days later, through a press interview with Louis Lyons of the *Boston Globe,* published on November 10, Kennedy proclaimed his views to the general public. "Democracy is all finished in England," he said. "It may be here. . . . It's the loss of our foreign trade that's going to change our form of government. . . . If we get into war . . . a bureaucracy will take over right off. . . . They tell me that after 1918 we got it all back again, but this is different. There's a different pattern in the world." He had supported Roosevelt in the election, he said, because Roosevelt was "the only man who can control the groups who have to be brought along on what's ahead of us. . . . I mean the have-nots." Amid the storm of angry public protest that these words immediately aroused in both England and the United States, he claimed he had been misquoted and demanded a retraction from the *Globe* (the newspaper would refuse, whereupon Kennedy would cancel thousands of dollars of advertising that had been scheduled for that paper by liquor interests he controlled); but he was not in the slightest deterred from what was evidently, for him, a crusade. On November 13 he was in Hollywood, California, where, during an impromptu speech at a luncheon in his honor, he "threw the fear of God into many of our [movie] producers and executives by telling them that the Jews were on the spot and they should stop making anti-Nazi pictures" or films sympathetic "to the cause of the democracies versus the dictators," as agitated actor Douglas Fairbanks, Jr., wrote in a confidential personal letter to Roosevelt. From Hollywood, Kennedy flew to northern California, where, at a wilderness vacation place owned by publisher Hearst, his forceful expression of his views angered and alarmed his fellow houseguests, John and Anna Roosevelt Boettiger (the latter the President's daughter), both of whom were employed by the Hearst-owned *Seattle* (Washington) *Post-Intelligencer.* A letter went from Boettiger to Roosevelt: "After our talk with Joe in California, both Anna and I were considerably worried by what we thought were Fascist leanings." Returning to New York, Kennedy called upon Herbert Hoover, Roosevelt's political arch-foe who, though not formally a member of the America First Committee, was, next to Lindbergh, the most influential of American isolationists.[21]

A weary and worriedly watching Roosevelt, abundantly warned of his ambassador's machinations, took Kennedy far more seriously as a threat to American freedoms than later historians would generally do. He knew that the "evil forces" that had evidently captured an ambition-distorted Willkie in the last stages of the Republican presidential campaign were by no means crushed or even much cowed by the election's outcome. They could be counted upon to pursue their goals relentlessly. There were plausible rumors that a powerful group of them—big American financiers and industrialists whose concern for their own privileged well-being far outstripped any commitment they might have to democratic values—were organizing a covert campaign to arrange, through the collaborationist government of Vichy, a negotiated peace between Great Britain and Germany. And in all probability, as it appeared to Roosevelt, Kennedy was about to become, if he were not already, an active leader of this enterprise. In such a role, he could be formidable. Though overly impetuous and generally maladroit as a democratic politician, he might well prove superbly equipped for the kind of conspiratorial, fearful, and distrust-breeding politics through which democracies are undermined and the ground prepared for totalitarian dictatorship. He had a charming magnetic personality, great energy, a shrewdly manipulative intelligence, a passionate will to power (his overriding ambition was to found a Kennedy family dynasty), and few scruples. Evidently he was busily gathering into his hands very powerful tools for mass persuasion. Already he "had had an interview with Hearst with a view to starting a campaign for appeasement," as Harold Ickes would soon say in his diary, reporting Roosevelt views, and "has seen, or is about to see, Roy Howard [appeasement-minded head of the Scripps-Howard newspaper chain] and Joe Patterson [appeasement-minded head] of the *New York Daily News* . . . which has the greatest circulation of any newspaper in the country." The *Chicago Tribune* and *Washington Times-Herald* would certainly "go along."[22]

So it was that Roosevelt, having talked with Eleanor about Kennedy's recent activities, wearily told her that "we'd better have him" come to Hyde Park as weekend guest to "see what he has to say." He asked her to invite him. Kennedy of course accepted, was met by Eleanor when his morning train arrived at the Rhinecliff station, was taken by her to the Big House, where he was at once closeted with Roosevelt in Roosevelt's small study off the library living room. Eleanor drove on to her Val Kill cottage a couple of miles away. She had barely arrived there, however, when a phone call summoned her back to the Big House. There, in the study with the door closed behind her (Kennedy had been asked to leave the room for a moment), she found herself alone with a husband whose coldly furious anger, being so rare an interruption of his normally placid temper, was frightening. His face was pale, his voice trembling.

"I never want to see that son of a bitch again as long as I live," he said. "Take his resignation* and get him out of here!"

Eleanor protested: Kennedy had been invited for the weekend, she had guests coming for lunch at her cottage, and the next train for New York did not leave until two o'clock.

"Then you drive him around Hyde Park, give him a sandwich, and put him on that train!" ordered her wrathful husband.

Thus began what Eleanor would remember twenty years later (with considerable exaggeration, in view of her childhood and marital experiences) as "the most dreadful four hours of my life."[23]

But it would be made obvious by subsequent events—indeed, it was evident at the time from Kennedy's unabashed demeanor, his continued frank expression of his foreign policy views, during his hours with Eleanor—that Roosevelt, with what must have been in his weary condition a stupendous effort of self-control joined with a phenomenal exercise of his role-playing talent, had given his guest no inkling of how he felt. His outburst to Eleanor was but an explosive release of the inner tensions this effort had involved; it did not mark a final break between himself and Joseph Patrick Kennedy—and Eleanor, with her intimate knowledge of her husband, almost certainly suspected at the time that this was the case. Roosevelt as President dare not, in the present circumstances, risk making Kennedy an open avowed enemy—or so Roosevelt felt. His concern must be to keep Kennedy "sweet" but off balance, a man uncertain of his standing with the White House but still hopeful of future appointment to a high government post. When the ambassador submitted his resignation to Roosevelt in a personal interview on December 1, Roosevelt, though he accepted it promptly, spoke with a disarming seeming frankness, as to a warm personal friend, of the complexities of the problems he faced, the heaviness of the bur-

---

*Evidently Kennedy, at the outset of this interview, had stated emphatically his wish to resign his ambassadorial post at the earliest moment convenient for the President.

dens he must carry as President of the United States, and begged Kennedy to help him by continuing to perform ambassadorial functions until a new ambassador could be named. Kennedy agreed to do so. The interview was wholly amicable. Immediately following it, Kennedy told White House reporters that "the President was good enough to express regret over my decision." He promptly added words, however, that might well have caused Roosevelt to wonder if a clean public break between the two of them might not have been preferable to the prevailing anomaly. Said Kennedy: "My plan is, after a short holiday, to devote my efforts to what seems to me the greatest cause in the world—and means, if successful, the preservation of the American form of democracy. That cause is to help the President keep the United States out of war."[24]

IV

MEANWHILE there mounted to a culmination the financial crisis whose essence was the continuing drain upon, the rapid diminution of, Britain's ability to pay in dollars for the American aid she so desperately needed. Relations between London and Washington were increasingly secretly strained by London's reluctance, if not inability, to provide the precise financial data that Washington demanded, and by Washington's consequent wishful reluctance to believe that Britain's financial situation was as dire as London claimed. We have noted Roosevelt's remark to his cabinet on November 8 that Britain still had, in his belief, some $2.5 billion in American credits and assets that could be quickly converted into dollars—enough to cover months more of British purchases. It was perhaps a rumor of this remark, coupled with a wish to block any administrative proposal of massive credit extensions to Great Britain, that caused North Dakota's isolationist and Anglophobic Senator Gerald P. Nye to introduce in the Senate, four days later, a resolution calling for a congressional investigation to determine how much property in the United States, real and otherwise, was owned by Britain and the British empire. This isolationist effort was bound to fail, of course; the resolution, promptly assigned to the Senate Foreign Relations Committee, was certain to die in committee; but it provided another encouragement of administration procrastination. And when London told Washington, though without public announcement at the time, that the British government was sending to the United States, in December, Sir Frederick Phillips of the British Treasury to discuss Britain's financial situation, White House postponement of decisive action was further encouraged. Presumably Sir Frederick would come armed with the full and precise information that was needed as a basis for American action; until he arrived, therefore, action *must* be postponed. In a personal letter to King George VI, on November 22, 1940, Roosevelt revealed his fearful distrust of the legislative process when dealing with matters of this kind. Had he gone to Congress with a proposal to give overage U.S. destroyers to Britain last summer, he wrote, as "legalists" demanded he do, the proposal "would still be in the tender care of the Committees of the Congress."[25] The remark indicates that if he were not still casting around at that time for some way to accomplish his purpose without going to Congress, he was determined not to go until he had in hand some means that was virtually certain of being congressionally approved.

But on the day following his writing to the King, his procrastinating hand was forced by the normally smoothly diplomatic Lord Lothian.

The British ambassador returned to America from lengthy and far-reaching consultations with Churchill and Sir Kingsley Wood, the chancellor of the exchequer, during which it had been decided, at Lothian's urging, that Churchill should write a lengthy personal letter to the President setting forth in the frankest terms the present British predicament and forecasting, from the Prime Minister's point of view, the main thrust of events through the coming year. ("I am writing you a very long letter on the outlook for 1941, which Lord Lothian will give you in a few days," telegraphed Churchill to Roosevelt on November 16.) The essential body of this letter had actually been composed by Churchill, in consultation with Lothian, by the time the ambassador boarded his return plane. But, as Churchill explains in his memoirs, "the document had to be checked and rechecked by the Chiefs of Staff and the Treasury, and approved by the War Cabinet"—a time-consuming process. Hence it remained unsent when Lothian, immediately upon landing at LaGuardia Airport in New York City on November 23, perpetrated what his biographer characterizes as a "calculated indiscretion." Cheerily greeting the newsmen who awaited him, he said bluntly: "Well, boys, Britain's broke; it's your money we want." He repeated the statement in effect before newsreel cameras a few minutes later, then refused to elaborate upon it. How was the needed money to be obtained? he was asked. Wouldn't the Johnson Act and the Neutrality Act have to be repealed? The ambassador wouldn't say, couldn't say. Americans must answer such questions. He could only reiterate that Britain, to continue fighting, would have to have massive American financial aid in the very near future, adding (his was effectively the first public announcement of the fact) that Sir Frederick Phillips of the British Treasury was coming to the United States in early December to discuss ways and means with American officials.[26]

These decidedly undiplomatic remarks were reported under big front-page headlines in papers all across the country. They shocked an American public that had had no idea Britain's financial plight was so dire. They angered Roosevelt, who always resented and stubbornly resisted perceived attempts to force him and who in his present weary state was more than normally inclined to do so. He was, moreover, sure the Lothian statement gave into the hands of congressional isolationists ammunition that could gravely, if not fatally, wound the aid program. He received the ambassador coldly when the two conferred at length on November 25, telling him that the request for financial help was "premature" and would remain so until the American public was thoroughly convinced that the British had liquidated their liquifiable assets in the Western Hemisphere, assets he estimated to total over $9 billion. (At his press conference immediately following this interview Roosevelt was asked if the ambassador had presented "specific requests for additional help." He replied: ". . . [N]othing was mentioned in that regard at all, not one single thing—ships or sealing wax or anything else." Within a day or so thereafter, Hans Thomsen of the German embassy cabled to Berlin: "I have learned from a reliable source that Roosevelt, in his long conversation with Lothian . . . , made no secret of his annoyance over the British propaganda pressure. He did not wish to be put under pressure by the English. He had assured the American people that he would not lead them into war and he intended to keep his word.")[27] Morgenthau, too, was angered; he told Lothian with some heat that the latter's words exposed him, Morgenthau, personally to serious danger as he perforce went ahead with the aid program. "If Senator Nye or any other [isolationist] senator called me on the Hill," said the Treasury secretary, "they would say, 'Well, on such and such a date Ambassador Lothian said the English were running short of money. By what authority did you let them place additional orders in this country?' "[28] Finally, the ambassador was reprimanded by the Prime Minister—conclusive evidence that Lothian's "calculated indiscretion" was wholly his and as surprising to London as to Washington. Churchill cabled Lothian on November 27: "I do not think it was wise to touch on very serious matters in a newspaper interview to reporters on the landing stage. . . . The Chancellor of the Exchequer complains that he was not consulted about your financial statements and Treasury does not like their form. While it is generally understood that you were referring wholly to dollar credits, actual words attributed to you give only too much foundation for German propaganda that we are coming to the end of our resources." Lothian, though evidently greatly depressed by this chastisement, remained unrepentant. In a message to London he revealed, defensively if not defiantly, his motives for acting as he had. The Americans, he said (and clearly he referred especially to Roosevelt), were "saturated with illusions that we have vast [dollar] resources available that we have not yet disclosed and that we ought to empty this vast hypothetical barrel before we ask for assistance."[29] It was absolutely necessary that they be stripped, promptly, of these illusions.

And it must be said that Lothian's airport interview did do what he intended: it jarred into action a White House that was at that moment extremely reluctant to act; it initiated "the beginning of the end of . . . [Roosevelt's] postelection slump," as William L. Langer and S. Everett Gleason have written.[30] Morgenthau, for all his temporary personal annoyance with Lothian, was moved to disabuse Roosevelt of the notion that the British could raise anywhere near $9 billion on her Western Hemispheric properties. Great Britain and the British empire had in foreign assets *over the world as a whole* approximately $9.5 billion, according to Treasury Department calculations; Britain's dollar deficit between November 1, 1940, and June 30, 1941, would total, it was estimated, something over $2.1 billion; and even if Britain managed to liquidate the whole of her dollar resources, she would be about $70 million in arrears at the end of the fiscal year. Much, indeed most, of the wealth of the British empire, though its value could be (and was) estimated in dollars, could not be converted into ready cash, Morgenthau pointed out; these possessions were immediately useful only as collateral for cash loans; and even as collateral their dollar utility was severely limited.[31] Hence the British were indeed running out of dollars, and very rapidly, as Lothian had so undiplomatically publicly disclosed. The President was forced to the conclusion that Stimson, Knox, Morgenthau, and others had reached weeks ago and that the war secretary especially had been pressing upon him ever since, namely, that on this matter he had stretched to its limit, if not beyond, the Executive's authority to operate without the specific approval of the Legislature. He must now go to Congress with any further proposal for doing what the situation demanded he do. *How* he should go, in what way he could go that would assure success, was now the only question.

And while he sought an answer to it he refused to slow in the slightest, he instead moved to increase, the flow of American supplies to Britain. With the boldness he had manifest several times before, reasserting leadership after lengthy passive periods in the face of crisis, he encouraged the British to go full speed ahead with matériel orders they had proclaimed they could never pay for. It was as if he literally took himself in hand, lifting himself—for the moment, at least—out of a morass. In a December 1 (Sunday) meeting with Morgenthau, he approved the orders from London for ships, airplanes, and munitions totaling $2.1 billion—orders the filling of which would require $700 million of an American plant expansion that could not possibly, in the prevailing circumstances, be privately financed. Government funding was required. Moreover, he devised an intricate, devious interim plan for the fulfillment of these orders and put it into handwritten shorthand language at Morgenthau's insistence (experience had taught the Treasury secretary not to rely too heavily on exclusively oral presidential instructions). In an initialed note at the bottom of the memo Treasury had prepared for him he wrote: "Planes, munitions, use . . . R.F.C. [Reconstruction Finance Corporation] funds for plant capital on United States orders," meaning that the American government would place the orders for what Britain needed, the RFC would finance the plant expansion required to fill these orders, and the British would pay upon delivery the cost of manufacture plus, as a surcharge, a proportionate share of the cost of plant expansion.[32] His justification of this, his defense of it against political attack, was that the resultant expanded plant was needed as standby; it would soon be manufacturing war goods for the vastly expanded U.S. armed forces to which the government was now committed.

A delighted Morgenthau, returning to his office, at once phoned Stimson to report what the President had done, whereupon Stimson told Morgenthau of a similarly heartening conversation he himself had just had with the President. In it, Roosevelt had expressed total dissatisfaction with current methods of getting aid to Britain. "We have just got to decide what we are going to do for England," Roosevelt had said, according to Stimson, indicating a realization that no finally effective decision had yet been made. "Doing it this way is not doing anything."[33]

The effect was that of a dam's being breached. Within forty-eight hours a new, growing, energizing wave of expectation was spreading from the White House through all the key administrative offices of the government and from these into the halls of Congress. There were excited meetings of key administration figures on December 3. In them, Stimson and Knox boldly asserted what others had dared barely whisper, namely, that U.S. destroyers must be used, inevitably and soon, to convoy supply ships across the Atlantic; Stettinius and Knudson agreed to use the upcoming annual meeting of the American Manufacturers' Association to stir into action the yet asleep "business people of the country"; and a reluctant Jesse Jones was moved toward provision of the RFC money ($700 million) for plant expansion that Roosevelt, with dubious legitimacy in the absence of congressional authorization, had called for in his meeting with Morgenthau. Jones, however, insisted that though the RFC could finance new plant construction for the War Department, it could not do so for Britain unless Congress clearly specifically approved. The conferees then unanimously agreed that the Executive must go *at once* to Congress, if the immense increase of aid to Britain that the situation demanded was to be achieved in time.[34]

Everyone assumed the immediate impendence of a historic White House legislative proposal, a proposal bound to raise a storm of controversy. . . .

V

IT therefore surprised and dismayed nearly all British officials and not a few American ones when Franklin Roosevelt, on this same Wednesday, December 3, left Washington for a two-week vacation. In blithe, seemingly utter disregard of time pressures, he embarked on the USS *Tuscaloosa,* the heavy cruiser on which he had vacationed for ten days immediately before Hitler's invasion of Poland last year. Its admiral's cabin (the *Tuscaloosa* was a flagship) remained prepared for his occupancy: the six-inch coaming at the doorway of the bathroom had been removed to permit access by his wheelchair, holding bars had been installed beside shower and water closet, and a wide comfortable bed invited the hours of deep sleep he so greatly needed. In 1939 he had cruised in northern waters to escape Washington's summer heat; he now headed in the opposite direction, away from the oncoming Washington winter into the warmth and sunlight of the Caribbean, where, Steve Early announced, he was to inspect bases acquired from Great Britain in last summer's destroyers-bases deal. He himself indicated to associates that he intended a working vacation, and he did take working papers with him—bundles of correspondence; notes for a major foreign policy speech that, he told Ickes, he planned soon to deliver.[35] But he took with him no working colleagues, only men he could easily relax with— three members of his immediate official staff (Pa Watson, personal physician Ross T. McIntire, naval aide Captain Daniel Callaghan) and, of course, Harry Hopkins, plus three press association representatives.

These last, whom he kept at a distance for the most part, were able to report some activity of a vaguely official nature during this fortnight at sea. British colonial officials came aboard ship with their wives at Jamaica, St. Lucia, and Antigua to lunch with the President. The Duke of Windsor, newly appointed governor-general of the Bahamas, came aboard at Eleuthera Island (the Duchess of Windsor was in the hospital in Miami, having just undergone major surgery; it was from Miami that the duke flew to Eleuthera). At Martinique the French aircraft carrier *Bearn* was anchored in the harbor of Fort-de-France with a hundred American planes still aboard her, the ship having been ordered there by Admiral Darlan when France fell; and off Martinique the President conferred at some length in the admiral's cabin with the U.S. consul and the naval observer stationed on that strategic island. (The conference was serious: Martinique, in the wavering hands of Vichy France, with the *Bearn* in its harbor and some twelve billion francs [$245 million] of gold bullion in her bank vaults [it had been transferred there from Quebec when France surrendered], presented a potentially grave threat to the approaches to the Panama Canal.) Otherwise, save for the perusal of mail and the signing of state documents delivered to the *Tuscaloosa* by navy seaplane at scheduled intervals, the President, within the sight or hearing of the newsmen, did precious little that could be called "work."

He did some desultory fishing, with little success. At night he played poker and watched movies, among them *Northwest Mounted Police,* starring Gary Cooper, Paulette Goddard, and Madeleine Carroll; *I Love You Again,* with William Powell and Myrna Loy; *They Knew What They Wanted,* with Carole Lombard and Charles Laughton; and *Tin Pan Alley,* with Alice Faye and Betty Grable.[36] There was much bantering talk and socializing. Those critical ones who watched and waited in Washington, had they been able to observe through eye and ear their President's trivial pursuits, would have been the opposite of reassured.

They would have been reassured, however, had they known what went on in Roosevelt's "well-forested interior" during his solitary hours aboard this cruiser—and he was alone by choice through a good part of each day, in his cabin or on deck in his wheelchair or deck chair, reading, dozing, smoking cigarettes, often merely gazing silently far across placid waters (the sea was generally calm in brilliant sunlight) to the faint line where the enormous seascape and yet more enormous skyscape came together.

For the effect of these long hours of restful solitude was to bestow upon this vacation cruise a historic importance insofar as it became, for the President of the United States, a voyage of self-renewal, even of self-discovery. He pulled himself together, or (to put it perhaps more accurately) was enabled by bright sunlight and forced by weariness to relax at long last into his natural shape. There was a personal renaissance. Empty space was all around him. The feel of distance was in the warm wind that fanned his tanning cheek. There was a heal-ing, cleansing tang in the salt air he sucked deep into his nicotine-tortured lungs. And as the days passed, lengthened in his experience of them by the unwonted peace and quiet, there passed also, draining away, the aching tiredness that, long in its making, had remained longer with him as a fog upon his mind and a dull weight upon his spirit than any other he had suffered since entering the White House. Resilience returned to him. Zestfulness returned to him. The dark future, brightening in his vision of it, was transformed from an overwhelming threat into a stirring challenge—and as of yore, his spirit rose to meet it.

On the morning of December 9, the seaplane mail delivery to the *Tuscaloosa* included the "very long letter" Churchill had told Roosevelt, more than three weeks before, that he was writing. It was indeed long, ten typewritten pages to-taling some four thousand words, and it was as boldly frank as it was lengthy.

"The form which the war has taken and seems likely to hold does not enable us to match the immense armies of Germany in any theater where their main power can be brought to bear," it said. "We can however by the use of sea power and air power meet the German armies in the regions where only comparatively small forces can be brought into action." For this purpose, and for island de-fense against invasion, "we are forming as fast as possible . . . between fifty and sixty divisions." Clearly, the "danger of Great Britain being destroyed by a swift overwhelming blow has for the time being greatly receded." But "[i]n its place there is a long, gradually maturing danger, less sudden and less spectacular but equally deadly." This "mortal danger" was "the steady and increasing diminu-tion of sea tonnage" consequent upon Nazi submarine, air, and warship attacks—a diminution that, should it continue, could cause Britain to "fall by the way" before the United States had time "to complete her defensive preparations." The annual tonnage of goods that must be imported "in order to maintain our war ef-fort at full strength" was 43 million, but in September imports were at a rate of only 37 million per annum. In October they were at a rate of 38 million tons per annum. "Were the diminution to continue at this rate it would be fatal, unless in-deed immensely greater replenishment than anything at present in sight could be achieved in time." (In Washington a few days later, Admiral Stark told the secretaries of state, war, and navy and General Marshall that at the current rate of her shipping losses Britain could not survive more than six months.) Hence the urgent need to increase both "the naval forces which cope with attacks" in the Atlantic and "the number of merchant ships" there. As regards the former, Churchill suggested alternative courses of possible action by the United States. *One* was "the reassertion . . . of the doctrine of the freedom of the seas"—that is, the freedom "to trade with countries against which there is not an effective legal blockade" and to protect such trade with "escorting battleships, cruisers, destroyers and air flotillas." This involved a risk that Germany would declare war upon the United States, but the risk was slight in Churchill's view since Hitler "does not wish to be drawn into a war with the United States until he has gravely undermined the power of Great Britain. His maxim is 'one at a time.' " The *alternative* was "the gift, loan or supply of a large number of American vessels of war, above all destroyers," coupled with the extension of U.S. "sea control over the American side of the Atlantic, so as to prevent molestation by enemy vessels of the approaches to the new line of naval and air bases which the United States is establishing in British Islands in the Western Hemisphere." Churchill also asked for heavy and continuous U.S. pressures upon the government of Eire "to procure for Great Britain the necessary facilities upon the southern and western shores of Eire for our flotillas, and still more important, for our aircraft working westward into the Atlantic." And as regards aircraft, Britain needed far more of them than she could obtain from her own plane-production capacity, even after this was increased to the maximum possible. To achieve "the massive preponderance in the air on which we must rely to loosen and disintegrate the German grip on Europe . . . we shall need the greatest production of aircraft which the United States . . . are capable of sending us. . . . May I invite you then, Mr. President, to give earnest consideration to an immediate order on joint account for a further 2,000 combat aircraft a month? Of these . . . the highest possible proportion should be heavy bombers, the weapon on which above all others we depend to shatter the foundations of German military power."

In closing, Churchill turned "to the question of finance," stating the British case with a forceful candor whose employment must have caused him some trepidation (he risked the displeasure of the man he sought to persuade) insofar as it challenged on moral grounds the position Roosevelt had thus far taken on this matter. "The more rapid and abundant the flow of munitions and ships which you are able to send us, the sooner will our dollar resources be exhausted," he wrote. ". . . Indeed, as you know, orders already placed or under negotiation . . . many times exceed the total exchange resources remaining at the disposal of Great Britain. . . . While we will do our utmost and shrink from no proper sacrifice . . . , I believe that you will agree that it would be wrong in principle and mutually disadvantageous in effect if, at the height of the struggle, Great Britain were to be divested of all saleable assets so that after victory was won with our blood, civilization saved and time gained for the United States to be fully armed . . . , we should stand stripped to the bone. . . . If, as I believe, you are convinced, Mr. President, that the defeat of the Nazi and Fascist tyranny is a matter of high consequence to the people of the United States and the Western Hemisphere, you will regard this letter not as an appeal for aid, but as a statement of the minimum action necessary to the achievement of our common purpose."[37]

The letter had upon Roosevelt a chastening as well as stimulating effect—an effect that was heightened three mornings later (December 12) when he learned that Lord Lothian, with whom he had formed a warm personal friendship but who had suffered his wrath during their last important meeting, had died the night before, suddenly, unexpectedly. (The cause of death was uremic poisoning; a fervent Christian Scientist, Lothian had refused to consult a medical doctor when his fatal illness came upon him.) Nor was it only the news of this death that stung Roosevelt, making him smart, at least a little, with a species of remorse; it was also the British ambassador's last public words, spoken for him, while he lay dying, by the first secretary of the British embassy, Neville Butler. Their immediate audience was a convention of the American Farm Bureau Federation in Baltimore; but it was to all Americans that Lothian spoke when he eloquently stressed the vital stake that the United States had in British victory and that this victory was assured (he phrased this last in words of utter confidence, boldly challenging the noisy defeatism of the isolationists), provided only that Britain received *now* the unstinted American aid that the current situation demanded.[38] The words echoed those of Churchill's letter, which Lothian had helped to compose, and by clear implication they joined with Churchill's to condemn as factually incorrect and morally callous the attitudes and opinions regarding Britain's dollar problem that Roosevelt had been expressing during the last several weeks in cabinet meetings and personal interviews.

At once, Roosevelt dispatched through the State Department a message to King George VI expressing his shock and grief at this abrupt loss of a personal friend who was also America's great friend; and barely had he done so than he received a message from Churchill describing Lothian as "our greatest ambassador to the United States. . . . We have lost a good friend and high interpreter."[39] Into both Churchill's and Roosevelt's minds now loomed the question of Lothian's replacement—a difficult question that would require much thought, for the now lost diplomat seemed at the moment, to both Prime Minister and President, virtually irreplaceable.

But by this time—indeed, even before he learned of Lothian's death—Roosevelt had revealed to Harry Hopkins a decision, along with a way of implementing it, whose mere public announcement, when he made it, would compensate for his earlier sins of passivity, of procrastination, with regard to this matter. . . .

During the two days following his receipt of the Churchill letter he spent a more than usual number of quiet, solitary hours on the *Tuscaloosa*'s deck, seated in a spot shielded from the wind. He had the Churchill letter always at hand, and sometimes he glanced at it or reread portions of it. But for the most part he simply sat there, his unseeing gaze sweeping the gently waved sea to the far horizon while his mind worked over his problem or, as one may say with equal accuracy, was worked upon *by* his problem. For his mind did not move along straight logical lines; it was instead moved in feeling, brooding ways over a jumble of personal memories, past sensations, and ideas that had long lain dormant within him, unconnected with one another. He remembered the smug certainty with which New York bankers and brokers, at the outbreak of the First World War, had predicted its early end—remembered specifically a group of them doing so in a parlor car of the *Bar Harbor Express* on which he rode southward from Ellsworth, Maine, toward New York in early August 1914. The war could not last more than three months, they had said flatly. Why? Because there was "not enough money in the world" to finance a conflict of these dimensions for more than three months. He remembered the equally smug if outraged certainty with which much of the American banking community had predicted the end of the civilized world if he dared take the United States off the gold standard. He mentally contemplated Adolf Hitler's utter disregard of money, or of Germany's lack of it, as an obstacle to his world-conquering ambition—contemplated Nazi Germany's substitution of a barter system for money transactions as she engaged in a very substantial international trade. He recalled a simile-metaphor Harold Ickes had used in a letter to him last August 2 in support of the destroyers deal. "It seems to me that we Americans are like the householder who refuses to lend or sell his fire extinguishers to help put out the fire in a house that is right next door," Ickes had written, "although that house is all ablaze and the wind is blowing from that direction." There rose up with renewed force and extended meaning his own notion of building cargo ships in American shipyards and leasing them to Britain—an action for which legal basis already existed, according to Treasury lawyer Oscar S. Cox: an 1892 statute authorized the secretary of war to lease army property for a period not longer than five years "when in his discretion it will be for the public good." Surely, then, this leasing device was a feasible one. And why should it be limited to cargo ships? Why not extend it to *all* munitions, *all* war matériel? Finally, if the leasing device were combined with the lending device—the lending of *things,* not money—might not the combine be an overall solution to the problem? Thus, gradually, the blur of impressions, memories, and ideas in his mind achieved a focus, assumed a logical form. And in the evening of the second day after the Churchill letter was received (that is, on the evening of December 11), as Hopkins later recalled, "he suddenly came out with it—the whole program. He didn't seem to have any clear idea how it could be done legally. But there wasn't any doubt in his mind that he'd find a way to do it."[40]

Nor was it only this specific problem that he brooded over during these hours of rare quiet and solitude. For it was impossible for him to do in this case what his collector's mind inclined him to do, namely, isolate the problem from all that surrounded it and then deal with it as a self-sufficient entity, exclusive of all else. Realism, his acute sense of objective realities, opposed this. He must deal with the problem contextually. He must see it (feel it) as an element of his over-all problem—handle it, not as a solid hard-bounded item, but as a fluid aspect of a flowing organic whole. And as he brooded over it in this way, he saw (felt) more clearly than ever before the way that he should go as President into a dark, flame-shot future wherein the Republic was threatened from the outside, as never before, with violent total extinction. He achieved a firmer mental grasp than ever before upon basic premises, upon underlying principles, and was con-firmed in (but with a greater understanding of) the general strategy, the overall strategical concept, that had been developed under the impact of events abroad and had increasingly guided the whole of his presidential endeavor through the last twelve months, despite his departures from it (forced departures, in his view) during his reelection campaign. If Great Britain and the British Com-monwealth were destroyed by the Nazi-Fascists, the world would be dominated by the endlessly aggressive present masters of Germany, Italy, and Japan. In such a world the American democracy and the human freedoms for which it stood could not long survive. Hence the preservation of the American democ-racy, and of the very idea of human freedom, required the destruction of Adolf Hitler, of Nazi-fascism, and, if less certainly, of Japan as an aggressive military power. Very probably, indeed almost certainly, this would require the United States to enter the war as an ally of Britain within a year or two. But such entry would lead to the kind of total victory that was necessary only if it were a full-scale entry by a truly *united* United States—an America prepared, materially and psychologically, to wage total war and also, after military victory was won, to join with other nations in international organization whereby peace could be assured throughout the world. Roosevelt's great fear was that war would be forced upon an America that remained deeply divided ideologically and in eco-nomic interest. His task as President, therefore, had similarities to that of Abra-ham Lincoln during the Civil War—the task of uniting the American people (the achievement of union) while at the same time making swift adequate active re-sponses to immediate individual challenges and presiding over the greatest mili-tary preparedness campaign in the nation's history. He must strive to make of himself the very personification of the kind of active American union that was vitally necessary, stressing the positive (all that made for union) while shun-ning, to the maximum possible degree, divisive words and deeds. He must encourage the pressures upon him to do what he knew must be done while dis-couraging the forces of isolationism, but without directly attacking those forces in ways that would increase their popular support. He must make upon the public mind a personal impression that was, overall, self-contradictory, being that of a strong, bold leader who is pushed, forced by circumstances, into actions he is reluctant to take. Above all, he must avoid like the plague what he saw as Woodrow Wilson's great mistake, especially in 1919, of going too far too fast in pursuit of his goals, outstripping his public support.

The *Tuscaloosa* had by now turned around and headed northward, toward Charleston, South Carolina, where Roosevelt was to debark; and official Washington, stirred by the import of the Churchill letter (a copy of it had gone to Morgenthau) awaited the President's return with increasing impatience and mounting excitement.

Indeed, a wave of suspenseful anticipation was sweeping the nation as a whole, encouraged by Lothian's farewell address and by a thick cluster of speeches made by top administration officials on December 12 and 13, these last in implementation of a propaganda effort ("we must instill a sense of urgency . . .") decided upon by the secretaries of state, war, and navy and by the members of the National Defense Advisory Commission when they met together on December 3. Stimson and Patterson of the War Department, Knudsen and Nelson of the National Defense Advisory Commission, gave forceful, nationally reported addresses (nationally radio broadcast also in the case of Knox and Stimson) during these two days, and so did Winthrop W. Aldrich, president of the Chase National Bank. "Let us meet the issue head-on without subterfuge or evasion," said Aldrich to a crowd of leading businessmen in Boston, "and put it directly up to Congress to provide Britain with the funds she will urgently need in the future."[41] Nevertheless, the *Tuscaloosa* made no hurried dash northward, nor did Roosevelt hurry on to Washington after he'd debarked on December 14. He paused for a day of casual relaxation with his "gang" of fellow polio victims at Warm Springs, telling the crowd gathered at the Warm Springs depot when he reboarded his train that he would be back in the spring for a longer stay "if the world survives."[42] He spoke these words flippantly (they would provoke bitter isolationist commentary upon the insouciance with which the President was leading the nation down the road to hell), but as he spoke to them he manifested not the slightest fear that the world would *not* survive. He exuded confidence—in himself and in the ultimate triumph of good over evil throughout the world.

It was the happy hearty suntanned Roosevelt of yore, jaunty, buoyant, eager for the fray, who in the evening of Sunday, December 16, returned to the White House. The fact was duly noted by the White House press corps and, with immense relief, by Roosevelt's administration colleagues. It appeared that what reporters had dubbed the President's "post-election slump" was at an end.

VI

NEXT day, lunching with Morgenthau, as he usually did on Mondays, Roosevelt outlined for the Treasury secretary the general British-aid formula he had arrived at during his vacation. Morgenthau endorsed it enthusiastically, despite the fact that "if I followed my own heart, I would say, let's give it to them."[43] And immediately thereafter, in one of the most momentous, if not actually the most important historically, of all his hundreds of press conferences, Roosevelt revealed the formula, in general outline, to all the world.

He opened the conference as he almost always did when he had important news to convey—that is, with the remark that he didn't have "any particular news." On the other hand, there was "possibly one thing" that might be worth his "talking about." Whereupon he spoke at length ("I am just talking background, informally; I haven't prepared any of this") about the "nonsense" he had been reading "the last few days" concerning aid to Britain—nonsense published "by people who can only think in what we may call traditional terms about finances." In all history, he asserted, not a single major war had been won through money in abundance, nor lost through the lack of it. Money was important, he implied, only to the extent that it enabled an accurate symbolic measurement of material things—guns, ships, planes, ammunition; and when the symbol was mistaken for the thing symbolized and thus substituted for it in mental operations, as "narrow-minded fellows" commonly did, dangerously absurd thinking ensued. What America needed for her defense against totalitarian aggressions, then, was not money, of which we had plenty, but "factories, shipbuilding ways, munition plants, et cetera, and so on." These facilities must be vastly expanded, and the necessary expansion had been and was being stimulated by British orders for war goods. But now, as Roosevelt did not explicitly say but emphatically said by clear implication, the United States must face the fact that the British were running out of money with which to pay for their orders, forcing upon Americans the necessity to choose among alternatives which he *did* state explicitly. One was to repeal the Johnson Act and the Neutrality Act to enable us "to lend money to Great Britain to be spent over here—either lend it through private banking circles, as was done in the earlier days of the previous war, or make it a loan from this Government to the British Government." Another possibility ("we may come to it, I don't know") was "for us to pay for all these munitions . . . and make a gift of them to Great Britain." He, however, was "not at all sure" this was "necessary" or that "Great Britain would care to have a gift from the taxpayers of the United States. I doubt it very much." A third possibility—and this one the crux of the matter he dealt with that day— was "for the United States to take over British orders, and, because they are essentially the same kind of munitions that we use ourselves, turn them into American orders." We could then lease or lend to "the other side" whatever portion of our total war production would best serve our security interests if they went to that "other side"—this "on the general theory that . . . the best defense of Great Britain is the best defense of the United States, and therefore that these materials would be more useful to the defense of the United States if they were used by Great Britain, than if they were kept in storage here." What he was "trying to do," he said, was "eliminate the dollar sign . . . get rid of the silly, foolish old dollar sign."

Thus he came to the inspired metaphor the very expression of which would be recognized, retrospectively, as a historical event.

"Well, let me give you an illustration," he said. "Suppose my neighbor's home catches fire, and I have a length of garden hose four or five hundred feet away. If he can take my garden hose and connect it up with his hydrant, I may help him put out his fire. Now, what do I do? I don't say to him before that operation, 'Neighbor, my garden hose cost me fifteen dollars; you have to pay me fifteen dollars for it.' What is the transaction that goes on? I don't want fifteen dollars—I want my garden hose back after the fire is over." He couldn't "go into details" about the legislation that, obviously, would be needed to effect this lending operation, he emphasized, "and there is no use asking legal questions . . . but the thought is that we would take over not all, but a very large number, of future British orders; and when they came off the line . . . we would enter into some kind of arrangement for their use by the British on the ground that it was the best thing for American defense, with the understanding that when the show was over, we would get repaid sometime in kind, thereby leaving out the dollar mark in the form of dollar debt and substituting for it a gentleman's obligation to repay in kind. I think you all get it."

He then answered or expertly dodged a barrage of questions from the reporters. This stuff we sent to Britain, would we retain title to it? That was the kind of legal-detail question he had told them not to ask, but personally he didn't think it "makes any difference" who had title to, say, a particular ship that went down American ways into British hands, just so the ship was "returned to us in first-class condition after payment [to us] of what might be called a reasonable amount for the ship during that time" it was in British use. When he spoke of ships, did he mean naval craft? "No, no! I'm talking about merchant ships." Wouldn't this leasing and lending program take us "more into the war than we are"? Of course not. "Even though the goods we own are being used?" the reporter persisted. One doesn't "go into a war for legalistic reasons," was Roosevelt's reply; and he didn't see how aiding Britain to the maximum of our ability, while simultaneously increasing that ability, would change anything fundamental since "we are doing all we can at the present time."[44]

There followed a number of questions based on an implicit recognition that the garden hose metaphor required considerable revision in order to fit the actual present situation. What America must direct toward Britain was not a garden hose, but a thick fire hose; this hose must be attached, not to a British, but to an American hydrant; and clearly the water pressure in the hydrant was at the moment much too low for the firefighting task at hand. Knudsen had indicated as much in recent statements—had said, in fact, that "the whole defense program was lagging pretty severely." And Roosevelt agreed that a speedup of defense production was needed—that "machines that will run seven days a week" must be kept "in operation seven days a week." But didn't this mean, a reporter asked, that the present defense setup must be greatly strengthened? Should not the currently headless National Defense Advisory Commission be given a head, someone with sufficient authority "to tell a manufacturer he should run two or three shifts a day"? At once Roosevelt went on the defensive. "After all, you have to follow certain laws of the land," he said; these laws said that war contracts must be signed by the secretaries or assistant secretaries of war or navy; and there "never has been one individual in this country, outside the army or navy, who could do anything more than recommend very strongly that they [private manufacturers] do thus and so, and supervise it—supervise keeping the program up-to-date." If the program was "not kept up-to-date, there are lots of things that have been done in the past, and would be done in the future"—but he didn't say what these "things" were, and he branded as "perfectly crazy" the assertions "made in the last couple of weeks by some people who didn't grow up until after the World War" that, during that war, certain American officials had vast authority, vast powers over American factory and farm production. This authority and these powers "never existed," he asserted misleadingly, save as a "figment of" their "imagination." He knew whereof he spoke, said he, because "I went through it." He was similarly evasive in his response to questions about "excessive" wage demands on the part of labor unions and about the maintenance of the forty-hour work week, as twin hindrances to war production. As for his own executive powers, he saw no need at this time for him to augment them by declaring a full-scale national emergency in place of the limited emergency he had declared by executive order at the war's outset—though this, again, was "largely a legalistic problem." It was "a great question" whether the Executive's exercise of full emergency powers would actually speed up production, he said—"a great technical question."[45]

The press conference ended. The reporters rushed from the room to file their stories, all of them acutely aware of the enormous immediate importance of the event they reported, a few of them conscious of the event's long-term world-historical significance. For clearly this lend-lease arrangement, if it achieved congressional approval, would tie the British and American economies so closely together as virtually to fuse them, as time went on, into a single planned economy—would consequently and simultaneously commit the United States so firmly to a British victory in this war that American entry into the war was certain if or when such entry became absolutely necessary to assure British victory. Already (in August 1940), a British scientific mission headed by Sir Henry Tizard had brought to America a black steamer trunk filled with British military secrets whose sharing with U.S. scientists working under Vannevar Bush's National Defense Research Committee* had been specifically approved by Prime Minister Churchill; it was a sharing that enormously stimulated American science devoted to national defense as it presaged the joining together of British and American scientists in a single secret military effort—the effort that Churchill would dub "the wizard war."[46] Already, in a formal agreement reached between Stimson and British special envoy Sir Walter Layton less than three weeks ago (November 29, 1940), Britain and the United States had agreed to standardize their basic designs for planes, tanks, guns, and military vehicles so that these could be used interchangeably by the two countries. And immediately before or immediately after this momentous press conference, Roosevelt at last approved Admiral Stark's long-pending request for highly secret military staff talks, to be held in Washington beginning in January 1941, between representatives of the British chiefs of staff and representatives of their American counterparts. The purpose of the talks, as stated in the Stark proposal, was tripartite: 1) to determine the best methods by which the United States and Great Britain could defeat "Germany and the powers allied with her, should the United States decide [Roosevelt changed 'decide' to 'be compelled'] to resort to war"; 2) to coordinate, in broad outline, plans for the employment of the two nations' armed forces; 3) to reach agreements between the two regarding "areas of responsibility, the major lines of strategy to be pursued . . . , the strength of the forces . . . , and . . . command arrangements."[47] Which is to say that the fusion of the two nations' economies was to be matched by that of their military science, their armed forces, and the strategies and tactics for the employment of these.

On the following afternoon (December 18, 1940), Secretaries Stimson and Knox, accompanied by Assistant Secretary of War Patterson and Assistant Secretary of the Navy James V. Forrestal (these two were to be elevated to the rank of undersecretary next day), met with Roosevelt in the White House Oval Study to discuss a proposed reformation of the present "defense set-up"—a reformation whose immediate necessity, especially stressed in the White House at that moment by Hillman's outrage over big business's use of the war emergency to render New Deal labor laws ineffective, Roosevelt had seemed to deny in his press conference. The plan for it had been long and arduous in the making. Stimson was its chief architect, but he had conferred at length with his cabinet colleagues; with Knudsen and Hillman; with Justice Felix Frankfurter of the U.S. Supreme Court; with Bernard Baruch; and with Jesse Jones, who in turn had undertaken to obtain the input and support of President William Green of

*See *FDR: Into the Storm*, pp. 561–62.

the American Federation of Labor. The outline plan that Stimson now handed the President was, of necessity, a compromise plan. It shied away from the "production czar" idea yet would repose in Knudsen as NDAC chairman an authority sufficient to achieve some coordination of the theretofore uncoordinated activities of the seven commissioners. And it had the pledged support of the key people who would be most affected by it. Nevertheless, Stimson approached this presidential interview with his usual fear that not much would come of it, thanks to Roosevelt's "grasshopper" mind—a mind that "does not follow easily a consecutive chain of thought, but . . . hops about from suggestion to suggestion."[48]

But again, as in his meeting with the President on November 12, Stimson was pleasantly surprised, and more surprised than he had been on the earlier occasion. For not only did Roosevelt pay close concentrated attention to what his visitors had to say, he also revealed that he himself had been brooding over the problem that concerned them, and brooding more deeply and in a wider context than their thinking had done. He had taken account, as they had not, of the danger of unlimited price inflation unless price-control devices were built into the industrial mobilization program (he had conferred on this with Leon Henderson). He had taken into account, as they had not been inclined to do (so we have seen), the need to prevent savage labor-management quarrels that would greatly slow defense production (here Hillman was influential). Moreover, taking these price and labor matters into account, he was prepared to go further and faster than they in the reformation of the industrial mobilization setup. The director of the budget, Harold D. Smith, had dug up for him an old statute "which nobody seemed to know about" authorizing the President to establish "a managing bureau for all kinds of emergencies." The statute was still on the books, and under its provisions Roosevelt proposed to establish a three-man board of Knudsen, Knox, and Stimson to replace the seven-member NDAC. He wanted to announce this or an equivalently drastic and effective reorganization of the defense-production setup as soon as possible, and not later than Sunday, December 22!

What ensued was the announcement on Friday, December 20, two days before the Roosevelt deadline, that an Office of Production Management (OPM) was to be established, partially replacing the NDAC whose members (those not incorporated into OPM) would henceforth advise OPM, not the Defense Council or the White House directly, on such matters as consumer protection, price controls, and transportation. Within OPM itself would be three divisions: a production division headed by Jack Biggers; a purchasing division headed by Donald Nelson; and a priorities division headed by Edward Stettinius. Knudsen was to be OPM's director general. The CIO's Sidney Hillman was to be OPM's associate director general. The secretaries of war and the navy were also to serve as members of OPM's board of directors but would have, necessarily, a merely ex officio and passive role in the new organization's direction. As Roosevelt later explained to reporters, Knudsen and Hillman with the two cabinet secretaries would "fix the policy" that Knudsen and Hillman would then execute—a blurred and blurring arrangement that improved upon the current situation, certainly, but still did not satisfy those who called for a single responsible head of the industrial mobilization effort. For as Roosevelt would confirm in the process of denying it, when asked about it in his press conference, Knudsen and Hillman were to operate as equals in power and authority; OPM would therefore be a double-headed, not a single-headed, enterprise. The arrangement was analogous to that of a law firm, said Roosevelt; and the firm of "Knudsen & Hillman" constituted the "single, responsible head" that people were crying for. (But it didn't! his critics asserted: OPM was *not* analogous to a law firm; law partnerships did not administer vast productive enterprises.) Hillman's addition to the original triumvirate had been made by Roosevelt to ensure a maximum cooperation between labor and management in the defense production effort and with the assurance, based on a shrewd Rooseveltian appraisal of psychological factors, that Hillman and Knudsen could and would work together as a team. The two promptly evinced their eagerness to do so. Hillman, though he had some private doubts about Knudsen's administrative ability, expressed publicly a personal liking and respect for this captain of industry and a conviction that he could work in tandem with him to ensure labor's full commitment to the defense effort as well as labor's fair treatment in the marketplace. Knudsen, who had accepted with some enthusiasm the original Stimson-Knox arrangement whereby he stood alone at the head of the production effort, manifested no dismay or any negative feeling whatever over this diminution or dilution of his authority. Instead he promptly issued a public statement calling upon the American people "to pull off their coats . . . roll up their sleeves" and go to work full force upon the production job. He made oblique reference to Hitler's most recent speech, to munitions workers in Berlin, wherein Der Fuehrer had declared that the war was an irreconcilable struggle for world power between totalitarianism and democracy whose end would be the utter destruction of democracy (this exercise of Hitlerian political "genius" pulled the rug out from under those American isolationists who claimed America had no stake in the European conflict); the struggle was indeed "irreconcilable in character," said Knudsen, and therefore could not be "terminated by methods of appeasement." The Office of Production Management, he concluded, was born of the realization that British democracy must triumph in this struggle if America's democracy were to survive.[49]

On that same day, in another exercise of his peculiar "genius," Hitler issued through a "Wilhelmstrasse spokesman" a statement that, in its virulent, if (in the circumstances) virtually impotent, threatfulness, was as if designed to solidify mass American support behind the President's anti-Nazi foreign policy. Said the statement: "We are watching with extraordinary interest the attitude of a nation which has shown only restraint and friendliness towards one warring nation, but whose attitude towards the other has consisted of a policy of pinpricks, injury, challenges, and moral aggression which has reached a point at which it is insupportable." If the United States turned over to Britain the seventy thousand tons of shipping now in American ports, as the United States was said to be about to do, Berlin would deem it a "warlike act," said the "spokesman" ominously. Even Roosevelt-hating Representative Hamilton Fish of New York, leader of the House isolationists, found this "insupportable." "The Government of the United States will decide on what action to take to protect American interests regardless of complaints emanating from Berlin," he said. And no major American public figure or newspaper reacted in the way obviously intended by the Hitlerian spokesman—that is, with a frightened cry for the cutting off of American aid to Britain—for none believed that Germany would in fact declare war upon the United States if present attitudes and policies remained unchanged. What Berlin's statement did do was swell the cry for a full-scale public statement by the President of the United States, giving his personal view of the current world situation and of the actions this nation must take in response to it.[50]

On December 23 it was reported that Roosevelt was preparing a major foreign policy address to be delivered to the nation as a fireside chat on December 29.

Meanwhile, Churchill, with Roosevelt's concurrence, dealt with the problem of Lothian's replacement as British ambassador to the United States. In a December 14 message to the President, the Prime Minister said he was "thinking of proposing . . . Mr. Lloyd George," who had been British Prime Minister during World War I and would "be very glad to know informally that this would be agreeable to you." Roosevelt, vividly remembering Lloyd George's publicly proclaimed admiration for Hitler after conversations with the dictator in the mid-1930s, and Lloyd George's shunning of Churchill's efforts to alert Chamberlain's Britain to the growing Nazi threat thereafter, was less than enthusiastic. He was "entirely agreeable," he said, but added: "I assume that over here he will in no way play into the hands of the appeasers." He was relieved when the ex–Prime Minister, enfeebled by age and illness, decided that "the strain would be too great"; whereupon Churchill, surprisingly, decided to appoint Lord Halifax, whom he had retained in his cabinet as foreign secretary, the post Halifax had held in the Chamberlain government, the appeasement policies of which Halifax had helped to shape and promote. Halifax accepted this evident demotion in good grace, perhaps because he felt as Churchill did that it was not actually, in the circumstances, a demotion. "I need not tell you what a loss this is to me personally and to the War Cabinet," wrote Churchill to Roosevelt on December 21. "I feel however that the . . . relationship between our two countries, and also the contact with you, Mr. President, are of such supreme consequence to the outcome of the war that it is my duty to place at your side the most eminent of my colleagues, and one who knows the whole story as it unfolds at the summit."[51] Anthony Eden, currently serving as secretary of state for war, was now shifted from that post to the Foreign Office as Halifax's replacement.

VII

THE White House Christmas of 1940 was somewhat less exuberantly Rooseveltian than most had been since the Roosevelts moved there. There was the usual large, noisy gathering of family, including the President's mother and numerous aunts, uncles, Roosevelt children and grandchildren, and close family friends. There was again a huge White House Christmas tree outdoors, over the lighting of which the President presided, and a smaller tree, yet a large one, in the White House itself. Again, on Christmas Eve, Roosevelt read aloud to family and guests an abridged version of Dickens's *A Christmas Carol,* virtually acting out the various scenes and roles; and there were the usual stuffed stockings fireplace hung, traditional feasts, and laughing gift exchanges and unwrappings. Everyone in the White House strove to "make this Christmas a merry one for the little children," as the President, in his Christmas greeting to the nation, said it should be. But through it all sounded a somber note ("For us of maturer years" this Christmas "cannot be merry," the presidential message also said)— a recognition that "the ideals of the Brotherhood of Man" were being challenged worldwide as never before in modern history. For adult Americans this could be a "Happy Christmas," said the President to the nation, only "if by happiness we mean we have done with doubts, that we have set our hearts against fear, that we still believe in the Golden Rule for all mankind, that we intend to live more purely in the spirit of Christ, and by our works, as well as our words, we will strive forward in Faith and in Hope and in Love."[52]

There followed four days of intense labor by Hopkins, Samuel I. Rosenman, Sherwood, and Roosevelt himself upon the drafting of the upcoming fireside chat. It was not completed until late in the afternoon of the day it was given. And, as completed, it was, in Robert Sherwood's words, "one of the most tightly packed" of all Roosevelt's speeches, necessarily ranging over "the map of the world," and with every phrase in it, almost every word, having been carefully weighed and tested, in consultation with the State Department, for implicative and inferential values.[53]

The diplomatic reception room of the White House was fairly crowded with people when Roosevelt was wheeled into it on the night of December 29. The group awaiting him was rather strangely mixed. His mother was there. Cordell Hull and other cabinet members were there. Some of his personal staff were there. But so, incongruously, were two Hollywood celebrities: actor Clark Gable, and his wife, actress Carole Lombard.[54] Roosevelt acknowledged the presence of all of them with a slight smile and nod before being seated beside a desk that was clustered with radio network microphones. He appeared grave, even a little grim, but perfectly poised and relaxed, as he opened the folder containing his speech manuscript.

And gravity, with calm confidence and determination, characterized every word he then spoke into the microphones.

"This is not a fireside chat on war," he began. "It is a talk on national security; because the nub of the whole purpose of your President is to keep you now, and your children later, and your grandchildren much later, out of a last-ditch war for the preservation of American independence and all the things that American independence means to you and to me and to ours." (Critical analysts of this sop to pacifists and isolationists might later ponder the significance of "last-ditch" in the artfully crafted statement; it prevented the statement's being of an unwavering "purpose" to "keep out" of any and all wars. A clearly winnable war in the near future was certainly preferable to a later one in which the American democracy was forced to defend itself, and probably without success, against the aggressions of a totalitarian Europe, a totalitarian Asia.) "Never before since Jamestown and Plymouth Rock has our American civilization been in such danger as now," he went on, justifying what he said by reference to the Tripartite Pact recently entered into by Germany, Italy, and Japan and obviously aimed against the United States—by reference also to Hitler's speech of "three weeks ago" in which the Nazi master of Germany declared that "there are two worlds that stand opposed to each other" and that the "world" he headed was bound to crush the other. "In other words, the Axis not merely admits but *proclaims* that there can be no ultimate peace between their philosophy of government and our philosophy of government. In view of the nature of this undeniable threat, it can be asserted, properly and categorically, that the United States has no right or reason to encourage talk of peace, until the day shall come when it is the clear intention on the part of the aggressor nations to abandon all thought of conquering the world."

For the moment, the forces of tyranny were "being held away from our shores"—on the Atlantic side "by the British, by the Greeks, and by the thousands of soldiers and sailors who were able to escape from the subjugated countries"; on the Pacific side "by the Chinese in another great defense" against Japanese imperialism, and by our own fleet. But if Britain went down, Axis powers would "control the continents of Europe, Asia, Africa, Australasia, and the high seas." They would be "in a position to bring enormous military and naval resources against this hemisphere. It is no exaggeration to say that all of us, in all the Americas, would be living at the point of a gun—a gun loaded with explosive bullets, economic as well as military. We should enter upon a new and terrible era in which the whole world . . . would be run by threats of brute force. To survive in such a world, we would have to convert ourselves permanently into a militaristic power on the basis of war economy." Indeed, the enemy was already within our gates. The Axis powers' "secret emissaries" were active here in the United States and Latin America, seeking "to stir up suspicion and dissension to cause internal strife. They try to turn capital against labor, and vice versa. They try to awaken long slumbering racial and religious enmities which should have no place in this country. They are active in every group that promotes intolerance." Their "one purpose" was "to divide our people into hostile groups and destroy our unity and shatter our will to defend ourselves." And their nefarious purpose was aided, albeit "unwittingly in most cases," by "American citizens, many of them in high places [the State Department tried to delete the 'in high places' phrase from the speech draft, according to Sherwood; Roosevelt irritably refused to do so]. . . . I do not charge these American citizens with being foreign agents. But I do charge them with doing exactly the kind of work that the dictators want done in the United States."

But having thus stressed the futility of attempts to appease the Axis ("there can be no appeasement with ruthlessness"), and the absurdity of pacifistic isolationism in the present crisis, he cast as many further sops as he could toward isolationists and all who would keep America out of war at all costs. "The people of Europe who are defending themselves do not ask us to do their fighting. . . . There is no demand for sending an American Expeditionary Force outside our own borders. There is no intention by any member of your Government to send such a force [Stimson and Knox, listening, may have cringed slightly]. You can, therefore, nail any talk about sending armies to Europe as deliberate untruth. Our national policy is not directed toward war. Its sole purpose is to keep war away from our country and our people." Of course, "there is risk in any course we may take. But I deeply believe that the great majority of our people agree that the course I advocate involves the least risk now and the greatest hope for world peace in the future." What the British were asking for were "the implements of war, the planes, the tanks, the guns, the freighters which will enable them to fight for their liberty and for our security. Emphatically we must get these weapons to them in sufficient volume and quickly enough, so that we and our children will be saved the agony and suffering of war which others have had to endure. . . . We must have more ships, more guns, more planes—more of everything. This can be done only if we discard the notion of 'business as usual.' " Those who feared "the future consequences of surplus plant capacity" must measure their fear against "the consequences of failure of our defense efforts now," consequences that were "much more to be feared." Indeed, "a proper handling of the country's peacetime needs," once the present defense needs "are past," would "require all the new productive capacity—if not more."

And so he came to the phrase that, italicized by the manner in which he delivered it, became the identifying tag for this speech in the public mind and in history.

"We must become the great arsenal of democracy," he declared. "For this is

an emergency as serious as war itself. We must apply ourselves to our task with the same resolution, the same sense of urgency, the same spirit of patriotism and sacrifice as we would show were we at war. . . . I have the profound conviction that the American people are now determined to put forth a mightier effort than they have ever made to increase our production. . . . As President of the United States I call for that national effort."[55]

The public reaction to this speech surprised and delighted Roosevelt by the swiftness with which it was manifested and the strength of its support of his policy. At once, letters and telegrams began pouring into the White House mail-room in astounding volume, and as Steve Early reported to the President, they ran 100–1 in approval of what the President had said. A Gallup poll, promptly taken, revealed that 59 percent of a representative sample of the American people had listened to the broadcast and that another 16 percent had read the speech in newspapers—"the highest number of readers and listeners of any of his [Roosevelt's] speeches for which there are polls," as Warren F. Kimball has written.[56]

VIII

ON Monday, December 30, 1940, in conference with Morgenthau and British purchasing agent Purvis, Roosevelt asked the latter for an estimate of the dollar value of the goods Britain would have to obtain from the United States, overall, if she were to wage successful war during the months ahead. Purvis had been refused an answer to this question when he'd addressed it to the Ministry of Supply in London—had been told that such an estimate was bound to be "misleading," meaning that it was bound to be so high that it would, in the ministry's view, "scare off " the Americans. But, fortunately for democracy's cause, especially at that moment, Purvis was a man remarkably free of the typical bureaucrat's self-protective timidity and consequent tendency toward circumlocutory duplicity. After futilely protesting the Supply Ministry's reticence, which he knew had already angered the Americans and would now if revealed outrage them, he set to work with his staff preparing a "balance sheet" estimate of his own, the balance sheet idea being a brainchild of Jean Monnet, former head of the French Purchasing Mission to America, who after the fall of his country had become a key member of the British Purchasing Commission. This estimate Purvis now, after anxious oral explanation, presented to the President. He did so with pardonable trepidation. The estimate was indeed high; it was $15 billion, a figure twice as great as the highest that had been mentioned before in this connection. The British purchasing agent was at once relieved of his anxiety, however. It is typical of Roosevelt's crisis leadership that he responded to the estimate with no sign of surprise, much less of dismay, and seemed tacitly to assume its accuracy (though later acts on his part would reveal that he had not really done so) by at once making tactical decisions that were evidently partially based upon it.[57]

Turning to Morgenthau, he said that he wanted the lend-lease legislation to be prepared by Treasury (the bypassing of State would, of course, be resented by Cordell Hull) and as quickly as possible after the "green light" for doing so came from the White House a few days hence. He wanted Purvis to be actively involved in the drafting process, an unprecedented participation by an officer of a foreign power in crucially important decision making at the highest level of the American government and a participation of which knowledge had best be denied the public at large. Finally and most emphatically, the legislation must be a very broad grant of authority to the President—the broadest possible in the circumstances. This was absolutely necessary if the legislation were to accomplish its purpose. Any close specificity as to what items might be ordered, in what quantities, and where sent by the Executive—any close specificity as to how the leased and lent items were to be returned or compensated for at war's end—would make a shambles of the law's administration. Morgenthau expressed frankly his fear that Congress might not "go along" with a new drastic shift of power from the Legislature to the Executive; the proposal to do so was bound to raise again a storm of angry voices shouting across the land that "that man in the White House" aspired to dictatorship. But Morgenthau agreed with Roosevelt that the attempt must be made and promised a draft bill that was, as he later put it to members of his staff, "as broad as the world, and then let somebody else tighten it up."[58]

Roosevelt himself, buoyed by the immediate popular and press response to his speech, was confident of ultimate success, his only great fear being that the success would be too long delayed. A furious political battle loomed, of course; but it had been looming larger and larger for several months, and in the shadow of its oncoming the basic issue between the opposing forces had been sharpened and clarified, Roosevelt felt, in ways that favored his cause. "Candor [on Roosevelt's part], emerging at last from the camouflage of the campaign, has been received with a calmness that adds to the regret that this approach was delayed at the expense of six months of vital preparation," said Arthur Krock (one of Roosevelt's least favorite columnists) in *The New York Times* on the last day of 1940. ". . . . Everyone seemed relieved to have had clearly posed an issue that has been forming since Munich."[59] But what *was* this issue, at base, and how "clearly" had it in fact been "posed" in this speech? Roosevelt's perception of it, also his sense of the immediately politically possible, a sense that militated against complete candor on his part, were revealed by his choice of the ground on which to wage the impending battle. It was, typically, a ground of ambiguity. It could be described as "middle," being located halfway between total American isolation and total intervention in the war. But such "middleness" was strictly temporary, as Roosevelt acutely sensed (though never publicly admitted), since, under the pressure of events, the ground shifted steadily, inexorably toward intervention. It yet contained a faint and diminishing possibility (which Roosevelt stressed publicly as a probability) that democracy could prevail over totalitarianism in this war without America's having actually to fight. It was therefore ground on which could stand those many millions of Americans whose dread of war, whose desperate wish to keep out of it, was yet a ruling passion. This pacifistic passion was, however, a waning one, for the millions increasingly realized that their truly *fundamental* commitment was not to peace at any price, but to democratic freedoms, and that for the latter they would, if necessary, fight. The basic issue, then, for Americans as for Europeans, was democracy vs. totalitarianism, and it must ultimately be decided through political struggle between those Americans who retained their democratic faith and those who had lost it—between those whose loathing of Nazi-fascism was visceral and those who saw merit in it or, at any rate, were willing to cooperate with it.[60]

The battle lines were hardening.

And as they hardened they squeezed out of their ranks those who were infirm of purpose or whose purpose was at odds with that, within each of the battle lines, was an increasingly dominant tendency.

A case in point was that of the greatly beloved folk hero of the American middle class, William Allen White, publisher-editor of the *Emporia* (Kansas) *Gazette,* who with some difficulty had been persuaded into the chairmanship of a so-called Non-Partisan Committee for Peace Through Revision of the Neutrality Act when this national pressure group was formed in the fall of 1939. The committee had at once been dubbed the White Committee—it had continued to be so known as, continuing beyond the repeal of the arms embargo, it became officially the Committee to Defend America by Aiding the Allies—and this fact had greatly increased the organization's effectiveness as an opponent of isolationism. Isolationism dominated the Middle West, and White was a Midwesterner. Isolationism dominated the Republican contingent in the Congress, and White was a Republican—a Progressive Republican of the Norris–La Follette stripe, but one whose loyalty to the party in election years was unwavering. He was known to the nation as a kindly ameliorating personality who abhorred extremes and never permitted himself to go to them. His acceptance of this chairmanship therefore testified in the popular mind to the committee's moderate commonsensical views on American foreign policy. Such testimony greatly augmented the committee's popular persuasiveness, and Franklin Roosevelt had reason to be grateful for this: under White's leadership, on crucial occasions during the last year, the committee had perfectly and persuasively expressed the President's aid-to-Britain policy as that policy stood at that moment and had done so more explicitly and emphatically than Roosevelt had felt himself able to do.

But White's leadership was by no means perfectly expressive of the increasingly dominant opinions and convictions of his committee's membership as these evolved and hardened in response to Hitler's lightning conquest of Norway, Denmark, Belgium, Holland, and France in the spring of 1940. Several of the most prominent committee members also became members of a so-called Century Group (it was formed and met in New York City's Century Club), which, as France fell, publicly proclaimed Britain's cause to be our own and called for an immediate declaration of war upon Germany by the Congress of the United States. These members assumed, as an overwhelming majority of the committee as a whole assumed, that an active purpose of their organization during the election would be to support congressional candidates who favored aid to Britain and to defeat those who opposed it. To this end they proposed to publish as an organization document the voting record of isolationist representatives and senators who were up for reelection. To their astonishment, anger, and dismay, White refused to permit this, saying that it would destroy the nonpartisan character of the committee! Why, virtually every Republican member of Congress had an isolationist voting record! Nor was this the full measure of White's divergence from his committee's majority opinion as election day approached. In mid-October he dashed off a letter to arch-isolationist appeasement-minded Representative Hamilton Fish of Roosevelt's home congressional district, saying: "However you and I may disagree about some issues of the campaign, I hope as Republicans we are united in our support of the Republican ticket from top to bottom in every district and every state." He added that the letter was "not private." And Fish was making good use of it when, forced by the furor it aroused, White wrote to candidates opposed to Fish's stand, saying that "our Committee is non-partisan," that it therefore "naturally wishes to see appeasers, isolationists and pro-Germans defeated irrespective of party," and that "you may make the widest use of this that you wish."[61]

Fish won reelection.

Immediately thereafter the leadership majority of the committee pressed hard for committee endorsement of the use of American convoys to insure delivery of supplies to Britain across the U-boat-infested Atlantic. From a November policy meeting in New York, with White presiding, came a published statement of committee policy: "The life line between Great Britain and the United States is the sea route to the Western Hemisphere. Under no circumstances must this line be cut and the United States must be prepared to maintain it. . . . We favor through Congressional action . . . a repeal or modification of restrictive statutes which hamper this nation in its freedom of action when it would cooperate with nations defending themselves against attack. . . ."[62] This statement, published on November 26, clearly implied the committee's advocacy of convoying and of repeal of the Neutrality Act, as White knew at the time. He worried about it, however. He believed the committee bearing his name was "getting out too far in front" of public opinion—was certainly moving considerably farther toward armed intervention than Roosevelt had done publicly or intended to do in any near future, as White had been assured in private conversation by the President himself. He was dead tired as he rode a Pullman back to Kansas, where, uninhibited by face-to-face contacts with New York committee leaders, his doubts about the announced policy statement grew toward an actual personal rejection of it. When he was warned that the powerful Scripps-Howard newspaper chain was preparing a full-scale attack upon him and the committee as warmongers, he dashed off a typically effusive personal letter to the chain's head, Roy Howard. "Look now, Roy," he wrote on December 20, 1940, "you and I have been buddies . . . The only reason in God's world I am in this organization is to keep this country out of war. . . . The story is floating around that I and our outfit are in favor of sending convoys with British ships or our own ships, a silly thing, for convoys unless you shoot are confetti and it's not time to shoot now or ever. . . . It is not true even remotely that we favor repealing [the Neutrality Law] to carry contraband of war into the war zone. That would be leading us to war and our organization and I personally am deeply opposed to it. If I was making a motto for the Committee to Defend America by Aiding the Allies, it would be 'The Yanks Are Not Coming.' " Howard, with White's permission, at once published this effusion, whereupon there broke about White's weary head (he approached his seventy-third birthday; he and his wife were both in failing health) a storm of criticism from those for whom he presumed to speak. New York City Mayor Fiorello La Guardia accused him of "doing a typical Laval." Simultaneously, Charles A. Lindbergh and General Robert E. Wood, the latter being chairman of the national America First Committee (it was formed in September 1940 precisely for the purpose of counteracting the White Committee's influence), issued statements of gratification that William Allen White agreed with them.[63]

On January 1, 1941, White wired to New York his resignation as committee chairman, to be effective immediately.

Within America First, too, there was disaffection as its battle lines began to harden on a theme of appeasement through a negotiated peace with Hitler. It was a theme of which one element was the pro-fascism of a portion of the big-business community (significantly, America First steadfastly refused to publish a list of its principal financial contributors, though the aid-Britain committee published such a list periodically and held its books open to inspection at all times). It was also a theme having at its heart an increasingly potent strain of anti-Semitism. Of course, many of the elite members of the White Committee were anti-Semites to the extent that they "disliked Jewishness," excluded Jews from their social clubs, and barred Jews in various ways from buying property in their neighborhoods. But anti-Semitism was no part of the White Committee's organizing principle, spoken or unspoken; if anti-Semites joined the aid-to-Britain effort, they did so despite their prejudice, while many others joined, in part, precisely because Hitler's anti-Semitism was utterly loathsome to them. The opposite was true of America First. From its inception, America First was attractive to people who sympathized with Hitler's "solution" to the "Jewish problem"—people who believed or professed to believe that Jews, dominating the financial community, had inveigled this country into World War I for profit-making reasons and were now engaged in the same nefarious enterprise during World War II. They constituted a growingly significant portion of America First's membership; anti-Semitism was a part of their motivation as they pressed for a negotiated peace, knowing full well that such a peace must be on Hitler's terms: the immediate official response of America First to Roosevelt's "arsenal" speech focused upon his assertion that the United States had "no right or reason to encourage talk of peace" so long as the Axis was bent upon world conquest; the assertion made Roosevelt personally responsible in large degree for the war's continuance, charged General Wood.[64] Yet Wood himself had recognized anti-Semitism as a threat to the new organization's integrity and persuasiveness when he, board chairman of Sears, Roebuck in Chicago, accepted the committee chairmanship in early September 1940. He had then insisted that J. Lessing Rosenwald, a Jew and a director of Sears, Roebuck, be placed on the new organization's executive committee. This gesture's effectiveness had been nullified, however, when, evidently at the insistence of the chairman of the Chicago branch of America First, there was simultaneously named to the executive committee the notoriously anti-Semitic Henry Ford, who, like Lindbergh, had accepted a Nazi decoration. The Ford appointment along with Rosenwald's would, it was argued, provide "a proper balance"! Rosenwald, naturally, found the arrangement intolerable. He soon resigned from the executive committee, whereupon, to maintain "balance," Henry Ford was quietly dropped from it.

Such machinations caused great unease among those America Firsters who abhorred racial and religious bigotry, and loathed Hitler's regime for that reason, but who opposed America's entry into the war because they were conscientiously opposed to war, or believed that Britain's cause was hopeless, or were convinced that American dictatorship would result from our entry and thus nullify the alleged reason (to preserve democracy) for our doing so. Among these were Norman Thomas, journalist John T. Flynn, advertising man Chester Bowles, University of Chicago vice president William Benton, actress Lillian Gish, former Wisconsin governor Philip La Follette, Mrs. Burton K. Wheeler, and novelists John P. Marquand, Margaret Ayer Fairbank, and Kathleen Norris. Such America Firsters as these were profoundly disturbed by the fact that a best-selling little book by Anne Morrow Lindbergh, wife of the aviator hero, entitled *The Wave of the Future* and published in the fall of 1940, was widely regarded as "the bible" of America Firsters, since the book was essentially an argument, if a series of poetically metaphorical assertions can be called an "argument," for totalitarianism.[65] Some of these people vigorously protested the growing influence in their ranks of anti-Semites and anti-Semitism—the fact, for instance, that Father Coughlin's violently anti-Semitic followers were the core group of America First's Boston chapter.

Epitomizing the national hardening process, while also pointing up the shifty ambiguity of the ground on which Roosevelt had chosen to fight the upcoming battle, was the mental experience in early December 1940 of the chairman of the Chicago chapter of the White Committee.

He was a forty-year-old corporate lawyer named Adlai E. Stevenson, a man of sensitive intelligence and remarkable effectiveness as a public speaker who was also a man of conscience, being profoundly committed to strict honesty and truth telling in his dealings with public issues. His conscience became increasingly uneasy as he bore the brunt of the battle against isolationism in Chicago, the capital of isolationism, through the spring, summer, and fall of 1940. He vehemently asserted in public speech that aid to Britain offered the "best chance" for the United States to keep out of the war—and this, he continued to believe, was true. But suppose that despite all our material aid, Britain tottered at the edge of defeat. We would then be faced with a choice between entering the war and permitting a final Nazi-Fascist triumph in Europe. Which of the two would he, Adlai Stevenson, choose? When he frankly admitted to himself that, in such a case, he would choose war, he was forced to face a further question: If Hitler's defeat were of such imperative importance, was it not the part of honorable men to assume the vital risks of ensuring that defeat? Was it not cowardice to hide from so terrible a menace behind the sacrifice, the valor, and the fortitude of Britain and the British Commonwealth?[66]

The question gnawed deeply into his conscience when, in the last month of 1940, he twice engaged in public debate with a spokesman for America First named Clay Judson—once before the Chicago Bar Association, once before a meeting arranged by the League of Women Voters. His growing realization that he stood on a ground of ambiguity was especially evident in his address to the bar association. "You hear it said that this is not our war," he said. "I don't care whose war it is—the enemy is our enemy, and if Britain can't . . . defeat that enemy now, then we can confidently look forward to the day when, perhaps alone in the world, we shall have to make our stand. . . . Great Britain can win, but I'm not sure she will win—and she cannot win without us." Even as he spoke these words they rang hollow in his ears; for was he not virtually admitting that this "best chance" to stay out of the war was also a long step toward armed intervention and that, insofar as it constituted a real chance to avoid the latter, it was cowardly—a disgraceful cowering behind walls of courage and sacrifice raised up by others against our enemy? His debate opponent stood on more solid ground than his own. Said Judson: "The question we must answer before it is too late is: 'Is this our war?' If it is our war, then we should be in it without delay, even though it will not be the comparatively simple job it was the first time we saved the world for democracy." It was an argument that would be made repeatedly by leading isolationists during the coming battle over lend-lease—their assumption was that if the issue of war or peace were faced squarely, most Americans would choose peace—and every time Stevenson heard it he would flinch inwardly. As regards the essential issue, he was becoming as self-contradictory, he felt, as William Allen White had been, and with far less personal excuse. . . .[67] (Something over six months later, in May 1941, Stevenson would seize an opportunity to escape his Chicago dilemma, offered him by his older friend Secretary of the Navy Knox. "I go to all these meetings," Knox grumbled. "Every day, important meetings with important people. There sit Hillman and Knudsen and Stimson, and the others—and every one of 'em has his own personal lawyer. Even Jim Forrestal has his own lawyer [James Forrestal was Knox's undersecretary], and I don't have one." Would Adlai come to Washington as his, Knox's, special assistant? Adlai would. He jumped at the chance. His Washington appointment would be publicly announced in early July 1941.)[68]

3

>>X<<

The Birth of
the Grand Alliance

I

THE "green light" for the drafting of lend-lease legislation came to Morgenthau from the White House on Thursday, January 2, 1941. It incited a drafting effort remarkable for its speed and efficiency. Treasury lawyers Edward Foley and Oscar Cox, working with a couple of young assistants, completed the initial rough draft shortly before midnight that night. In the following days there were repeated redrafting conferences in which active roles were played by both Purvis and Roosevelt's longtime personal friend and adviser Felix Frankfurter, now a Supreme Court justice—also by Benjamin V. Cohen, who, with his close friend Thomas Corcoran, had been one of the principal legal draftsmen of the New Deal and held now the official title of counsel to the National Public Power Committee in the Interior Department. Through Cohen, Roosevelt transmitted to the bill drafters his views on the bill's provisions and language, and upon legislative strategy insofar as this was determined by the bill's form. On Tuesday afternoon, January 7, the draft was in final shape, as attested to by the initials of Hull, affixed at 3:25 P.M.; of Knox, affixed at 4:20; of Stimson, affixed at 4:29; and finally of the President, who remarked that the drafting had been "really a fast piece of work for Washington" as, broadly smiling, he scrawled "OK, FDR" upon the draft at 5:15 P.M. Certainly he, the President, could not complain that the drafters had not followed his instructions as to the broadness of the grant of authority required: the economic and foreign policy powers the proposed legislation would vest in him were sweeping beyond any precedent in U.S. history. "Notwithstanding the provisions of any other law," he would be empowered "to manufacture or otherwise procure" any "defense article" for the government of "any country" (none was named specifically) whose defense he deemed "vital to the defense of the United States." He would be empowered "to sell, transfer title to, exchange, lease, lend, or otherwise dispose of to any such government any defense article." And to the term *defense article* was given a very wide definition. A defense article was not only any weapon and munition, any airplane or ship, but also "any machinery, facility, tool, material or supply" necessary for the making or repairing of these, along with "any agricultural, industrial or other commodity" that was usable or necessary for defense purposes.[1]

Two days later, final decisions about the strategy to be employed for the bill's introduction were made in a large White House conference attended, among others, by Jesse Jones in his capacity as director of the RFC, by William Knudsen of the new OPM, and by Morgenthau, Hull, Stimson, Knox, House Speaker Sam Rayburn, House Majority Leader John W. McCormack, Senate Majority Leader Alben Barkley, Senate Foreign Relations Committee chairman Walter George, Senator Tom Connally, who was soon to replace George as committee chairman, and Representative Sol Bloom, chairman of the House Foreign Affairs Committee. It was agreed that the act's title would be "to promote the defense of the United States [Frankfurter had proposed this in place of Cohen's suggested 'an act to aid nations whose defense is related to the defense of the United States'] and for other purposes": that the bill would be introduced simultaneously in House and Senate by the majority leaders, McCormack and Barkley, though Roosevelt wanted to spread abroad the impression that it had House origin since the House originated all appropriations bills, and that because House rules required the bill as written to be assigned to the Foreign Affairs Committee, or so Speaker Rayburn insisted, it would have to be assigned to the equivalent committee, the Foreign Relations Committee, in the Senate.

This last decision was made reluctantly: the Senate committee was stacked with isolationists, thanks to the appointments to it made by Vice President John Nance Garner during his eight-year presidency over the upper house; the conferees would therefore have much preferred to assign the bill to the Senate Military Affairs Committee, whose majority favored aid to Britain—a preference responsible, in part, for the bill's title. There happened at that time to be two vacancies on Foreign Relations. Even if these were filled with supporters of the measure, said George, getting the bill reported out favorably would be extremely difficult; if they remained unfilled, a favorable report might prove impossible. Whereupon Roosevelt asked soon-to-be chairman Connally about the possibility of filling the vacancies with South Carolina's Senator James F. Byrnes and Virginia's Senator Carter Glass; Connally said this could be done (in the event, it was done, Byrnes becoming an effective leader of the fight for the bill in committee and on the floor). The conferees then talked of the opposition that the broadness of the grant of authority to the President was bound to arouse. When Texas's Senator Connally was confirmed in his impression that the battleship *Texas* could legally be transferred to Britain under this bill, he suggested that a provision be added limiting the bill's application to things produced from now on. Roosevelt emphatically rejected the suggestion: Britain's immediate needs required "old" as well as "new" American products; people would simply have to trust their President not to give away the U.S. Navy, of which he was known to be especially fond.[2]

By that time, the first session of the Seventy-seventh Congress had been formally opened and the President had delivered to it, and to the nation, both his annual budget and his annual State of the Union messages.

His annual budget message, delivered on January 3, 1941, was remarkable among such documents for the extent to which its statistical information was imbedded in, and expressive of, a philosophy of government. During the fiscal year ending June 30, 1942, the administration proposed to spend nearly $11 billion for national defense, a 67 percent increase over the defense spending for the current fiscal year, making a grand total defense expenditure since June 1940 of well over $28 billion. Of this, nearly $14 billion went to the army, which was expanding from 250,000 in June 1940 to 1,400,000 in 1942; approximately $11.5 billion went to the navy, which was doubling its personnel; nearly $2 billion went for industrial plant expansion; and over $1 billion went for other defense activities. "This is a vast sum," the President admitted, but was not all that our circumstances required to be spent. "It is dangerous to prepare for a little defense," he went on. "It is safe only to prepare for total defense." And total defense meant "more than weapons," more than "an industrial capacity stepped up to produce all the matériel" for war with all possible speed. It meant also "people of health and stamina, conscious of their democratic rights and responsibilities." It meant "an economic and social system functioning smoothly and geared to high-speed performance." For it was not only our existence as a sovereign state that was at stake; democracy "as a way of life" was "equally at stake." Which led to the conclusion that mere survival as a nation-state was not our purpose in the present crisis; our purpose was to survive and prosper *as a free and open society*. We were challenged to prove that our democracy's linkage of practical efficiency to moral values—that is, our insistence that means and ends be consistent with one another—enabled us to mobilize our resources "of manpower and skill and plant" for armed defense without sacrificing the "governmental services, social security, and aid to those suffering through no fault of their own" that made national survival humanly valuable. Indeed, such sacrifice would reduce overall efficiency. "Only by maintaining all these activities can we claim the effective use of resources which our democratic system is expected to yield, and thus justify the expenditures required for its defense," said Roosevelt. To this end, he recommended not contraction, but instead an expansion "of the social-security programs. . . . I deem it vital that the Congress give consideration to the inclusion in the old-age and survivors insurance system and the unemployment compensation system of workers not now covered." Such increase would be offset by a cut of $400 million in the appropriation for work relief and by "a reduction of $45 million in the agricultural programs" that was made possible by the "increased domestic market for farm products resulting from defense expenditure." Nor was this the sum total of the work relief reduction that might become possible. Though he proposed a $995 million appropriation to the Works Progress Administration (WPA) for fiscal 1942, as compared with the $1.25 billion that had been appropriated for fiscal 1941, it "will not be necessary to use this full amount if the defense program should result in more general reemployment than is presently indicated."

The fact that full employment did not yet obtain, that pockets of severe unemployment were yet scattered across the land, conditioned Roosevelt's approach to the problem of financing the vast defense expenditures. These last would in some part finance themselves, even at current rates of taxation, insofar as they lifted personal and corporate incomes to new highs and so enlarged income tax revenues. They would also, for the same reason, facilitate borrowing through the sale of government securities to both small and large investors. But, of course, "in the case of most taxes, there is . . . a time lag"—the full impact of defense expenditures on government revenues would "not be felt before the fiscal year 1943"—and even if the full impact were felt at once, the existing tax structure could not bear the strains that war finance imposed upon it. "We cannot yet conceive the complete measure of extraordinary taxes which are necessary to pay off the cost of emergency defense and to aid in avoiding inflationary price rises which may occur when full capacity is approached," said Roosevelt, but "extraordinary taxes" would certainly be necessary. There was "no agreement," he admitted, "on how much . . . should be financed on a pay-as-you-go basis and how much by borrowing." He himself had favored, in the not distant past, a nearly total financing of armaments expansion on a pay-as-you-go basis. But the expansion was now so swift and huge that such financing would require "drastic and restrictive taxation," taxation that would "I fear . . . interfere with the full use of our productive capacity." We were presented with "a choice between restrictive tax measures applied to the present national income and a higher tax yield from increased [future] national income under less restrictive tax measures." He chose the latter. He was "opposed," he said, "to a tax policy which restricts general consumption so long as unused capacity is available and as long as idle labor can be employed." Nevertheless, "a start should be made this year" toward meeting "a larger percentage of defense payments from current tax receipts." And to this end he suggested the adoption of "additional tax measures . . . based on the principle of ability to pay." He placed heavy stress upon the "principle" because of its causal relationship to "the fixed policy of the Government that no citizen should make any abnormal net profit out of national defense." He was, he said, far from "satisfied that existing laws are in this respect adequate."* Indeed, he was convinced that a major reform of the entire tax structure was needed, a reform in which both a closer "Federal-State-local fiscal relationship" and a steeper progressivity of personal income taxation were

---

*As he spoke these words, did he feel a twinge of conscience, remembering his capitulation to big-business interests during the writing of the second Revenue Act of 1940? See pp. 18–20.

achieved (after all, he reminded Congress and nation, "our tax burden is still moderate compared to that of most countries"). He hoped "that action toward these ends" would "be taken at this session."

He closed on the philosophical note that had sounded through the message as a whole. "The Budget of the United States . . . is a preview of our work plan, a forecast of things to come," he said. "It charts the course of the Nation." But this present budget, whose "loading . . . with armament expenditures" was "regretted by every American," had "been prepared at a time when no man could see all the signposts ahead." Only one "marker . . . stands out all down the road" and "that marker carries not so much an admonition as a command to defend our democratic way of life."[3]

Earlier on that same day, Roosevelt had made two announcements at his press conference. One, to which he ascribed major importance, was of the launching of a government shipbuilding program whereby some two hundred merchant vessels of some 7,500 tons each would be produced at high speed "in a number of new plants," at a cost of something over $300 million—this to offset the tonnage that was currently "going to the bottom" at a rate that, if not offset, must "sooner or later" result in a "world shortage" of tonnage. The design of the new vessels, which would be government property (they were destined for fame as "Liberty Ships"), was decidedly unhandsome; they were "the kind [of vessel] that is built by the yard or foot." Anyone who "loves a ship would hate them, as I do." But "the difference . . . in time between building a ship that is . . . like a square, oblong tank and a ship that is really a ship is six or eight months. In other words, by building this dreadful-looking object you save six or eight months." And time was of the essence.

His other announcement was that he planned to send to the Senate next week the name of the new ambassador to Great Britain but that "in the meantime I am asking Harry Hopkins to go over [to England] as my personal representative" for a short visit, leaving "very soon." Was it "safe to say Mr. Hopkins will not be the next ambassador?" a reporter asked. Replied the President: "You know Harry isn't strong enough [well enough] for that job." And he went on to downplay the importance of the Hopkins trip. No staff would accompany the envoy. He would have no title and no special mission ("he's just going over to say 'How do you do?' to a lot of my friends"). He would have no powers. And he would return to America in a couple of weeks. . . .[4]

Three days later, Roosevelt presented to Congress and nation his report on the State of the Union. It echoed his fireside chat of December 29. Again he stressed that "at no previous time has American security been threatened from without as it is today." Again he stressed that our nation would "never . . . acquiesce in a peace dictated by aggressors and sponsored by appeasers." Again he stressed "the immediate need" for vastly increased armaments production, not only to equip our own immensely growing armed forces, but also to supply the embattled democracies abroad (he repeated the gist of his lend-lease proposal for assuring supply deliveries to nations unable to pay cash for them). Again he stressed that a "greater portion of this great defense program" should be immediately paid for by increased taxation ("no person should . . . be allowed to get rich from this program; and the principle of tax payments in accordance with ability to pay should be constantly before our eyes to guide our legislation").

Finally, he again stressed, and most emphatically, that our stake in this crisis was not merely our survival as a nation-state, but our survival as a *democratic* nation-state. "As men do not live by bread alone," he said, "they do not fight by armaments alone. Those who man our defenses, and those behind the lines who build our defenses, must have the stamina and the courage which comes from unshakable belief in the manner of life which they are defending. The mighty action that we are calling for cannot be based on a disregard of all things worth fighting for." Therefore, this was no time "for any of us to stop thinking about the social and economic problems which are the root cause of the social revolution which is today a supreme factor in the world." There was, he went on, "nothing mysterious about the foundations of a healthy and strong democracy. The basic things expected by our people of their political and economic systems are simple." He listed them: equality of opportunity; jobs for all who can work; security "for those who need it"; "an end to special privilege"; the preservation of civil liberties; the "enjoyment of the fruits of scientific progress in a wider and constantly rising standard of living."

And so he was led to his closing words—the words whereby this address would be remembered in history.

He said:

"In the future days, which we seek to make secure, we look forward to a world founded upon four essential freedoms.

"The first is freedom of speech and expression—everywhere in the world.

"The second is freedom of every person to worship God in his own way—everywhere in the world.

"The third is freedom from want—which, translated into world terms, means economic understandings which will secure to every nation a healthy peacetime life for its inhabitants—everywhere in the world.

"The fourth is freedom from fear—which, translated into world terms, means a worldwide reduction of armaments to such a point and in such a thorough fashion that no nation will be in a position to commit an act of physical aggression against any neighbor—anywhere in the world.

"That is no vision of a distant millennium. It is a definite basis for a kind of world attainable in our own time and generation."[5]

II

THE lend-lease bill, stamped "H.R. 1776" by the House clerk, was introduced in the House by Majority Leader McCormack and in the Senate (as S. 275) by Majority Leader Barkley on January 10, 1941. The "significance" of the House number it bore was at once loudly commented upon. For proponents of the bill, its number signified its patriotic nature—a nature that made voting for it a patriotic duty. For Anglophobic opponents, the number symbolism was bitterly ironic: we who had declared our independence from Britain in 1776 proposed in 1941 to repudiate that declaration and, through H.R. 1776, rejoin the British empire![6]

But what chiefly angered leading isolationist spokesmen, as it also disturbed many of the supporters of all aid to Britain, as we have seen, was Roosevelt's choice of ground on which to fight the legislative battle over the bill—the ground he had defined with his insistence, in his last fireside chat, that the "whole purpose" of his "arsenal of democracy" proposal was to keep this country out of war. It was false ground, cried some of the most respected isolationists; the statement of purpose was craftily designed, as the stated purpose of "court reform" in 1937 had been designed, to obscure the bill's real purpose, which was to get us *into* the war, not with brave bold directness, but through a furtive cowardly step-by-step. The wily, slippery politician in the White House refused frankly to state the only logical and honorable conclusion to his premise that our survival depended upon British victory because he knew that if he did so, the American people would repudiate him. But would they? Or would they for very long? The more politically astute of the isolationists began to doubt it. Their doubt added a desperate urgency to their present opposition.

Montana's Senator Burton K. Wheeler was especially angered. A notably liberal Democrat when the New Deal began, Wheeler, who was himself abnormally addicted to blunt candor of speech and straightforward action, had been repeatedly dismayed during the administration's first term by what he saw as Rooseveltian deviousness, Rooseveltian deceitfulness. He became finally convinced by the White House's court-packing scheme, against which he led the victorious charge, that Roosevelt was an unscrupulous, vindictive double-dealer whose lust for power threatened the very foundations of liberal government. Since then the senator's disaffection had become a personal hatred—a hatred so bitter and pervasive that it distorted his vision, flawed his judgment, and caused him to ally himself, in political battle, with people he knew to be enemies of democracy. "Never before has this nation resorted to duplicity in its conduct of foreign affairs," he now said to a national radio audience during a debate (it was broadcast January 12 over the Mutual Broadcasting System) on the just introduced bill. "Never before has the United States given to one man the power to strip this nation of its defenses. The lend-lease-give program is the New Deal's triple-A foreign policy; it will plow under every fourth American boy!"[7]

Roosevelt, whose normal procedure was publicly to ignore attacks upon him, was moved by this one to reply immediately and heatedly. At his press conference on January 14, a reporter questioned him concerning the allegation that H.R. 1776 would give him a "blank check" on which to write his will. (General Wood, announcing on January 11 that the America First Committee would oppose lend-lease "with all the vigor it can exert," had added that the President was asking not merely for a "blank check," but for "a blank check book with the power to write away our man power, our laws and our liberties.")[8] He challenged those who made this allegation to "write me another [bill] that you would not put that label on but which would accomplish the same objective." This was "a perfectly good answer," he went on; but of course it would never satisfy (and his voice rose) "those who talk about plowing under every fourth American child, which I regard as the most untruthful, as the most dastardly, unpatriotic thing that has ever been said. Quote me on that. That really is the rottenest thing that has been said in public life in my generation."[9]

But if the "most dastardly" of the published attacks upon the bill and the man who inspired it, Wheeler's was little if any more vehement than dozens of others launched by isolationists as the lend-lease debate mounted to heights of frenzy not reached since the 1937 struggle over court reform. Former Undersecretary of State (under Hoover) William R. Castle said the bill "signs away our freedom, creates a dictatorship, . . . [and] permits the President to ignore such laws as he pleases [Castle evidently had in mind the Johnson Act, the Neutrality Act] and thus make war." Hanford MacNider, a former national commander of the American Legion, was similarly convinced that lend-lease enactment "would mean the beginning of the end of the Republic with consequent disaster not only to the American people but to free men everywhere." Most of the leading Republican politicians—Alf Landon, Thomas E. Dewey, Ohio's Senator Robert Taft, Michigan's Senator Arthur Vandenberg, ex-President Hoover—announced their opposition to the bill, some of them in doomsday language. Colonel McCormick's *Chicago Tribune* proclaimed lend-lease to be "a bill for the destruction of the American Republic," a "brief for an unlimited dictatorship with power over the possessions and lives of the American people, with power to make war and alliances forever"—and the opposition of the Hearst newspapers was equally loud and shrill.[10]

Yet Roosevelt had no reason for dismay and felt none as he surveyed the stormy scene. Public opinion polls showed a majority of the American people in support of the bill—a small majority, but one that could confidently be expected to grow, and have impact on Congress, as the debate continued in circumstances that almost certainly would add weight in the public mind to the arguments of the bill's supporters. The isolationist press opposition to the bill was more than offset by the support of newspapers, *The New York Times,* the *New York Herald-Tribune,* and the *Christian Science Monitor* among them, that were highly influential of people who in their turn were highly influential of the public opinion of their communities. The well-organized and abundantly financed opposition of the America First Committee was offset by the persuasive support of the White Committee (so the aid-Britain committee continued to be called, William Allen White having been persuaded to accept the committee's honorary chairmanship—this by the very people in New York, in Chicago, who had most condemned his recent actions). Best of all, the massive and seemingly carefully orchestrated frontal assault upon the bill by leading Republican politicians was offset, and more than offset, by the immediate and fervent support of it, in principle, by the Republican Party's titular head, Wendell Willkie.

For Willkie, emerging from the slough of despond into which his ambition-distorted self had been cast on election night, then snapping back into his natural shape, had swiftly recovered the principled commitments he had violated in the closing weeks of the campaign. He had welcomed and promptly responded to the approach made to him, two weeks after the election, by fellow Republican Henry Stimson; gratefully, he had resumed the close friendly relations that had formerly obtained between him and the secretary of war. He now made banner-headline news with two announcements, on January 12, from his New York City headquarters in the Commodore Hotel: *first,* that he strongly supported the President's aid-to-Britain proposal, though favoring some modifications of it; *second,* that he was leaving shortly for England to see for himself how the British fared in their defense of human freedom. Six days later, January 18, addressing the Women's National Republican Club, than which there was no body more filled with a virulent hatred of Franklin Roosevelt, he denounced those in his party who "blindly" opposed the bill simply and solely because it was a Roosevelt bill. "If the Republican Party . . . allows itself to be presented to the American people as the isolationist party, it will never again gain control of the American government," he prophesied, adding that, because developments in the "art of transportation" and the "art of communication" had made the world now "actually no larger than the thirteen original colonies," American freedoms could not survive the total conquest of Europe by totalitarianism. The warriors of Britain, he said, were "defending our liberty as well as theirs."[11]

All this brightened Roosevelt's vision, lifted his spirits, and confirmed in his mind the wisdom of his choice of ideological battleground. He had cabled Churchill via the State Department on January 16: "My best information is that Bill at present has safe majority in both Houses. No accurate guess as to date of final passage can be made, but I hope for February 15th." This "hope" was now strengthened, though there remained a regrettable possibility that, as Roosevelt had added to his Churchill message, "a Senate filibuster might delay" things.[12]

III

THE two men whose bitter political war upon one another had sharply divided the country less than three months ago now set before the country a potent example of national union against foreign threat, though one that outraged and embittered the dominant politicians of the Republican Party.

On January 19, the day after his Women's Republican Club speech and the day before the presidential inaugural, Willkie had a brief but cordial and hugely publicized visit with Roosevelt in the White House, this in response to an invitation issued by Roosevelt as soon as he learned of Willkie's travel plans. Robert Sherwood has told how the President was in the Cabinet Room, putting the final touches on his third inaugural address with the aid of Sherwood and Sam Rosenman, when word came that Willkie had arrived in General Watson's presidential secretarial office. Roosevelt "shifted into his wheelchair and was going through Missy LeHand's office into his own," writes Sherwood, when "he saw that his desk was clean of papers." He called back to his two speechwriters, asking them to give him a handful of papers from the litter on the cabinet table; any papers would do, he simply wanted to spread them around on his desk so that he would "look very busy" when Willkie came in.[13] He was thus obviously very busy, but just as obviously delighted to be interrupted, when he heartily greeted "Wendell" and entered at once into a conversation for which he set a light and bantering tone. He laughingly "wished" that it were Wendell and not himself who must stand up in the wintry cold tomorrow noon to take the oath of office. Willkie replied in kind, saying that the President must also wish it were he, not Willkie, who now departed for England, "where the excitement is." But there was a sense in which Roosevelt already *was* in England, insofar as Harry Hopkins was a vital extension of himself, and, reminded of this, he said that Willkie must "be sure to look Harry up" in London.

The remark jarred the conversation momentarily from its prevailing line of light repartee. For it happened that Willkie, who knew Hopkins only as a public figure, had a special loathing of him as a Machiavellian manipulator, the sinister embodiment of all that was most reprehensible in the New Deal. He had long been puzzled and disturbed by the Roosevelt-Hopkins relationship. He now asked bluntly why Roosevelt kept Hopkins "so close" to him: "You must surely realize that people distrust him and . . . resent his influence." Roosevelt's reply, as recorded by Sherwood, was destined for endless quotation. He kept "that half-man around" because he needed him, he said—"half-man" being a reference to Hopkins's wretched health that was as insensitive to Hopkins's feelings, should Hopkins ever learn of it, as it was sensitively deferential to Willkie's bias. Someday Willkie might well "be sitting where I am now as President of the United States," Roosevelt continued. "And when you are, you'll be looking at that door over there and knowing that practically everybody who walks through it wants something out of you. You'll learn what a lonely job this is, and you'll discover the need for somebody like Harry Hopkins, who asks for nothing except to serve you."[14]

At the close of the interview Roosevelt asked his guest to deliver personally a message from him to Winston Churchill—a message he promptly wrote out

on a sheet of personal stationery, sealed in an envelope inscribed "Kindness of
the Honorable Wendell Willkie," and addressed to "A Certain Naval Person."
"Dear Churchill," it began, "Wendell Willkie will give you this—He is truly
helping to keep politics out over here." Its substance was a quotation from
Longfellow's "Building of the Ship" (though the poet and title were not
named), which "I think . . . applies to you people as it does to us:

> Sail on, Oh Ship of State!
> Sail on, Oh Union strong and great.
> Humanity with all its fears,
> With all the hope of future years
> Is hanging breathless on thy fate.[15]

Roosevelt dated this missive January 20, 1941.

On that same date, Churchill wrote Roosevelt, saying that Lord Halifax, the
new ambassador to the United States, would "arrive at Annapolis in our new
battleship HMS *King George V*" which was "due at the entrance of Chesapeake
Bay at seven A.M. January 24." By law, the warship of a belligerent power could
remain no longer than twenty-four hours in a neutral country's port, but during
that time "we should be proud to show her to you or to any of your high naval
authorities." To this Roosevelt replied on January 22: "If I can manage it I will
go there [to Annapolis] Friday afternoon and meet Halifax off harbor. Destroyer
will meet her [the battleship] off Capes and act as escort. Would greatly appreciate it if two of our rear admirals and an aide could go up bay on her."[16]

Coming as it did hard upon a succession of ringing presidential declarations (the
"Arsenal of Democracy" speech, the philosophical budget message, the "Four
Freedoms" speech), Roosevelt's third inaugural address on January 20 was "almost anticlimactic," as James MacGregor Burns has written.[17] It was uncharacteristically "literary" and "high-toned," the latter term being the one Roosevelt
had used as he described to poet Archibald MacLeish, now Librarian of Congress, the kind of address he wanted. Its initial draft, which MacLeish had then
composed, was carefully integrated around a central theme and was replete with
lyrical abstractions; but during draft revisions by four minds having no gift for
soaring eloquence, or much appreciation of it, the original speech's unity was
destroyed, many of its most lyric phrases were removed, and several of those
that remained were tortured into meaninglessness.

Thus Roosevelt told the huge multitude shivering upon the Capitol Plaza (the
sky was clear, a bright sun shining, but a bitterly cold wind drove in from the
north), "Lives of Nations are determined not by count of years, but by the lifetime of the human spirit"; that the "life of a Nation is the fullness of the measure of its will to live"; that a "Nation, like a person, has a body" and "a mind"

and "a spirit" that "is something deeper, something more permanent, something larger than the sum of all its parts"; and that "the spirit—the faith of America" was born of a "democratic aspiration" that had very ancient lineage, having "permeated the life of early peoples," "blazed anew in the Middle Ages," and "been written in Magna Carta." Roosevelt closed: "It is not enough to clothe and feed the body of this Nation, to instruct, and inform its mind. For there is also the spirit. And of the three, the greatest is the spirit."[18]

The words rode out on Roosevelt's mellifluous tenor voice, were spread by amplifiers to the farthest reaches of the assembled shivering thousands, and, alas, fell flat upon them out of the freezing air. Of all the major speeches Roosevelt made as President, this one aroused the least response on the part of its immediate audience. "[P]erhaps the very solemnity of the theme hushed public reaction," commented Rosenman in a later year. "In any event, the President was disappointed at the apparent failure of his words. . . ."[19]

IV

By that time, hearings on the bill before the House Foreign Affairs Committee were well under way. They had been opened on Wednesday, January 15, in the Ways and Means Committee room of the Longworth Building (the House Office Building)—a large room that, on that day and on every day of hearings that followed, was packed by some five hundred intensely interested spectators.

The leadoff administration witness was Secretary of State Hull. This was to be expected. The expectation had been fulfilled in this case with difficulty, however, thanks to Hull's hurt resentment of Roosevelt's assignment of the bill's drafting to Treasury. When Treasury's Foley initially proposed the role Hull would ultimately play, Hull's resentment fed on the fact that Foley came to him as Morgenthau's emissary, not the President's. He petulantly demurred, protesting that he was ill informed about the bill's financial detail (he himself continued to insist that the British had far greater financial resources than they chose to disclose) and about its technical sections also (though, as he was reminded, a competent State Department representative had been present at every important conference on the measure). Why didn't Morgenthau lead off? asked Hull. The reason why was obvious to Morgenthau, as to others. The bill was a foreign policy measure, and Hull was the administration's chief foreign affairs officer. Hull's standing with Congress, of which he had formerly been a leading member, and with the national electorate, was higher than Morgenthau's. And Hull was of "old American" stock, whereas Morgenthau was a Jew and, as Morgenthau himself stressed in private argument, might be perceived to be testifying as much out of a blind personal fear of Hitler's anti-Semitism as out of a sober, reasoned commitment to the national interest. It would be best if Morgenthau limited his testimony strictly to financial matters, of which he was a presumed and ex officio authority, eschewing the kind of general philosophical statement with which the discussion should be opened. In the end, Morgenthau had to persuade Roosevelt to persuade Hull into the leadoff testimony, of which a portion of the opening statement was written by Roosevelt himself.[20]

Despite all this, Hull, confining himself to the basic theme of America's peril and the desperate need to get war stuff to Britain *fast,* performed his task well, his testimony laying a solid foundation for the administration testimony that followed. "We are in the presence of forces which are not restrained by considerations of law or principles of morality," he said, and "the most serious question before this country" was whether "control of the high seas" was to be permitted to "pass into the hands of the powers bent on a program of unlimited conquest." It was "in this light . . . that we should order" our "thinking and action" regarding "the amount of material assistance which our country is prepared to furnish Great Britain." Under critical questioning, he made no claim that lend-lease would keep America out of war ("I want you to know that in my view there is danger in either direction") but insisted that it was "the safest course" available to us. He admitted that major portions of the Neutrality Act would be superseded by this new act but flatly denied that the Johnson Act would be affected by it. The latter, he asserted with dubious accuracy, forbade *private* lending to debt-defaulting nations but did not "apply to this Government or to a public corporation."[21]

Morgenthau followed.

Over his testimony, too, as it was being prepared, there was disagreement between Hull and Morgenthau. Though the secretary of state protested a lack of information about Britain's financial situation, he claimed to know that Britain had $18 billion in total assets worldwide and therefore could and should put up collateral worth $2 billion, or $3 billion, for the loans we would make to her under lend-lease. He enlisted in support of this proposal Vice President Garner, Jesse Jones, and initially Frank Knox, who later admitted, somewhat sheepishly, that he had been misled by his ignorance of the distinction between dollar reserves and sterling assets. And from this position, Hull could not be budged by Morgenthau, by Treasury economist Herbert Feis, or by any Treasury document. Neither was he moved by a January 2 message from Churchill to Roosevelt (a copy of it went to Hull) wherein the Former Naval Person worried about how Britain was "to live through" a period of financial drought that might extend to February 15 or even beyond. "What would be the effect upon the world situation if we had to default in payments to your contractors who have their workmen to pay?" asked Churchill. "The idea that in the interval we shall either have to default or be stripped bare of our last resources is full of danger and causes us profound anxiety." Referring to this message, Roosevelt said in a letter to Hull from Hyde Park, on January 11, that while the "situation in regard to British payments for materials already ordered in this country is not clear," he was very sure that British assets "all over the world" amounted to much less than $18 billion. "My figure would be 9 to 10 billion dollars." He expressed himself as "sympathetic" to the idea of stipulating "some form of security" if that proved absolutely necessary "to get the bill through," but he had "real doubt" about the value to the United States of the collateral the British might put up—"assets in India, Straits settlements, China, etc. . . . for instance, British property in Singapore." There was, of course, "the possibility of their putting up their sovereignty . . . over certain colonies" in the Western Hemisphere, but he, Roosevelt, feared that U.S. sovereignty over these territories would prove "a distinct liability" to us. "If we can get our naval bases why, for example, should we buy with them two million headaches, consisting of that number of human beings who would be a definite economic drag on this country . . . ?" Nevertheless, Hull continued to argue for collateral. He did so in strategy meetings held on January 14, the very eve of the hearings' opening. At the same time, in evident tacit recognition that Britain's actual financial condition was much more dire than he claimed, he vehemently opposed Morgenthau's full disclosure of this condition to public view in hearings testimony because, he said, doing so would hearten Britain's enemies and dishearten the British people.[22]

His confused argument was ineffective.

Morgenthau, as he was about to depart for the Capitol to give his testimony, received a phone call from the President admonishing him, in a jocular tone, not to be "too definite" and, above all, not to let the British saddle us with any West Indian islands! Arrived in the committee room, he proceeded according to plan. "I come here prepared to give you all the information which the British Treasury has furnished me," he said, "and I give it to you with their consent. . . . And so far as I know, this is the first time in history that one government has put at the disposal of another figures of this nature." He presented the information in four separate documents, three of them dealing in detail with Britain's present and prospective financial condition. The fourth was a comparison of British with American taxes—this is evident support of Roosevelt's budget message implication that Americans, measured by the demands of the world crisis they faced, were now greatly undertaxed. Since the war's outbreak, the British Purchasing Commission had paid for and taken delivery of $1,337,000,000 in supplies, Morgenthau continued; on order were an additional $1,400,000,000 of supplies, more than the British now had dollars to pay for but for which they might be able to pay by the end of 1941. (The question implicitly raised was, How could the American suppliers pay their own costs for labor and materials during an interval of weeks or months between supply delivery and payment?) "But when it comes to finding dollars for anything like what they need in the future," said Morgenthau, "they just have not got it." Under questioning, he denied that lend-lease, having been prepared by Treasury, was therefore a Treasury bill, not a foreign policy bill (indeed, he played down Treasury's bill-drafting role to a rashly mendacious degree): and he refused to estimate what the ultimate cost of lend-lease might be to the United States. Any such "estimate," in these times of swift turbulent change, could be only a wild guess, he indicated.[23]

Stimson followed Morgenthau to the witness table. Because he was a prominent Republican serving in a Democratic administration, hence branded a "renegade" by leading politicians of his party; because of the reputation for absolute integrity and truth telling that he had acquired through decades of public life; and because early last summer (before his cabinet appointment but after the fall of France) he had joined other prominent Americans in a public call for an immediate declaration of war upon the Axis powers, Stimson's testimony attracted a closer and wider attention across the land than did that of any other administration witness. It was also more effective than any other in support of the bill. The central thrust of his prepared statement was that the legislation would result in an expanded, more expeditious American arms production and enable the establishment of rational, orderly procedures for the distribution of that production among the American armed services and those of Britain and other friendly powers. At the moment, with regard to this matter, chaotic conditions prevailed. To the charge that lend-lease violated international law, he made so effective an answer that no later administration witness had to deal with it. He accomplished this by citing the International Law Association's interpretation of the 1926 Kellogg-Briand Peace Pact—a pact that the United States along with every nation now at war had signed. Said the interpretation: If any signatory state violated the pact (as the Axis powers had certainly done), the other signatory states were no longer bound "to observe toward" that state "the duties prescribed by international law, apart from the pact, for a neutral in relation to a belligerent."[24]

Only somewhat if any less effective was Stimson's response to the charge by leading members of his own party that lend-lease would give dictatorial powers to a President who (it was unmistakably implied when not explicitly stated) could not be trusted. Any "government or law which is so constructed [that is, based on the premise] that you cannot trust anybody [with power] will not survive the test of war," said Henry Stimson. Actually, the present legislation did only what had always been done, and must be done, by Americans in a national emergency: it delegated to the President a power to act that was proportionate to the crying need for swift, untrammeled action. In the present crisis, the President *had* to be trusted. Moreover, in Stimson's opinion, he could be safely trusted. He, Stimson, had had "the privilege and honor of observing at close range" several Presidents during his seventy-four years of life, and "I have been impressed always with the tremendously sobering influence that the terrific responsibility of the Presidency will impose on any man, and particularly in foreign relations. . . . I feel that there is no one else, no other possible person in any official position who can be trusted to make conservatively and cautiously such a tremendous decision as the decisions which would have to be made in a great emergency involving a possible war. . . ." Though repeatedly and sometimes in-sultingly pressed to do so by committee isolationists, he flatly refused comment upon any controversial matter not explicitly covered by the bill's language—the U.S. naval escort of convoys, for instance, or the sending of American merchant ships into war zones, despite the fact that these matters must soon be dealt with if lend-lease were to accomplish its purpose. When Congressman Hamilton Fish asked him if it were "not rather cowardly of us, if England is fighting our battle, not to go into the war," he replied that he would not "pursue this line of argument" because "[w]e are not concerned with it in this bill."[25]

Secretary of the Navy Knox, the next administration witness, stressed the in-dispensability of the British navy to American security. The Monroe Doctrine had been largely implemented by the British navy; this navy had constituted, in effect, half the two-ocean navy required for our security after Japan's rise to great sea power; and Britain's continued resistance to Nazi-fascism bought time we desperately needed for the completion of our own two-ocean defenses. If Britain's sea power were destroyed within the next few months, we would face a combined Axis naval strength considerably stronger than our own—an omi-nous fact that Knox demonstrated with a statistical table. Questioned about the use of armed escorts for convoys, the navy secretary did not refuse to answer, as Stimson had done, on the ground that this matter was not covered in the bill. In-stead, having stated his opposition to a proposed bill amendment that would ex-plicitly prohibit armed convoys, he was driven by hostile questioning to say (Stimson was appalled by Knox's saying, as Knox was later appalled at his hav-ing said) that he personally opposed the escorting of convoys because it was an act of war and was even more strongly against the sending of American "man-power" to Britain should lend-lease aid prove "insufficient."[26]

Knudsen of OPM, the last of the key administration witnesses, was also the least controversial of them, being less closely identified with the administra-tion than any of the others and, of course, far more closely identified with the big-business interest to which the top leadership of the Republican Party was committed (he had been a member of the Liberty League, which vehemently opposed Roosevelt's reelection in 1936). His prepared statement, and his an-swers to questions, which were put to him more gently than they had been to his predecessors at the witness table, were mostly a repetition of what had already been said. He did admit, under questioning, that no significant amount of lend-lease matériel could reach Britain before the end of 1941 unless there were a swift acceleration of American war goods production, which is to say that lend-lease would not materially affect the outcome if Britain were invaded within the next sixty to ninety days, as it was then widely believed she might be. But Knudsen vaguely indicated, and others were quick to assert, that American in-dustry *could* and *would* increase its production vastly and quickly as necessary organizational "adjustments" were made.[27]

The private citizens who gave House committee testimony in favor of the bill included columnist Dorothy Thompson; William Green of the American Federation of Labor; ex-ambassador Bullitt; General John F. Ryan; Ernest W. Gibson, who had replaced White as active chairman of the White Committee; and Mrs. J. Borden Harriman, who had been U.S. minister to Norway when that country was invaded. They generally based their testimony on wider ground than Rooseveltian policy had permitted administration witnesses to occupy. They were also generally more frank and fervent in their statements than the administration spokesmen had been. Thus Dorothy Thompson expressed with passionate eloquence the loathing of Nazism that she shared with millions of Americans. Bullitt inveighed in typically dramatic style against America's "Maginot line mentality," saying that the complacency with which our citizenry now huddled behind the ramparts raised by British valor (though Bullitt was no lover of Britain) would, if continued, lead to such tragedy as had overwhelmed France. General Ryan, a frank advocate of immediate U.S. entry into the war, pointed out that it did not require two or more to make a war; one sufficed— the aggressor. Mrs. Harriman reinforced General Ryan's point as she spoke of Hitler's surprise attack upon Norway.[28]

The first of the opposition witnesses to appear before the committee was Joseph P. Kennedy—and he proved, from the opposition's point of view, remarkably unsatisfactory.

A principal reason for this was a ninety-minute interview Kennedy had had with the President on January 16—an interview arranged by the White House within hours after it learned that Kennedy would address the nation over a national radio network on January 19.

Roosevelt had carefully refrained from public comment, during the last seven weeks, upon Kennedy's repeated assertion that he "helped the President" in the "greatest cause in the world today" (that of keeping America out of war) as he spread across the land the view that Britain was doomed and that an accommodation must therefore be reached with the Axis powers. Nor did Roosevelt now, in this White House interview, give the slightest sign of that personal loathing of Kennedy he had expressed to Eleanor in Hyde Park. Indeed, it was as a warm personal friend of Joe's and Joe's family, eager to help Joe Jr.'s political ambition, that he greeted Kennedy and, as before, spoke to him with beguiling candor of the crushing burdens that must be carried, the complex problems that must somehow be solved, by a President of the United States in times like these. He sympathized with Kennedy's bitterness over press attacks upon him by administration "hatchet men"; he even deplored such attacks; but they were part of the price one paid for any real activity in a democracy's high office, he indicated, and, in any case, were nothing he personally could do anything about without violating free speech principles. He himself had to endure worse press attacks almost every day. He then presented, in terms of a personal plea for help, the reasons why lend-lease was essential to Britain's survival, argued persuasively on the basis of factual information that with lend-lease help Britain could not only survive, but actually win the war, and managed to coax from Kennedy an admission that such survival, such victory, was greatly in the interest of the United States. He went further, according to Kennedy's own recollection. The ex-ambassador, in violation of his private convictions but in close pursuit of his ambition, had recently suggested to the British embassy in Washington that he, as a leading American Irish Catholic, might be able to persuade Eamon De Valera's government to open Irish seaports and airports to British use if he went there in a semiofficial capacity. The personal prestige and publicity thus obtained might restore him to popular and administration favor. The President now encouraged him to believe that this stratagem was producing results, saying to him, as Kennedy wrote years later, that "he [the President] would like to have a long talk with me about the Irish situation, which, according to Welles, I was the only one who could help in straightening it out." (The "long talk" was never held.)[29]

Kennedy left the White House that day glowing with friendly feelings for Franklin Roosevelt and, three days later, delivered a radio address so confused in its reasoning and so carefully "fair-minded" that no critical listener could tell for sure just where the speaker stood on the matters discussed. He favored aid to Britain even though Britain could not pay for it but insisted that the aid must not be so great that it committed this country to intervention in the war. "We want to preserve democracy," but the American democracy could not, in his opinion, survive a long war, and our getting in would "practically leave Russia alone outside the war area, getting stronger, while the rest of the world approached exhaustion." In the face of published evidence to the contrary, he denied he had ever said that Britain's cause was hopeless. It was not hopeless. But "England" was not "fighting our battle." He closed with the statement that he was opposed to the Lend-Lease Act.[30]

Kennedy's testimony before the House committee on January 21 was similarly confused. He favored all aid to Britain short of war that could be constitutionally given but seemed to imply that lend-lease in its present form was an unconstitutional delegation of powers to the President. At any rate, he opposed lend-lease in its present form. He admitted that efficiency required a concentration of executive power and expressed utter confidence in Roosevelt's competency in the field of foreign policy, but he said that Congress must not be permitted to become "a rubber stamp" and should have an active part in lend-lease administration. England was at war "against a force which seeks to destroy the rule of conscience, and reason, a force that proclaims its hostility to law, to family, even to religion itself," but nevertheless, this was "not our war." He did "not want to see this country go to war under any circumstances unless we are attacked." Under questioning, to the dismay of some of his interlocutors, he refused to say that lend-lease would bring us any closer to intervention than we now were and refused to describe himself as an isolationist.[31]

More satisfactory by far to the isolationists who constituted a majority of the audience in the committee room on January 23 was the testimony that day of Charles Lindbergh. Adhering strictly to the line he had been following ever since his first radio broadcast, the aviation hero was, in his testimony, perfectly straightforward and self-consistent. He favored the strengthening of America's air arm (he deemed sufficient "an air force of about 10,000 . . . modern fighting planes plus reserves") and of all else necessary to ensure hemispheric defense, but he was implicitly opposed to any arms strengthening beyond this point, since once adequate hemispheric defenses were in place, we would be in absolutely no danger of invasion. Though most isolationists, while against lend-lease, now professed support of aid to Britain, Lindbergh did not. Such aid could not change the outcome of the war, he said; it merely prolonged the bloodshed abroad and reduced our strength at home. "[W]e are strong enough [now] in this nation and in this hemisphere to maintain our way of life no matter what the attitude is on the other side. I do not believe we are strong enough to impose our way of life on Europe and Asia." He was flatly opposed to H.R. 1776 because it was a step away from democracy (though his commitment to democracy was, on the evidence, dubious) and a step toward war. He professed an absolute neutrality of attitude toward the conflict; the "two sides" were equally to blame for the catastrophe. When an exasperated congressman asked him (and was loudly hissed for daring to ask) which side he personally *wanted* to win, Lindbergh replied with icy calm that he wanted neither to win: he favored a negotiated peace and was sure one could be arranged by the United States government if that government but tried. Of course, it would probably not be "what we here think of as a just peace . . . , but I ask what the alternative is." A "complete victory on either side would result in prostration in Europe such as we have never seen."[32]

What Lindbergh here testified to with perfect consistency was the opinion of that hardest inner core of American isolationism that, in the months ahead, would stand firm under whatever pressures were brought against it by hostile event or logical argument. It was an opinion that was coldly calculating in its implementation but, in essence, anti-intellectual, even literally irrational, insofar as it was grounded in the romanticism (the assertion that feeling is superior to thinking as a guide to truth) that Rousseau initiated in the Western world, which leads naturally to a worship of Great Men and from which sprang the ideology of Nazi-fascism. Of very different nature and significance was much of the opposition testimony that followed. It was characterized not by self-consistency, but by self-contradiction; it expressed not an opinion, but a wide variety of opinions between which were wide areas of disagreement.

Some of this testimony was scholarly and high-minded. Eminent constitutional lawyers John Basset Moore and Edwin Borchard made closely reasoned, scholarly presentations "proving" that H.R. 1776's transfer of power from the Legislature to the Executive was both unwise and unconstitutional. In what was certainly not his happiest contribution to the national dialogue (if just as certainly high-minded), Norman Thomas argued with characteristic eloquence that since America's entrance into the war would mean the death of an already dangerously ill American democracy, our historic challenge was to concentrate upon the cure of our own social and economic ills and, in the process, so uplift our democracy that it became a beacon light for all the world. He went so far as to suggest that if we performed our task well, the example of social justice and human decency that we provided the world would be persuasive enough to cause even Nazi Germany to mend its evil ways. (No such hope animated University of Chicago president Robert Maynard Hutchins as he joined the national debate of the bill; in a speech condemning H.R. 1776 as suicidal, he asserted that the American democracy was so sick morally and intellectually that it could not exercise world leadership of any kind against totalitarianism.) But neither scholarship nor high-mindedness characterized much of the rest of the House opposition testimony. Prominent in it was a profound distrust of Great Britain— this an element of the continuing bitter disillusionment resulting from the nationalistic machinations of Versailles, from the disclosure of the murderous command stupidities that had been hidden by a wall of censorship during the Great War, and from the revelation that a large part of the Great War's official propaganda was wholly false. Detroit's Gerald L. K. Smith, a fundamentalist preacher and racial bigot, testified nastily on behalf of a highly questionable Committee of One Million (its actual membership was unknown), organized by himself. The notoriously Anglophobic William R. Grace of Chicago, speaking for a Citizens Keep Out of War Committee, was sure lend-lease was a traitorous sacrifice of American interests to those of Perfidious Albion. And but little more elevated in tone or content was the testimony of others who were asked or permitted by isolationist congressmen to appear before the committee.[33]

In sum, as Langer and Gleason have written, this opposition testimony "served chiefly to emphasize the diverse sources and inspiration of the opposition group, and to reveal how seemingly hopeless was the task of uniting them on any workable program."[34]

The last of the House committee witnesses to appear in the public hearings did so on January 29. The committee then went into executive session to hear secret testimony given by Hull and General Marshall. There were signs that Vichy was being pressured to permit Axis use of French North African port facilities (German dive bombers had been seen over the Mediterranean), said Hull; and the invasion of Britain was likely to come within ninety days—a prediction supported by, if not derived from, cables and letters to the President from Harry Hopkins in London. Marshall made a factual depressing report of the state of American preparedness, or unpreparedness at that moment, for war.

Next day, the committee members debated nineteen proposed amendments to the bill, of which only four were adopted. These four, part of the "tightening up" that Morgenthau had allowed for during the drafting process, had been readily agreed to by the President in a bipartisan White House conference (Senate Minority Leader Charles McNary of Oregon and House Minority Leader Joseph Martin of Massachusetts were present, along with the majority party leaders of both houses) on January 27. One of them would set a specific limit upon the time during which the President could authorize the making of lend-lease agreements by the secretaries of war and navy. Another would say that nothing "in this Act shall be construed to authorize or permit the authorization of convoying vessels by naval vessels of the United States" or "to authorize or permit the authorization of the entry of any American vessel into a combat area in violation of section 3 of the Neutrality Act of 1939." (Stimson contended, and would soon persuade Knox, that congressional approval of naval escorts for convoys was not necessary—the Constitution gave the President authority to order such action, for national defense, on his own.) The third amendment would require the President to consult with the chief of staff and the chief of naval operations before authorizing the release to foreign nations of defense materials already on hand. Another would require the President "from time to time, but not less frequently than once in every ninety days," to report to Congress all information about operations under the act that were deemed by him not "incompatible with the public interest to disclose." Roosevelt's agreement to these changes was no forced concession on his part: obvious to all was the fact that the administration had the votes to pass an unamended measure through House and Senate. But, while giving away nothing vital, the amendments would appear a gesture of magnanimity on the part of the White House; their adoption would speed the measure's passage.[35]

And speedy action continued.

The Foreign Affairs Committee reported the amended bill favorably by a vote of 17–8 on January 30, within hours after Adolf Hitler had helped the cause along by threatening to sink every ship that attempted to carry supplies to Britain. House floor debate of the measure opened four days later. During it, other amendments were adopted, only one of which was of importance: it provided that the President could at any time, during the tenure of the act, be stripped of his lend-lease powers by congressional resolution. But since such action, once the lend-lease program was under way amid increasing world crisis, was unlikely in the extreme, it little worried the Executive. On February 8, the House passed its version of lend-lease by a vote of 260–165 (236 Democrats and 24 Republicans voted for it; 135 Republicans and 25 Democrats, plus pro-Communist Vito Marcantonio of the American Labor Party, voted against).

By then the Senate hearings on the bill had been under way for more than a week, having been gaveled into order by Foreign Relations Committee chairman Walter George on January 27. (As soon as the House acted on the bill, the

Senate committee dropped S. 275 and adopted H.R. 1776 as its own.) Hull, Morgenthau, Stimson, and Knox had substantially repeated as administration spokesmen the testimony they had earlier presented to the House committee. Opposition testimony, somewhat more weighty than that given the House committee, had been presented by, among others, historian Charles A. Beard (he described lend-lease as "an Act to place all the wealth and all the men and women of the United States at the free disposal of the President"); Joseph Curran, head of the Communist-influenced National Maritime Union (he described the proposal as "downright Fascist"); the Communist-dominated American Youth Congress (it begged the senators, by letter, "not to lend or lease our lives"); the editor of the *Christian Century* (Dr. Charles Clayton Morrison denounced "the angry and futile sentimentalism" of theologian Reinhold Niebuhr's assertion that the present war was one for the preservation of Christian civilization); again, Charles Lindbergh (he claimed that the American army and air force were poorly equipped by "modern standards," that "even our navy is in urgent need of new equipment," that "if we deplete our forces still further, as this bill indicates we may, and if England should lose this war, then, gentlemen, . . . we may be in danger of invasion, though I do not believe we are today"); and *Chicago Tribune* publisher Colonel Robert McCormick, who said that the geographic and strategic position in the United States was such that any talk of foreign invasion was ridiculous.[36]

V

"DID he speak as an expert?" was Roosevelt's interruptive, laughter-provoking, and dismissive comment upon the McCormick testimony when a *Tribune* correspondent attempted to question him about it in a press conference on February 7, the day after the testimony was given.[37]

He commented at length, however, when queried that day about his appointment of Kennedy's successor as ambassador to Great Britain, an appointment just announced, many weeks after Roosevelt had "expected" to do so.

The appointee was John G. Winant, a man widely different in every way from his predecessor. A New Hampshire Republican, he was of that party's progressive wing whose members, in the 1930s, found Roosevelt's New Deal more attractive than old guard Republicanism had ever been to them. He was commonly described as Lincolnesque. He was certainly so in appearance, being tall and heavy boned, with a craggy countenance; he was also Lincolnesque in general character, impressing his associates as a remarkably *good* man, selfless, kind, utterly committed to the general welfare, and, like Lincoln, a man of sorrows, conscientious to a fault and consequently subject to fits of melancholy. Like Lincoln, too, he was not slavishly addicted to the neat and orderly in his professional life—was, indeed, a haphazard, highly disorganized administrator, so much so that his effectiveness often suffered from it. He had served three terms as governor of New Hampshire (1927–1929, 1931–1933, 1933–1935), during which he had dealt fair-mindedly with the abundant labor problems of New Hampshire's ailing textile industry. He had also become actively concerned with national problems when the New Deal began—had been called to Washington to serve on the committee that drafted the original Social Security legislation, had also served on the three-man board appointed by Roosevelt to inquire into and arbitrate the issues of the great national textile strike of 1934. In 1935 Roosevelt had named him chairman (the first chairman) of the three-member Social Security Board, a post he resigned during the presidential campaign of 1936 in order to defend Social Security against the misinformed charges brought against it by Republican presidential candidate Alf Landon. Subsequently he had served in Geneva as assistant director, then as director, of the International Labor Organization (ILO), one of the few actively surviving agencies of the defunct League of Nations), and had managed with much difficulty to transfer ILO headquarters to Montreal shortly after the fall of France.

Winant was summoned from Montreal by Roosevelt for a White House interview on the morning of Friday, January 24. This was the day when, in the afternoon, Roosevelt went to Annapolis, as tentatively promised, to greet in person the arriving Lord Halifax, also to inspect HMS *King George V*—a greatly publicized gesture that was deliberately significant of the increasing intimacy of British-American relations. Winant's morning visit came amid a flurry of published rumors that he was slated to be Halifax's counterpart in London, but according to Winant himself, the President made no mention of the ambassadorship that day. Instead he quizzed Winant concerning the latter's personal observations of the Battle of France and the Dunkirk evacuation.[38] What seems probable is that this interview finally solidified in Roosevelt's mind a decision theretofore tentatively fluid and that Winant, having sensed as much, was not at all surprised when he read in the Canadian press on February 7 that he, though he had received no official notification of the fact, was to go to the Court of St. James.

Why was he chosen?

Not because he was a Republican, replied Roosevelt at his press conference. It would be "a great mistake to make" Winant's party affiliation the "lead in any story." He was chosen because he was a truly representative American, having had statewide executive experience, national Social Security experience, and international experience in labor matters. "In other words, he had a lot of experience that fitted him for the job" of representing *all* Americans. The questioning reporter protested that what he "had in mind" was not party politics, but the fact that Winant had been "out in front" on matters of social reform, of changing "social structure." Did this have "anything to do with" Winant's selection? "I don't think so," Roosevelt said cautiously. Of course Winant did "represent . . . pretty well" a changing America in which the changes were "worked into the constitutional and democratic form of government that we happen to live under, and without the necessity of revolution or dictatorship. He represents that . . . *fact* that is going on in our midst and in a great many other places in the world—he represents that fact pretty well."[39]

Actually, as was widely surmised at the time, and as Roosevelt sought to play down in the public prints for political reasons, Winant's liberalism, his having "a sense of social service which amounts almost to a religious conviction" (so a British Foreign Office minute observed), was a dominant factor in Roosevelt's choice of him for this post. And what had been widely surmised became a virtual certainty in the public mind when announcement was made that Benjamin V. Cohen, than whom there was a no more fervent and intellectually brilliant New Dealer in the whole of the administration, would accompany Winant to London as embassy counsel. Clearly Roosevelt sought with this appointment to extend the New Deal to Britain, wrote Arthur Krock in *The New York Times*. He did so because he "sees the possibility (even probability) of a 'new order' in England," wrote Breckinridge Long in his diary after conversing with Roosevelt. "The Country Gentleman type, the landed and industrial aristocracy [personified by the former appeaser, Lord Halifax], are being jolted out of position. If Churchill should fall, a new government would be drafted from a new type." And Roosevelt frankly indicated the same thing to Willkie when the two men conversed shortly after Willkie had returned from his European trip; Roosevelt then said he had named Gil Winant ambassador because there was likely to be "a social revolution" in England as a result of this war and Winant, with his profound sympathy for the underdog, was sensitively attuned to such developments.[40]

This assessment of historic trend was one in which Willkie concurred.

Willkie's visit to England had been more than a huge personal public relations triumph, though it was certainly that. He had toured the bomb-ruined portions of London, Birmingham, Dover, Coventry; had had interviews with Churchill and the top members of the Churchill cabinet; had conversed at length with Labour intellectual Harold Laski; had socialized with some of Britain's most prominent literary figures at a dinner party hosted by Rebecca West; had submitted to numerous press and radio interviews. But he had also mingled much with ordinary citizens, had talked with them face-to-face on the street and in air raid shelters while bombs fell from the skies, had visited with them in pubs, where he engaged, with a notable lack of expertise, in dart throwing. As he did these things he had become convinced that England's historic class structure was indeed cracking, was breaking down bit by bit under the hail of German bombs and the leveling pressures of an immense common danger. He concluded that a principal motivation of Chamberlain's appeasement policy had been fear on the part of Tory businessmen that war would cause labor upheaval in England and social revolution on the Continent, had concluded also that what these privileged few had feared was in process of occurring—a conclusion that increased his admiration for those Tories who, like Churchill, recognized this risk but measured it small against that of a total loss of human freedom. While Willkie thus learned, he "earned more newspaper, radio, and newsreel space than almost anything in the war," according to a leading mass-circulating British periodical. The sober-sided *Times* of London said that "the impression" Willkie made upon the British people "of sincerity, friendship, boundless energy, and radiant high spirits" had been "immensely heartening." In sum, though his trip achieved no tangible results (he tried but wholly failed to persuade De Valera, during a visit to Ireland, to open Irish ports and airfields to the British), "his effect both on Europe and the United States was enormous," as Joseph Barnes has written.[41]

He now made a further important contribution to the developing British-American alliance by responding affirmatively to pleas by proponents of lend-lease that he return to America to testify in person before the Senate Foreign Relations Committee hearings. He cut short his European trip and flew on a British Overseas Airway clipper from England to Lisbon, then on a Yankee clipper from Lisbon to New York,* landing at LaGuardia on Sunday, February 9.

That same Sunday, Winston Churchill broadcast from Chequers, the official country estate of the British Prime Minister, one of the most memorable of his radio addresses—a carefully crafted (not to say crafty) composition whose tone and content were much influenced by what Churchill had learned of the American political situation from Willkie and Hopkins—especially Hopkins, who, on the eve of his return to America, actually helped draft it. Said the Prime Minister: "It seems now certain that the Government and people of the United States intend to supply us with all that is necessary for victory." But, he emphasized, this necessity did not include the sending of "two million men across the Atlantic," as America had done "in the last war." The present war differed from the last. It was not one of "vast armies, firing immense masses of shells at one another" (to prevent its becoming so, in repetition of the horrors of the Great War's stalemate, was a principal aim of Churchill's war strategy). There would therefore be no call by Britain upon "the gallant armies which are forming throughout the American Union"—not "this year, nor next year, nor any year that I can foresee." What Britain did need, however, and "most urgently," was "an immense and continuous supply of war materials and technical apparatus of all kinds," which only America could supply. America must also help in supply delivery; there would be required "a great mass of shipping in 1942, far more than we can build ourselves, if we are to maintain and augment our war effort in

---

*U.S. neutrality law at that time forbade any U.S. commercial plane from going to any airport in a belligerent nation.

the West and in the East." The address closed with a reference to the handwritten personal message from the President of the United States to the Prime
Minister of Great Britain, hand-delivered by Willkie at No. 10 Downing Street
a couple of weeks ago. Churchill read dramatically the Longfellow verse that
Roosevelt had included. Then: "What is the answer that I shall give, in your
name, to this great man, the thrice-chosen head of a nation of a hundred and
thirty million? *Give us the tools and we will finish the job.*"[42]

Willkie's testimony before the Senate committee was presented two days
later, on Tuesday, February 11, before 1,200 people, the largest crowd ever assembled, or that it was physically possible to assemble, in the marble-walled
caucus room of the Senate Office Building. The opponents of the measure had
by then completed their testimony, some of which made embittered reference
to Willkie's apostasy, as isolationist Republicans saw it. One Cathrine Curtis,
for instance, chairman of a Women's National Committee to Keep the U.S. Out
of War, had spoken sneeringly of "Indiana's wandering—and wondering—
son . . . just returned from his circus tour of British pubs and London slums [one
senses Ms. Curtis's class bias]." Thus was prepared a dramatic psychological
setting for an appearance that in itself, at its outset, was not at all dramatic. The
usually somewhat rumpled Willkie presented a well-groomed appearance, his
new blue suit neatly pressed, his abundant dark hair neatly combed (initially,
that is; it became somewhat tousled as he ran his hand through it during the
question period). His manner was frank and open but less exuberant than usual,
for he aimed to give an impression of quiet confidence and self-control. His
opening statement contained no surprises. He declared again his firm support of
the lend-lease principle, also of its embodiment in the present bill as amended
in the House. He found self-contradiction in those who said they favored an aid-
Britain policy but opposed this particular measure on the ground that it would
get us into war. Actually, lend-lease simply implemented effectively the aid-
Britain policy that the country had already adopted, with overwhelming popular
approval. If this policy was bound to get us in, we already *were* in, practically
speaking. But he himself remained convinced that lend-lease, far from assuring
our full-scale entry into the war, represented a last best chance for us to avoid it.
For Hitler, who would not hesitate to attack us whenever he thought it would advantage him, was highly unlikely to do so while Britain yet stood firm and
strong against him, and Britain would stand more firm and strong than ever
when provided with the material help this measure would give her. Moreover, as
her Prime Minister had just said, material help was *all* she would need from us.
Willkie's own observations abroad testified to the truth of Churchill's assurance: the British desperately needed from America the tools of war; they didn't
need or want American manpower.[43]

The only dramatic surprises in this testimony came when Willkie responded
to the committee members' questions. A senator asked him about the naval pro-

tection of convoys. The United States would not need to provide such protection, replied Willkie, if the British were given enough destroyers to guard the convoys themselves; he proposed, therefore, that the United States give the British five to ten destroyers *a month*! This shocked and dismayed Frank Knox, who, only a few days before, had told this Senate committee that he opposed any further transfers of American naval vessels (the navy secretary suspected that what Willkie proposed had been suggested to him by Roosevelt during the conversation the two men had had immediately following Willkie's return).

Even more dramatic was Willkie's response when a committee isolationist, in support of his contention that Roosevelt could not be trusted with the vast power this bill would give him, referred to things Willkie had said about his opponent's deviousness and mendacity during the presidential election campaign. The initiation of this line of questioning provoked a chorus of groans among that considerable majority of the audience that was sympathetic to Willkie. It caused Willkie himself to shift uncomfortably in his chair, run his fingers through his hair, and fumble for words. "I struggled as hard as I could to defeat Franklin Roosevelt," he finally said, "and I tried not to pull any of my punches. He was elected President. He is my President now." Loud applause and muffled cheers came from the audience. Committee chairman George threatened to clear the room. Then came the turn of arch-isolationist Nye, who read a sentence from a campaign speech Willkie had delivered in Baltimore a few days before the election. The Republican candidate had there referred to Roosevelt's allegedly long list of broken promises before saying with hoarse and heavy emphasis: "On the basis of his past performances with pledges to the people, you may expect we will be at war by April 1941, if he is elected." Nye wanted to know if Willkie was of the same opinion still. Willkie hedged with a question of his own: "You ask me whether or not I said that?" Said Nye: "Do you still agree that that might be the case?" "It might be," Willkie began, then broke off. With a shrug of his heavy shoulders, a wide sheepish grin, and a hand gesture of helplessness, he confessed: "It was a bit of campaign oratory."[44] Laughter swept the room. (It must be said that Willkie's rueful frankness, while delighting most of his immediate audience, and most of the country when the country learned of it, ill served his ambition to remold the Republican Party along more liberal lines, for it greatly augmented and hardened the hatred of him by the ruling powers of Republicanism and gave into their hands the means of discrediting, as mere "campaign oratory," whatever policy statements he might issue.)

Two days later, on February 13, the Senate Foreign Relations Committee reported out the lend-lease bill favorably by a vote of 15–8. A single Republican committee member, Senator Walter H. White, Jr., of Maine, voted for the bill; two isolationist Democrats, Guy Gillette of Iowa and Champ Clark of Missouri, voted against it, as did Progressive Senator Robert La Follette of Wisconsin. On February 17, two days after the date on which Roosevelt had hoped (as he said to Churchill) that the bill would be passed, Barkley opened Senate floor debate on the measure.

VI

WHEN announcement was made in early January that Harry Hopkins was going to England as the President's personal representative, several press and radio commentators ascribed to the event a sinister significance. Comparisons were made between the Hopkins mission and that of Woodrow Wilson's close friend Colonel Edward M. House in 1915.* Most explicit was the Communist *Daily Worker;* it editorially reminded its readers that House had pledged "American entrance into the first imperialistic war on the side of the Allies while Woodrow Wilson was assuring the American people that he would keep the country out of war. . . . The secret diplomacy involved in the Hopkins appointment can put the American people on the alert—in insisting that no further aid be given British imperialism, since such aid brings the shadow of war closer and closer to our homes."[45] And it must be said that the dark suspicions of this *Worker* editorialist, and of all those isolationists for whom Lindbergh spoke, were abundantly justified by Hopkins's words and deeds from the moment he arrived in England, though in his case (unlike House's) these expressed with accuracy the actual as distinct from the ostensible will of the President of the United States.

He, who frankly admitted that air travel "scared" him, was five days en route, with much rough air, and was so tired and ill when his plane landed at an airport near Poole, some seventy miles from London (the London airports were closed by the Blitz), on Thursday, January 9, that he was unable to debark when the other passengers did. Brendan Bracken, the British minister of information, whom Churchill had sent to greet this American VIP, was appalled when, boarding the plane, he found a shockingly thin, frail creature, pale of face, his dark eyes glittering as if with fever, who lay back in his plane seat in a state of total collapse, too weak even to unbuckle his safety belt. Hopkins's mission to England was coming to an end, Bracken surmised, before it had begun. Some time passed before the visitor felt strong enough to start the journey to London. But once he was on the train of Pullmans that had been assembled in pursuance of Churchill's order to accord this visiting American the honors due a foreign potentate (the train conductors wore white gloves), he rapidly, remarkably revived. It seemed to him delightfully incongruous that he, "the son of a harness-maker from Sioux City, Iowa," as he was fond of describing himself, should be

---

*In England as Wilson's personal emissary in May 1915 when the *Lusitania* was sunk by a German submarine, House immediately told his English hosts that "we [the United States] shall be at war with Germany within a month." See *FDR: The Beckoning of Destiny,* pp. 404–05.

dealt with in such royal fashion; and the revivifying effect of this sensed incongruity was joined with the intense interest he took in what he saw through his train window, namely, the bomb damage along the tracks in the port towns of Poole, Bournemouth, and Southampton. Then, as the train slanted northeastward through rural Hampshire, he made a first blunt effort to ascertain the nature and strength of the British will. Gesturing toward a window-framed landscape whose tranquility, undisturbed for centuries, contrasted sharply with the war ruins of the port towns, he asked the bespectacled carrot-haired Bracken point-blank: "Are you going to let Hitler take these fields away from you?" Bracken was somewhat taken aback. But he answered with a flat "No" and thereafter regarded his strange companion with a more hopeful interest. As the train conversation continued, Bracken was impressed by the depth of this unique envoy's commitment to the total destruction of Adolf Hitler, also by the quick shrewdness and direct honesty of his mind. By the time the train drew into Waterloo Station at seven o'clock in the evening (an air raid was under way; incendiary bombs by the hundred were falling on the line between Clapham Junction and Waterloo, over which the train had just passed), Brendan Bracken was utterly "sold" on Harry Hopkins.[46]

The latter had an even more tonic effect upon Herschel V. Johnson, who as chargé d'affaires was the ranking official of the American embassy, pending the arrival of the new ambassador, and had become despondent over Washington's evident incapacity or unwillingness to recognize the direness of Britain's plight. Hopkins pleaded weariness as an excuse for not accepting Churchill's invitation to dine at No. 10 Downing on the evening of his arrival; he instead dined with Johnson in the latter's Claridge's hotel room; and by dinner's end (it had as background noise the banging away of antiaircraft guns in Hyde Park), Johnson was greatly "heartened by the sincerity and the intensity" of Hopkins's "determination to gain firsthand knowledge of Britain's needs and of finding a way to fill them." Other official visitors from America had come to determine whether or not "the British really needed the things they were asking for. Harry wanted to find out if they were asking for *enough* to see them through. . . . He made me feel that the first real assurance of hope had at last come."[47]

By dinner's end, too, Hopkins had learned from Johnson of Churchill's speech at a luncheon that day honoring Lord Halifax, who was to sail for America aboard the *King George V* from Scapa Flow, Scotland, on the coming Tuesday. Johnson, a guest at that luncheon, had heard Churchill's orotund praise of the President whom Halifax sailed to meet—a praise deliberately designed by the Prime Minister to appeal to Hopkins's reportedly worshipful attitude toward Franklin Roosevelt, abolishing any lingering resentment Hopkins may have felt, on behalf of his chief, over Churchill's failure to send an encouraging word to Roosevelt during the difficult closing weeks of the presidential election campaign. Said Churchill at the luncheon: "I hail it as a most fortunate occurrence that at this awe-inspiring climax in world affairs there should stand at the head of the American Republic a famous statesman, long versed and experienced in the work of government and administration, in whose heart there burns the fire of resistance to aggression and oppression, and whose sympathies and nature make him the sincere and undoubted champion of justice and freedom, and of the victims of wrongdoing wherever they may dwell." Churchill had also felt "able" to say, now that "the party struggle in the United States" was over, how happy he was that "this preeminent figure should newly have received the unprecedented honor of being called for the third time to lead the American democracies in days of stress and storm."[48]

After dinner, the embassy military attaché, General Raymond E. Lee, came from his own Claridge's suite to Johnson's room, on Johnson's invitation, to meet Hopkins, of whom he had theretofore had no high opinion. Born to prosperity, Lee, a remarkably handsome man, was also a remarkably well-informed officer, greatly interested in history and literature; but he had an aristocratic disdain for the untidy, unhandsome, unhealthy, and overly ambitious "do-gooder" he deemed Hopkins to be. Five days before, commenting in his diary upon the news that Hopkins was coming, he had written: "Here is a man who eight or nine years ago was only an obscure social worker, who managed to prevail upon the President and the New Dealers to such an extent that he was put in charge of the Works Progress Administration. . . . He was not a success at this. . . . [He then] went to be Secretary of Commerce, where he was of no consequence at all. . . . When he left this job after some public protest, he moved into the White House. . . ."

Lee's diary entry immediately following this evening meeting was different in tone; it noted that "Hopkins is quiet, unassuming, and very much to the point," the point being the destruction of Hitler. Hopkins had responded approvingly to Lee's remark that lend-lease should not "be labeled . . . 'a Help Britain' proposition" because our real aim was "to knock Hitler on the head," and we helped the British "only because they are . . . interested in doing the same thing." Lee also noted "that Hopkins after a very rough trip up here by air from Lisbon" had, according to one of Bracken's welcoming party, "looked . . . green and ill" when he arrived, but "when he went to bed at a quarter to one he did not look exhausted at all."[49]

Next morning Hopkins phoned the Columbia Broadcasting System's chief European correspondent, Edward R. Murrow, whose dramatic reports of England's ordeal (each broadcast beginning, "This—is London," in a vibrantly portentous voice), had been daily listened to avidly by tens of millions of Americans for the last year and a half. He asked Murrow to come to his Claridge's suite, and Murrow, eagerly anticipating a news-making interview, promptly came. He quickly realized, however, that he had been summoned to provide rather than obtain information. Hopkins plied the journalist with probing questions about Churchill and the other leading political personalities with whom Hopkins must soon deal, about the state of British morale, and (though this was little emphasized) about physical and economic conditions in England as Murrow had observed these. Murrow's inquiry into Hopkins's mission received, however, no reply that could be broadcast. "I suppose you could say [but not out loud] that I've come to try to find a way to be a catalytic agent between two prima donnas," said Hopkins—an offhand but revealing remark. For though Hopkins, within hours of his first meeting with Churchill, yet remained unconvinced by Churchillian rhetoric that the Prime Minister had the substance of greatness, he was absolutely convinced that Churchill's ego was a match for Roosevelt's very formidable one and that, in the prevailing circumstances, two such egos would or could clash in ways dangerous to freedom's cause. "I want to try to get an understanding of Churchill and of the men he sees after midnight," Hopkins added, referring to Churchill's well-known daily work schedule, which, fueled by an afternoon nap and a steady intake of alcohol (whiskey, Champagne, brandy), continued until two or three hours after midnight.50

Hopkins also saw that morning both Foreign Secretary Anthony Eden, who made no favorable impression upon him (the two would later become good friends), and Halifax, "a tall stoop-shouldered aristocrat" whom he liked. He was, in fact, greatly and (surprisingly) very favorably impressed by Halifax. He contrasted this new ambassador to Washington with the British ambassador in Lisbon, Sir Ronald Campbell, whom he had found offensively aristocratic ("the morale of the lower classes is wonderful," was a typical Campbell remark); Halifax he found to be far too sincere a Christian to indulge personally the attitudes of privilege—a devout Anglican, as Hopkins knew Roosevelt to be at heart, whose wide range of interests would, he knew, appeal to Roosevelt. "He has no side," wrote Hopkins that evening in a longhand letter to Roosevelt, "—has been about—I presume is a hopeless Tory—that isn't too important now if we can but get on with our business of licking Hitler. I would not like to see him have much to say about a later peace—I would like to have Eden say less."51

An hour later he was at No. 10 Downing Street, which, as he wrote Roosevelt that evening, "is a bit down at the heels because the Treasury next door has been bombed more than a bit." Most of the windows of the Prime Minister's residence had been blown out, the Prime Minister himself was no longer permitted to sleep there (he slept in a safer place across the street, pending the completion of an absolutely safe shelter for him and the cabinet deep beneath the cabinet office building on Great George Street), and since dozens of men were at work repairing bomb damage to the main and upper floors of the house, the first meeting of Hopkins and Churchill took place "in a little dining room in the basement." It lasted for three hours and was, in itself and in what flowed from it, an event of major world-historical importance.

Hopkins told Churchill, according to Churchill's memoirs, that the "President is determined that we shall win the war together. Make no mistake about it. He has sent me here to tell you that at all costs and by all means he will carry you through, no matter what happens to him. . . ." When Hopkins said that the President was eager to confer with the Prime Minister face-to-face, Churchill made it emphatically clear that he was equally eager for the same thing, the sooner the better. Churchill then presented his guest with one of those vividly eloquent and comprehensive overviews of the war situation for which he had become famous during the last year and a half. He doubted that Hitler would attempt an invasion of England (this contradicted what "most of the Cabinet and all the military leaders" later told Hopkins; they believed "invasion is imminent"); but if invasion came, he would welcome it, for Britain's coastal defenses were excellent and her twenty-five divisions, "trained only in offensive warfare," would drive the invaders into the sea. The initially wide gap between Britain's air strength and Germany's was being rapidly closed; ultimately, with America's help, Britain would achieve air mastery; and when that happened, the Nazi-Fascists would be doomed without the necessity to employ huge armies against them. This war, Churchill believed, would "never see great [land] forces massed against one another"—an assertion prophetic of profound differences soon to develop between British and American concepts of military strategy. Greece, alas, was a probably lost cause. Churchill, however, largely for political strategic reasons (bringing Turkey into the conflict as an ally was then much on his mind), was diverting troops from North Africa to Crete to help Greece resist the Germans, who, coming down through (probably) Bulgaria, would almost certainly be reinforcing or replacing the wavering Italians in Greece very soon. This diversion weakened the British forces of General Archibald P. Wavell in Egypt just as Wavell was launching a drive westward that, Churchill believed, would nevertheless sweep the Italians off Africa's Mediterranean coast (that is, out of Cyrenaica) before Germany could reinforce them. That Germany was now preparing effectively to replace the Italians in North Africa, and perhaps for an assault upon Gibraltar, was indicated by the current appearance in force of German bombers over the Mediterranean: on that very day, Churchill would receive reports that the British cruiser *Southampton* was sunk and the British aircraft carrier *Illustrious* badly crippled by bomb hits from some twenty Luftwaffe Ju-87s and Ju-88s, these ships being part of the naval guard for a convoy bringing supplies to Malta. Taking Hopkins upstairs to the cabinet room, Churchill showed him "on the map where the convoys are coming thru [from America] to Liverpool and Glasgow—and . . . the route the German bombers are taking from France to Norway to intercept the ships."[52]

A press conference with Hopkins by British journalists was scheduled to begin in the U.S. ambassador's office at three o'clock that afternoon, but it was four o'clock before Hopkins arrived at the embassy from No. 10 Downing. And after the journalists were seated before him, who sat "solemnly in the ambassador's chair" (to quote General Lee's eyewitness account), "there ensued a long pause." Finally Hopkins said he didn't know "how to start one of these things," whereupon, after another embarrassing pause, a correspondent asked him what he had done that day. Hopkins, having visibly gathered his thoughts together, answered fully and precisely: "I got up this morning about eight o'clock and took a look out the window for the weather. Then I went into the bathroom and turned on my bath and when the tub was full I got into it. Then the telephone began to ring and I got out of my bath, and as the telephone continued to ring I never got back into it. So after I had talked on the telephone for a while, I went into the other room and rang for the waiter, and ordered some coffee, American coffee, and after a while it was brought up and I found it was very good coffee indeed. I also had an egg [eggs were severely rationed in England that year; the average Englishman was permitted but one or two a month], and after breakfast I rang for the valet, who laid out my clothes and told me I must get some shirts with separate collars—white stiff collars. I asked him if I had to have them. He told me that I did and so that is one of the things I am going to try to do here." His listeners, initially surprised and disconcerted by this, became highly amused, and by the time he was done he had established what Lee described as "a common meeting ground" with his interlocutors. He declined to answer their substantive questions, however, saying only that "he was here on urgent business of the greatest importance to both our countries."53

After the press conference, Hopkins made to Lee a brief but emphatic reference to his meeting with Churchill. Seldom had he had "such an enjoyable time as I had with Mr. Churchill," he said, lighting a cigarette, then added in an awestruck tone, "But God, what a force that man has!" He gave similar testimony when, a few days later, after a weekend with Churchill at Ditchley, the grand country home of Ronald Tree north of Oxford, he was accompanying Churchill, Mrs. Churchill, General Lee, Rear Admiral Robert Ghormley (the U.S. naval observer in London), and several high officials of the British government, on a train journey northward into Scotland. At one stop, Sir Oliver Lyttelton, president of the board of trade, "crept to bed" exhausted at two o'clock in the morning (that is, near the end of a typical Churchill workday) "but was prevented from sleeping" by Hopkins, "who slunk into his room and ensconced himself in a chair in front of the fire, muttering at intervals, 'Jesus Christ! What a man!' "54

During the Ditchley weekend an incident occurred (it, too, was first reported by Lyttelton) revelatory of a basic difference between the minds of Churchill and Hopkins—a difference historically important insofar as these two represented national governing minds (Hopkins's an extension of Roosevelt's) that would determine in the years ahead, through cooperation and conflict, the conduct of the war and the making of the peace.

It was after dinner in the stately, candlelit Ditchley dining room on Saturday evening, January 11.[55] "The ladies" had "retired," leaving "the gentlemen" to their tobacco, their brandy, their manly talk. Hopkins started things off with a graceful, obviously sincere tribute to the Prime Minister's speeches of last summer, which, he said, had deeply moved Americans of all classes and regions. Churchill, having lit an enormous dark cigar, replied that he hardly remembered what he had said last summer but knew he had expressed the feeling of the British people "that it would be better for us to be destroyed than to see the triumph" of Hitler's barbarous regime. It heartened him to learn that this feeling was evidently shared by a considerable portion of the great American people. He then launched upon a "majestic monologue," as Lyttelton called it, which was influenced in some degree by advice he had received in memorandum form, a day or so before, on how best to "handle" Harry Hopkins. ("Hopkins," said the unsigned memorandum, "is the old noncomformist conscience of Victorian liberalism arisen in our midst. He does not believe that a world in which some live in the sun and others in the shadow makes sense" and would try "to find out if we have similar views and aspirations." His perception of an identity of war aims between the two countries might well affect "how quickly and how much America comes in" while giving "a great tilt towards" the postwar "alliance between England and America" that was essential to the creation and maintenance of a just and peaceful world order.) Said Churchill: There must be established after the war a United States of Europe, and England must be the primary builder of it.* Neither Germany nor the Soviet Union was morally qualified to do so. Under Germany, "tyranny and brute force" would be institutionalized; under the Soviet Union, "communism and squalor." England, however, was committed absolutely to human freedom and would make this the central theme and purpose of European union. Whereupon Churchill described with typical Churchillian grandiloquence his country's vision of the coming peace: "We seek no treasure, we seek no territorial gains, we seek only the right of man to be free. . . . As the humble labourer returns from his work when the day is done, and sees the smoke curling upwards from his cottage home in the serene evening sky, we wish him to know that no rat-a-tat-tat [Churchill here rapped upon the table] of the secret police upon his door will disturb his leisure or interrupt his rest. We seek government with the consent of the people. . . ." Etc., etc.

What would the President say about this? asked Churchill of Hopkins when, at last, his flow of eloquence ceased.

There are two eyewitness versions of Hopkins's reply. According to Lyttelton, Hopkins said: "Well, Mr. Prime Minister, I don't think the President will give a damn for all that. You see, we're only interested in seeing that that god-

---

*Churchill, though of course he did not say so that night, had said privately on an earlier occasion that he envisaged Britain, not as a part of the European Federation, but as "the link connecting [it] . . . with the new world and able to hold the balance between the two." Was this a "new conception of the balance of power?" he had been asked. "No," Churchill had replied, "the balance of virtue."

damn sonofabitch Hitler gets licked." According to John Colville, one of Churchill's private secretaries, Hopkins, speaking "slow, deliberate, halting" words that contrasted remarkably with Churchill's eloquence, replied, in effect, that Roosevelt "refused to listen to those who talked so much of war aims and was intent only on one end: the destruction of Hitler." Both versions clearly indicate that Churchill was taken aback. According to Colville, the Prime Minister "hastily" protested that he "would be the first to agree that the destruction of 'those foul swine' is the primary and overriding objective," but that he had spoken as he had because he wanted Hopkins to know that "we were not devoid of all thoughts of the future."[56]

What this indicates is the difference between a mind that thinks most naturally in strategic terms and a mind that thinks most naturally in tactical ones. Churchill's was a mind that emphasized the connections of things in and through the ceaseless flow of time; he was acutely aware of how one thing leads into and merges with another, determining it—hence of the need for designs upon a future beyond the immediate objective if action toward this objective is to be truly beneficently purposeful. (Yet he was also distrustful of attempts "to dominate [the unfolding event]" through overly rigid plans shaped by "logic and clear-cut principles," as most Americans [*not* Roosevelt or Hopkins] were, in his view, inclined to try to do. Account must be taken, especially in war, of the "swiftly changing and indefinable.")[57] The Roosevelt-Hopkins mind, on the other hand, emphasized the separateness of things in the immediate present— was acutely aware of limitations, boundaries, the necessities of the moment (the need to act *now*), hence of the need for temporal priorities; it was impatient of any conception of the long term, any sense of connectedness, that might inhibit, since a severing of connections might be required for, the immediate practical use of any particular piece of information. "People don't eat 'in the long run,' they eat every day," had been Hopkins's disgusted reply to those who argued that free market forces were bound to bring back prosperity in the long run provided the federal government did nothing to interfere with these forces.[58] Similar in essential nature was his response to the challenge of the present crisis. His compartmentalizing mind, closely akin to Roosevelt's in this respect, divided the challenge into distinct and mutually exclusive segments, then graded these by a single definite order of priorities that was itself rooted in a basic commitment to human freedom. The top priority was the utter destruction of Hitler and Nazi-fascism. Subordinate to it, being essentially distinct from it, were domestic social reforms and the development of plans for the postwar world save insofar as such reforms and plans contributed obviously, immediately, directly, to the war effort. Roosevelt paid lip service to the proposition that Social Security and similar reforms should be retained and even expanded during the war because they were of the essence of what we were fighting for, but in practice he dealt with socioeconomic matters as distinct and separate from the fighting war and subordinated them wholly to the success of the war in his scheme of priorities. His and Hopkins's governing mottoes were "One thing at a time" and "First things first," joined with the optimistic assertion "We can cross that bridge [whatever or wherever it is] if or when we come to it."

The main ostensible purpose of the train journey to the north was to bid bon voyage to Lord Halifax, for whom the *King George V* was waiting in Scapa Flow—a send-off calculated to impress upon the American public the eagerness with which Britain extended her hand of friendship across the Atlantic. Also sailing on the new battleship, wholly unpublicized, were the British officers who were to engage with their American counterparts in the secret planning of overall British-American military strategy—these along with General Lee and Admiral Ghormley, who returned to Washington for conferences and would have an important advisory role in the strategic planning. On the last leg of the train journey into northern Scotland, Hopkins and Lee sat across from each other in the compartment they shared with others, giving Lee "a better chance to study him," as Lee wrote in his diary that night. He did so with an eye still highly critical and inclined toward disapproval. Hopkins, he recorded, was decidedly unattractive physically, having "sallow skin and [a] rather crooked chin." He "listens most of the time and gives the impression of being shrewd if not [suggesting, 'but not'] sagacious." His "occasional sidelong glance, glinting suddenly, does not create a feeling of complete confidence in him, but now and then he breaks out into forthright conversation which . . . seems quite frank."[59]

To Lee, Hopkins confided a sealed longhand letter to the President of the United States, along with several pages of handwritten notes ("Will you save them for me until I get back, when I shall try to put them into readable form?" asked Hopkins of Roosevelt), to be delivered in person to the White House—a letter designed, as per Hopkins's self-described role as "catalytic agent," to "sell" Churchill to Roosevelt as effectively as he was "selling" Roosevelt, he hoped, to Churchill. He wrote, in part:

"The people here are amazing from Churchill down and if courage alone can win—the result will be inevitable. But they need our help desperately and I am sure you will permit nothing to stand in the way. Some of the ministers and underlings are a bit trying but no more than some I have seen."

"*Churchill* is the gov't in every sense of the word—he controls the grand strategy and often the details—labor trusts him—the army, navy, air force are behind him to a man. The politicians and upper crust pretend to like him. I cannot emphasize too strongly that he is the one and only person over here with whom you need to have a full meeting of minds.

"Churchill wants to see you. . . . I am convinced this meeting . . . is essential—and soon. . . .

"I cannot believe that it is true that Churchill dislikes either you or America—it just doesn't make sense."[60]

The trip to Scapa Flow was hard on Hopkins, especially the last part of it, when he and Churchill rode a destroyer in rough seas while a blizzard raged along the north coast of Scotland; but he endured it without complaint or attempt to escape its rigors—a fact duly noted by Winston Churchill. The Prime Minister's sympathy for Hopkins's physical frailties did not, however, cause him to reduce in the slightest his demands upon this strange emissary's strength and endurance. He insisted upon keeping Hopkins at his side constantly as, at various stops along the way back to London, he showed himself to crowds of cheering, hero-worshipful people. Invariably he then pushed Hopkins forward, identifying him as the "personal representative of the President of the United States"—an identification calculated to have a tonic effect upon British morale; and invariably Hopkins increased this tonic effect by his public words, which were always few, succinct, in perfect accord with the mood of the occasion, and spoken in a manner disarmingly simple, direct, self-effacing. At Glasgow, for instance, called upon to speak, he expressed the President's commitment to Britain's cause by quoting from the Bible's Book of Ruth: "[W]hither thou goest, I will go; and whither thou lodgest, I will lodge: thy people shall be my people. . . ." He had been assured that what he said on this occasion would be kept off the record by wartime press censorship, but somehow all England seemed to know of it within a few days. The fact was disconcerting to Hopkins insofar as the stimulative effect of his words was greater, and less congruous with actual possibility, than the effect he intended. The popular morale-boosting conclusion drawn from Hopkins's words was that the United States would very soon become Britain's fighting ally in the war, perhaps as early as April (had not April been the month in which Woodrow Wilson's America entered World War I?)—a conclusion Hopkins had thereafter to correct, or try to correct, by emphasizing over and over again that though he spoke the mind and will of the President of the United States, these alone were not decisive of the event. The President had no constitutional authority to declare war; only Congress could do so. He was not deterred, however, from a further frank speaking of a presidential mind that was also emphatically his own. He did so most influentially ten days later when he was guest of honor at a large dinner at Claridge's given by Lord Beaverbrook, the immensely energetic, ruthlessly acquisitive, and highly controversial newspaper publisher (as publisher, he was somewhat analogous to Hearst in the United States; he had pressed hard for the appeasement of Adolf Hitler all through the late 1930s) who was now minister of aircraft production in the Churchill cabinet.

The dinner was attended by dozens of the editors, reporters, managers, and publishers of the most important newspapers in the United Kingdom, men who were "more important" than the high government with whom Hopkins had been theretofore conferring, Beaverbrook said jocularly to the President's envoy, for they were "the masters of the Government." Hopkins was to them an object of intense curiosity—he was so utterly different from any other American official they had ever seen; he had been so mysteriously reticent about his mission—and they watched in almost breathless silence as, according to an account written by one of the editors years later, Hopkins stood up, "looking lean, shy and untidy, grasping the back of his chair." He "continued to look shy throughout his speech." Because his words were "private . . . no notes were taken. But if it had been possible to record the sentences that came quietly and diffidently from the lips of Harry Hopkins they would have compared well . . . with the splendid oration which Mr. Roosevelt had delivered two days earlier when he was sworn in for the third time as President of the United States." Hopkins's speech, however, was devoid of conscious eloquence; it went directly, simply, and plainly to the point. "Where the President had spoken of America's duty to the world, Hopkins told us how the President and those around him were convinced that America's world duty could be successfully performed only in partnership with Britain. He told us of the anxiety and admiration with which every phase of Britain's lonely struggle was watched from the White House and of his own emotions as he travelled through our blitzed land." His listeners were left "with the feeling that though America was not yet in the war, she was marching beside us, and that should we stumble she would see we did not fall." Afterward, with Beaverbrook's encouragement, Hopkins went around the great table to converse with the guests individually, displaying as he he did so "a grasp of our newspapers' separate policies and problems" that "astonished us all." When the meeting ended, "[n]one of us . . . who had been listening to the man from the White House had any illusion about the peril which encompassed our island. But we were happy men all; our confidence and our courage had been stimulated by a contact for which Shakespeare, in *Henry V,* had a phrase: 'A little touch of Harry in the night.' "[61]

The Hopkins visit, initially intended to last no more than two weeks, stretched out over nearly six. They were daily crowded with activities that would have taxed the strength of a man in robust health; much of the time he operated near the point of utter exhaustion; but he did so with a commitment to what he was doing so intense, so stimulating, that it carried him through, his efficiency seemingly unimpaired. On most days he was in the company of Churchill, often for hours—in London, at Chequers, on tours of military and naval bases and of bombed cities. He had extensive interviews with all the cabinet ministers; most of the undersecretaries; Chief of the Imperial General Staff Sir John Dill; First Sea Lord Admiral Sir Dudley Pound; Chief of the Air Staff Sir Charles Portal; and the chiefs of the fighter and bomber commands. He lunched with the King and Queen of England in Buckingham Palace (actually, in an air raid shelter in the palace basement; an air alert was on) and had a long morning talk with the exiled King of Norway in the Norwegian embassy. He filled scores of pages of cable form with detailed information about British needs ("10 destroyers a month beginning April 1. . . . More merchant shipping at once; British cannot wait until new ships are built. . . . 50 PBY planes fully equipped with radio, depth charges, bombs, guns, and ammunition. . . . 20 million rounds of fifty caliber ammunition and as many extra fifty caliber gun barrels as are available", etc., etc.), supporting the requests with highly personal and impressionistic judgments of situations and people. "I believe that I have in no way overstated Britain's need," said the last of his cables, written at Chequers, where he was assisting Churchill in the preparation of the latter's February 9 broadcast. ". . . It has been emphasized more than ever in my mind that Churchill is leading this country magnificently in every respect and that the whole nation is behind him. I hesitate to urge you in matters about which I know you are already convinced. . . . But I feel sure that there has been no time in your Administration when the actions that you have taken and the words that you have spoken have meant so much to the cause of freedom. Your decisive action now can mean the difference between defeat and victory. . . ."[62]

When, late in the night of Saturday, February 8, he boarded at Chequers the special train that would take him to Bournemouth, whence he would fly to Lisbon, he took with him a mass of top-secret British documents. These included technical scientific papers, obtained through Churchill's scientific adviser and close friend Professor Frederick Lindemann (soon to become Lord Cherwell), that would be immensely helpful to the American war science effort. The total mass was so large and vitally important that a British security officer was assigned to carry and guard it, as Hopkins's companion, all the way to Washington.

At Bournemouth, where bad weather prevented the immediate takeoff of his clipper, he had time to scribble on that Sunday, February 9, a farewell note:

"My dear Mr. Prime Minister—

"I shall never forget these days with you—your supreme confidence and will to victory. Britain I have ever liked—I like it the more.

"As I leave for America tonight I wish you great and good luck—confusion to your enemies—victory for Britain.

Ever so cordially,
Harry Hopkins"[63]

VII

THUS was initiated a personal friendship that remains unique, and of (literally) immeasurable importance, in the history of our times.

Four days after Hopkins's arrival in England, the Former Naval Person cabled the President: "Hopkins and I spent the week-end together. . . . I am most grateful to you for sending so remarkable an envoy, who enjoys so high a measure of your intimacy and confidence." Three weeks later (January 28, 1941), he cabled: "It has been a great pleasure to me to make friends with Hopkins who has been a great comfort and encouragement to everyone he has met. One can easily see why he is so close to you."[64] Nine years later, in the course of as glowing a tribute as any great man of history has ever paid another, Churchill would tell of his first meeting with "Harry Hopkins, that extraordinary man, who played, and was to play, a decisive part in the whole movement of the war." He would tell of Hopkins's sitting at the luncheon table "slim, frail, ill, but absolutely glowing with refined comprehension of the Cause," and of how in that hour "began a friendship that sailed serenely over all earthquakes and convulsions." Harry Hopkins was to become "the most faithful and perfect channel of communication between the President and me"; but, more important, he was also "the main prop and animator of Roosevelt himself" for several years. These two men, "the one a subordinate without public office, the other commanding the mighty Republic," functioned at the fulcrum of world power as a single directive unit, "taking decisions of the highest consequence over the whole area of the English-speaking world." Of Hopkins's mental qualities, one stood out, in Churchill's view, as of the greatest importance, namely, his ability to go "always . . . to the root of the matter. I have been present at several great conferences, where twenty or more of the most important executive personages were gathered together. When the discussion flagged and all seemed baffled, . . . he [Hopkins] would rap out the deadly question: 'Surely, Mr. President, here is the point we have got to settle. Are we going to face it or not?' Faced it always was, and, being faced was conquered."

The "soul" of Harry Hopkins "flamed out of a frail and failing body," writes Winston Churchill. He was a "crumbling lighthouse from which there shone the beams that led great ships to harbour." He was "a true leader of men, and alike in ardour and in wisdom in times of crisis he has rarely been excelled."[65]

VIII

IN the House of Representatives, the major battle over lend-lease had been fought in the Foreign Affairs Committee; House floor debate of the measure had been limited and perfunctory. The reverse was true in the Senate. Opponents of the measure, having done what they could to prolong the Foreign Relations Committee hearings, were prepared by the time the bill was reported to take full advantage of the Senate's tradition of unlimited debate. Their forlorn hope was that, during a long postponement of final action, things would happen that reversed the tide of public opinion, causing it to rise against this presidential "warmongering" as it had risen against presidential "court-packing" four years before. To this end they deliberately strung out their opposition argument to several times the length of the supportive one—a near filibuster that would become a full-fledged one, they threatened, if Majority Leader Barkley succeeded in extending each daily Senate session into the night hours until this measure was disposed of, as Barkley proposed to do. Barkley, perforce, backed down; and Senators Nye, Wheeler, Bennett, Champ Clark, and others of the isolationist minority contrived to fill most of the last two weeks of February with fervently denunciatory, endlessly repetitious oratory. North Carolina's "tobacco senator," Robert Reynolds, for one notable instance, inveighed for literally hours on end against the millionaires of Great Britain, the exploiters of India, who clung stubbornly to riches they should be devoting to their country's defense. Not until these plutocrats had divested themselves of their castles, their jewels, their horses, their foxhounds, should the "one-gallused, overall-clad farmer or laborer" of America be called upon to finance the British government, cried Reynolds, whose own passion for private wealth (his own, his family's, his class's) was notoriously the mainspring of his politics.[66] The isolationists also introduced and compelled the Senate to deal in time-consuming ways with one amendment after another designed to eviscerate the bill, drastically reducing the grant of power to the Executive.

It was to a White House anxiously anticipating this needlessly prolonged Senate debate that Harry Hopkins returned in mid-February. And it was to a President whose capacity to deal with manifold pressing problems was impaired by physical illness that Hopkins made oral report of his trip, supplementative of those he had made by letter and telegraph. For Roosevelt, having been struck down by an especially virulent flu virus a fortnight after Hopkins's arrival in England ("I read in the papers that you are sick in bed with flu," Hopkins had said in his first full cabled report from London),[67] had not been able to "shake" the stubbornly persistent "bug." There had been days when he seemed to be recovered, but then the infection flared up again, rendering him utterly miserable, sometimes again bedridden, and consequently in no shape to wage a normally active and zestful behind-the-scenes war against lend-lease's senatorial enemies. The main burden of the administration's battle for aid to Britain was therefore carried at the top level of the administration by Henry Morgenthau, who indeed had been carrying it with valiant and unflagging energy ever since Roosevelt assigned him the task of facilitating the purchase of American aircraft by the French and the British a few weeks after Munich.

At the present moment, the battle required of the Treasury secretary— ironically, and to his profound distaste—adversarial proceedings against the very people he sought to aid. Such arguments as North Carolina's Reynolds was making had persuasive appeal to all American Anglophobes and to a good many who, though not actually Anglophobic, deplored and were made wary by Britain's class structure, Britain's colonialism, and Britain's reputed penchant for sharp dealing. Such arguments must therefore be countered; the American people must be absolutely convinced that the British sought American aid solely for national survival and not for the preservation of personal wealth and privilege. So argued Morgenthau as he increased his pressure upon the naturally reluctant British for a virtually total liquidation of their American holdings in such companies as Lever Brothers, Shell Oil, Dunlop Tire, and the Viscose Corporation of America. These holdings had been considerably reduced in recent weeks, sold for desperately needed dollars; but the British argued that "there should certainly be other ways of putting up the necessary security [collateral for loans], or at least of assuring that the pledge of such assets for security for supplies does not involve an outright change of ownership,"* and they yet retained some American properties of substantial size, including ownership control of Viscose. Morgenthau insisted that these, too, must be liquidated, if lend-lease aid were to be assured.

Halifax yielded to the pressure. It was "of the utmost importance that we should without delay hand over to the Americans our remaining financial resources in that country," the new ambassador cabled Churchill on February 18. On the same day, at Morgenthau's behest, Hopkins cabled Churchill asking for "full details on British taxation," with emphasis upon the increased taxation imposed since war began. The request clearly implied that the administration was preparing to ask of Congress a great increase in American taxation rates (the British were imposing, in addition to a 100 percent tax upon all business profits exceeding the prewar standard, an approximately 100 percent increase in all personal income taxes), and it caused Churchill to react positively to Halifax's recommendation. "We should resign ourselves to meeting American wishes," he told the British cabinet on February 20; the fact that the Americans were about to impose upon themselves vastly increased taxation made it "all the more necessary that we should show that we are willing to make the sacrifice." Shortly thereafter he perused a memorandum sent him on that same February 20 by his minister of aircraft production, Lord Beaverbrook. After citing half a dozen instances in which Britain had yielded to Washington's demands with, as Beaverbrook saw it, no quid pro quo from the United States, the air production minister protested vehemently: "If we give everything away, we gain little or no advantage over our present situation. [Or, 'If we give everything away, what are we fighting for?' as Beaverbrook seemed to be saying]. Stand up to the Democrats!" Churchill was unmoved.[68]

Five days later, an ailing Roosevelt departed from his policy of nonintervention in the Senate debate to the extent of expressing, at his press conference, disapproval of an amendment to the lend-lease bill offered by Democratic Senator Allen J. Ellender of Louisiana. The language of the amendment, evidently designed to blunt the charge that the bill would create presidential dictatorship, seemed innocuous enough, and it was certainly in accord with Roosevelt's as-

---

*In the end, many weeks later, "other ways" were indeed found. Direct loans to the British government by the Reconstruction Finance Corporation enabled them to obtain dollars without further disvestiture of their American holdings.

sertion that lend-lease's primary purpose was to keep this country out of "foreign war." It simply said that nothing in the proposed act "shall be deemed to confer [upon the President] any additional powers to authorize the employment or use of persons in the land or naval forces of the United States at any place beyond the limits of the Western Hemisphere, except in the territories or possessions of the United States, including the Philippine Islands." A reporter asked how this could hamper a government that, as Roosevelt insisted, had no intention of sending troops abroad. The reply of Roosevelt—and of Barkley, George, Rayburn, and other leading congressional supporters of the measure—was that the amendment might prevent the use of military and naval personnel to facilitate aid to Britain; moreover, it seemed to imply a distrust of the Executive, a lack of unity among the people of the United States, that would weaken what Senator George termed the "moral effect" of the bill upon our friends and foes abroad. Indeed, according to Far Eastern expert Stanley Hornbeck in the State Department, the militarists of Japan would view the amendment as a "go ahead" signal; they would be encouraged into acts of aggression in Southeast Asia that we as a nation could not tolerate. The flurry of anxiety rose high. It soon subsided, however. Within a couple of days, administration forces managed to substitute for Ellender's original language a revision that rather strengthened than weakened the President's hand; it said that "nothing in this Act shall be construed to change existing law relating to the use of the land and naval forces of the United States, except in so far as such use relates to the manufacture, procurement and repair of defense articles, the communication of information, and other noncombatant purposes enumerated in this Act."[69]

Not so easily dealt with was an amendment proposed by Senator Byrnes, joined by Virginia's Democratic Senator Byrd and Ohio's Republican (and isolationist leader) Senator Robert A. Taft. There was nothing in the language of lend-lease's original draft to prevent the President from transferring to friendly foreign powers whatever he deemed necessary of defense articles that Congress, when appropriations for them were made, intended for the use of the armed forces of the United States. Clearly a flat prohibition of transfers from existing stocks would defeat the purpose of the act, though the Senate Foreign Relations capped at $1.3 billion the value of such stock that could be transferred. But what of the future? Was it wise policy, as it seemed certainly a violation of the constitutional separation of powers, to permit the President to decide on his own, without congressional authorization, what and how many items to transfer from those purchased in the future with appropriations made by Congress specifically for the U.S. Army and Navy? Byrnes thought not; his amendment said that the President, before disposing of defense items bought with funds appropriated from now on specifically for the army and navy, must obtain congressional authorization. Senator Byrd then went further along this line. He added a clause saying that all future aid to foreign governments must be supplied from funds appropriated specifically for that purpose; none could be supplied out of funds appropriated for the U.S. armed forces.

This spread dismay and confusion through the top echelons of the Treasury, War, and Navy Departments. A highly agitated Morgenthau led the attack against it, saying it would eliminate joint procurement, compel the adoption of wholly separate military and foreign aid production programs, and deny to lend-lease administration the flexibility essential to its swift effectiveness. An equally agitated Stimson and Knox agreed with this and, after trying in vain to get Hull to exercise his persuasive powers on the Hill against the amendment, turned desperately to the just returned Harry Hopkins, begging him to persuade the President to put pressure upon Hull to do what needed to be done. A hurried conference of Stimson and Hull with the President was then arranged (it was a bedside conference; Roosevelt was again down with the flu) during which Stimson vehemently pressed the case against the amendment and Hull continued to resist the suggestion that he use his congressional connections against its passage. The secretary of state said he found the Morgenthau-Stimson-Knox protest "a little hard . . . to get my teeth into," meaning he didn't see what all the fuss was about. Neither, it would seem, did the President. Certainly Roosevelt did not deem the matter to have the crucial importance assigned it by the pro-testers; he deemed more important the maintenance of close friendly ties be-tween Byrnes and himself; and in any case, with his eyes watering, his nose running, his voice hoarse with coughing, he was in neither shape nor mood to do battle with a recalcitrant Senate. He finally wearily asked the reluctant Hull to arrange promptly a meeting with Morgenthau, Stimson, Byrnes, Barkley, and George to try with them to "work things out."

The meeting in Hull's office next day (Sunday, March 2) accomplished little or nothing. More productive was a meeting two days later—a larger meeting that included budget director Harold Smith. Smith came armed with a compro-mise amendment he had worked out with Treasury's Foley. It somewhat weak-ened the addition Byrd had made to the original Byrnes proposal, but Byrnes and the other senators involved readily agreed to it; whereupon it was written into paragraph (a) (2) of section 3 of the bill as follows: "Defense articles pro-cured from funds hereafter appropriated to any department or agency of the Government, other than funds authorized to be appropriated under this Act, shall not be disposed of in any way . . . except to the extent hereafter authorized by the Congress. . . ."[70]

By this time, the Senate majority was sick and tired of the prolonged and now meaningless debate. Groans and cries of "Vote! Vote!" greeted last-ditch oppo-nents of lend-lease when they rose to propose repetitious amendments, and amendments of amendments, all of them foredoomed, all of them swiftly re-jected; and on Saturday, March 8, the bill was at last passed by a weary Senate, 60–31, with only 14 out of 65 Democrats voting against the measure, while 10 of 28 Republicans voted for it. Harry Hopkins at once phoned Chequers, where Churchill was spending the weekend and where it was early in the morning of March 9—past even Churchill's bedtime. Not until the Prime Minister awoke on Sunday was he given Hopkins's message, along with a cable from the President saying that "final concurrent action by the House followed by my signature should take place Tuesday." Churchill at once cabled Hopkins: "The strain has been serious so I thank God for your news." To the President, he said: "Our blessings from the whole of the British Empire go out to you and the American nation for this very present help in time of trouble." (He would later describe lend-lease to Parliament as "the most unsordid act in the history of any nation.") Thereafter things moved as Roosevelt had predicted. The House leadership proposed to the membership a resolution accepting the Senate amendments, thus obviating the necessity for a joint conference committee, and succeeded in limiting an utterly futile floor debate of the resolution to two hours. Whereupon, at 3:20 in the afternoon of Tuesday, March 11, the House passed the amended bill by the overwhelming margin of 317–71.[71]

Roosevelt was of course gratified by his legislative victory. The size of the majority by which the bill was passed testified, in his view, to the wisdom of his legislative strategy—that is, of his choice of battleground, his "hands-off" policy once the battle was joined. But his joy of victory, on this Tuesday afternoon, was far from unalloyed. He bitterly resented what he felt was a grossly unfair advantage taken, by the measure's opponents, of his displayed magnanimity and willingness to compromise; was thoroughly exasperated by the length of time Congress had consumed; and was unwontedly full of rancor over the personal attacks that had been made upon him during the legislative battle—a rancor stemming in part, no doubt, from a purely physical irritability, for he still felt physically "lousy." He revealed nothing of his bitterness, however—he smiled his famous broad, happily confident smile while news cameras focused upon him—as at 3:50 in the afternoon of that same Monday he signed the lend-lease bill into law.[72]

Next day, in the evening, after dining with Missy, Hopkins, and Sherwood off a card table in the Oval Room, and after Missy and Hopkins had left the room, Roosevelt poured his rancor into the initial draft of a speech he was scheduled to make to the annual dinner of the White House Correspondents Association on the coming Saturday evening. An increasingly horrified Sherwood listened as the President of the United States, in what should have been for him (Sherwood thought) an hour of happy triumph and gratitude to the American people for their acceptance of a revolutionary executive proposal, dictated to a stenographer a scathing, petulant, vindictive tirade against his political enemies, replete with references to "a certain columnist," "a certain senator," and "certain Republican orators." He kept at it for more than an hour, while Sherwood grew more and more depressed; then he broke off, bade the stenographer and Sherwood a cheery good-night, and wheeled himself into his bedroom next door. Highly agitated, Sherwood went at once to Hopkins's room down the hall to warn him of the ghastly mistake Roosevelt was about to make. Hopkins dismissed Sherwood's fears with a show of irritation. Sherwood ought to know, he said, that Roosevelt had "no intention of using" any of the "irritable stuff." He was "just getting it off his chest." It had "been rankling all this time and now" he was "rid of it." He felt "a lot better" and, no doubt, would "have a fine sleep."[73]

Nor *was* there any explicit show of rancor over needless delay when Roosevelt addressed the correspondents, and the nation as a whole via radio, four days later. Instead, in a speech written in collaboration with Hopkins and Sherwood, and in which at Hopkins's suggestion he incorporated a personal tribute to Winston Churchill ("In this historic crisis, Britain is blessed with a brilliant and great leader"), he spoke of the "vast difference" between obedience and loyalty as attitudes, as forms of behavior, on the part of individual citizens toward government. Obedience could be obtained through coercion, terror, censorship, and bribery and was so obtained by dictators. But true loyalty must be freely given; it "springs from the mind that is given the facts, that retains ancient ideals. . . ." Nourished by truth, it issues in a willing obedience of laws and legal orders. And Roosevelt extolled the virtues of that free and open discussion of issues through which the laws of the American democracy are (in theory) arrived at, saying such discussion prevented Americans from being "confounded [here was a hint of the bitterness he felt] by the appeasers, the defeatists, the backstairs manufacturers of panic." We Americans had "just now engaged in a great debate," one that had "not [been] limited to the halls of Congress" but "argued in every newspaper, on every wavelength, over every cracker barrel in the land" before being "finally settled and decided by the American people themselves. Yes, the decisions of our democracy may be slowly arrived at. But when that decision is made, it is proclaimed not with the voice of any one man but with the voice of one hundred and thirty millions. It is binding on us all." Moreover, once made, the decision could be swiftly acted upon, as it was in the present case. Five minutes after signing lend-lease, "I approved a list of articles for immediate shipment" to Britain and Greece and "today—Saturday night—many of these are on their way. On Wednesday [March 12], I recommend an appropriation for new material to the extent of seven billion dollars; and the Congress is making patriotic speed in making the money available." (We may say here that, though most Republicans agreed that the enactment of a bill necessarily implies its implementation, a handful of mostly Republican isolationists led by Senators Wheeler and Nye would wage a futile last-ditch fight against this initial appropriation for lend-lease. They would fail to delay action for long. The "Defense Aid Supplemental Appropriation Act, 1941," providing the requested $7 billion, would be passed by a vote of 336–55 in the House, 67–9 in the

Senate, a fortnight after its introduction, and the President would sign it on March 27.) "This decision is the end of any attempts at appeasement in our land," Roosevelt told the correspondents; "the end of urging us to get along with the dictators; the end of compromise with tyranny and the forces of oppression. And the urgency is *now*. . . . The great task of this day, the deep duty that rests upon each and every one of us is to move products from the assembly lines of our factories to the battle lines of democracy—*now!*"[74]

The immensely favorable popular response to this address, delivered with "an unusual amount of emotion," as Sherwood says, seemed to confirm the truth of Roosevelt's wishful assertion that the passage of lend-lease marked the end of isolationism as a potent force in American political life. Halifax was sure of it. "With the passage of the Bill, it can be said that except for a small number of irreconcilable isolationists the whole country is united in its support of the Allies against the totalitarian powers," the British ambassador told London, adding that Roosevelt's political hand had been greatly strengthened (the latest Gallup poll showed 72 percent of the poll sample in support of the President) and that "thinking people are more and more coming to the view that the United States and the British Empire will have to stand very close and share responsibility for keeping peace in the world."

But other British observers, more intimately acquainted with American psychology than newcomer Halifax could yet be, remained doubtful. T. North Whitehead (he was the son of philosopher Alfred North Whitehead), who had returned to England from a professorship at Harvard to serve in the Foreign Office, found Halifax's assessment uncritically optimistic. The Americans, he said in a lengthy and influential commentary on the Halifax telegram, were "a mercurial people" who could not be counted upon to eschew isolationism once and for all "until they are finally committed to actual warfare." What lend-lease passage signified was but another step in what Britain must view as the right direction; it was not an arrival at the desired destination. The "most numerous and influential group of Americans" had formerly favored "aid short of war," wrote Whitehead; they now favored aid "at some risk of war"; but "it would be unwise to assume that, in certain circumstances, the Americans would be incapable of checking their present helpful trend."[75]

IX

SIMULTANEOUS with the hugely publicized debate of lend-lease, and of its funding, were the discussions of military and naval strategy engaged in by planning representatives of the American and British chiefs of staff. These were not publicized at all—were, in fact, conducted behind a thick, carefully arranged veil of secrecy. They were formally dubbed the American-British Conversations (ABC) and opened in Washington on January 29. They concluded on March 29,

1941, two days after Roosevelt signed the $7 billion lend-lease appropriation bill into law, at which time a top-secret joint report, known in military history as ABC-1, was issued.

The British representatives had been invited to Washington by Admiral Stark in the third week of December, immediately after Roosevelt's long-delayed and highly qualified approval of such discussion.* They were, it will be remembered, fellow passengers of Halifax's aboard HMS *King George V* when this new battleship sailed from Scapa Flow, and they were as unnoticed by news reporters when they arrived in America as they had been when they departed Scotland. All public attention was focused upon the presidential yacht *Potomac,* which, with Roosevelt aboard, awaited the battleship when it arrived off Annapolis in Chesapeake Bay on January 24; for it was on the *Potomac* that the President of the United States, in an unprecedented gesture of British-American solidarity, personally welcomed to America the British ambassador (Lord and Lady Halifax were served tea aboard the yacht) after the battleship had anchored.[76] The few reporters who inquired about the British army and navy officers who debarked at Annapolis that day were told that the officers came as military advisers of the British Purchasing Commission, an identification evidently unquestioned by the reporters, though some of them may have wondered why officers of so high a rank (two of them were vice admirals, one a major general) were employed on so humble a mission.

Their actual mission, if far from humble, was also far from grand. Impressed upon the conferees was the fact that theirs was no commanding role but a strictly subordinate one. The British delegation was received by neither Secretary Hull nor the President; the staff conversations, after their initial session, were attended by neither the U.S. chief of naval operations nor the U.S. Army chief of staff; and frustratingly severe limits were placed, by circumstance and by presidential edict, upon what the conferees could legitimately talk about and what conclude. The conversations, Roosevelt insisted, must be rigorously "nonpolitical," and no specific commitments could be made by the Americans, even in the exclusively military field, save as regards "methods of cooperation." Admiral Stark therefore stressed, in his prepared conference opening statement on January 29, that, though obviously the United States and Britain would become "associates" (this Wilsonian word had been substituted for "allies" by Roosevelt) in the event of war, a majority of the American people currently wished to confine their support of Britain exclusively to economic and material aid. The majority wish was binding law: only very general and highly tentative contingency plans for joint military action could issue from the strategical discussions, and these could become valid, even as contingency plans, only if approved by the British and American staff chiefs.

*See p. 77.

Yet despite these restrictions, the talks proved fruitful of strategic decision, valuable in their definition of areas of agreement and disagreement, and portentous in their revelation of the differing motives, the differing mental processes, whereby the strategic concepts of the two powers were shaped.

The British were of course in total agreement with Stark's Plan Dog— no matter what Japan did in the Pacific, the *major* U.S.-British effort must be directed against the European Axis until this was defeated—but they insisted that an essential linchpin of the British empire and commonwealth was Singapore. If Singapore were lost to the Japanese, Australia would be threatened and the cohesiveness of the commonwealth destroyed. And since the defense of Singapore was thus of vital importance to the success of any overall British-American war effort, the Americans should assume some active responsibility for it. With the premise of this argument, the Americans expressed no disagreement: Singapore might indeed have the importance the British ascribed to it. But since this importance was measured by British imperial interests, and since these by no means coincided with American national interests, the Americans refused to accept the British argument's conclusion. They were here forced to cross the arbitrary line that Roosevelt had drawn between "political" and "military" considerations. As strategic planners, they necessarily operated in the world of the "Big Picture," not the world of "mere detail," to use Rooseveltian language, and it was only in the latter—the world of close-up views and immediate physical experience; the world dubbed "real" and "practical" by common sense—that a sharp distinction could be made between military and political activity. In the "Big Picture," military and political considerations blurred into one another inseparably. "At the summit," writes Churchill, "true politics and strategy are one."[77] Thus, the United States was concerned equally with the British to prevent the expansion of the Japanese empire southward. The United States desired equally with the British to postpone if not prevent Japan's entrance into the shooting war and would do what it could, with Britain, to achieve this objective. But the United States was not and would not permit itself to become committed to the preservation intact of Britain's imperial interests in the Far East save insofar as these were joined with the American commitment to the Philippines. If American naval forces at Pearl Harbor must be weakened in order to strengthen naval forces elsewhere, that "elsewhere" had far better be the Atlantic, in defense of the lifeline from America to Britain, than Singapore. The latter bastion of British power in the Far East was Britain's problem, Britain's responsibility.

The debate on this point revealed a fundamental difference between the British and the American approaches to grand strategy—a difference destined in the future to strain very near to the breaking point, on at least one crucial occasion, the now aborning grand alliance.

Great Britain's strategic doctrine, of which Churchill was a principal author, was shaped and colored by memories of the Great War. They were ghastly memories of masses of men advancing in line across open fields against prepared defenses and being cut down, as wheat is scythed, by machine-gun fire—memories of four years of bloody stalemate in which millions of men were killed and maimed for no strategic or even tactical gain—memories of which the dominant fact was that in 1914–1918, given an equivalence in modern weaponry, and measured in terms of casualties, offensive warfare was at least twice as costly as defensive warfare. "It is certain, surveying the war as a whole," writes Churchill in his *The World Crisis,* "that the Germans were strengthened relatively by every Allied offensive . . . launched against them, until the summer of 1918."[78] Joined with these memories was an awareness, never openly admitted, that Britain, in part because of the Great War, no longer stood in the first rank of major world powers, militarily or economically. Especially did she stand in the second rank economically. Her actual and potential economic strength measured smaller than Germany's or the Soviet Union's, smaller still against that of the United States. And as a result of this loss of power her hold upon her imperial possessions was increasingly a slippery one (indeed, her moral *will* to hold India was being steadily eroded by Gandhi's relentless campaign of passive resistance). Small wonder, then, that the British planners in Washington proposed to continue, even after (as they hoped) the Americans entered the war, a Fabian strategy in which no finally decisive battle would be sought, indeed would be studiously avoided, until Hitler had been brought to the verge of collapse by blockade, air bombardment, and internal dissension. For the time being, which admittedly might last many years, the British proposed no massing of their forces in the British Isles for a direct frontal assault upon *Festung Europa,* but instead to retain at home only such forces as were needed to repel invasion. The rest would be distributed among imperial bases in Malaysia (to block Japan), the Mediterranean, North Africa, and the Middle East, where they could be used not only to prevent Axis expansion into these areas, but also to launch offensives against the fringes of the Axis empire, forcing Hitler to spread himself more thinly.

The American planners, however, had neither the horrid memories nor the sense of irremediable national weakness that gnawed at the root of British morale. Their nation's military experience of the Great War had been limited virtually to the spring, summer, and fall of 1918, the period during which trench warfare at last gave way to a war of maneuver whereby decisive results could be achieved; and unlike any other major participant, the United States had emerged from the war with a minimal loss of manpower and a greatly increased economic strength. This strength had continued to grow rapidly through the 1920s.[79] True, the world depression of the 1930s, largely the result of American business and governmental policies and practices, had had greater adverse effect upon the U.S. economy than upon Britain's (American manufacturing pro-

duction was almost halved between 1929 and 1932, whereas Britain's was reduced just one-fifth); but this was mostly because Britain's economy was depressed to begin with. True, too, the New Deal recovery program, badly jarred
by a 1937 recession triggered by an ill-timed reversal of fiscal policy, had not
promoted anything like full national recovery. Ten million American workers
remained unemployed. Much of America's industrial plant stood idle. But this
meant that the decline in production was due to a vast underutilization of existent productive capacity, not to a lack of such capacity—and, even so, the
United States on the eve of new world war remained the most productive industrial power in the world by far.* Since then, stimulated by war goods demands, production had increased rapidly and the number of unemployed had
begun, if less rapidly, to decline.

It was therefore with a sense of immense national strength, and a determination to take full advantage of it, that the American war planners negotiated and
cooperated with their British counterparts. Given their country's immense actual capacity and seemingly limitless potential for war matériel production,
given also manpower resources greater than those of Germany and far greater
than Great Britain's, they found it unthinkable that Hitler's power center should
not be directly attacked just as soon as America's resources were sufficiently
mobilized to assure the attack's probable success. They were impatient with any
"nibbling-around-the-edges," any strategy of "indirect approach" (as Liddell
Hart dubbed it), which would disperse Allied power and so delay the buildup of
a massive striking force in the British Isles.

This impatience added emotion to the adamant stand that the Americans took
against sending capital ships from Pearl Harbor to Singapore rather than (if necessary) to the Atlantic; and their stand, coming hard against an equally emotional British stand, came close to ending the conversations in futile quarrel.
Fortunately, both sides saw that politics and strategy were fused upon the point
at issue; the Americans remembered that they most emphatically had no authority to make political decisions; and both sides consequently decided, wisely,
to refer the matter to political authority for arbitration. Otherwise, and in general, the Americans, in this initial essay in joint planning, were forced by existing circumstances into a large measure of agreement with their British
colleagues as regards the immediate future. There was no blinking the fact that
the United States had made thus far but a fumbling, bumbling start toward a full
mobilization of its resources; for many months if not years to come a British-
American alliance would not be physically able to mount a major assault upon

---

*Take, for example, that crucially important armament material, steel: Using just *one-third* of its steel
plant capacity, the United States produced 26.4 million tons of steel in 1938 compared with Germany's
20.7 million, the Soviet Union's 16.5 million, and Japan's 6 million, though these other countries were
straining their steel-making capacity to the utmost.[80]

the Continent. During this period the only alternative to no military action at all (and prolonged inaction would severely strain national morale) would be the kind of "nibbling-around-the-edges" action that the British were currently taking in North Africa, Crete (alas), and the Middle East. The Americans therefore concurred in such action for the opening months of U.S. "association" with the British in active warfare, with the stipulation that it not prevent a buildup of decisive striking force as rapidly as possible. They accepted into the final joint report large portions of typically Churchillian strategy—operations focused upon Mussolini's empire and designed to force Italy out of the war, hit-and-run amphibious raids against German positions, a major air offensive against Germany, and covert activities to encourage resistance movements in the countries Hitler had occupied. Of greater long-run importance than these decisions was ABC-1's proposal of continuing consultations between the British and American staff chiefs. This proposal would not only lay the foundation for an actual fusion of the two nations' general staffs; it would also enable ABC-1 to serve as a guide, substituting rational process for hit-or-miss improvisations, in the allocation of available resources, and in the distribution of responsibility among the personnel of the two nations.

As has been said, ABC-1 was dated March 29, 1941. It became the basis for the Rainbow-5, which the Joint Army-Navy Board at once ordered prepared. In mid-May, the Joint Board formally approved both ABC-1 and Rainbow-5. So did Secretaries Stimson and Knox soon thereafter. But when the two documents went to the White House in early June, the President, having studied them carefully, refused to approve them "at this time," his reason being, as Pa Watson told the board, that the British government had not yet approved ABC-1, and Rainbow-5 was based on ABC-1. "However, in case of war," Watson concluded, "the papers would be returned to the President for his approval."[81] Actually, his refusal seemed to informed observers to be motivated by political considerations; he seemed to fear that knowledge of his commitment to the plans, if he did commit, might somehow spread into circles hostile to him, exposing him to renewed charges of warmongering. Certainly, in contradiction of the central thrust of his speech of March 15, wherein he seemed to say that the passage of lend-lease marked the end of isolationism's political potency, he continued to measure far greater than many of his subordinates did the strength of his isolationist opposition. He continued to be inhibited, in overt action, by his fear of it. And the army and navy decision makers were in turn inhibited by their lack of that authority, which Roosevelt's formal blessing of ABC-1 would have conferred upon them.

They would have been much more so had it not been for George C. Marshall, who here demonstrated qualities that would make him uniquely valuable to freedom's cause during the months and years ahead. At a weekly meeting in Stimson's office of the informal "war council" (it may be remembered to have consisted of the secretaries of state, war, and navy) on June 10, there was agitated discussion of the quandary in which the American staff chiefs were seemingly placed by their commander in chief's ambiguous response to the two planning documents. These plans required a considerable measure of immediate implementation. Certain arrangements must be made, certain actions must be taken *now,* if the agreed plans were to guide America into an adequate preparedness for belligerency. Could the army and navy do so in the absence of explicit authorization from their commander in chief? Marshall answered with an emphatic "Yes." The army chief of staff continued strictly to adhere to the principle of military subservience to civilian authority, but he had had by this time a considerable experience of Roosevelt's psychology and ways of administration—had developed, also, a considerable sympathy and respect for Roosevelt's political acumen and skills—and on the basis of this experience, this sympathy, he confidently proposed that they all go ahead full speed on the assumption that the plans, though not approved in form, had been approved in fact. In the prevailing circumstances, they *had* to be either approved or disapproved; there was no open middle way; and Roosevelt had not *dis*approved either ABC-1 or Rainbow 5. Ergo, they were approved. Had not the President specifically directed that both documents be brought to him *for* formal approval in case of war? Coming from Marshall, this argument convinced Stimson, Knox, Stark, and, to the minimum necessary degree, cautious Cordell Hull. The necessary work went forward, less expeditiously than it might otherwise have done, perhaps, but expeditiously all the same.[82]

BOOK TWO

→≫✖≪←

Through War Undeclared
to War Declared

4

-->>)(<<-

Black Spring 1941

I

IN retrospect, no season in all the years of stupendous global conflict, not even the furiously flaming spring of 1940, would appear to British and American leaders more fraught with fatal danger to freedom's cause, more crowded with insoluble anxiety-breeding problems, and less lighted by a belief in ultimate victory, than the black spring of 1941. Nor did this retrospective belie the reality actually experienced at the time. A sense of doom invaded responsible minds and spirits in London, in Washington.

II

THE new year had opened well enough militarily from the Allied point of view in the only war theaters where Allied ground troops directly engaged the enemy—that is, the Greek-Albanian, the North African, the East African—and had remained well enough through much of the year's first three months. The Greek army continued everywhere victorious over the Italians, though it was now more greatly outnumbered than it had been in the fall and though massive attacks were launched against it by reorganized forces under new command in early February. By March 3, having driven all the invaders off the soil of their country, the Greeks occupied approximately one-third of Albania, their farthest advanced units standing just twenty-five miles from the Albanian capital of Tiranë. Simultaneously, in the vast desert regions of North Africa, the British Army of the Nile, under the supreme command of General Archibald P. Wavell, scored an uninterrupted series of triumphs over the best troops of the Italian army. Driving westward from an original position a hundred miles east of the Egyptian border, British Commonwealth and colonial troops, armored and motorized, advanced four hundred miles into Libya between December 6 and February 7, capturing in swift succession the Mediterranean coastal towns of Sidi Barrâni, Bardia, Tobruk, Derna, Benghazi, and destroying an entire Italian army (the Tenth) in a battle at Bedafomm some fifty miles south of Benghazi, at which point all Italian resistance in the area ceased. Thus the whole of Cyrenaica was torn from Italy's grasp and more than 130,000 Italian troops captured in a two-month campaign at a cost of fewer than 2,000 British casualties. British armor then stood at El Agheila, on the border of Tripolitania, poised, as it seemed, for a drive toward distant Tripoli.

Equal success at even less cost attended British operations in Italian Somaliland, some two thousand miles to the southeast. South African and African colonial troops under the command of Lieutenant General Sir Alan Cunningham (he operated under Wavell's direction), striking eastward from Kenya, captured the Indian Ocean port of Kismayu on February 16, then immediately fought a battle along the river Juba north of Kismayu against the only effective Italian fighting force between Kismayu and the Somaliland capital of Mogadishu. The Italians were routed; Italian resistance in Somaliland totally collapsed. And these East African successes continued well into the spring, as we may here anticipate. After the most stubbornly fought of all the battles against the Italians in Africa, at Keren in Eritrea, some fifty-odd miles west of the Red Sea, the British thrust southward into Ethiopia, also northward and eastward into that country from Mogadishu in Somaliland, and, encountering little effective Italian opposition, swiftly liberated from Italian rule this largest component of Mussolini's new Roman empire. Some two hundred thousand Italian troops surrendered. The exiled Ethiopian Emperor Haile Selassie, who had reentered his kingdom on January 20, returned in triumph to Addis Ababa, his capital, on May 5, 1941, five years to the day after Mussolini's troops had seized the city.

There was also a decisive British victory at sea. On March 28, in a battle fought mostly at night off Cape Matapan at the southern tip of Greece, British warships sank by gunfire and bombardment three Italian cruisers and two destroyers (more than 2,400 Italian lives were lost) at the cost of a single British torpedo bomber flying off the aircraft carrier *Formidable*. An intimidated Italian fleet retreated to its Italian bases, assuring British naval mastery of the eastern Mediterranean when the lack of it would have exposed to fatal danger transports bringing British troops from Africa to the aid of Greece. . . .

But even while the earliest of these triumphs were being achieved, the victor's joy in them was overshadowed by anxiety over Hitler's response.

We have mentioned the abrupt and devastating appearance of Nazi warplanes in the Mediterranean in mid-January 1941—how, flying from bases in Sicily, they sank the British cruiser *Southampton* and damaged the British carrier *Illustrious* so seriously that she was out of action for months.[1] Britain lost in this single action its command of the central Mediterranean. An almost defenseless Malta was exposed to continuous air assault, and the Germans were enabled to transport and supply, with little hindrance and in a remarkably short time, a sufficient Axis force in North Africa to mount a counterattack toward Egypt. The force consisted of two panzer divisions that, later joined by German infantry units and several Italian divisions, constituted an Afrika Korps, which, under a remarkably audacious and skillful general, Erwin Rommel, was soon world famous. Rommel was in direct contact with the British west of Agheila by February's end. A little over three weeks later, defiantly and successfully challenging logistical difficulties that his opponents had deemed it impossible for him (or anyone) to overcome, and with the aid of far greater airpower than the British could muster, he launched his offensive.

And from that moment on through all of that black spring, the British were forced everywhere onto the defensive, their every move a response to an enemy initiative and harshly limited by the meagerness of their fighting strength. Nothing could be done by them anywhere without risk of disaster elsewhere, for nowhere did they have a margin of safety. Thus their decision to aid Greece required a reduction of Wavell's already slender strength in Africa, for he dared not transfer British troops out of Palestine (it was part of the huge war theater under his command); the Palestine force was barely strong enough to keep the quarrel between Arabs and Jews, also the eagerness of both to cast off British rule, from erupting into Axis-encouraged violence that could result in Axis domination of the entire Middle East. But hardly less risky was the transfer of troops from Africa to Greece; it was in good part responsible for the disaster that now befell the Army of the Nile. Within six weeks Rommel's offensive had recovered for the Axis all the ground and port facilities that Wavell's winter offensive had wrested from the Italians, save only the crucial port of Tobruk— and Tobruk was closely besieged, gravely threatened. By the last of April, the Desert Fox (so Rommel was dubbed) had pushed the British all the way back to the Egyptian base from which their drive had been launched in December. Reinforced and supplied from ports west of Tobruk, he threatened to grow strong enough to mount soon a drive upon the great naval base of Alexandria.

Meanwhile, far to the north, as Hitler came to the rescue of Mussolini's failing Greek venture, the other arm of what appeared on the map as a giant Axis pincers closing upon the Middle East was pushing down through the Balkans with a force, speed, and efficiency that was terrifying.

The way had been prepared by a typically Hitlerian combination of threat, bribe, and treason. Romania had by January already joined the Axis; German troops were being massed there. Hungary and Bulgaria were soon persuaded to do so in effect, granting transit rights across their countries to the Germans. Likewise with the Yugoslavian government headed by Prince Paul as regent for the seventeen-year-old Prince Peter; on March 25, in Vienna, in the presence of Hitler and Joachim von Ribbentrop, the Yugoslav Premier and foreign minister formally committed their country to the Tripartite Pact. But then came a hitch. The Belgrade government had failed to take adequately into account an army and Serbian public opinion (the Croatians, less numerous than the Serbs, were pro-Nazi) that was bitterly hostile to any Hitler alliance. This hostility had been encouraged by the British, of course, also by a message from Roosevelt (February 14) and, far more, by the very active presence in Belgrade at that time of a Colonel William ("Wild Bill") Donovan, a strong, vivid personality with a talent for undercover operations who had come to the Balkans in December, allegedly on a fact-finding mission for the President. Through Donovan, promises had been made of material U.S. aid for Yugoslavia, if Hitler's demands were resisted, via lend-lease, the passage of which then still pended but could be confidently assumed. Thus encouraged, the government's opposition had made secret plans. These were now carried out. On March 27, army and air force officers seized control of the Belgrade government in a swift, bloodless coup that had immediate overwhelming popular support. Prince Paul was forced to abdicate. Young King Peter was installed as head of state. And the signature of the Tripartite Pact was declared invalid.

Hitler's response to this wholly unexpected (by him) development, which he took as a personal affront, was an outburst of raving fury reminiscent of that in which he had proclaimed to his generals, in 1938, his "unshakable will to wipe Czechoslovakia off the map."[2] Now as then he abruptly summoned his top generals to a meeting (March 27) in the Berlin Chancellory, wherein he issued flat orders and brooked no discussion of them. The generals were to launch without further warning to Yugoslavia, as soon as preparations could be made, an attack that would "destroy Yugoslavia militarily and as a national unit . . . *with unmerciful harshness.*"[3] The orders were promptly fully obeyed. On April 6, in the first light of day, coordinated attacks upon an as-yet not fully mobilized Yugoslavia were launched from Austria, Hungary, and Romania, with the brunt of the assault being borne by the German Twelfth Army of fifteen divisions, four of them armored. Simultaneously, in what Hitler dubbed "Operation Punishment," waves of German aircraft flying at rooftop level began a systematic bombing and strafing of Belgrade, which had no antiaircraft guns or other defenses against such attack, continuing it for three horrible days and nights, at the end of which the city was reduced to rubble and more than seventeen thousand civilians lay dead among the ruins. By then, Hungarian and Italian troops having joined the Twelfth Army's attack, all southern Serbia was in Axis hands. On April 13, the Germans entered Belgrade. On April 17, the Yugoslavian army surrendered. And two days after that, German panzer units attacking from Macedonia occupied the Pindus Mountain passes, cutting off the only lines of retreat from Albania for the bulk of the Greek army. When it was obvious that Greece's position was hopeless, the Greek Premier, M. Korysis, committed suicide. On April 20, the Greek government surrendered. There followed the evacuation from Aegean Sea ports of as many as possible (about 80 percent) of the fifty-five thousand British and Commonwealth troops who had come to Greece's aid—an evacuation more difficult and costly in percentage of casualties than Dunkirk had been, for there the Royal Air Force had provided effective air cover, whereas here the Axis had complete command of the daylight air. Twenty-six Allied ships were lost to air attack, including five hospital ships, as twenty-six thousand British troops were transported to Crete and over fifteen thousand, including wounded, to Alexandria.

At sea, all through this period, the threat to Britain's lifeline not only continued, but grew more ominous. "Even now," Ribbentrop had told the Japanese ambassador in Berlin in late February, "England is experiencing serious trouble in keeping up her food supply. Meat and fats are already in very short supply. The important thing now is to reduce England's imports to below the absolute minimum needed for existence." This same "importance" was being stressed to Hitler by Admiral Erich Raeder, commander of the German navy, at that time, as the British more than suspected.[4] The admiral begged Hitler to invalidate the American-declared neutrality zone in the North Atlantic by boldly extending the German-declared combat zone to Greenland waters and then giving top priority to the severing of Britain's Atlantic lifeline; he made this recommendation with redoubled force after the lend-lease bill had passed; and Hitler seemed to be accepting it when, on March 25, 1941, he did extend the combat zone to Greenland.[5] U-boats had begun to hunt together in so-called wolf packs and to concentrate their attacks farther west in the North Atlantic than they had formerly done. They thus took advantage of the total lack of air cover and the dearth of convoy flotilla escort that was imposed upon the British over a thousand-mile-wide area by Ireland's refusal to permit their use of Irish seaports and airfields. Shipping losses to U-boat attack climbed steeply: 142 ships totaling 818,000 tons would be sunk in the North Atlantic in the three months ending May 1 as compared with 688,000 tons of merchant shipping sunk by U-boats in all the first seven months of the war. The sea approaches to British ports continued to be harassed by land-based German planes. To these hazards was added that of powerful surface-vessel attacks. The German battle cruisers *Scharnhorst* and *Gneisenau,* taking advantage of winter fog that prevented air surveillance, escaped from their home ports into the North Atlantic at the end of January and in the two following months sank or captured twenty-two ships totaling 115,000 tons, coming then safely into port at Brest. Equally destructive in the South Atlantic was the Brest-based battle cruiser *Hipper,* which in one attack, near the Azores, sank nineteen of twenty-two ships in a convoy bound for Freetown in Sierra Leone. And by May 1941 a great new German battleship, the *Bismarck,* which carried fifteen-inch guns and was larger, more heavily armored, and perhaps faster than any British warship, would be poised in the Norwegian port of Bergen for what might become, if simultaneous raids were conducted by *Gneisenau* and her sister cruisers, an assault upon the Atlantic lifeline too powerful for the Royal Navy to cope with.

German bombers continued to rain death and destruction upon England on every night of permissible weather, with a continued concentration on London but also, as spring came on, with a new and frightening concentration upon shipyards and port facilities elsewhere. Some of the latter attacks were prolonged through a whole week. Portsmouth, Liverpool, Plymouth, Bristol, Hull, the shipyards of the Clyde and the Mersey—each in its turn suffered severe damage and heavy casualties, with Liverpool and the Mersey suffering so greatly that after seven successive nights of bombing, the import tonnage that could be unloaded there was reduced by three-fourths for weeks. The fury of these massive air attacks, each in itself an invasion of England, pointed up the continuing threat of a full-scale invasion with ground troops and armor, a possibility that measured small in Churchill's eyes but which members of the imperial general staff deemed, with the coming of warm weather, increasingly likely.

By May 1941 it was clear that Britain was rapidly losing what Churchill, in a directive he issued as minister of defense on March 6, 1941, called the Battle of the Atlantic—was in fact losing the war as a whole. Its only hope of survival was a far more direct and energetic intervention in the struggle by the United States than had thus far obtained—at the very least, U.S. naval vessels must provide escort for convoys—and the involvement must come very soon.

This meant that now as never before in history, certainly far more than in 1915 or 1916 or 1917, the fate of Western democracy, indeed the very survival of Western civilization, depended upon the mental operations and decisive will of the President of the United States. In part by pure accident, in part through the exercise of his own peculiar genius for locating and holding balance of power points, in part because Britain's increasingly desperate leaders insisted upon it, Franklin Roosevelt had become the central pivotal figure of the whole free world. Almost his every word, deed, gesture—his every act or refusal of action in response to a specific challenge—had worldwide consequence. Yet with the passage of lend-lease, which he himself had described as the death of isolationism, the birth of national unity, and the beginning of a redoubled national effort toward Nazi-fascism's destruction—an event that had therefore been expected to be followed by a burst of executive activity—there began instead what most knowledgeable observers saw as a strange, prolonged, exceedingly dangerous pause in presidential leadership.

Why?

III

WE have told of the fog of weariness that clouded Roosevelt's mind and oppressed his spirit during the weeks immediately following election day, and of how this was dispelled and a surge of decisive energy initiated during his restful Caribbean cruise, with Harry Hopkins at his side, in early December. But the surge had not long continued. It was drastically slowed barely a month later when Roosevelt was struck down by a flu attack in the last week of January, while Hopkins was in England; it was soon seen to have ended altogether by the second week of March, when lend-lease was finally passed.

So much is clear.

But it is a difficult question of psychosomatics whether, or to what extent, Roosevelt's failure to exercise leadership through March, April, and most of May was cause or effect of the recurrent physical illness that plagued him. If there was no important causal relation between the two, what *did* cause his failure to exercise leadership? Was it simple inability to choose among courses of action that, though contradictory of one another, presented themselves to his mental vision as approximately equal in merit and peril? Or had he carefully weighed the probable cost of passivity against the probable cost of any possible action and, finding the probable cost of action to outweigh that of passivity, decided to wait upon "the logic of events" to produce clear and solid conclusions?

If this last was his decision, we can surmise the way in which the decision was reached.

Hopkins in England, responding to a Churchill question, had said there were at the present moment (January 1941) "four divisions" of American public opinion: "a small group of Nazis and Communists, sheltering behind Lindbergh, who declared for a negotiated peace and wanted a German victory; a group, represented by Joe Kennedy, which said 'Help Britain, but make damn sure you don't get into any danger of war'; a majority group which supported the President's determination to send the maximum assistance [to Britain] at whatever risk; and about 10% or 15% of the country, including Knox, Stimson, and most of the armed forces, who were in favour of immediate war."[6] What gave Roosevelt pause was, of course, the group "sheltering behind Lindbergh" joined with the group "represented by Joe Kennedy" (dubiously represented, some would say). They yet constituted, by his estimate, approximately a third of the American people. They were thus a minority far too large to be ignored in the decision making of a President who, if not yet *absolutely* convinced that the United States must enter the fighting war, *was* convinced that such entrance, if made, must be by a truly united people. Moreover this stubbornly persistent minority contained, incongruously, its full share of the most influential opinion makers of the liberal Left, especially in the West, Midwest, and South. The fact was profoundly troubling in that it continued, if with diminishing intensity, a dilemma Roosevelt had faced ever since his "quarantine the aggressor" speech of October 1937. Conservatives who strongly opposed his domestic policy were far more inclined to support his foreign policy than were liberals who supported his domestic reforms. Many of the most influential conservatives seemed perfectly willing to risk the totalitarian dictatorship that, according to many liberals, must "inevitably" accompany total war, provided such dictatorship was

organized around their special economic interest—and prevailing circumstances (the desperate shortage of time, especially) encouraged it to be so organized. By the same token, many liberals, loathing both war and fascism, were
profoundly suspicious of a foreign policy that seemed likely to lead to both—a
foreign policy expressive, they feared, of Rooseveltian attractions toward militarism (was not his love of a Big Navy notorious? had he not placed unemployed youth under army control via the CCC?) and toward limitless personal
power (his threatfully proclaimed determination to "master" the "forces of selfishness," during the 1936 election campaign, came to mind). Thus Roosevelt
was presented, as he saw it, with a Hobson's choice. His primary present concern was to lead into war, should this prove necessary, an American citizenry
that was of one mind as regards the destruction of the Axis and the setting up of
effective peacemaking machinery afterward—an American citizenry that willingly and even ardently embraced the kind of militarism and authoritarianism
that victory in total war demanded—yet a citizenry that retained in its heart the
commitment to personal freedoms and to economic and social justice that had
animated the New Deal. The leader of such a citizenry must be eternally vigilant against the usurpation of power by any special interest—must be especially
vigilant against the overweening ambition of the conservative big-business
community closely linked, as it had always been, with the career interests of top
officers of the army and navy—yet must reach unprecedentedly huge production and rearmament goals within a severely limited time span. He must, in sum,
shape the necessary war organization in a way that not only achieved maximum
efficiency, but also enabled the necessary authoritarianism to be cast off, as a
cloak no longer needed, once the storm of war was over. And for the life of
him, Roosevelt could not see how the cardinal choices so loudly demanded of
him could now be made by him, an extremely controversial public figure, without disastrously disuniting the American people. What could he now do, therefore, save wait and hope, with a waning strength of hope, that events would
soon mold the public opinion that made decisive leadership possible? It was an
ordeal of helpless waiting too severe for even his immense patience to survive.
He fussed and fumed inwardly, as he coughed and sneezed outwardly, in frustration. . . .

But this, to repeat, is surmise, if surmise of highly probable accuracy.

All we can be absolutely sure of is that Roosevelt did fail to lead at this time.
He did stubbornly resist efforts to persuade him to do so. He did have at hand an
abundance of plausible justifications for inaction.

And he did continue to be plagued by ill health.

It is true that he was suspected by his intimates of faking an illness now and
then, or exaggerating its seriousness, in order to avoid disturbing importunities
(very few people were permitted into his sickroom). For instance, he was
bedridden with what was reported to be another attack of the grippe through

most of the middle weeks of May; yet when Robert Sherwood had a "long talk" with him in his bedroom at that time, its subject an eagerly anticipated foreign policy speech that had been announced for May 14 (Pan-American Day) but then postponed until May 27, he seemed to Sherwood completely recovered. "He didn't cough or sneeze or even blow his nose the whole time I was in there," said a puzzled Sherwood to Missy LeHand. "What's really the matter with him?" Missy replied, with a shake of her head and a rueful smile, that what the President mostly suffered from at that time was "a case of sheer exasperation."[7]

But though he was certainly exasperated, and with reason, this was by no means all that was wrong with him, as Missy well knew. He was no chronic complainer. He possessed almost incredible stoic courage and a unique ability to mask grievous hurts with cheerful smiles. Yet by mid-May he was sometimes almost querulous when with intimates. He complained with increasing irritability that never before had a cold hung on as this one did, continuously if with varying intensity, through four solid months! And Missy grew worried not only over his sickness's longevity, but also over the effect it was having on his psychology. She had been at his side through the whole of his long struggle back to health after his polio crippling; she was among the very few who had personally witnessed the despondency that had sometimes overwhelmed him in the period from 1922 to 1924.

But not since 1924 had ill health come as close to total triumph over his sunny disposition as it now did. Missy's anxiety would have been greatly increased had she known what medical examinations discovered at this time, namely, that Roosevelt was suffering from a potentially dangerous diastolic hypertension along with, in May and early June, a serious iron deficiency due to bleeding hemorrhoids. His hemoglobin count sank at that time to just one-third of what it should have been. He was treated with iron to build up the blood cells. This information was not given the Roosevelt family by White House physician Ross T. McIntire, nor, it would seem, was it given to Roosevelt himself—at least not with a frankness and force commensurate with its importance. To the world at large, McIntire proclaimed that the President's health, though he was for the moment a bit "run down," was fundamentally sound, was indeed remarkably good for a man his age.[8]

Some of Roosevelt's close associates believed there was causal connection between Roosevelt's bad health and the White House's notoriously poor cuisine. One who did so was handsome, forty-nine-year-old W. Averell Harriman, who in the spring of 1941 began to play an important role in America's wartime foreign affairs.

The son of railroad magnate E. H. Harriman, whose panic-breeding financial manipulations in the early 1900s had caused Theodore Roosevelt to brand him an "enemy of the Republic," Averell Harriman was immensely wealthy. Like

Franklin Roosevelt, he had gone to Groton, where he was fully exposed to Rector Endicott Peabody's gospel of public service for the rich and well-born. But he had then gone to Yale, where he was exposed to a different virus, one that evidently "took" and infected him through most of his young manhood. In the 1920s, though nominally a railroad executive and banker, he had been a fairly typical rich man's son, a playboy of the Jazz Age, notorious in his social circle for dalliance with other men's wives, though himself married, and known to the general public chiefly as an excellent horseman and polo player. But in 1928, influenced by his liberal, reform-minded sister, Mary Harriman Rumsey, who was an ardent friend and admirer of Eleanor Roosevelt's, he evidently experienced a conversion: he abandoned the Republican Party to become a strong supporter of Al Smith for President and Franklin Roosevelt for governor of New York and to dedicate himself to public service as a first priority. He came to Washington as a National Recovery Administration official in 1933, chaired the Business Advisory Council from 1937 to 1940, and formed at this time a warm personal friendship with Harry Hopkins. He was serving as a dollar-a-year man in the OPM when, in mid-February 1941, at Hopkins's behest, he was asked by Roosevelt to go to London as the President's personal representative on all matters having to do with aid to Britain. He was to deal with Churchill and Churchill's top people directly, not through Winant and the American embassy; he was to communicate with the President directly, not through the State Department; and his terms of reference were sufficiently vague and broad to give him great freedom to decide and act. It was a typically Roosevelt arrangement in that it insured immediate responses to pressing demands and satisfied Roosevelt's felt need to keep as many reins of power as possible in his own hands, but did so by reducing the prestige, the authority, and the effectiveness of John G. Winant in London and by increasing the hurt in the chronically hurt feelings of Cordell Hull in Washington. Harriman's appointment was announced in Roosevelt's press conference on February 18, he then bestowing upon his new envoy the theretofore unknown title of "defense expediter." As such, Harriman would handle the London end of whatever program was established under the then-pending Lend-Lease Act, the President said.[9]

It was on March 7, three days before he boarded a Pan-American clipper for his flight to England and four days before lend-lease was signed into law, that Harriman personally experienced what seemed to him a serious food crisis in the White House. He lunched with Roosevelt that day in the Oval Room. There, at Roosevelt's desk, the two were served what Harriman described in his notes as "an extraordinary meal." It consisted of spinach soup, which "didn't taste bad" but "looked like hot water poured over chopped-up spinach"; white toast and hot rolls; a main dish of "cheese souffle with *spinach!!*"; and, for dessert, "three large fat pancakes, plenty of butter and maple syrup." It seemed to Harriman just about "the most unhealthy diet" possible for a man who "was just recovering from a cold" and "was obviously tired and mentally stale." The two men discussed over lunch "the British food situation and their increasing need for vitamins, proteins and calcium," but "it struck me [Harriman] that, in the British interest, fortification of the President's diet should be first priority."[10]

No improvements were made, however, either in Roosevelt's diet or in his health, as spring came on and a multitude of interrelated problems marched inexorably into the White House, where they were dealt with, if at all, individually, disconnectedly. The consequence was an increased clutter in what had always been an extremely cluttered administrative apparatus. Again, as in the earliest days of the New Deal, emergency agencies were set up in response to immediate challenges and jammed willy-nilly into the governmental structure with little regard for long-term purposes or overall efficiency. There was a widening of the discrepancy, which had always been wide in Roosevelt's Washington, between the administrative structure described on organization charts and the actual loci and flow lines of effective power. Loose ends abounded. Huge energies clashed where they should have meshed. Quarrels sprang up as weeds in an untended garden. "I do not think the president ties up awfully well," complained British Ambassador Halifax, understating his actual thought, in a message to Churchill in March 1941; "I am quite sure Harry Hopkins doesn't, and as for the Government departments they might almost as well be the administrations of different countries. The result is . . . that a great deal of what we try to do from the outside seems like hitting balls of cotton wool."[11] The ambassador's sentiments would be echoed by British economist John Maynard Keynes when, in May 1941, he came to Washington to try to straighten out a serious financial tangle involving payments for war goods shipped to Britain on contracts signed before lend-lease went into effect.* In Roosevelt's Washington, "everything is done, so to speak, backstairs," he wrote in a letter to London on June 8, 1941, "and unless one spends three quarters of the day seeing people on one pretext or another, one knows nothing and can effect little."[12] All the same, if with much wasted time and energy, a great deal of useful work was getting done, as both Englishmen admitted.

A crucial case in point (it indeed was the case with which both Halifax and Keynes were primarily concerned) was the administration of lend-lease. The

---

*The tangle was a consequence of Roosevelt's failure to "tie up"—that is, his ad hoc, hence fragmentary dealings with lend-lease financing by Congress. Because budget director Harold Smith was highly respected by House members as a fiscal expert, Roosevelt employed him to make the administration argument for a $7 billion lend-lease appropriation but failed to consult either Hopkins or Morgenthau before instructing Smith regarding the latter's testimony. The result was that Smith assured Congress that lend-lease moneys would *not* be used to pay for some $400 million worth of goods contracted for by the British prior to lend-lease's passage, an assurance flatly contradictory of promises Hopkins and Morgenthau (the latter most specifically) had made to the British.

main outlines of the setup for this had been established well before the bill was finally passed. Originally, Morgenthau and others had assumed that he, having borne the main burden of aid to the Allies and China ever since the war's beginning, would exercise major executive control over whatever lend-lease agency was established. He had stated his assumption to Roosevelt early on, and Roosevelt had expressed agreement with it. But Stimson's top assistants in the War Department, anxious to end Treasury's intrusion upon territory properly belonging (so they believed) to the military and its industrial contractors, had a different idea. Stimson proposed to the President a four-man cabinet committee for the overall supervision of the new aid program, the actual administration of it to be in the hands of this committee's executive secretary; and in late February, as the lend-lease bill was entering the final stage of its congressional journey, the President adopted this plan. He did so, however, with one highly important change. "I propose to administer the bill through . . . an Advisory Committee consisting of the Secretary of State, the Secretary of War, the Secretary of the Navy and you," he wrote Morgenthau on February 25; but whereas Stimson had proposed for the post of committee secretary General James H. Burns, a highly respected career officer who had formerly headed the army ordnance department, Roosevelt was "going to ask Harry Hopkins to act as Secretary of this Committee. . . . I do this," he told Morgenthau, "because of his intimate acquaintance with the needs of Britain and his understanding of governmental relations here." This meant, of course, that lend-lease would be neither a Treasury nor a War Department operation, but a White House one. Its administrative headquarters would be Hopkins's White House living quarters, where, operating as the President's alter ego while undergoing rigorous medical treatment for his deranged digestive tract, he would do much of his work while lying in bed. There was implicit derision in the name bestowed on the advisory committee by Washington insiders, who called it the "plus four"—that is, a superfluous appendage whose relationship to real work was as that of plus fours (golfing knickers) to overalls. A derisive note was also discernible in the labeling of Hopkins's top assistants, by Morgenthau, as "Hopkins' bedroom boys."[13]

Morgenthau's initial response to the Hopkins appointment was one of dismay, though he confined his expression of it to his personal staff. "I am just worried sick over it," he said, "because . . . Hopkins isn't well enough. . . . I think just at this time . . . it is very, very unfortunate that there is going to be a swapping of forces." Chief British purchasing agent Arthur Purvis thought so, too, and said so in a handwritten letter to Morgenthau (dated March 13, 1941), which he treasured for the rest of his life: "Your note with its—to me—sad confirmation of the break with your arduous work in the field of war supplies for Britain, has reached me today. I can only hope . . . that that break will not extend to the policy field. . . . You have from the start been a consistent and persistent friend . . . [and the] fact that your guiding skill was available to us in the time of trial is far from the least of the debts we owe to the President." Ickes, who would not have been averse to administering lend-lease himself, had by mid-February heard rumors that Hopkins would do so and reacted sourly. He told his diary March 13, with little concern for strict accuracy, that "Harry has not success-fully operated any government enterprise since he came to Washington. People have no confidence in him and, I believe, justly so."[14]

In this same March 13 diary entry, Ickes fretted over executive inaction on a number of matters he deemed of crucial importance, adding: "And permeating all of this unease and apprehension is the indisputable fact that the President is an exceedingly tired man. He looks as tired as I feel and I know I am in no con-dition to play an important part in what this country must do if we are to save our lives and souls." He was therefore glad that the President planned a fishing cruise in the Caribbean as soon as possible after lend-lease passed and that he himself would be one of the cruise party. His anticipatory pleasure was consid-erably lessened, however, when Roosevelt told him, on February 20, that the cruising vessel would be the shallow-drafted presidential yacht *Potomac,* upon which he with Hopkins, and even the President himself on one rough day and night, had been miserable in these same waters in early December of 1937.* Wouldn't it be advisable to select a cruise ship "that would not rock so much?" Ickes had asked plaintively, and had not been much comforted by Roosevelt's soothing reply that "at this time of the year the water would be smooth."[15]

In the event, Ickes's fears for the cruise, the timing of which (that is, during the mounting Yugoslavian crisis) seemed to some unfortunate, proved justified. The small presidential party, which included Hopkins, Ickes, Attorney General Robert H. Jackson, Steve Early, Ross McIntire, and Pa Watson, boarded the President's special train in Washington late in the afternoon of Wednesday, March 19, for the trip to Florida, where, in the harbor of Fort Lauderdale, the *Potomac* awaited them. On Saturday, March 22, the *Potomac* set out for a small Bahamas island called Great Isaac, sailing slowly so that the party could fish all the way. On that day, and for three days thereafter, the skies were bright, the seas calm, the fishing excellent, and the company congenial despite Ickes's barely concealed jealousy of Hopkins. The President's days were largely given over to fishing, he catching more fish than any of his companions, and to working on his stamp collection. There was poker almost every night. But on Wednesday, March 26, the sea suddenly roughened and the *Potomac* began to roll alarm-ingly, listing sometimes as much as thirty-two degrees, putting Hopkins, Ickes, and Watson to bed with, or to avoid, seasickness through much of the rest of the cruise, and raising in the minds of those aboard, even in the President's, ques-tion of what would happen should the unseaworthy craft actually capsize. The

*See *FDR: Into the Storm,* pp. 147–51.

danger was real. Jackson, who shared a cabin with Ickes, remarked matter-of-factly to his cabin-mate one night that "there wasn't a chance for a single one of us" if the vessel foundered; the accompanying navy destroyer *Benson* would not be able to launch lifeboats in so angry a sea; and Ickes voiced his disgust over the running of such needless risks by the President, especially the risk of his own (the President's) precious life.[16]

It was on rough seas that the President signed on March 27 the $7 billion lend-lease appropriation bill, flown down from Washington on a navy plane (it landed with difficulty), and then handed Hopkins a letter formally designating him "to advise and assist me in carrying out the responsibilities placed upon me" by the Lend-Lease Act. For his services, Hopkins would be paid $10,000 per annum—his first government pay since he resigned his $12,000 post of secretary of commerce in August 1940.[17] On that same day, *Potomac*'s radios told those aboard of the overthrow of Prince Paul's appeasement government in Belgrade and its replacement by a determinedly anti-Nazi one. A message came to Roosevelt from Stimson and Knox, jubilant in tone, suggesting that he issue at once a statement of support of the new government along with an order for the immediate loading of munitions upon Yugoslavian ships now in U.S. ports, munitions to go to the Yugoslavs, the Greeks, and the British in Greece, North Africa, and the Middle East. This message, combined with the continuing rough weather, caused Roosevelt to order the *Potomac,* then anchored again at Great Isaac, to sail at top speed (which was not very fast in the *Potomac*'s case) for Fort Lauderdale, where, on Friday evening, March 28, the vessel was at last in quiet waters. All those aboard would have been content to remain in safe harbor next day, save only Roosevelt, who wanted another day of fishing and whose wish was the vessel's law. Accordingly, the weather having moderated, the *Potomac* ventured out into the open sea late in the following morning and slowly coasted the Florida shore while Roosevelt and the others fished with little luck through most of the rest of the day. At sunset, the yacht was again anchored in Fort Lauderdale's harbor.

There, from his cabin, the President broadcast to the nation that evening a Jackson Day speech notable among such addresses for its total lack of partisanship but otherwise notable only for personal revelations made in an unwontedly apologetic tone. (He made no reference to Yugoslav developments, having been told that the American ambassador in Belgrade, Arthur Bliss Lane, had already, on his own authority, informed the new Belgrade government of the United States' firm support.) He needed a saltwater holiday a couple of times a year, he said, because only at sea could he escape the unremitting pressures, the fifteen-hour workdays, which the emergency imposed upon him in the White House. "Even when I go to Hyde Park or to Warm Springs, the White House office, the callers, the telephones, all follow me. But at sea the radio messages and the occasional pouch of mail reduce the official work to not more than two or three hours a day." He could loaf in sunlight, fish, nap, read "a biography or a detective story." Most important, "there is the opportunity for thinking things through—for differentiating between principles and methods, between the really big things of life and those other things . . . which may seem all-important today and are forgotten . . . in a month. . . . Yes, you recapture your philosophy. . . ." But in so seeking "peace of mind and spirit," he realized that such peace "will become a mere unattainable dream" unless he and all Americans worked today "harder than ever before." In the "quiet of this week, I have become more clear than ever that the time calls for courage and more courage—action and more action."[18]

Next day, the presidential party debarked and boarded the special train for Washington, with Roosevelt little if any less tired than he had been when his holiday began.

Returned to Washington, he announced the Hopkins's appointment in a calculatedly offhand manner, as if it were of no real importance. Hopkins's function, he told his press conference, would be primarily that of "bookkeeper, recording the expenditures and remaining balances of the Lend-Lease funds." This failed to deceive those who remembered that WPA, with Hopkins as its head, had been initially announced by Roosevelt in May 1935 as essentially a bookkeeping enterprise;* and it failed to prevent a resurgence of the virulent personal attacks upon Hopkins, in the press and in Congress, that had been a drumbeat accompaniment of his operations ever since his arrival in Washington at the outset of the New Deal. With stuttering fury, Republican Congressman John Taber of New York asserted that Hopkins as WPA administrator had made "the grossest record of incompetence of any of the notorious incompetence that this Administration has produced" and that his present appointment was "the worst blow the President has struck [thus far] at national defense."[19] No less vituperative, and often more so, were the comments of editorialists and columnists in the press, and of such radio pundits as Lindbergh's friend Fulton Lewis, Jr. Hopkins, though he had learned to expect unfair criticism, had not always (or often) been able to ignore it; he managed to do so in this case by immersing himself totally in a job he knew to be of vital importance.

And within weeks his performance was confounding not only those observers who deemed him personally incompetent, but also those who damned lend-lease's amorphous, ambiguous, utterly untidy administrative setup as unworkable by anyone. He did so in good part through a circumvention of that key portion of the announced setup that was indeed unworkable, namely, the cabinet "advisory committee" of which he was "secretary." On the very day (March 12) the lend-lease bill was signed he had moved to render the committee ineffective as lend-lease supervisor. He had then said to Roosevelt with all possible

*See FDR: *The New Deal Years,* pp. 468–69.

emphasis: "You've just got . . . to have this committee together [in the President's office] once a week. Otherwise . . . I've got to go each week and spend a great deal of time with each member of the committee" separately—a drastic needless drain upon his severely limited time and energy. He knew full well that Roosevelt, though he nodded his agreement with Hopkins's words, would find it more convenient to assume for himself all supervisory authority over Hopkins's work, which meant in effect that Hopkins would be free, as the President's right arm, to commit lend-lease money and arrange transfers of existing war matériel virtually on his own. (The advisory committee, though serving as Roosevelt's "war cabinet," never for one moment performed on lend-lease matters as it had been initially intended to do.) Hopkins had also moved, before embarking on the *Potomac,* to reduce to the maximum degree possible the inevitable competition between U.S. and British government military chiefs for a yet severely limited war material supply. He did so through a "both ends against the middle" strategy whose lack of candor was dictated by an acute sense of realities. He warned the British against expecting more aid than could be delivered, persuading them to form a small committee of production and military advisers to draw up a list of priorities. But he also, in a seemingly casual conversation with Army Chief of Staff Marshall, expressed concern that the British might be asking for more than they actually needed and suggested that Admiral Stark, General Henry H. ("Hap") Arnold, and Marshall—or at least one of the three—go to London to determine "actual necessities." When Arnold left for London in early April, however, Hopkins warned Churchill that though Arnold was an "excellent" officer who should be given all relevant information, he was committed "at all costs" to building up the American army and "had a [consequent] tendency to resist efforts to give adequate aid to Britain."[20]

And by that time Hopkins was fully exercising his unique talent for personal administration, its essence a sensitivity to, an empathic understanding of, other people. He, perhaps even more than role-playing Roosevelt, seemed able to feel what those he dealt with felt—seemed able to feel himself *into* them, actually *becoming* them to a degree (he sometimes knew Roosevelt's mind before Roosevelt knew it himself)—and he now shrewdly implemented the resultant accurate perceptions with a shifting combine of cajolery, flattery, subtle threats, subtle bribes, and appeals to the "better angels of our nature." He saved desperately needed time and energy by dealing directly with those who performed specific tasks, eschewing bureaucratic channels, and so made a virtue out of what others deemed a colossal defect in his situation. At the outset, he mollified the War Department by appointing as his second in command the highly efficient and wholly dedicated General Burns of the army ordnance department while permitting him to remain on Undersecretary of War Robert Patterson's staff— an arrangement that violated every principle upon which organization charts are based but enabled him to maintain direct intimate contacts with the army's procurement program. He mollified Morgenthau, who had objected to the Burns appointment on the ground that Burns was bound to give higher priority to the U.S. Army's needs than to Britain's—he also obtained two brilliant aides—when he brought in as his other top assistants Philip Young and Oscar Cox. Both men were close and highly valued associates of Morgenthau's, and both promptly let the Treasury secretary know that Hopkins, despite his physical frailties, was more than up to his job. His closest personal aide, constantly at his side in the White House bedroom, was intellectually brilliant Isador Lubin, borrowed from the Labor Department, where he had been chief of the Bureau of Labor Statistics since 1933; Lubin was as focused as Hopkins was upon the immediately practical, had an immense capacity for concentrated mental labor, maintained an invaluable close liaison between Hopkins and Sidney Hillman of OPM, and in general, being physically mobile as Hopkins was not, provided the latter with "exceptionally acute and accurate pairs of eyes and ears," as Sherwood has said.[21] Quickly assembled under these men was a staff as efficient as it was remarkably small for so huge a job (it totaled at its largest some one hundred people, all of whom were housed in the Federal Reserve Building)—a staff that was soon bound to Hopkins with steel-strong ties of personal loyalty, as had been the staffs of the Civil Works Administration and the Works Progress Administration.

Thereafter the hard, swift, compartmentalized Hopkins mind was so intensely and exclusively concentrated upon obtaining quick results that he irritably dismissed all ideas and requests that were, in his opinion, hostile or not immediately relevant to his doing so. Most such ideas and requests came from former associates of his in liberal causes, people who saw in the war emergency not only grave threats to these causes, but also shining opportunities to advance them; his dismissals of them therefore offended and sometimes permanently alienated people who had long been his personal friends. There was, for instance, a weakening of the formerly close sympathetic ties between Hopkins and some of the top national leaders of organized labor (he "would have thrown the whole labor movement overboard at this stage if it would help Lend-Lease," Lubin later said). There was also a further cooling of Hopkins's formerly warm friendship with Eleanor Roosevelt—a friendship that had already cooled almost in proportion to the increase in the warmth and closeness of Hopkins's relations with Eleanor's husband. She now increasingly felt, as many other liberals felt, that "Harry," though "deep down a fine person who had the courage to bear pain and who loved his country enough to risk the curtailment of his life in order to be of service," had "lost his sense of values. . . ." If Hopkins deeply regretted this loss of friendship, his absorption by his work permitted few signs of it. Instead: "I'm getting sick and tired of having to listen to complaints from those goddamn New Dealers!" he exclaimed one day that spring to Robert Sherwood, who could hardly believe his ears.[22]

As Hopkins and Roosevelt saw it, big-business men, though they had proved themselves generally unfit for key roles in a government dealing with Depression problems (witness their NRA performance),* must become active policy-making participants in a government dealing with war-waging problems. They must, because they had under their control a disproportionate share of the means to produce and deliver goods *now.*

IV

YET there were many who, that spring, saw big-business dominance of the industrial mobilization program as a threat, not just to liberal democracy, but to industrial mobilization itself. Roosevelt had dramatically announced a few months before the goals of fifty thousand airplanes a year, a two-ocean navy in five years, great stockpiles of rubber, aluminum, and other needed raw materials, and so forth. Measured against its stated goals, the progress appeared meager; indeed, the whole rearmament and aid-to-Britain program appeared to be in a mess. And this was largely due, many felt, to the mind-set and profit motivation of those who had industrial mobilization in their charge.

For instance, aircraft production was curtailed by a severe shortage of aluminum. The monopolistic Aluminum Company of America (Alcoa) had for decades severely limited aluminum production in order to achieve for itself the highest possible total profit. In 1931, Alcoa had made cartel arrangements with foreign producers to limit world production and fix aluminum's world price. Somewhat similar to the aluminum situation was that of steel. A chief reason for this was a dearth of steel, which also, of course, curtailed the production of tanks, military vehicles, guns, and ammunition. The failure to adequately stockpile rubber was of at least equal potential seriousness. It was clear that major sources of America's rubber supply would be cut off if a conquering Japan moved southward into Indo-China and the East Indies. All of this pointed up the necessity for the swiftest possible stockpiling of raw rubber *now* in the United States. There was an increasingly severe shortage of electricity, due to the profit-motivated decisions of businessmen—though the utilities industry, loath to increase greatly its generating and delivery capacities, and also bitterly hostile to any expansion of government-owned and -controlled hydroelectric facilities, loudly denied that an energy shortage existed.

Simultaneous with the above hinderings of industrial mobilization, and rooted in the same concern for private profit, was the continuing active hostility of key members of the big-business community to industrial unionism, manifest by the stubborn refusal of these key members to obey the Wagner and Fair Employment Practices Acts. It was a hostility countered by the equally stubborn insistence of the CIO, and the somewhat less stubborn insistence of the AFL,

---

*See pp. 242–69, 314–22, of *FDR: The New Deal Years.*

upon labor's right to organize and bargain collectively under New Deal labor law, also upon wage increases proportionate to the war-stimulated increase in corporation profits. The inevitable result was labor-management strife that slowed industrial mobilization's progress. We have noted that in this field, unlike those of war profits taxation and the financing of war plant expansion, big business had not had all its own way in 1940, thanks to Roosevelt's realization of the need for labor support during the 1940 election campaign and also for reaching the production goals he had set. But we have further noted that even in this field big business had won more battles than it lost in 1940's spring, summer, and fall and continued to do so after the election had ended in a solid Roosevelt victory. Indeed, within twenty-four hours after this victory was confirmed, as has been said, the War Department had announced the granting of a huge contract for the making of airplane engines to the notoriously violently anti-union Ford Motor Company, whose refusal to obey the Wagner Act continued adamant.* And the vehement protest of the contract by NDAC labor commissioner Sidney Hillman had not deterred the War Department from issuing another to Ford some six weeks later, this one so small (it amounted to a mere $1,387,000, for making midget scout cars for the army) that the department could not defend it on the ground that only big and famously "efficient" Ford could handle it expeditiously. It could have been handled expeditiously by any number of other manufacturers who were in compliance with labor law. This gave to the incident the quality of a deliberate slap in the face for Hillman and brought him, normally only too patient and even tempered, fuming to the White House with a clearly implied threat to resign his post as labor commissioner on the NDAC if the helpless, humiliating situation in which he had been placed were not at once rectified. Roosevelt had mollified him by committing himself to the proposal, in the making of which Hillman had a hand, to abolish the NDAC as the chief agency for industrial mobilization, replacing it with the two-headed OPM, Hillman and Knudsen to be the equally responsible and authoritative heads.

Barely had Hillman been installed as OPM's co-head than army procurement officers challenged his authority with an attempt to grant another large contract to Ford, this one for $67 million worth of army trucks, despite the fact that Ford remained in defiance of a National Labor Relations Board (NLRB) order, which it was challenging in the courts, and that increasing numbers of Ford workers, frustrated in their efforts to organize, were going on strike. An angry, determined Hillman promptly confronted Undersecretary of War Patterson, who, though intensely annoyed, felt forced to yield: the contract was shifted to Chrysler, which was in compliance with labor law. Nor was this the full extent of the public (and pocketbook) humiliation that aged, tyrannical, bigoted

*See pp. 16–24, 45–46.

Henry Ford had now to suffer. Within days thereafter, the U.S. Supreme Court sustained the NLRB ruling that Ford had challenged. This jarred, if it did not crack, the Ford Company's rigid corporate mind. For clearly the company's labor policy was beginning to cost it money; clearly the company's cozy and extremely profitable relationship with the U.S. Army Quartermaster Corps was being threatened; and so, abruptly, at long last, the labor policy was changed. In early May, yielding to the Supreme Court ruling, Ford opened negotiations with the CIO's (and young Walter Reuther's) United Auto Workers (UAW); soon it signed an agreement whereby UAW became the single collective bargaining agency for Ford's 140,000 workers.

Somewhat the same thing happened, and at the same time, in the case of that other giant opponent of unionization and New Deal labor law, Bethlehem Steel. In February 1941, a majority of the workers in the company's great Lackawanna, New York, plant prepared a strike that, if it spread to other Bethlehem plants, would cripple the whole mobilization effort. Bethlehem executives in Pennsylvania, reflecting the attitude of Bethlehem's head, Eugene Grace, initially told Hillman bluntly that troops would be called out to break such a strike; but the company's executive vice president, Joseph Larkin, and others of Bethlehem's top management had begun to realize, as Ford was realizing, that opposition to industrial unionization had passed the point of diminishing returns. After Philip Murray had wired the President an appeal for federal enforcement of federal law in the Bethlehem plants and Roosevelt had replied with a letter drafted by Hillman that indicated White House sympathy with the workers in this dispute, Bethlehem at last gave up. In March, the company agreed to permit the holding of an NLRB election among the workers in its plants, and not long afterward a collective bargaining agreement between Bethlehem and the United Steel Workers was signed.

V

IT was not solely with a recalcitrant management that Hillman had to deal adversarially as he strove for a just and nation-serving labor-management equilibrium. He had also to deal with labor leaders who, if not Communist Party members, accepted as true the then-current Moscow line that this war was but another bloody imperialist adventure into which an American administration, ultimately representative of only capitalist interests, sought to lead the deceived American masses. The Communist influence seemed evident in a strike that closed the great North American Aviation Company plant in the Los Angeles suburb of Inglewood in early June 1941: a key official of the CIO-UAW local in Inglewood openly avowed his membership in the Communist Party, and a number of the local's other leaders were at least "fellow travellers."[23] North American's eleven thousand workers had legitimate grievances, certainly. The company held contracts for approximately 20 percent of America's warplane production (it had fully 25 percent of the nation's total fighter aircraft production capacity); its 1940 profits, mostly from government contracts, had amounted to 57 percent of its net worth; yet the company paid its assembly line workers a mere 50 cents an hour, or $20 for a forty-hour week (other plants with government contracts in the Los Angeles area paid 75 cents), and flatly refused to grant the across-the-board 10-cent-an-hour increase that the UAW local demanded. The company still refused to do so when the union's wage increase demand was tentatively endorsed by the National Defense Mediation Board (NDMB) after a meeting between UAW representatives and those of North American held under NDMB auspices in Washington. The UAW representatives from Inglewood, under pressure from the UAW International, left Washington promising to postpone strike action until further investigation of the situation had been conducted. Instead, defying their union's national headquarters, the UAW local leaders ordered an immediate strike. On June 4, North American's employees poured out of the plant and onto picket lines in sufficient force to fight off the Los Angeles police, who were promptly called in to "restore order."

The negative reaction to this in Washington, on the part of both the government and the UAW International, was immediate and extreme. In a cabinet meeting on Friday, June 6, Attorney General Jackson likened the strike to an "insurrection." Secretary Hull proposed that Justice deport labor agitators who had demonstrated that their primary commitment was not to the United States, but to Russia, prompting Jackson to ask how one could deport "aliens" to a country that refused, as the Soviet Union would almost certainly refuse, to accept them. Roosevelt wished out loud that the agitators could just be forced aboard a ship that deposited them on some remote beach with only enough supplies to suffice them for a few weeks. Secretary Stimson was impatient of such fantasizing. He called for immediate seizure of North American by the army and the employment of stern coercive measures (drafting workers into the army if necessary) to restore production—a proposal with which Roosevelt, who had the week before augmented his executive powers by proclaiming the existence of an "unlimited national emergency" (we will tell of this later), indicated his agreement. Certainly this kind of "wildcat" or "outlaw" strike could not be tolerated for one minute in key defense industries. However, he decided not to act in the present case until, as Sidney Hillman advised, the UAW International had had time to bring, or attempt to bring, its local chapter back into compliance with International policy.

A few hours later he embarked on the *Potomac*, with Hopkins, for a weekend cruise. By then, Richard T. Frankensteen,* the UAW International vice presi-

---

*Frankensteen, with Reuther, was a hero of the struggle to organize Ford. A photograph of Frankensteen and Reuther, groggy and bloody after a beating just administered by Ford's hired thugs, has become a standard illustration in histories of American labor.

dent who had charge of the effort to unionize the airplane industry, was in Los Angeles, where he pleaded with the North American workers, in mass meeting assembled, for a return to work while the dispute issues were arbitrated by the NDMB. He was booed and shouted down. The local's UAW charter was then canceled by Frankensteen; its negotiating committee was suspended; five UAW International representatives who sided with the strikers were discharged. And Hillman, who had returned to Washington from Florida, blaming the strike's continuance upon a "small band of irresponsibles," now agreed with Stimson that strong government action was immediately necessary.

On Monday, June 9, after conferring in the Oval Office with Hillman, Stimson, Patterson, Assistant Secretary of War John J. McCloy, and Jackson, Roosevelt ordered the army to take over and reopen the North American plant. The order was executed at dawn of the following day: army trucks by the score roared through Inglewood's streets to disgorge at the plant site some 2,500 fully armed troops. They advanced in rank with fixed bayonets upon the picket line, which promptly dissolved, though not before one striker was seriously wounded by a bayonet thrust. The workers returned sullenly to work, having been warned that if they didn't, they would be reclassified for immediate draft under the Selective Service Act. Weeks passed, however, before the factory's production was back on schedule, by which time great events abroad had caused all American Communists to discover abruptly that this war was *not* "imperialist" after all, but a struggle of Freedom against Tyranny, and that, therefore, a full and uninterrupted production of American war goods was of paramount importance. . . .*

The spectacle of American soldiers marching against unarmed American workers, mirroring the way in which Nazi-Fascists dealt with labor disputes, chilled every heart that beat ardently for democracy. It brought to a climax the storm of hateful abuse and vituperation that had swirled about Hillman ever since he'd first asserted himself as NDAC labor commissioner, though now it blew more strongly from the Left than from the Right as labor leaders, with John L. Lewis in the van, blasted him as "spineless," "cowardly," "traitorous." Even among the moderates of the Left there was sharp criticism of Hillman's failure to support a proposal made months ago by Walter Reuther for the establishment of labor-management committees in defense plants. Why hadn't he? Of *course* the big-business men of NDAC and OPM bitterly opposed as "social revolutionary" the idea of giving labor a voice in management; of *course* a determined effort to implement the idea would stimulate counterefforts by con-

---

*During those weeks, it should be added, the government moved to correct the situation that the strike had protested. After the Inglewood UAW had been reorganized and its charter restored, the NDMB ruled that all of the union's original wage demands, and its demand for payroll deductions by management for union dues (a key closed-shop provision), must be granted—and management, acutely aware that otherwise bayonets just might be pointed at its breast, complied.

servatives to enact anti-labor congressional legislation. But wouldn't such committees heighten worker morale, prevent strikes and slowdowns, and so increase defense production? And wouldn't this beneficent effect stymie the efforts of the conservatives to (in effect) legislate labor unions out of existence? Affirmative answers to such questions pointed toward the conclusion that Hillman wasn't tough enough, that he was too conciliatory, too accommodating, too deficient in fighting courage, to deal with businessmen whose single-minded devotion to their special economic interest made them very tough indeed in adversarial situations. Nor was the increased virulence in the attacks upon him from the Left offset by any perceptible decrease in the virulence of the attacks upon him from the Right. If the businessmen and their conservative allies over the country felt any gratitude to Sidney Hillman for services that others claimed he rendered them, they gave no public sign of it. In press and radio statements tinged often with anti-Semitism, they continued to portray him as a figure of great and sinister power, an immigrant Jew trained in Russian revolutionary tactics and strategy whose overall purpose, a purpose that determined his every move, was to advance a secret social revolutionary agenda for America.

He remained for them symptomatic of all they loathed and feared in the administration, all that prevented the elevation of their spirits, the surge of hopeful expectation, that would otherwise have come to them out of their economic circumstances.

For it must be here remarked, since it is indeed remarkable in retrospect, that the morale of the business community remained very low through all these first six months of 1941 and indeed through the year as a whole. The special business interest had scored one triumph after another over the general welfare as the New Deal had defined it. Published statistics showed that a hugely profitable market for both industrial and agricultural products was rapidly developing, with no end to the development in sight. Every credible sign said that a great business boom had been gathering momentum for months and would soon assume unprecedented proportions. Yet the American businessmen remained anxious, uneasy of mind, gloomy of outlook.

"Almost daily the newspapers were filled with rumors concerning heavy increases in taxation and regimentation of business of one kind or another to advance the defense program, to step up the war activity, and to curb the hazard of inflation," explained economics professor S. S. Hueber of the University of Pennsylvania in a summary of the year's financial market activity. "All this news, together with the increasing belief that business troubles along all the lines indicated would be steadily worse with respect to the future, was bound to cause fear and hesitancy and even gloom. . . ."[24] In other words, despite abundant evidences to the contrary, the businessman feared that the administration would still do what Roosevelt had publicly said should be done, namely, maintain in full force the New Deal's labor, business, and social welfare laws, and might even socialize the whole economy as a defense necessity. Were not some of the most influential of the hated liberals saying in public speech that the total war into which we were heading meant inevitably total national economic planning and control? The businessman also sensed grave threats lurking in the massive investigative report on American business that the Temporary National Economic Committee (TNEC) was completing during 1941's first six months, a report that revealed cartel arrangements that disadvantaged the United States relative to Germany. Had not the President plainly said, when this TNEC investigation was launched in the spring of 1938, that drastic changes *must* be made in the nation's overall business structure? The control of American enterprise was concentrated in too few hands, he had said, and must be redistributed, either by the forcible breakup of huge corporations and the restoration of competition or by a shift of economic power from business to government. The latter possibility was, of course, horrifying. And, hearing and reading all the above horrid news, the businessman was deafened and blinded to clear signs that the Executive would never permit New Dealers ("governmental cliques that mix defense with politics," as *Newsweek* called them)[25] to implement the views that gave a reddish tinge to their public speech—clear signs that Roosevelt's commitment to, and even his interest in, Thurman Arnold's anti-trust activities was being rapidly eroded away by current events—clear signs that such business regulation as was in the offing would almost certainly be self-regulation of the NRA code-authority variety, since virtually every one of the business executives now serving as "dollar-a-year" men had had a role in the making and application of NRA codes.

In sum, looking at the White House, the businessman did not see the President who actually lived there, "the best friend the profit system ever had,"[26] but instead "that man," the enemy of free enterprise, the promoter of socialism, who was a figment of the businessman's own fevered imagination, being shaped out of his furious reactions to the most fervid rhetoric of the New Deal.

VI

THE storm that now swirled around and focused upon Franklin Roosevelt as April gave way to May and May advanced toward June was far wider, and more intense, than the storm that swirled about Hillman. Liberals assailed him for letting big business take over the country as a national defense "necessity." Conservatives assailed him for alleged designs to use the war emergency to impose liberal reforms through executive decree. Isolationists assailed him with growing vehemence for deviously, covertly leading the nation into war. Interventionists assailed him for not leading at all in a time when, as never before, national survival required decisive leadership. ("I cautioned him . . . that without a lead on his part it was useless to expect the people would take the initiative in letting him know whether or not they would follow him . . . ," Stimson reported, in his diary, of a private meeting between himself and the President on April 22, 1941.)[27] Almost everyone who was well-informed assailed him for lack of candor in his current dealings with the American people. Ardently interventionist Stimson did so, begging the President to give fully and frankly to the American people his assessment of the importance of the Battle of the Atlantic, the current parlous condition of this battle, and the consequent need to assign Atlantic convoy duty to U.S. naval and air forces. Ardently isolationist Charles Lindbergh did so by inveighing in public speech against "government by subterfuge" and, more specifically, by asserting that this President who preached the "Four Freedoms" to the world simultaneously denied Americans "freedom of information—the right of a free people to know where they are being led by their government."[28]

The quoted Lindbergh words are from a speech he gave in Minneapolis on May 10, 1941—his third address under the auspices of the America First Committee, he having formally joined that organization in April 1941. His first had been in Chicago on April 17, four days after Ickes, encouraged to do so by the President, had delivered a slashing public attack upon him in that same city (Ickes had called the aviator the "No. 1 Nazi fellow traveller in the United States . . . the proud possessor of a Nazi decoration," which, from Hitler's point of view, he richly deserved).[29] The second had been in New York on April 23. The argument both speeches made—that Britain's defeat was inevitable, that even full American intervention in the war could not now save her—gained plausibility from the dire news that poured uninterruptedly out of the eastern Mediterranean even as he spoke. Yugoslavia conquered! Greece conquered! Defeated British troops under heavy air attacks as they embark miserably from Greek ports! The last desperate hope of Britain's leaders was to persuade us "to send another American Expeditionary Force to Europe," said Lindbergh, but "look at the map of Europe today and see if you can suggest any way in which we could win this war if we entered it." If we took our navy from the Pacific and used it to convoy shipping to Britain, it "would not win the war for England," but only prolong the agony of inevitable defeat. And if "we had an air force that we could send to Europe," which we did not, where would it operate? "Some of our squadrons might be based on the British Isles; but it is physically impossible to base enough aircraft in the British Isles alone to equal in strength the aircraft that can be based on the continent of Europe."[30]

The absurdity of that last argument provoked smiles from some.

But Roosevelt, who had hoped that Lindbergh would not formally identify himself with America First, which had seemed about to be torn apart by internal dissensions, was not amused. He saw Lindbergh's heroic leadership as a force that could now hold intact, impervious to all counterargument, a hard core of organized, well-financed isolationism sufficiently large and strong to frustrate administration purposes in the months to come as it had in months past. He was prepared with a forceful bitter answer when asked at his press conference on Friday, April 25, 1941, a question he himself had planted through Steve Early: Why was Lindbergh, a colonel in the air corps reserve, not now called into active service as so many other reserve officers had been? Roosevelt referred to the Lincoln administration's handling of "the Vallandighams" of the Civil War period (Congressman Clement L. Vallandigham of Ohio was the leading spokesman for those in the North, dubbed "Copperheads," who violently attacked the Lincoln administration for prolonging a war the North could not win). Such men were not called into service in the Union Army because, being defeatist, if not disloyal, they were unfit for service. He also spoke of Thomas Paine's *Crisis* pamphlet of December 1776 with its acid references to "the summer soldier" and "the sunshine patriot" who, in the hard winter of Valley Forge, shrank "from the service of their country." Asked a reporter, "Are you still talking about Colonel Lindbergh?" Replied Roosevelt, emphatically, "Yes." This made front-page news in next morning's papers, causing a furor amid which, on the following Monday, Lindbergh dispatched a letter to the President and simultaneously released it to the press (the "second time" Lindbergh had shown the President "discourtesy" by publishing a letter before the President had received it, complained Steve Early). Hurt and angry, the hero wrote that since his President and commander in chief deemed him unworthy of service and impugned "my loyalty . . . , my character, and my motives, I see no honorable alternative to tendering my resignation as colonel in the United States Air Corps Reserve." He was therefore at once "forwarding my resignation to the Secretary of War."[31]

Stimson, Knox, and a great many others were very sure that Roosevelt overestimated Lindbergh's potency as a molder of public opinion—that he overestimated greatly the strength of isolationist sentiment in general. Most of such strength as isolationism had was due to Roosevelt's obviously fearful respect for it, they said. He conceded far more than was necessary in his public speech, blurring issues that should be sharply defined; he continuously waffled on the convoy issue, for major example; and through the cloud of doubt and confusion thus raised in the public mind, isolationism loomed a far larger phenomenon than it actually was. The illusion would be instantly dissipated, reality would be revealed in the clear light of frank and honest discourse, if ever the President again performed his sacred duty *to lead*. The truth of their assertion was seemingly confirmed by a Gallup poll taken in April the previous week. Asked by Gallup whether they would favor U.S. entrance into the war "if it appeared certain that there was no other way to defeat Germany and Italy," three-fourths of those who replied said yes, they would. Asked if they thought the United States would enter the war sooner or later, four-fifths said yes, they did. Asked if the United States should enter the war *now,* however, four-fifths said no (a Gallup poll taken earlier that month showed a majority of the people opposed to con-voying on the grounds that convoying was an act of war)—which clearly meant that these four-fifths were not *yet* convinced that American entrance was an absolute necessity for Nazi-fascism's defeat. It was the President's moral obli-gation to convince them, cried the interventionists.

Why did he refuse even to try?

The most perceptive answer to this question, and the most accurate descrip-tion of Roosevelt's political situation as Roosevelt himself saw it that spring, was given at the time by newspaper columnist Raymond Gram Swing, who, on the evidence, based his conclusions on a lengthy White House interview, proba-bly with his good friend Harry Hopkins: "The great agitation in the United States today is over the President's leadership," wrote Swing in an article writ-ten for the *Sunday Express* of London and published on May 10, 1941. "He is being snarled at, shouted at, prayed at, blasted at to tell the country the whole truth, and to lead the country right off into convoying, which is a new word meaning war. . . . One catchword of the hour is that the President is behind pub-lic opinion, that in not leading it he may lose it, and the opinion may then drift off, say to Lindbergh and the appeasers." Swing was sure it would not. But: "If he [Roosevelt] should assume the leadership now, and appear to be 'taking' the country into war, the public would turn on him later. . . . At such times, the only possibility of maintaining unity and morale is that the President shall not have whipped up sentiment for war, that he should appear to have yielded to public insistence, and that the war should be an enterprise of partnership rather than something entered into at his behest." Swing believed that the President could "get convoying now if he asked for it," and perhaps by a 55 percent to 45 per-cent congressional vote. But a 10 percent margin of approval was just not wide enough on a life-or-death issue; the President needed the support of at least two-thirds of the Congress. "What is important . . . is not American entrance into the war now but American effectiveness [if or when we *do* enter]. . . . America must come in, if it comes, with a feeling of having . . . been allowed to make up its own mind. . . . [The President] must choose a time for assuming leadership which makes for strength and reliability later on." Meanwhile: "Impatience with Roosevelt . . . now paradoxically becomes a part of the Roosevelt strategy. He needs all the impatience that can be mustered. The more his friends are in anguish about his inscrutable delay, the better they serve him. . . . That is not to say that he is egging his associates on to create a demand." He "does not under-take to instruct the public himself " because to do so would be to compromise fatally his position at the center of national unity; he would destroy himself as the symbolic figure around whom a solid national opinion could cohere. Others must do the instructing. And they were doing it. "Hull, Knox, Stimson, and Willkie, the four most authentic secondary leaders in the country, are hammer-ing and teaching. Three of them, by the way, are Republicans. This is a national

movement. And the nation is responding, no question about that, not with enthusiasm but with reluctance, which is the only way a free, civilized nation can
enter a war."[32]

None of which was persuasive of the four stalwarts who, according to Swing,
were carrying the ball for Franklin Roosevelt. In their view, and that of the interventionists as a whole, there simply was not time enough to permit a politically safe, rudderless national drift, even a fairly swift drift, toward ultimate
decision. Roosevelt no doubt hoped that Hitler, sufficiently provoked, would
provide an "incident" that united the American people in a call to arms. But to
trust blind chance to make a decision whose necessity was obvious to clear-eyed
reason was, in the circumstances, as foolhardy as it was cowardly. The Swing-
Roosevelt argument was but a plausible yet flawed excuse for presidential
timidity, there being no such necessity as Swing alleged for so slow a working
of "democratic" processes. Bold, frank executive leadership could unite the
people almost at once to defend their liberties, whereas every week, every day,
every hour of delay increased the risk to the life of the nation, the life of freedom itself. . . .

VII

As May opened, Hitler stood at the apex of a conquering power far greater than
Napoleon had had in the spring of 1810, with a capacity to choose, and to implement his choice, that was immense. Two options, especially, were glaringly
open to him, either of which, promptly exercised, seemed certain to give him
final victory over the British within months—that is, long before American aid,
at its current rate of production, could become substantial enough to count in the
equation.

One option was to move at once, with a major portion of the overwhelming
force that was at his disposal, upon Alexandria and the Suez Canal. Rommel
and Admiral Erich Raeder, commander of the German navy, were begging him
to do this, as was suspected at the time and as we now know. It was something
he could do while simultaneously fomenting and supporting political upheavals
in Iraq, Syria, and Palestine, whose inhabitants, Jews and Arabs alike (if for
very different reasons), violently resented their Versailles-imposed domination
by France and Britain; and it "would be more deadly to the British Empire than
the capture of London!" as Raeder said to him.[33] Churchill had touched on this
fateful possibility in a message to Roosevelt a few days after the British evacuation of Greece. "At this moment much hangs in the balance," he wrote on April 29.
"We must expect dangerous demands will be made upon Turkey. They [the
Turks] will try their best to have themselves let alone and may go a long way to
meet German wishes short of actually giving passage to large quantities of German troops [which meant, in Churchillian language, that the Turks would

probably ultimately feel compelled to grant such passage]. . . . Meanwhile at the western end of the Mediterranean I must regard the Spanish situation as most critical. Hitler may easily be able to get control of the batteries on the Africa shore. The [Nazi] infiltration into Tangier is continuous and both Morocco and Algeria may soon be infected. Once the German air force is well established in Morocco it will not be long before Dakar becomes a German U-boat base." Thus, while the Mediterranean became an Axis lake, the already abundant Atlantic dangers would be greatly increased. "All this comes back to Vichy. . . . I trust therefore that you will be able to put the most extreme pressure upon Vichy to break with the Germans if they violate Syria, Morocco, Algeria or Tunis [Roosevelt's justification for diplomatic recognition of Vichy was that it would enable U.S. pressure to be exerted upon the Pétain government]. I feel Hitler may now quite easily gain vast advantages very cheaply and we are so fully engaged that we can do little or nothing to stop him spreading himself."[34]

The *other* option open to Hitler was to shift troops, armor, and airpower from the Balkans westward to augment the forces now occupying the Low Countries and northern France, then use them in a massive invasion of the British Isles while at the same time focusing his U-boat, surface fleet, and air force more concentratedly than ever before upon the severance of Britain's Atlantic lifeline. It was this option that General Sir John Dill, chief of the imperial general staff, stressed in a paper sent to Churchill on May 6, 1941. ". . . German land and air forces could be concentrated for invasion within six to eight weeks of their release from the Balkan theater," said Dill; and "after exhaustive inquiry" the general staff calculated "the [probable] scale of [Germany's] armoured attack upon this country at six armoured divisions, a total of some 2400 tanks." These would operate in coordination with "a powerful air force." To be reasonably assured of countering this successfully, the British should be able to deploy "six armoured divisions and four army tank brigades (i.e., some 2,600 tanks)" but had now on the home island only "the equivalent of three fully effective armoured divisions" deploying some 1,250 tanks. As for the comforting belief that Germany could not successfully assault the island because it lacked command of the sea approaches, Dill deemed it "dangerous" because false. "It would take five to seven days for us to concentrate adequate naval forces in home waters," he said. "Our bombers cannot deal with more than six invasion ports [at once] effectively, and then only if the weather is favorable. Air attack cannot be counted upon to break up a disembarkation, any more than it did . . . at Dunkirk." Dill therefore opposed any further buildup of armor under Wavell's command until Britain's home defenses were far more secure than they now were. Of course, the loss of Egypt "would be a calamity, and one we would not accept without a desperate fight; but it would not end the war." A "successful invasion," on the other hand, "spells our final defeat." Hence "the defence of the United Kingdom must take first place." Indeed, Egypt was "not even second in order of priority, for it has been an accepted principle that in the last resort the security of Singapore comes before Egypt [Churchill most emphatically disagreed with this assessment of priorities]. Yet the defences of Singapore are still considerably below standard." He concluded with a statement of general principles: "Risks must of course be taken in war, but they must be calculated risks. We must not fall into the error of whittling away the security of vital points. If need be, we must cut our losses in places that are not vital before it is too late."[35]

Churchill was "astonished" by this "grave pronouncement by the the highest professional authority"—a pronouncement before which many a government "would have wilted," as he says in his memoirs.[36] He was also badly jarred by it. For what Dill had to say dovetailed all too neatly with an estimate of the situation he had just received (on May 1) from the President of the United States—the one man in the world upon whose judgment and will now depended Britain's fate and freedom's cause as never before.

Replying to Churchill's message of April 29 after having conferred with the four members of what he had come to call his "war cabinet" (Hull, Stimson, Knox, Morgenthau), Roosevelt not only tacitly accepted as a foregone conclusion the British loss of Egypt, the Canal, and the Middle East, but also deprecated the importance of this loss in language that, if determinedly optimistic, was gallingly (all the more so for being unconsciously) patronizing. "You have done not only heroic, but very useful work in Greece and the territorial loss is more than compensated for by the necessity for enormous German concentration and resulting enormous German losses in men and material," the President wrote. "Having sent all men and equipment to Greece you could possibly spare, you have fought a wholly justified delaying action and will continue to do so in other parts of the Eastern Mediterranean, including North Africa and the Near East. Furthermore . . . if additional withdrawals become necessary they will all be part of a plan which at this stage of the war shortens British lines, greatly extends the Axis lines, and compels the enemy to expend great quantities of men and equipment. I am satisfied that both here and in Britain public opinion is growing to realize that even if you have to withdraw further in the Eastern Mediterranean, you will not allow a great debacle or surrender, and that in the last analysis the Naval control of the Indian Ocean and the Atlantic Ocean will in time win the war." If Churchill was not irritated by this evident assumption of Roosevelt's that an approving "public opinion" was a ruling concern at a time when England's very life was at stake, he was certainly perturbed by the words that followed. They replied negatively, not only to Churchill's implicit request for U.S. action to "stiffen" the Turks, but also to the explicit request for concrete U.S. pressure upon Vichy, whereby the Pétain government might be persuaded "to break with the Germans" should the latter "violate" French-controlled territory in North Africa and the Middle East. "In regard to Turkey, I fear there is little we [the United States] can do" save offer moral support, said Roosevelt.

As for Vichy France, "I do not think there is any chance of persuading Vichy to break with the Germans." And the perturbation these words caused was certainly not reduced by those with which the message was concluded. They struck Churchill as, in the circumstances, fatuous. "Personally, I am not downcast by more spread of Germany for additional large territories," the President declared. "There is little of raw material in all of them put together—not enough to maintain nor compensate for huge occupation forces. The exception is the oil in Mossul and Iraq and I assume production there will be practically destroyed by you in event of necessity."[37]

Thus this missive, overall, in part because it seemed designed to "cheer up" the Prime Minister as if he were a disappointed little boy, had upon him an opposite effect. It triggered a sharp attack of the "black dog," as Churchill dubbed the psychological depression that had recurrently hounded him since childhood and that, in this season of gloom, had an abundance of stuff to feed upon. He moved at once to fight it off, as he had learned to do, by directly addressing its immediate incitement. He let Ambassador Winant know within hours how unhappy the President's letter had made him, and Winant promptly reported this to the White House. Churchill minuted Foreign Secretary Anthony Eden on May 2, "It seems to me as if there were a considerable recession across the Atlantic, and that . . . we are being left very much to our fate."[38] But he simultaneously publicly asserted with great force the very opposite of the near despair such abandonment aroused in him; he broadcast to the world on this same May 2 a speech as determinedly optimistic in tone and in this respect as contradictory of stern realities as, in his opinion, the President's message had been. Roosevelt had announced on April 25 that the U.S. Navy would henceforth patrol much farther out into the Atlantic than it had formerly done, saying this was necessary for "the protection of the American hemisphere," now that "American lives and American property" were at stake in Greenland, Newfoundland, and Bermuda. The announcement had been very cautiously worded. Roosevelt had refused to say whether "protection of the hemisphere" meant the "protection of shipping" or what a patrolling vessel was authorized to do if it encountered an "aggressive ship."[39] Nevertheless, Churchill described the announcement, in his speech, as a "tremendous decision . . . by the President and people of the United States" that presaged the inevitable "total defeat of Hitler and Mussolini," then closed by quoting the two stanzas of Arthur Hugh Clough's poem that end with

> In front the sun climbs slow, how slowly,
> But westward, look, the land is bright.[40]

No such optimistic warmth characterized the message he dispatched on the following day (May 3) to the President of the United States. It was of unwonted brusqueness.

"We [you] must not be too sure that the loss of Egypt and the Middle East would not be grave,"* he wrote. "It would seriously increase the hazards in the Atlantic and Pacific. . . . We shall fight on whatever happens, but please remember that the attitude of Spain, Vichy, Turkey, and Japan may be finally decided by the outcome of the struggle in this theater of war." He rejected "the view that the loss of Egypt and the Middle East would be a mere preliminary to the successful maintenance of a prolonged oceanic war. If all Europe, the greater part of Asia and Africa became . . . a part of the Axis system, a war maintained by the British Isles, the United States, Canada, and Australia against the mighty agglomeration would be a hard, long, and bleak proposition. Therefore, if you cannot take more advanced positions now or very soon, the vast balances may be tilted heavily to our disadvantage. Mr. President, I am sure you will not misunderstand if I speak to you exactly what is in my mind. The one decisive counterweight I can see to balance the growing pessimism in Turkey, the Near East, and in Spain, would be if the United States were immediately to range herself with us as a belligerent power. If this were possible I have little doubt that we could hold the situation in the Mediterranean until the weight of your munitions gained the day."[41]

This missive was considerably milder, less ominous in tone, than had been the original draft reply that Churchill submitted to the British cabinet and Foreign Office for review. With difficulty, Eden, Deputy Prime Minister Clement Attlee, and the American Department of the Foreign Office had persuaded Churchill to "tone it down," weakening the first draft's implication that if Egypt and the Middle East were lost, the British government might feel forced to open negotiations with Hitler.[42] More than a hint of this possibility remained, however, in the message Roosevelt received, and he, too, was now badly jarred. He realized the imperative importance of an immediate response and, within hours, had one drafted in the State Department. He found this draft unsatisfactory, however, when he received it on May 4—also he was again feeling so "lousy" physically that his ability to concentrate was impaired—so it was not until six days later, after a considerable redrafting effort, that the reply was finally dispatched.

In it, Roosevelt made no reference to the Prime Minister's call for U.S. belligerency, but he was in other respects reassuringly responsive. He had not intended "to minimize in any degree the gravity of the situation particularly as it regards the Mediterranean," the "great strategic importance" of which he fully recognized; nor had he intended to suggest that U.S. support of the British effort there would be reduced. On the contrary, knowing "your determination to win on that front . . . we shall do everything that we possibly can to help you do it." He had "issued instructions that supplies insofar as they are available are to be rushed to the Middle East." Thirty ships were "to go within the next three

---

*"Mortal" was the word used in the first draft, "overwhelming" in the second.

weeks." He had in his "previous message merely meant to indicate that should the Mediterranean prove . . . an impossible battleground I do not feel that such fact alone would mean the defeat of our mutual interests. I say this because I believe the outcome of this struggle is going to be decided in the Atlantic and unless Hitler can win there he cannot win anywhere in the world in the end." He concluded: "Our patrols are pushing farther out into the Atlantic. I have just added all our heavier units of the Coast Guard to the Navy for this purpose. Other steps to strengthen that patrol will be taken soon."[43]

Some half dozen hours before this message was dispatched (it left the White House at eleven P.M. of that May 10), while Washington yet basked in warm late afternoon sunlight, an unarmed Messerschmitt-110 fighter plane roared through the chill darkness of night high above Scotland's Lammermuir Hills and Pentland Hills before being deliberately crashed in flames. Thus ended a flight that had begun in Augsburg, Germany, some eight hundred miles to the southeast. The pilot, a stocky, beetle-browed, youngish man, (actually thirty-seven years old) clad in the uniform of a Luftwaffe lieutenant, parachuted onto a farm within twelve miles of the estate, near Glasgow, of the Duke of Hamilton. To those who took him at once in charge, and to whom he seemed remarkably calm and self-possessed, considering his circumstances, he identified himself at first as "Alfred Horn." But a little later, while being treated in a nearby military hospital for a slight injury received in his bailout, he confessed that his real name was Rudolf Hess. This true confession was so astounding that it was at first disbelieved. For Rudolf Hess was Deputy Fuehrer of the Reich, administrator of the Nazi Party, a member (without portfolio) of the Reich cabinet, and, by general repute, Hitler's closest longtime personal friend; he was said to know Hitler's mind as did no other.* He now asked for an immediate interview with the Duke of Hamilton, whom he had met, he said, during the 1936 Olympic Games in Berlin, and whom he had then judged to be a man of good sense and goodwill, sympathetic with Hitler's Germany, anxious to promote friendly relations between the British and German governments.† It was as a peacemaker that he had come, he told the duke the next day, for "the Fuehrer did not wish to defeat England and wished to stop the fighting." He had come, however, altogether on his own initiative and without Hitler's prior knowledge, as was developed in the duke's interview and in subsequent ones with Ivone Kirkpatrick, a former first secretary of the British embassy in Berlin. His motives were pure, selfless, hu-

---

*It was to Hess that Hitler, while imprisoned following the failed 1923 Munich putsch, dictated most of the manuscript of *Mein Kampf.*
†It was later denied by the Duke of Hamilton, or by someone speaking for him, that he had ever met Hess personally. But Churchill says that he did, in *The Grand Alliance,* page 50, and the duke was no doubt concerned to mitigate to the fullest possible extent what must have been for him a peculiarly galling embarrassment.

manitarian. He had been horrified by the 1940 German air assault upon London, with its indiscriminate slaughter of women and children. They were made necessary by the stupid intransigence of the present British government, as were the U-boat attacks that were bound to produce wholesale starvation of the British people. And far worse was in store for the British if they persisted in their hopeless struggle. Hitler would never negotiate with the Churchill ministry, Hess further indicated; Churchill must be removed from office; but with that done, Der Fuehrer, dealing with a government representative such as Hamilton, the Duke of Windsor, and those who had dominated the British government during the Chamberlain years, would gladly permit Britain to retain and manage its empire intact while he took charge of the Continent. This suggested to the British cabinet that arch-appeaser Lord Simon, who had demonstrated much sympathy with Nazi-fascism while serving in the Baldwin, MacDonald, and Chamberlain cabinets, might be of all Englishmen the best equipped to obtain information from Hess. Assigned to interview this strange visitor, he, however, learned nothing new. By then, Churchill had ordered that Hess be treated as a high-ranking prisoner of war, "strictly isolated in a convenient house not too far from London," and that "every endeavor . . . be made to study his mentality and get anything worthwhile out of him."[44]

Insofar as it seemed revealing of weakness, if not disarray, in the uppermost ranks of the Nazi hierarchy, the British and American public derived hopeful inspiration from Hess's adventure. Pleasure was derived in both Britain and America from Hitler's acute embarrassment and consequent fury, during which he publicly stripped Hess all offices, replaced him as deputy leader of the party with Martin Borman, arrested plane-maker Wilhelm Messerschmitt for having facilitated Hess's obtaining of a plane and learning to navigate, and secretly ordered Hess's immediate execution if he returned to Germany. "It seemed that Party Member Hess lived in a state of hallucination," said an official press release in Berlin, "as a result of which he felt he could bring about an understanding between England and Germany. . . . This, however, will have no effect on the continuance of the war, which has been forced upon the German people." From Roosevelt to Churchill went a message on May 14: "If Hess is talking . . . it would be very valuable to public opinion over here if he can be persuaded to tell your people what Hitler has said about the United States or other parts of the Western Hemisphere, including commerce, infiltration, military domination, encirclement of the United States, etc. . . . I can assure you that the Hess flight has captured the American imagination and the story should be kept alive for just as many days or even weeks as possible." Replying three days later, Churchill briefly summarized for the President the meager information thus far obtained from Hess's volubility. As regards the United States, "not much emerged save incidentally some . . . disparaging remarks about . . . the degree of assistance you will be able to furnish to us," said Churchill. "I am afraid in particular he is not sufficiently impressed by what he thinks he knows of your aircraft types and production. Hess seems in good health and not excited and no ordinary signs of insanity can be detected. . . ." As regards publicity: "[I]t is desirable that the press should not romanticize him and his adventure. We must not forget that he shares responsibility for all of Hitler's crimes and is a potential war criminal whose fate must ultimately depend upon the decision of the Allied Governments."[45]

Alas, the lift that the Hess flight gave to British and American spirits was not long sustained. It was all too soon apparent that the bizarre episode was but an aberration; it would have, as Hitler had so emphatically said, no influence whatever upon the course of events.

And this course continued downward, from the British-American point of view, toward black despair.

There was great anxiety at this time over Britain's sea lifeline, for the great new battleship *Bismarck,* accompanied by the powerful new cruiser *Prinz Eugen,* had escaped from her berth at Bergen and, eluding the British warships that desperately searched for her, now threatened to wreak havoc upon Allied shipping in the North Atlantic. Eleven convoys, including a troop convoy, were then at sea, or about to sail, in the North Atlantic. None of them could defend itself against the *Bismarck*'s fifteen-inch guns. Anxiety mounted when, on May 24, in the Denmark Strait between Iceland and Greenland, the British *Hood* and new *Prince of Wales* managed to intercept the German vessels and engage them in a classic gun duel. In a furious half hour, the *Prince of Wales* was severely damaged and the *Hood* sunk (a shell exploded her magazines and she went down in four minutes, taking with her all save 3 of her crew of 1,419), following which the two German ships, seemingly little damaged, got away. The direction of their flight was ominous; they headed southeastward toward sanctuary at Brest but also toward the main convoy route across the Atlantic. Special anxiety was felt over the threat to the troop convoy that approached Ireland from the southwest, for this convoy could make, at most, twelve knots as against the *Bismarck*'s reputed twenty-five. The *Bismarck,* however, as was soon discovered, had *not* got away without grave wounds; shell hits had damaged her steering mechanism, reduced her speed, and ruptured an oil tank. She left behind her a trail of leaked oil highly visible from the air. Following it, a British Catalina flying boat based in Lough Erne of Northern Ireland found her on the morning of May 26 as she was approaching, but had not yet reached, the area sheltered by the wide, massive, land-based air umbrella that opened for the Germans out of Brest. She was very soon under attack by torpedo planes launched from the carrier *Ark Royal* and, by nightfall, was badly crippled. On the following morning, May 27, she was finished off by torpedoes and gunfire from the British *Rodney* and *King George V,* going down shortly before eleven in the morning. Nearly two thousand Germans died with her. (The *Prinz Eugen,* escaping British detection, managed to reach Brest safely nine days later.) News of this triumph was received with great relief and thanksgiving in London and Washington. A message flashed from the President to the Former Naval Person said: "All of us are made very happy by the fine tracking down of the *Bismarck* and that she has literally gone for good."[46]

But such happiness was mitigated by grief over the loss of the *Hood.*

And it was more than offset by the gloom that enshrouded news currently pouring, a dark flood, out of the eastern Mediterranean.

For tragic events continued to mock Churchill's "determination to win" on Crete, which, he had repeatedly said, must be held at all costs. Taking full advantage of their overwhelming air superiority, the Germans had launched on May 20 an unprecedentedly massive assault with airborne troops (they came down by parachute and glider) upon that strategically important island and attempted to follow this up with ground troops transported from Greece in, mostly, those lightweight, shallow-drafted vessels, usable only in narrow seas, called caïques. The British managed to frustrate the latter portion of this design. In a night-and-day action northwest of Crete on May 21–22 two large German convoys were attacked, scattered, and forced back to the Greek mainland by Royal Navy units. A dozen caïques and three steamers were sunk and many thousand Germans drowned. But the cost to the British was considerable—a destroyer sunk, a battleship and four crusiers damaged, by air attack—and the sea action did not slow the German conquest of Crete. The paratroopers and glider forces suffered heavy casualties as they hurled themselves recklessly against the island's stubborn defenders; indeed, the German parachute division, which was the only one in Reichsmarshal Goering's air force (though the British did not then know this) and which, properly employed, might well have won lightly defended Syria and Iraq for the Germans in the weeks that followed, was crippled by its Cretan losses. The immediate objective of the Germans was, however, quickly achieved. On the seventh day of the attack (May 26), New Zealand General Bernard Freyberg, the British commander on Crete, had to inform Cairo and London that "the limit of endurance has been reached by the troops under my command" and that "our position here is hopeless."[47] All that remained possible for the British command was another humiliating evacuation— an extremely difficult casualty-prone operation that, again, had to be carried out at night because of German air domination. It began on May 28 and ended four days later, by which time 16,500 troops, including 2,000 Greeks, had been rescued. Some 7,000 of the Allied defensive force were dead or prisoners of the Germans on Crete.

In this dark Middle Eastern picture a single bright spot appeared as May gave way to June: British troops from Palestine, supplemented by troops sent from India, managed to defeat by a narrow margin an Axis-fomented revolt in Iraq. British troops occupied Baghdad on May 31. Immediately thereafter, in cooperation with de Gaulle's Free French, the British would frustrate, again narrowly, an Axis attempt to take over Syria. But this bright spot was too isolate and uncertain to give any high lift to the spirits of those leaders in Cairo, London, and Washington who anxiously studied the scene, viewing it in its global context. The Allied grasp upon North Africa and the Middle East remained far from firm; Hitler had strength enough to break it and seize the whole of this crucial strategic ground, and soon, should he choose to do so. There would then be opened to him a third option: He might use North Africa and the Middle East as a vast springboard from which to launch a powerful drive eastward, counting upon his naval and air forces to complete, meanwhile, the process of starving Britain into submission. His military forces would then constitute the western arm of a pincers more gigantic than the one that seemed now about to close upon the Middle East—a pincers that would close upon India and, as an isolated America was thus reduced to the status of a second-class power, assure Axis domination of the globe.

The other arm of this pincers was being forged in the Far East as Japan prepared, with Hitler's blessing, to extend its empire over Indonesia and Southeast Asia. Such preparation obviously included immediate hostile designs upon Singapore; these designs must certainly have been encouraged by Hitler in his talks with Japanese Foreign Minister Yosuke Matsuoka when the latter visited Berlin in April 1941; and a major obstacle to Japan's southward drive was removed or greatly reduced when, in Moscow on his way home from Berlin, Matsuoka signed on behalf of Japan a neutrality pact with the Soviet Union, having hurriedly requested and received specific permission from Tokyo to do so. In the pact, Japan and Russia promised to respect each other's territorial integrity and maintain peaceful relations with one another; they also promised that if either of them became "the object of hostilities on the part of one or several third powers," the other would "observe neutrality throughout the duration of the conflict" (Stalin hastened to inform Chinese leader Chiang Kai-shek that this meant no lessening of Soviet support of China's resistance to the invading Japanese).[48]

VIII

THE Roosevelt sentence apropos the *Bismarck* quoted above is the second of a two-sentence message sent Churchill by the President on the morning of Tuesday, May 27, 1941. The first said: "I hope you will like the speech as it goes further than I thought it was possible to go even two weeks ago and I would like to hope that it will receive general approval from the fairly large element which has been confused by details and allow them to see the simple facts."[49]

The speech referred to, and already mentioned, had been originally scheduled for delivery on Pan-American Day (May 14) but then postponed because, it was announced, the President was ill.* It was the first major policy address since the

*See pp. 154–55.

"Arsenal of Democracy" speech of last December 29, and its delivery had been awaited with mounting excitement and anxiety on the part of those who, in England, in America, and especially in Washington, were longing and begging for a clear, emphatic statement of policy, as regards the war, by the President of the United States. Typical of the felt urgency, if uniquely Stimson's in expression, was a letter that came to Roosevelt from the secretary of war on Saturday, May 24. "From what has come to me on all sides," wrote Stimson, "I feel certain that the people of the United States are looking to you to lead and guide them in a situation in which they are confused but anxious to follow you." The whole world, Stimson went on to say, was divided "into two camps separated by fundamental principles and methods." Roosevelt was "the leader of one camp." And the "momentous decision" to "oppose forcefully . . . the evil leaders of the other half of the world" should be made by the American people, "not because by some accident and mistake American ships are fired upon by soldiers of the other camp," but instead "by your leadership in explaining why any other course . . . would be forever hopeless and abhorrent to every honorable principle of American independence and democracy." Stimson enclosed with his letter the draft of an "imaginary resolution of Congress" that might follow upon such presidential leadership, a lawyerly document that, after four lengthy "whereas" clauses sharply defining the grave danger the country was in, concluded: "BE IT RESOLVED that the President is hereby authorized to use the naval, air, and military forces of the United States (1) to prevent . . . control of the sea by . . . aggressor nations or by any other nations acting in cooperation with them; (2) to secure the successful delivery of the supplies, munitions, and other assistance sent by the United States to the warring democracies of Europe pursuant to the Act of Congress [the Lend-Lease Act] above mentioned; (3) pursuant to the historic policy of the Monroe Doctrine, to take all steps necessary to keep away from the Western Hemisphere the power of such aggressor nations and thus to preserve the safety of the United States and its institutions."[50]

The initial drafting of this Roosevelt speech, by Sam Rosenman and Robert Sherwood, with remarkably little direct input by Roosevelt, was an anxiety-ridden enterprise whose first fruit was "calculated to scare the daylights out of everyone . . . but . . . did not do much else," as Assistant Secretary of State Adolf Berle said in his diary entry for May 26. He and Undersecretary of State Welles had reviewed the draft on behalf of Hull on Saturday, May 24, Berle suggesting then to Hopkins that the speech be given more point, more substance, by concluding it with the statement that a presidential proclamation of an "unlimited national emergency," enabling a marked increase of executive powers, was being issued—this to replace the "limited emergency" that had existed since Roosevelt proclaimed it on September 8, 1939. Hopkins soon thereafter told Sherwood and Rosenman that the President did wish, Hopkins believed, to conclude his speech in this way and that the two should insert an announcement of it into the draft conclusion. The two writers did so. The announcement was in the draft that Roosevelt, after dinner on Sunday evening, May 25, read aloud in the Oval Room in the presence of Rosenman, Sherwood, Berle, Welles, and Hopkins. Hopkins, however, happened not to be in the room (he had gone to his own room down the hall to take a dose of the medicine that helped keep him slenderly alive) when Roosevelt came to the crucial insertion. "What's *this*?" he exclaimed. He fixed upon Sherwood a seemingly stern gaze. Someone, he opined, had been "taking liberties." But he accepted Sherwood's stammered explanation without comment; the insertion remained in the penultimate draft. It remained also in the final draft, which was completed on Monday evening, Roosevelt making then his most extensive direct contribution to this enterprise. He redictated considerable portions of the speech, making no substantial changes but a good many changes of language, of phrasing, in the interests of ease of delivery, while further cluttering with non sequiturs a speech whose penultimate draft was already typically Rooseveltian in its disorderliness, its failure to develop a logically coherent argument.[51]

Little of the excitement with which this address was listened to by a huge international radio audience was evident in those who saw and heard its delivery in the East Room of the White House on the night of May 27.[52] The occasion was still ostensibly a celebration of Pan-American solidarity, postponed from two weeks earlier, so the immediate audience consisted mostly of Latin American ambassadors and ministers, with their families, many of whom had a very imperfect command of the English language. They were uncomfortably seated on straight-backed gilded ballroom chairs; the room, without air-conditioning, was so stiflingly hot that news photographers were asked not to turn on their lights while the speech was being given (Roosevelt would repeat key portions of it later for picture taking); and almost the only thing in the speech directly relating to Latin America was its opening statement that "now, as never before, the unity of the American Republics is of supreme importance to each and every one of us and to the cause of freedom throughout the world"—also a later assertion that the Nazis planned, upon their victory, "to treat the Latin American Nations as they are now treating the Balkans." No bursts of applause punctuated the speech's delivery, and at its conclusion, the applause was little more than polite.

Indeed, the speech was not of the kind that invites a hearty interruptive applause. While carefully avoiding any new explicit commitment, it defined America's present situation in terms of the most ominous significance, terms implying that decisive action of the gravest import immediately impended.

This war, he began, "has developed, as the Nazis had always intended it should develop, into a world war for world domination." He described the development, and the American responses to it (the shipment of war matériel to beleaguered Britain, the destroyers-for-bases deal, the Lend-Lease Act), in swift summary, stressing that our "whole program of aid for the democracies has been based" not on a soft-hearted (or generous) concern for a friend in des-

perate need, but "on a hard-headed [that is, selfish] concern for our own security. . . . Every dollar of material that we send helps keep the dictators away
from our own hemisphere, and every day that they are held off gives us time to
build more guns and tanks and planes and ships. We have made no pretense
about our self-interest in this aid. Great Britain understands it—and so does
Nazi Germany." It was now more obvious than ever before that America's national security, indeed the nation's very survival as a free society, depended absolutely upon the defeat in this war of the Axis powers. It was also obvious to
the leaders of the democracies that at the present moment the war was going
badly for them in the Atlantic. "The blunt truth is this—and I reveal this with
the full knowledge of the British Government: the present rate of sinkings of
merchant ships is more than three times as high as the capacity of British shipyards to replace them; it is more than twice the combined British and American
output of merchant ships today." If Hitler conquered England, capturing or destroying the British navy, he would have full control of the oceans of the world
or be so far along the way to achieving it that he could "dictate to the Western
Hemisphere." He would of course say to the Americas, as he said to France and
England after the seizure of Austria, after Munich, and after the seizure of
Czechoslovakia, that " '[t]his is the last territorial adjustment I will seek' " and
" '[a]ll we want is peace, friendship, and profitable trade relations with you in
the New World.' " But "[y]our Government knows what terms Hitler, if victorious, would impose. They are, indeed, the only terms on which he would accept
a so-called negotiated peace." Under them, "Germany would . . . parcel out the
world—hoisting the swastika itself over vast territories and populations, and
setting up puppet governments of its own choosing, wholly subject to the will
and policy of the conqueror." The Nazis would then, according to plan, "stran-
gle the United States of America and the Dominion of Canada." American labor
"would have to compete with slave labor in the rest of the world. . . . Wages and
hours would be fixed by Hitler. . . . The American farmer would get for his
products exactly what Hitler wanted to give. . . . The whole fabric of working
life . . . would be mangled and crippled. . . . Yet to maintain even that crippled
condition would require permanent conscription of our manpower; it would curtail the funds we could spend on education, on housing, on public works, on
flood control, on health and, instead, we would be permanently pouring out our
resources into armaments. . . . Yes, even our right of worship would be threatened. The Nazi world does not recognize any God except Hitler. . . . Will our
children, too, wander off goose-stepping in search of new gods?"

But having thus forcefully indicated that the United States must do *whatever*
was necessary to ensure Britain's survival and Nazi-fascism's defeat, he carefully avoided the logically implied conclusion. Instead: "I have said on many
occasions that the United States is mustering its men and its resources only for
the purposes of defense—only to repel attack. I repeat that statement now."
Technological advances had blurred the distinction between offensive and de-

fensive warfare, however—or so he indicated rather than plainly said. The "word *attack*" must be now defined in terms of "the lightning speed of modern warfare. . . . When your enemy comes at you in a tank or bombing plane, if you hold your fire until you see the whites of his eyes, you will never know what hit you. Our Bunker Hill of tomorrow may be several thousand miles from Boston." Hence the extension of "our patrol" far out into "North and South Atlantic waters," a patrol to which "we are steadily adding more and more ships and planes. It is well known that the strength of the Atlantic Fleet has been greatly increased during the past year, and that it is constantly being built up." Its purpose, he stressed, was wholly defensive. The "ships and planes warn of the presence of attacking raiders, on the sea, under the sea, and above the sea. We are thus [put on] . . . our guard against efforts to establish Nazi bases closer to our hemisphere." All the same, he hinted, defense in this case might require action that was hard to distinguish from attack. "It does not make sense . . . to say, 'I believe in the defense of all the Western Hemisphere,' and in the next breath say, 'I will not fight for that defense until the enemy has landed on our shores.' If we believe in the independence and integrity of the Americas, we must be willing . . . to fight to defend them. . . . And that danger has recently been heavily underlined by the presence in Western Hemisphere waters of a Nazi battleship of great striking power." These words, if they had meaning, surely meant that we must fight at sea far off our shores, if not in foreign lands, for self-preservation—that we must, in self-defense, attack our attackers before they mounted a full-scale attack on us—whereupon he changed the subject, turning his attention to "the very great social progress" that had been made in "recent years" and to his determination "to maintain that progress and strengthen it," also to prevent disruptive strife between capital and labor. "The future of all free enterprise—capital and labor alike—is at stake. This is no time for capital to make, or be allowed to retain, excessive profits. A nation-wide machinery for conciliation and mediation of industrial disputes has been set up. That machinery must be used promptly—and without stoppage of work." There followed a long series of non sequiturs whose utter disconnectedness was hidden from his listeners by the intimately singing tone, the passionate emphatic earnestness, with which they were spoken.

He closed:

"As President of a united and determined people, I say solemnly:

"We reassert the ancient American doctrine of freedom of the seas.

"We reassert the solidarity of the twenty-one American Republics and the Dominion of Canada. . . .

"We have pledged material support to the other democracies of the world—and we will fulfill that pledge.

"We in the Americas will decide for ourselves whether, and when, and where our American interests are attacked. . . .

"We are placing our armed forces in strategic military position.

"We will not hesitate to use our armed forces to repel attack.

"We reassert our abiding faith in the vitality of our Constitutional Republic as a perpetual home of freedom, of tolerance, and of devotion to the word of God.

"Therefore, with profound consciousness of my responsibilities to my countrymen and to my country's cause, I have tonight issued a proclamation that an unlimited national emergency exists and requires the strengthening of our defense to the extreme limit of our national power and authority.

"The nation will expect all individuals and all groups to play their full parts, without stint, without selfishness, and without doubt that our democracy will triumphantly survive."[53]

This prolonged peroration, save for the sentence announcing the emergency proclamation, said actually explicitly nothing; but the manner of its delivery, conjoined with the eager longing of its hearers for leadership, made it sound to most of its radio audience as a ringing call to arms (many heard in it faint echoes of Woodrow Wilson's eloquence when, on April 2, 1917, he asked Congress for a declaration of war upon Germany). Scarcely had its last word been spoken than a flood of telegrams began pouring into the White House mailroom. A huge bundle of them awaited Roosevelt in his bedroom when he, after socializing with a small party of family and friends in the Monroe Room,* went upstairs to bed shortly before midnight.

"They're ninety-five percent favorable!" he said to Sherwood of the telegrams that littered his bed when Sherwood came in to bid him good night. "And I figured I'd be lucky to get an even break on this speech."[55] His great relief was evident, also surprising in view of the fact that the earliest expressed responses to a White House speech were almost always overwhelmingly favorable, and that he had been at great pains in this address, more so than in some others, to stay precisely in step with what he perceived to be the main body of public opinion as it marched to history's drumbeat. Evidently, during his rehearsals of his speech, he had felt that he marched in the very front rank of this main body, uncomfortably close to such advanced skirmishers as Stimson, and thus exposed himself to frontal fire from isolationist opponents.

As approving as the telegrams were the newspaper comments sampled by Roosevelt while breakfasting in bed next morning. The lead editorial in *The New York Times* began, "President Roosevelt struck a mighty blow last night for freedom," and went on to say that "the course" to which the President had "pledged the country, and the action taken, will have the endorsement of the vast majority of our people." Similarly enthusiastic were the *New York Herald-*

---

*One of the friends was Sherwood, who brought with him his guest for the evening, Irving Berlin. Roosevelt was, to quote Sherwood, "delighted to see" the songwriter, whom he "begged . . . to go to the piano and play and sing 'Alexander's Ragtime Band' and many other songs."[54]

Tribune, the *World-Telegram, The Washington Post,* and, as Steve Early would report to him later that day, a score of other papers scattered from coast to coast, including such normally fervent critics of Roosevelt as the *Kansas City Star.* Nearly all of them agreed with *The New York Times* that the President had "seized a great moment to speak to his countrymen with candor and courage." From Winston Churchill came that evening (it was received at six-thirty) a "personal and secret" message to the President that began: "We are uplifted and fortified by your memorable declaration and by the far-reaching executive measures involved in the state of emergency you have proclaimed. Pray accept, Mr. President, my heartfelt thanks. It was very kind of you to let me know in advance of the great advance you have found it possible to make."[56]

But by that time, Roosevelt, in inexplicable reversal (it was as if he were terrified to find himself actually leading those whom it was his office to lead), had taken back all or most of the climactic gist of what he had just publicly said.

Steve Early had told him that the Washington press corps would be clamoring for presidential elucidation of various points he had raised; they expected the special press conference set up for Wednesday morning to be one of the most newsworthy he had ever held. It was, instead, the most disappointing, not only to the newsmen who attended it (some two hundred were jammed into the executive office), but to the millions who had been uplifted by his words of the night before and now anticipated a surge of executive action. The proclamation of an "unlimited national emergency" didn't really mean much, after all, said the President and commander in chief in effect. The proclamation could be made effective only through "a series of executive orders carrying into force a long list of emergency laws passed in the last forty years," and he, Roosevelt, "had no plans for issuing any of these orders at the present time." Neither did he have any plans for new legislation regarding foreign affairs. He stood "unequivocally" by the statement he had made regarding freedom of the seas "but had no immediate intention of seeking repeal or substantial revision of the Neutrality Act through which the government has purposely foregone the exercise of that doctrine [freedom of the seas] to date in an effort to keep out of the European war," to quote Turner Catledge's story in *The New York Times.* He "scouted the idea that this government had any notion of convoying these goods under the protection of the navy."[57]

Henry Stimson and his fellow interventionists were both astonished and dismayed. Everyone who had been inspired toward noble risk and action by last night's words felt terribly let down. Even Harry Hopkins, who thought he knew Roosevelt's mind, and sometimes made up that mind by acting in accordance with his understanding of it, was utterly nonplussed.

Subsequent efforts to explain conclusively how and why Roosevelt, overnight as it seemed, so completely changed his mind were both strenuous and futile. Sherwood, five years later, having remarked that Roosevelt in the late spring of 1941 stood "almost alone [within the administration] in his reluctance to take decision and action," thought he saw the reason for it in "the isolationists' long and savage campaign against the President," a campaign that had "failed to blind American public opinion" but had certainly "exerted an important effect on Roosevelt himself: *whatever the peril* [present author's italics], he was not going to lead the country into war. . . ."[58] But the fact was that Roosevelt's every clear advance toward intervention thus far had been followed by a proportionate retreat of expressed isolationist sentiment in the American body politic as a whole; his every retreat from the logical conclusion of his stated foreign policy argument had been followed by a proportionate strengthening of isolationist sentiment in the body politic as a whole; and surely so astute a politician as he was fully aware of this fact. It would seem that he himself, even at this late date, must have remained undecided, his mind confused. And debilitating ill health, to the extent that it had ever been responsible for his evident indecision, may still have been playing its part. For though he rose from his mid-May sickbed fully recovered from the "flu bug" that had plagued him for so long, there was not yet returned to him the zest, the joie de vivre, the immense energy and seemingly inexhaustible patience that were normally his. He remained seriously anemic, because of the bleeding hemorrhoids already mentioned, and in early June suffered a temporary flare-up viral infection, developing a severe sore throat with accompanying fever. Churchill referred to this at the conclusion of a message to him on June 14: "Kindest regards and every wish that your indisposition may soon pass."[59]

The main substance of this last Churchill message had to do with the single important decision taken by the President at this time that was consistent with the explicit meaning and conveyed general impression of the May 27 speech. He took it at the insistence of Admiral Harold ("Betty") Stark, chief of U.S. naval operations. For weeks Stark and others had been arguing the case for a U.S. military presence on Iceland, since Iceland flanked the main British lifeline across the Atlantic and its occupation by an enemy would directly threaten the American mainland. Iceland was an independent republic, the proud possessor of the oldest continuously functioning elective legislative body in the Western world, but it was tied to Denmark with bonds of blood, tradition, and legal unity; there was consequently a possibility that Hitler, having occupied Denmark, might attempt forcibly to claim Iceland as his own. Hence the stationing of British forces on the strategic island, with the islanders' willing consent, immediately following Denmark's fall—troops that were desperately needed elsewhere. Hopkins and Sumner Welles had opened highly secret negotiations with Iceland's consular general in Washington in mid-April; the negotiations had resulted a few weeks later in an equally highly secret invitation of U.S. troops from Iceland's Prime Minister; and in the second week of June, Stark, with Knox's concurrence, wrote out an order to Admiral Ernest J. King, commander of the U.S. Atlantic Fleet, to land four thousand U.S. Marines in Iceland as the spearhead of an American force that would "eventually . . . replace the British forces. . . ." Initially, however, twenty thousand British troops were to remain on the island, and with these the marine general in charge of the U.S. operation was told to "coordinate" his operations through "mutual cooperation."

But before dispatching the order to King, Stark, acutely aware of "the potential dynamite in this order," sent it by special messenger to Hopkins in the White House with a cover note saying that though he knew the President had been kept fully informed of what had been done thus far, and had approved it (Hopkins had operated as the President's arm), he also knew that what was being ordered was "practically an act of war" and should therefore be specifically approved by the President. Roosevelt promptly did so, with an "Okay, F.D.R." scrawled upon the document. Said Churchill in his June 14 message: "I am much encouraged by . . . your marines taking over that cold place, and I hope that once the first instalment have arrived you will give full publicity to it. It would give us hope. . . . It would also produce the best effects in Spain, Vichy France and Turkey." The act was at once fully publicized. It provoked a storm of isolationist outrage but, from Berlin, no declaration of war, and it was calmly and approvingly accepted by the great majority of Americans as something necessary and to be expected, in view of what the President had said in his speech. Equally calmly accepted were Roosevelt's executive order of June 14 freezing all German and Italian assets in this country, including those of countries Hitler had occupied, and his order of June 16 closing all German consulates and agencies. The "reaction here is, I should say, 90% favorable," Roosevelt told Churchill on June 17.[60]

But he reverted to supercautiousness in his response to a direct challenge to his "freedom of the seas" policy made in late May and learned of in Washington in mid-June.

On May 21, far out in the Atlantic but very near the Equator, an American merchant ship, the *Robin Moor*, en route to South Africa, encountered a surfaced German submarine. Though the ship's flag and markings clearly identified it as American, and though international law required a belligerent to provide a maximum possibility of safety for the passengers and crew of any ship it sank, the submarine commander gave those aboard the *Robin Moor* a scant thirty minutes in which to take to lifeboats before he sent it to the bottom. The survivors, soon widely scattered across the ocean, spent from two to three weeks in their open boats under a broiling equatorial sun before passing ships chanced upon them. The story of their ordeal, flashed northward in driblets from the South American ports where they were landed, provoked a surge toward interventionism in the American public mind. Hopkins felt that the incident was the kind his chief had been waiting for, hoping for, to justify a further long step toward U.S. belligerency. He promptly addressed a memorandum to Roosevelt saying that since the merchantman's sinking clearly "violated international law" as well as "your policy of freedom of the seas," the present "observation patrol of the Navy" might well "be changed to a security patrol" authorized to provide "security for all American flag ships" sailing on seas outside the American-designated combat zones. "It occurred to me that your instructions . . . could be that the . . . patrol forces . . . are . . . to . . . establish freedom of the seas, leaving it to the judgment of the Navy as to what measures . . . are required to achieve that objective," he concluded.[61] Roosevelt, however, issued no new directive to the navy. He confined himself to a special message to Congress (June 20, 1941) in which he denounced the sinking as "the act of an international outlaw." The U.S. government could "only assume that the Government of the German Reich hopes through the commission of such infamous acts of cruelty . . . to intimidate the United States" and "drive American commerce from the ocean wherever such commerce is considered a disadvantage to German designs," he said. ". . . Were we to yield on this we would inevitably submit to world domination at the hands of the present leaders of the German Reich. We are not yielding and do not propose to yield."[62]

He also continued supercautious in his dealings with London and Lisbon about the Azores, the strategic North Atlantic islands owned by Portugal that "would in enemy hands have proved as great a menace to our shipping movements in the south as Iceland [would have] in the north," to quote Churchill. In April he had refused Churchill's request for a "friendly visit" by an American warship to the islands unless a specific request for it came from the head of the Portuguese government, Premier Salazar. He had since refused to commit the United States to any Azores action not requested by Lisbon. Yet in his May 27 speech he spoke of the Azores as "island outposts of the New World" whose occupation or control by the Germans "would directly endanger the freedom of the Atlantic and our own physical safety. . . . We insist upon the vital importance of keeping Hitlerism away from any point in the world which could and would be used as a base of attack against the Americas." The statement was immediately strongly protested by the Lisbon government, which feared it might provoke Hitler into preventive action against what he perceived as an imminent American occupation of the Azores. Portugal had maintained a policy of strict rigid neutrality in this war, said a Portuguese note to Washington on May 30, 1941. Its "territories have not . . . presented any harm, hindrance, or menace to any of the belligerents or their allies." And Portugal "therefore" found it impossible "to understand the [President's] specific reference by name" to the Azores, a reference "which by itself could not fail to surprise the Portuguese people and Government." To this the State Department responded with typical State Department gobbledygook: "The strategic importance of these islands . . . was stressed by the President solely in terms of their potential value from the point of view of attack against this hemisphere." This naturally failed to satisfy Lisbon, nor did subsequent "clarifying" State Department messages (it seems to have been outside the capacity of the State Department of those days to say anything on any subject with absolute clarity), but the Lisbon reaction determined Roosevelt to let London carry the responsibility for whatever was done in the Azores.[63]

IX

PERHAPS something of the root of Roosevelt's vacillations in this late spring of 1941 can be seen in a conversation he had had with his wife a year before, on an evening in early June 1940. During after-dinner talk, Eleanor then told her husband of a conversation she had had that day with their son James (or Jimmy, as his father always called him), erstwhile presidential secretary, erstwhile executive in Samuel Goldwyn Productions in Hollywood, currently president of his own film company (Globe Productions). Hitler's blitzkrieg in the West was then at its height. Holland and Belgium were German conquests. The whole of the British Expeditionary Force was backed into a narrowing pocket at Dunkirk, whence its perilous evacuation, the success of which was then doubtful, was under way. Hitler readied his forces for the drive toward Paris, the fall of which was expected (and would occur) within two weeks. And Jimmy "supposed" that, in the lurid light of all this, he'd best be getting his Hollywood business affairs in order preparatory to going soon into uniform, for he was an officer in the marine reserve (he in fact went into active service in November 1940). His pacifistic mother gloomily agreed that early U.S. entry into the war seemed likely. James said he would do his duty, of course, but with no real belief that it would prove in the end worth doing; he saw no reason to believe that America's entry into this war would be any more productive of permanent good than its entry into the last world war had been—no reason to believe that the brutal cycle of war, an interval of uneasy peace, then war again, would not continue to the end of civilization.

And what James felt on this matter was what millions of America's youth were feeling, said Eleanor that evening to her husband. Could he, the President, give her any convincing reason why they should feel otherwise? Did he himself know of a single "practical plan" for ensuring "permanent peace"? Her husband made a lame reply. "Perhaps next time we shall have the sense to say there will be no more armaments," he said.[64]

The conversation ended with no sign from Roosevelt that his wife's impassioned words had greatly disturbed him. But next day he confessed to her, who felt guilty about it, that some of the things she had said had kept him awake in his bed, tossing and turning, well into the wee hours of that morning—he whose ability to drop off instantly into eight hours of restorative sleep amid the most nerve-straining circumstances had repeatedly amazed his associates. Eleanor continued to operate for him as image and voice of his own sense of justice and morality, troubling his mind, his conscience, to the extent that what she said and exemplified suggested a failure on his part to do what he felt, deep down, he should have done and should now be doing but couldn't do, he also felt, without incurring fatal losses of time and governing capability. Thus did she continue to exercise the power given into her hands by his guilt feeling over his betrayal of her and of all his basic principles of conduct in the Lucy Mercer affair—a power of which she could not but have been aware, though her exercise of it may have been, for the most part, unconscious. She was, for him, in this instance, an image and voice that contributed to his profound reluctance to assume the responsibility for war making forced upon him by his office and circumstances; for it was indeed true, as Eleanor surmised, that he had neither shaped nor received from On High, as he felt he ought to have done, any clear, definite ideas regarding the peace that should follow this war.

And through all this black spring of 1941 Eleanor had continued to be the relentlessly nagging image and voice of his sense of right and wrong. Her greatest anxiety in that season was that her husband, under the immense pressure that the mounting war crisis enabled conservative businessmen to focus upon him, was yielding to them piece by piece the social and economic ground that the New Deal had been enabled by the Great Depression to conquer. (There was bitterness for her in the fact that the market operations and governmental policies of these same conservative businessmen had brought on the Great Depression out of which, or out of the mass misery it had bred, Nazi-fascism's power and war itself had come.) Far from pointing the need for a retreat on the social front, the war emergency pointed the urgent need for further advances, she argued. For instance, there was the deplorably high number of draft inductees who were failing to pass army and navy physical examinations. Clearly the nation's current health care delivery system was at fault; there was urgent need for drastic improvements in it to make sure of adequate manpower in the years just ahead, if not an immediate need for the kind of national health insurance that other industrialized nations (Germany, for one) had long provided.

At the very least, "the groundwork should be laid [now] for a wide health program *after* the war," she said to Harry Hopkins, who back in 1934 had fervently supported national health insurance and been convinced it would pass as part of the Social Security legislation then being prepared, if only Roosevelt pressed for it.* But the Harry Hopkins of 1941 had priorities different from those of the Hopkins of 1934, and unlike Eleanor's, his priorities were rigidly mutually ex-

---

*Instead, Roosevelt had heeded the business types who dominated the American Medical Association and were, of course, opposed to any legislation that might curtail their private profit or freedom of the market. They would not have doctors become purely professional people; they preferred to have them remain part professional, part business, in their working lives and saw no contradiction between the two. See *FDR: The New Deal Years, 1933–1937*, pp. 452–53.

clusive. In this black spring he "could not be bothered" with national health problems, as Eleanor later, with some resentment, recorded; in common with the conservatives with whom he now chiefly worked, he felt "that money could not be diverted to anything which did not have a direct bearing on the fighting of the war."[65]

Eleanor was even more immediately concerned over the threat to the National Youth Administration (NYA) and the Farm Security Administration (FSA) that was posed by the efforts of business conservatives to eliminate all governmental agencies not "essential" to national defense. (Their definition of "essential" was indicated by the move of some of them that spring toward abolition of the school lunch and food stamp programs; these they deemed "non-essential," though millions yet remained unemployed and destitute.) NYA was the creature of a June 1935 executive order placing it in, and as an integral part of, the then newly established Works Progress Administration. Under the leadership of Aubrey Williams, a Southern liberal dedicated to racial equality, the agency had enabled millions of young Americans to receive an education they could not otherwise have received—this through grants given in return for work on WPA-NYA projects. It had provided other millions with vocational training that enabled them to obtain jobs in industry as, slowly, gradually, with a major interruption of the process in 1937, such jobs opened up. Since 1939, the agency had concentrated more and more on training young people for defense industry work. Its success in this endeavor was being enthusiastically attested to by thousands of businessmen (generally by small-business men who had managed to obtain defense contracts) across the land. Yet the attack by conservatives upon the agency, because of its liberal leadership and because its example encouraged liberal views, was increasing, and Eleanor was sure that only firm and even aggressive support of it by the President could ultimately save it. On that ground, her husband assured her, NYA was safe; he deemed it an essential defense agency. (In mid-May he asked Congress for a supplemental appropriation of $22,500,000 to the NYA for fiscal 1941.)[66]

No such assurance could he truthfully give her regarding the FSA. This agency was, in essential substance, the Resettlement Administration that Roosevelt had established by executive order, in May 1935, under the vast enabling authority granted him by 1935's Emergency Relief Appropriations Act. It had been integrated into the Department of Agriculture as the FSA in 1937. Under its first head, Rexford Tugwell, and his successors, Will W. Alexander and C. B. "Beanie" Baldwin, it had engaged in many frankly experimental projects—projects for retiring from production marginal and submarginal land; resettling rural and urban destitutes on land fertile enough to provide subsistence to them; establishing or continuing subsistence homestead communities for people currently living in miserable rural slums (one such, which Tugwell regretted having to handle, was Arthurdale, Eleanor's "baby" in West Virginia);

providing housing, subsistence, and medical care for unemployed migratory workers; developing so-called greenbelt communities that mingled urban and country living; and establishing an information branch staffed with remarkably able writers and photographers who invented the documentary as an art form and whose productions remain the most vivid and authentic record of what life was like for millions of Americans during the Great Depression. From the first, the agency's main focus had been upon the rural poor, the rural dispossessed— tenant farmers, sharecroppers, migrant agricultural workers. From the first, it had paid special attention to the improvement of race relations in the South. And from the first, it itself had been the focus of virulent opposition from Southern whites, from the well-off farmers and agribusinessmen of the Farm Bureau, from personnel of the land-grant colleges and USDA extension service whose career interests were intertwined with those of the Farm Bureau, and from conservatives in general. This opposition was growing, was increasingly effective, and, as the war crisis mounted, was increasingly hard to defend against; the prospect before the agency by the late spring of 1941 was poor indeed. Roosevelt, however, in his conversations with his wife, refused to admit it. As late as January 12, 1942, after his budget request had trimmed 27 percent off FSA's financing of the year before, he would tell Eleanor that "neither farm security nor NYA was being curtailed" (the quote is from a letter she wrote to Aubrey Williams that night).[67]

Yet on this all-important home front, Eleanor won that spring one victory that initially appeared to be complete.

Among her longtime English friends was Lady Stella Reading, whose husband had been British ambassador to the United States during the Great War (Eleanor had first met her then) and who in this Second World War had become the administrator of Britain's Women's Voluntary Services for Civil Defence. Lady Reading's definition of "civil defense" included the protection and advancement of social justice as well as the enlistment of British women in useful war work, and the organization she headed was therefore, in Eleanor's view, a model that the U.S. government might follow if it would make social justice, as it certainly should, an integral part of America's overall defense program. Soon after the 1940 election, acting on his wife's suggestion, Roosevelt asked Mrs. Florence Kerr, who headed WPA's Community Service Projects, to develop a plan for mobilizing American "womanpower" for national defense, a task in which a number of prominent women, including both Eleanor and Secretary of Labor Perkins, became involved. These women quickly decided that the "home defense" organization they contemplated ought *not* to be a "women's movement," though in the circumstances women were bound to play key roles in it. It should be something much broader, namely, "a social defense organization." And the plan they finally came up with, in mid-January 1941, was certainly very broad. Harold Ickes, whose bitterly unhappy first marriage and gloriously happy second one had both confirmed him in the conviction that a woman's proper place was in the home, described Mrs. Kerr's final product as "one of the most elaborate and finical plans of organization that I have ever seen . . . cockeyed . . . an overall Federal organization to be financed by the Federal Government which would cut through and totally ignore state and local defense groups." Silver-haired though yet youthful Paul McNutt, the conservative Indiana Democrat whom Roosevelt had made head of the Federal Security Agency, also damned the Kerr proposal. Under typically duplicative presidential orders, he himself had for weeks been struggling with a civil defense organization plan, one that integrated with the state and local programs already in place; to "go ahead" with this "scheme" of Mrs. Kerr's would cause vast "confusion, and extra expense," he said.[68]

As for Roosevelt, he took no action on the matter for months, partly because ill health severely limited his activity at this time, but also because this "home defense thing," as he told his March 4 press conference, was "one of the most difficult things to put together . . . that I have had yet. . . . It's sort of a general endeavor on the part of men, women, and children in every State of the Union, and it is very hard to set up the right kind of administrative machinery that at the same time will allow it to be decentralized and run primarily by the various communities themselves."[69] But in the end, prodded by his wife, who was of course well aware of his penchant for omnibus "weaving together" measures, he accepted virtually in toto the women's plan. On May 20, 1941, he established in the President's Office of Emergency Management (OEM) an Office of Civilian Defense (OCD) "to assure effective coordination of Federal relations with State and local governments engaged in defense activities," to help effect "adequate protection of the civilian population in emergency periods," and "to facilitate constructive civilian participation in the defense program, and to sustain national morale."[70] New York City Mayor Fiorello La Guardia, a volatile, voluble, colorful, temperamental Italian American, was named the new agency's first director, and after his top subordinate Florence Kerr had found it impossible to interest him in the volunteer participation program she nominally headed, Eleanor Roosevelt reluctantly accepted appointment (September 1941) as the OCD's deputy director.

During the years of its operation, the office accomplished much that would have been invaluable to the nation's defense had the United States been directly attacked by hostile aircraft or invading ground troops. It created a civilian air raid warning system, enlisted civilian airplane pilots in a Civil Air Patrol, organized civilian volunteers to provide services to draft boards and draftees, organized civilians in defense against industrial sabotage, established a volunteer messenger service, established a Forest Fire Fighters Service as an auxiliary to the regular firefighting apparatus of the U.S. Forest Service, and so on. But it was destined never to become the kind of "social defense organization" that

Eleanor Roosevelt and Florence Kerr had originally envisaged. La Guardia's lack of interest in this aspect of the program and the actual hostility to it by many of the key men in national defense proved ultimately fatal to it.

X

ONE important reason for Eleanor's commitment to the National Youth Administration and the Farm Security Administration was that both, in their operations, were totally color-blind. Black tenant farmers equally with white were aided by FSA programs; in proportion to their numbers, black youth benefited equally with white in the job training programs of the NYA, which had a specific Negro program headed by Mary McLeod Bethune. This was emphatically not true of other government civilian agencies. With the notable exception of the Department of the Interior, which Ickes had desegregated completely, the departments and their bureaus were segregated and in other ways practiced racial discrimination as a matter of policy. The armed services did so flagrantly, with self-justifying assertions of the Negro's natural and hence ineradicable inferiority to whites as warriors on land, on sea, or in the air (especially on the sea and in the air): blacks might sometimes fight well as infantrymen, it was conceded, but only under white officers; they were best fitted for menial jobs. Equally denigrating of blacks were the defense industries, the business world generally, and, most disappointingly, organized labor, especially the old-line craft unions of the AFL.* This last fact was reflected in Sidney Hillman's otherwise somewhat surprising refusal to press, as co-director of OPM, for specific anti-discriminatory clauses in government defense contracts. He was urged to do so by black Robert Weaver, whom he had named chief of a Negro Employment and Training Branch but who had little influence within OPM. He was urged to do so by Will Alexander, who, because Hillman shied away from this (also for other reasons), concluded that Hillman was too "timid" and lacking in "confidence in himself in the field of politics" to be a truly effective leader.[71]

We have mentioned black Mary McLeod Bethune as one of the key officials of the NYA; she helped make policy as head of NYA's program for blacks and as a member of the agency's advisory committee. Educator, civil rights leader, political activist, founder (in 1935) of the National Council on Negro Women, a

---

*Said a retrospective article in *American Labor* magazine in the August 1968 issue: "When Negroes of Seattle [in 1942] . . . demanded the elimination of the union color bar at the Boeing Aircraft plant, the district organizer of the International Association of Machinists declared: 'Labor has been asked to make many sacrifices in this war and has made them gladly, but this sacrifice . . . is too great.' " The same article has the president of North American Aviation declaring at a press conference that "regardless of training, we will not employ Negroes in the North American plant. It is against company policy." The Kansas City Urban League was told by Standard Steel Corporation: "We have not had a Negro worker in twenty-five years and do not plan to start now."

woman of sound common sense, strong character, and immense personal force, Mrs. Bethune was greatly respected by the national Negro community and had become one of Eleanor Roosevelt's close personal friends. A frequent visitor in the White House, where a half dozen or more times a year she conferred with the President himself on various matters, she had come to Eleanor in mid-July 1940 with a bundle of official documents showing in detail the gross discrimination against Negroes in the armed forces—these along with a cover memo citing "grave apprehension among Negroes lest the existing inadequate representation and training of colored persons in the armed forces may lead to the creation of labor battalions and other forms of discrimination against them in the event of war." To counter the effect this would have upon the Negro vote in that presidential election year, a vote that just might be decisive in view of the expected closeness of the race between Willkie and Roosevelt, Mrs. Bethune strongly recommended the appointment of a prominent Negro to serve as civilian aide to the then newly installed Secretary of War Stimson, the aide's specific assignment to be that of protecting and advancing fair treatment of blacks by the armed services.[72] She mentioned Judge William Hastie for this post. She also urged the immediate promotion of Colonel Benjamin O. Davis, the highest-ranking Negro officer in the army, to the rank of brigadier general, he having been long on the promotion list but repeatedly passed over because of his color. Both these recommendations were soon carried out, provoking cries of outrage from white supremacists across the land but soothing somewhat the outrage felt by blacks across the land.

Much, much more needed to be done, however, in the opinion of black leaders.

Of these, one of the most effective was A. Philip Randolph, head of the Brotherhood of Sleeping Car Porters, whose character and personality are here worth a glance from us since he was about to effect a definite and historically significant elevation of his race's status in the American marketplace. He was a tall man (well over six feet) and, standing or sitting, always held himself rigidly erect. His manners and speech were so formal that some, on first acquaintance with him, felt he was putting on airs and were tempted to dismiss him as a phony. He used such words as "verily," "vouchsafe," and "behoove" in ordinary conversation, speaking with an accent that, once his integrity and sincerity were recognized, as they always soon were, made plausible the suspicion, which ultimately became a widespread belief, that he had been educated at Harvard. Actually, though none who dealt with him could doubt his high intelligence, his only formal education beyond high school had been in evening classes at the City College of New York; he held no academic degree. His voice was deep and musical, "almost like an organ," and in public speech he employed language "biblical in its eloquence," seeming never to direct his words "to his immediate audience, but [instead] somewhere out beyond, perhaps to the whole human race," as an obviously impressed *New York Times* reporter once wrote.[73] His dignity, imperturbable, bespoke immense self-control and was of itself alone rather intimidating, yet his sincerity and loving concern shone through it and caused him to be beloved of those he led. What he asked of his followers he almost invariably obtained.

In mid-September 1940 what he asked for and obtained from the annual convention of the brotherhood, held in the Harlem YMCA, was a resolution calling upon the President, Congress, and governmental departments "to see to it that no discrimination is practiced against American citizens entering all departments of the Army, Navy, and Air Corps on account of race or color." An honored guest of the convention was Eleanor Roosevelt, who, addressing it, promised her full cooperation in any effort "to make this a better country, not for you alone but for all of us." Returned to Washington, she persuaded the President, who worried increasingly about the upcoming election, to meet in the Oval Office, on the morning of September 27, with Randolph; Walter White, head of the National Association for the Advancement of Colored People (NAACP); T. Arnold Hill of the National Urban League; Secretary Knox; and Undersecretary Patterson. The meeting was, in her words, "to discuss the rights of Negroes—their rights to volunteer, their rights under the Conscription Act, their general rights to participate in the whole structure of national defense, but particularly the Army and Navy." To the meeting, White, Hill, and Randolph brought a memo calling for an immediate end to segregation in the armed services and in defense industries.[74] As usual, the President presided with force and charm. As usual for such meetings, there was no decision on the central issue; the memo remained unanswered. But Patterson promised a new War Department policy statement drafted in the light of this discussion, and the meeting ended, as meetings with Roosevelt commonly did, in a glow of goodwill.

From it came, however, no improvement of relations between the black community and the President's office. Instead, harm came. This was due in good part to the ingrained racial prejudices of Stimson, Patterson, and Steve Early, and to the failure to guard against these by a President whose own commitment to civil liberties was far from absolute. Patterson's conception of the Negro's character and ability was consistent with his conviction that racial integration in defense industries would fatally disrupt defense production. Stimson often claimed that his abolitionist parents ("my father fought in the Civil War") had instilled in him a commitment to "justice for the Negro," but he was convinced "of the incompetency of colored troops except under white officers" and that "what these foolish leaders of the colored race are seeking is at bottom social equality," which would lead toward "the basic impossibility of race mixture by marriage" (he inveighed in his diary against "Mrs. Roosevelt's impulsive and intrusive folly").[75] As for Steve Early, had he been a contemporary of Chief Justice Taney, he would have agreed with the latter's opinion, in the Dred Scott case, that under the Constitution a Negro had no rights a white man was bound to respect. On October 9 Early summoned White House press correspondents to his office. He reminded them that nearly two weeks before, the President had met "with Walter White and, I think, two other Negro leaders." He said that "as a result of that conference the war department has drafted a statement of policy with regard to Negroes in national defense." He read the statement aloud and passed out copies of it to reporters. The key phrase in it said that "the policy . . . is not to intermingle colored and white enlisted personnel in the same regimental organizations." The clear implication was that White, Hill, and Randolph had concurred in this ("the segregation policy was approved after Roosevelt had conferred with White and two other Negroes," said press reports), and it exposed the three to angry charges of betrayal, of "sellout," of "Uncle Tomism," by those they led.

The three at once demanded from Early a "clarifying" statement specifically denying the implication. Early refused to issue one; he confined himself to an "emphatic" assertion, in a letter to White, "that there was no disposition or intention on my part . . . to cause you or your colleagues any embarrassment whatsoever." But Roosevelt responded to the uproar, a little more than a week before election day, with a letter to the three Negro leaders, which he permitted to be published, expressing his regret over the "misinterpretation" of the War Department policy statement and the "misunderstanding" of the "position" of the three Negro leaders. "The plan . . . on which we are all agreed," he said, "is that Negroes will be put into all branches of the service, combatant as well as supply." He said nothing, however, about segregation and the exclusion of Negroes from defense industry employment, which were the key points at issue, and the three Negro leaders, Randolph especially, remained unsatisfied. Proud Early's guilty realization that he had badly mishandled White House public relations in this matter no doubt increased his resentment of Negro pressure upon him and may have contributed to his loss of self-control on the night of October 28, 1940, when he kneed in the groin a black policeman in New York City's Pennsylvania Station. *76

All this failed to reduce measurably black support of Roosevelt on election day. White and Randolph were at some pains to ensure that it did not, pointing out to their followers that Negroes had made greater solid social and economic gains under the Roosevelt administration, and had received more sympathetic treatment from the White House, than they had under any earlier administration—pointing out, too, that the alternative to Roosevelt's reelection, in the present world situation, and in the present state of the Republican Party, would be horrendous for Negroes. But Randolph remained unhappy over what had happened. He brooded over it while riding a train into the South a few

*See p. 40.

weeks after the election and came to a conclusion. Obviously, appeals to the President and conferences in the White House were not going to achieve justice for the Negro. A helpless dependence upon the goodwill of white people, even upon such as Eleanor Roosevelt, was futile beyond a point that had now been passed. Blacks must take their destiny into their own hands. And when he arrived at Savannah, Georgia, where institutionalized racial bigotry had ruled supreme since Reconstruction days, he frightened and at the same time exhilarated local Negro leaders by announcing in a public meeting that he planned to organize a March on Washington by ten thousand Negroes "to demand jobs in the defense industry." He made the same announcement to Negro leaders in Jacksonville, Mississippi, and in Tampa and Miami, Florida. The Negro press reported this under imposing headlines, with the result that Randolph found waiting for him, when he arrived back in his New York City headquarters, messages of enthusiastic approval of his proposal from all over the country. Thus encouraged, he issued (January 15, 1941) a national press statement ("How to Blast the Bottlenecks of Race Prejudice in National Defense") in which he not only called for the march, but also expressed the thought that led him to do so.[77]

This thought, born of despair, accorded well with Marxist ideology in its rejection of persuasive argument and its embrace of force as the means of social change. ". . . [O]nly power can effect the enforcement and adoption of a given policy, however meritorious it may be," he wrote. "The virtue and rightness of a cause are not alone the condition and cause of its acceptance. Power and pressure are at the foundation of the march of social justice and reform." And these, he went on, "do not reside in the few, and intelligentsia, they lie in and flow from the masses." Not, however, from "the masses as such." Power was "the active principle only of the *organized* masses [present author's italics], the masses united for a definite purpose. Hence, Negro America must bring its power and pressure to bear upon the agencies and representatives of the Federal Government to exact their rights in National Defense employment and the armed forces of the country." He made then his proposal that "TEN THOUSAND Negroes march on Washington, D.C. . . . with the slogan: WE LOYAL AMERICAN CITIZENS DEMAND THE RIGHT TO WORK AND FIGHT FOR OUR COUNTRY." He concluded: "One thing is certain and that is if Negroes are going to get anything out of this national defense, which will cost the nation 30 or 40 billions . . . that we Negroes must help pay for in taxes . . . WE MUST FIGHT FOR IT AND FIGHT FOR IT WITH GLOVES OFF."[78]

Randolph himself was astonished by the amount of enthusiastic active support his proposal now received from the Negro "masses." Into the national office of the promptly established March on Washington Committee flowed (mostly in small donations) some $50,000 with which to pay for propaganda mailings and hire trains and buses. From that office fanned out brotherhood organizers who set up local March on Washington Committee branches across the country. Aware that his activities were being monitored by J. Edgar Hoover's FBI and that reports of this surveillance would go to the White House, where they would heighten the Executive's sense of the seriousness of this endeavor, Randolph personally canvased Harlem, speaking to Negro crowds on street corners, in bars and poolrooms, in beauty parlors. Everywhere his message continued to be received enthusiastically. In March, he officially announced that the mass demonstration would take place on July 1. ". . . [B]e not dismayed in these terrible times," said this announcement to Negro America. "You possess power, great power. Our problem is to hitch it up for action on the broadest, daring and most gigantic scale. In this period of power politics, nothing counts but pressure, more pressure, and still more pressure. . . . Mass power can cause President Roosevelt to issue an Executive Order abolishing discrimination." He now ceased to speak of a march by ten thousand. The number doubled, then tripled, then quadrupled. By late May, Randolph's call was for a march by one hundred thousand Negroes upon the capital of the United States, and signs were multiplying that this number would actually be attained.[79]

The President was now thoroughly alarmed. For health and other reasons, he had through that spring repeatedly refused requests from Walter White and other Negro leaders for another conference about Negro grievances. He was still reluctant to confer. But he was only too aware that, at best, the impending demonstration would complicate his problems with Congress; at worst, Negro blood would flow copiously down Washington's streets, for the capital was a Southern town whose natives, including most of the police, had their full share of the white Southerner's guilt-burdened fear of "uppity niggers." He sent Aubrey Williams to New York to "try to talk Randolph and White out of the march" ("Hell, Williams will join them!" was Southerner Pa Watson's comment upon Roosevelt's choice of emissary). He asked Eleanor to use her influence with the black community. She did so despite, or because of, her commitment to Randoph's objective, for, as she said in a letter to Randolph, she felt "very strongly that your group is making a grave mistake. . . . I am afraid it will set back the progress which is being made, in the Army at least, toward better opportunities and less segregation." She feared a tragic "incident" that would "create in Congress even more solid opposition from certain groups than we have had in the past." She made the same argument, expressed the same fear, when, journeying to New York, she met in City Hall with New York City Mayor Fiorello La Guardia, Aubrey Williams, labor and personnel relations expert Anna Rosenberg,* and Randolph and White. The last two refused to back down, whereupon La Guardia urgently recommended, and Eleanor concurred in the recommendation, that Roosevelt arrange an Oval Office conference in which

---

*A strong personality with a keen mind and much charm, Mrs. Rosenberg functioned often through this period as creative liaison between the White House and labor unions.

the President, the secretary of the navy, the secretary of war, and the two heads of OPM would meet with the two Negro leaders. Anna Rosenberg phoned this recommendation to Watson, who reported it to Roosevelt, saying: "Fiorello thinks this will stop the march and nothing else will. . . ." Roosevelt replied at once: "I will see Stimson, Knox, Knudsen, Hillman, White and Randolph on Friday next—or, if I do not go away and feel well enough, I will see them on Wednesday or Thursday."[80]

He saw them, together with Williams, La Guardia, and Mrs. Rosenberg, on Wednesday, June 18. He immediately focused his famous charm upon Randolph, whom he greeted as "Phil" and at once asked: "Which class were you in at Harvard?" Informed that Randolph "never went to Harvard," he was for a moment taken aback. "I was sure you did!" he said. But he then went on to say that, in any case, he and Randolph had something in common, sharing "a great interest in human and social justice." To this, Randolph readily assented. There followed a duel between Roosevelt's manipulative charm and Randolph's courteous but iron-hard determination, with the others as almost silent witnesses. Roosevelt pursued the diversionary tactics he generally employed, and generally successfully, when he wished not to do what the person calling upon him wanted him to do. He attempted to engage Randolph in small talk. This failing, he began to exercise his considerable talents as raconteur. But not for long. Randolph soon broke in, politely but firmly, to say he knew how valuable was the President's time and that "what we want to talk with you about is the problem of jobs for Negroes in defense industries." Negroes were "being turned away at factory gates because they are colored," and they wanted the President to do something to stop it. Roosevelt wanted it stopped also, he told "Phil," and he would let the heads of defense plants know that Negroes should be given the same rights to work as other citizens had. That was not enough, said Randolph.

"Mr. President, we want you to issue an executive order making it mandatory that Negroes be permitted to work. . . ."

"Well, Phil, you know I can't do that. If I issue an executive order for you there'll be no end to other groups coming in here and asking me to issue executive orders for them, too."

Certainly, no executive action of any kind could be taken unless and until "you call off this march of yours." That couldn't be done, said Randolph. Roosevelt, indicating his doubt that Randolph could deliver on his published promise, or threat, wanted to know how many people Randolph "really" planned to bring.

"One hundred thousand, Mr. President."

Shaking his head, Roosevelt turned to White, asking "Walter" how many would "really march."

"One hundred thousand, Mr. President," said Walter White.

But that, cried Roosevelt, would create an absolutely impossible situation.

Somebody was likely to be killed. Not if it were known that the President planned to "come out and address the gathering," said Randolph, smiling. Abruptly, Roosevelt's cajoling affability disappeared. The President of the United States did not negotiate with "a gun at his head," he said curtly; there could be no further talk with him on this subject until the march was called off.

"Then I shall have to stand by the pledge I've made to the people," said A. Philip Randolph.

At which point, Fiorello La Guardia interposed, saying it was clear that "Mr. Randolph is not going to call off the march, and I suggest we all begin to seek a formula."[81]

Obviously relieved by this suggestion, Roosevelt asked Anna Rosenberg, La Guardia, and Williams to take the group into an anteroom and work out a formula. It turned out to be the executive order Randolph had called for, an order "with teeth in it," and after some backing and filling Roosevelt perforce accepted it, assigning one of his executive assistants, a young lawyer named Joseph L. Rauh, to the drafting of it.

The drafting and redrafting took several days, for Randolph refused to call off the march until an executive order satisfactory to him was issued, and he rejected one after another of Rauh's early efforts as insufficiently clear and strong. But on June 25, just five days before the scheduled date of the march, Roosevelt signed and issued Executive Order No. 8802. It admitted in a "whereas" "that available and needed workers have been barred from employment in industries engaged in defense production solely because of consideration of race, color," etc. It mandated the inclusion in all defense contracts of "a provision obligating the contractor not to discriminate against any worker because of race, creed, color, or national origin." It ordered all government departments and agencies to "take special measures to assure that . . . programs are administered without discrimination because of race, creed, color, or national origin." And it established in the labor division of OPM a Fair Employment Practices Committee (FEPC) consisting of a chairman and four members (in March 1942 the membership would be increased by another executive order from five to seven) with authority to "receive and investigate complaints of discrimination in violation of the provisions of this Order" and to "take appropriate steps to redress grievances which it finds to be valid."[82] Randolph then, at almost the last moment, canceled, with an explanatory statement, the Negro march on Washington.

The order did not end discrimination in the defense industries. Far from it. For one thing, contracts already signed before the order's issuance contained no anti-discriminatory clause. For another, racial prejudice was so deeply ingrained in much of the American white community that, law or no law, it would continue to express itself in action. But blatant racial discrimination in employment was thereafter markedly reduced and, most important, the success that crowned Randolph's efforts justified the premise on which he had acted and the strategy he had employed. Thus was pointed the way that American Negroes would follow in the future to gain in actuality the rights that had been legally theirs under the Constitution of the United States since the ratification of the Fourteenth and Fifteenth Amendments in 1868 and 1870.

XI

BUT the length and difficulty of the road that yet lay ahead for Negroes in quest of their rights was indicated for them by an event that occurred simultaneously with the Randolph triumph—an event that was, in the view of Negro leaders, a sad offset to that triumph—namely, Roosevelt's appointment of South Carolina's Senator James F. Byrnes to the U.S. Supreme Court.

Long gone by the summer of 1941 were the days when the White House faced, as Roosevelt had faced from 1933 through 1936, a Supreme Court of old men (average age seventy-one) dominated by conservatives whose supreme judicial goal was to frustrate, on grounds of unconstitutionality, every executive and legislative effort toward socioeconomic reform. A President who had been unable to make a single Court appointment during his first term had made five of them in his second. The justices' average age now was in the mid-forties; the Court of 1941 was the most youthful of all those since the Civil War. It was also the most liberal minded. The Court's balance between liberalism and conservatism had been definitely shifted toward liberalism when the reactionary Justice VanDevanter retired and was replaced in 1937 by Hugo Black. The shift had been confirmed with the appointment in January 1938 of Stanley Reed to succeed the reactionary Sutherland. The new balance had been maintained with the appointments of Felix Frankfurter to succeed Cardozo in July 1938 and William O. Douglas to succeed Brandeis in March 1939, and then, in January 1940, the Court had become emphatically a Roosevelt Court when Frank Murphy was appointed successor to the reactionary Pierce Butler in January 1940. So it was that, when Mr. Justice McReynolds, the sole remaining member of the Court's former old guard, at last retired at age seventy-nine in January 1941, Roosevelt was under no strong compulsion to fill the vacancy with a tried-and-true liberal. He could instead use the appointment of a conservative to pay off personal political debts and forestall future political troubles, and this is what he did with the Byrnes appointment.

James Byrnes in 1941 was Roosevelt's own age of sixty-one. A man of small physical size (five feet seven in height, 140 pounds in weight) but of immense ambition, possessed of an Irish charm that enabled him to ingratiate himself with those who could advance his career, he was first a protégé of the racially bigoted populist demagogue of South Carolina, "Pitchfork Ben" Tillman; then of the aristocratic Virginia conservative Carter Glass; then of the urbane, wealthy, covertly manipulative Bernard Baruch. Though never a New

Dealer—indeed, in part *because* he was not—he had been enabled over the years to render Roosevelt several signal political services. He was a remarkably adroit politician. It was said that the President had never lost a battle in the Senate when Byrnes fought prominently on his side, nor won one in which Byrnes fought prominently on the opposing side—and in some of the most crucial instances, Byrnes had been instrumental in bringing victory to the President. He had played an important role in the battle over lend-lease, as we have seen. During the 1940 Democratic National Convention, though himself a disappointed candidate for the vice presidency, he had loyally corraled votes for Roosevelt's choice, Henry Wallace, to whom most of the convention delegates were vehemently opposed.* He would certainly be a strong candidate for the vice presidency again in 1944, no matter who headed the Democratic ticket, but this was a potential political embarrassment that would be avoided if Byrnes were an associate justice of the Supreme Court; never had a Court member given up his prestigious lifetime post in order to participate in ("descend" into) elective politics.

The appointment outraged Negro leaders. When news stories first announced in mid-March 1941 that Roosevelt might send Byrnes's name to the Senate for confirmation, Walter White sent a lengthy telegram to the President begging him not to do it. "If Senator Byrnes at any time in his long public career failed to take a position inimical to the human and citizenship rights of thirteen million American Negro citizens, close scrutiny of his record fails to reveal it," wrote White. "We are sending to the White House a detailed record of Mr. Byrnes' opposition to educational, economic, and citizen rights for Negroes as well as material on his savage attacks on legislation to stop lynching and mob violence."[83] The record included attacks upon civil liberty proposals delivered by Byrnes on the floor of the House of Representatives in 1919 and 1920, speeches that obviously expressed his own passionate convictions and that, in their virulent racism, were vicious even for white Southerners of conservative views. The four-page report that White sent to the White House contained excerpts not from these, however, but from a speech Congressman Byrnes had made in 1925 against federal funding for Howard University (Negroes educated at Howard, returning to South Carolina, would foment trouble, he argued) and from Senator Byrnes's filibustering attack upon the anti-lynching bill of 1938.

This may have given Roosevelt pause, for he did not formally nominate Byrnes in March, or in April, or in May. He did not do so until the second week in June, after the Republican leadership in the Senate had informed him that the Republicans of the upper house were so enamored of Senator Byrnes's ability and integrity that they would join in a confirmation of Byrnes's appointment by unanimous consent, without referring it for hearings by the judiciary committee.

---

*See pp. 599, 600, of *FDR: Into the Storm.*

By then (actually on June 2), Chief Justice Charles Evans Hughes had resigned from the Supreme Court, saying that "considerations of health and age made this necessary." Thus Roosevelt had now not one, but two Court vacancies to fill: he could balance the Byrnes appointment with one of a solid liberal. The formal Byrnes nomination went before the Senate on June 12, 1941. It was approved unanimously eight minutes later.

Six days later, Associate Justice Harlan Fiske Stone was named Hughes's successor as chief justice—an appointment that was almost universally applauded and would prove fortunate for the nation in that it resulted in a more rational balance between progress and tradition, among the three branches of government, than had earlier existed. Shortly thereafter, the Byrnes appointment was compensated for, in the view of many, by the appointment to the Court of Attorney General Robert Jackson, whom Roosevelt had originally intended, or had said to Ickes and others that he intended, to name chief justice.

Seven of the Court's nine members were now Roosevelt appointees.

XII

MEANWHILE, Ambassador Winant had returned to Washington to report in person to the President on his mission to the Court of St. James; and Averell Harriman, at Churchill's request and with Roosevelt's approval, had gone to North Africa to see what the United States might do to strengthen the British position there. From both men, Roosevelt received messages of alarm over what each saw as a widening gap between what America was doing and what desperately needed to be done to assure Britain's survival.

Winant's message, aside from the one he delivered orally in the White House, had been written by his embassy's military attaché, General Raymond E. Lee, whom we have met. Lee still believed "the British can resist invasion" but was far less sanguine about their long-term survival without far greater help from the United States than was now being given. "The equation at present is too unbalanced: 80,000,000 Germans in one lump + the labor of n slaves + 8 years of intense rearming and organization + frenzied fanaticism > 70,000,000 British in 4 continents + zero slaves + only 3 years of real rearmament and no industrial mobilization + dogged determination. It is another example of the old prize ring rule: 'A good big man will beat a good little man every time.' What our position and policy are at home, it is difficult to discern at this range. From here our steps [in support] of Britain appear to follow along well behind the development of events. The lag is great and may prove too much."[84]

Harriman's appreciation of the situation was given in a letter to Hopkins written in Lisbon, where Harriman paused en route to the Middle East: "It is awfully hard for me to understand what is going on in the mind of America from this distance. Recent polls seem to indicate that 80 percent or 85 percent of the people believe we are eventually going to be in the war, and over two-thirds that we should be in the war, if necessary to save Britain, but only a minority think we should go in now. My conclusion after three months in London is that England cannot win without our direct intervention . . . and that every week America waits the difficulties of the job when we do come in will be multiplied. Are the facts being properly presented and interpreted to America? After all, the British stopped the Germans from daylight bombing by taking a toll of about 10 percent. Why, then, is Washington so complacent over the Germans' taking a similar toll of merchant ships and their cargoes in the Battle of the Atlantic?"[85]

Winant was back at his London post in the third week of June. Harriman did not return to London from the Middle East until mid-July.

XIII

WHILE Winant was in Washington there occurred in Roosevelt's personal life, as a culminating darkness of that black spring, an event of major and sad importance. . . .

Each June for the last several years the manager of Washington's Willard Hotel had hosted a dinner for members of the President's personal staff. Always before he had given it at his hotel, but in 1941 it was arranged that he do so in the White House, on June 4, a Wednesday, so that the President himself could attend. As the dinner drew to a close, Missy LeHand confessed to Grace Tully that she felt ill and very tired. There were obvious reasons why she should. Her physical strength had never been great (rheumatic fever in childhood had seriously weakened her heart), she had always worked near the limit of that strength (Roosevelt "had no idea of the demands made upon people close to him," she once remarked to a close friend), and the physical strain upon her these last months had been greater than usual, thanks to Roosevelt's prolonged indisposition. She now refused, however, to go at once upstairs to bed, as Grace Tully urged her to do: she would not, at a White House social function, precede the President from the room. He left at nine-thirty, and barely had he done so than she, with a loud moan, fell heavily to the floor, unconscious. She was carried at once to her third-floor bedroom, where Dr. McIntire, a nose and throat specialist, tentatively diagnosed her illness as a combination of heart trouble and nervous collapse. He sedated her and ordered complete rest.[86]

Twice before she had suffered nervous breakdowns. On each occasion the immediate incitement may have been a perceived threat to her relationship with Roosevelt, in whom virtually the whole of her emotional life was invested. The first had been in June 1927, in Warm Springs, when Roosevelt's sale of the hurricane-wrecked houseboat *Larooco* marked the end of what had been, for her, an idyllic life with the man she loved—a life during which she had been Roosevelt's sole close companion, in relaxing pursuits conducive of intimacy, for months at a time, both in Warm Springs, where Eleanor, after a single unhappy visit, never came, and aboard the *Larooco,* on which Eleanor, save for a single unhappy cruise, never set foot. In 1927 as in 1941, her illness had been initially diagnosed as a combination of mild heart attack with nervous collapse. But the latter had been by far the more serious. Her heart function soon returned to normal, whereupon Roosevelt went north for his summer months at Hyde Park, leaving her under the expert care of Dr. Leroy Hubbard, whom he had persuaded in the spring of 1926 to head Warm Springs' medical services. But thereafter her mental condition swiftly worsened. She became delirious, she had hallucinations, she suffered attacks of depression so severe that her doctor ordered removed from her room all objects with which she might harm herself. Only slowly did she recover her usual radiantly cheerful, selfless disposition; not until November was she able to return to her secretarial duties.

The second breakdown was less serious than the first, but serious enough. It occurred a year later, after Roosevelt, in Warm Springs, permitted himself to be persuaded into the 1928 race for governor of New York. He had vowed he would *not* enter this race, had solemnly promised Louis Howe that he would not, and Missy was passionately opposed to his doing so because she feared what it would do to his health and, even more, what it might do to her relationship with him.* Within a few days after his gubernatorial nomination, she had again fallen ill with what was seemingly a recurrence of the earlier illness. She had been unable to play any part in the campaign that followed.[87]

During the last year, a new anxiety had entered her life (also Eleanor's, if to a considerably lesser degree) in the person of Crown Princess Martha of Norway. Roosevelt took what some of his associates deemed an almost adolescent pleasure in the company of royal personages; he seemed to find royalty per se glamorous; and he had been especially taken with this princess when she and her husband, Prince Olav, who was also her cousin, came to the United States in the spring of 1939 to dedicate the Norwegian exhibit at the New York World's Fair. When the Norwegian royal family fled their native land in the summer of 1940 to escape capture by the Nazis, the King and Prince Olav had gone to London to establish there a Norwegian government-in-exile. But Princess Martha with her three children, whose welfare was her paramount concern, accepted Roosevelt's invitation to come to the United States, where she was herself at once accepted into the bosom of the Roosevelt family. She had actually lived with that family in Hyde Park, then in the White House, for several weeks before finding, with Roosevelt's personal help, a suitably magnificent estate, a twenty-five-room stone mansion with 105 scenic acres around it, in Bethesda, Maryland. She was of the feminine type that had always greatly pleased Roosevelt. She was tall, willowy, regal of bearing yet vivacious, with gaiety in her

*See pp. 843–53 of *FDR: The Beckoning of Destiny.*

smile, a glint of mischievous flirtatiousness in her large brown eyes, and a fully exercised ability to focus adoring attention upon Franklin Roosevelt and hang breathlessly on his every word. Throughout the fall of 1940, to Missy's increasing dismay, she had occupied more and more of the vital space next to him, space that had formerly been Missy's virtually exclusive territory. On afternoon automobile rides, she sat on the seat beside Roosevelt that had always before been Missy's; during the evening "Children's Hour," she absorbed more of Roosevelt's delighted attention than Missy did; she took precedence over Missy at the dinner table. The onset of Roosevelt's illness, and his long bout with it, restored to Missy her former role in his life throughout the winter and spring, but with his return to better health in late May had come a return of Princess Martha into his life (on Friday evening, June 6, just forty-eight hours after Missy's collapse, the princess was his companion as he boarded the *Potomac* for a weekend cruise). His relationship with his personal secretary had always been a mixture of work and play; his relationship with the flirtatious Martha, who was obviously fascinated by him, was pure pleasure. . . .

It became almost at once evident that Dr. McIntire had misdiagnosed Missy's illness. Bed rest did not improve her condition. Instead, her condition worsened alarmingly, and the fact that her speech was now noticeably slurred indicated that what she had suffered was a small stroke.

In mid-June she suffered a major one.

She was partially paralyzed, her speech became almost unintelligible, and her personality was sadly changed: her normally brightly optimistic disposition became sour and depressed, to the dismay of those who loved her—and virtually everyone who knew her loved her. She grew irritable, she became complaining, who had formerly been notable for her patience and her sweet, even temper. Clearly her full recovery, should it ever occur, would be a long-drawn-out process. She was moved from the White House to Doctors Hospital, where she could have round-the-clock nursing care and where it was at once realized by those who attended her that, at age forty-three, her duties as Roosevelt's confidential assistant, her role as White House hostess during Eleanor's absences, and whatever personal intimacies had developed between her and Roosevelt during her two decades of devoted service to him were forever ended.

To members of his close-knit "official family"—even to those most acutely aware of his role-playing, emotion-hiding genius—Roosevelt's overt emotional response to this tragedy seemed astonishingly cool and meager. He evinced concern and regret but spoke little to others of what had happened, said nothing of what he felt, gave no sign of great grief. Ickes complained in his diary of Roosevelt's coldness in this instance, saying that the President was now "all President," devoid of human feeling and thus able to discard without a qualm those who, however close to him they had formerly been, were of no further use to him in his presidential role. (Missy herself had once surprised her friend Fulton

Oursler with the remark that Roosevelt was "really incapable of a personal friendship with anyone.")[88] Yet he suffered a setback of his own recovery of health at this time, as we have mentioned*—a throat infection accompanied by fever, which Eleanor believed was probably caused by anxiety over Missy (Eleanor said so in a letter to her daughter Anna Boettiger). While Missy remained in her White House bedroom he visited her every day, coming armed with encouraging words and a great show of smiling confidence in her quick recovery. He also visited her in Doctors Hospital as often as his schedule permitted, during the first part of her stay there. But others were made aware that he dreaded her emotional outbursts. When she wept, as she did during many of his visits, he fled her room quite abruptly. And not long after her removal to the hospital his visits became more seldom, also more brief. He gave signs of being pained and sometimes annoyed by her occasional pitiful efforts to restore their old relationship.

None of this last is clear evidence of insensitivity, however. Indeed, it may well be evidence of a sensitivity greater than most—evidence that his empathy with Missy in her suffering, and his sense of responsibility for that suffering, were so great that they would wholly destroy his capacity to function as a public man if they were not cut off, ruthlessly put aside. He dared not give way to personal feeling. He must resist debilitating assaults upon his emotions. He must prevent the rise of any overwhelming sense of personal guilt. His deeply felt but simplistic religious faith (alas, a limitation of thought as well as of moral responsibility) commanded him to do so. One must bear what God imposed, and God had willed this affliction upon Missy, upon himself—the same God Who had assigned him his great role in the drama of history. He *was,* after all, President of the United States in a time of extreme danger for the Republic; his immense obligation to the American people, and to the cause of freedom throughout the world, had been divinely ordered; he must, by divine order, fulfill it, though it require of him a suspension of empathy, a deliberate callousness, a continued indulgence of his need for pleasurable diversions whereby his staying power and ability to remain on even keel in rough waters were sustained.

More solid evidence of his deepest personal feeling is the fact that Roosevelt paid all of Missy's very considerable medical expenses out of his personal income and, as the world would later learn, soon altered his will to provide that should he precede her in death, her expenses would continue to be paid out of the income from his estate, up to 50 percent of that income, for as long as necessary. All the rest of the estate income was to go to Eleanor.[89]

*See p. 197.

5

⇢⤳✕⤷⤸

The Grand Alliance Is Enlarged and Strengthened

I

EXECUTIVE Order 8802, though in final form, remained as yet unsigned when on Sunday, June 22, Robert Sherwood, in New York City, taxied uptown to Harlem to attend a rally sponsored by the interventionist Fight for Freedom Committee. The rally was held in a great ballroom, the Golden Gate, before which paraded, under the blazing sun of one of that summer's hottest days, a picket line organized by the American Communist Party. That it had been so organized was obvious from the wording of the placards the picketeers carried and of the pamphlets they distributed. The placards proclaimed Fight for Freedom to be composed of warmongering lackeys of Wall Street and British imperialism, their purpose to inveigle the innocent masses into shedding blood out of which bloated capitalists would coin money. The pamphlets urged all Negroes to join the March on Washington to demand not only equality but also peace. Sherwood, who seldom crossed strike picket lines, crossed this one without a qualm, then suffered through an hour and a half of speechifying (he made one of the speeches) in sweltering heat. The ballroom had no air-conditioning. He was limp and soaked with perspiration when he at last emerged on the street to find that the picket line had disappeared. The March on Washington, he was told, was being canceled, an action he assumed to have been taken by the Communists. He at once suspected that whether or not it was Communists who had called off the Washington march, it was certainly the American Communist headquarters that, during the ninety minutes of his sweltering in the ballroom, had ordered a halt to the picketing, this because there had been a total reversal of the main policy line of the American Communist Party. On the following day he knew this was true: the Communist *Daily Worker* "was pro-British, pro-Lend-Lease, and, for the first time in two years, pro-Roosevelt."[1]

In retrospect, the most astonishing thing about this episode is that the Communist demonstration had been permitted to begin. It would not have been had there not been a failure of communication between Moscow and the New York

Communist headquarters, a failure consequent upon a failure of nerve at the Moscow source of American Communist policy, that was in turn consequent upon a nearly fatal miscalculation by the Soviet Union's supreme authority. For the mighty event that determined the sudden policy reversal had come as a literally stunning surprise to Josef Stalin, who was not even at his Kremlin command post when the event began to unfold in the earliest light (three-thirty in the morning in that northern latitude) of June 22 (eight-thirty on the night of June 21 in Washington). He had retired to his weekend villa in the Moscow suburb of Kuntsevo. And when he rushed back to the Kremlin he was in a highly agitated state that soon became an actual nervous breakdown. Under the pressure of catastrophic news that poured in upon him from the West he became distraught, disoriented. He gave orders that made no sense, orders that could not possibly be obeyed, then again retired to Kuntsevo, where he remained utterly secluded and incommunicado for more than a week—an eight-day period during which a rudderless Soviet Union was driven to the very edge of total collapse.[2]

Yet Stalin had been repeatedly and urgently warned of what impended. . . .

Nearly half a year before, on a night early in January 1941, the commercial attaché of the U.S. embassy in Germany, one Sam E. Woods, had entered a motion picture theater in Berlin and seated himself as if by accident, though actually by prearrangement, beside a highly placed official of the German government. This official was secretly fervently anti-Nazi; with him, Woods had developed relations of personal friendship and mutual trust. While both men stared at the picture screen, giving no sign that they knew one another, the German slipped into the American's hands a document that, upon its careful examination in the U.S. embassy an hour or two later, seemed to be an authentic digest of a top-secret directive, headed "Operation Barbarossa," issued by Hitler to his armed forces command on December 18, 1940. "The German armed forces must be prepared to *crush Soviet Russia in a quick campaign* before the end of the war against England," the directive began. ". . . Preparations . . . are to be completed by May 15, 1941." There followed a fairly detailed description of a blitzkrieg operation designed to break into pieces and then destroy piecemeal the "mass of the Russian *Army* in western Russia," thereby preventing "the retreat of intact, battle-ready troops into the wide spaces of Russia."[3] That such an attack would actually be made was initially hard for Washington to believe. The congenitally suspicious and cautious Cordell Hull was at first convinced that the alleged directive was a phony, a "plant" designed to mislead American policy. For why on earth would Hitler, who with a single hard knock, well within his power to administer, could now send Britain tottering into her grave, turn instead upon his Soviet partner and so open, needlessly, what might become a dangerously prolonged two-front war? During the following weeks, however, intelligence reports of the movement of German troops to the Russian frontier and of the accumulation of stockpiles of matériel there persuaded London and Washington that the document was what it purported to be; whereupon Roosevelt ordered the State Department to report the substance of it to Soviet Ambassador Constantine Oumansky. Sumner Welles did so on March 20. The ambassador was evidently profoundly shocked by what he heard; he "turned very white," as Welles later wrote, and was silent for a long moment before acknowledging "the gravity of the message" and saying his government would be "grateful for your confidence."[4]

A few days later, British intelligence reported that when the Yugoslav government of Prince Paul formally joined the Axis, three of five panzer divisions theretofore poised near Bucharest for an evident thrust westward into Yugoslavia had been abruptly moved northward by rail, toward Kraków in southern Poland—reported also that this movement had then been as abruptly halted and the panzers returned to Romania, when, on March 27, the Belgrade coup overthrew Prince Paul. Churchill, desperately grasping at straws of hope, saw this as conclusive evidence that Hitler, having designed a spring invasion of the Soviet Union, now felt compelled to postpone it in order to secure first the southern (Balkan) flank that his drive eastward would expose.* The conquest of Yugoslavia and Greece was in that case *not* the prelude to an immediate conquest of Egypt, Suez, the Middle East. Britain was being granted a reprieve! And to prolong that reprieve as much as possible—above all, to prevent an overwhelming surprise attack upon an unprepared Soviet Union—became for Churchill a prime concern. On April 3 he instructed the British ambassador in Moscow, Sir Stafford Cripps, to hand-deliver a three-sentence personal message from the Prime Minister to Stalin saying that the Germans had begun their panzer movement northward "when they thought they had got Yugoslavia in the net," that the "moment they heard of the Serbian revolution this movement was countermanded," and that "Your Excellency will readily appreciate the significance of these facts." Churchill believed that this personal communication from one head of government to another, its significance enhanced by its cryptic brevity, would "arrest Stalin's attention," lay foundations for British-Soviet cooperation against Hitler, and stimulate Russian defense preparations. Cripps, however, permitted a full week to elapse before informing British Foreign Secretary Eden that Churchill's note remained undelivered because it would "probably . . . weaken" the effect of a much more detailed and "emphatic" warning message that he himself had just sent to Andrei Vyshinski, deputy commissar (under Molotov) for Soviet foreign affairs—a message in which Cripps urged USSR cooperation with Yugoslavia, Greece, and Turkey to thwart Hitler's Balkan ambitions. The ambassador had in the end to be flatly ordered to

---

*We now know that an infuriated Hitler did indeed postpone the launching of "Barbarossa" from May 15 to mid-June 1941 immediately upon learning of the Belgrade coup, later postponing it to June 22.

deliver the Churchill message. He finally did so on April 19, though even then he did not deliver it in person, as Churchill had originally specified, but instead gave it to Vyshinski, who on April 23 told Cripps that Stalin had received it.[5]

It is doubtful that a prompt and strict obedience of Churchill's instructions would have made any difference. Certainly, in the event, none of the warnings from the West—not Roosevelt's via Oumansky, not Cripps's, not Churchill's—had any perceptible effect upon Moscow's attitude toward, or dealings with, Berlin. Even very explicit warnings from the remarkably efficient Soviet spy apparatus in Tokyo,* warnings that gave June 22 as the invasion date, failed of their intended effect. The Soviet government refused to believe that Hitler would have the "madness . . . to undertake a war in the East . . . before finishing off the war in the West," as Maxim Litvinov confessed eight months later, after he had succeeded Oumansky as Soviet ambassador in Washington.[6] Instead, though Hitler's invasion of the Balkans was an invasion of the Soviet sphere of influence in Eastern Europe and provoked strong Soviet protests to Berlin, the government-controlled Soviet press dismissed with contempt what it viewed as a desperate effort by the Western democracies to save Britain by fomenting strife between Germany and Russia—a desperate pursuit, in other words, of the strategic goal (the destruction of communism) that had been Britain's ever since Hitler came to power. The danger that the Soviet Union would be surprised by Hitler therefore remained acute, and surprise would simply make easier what seemed likely to be in any case another swift, overwhelming Hitler triumph.

For though the prospect of Hitler's turning to the East was in the eyes of London and Washington another beam of light thrust into the general gloom, the beam was rendered dim and flickering by the universal belief on the part of top British and American military experts that Hitler's obviously low opinion of the Soviet Union's capacity to wage war was abundantly justified. The dismal initial performance of Soviet armies in Finland seemed clear evidence that Stalin's massive purges of the 1930s had disastrously lowered the effectiveness of his army's officer corps. Hitler's armed forces, on the other hand, had demonstrated apparent invincibility time and again. It seemed likely, therefore, that the Soviet Union would be eliminated from the ranks of the great powers, if not (as seemed more than possible) utterly destroyed by early autumn.

Certainly this was Hitler's own expectation.†

The West would later learn that not until the afternoon of June 21, barely twelve hours before the invasion began, did the Nazi Fuehrer inform his Fascist

---

*Comintern espionage agent Richard Sorge in Tokyo, "who was privy to the dispatches of the German ambassador (which he helped him compose)," informed Moscow as early as April 1941 that preparations for the invasion were complete, according to John Keegan in his *The Second World War* (New York, 1989), p. 179.

†He need only "kick in the door" to assure the collapse of the whole rotten structure of the Jewish-Bolshevist state, he told his close associates at this time.

partner, Mussolini, of what impended. He did so then at length, however, stressing the "months of anxious deliberation and continuous nerve-racking waiting" that had accompanied "the hardest decision of my life" and claiming that he had waited so long to inform his friend only because the "absolutely final decision will not be made until 7 o'clock tonight." He gave his reasons for the decision. "England has lost the war," he wrote, but "some of her hopes of survival" had "a certain logic" insofar as they focused upon Soviet Russia . . . "the place from which they tried to start the war" and whose immense air force, he recognized, would be a serious threat to what would become the rear of the main German force should he launch a full-scale attack upon the British Isles. "Really, all available Russian forces are [now] at our border," Hitler continued; a commitment of his own forces to the West would consequently inevitably expose him to a Soviet "strategy of extortion, to which I would have to yield in silence simply from a feeling of air inferiority." Therefore, since "it . . . [lies] within our power to exclude [eliminate] Russia," and since this elimination "would mean tremendous relief for Japan in East Asia and thereby the possibility of a much stronger threat to American activities through Japanese intervention," he proposed to take the offensive immediately against Russia. "So far as the air war on England is concerned, we shall, for a time, remain on the defensive. . . ." If England failed to give up after Russia was conquered, "we can, with our rear secured, apply ourselves with increased strength to the dispatching of our enemy."[7] He ("we") could then do this, he clearly implied, well before support from the United States, no matter how determined this was (it would almost certainly be, in such circumstances, a weak and wavering support), could become strong enough to be decisive.

This optimistic view from Berlin, which was also the pessimistic view from London and Washington, seemed abundantly justified by the mighty event as it unfolded.

What began in that flaming dawn of June 22 was by far the most gigantic collision of military forces in all of world history. It was also symbolic, if not actually expressive, of a profound schism of the soul of Western civilization, namely, the divorce of intellect from emotion, of the thinking self from the feeling self, with crippling injury to both.* In Nazi Germany, dark romanticism dominated the state; cruel passions, escaped from reasonable controls, dictated action. In Soviet Russia, scientific materialism dominated the state (though Marxist "science" perverted the real thing); cold logic, turning its back upon the emotions where humane values are rooted, dictated action. And in the head-on

---

*The author believes the schism to be a result of the impact of a relentlessly advancing scientific technology upon individual human beings, cultural attitudes, and socioeconomic institutions that are unable to cope with it in ways conducive of human freedom and humane values. See pp. 370–80 of *FDR: The Beckoning of Destiny,* and pp. 218–19 of *FDR: The New Deal Years.*

clash of the two there would be no vestige of "civilized" warfare; neither of the warring nations had formally subscribed to the Geneva Convention, and savagery would rule supreme over their conflict. The battlefront stretched an unprecedented 1,800 miles, from the Baltic to the Black Sea. Along it, more than 3,000,000 superbly led German troops, organized into three army groups and armed with 3,000 tanks, 2,000 planes, and 7,200 guns, hurled themselves upon Russian armies of even greater size and possessing even more planes, tanks, guns. The defenders were everywhere confused, disorganized, surprised—they were also often incompetently led on both the tactical and strategic command levels in these opening days—thanks to Stalin's purges and his refusal to believe the warnings that had been given him. Within twenty-four hours, the air cover for the central German army group whose immediate objective was Minsk had destroyed 528 Soviet planes on the ground and 210 in the air; along the whole of the front, the Soviets had lost 1,200 planes, which was a fourth of their total front-line air strength; and panzer units were thrust fifty miles and more eastward on every vast segment of the total front, cutting off and isolating large pockets of Soviet troops, who were quickly surrounded by the advancing German infantry and blasted by German artillery. By July 2 the Germans claimed the capture of 150,000 Red Army troops along with 1,200 tanks and 600 big guns.

Small wonder that when Stalin on July 3 at last broke with a radio address what had been to his countrymen a mysterious and ominous silence, he did so "badly" as far as delivery was concerned, according to a later account by Ivan Maisky, the Soviet ambassador to Britain, who personally witnessed Stalin's performance. "Stalin spoke in a dull, colorless voice, often stopping and breathing heavily. . . . He seemed ailing and at the end of his strength."[8] Yet the very fact that he was there at the microphone, addressing his "brothers, sisters . . . friends," was, to the theretofore puzzled and frightened Russian masses, immensely reassuring. A sense of certainty, a feeling that solid realities yet obtained, was restored to them—a conviction that there yet remained, amid monstrous change and ghastly turmoil, a basis for social order, a firm framework for coherent thought—a sense of their country as a yet living organism with a heart that beat passionately and a brain that directed rationally. The words that Stalin spoke were unwontedly eloquent (one suspects that Maxim Litvinov, influenced by Churchill's oratorical style, had a hand in their drafting) and, despite the ominous tidings they bore, heartening to a people who yearned for truth after a long week of clumsily lying press and radio propaganda. Stalin frankly admitted that Latvia, Lithuania, considerable portions of Byelorussia, and considerable portions of western Ukraine were already in the enemy's bloody hands; that the enemy continued his advance toward Leningrad, toward Minsk (with Smolensk and Moscow beyond), toward Kiev; that "our country is in serious danger." The utmost of courageous, devoted fighting effort was demanded of a Russian people who, however, were not now alone, friendless in a wholly hostile world. "In this great war we shall have true allies in the peoples of Europe and America," he said. ". . . Our war for the freedom of our country will merge with the struggle of the peoples of Europe for their independence, for democratic liberties [*sic*]. . . . In this connection the historic statement of the British Prime Minister, Mr. Churchill, . . . and the declaration of the United States Government signifying readiness to render aid to our country, which can only evoke a feeling of gratitude in the hearts of the people of the Soviet Union, are fully comprehensible and symptomatic."[9]

For by that time, Churchill had told the world of his response, and the response of his government, to what was happening in and to the Soviet Union. The Roosevelt administration had also spoken. . . .

II

ON Saturday evening, June 21, 1941, Churchill and his wife had dined at Chequers with, among others, the U.S. ambassador to Britain, John G. Winant, and Mrs. Winant;* British Foreign Secretary Anthony Eden and Mrs. Eden; Churchill's youngest daughter, Mary; Edward Bridges (he, the son of British poet laureate Robert Bridges, had succeeded Sir Maurice Hankey as secretary to the British cabinet); and the Prime Minister's private secretary, John Colville. During dinner, Churchill said that a German attack on Russia was certain and that, just as certainly, Russia would be defeated. Hitler counted upon right-wingers in Britain to support Germany's attack upon Communist Russia and to frustrate, therefore, any effort the British government might make to ally itself with Moscow, but in this, said Churchill, Der Fuehrer was badly mistaken. He himself was absolutely determined to "go all out to help Russia." (He had said so, though this went unmentioned at the dinner table, in a message to Roosevelt a week ago: "From every source at my disposal . . . it looks as if a vast German onslaught on Russia was imminent. . . . [W]e shall, of course, give all encouragement and any help we can spare to the Russians, following the principle that Hitler is the foe we have to beat. I do not expect any class political reactions here, and trust a German-Russian conflict will not cause you any embarrassment.") He turned to Gilbert Winant. The ambassador had already reported

---

*Winant, almost immediately following his arrival in London, had become a personal friend of the Churchills' and was generally a weekend guest at Chequers. Lincolnian in both appearance and (to a considerable degree) temperament, as we have said, his natural introversion and melancholy were augmented by the fact that he was unhappily married, as Lincoln had been. By the summer of 1941 he at age fifty-two was falling helplessly, hopelessly in love with Churchill's actress daughter, the vivacious, highly intelligent, dark-red-haired Sarah, aged twenty-six, who was herself enmeshed in a marriage (to a Vic Oliver) destined to end in divorce. But Winant was a painfully conscientious man, and according to Colville, his love for Sarah was and forever remained "innocent."

orally to his host the President's answer to the Churchill message, which was that he, the President, would support "any announcement that the Prime Minister might make welcoming Russia as an ally." Winant now told the dinner assembly that what Churchill had proclaimed as the British view would be also the official view of the United States.[10]

After the dinner party had broken up, Churchill and Colville strolled together on the lawn in evening light, and as they did so Colville mildly but pointedly baited his superior, remarking on Churchill's ardent support of the Allied invasion of Lenin's Russia in 1918, Churchill's siding with Franco against an allegedly Communist-dominated government during the Spanish Civil War, Churchill's repeated public denunciations of the "wickedness" of communism during the last quarter-century. In view of all this, was not the Prime Minister now "bowing down to the House of Rimmon"? Churchill was unperturbed. He told Colville (so Colville recorded in his diary) that he "had [now] only one single purpose—the destruction of Hitler—and his life was much simplified thereby; if Hitler invaded Hell he would at least make a favorable reference to the Devil [in the House of Commons]!"[11]

He made no favorable reference to hell (communism), however, when he broadcast to the world from BBC microphones less than twenty-four hours later. "No one has been a more consistent opponent of Communism than I have," he said, and he would now "unsay no word that I have spoken about it." But "all this fades away before the spectacle that is now unfolding." What he now saw was the Russian people of "ten thousand villages where the means of existence is wrung so hardly from the soil, but where there are still primordial human joys, where maidens laugh and children play"—a people upon whom advanced "in hideous onslaught the Nazi war machine with its clanking, heel-clicking, dandified Prussian officers," its "dull, drilled, docile, brutish masses of . . . Hun soldiery." And "[b]ehind all this glare, behind all this storm," he saw "that small group of villainous men who plan, organise, and launch this cataract of horrors upon mankind. . . ." Responding to all this, "can you doubt what our policy will be? We have but one aim and one single, irrevocable purpose. We are resolved to destroy Hitler and every vestige of the Nazi regime. From this nothing will turn us—nothing. We will never parley, we will never negotiate with Hitler or any of his gang.* We shall fight him by land, we shall fight him by sea, we shall fight him in the air, until, with God's help, we have rid the earth of his shadow and liberated its peoples from his yoke. Any man or state who fights on against Nazidom will have our aid. Any man or state who marches with Hitler is our

---

*The "unconditional surrender" formula that Roosevelt would announce at Casablanca in January 1943, allegedly to Churchill's complete surprise, is here clearly implied, if not actually stated, by Churchill himself. If it "prolonged the war," as is commonly charged (mistakenly, in this author's opinion), Churchill is equally with Roosevelt "to blame" for it, though the burden of this complaint has generally been placed exclusively upon Roosevelt's shoulders.

foe. . . . That is our policy and that is our declaration. It follows, therefore, that we shall give whatever help we can to Russia and the Russian people. We shall appeal to all our friends and allies in every part of the world to take the same course and pursue it, as we shall, faithfully and steadfastly to the end. . . . [Hitler] wishes to destroy the Russian power because he knows that if he succeeds in this he will be able to bring back the main strength of his army and air force from the East and hurl it upon this island, which he knows he must conquer or suffer the penalty of his crimes. He hopes . . . that all this may be accomplished before winter comes, and that he can overwhelm Great Britain before the Fleet and air power of the United States may intervene. . . . [T]hen the scene will be clear for the final act, without which all his conquests would be in vain—namely, the subjugation of the Western Hemisphere to his will and to his system. The Russian danger is therefore our danger and the danger of the United States, just as the cause of any Russian fighting for his hearth and home is the cause of free men and free peoples in every quarter of the globe."[12]

This ringing declaration, though it was persuasive of millions of fervently anti-Communist Americans, was but feebly echoed, publicly, by the Roosevelt administration. The President's extreme caution continued. He anticipated the isolationist reaction that would in fact be expressed during the coming week. Senator Burton K. Wheeler would say: "I don't think the American people will stand for us to tie up with the Communists. . . . Now we can just let Joe Stalin and the other dictators fight it out." Senator Bennett Clark would say: "Stalin is as bloody-handed as Hitler. I don't think we should help either one." Senator Taft would say: "The victory of Communism in the world would be far more dangerous to the United States than a victory of Fascism." Taft's fellow Ohioan, Representative Frederick C. Smith, would say: "There is no doubt that any union between ourselves and Russia will operate strongly to encourage the further development of Communism in this country." And the same sentiments would be voiced in chorus by isolationist newspapers, one of which (Hearst's *New York Journal-American*) would go so far as to "hope that Occidental peace can still be made and Europe united against the expansion of Asiatic Communism." Roosevelt was uncertain of how widely such opinions as these were shared by his fellow countrymen. He was determined to preserve his own self-perceived position as the necessary focus of an ultimate "national unity." He was unwilling to commit himself to any of the options he perceived as open to him until one of them (in itself and in the timing of his action upon it) *felt* right to him. None of them now did. In typical fashion, therefore, he decided *not* to decide but instead to "wait and see" how things developed. He made no radio broadcast about the Nazi-Soviet clash. He issued no formal press statement of his own on the subject. He contented himself with approving an utterly innocuous statement of the U.S. "position" drafted in vacuous, repetitious State Department prose by Sumner Welles (he was then acting secretary; Hull was again ill) and brought to the presidential bedroom by its drafter early in the morning of June 23. Roosevelt read it while still in bed. The "immediate issue" facing "the people of the United States" was whether or not Hitler's "plan for universal conquest" was "to be successfully halted and defeated," it said. "That is the present issue which faces a realistic America. It is the issue at this moment which most directly involves our own national defense and the security of the New World in which we live." The "opinion of this Government, consequently," was that "any defense against Hitlerism, any rallying of the forces opposing Hitlerism . . . will hasten the eventual downfall of the present German leaders, and will therefore redound to the benefit of our own national defense and the security of the New World in which we live." To this banality Roosevelt added in his own handwriting what Welles later described as "perhaps" the document's "most salient point"—a single sentence saying, "Hitler's armies are today the chief dangers of the Americas." Welles then hurried across the street to his State Department office, where the draft was put into final form for issuance at the department's regularly scheduled press conference a couple of hours later.[13]

Almost equally noncommittal as regards aid to Russia were Roosevelt's published words and deeds in the immediately following days. He ordered unfrozen some $40 million of Soviet funds in the United States that had been frozen when those of the European Axis powers were. He told his press conference on June 24 that he favored giving the Russians whatever aid it was possible for the United States to give but that Britain would continue to have first call upon American resources and that, having received no Russian request for aid, he had no idea what the Russians might need. He added that, in any case, American aid could become important only if the war on the eastern front were a long one, thus obliquely indicating an argument against the rushing of war material to Russia: such material seemed likely to become Nazi property in short order. On June 25 he announced that the Neutrality Act would not be applied by him to the Soviet Union (the legal justification for such non-application was dubious), which meant that American ships might legally deliver goods to such Soviet ports as yet remained in Soviet hands; but this in turn meant relatively little since the all-season Baltic Sea ports were now in Hitler's hands, the approaches to Soviet Black Sea ports were effectively closed off by German aircraft based in Greece, and the approaches to the Barents Sea port of Murmansk, which itself was icebound for many months each year, were rendered hazardous in the extreme by German aircraft based in Norway.[14]

III

MEANWHILE Roosevelt, directly and through Hopkins, was receiving much expert opinion and advice out of which, joined with his own intuitive judgments, his mind was being gradually made up.

On June 23, Secretary Stimson reported to him the conclusions unanimously reached during a conference that day with Chief of Staff Marshall and top officers of the general staff's War Plans Division. Germany would "be thoroughly occupied in beating Russia for a minimum of one month and a possible maximum of three months," wrote Stimson, which meant a one- to three-month "breathing spell" for the West. During it there would be no attempt to invade the British Isles, no determined effort to prevent the U.S. occupation of Iceland; there would be a reduction of German "pressure" on West Africa, Dakar, South America, and "probably . . . Libya and the Mediterranean." The military experts "were unanimously of the belief that this precious and unforeseen period of respite should be used to push with utmost vigor our movements in the Atlantic theater of operations. They were unanimously of the feeling that such pressure on our part was the right way to help Britain, to discourage Germany, and to strengthen our own position of defense against our most imminent danger." A few days later, Hopkins received and passed on to Roosevelt an estimate of the Russian situation by top British military authorities. It accorded closely with the American appreciation but was somewhat more tentative in its conclusions, being slightly less certain of a quick Russian collapse. "It is possible that the *first phase* [present author's italics], involving the occupation of Ukraine and Moscow, might take as little as three, or as long as six weeks, or more," the British wrote, which meant that an "attempted invasion of the United Kingdom may now be considered to be temporarily postponed." But only temporarily, they emphasized. If the German campaign were "a lightning one, say from three to four weeks' duration," the Germans might be regrouped in the West for an invasion attempt within seven to ten weeks from now. Nothing was said by either set of experts about aid to Russia. If their estimates were accurate, it would be impossible for such aid to be got to its destination in time, and in sufficient quantity, to affect the outcome, and whatever was sent would be wasted or, worse, would feed the Nazi war machine.[15]

But Roosevelt was not inclined to accept such expert advice uncritically; he felt it to be colored, if not in good part determined, by strong prejudices against communism and the Communist state, prejudices he himself did not share to anything like the same degree. He believed and told close associates that the ultimate differences between an industrialized Communist state and an industrialized capitalist state were not as great as was commonly believed and that, as decades passed, the differences were likely to shrink; as the United States became increasingly a planned economy and the Soviet Union increasingly democratic, the two systems would come to resemble one another more and more closely.[16] Meanwhile, and certainly at this moment, totalitarian communism was not a threat to American survival; Nazi-Fascist totalitarianism most emphatically was. Roosevelt therefore listened sympathetically to advice, radically different from that of the military men, which came to him, again most often through Hopkins, from the former ambassador to the Soviet Union, multimillionaire Joseph E. Davies, who was currently a special assistant to Secretary Hull dealing with war emergency problems and policies.

During his Moscow tenure, from November 1936 to June 1938, when the great Stalin purges were at their height or hideous depth, Davies had pleased Roosevelt and earned the bitter contempt of his own foreign service staff (it included Soviet experts Charles E. Bohlen and George F. Kennan) by presenting the President with admiring reports and approving appraisals of the Soviet government and its acts—the kind of reports and appraisals that the President wished to believe true, as Davies knew.* He was persuaded, or persuaded himself, that the forced "confessions" of treason by Old Bolsheviks in staged trials were valid and that the sentence of death passed on each of them was therefore justified under Soviet law; he said so in his reports to Washington. Of Stalin the man he wrote, "His demeanor is kindly, his manner . . . simple, his . . . expression of reserve strength and poise very marked. . . . He gave me the impression of being sincerely modest." But this impression, the one Stalin aimed to make, did not differ from that made on the much more knowledgeable and highly critical George Kennan, who described Stalin's manner as "simple, quiet, unassuming" with "no striving for effect." ("An unforewarned visitor would never have guessed what depths of calculation, ambition, love of power, jealousy, cruelty, and sly vindictiveness lurked behind this unpretentious facade," Kennan added. "Stalin's greatness as a dissimulator was an integral part of his greatness as a statesman.") In general, Davies was a shrewd observer and a succinctly accurate reporter of what he saw, especially in his reports of the swift industrialization progress being made under the Five-Year Plans and in his consequent assessments of Soviet material and military strength. Even his assessments of the personalities, the primary motivations, and the thought processes of top Soviet officials had proved more accurate, in Roosevelt's view, than many made by people reputed to be Russian "experts." His vision unblinkered or distorted by ideological preconceptions, he had clearly seen what others had failed to see, namely, that a Nazi-Soviet non-aggression pact was almost certain to result from Chamberlain's repeated rebuffs of Litvinov's efforts toward a "united front" against Hitler. And of all this, Roosevelt was gratefully appreciative, writing Davies in January 1940: ". . . your reports . . . from Moscow were extremely valuable. You exercised a happy faculty in evaluating events at hand and determining with singular accuracy their probable effect on future developments."[17]

---

*In this summer of 1941, Davies was preparing for publication in late autumn a collection of his official dispatches to Washington, along with diary excerpts and letters and memoranda he'd written since leaving Moscow, all of them carefully edited to remove material that might discredit the Kremlin. Entitled *Mission to Moscow,* it would become a huge best-seller and the basis of a commercially successful motion picture that could not have been more glowingly admiring of the Stalin regime had it been produced by the propaganda arm of the Comintern. Stalin and his colleagues were reportedly much amused by the movie when it was screened for them in the Kremlin.

Hence the respect with which the White House listened to Davies's emphatic prediction, immediately following the Russian invasion, that "the extent of the resistance of the Red Army will surprise and amaze the world" and that "even though Hitler takes a substantial part of the Ukraine his troubles will then just begin." A few days later, lunching with Acting Secretary Sumner Welles, Davies "urged that the United States" follow "promptly and vigorously" Churchill's lead in promising and expediting "all-out" aid to Russia "as allies" in order to strengthen Stalin's resistance to any peace overtures Hitler might make if he managed to take White Russia, Moscow, and the Ukraine. Stalin's yielding to Hitlerian blandishments was unlikely in the extreme, in Davies's opinion—he stressed "the tendency of the people to rally around the Government in power in the face of an attack upon their homes and 'Holy Mother Russia' "—but "human nature is human nature," and if all or most of European Russia were in the conqueror's hands, Stalin, despite his experience of the worthlessness of Hitler's pledged word, just might be tempted to listen to Hitler's offer of a peace based on the "then status quo," a peace that would permit Stalin "to find his outlet" to the rest of the world through "China, possibly India." Such temptation would *certainly* be resisted if Stalin were absolutely convinced that the Soviet Union was not being used "to pull our chestnuts out of the fire" but was being treated as a highly respected champion of a cause shared with the Allies. ("Vis-à-vis Japan," Davies would write in a later memo to Hopkins, "it is obviously to our advantage to have a friendly Russia at Japan's rear.")[18]

On the following day, July 8, Davies was in the Oval Office as witness to the swearing-in of his "old friend Jim Byrnes" as associate justice of the U.S. Supreme Court, following which he went with Harry Hopkins to Hopkins's White House room "to talk about this Russian situation." On the wall "was a large military map of Europe," and Davies pointed out on that map "where the various industrial military manufacturing plants were located back of the Urals as long ago as 1937," this in support of his contention that if there were no "internal revolution which would overthrow Stalin and . . . put a Trotzkyite Pro-German in power," an eventuality rendered highly unlikely by the purges, the Stalin regime could maintain itself from behind the Urals and almost certainly would, provided Stalin was firmly assured of full U.S. and British support. "Word ought to be gotten to Stalin direct [from the President] that our attitude is 'all out' to beat Hitler and that our historic policy of friendliness to Russia still exists," Davies told Hopkins.[19]

Roosevelt entered into no direct correspondence with Stalin at this time, but Davies's influence upon him seems evident in the important interview he had with Soviet Ambassador Oumansky on July 10. Eleven days earlier, during the period of Stalin's incapacitation, Soviet Foreign Minister Molotov had presented the U.S. ambassador in Moscow, Laurence Steinhardt, with a first schedule of Soviet requirements while simultaneously expressing doubt that, despite Roosevelt's press conference statement of two days before, any significant

American aid would actually be forthcoming. This first schedule was impressive both in size (its estimated total cost was $1.8 billion) and in its inclusion of rolling mills for light alloys and machinery for airplane manufacture, cracking plants for aviation gasoline, machinery for tire manufacture, and other items indicative of a Soviet intention to continue fighting even though the industrial cities of western Russia were overrun. Roosevelt now told Oumansky, in the form of a pledge, that whatever orders of an urgent nature the Soviet government immediately placed in the United States would be filled to the fullest possible extent consistent with the need for also supplying Britain. He simultaneously stressed that whatever was sent now of such urgent nature should (must) actually be delivered in Russia by October 1. Clearly, if Roosevelt were not "staking everything on the chance that the Red armies could hold out until the onset of winter," as William L. Langer and S. Everett Gleason have written,[20] he was staking far more than his professional military advisers thought wise.

For at that moment and as July further advanced, it did not appear to most Allied military experts that their initial assessments were mistaken to any high degree. The Germans' grand strategical aim of annihilating the bulk of the Russian army as near the western Russian frontier as possible through a series of giant lightning encirclements, thereby preventing Russia's trading of "scorched earth" for time until the fearsome Russian winter came on, the strategy Napoleon had found catastrophic*—this aim was, it seemed, being achieved. By mid-July the Stalin line of defensive fortifications, stretching and twisting from Narva on the Gulf of Finland to the Black Sea near Odessa, had been breached by all three German army groups. In the north, German armored columns had thrust well beyond Ostrov toward their ultimate objective, Leningrad. In the center, 290,000 Russian troops trapped in the Minsk pocket had surrendered with a loss of 2,500 tanks and 1,500 artillery pieces while German armor pushed far beyond Minsk to complete an even larger encirclement, pocketing at least twenty-five Russian divisions centered on Vitebsk, Mogilev, Smolensk. Here the Germans soon had in hand another 310,000 prisoners, 3,200 tanks, 3,100 guns. This center army group had in less than four weeks covered half the distance between their Polish launching line and Moscow, whose capture in 1941 would have a far more devastating effect upon the Soviet Union than its capture by Napoleon had had upon the Russia of 1812; Moscow was now a major industrial center as well as the hub of western Russia's rail transport system. To the south, German armor was within ten miles of Kiev and was arching southward toward Odessa. It was estimated by the German command, in the

---

*One of the great American publishing successes of the early spring of 1942 would be a new edition of Tolstoy's *War and Peace,* with a foreword by literary critic Clifton Fadiman that vividly analogized the Hitlerian and Napoleonic invasions of Russia.

second week of July, that they had destroyed 89 of the 169 identified divisions they had encountered since the attack began—and Hitler, it will be recalled, had told Mussolini on June 21 that "all available Russian forces are [now] at our border."

But had they been?

To the Germans' surprise and growing unease—to the Allied observers' equal surprise but growing hope—the Russian military effort, despite frightful losses, showed no signs of collapse as July wore on. Indeed, resistance grew stronger as the Russian armies were driven eastward. There were reports of massive atrocities behind the German lines, atrocities of which the victims were not only Jews but also Slavs and which were carried out not by gangs of soldiers out of control, but coldly, deliberately, on orders from supreme headquarters, by special units trained to torture and murder. The survival chances of Russian troops taken prisoner were said to be low. And the spreading knowledge among the Russian troops that this was so could not but increase the stubbornness, the ferocity, of their resistance, their determination when surrounded never to surrender, but either to fight their way out or fight to the death. Moreover, new Russian formations, theretofore unidentified, began to show up in the front lines. When these were used up by the furious battle, as many of them soon were, they were replaced by still other new formations. New regiments, even whole new divisions, suddenly appeared as if conjured up, magically, out of nothing. It became increasingly clear that Hitler and his top officers had been badly mistaken: far from concentrating all available troops at the frontier, the Russian high command had maintained in the east reserve forces of unknown but evidently great size. ("I realized soon after the attack was begun that everything that had been written about Russia was nonsense," German Field Marshal Rundstedt would tell Allied interrogators after the war; and German Army Chief of Staff Halder would write into his diary on August 11, 1941: "At the beginning we reckoned with some 200 enemy divisions and we have already identified 360.")[21]

Nor did the enormous quantities of matériel destroyed or captured by the Germans prove immediately irreplaceable. Moscow's urgent pleading for great material aid from the West indicated needs that must be supplied to assure Russia's long-term survival; it seemed evident that her unaided material strength would not permit the launching and maintaining of any massive counteroffensive; but it appeared that for some years past there had been under way a strategic relocation of factories whereby much of the industrial might formerly concentrated west of Moscow had been transported by rail eastward and reestablished beyond the Urals and that there had been a furious acceleration of such relocation since the invasion began. Also there had obviously been since 1939 a massive stockpiling of weaponry and strategic goods east of Moscow. New fighter and bomber formations began to make their appearance in the Russian skies. New artillery pieces amply supplied with ammunition took their toll of the advancing Germans; the antiaircraft defenses of Moscow proved so strong and the German plane losses over that city so heavy that the Germans would soon abandon their effort to reduce the city from the air.

IV

AT this juncture—that is, during the first six or seven weeks of the Russian invasion—the fate of the Allies and world democracy depended as heavily upon the workings of the Roosevelt mind and spirit as it had ever done. But at this juncture, as was not the case at several others, the persistence of his caution and suspension of judgment, which was still to some extent determined by ill health,* worked in a way fortunate for the cause of freedom. He did not commit American resources immediately, in the amount urged by the British high command, to the defense of the Middle East, but neither did he accept and act upon the American high military command's view that Britain's Middle Eastern position was indefensible (the Germans might seize Gibraltar, might block the Suez Canal, at any moment) and that therefore the whole of the British-American effort should be concentrated in the Battle of the Atlantic. "He shares the belief that British chances in the Middle East are not too good" but "is inclined to support continuing the campaign" there, Hopkins would tell Churchill and the British chiefs of staff in late July; his opinion on the matter remained tentative because he didn't fully understand "your problems" in that region, having "never been given a comprehensive explanation of " Britain's "broad" Middle Eastern strategy.[23] As we have seen, he committed himself to aid to Russia, but in a way and amount that would not dangerously compromise either the Atlantic effort or the Middle Eastern effort should Russia collapse before the dread Russian winter closed down. In sum, he kept all his major options open pending his receipt of information on which to base decisions that were final, irrevocable—and he now moved to obtain that information in a form he could absolutely trust.

He sent Harry Hopkins again to Europe to gather it.

---

*When Stimson chided him on June 29 for depending excessively on Gallup polls for decision making, he replied defensively that he "had been feeling so mean" and had no "pep." His lack of zest seemed evident in his perfunctory delivery of an informal address dedicating the Franklin D. Roosevelt Library at Hyde Park on the following day—a library that, beginning at midnight of that June 30, was to be administered through a presidentially appointed board of trustees by the National Archivist of the United States. The dedication of any library is "an act of faith," he said. Since this one was a national library, it testified to this nation's belief "in the past . . . in the future" and "above all . . . in the capacity of its own people so to learn from the past that they can gain in judgement in creating their own future." Among the appointed library trustees were Secretary of the Treasury Morgenthau, Postmaster General Frank Walker, historian Samuel Eliot Morison, and Harry Hopkins.[22] Two weeks later Roosevelt felt better but was still not fully recovered.

. . .

After dinner on Friday, July 11, Roosevelt and Hopkins, alone together in the Oval Room, talked far into the night about the world situation, with particular attention to a) the Nazi threat to the Atlantic lifeline; b) loud isolationist charges currently being made that the British illegally used lend-lease goods for lucrative trade with South America, charges that Hull with his religious devotion to free trade was disposed to listen to with a remarkably sympathetic ear; c) industrial production problems that were adversely affecting lend-lease shipments; d) difficulties stemming from the ill-defined official relationship in London between defense expediter Averell Harriman and Ambassador Winant; and e) the desirability, which Roosevelt felt was great, of his meeting Churchill face-to-face in some out-of-the-way place as soon as possible. As regards point a), Roosevelt tore from a *National Geographic* magazine a map of the North Atlantic and drew upon it a thick penciled line that ran northward along Longitude 26 through the Azores to a point some two-hundred-odd miles southwest of Reykjavík, Iceland, then curved east and north two hundred miles out from the Icelandic shore. It very liberally defined the Western Hemisphere that Roosevelt proposed to police with American warships. "Police," however, remained still undefined save by its implied intent to free British convoy escorts for use on what would soon become famous as the "Murmansk run."[24] (This sea route around Norway through the Barents Sea whereby supplies were just beginning to be moved from Britain to the Soviet Union was extremely dangerous, as has been indicated, since in the Arctic at the height of summer there was no cover of darkness and virtually the whole of the route was within striking distance of land-based German planes.) As regards point d), it will be recalled that when the Harriman mission was established to handle lend-lease affairs at the English end, Roosevelt had instructed Harriman to report to him and the State Department directly and not through the U.S. embassy, though the mission was headquartered in the embassy building on Grosvenor Square. This meant that Churchill and his government also dealt with Harriman directly and did not confine such dealings strictly to lend-lease matters, since Harriman was in more direct and intimate contact with the White House than the ambassador was. The ambassador was merely "kept informed," and not always promptly or fully. This led inevitably to confusions of political with economic considerations, of policy making with policy implementation (the two were practically inseparable in the economic field), and to personal tensions between Harriman and Winant despite the fact that the two men greatly liked and respected one another and were at great pains to avoid frictions.[25]

On the following morning, Saturday, Hopkins breakfasted with Sidney Hillman. No record has been preserved of what the two men said over their breakfast food, but their subject was production and they must at least have touched upon the failure of OPM thus far to achieve anything close to the degree of industrial mobilization that the President had called for and that was so urgently necessary. A huge portion of America's productive capacity was not now being used for defense at all because it resided in small factories that, when defense contracts were handed out, had been ignored by procurement officers of the U.S. Army, by OPM's dollar-a-year men (most of them remained on the payrolls of the companies that had granted them leave and that now received hugely lucrative government orders), and by the big contractors when they subcontracted. An official OPM press release just last week had revealed that fifty-six corporations held three-fourths of the dollar value of all the government contracts thus far let, this despite the fact that the bulk of America's total industrial production had come in preceding years not from these few dozen huge corporations, but from many hundreds of plants too small to be noticed by the army or by Knudsen's side of OPM. A good many of these smaller plants had actually been forced to close down in recent months, idling thousands of workers, because they could not obtain the raw materials they needed for continued non-defense manufacture.[26]

Sometime after breakfast Hopkins talked again briefly with the President, who left the White House shortly before noon for his usual weekend cruise on the *Potomac*. Hopkins, who had expected to go with him, lunched instead with Sumner Welles in the White House, reviewing with him the Harriman-Winant situation and some of the diplomatic issues that had lately arisen between Washington and London. He filled the rest of his day with a conference on supplies with his lend-lease second in command, General Burns; a conference on shipping with Admiral H. L. Vickery; and dinner at the British embassy as guest of Lord Halifax. He got no extra rest that night in preparation for what was bound to be an extremely arduous journey. He was physically tired, if spiritually energized, by the excitement of his mission when, on Sunday morning, July 13, he boarded a B-17 (Flying Fortress) bomber that took him via Montreal to Gander, Newfoundland, where his flight eastward was delayed by bad weather. He had a day of relaxation during which he fished for rainbow trout with Colonel Elliott Roosevelt of the U.S. Army Air Force; Elliott was stationed at Gander.[27] From Gander he flew aboard a B-24 (Liberator) bomber, one of twenty-one that were being ferried across the Atlantic to Prestwick, Scotland, where he arrived in almost as bad shape as he had been in when Brendan Bracken met him at the airport near Poole the previous January. But now as then he made no concessions to his ill health; he insisted upon immediate departure by train southward to meet Churchill in London on July 16.

He was accompanied on the train by Harriman, who, having just returned from his inspection trip to the Middle East, had come to Prestwick to meet his friend. One may be sure that as the two rode southward together, Hopkins brought up the ticklish question of the working relationship between Harriman and Winant. (Several days later he told the U.S. embassy's military attaché,

General Raymond Lee: "I have given Harriman the most strict and explicit in-structions not to touch anything which is in any way political. That is the am-bassador's business, and his alone. I also told Churchill that we had at that moment in England the best, the finest, and most highly qualified man for am-bassador that we have had for twenty-five years, and a man who is a sincere friend of Great Britain, and that therefore he [Churchill] must deal with Winant direct and fully in all matters which have any political aspect whatever."[28] This, alas, would effect little improving change in the situation because the adminis-trative arrangement in which the situation was rooted remained unchanged.) We may be sure, too, that Harriman spoke at length of the Middle Eastern situation as he assessed it: "the need for a definite commitment of American aid to the Middle East; the overall shortage of spare parts; poor road and rail transporta-tion; the incredible waste of equipment the British troops had never been trained to use; and above all else, the need for a single commander with overall respon-sibility for the defense of the Middle East."[29] Churchill had relieved the ex-tremely tired Wavell of his Middle Eastern command while Harriman was in the Middle East, in good part because of the failure of a Wavell offensive against Rommel ("Battleaxe") designed to relieve besieged Tobruk, a failure that was itself due in good part to tank and armored vehicle failures resulting from inade-quate technical maintenance (Harriman stressed to Hopkins the urgent need in the Middle East for American technicians). Wavell had been sent to command British forces in India. General Sir Claude Auchinleck had been brought from the Indian command to take Wavell's former place. But, like Wavell, Auchin-leck had no command authority over the British Middle Eastern naval com-mander (Admiral of the Fleet Sir Andrew Cunningham) or the British Middle Eastern air force commander (Air Marshal Arthur Tedder), nor did either of them have authority over him. Each was his own boss. Each was critical and suspicious of the others. Clearly, that close intermeshing of ground, sea, and air forces that was essential to victorious warfare could be achieved only if all the services were placed under a single strong supreme commander.

Hopkins arrived in London, somewhat less ill but even more tired. He went directly from the train station to No. 10 Downing Street, where Churchill greeted him as a personal friend. It was a warm sunny day. Churchill suggested that he and his American guest repair to the garden behind the Prime Minister's official residence, where the two had a long, wide-ranging conversation. At the outset Hopkins told his host that the long preparations for a face-to-face meet-ing between President and Prime Minister were, on the American side, con-cluded. The President, advised on this by the commander of the American Atlantic Fleet, Admiral Ernest J. King, proposed that the meeting be held in the second week of August on Placentia Bay, Newfoundland, where an American naval base Argentia was being established as one result of the 1940 destroyers-for-bases deal. Churchill promptly agreed to the meeting, though saying that the "actual secret rendezvous need not be settled till later."[30] He added that the British cabinet would, he was sure, approve. Hopkins then showed the Prime Minister the map page Roosevelt had torn from *National Geographic,* whereupon Churchill, though pleased by this evidence of another step toward U.S. belligerency, stressed the need for a precise definition of "policing," a definition to be arrived at through discussion between British and American naval officials. Later that afternoon Hopkins, at Churchill's invitation, became the first foreigner ever to attend a meeting of the British cabinet, going from that meeting to Claridge's, where, at long last, he had a full night of sleep.

There followed, for him, ten days of whirlwind activity. He attended other meetings of the British cabinet as Churchill's guest, somewhat to the disgust of Alexander Cadogan, the permanent undersecretary for British foreign affairs. ("Cabinet at 5," noted Cadogan in his diary on July 24. "Hopkins there again. This is rather absurd, and we had to get rid of him before the end on the excuse that we were going to discuss home affairs, and then discussed America and the Far East!")[31] He obtained, with Winant, information to refute the charges of British misuse of lend-lease matériel and cabled Oscar Cox, who was functioning as his lend-lease "brain trust" in Washington, requesting the drafting by Cox of a presidential letter addressed to Churchill stressing that "section 4 of the Lend-Lease Act requires my [the President's] consent to any retransfers of lend-lease items by His Majesty's Government" and that any distribution "through commercial channels in the United Kingdom and in other parts of the Empire of necessity involves a retransfer and my consent."* He conferred on a widely various host of problems with, among others, Lord Beaverbrook, the minister of supply; Ernest Bevin, the minister of labor; Field Marshal Sir John Dill, chief of the imperial general staff; General Sir John Kennedy, who headed the British equivalent of the U.S. Army's War Plans Division; and numerous other high British officials. He very actively participated in two conferences on grand strategy attended by Churchill, the British chiefs of staff, and the U.S. Navy and Army observers stationed in England—conferences in which differences between the American and British points of view on the Middle East and on the proper response to Japanese aggression in the Far East were thoroughly explored. He was alone with Churchill, often for hours, each day—was twice a weekend houseguest at Chequers, where he came under the maternal care of

---

*In the event, neither a first nor a second draft of this letter was actually signed and sent by Roosevelt, who was uneasy over the effect it might have upon his personal relationship with the Prime Minister. Under heavy pressure by the State Department, however, the British on September 10, 1941, issued a white paper "in which they accepted a wide range of controls over the re-export of lend-lease goods," as Warren Kimball writes in his editorial note on page 232 of *Churchill and Roosevelt: The Complete Correspondence* (on that page and the two following, both drafts are printed). "Many of the restrictions would apparently aid American business in penetrating markets in the British Empire which London merchants had previously dominated. In this case political necessity outweighed economic considerations and Britain acceded to American demands."

Churchill's wife, Clementine, who saw to it that he received as much rest and relaxation as his circumstances permitted.

These last permitted much relaxation on only the first of these Chequers weekends—the second was crowded and straining in the extreme, as we shall see—but even this relatively quiet first weekend was by no means free for him of important business.

For one thing, Ivan Maisky, the Soviet ambassador in London, came on Saturday, July 19, to hand-deliver Stalin's long-awaited reply to two personal messages Churchill had sent him (the first nearly two weeks ago), and Churchill promptly involved Hopkins in the ensuing transaction. Stalin, after expressing "gratitude for the two personal messages," pleaded for the immediate establishment by the British of a fighting front in northern France that "besides diverting Hitler's forces from the East, would make impossible the invasion of Britain by Hitler."[32] The plea, which Maisky urgently orally endorsed, was so at odds with realistic possibility that Churchill received it with some impatience. (In his written reply to Stalin he would point out that the Germans had "forty divisions in France alone"; had air superiority over a coast that "bristles with cannon, wire, pill-boxes, . . . beach-mines"; that there were at the height of summer "less than five hours" of a "darkness" that was itself nominal since the crucial areas were illuminated by masses of searchlights; and that, in consequence, any "attempt to" land "in force would . . . encounter a bloody repulse" while "petty raids would lead to fiascos doing far more harm than good to both of us.")[33] His impatience evidently showed. For when, following his talk with Maisky, he introduced the ambassador to Hopkins and left the two alone to converse in the Chequers drawing room, the ambassador quickly concluded that the American was more committed to all-out aid to the Soviet Union than the Prime Minister was and should therefore be further cultivated.

Returned to London, Maisky arranged through Winant a luncheon meeting with Hopkins, hosted by Winant in the American embassy on Tuesday, July 22—a meeting during which the Russian, though denying that his country's battle losses thus far presaged inevitable ultimate defeat, stressed that the current strain was dangerously great and could be relieved only by a "second front" in northern France. According to Maisky's later account, Winant fully openly agreed that such a front should be opened at the earliest possible moment. Hopkins was less committal. He said that the United States, being a "nonbelligerent" at that moment, was in no position "to help you in regard to a second front" but might be able to do a good deal "as regards supplies." "What do you require?" he asked. "Couldn't you tell me?" Maisky could not; information about war needs and progress on the eastern front was tightly controlled in Moscow; and the ambassador therefore suggested that Hopkins go there, where he would be warmly welcomed, to obtain it. Obviously intrigued, Hopkins said he would think about it.[34]

He did think much about it in the following hectic days, during which he became increasingly convinced that none of the great decisions in the making of which he as the President's agent was involved—decisions about the Battle of the Atlantic, the Middle East, the Far East, and the relative emphasis to be given each of these—could be wisely, realistically made in the absence of solid accurate information about the fighting strength, fighting will, and survival chances of the Soviet Union. The accuracy of every calculation made at the forthcoming meeting of Churchill and Roosevelt depended upon such information. And the number and importance of these calculations grew in proportion to the expansion, as the days passed, of the conference's purpose and implied agenda. Roosevelt's initial idea had been that he and the Prime Minister would be accompanied to Placentia Bay by a minimum of staff—that the conference would be a very intimate simple informal meeting of their two minds—and with this Churchill had at first agreed.

But the Prime Minister soon decided, and persuaded Hopkins, that to do what the President suggested would be to miss a shining opportunity to advance greatly the developing alliance between Britain and the United States. He was to cross the Atlantic on the great battleship *Prince of Wales,* which was just returning to sea duty following repair of the considerable damage done her during the *Bismarck* encounter; there would be plenty of room aboard for a considerable company and plenty of time, as the battleship sailed westward, for the development of expert ideas on the subjects to be discussed. On July 25, Churchill cabled Roosevelt: "Cabinet has approved my leaving. Am arranging, if convenient to you, to sail August 4, meeting you sometime 8th-9th-10th. . . . Am bringing First Sea Lord Admiral Pound, . . . Dill, and Vice-Chief Air (Marshal, Sir W.) Freeman. Am looking forward enormously to our talks. . . ."[35]

Roosevelt, at Hopkins's urging, had by then decided that he, too, should be accompanied by military advisers; he would bring with him Marshall, Stark, King, and Army Air Corps Chief Henry H. ("Hap") Arnold. Ultimately the American company would total twenty, including Sumner Welles (Hull was still in Sulphur Springs, recuperating from his illness, but would not have been included in the party had he been well), Harriman (he was to fly home at once to report on the latest English developments, then go with Welles from Washington to Argentia), and Hopkins (he was to come with Churchill aboard the *Prince of Wales*). The British party, ultimately, would total twenty-one, including Cadogan and scientific adviser Lord Cherwell (Professor Frederick Lindemann), who was one of the closest of Churchill's personal friends and upon whose ability to gather, organize, and analyze scientific and production data the Prime Minister greatly depended. This meeting's potential value and importance to the free world were obviously enormous. But how could the potential be realized if every conference deliberation was rendered tentative and dubious by ignorance of what was happening and likely to happen in Eastern Europe? How, behind such a veil of ignorance, could Hopkins himself deal effectively with the lend-lease operation for which he yet had primary responsibility? Realistic decisions concerning the allocation of available American resources between Britain and the Soviet Union were impossible in the absence of information only Moscow could supply and had thus far withheld. . . .

On the same day (Friday, July 25) that Churchill told Roosevelt of the British cabinet's approval of his westward voyage, Hopkins addressed to the President a lengthy cable drafted cooperatively by him and Winant.

Hopkins had by that time ascertained that the Royal Air Force Coastal Command had established an air route to Archangel in the Soviet Union from Invergordon in Scotland, using American PBY (Catalina) flying boats. It was a lengthy flight around northern Norway, rendered hazardous by the fact that when severe storms, which were frequent, were not buffeting the plane, it would run the risk of attack, in the virtually perpetual summer daylight of that northern region, from Norwegian-based German planes. To secure the Prime Minister's expediting blessing upon this enterprise, Hopkins had had to overcome Churchill's initially grave doubts that the object to be gained was worth the risk of the American's frail but exceedingly precious life (the Prime Minister deemed Hopkins's presence at Placentia Bay of vital importance to a true meeting of minds between himself and Roosevelt); only reluctantly had Churchill yielded to the argument that the wall of secrecy behind which the Stalinist government operated simply *must* be penetrated, and soon, and that Hopkins, speaking and acting for the President of the United States, was of all men the most likely to penetrate it. In his cable to Roosevelt, the one drafted cooperatively with Winant, Hopkins made a somewhat different argument in a studiedly casual tone. "I am wondering whether you think it important and useful for me to go to Moscow," he wrote. "Air transportation good and can reach there in twenty-four hours. I have a feeling that everything possible should be done to make certain that the Russians maintain a permanent front even though they be defeated in the immediate battle. If Stalin could in any way be influenced at a critical time I think it would be worth doing by a direct communication from you through a personal envoy. . . . Stalin would then know in an unmistakable way that we mean business on a long term supply job. . . . Am spending weekend with Prime Minister but message through Navy will reach me quickly. . . . Everyone here asks about you and are delighted to know that you are [at long last] in good health."[36]

The weekend at Chequers was, for Hopkins, crowded and stressful. "He had been working very long hours . . . and he showed it," remembered (years later) Quenton Reynolds, the then famous American foreign correspondent who had been invited to Chequers to help draft a speech, a very important one, which Hopkins was scheduled to deliver Sunday evening over the BBC, using the Prime Minister's Chequers microphone. "He was dog-tired" and had "a touch of grippe" (he thus invariably deprecated the flare-ups of his chronic illness) as, on

Saturday afternoon, in the bedroom assigned him and to which Reynolds had brought a typewriter, he outlined the substance and indicated the desired tone of his speech. He then lay down on his bed and took a desperately needed nap while Reynolds pounded out a rough speech draft. It seemed to Hopkins, when he awoke and read it, much "too strong" ("Hell, Quent," he complained with rueful grin, "you've got me declaring war on Germany," to which Reynolds replied, "We should have done that long ago"); he spent an hour or two "toning it down." Yet the final draft, as spoken the following evening by this closest of Roosevelt's associates, proved sufficiently "strong" to outrage American isolationist sentiment while, by the same token and to the same extent, inspiring and uplifting those to whom it was directly addressed. "I arrived here from America one week ago on business," Hopkins would say. "That business . . . the same as that of every other American . . . is the safeguarding of our heritage of freedom of thought and action. Right now, Hitler is seriously threatening this heritage of ours, a heritage which is yours." He had not come from America "alone," he would go on to say, but "in a bomber plane" accompanied by "twenty other bombers made in America," planes that "tonight may be dropping bombs on Brest, on Hamburg, on Berlin, safeguarding our common heritage. . . . The President is one with your Prime Minister in his determination to break the ruthless power of that sinful psychopath in Berlin."[37]

Roosevelt's reply to Hopkins's cable arrived at Chequers late that Saturday night and was read by Hopkins early Sunday morning. It was a further revelation of the absolute trust that Roosevelt placed in Hopkins as an extension of his own mind and purpose, a trust as great as that he had reposed in Louis Howe in prepresidential years and whose only precedent in American presidential history was Woodrow Wilson's use of Colonel House in 1912–1919. The missive said: "Welles and I highly approve Moscow trip and assume you would go in a few days. . . . I will send you tonight a message for Stalin." Hopkins at once took this to Churchill's bedroom, where the Prime Minister read it in bed and then immediately issued by phone to London the necessary expediting orders: Hopkins was to depart by train for Invergordon immediately following his radio broadcast, scheduled for nine-fifteen that evening; the PBY that was to fly him to Archangel would take off as early as possible on Monday.

The rest of that Sunday passed, for Hopkins, in a flurry of activity as he prepared for his trip and intermittently socialized with other Chequers guests (one of them was American newspaper columnist Dorothy Thompson), who had no notion the trip was being made. He arranged for his checkout in absentia from Claridge's and the delivering from his hotel suite to London's Euston Station of the small amount of personal luggage he deemed necessary. He arranged, through Winant's office, for a Russian visa on his passport, a task that required the tracking down of Ambassador Maisky, who was out of London for the weekend, also a task that would prove wholly unnecessary since no Russian official would so much as glance at the Hopkins passport. More important, he arranged to take with him to Moscow two American military experts whom Marshall, at Hopkins's request, had named, to provide and help gather technical information; they were Colonel [later General] Joseph T. McNarney, a reputed army organization and administrative genius, and Army Air Force Lieutenant John R. Alison, who was fully informed regarding the latest American plane developments and fully capable of digesting such technical information about Soviet airpower as was made available to him in Moscow.[38]

Early in the evening he received Roosevelt's promised message to Stalin. It said, in the flatulent style characteristic of State Department drafting: "Mr. Hopkins is in Moscow at my request for discussions with you personally and with such other officials as you may designate on the vitally important question of how we can most expeditiously and effectively make available the assistance which the United States can render to your country in its magnificent resistance to the treacherous aggression by Hitlerite Germany. . . . The visit will . . . , I feel, be invaluable by clarifying for us here in the United States your most urgent requirements so that we can reach the most practicable decisions to simplify the mechanics of delivery and speed them up. . . . I . . . think the immediate concern of both governments should be to concentrate on the matériel which can reach Russia during the next three months." There followed two sentences evidently penned by Roosevelt himself: "I ask you to treat Mr. Hopkins with the identical confidence you would feel if you were talking directly to me. He will communicate directly to me the views you express to him. . . ." Then: "May I express, in conclusion, the great admiration all of us in the United States feel for the superb bravery displayed by the Russian people in the defense of their liberty. . . ."[39]

The envelope containing the message was in Hopkins's inner breast coat pocket when, having broadcast his speech and been driven by Harriman to the station, he boarded his train in the last hour of that July 28. He was at that moment greatly agitated by the fact that he had with him no passport, having given it to Winant for the purpose of obtaining a Russian visa. But then, just as the train began its slow pullout from the smoky, gloomy train shed, Winant dashed up to thrust the visaed passport through the compartment's open window into the traveler's eager hand.

v

To Hopkins, as to others who watched from London and Washington, Red Russia, thickly veiled in a secretiveness rooted in fearful suspicions, had long seemed almost as remote and strange as the red planet Mars. His flight to Moscow was therefore, for him, a flight into the heart of a mystery that rendered memorable every detail of his journey. It was also a flight as devoid of creature comforts as it was full of danger, for the Catalina that took off in fouler weather than its pilot cared to fly in (he was ordered by London to do so) was an operational warplane having no accommodations for non-operational passengers. Its cabin was unheated, and Hopkins suffered much from the chill. He spent most of the twenty-four-hour flight in the machine gunner's seat in the "blister" near the tail end of the fuselage, looking for and half hoping to see (so that he might shoot down) a German plane. Small wonder that when the plane at last came down, late in the day, upon the harbor water at Archangel, Hopkins "was looking very tired," as the Catalina's pilot, Flight Lieutenant D. C. McKinley, wrote in his report of this mission. The Russian plane (actually it was an American Douglas, with Russian crew) that was to fly him to Moscow was not to take off until the following morning; but the full night's sleep he badly needed was denied him by the overwhelming hospitality of the admiral who commanded the Archangel naval base. He invited Hopkins and his companions to dine aboard the admiral's yacht, anchored in the azure Dvina River, where the dinner proved to be a multicourse banquet replete with fresh vegetables grown on farms around Archangel, fish, caviar, several meat dishes, and vodka, a great deal of Russian vodka, which has a higher alcoholic content than American whiskey and of which Hopkins partook as meagerly as possible, using bread thickly coated with caviar to cushion the fiery stuff's burning impact upon his remnant of a stomach. The banquet lasted four hours. Hopkins had had but two hours of fitful sleep when he boarded the plane next morning for the flight to Moscow.[40]

Yet he was wide awake, alert, eagerly observant, made so by the stimulating novel excitement of his mission, during the four hours of his flight due south. He looked down upon seemingly endless forests of pine and birch amid which lakes and ponds glinted and glittered here and there in slanting sunlight; then upon an agricultural country dotted with towns and villages; finally, excitingly, upon the great city that was his destination, spread out maplike below him. Moscow, capital of an atheistic state, was a city of churches; hundreds of gilt-domed churches gleamed in what was now a noonday sun. It was also a fortress city; scores of miles of brick wall traced in dull red lines a series of concentric circles, so that the city appeared to Hopkins's eyes as the gigantic hub of an immensely more gigantic wheel. Railroads and highways thrust outward from it, spokelike, in every direction. At the airport an imposing number of Soviet dignitaries made him welcome. Here, as at the outset of his direct contact with Soviet officialdom, there was an enormous amount of handshaking ("In Russia I shook hands as I have never shaken hands before," he later wrote); but here he was protected against an excess of Russian hospitality by the U.S. ambassador, Laurence A. Steinhardt, who whisked him off as soon as possible to Spasso House, the U.S. embassy, where, alarmed by Hopkins's evident near exhaustion, he insisted that his guest go at once to bed.

Within a couple of hours or so after he lay down, however, Hopkins was on his feet again, seeking out the ambassador. The two had then a long conversation, at the outset of which Hopkins said that the main purpose of his visit was to find out whether Russia's situation was as dire, as utterly hopeless, as it was deemed to be by the American military, including especially Major Ivan Yeaton, the embassy's military attaché. Steinhardt seemed inclined to believe it was not, that Russians fighting in defense of Holy Mother Russia against invaders of her sacred soil might well prove as unconquerable in 1941 as they had been in 1812; but he stressed that it was impossible for him or his military attaché or any other foreigner to know what was really happening. No foreign observers were permitted on the Russian front. The daily dole of official news contained more propaganda than reliable information, and no other channels of information were open to any foreign national. The embassy compound was a narrow island in a sea of distrust and suspicion or, more accurately, a luxurious prison (Spasso House was palatial) closely guarded by secret police and infiltrated by police spies. Embassy officials were trailed when they went anywhere, by car or on foot; no ordinary Russian citizen dared communicate freely and frankly with them; it was necessary to assume that every native servant hired in the embassy was an espionage agent. Hopkins nodded his sympathetic understanding (he knew that the British airmen who had flown him from Scotland were now confined on a houseboat in the Dvina; he would later learn that their every request to go ashore was brusquely denied), but he reiterated his determination to find answers to his questions. They would *have* to give him the information he wanted if they were to receive the American aid for which they pleaded. Steinhardt hoped Hopkins was right. At any rate, he said, they'd find out, or begin to, in a little more than twenty-four hours: they were scheduled to meet Stalin in the Kremlin at six-thirty tomorrow evening.

After a long night's sleep, his first sound sleep in forty-eight hours, Hopkins spent a relaxing day, a good portion of it in sight-seeing with Steinhardt and American photographer Margaret Bourke-White, who was in Russia on assignment from *Life* magazine. At a dress shop he bought, under Bourke-White's guidance, a dress for his daughter Diana and another for Betsey [Mrs. James] Roosevelt. At an antique shop specializing in old silver, he himself was presented by Steinhardt, as a souvenir gift, a silver teapot on which was engraved a picture of the Kremlin.[41] He was in the best physical shape possible for one who suffered such chronic disabilities as his when, shortly before the appointed hour, he rode with Steinhardt in an embassy car through late afternoon light to the multi-towered Kremlin wall and through a gate in that wall up a narrow street to a three-story yellow house whose plainness was accentuated by its location in the shadow of a great and ornate palace.

The room of that house into which Hopkins and Steinhardt were ushered a few minutes later was as plain as the house's exterior. It was a large room, but of no such intimidating size as Mussolini's famous office in Rome. A death mask of Lenin, under glass, adorned one wall. Much wall space was covered by maps—the best, thought Hopkins, that he had ever seen. Bookshelves near the desk contained what appeared to be statistical reference books. There were some plain armchairs and a plain, almost bare desk on which reposed a single telephone and a single pushbutton device for the summoning of secretaries.

And at first glance the man who now advanced upon his visitors, hand outstretched in greeting, was no more impressive than his immediate surroundings. Josef Stalin, clad in a plain gray jacket that bore no ornament of any kind and matching gray trousers that bagged at the knees above highly polished knee-high boots, was much shorter than he appeared to be in photographs; Hopkins was surprised to find himself looking down from his height of six feet upon a blocky figure standing, at most, five feet six. Yet at second glance the general visual impression this figure gave was of strength and toughness: heavy-boned, heavily muscled, broad of chest and shoulders, Stalin was "built like a football coach's dream of a tackle," as Hopkins later wrote. He appeared in excellent physical shape, hard as nails, though when Margaret Bourke-White photographed him next day standing beside Hopkins, each man with a cigarette in hand, the picture revealed him to have a paunch, small but sufficient in size to bulge his jacket perceptibly. His face fitted his figure, being also broad and heavy looking. It was far from handsome; it was the opposite of mobile. Sallow of complexion and pockmarked, with narrow-lidded eyes and a mustache thick enough to mask whatever expressiveness his lips might otherwise have had, it was a face that in repose appeared wooden, insensitive, as if carved from an oaken block. Bad teeth were revealed on the rare occasions when he laughed, generally sardonically, or spread open his lips in what impressed Hopkins as a "managed smile," also generally sardonic. These teeth were yellowed by tobacco smoke, for Stalin, though a pipe smoker, was also, like Hopkins, a chain-smoker of cigarettes; at the very outset of their interview he offered his guest a Russian cigarette, accepting an American cigarette in return. Though his present manner was affable and cordial, his voice was harsh, perhaps roughened by the effect upon his throat of constant smoking but also possibly expressive, one felt, of a harshly authoritarian temperament. He used this voice economically. His welcoming speech was succinct, nor did he use an unnecessary word, he never once repeated himself, during the conversation that began as soon as everyone was seated.[42]

With their sitting down, Hopkins lost whatever psychological advantage he might have gained from a continual "looking down" upon his host. Though short legged, Stalin was long of waist; when he was seated, his face was on a level with Hopkins's. And he looked into Hopkins's eyes with an initially rather disconcerting directness as the American stated that his purpose as the President's "personal representative" was simply to facilitate mutual understandings of their two governments at the highest level, which would in turn facilitate their cooperation in the crushing of Hitler. The President was convinced "that the most important thing to be done in the world today is to defeat Hitler and Hitlerism," and to this end he personally and "our Government" as a whole were determined "to extend all possible aid to the Soviet Union at the earliest possible time." Stalin did not so much as glance at the interpreter; he kept his hard gaze fixed upon his visitor as, replying to what had been said, he stressed the necessity to maintain a "minimum standard of morality" in the conduct of international affairs. Nations could not coexist that did not share such a standard. Pledged words must be honored, treaties must be adhered to; and since Germany knew "no such minimum moral standard," it was an "anti-social force in the world." It must be overcome. "Therefore," concluded Stalin, "our views [the American, the Russian] coincide." These introductory formalities out of the way, the two settled down to business with a single-minded concentration upon essentials that gave Hopkins an exhilarating sense of much important business being disposed of in the shortest possible time. Stalin answered questions quickly, unequivocally, with a frankness and fullness that were astonishing to the listening Steinhardt. Within a couple of hours, Stalin had provided the Americans a clearer sense of the Soviet Union's ruling intentions and attitudes than the embassy, for all its trying, had been able to achieve in the weeks since the invasion began.

Stalin stressed his immediate need for twenty thousand antiaircraft guns, the bulk of them highly mobile rapid-fire weapons of medium caliber (20 to 37 millimeters). These would enable him to release for front-line duty some two thousand fighter planes at present engaged in protecting behind-the-lines military objectives. He also needed large-caliber machine guns "for the defense of his cities" and a million rifles, of which, he had been told, the United States had a large supply of the same caliber as his own troops used. There was no need for American ammunition for these rifles; "we have plenty." Of long-term needs, he mentioned high-octane aviation gasoline and aluminum for airplane construction, these along with items on the list of needs already presented the American government by the Soviet ambassador. "Give us anti-aircraft guns, and the aluminum, and we can fight for three or four years," he said significantly. He laid somewhat less emphasis on the need for warplanes than Hopkins had expected him to do. The Russian air force, after the first few days, had more than held its own, he said, and its initial losses were far less than the German claimed. But he did badly need short-range bombers capable of operating 600 to 1,100 kilometers from their bases (that is, with a total range of 1,200 to 2,200 kilometers). As regards supply delivery routes, Stalin deemed the Archangel one the most practicable, despite its abundant hazards; it could be kept ice-free the year around by means of icebreakers, he said. The Persian Gulf–Iranian alternative was rendered dubious by Iran's inadequate railroads and highways and by the uncertain attitude of the Iranian government. Vladivostok was even less satisfactory because of its immense distance from the battle line, also because it and its approaches were vulnerable to attack from Japan—and Japan's attitude toward Russia, despite the non-aggression pact that Matsuoka had signed in Moscow, was as uncertain as Iran's. Hopkins then referred to two hundred Curtis P-40 planes now being delivered from America to Russia, most of them via England, and asked if Stalin would "care to have Lt. Alison," the aviation expert Hopkins had brought with him, "stationed in Archangel" for a time "in an advisory capacity." Stalin welcomed the suggestion. The remainder of the interview was concerned with the best use of Hopkins's severely limited time in the Soviet capital, it being decided that he would confer with Soviet General Yakovlev at ten o'clock that night, with Foreign Minister Molotov at three o'clock tomorrow afternoon, and with Stalin again at six-thirty tomorrow evening.

Hopkins, who had taken sufficient notes of the conversation to sustain his remarkably retentive memory when he wrote lengthy and detailed reports to the President of what was said, was by then enormously impressed by Stalin's intelligence and mastery of detail, his decisiveness and tough efficiency. He was heartened by Stalin's calm, seemingly absolute conviction that the present battle on Russian soil would not be decisive. Yet he still had doubts about Stalin's willingness to disclose the kind and amount of information, as regards the actual war situation, that Washington needed if it were to make up its own mind about Russia's survival chances—and these doubts were reinforced when, an hour later, accompanied by General McNarney and Major Yeaton, he engaged in technical discussions with General Yakovlev.

For Yakovlev obviously operated under rigid and severely limiting instructions from which he was afraid to deviate to the slightest degree. When asked for additions to the list of items Stalin had said were needed, he could think of none. To Hopkins's expressed surprise that no mention was made of tanks and anti-tank guns as a Russian need, he replied: "I am not empowered to say whether we do or do not need tanks or anti-tank guns." He refused to comment upon Hopkins's suggestion that a Soviet technical mission be established in Washington for the war's duration; that was something that must be taken up with Comrade Stalin, he said. Asked how heavy was the heaviest Russian tank, he said: "It's a good tank." Asked if Russian artillery had been able to stop German tanks, he said, "[O]ur artillery shoots any tank—conditions vary."[43]

More satisfactory was the interview the following afternoon with Molotov (Steinhardt accompanied Hopkins), this after Hopkins had had a long talk with British Ambassador Sir Stafford Cripps, most of which was devoted to the upcoming Argentia Conference. Yet during this Molotov interview, too, Hopkins had a sense of the deindividualizing, hence dehumanizing, effects of totalitarianism—a sense that when one talked on public matters to anyone not at the very apex of power in Moscow, one talked not to a human person, but to a machinelike element of the state. Even when talking to Stalin, as Hopkins would say a few months later, one felt one was talking "to a perfectly coordinated machine, an intelligent machine." The Soviet dictator, however, seemed almost vibrantly, humanly alive compared with his foreign minister. Stalin laughed now and then, if a short barking sardonic laugh, and some of his words revealed a "keen, penetrating" sense of sardonic humor. Molotov laughed not at all, seldom smiled, seemed utterly humorless; his bland, mustached, bespectacled countenance was wholly without expression; and though his intelligent eyes looked out hard through the glasses he wore, no one could look into them to discern any inner self, to glimpse inward thoughts or actual emotions. One soon doubted that Molotov had any.

The chief topic of their conversation was the rising menace of Japan. Hopkins, speaking the President's mind, stressed "the long-standing amicable relations between the United States and Russia, which the American public had come to accept as assuring stability in the north Pacific," and indicated, vaguely, tentatively, that the United States would act if Japan attempted a movement upon Siberia. He said he had "reason to believe" that such a move might be made if Russia lost the huge battle now raging on its soil. Molotov replied that Soviet-Japanese relations had "presumably" been defined by Matsuoka's conversations in Moscow in April, and by the pact that Matsuoka and Stalin had then signed, but he noted that there was governmental turmoil over foreign policy in Tokyo and that "the attitude of the new Japanese Government toward the Soviet Union" was "uncertain." (We now know that when the invasion of Russia began, the erratic, unstable Matsuoka pressed for immediate war upon the Soviet Union in accordance with the Tripartite Pact and that to get rid of him, the entire Konoye cabinet resigned on July 16, reconstituting itself two days later with almost the same personnel save that Admiral Toyoda was now foreign minister. But since Toyoda sided with bellicose General Hideki Tojo, who remained minister of war, the cabinet remained almost evenly divided between the nation's civil and military authorities as regards foreign policy. A policy statement that had issued from an Imperial Conference held on July 2, itself revelatory of sharp division between moderates and warmongers, remained in force. A key article said: "Our attitude with regard to the German-Soviet War will be based on the *spirit of* the Tri-Partite Pact [emphasis added]. However, we will not enter into the conflict for some time but will steadily proceed with military preparations against the Soviet and decide our final attitude independently.")[44] The Soviet government was "watching the situation with utmost care," said Molotov. As for actions the United States might take, none would be more likely to deter Japan from a Siberian adventure than a flat warning to the effect that the United States "would come to the assistance of the Soviet Union" if the latter were attacked. To this, Hopkins could reply only that Washington was greatly disturbed by Japan's Far Eastern aggressions and that, while the American people would certainly "not look with any favor on Japan gaining a further hold on Siberia . . . our attitude towards Japan is a reasonable one and . . . we have no desire to be provocative. . . ." He asked whether the Soviets would or could continue "rendering the substantial material assistance they had been giving Chiang Kai-shek." Molotov replied that aid to China would continue to the utmost extent permitted by the demands of the Hitler war but must, of course, be reduced; he hoped that the United States would be able to supply the difference.

Hopkins's second interview with Stalin at six-thirty that evening was by far the most important of all his Moscow conversations. This time neither Steinhardt nor anyone else accompanied him; for almost four hours he and Stalin were alone together, save for the interpreter and, for a minute or so on two or three occasions, a secretary summoned to answer a specific question; and by the interview's end, Stalin, stimulated and guided by an occasional Hopkins question, had presented with a gratifying frankness and fullness his personal "appreciation and analysis" of the Russo-German war.

Some 125 German divisions had attacked on June 22 a considerably smaller number of Russian divisions, said Stalin, for though the Russians had 180 divisions available at the start of the war, a great many of them were "well back of the line of combat" and could not immediately be brought forward. Hence the initial German successes. The Germans now had, he believed, 232 divisions in Russia and could mobilize, altogether, 300. He himself now had 240 divisions at the front, with 20 in reserve, and could mobilize 350. The Germans were believed to have had 30,000 tanks at war's outbreak; the Russians had had 24,000 and were now producing them at the rate of 1,000 a month, half of them heavy and medium tanks, the other half light. But during the winter months the Germans could produce more tanks than the Russians, who needed more steel for tank production and hoped the United States would be able to supply it. Stalin said he also would like to have tanks produced to Russian specifications in the United States and would gladly send a Russian tank expert to Washington to facilitate this. There were 60 Russian tank divisions, each with 350 to 400 tanks, and every infantry division had "about 50 tanks." Only a few of the much touted 70-ton German tanks had been encountered at the front; Russian roads and bridges were not constructed to bear such giant machines, the Russian terrain was ill suited to their deployment, and they were vulnerable to Russian 75-millimeter guns. Stalin was convinced that Russia's own heaviest tanks were superior to the Germans'—had proved to be so repeatedly in battle action.* These heaviest tanks, of which Russia had 4,000, were of two types, one weighing 48 tons, the other 52, the former armed with 75-millimeter guns, the latter with 85-millimeters. The medium Russian tank, of which there were 8,000,

---

*As a matter of fact, and as later battle action would prove, the Russian tanks in general were superior to those mass-produced for the U.S. Army.

weighed a little over 30 tons; its armor was 33 millimeters thick, and it was armed with 75-millimeter guns. The Russian infantry tank, of which there were 12,000, weighed 13 tons; it had 37-millimeter armor and 45-millimeter guns.

As for warplanes, Germany currently had more of them at the front than Russia had. Many of these, however, thanks to Germany's initial underestimation of the Russian air force, were of outmoded types no longer manufactured and were flown by pilots who had had a minimum of training. Russia, too, had older-type planes at the front, 7,000 or 8,000 of them that had a maximum speed of only 440 kilometers an hour, but these had proved "very useful against many of the planes that the Germans had been using." Stalin believed that German plane losses in current battles exceeded the Russian. The Germans were now producing 2,500 to 3,000 warplanes of all types per month, the Russians only 1,800, but Russian production would increase to 2,500 a month by January 1942 despite the considerable damage German air raids had done to Soviet plane-manufacturing plants (Steinhardt had shown Hopkins two totally destroyed airplane factories just outside Moscow). Save for the German Junkers 88, which "was as good or better than anything of that type" that the Russians had, the new planes the Russians were producing were more than a match in design and overall quality for those they fought.

Relevant to any estimate of Russia's chance to survive was information as to the locations of Russia's munitions plants, but to Hopkins's request for this information Stalin made no such factually detailed reply as he made to other questions. He merely "indicated that about 75% of the sum total . . . , the percentage varying depending on the type of plant, were in the general areas of which Leningrad, Moscow, and Kiev were the centers," Hopkins would write in his report to the President. "I [therefore] gained the impression that if the German army could move some 150 miles east of each of these centers, they would destroy almost 75% of Russia's industrial capacity." But Stalin also said "they had dispersed a good many of their larger factories and were moving many machine tools eastward" and that, though "he did not under-rate the German army" and believed this army fully capable of a Russian winter campaign, he was confident "that the line during the winter months would be in front of Moscow, Kiev, and Leningrad—probably not more than 100 kilometers away from where it now is." He thought the front would probably be stabilized by October 1, when autumn rains would begin to hamper offensive operations. This prompted Hopkins to say, with regard to long-term supply, that the United States, and (he believed) the British government also, would be "unwilling" to commit heavy munitions (tanks, planes, antiaircraft guns) to the Russian front in the quantity needed for the long term "unless and until a conference had been held between our three Governments at which the relative strategic interests of each front, as well as the interests of our several countries, was [sic] fully and jointly explored." He, Hopkins, was not authorized officially to propose such a conference but gave it as his opinion that it should be held immediately after, not before, the present battle had been decided. He suggested early October. Stalin, though noncommittal about the date, said he would "welcome such a conference" provided it was held in Moscow; it would be impossible for him to leave his command post there for even a few days.

Hopkins divided into three parts his lengthy report to the President of this final conversation. The first two, copies of which went to the secretaries of state, war, and navy, covered the information condensed above. The third part, labeled "FOR THE PRESIDENT ONLY" (though Hopkins suggested an oral communication of its gist to Secretary Hull), summarized what Stalin called a "personal message" to Roosevelt. Hitler's "greatest weakness," said Stalin, lay in the bitter hatred he had aroused, not only among the masses of people he had oppressed, but also among the "countless millions" in nations "still unconquered." This weakness was enhanced by the fragility of "the morale of the German army and the German people, which he [Stalin] thinks is already pretty low." The great masses "can receive the kind of encouragement and moral strength they need to resist Hitler from only one source, and that is the United States." The "world influence of the President and the Government of the United States is enormous." It was "inevitable" that the United States "come to grips with Hitler on some battlefield" sooner or later, in Stalin's belief, since Hitler's defeat was in the vital interests of the United States, and the combined strength of Britain and Russia, of itself alone, was (probably) not great enough to achieve it. Why, then, delay? It was just possible that the announcement *now* "that the United States is going to join in the war against Hitler" would have such galvanizing effect upon the world masses and such demoralizing effect upon the German army and citizenry that Hitler's defeat would be accomplished "without [the United States'] firing a shot." If, however, the war proved "bitter" and "long," as Stalin thought it was likely to be, he was convinced that "the American people would insist on their armies coming to grips with German soldiers"; and he wanted the President to know that he (Stalin) "would welcome the American troops on any part of the Russian front under the complete command of the American Army."

That last astonishing statement was evidently not felt by Hopkins to be, as in retrospect it would appear to some historians to have been, a tacit admission by Stalin that the Russian army was at that moment *in extremis* (Stalin himself quickly reiterated his confidence "that the Russian Army could withstand the German army"). The American simply replied that the question of our joining the war was not one he was authorized to discuss, though he ventured the opinion that it would be answered "largely by Hitler himself and his encroachment upon our fundamental interests." He doubted that if we *did* enter the war, we "would want an American army in Russia" but would of course tell the President what Stalin had said.

Before he boarded his plane for the flight back to Archangel next day, Hopkins cabled Washington that he felt "ever so confident about this [Russian] front," adding, on an obviously very limited basis of personally observed fact, that the "morale of the population is good" and there "is unbounded determination to win." He carried away with him a favorable impression of Stalin the man. If the dictator seemed but "an intelligent machine" and, as such, almost devoid of such human emotions as love or hate, cruelty or compassion, vindictiveness or charity, he also possessed, obviously, rare and great abilities; Hopkins wholeheartedly admired his iron self-control, swift tough mind, ability to concentrate on essentials, and consequent work efficiency.[45]

He had no such favorable impression of the Soviet regime. He believed the Russians would, with help, prevail in this war, but they must do so despite the Communist system.[46]

As a "man of action," Hopkins, like Roosevelt, was the opposite of ideological, and like Roosevelt, he thereby avoided a typical fallacy of the ideological mind, namely, the conclusion that what people do (history, that is) is wholly determined by forces—economic, in Marx; organismic in Spengler; Christian in Toynbee—that are themselves ahistorical and beyond human control. In both Hopkins's and Roosevelt's conviction, if more vividly in Roosevelt's than in Hopkins's, human beings were by God's will free to choose; though they worked out God's grand design, they must do so through the anguish of personal choice, guided by such signs of His will as He permitted them, human freedom being integral to God's design. But in eschewing both ideology and the quest for fundamental causes, Hopkins, like Roosevelt, also eschewed coherence and fundamental consistency in his dealings with current event. The whole of his mental concern was with the event itself, and about this he asked questions of "what" and "how" to the virtual exclusion of "why."

Hence his brief but vivid experience of the Russian regime did not now cause him to view that regime in historical context. There entered his mind no hint of the question of *why* communism, and the fascism it incited and inspired, had arisen. Had there done so, he might conceivably have seen and judged what he had just witnessed in somewhat the same way as the present author sees and judges it—as a grievously mistaken response to the challenge that scientific technology, its applications uncontrolled and uncontrollable by humane intelligence within a competitive private profit system, makes to the system's institutions and values. He might thereby have been led toward some basic conclusions about the way the Western world *ought* to respond to this challenge, conclusions that would have guided his dealings with specific war problems and his thinking about U.S. domestic and foreign policy in general. As it was, Hopkins saw Russian communism, accurately but superficially, as a way of governing that—by concentrating overwhelming coercive power at the summit of the social structure and attempting to direct every operation of society in detail from that summit, relying heavily on coercion and terror to do so—was hugely wasteful of human resources, destructive of human personality, and consequently grossly inefficient.

Witness the waste of individual initiative, energy, information, and skill manifest during the Yakovlev interview! The general's expert knowledge and judgment of the matters Hopkins had discussed with him were rendered useless to Hopkins, to Stalin himself in the circumstances, by his awful fear of superior authority. And the impression of terror as a dominant ruling force in Moscow had been deepened by Stalin himself, inadvertently, one was sure, during Hopkins's two conversations with him. At the second of these the interpreter had been none other than Maxim Litvinov, the former Soviet commissar of foreign affairs who was seen by millions in the West as the chief implementer, if not the principal author, of United Front collective security policies that would have averted World War II had Britain, France, and the United States accepted and acted upon them. He was a man whose mind and character and talents were consequently greatly admired in the West; and it was obviously for this reason, as a show of courtesy to the visiting American, that he had now been snatched from the obscurity in which he had been buried since the spring of 1939 (some in the West had thought him literally buried, shot when the Stalin-Hitler pact was made). But the effect of the gesture upon Hopkins was opposite the one intended. Instead of complimenting, it faintly disgusted him. For Litvinov "seemed like a morning coat that had been laid away in mothballs . . . but which had now been brought out, dusted off," as Hopkins later said—and throughout the long evening this highly capable and distinguished diplomat was treated by Stalin as a mere thing. Not once was his opinion asked for; not once did he volunteer a statement of his own; he functioned exclusively as a machine, and a machine fueled and lubricated by pure terror, as Hopkins sensed with revulsion. Fear and trembling seemed evident in Litvinov's shrinking, self-effacing demeanor. They seemed manifest, too, in Stalin's secretarial help. When asked a question he couldn't answer to his own satisfaction, the dictator "touched a button. Instantly, as if he'd been standing alertly at the door, a secretary appeared, stood at attention. Stalin repeated my question. The answer came like a shot. The secretary disappeared. . . ."[47] But at what long-term cost came such immediate "efficiency"? Would not Stalin and Stalin's office have been better served by a secretary less rigidly subordinate and robotlike—a free human being who served, as Missy LeHand served, not out of fear or power lust, but out of personal devotion to a job and a man? One could not imagine a Stalin secretary giving wise counsel or using independent judgment to prevent grave error, as Missy had often done.

In the weeks and months ahead, Roosevelt in private communications with Hopkins and Churchill would take to calling Stalin "Uncle Joe," as if the Russian dictator were basically a kindly, salty, lovable man whose chronic suspiciousness and flashes of harsh temper were merely irritating, though sometimes also amusing quirks of an otherwise sympathetic personality. Hopkins probably initiated the practice: in a letter to Brendan Bracken dashed off during his westward voyage on the *Prince of Wales* he said, "I would have liked so much to tell you about my visit to Uncle Joe. . . ."[48] But Stalin was never actually for him an avuncular figure. The Russian dictator was formidable. He was decidedly *not* lovable. He lacked human quality. There even emanated from him, faintly but unmistakably, an odor of contempt for humanity. . . .

When Hopkins arrived back at Scapa Flow on August 2 after a storm-buffeted thirty-hour flight from Archangel, he was desperately ill as well as exhausted. By some horrid mischance the satchel containing the medicines without which he could not long live had been left in Moscow. It was with almost his last strength that, the flying boat having landed on rough water, he jumped from it onto the slippery deck of the launch that was to take him to the *Prince of Wales*. His luggage containing his precious papers was tossed after him. On the launch, one sailor hauled him, sprawling, to safety while another retrieved his luggage. Yet he laughed! So ludicrous a reception by the British, aboard a British boat, of a personal representative of the President of the United States struck him as hilarious. He waved a cheery farewell to Flight Lieutenant McKinley, who would later write in awestruck tone of his passenger's "unbelievable courage" and "unparalleled devotion to duty."[49] Aboard the *Prince of Wales,* he was put to bed in the admiral's cabin by Sir John Tovey, commander of the home fleet, who at first sight of him seriously wondered if he would live through the night. Doctors were summoned, the medication he so desperately needed was supplied, and emergency blood transfusions were given him. Whereupon, under heavy sedation, he slept for eighteen hours. He did not come on deck again until the Prime Minister's party came aboard on August 4.[50]

That midnight a message was addressed by Churchill to Roosevelt: "Harry returned dead beat from Russia but is lively again [actually he remained very feeble]. We shall get him in fine trim on voyage. We are just off. It is just 27 years ago that the Huns began the last war. We must all make a good job of it this time. Twice ought to be enough."[51]

VI

ROOSEVELT received the message on the morning of August 5 when he, too, was at sea. At 6:17 A.M. he had boarded the heavy cruiser *Augusta,* flagship of the U.S. Atlantic Fleet, which, accompanied by the *Tuscaloosa* and five destroyers, now sailed northeastward out of Nantucket Sound, bound for Newfoundland.

Two days before, the world having been told that he was going on a holiday fishing cruise along the New England coast, Roosevelt had left Washington by train for New London, Connecticut, where the presidential yacht *Potomac* awaited him. His party consisted only of Pa Watson, naval aide Captain John Beardall, and Dr. McIntire, all of whom were former fishing partners of his and none of whom knew at the outset that this trip would be other than it was purported to be. Before leaving Washington, he had arranged with Princess Martha, who with her three children was vacationing in the New Bedford area, to take her and her brother Prince Carl on a day of cruising and fishing in Buzzards Bay. On August 4, a day of blue skies and brilliant sunshine, he did so. The royal guests came aboard from the New Bedford Yacht Club pier in the morning, and by evening Roosevelt had been seen with them, obviously greatly enjoying himself, by some dozens of people. This was reported in the morning newspapers of August 5. The evening papers of that same day told of the *Potomac*'s slow progress through the Cape Cod Canal from Buzzards Bay to Cape Cod Bay, with the vacationing President visibly relaxing on the yacht's deck. This last story was, of course, part and parcel of the elaborate hoax Roosevelt had devised, and (typically) delighted in devising, to make sure that this historic journey was shrouded in absolute secrecy until its successful, dramatic conclusion could be announced. By Roosevelt's order *Potomac* crew members, dressed in casual civilian clothes, one of them wearing rimless glasses and gesturing with a cigarette in a long holder, lounged on the yacht deck—and Roosevelt derived particular pleasure from the fact that this ruse took in Colonel Edward W. Starling of the Secret Service, whose men, stationed along the canal shore, kept a close and anxious eye upon the *Potomac* as she passed.[52]

During the week that followed, while the yacht coasted New England, terse communiqués issued from her now and then saying that "all on board" were having a good time.

This elaborate secrecy exceeded necessity, and the excess limited the effectiveness at the conference of the President's military advisers, in the opinion of these advisers themselves. Marshall and Admiral Stark received their orders for the trip only three days before it began and were not permitted to tell anyone, not even their cabinet officer superiors, why they left the capital at that time. The chief of the newly created U.S. Army Air Corps, "Hap" Arnold, was not told the nature of his trip until he arrived in Nantucket Sound aboard the *Tuscaloosa,* just an hour before Roosevelt's party transferred to the *Augusta* and the voyage north began. During the two-day voyage they talked among themselves of what they might say or do in the conference, but they were unprepared to make firm national proposals or take firm national positions regarding grand strategy and its accompanying logistical problems. The situation was different with their British counterparts. The people the Prime Minister brought with him were early told the general nature and purpose of the upcoming meeting. They had some, if little, time in which to obtain information materials they might need for meaningful discussions. And aboard the *Prince of Wales,* as it thrust its way through storm-tossed seas, they talked and arrived at conclusions about the positions they should take with regard to the Far East, North Africa, the Battle of the Atlantic, and aid to Russia and about the most effective way to articulate these positions. It must be said that they did so with little help from Churchill, who, badly needing a vacation, treated the westward voyage as a holiday outing. He wished his military advisers to be prepared to impress their strategical concepts and sense of priorities upon their American counterparts in such a way as to strengthen Anglo-American military cooperation; but in his view, as in Roosevelt's, the main purpose of this expedition was to enable him to know Roosevelt personally and enable Roosevelt to know him, in ways that would enlarge and solidify the developing Grand Alliance. All else was secondary, relatively unimportant. To this end, as he involved Harry Hopkins in his relaxing pursuits, including hours of backgammon at a shilling a game (the American took the Prime Minister for several pounds), Churchill closely questioned the Roosevelt intimate concerning the President's disposition, his likes and dislikes, his "real" feelings about Hitler's Germany, his "real" opinion about the way the war was going, his "real" attitude toward Churchill personally. Roosevelt, in Washington, had questioned in somewhat the same way Frances Perkins, who had known Churchill, not well, as a young man.[53]

After his long months of close confinement in the White House, Roosevelt was as exuberant as a schoolboy unexpectedly released from classroom drudgery. There was nowhere he would rather now be than aboard a warship on the high seas heading for an exciting, historic rendezvous with the one man in the whole free world who was his match in prestige and governing authority, and concerning whom he had intense personal curiosity. He felt really well, at long last, both physically and mentally. In early July he had begun to recover from the viral infection that had again laid him low in mid-June; by mid-July he was again fully restored to physical health; and his mind was now also considerably relieved of unadmitted guilt feelings born of his long failure to address problems that, because of his neglect of them, had grown to crisis proportions. During the last two weeks he had begun to exercise leadership with a good deal of his old-time zest and vigor.

One of the problems, if left unsolved, would soon quickly destroy the bulk of what had been thus far accomplished toward the creation of an adequate U.S. Army. The threat of this was posed by the provision in last year's Selective Service Act limiting to one year the term of service for draftees and for the National Guard and reserve personnel who, under the act, had been called into service. This meant that the hundreds of thousands who had entered the army last fall and were just beginning to compose the basis for an effective national fighting force must be discharged this coming fall, beginning in October, and replaced by raw recruits. Another of the act's unfortunate provisions prohibited the service of any of these troops outside the Western Hemisphere. The hemisphere had been given an expansive definition by Roosevelt in his latest naval patrol proclamation. Even so it did not comprehend the Azores or Cape Verde Islands. These islands were Portuguese possessions. And all Allied leaders must assume that Hitler intended to occupy Portugal, if not Spain also, in a lightning movement that might be launched at almost any moment and that he would then claim as his own Portugal's island possessions, if not also Spain's Canary Islands. In his hands they would greatly facilitate his domination of the South Atlantic, consequently his penetration of South America. The islands *must* be deemed outposts of the American defense system, the seizure of which would be tantamount to an invasion of American soil, in Marshall's professional judgment; the American military command *must* be free to send troops there immediately upon any move by Hitler into the Iberian Peninsula.

Marshall and Stimson had begun in early spring to press the President for permission to propose to Congress the elimination of the two hazardous provisions. Roosevelt had reluctantly granted this permission on June 21. He did not then publicly endorse the proposal, however, nor did he do so for weeks thereafter, being wary of the outburst of wrathful opposition that immediately ensued. Even House Speaker Rayburn and House Majority Leader McCormack, each of them an administration stalwart, opposed draft-term extension as a breach of contract between the government and the present conscripts. Both were acutely aware that congressional members, those in the House from the West and Midwest especially, risked their seats if they voted as the administration wished (some of the President's most emphatic past pledges concerning "our boys" and "foreign wars" now helped fuel a popular protest that was loud and passionate); both were absolutely convinced that term extension could not possibly pass unless the proposal to lift the restriction upon extrahemispheric service were dropped. So Roosevelt decided to drop it (he compensated by redefining the Western Hemisphere to include *both* Iceland and the Azores, as we have seen) and announced that he was dropping it in a White House meeting on July 14 with key congressional members. The assembled senators and representatives promised in return to try for service-term extension.

So far, Marshall had been compelled to bear the heavy burden of argument in congressional halls with no overt help from the White House, testing as he did so the outer limits of his prestige, his self-control, his capacity for fact-loaded logical argument. He continued so to operate for a week longer. Then, on July 21, Roosevelt went public with his support of term extension in a strongly argued, superbly delivered radio address. "The legislation of last year provided definitely that if national danger later existed, the one-year period of training could be extended by action of the Congress," he said. The "danger today" was "infinitely greater" than it was a year ago; none could deny the reality of the "unlimited national emergency" he had recently proclaimed. He realized that extending the service period involved "personal sacrifices" by those inducted last year, but "provision . . . can and will be made . . . to relieve individual cases of undue hardship," and he was "confident that the men in the ranks of the Army realize far better than does the general public the disastrous effect which would result from permitting the present Army . . . to melt away. . . ." We as a nation were accepting "at great cost . . . the material burdens necessary for our security." We must accept the human burdens as well. For if "in modern war men without machines are of little value . . . machines without men are of no value at all."[54] His words were effective. An overwhelmingly favorable response to them was indicated by both press commentary and White House mail. A Gallup poll published on July 29 had 51 percent of those sampled favoring the revision bill as originally proposed and, upon analysis, indicated that a much greater majority would do so if the restriction of service to this hemisphere were retained, as Roosevelt had already decided must be done.[55] A furious debate of the issue now raged in the Congress, the most important since lend-lease, said *The New York Times,* but Roosevelt aboard the *Augusta* was sanguine over its outcome; he expected the measure to pass with as comfortable a majority as lend-lease had obtained.

During the last two weeks he had also exerted leadership with regard to Russian aid.

He had only mildly and tentatively committed himself to aid to Russia immediately following Churchill's June 22 broadcast, as we have seen. But he had definitely, significantly done so during his historic interview with Oumansky on July 11, pledging then that the United States would supply by October 1 all that it could possibly supply of those urgent needs listed on the schedule Molotov had earlier given Steinhardt. The President had promptly issued the necessary orders to his lend-lease administrator and the State and War Departments, the last of which must supply the needed items from the military's stockpiles. His orders had been only reluctantly and imperfectly obeyed, however, in part because of the confused administrative setup of lend-lease, but also because the military resented and resisted the denial of desperately needed munitions to the U.S. Army in order to give them to despised Red Russia: a mere $6,522,000 worth of goods had gone to Russia by the end of July, and the War Department estimate at that time was that the Soviets would receive only $29 million of U.S. exports by October 1—an amount too tiny to have any impact at all upon Soviet fighting strength and will. Roosevelt reacted with unwonted anger when informed of this by Morgenthau, who had himself been outraged when he learned of it. The President vented his anger in a forty-five-minute outburst at the cabinet meeting of Friday afternoon, August 1, making painfully clear to Stimson his conviction that the War Department was purposely "dragging its feet" on this matter. "I am sick and tired of hearing that they are going to get this and they are going to get that," he fumed; "the only answer I want to hear is that it is under way." (A delighted Ickes, who had for months been complaining of Roosevelt's loss of grip, noted in his diary on August 3 that "the President . . .

seemed to be very alert and very much on the ball on Friday.") Immediately following the meeting, he summoned presidential assistant Wayne Coy, whom he regarded as a first-class administrator, and told him to take charge of Russian aid, writing him next day: "Please get the list [of Russian needs] and please with my full authority use a heavy hand—act as a burr under the saddle and get things moving!"[56]

He had also, during the last two weeks, dealt with crucial problems on the economic front, somewhat less decisively than he had with Russian aid but more so than he had done through the months immediately following his "Arsenal of Democracy" speech.

Lingering effects of the Great Depression had served as a bulwark against inflation during the first year and a half of the European war. So much of the United States' productive capacity lay idle in September 1939 that large war orders could be filled in the following months without creating serious market scarcities and thus upward pressures on prices. But beginning in February 1941 prices began rapidly to rise as the combine of military and civilian demand for goods began to exceed the supply. The prices of food and clothing rose most steeply of all, provoking increasingly loud consumer protests along with labor unrest harmful to defense production. Roosevelt's initial response had been to establish by executive order last April 11 an Office of Price Administration and Civilian Supply (OPACS), transferring to it the functions originally assigned to OPM's price stabilization and consumer protection divisions. Hard-hitting, hard-driving Leon Henderson was named head of the new agency (Harriett Elliott remained in charge of consumer protection in the new agency). Henderson was a remarkably effective administrator, but as OPACS head he was empowered to do little more than beg producers not to raise prices excessively. He achieved some success with the producers of goods directly related to the defense effort. He had no success at all in the area of civilian consumer goods.

The cost of living was still shooting upward when, on July 30, 1941, Roosevelt in a special message, of which the first draft was prepared by Henderson, asked Congress to enact price control legislation with teeth in it. He stressed the magnitude of the inflationary pressure exerted upon "an already limited supply of goods" by defense expenditures now totaling more than $30 million a day and bound greatly to increase. The pressure was augmented by the simultaneous increase in civilian consumer purchasing power. "In such a situation" price rises did not increase available supply, they "merely" determined "who gets the scarce materials." In other words, the nation was threatened with runaway inflation whose disastrous consequences were perfectly predictable. Manufacturers, unable to calculate their costs, would hesitate to enter into defense contracts; speculators anticipating price rises would withhold scarce materials "from essential military production"; labor-management friction would increase as the manufacturer made "excessive profits" while his workers' wages shrank in inverse proportion to the rise in living costs; government costs would balloon, along with the public debt; and a future catastrophic economic depression would be made inevitable. Hence the immediate need for legislation that included "authority to establish ceilings for prices and rents, to purchase materials and commodities when necessary to assure price stability, and to deal more extensively with excesses in the field of installment credit." Such authority should be flexible and should, of course, "expire with the passing of the need." He stressed that the concept of a price ceiling did not include the fixing or freezing of prices; these last would not be permitted to rise above a prescribed level, but below that they would be free to fluctuate in response to market pressures. "I recognize that the obligation not to seek an excessive profit from the defense emergency rests with equal force on labor and on industry . . . ," he concluded. "I also recognize that we may expect wholehearted and voluntary cooperation from labor only when it has been assured a reasonable and stable income in terms of the things money will buy, and equal restraint or sacrifice on the part of all others who participate in the defense program. This means not only a reasonable stabilization of prices and the cost of living but the effective taxation of excess profits and purchasing power. In this way alone can the nation be protected from the evil consequences of a chaotic struggle for gains which must prove either illusory or unjust, and which must lead to . . . disaster. . . ."[57]

On that same July 30, he established by executive order an Economic Defense Board, destined to play a highly important and controversial role in the national defense effort. Its sweeping assignment included the prevention of direct or indirect shipments of critical war materials from the United States to Axis nations, the purchase by the United States of such materials from foreign countries, the control of "foreign and international investments and patents," and the bringing of "the full power of economic controls to bear on strengthening the national defense." The board was nominally another cabinet committee. Vice President Henry Wallace was named chairman of it; the other designated members were the secretary of state, the secretary of the Treasury, the secretary of war, the attorney general, the secretary of the navy, the secretary of agriculture, and the secretary of commerce. These, of course, would do little or none of the board's actual work. "The Chairman may, with the approval of the President, appoint additional members," said the executive order. "Each member of the Board, other than the Chairman, may designate an alternate from among the officials of his Department, subject to the continuing approval of the Chairman, and such alternate may act for such member in all matters relating to the Board."[58] Ultimately the board, reorganized, expanded, and renamed the Board of Economic Warfare, would employ nearly three thousand extremely busy people who operated not only in the United States, but also in more than a dozen other countries.

As a final act in the economic field, just as he was leaving for his great northern adventure, Roosevelt signed an executive order (it was not formally issued until August 9) directing and authorizing the Federal Reserve Board to curb installment buying. Such extension of credit to consumers, uncurbed, "tends to generate inflationary developments of increasing consequence as the limits of productive capacity are approached in more and more fields," the order explained. And we may forecast here that Federal Reserve under Marriner Eccles would very effectively implement this order: by early 1944 the total volume of consumer credit in the United States, which approximated $10 billion in July 1941, would be more than halved. Thereafter, as a veritable miracle of war production enabled a gradual increase in the availability of civilian goods and a consequent relaxation of civilian price controls, the installment credit volume would be permitted slowly to expand until, by the end of 1945, it amounted to $6.7 billion.[59]

VII

THE *Augusta* with her accompanying heavy cruiser *Tuscaloosa* and flotilla of destroyers arrived at eleven o'clock in the morning of Thursday, August 7, in Argentia's harbor—"a really beautiful harbor," as Roosevelt wrote in a brief diary letter about this memorable trip, "high mountains, deep water, & fjord-like arms of the sea."[60] Soon thereafter he was delightfully surprised when Ensign Franklin D. Roosevelt, Jr., whom he had not seen for many months, came aboard the cruiser. Admiral King had arranged this happy reunion: Ensign Roosevelt was assistant navigator on the destroyer *Mayrant,* and King, for this reason, had ordered the *Mayrant* off Atlantic convoy duty and into Placentia Bay. Through Arnold, Roosevelt then at once ordered Air Corps Colonel Elliott Roosevelt, whom he had also not seen for months, to fly down (an eighty-mile flight) from the Gander Lake air base, Elliott having just returned there from a survey flight to Baffin Island. Elliott was formally designated the President's junior military aide and Franklin his junior naval aide for the duration of the conference; and with Franklin Jr. the President fished and cruised in a small boat along the Newfoundland shore that afternoon, catching dogfish, halibut, and one large fish no one could identify and which, for that reason, was ordered shipped to the Smithsonian.[61]

Next day, Friday, August 8, in the afternoon, after a morning of relaxation for Roosevelt, a flying boat having Welles and Harriman as passengers landed in the bay, whereupon Roosevelt summoned what he called in his diary letter a "dress rehearsal" conference attended by the two new arrivals and by Marshall, Stark, Arnold, and King—a conference, however, that did little to clarify or solidify either the diplomatic or military positions, as regards strategy, which the Americans should take in their upcoming discussions with the British. Clearly Roosevelt deemed these Anglo-British staff discussions to be primarily "get acquainted" sessions, not decision-making enterprises, and of minor importance compared to the "get acquainted" meeting of Prime Minister and President—though he, like Churchill, also wanted the conference to issue a statement of mutual national aims that would tangibly, dramatically evince the increasingly close collaboration of the American and British governments. It was in a happily anticipatory mood that the President of the United States went to bed that night, writing then into his diary letter: "All set for the Big Day tomorrow!"[62]

The Big Day (Saturday, August 9, 1941) had a rather dismal dawn. Heavy mist blanketed Placentia Bay, muffling sounds, blurring vision; it still did so at nine o'clock when the *Prince of Wales* loomed through it into the fogged vision of those who eagerly watched from the quarterdeck of the *Augusta*—loomed as a shadowy, turreted, gun-bristling, gray blue monster, its fog-dimmed visibility yet further reduced by camouflage paint as it slowly swung into her assigned berth beside, yet some distance away from, the American heavy cruiser. Then, abruptly, as Roosevelt remembered had happened back in June 1933* when he sailed up the Bay of Fundy to Campobello Island aboard the schooner *Amberjack,* the curtain of fog lifted (now as then it seemed to him a sign of blessing from On High) to reveal a dramatic scene in brilliant sunlight—a harbor fairly crowded with vessels of widely various shapes and sizes, though this time all were warships anchored under a deep blue sky, across which constantly patrolling warplanes traced a pattern of circles. Harry Hopkins at once crossed over to the *Augusta,* where Roosevelt greeted him warmly but, since he appeared far from well, somewhat anxiously. "How are you, Harry?" he asked. "Are you all right? You look a little tired." Hopkins asserted he was perfectly "all right," indicated his eagerness to report orally in full his Russian observations, and then, realizing that Roosevelt's primary interest was not Russia at that moment, promptly reassumed his role of intermediary, giving Roosevelt the latest information about Churchill's mood and wishes and so preparing for both President and Prime Minister the final steps toward their momentous meeting. The meeting itself did not take place for another hour and a half. During this waiting period Hopkins was at pains to blunt and render innocuous what could have been sharp discord between the two leaders. It had been agreed between them that no press representatives, no news reporters or photographers, would be permitted to be present at Argentia; the conference's leading participants would give out such information of it as was necessary after the conference ended. Churchill, however, had included in his party two freelance writers, travel writer H. V. Morton and novelist Howard Spring (his *Oh Absalom,* a current best-seller in England, was also a best-seller in the United States under the title *My Son, My Son*). He had also brought with him photographers so that there would be a photographic record of the historic event. He deemed all this to be

*See *FDR: The New Deal Years,* pp. 185–86.

simply a means of assuring accurate later accounts of the event (neither Spring nor Morton was a working journalist, though both had journalistic experience). But Roosevelt, learning of this from Hopkins, deemed it a violation of agreement that could gravely embarrass him with the American press, whose representatives were already resentful of their total exclusion from the President's supposed pleasure cruise, since always before they had been permitted to tag along, at some distance, in a separate vessel and had been granted at least one interview with the vacationer. The threatened breach, however, became with Hopkins's help an easily repaired misunderstanding: he told Roosevelt he was sure that Churchill, informed of the President's displeasure, would (as in fact he did) promptly order Morton and Spring not to board an American ship or attempt an interview with any American or write anything for publication until well after the conference had ceased to be current news. Roosevelt then had Arnold order U.S. Army Air Corps photographers down from Gander Bay so that there would be an American as well as a British photographic record. Meanwhile, the boarding calls demanded by custom were exchanged between the *Augusta* and the *Prince of Wales*. When Roosevelt's naval aide, Captain Beardall, crossed over, he carried a note from Hopkins to Churchill: "I have just talked to the President and he is very anxious, after dinner tonight [Churchill was to lunch and dine that day aboard the *Augusta*], to invite in the balance of the staff and wants to ask you to talk very informally to them about your general appreciation of the war, and indeed to say anything that you would be disposed to say to a group as large as will be present. I imagine there will be twenty-five people altogether."[63]

Not until an hour before noon did Winston Churchill, clad in the plain blue uniform of the Warden of the Cinque Ports, come at deliberate pace up the *Augusta*'s gangway while the American naval band played "God Save the King." He was received by Franklin Roosevelt who, clad in a light brown Palm Beach suit, an imperfectly blocked felt hat on his head, stood rigidly upright under an awning below the *Augusta*'s bridge, supported at his left arm by son Elliott and at his back, should he need further support, by the deck rail. There was ceremony. The band played "The Star-Spangled Banner" while all stood at attention. A U.S. Marine color guard resplendent in dress blues presented arms. Then His Majesty's first minister presented to the President of the United States, with a slight bow, a sealed envelope containing a letter from King George VI. (Churchill on formal occasions was always respectful of the fact that he was a "mere" head of government, under the King, whereas Roosevelt was both head of government and head of state.) The letter itself, as Roosevelt gladly noted when he read it, was informal: "This is just a note to bring you my best wishes, and to say how glad I am that you have an opportunity at last of getting to know my Prime Minister. I am sure you will agree that he is a very remarkable man, and I have no doubt that your meeting will prove of great benefit to our two countries in the pursuit of our common goal." What immediately followed was equally informal. Roosevelt and Churchill lunched together, a luncheon of which Roosevelt wrote in his diary letter: "He [Churchill] is a tremendously vital person & in many ways is an English Mayor La Guardia [one doubts that Churchill would have relished this comparison, the ebullient La Guardia being often regarded as a somewhat comic character]. . . . I like him—& lunching alone [actually Hopkins was also present] broke the ice both ways." The official dinner for sixteen hosted by Roosevelt in his cabin that evening was "very grand" according to his letter diary: "All the head Americans & British—toast to the King by me and to me by Churchill— Then I asked him to sum up the war & later called on Pound & Dill & Freeman to say a few words— A very good party & the 'opposite numbers' are getting to know each other— We broke up at I I P.M."[64]

There were two high points during that Saturday night dinner and its immediate aftermath. One was Hopkins's conversational question-answering presentation to the company of his Moscow observations, a presentation that, since it was made by a man known to be uniquely trusted by both President and Prime Minister, finally convinced the reluctant, skeptical chiefs of staff that all-out aid to Russia would be from now on a firm Anglo-American policy, a policy to which they would have to adapt. The other high point was reached after the table had been cleared and those senior officers of the warships who had not been invited to the dinner were called in to hear one of Churchill's famous overviews of the war. Some of the British who had heard him before felt that the Prime Minister was not at his absolute best on this occasion, but none who listened could fail to be impressed by the sweep, the fervor, the eloquence, of his discourse. He defended British war policy for the Middle East as part of his familiar overall argument that this war, unlike the Great War, was one of mechanized mobility, not of huge mass-army confrontations (he evidently failed to take into account what was happening on Russia's battlefields), and would be won by an Allied strategy of heavy bombing, subversion, blockade, and constant pressure along the margins of Axis empire, places where the enemy could be met on more or less even terms. He stressed the importance of Singapore in this connection while at the same time arguing that Japan might yet be deterred from a major forceful drive into the Dutch East Indies and Southeast Asia by a stern, unequivocal warning from the United States and Britain, perhaps concurred in by the Soviet Union, that further aggression in that direction would at once bring these nations in arms against her. Not directly but by unmistakable implication he pleaded for America's early entry fully into the war, no doubt counting on his argument for a war strategy of subtle indirection and swift mechanized mobility, this instead of massive bloody confrontations, to make such entry more palatable to his American listeners. America's *primary* role as belligerent, he implied, would be but an intensified continuation of its present role as a producer of munitions, of war matériel.[65]

Of the conference as a whole, the emotional high point was reached on the following morning, Sunday, August 10, in a religious service aboard the *Prince of Wales* attended by all the conferees, by some three hundred sailors from the *Augusta,* and by the full crew of the great British battleship. It was a service in whose planning Churchill had been personally much involved, this to ensure that it was "fully choral and fully photographic," as he said. He had selected the hymns "O God Our Help in Ages Past," "Onward Christian Soldiers," and "Eternal Father Strong to Save." He had approved the rather strange, enigmatic choice of Bible lesson, which was from the first chapter of Joshua: "There shall not any man be able to stand before thee all the days of thy life: as I was with Moses, so will I be with thee: I will not fail thee nor forsake thee. Be strong and of good courage. . . ." He had even vetted the prayers, having had them read to him, as he lay naked in his bath, by his private secretary, John Martin—prayers for the President, for the King and his ministers and his armed services, for the millions who suffered from war injury and Nazi-Fascist oppression, and a closing prayer that "we may be preserved from hatred, bitterness and all spirit of revenge." The event fully justified its careful preparation. The fine weather of the day before, rare in Newfoundland even at the height of summer, continued. "None who took part in it will forget the spectacle presented that sunlit morning on the crowded quarterdeck," wrote Churchill in a later year, "—the symbolism of the Union Jack and the Stars and Stripes draped side by side on the pulpit; the American and British chaplains sharing in the reading of the prayers; the highest naval, military, and air officers of Britain and the United States grouped in one body behind the President and me; the close-packed ranks of British and American sailors . . . sharing the same books and joining fervently in the prayers and hymns familiar to both. . . . Every word seemed to stir the heart. It was a great hour to live."[66]

Since Churchill and Roosevelt had agreed that such organization as the conference had should be along "functional" lines, what followed—what, indeed, had begun the day before with a lengthy meeting between Welles and Cadogan—was actually three imperfectly coordinated conferences held simultaneously. There were no plenary sessions. One conference, and of course by far the most important, consisted of the meetings between the two heads of government. Another consisted of diplomatic strategy talks between the undersecretary of state and the permanent undersecretary of the British Foreign Office. The third was of the naval, army, and air chiefs of staff. Hopkins participated largely in the summit conference but also spent considerable time and energy impressing upon the military-naval men his view of the Russian war and of what the British and Americans should do about it. Churchill's close friend and scientific adviser, Lord Cherwell (Professor Lindemann), served all three conferences, when called upon, as technical information resource.

The chief topic of the initial conversation between Welles and Cadogan, and a major subject of the conversations between Churchill and Roosevelt, was the Far Eastern situation. . . .

Both Britain and the United States were anxious to postpone for as long as possible, if unable to prevent, Japan's entrance into the war as a full-scale Axis partner. There were obvious reasons. Japan as fighting enemy would not only force a diversion of American products, of which the supply was as yet severely limited, from the Atlantic, where they were desperately needed, to the Pacific; it would also force a diversion of American naval power, since the two-ocean navy that Roosevelt had called for was yet abuilding. Japan at war with the West might do as Hitler wished, namely, attack Siberia; no informed person believed that the recently signed Russo-Japanese pact would prevent this event if, from Tokyo's point of view, other factors favored it. Worst of all, the major focus of American hostility might be shifted by uncontrollable political forces away from Germany onto Japan; a considerable if indeterminate number of Americans who bitterly opposed intervention in the Nazi-Fascist war seemed more than willing to fight for white civilization against a perceived rising Yellow Peril.

Such a shift would be equally catastrophic for Britain and the United States, in the belief of both Roosevelt and Churchill. It was for these reasons that State Department and White House had, since the war's beginning, been wary of the imposition of severe economic sanctions upon Japan (iron and steel scrap iron *had* been embargoed in September 1940 because our steel plants were not then supplying our own urgent needs) and had made repeated efforts toward a modus operendi that put off, if it did not preclude, that southward extension of the Japanese empire, to assure vitally necessary supplies of oil and rubber, which the Western democracies could not tolerate. These efforts had latterly centered on direct conversations in Washington between Hull and special Japanese envoy Admiral Nomura, begun last March and continued until interrupted by Hull's illness in mid-June. By that time some fifteen or twenty had been held, mostly at night. In them, Hull had had a great advantage over the admiral: in September 1940 a small group of brilliant cryptologists of the U.S. Army Intelligence Service, headed by Colonel William Friedman, had broken Japan's top-secret code, enabling Americans to read, simultaneously with their transmission, every message sent between Tokyo and Japanese embassies throughout the world (the decrypts were code-named "Magic") along with much of the radio traffic between Tokyo and military-naval commanders and between those commanders themselves. Hence Hull, knowing precisely what Tokyo was telling Nomura and Nomura Tokyo, knowing also some of what Tokyo was telling its army-navy command but *not* telling Nomura, was enabled to avoid every trap laid for him while revealing no secrets of his own.

Nevertheless, the conversations had been so far productive *only* of postponement, if indeed they were actually responsible even for this, and the secretary had little hope of their being more productive in the future. Yet he was wearily inclined to favor their continuance as he prepared, in the last days of his convalescence at White Sulphur Springs, to return to his office on August 5. He was also inclined to continue the policy of restraint upon provocative acts—and of these the most provocative, since it threatened Japan's very survival as a world power, would be the total embargo of American oil shipments. Deprived of imported oil, the bulk of it coming from the United States, Japan's economy would collapse within a couple of years, for it had stockpiled on its home island a two-year supply at most.

But ever since the war began, the general American public had been demanding with increasing fervor the imposition of precisely those economic sanctions that Hull with White House backing (silent backing for the most part) opposed. The popular clamor for an oil embargo was especially vehement, swelled by an infuriating belief that the greed of American oil companies was dictating American policy in this matter. The clamor had grown deafening when petroleum administrator Ickes, who personally favored the embargo, was compelled by shortages of gasoline and oil on the East Coast to order a curtailment of the consumption of these in that area in early June. Oil shipments to Japan from the East Coast had been halted at that time. Those from the West Coast had simultaneously increased, however, and rather more than proportionately. So had the popular outcry. Clearly this last, if unanswered, would become politically overwhelming when the public learned what the government through "Magic" knew in the third week of July was about to happen, namely, a movement of Japanese military forces into French Indo-China with the consent, openly proclaimed, of Vichy France. The event, scheduled for July 24, would be doubly embarrassing to the White House, for its full diplomatic recognition of Vichy, highly unpopular with the general public, had been justified by Roosevelt on the ground that it would enable us to discourage, if not wholly prevent, just this kind of Vichy-Axis collaboration.

The appointed day came.

Early in its morning there were radio reports of Japanese warships in Camranh Bay, of twelve Japanese troop transports on their way down from Japanese-occupied Hainan, and of the evidently friendly cooperation of French officials in this enterprise. Whereupon, later in the same morning, Roosevelt moved to muffle the expected new outburst of popular anger. For the first time he frankly publicly explained his policy (had he done so at the outset, he might have greatly reduced the political danger he now faced) in homely words that, though initially addressed to a group of civilian defense volunteers brought to the White House by La Guardia, were clearly intended for that full report of them that they promptly received in the mass media. "[I]t was essential for Great Britain [in 1940] that we try to keep the peace down there in the South Pacific," he said. ". . . Whether they [the Japanese] had at that time aggressive purposes to enlarge their empire southward, they didn't have any oil of their own up in the north. Now if we [had] cut the oil off, they would have gone down in the Dutch East Indies a year ago, and you would have had war. Therefore, there was . . . a method in letting this oil go the Japan, with the hope . . . of keeping war out of the South Pacific for our own good, for the good of the defense of Great Britain, and the freedom of the seas."[67] Later on that same day, Roosevelt personally proposed to Nomura in an Oval Office meeting with him (Welles and Admiral Stark were also present) that Indo-China be declared "neutral" ground. According to Welles, the President said that "if the Japanese Government would refrain from occupying Indo-China . . . or, had such steps actually been commenced [he knew, of course, they had been], if the Japanese Government would withdraw such forces," he "would do everything in his power to obtain from the Governments of China, Great Britain, the Netherlands, and of course the United States itself a binding and solemn declaration, provided Japan would undertake the same commitment, to regard Indo-China as a neutralized country. . . ."[68] In the evening of the following day, when the President was in Hyde Park, his local office in Poughkeepsie announced in a press release that an executive order was being issued whereby all Japanese assets in this country would be frozen, that is, could be used by Japan only under specific licenses from the U.S. government. Thus an impression of firm decision was made upon the public mind while leaving open to the administration the question of how much, if any, American oil Japan would be permitted, under license, to buy.

The freeze order was duly issued the following morning. A few hours later, in his cable to Hopkins authorizing the latter's trip to Moscow, Roosevelt said: "Tell Former Naval Person our concurrent action in regard to Japan is, I think, bearing fruit. I hear their Government much upset and no conclusive policy has been determined on."[69] Actually, as we know and as Churchill seems to have suspected at the time, a "conclusive policy" *had* been decided in Tokyo, this on July 2, and the decision remained firm despite the great agitation provoked in Japanese officialdom by the American freeze and neutralization proposal. The fact was evinced in the reply Tokyo made to the latter, through Nomura, on August 6, and of which Roosevelt received from Hull a summarizing memorandum, at Placentia Bay, on August 8. Tokyo treated its troop movement into Indo-China as a fait accompli, non-negotiable; it promised not to station troops anywhere else in Southeast Asia provided the United States didn't engage in military operations in that area, but the troops now in Indo-China could be withdrawn only after the China "incident" had been concluded, and the United States should employ its "good offices" with Chiang Kai-shek to achieve such conclusion. Normal trade relations between the United States and Japan must be restored, and the United States must cooperate with Japanese efforts to obtain the raw materials Japan had to have from Southeast Asia and the Indies. The United States must also recognize a special status for Japan in Indo-China even after Japanese troops were withdrawn.[70] Roosevelt found this an unresponsive reply. It said in effect that the United States and Britain could have peace in the Far East only if they sanctioned Japan's conquest of China. This was so unacceptable that Roosevelt was hard put to defend his temporizing Japanese policy—that is, his further continuance of it—against the strong argument that Churchill made at Argentia for a harder, sterner line.

Possibly influenced by Hopkins's report to him of the Stalin-Molotov call for a firm U.S. stand in the Far East, Churchill had in hand when he arrived at Argentia a two-sentence draft statement that, with only such differences in wording as were made obviously necessary by differences in governmental structure and circumstances, could be simultaneously addressed to Tokyo by Washington, London, and the Netherlands government-in-exile (in London, this government continued to be the national authority over the Dutch East Indies). The first sentence of the proposed Washington statement said: "Any further encroachment by Japan in the Southwestern Pacific would produce a situation in which the United States Government would be compelled to take countermeasures even though these might lead to war between the United States and Japan." The second sentence, written with Soviet Russia in mind, said: "If any third Power becomes the object of aggression by Japan in consequence of such counter-measures or of their [the third Power's] support of them, the President will . . . seek authority from Congress to give aid to such Power." Churchill vehemently argued in personal talk with Welles and Cadogan as well as Roosevelt that a declaration of this sort, concurred in by the British Dominions, the Netherlands, and possibly the Soviet Union, would have a deterrent effect upon Japan and that nothing less forceful and definite would now have any effect at all. As for the effect of Japan's continuation on its present course, it was horrible to contemplate from the British point of view. "He said in the most emphatic manner," reported Welles of his conversation with the Prime Minister, "that if war did break out between Great Britain and Japan, Japan immediately would be in a position through the use of her large number of cruisers to seize or destroy all of the British merchant shipping in the Indian Ocean and in the Pacific, and to cut the life-lines between the British Dominions and the British Isles unless the United States herself entered the war."[71] One may be sure that Churchill was no less vehement in his unrecorded conversations with Roosevelt.

But Roosevelt's innate aversion to the decisive and clear-cut was no less operative at Argentia than elsewhere. He was clearly influenced toward increased firmness yet reluctant to go as far as Churchill proposed; to do so, he felt, would force a showdown whose outcome might be opposite the one desired: it might incite rather than deter immediate further Japanese aggression. "President's idea is to negotiate about these unacceptable conditions [those in Tokyo's reply to the neutralization proposal] and thus procure a moratorium of, say, thirty days in which to improve our position in Singapore and the Japanese will have to stand still," said a Churchill message to Foreign Secretary Eden on August 11. "But he will make a condition that the Japanese . . . do not use Indo-China as a base for attack on China. He will also maintain in full force the economic measures directed against Japan." Churchill believed this unlikely to have effect even upon Japan's timetable, much less upon her basic decision. "I pointed out of course that the Japanese would double-cross him and would try to attack China or cut the Burma communications," he continued in his message to Eden. "However, you may take it that they consider it right to begin negotiations on these lines, and in view of what has passed between the United States and Japan it will be necessary to accept this fact." Besides, the Roosevelt tactic, as Churchill understood it, did not actually exclude the Churchill one; it contained the latter while surrounding it with time-absorbing cushions of continued talk. For at the end of the note he would hand Nomura when he returned to Washington, the President promised to place the first sentence of the proposed parallel declaration that Churchill had penned on his way to Placentia Bay—the sentence saying that any further encroachment by Japan in the Southwest Pacific would compel the United States to take counter-measures, "even though these might lead to war. . . ." Roosevelt also promised to add "something to the effect" that, "Soviet being a friendly Power," the United States might be compelled toward similar action in the Northwest Pacific, should Japanese "encroachments" be made there.[72] Churchill was thus encouraged to carry back with him to England the distinct impression that (in Churchill's own words) "the United States, even if not herself attacked, would come into a war in the Far East" should such war break out.[73]

Those who knew Roosevelt better than Churchill then knew him would have been less certain at Argentia than Churchill seems to have been that he would actually do what he said (or, more probably, indicated or implied ambiguously) he would do. In the event, he didn't do it, as we may here forecast. To the note he handed Nomura on August 17 he appended, not the language Churchill had supplied him, but a typical specimen of State Department gobbledygook that, in substance, said only that the United States was a sovereign power and proposed to perform its sovereign duty. "This Government now finds it necessary to say to the Government of Japan," said the note, "that if the Japanese Government takes any further steps in pursuance of a policy or program of military domination by force or threat of force of neighboring countries, the Government of the United States will be compelled to take immediately any and all steps which it may deem necessary toward safeguarding the legitimate rights and interests of the United States and American nationals and toward insuring the safety and security of the United States."[74] Economic sanctions *were* kept in place, and all requests for licenses to use the frozen Japanese funds remained in suspension through the weeks after Roosevelt's return to Washington—the domestic political repercussions of doing otherwise would have been immense—but as late as August 28 the President was telling Nomura that Japan might still obtain its full quota of American oil![75]

Obviously closely linked to the Far Eastern crisis, and receiving as much attention from the two heads of government, was the problem of aid to Russia (even as Roosevelt and Churchill conferred, tankers carrying American oil for Russia were passing through Japanese waters on their way to Vladivostok, a fact that of course augmented Japan's resentful anxiety over the embargo and might tempt her to seize such tankers in the near future). The problem of allocating available resources between the British and American armed forces had been difficult enough. Immensely more difficult was the problem of allocation among Americans, British, and Russians at a time when the Russians engaged the bulk of Hitler's armed strength in a battle of doubtful outcome. Churchill on his way to Placentia Bay had therefore agreed at once to Hopkins's suggestion, originally made to Stalin, that an international conference on the supply problem be held in Moscow in early October, by which time the situation on the Russian front should be clarified. He had already decided that Lord Beaverbrook should deal for the British with the question of American aid to Russia. Beaverbrook was therefore the logical choice for British representative at the Moscow conference. And Churchill, while yet at sea, had invited that fervent imperialist (Beaverbrook was also for the moment, somewhat incongruously, a fervent Russophile) to fly to Newfoundland, arriving on the afternoon of August 11 or the morning of August 12. He had also asked the immensely able Arthur Purvis, head of the British Purchasing Commission to the United States, who was then in London, to return to the United States from London via Newfoundland, arriving at Argentia at the same time as Beaverbrook. Roosevelt, too, had accepted Hopkins's suggestion by the time he arrived at Argentia and had decided that since Hopkins's health was too frail to bear the strain of another trip to Russia, Hopkins's good friend Averell Harriman should represent the United States there. Hence the joint message to Stalin from Roosevelt and Churchill on August 12, which was the conference's last day: "We have taken the opportunity afforded by the consideration of the report of Mr. Harry Hopkins on his return from Moscow to consult together as to how best our two countries can help your country in the splendid defense that you are making against the Nazi attack. . . . In order that all of us may be in a position to arrive at speedy decisions as to the apportionment of our joint resources, we suggest that we prepare for a meeting to be held at Moscow, to which we would send high representatives who could discuss these matters directly with you. If [you agree] . . . we want you to know that, pending the decisions of that conference, we shall continue to send supplies and materials as rapidly as possible."[76] There was, of course, no question that Stalin *would* agree since, as Roosevelt and Churchill knew, he had told Hopkins he welcomed such a conference.

The meetings of the British and American staff chiefs served well their primary purpose, as conceived by Roosevelt and, if less exclusively, Churchill. The two countries' "opposite numbers" became personally acquainted with one another in circumstances that revealed, in terms of the job to be done, much of their minds and motives, their character strengths and weaknesses. Without consciously endeavoring to do so, Marshall quickly established himself as the dominant personality among the conferees—and probably the most important single development, historically, of all the military talks was the warm personal friendship he formed with Chief of Imperial General Staff (CIGS) Sir John Dill, a man who resembled him "in sincerity, frankness, and self-discipline" (to quote Marshall biographer Forrest Pogue), but whose sweetness of disposition and conciliatory temper were ill suited to close continued collaboration with the strong-willed, continuously brilliant, but often erratic Winston Churchill.[77] Dill had begun slipping out of Churchill's favor last May 6* with his "astonishing" paper on the relationship between the Middle East and British Isles security. He was probably already marked down in Churchill's mind for early removal from the post of CIGS. He was certainly marked down by destiny† for a crucially important future role in Washington, where, again and again, he would moderate clashing points of view, lubricate relations between abrasive personalities, and mediate what could otherwise have been disastrous quarrels between the American and British military.

As for the military-naval discussions themselves, the emergence from them of agreements on grand strategy, for which the British staff chiefs had prepared and hoped, was militated against by the unpreparedness of the Americans. There could only emerge a clearer definition of the differences between the two countries—and even between the American land, sea, and air commands to a much lesser degree—as regards basic strategic concepts. The British had brought with them a lengthy document entitled "Review of General Strategy," which was an elaborate exposition of the position they had taken during the ABC talks of last March and that Churchill had outlined repeatedly. It stressed sea blockade, the fomenting of subversion in Nazi-occupied lands, and, above all, a massive bombing offensive against Germany. "It is . . . bombing, on a scale undreamt of in the last war . . . on which we must principally depend for the destruction of German economic life and morale," asserted the "Review." As the German people suffered and died under a rain of bombs that devastated their industry and their cities, their morale would collapse; the "whole structure upon which the German forces are based . . . will be destroyed."[78] And only after this had happened, subversion having also done its work, would any major invading army be sent into Hitler's Europe. By then, the invasion need be little more than a "mopping up" operation. Meanwhile, direct fighting contact would be maintained with the enemy on the ground only where he was weakest, namely, at the outermost frontiers of his empire. The major overall role of the United States in all this would be to supply not masses of troops, but masses of

---

*See pp. 175–76.

†"Destiny" being here the name assigned a presumed author of what is revealed to us in hindsight.

matériel—the huge masses of munitions and other goods upon which victory depended.

It was a strategic concept which only Airman Arnold among the American staff members could find attractive, and even he could not accept it. Marshall, whose primary concern at the moment was the building of a huge American army, disagreed with it totally. The heavy long-range bomber was, for him, no finally decisive weapon, but only one of many necessary tools of war, all of which must be used in balance; and he feared that the emphasis the British concept placed on heavy-bomber production at the expense of other production would grievously, perhaps fatally, distort the whole logistical picture. For he was convinced that ultimate victory would require a direct massive confrontation of Hitler's armed forces, casualty prone though such confrontation was bound to be, and he noted that British Field Commanders Wavell and Auchinleck evidently agreed with him. Certainly they seemed in flat disagreement with Churchill and the imperial general staff regarding the need for American troops. "We are certainly going to need American manpower, *just as we did in the last war* [emphasis added]," Auchinleck had told a *New York Times* reporter a few weeks ago; and Wavell, asked at that same time if he thought the tools Churchill called for from America would by themselves ensure victory, had replied with an emphatic negative. "[W]e shall need [American] manpower if the war continues long enough," he had said, "and I have no doubt it will."[79] As regards bombers, the use of them as sky artillery in close coordination with tanks, cannon, machine guns, and rifles in the hands of infantrymen would contribute more to ultimate victory, in Marshall's belief, than "strategic bombing" with its morally outrageous slaughtering of unarmed civilians could ever do. Did not the reaction of London's citizenry to the mass bombing of their city give the lie to the assertion that such bombing destroyed morale? It was more likely to enhance the bombed populace's hatred of the enemy and determination never to yield to him. Marshall also continued to regard askance the emphasis the British placed upon the Middle East. He assigned far less strategic importance to the Suez Canal than the British did and, in view of the demands that Russian aid made upon limited war supplies, deemed intolerable the loss and wastage of matériel in North Africa, which was graphically described in Harriman's report of his recent trip to that region. He and his American colleagues did not, however, oppose the British proposals in forceful argument. They were in no position to do so. As Marshall put it, the British "were at this business every day—all day" whereas the Americans, operating under strict orders to avoid anything "political," were wholly engaged in building up their country's armed forces, had no definite detailed plans for the use of them, and were therefore (in Marshall's words) "not prepared to give them [the British] fixed advice."[80]

VIII

ON the chill misty morning of the conference's last day, Tuesday, August 12, Lord Beaverbrook arrived at Argentia. There, as he was greeted by Churchill, he learned from the Prime Minister's lips news of sad import for the Allied war effort and of sobering personal import for Beaverbrook himself. He and Arthur Purvis had traveled together from London to Prestwick. There, as a risk-spreading measure, they had boarded separate planes for the transatlantic flight. It had been a matter of pure chance who took which plane. And as tragic chance had it, the plane bearing Purvis crashed into a Scottish hillside within minutes after takeoff, killing all aboard. Churchill later wrote that "Purvis was a grievous loss [he was especially so at that moment, when crucial decisions of supply allocation had to be made] as he held so many British, American, and Canadian threads in his hands, and had hitherto been the directing mind of their harmonious combination." Churchill also wrote that Beaverbook, when he received this news, "was silent for a moment, but made no comment. It was wartime."[81]

But imperialist Beaverbrook was most emphatically not silent, even for a moment; he instead burst out with vehement comment in accents of outrage, when he read a few hours later the document, known as the Atlantic Charter, which was being finally readied for signature by Roosevelt and Churchill this day and for which the Argentia Conference is now chiefly remembered in history. . . .

In the very first of his conversations with the Prime Minister, aboard the *Augusta* on August 9, the President had stressed the importance he placed upon a joint declaration of general principles for the guidance of war- and peace-making, a declaration to be signed by the two of them as heads of government and issued as soon as practicable after the conference's end. Churchill, who was eager for a document whose publication would proclaim the growing closeness of the Anglo-American alliance, had next day handed Roosevelt a draft declaration of his own composition, to serve as the basis for discussions. It was a five-point declaration of mutual purpose, of which only one, point four, initially provoked serious discussion. It said: "*Fourth,* they [Britain and the United States] will strive to bring about a fair and equitable distribution of essential produce, not only within their territorial boundaries, but between the nations of the world."[82]

Roosevelt and Welles, especially Welles, felt that this Churchill wording did not go far enough. The President wished to insert after the sentence's first clause the phrase "without discrimination and on equal terms." The undersecretary argued that doing so was a necessary confirmation of the ardent free trade stance that the State Department, under Hull, had maintained for the last nine years. The Prime Minister countered that the Ottawa Trade Agreements, providing that countries within the British Commonwealth give each other preferential treatment in trade with one another (they were agreements, incidentally, that

Cadogan and Churchill himself had opposed when they were made nine years before), made it impossible for him to sign an agreement with the proposed words in it unless and until the British Dominions agreed to it—and the obtaining of such agreement, even if that were possible (Churchill doubted it was), would delay the signing of the document far beyond the date of August 14 set by Roosevelt for its publication. He pointed out that Britain's commitment to free trade greatly predated and was far more firm, historically, than that of the United States. "I could not help mentioning the British experience in adhering to free trade for eighty years in the face of ever-mounting American tariffs," he writes in his war memoirs. "We had allowed the fullest importations into our colonies. Even our coastwise traffic around Great Britain was open to the competition of the world. All we had got in reciprocation was successive doses of American Protection." Hopkins intervened, saying it was "inconceivable that the issuance of the joint declaration should be held up by a matter of this kind" and suggested the drafting of new language by Welles and Cadogan "to prevent the delay of which Mr. Churchill spoke"—a suggestion, incidentally, that infuriated Welles. In the end, the words "without discrimination" were removed and the words "with due respect for their existing obligations" were substituted for them.[83]

But there was further disagreement when, in redrafting, Roosevelt with Welles substantially changed the last point of Churchill's original document: "*Fifth,* they seek a peace which will not only cast down forever the Nazi tyranny, but by effective international organization will afford to all States and peoples the means of dwelling in security within their own bounds and of traversing the seas and oceans without fear of lawless assault or the need of maintaining burdensome armaments." The Roosevelt-Welles redraft eliminated from this the call for "a peace" to be achieved and maintained through "effective international organization" and the words pertaining to the "traversing of the seas and oceans." The substance of this last was contained in a proposed point six calling for a peace "to establish for all safety on the high seas and oceans." Also proposed was a point seven calling for "the abandonment of the use of force" by the nations of the earth, "the disarmament [by the victors in this war] of such nations" as had committed acts of aggression, and "the adoption of all other practicable measures which will lighten for peace-loving peoples the crushing burden of armaments." Churchill deplored the removal of all reference to "international organization," saying that the people of England would be "disappointed" by it; but Roosevelt, concerned as always to placate his country's isolationists, shied away from any suggestion that he favored a restoration of the League of Nations. A compromise was worked out. At Churchill's suggestion, there was inserted in the sentence dealing with the disarmament of aggressors the phrase "pending the establishment of a wider and permanent system of general security." The penultimate draft statement was telegraphed to

London, for the consideration of Churchill's war cabinet, at two o'clock in Newfoundland's afternoon of August 11. It did not arrive until after midnight in England, when most of the ministers were in bed. Yet the document had been reviewed carefully by the cabinet in London and received back in Argentia, with a few minor changes and additions made in it, by the early morning (in Newfoundland) of August 12. A few hours later, the soon-to-be-famous Atlantic Charter was in final shape. As signed by Roosevelt and Churchill that day and published to the world two days later, it proclaimed the end of American isolationism even more emphatically than lend-lease had done. Later "explanatory" statements employing qualifications, disclaimers, and subterfuge would be unable to hide the immense fact that with this document the British and American heads of government committed their two countries before the eyes of the world to an alliance not only for the waging of war, but also for peace-making and -keeping after the war ended. They did the latter with the phrase "pending the establishment of a wider and permanent system of general security," which Churchill had insisted upon inserting in point eight: it opened the way to the United Nations of the future.

Said the Atlantic Charter:

"The President of the United States of America and the Prime Minister, Mr. Churchill, representing His Majesty's Government of the United Kingdom, being met together, deem it right to make known certain common principles in the national policies of their respective countries on which they base their hopes for a better future for the world.

"*First,* their countries seek no aggrandisement, territorial or other.

"*Second,* they desire to see no territorial changes that do not accord with the freely expressed wishes of the peoples concerned.

"*Third,* they respect the right of all peoples to choose the form of government under which they will live; and they wish to see sovereign rights and self-government restored to those who have been forcibly deprived of them.

"*Fourth,* they will endeavor, with due respect to their existing obligations, to further the enjoyment by all States, great or small, victor or vanquished, of access, on equal terms, to the trade and to the raw materials of the world which are needed for their economic prosperity.

"*Fifth,* they desire to bring about the fullest collaboration between all nations in the economic field, with the object of securing for all improved labor standards, economic advancement, and social security.

"*Sixth,* after the final destruction of the Nazi tyranny they hope to see established a peace which will afford to all nations the means of dwelling in safety within their own boundaries, and which will afford assurance that all men in all lands may live out their lives in freedom from fear and want.

"*Seventh,* such a peace should enable all men to traverse the high seas and oceans without hindrance.

"*Eighth,* they believe that all nations of the world, for realistic as well as spiritual reasons [the 'spiritual' is *not* 'realistic'? the 'practical' is *not* 'moral'?], must come to the abandonment of the use of force. Since no future peace can be maintained if land, sea, and air armaments continue to be employed by nations which threaten, or may threaten, aggression outside of their frontiers, they believe, pending the establishment of a wider and permanent system of general security, that the disarmament of such nations is essential. They will likewise aid and encourage other practicable measures which will lighten for peace-loving peoples the crushing burden of armaments."[84]

It was to this final draft that Canadian-born newspaper magnate William Maxwell Aitken, first Baron Beaverbrook, reacted explosively when Churchill showed it to him on August 12.

A puckish- and foxy-appearing little man, possessed of a fiery temper, a stubborn will, an abnormally strong acquisitive instinct, and a naturally pugnacious bullying disposition joined with a considerable ability to charm when he chose to do so, he had become England's most powerful newspaper publisher. As such, he had long exercised what many deemed a baneful reactionary influence upon the country's political life. He had been one of the most ardent supporters of appeasement policy, had hailed the Munich Agreement as a guarantor of "peace in our time," and as late as the early summer of 1939 had loudly asserted, in person and in his newspapers, that there would be no new world war. But Churchill, who shared with him a religious devotion to the British empire, greatly liked him personally, believed him to have a genius for large-scale organization and administration, and so had brought him into the cabinet, where, as minister of aircraft production and then of supply, he had indeed performed well.

He now damned the Atlantic Charter as a shameful betrayal of British imperial interests.[85] Only with difficulty did Churchill mollify him and then persuade him, with Hopkins's help, to proceed by plane to Washington, with Harriman, instead of returning on the *Prince of Wales.* Hopkins argued persuasively that in Washington Beaverbrook could impress upon the President and other key officials the magnitude of Britain's supply needs, which immensely exceeded Washington's current conceptions, while he himself learned at "first hand just what might be expected of our American production—now and in the future." Certainly both London and Washington were in urgent need of the information Beaverbrook could develop, Hopkins pointed out, for the Americans grossly underrated Britain's needs while the British, misled by overly optimistic OPM reports, greatly overrated current American production. (Air Vice Marshal Freeman at Argentia had staggered the Americans by requesting for the British six thousand more heavy bombers than the Americans had scheduled for production, these plus four thousand planes of other types. He had been led to believe that American hangars were bulging with new warplanes.)[86]

The Beaverbrook incident brought Roosevelt to a clearer realization and a more sympathetic understanding of Churchill's domestic political problems.

Simultaneously, disturbing news from Washington brought Churchill and his British colleague to a clearer and very sobering realization of Roosevelt's domestic political problems.

For on that August 12, 1941, the draft-extension bill, having handily passed the Senate, came within a single vote of going down to defeat in the House of Representatives! Voting in favor of the measure were 203 representatives, 182 of them Democrats, 21 Republicans; voting against were 202, 133 of them Republicans, 65 Democrats. Actually the measure might well have gone down to defeat had not Speaker of the House Sam Rayburn instantly proclaimed, when the tally was 203–202, that the measure was passed and brought down his gavel with a loud bang; several congressmen were at that moment waiting to approach the well below the Speaker's rostrum to announce a change in their vote, as House rules permitted them to do. The Republicans' protest of the Speaker's action was loud, long, bitter—and futile.

Analysis of the vote would later reveal it to be no accurate reflection of the sentiment of the country as a whole or even of the House itself. A considerable number of the Democratic opposition votes had been cast by congressmen who, though personally in favor of the measure's passage, felt that it would do so despite their recorded opposition, a record that would protect them against the wrath of constituents in the elections of 1942.[87] The direness of the vote news from Washington that arrived at Argentia on August 12 was unmitigated by such analysis, however. It cast a dark pall over the meeting's last hours. The British, especially, were shocked by this seeming show of American isolationist strength at this late date. They were inclined to equate the House of Representatives with the House of Commons and thus to see the event as a vote of no confidence in Franklin Roosevelt. Such a vote on an issue of this magnitude in the Commons would have presaged the downfall of the Churchill ministry.

Nevertheless, the conference ended on the afternoon of August 12 in, for the British, a glow of good feeling and renewed hope. Aboard the *Augusta,* Churchill and Roosevelt said good-bye with a warm handshake shortly before three-thirty P.M., following which came what Roosevelt described in his diary letter as "a very moving scene," Churchill and his colleagues receiving "full honors going over the side." Then: "At 5 P.M. sharp the P. of W. passed out of the harbor, past all our ships. All crews were at quarters. She was escorted by her two corvettes & 2 Am. destroyers, F Jr aboard one of the latter [the President's son was named a naval aide to the Prime Minister during the latter's homeward voyage]. Elliott left on a different secret mission, flying over Greenland's ice cap to Ireland." Ten minutes later the *Augusta,* too, "stood out of the harbor with our escort, homeward bound."[88]

And the glow of optimism remained with Churchill when he made his personal report of the conference to the war cabinet upon his return to London on August 19. He had "got on intimate terms with the President," who, he said, "had shown great activity, considering his physical disabilities, and on one occasion [this when he came aboard the *Prince of Wales* for the Sunday service] had walked (every step causing him pain) a considerable distance in front of Marines drawn up on parade. . . ." Roosevelt personally "was obviously determined that they [the Americans] should come in" to the war and, despite the fact that he "was skating on pretty thin ice in his relations with Congress, which, however, he did not regard as truly representative of the country," had told Churchill "he would wage war, but not declare it," that he "would become more and more provocative," and that the Germans, if they "did not like it, could attack American forces!" Churchill had warned the President that if, say, next spring, Russia "was compelled to sue for peace" and "hope died in Britain that the United States were coming into the war," he, the Prime Minister (Churchill), "would not answer for the consequences." Roosevelt in reply had "made it clear that he would look for an 'incident' which would justify him in opening hostilities" within the next few months.[89]

Fortunately for the President none of this, which would have confirmed the darkest suspicions of his political opposition, leaked from the war cabinet minutes into the British press. He himself, in public statement, lent no credence to the Prime Minister's report of his personal feelings and intentions. On the contrary, he seemed determined to downplay the conference's actual as distinct from its undeniably great symbolic importance. The initial stage of his homeward voyage was leisurely—he wanted to discourage speculation as to the meeting's whereabouts until the *Prince of Wales* was safely out of the Western Hemisphere. He was also not personally averse to some loafing days at sea, some fishing off the coast of Maine—so it was not until the morning of Saturday, August 16, the day the *Prince of Wales* arrived at Iceland, that he, having transferred from the *Augusta* to the *Potomac,* anchored off Rockland, Maine, held his first press conference since before his northern trip began. By then, the Atlantic Charter had been published. A reporter asked if anything had been decided about "the actual implementation of these broad declarations." Roosevelt replied that there had been an "interchange of views, that's all." He was asked, "Are we any closer to entering the war, actually?" He replied, "I should say, no." Might he be quoted directly on that? "No," Roosevelt replied, "you can quote indirectly." He even refused to say that in view of the aid-to-Russia policy and the continuing need to aid Britain, there must be another, and a larger, lend-lease appropriation. "We are still studying it," he said.[90] (At his next press conference, in Washington on August 19, Roosevelt would be asked whether the Prime Minister at Argentia had "seemed confident that Britain can win the war, without our entry." Roosevelt would refuse an on-record reply but say off the record that "yes— . . . he is extremely confident, in the long run—in the very long pull."){91}

LATER on August 16 Roosevelt set foot on land for the first time in nearly two weeks. He came ashore at Rockland, Maine, where his special train awaited him. A couple of hours later, when his train paused at Portland, he was reintroduced to the kinds of pressures, the kinds of crisis excitements, from which he had been blissfully detached during his last days at sea but which, on land, he must continuously relieve and soothe through a process of personal absorption ("if you run into problems, bring them to me; my shoulders are broad"). There came into his stateroom, while he was at dinner, a highly agitated Adlai Stevenson, Secretary Knox's personal assistant, bringing an executive order that it was imperative the President sign at once—bringing also secret information of such overwhelming importance that it must be conveyed to the President's ear, and that ear alone, at once!

The order was for the taking over by the Navy Department of the huge shipyard of the Federal Shipbuilding and Dry Dock Corporation at Kearny, New Jersey. The shipyard employed sixteen thousand people, held contracts for $493 million worth of warships and merchant marine vessels, and had been shut down on August 7 by a dispute over a union maintenance-of-membership clause that the CIO Union of Marine and Shipbuilding Workers insisted must be in its work contract in return for a union pledge not to strike for the duration of the emergency. The shipyard's management, adamantly opposed to industrial unionism, refused to agree. After eleven days of work stoppage, Knox and Undersecretary of the Navy Forrestal (especially Forrestal) were convinced that the shipyard must be forced to resume work at once. Even a further twenty-four-hour delay was intolerable. Hence Adlai Stevenson must fly by navy plane out to the *Augusta,* explain the situation to the President, show him the necessary documents, and obtain the crucially important presidential signature.

As for the highly secret information, it had then been imparted to Stevenson, in Knox's presence, by a tense, stern Admiral Chester Nimitz, chief of the Navy Department Bureau of Navigation. "Tell him [the President] I have learned today, from a heretofore reliable source, that Stalin has opened negotiations with Hitler," said Nimitz, who for secrecy's sake forbade Stevenson to put the message into writing.

Bad weather had prevented Stevenson's flight from Quonset to the *Augusta.* The admiral in charge, despite Stevenson's pleas, flatly refused to permit any of his seaplanes to attempt a flight to a ship at sea; he was only with great difficulty persuaded to permit a small plane to fly Stevenson to Rockland, where he arrived just as the President's train was pulling out. He then flew to Portland, where, when the special train arrived, he managed, also with great difficulty, to talk his way onto it. What then ensued was highly educative of young Stevenson. Hopkins, Marvin McIntyre, Eleanor Roosevelt, and Grace Tully were all at the dinner table with the President. Roosevelt listened calmly, the others restively (the President's dinner was growing cold), to Stevenson's explanation of the Kearny situation, then asked him to hand over the necessary papers, saying he'd "look them over tonight." He also asked Stevenson to fly back to Washington and arrange a meeting for nine o'clock tomorrow morning, in the White House, of Knox, Myron Taylor (former chairman of U.S. Steel and Roosevelt's special ambassador to Pope Pius XII), and the attorney general—"and you be there too." He blandly dismissed Stevenson's protest that the executive order was "supposed to be signed right now," saying he thought it would "work out all right this way." A flustered Stevenson then said he had something else, a message from Admiral Nimitz, who insisted that absolutely no one but the President should know of it. Might he write it down? he asked desperately, since four people besides the President were present. Roosevelt nodded his consent. Stevenson then wrote his message on the back of a dinner menu, using precisely the words Nimitz had spoken. Roosevelt read it with close attention, then looked up.

"Adlai," he said, "do you believe this?"

Stevenson, taken aback, replied that he "didn't know" what he thought about it.

"I don't believe it," Roosevelt said. "I'm not worried at all. Are you worried, Adlai?"

Stevenson "guessed" he wasn't if the President wasn't.

On the following morning, at the meeting in the Oval Office, Roosevelt "settled the whole business [that is, as regards the Kearny labor dispute] in fifteen minutes and signed the executive order," to quote Stevenson's later account of the episode.[92]

6

-->>X<<-

Toward Culmination:
The Day of Infamy

I

ROOSEVELT had indicated to Churchill his determination to "look for an 'incident' " that would justify American hostilities. His felt need for one was intensified when, at the end of August, he decided to permit the U.S. Navy to escort as far as Iceland any ship, American or not, carrying goods bound for Britain or Russia. The decision was being implemented but remained unannounced as September opened.

On Thursday, September 4, 1941, in that wide area of the North Atlantic where the Hitler-proclaimed German war zone and the Roosevelt-proclaimed Western Hemispheric defense zone overlapped, an American destroyer, the USS *Greer,* was speeding toward Iceland, bearing mail for U.S. troops, when told by a British patrol plane that a German submarine lurked beneath the waves about ten miles ahead of it. The submarine, we now know, was U-652. The destroyer's commander at once sounded general quarters and began a zigzag course at increased speed while seeking sonar contact with the submerged vessel. Such contact was soon made. Thereafter, the destroyer trailed the U-boat and continuously reported its location to the British, this in accord with the policy the President had announced, if publicly in rather vague terms, last May. After an hour or so the British plane was in position to drop depth charges in the U-boat's close vicinity and dropped four of them, with no evident effect, before turning back to Iceland to refuel. For two hours more the *Greer* tracked the submarine and reported to the British. Finally the harassed U-boat, its desperate commander probably believing that the destroyer had made the depth-charge attack actually made by the British plane, suddenly fired a torpedo at the destroyer, then a second one, perhaps a third. The *Greer* dodged them and began to circle, dropping depth charges but losing contact with the submarine as it did so. When the resumed sonar search found the submarine after another two hours or so, the *Greer* again dropped depth charges, no fewer than eleven of them, before breaking off an engagement in which neither side had inflicted casualties or material damage on the other.[1]

Who was the aggressor in this episode? To a dispassionate judgment the weight of evidence would seem to tilt toward the *Greer* as aggressor, for it was only after hours of threatful surveillance by the destroyer, every minute of which increased the submarine's fatal danger, that the submarine took what it had a right to regard as defensive action. Roosevelt, however, had concerns other and, to his mind, far more important than absolute factual accuracy concerning this single episode. The salient point for him was that, for the first time, a Nazi war vessel had fired upon an American,* provoking retaliatory action, and it was upon this point that, on September 5, having been imperfectly informed of what had happened, he told the press that orders had been issued to the U.S. Navy to "eliminate" the guilty submarine. With Hopkins, he conferred over lunch that day with the secretary of state. He was gratified to find the normally supercautious Hull in a mood more wrathful, and far more full of moral indignation, than his own. He at once capitalized on it, asking Hull to have a draft radio address dealing with the event prepared at once in the State Department, a draft that White House speechwriters Rosenman and Hopkins could, with Roosevelt (Robert Sherwood was in England, studying Britain's war information organization), work into final form for presidential broadcast as a fireside chat on Monday evening, September 8.

Shortly thereafter Roosevelt replied to a September 1 message from Churchill. In that message the Prime Minister had exulted over a triumph of diplomacy that, he believed, had just been consummated in Teheran: The Shah of Iran had been persuaded to expel the sizable German colony that had settled in his country (Churchill persisted in calling the country "Persia") and to grant transit rights to Britain and the Soviet Union, thus enabling the Persian Gulf and the Iranian transport system to be used as a Russian supply route.† "[W]e propose to double or at least greatly improve the railway from the Persian Gulf to the Caspian, thus opening a sure route by which long-term supplies can reach the Russian reserve positions in the Volga basin," Churchill had written. To protect this supply route, it was of the utmost importance that Turkey "stand as a solid block against German passage to Syria and Palestine"; and to encourage Turkey's doing so, Churchill proposed "to reinforce the Middle East armies with two regular British divisions, 40,000 men, in addition to the 150,000 drafts and units which we are carrying ourselves between now and Christmas." Britain had not enough available shipping to do this by itself, however. American shipping was needed. Churchill asked for the loan of "twelve United States liners

---

*There was no certainty that the German commander knew whether the destroyer was American or British.

†Churchill's exultation was somewhat premature. The Shah proved slippery in this matter. On September 17, Soviet and British troops abruptly occupied Iran, forced the Shah to abdicate, and replaced him with his son, who was firmly pro-Ally. It was the son who then guaranteed the urgently desired transit rights, whereupon the Soviet and British troops were withdrawn.

and twenty United States cargo ships manned by American crews from early October till February." In his reply, Roosevelt, acting in accord with the recommendations on the Middle East made to him by Harriman and Hopkins, promised to provide the British with transports for 20,000 men—U.S. Navy transports manned by navy crews. He also said that the U.S. Maritime Commission was arranging "to place 10 or 12 additional [cargo] in the North Atlantic run between American ports and Great Britain so that you can release 10 or 12 of your cargo ships for carrying cargo to the Middle East." He added: ". . . I am delighted that you are going to reinforce the Middle East." He closed: "For your private and very confidential information I am planning to make a radio address on Monday night relative to the attack on our destroyer and to make perfectly clear the action we intend to take in the Atlantic." Churchill's thank-you note of September 7 said, "We all await with profound interest your promised statement for Monday."[2]

There was no fireside chat on Monday evening, however. Personal sorrow supervened. . . .

Soon after Roosevelt had dictated his message to Churchill he received a phone call from Eleanor. She was at Hyde Park. She had gone there to meet her mother-in-law upon Sara's return from a summer spent, as her summers always were save when she traveled abroad, in the cottage she and her husband had built on the Canadian island of Campobello, in the Bay of Fundy, in 1883. Eleanor, too, had been much on the island that season, as she was every year, in the house, next door to her mother-in-law's, where Franklin had suffered his polio attack in 1921 and to which he had returned but twice (in 1933, in 1939) in all the years since. For Sara Delano Roosevelt, however, this last summer had been sadly different from any other in that, at its very beginning, her health, theretofore remarkably robust for a woman of eighty-six years, had suddenly broken: in June she had suffered a stroke that, though nonparalyzing, seriously impaired her circulatory system and confined her to her bedroom. She was too weak adequately to care for herself but, characteristically, resented and resisted Eleanor's insistence upon a full-time nurse for her. She persisted in this until her son in the White House let her know that her stubbornness was seriously disturbing his "peace of mind," whereupon she at once yielded ("Of course you are right. . . . I am sorry you got alarmed"). Under the nurse's care, her condition seemed to improve—so much so that when she left her cottage at season's end, she insisted upon walking unassisted down the front steps to the waiting automobile. This was overdoing it, however; she barely made it to the car, was desperately short of breath by the time she was settled in its backseat. And at breakfast in the Big House on Friday, September 5, the morning after her arrival at Hyde Park, she seemed very ill indeed to Eleanor, who breakfasted with her. Her skin was paper white, her breathing labored, her voice weak, and the absolute self-assurance that normally shaped her facial expression was replaced by a flickering hesitancy, a pale, weary resignation. Contemplating her mother-in-law's broad countenance, Eleanor saw death upon it, and this premonition grew stronger as the hours passed. Hence, finally, her afternoon phone call to the White House.3

Immediately Roosevelt canceled his plans for a weekend of work in Washington, unusually urgent though this work was at that moment. He ordered Hopkins and Rosenman to deal with Hull's speech memorandum when it arrived; he sent a telegram to the Big House at Hyde Park saying he would arrive there at nine-thirty on Saturday morning.

Sara, overjoyed at his coming, announced on Friday evening her intention to be under the colonnade on the front porch to greet her son when his car drove up next morning. She was far too weak for that, however. It required all her strength to don her most elegant lace-trimmed bed jacket, have a bright blue ribbon tied into her braided hair, and move herself with help from her bed to a chaise longue, where she lay, propped up by pillows, as her son wheeled himself through the doorway of her spacious, sunlit, second-story room. They greeted each other, as always, with kisses. He spent all the morning and much of the afternoon alone with her, telling her about his meeting with Churchill, telling her of some of the things he was doing in Washington, sharing remembrances with her—and when he left her in midafternoon she seemed better than she had been when he came. At nine-thirty that night, however, a blood clot lodged in her lung, and she sank abruptly into a coma from which it was impossible to rouse her. Her son, who had often clashed with her but with whom the whole of his life was intermeshed as it was with none other, sat at her bedside through most of the night, gazing upon her immobile face, listening to her shallow breath, and feeling such rending emotion, thinking such memory-soaked thoughts, as none other would ever be given any inkling of by him, save inadvertently. He was again seated silently at this bedside, his somber gaze again fixed upon his mother's now bloodless countenance, when, shortly before noon on Sunday, September 7, precisely two weeks before her eighty-seventh birthday, she died.4

A few minutes later, a great crashing sound from the mansion yard startled everyone in the Big House and alarmed Michael F. Reilly, chief of the Secret Service detail that guarded the President. He with others rushed outdoors. They were awestruck by what they saw: Though there was no storm, no wind, and no lightning to account for the fact, the tallest tree on the estate, a huge ancient oak, prominent in some of Franklin Roosevelt's earliest memories, had toppled to the ground! Soon thereafter, geologists assured an anxiously questioning Reilly that the event was neither unnatural nor unusual: only a thin mantle of soil was spread over the granite undergirding of this portion of the Hudson Valley, and in consequence the greatest trees growing there were likely to have root systems too shallow to support steadfastly the leveraged weight placed upon them; in some circumstances the slightest breath of air could blow one down. But this mundane explanation "was never the true explanation to a lot of us," Reilly later wrote—and the "lot of us" undoubtedly included the President of the United States, whose eyes and ears were always attuned to signs, messages, cues from On High, and whose mother had been from his earliest memory the great oak of his familial forest. Not long after the tree crash he had himself carried out to its site, where he sat for a while gazing silently at the hole torn in the earth by the uprooting, and at the fallen giant itself with its huge trunk, its tangle of roots, its extensive foliage and broken branches.[5]

Sometime that afternoon Harry Hopkins found it absolutely necessary to phone Roosevelt about the *Greer* speech draft that had been received from Hull. It was as unsatisfactory as most State Department drafts were. Evidently Hull had naturally reverted to, or permitted himself to be talked back into, his customary timorousness; for though the draft made a fairly strong case for American action of *some* kind, it stated the case in flatulent, equivocating State Department language, was not explicit about the action that would be taken, and wholly lacked the fiery indignation that Hull had expressed during his September 5 luncheon talk. Roosevelt, having listened to Hopkins's review and to the salient parts of the draft that were read to him, at once agreed that it would not do at all what he wanted this speech to do. There would now, however, be plenty of time in which to work up a usable draft, he added, for of course he would not now be broadcasting on Monday night; the delivery date must be postponed until September 11. His mother's funeral was to be in Hyde Park on Wednesday, he said. He would remain in Hyde Park until it was over, then immediately board his train at the Hyde Park station. Hopkins with Rosenman should meet his train at the 138th Street station in New York City so that the three of them could work on the speech while returning to Washington.[6]

From that moment until after the funeral, Roosevelt "shut himself off from the world more completely than at any time since" he had become President, according to *The New York Times*. Even the Secret Service men respected his wish, his need, for solitude, doing so at some risk to their congressionally mandated duty of guarding him closely through every moment of his day or night. When on Tuesday afternoon, feeling he simply had to get away from the soft-speaking obsequious strangers who prepared the funeral in the Big House, he took a long, lonely drive in his hand-controlled Ford through the beloved memory-haunted woods of the estate, Reilly felt duty-bound to sit beside him in the front seat; but the Secret Service man neither spoke nor looked at the big, silently brooding man behind the wheel. He kept his trained, watchful eyes focused always (as, indeed, his job required his doing) upon the trees and shrubbery along the road. As for the Secret Service car that trailed the Ford, it did so from a greater distance than ever before, though that distance, we may be sure, was an anxious one for the men in it.[7]

On Wednesday, the funeral and interment ceremonies were the brief, formalized, utterly impersonal rites of the Episcopal Church, conducted in the Big House library and then in the St. James Church graveyard three miles to the north. The Reverend Frank R. Wilson, the St. James rector, officiated. At neither ceremony did Roosevelt display emotion. He stood upright on his steel-braced legs in the churchyard, one hand grasping the door of the car that had carried him there, as the Reverend Wilson intoned the ritual "ashes to ashes, dust to dust"; it was remarked that he did not once look at the casket as it was lowered into the brick-lined vault in which his long-dead father lay, "nor did he return an anxious glance cast his way by his wife."[8] Not long afterward he boarded his train at Hyde Park station and, two hours later, being met by Hopkins and Rosenman in New York City, was abruptly returned, willy-nilly, to his hectic, highly pressurized public life.

The only sign of personal grief that he gave the watching public in the following weeks was the black mourning band he wore on his left sleeve everywhere he went and would continue to wear for more than a year. The only sign he gave his closest associates was inadvertently given Grace Tully one day soon after the funeral when, in the office he had designed for himself in the Franklin D. Roosevelt Library at Hyde Park, the two of them were sorting through cartons of books and papers that had been stored in cabinets along one office wall. Most of the cartons had been packed and shipped from Washington by Grace herself, but among them was a box neither she nor Roosevelt had ever seen before. Opening it, they found a number of packets wrapped in tissue paper, each labeled in Sara's large, bold handwriting. One contained the gloves she had worn at her wedding, another locks of her and her son's brown hair, a third his baby shoes, a fourth his christening dress. There were also packets of letters he had written his parents when separated from them as a young boy, and from Groton and Harvard when he was in school there. Suddenly, unexpectedly, Roosevelt was overcome. Tears filled his eyes—the only tears any of his staff members, save possibly Missy, had ever seen him shed—as he said quietly to Grace that he wished to be alone for a while.[9]

As for Eleanor, who over the years had suffered much deep hurt from the imperious, overwhelming Sara, she frankly admitted in a letter to her daughter Anna that, though "appalled" by the fact, she "couldn't feel any real grief " over this death. To her young friend Joseph P. Lash she wrote: "It is dreadful to have lived so close to someone for 36 years & to feel no deep affection or sense of loss." But, she added, "It's hard on Franklin. . . ." And to Franklin, as son James later wrote, she "showed . . . more affection during those days than at any other time I can recall."[10]

It was with no such detachment that Eleanor viewed, at this same dark time, the long hard dying of her brother, Hall. Hall had displayed brilliant qualities as a boy and youth but, like her father and two of her maternal uncles, had become a chronic alcoholic while yet a young man. Through the last few years he had been literally drinking himself to death, daily consuming fantastically large quantities of whiskey, gin, and wine. He was doing so in his little house at Hyde Park on the last full day of Sara's life—and that night, as Sara sank into a coma, he, too, collapsed, mortally ill of cirrhosis. He was rushed to Vassar Hospital in Poughkeepsie. Three days later, on the Wednesday of Sara's funeral, he was moved, at his request and by Eleanor's arrangement, to Walter Reed Hospital in Washington, where he lay, unconscious much of the time, in agony at others, for nearly three weeks. Eleanor was at his bedside most of that time, day and night. "My idea of hell, if I believed in it," she wrote Joe Lash, "would be to sit or stand & watch someone breathing hard, struggling for words when a gleam of consciousness returns & thinking 'this was once the little boy I played with & scolded, he could have been so much & this is what he is.' " He was six years her junior. Her loving relationship with him had always been more maternal than sisterly (". . . Hall was always a little my child & the waste . . . seems a bitter thing," she wrote Lash), and this love had sometimes assumed forms fiercely, even ferociously, protective of him.* When at last he died, aged fifty-one, at five o'clock in the morning of September 25, she drove at once from hospital to White House and went to her husband's bedroom, where breakfast had not yet been served (very rarely in recent years had she and her husband breakfasted together). Son James was there and, long after, described a scene he would never forget. "[S]he went to father and said simply, 'Hall has died.' Father struggled to her side and put his arm around her. 'Sit down,' he said, so tenderly I can still hear it. And he sank down beside her and hugged her and held her head to his chest. I do not think she cried. I think mother had forgotten how to cry."[11]

Hall was given a White House funeral and his body taken for burial in the Hall family vault at Tivoli, near Oak Terrace, the gloomy, doomful mansion where he and Eleanor had spent most of each of their turbulent childhood years.

II

WHEN Roosevelt arrived back in Washington in the late afternoon of September 10, having worked with Hopkins and Rosenman during the trip from New York City on the speech draft that, with input from Assistant Secretary of State Berle, they had crafted, he had in hand a draft he was willing to accept as final. It was truculent in tone, and some of its most truculent phrases had been penned by Roosevelt himself. He read the draft aloud that evening, after dinner, to Hull, Stimson, and Knox, all of whom heartily approved it (the speech was "the most decisive . . . which he [the President] had made," a pleased Stimson told his

*See *FDR: Into the Storm*, pp. 302, 304–05.

diary that evening). By the following morning, Hull had again reverted to his normal supercautiousness; he now argued for a speech loud in its expressions of moral outrage but muffled in, or totally omissive of, statements about proposed retaliatory action. However, of the group of congressional leaders to whom Roosevelt read the draft that morning, only Republican isolationist Joseph Martin of "Martin, Barton, and Fish" fame took exception to it. In any case, Roosevelt's mind was now made up.[12]

He opened his broadcast that evening with a carefully edited account of the *Greer* incident. The destroyer was "proceeding in full daylight toward Iceland" on the morning of September 4 last, "flying the American flag," her "identity as an American ship . . . unmistakable," when she "was attacked by a submarine" that "Germany admits was a German submarine." This submarine "deliberately fired a torpedo at the *Greer,* followed by another torpedo attack. In spite of what Hitler's propaganda bureau has invented, and in spite of what any American obstructionist organization may prefer to believe, I tell you the blunt fact that the German submarine fired first upon this American destroyer without warning, and with the deliberate design to sink her." This, said the President of the United States, "was piracy—piracy legally and morally. It was not the first nor the last act of piracy which the Nazi Government has committed against the American flag in this war. For attack has followed attack." He referred to the sinking of the *Robin Moor,* to an aborted Nazi submarine attack upon "an American battleship in North American waters" last July, to the sinking of an American-owned ship flying the Panamanian flag (the *Sessa*) on August 17, of which there were but three known survivors, and to the sinking "five days ago" in the Red Sea of a "United States merchant ship, the *Steel Seafarer."* Clearly "these acts of international lawlessness" manifested "a design . . . the Nazi design to abolish the freedom of the seas and to acquire absolute control and domination of these seas for themselves." Hitler's "intention" had been made obvious. "The American people can have no further illusions about it. No tender whisperings of appeasers that Hitler is not interested in the Western Hemisphere, no soporific lullabies that a wide ocean separates us from him, can long [did he mean 'now'?] have any effect on the hard-headed, far-sighted, and realistic American people." He was "sure that even now the Nazis are waiting to see whether the United States will by silence give them the green light to go ahead on this path of destruction." The answer was an emphatic "No": "No act of violence, no act of intimidation will keep us from maintaining intact two bulwarks of American defense: First, our line of supply of matériel to the enemies of Hitler; and second, the freedom of our shipping on the high seas. No matter what it takes, no matter what it costs, we will keep open the line of legitimate commerce in these defensive waters. We have sought no shooting war with Hitler. We do not seek it now. . . . But when you see a rattlesnake poised to strike, you do not wait until he has struck before you crush him. These Nazi submarines and raiders are the rattlesnakes of the Atlantic. . . ."

Came then that explicit announcement of new policy that the secretary of state opposed but that most others in the administration deemed long overdue.

"In the waters which we deem necessary for our defense," said Roosevelt, "American naval vessels and American planes will no longer wait until Axis submarines lurking under the water, or Axis raiders on the surface of the sea, strike their deadly blow—first. Upon our naval and air patrol—now operating in large number over a vast expansion of the Atlantic Ocean—falls the duty of maintaining the American policy of freedom of the seas—now. That means, very simply and clearly, that our patrolling vessels and planes will protect all merchant ships—not only American ships but ships of any flag—engaged in commerce in our defensive waters. They will protect them from submarines; they will protect them from surface raiders. . . . From now on, if German or Italian vessels of war enter the waters, the defense of which is necessary for American defense, they do so at their own peril. The orders which I have given as Commander in Chief of the United States Army and Navy are to carry out that policy—at once. . . ."

He concluded:

"I have no illusions about the gravity of this step. I have not taken it hurriedly or lightly. It is the result of months and months of constant thought and anxiety and prayer. In the protection of your Nation and mine, it cannot be avoided. The American people have faced other grave crises in their history—with American courage, and with American resolution. They will do no less today. They know the actualities of the attacks upon us. They know the necessities of a bold defense against these attacks. . . . And with that inner strength that comes to a free people conscious of their duty, and conscious of the righteousness of what they do, they will—with Divine help and guidance—stand their ground against this latest assault upon their democracy, their sovereignty, and their freedom."[13]

Newspaper headlines next morning proclaimed in banner headlines that America's theretofore undeclared war in the Atlantic had now become, by presidential edict, a shooting war—a fact confirmed when on September 13 Admiral King formally ordered the U.S. Atlantic Fleet to defend "against hostile attack" not only United States, but also "foreign flag shipping (other than German and Italian shipping)" between U.S. ports and Iceland "by escorting, convoying and patrolling as circumstances may require, or by destroying German and Italian naval, land, and air forces encountered."[14] SHOOT ON SIGHT! screamed the headlines. And the isolationists who dominated the Republican Party reacted in their expected way to this final erasure of the ever-thinner and -vaguer line that had separated "acts short of war" from war itself in the North Atlantic. On September 16, former President Herbert Hoover inveighed in a radio address against Roosevelt's deliberate pushing of American warships into "danger zones" and effectively usurping the authority to declare war, which the Constitution assigned exclusively to Congress. On the following day, Republican Senator Charles Tobey of New Hampshire, at an America First rally in New

York City, inveighed against "a gigantic conspiracy," spearheaded by Roosevelt, "to drive" the American people "into war." The President and the "belligerent old men in his Cabinet" were deliberately trying to create an incident that would involve us in war without a constitutional congressional declaration of it, said the *Chicago Tribune* after both Stimson and Knox had publicly fervently approved what the President had said—and the *Tribune*'s sentiments were substantially echoed next day by Hearst's *New York Journal-American.* Much was made of discrepancies between the President's account of the *Greer* incident on September 11 and that given to a congressional committee by Admiral Stark on September 20. These discrepancies were due to Stark's possession of information not available to the President nine days earlier, explained Knox—an explanation that did nothing to defend the President against the charge that he, in his eagerness for an "incident" and in flagrant violation of his moral obligation, had acted precipitously upon a matter of life-and-death importance to the American people.[15]

But fortuitous simultaneous events reduced considerably the effectiveness of this isolationist attack, and especially of the America First portion of it.

On the very evening of Roosevelt's fireside chat, Charles A. Lindbergh delivered to an America First rally in Des Moines, Iowa, a nationally broadcast address in which he declared that "the three most important groups who have been pressing this country toward war are the British, the Jewish and the Roosevelt Administration." These "war agitators" comprise "only a small minority of our people," he went on; "but they control a tremendous influence." And he proceeded to elaborate ominously: "It is not difficult to understand why Jewish people desire the overthrow of Nazi Germany. The persecution they suffered in Germany would be sufficient to make bitter enemies of any race. No person with a sense of the dignity of mankind can condone the persecution the Jewish race suffered in Germany. But no person of honesty and vision can look on their pro-war policy here today without seeing the dangers involved in such a policy, both for us and for them." He then rendered explicit the threat he had implied, saying: "Instead of agitating for war the Jewish groups in this country should be opposing it in every possible way, for they will be among the first to feel its consequences. Tolerance is a virtue that depends upon peace and strength. History shows that it cannot survive war and devastation. A few far-sighted Jewish people realize this and stand against intervention. But the majority still do not. Their greatest danger to this country lies in their large ownership and influence in our motion pictures, our press, our radio, and our government."

The uproar this provoked was gravely injurious to the prestige and credibility of America First in particular, of isolationism in general—and it was loud enough to drown out a significant portion of the criticism of Roosevelt's speech and policy. Space that the press would normally have devoted to condemnation of the President was filled instead with adverse comment upon the Lindbergh address. Isolationist William Randolph Hearst, whose newspapers were notoriously careless of the truth and unheeding of the claims of justice, editorialized, somewhat surprisingly: "Charles A. Lindbergh's intemperate and intolerant address in Des Moines, in which racial and religious prejudices were incited—especially against the Jewish faith*—should arouse universal protest and denunciation." The *Des Moines Register* said that Lindbergh's speaking "his mind" at this place and time was "so lacking in . . . appreciation of consequences [Father Coughlin's followers were then beating up Jews every day on city streets] . . . that it disqualifies him for any pretensions of leadership in this republic in policy-making." The speech as a whole, said the *Register,* "was so intemperate, so unfair, so dangerous in its implications that it cannot but turn many spadefuls in the digging of the grave of his influence in this crisis." Thomas E. Dewey was of the same mind. "Charles A. Lindbergh, in a national broadcast, injected religious and racial prejudice into a discussion of our foreign policy," said he. "That, I declare, is an inexcusable use of the right of freedom of speech, which 130,000,000 Americans, regardless of their views, will wholly reject." Wendell Willkie damned the address as the "most un-American . . . in my time by any person of national reputation." Alfred E. Smith said that Lindbergh "had seen fit to inject anti-Semitism into his campaign against our foreign policy" and that his doing so "strikes at the very basis of our national unity. . . ." Some journalists compared what Lindbergh had just said with what Hitler had said in a speech to the Reichstag on January 30, 1939, to wit: "At the moment, Jews of certain countries may be fomenting hatred under the protection of the press, of the film, of wireless propaganda, of the theater, of literature, etc., all of which they control." It was pointed out in printed and publicly spoken words that neither in Germany nor in the United States had the Jews ever operated as a tightly organized cohesive force in national life, nor had they ever individually exercised anything like as much control over press, radio, and government as Hitler and Lindbergh alleged. In the United States, far from "controlling" press and radio, the Jews, insofar as they constituted a pressure group at all, had considerably less influence over them than had several other pressure groups—a fact it would have been easy for Lindbergh to ascertain.[16]

It took America First's national leadership two weeks to decide its response to the clamor. During those two weeks, a few influential members of local chapters of America First resigned in protest of the Lindbergh speech; but the speech was strongly defended and approved in a huge majority of the letters (some 85 to 90 percent of them) received by the national headquarters from rank-and-file membership. A significant number of these letters were so ugly and vicious in their anti-Semitism that the headquarters staff stamped them "Crank-

---

*Note the substitution of "faith" for Lindbergh's "race." Those who call Jews a "race" often tend to be anti-Semitic in basic attitude.

Ignore." The official committee statement finally issued on September 24 was singularly unpersuasive. It asserted that Lindbergh and "his fellow members of the America First Committee" were "not anti-Semitic," that they deplored "the injection of the race issue into the discussion of war or peace," but that it was "the interventionists who have done this," not Lindbergh.[17]

All of which, to repeat, by exposing the racial and religious bigotry that were an important part of isolationism's motivation, considerably reduced opposition to Roosevelt's speech and policy. Indeed, the national public accepted this new and crucial turn of events with a calm and general approval that may have been somewhat surprising to Roosevelt, though it had seemed perfectly predictable to such interventionists as Stimson, since, after all, it was an inevitable development of the policy established with lend-lease. Even before the *Greer* incident and the fireside chat, public opinion polls had showed a majority of the American people in favor of U.S. convoying. After the speech, a Gallup poll had 62 percent of those sampled approving the President's policy. True, context indicated that much of this approval continued to derive from a Roosevelt-induced belief that the purpose of his policy was to keep the United States out of the war; but clearly most Americans would now rather fight than permit Hitler to triumph. Indeed, in a Gallup poll on October 5, 70 percent of the poll sample said they believed it more important to defeat Hitler than to keep America out of the war. Clearly Americans were prepared to fight if necessary, were increasingly persuaded that it *would* be necessary, and now awaited without trepidation Hitler's reaction to the new U.S. policy.

Hitler, however, declined to react. As we know, Admiral Raeder, the Nazis' chief of naval operations, had begun urging Hitler the previous spring to permit unlimited U-boat warfare upon Anglo-American supply lines. He now seized upon Roosevelt's speech as a declaration of war to which Germany simply *had* now to respond: every resource of the German navy must be devoted at once and without stint to the Battle of the Atlantic! But Hitler, though infuriated by this latest Roosevelt move, continued deaf to Raeder's pleas. He told Raeder that before taking on the United States Navy, if not the United States as a whole, in all-out war, Germany must complete its conquest of the Soviet Union. This, he added, should not unduly postpone the action Raeder wished to take: Russia was on the verge of collapse and might well be crushed before the end of September.[18]

III

WELL and good was Roosevelt's (America's) determination to defend the supply line, but to what purpose was a supply line if it remained empty or insufficiently filled with supplies?

There was a growing demand that the decisiveness with which the Executive now dealt with the Battle of the Atlantic be at once matched by him in the field of American industrial mobilization. No such match occurred; confusion and division were only somewhat diminished by presidential action as autumn advanced into winter. For Roosevelt continued not to know how to accomplish, he had not even a vague general plan for doing, what he repeatedly said he wanted to do, namely, mobilize fully the nation's resources for defense while also preserving and even extending the social gains that the New Deal had made. He was sure only of what he did *not* want to do, and would do only to the extent that circumstances forced him, namely, designate an economic "czar" and delegate to him large portions of the authority now residing in the White House. He remained convinced that this authority should stay in the White House and be exercised by himself, that his relinquishing it to the wrong man (and how could he be certain to choose the right one?) would gravely imperil the general welfare and could be fatal to representative government. Liberals, on the other hand, along with some leaders of the small-business community, cried out that prevailing arrangements were more damaging to national defense, hence to democratic government and the general welfare, than the operations of a presidentially appointed and supervised "czar" could possibly be!

In late August Roosevelt had admitted in action what it was impossible to deny, namely, that war production, and especially those portions of it dependent upon plant expansion and plant conversion, continued to lag far behind what was absolutely necessary for the preservation of the British and American democracies—admitted also that the existing governmental administrative arrangements were in some degree responsible for the lag. His answer in action, however, was not to scrap OPM and set up an administrative structure whereby finally decisive power was shifted from profit-motivated people to people whose prime commitment was to national defense and the general welfare. It was, instead, to interpose between OPM and White House a new agency having administrative authority over OPM but also sharing most of its top key personnel with OPM, thereby complicating beyond the possibility of comprehension the relationship between governors and governed within this vital area of national defense.

The new agency, created by executive order on August 28, was a Supply Priorities and Allocation Board (SPAB). The huge task assigned it was to "determine the total requirements of materials and commodities needed respectively for defense, civilian, and other purposes, establish policies for the fulfillment of such requirements, and where necessary make full recommendations to the President relative thereto." How this was to be done, the order did not say. It did say that the board was to be "the coordinating center" for all governmental defense production activities "relating to priorities" and was "in this connection" to "review, clear, and approve for execution all requests or proposals" from federal agencies or private industry having to do with the "procurement, production, transmission, or transportation" of materials, fuel, or energy. But this state-ment, taken by itself and literally, made no sense: Why should the agency bother to review requests that it must in any case "clear, and approve for execution"? Context revealed the true intent, which was to impose rational purposeful order upon what must otherwise be a blindly selfish and vicious competition for ma-terials in short supply—in other words, to replace a "free market" economy with a governmentally planned one to the extent necessary for defense. To this end, the agency was not to "approve," but was instead to refuse or drastically alter specific "requests or proposals" whenever the granting of them was deemed detrimental to national defense. Such meaning was implicit in the agency's stated authority to issue "priority orders, warrants, certificates, or rat-ings" whenever and wherever "preferential treatment" with regard to "certain materials, commodities, facilities, or services" was deemed by OPM to be "nec-essary for national defense." The meaning became explicit in the statement that OPM's "general plans and programs providing for allocations and priorities . . . shall be submitted to the Supply Priorities and Allocations Board (SPAB) for approval or modification."[19]

The board's membership, presidentially appointed, consisted of William Knud-sen, who also continued as director general of OPM; Sidney Hillman, who also continued as associate director general of OPM; Vice President Henry Wallace in his capacity as chairman of the Economic Defense Board; Secretary of War Stimson; Secretary of the Navy Knox; Harry Hopkins, as special assistant to the President in charge of the defense aid program; and Leon Henderson, as admin-istrator of the Office of Price Administration. Wallace was named board chair-man. Donald M. Nelson was named executive director, that is, the actual boss of SPAB as an operating policy-making agency. The official working relationships among these people were hopelessly scrambled. Price administration, it will be remembered, was originally one of two functions of the Office of Price Admin-istration and Civilian Supply, which Roosevelt had established the previous April as an agency separate from OPM and on a par with it in terms of authority. OPACS was now split in two, with OPA remaining an independent agency within the Office of Emergency Management while CS became a division of civilian supply in OPM; and since Henderson was named head of the civilian supply division while remaining administrator of OPA, he too was officially split in two. As OPA chief he was ex officio a member of SPAB, where his au-thority was the equivalent of Knudsen's, but as a division chief in OPM he was subordinate to Knudsen. As for Knudsen, he as OPM boss was subordinate to himself as SPAB member insofar as SPAB had authority over OPM. He was also subordinate to Nelson in SPAB, while Nelson, who remained head of the priorities division of OPM, was in the latter capacity subordinate to Knudsen. Perhaps a primary concern of Roosevelt's in all this was to prevent or at least muffle the violence of such head-on clashes as had recently occurred between

Knudsen (OPM) and Henderson (OPACS) with regard to cutting automobile production. He may have felt that he would do so by mixing up together production personnel with priorities and allocations personnel, also mixing up their separate functions and responsibilities in ways that confused policy making with policy execution, and that the cost of this in reduced efficiency would not be high. If so, he was mistaken.

Yet for all its entanglement of functions and scrambling of lines of authority, SPAB was an improvement upon what had gone before. It had more real power than any earlier economic defense agency had had; it was more broadly representative of the American economy than any earlier agency had been; and many of the confusions and fractions inherent in its makeup, and in its relationships with other agencies, were clarified and lubricated by Roosevelt's exercise of personal leadership and charm, now that he was again in a full tide of health and vigor. There was also, in the business community as in the country as a whole, an increase of genuine patriotic feeling, of concern for the general good, proportionate to the increased realization that the United States really was in grave danger and must, sooner or later, fight for its life. Thus aided, SPAB during the next three months brought more order out of chaos, and accomplished more in the way of economic mobilization, than anyone could have reasonably expected it to do. It effected both expansions of plant and curtailments of civilian production that were badly needed. On October 2 it ordered an increase of ten million tons per year in the nation's steel production capacity—an order whose carrying out would prove immensely helpful to freedom's cause during the months ahead. A week later it restricted non-essential building and construction. And a week after that it limited the use of copper to essential war production, denying it to most civilian products. It also facilitated, as no earlier agency would have been able to do, the swift supply of American defense materials to the Soviet Union in fulfillment of the terms of the Moscow Protocol.[20]

This last was the fruit of the conference in Moscow, originally suggested by Hopkins during his Moscow visit, to which Harriman as Roosevelt's personal envoy, and Beaverbrook as Churchill's, journeyed the last of September, accompanied by considerable staffs of experts. . . .

The conference was held in the dark red shadow of dire events immediately past and evidently immediately impending. Despite stubborn Russian resistance and autumn rains that turned battlefields into quagmires, the German armies pressed relentlessly eastward, and more rapidly, more disastrously, for Russia than Stalin, in his conversations with Hopkins, had predicted. The winter battle line would remain in front of Kiev, he had said—but as early as September 1 the Germans were fifty miles east of Kiev, capital of the Ukraine, where Soviet troops, ordered by Stalin to "stand and die," were surrounded. On September 16, in what would prove to be the greatest single capitulation of the war, more than half a million Russians in the Kiev area surrendered, and two days later Kiev itself fell after a battle that cost 350,000 Soviet casualties along with 3,718 guns and 884 armored vehicles.* In the far north, the Germans reached the south shore of Lake Ladoga on September 22, cutting off Leningrad from the remainder of the Soviet Union and seemingly making it certain that Leningrad, no matter how valiantly the Russian troops fought in its defense, would be starved to death before the coming winter ended. In the center of the 1,500-mile front, the Germans, though slowed by Hitler's insistence upon diverting troops and matériel to the conquest of the Ukraine, drove ever closer to Moscow, where, by the time the Harriman-Beaverbrook mission arrived there, factories were beginning to be disassembled for evacuation eastward (two weeks hence, Soviet governmental officialdom would leave Moscow for Kuibyshev, 525 miles to the east, though the central government itself, in the person of Josef Stalin, would remain in Moscow). Hence the sense of extreme urgency that animated the Moscow conferees.

Beaverbrook's volatile gamecocky temperament and bullying disposition grated on Harriman, as it did on most who had to work with him, but the two men were equally eager to provide Russia with all the aid possible, and they managed to function well as a team during their meetings with Molotov and Foreign Trade Commissar Anastas Mikoyan. They did so especially during their decisive sessions with Stalin. There were three of these, on the nights of September 28, 29, and 30—sessions at which Molotov was in attendance and Litvinov was again interpreter† but from which U.S. Ambassador Steinhardt and British Ambassador Sir Stafford Cripps were excluded. (Harriman had been advised by Hopkins to bypass Steinhardt on this mission because Steinhardt was disliked and distrusted by both Stalin and Molotov. Beaverbrook had been told that Cripps, too, was disliked and distrusted, and he himself disliked him, Cripps being a fervent and highly moralistic Laborite.) The first of the three sessions went very well, with much business accomplished. The second became little short of disastrous as Stalin revealed in full force a side of his character he had not revealed to Hopkins, a side decidedly at variance with the "Uncle Joe" image of him. He was surly, pugnacious, insultingly suspicious, and even willing, it incredibly seemed, to break off negotiations altogether. When

---

*On September 29 and 30 occurred the infamous Babi Yar massacre, wherein thirty-four thousand men, women, and children, nearly all of them Jews, were shot to death at a ravine near Kiev by one of four *Einsatz* (Special Action) groups of the SS. These special groups were organized for the specific purpose of following closely the advancing German troops and eliminating "undesirables" from the areas conquered. They soon developed ways of killing more efficient than bullets and managed to murder some two million Jews in Poland and Russia by war's end.

†Harriman was "somewhat shocked by Litvinov's appearance," as he later said. "His clothes and shoes were shoddy and . . . his waistcoat and trousers did not meet to cover the expanse of his shirt front." Clearly he had been long out of favor with the regime.[21]

Beaverbrook presented him with a personal letter from Churchill, he threw it contemptuously on the table unread. He expressed disgust over the paucity of the Anglo-American aid being offered, asserting that it "clearly shows that you want to see the Soviet Union defeated." So little was accomplished at this session, which had been originally intended to be the last with Stalin, that Harriman and Beaverbrook felt compelled to propose a third meeting for the following night. They did so with trepidation. They were immensely relieved when Stalin agreed to it. And at this third meeting Stalin was again courteous, affable, cooperative. He agreed with Harriman at its outset that the work they were doing must be concluded swiftly "with [public] expressions of satisfaction by all concerned," adding that the Berlin radio was already telling the world the conference had failed—and in the arduous hours that followed he, in Harriman's words, clearly tried to be "reasonable and not too exacting."[22]

There was finally drawn up a seventy-item list of things the Russians needed along with a specific commitment of Anglo-American supply for each, a commitment of date and rate of delivery as well as of quantity. At suspicious, distrustful Molotov's insistence, concurred in by Stalin, these commitments were incorporated in a formal international agreement, the First (Moscow) Protocol (there would be a Second [Washington] Protocol a year later). Harriman, Beaverbrook, and Molotov signed it in Moscow on October 1. Roosevelt formally approved it on October 7. By its terms, the United States was pledged to supply the Soviet Union with a billion dollars' worth of goods by June 30, 1942. And as has been said, SPAB, at once issuing the necessary orders for the allocation of equipment and materials, was able to facilitate this Russian aid as none of the earlier defense production agencies could have done.

But SPAB's greatest contribution to national defense came through its effort to determine the total material requirements for defense, and to establish policies for the fulfillment of these, in accord with the huge overall assignment given the agency by the executive order creating it. The effort stimulated and guided the development of a huge planning project that had already begun and would ultimately issue in what became known as the Victory Program.

The program may be said to have had its genesis in the collaborating minds of Jean Monnet, whom we have met several times before,* and Stacey May, who had entered the government defense effort (in June 1940) not from the ranks of big business, but as a political economist in the Rockefeller Foundation. May had headed the Bureau of Research and Statistics in NDAC, he continued to head that bureau in OPM, and he had been early and wholly persuaded, as Arthur Purvis was, by Monnet's vehement argument for a consolidated "balance sheet" of British-American war needs and war goods supplies—a sheet

*See p. 84; also *FDR: Into the Storm,* pp. 354–55, 399–40, 559–60.

(actually it would be a very thick tome) that included full information about what was presently available, what was immediately needed, and what would be needed for as far ahead as projections could be reasonably made, along with exact information about actual and potential production capacities. Only on the basis of such information could rational war planning proceed. But supply needs were determined by military strategic and tactical concepts; and the armed services of warring Britain were reluctant to share with an American civilian the British information that the balance sheet must contain. May managed to pry some of the information loose and onto paper during consultations in London in the spring of 1941. He pried out much more when, within a week or so after the invasion of Russia had upset all earlier calculations of foreign aid needs, he was again in England, this time on special assignment from the War Department (he took leave from OPM). He returned in early September with what he himself deemed "the most important papers in the world" (they weighed thirty-five pounds), information that would have been of inestimable value to Hitler had Nazi secret agents managed to get hold of it, though, strange to say, May was given no special security protection as he carried it home.[23]

This second May trip was arranged by Stimson after he and Knox had received a letter from Roosevelt dated July 9, 1941, requesting them to "explore," with Hopkins's assistance, "the overall production . . . required to defeat our potential enemies." The President realized "that this . . . involves the making of appropriate assumptions as to our probable friends and enemies and to the conceivable theaters of operation which would be required." It involved, in other words, entry by U.S. Army and Navy planners into political country they had been explicitly barred from entering during the ABC sessions of last winter and early spring, for the grand strategic concepts that determined production requirements were in turn determined by grand political aims. If the aim was the maintenance of Britain's present world status and the preservation intact of the British empire on the assumption that these were in the vital American interest, then the grand strategic concept that the British military had presented during the ABC talks and at the Argentia Conference should be seriously considered. But as we know, this concept had been rejected by the American military on the ground that the long, long war it indicated—a war of blockade, air strikes, raids "around the edges," and subversive infiltration, with America supplying only such troops as were needed to maintain a slowly increasing pressure—could not bring victory over Hitler. Only an invasion of the Continent, on a scale beyond Britain's capacity, could do so. And to this end, Marshall and his colleagues were contemplating by July 1941 an eventual American army of eight million men organized into five field armies totaling 215 divisions. "I wish you would explore," Roosevelt's letter continued, "the munitions and mechanical equipment of all types which in your opinion would be required to exceed by an appropriate amount that available to our potential enemies." The report of this exploration, he added, should enable the establishment of "a munitions objective indicating the industrial capacity which this nation will require."[24]

When after seven weeks of waiting he had not received the requested report, Roosevelt on August 30, 1941, addressed a memorandum to Stimson, with a copy to Knox, reminding him that representatives of the United States and Britain were to meet in Moscow with USSR representatives by October 1 to determine what Russian war needs Britain and the United States could supply. "I deem it of paramount importance for the safety and security of America," wrote Roosevelt, "that all reasonable munitions help be provided for Russia, not only immediately but as long as she continues to fight the Axis powers effectively." Obviously the immediate help would have to come mostly "from production already provided for" and "I desire that your Department working in cooperation with the Navy Department, submit to me by September 10 next your recommendations of distribution of expected production of munitions of war as between the United States, Great Britain, Russia and the other countries to be aided—by important items, quantity time schedules and approximate values, for the period from the present time to June 30, 1942." He also wanted "your general conclusions as to the overall production effort of important items needed for victory, on the general assumption that the reservoir of munitions power available to the United States and her friends is sufficiently superior to that available to the Axis powers, to insure the defeat of the latter."[25] The task thus assigned, however, immense and difficult in any case, was so complicated by differences between the army and navy (for one thing, the army had a well-developed statistical function; the navy did not) that it remained incomplete on the deadline date of September 10. The requested information did not arrive on the President's desk until September 25. But it arrived then in an unprecedentedly concise and unambiguous, though necessarily lengthy, form—not as a single document, but as several documents (they bore different dates) that were closely interrelated and consistent with one another.

The major premise of the argument developed in the report as a whole—the argument that underlay all the statistical estimates of overall production needs—was stated in blunt, unequivocal, hence highly un-Rooseveltian language in a paper entitled "Joint Board Estimate of United States Over-all Production Requirements,"* dated September 11, 1941, and signed by General Marshall and Admiral Stark. "It is the opinion of the Joint Board that Germany and her European satellites cannot be defeated by the European powers now fighting against her," the paper said. "Therefore, if our European enemies are to

---

*It will be remembered that the Joint Army-Navy Board functioned in those days as coordinator of policy on all matters requiring joint action by the two services. It often did so imperfectly, arriving at flawed conclusions more reflective of interservice rivalry than of interservice cooperation. But in this case it worked well.

be defeated, it will be necessary for the United States to enter the war, and to employ a part of its armed forces offensively in the Eastern Atlantic and in Europe or Africa." Similarly with regard to Japan and the Pacific: the British and Dutch were not strong enough to defend Southeast Asia against the Japanese advance. Here, too, if Japan were not to be permitted to dominate absolutely the Western Pacific, the United States must actively intervene. In other words, the United States must plan to wage two wars simultaneously, one against Germany, the other against Japan, and must be very clear at the outset as regards the relative emphases between the two. The armed services had already made their decision on this matter, as we know. So had Roosevelt, implicitly, in the extreme privacy of his own mind. But Roosevelt as President and commander in chief had not yet done so explicitly and officially, in consequence of which the Joint Board deemed it wise to review the case for Plan Dog in terms of stark, harsh realism. Germany was the primary enemy, Japan the secondary, because "if Germany were defeated, her entire European system would collapse, and it is probable that Japan could be forced to give up much of her territorial gains, unless she had already firmly established herself in such strength that the United States and its associates could not afford the energy to continue the war against her." But the defeat of Germany must be a total military defeat, since an "inconclusive peace . . . would . . . give Germany an opportunity to reorganize continental Europe and to replenish her strength. Even though the British Commonwealth and Russia were completely defeated," the paper continued, "there would be important reasons for the United States to continue the war against Germany, in spite of the greatly increased difficulty of attaining final victory. From this it follows that *the principal strategic method employed by the United States in the immediate future should be the material support of present military operations against Germany, and their reinforcement by active participation in the war by the United States while holding Japan in check pending future developments* [italicized in the original]." The statement of major premise concluded in a way revelatory of Marshall's persuasive power and of Stark's ability to subordinate his special professional interest to his commitment to objective truth: "Except in the case of Russia, the principal strength of the Associated Powers is in naval and air categories. Naval and air power may prevent wars from being lost, and by weakening enemy strength may greatly contribute to victory. By themselves, however, naval and air forces seldom, if ever, win important wars. It should be recognized as an almost invariable rule that only land armies can finally win wars."[26]

The challenge thus presented to America's productive capacity was, in Stimson's word, "staggering." The word had previously been applied to the $49 billion munitions program called for by the Stacey May report of last spring; but it was now clear that a program several times as large would be required—and Donald Nelson's overall primary concern as SPAB executive was to spur the development of it. At a full board meeting chaired by Wallace on September 9, he was instructed to compile full schedules of both military and civilian requirements for as far into the future as possible. A week later he officially requested from the army, the navy, and the maritime commission statements of estimated requirements, based on military objectives, for the next two years. And by late November, after a monumental labor involving much conjecture, much educated guesswork (neither the navy nor the maritime commission submitted specific programs of their own, claiming it was impossible to determine what needs they might have)—a labor shaped largely by Robert Nathan, one of May's aides, a brilliant mind whom army procurement officers had already begun to hate with a passion—SPAB had shaped an estimate of total "victory" requirements costing $150 billion by September 30, 1943, a date chosen arbitrarily simply because a terminal one was necessary.[27] Thus was finally destroyed absolutely the illusion that a normal civilian production could be maintained with an adequate defense production superimposed. Only unlimited time and manpower could have made this possible, and since both were limited, a flat choice must be made between "guns" and "butter," with the butter wholly subordinate to the guns from now on through the war emergency. Nor could even the absolute minimum of war production needed be achieved through the blind chances of an allegedly freely competitive marketplace. Purposeful, detailed, and total economic planning by the national government (even by an international government to a considerable degree) was emphatically called for—planning that harnessed scientific technology to human purpose (albeit a narrowly focused purpose) as never before and that realized the productive potential of modern technology as never before.

This planning, however, was not to be of a democratic socialist variety, with a major stress on cooperation, disinterested commitment to the common good, an equal sharing of burdens, and the preservation and ultimate enhancement of human freedom. It would not be done predominantly by freely chosen representatives of the people whose whole responsibility, systematically enforced upon them, was *to* the people. It would continue to be done predominantly by big-business men and high officers of the army—men who were generally highly competent in their respective fields, also strongly motivated by what they conceived to be patriotism, but who were also generally authoritarian in temper, coercive in tactics, and inclined (as has been said) to identify "patriotism" with "profit." *Their* profit. They made this identification in ways as various and extensive as they were probably, for the most part, unconscious (their published statements reveal a genius for self-serving rationalization), and they would now continue to do so throughout the war years, at the end of which democracy in America would be gravely injured at its roots.

Consider, as significant example, the fate of the aforementioned idea of pooling resources at the local community level for participation in war production.

The idea had occurred to many at the so-called local level by the fall of 1940. It was by then already clear that defense production would create raw material shortages that, if no remedial action were taken, would force the closure of small plants now engaged in civilian production, adding these to the large numbers of such plants that were yet idled, or partially so, by lingering depression. There would result a wastage of manpower (the ranks of the unemployed would be swelled) along with the forced transfer of the used portion of that manpower from present locations to already overcrowded industrial centers, where, because of acute housing shortages, rents and real estate prices were rising to ruinous heights. Clearly it was in the interest of national defense as well as of the small businesses and local communities themselves to find some way to achieve for the communities a much larger share of the government's defense business than they were now receiving. The fact stimulated efforts of a kind a truly representative national government would have welcomed and encouraged, efforts that were of the very essence of democratic process insofar as their substance was an energy of mind and purpose that surged upward from the people instead of thrusting downward coercively from an unrepresentative bureaucracy. Many hundreds of people in dozens of counties and towns across the land—free individual human beings exercising their rights and fulfilling their responsibilities as the rulers as well as the ruled of a self-governing society—joined together to make plans and develop programs for harnessing their local resources to a national will of which their own individual wills were integral parts.

One of the earliest and most energetic of these efforts was that of Beaver County in western Pennsylvania, which had been harder hit by the Great Depression than most areas.[28] Here the local people set up a carefully chosen county committee to make a detailed survey of local industrial resources. The survey listed the number and kind and size of the county's manufacturing plants, determined the extent of their present use (not a few were yet idle or partially so), indicated the kind of defense production in which plants could now or could readily be prepared to engage, and estimated the local availability of skilled and unskilled labor. Emissaries were then sent to Washington, where, according to recent NDAC press releases, government officials were anxiously searching for ways of recruiting idle plants for defense work. The emissaries perceived no sign of such anxiety, however, in those NDAC officials whom they initially consulted, officials having to do with materials supply and industrial production. These listened politely but indifferently to what the emissaries had to say; they made no affirmative response. Not until the emissaries encountered an NDAC official who served not under Stettinius or Knudsen, but as a key member of Sidney Hillman's labor division, did they receive encouragement.

This single interested official was Morris L. Cooke, the Philadelphia management engineer and power expert whose creative administration of the Rural Electrification Administration (REA) at that agency's outset had resulted in one of the New Deal's most solid triumphs. Cooke as REA administrator had become enamored of the cooperative idea (rural America was being electrified through cooperatives after privately managed utilities had flatly refused to do it),* and he immediately saw in this Beaver County pooling idea a means of democratizing efficiently a very considerable portion of the whole defense production effort, involving directly in it tens of millions of Americans who, under existing arrangements, could contribute to it nothing, or at most but a small fraction, of the skill, the energy, and the brainpower that were theirs. (Certainly the wastefulness of the existing arrangements became more glaringly evident with every passing day. When OPM replaced NDAC, it conceded that a large majority of the nation's 45,000 metal-working plants were currently excluded from the defense production effort: of 27,000 small establishments, 4,000 had been given government contracts averaging $50,000 apiece, while 6,000 had managed to obtain subcontracts; 17,000 were in danger of going under for lack of the metal they needed to continue production and would thereby contribute to the phenomenon of small-town and small-city depression amid a hugely developing economic boom.)[29] But, alas, Cooke's division of NDAC had nothing directly to do with the placing of government contracts, and the divisions that did were at that time doing all they could to frustrate the labor division's efforts to influence contracting policy affecting labor, as we have seen. Relations between the two divisions were consequently far from cordial. Cooke's persuasive power with the Knudsen-Stettinius people was severely limited, and his efforts to obtain action on the Beaver County program came to nothing. The "boys at the top [of the procurement system] just weren't going to play it that way," to quote Bruce Catton.[30]

The program was given what initially seemed like an excellent second chance in August 1941 when Roosevelt, at the same time as he created SPAB, established through executive order a so-called division of contract distribution in OPM.

Various pressures had moved Roosevelt toward this act.

A chief one of them was the bold stubborn energy, sparked by angry outrage at the way things were going, of Missouri's Senator Harry S. Truman. His countryman's distrust of Wall Street and big business in general had been abundantly encouraged by his remarkably thorough 1937 investigation of railroad financing—an investigation that exposed to the public gaze the devious ways in which great bankers and their allied corporate law firms were deliberately ruining, for their own profit, the nation's railroads.† He now fully shared the conviction of such as Morris Cooke that the government's failure to enlist small

---

*See *FDR: The New Deal Years,* pp. 491–92.
†See pp. 76–77, 208, of *FDR: Into the Storm;* also K. S. Davis, "Harry Truman's Attempt to Halt the Ruination of America's Railroads," *Gettysburg Review,* Summer 1989, pp. 457–475.

business in the defense program was a blow both to the defense effort and to the democracy that was supposedly being defended. He was thus prepared to listen with sympathy to complaints that came to him from his constituents about huge waste, gross inefficiency, and wholesale profiteering in the construction of Fort Leonard Wood in south-central Missouri. In late 1940 he conducted a personal investigation of army base construction and found the complaints to be justified. The contractor to whom the Army Quartermaster Corps had awarded the building contract was wholly inexperienced in large construction but highly skilled at exploiting the profiteering possibilities of unsupervised cost-plus. Expensive equipment sat unprotected and unused in the snow and rain; hundreds of workers stood around doing nothing, being encouraged by their employers to do nothing save draw their pay. Truman then embarked upon a personal tour of army bases under construction, driving his Dodge from Washington into the Midwest, going as far north as Michigan, as far south as Florida, and everywhere finding in various degrees the business-profiting waste and inefficiency that characterized the Fort Leonard Wood construction. Returned to Washington, he sought an appointment with the President, received one on February 3, 1941, and during it presented not only the findings of his trip, but also a small-business mobilization plan having similarities to Beaver County's, which he had devised with a longtime friend of his, a small-town banker named Lou Holland. It called for the formation, in each suitable geographic region, of a consortium of small manufacturers that could then contract as a unit with the army and navy, thus obviating the necessity of multitudinous contracting. Truman left the Oval Office dissatisfied, having been so overwhelmed by Roosevelt's personally flattering, loquacious cordiality that he doubted his presentation had made any affirmative impression upon the presidential mind.[31] He decided to go ahead anyway, on his own.

On February 10, 1941, he proposed to a receptive Senate the establishment of a special Senate committee to investigate the awarding of defense contracts. The proposal was assigned to the Senate Committee on Military Affairs, of which Truman was a member and which promptly reported it unanimously and favorably. But the proposal had then to pass, for funding, through the Committee to Audit and Control the Contingent Expenses of the Senate, and there it was stalled by the committee chairman, Senator Byrnes, who operated in this instance as agent of the administration. For Truman's proposal was decidedly unwelcome in a White House where dwelt vivid memories of the great trouble given Abraham Lincoln in Civil War days, and the great harm done the Union war effort, by a highly politicized Joint Committee on the Conduct of the War— where dwelt also a Roosevelt who gave speed of war mobilization top priority, believing that national survival depended upon this and was willing to accept such loss of economical efficiency as headlong speed inevitably involved. The Truman proposal might have died of Byrnes's inaction had not a bigoted reactionary southern Democrat, Representative Eugene Cox of Georgia, who

passionately hated Roosevelt, then proposed the establishment of a joint investigative committee having the wide unspecified powers granted the aforementioned Civil War committee. Byrnes was then persuaded, and had no difficulty
persuading Roosevelt, that Truman's committee would be infinitely preferable
to the one Cox proposed, whereupon the enabling resolution went to the Senate
floor. There a unanimous vote of the members assembled (only sixteen members happened to be present at the time) established a Senate Special Committee to Investigate the National Defense Program, with Truman as chairman.
Known at the time, and to history, as the Truman Committee (on it were five Democrats, two Republicans, most of them freshman senators), it began operations
on April 15, 1940, with an insultingly small initial appropriation of $15,000—
this for overseeing defense expenditures that, after the lend-lease appropriation
was made, totaled some $20 billion: Truman was naturally angered by this, but
not dismayed. He was confident that if the committee worked as diligently and
fair-mindedly as he was determined it would, the popular approval it gained
would assure adequate future funding.[32] This happened. The committee's natural first target was waste and fraud in army base construction, and by late summer of 1941 this target had been repeatedly explosively hit (one army camp
ended up costing ten times its originally estimated cost; another, estimated to
cost $480,000, actually cost $2,539,000). The committee, firmly established in
the public mind as a highly effective watchdog, received thereafter sufficient
funding with no difficulty—and its findings, fueling a growing popular disgust
with the way defense contracts were being handled, were forcing reforms (for
one thing, supervision of army base construction was transferred from the Army
Quartermaster Corps to the Army Corps of Engineers).

Hence Roosevelt's order establishing OPM's contract award division.

And certainly a governmentally sponsored formation of such small-business
consortia as the Beaver County people and Harry Truman proposed was well
within this division's province. "Through this new division, it was hoped the
Office of Production Management would be enabled more effectively to adjust
the dislocations and alleviate unemployment resulting from priorities and material shortages, and bring about maximum use of the nation's factories and industrial plants, especially the smaller ones," Michigan University Professor
Everett S. Brown would report in the 1941 *American Year Book.*[33] Of course,
the practical realization of this hope would have meant a radical change in war
production and procurement policies and procedures that were by that time very
deeply rooted in the big-business interest. Much ruthless uprooting and replant-
ing in new soil would have been required. And Roosevelt seems to have recognized, or to have been willing to accept, at least, that this was possibly so. The
man he appointed to head the division, evidently at Harry Hopkins's behest,
was yet another big-business man, namely, Floyd B. Odlum of the Atlas Corporation; but Odlum was reputed to be a "different kind" of businessman, a
"financial genius" who was imaginative and innovative. Moreover, the grant of

presidential authority under which Odlum was to operate was remarkably broad and was defined with a vagueness that assured great freedom of administrative interpretation. Odlum was authorized "to formulate and promote specific programs for the purchase of munitions and supplies by the armed services from the smaller units of industry; to make such changes as he desired in government procurement practices and procedures; to develop and activate plans for the conversion to war production of peacetime industries; to organize and use community 'pools' after the Beaver County model; [and] to provide both financial and engineering aid for small manufacturers, needed in defense production. . . ."[34]

We who know how Hopkins operated under the mere "bookkeeper" assignment publicly given him by the executive order that established a Works Progress Division in the National Emergency Council in 1935—who know, too, how Hopkins was fulfilling the similar "bookkeeping" assignment publicly announced for him a few months ago when he was named secretary of the lend-lease advisory committee—can imagine what Floyd Odlum might have done with the authority now given him, had he possessed half the focused will, the courage, the practical imagination, and the understanding of Roosevelt's mind that Hopkins, despite desperate illness, yet actively manifested. The most cursory examination of Roosevelt's administrative habits should have enabled a reputed genius to recognize in the wording of this executive order an urgent desire for *action now* to stem the rising tide of bitter popular dissatisfaction with the way industrial mobilization was going. Odlum would almost certainly have had uncommonly solid White House backing for almost any reasonable program he devised. He might conceivably have made himself master of the army-navy procurement system while developing and administering the efficient democratization of America's production potential that was epitomized by the Beaver County plan. He might thereby have gathered into his hands ultimately a very considerable portion of the governing power of the "economic czar" who was so loudly called for, though Odlum's would then have been a czardom that operated far more in the general public interest than the one Baruch and his conservative colleagues envisaged. To do this, however, Odlum would have had to conceive his fundamental purpose to be that of enlisting in the defense effort, in a cooperative rather than a coercive way, the vast energies now scattered futilely among a multitude of small, deprived units. Instead, big-business man Odlum conceived his role to be that of reaching down from Washington to help the "little fellow" obtain a "fair share" of the profits being generated by the national defense effort. In the prevailing situation, the helping hand must be that of big business. But since "fair share" remained undefined, and to the extent that small-business pressure was being felt by dollar-a-year men, Odlum's OPM colleagues very willingly cooperated with him in what became primarily a public relations campaign.

It was gaudy in appearance and loud in sound, this campaign (it involved much public speechifying, an activity in which Odlum himself participated fully), the evident hope being that it would prevent popular perception of the fact that nothing was being done, really, about the problem allegedly addressed. The campaign's announcement was made in late October 1941 through a press release from OPM's Division of Contract Distribution. "To make sure that no qualified manufacturer—no matter where he is—misses an opportunity to get a defense contract for lack of information," the release said, "officers of the Army, Navy, Maritime Commission, and the OPM will tour the country beginning November 10 in three special trains, painted red, white, and blue. The specials will carry exhibits consisting of samples of defense equipment and parts needed by the services to give prospective defense manufacturers a clear idea as to the type of articles needed." Each train was to have six cars, four of them containing samples, two of them the government officials.[35]

Shortly after these flamboyantly patriotic trains had departed their initial stations, Odlum proposed a plan to set aside 2 percent of all the nation's available "critical" materials to form a supply pool upon which small manufacturers who were unable to obtain war contracts might draw what they needed to stay in business. Measured against the demands of the Victory Program, practically all the available materials in America could then be classified as "critical," though aluminum, rubber, steel, copper, and zinc were in especially short supply—and the acceptance of Odlum's proposal would have sabotaged the priorities system that Nelson and SPAB were at that moment painfully setting up.[36] But the proposal itself was destined to be sabotaged by historic event within a few weeks after its announcement, whereupon Floyd Odlum would fade out of the national scene, not to be seen there again. Nor would the Beaver County plan, or Truman's consortia plan, be heard of again.

IV

ON the morning of Thursday, October 9, 1941, a small meeting of enormous consequence was held in the Oval Office. During it Roosevelt departed sharply from the strategy of drift and compromise he was then employing in his dealings with basic economic problems. Swiftly, amid great secrecy, and in the utter solitude that obtains at the apex of any great pyramid of power, he made a flat yes-or-no decision destined to affect profoundly the course of world history. . . .

Only two men sat across the desk from the President.

One was spare, lean Vannevar Bush, the archetypal Yankee whose background as inventor, engineer, and experienced administrator, coupled with great energy, a perhaps excessive self-confidence, a rare mastery of the intricacies of the Washington power structure, and a shrewd, imaginative, yet wholly practical mind, equipped him wonderfully well for the recruitment of scientists into government service and as bridge man between them and the executive and legislative branches of government (his talent for effective testimony before congressional committees was remarkable). He had been the architect of the National Defense Research Committee (NDRC), through which the first direct active linkage of American government with American science had been effected, and had become its first chairman when the President created it in June 1940. When at his behest an Office of Scientific Research and Development (OSRD) was established in June 1941, incorporating the NDRC in an expanded organization that included engineering developments and research in military medicine, he had been named its head, while another spare, lean New Englander, James Conant, organic chemist and president of Harvard University, who had been Bush's second in command of NDRC, became NDRC chairman. Conant continued as Bush's second in command—and among his responsibilities as committee chairman was oversight of federally sponsored uranium research. It was with regard to this last that Bush as OSRD director had instigated this Oval Office meeting.

The other man in the room was Henry Wallace. He came here at Bush's urgent request, not because he was Vice President of the United States, or even because he was chairman of the National Defense Board, but because he was a scientist (a plant geneticist), the only one in the cabinet, and Bush had found him to be a highly intelligent and contributive consultant on the matters with which OSRD was concerned. The President, too, had found him so.

The single subject discussed at this meeting was the atomic bomb, already so called by the very few, nearly all of them physicists, who were aware of it as a possibility. The possibility had seemed to Roosevelt real but remote when he first learned of it and promptly decided upon a governmental effort to explore it. That had been almost precisely two years ago: it was on October 11, 1939, that a letter written by Leo Szilard and signed by Albert Einstein was hand-delivered to the President, with extended commentary, by the astute but almost intolerably voluble Alexander Sachs. The question now to be answered by Roosevelt was whether the slender possibility then perceived had grown sufficiently strong during the intervening years to justify a greatly intensified governmental effort to realize it.

If it had, little credit for the fact was due the exploratory activity that initially resulted from Roosevelt's decision of October 1939. A presidential Advisory Committee on Uranium was then established consisting of an army ordnance expert, a navy ordnance expert, and, as chairman, Dr. Lyman J. Briggs of the National Bureau of Standards.* The three committee members were ill equipped for the task assigned them. Neither ordnance officer had any competence in the field of nuclear physics; both were predisposed to regard the "fantastically powerful" new explosive of which the physicists spoke as a pipe

*See *FDR: Into the Storm,* pp. 482–85, 509–10.

dream of overly enthusiastic and utterly impractical theorists. As for Chairman Briggs, he had begun his governmental career some forty years before as a soils physicist in the Department of Agriculture but had done no physics of any kind for decades and, as he neared retirement age, fitted all too well the stereotype of bureaucrat. He had the typical bureaucrat's religiously self-denying devotion to established routines and proper channels—was cautious, slow moving, unimaginative, and, encouraged in this by his presidential instructions, obsessed with and inhibited by the necessity for extreme secrecy. The consequence was that, from late October 1939, when an inadequate grant of $6,000 for the purchase of purified graphite was made to Columbia University physicists, until mid-June 1940, when the Briggs Committee, as it was called, became a subcommittee of the NDRC, it did precisely nothing to stimulate uranium research in the United States. Indeed, by its very existence, it retarded American atomic research, for the nation's physicists assumed that research activity was going forward secretly and that those of the physicists who could contribute to it were being called upon when needed—an assumption that discouraged university physics department work that might otherwise have been pressed.

There had been some speedup of government-sponsored atomic research after the Briggs Committee became a section of the NDRC. The committee was then enlarged and, with the removal from it of the army and navy ordnance representatives, became wholly a subcommittee of scientists. The speedup, however, was slight.

By that time laboratory experiment had determined that, as Niels Bohr and Princeton's John Wheeler had theorized in early 1939, it was only the rare light isotope of uranium, U-235, that fissioned under slow neutron bombardment; slow neutrons did not fission the slightly heavier isotope U-238, which made up 99.3 percent of all natural uranium. Further, it had been determined experimentally that when a slow neutron was captured by a U-238 atom, the atom, instead of fissioning, shot out two beta particles or rays in the process of becoming a new, heavier "transuranium" element, element number 94, atomic weight 239. This new element, soon to be officially dubbed plutonium, was bound to be even more unstable (radioactive), hence fissionable, than U-235 and, since it was a different element from uranium, could be separated by chemical means out of the uranium in which it was originally imbedded. These established facts confirmed absolutely the theoretical possibility of creating a self-sustaining, controllable chain reaction in natural uranium. This pointed, somewhat hesitantly, toward, in the present state of the world, the profoundly ominous possibility of creating a uranium explosive many thousands of times more powerful than any now in existence. Equally strongly indicated was the possibility of a yet more powerful plutonium bomb.

Briggs, when he came under Bush's jurisdiction, proposed to him a modest government expenditure of $240,000 for a research attack upon two basic problems, that of separating U-235 from U-238 and that of achieving a chain reaction in natural uranium. Bush approved the aim of the attack, but not the whole of the appropriation Briggs asked for. He reduced it significantly. Advised on this by Conant, he had at that time small expectation of an atomic weapon that would be useful in this war. A bomb of natural uranium, if possible at all, would surely be too large and heavy to be practically deliverable to a target area. As for a smaller bomb of U-235–enriched uranium, if *that* were possible, its development by either Germany or its opponents within the next half decade, the period during which the war's outcome would almost certainly be decided, was extremely unlikely: the immensity and difficulty of the technological effort required for any large-scale uranium isotope separation had been deeply impressed upon Bush's mind. Nor was Briggs himself much, if any more, hopeful of useful results. Consequently, through the remainder of 1940 and the first half of 1941, American research toward atomic bomb development had been given a much lower priority than radar research, since radar's huge war value (without it the Battle of Britain would almost certainly have been lost) was being daily and nightly demonstrated in Europe and on the Atlantic. During this period, Briggs's obsession with total secrecy operated to deprive American physicists of information that, had they possessed it and impressed its significance upon Bush and Conant, would have drastically altered the Bush-Conant conception of priorities.

Through the winter and spring of 1941, in accordance with the principle of full disclosure to the Americans that Sir Henry Tizard* championed, MAUD progress reports, incorporated in the minutes of committee meetings, were sent to the United States, arriving at frequent intervals on the desk of Lyman Briggs. The draft final report, whose last recommendation was that "the present collaboration with America . . . be continued and extended," also went to him. But none of the progress reports had elicited a U.S. response, a fact that increasingly puzzled and troubled the British scientists; and when the draft final report, which most certainly called for an American answer, was also received silently, anxiety became streaked with dismay. So when MAUD committee member M. L. E. Oliphant† flew to America in late August 1941 for consultations on

---

*Tizard was chairman of the British Committee of Air Defense and in April 1940 had established a subcommittee of scientists, known as the MAUD committee, to study the feasibility of a uranium bomb.[37]

†Oliphant, head of the University of Birmingham Department of Physics, had sent the findings of two refugee German physicists to Tizard in April 1940. The two, Otto Frisch and Rudolf Peierls, told how "a 'super-bomb' based on a nuclear reaction in uranium" was possible by the isolation of U-235, which was in turn made possible by already developed isotope separation techniques. They estimated the explosive force of a five-kilogram (eleven-pound) bomb would equal that of several thousand tons of dynamite. The conclusion seemed to them inescapable: An atomic bomb so light that it could be air delivered was not only merely possible, it was in the prevailing circumstances virtually inevitable! The only real questions were: Would it be made in time for use in the present war? If so, would the Allies or Germany have it first? The Frisch-Peierls memorandum was the impetus for the creation of MAUD.

radar with the NDRC, he made a point of finding out the why of the American silence. "I called on Briggs in Washington, only to find that this inarticulate and unimpressive man had put the reports in his safe and had not shown them to members of his Committee," he would remember in 1982, adding that he was "amazed and distressed."[38] He at once set about rectifying the deplorable situation. He emphatically presented the MAUD conclusions at a Briggs-chaired committee meeting, whose members, most of them, were astounded by what they heard; Briggs had led them to believe that the purpose of their uranium work was to develop a power source for submarines. Oliphant then flew out to California for the sole purpose of impressing the importance of the MAUD findings upon Ernest Lawrence, the dynamic and forceful inventor of the cyclotron, who directed Berkeley's Radiation Laboratory. But at Berkeley he found to his delight that he preached to the converted. Lawrence was already convinced of the feasibility of an atomic bomb using plutonium.

What Oliphant did not know was that Briggs, though he kept the MAUD findings secret from his own subcommittee's members, had, like the good bureaucrat he was, promptly passed the MAUD draft final report upward to his superiors, Conant and Bush, neither of whom had seen fit to say so to the visitor from England. Indeed, by that time a good many increasingly strong pressures for action were focused upon these two, and the two were increasingly moved by them. American physicist Charles C. Lauritsen had taken full notes at the MAUD committee meeting when the final draft report was discussed and approved and, upon his return to America, had given a persuasive written report to Bush. The MAUD draft report had been even more persuasive, so much so that Bush in July, on the basis of it, "had a discussion with Vice President Wallace about the question of spending a large amount of government money on the uranium program," to quote Conant.[39] Lawrence not only directly pressured the OSRD director and the NDRC chairman, but also enlisted the support of Arthur Compton, the Nobel laureate who headed the University of Chicago Department of Physics and also chaired a special uranium research review committee of the National Academy of Sciences, a committee established at Bush's request. Compton applied strong pressure of his own toward faster action.

He did so especially on a chilly September night when Conant and Lawrence (they had come to Chicago to receive honorary degrees from the university) were guests in his home. The three sat, coffee cups in hand, before the Compton fireplace, in which a wood fire blazed cheerfully, and as the flame light flickered across Conant's bespectacled, wide-mouthed countenance, the other two men bombarded him with what they assumed to be, for him, new information. *Item:* Extremely cautious and careful Enrico Fermi, experimenting at Columbia University with a lattice structure of pure graphite into which lumps of natural uranium were inserted at regular intervals, was convinced that his chances of thus achieving a chain reaction were considerably better than fifty-fifty. *Item:*

Lawrence's brilliant Berkeley colleague, young physical chemist Glenn Seaborg, using Berkeley's sixty-inch cyclotron, had produced traces of U-239 (plutonium) and was convinced it would be made in quantity by Fermi's "chain-reactive pile." *Item:* Dunning and Urey at Columbia were making definite progress with their gaseous diffusion method of uranium isotope separation, and what they were finding confirmed what, according to Oliphant, the British had found. Finally, it was "known" (so Lawrence and Compton asserted) that the Germans, with the brilliant Werner Heisenberg in the van, had been working hard on this uranium problem and were probably well on the way to acquiring a weapon that, in their exclusive possession, would enable them to dominate the world.

It was Compton's conviction ever after that Conant, when he sat down before the fireplace, believed "the time had come to drop the support of nuclear research as a subject for wartime study" because every competent physicist was needed for work more certain of "useful results," and that what he heard from his host and Lawrence produced a revolutionary change in his mind.[40] Actually, Conant was by then already persuaded, and had persuaded Bush, that a major governmental effort along the lines Compton recommended should probably be made, the clincher for him having been the judgment expressed to him by his longtime friend and fellow Harvard chemist, George Kistiakowsky. He had asked Kistiakowsky to explore for him the question of whether an atomic bomb was feasible, and Kistiakowsky, having done so with Compton and others, reported unequivocally: "It can be made to work. I am one hundred percent sold."[41] But on that September night in the Compton home the MAUD committee's final report had not yet been *officially* transmitted to the United States; Bush had decided to wait for the official transmittal before going to the White House with the recommendation he, upon Conant's advice, was prepared to make; and Conant saw no reason to shut off a Lawrence-Compton argument that bolstered the position he had already decided to occupy.

The final MAUD committee report came officially to the United States on October 3. Chairman G. P. Thomson himself brought it to Washington and talked it over with Conant. Immediately thereafter, Bush arranged the White House interview.

BUSH had a copy of the MAUD report with him when he and Wallace entered the Executive Office on Thursday morning, October 9, 1941. It is unlikely, however, that Roosevelt actually read any of it, then or later. His formal education had included nothing of physical science, almost nothing of science of any kind, nor had he, after his formal education was concluded, evinced any active curiosity about scientific subjects. He probably knew less of physics and chemistry than the average graduate of a liberal arts college, certainly less than the average graduate of a technical school, and he frankly admitted to himself, without shame or regret, his incompetence in these fields. Others existed who could supply his deficiency; by God's will (so he felt, deep down), others existed *for the purpose* of supplying his deficiency. Among these were Vannevar Bush and Henry Wallace. He therefore could and did rely totally at this moment upon Bush's knowledge and judgment and upon his own capacity to absorb quickly, with remarkable completeness, information that came to him through his ears. He listened closely to Bush's crisp, clear summary of what the report said. He took very largely into account Bush's policy conclusions concerning the matter in hand, conclusions strongly supported by Wallace. He asked clarifying questions. Bush stressed risks: What he was presenting, what the British were presenting, was "not a proved case," but a carefully calculated definition of possibilities and probabilities. There was no absolute guarantee that the bomb would do what these scientists predicted. It might not work at all. And to find out whether it would might require dangerously large diversions of scarce scientific manpower and material resources from war projects whose efficient ends were known.

So Roosevelt was, at that moment, acutely aware of grave risks.

Nevertheless he did not hesitate to make the decision that only he could make.

He made it within a few minutes after Bush had completed his exposition. He made it not as political leader or chief magistrate, in which roles he would have had to consult or at least take careful account of congressional and court opinions, but solely, exclusively, in utter secrecy,* as commander in chief of the armed forces of a nation at war, and this despite the fact that the nation was *not* formally at war, no declaration of it having yet issued from Congress. Perhaps he told himself that should he be challenged later, he could claim that he operated under the grant of large unspecified powers given the Executive by an officially proclaimed "unlimited national emergency." But if he told himself this, it was with an awareness that should the gamble he now admittedly took be lost, it would be very forcefully pointed out to the world that the extraordinary power he now exercised was not a distinct free grant to him by the people, made in constitutionally prescribed ways, but had instead been seized by him; it was Franklin Roosevelt who had suspended the Constitution to this extent by formally proclaiming that an unlimited emergency existed.

His decision was, therefore, a lonely and fearsome one.

But this is not to say that Roosevelt's actual experience of it was characterized by fearful loneliness. His, as we know, was an imperious nature, animated by an instinct for power and possessing no talent whatever for subordination (witness his behavior during his years as assistant secretary of the navy). In such

---

*Secrecy eased the decision, of course, by protecting him against any immediate political repercussions.

natures, at moments of crucial decision, the ache of loneliness and the dreadful sense of risk are offset by the exhilaration, the self-gratification, that derives for them from the exercise of great power. And fear is more than offset, the sense of aloneness is immensely reduced, when he who exercises power believes, as Roosevelt believed, that he does so under God's guidance, as God's chosen agent. For the power then is, in his feeling, not ultimately *his,* a personal property, but belongs to God, which means that the ultimate responsibility for the consequences of power's exercise also belongs to God. It is God—*not* God's agent, *not* Franklin Roosevelt—who determines consequences.

Of course, there were incorporated in this decision the maximum possible of tentativeness and open options. Roosevelt authorized a crash research program aimed at ultimate atomic bomb production, to be federally funded to whatever extent was necessary, but he stipulated that the research findings be exhaustively reviewed and the results of the review presented him before he, and he alone, decided whether or not actually to manufacture the bomb. Yet he could not but sense that the decision he made now was essentially a final one. In the ominous shadow of Germany's work with uranium (like Sachs, like MAUD, Bush and Wallace stressed this threat), he launched a process that was irreversible; it must inevitably proceed under the thickest possible cloak of secrecy to involve—eventually, probably—immense expenditures of scientific effort and industrial material that were needed elsewhere. We know he had this sense of inevitability and irreversibility because he mentioned to Bush on this Thursday morning that the funding of the project "would have to come from a special source available for such an unusual purpose" (he said "he could arrange this") and discussed also at some length with Bush and Wallace questions of "after-war control" of the atomic weapon (one yearns to know what each of the three said on this subject, but, alas, none of the three made a written record of this conversation).[42] Obviously Roosevelt realized thus early that the immensity of this new weapon's power, if the weapon worked, would alter all the proportions of statesmanship and effect a profound change in the relations among nations.

Further, there was a discussion that morning of ways and means of cooperating with whatever program the British government launched on the basis of the MAUD report—a discussion the consequences of which would prove almost as important historically as the bomb-making decision itself.

Bush, in the opening sentences of a memorandum he addressed to Conant immediately following the presidential interview, says he "told [the President] of the complete interchange with Britain on technical matters" (it was an interchange of which Roosevelt was probably already aware) and that Roosevelt "endorsed" the continuation of this. Roosevelt also agreed that when the time came for actual production of the atomic explosive, and the bomb itself, the whole enterprise should come under the administration of the U.S. Army. Bush then pointed out a significant difference between the way governmental war science was being currently handled in England and the way it was being handled in the United States. *In the United Kingdom* "technical people" did not hesitate to formulate policy and directly transmit policy arguments to the British war cabinet; they had most emphatically done so in this final MAUD report; and Oliphant, visiting this country, had even pressed his policy views upon American citizens before his own government's policy was officially decided.* *In the United States,* the "technical people" of the NDRC's S-1, along with Compton's special committee of the National Academy, were rigorously excluded from policy making, rigorously confined to technical matters; they might express their personal policy views to Conant and Bush, but these last two were alone authorized to decide policy at their level of operation, and they alone (Conant to a lesser extent than Bush) were authorized to make national policy recommendations to the President.43

Those who view all this in the light of history may see an analogy between a) the advantageous lack of compartmentalization of technical work in Britain that enabled British physicists to know what chemical engineers were doing; and b) an equally advantageous lack in Britain of sharp distinctions between the acquisition of new scientific knowledge and the working out of the policy implications of such knowledge. In England the same people were involved in both the latter enterprises. Bush saw no such analogy or, if he did, perceived no advantage shared by the two analogues. To his engineer mind, the difference between the two ways of operating was a difference between sloppiness and tidiness, between a wasteful looseness and an efficient tightness, of administrative organization—and he was most emphatically aware that if the British way were substituted for the American, he personally would lose a good deal of the administrative authority and governing power that were now his.

An awareness of similar kind, relating to Roosevelt personally, was incited in the presidential mind when Bush, having presented the British-American difference of operation, asked for a presidential decision on how the matter was to be handled here from now on. Roosevelt's instinct for power was at once alerted. All final policy decisions, on this as on other matters, must be made by himself; he preferred in this instance, for secrecy's sake, to have a single line of authority lead up to him; therefore the present American way of handling things, the one Bush had worked out, should be continued and extended. Whereupon Bush evinced his sophisticated knowledge of bureaucratic politics, his awareness of a need for self-protection in bureaucratic wars, by suggesting that there be appointed a top policy committee with which he could discuss policy matters and from which he could gain approval of policy recommenda-

---

*This had outraged Bush, who would have been yet more outraged had he known that Oliphant, when he argued vehemently for an all-out American atomic bomb effort, did precisely what Cherwell had told Churchill ought not be done.

tions before he presented these to the President. Roosevelt responded by naming such a committee then and there. On it he placed the two men seated before him, Bush and Wallace; Conant as Bush's deputy; Secretary of War Stimson; and Army Chief of Staff General Marshall. To these five and the President *all* policy consideration was to be confined; there must be maintained for the whole enterprise the utmost secrecy. And we may forecast here that this top policy committee would serve, in actuality, no other purpose than the protection of Bush and the strengthening of his position. Its five members held few meetings, possibly only one, chaired by Wallace, they never met as a group with the President; and Bush used the committee primarily to bolster his proposals to the White House, saying to the President now and then that, by the way, "this report has been approved by your Top Policy Committee."[44]

Thus it was made virtually certain, at the very outset of the atomic bomb project, that the scientists whose genius created the bomb would have little or nothing effective to say about whether, or how, or where, their creature was used. They were to be the victims of that glorification, by administrators, of mere administration (the allocation of material resources, the distribution of human effort according to plan) whereby almost every American enterprise is needlessly complicated and distorted. The typical American administrator evidently justifies with a non sequitur his satisfaction of a large appetite for power, to wit, that since means realize ends, he who administers means determines ends and must, in the very nature of things, do so—in other words, that the final determination of policy must be exclusively an administrative prerogative. The atomic scientists were creative men who, most of them, were acutely conscious of the social implications of what they were doing and greatly worried over the moral implications of what they were doing. Only reluctantly had they come to the conclusion that the bomb must be made. Only with difficulty had they then persuaded administrators that the bomb must be made. Yet they were now to become in effect the servants, the hired hands, of these same administrators and of others (after the army took over) considerably more obtuse and less morally sensitive— men who would often deal with them as if they were children, very bright and clever, of course, but too immature to operate in the adult world of hard practicalities and harsh realities. It has been remarked before in this work that the gap between power and intelligence, generally existent throughout history, is continually widened in our time by a rampantly advancing scientific technology because the amount of physical power thus placed in men's hands is multiplied within a socioeconomic system that, unchanged, is unfit to cope with it in ways conducive of human freedom and humane values. In the present instance, the gap was to be somewhat narrowed. But thanks to this decision in the White House on October 9, 1941, the gap would remain sufficiently wide to ensure the issuance through it of catastrophic, world-threatening errors.

V

AT Argentia in August, it will be remembered,* Roosevelt had declined Churchill's proposal that Britain, the United States, and the Netherlands government-in-exile jointly address to Japan a two-sentence warning that any further Japanese encroachment in the Southwest Pacific would compel countermeasures "even though these might lead to war. . . ." Roosevelt had feared that so explicit a threat would have an effect opposite the one Churchill wanted, that instead of deterring Japan it would spur the onset of a Pacific war whose outbreak, if it could not be prevented, Britain and the United States were anxious to postpone for as long as possible. The event could be put off, the time thus gained could be used to improve U.S. and Allied military positions in the Far East, if the talks between Hull and Ambassador Nomura that had begun last spring were continued, Roosevelt had argued. He had had his way. Immediately upon his return to Washington he personally presented to Nomura in a White House meeting the innocuous statement that the State Department had prepared as a substitute for Churchill's emphatic warning. He coupled with it a statement of U.S. willingness to resume the interrupted conversations. He encouraged Nomura to believe that agreements enabling the lifting of the oil embargo were still possible and might be soon achieved. For weeks the Konoye government in Tokyo had been urging, with growing desperation, a personal meeting between the American President and the Japanese Premier, possibly in Juneau, possibly in Honolulu, to iron out differences between the two countries, and Roosevelt now indicated his more than willingness to have such a meeting, provided the probability of its success was assured beforehand. Whereupon the gaining of such assurance became a prime motivation and purpose of the renewed Hull-Nomura talks. The effect in Tokyo had been a slight temporary slowing of the erosion of Konoye's position vis-à-vis the warmongers of his cabinet, headed by the war minister, General Hideki Tojo, who insisted that Japan's situation was worsening day by day and necessitated an immediate flat decision for war as soon as possible.

No amount of Rooseveltian charm and manipulative skill could change Japan's realization of its actual situation, which, thanks to the trade embargo, was indeed dire. Especially was this so with regard to oil. Considerable progress had been made in the production of synthetic oil in Japan, but this production was nowhere near great enough to supply the deficiency of natural oil on the home islands: home-produced oil, natural and synthetic, would total only some 3 million of the 33 to 38 million barrels of crude and refined petroleum needed to satisfy Japan's estimated 1941 needs. Before the oil embargo was imposed, 90 percent of this need had been supplied by imports from the Caribbean, the

*See pp. 264–65.

East Indies, and (the bulk of it, 70 or 80 percent) the United States. Now the need must be supplied from oil reserves that had shrunk since 1939 from 55 million barrels to (probably) less than 50 million. The reserve of aviation gasoline, a good deal of it coming directly or indirectly from the United States, had been increased from 1 million to 4 million barrels since 1939 but remained inadequate for a long war. Nor was oil all that was in dangerously short supply. There were also, for a long war, insufficient reserves of rubber, rice, bauxite, and iron ore. The recognized shortages had a determinative effect upon the war plans devised by the imperial military headquarters. These called for war action preferably in October or November, but before the end of the year at the latest (by January weather conditions would make operations difficult, if not impossible)—action having as its objectives the swift conquest of Java, Sumatra, Borneo, and Malaya; the expulsion of the British from Singapore; and the seizing of the Philippines, Guam, and Wake from the United States. In the view of the Japanese army, the diplomatic talks with the United States ought to be broken off but, since they continued, should be used as a smoke screen behind which to hide the preparations for attack—and one of the things to be hidden was a simulated surprise attack, during that late summer's Japanese naval war games, upon the great U.S. naval base at Pearl Harbor.[45]

In Tokyo on September 18 an attempt was made by four pro-war fanatics to assassinate Konoye. The attempt, seemingly presaging a violent seizure of governing power by the war party if its policy demands were not now met, left the Premier physically unhurt but spiritually weakened. Nothing of this foiled assassination attempt was known in Washington. The event was wrapped in thick secrecy by the Japanese government. But all who read Magic intercepts and Ambassador Grew's coded messages, as September gave way to October, were aware that Konoye was losing his nerve as well as his power, that the breach between him and the powerful Tojo widened steadily, and that this breach was becoming filled with a personal animosity, especially on Tojo's part, which made Konoye's long continuation as Premier unlikely. As for the Japanese navy, it was maintaining, as regards the policy crisis, a noncommittal silence. Its leadership evinced no enthusiasm for the greatly expanded war that the army proposed. Its top officers (Nomura was at one with them in this) were acutely conscious of the risks and probable tragic consequences of what the army proposed to do. But these naval officers were too concerned with saving face, too afraid of the charge that they were weak and cowardly, to express forthrightly their misgivings in public councils. They insisted instead that questions of war or peace must be decided by the Premier, that their own sole duty was to carry out whatever orders the imperial government issued, and that this they would faithfully do.

Ambassador Grew, all through these September and early October weeks, pleaded fervently for a greater flexibility of diplomatic stance by Washington officialdom. He was no "appeaser" in the sense in which that word, thanks to Chamberlain, had come to be known. He was convinced, as his "green light" telegram showed, that aggressive militarism increasingly dominated the Japanese government and must be firmly opposed by the United States. But he was a diplomat who knew that such militarism yet had strong opposition within Japan itself, that a large amount of democratic freedom yet existed in Japan, and he was consequently sure that the resources of diplomacy had not yet been utterly exhausted in the present crisis. He was convinced of the sincerity of Konoye's acceptance of the general principles of international order that Hull continually preached, convinced also that Konoye with the Emperor's backing was yet politically strong enough in late October and early November to keep whatever promises circumstances permitted to be explicitly made, and he was sympathetically aware of the Prime Minister's difficulties. It was simply politically impossible for Konoye to make all at once the unambiguous, finally conclusive statement that Washington demanded. Grew therefore proposed that Washington stop making this demand and instead adopt a step-by-step approach, enabling Japan to reverse step by step, in orderly, dignified fashion, the course of action into which it had been initially forced, as it felt, by American tariff and trade policies of the 1920s and early 1930s. Herbert Feis sums up Grew's judgment on America's operations in the fall of 1941, a judgment made in retrospect: "Wise American statesmanship . . . would have bartered adjustment for adjustment, agreeing to relax our economic restraints little by little as Japan, little by little, went our way. Instead . . . [b]y insisting that Japan promise in black and white, then and there, to conform to every American requirement, it [American statesmanship] made Konoye's task impossible." Whether or not this is so,* Grew's argument failed to persuade Roosevelt when it was first made—which seems strange in view of Roosevelt's strong desire to stall Tokyo for as long as possible. Less surprising is the refusal of Hull to countenance the slightest departure from the path of righteousness as he defined it. The secretary of state continued to demand that Japan immediately totally reverse its foreign policy—that it withdraw at once and totally from China and Indo-China, that it renounce its treaty ties with Berlin and Rome (by these it was pledged to go to war with the United States if Germany did), and that it in effect pledge itself now to go and sin no more.

On October 16, the news came to Washington that the Konoye cabinet had fallen. Two days later, General Tojo became Japan's Prime Minister while remaining on active army service, enabling him to continue also as minister of war.

---

*It seems unlikely that Grew's "wise statesmanship," had it been employed during these weeks, would have made any significant difference. Events were moving along the course already set with such momentum that they probably could not have been substantially rechanneled at that late date.

At this point Admiral Nomura tried to resign his ambassadorship, as Hull and Roosevelt promptly learned from Magic decrypts. With the change of cabinet he no longer knew what his government wanted him to do, and he himself did not know what could or should be done. His mission had clearly failed thus far. He was at the end of his tether ("I cannot tell you how much in the dark I am"), he was without influence either in Tokyo or Washington ("I am a dead horse"), and he did not "wish to continue this hypocritical existence, deceiving myself and other people." But the Tojo government begged him to stay on, promising to send out to him, as he had requested, a professional diplomat to help him with the continued talks, and his patriotism, his honor as a naval officer, persuaded him to do as his government desired. Ambassador Grew, too, thought that the talks, even now, should continue and had best be continued by the honest and, by nature, forthright admiral. For Grew yet perceived faint glimmers of hope: the members of the new Japanese cabinet were not all of one mind (Tojo's mind) on the question of war and peace; Emperor Hirohito was intervening on behalf of continued negotiations. There should be no compromise of principle by the United States, he said in a long telegram to Hull on November 3, but cognizance must be taken of the fact that the economic sanctions that Grew himself had favored had not produced the desired effect and might, if carried too far, drive Tokyo into an "all-out, do or die attempt to render Japan impervious to foreign economic embargoes." Certainly there was no reason, in Grew's opinion, for the United States to "rush headlong into war," because when Hitler was defeated, "as he eventually will be," the "Japanese problem will solve itself."[46]

A contrary pressure upon Washington was exerted by China's Chiang Kai-shek, who had felt as a snub his lack of representation at the Argentia and Moscow Conferences and was understandably thrust into the greatest anxiety by the change of cabinet in Tokyo, an anxiety added to that he felt over the influence the Chinese Communists in North China were having with the peasants and workers there. This last waxed as Chiang's military fortunes against the Japanese waned. For though nationalist China yet stood against the invaders, it stood precariously upon quaking ground. It was almost wholly lacking in air cover (Chiang's capital, Chungking, defenseless against air raids, was being savagely bombed every day), and it was desperately short of virtually everything else needed for self-defense, much less for offensive action. An American Volunteer Air Force of some three hundred pilots and planes had been organized by Colonel Claire Chennault, but it was still training in Burma. Only a fraction of promised lend-lease supplies had actually been received by Chungking. And Japan, Chiang was convinced, was about to launch from northern Indo-China a massive offensive into Yunnan province, its objectives the capture of Kunming and the severing of the Burma Road, China's only major supply line. The success of this offensive would mean the encirclement of China's fighting forces, the end of China as a nation-state. As October ended and November began, a series of excited telegrams went from Chiang to Washington. They called for the immediate supply of bombers and pursuit planes and for the issuance of what amounted to an ultimatum to Tokyo, saying in effect that a march into Yunnan would mean war with the United States.* The last of these urgent telegrams was read in Washington in the light of one that had been sent by Tokyo to the Japanese command in Nanking on October 31 and deciphered in Washington on November 2. It said that on November 25 two things would happen: the negotiations in Washington would be broken off and the Tripartite Pact between Germany, Italy, and Japan would be renewed for five years.[48]

Clearly time was running out.

Roosevelt asked for the advice of the Joint Board of the Army and Navy. He received in reply a lengthy memorandum dated November 5, 1941, signed by Marshall and Stark, in which the recommended response to Chiang's plea was defined in terms of the "world strategy" (Plan Dog its essence) already agreed upon by the leadership of America's and Britain's armed forces. Marshall and Stark were sure Chiang was mistaken about the imminence of a Yunnan offensive. The necessary concentration of forces "cannot be completed in less than about two months." Moreover, the "advance towards Kunming, over nearly three hundred miles of rough country, with poor communications," would be "extremely difficult." The Chinese, if able to wage war at all, should be able to defeat it. The United States must constantly, consistently act upon the premise that Germany was the primary enemy, Japan the secondary, which meant that war with Japan should be avoided "until Japan attacks or directly threatens territories whose security to the United States is of very great importance." Such "territories" were New Caledonia, Portuguese Timor, and those portions of Thailand (Siam) that lay "west of 100 degrees East or south of 10 degrees North," this last because such an attack would have Singapore as its objective. Considered in terms of world strategy, "a Japanese advance against Kunming, into Thailand except as previously indicated, or an attack upon Russia, would not justify intervention by the United States against Japan." Specifically, the two chiefs of staff recommended "that the dispatch of United States armed forces for intervention against Japan in China be disapproved; that material aid to China be accelerated consonant with the needs of Russia, Great Britain and our own forces; that aid to the American Volunteer Group be continued and accelerated; that no ultimatum be delivered to Japan."[49]

---

*Essentially the same Chinese appeals went to London, whence Churchill cabled Roosevelt on November 5, 1941: "The Chinese have appealed to us, as I believe they have to you, to warn the Japanese against an attack on Yunnan. I hope you might think fit to remind them that such an attack ... would be in open disregard of the clearly indicated attitude of the United States Government. We should of course be ready to make a similar communication. No independent action by ourselves will deter Japan because we are so much tied up elsewhere."[47]

By this time, U.S. defenses of the Philippines were being reinforced by the dispatch to Manila of several squadrons of B-17s (Flying Fortresses), to be followed soon by squadrons of the B-24s then being built; the latter were expected to have an operating radius of 1,500 miles carrying a seven-ton bomb load. Great risk attended this commitment of heavy bombers unaccompanied by pursuit planes to an area wholly lacking in early warning or interception capability, but since the ports and airfields whence Japan must launch her southward drive would thus be brought within bombing range, and since pursuit planes sent out by sea would arrive in Manila within weeks after the bombers did, the risk seemed well worth taking. Indeed, Stimson viewed this as a "strategic opportunity of the first importance" and said so in an October 21 letter to Roosevelt. "From being impotent to influence events in that area [the Southwest Pacific]," he wrote, "we suddenly find ourselves vested with the possibility of great effective power. . . ." Admittedly the power was "imperfect," but "even this imperfect threat, if not promptly called by the Japanese, bids fair to stop Japan's march to the south and to secure the safety of Singapore. . . ."[50] For, simultaneously, construction was beginning of an ocean-spanning chain of U.S. airfields, located on islands between Hawaii and Australia, and between Australia and the Philippines, to accommodate the long-range bombers. There was a downside to all this, however, that Stimson did not mention: Though its specifics remained unknown by the Japanese, strenuous American military preparations were known by them to be under way in the Pacific, which meant that Japan's military situation vis-à-vis her opponents grew steadily worse and that Tojo's argument for war at the earliest possible moment was supported by hard facts.

On November 5 the decision was made in Tokyo to present to Washington two more proposals for the aversion of conflict. Designated Plan A and Plan B, Plan B was to be presented only if or when Plan A was rejected. It was to be the absolutely final proposal that Japan would make; if no accord had been reached by November 25, the war decision would go to the Emperor; and meanwhile, preparations were to be rushed by the Japanese army and navy for the outbreak of hostilities on or about the first of December. Already approved (on November 3) by Admiral Isoruku Yamamoto, commander in chief of Japan's combined fleet, was an operations order, labeled "secret," saying that Japan "is expecting war to break out with the United States, Great Britain and the Netherlands" and would "be declared on X day" with the present order to "become effective on Y date," with X and Y to be specified later. This order was now (November 5) dispatched to the Japanese fleet commanders.[51]

On the evening of November 7, Nomura came to Hull's Wardman Park Hotel apartment to present two key portions of Plan A to the secretary of state, who thanks to Magic was already familiar with the whole of the document's contents. These differed but slightly from the proposal Roosevelt had found wholly unresponsive in early August. Japan would accept the "principle of economic equality" (the so-called Open Door policy) in China and throughout the Pacific area provided that same principle was applied worldwide; it would begin withdrawing its troops from China within two years following "the firm establishment of peace and order" there but would maintain armed forces of unspecified strength in north China, Mongolia, and Hainan island for a "necessary period" (defined as "about twenty-five years," Nomura was instructed to say if asked); the Japanese forces in Indo-China would be withdrawn at some unspecified time following the end of hostilities in China. In return for these vaguely defined "concessions," the United States was to restore normal trading relations with Japan and pressure Chiang Kai-shek into a settlement with Japan, in effect placing its seal of approval upon the gains bloodily made by Japan during the prolonged "China Incident." It happens that Hull, when he glanced over the paper Nomura presented him, was only a few hours returned from a cabinet meeting in the White House. During that meeting he had told his fellow cabinet members that Japan might attack at any time, and Roosevelt had orally pondered the question of whether or not the American people would support war action by the United States if Japan, without attacking the Philippines or any other American possession, moved against southern Indo-China, the Dutch East Indies, and Malaysia. It was, for the President, an anxious question, and he had put it to each cabinet member individually, in pollster fashion. Each had assured him that, in his or her opinion, the American people *would* support such action, though how strongly, how fervently, none could say. All could and did reiterate that the outbreak of hostilities should be postponed for as long as possible. So Hull in his evening talk with Nomura, instead of commenting directly on the paper before him, abruptly introduced an idea of his own (he claimed it was a sudden inspiration on his part) whose sole merit was that its discussion might prolong the conversations. "Supposing the Chinese were now to say that they desired a real friendship with Japan and would do everything in their power to work together [with Japan] along peaceful ways," said Hull, according to the official U.S. account of this meeting. "Would not this be a wonderful opportunity for Japan to launch forth on a real new order, an order from which Japan would gain her real moral leadership in the Far East?" Asked if China's "intentions had already been ascertained" on this matter, Hull said they had not, the idea was solely his own (he must have known there was a slight chance that Chiang would agree to it), but he wanted it "conveyed to the Japanese Government for an expression of its views thereon."[52]

Three days later, Nomura was received by Roosevelt, who had Hull by his side, for a conversation at which the whole of Plan A was formally presented and, to all intents and purposes, pronounced dead on arrival by its recipients. Four days after that (November 14), a Magic decrypt of a message from Tokyo to Nomura told Hull and Roosevelt that "in the event of the United States' participation in the European War, Japan shall automatically carry out *what she un-*

derstands to be [present author's emphasis] the obligations which befall her as a party to the Three Power Agreement."[53] And on November 17 professional diplomat Saburo Kurusu, having flown from Japan to help Nomura with the final negotiations, was received with the Japanese ambassador by the President and Hull in the Oval Office. The professional diplomat proved at once a far less effective negotiator with the Americans than Nomura the amateur had been and continued to be despite a palpable confusion of mind. Both Roosevelt and Hull, Hull especially, took an instant dislike to Kurusu the man. He was much more stereotypically Japanese in physical appearance than Nomura was, being short (Nomura was six feet tall) and slight of build. He wore glasses, as did so many Japanese, and he peered through them with, in Hull's opinion, shifty eyes. There seemed to Hull nothing in him of the simple, the direct, the forthright, and much that was sly, slippery, and deceitful as he argued in fluent (all-too-fluent) English a case that was itself known to all Magic readers to be disingenuous.

The meeting was predictably unproductive.

Immediately before or after it, Roosevelt scribbled in pencil a note to Hull, undated, whose contents were in line with the step-by-step approach for which Grew had pleaded in September and early October. It outlined a temporary arrangement, a modus vivendi to last six months, during which a final settlement of issues might be worked out, thus: "Six Months. 1. U. S. to resume economic relations—some oil and rice now—more later. 2. Japan to send no more troops to Indo-China or Manchurian border or any place south (Dutch, Brit. or Siam). 3. Japan to agree not to invoke tripartite pact if U.S. gets into European war. 4. U.S. to *introduce* Japs to Chinese to talk things over but U.S. take no part in their conversations."[54] Before this could be worked into a form presentable to the Japanese, they, through Nomura and Kurusu, presented to Roosevelt and Hull (on November 20) their Plan B. It was itself in the nature of a modus vivendi, as Magic readers already knew: Pending a final settlement, Japan would make no further military advance, nor would the United States take military action "in the Southeastern Asia and the Southern Pacific area except the part of French Indo-China where the Japanese troops" were presently stationed; Japan would move its troops now in southern Indo-China to northern Indo-China "upon the conclusion of the present arrangement" and withdraw altogether from that country as soon as peace was restored between China and Japan; the United States would cooperate with Japan in "securing the acquisition of those goods and commodities which the two countries need in Netherlands East Indies"; the commercial relations between the United States and Japan that had prevailed prior to the freezing order would be restored, with the United States supplying Japan "a required amount of oil"; the United States would "refrain from such measures and actions as will be prejudicial to the endeavors for the restoration of general peace between Japan and China."[55] Plan B's final point was, of course, absolutely unacceptable to the United States and was known to be by those (General Tojo was a chief one of them) who insisted upon its inclusion.

By this time the Americans knew via Magic that Nomura had pleaded with Tokyo (in a November 14 telegram) for more negotiating time and been turned down. "[T]hough I know I will be harshly criticized for it," he had written, "I . . . would like to caution patience for one or two months. . . ." Foreign Minister Tojo's prompt and irritable response (on November 16) had been that "the situation renders this out of the question. The deadline for the solution of these negotiations is set . . . and there will be no change. Please try to understand that."[56] Nevertheless, when, responding to Plan B, the modus vivendi Roosevelt had outlined in his penciled note to Hull was shaped into a formal proposal and presented to Nomura, this on November 22,* Nomura, with Kurusu in support, had the temerity to send another request to Tokyo for negotiating time beyond November 25. His request had the urgency of desperation. Tojo stressed in his reply the extreme difficulty ("for reasons beyond your ability to guess") of any deadline postponement whatever, but "if you can bring about the signing of the pertinent notes we will wait until November 29. After that," he concluded, "things are automatically going to happen." These exchanged messages were promptly read by the Americans via Magic. On that same day, in a top-secret message that was *not* intercepted and so did *not* become a Magic decrypt, the supreme commander of the Japanese fleet, Admiral Yamamoto, sent a highly secret signal to a task force that had been assembled in Hitokappu Bay at windswept and desolate Etorofu island in the Kuriles northeast of the Japanese homeland: "The Task Force will move out . . . on 26 November and proceed without being detected to Rendezvous set for December 3. X-day will be December 8 [Japanese time]."[58]

VI

At no time during his presidency was Roosevelt under greater, more various public pressures than during this long autumn of 1941, and in no other extended period, not even during the months immediately preceding the outbreak of the war in 1939, did he feel in general more helpless, less able to effect significant change in the course of onrushing events. The pressures of impending war in the Pacific mingled inextricably with those of the continuing Battle of the Atlantic, and these with the pressing interconnected problems of aid to Russia, of lend-lease administration, of Neutrality Act revision, of inflation control, and of

---

*It was, of course, presented also, on November 24, to Churchill, who gave it a lukewarm reception. "Of course, it is for you to handle this business," he replied on November 26, but, "What about Chiang Kai-shek? Is he not having a very thin diet? . . . If they [the Chinese] collapse our joint dangers will enormously increase."[57]

defense-threatening labor strife managed by perhaps the bitterest of Roosevelt's many bitter enemies, the isolationist power-lustful John L. Lewis. Again, as in the spring and summer of 1939, his general experience was that of a man whose major effort and purpose are simply to keep his balance, a precarious balance, as he rides an all-too-flimsy raft down a narrowing turbulent river toward the roar of a rock-strewn rapids or, perhaps, of a death-dealing waterfall. Nor was he permitted only to keep his balance and ride passively. He must instead constantly act, must tilt this way and that, must prod and nudge and pull, all the while feeling that what he did was essentially a strenuous passivity, a helpless waiting upon a culminating event over which he had no control.

On October 9,* 1941, he addressed to Congress a request that the Neutrality Act be revised to permit the arming of American merchant vessels and the delivery of war goods to belligerent ports. Such revision, consistent with the stated purpose of lend-lease, was necessary for lend-lease's effective implementation, as Roosevelt in his congressional message pointed out. "I earnestly trust that the Congress will carry out the true intent of the Lend-Lease Act by making it possible for the United States to help deliver the [war] articles to those who are in a position effectively to use them," he said. "In other words, I ask for Congressional action to implement Congressional policy." And such revision, as regards the arming of merchantmen, would be but a return to traditional American practice. "Until 1937 [arming merchant ships for civilian defense] ... had never been prohibited by any statute of the United States. Through our whole history American merchant vessels have been armed whenever it was considered necessary for their own defense." He hastened to add that he "would not go back to earlier days when private traders could gamble with American lives and property in the hope of personal gain, and thereby embroil this country" in a war-breeding incident of no "direct interest" to the American public. But there were now safeguards against this. "[T]oday no ship and no cargo can leave the United States, save on an errand which has ... been approved by governmental authority." He concluded his plea with naked assertions: "We will not let Hitler prescribe the waters of the world on which our ships may travel. ... We intend to maintain ... the freedom of the seas against the domination by any foreign power which has become crazed with a desire to control the world. We shall do so with all our strength and all our heart and all our mind."59 These assertions were promptly implicitly challenged across the land, though especially in the Middle West, by a storm of isolationist opposition to what the President proposed—an opposition, dominated by Republicans, no less adamant and even more bitterly forceful than that provoked by each earlier major national defense proposal made by the President. For isolationism, now stripped down to its hard core, made up in increased stridency and solidity for the loss of general prestige

*The day of Roosevelt's fateful meeting with Bush and Wallace.

it had suffered in recent months. It remained as a boulder too large to be moved and impossible to shatter athwart the only path toward intervention that Roosevelt perceived as possible for him to follow.

To his press conference on the day following his congressional message Roosevelt presented disturbing statistics, derived from Selective Service, concerning the fitness of young American men for the rigors of war or even the rigors of ordinary life. Fifty percent of the two million men called up in the draft thus far had been "disqualified for physical, mental, or educational reasons." One of every ten had been rejected because he couldn't meet the fourth-grade educational requirements. Of the remaining nine hundred thousand rejectees, something over 20 percent were rejected for dental reasons, a little over 13 percent for poor vision, 10 percent for cardiovascular diseases, a little less than 7 percent for musculoskeletal defects, 6.3 percent for venereal disease, 6.3 percent for mental and nervous illness, 6.2 percent for hernia, a little less than 6 percent for hearing defects, 4 percent for foot defects, nearly 3 percent for defective lungs (including tuberculosis), and 17 percent for a miscellany of reasons, the chief being accidental injury. Clearly indicated was a serious long-range health problem for the nation, said Roosevelt, who then vaguely suggested, as "one of the phases" of an answer, the mandating of periodical physical checkups for everybody. "I suppose, under the Constitution, a person has a right to die at an early age," he went on. "But I think . . . government, local government, state government, has a right to say to that fellow, 'Now, look, don't die. Why don't you get better?' . . . and know . . . whether that individual insists on dying or not." He did *not* indicate any realization (Eleanor Roosevelt stated it as a fact) that America's health care delivery system was faulty and should be reformed. He did *not* suggest, even vaguely, what his wife argued for vehemently, the need for instituting a national health program, or at least laying the foundations for it, as an integral part of the defense effort. Nor would he say, when prodded to do so by a reporter's question, that the dismayingly large number of rejections because of educational deficiency, the bulk of them in the South, argued for a program of federal aid to education. "[P]erhaps some day we may come to some form of . . . [federal] aid for . . . the poorest sections of the United States," he said, ". . . but I don't think the federal government ought to undertake running the educational field. A great majority of states have pretty good educational systems."[60]

Six days later (October 16) came an episode in the North Atlantic of the kind for which Roosevelt had long been waiting, since it had all the earmarks of a truly galvanizing incident (the *Greer* episode had served as a poor substitute). A slow convoy of forty merchantmen, guarded meagerly by four British corvettes, encountered a wolf pack of U-boats as it sailed eastward some four hundred miles south of Iceland. Ten of the convoy's vessels were sunk before five U.S. destroyers, dispatched from Reykjavík in response to the convoy's urgent plea for help, arrived on the scene as night was falling. One of the destroyers was the USS *Kearney,* and in the confused night action that followed she was struck by a torpedo, which killed eleven of her crew, wounded several others, and for a time disabled her power system. Power partially restored, she barely made her painful way back to Iceland. The immediate effect of this in Congress was gratifying to the President: On the morrow of the fatal action the House approved 259–138 the arming of merchant vessels and sent the Neutrality Act revision bill to the Senate, which was considerably more inclined toward the further revising amendments that Roosevelt wanted than the House was. This, however, was the limit of an effect Roosevelt had hoped would be much greater. There was no huge outpouring of popular outrage and wrath.

He tried hard to overcome the lethargy, the apathy, or whatever it was that had America in its grip, when he delivered a nationally broadcast speech on Navy Day, October 27. He exploited to the full the wrath-inducing potential of the *Kearney* attack. "The shooting has started," he cried into the microphones. "And history has recorded who fired the first shot. . . . America has been attacked! The USS *Kearney* . . . belongs to every man, woman, and child in this country." He claimed to have in his possession two highly secret Nazi documents dealing with the postwar world. One was a map showing how the Nazis proposed to reorganize Central and South America; fourteen presently existing nations were to be replaced by five vassal states, one of them including Panama "and our great life line—the Panama Canal." The other document was "a detailed plan . . . to abolish all existing religions," replacing them with "an International Nazi Church" having as its Bible *Mein Kampf* and as its symbols, in place of the cross of Jesus, "the swastika and the naked sword." He excoriated the "Americans—not many" who continued "to insist that Hitler's plans need not worry us" and whose "protestations" would "as usual be paraded through the Nazi press and radio during the next few days." These people did not speak the mind and will of their country, they spoke the mind and will of America's enemies ("the motive of such Americans is not the point at issue"), and their efforts to disunify the American people and breed distrust of the American government had failed and would forever fail since "we Americans have cleared our decks and taken our battle stations."[61] But if they had, they waited there— disturbingly quiet, disturbingly passive—for battle orders their commander in chief refrained from issuing. They had heard before from his lips that Hitler was the enemy of mankind and of all that America stood for. They had been told by him again and again in fervent words that American survival required Hitler's defeat. But the Executive action logically implied by Executive words had not been taken. The head of the America First Committee, General Robert E. Wood, had dared Roosevelt, a few days after the *Kearney* incident, to present the issue of war or peace unequivocally to Congress, as Stimson had repeatedly urged him to do, and Roosevelt dared not accept the challenge. Nor was such ineffectiveness limited to the American domestic scene: as Robert Sherwood writes,

Roosevelt's "brave words" unbacked by brave action "may well have been greeted with derisive laughter by the war lords in Berlin and Tokyo."[62] Certainly Hitler's navy was undeterred by them. On October 31, just three days following the Navy Day speech, the destroyer USS *Reuben James,* escorting a British convoy that had sailed from Halifax, was torpedoed and sunk off the west coast of Iceland—the first American fighting ship to be lost in combat in World War II. One hundred and fifteen of the crew, including all the officers, were killed. Yet the popular reaction in the United States was, if anything, more fatalistically passive than that which followed the *Kearney* episode—and Roosevelt issued no public statement concerning it, having already "said everything 'short of war' that could be said," as Sherwood notes.[63]

On November 7 the Senate passed by a distressingly close vote (50–37) the Neutrality Act amendment in the form proposed by the President (the House would pass it by an even closer vote, 212–194, a week later, after Roosevelt had sent an urgent written appeal to the House Speaker and majority leader). On that same day, Roosevelt announced that, "pursuant to the power conferred upon me by the Lend-Lease Act," he had found the defense of the Soviet Union to be vital to the defense of the United States and was therefore authorizing and ordering the delivery of lend-lease supplies to that country.[64] This move greatly facilitated aid to Russia, whose ability to pay cash for what she needed was, as in the case of Britain last year, swiftly draining away. It facilitated with unprecedented efficiency because of a change in lend-lease management that Roosevelt had just made. Ten days before (on October 28), he had established by executive order an Office of Lend-Lease Administration as an integral part of the Executive's Office of Emergency Management, thus at last formally incorporating in the national defense structure what had theretofore been an almost wholly ad hoc operation directed by Harry Hopkins from his White House bedroom. Hopkins himself had instigated the change. In the weeks following his arduous Moscow trip and the Argentia Conference his physical strength had not been restored to even the meager extent normal for him. Lend-lease was now a going and steadily growing operation, the day-by-day direction of which, he told Roosevelt in September, should be turned over to a full-time administrator. He proposed for that post Edward R. Stettinius, Jr., with whom he was on personally friendly terms and who could be counted upon to adhere to the policies that he, as Roosevelt's right arm, would continue largely to shape. It was to Stettinius, therefore, that this executive order went—and it was to the Navy Hospital that Hopkins went (on November 4) for what turned out to be a four-week stay. He, Hopkins, would be by no means completely out of action during these four weeks: there was a phone in his hospital room, and through it he remained in constant touch with Stettinius and General Burns on lend-lease matters; also, his doctors permitted him to leave the hospital occasionally to dine with the President in the nearby White House.

A running accompaniment of the above various troubles for Roosevelt—

indeed, the major absorbent of his time and energy as the Pacific crisis entered its final, culminating stage—was the labor dispute in which the key figure was John L. Lewis, the lion-maned, beetle-browed boss of the United Mine Workers (UMW) who had launched the CIO. Two factors governed it. *One* was a compound of the power lust, the stubborn and extreme isolationism, and the Roosevelt hatred of the combative, utterly ruthless, yet immensely able Lewis. The *other* was the chronic furious anger bred in America's coal miners by the horrendous conditions of their labor. Hazardous under the best of conditions, their work under those that prevailed in the United States was little less dangerous than a soldier's in combat; almost 1,300 of them had been killed on the job in 1940, and thousands more had been permanently injured. There was no national mine safety law, and such laws as were adopted by the states were commonly flouted by mine operators powerful enough to have their way with state and local governments. The fatal accident rate in American coal mines was three times that in England, four times that in France, six times that in Holland; mine disasters were so frequent in the United States that none that killed less than a score was deemed nationally newsworthy.[65]

The specific issue now in dispute was the "union shop" in the so-called captive coal mines (mines owned by and producing coal only for a steel company), a union shop being one in which all who accepted employment must also accept union membership. This specific issue was, however, but an instance of a general and fundamental one, namely, union security in the face of the vast expansion of the industrial labor force that resulted from huge government defense contracts. In the view of labor leaders, union security and simple justice required the forced enrollment of the newly employed in the unions that had fought for and obtained the worker benefits they now enjoyed. Otherwise business management, which had fought tooth and nail against unionization and collective bargaining, could be counted upon to use the great increase in unorganized labor to weaken or destroy the labor movement. Indeed, business management was currently fighting tooth and nail against the union shop in defense industries. At the center of the controversy was the eleven-member National Defense Mediation Board. It had generally opposed the union shop, though on one occasion it had granted a closed shop (a shop in which union membership was a condition of initial employment); it had sometimes plumped for the "maintenance of union membership" clause that Sidney Hillman had worked out as a compromise arrangement;* it had shifted from one side to the other on issues involved in the jurisdictional war between AFL and CIO, though inclining (or so thought the CIO) toward AFL; and many of its decisions had been

---

*This did not make union membership a condition of employment but required every employee who was a union member when employed, or who became a union member after his employment, to remain in the union for the duration of the defense contract or lose his job.

weighted heavily on the side of employers (or so the leaders of organized labor believed).[66]

Last summer, as the time approached for the signing of a new labor contract, Lewis, whose union already comprised 95 percent of the captive mine labor force, had promised labor peace in the captive mines if steel management agreed to a union shop in the upcoming contract. Steel management had refused the offer, feeling secure in the knowledge that it had the firm support of a business-dominated defense bureaucracy, that uninterrupted steel production was essential to defense, and that a general public informed through business-dominated mass media was automatically inclined to blame unions, not management, for any work stoppage. So in mid-September, Lewis had called some fifty-three thousand UMW captive mine workers out on strike, provoking screaming headlines to the effect that he had declared a personal war on Roosevelt that fatally threatened national defense. Hearings on the matter were promptly begun by the National Defense Mediation Board. On September 19, the board asked the strikers to go back to work for thirty days while hearings continued before a panel of the board. They did so on September 22. But they were called out again by Lewis on October 27, after the board panel had announced its unwillingness to enforce its own recommendations and had urged the miners to remain on the job while the full eleven-man board (not just the panel, as theretofore) considered the matter and made a final decision. On October 29, in a White House conference called and presided over by Roosevelt, Lewis reluctantly agreed with National Defense Mediation Board chairman William H. Davis and U.S. Steel representative Myron C. Taylor (he had formerly been chairman of the board of that corporation) that the dispute be submitted to the full mediation board and that the miners return to work pending the board's final decision. They did so on November 3. But a week later the full board voted 9–2 against the union shop, the two dissenters being the two CIO representatives, Philip Murray and Thomas J. Kennedy (he was UMW secretary), whereupon Lewis announced that the strike would resume. Both Murray and Kennedy, in the interests of labor solidarity on the fundamental issue, then resigned in protest from the board, and so did the board's five CIO alternates, which meant that the CIO's five million members were no longer represented. The board's effectiveness was thus totally destroyed.

Roosevelt reacted swiftly, not by issuing orders as chief executive or commander in chief, but by assuming personally the mediating role the board had been established to perform. He summoned mine union officials and steel executives to the White House on November 14, stressed to them the absolute necessity for uninterrupted coal production, and warned them (a warning obviously aimed chiefly at Lewis) that "if legislation becomes necessary toward this end the Congress . . . will without question pass such legislation." He added that the pressure upon him "to ask for legislation during the last couple of months" had been "not only constant but . . . very heavy." Of course, there was "absolutely no element of threat" in his "telling you this"—but he went on to say emphatically "that the Government of the United States will not order, nor will Congress pass legislation ordering, a so-called closed shop." He concluded by asking them ("I never threaten—I am asking you") to resume collective bargaining immediately following this meeting, and if "you can't agree today, please keep on conferring tomorrow and Sunday."[67] There followed three days of fruitless wrangling among the conferees that ended acrimoniously on Sunday afternoon. Next day, November 17, the day on which special Japanese envoy Kurusu was received by Roosevelt in the Oval Office, the coal strike resumed—and this time it was not only the captive mines that were struck, but also, in sympathy, many commercial ones in Pennsylvania, West Virginia, and Kentucky. Roosevelt at once (Tuesday, November 18) addressed to Lewis and the steel executives a lengthy letter asking them "as patriotic Americans" to accept one or the other of alternative proposals: "(a) Allow the matter of the closed shop in the captive mines to remain in status quo for the period of the national emergency . . . or (b) Submit this point to arbitration, agreeing in advance to accept the decision so made for the period of the national emergency without prejudice to your rights in the future." Within an hour after receiving this missive, the steel executives agreed to binding arbitration. Lewis replied simultaneously that he could not do so without consulting the UMW's national policy committee. Roosevelt refused to wait. On November 22, he presented Lewis with a fait accompli, informing him by letter that, the steel executives having accepted his proposal, "I am today appointing a board of three members consisting of Dr. John R. Steelman [director of the U.S. Conciliating Service of the Labor Department], Mr. Benjamin Fairless [president of U.S. Steel], representative of the steel industry, and Mr. John L. Lewis. . . ." On that same November 22, Lewis informed the President in writing that the UMW's national policy board had voted unanimously to accept binding arbitration. The miners then returned to work.[68] Roosevelt had "suggested" that the board "begin its work immediately and remain in continuous session until this task is completed." The "suggestion" was followed. For two long weeks there was a flat and far from amicable confrontation of Lewis and Fairless, between whose unyielding positions Steelman was evidently unwilling or unable to decide. He finally did so on the morning of Sunday, December 7, 1941, when the board by a vote of 2–1, with Fairless in dissent, ruled in favor of the union shop for captive mines. News of the event was so overshadowed by simultaneous news of a far greater event that the general public scarcely noticed it, fortunately for the public relations of both Lewis and the administration—but the fact remained that Lewis, at the cost of making himself perhaps the most hated man in the United States, had won for the miners and for the labor movement as a whole a solid victory. He had won it in the only way, seemingly, any such victory could now be won, through unyielding combative confrontation.[69]

VII

IT was with almost incredible patience, fortitude, and self-control that Roosevelt bore these various heavy burdens, giving no sign to the general public and few to his most intimate associates of the anxiety, the frustration, and the sense of utter helplessness in the face of great event that were his. Indicative of the general tenor of his demeanor was the good humor, the warm camaraderie, the uninhibited give-and-take punctuated by inordinate laughter at rather crude jokes, which continued to characterize his twice-a-week press conferences. (In his October 24 press conference, asked about stories of wildly inaccurate Nazi bombing of ships in the Red Sea, he replied that the only relevant thing he had heard was that Hitler was trying to get "one of the few prominent Jews left in Germany" to explain how Moses managed to part the Red Sea waters. The sally provoked gales of laughter. In his November 3 press conference, a reporter told him "of a time Tuxedo Park [rich, therefore Republican] voted unanimously the Socialist ticket" due to a voting machine error. "I love it!" he proclaimed with a loud laugh. In his December 2 press conference, a reporter presented him with a heavy ash walking stick, saying that if ever the President needed a "big stick," it was now. Without the blink of an eye, he who could not walk replied that this was "one thing" he had "longed for" and held it up before the reporters, saying that it had "an awfully nice balance." Again there were gales of laughter.)[70] The maintenance of this facade of cheerfulness and confidence was all the more remarkable in that the outer props for it in his immediate environment were now fewer than at any earlier time in his presidency, his personal life being lonelier than at any earlier time.

Among the few elements of personality he shared with Woodrow Wilson, repeatedly manifested in the past, as we have seen, was an uncommonly great dependence, for his psychological security, upon the adoration of women. This must be, as in Wilson's case, a certain kind of adoration, essentially uncritical, having little or nothing in it of physical sex—a kind of spiritual subservience that Eleanor had never been able to give him save in scattered moments during the early years of their marriage. Such adoration had been given him in huge quantities by his mother, despite her general imperiousness and frequently expressed will to dominate his life. It had been given him in equally huge quantities by Missy, despite her unhappy awareness of a coldness, an untouchable aloofness, at the very core of him. But now both these adoring women were gone from his personal life. And gone also, or sadly diminished, were personal relationships that had formerly enriched his official, working life. The replacement of liberal New Dealers by conservative businessmen had meant a departure from him of lively sympathetic company. He could not enjoy half as much (if at all) the relatively stodgy personalities and narrowly focused minds of men whose ruling passion was moneymaking and the gaining of economic power; he had with these men few or none of the relaxed human contacts (through luncheons, cocktails, poker sessions, Val Kill picnics, cruises) that had with other men lightened and lubricated his working life.

Representative of this general loss was the departure from government of Tom Corcoran. As we know, he with his great friend Ben Cohen, both of them protégés of Felix Frankfurter, had been very much a part of government's vital center during the New Deal years. Roosevelt had delighted in Corcoran's exuberance, wit, warming Irish charm, and accordion playing and ballad singing in a rich tenor voice. But, inevitably, Corcoran had been found steadily less useful and more expendable operationally by Roosevelt as the President shifted to the political Right following the 1938 midterm elections. Naturally, Corcoran, whose frequent ruthlessness in the service of the President had made him many enemies, resented this. As for the placing of a corporation executive flanked by corporate lawyers in virtually every key position of the national defense effort, a move deemed a practical necessity by Roosevelt, it was seen by Corcoran as a moral outrage, an unforgivable abandonment of fundamental principles. And outrage was joined to deep personal hurt when Roosevelt rebuffed Corcoran's efforts to play in the 1940 election campaign a role equivalent to that he had played in 1936. The hurt was compounded when Roosevelt, evidently anxious to get him out of the way, urged him to go to New York and work there with Mayor La Guardia as a member of the Citizens' Committee for Roosevelt. Nor had Roosevelt, dead tired, done anything to soothe Corcoran's wounds in the weeks immediately following election day. As a result, and as Justice Frankfurter wrote in a confidential memorandum to the President on January 8, 1941, "Tom lacks mental health just now. He is," Frankfurter continued, ". . . in great danger of making a wrong turning, with possibilities of vast harm to himself and of undoubted serious damage to the present national effort. For, were Tom to leave Ben would also go [though] [t]hat is the last thing Ben wants to do." Frankfurter recommended the "absorption of Tom in a defined adequate task, intimately related to the program for national defense," where his "energies and resourcefulness would . . . have ample outlet and could produce material results of which few people are capable. Ben, on the other hand, is almost indispensable in a variety of ways. . . . [I]t ought not to be too difficult to have him [Tom] temporarily made a Special Assistant to the Attorney General." He urged a "command" by Roosevelt "showing affection that would compose [Tom's] . . . troubled soul. . . ."[71] But Roosevelt, for whatever reason, did not follow Frankfurter's advice. Corcoran, utterly disillusioned and permanently embittered, soon thereafter quit the government. (In later years he would establish a lucrative "influence-peddling" law practice in Washington, violating the passionate idealism [it was in his case a "pragmatic" idealism] that had been nourished in him by Alexander Meiklejohn during his student days at Brown. His personal commitment to Meiklejohn remained strong, however.) Ben Cohen had been persuaded, with difficulty, to remain in the government after his friend's departure, but he wanted no further part in domestic political affairs, at least for the time being. Hence his temporary assignment as Ambassador Winant's chief assistant in London, an assignment from which he returned in June 1941.

Another in Roosevelt's official life with whom contact had been for him pleasurable and stimulating but from whom he was now alienated was William Bullitt, who since his resignation as ambassador to France* had awaited with growing impatience his appointment to another high government post.

Last April 23, on a day when Roosevelt was feeling especially "lousy" physically, Bullitt had come to him with a written report that a drunken Sumner Welles (whom Bullitt, for reasons unknown, hated virulently) had made repeated homosexual advances upon Pullman car porters while returning to Washington from the Alabama funeral of former House Speaker William B. Bankhead in September 1940. One of the porters had filed a complaint with the railroad. Bullitt claimed that the late Judge J. Walton Moore, former counselor of the State Department, had on his recent deathbed charged him, Bullitt, with the duty of informing the President of this highly sensitive and dangerous matter. Actually Roosevelt had learned of the incident through a top railroad executive not long after it occurred and had had FBI director J. Edgar Hoover investigate; Hoover's detailed report reposed in Roosevelt's most secret file (Hoover had been told that it must be shown to absolutely no one else). So Roosevelt merely glanced through the document Bullitt handed him before saying he knew "all about this already" and that there was "truth in the allegations." Obviously, then, cried Bullitt, Welles must be removed from office at once. His "maintenance" there "was a menace to the country," since he was not only vulnerable "to blackmail by foreign powers," but also likely at any moment to become the subject of "a terrible public scandal . . . which would undermine the confidence of the country in . . . the President." Roosevelt demurred. No newspaper would print material so scandalous, he said, and there was no danger that the porter or anyone else would initiate criminal proceedings. Neither was there serious danger that Welles would repeat his admittedly criminal act; he was now being watched "night and day," on Roosevelt's orders, by a professional guardian operating under the guise of bodyguard. Moreover, for the episode itself, there were mitigating circumstances. Welles had been under excessive strain through overwork, had felt ill on the train, had taken medication that caused him to become unexpectedly intoxicated after a cocktail or two, had then become very drunk indeed; when he arrived in Washington next morning he had absolutely no memory of what had happened.

Bullitt was unpersuaded. Coldheartedly but hot-temperedly, he rejected what amounted to a personal plea by Roosevelt that the matter be simply dropped. When Roosevelt said that Welles in his present position was highly useful to

*See pp. 52–53.

him, being the one top man in the State Department with whom he could work most easily, Bullitt flatly "questioned" this "utility," asserting that the morale of the foreign service, of the State Department as a whole, was being undermined "by the knowledge [widespread?] that a man of the character of Welles was in control of appointments and transfers." Bullitt himself, though he "wanted to do all" he "could to accelerate our preparation for war," would "under no circumstances . . . take any position in the department of state or the foreign service" unless or until Roosevelt "dismissed Welles."[72]

It is a measure of Roosevelt's patience, tolerance, and self-control, also of the fondness he had long had for Bullitt personally, the pleasure he had taken in Bullitt's company, the understanding he had developed of Bullitt's theatrical temperament, the respect he had for Bullitt's abilities joined with a realization of Bullitt's capacity in this instance to cause trouble—it is a measure of all these that he did not then and there tell Bullitt the government would somehow manage to stagger along without him. Instead he simply terminated the interview by ringing for Pa Watson, saying to Pa as Bullitt rose to leave: "Pa, I don't feel well. Please cancel all my appointments for the rest of the day. I want to go over to the House." From then on his personal contacts with Bullitt, though they remained cordial in tone, were less frequent and warm. He could find in the whole of the huge defense apparatus no place of adequate size and importance for Bullitt to occupy and paid little attention to the copious advice on foreign policy, much of it sound advice, that Bullitt continued to give him. He did employ Bullitt now and then on special assignments of importance. Thus in late November 1941 Bullitt was sent abroad as the President's personal representative, with the rank of ambassador, to report directly to the White House on the situation in North Africa, the Near East, and the Far East—though supervening event caused the cancellation of the last portion of this assignment.[73]

Escapist impulses were manifested by Roosevelt during this tense, helplessly waiting period. He went to Hyde Park more frequently and for longer periods than he had ever before done since entering the White House; he conducted the presidency from his boyhood home for as long as five days at a time. He spent more time than ever before in talk with intimate associates about things past and things possibly future, eschewing the ghastly present. It was during this period that he made with Hopkins the aforementioned elaborate and various plans for his and Harry's retirement, going so far as actually to initiate negotiations for the purchase of the Florida Key on which he proposed to build a hurricane-proof house. With extreme reluctance, forced by the mounting Pacific crisis, he canceled his planned annual Thanksgiving holiday at Warm Springs (Thanksgiving Day was November 20 that year), but he abruptly reinstated it for the following weekend when it appeared that war would probably not erupt for a few days hence. He entrained for Warm Springs on the afternoon of Friday, November 28, and on the following evening, in extemporaneous remarks at a belated

Thanksgiving dinner, told his audience of patients and hospital staff that he hoped to stay with them until the coming Tuesday. He stayed barely twenty-four hours. An urgent phone call from Hull prompted his boarding of his special train in the late afternoon of Sunday, November 30, and he was back in Washington on Monday, December 1.

VIII

WHAT had made it seem possible to Roosevelt that he, during this time of intense crisis, could be away from Washington for several days?

On November 25—moved by the lukewarmedness of Churchill's response to its terms, moved even more by Chiang Kai-shek's anguished outcry against those same terms—he had decided to shelve the modus vivendi he had been about to propose formally to Japan. Informed of this fact, Hull had then ordered the drafting in his department of a very different kind of proposal. On the following morning, early, Stimson informed Roosevelt over the phone that a large convoy of Japanese troop transports, escorted by cruisers and destroyers, was moving south past Formosa (where was it headed? the Philippines? Indo-China? the East Indies? Siam? Malaysia?)—this while the Japanese were ostensibly, in Roosevelt's words as noted by Stimson, "negotiating for an entire . . . withdrawal" from Southeast Asia. The President had reacted with rare anger to what he saw as Tokyo's "bad faith" (he "fairly blew up—jumped into the air, so to speak," Stimson told his diary that evening). A few minutes later, Hull came to him with the document his department had just drafted—a lengthy document consisting of two parts to be presented to Japan in place of the discarded modus vivendi. Part one was a statement of general principles to be agreed upon by the two countries. Part two was a list of ten specific "steps to be taken by the Government of the United States and the Government of Japan." Of these ten, the two crucial ones were "3) The government of Japan will withdraw all military, naval, air and police forces from China and from Indo-China"; and "4) The Government of the United States and the Government of Japan will not support— militarily, politically, economically—any government or regime in China other than the National Government of the Republic of China with capital temporarily at Chungking." These words, stating proposals known to be impossible of acceptance by those now dominating the government of Japan, gave the document as a whole the character of an ultimatum. Roosevelt, however, was at the end of his own vast patience that morning and, after listening carefully to Hull's reading of the document aloud, "promptly agreed" (Hull's words) that it be at once presented to the two Japanese ambassadors, though with the stipulation that it be headed "Tentative and without Commitment."[74]

There was, of course, no chance that the proposed terms would be accepted (Magic intercepts had revealed that Tojo's government would not now agree even to a modus vivendi). Indeed, when Stimson on the morning of November 27 asked Hull about the latest diplomatic move, the weary and depressed secretary of state thought so little of the ten-point program's efficacy that he made no mention of it. Instead he indicated that all the resources of diplomacy were now exhausted. "I have washed my hands of it," he said, according to Stimson's diary, "and it is now in the hands of you and Knox—the army and the navy." Immediately thereafter, via Admiral Stark and General Marshall, explicit war warnings had been sent to the American armed forces commanders in the Pacific. Said the navy warning: "Negotiations with Japan . . . have ceased and aggressive move by Japan is expected within the next few days. The number and equipment of Japanese troops and the organization of naval task forces indicates an amphibious expedition against either the Philippines, Thai or Kra peninsula or possibly Borneo. . . ." Said the army warning, issued after Stimson had, upon his further inquiry, been told by the White House of the ten-point program: "Negotiations with Japan appear to be terminated to all practical purposes. . . . Japanese future action unpredictable but hostile action possible at any moment. If hostilities cannot, repeat cannot, be avoided the United States desires that Japan commit the first overt act. . . ."[75]

All the same, the Japanese would have to pretend, at least, to consider the ten points, then reply formally to them. This would take time—several days, in all probability—during which war was unlikely to break out. It was a portion of this small piece of bought time that Roosevelt had felt it reasonably safe for him to spend in Warm Springs. But he was prepared to return at once to Washington if things took a turn for the worse. This they had done by Sunday, November 30. Hull's phone call informed the President of belligerent words General Tojo had addressed on November 30 (Japanese time) to a great popular rally in Tokyo. Britain and the United States, Tojo had said, were determined to prevent development of the East Asia Co-Prosperity Sphere (the name Japan gave the new empire it was aggressively creating) so that they could "satisfy their greed . . . at the cost of 1,000 million East Asiatic peoples," Tojo had said. "[W]e must purge this . . . practice from East Asia with a vengeance."[76] Moreover, Japanese troop movements to the south were not only continuing, they were increasing in volume, accompanied by feverish mysterious activity on the part of Japanese naval forces as a whole.

Hence Roosevelt's first official act, early in the morning of December 2, was to ask Welles to inquire of the Japanese government, through their Washington emissaries, the meaning of the southward troop movements. He explained the inquiry at his press conference later that day. Japanese forces now in Indo-China greatly exceeded "the original amount that the French Government had agreed to," he said, yet "other [large] forces were on the way," and the Japanese government was being asked "very politely . . . what the purpose of this was." It obviously could not be "for the policing of Indo-China, which was an exceedingly peaceful spot beforehand." A reporter asked if a time limit had been put upon the Japanese reply; he was promptly rebuked, as any reporter was likely to be whose question cut too near the bone. The question was "silly," said Roosevelt: "One doesn't put a time limit on things any more. . . . We are at peace with Japan. We are asking a perfectly polite question . . . that's all."[77]

There followed several days of waiting for the Japanese replies, a period of nerve-racking suspense for Roosevelt. At his press conferences he steadfastly refused to deal with hypothetical questions—"iffy" questions, as he called them. He dubbed them "silly." But now his psyche was pierced and torn by an "iffy" question whose "if" might at any moment be replaced by brutally challenging fact. It was a variation of the question he had asked his cabinet on November 7: If Japan now attacked British and/or Dutch possessions but left the Philippines alone for the time being, would the American people support war action against Japan? The cabinet had unanimously answered "yes." But how would a Congress that had only narrowly endorsed the arming of American merchant vessels in the Atlantic less than two months ago, this after two American destroyers had been attacked and one of them sunk, with a total loss of 126 American lives—how would such a Congress respond to a presidential call to arms in defense, as the isolationists would loudly cry, of British and Dutch colonial interests? Certainly there would be prolonged and bitter congressional debate during which the Japanese would be able to pursue their aims with little interference and following which, if the debate issued in the requested war declaration, Roosevelt as President and commander in chief would have to lead into war a sadly divided America. And what if, on the other hand, Japan did attack the Philippines? In that case, the declaration of war against Japan would be immediate. Isolationists of the Lindbergh stripe saw no danger in Hitlerism, they even saw merit in Hitlerism, but they were more than willing to take up arms against the rising Yellow Peril. Would there not then be grave danger that this isolationist view would so permeate the body politic that Japan would displace Germany, in the popular mind and mood, as the nation's primary enemy, thereby frustrating the agreed American-British grand war strategy? The anguish of this question was increased by the possibility that Hitler, with that contempt for solemn promises that was the hallmark of his human and international relations, would fail in this instance to honor the Tripartite Pact. He might *not,* as Japan's ally, declare war on the United States! Would Congress then respond affirmatively, with the necessary unanimity, to a call from the President for a declaration of war upon Germany—a call issued *after* we were at war with Japan? Would not such a call provoke another extended and divisive congressional debate? Should Roosevelt therefore anticipate and seek to prevent this mortal danger by calling for a declaration of war on Germany at the same time as he called for one on Japan?

Added point was given these soul-piercing questions on Thursday, December

4, when Colonel Robert McCormick's *Chicago Tribune* published in the most sensational possible fashion the top-secret estimates that had just been made of the U.S. production necessary for the waging of global war—the whole of the so-called Victory Program—and published also Roosevelt's letter ordering that the estimates be made.* This was an astounding, alarming revelation not only of intelligence of immense value to America's enemies (it clearly violated the Espionage Act, in the opinion of Attorney General Biddle), but also of the ruthless daring, the arrogant confidence in their own continued influence with the general public, of Roosevelt-hating isolationists. There was much discussion of this outrage at that afternoon's cabinet meeting. During it, Ickes, Stimson, and Biddle urged the criminal prosecution of McCormick and his responsible hirelings. But no conclusion was reached. "It did not seem to me," a disgusted Ickes told his diary three days later, "that the President and other members of the cabinet were particularly interested in the matter although they were all very angry. . . ."[78] To Roosevelt, who in the end did nothing about what amounted in the circumstances to treasonable behavior, the episode was dramatic evidence that the kind of national unity he deemed essential to the waging of successful war was far from being realized.

And war now immediately impended!

On the morning of Saturday, December 6, word reached Washington that British reconnaissance planes, flying to the very last mile of their range from their Malayan base, had spotted on the day before three Japanese convoys entering the Gulf of Siam. They were of formidable size: forty-six troop transports, a battleship, and seven cruisers had been counted, accompanied by an unspecified number of destroyers. Stormy weather had prevented any further tracking of these convoys, which might be headed either for Siam or Malaya. Roosevelt hoped they were headed for Malaya: it would be much easier to convince the American people that the defense of Singapore was of vital interest to the United States than that the defense of Siam was. That afternoon, to prepare the public mind for whatever stern action he might be forced to take, he ordered released to the press the latest U.S. estimate of Japanese military forces in Indo-China, including those on transports that had just entered Camranh Bay. They totaled, according to the hasty estimate, 80,000 troops in northern Indo-China and 98,000 in southern Indo-China, including 18,000 still on transports.

Simultaneously, Roosevelt decided in favor of a project that had been under consideration for several days, namely, a personal appeal for peace made directly by him to Emperor Hirohito. He realized that this was almost certainly a

---

*The question of precisely who in the defense establishment leaked this vital information has never been answered conclusively. Isolationist Senator Burton K. Wheeler says in his *Yankee from the West* (Garden City, 1962), pp. 32–36, that an unnamed army captain brought a copy of the Victory Program to him and that he passed it on to Chesley Manly of the *Chicago Tribune*.

futile gesture at so late a date, but the formal Japanese reply to the last American proposal had not yet been received, the gesture had been prepared, and making it could do no harm. As for the appeal itself, it was indeed personal in that Roosevelt personally had done the drafting of it, with a few unimproving revisions by the State Department—a fact evinced by the message's discursive, adjectival style. "During the past few weeks," said the appeal, "it has become clear to the world that Japanese military, naval, and air forces have been sent to Southern Indo-China in such large numbers as to create a reasonable doubt on the part of other nations that this continuing concentration in Indo-China is not [*sic*] defensive in character."* Naturally, these concentrations alarmed "the people of the Philippines, of the hundreds of islands of the East Indies, of Malaya, of Thailand itself. . . ." And the President "was sure that Your Majesty will understand that the fear of these people is legitimate." Obviously the "continuation of such a situation" was "unthinkable." No one could "sit either indefinitely or permanently on a keg of dynamite." There was "absolutely no thought on the part of the United States of invading Indo-China if every Japanese soldier or sailor were to be withdrawn therefrom," he continued. "I think that we can obtain the same assurances from the Governments of the East Indies, the Governments of Malaya, and the Government of Thailand." Thus the withdrawal of Japanese forces from Indo-China would assure "peace throughout the whole South Pacific area." He closed: "I address myself to Your Majesty . . . in the fervent hope that Your Majesty may, as I am doing, give thought in this definite emergency to ways of dispelling the dark clouds."[79]

Roosevelt deemed it possible, even likely, that Hirohito would make no reply to this message—that, instead, Japan would open hostilities, attacking first either Siam or Malaya, or both. He was therefore also preparing (the State Department was working on the initial draft of) a presidential message to Congress to be delivered either on Monday, December 8, or Tuesday, December 9. Its purpose, admittedly highly difficult to achieve, was to convince Congress and the general public that aggression against Siam or Malaya or the Dutch East Indies was tantamount to aggression against the United States.

Meanwhile, beginning in the morning hours, there had arrived in the Magic decrypting room the anxiously awaited Japanese reply to Washington's ten-point proposal. A lengthy reply, it was divided into fourteen parts that restated the Japanese position and the argument for it in a tone of defiance (clearly the heading placed upon the last American message had not prevented Tokyo's viewing that message as an ultimatum). Only the first thirteen parts arrived in

---

*One suspects that this was an original Roosevelt sentence worked over by Welles. The undersecretary of state customarily employed unpunctuated periods extending well beyond an ordinary reader's attention span. The one quoted may have extended beyond Roosevelt's, resulting in the indicated double negative of the final product.

Washington that day; the fourteenth would come on the morrow, Nomura was told; and until it came, with instructions, the message was to be kept secret. Decrypted, the first thirteen parts were in Roosevelt's hands at nine-thirty that evening. He was then at his desk in the Oval Room, having shortly before excused himself from a dining table at which had been seated thirty-two guests—a not uncommonly large number for a Saturday evening in the Roosevelt White House. Harry Hopkins was the only other person in the Oval Room. The two were discussing in desultory fashion the domestic political repercussions of the *Chicago Tribune*'s exposé when Commander L. R. Schulz entered.[80] Schulz was assistant to the President's naval aide, Captain Beardall; he regularly delivered Magic to the President personally; he now placed some fifteen typewritten pages of it in the President's big hand. Roosevelt read them carefully while Hopkins, pale, thin, and wan after his lengthy hospital stay, paced the room restlessly. The pages were then handed to Hopkins, who also read them carefully before handing them back to Roosevelt.

"This means war," said Roosevelt.

Hopkins agreed it did. The Japanese would attack as soon as their forces were deployed to their utmost advantage, said Roosevelt—and the two then discussed for several minutes the current deployment of those forces. Neither man was at all surprised by the Tokyo message's contents, both having expected something of the sort. But since war was now absolutely inevitable, commented Hopkins, it was a pity that all choice as to the time and place of its outbreak was Japan's. Would that we could strike the first blow, robbing Japan of the advantage of surprise.

"No, we can't do that," said Roosevelt. "We are a democracy and a peaceful people." His voice rose as he added: "But we have a good record."

He tried to phone Harold ("Betty") Stark, was told by the White House phone operator that the admiral was attending a production of *The Student Prince* at the National Theater, then canceled the call, saying he would reach Stark later. He didn't want Stark paged at the theater because that would alarm the public— evidence that although he deemed war both inevitable and imminent, he had no sense that it would break out within the next twenty-four hours.

At that point Roosevelt handed the fifteen-page document back to Commander Schulz, who locked it in the pouch he carried and left the room. . . .

On the following morning, Sunday, December 7—a brisk cold day in Washington— part fourteen of the Japanese reply arrived. Decrypted, it was in Roosevelt's hands by ten A.M.; it simply confirmed the conclusion already reached. "Obviously it is the intention of the American Government," it said, "to conspire with Great Britain and other countries to obstruct Japan's efforts toward the establishment of peace through the creation of a New Order in Asia. . . . Thus the earnest hope of the Japanese Government to adjust Japanese-American relations and to preserve and promote the peace of the Pacific through cooperation with the American Government has been lost. The Japanese Government . . . cannot but consider that it is impossible to reach an agreement through further negotiations."[81] That the transmission of these final words should have been deliberately delayed for twelve hours was an ominous fact, and the ominousness was increased by the precision with which Tokyo was timing the formal delivery of the whole fourteen-part reply: Nomura and Kurusu were to hand it personally to the secretary of state at precisely one o'clock; they had arranged an appointment with Hull for that time. One o'clock of December 7 in Washington coincided with one A.M. of December 8 at Kota Bharu on the Malay Peninsula, which the Japanese were expected to attack, as the naval officer who delivered Magic to Stark pointed out.

Hopkins was again alone with Roosevelt in the Oval Room, having just lunched with him, when at 1:40 P.M. a phone call from Knox told them of a radio report from Honolulu saying that Pearl Harbor, where the Sunday dawn had just broken, was being attacked from the air and that the military command emphatically described the attack as "no drill." Hopkins was dumbfounded. The report must be mistaken, he said; it may have come from Hawaii, but surely the attack itself was on the Philippines. Roosevelt disagreed. He thought the report probably true: to attack the least likely target, also the most important to the U.S. Pacific defense, being the home base of the U.S. Pacific Fleet, while negotiations yet continued between Washington and Tokyo—this kind of totally unexpected thing was precisely what the Japanese *would* do if they could. He assumed that a prepared Pearl Harbor was giving them a hot reception. A few minutes after two o'clock he phoned the Pearl Harbor news to Hull, who told him the two Japanese ambassadors, having asked for a postponement of their meeting with him,* were only now arriving at the State Department. Say nothing to them of the Pearl Harbor news, ordered Roosevelt; just "receive their reply formally and coolly and bow them out." A quarter of an hour later, Admiral Stark phoned the President to confirm the accuracy of the initial radio report from Honolulu and add dismaying details: Grave damage was being done the fleet, and there was a considerable loss of life—news indicative of complete surprise achieved by the Japanese and woefully incomplete preparation for the event by the Pearl Harbor command. It jarred the commander in chief but failed to dissipate a great calm, a sense of relief, that, with the earlier news, had flooded into him.

Meanwhile, Hull was receiving the Japanese envoys. He did so not coolly but coldly. He kept them standing while he pretended to read the document they handed him. As he read, fury rose in him out of his remembrance of the endless wearing hours he had spent talking in circles with Nomura, latterly with Kurusu

---

*Decoding the message had taken the Japanese embassy's code room far longer than it took Magic to decrypt and translate it into English. Hence the forced delay of the Hull office meeting.

also, while they lied and pretended in accordance with Tokyo instructions known to him. He addressed Nomura, fixing upon that unhappy honest man a withering gaze. "I must say that in all my conversations with you during the last nine months I have never uttered one word of untruth," he said. ". . . In all my fifty years of public life I have never seen a document that was more crowded with infamous falsehoods and distortions—infamous falsehoods and distortions on [a] scale so huge that I never imagined until today that any government on this planet was capable of uttering them."[82] Nomura, obviously miserable, struggled for replying words. Hull refused to hear them. He nodded toward the door dismissively, and the two left the room silently.

For Roosevelt, the following hours, during which a steady stream of unrelieved bad news poured in from Hawaii and the Far East, were crowded with activity.

He met with his war cabinet (Hull, Stimson, Knox, Stark, Marshall) at three o'clock to discuss military and naval force dispositions, with special emphasis on the air force—to discuss also the immediate need for some kind of censorship of public information and for keeping the Latin American republics informed and in line with U.S. policy. During this meeting he received a phone call from Churchill, whom he told that the radio report just heard at Chequers, where the Harrimans and Winants were the Prime Minister's weekend guests, was "quite true. They have attacked us at Pearl Harbor," said Roosevelt. "We are all in the same boat now." He added that tomorrow he was going to Congress for a declaration of war. "This certainly simplifies things," commented Churchill, evincing a relief from helpless uncertainty and indecision that Roosevelt, despite the increasingly dismaying news, fully shared.[83]

There followed a meeting of the full cabinet during which the speech Roosevelt was to make tomorrow to Congress and the American people, its tone and content, was the chief topic of discussion. Hull urged a half-hour speech reviewing the history of Japanese-American relations. Others urged a call for war on Germany as well as Japan. But Roosevelt had already made up his mind. According to Hopkins, he "expressed himself very strongly that he was going to submit a precise message [that is, one limited to Japan's immediate aggression] and had in mind . . . a longer message later."

Immediately following this meeting he dictated his short speech to Grace Tully.

At eight-thirty that evening he met with Vice President Wallace and eight selected congressional leaders—an unhappy meeting, because more bad news had by then arrived from Pearl Harbor, and Roosevelt's report of it clearly indicated that neither the army nor the navy had been on the alert at Pearl Harbor. The Japanese had achieved total surprise, had not been effectively resisted, and the American "casualties were extremely heavy . . . we have lost the majority of the battleships there." Texas Senator Tom Connally of the Foreign Relations

Committee voiced the group's general feeling when he burst out: "They [the navy] were all asleep! Where were our patrols? They knew these negotiations were going on." Roosevelt, who had of course asked this question of himself over and over, replied rather miserably: "I don't know." But he did know this was no time for recriminations. We all had a big job to do, a job requiring our full attention and effort. We could afford to waste no energy in useless anger.[84]

Actually, as Roosevelt would know by late tomorrow morning, not one of the eight battleships at Pearl Harbor, constituting the whole battleship strength of the U.S. Pacific Fleet, was now able to put to sea. Seven of them had been lined up, mostly two by two, along Ford Island in the harbor. Of these, the *Arizona* had been blown up when a bomb went down one of her stacks; the *Oklahoma* was totally destroyed; the *West Virginia, California,* and *Nevada* were beached or sunk (perhaps they could be ultimately salvaged, but they were certainly out of action for many months); the *Maryland*'s damage was such as might be repaired in a few weeks, but the *Tennessee,* though not much more seriously damaged, had been so jammed against massive blocks of concrete by the sunken *West Virginia* that her repair could not begin until those blocks were blasted out of the way, which meant that she, too, was probably out of action for months. The *Pennsylvania* was the least seriously damaged of all the battleships, and since she was already in dry dock on the Oahu mainland when she suffered a direct bomb hit, her repair should be relatively swift but would take several weeks at least. In addition, two destroyers and a target ship had been totally destroyed; three cruisers, a destroyer, and three auxiliary vessels had been severely damaged. Equally catastrophic had been the damage done the Hawaiian air force. It had been virtually wiped out: 188 planes (96 army, 92 navy) had been destroyed, 159 (128 army, 31 navy) had been severely damaged. Altogether 2,403 American lives had been lost, 1,102 of them when the *Arizona* blew up. And the Japanese strike force that inflicted these grievous wounds had suffered very little from the American defense! Of the 343 planes that had been launched from Japanese carriers some two hundred miles north of Oahu, only 29 with 55 men in them had failed to return. In sea action, a Japanese submarine and 5 two-man midget submarines had been lost.

But for a single fortunate circumstance, this crippling strike at Pearl Harbor would have rendered the United States utterly helpless to interfere for many months to come with Japanese expansionism in Southeast Asia and the South Pacific. This circumstance was the absence from Pearl Harbor of all three of the aircraft carriers assigned the U.S. Pacific Fleet. The *Saratoga* was undergoing repairs at the San Diego naval base. The *Enterprise* was at sea with a task force that included three heavy cruisers and nine destroyers, its mission the reinforcement with marine fighter planes of the air strength on Wake Island. The *Lexington* with three cruisers and five destroyers constituted a task force headed for Midway island, its mission to reinforce the patrol plane strength there. Both these missions were, in part, responses to the "War Warning" message sent Admiral Husband E. Kimmel, commander of the U.S. Pacific Fleet, on November 27. Yet, incredibly, the Midway task force, which sailed directly toward Japan, had not been informed of it, and the vice admiral commanding the Wake Island task force knew of it only because he had happened to be with Kimmel when the message was delivered. The commander of the Japanese task force attacking Pearl Harbor knew the American carriers were at sea. He was greatly worried by that fact; he had search planes out looking for them. Luckily, from the U.S. point of view, he never found them. For as the Pearl Harbor strike itself indicated, and as immediately impending events in the Far Pacific would conclusively demonstrate, aircraft carriers with their plane complements would be far more important to victory in this war than battleships could be.

It was the inglorious fate of the Hawaiian air force that seemed most to disturb Roosevelt when, very late that night, too wound up to go at once to bed, he unwound in a private interview, over beer and sandwiches, with CBS news broadcaster Edward R. Murrow. Murrow and his wife had been dinner guests at the White House that evening (when Mrs. Murrow phoned in the afternoon to confirm her expectation that the long-standing invitation would be canceled by the events of the day, Eleanor refused to hear of it: "We still have to eat," she said)—and to him Roosevelt poured out in anguish the ghastly information he'd received that day from Pearl Harbor. He emphasized the loss of vital air cover. "Our planes were destroyed on the ground, by God, on the ground!" he cried, bringing his fist down on the table.[85]

IX

IT was a grimly determined Franklin Roosevelt who, a few minutes after noon next day, addressed to Congress in joint session the briefest of all his personally delivered messages.

"Yesterday, December 7, 1941—a date that will live in infamy—the United States of America was suddenly and deliberately attacked by naval and air forces of the Empire of Japan," he began. The attack had severely damaged American naval and military forces and "very many American lives have been lost." Simultaneously, "the Japanese Government . . . launched an attack against Malaya."

He continued:

"Last night Japanese forces attacked Hong Kong.

"Last night Japanese forces attacked Guam.

"Last night Japanese forces attacked the Philippine Islands.

"Last night the Japanese attacked Wake Island.

"And this morning the Japanese have attacked Midway Island.

"Japan has, therefore, undertaken a surprise offensive extending throughout the Pacific area. . . .

"Hostilities exist. There is no blinking the fact that our people, our territory, and our interests are in grave danger.

"With confidence in our armed forces—and with the unbounding determination of our people—we will gain the inevitable triumph—so help us God.

"I ask that the Congress declare that since the unprovoked and dastardly attack by Japan on Sunday, December 7, 1941, a state of war has existed between the United States and the Japanese Empire."[86]

Within an hour thereafter Congress had done so, unanimously in the Senate, with only one dissenting vote in the House.*

---

*The lone dissenter was pacifist Representative Jeannette Rankin of Montana, who in 1917, during her only other term as congresswoman, had voted against U.S. entry into World War I. Nebraska Senator George Norris, who had also opposed U.S. entry into the last war, voted for it this time.

BOOK THREE

➤➤✕◀◀

The Hazards
and Tumult of 1942

7

———>>X<<———

Arcadia: The Birth of the United Nations

I

IT was of the essence of Franklin Roosevelt's leadership capacity, an essence rooted in his peculiar brand of religious fatalism, that he in a crisis invariably displayed utter calm. "His reaction to any event was always to be calm," said Eleanor Roosevelt. "If it was something that was bad, he just became almost like an iceberg. . . ." So it was when she came to him in the Oval Room soon after the first news from Pearl Harbor arrived. She remarked on the contrast between his demeanor and that of his aides and cabinet members, who were tense with excitement. They rushed in and out of the room agitatedly, evincing extreme irritability. He sat quietly at his desk, absorbing with what she curiously termed a "deadly" calm the dreadful news that poured in upon him, his attention wholly focused on what must now be done. He was grim. He had tried hard to avoid a two-front war, he told Eleanor, because "we haven't got the navy to fight in both the Atlantic and the Pacific"—and since we didn't we would have now "to take a good many defeats" while our naval and military strength was "built up." But of "inevitable" ultimate triumph he had not the slightest doubt. His eldest son, James, was then in Washington serving as liaison officer between U.S. Marine Corps headquarters and the Office of Facts and Figures (the government's emergency information agency, headed by Archibald MacLeish). James was summoned by phone from his suburban home to his father's side a few minutes after the first Pearl Harbor news came in. When he entered the Oval Room, "I saw right away [from his father's demeanor] that we were in deep trouble." But his father showed no excitement, "he simply and calmly discussed who had to be notified and what the media campaign should be for the next forty-eight hours."[1]

There had been times when this crisis calm was a facade, effortfully maintained, behind which fear-soaked anxieties had had to be sternly repressed. He had anxiety enough now: by Tuesday afternoon, December 9, a full two days after the Pearl Harbor attack, Hitler had not yet declared war on the United

States, and if he continued to refuse to do so, the action the President would have to take might seriously endanger the overall war effort. But this anxiety was not sufficiently strong to require its harsh repression. Roosevelt could admit it fully to his calculating mind without disturbing a basic inward mood that perfectly harmonized with the one he outwardly displayed. His colleagues were aware of the harmony. "You know," said Frank Knox to Frances Perkins, "I think the boss must have a great load off his mind. I thought the load on his mind [during the preceding weeks and months] was just going to kill him, going to break him down. This must be a great sense of relief to him. At least we know what to do now."[2] And relief *was* what Roosevelt chiefly basically felt. For not only was his long period of helpless waiting ended, there had also been achieved the overriding purpose of the political strategy, as regards foreign policy, in which he had stubbornly persisted since 1938—that cautious wavering reluctant advance, that equivocating step-by-step approach (with frequent steps backward), that Stimson and others had found so exasperating. Whether the achievement was due to the strategy, or the extent to which it was, might be debated. Certainly, by November, the strategy had reached the limit of whatever effectiveness it had had. As Robert Sherwood would write: "The hat from which he [Roosevelt] had pulled so many rabbits was [by then] empty. The President of the United States was now the creature of circumstance which must be shaped not by his own will or his own ingenuity but by the unpredictable determination of his enemies."[3] But now circumstance in the form of his enemies' determination had decided in favor of his cause. He at once recognized that the sneak attack by the Japanese, a tactical triumph for them, was also for them a catastrophic strategic defeat, since its effect was to unite the American people behind presidential leadership as they had never been united before when entering a foreign war. There had been strong domestic opposition to American participation in the War of 1812, the Mexican War, the Spanish-American War, and the First World War. There was none to our entrance into war with Japan.

A huge wave of patriotic emotion permeated with grim determination swept across the land. Army and navy recruiting offices were thronged with young men eager to enlist; by the Monday night following Pearl Harbor Day, there had been three times as many enlistments at the New York City army recuitment center as there had been on April 6, 1917, when the United States entered the First World War. And there was an equivalent thronging of Civilian Defense Volunteer offices.[4] Wiped out of existence were national political divisions that, if continued, would have hampered war making and prevented real peace making. Isolationists who only three days ago had been the loudest voices of opposition to war spoke now only of unity in war—and if these voices were rendered somewhat quavering in the general public's ear by memories of what they had been saying up till now, they clearly spoke the present feeling of those who had formerly found them persuasive. "We have been stepping closer to war for many months," said Charles Lindbergh in a statement released through the national headquarters of America First. "Whether or not that policy has been wise, our country has been attacked by force of arms and by force of arms we must retaliate." ("Our own defenses and our military position have already been neglected too long," he added, though with his fellow isolationists he had ridiculed Roosevelt's call for a vast increase in warplane manufacture and had stubbornly opposed the President's every effort to build an adequate American defense.) Said Herbert Hoover: "American soil has been treacherously attacked by Japan. Our decision is clear. It is forced upon us. We must fight with everything we have." Even Representative Hamilton Fish, whose personal animosity toward Roosevelt was fully matched by Roosevelt's personal loathing of him, called upon the American people "to present a united front in support of the President."[5]

So it was with a consciousness of himself as personification of American union that Roosevelt on Tuesday, December 9, worked with his speechwriters on the fireside chat he would deliver, as he had announced, that night. His opening remark to his regular Tuesday morning press conference was that he had "darn little news, except that I haven't finished my speech." The typewritten pages on the desk before him were "old stuff . . . the third draft," he told the reporters; he was working now on the fifth. Two things made this composition difficult. *One* was the initial felt necessity to incorporate in it the lengthy history of Japanese-American relations that the State Department had prepared, something Roosevelt finally decided not to do (he would instead present the history in a special message to Congress; he did so on December 15) because this history, tediously fact laden, contradicted his purpose, in this address, of inspiring his listeners and realistically dedicating them to the great task ahead. The *other* difficulty arose from the felt necessity to convince the American people that in going to war with Tojo's Japan, they entered also into war with Hitler's Germany, with Mussolini's Italy—for if these two did not formally declare war upon us, Congress simply *must* declare war on them promptly, without divisive debate.

It was ten o'clock that night in Washington (seven o'clock on the West Coast, where fears of direct Japanese attack were rife) when Roosevelt began his address to a radio audience of some sixty million. The "criminal attacks" of the Japanese climaxed "a decade of international immorality," he opened. They were the culmination of a course Japan had followed "for the past ten years in Asia" and that "paralleled the course of Hitler and Mussolini in Europe. Today it has become more than a parallel. It is actual collaboration so well calculated that all the continents of the world, and all the oceans, are now considered by the Axis strategists." The 1931 invasion of Manchukuo by Japan "without warning," the 1935 Mussolini invasion of Ethiopia "without warning," the 1938 occupation of Austria by Hitler "without warning," the 1939 invasions of Czechoslovakia and Poland by Hitler "without warning," the 1940 invasions of Scandinavia and the Low Countries by Hitler "without warning," the 1940 at-

tacks upon France and Greece by Mussolini "without warning," the Hitler invasion of Russia "without warning," and now the Japanese attacks upon Malaya
and Thailand and the United States "without warning"—all these were elements
of "one pattern." Our government "knows," he said, that "for weeks Germany
has been telling Japan that if Japan did not attack the United States, Japan would
not share in dividing the spoils with Germany when peace came. . . . We know
also [we didn't, of course, because it was not true] that Germany and Japan are
conducting their military and naval operations in accordance with a joint plan."
And Americans, as they developed their own war strategy, must therefore think
globally. We must realize "that Japanese successes against the United States in
the Pacific are helpful to German operations in Libya; that any German success
in the Caucasus is . . . an assistance to Japan in her operations against the Dutch
East Indies; that a German attack against Algiers and Morocco opens the way to
a German attack against South America, and the Canal." Turning to the domestic front, he warned against hysterical rumormongering and emphasized, as he
had emphasized in his press conference that morning, the duty of journalists to
publish as war news only authoritatively confirmed facts. "To all newspapers
and radio stations . . . I say this: You have . . . no right in the ethics of patriotism
to deal out unconfirmed reports in such a way as to make people believe they are
gospel truth." He stressed that the war would be long and difficult. It would demand of all Americans "hard work—grueling work—day and night, every hour
and every minute." But he refused to characterize this effort, whether on the
fighting front or the home front, as "sacrifice." It was a privilege to serve in
the army or navy. It was a privilege and "not a sacrifice for the industrialist or
the wage earner, the farmer or the shopkeeper, the trainman or the doctor, to pay
more taxes, to buy more bonds, to forgo extra profits, to work longer or harder
at the task for which he is best fitted." For "[w]e are in . . . war, not for conquest,
not for vengeance, but for a world in which this nation, and all that this nation
represents, will be safe for our children. We expect to eliminate the danger from
Japan, but it would serve us ill if we accomplished this and found that the rest
of the world was dominated by Hitler and Mussolini." His voice rose as he concluded, speaking slowly and emphasizing every word: "We are going to win the
war and we are going to win the peace that follows. And in the difficult hours of
this day—through the dark days that may be yet to come—we know that the
vast majority of the members of the human race are on our side. Many of them
are fighting with us. All of them are praying for us. For in representing our
cause, we represent theirs as well—our hope and their hope for liberty under
God."[6]

Next day, Wednesday, December 10, as an overwhelmingly favorable response to Roosevelt's words was evinced in press and radio commentary, and in
the telegrams and letters that poured into the White House mailroom, it appeared to him that most Americans did consider themselves to be now at war
with all the Axis powers and not just with Japan.

Yet there also came that day from the South China Sea news that, following hard upon Pearl Harbor, might offset the fireside chat's effect insofar as it persuaded millions of a Japanese power currently so overwhelming that our dealings with it must be given top priority.

The news was of Britain's battleship *Prince of Wales* and her accompanying battle cruiser, *Repulse*. They had arrived in Singapore on December 2, having been sent there to strengthen the defense of that base and the Dutch East Indies. On December 8 they sailed north from Singapore without air cover to oppose Japanese landings on the east coast of Malaya. They were sighted by Japanese air reconnaissance in the late afternoon of December 9, and, being then far within the range of enemy planes land-based near Saigon, prudently reversed their course as night fell. Having sailed southwestward full speed through the night of December 9–10, they were off Kuantan, Malaya, when, shortly after eleven o'clock in the morning of December 10, they were accidentally come upon by a homeward-bound Japanese air fleet of eighty-four bombers and torpedo bombers that had been sent out from Southern Indo-China to intercept them. These promptly attacked and within two hours had sent both great ships to the bottom of the sea. It was the first battle ever fought on the high seas between planes and capital ships, and it ended forever the theretofore dominant role of the battleship in modern naval warfare (the aircraft carrier took its place). Churchill, who had journeyed to and from the Argentia Conference on the *Prince of Wales,* received the news by phone while yet in bed on that Wednesday morning. "In all the war I never received a more direct shock," he later wrote. "As I turned . . . and twisted in bed the full horror of the news sank in upon me. There were no British or American capital ships in the Indian or Pacific oceans except the American survivors of Pearl Harbour, who were hastening back to California. Over all this vast expanse of waters Japan was supreme and we everywhere weak and naked."[7]

Roosevelt, too, was badly jarred. The news was bound to strengthen the hand of those hard-core congressional isolationists who, though they spoke now for unity in war against the Yellow Peril, were uncommitted to war against white Nazi-fascism and who retained, despite their small number, a large capacity to obstruct and delay. The problem of how best to deal with them loomed ever larger in Roosevelt's mind as Wednesday's hours passed with no official word from Berlin or Rome. Indeed, Berlin's silence was now total, for in the late afternoon of Tuesday (Berlin time), every phone in the U.S. embassy there had suddenly gone dead.* With the fall of night rose anxiety in Washington's highest officialdom, and anxiety remained as a dark cloud upon the dawn, in Washington, of Thursday, December 11.

---

*It will be remembered that the U.S. ambassador to Germany, Hugh Wilson, had been called home "for consultations" following *Kristallnacht* in 1938 and had never returned. Diplomatic ties had not been broken, however; the U.S. embassy in Berlin had remained open under a chargé d'affaires.

But then, abruptly, it was dissipated.

Hitler on Pearl Harbor Day had been at his East Prussian headquarters, his so-called Wolf's Lair in a forest near Rastenburg, where he, having theretofore refused to permit obviously necessary tactical retreats in the face of a sudden unexpected resurgence of Russian military power before Moscow, had at last ordered a retreat that was occurring anyway. But he was now back in Berlin. Ever since the war began, he had been forced passively to endure one insult and provocation after another from Roosevelt. Addressing the Reichstag early in the German afternoon, he vented his long-pent fury against "that man who, while our soldiers are fighting in snow and ice, . . . likes to make his chats from the fire-side, the man who is the main culprit in this war. . . ." He contrasted Roosevelt's privileged upbringing with his own harsh one, Roosevelt's safe and easy war of 1917–1918 with his own dangerous service as an "ordinary soldier" in the front lines, Roosevelt's financial speculations in the early 1920s (he "made profits out of inflation, out of the misery of others") with his own hard "work and industry," Roosevelt's failure to achieve economic recovery in the United States with his own "success" in that same enterprise in Germany. It was because of Roosevelt's domestic failures, cried Hitler, that he, prodded by American Jewry, whose "full diabolical meanness . . . rallied around this man," now turned to war as a solution of his difficulties. The aim of "the President of the United States," he closed, "is to destroy one state after another. . . . I have therefore arranged for passports to be handed to the American chargé d'affaires today. . . ." (Actually, the American embassy personnel, of whom George Kennan was a leading one, were promptly confined by the Gestapo in a building on the outskirts of Bad Nauheim, where they remained incommunicado until the State Department finally arranged for their exchange five months later.) "Although Germany . . . has strictly adhered to the rules of international law in her relations with the United States," said the note delivered to the American chargé d'affaires in the Berlin afternoon and simultaneously to the State Department by the German chargé d'affaires in the Washington morning, ". . . the Government of the United States from initial violations of neutrality has finally proceeded to open acts of war against Germany. . . . The German Government, consequently . . . considers herself . . . in a state of war with the United States of America."[8]

Immediately thereafter Italy declared war upon the United States.

Whereupon a much relieved Roosevelt called upon Congress in a written message "to recognize a state of war between the United States and Germany, and between the United States and Italy." At 3:05 that afternoon of December 11, 1941, Congress did so unanimously, by recorded vote in the Senate, by voice vote in the House (a possible negative recorded vote by Representative Rankin was thus avoided).[9]

II

BY then there had been changes in White House arrangements and routines and atmosphere that militated against the easy informality of Roosevelt's preferred lifestyle while also abolishing certain formalities that Roosevelt was quite willing to do without. For instance, the official White House social season for 1941–1942 was canceled and would remain canceled for the duration of the war. The elderly but competent Colonel Ed Starling, head of the White House Secret Service detail, had been abruptly replaced by the younger Michael F. Reilly, formerly Starling's second in command—this on a December 8 order from a then almost hysterical Treasury Secretary Morgenthau, in whose department the Secret Service was located. Blackout curtains, hung at each White House window, were drawn tight every evening. New dim lighting, so directed as not to shine upon White House walls, was installed on the White House grounds. Sentry boxes were set up at driveway entrances and at intervals along the White House fence. The White House guard was doubled; police patrolled the hallways day and night. Identity cards were issued to all whose work required White House access, and only by appointment could visitors approach the Executive Office Building where, in the Oval Office, bullet-proof glass reaching halfway up the three south windows was installed. For an appointment that was to be kept in the White House itself, the visitor was required to enter through the Diplomatic Reception Room and ride the elevator to the second floor. When Roosevelt wished to see someone "off the record," that someone's automobile must be entered by a Secret Service agent at a designated point just south of the Treasury Building and be driven by him through the White House ground's southeast gate.[10]

And in this very different White House, Roosevelt by December 11 was preparing secretly to receive, for the second time in his administration, a British Prime Minister.*

"Now that we are as you say 'in the same boat' would it not be wise for us to have another conference?" Churchill had asked in a December 9 message to Roosevelt. "We could review the whole war plan in the light of reality and new facts, as well as production and distribution. I feel that all these matters, some of which are causing me concern,† can best be settled on the highest executive level." He could "if desired" leave "in a day or two," he added, coming "by war-

---

*It will be remembered that Prime Minister J. Ramsey MacDonald came to Washington at Roosevelt's invitation in the spring of 1933 to confer on international currency stabilization and other subjects that were to be considered in the World Monetary and Economic Conference, which opened in London in mid-June of that year. See *FDR: The New Deal Years*, pp. 105, 123.

†Churchill's greatest overall concern was that Roosevelt might be persuaded or compelled by domestic political pressures to abandon or drastically modify the Plan Dog grand strategy, substituting Japan for Germany as the enemy to be disposed of first.

ship" and bringing with him top British army, navy, and air staff chiefs, also Lord Beaverbrook, "with necessary staffs."[11]

In Washington this missive was received with some consternation. Roosevelt, though as convinced as Churchill was of the need for another face-to-face meeting, would have much preferred its delay "until early stages of mobilization complete here and situation in Pacific more clarified," as he said in a telegram drafted on December 10 but never sent. "Believe developing war will give both you and me a much clearer picture as to . . . when a conference should be held. . . ." In a second draft reply prepared that day but also unsent, he said: "My first impression is that a full discussion would be more useful a few weeks hence than immediately. However, I will wholeheartedly and gladly accept your opinion on timing." His wish for delay agreed with, if it was not determined by, the opinions of Marshall and Stark, both of whom (Stark perhaps more than Marshall) were suspicious of "perfidious Albion." They were far more so in this instance than they should have been, as Marshall would confess after the war. They feared that the Prime Minister and his military and naval colleagues would come to Washington as they had come to Argentia thoroughly well prepared with strategic proposals and arguments for those proposals that, though they served the British interest as distinct from the American, could not be effectively countered by the less well-prepared and -experienced Americans. They feared that Roosevelt was far too susceptible to the Prime Minister's formidable persuasive powers. (Their worst suspicions of British motives would have seemed to them confirmed had they known what Churchill said to his war cabinet on December 8 apropos the conference-proposing message he was about to send to Washington. Someone remarked that the message's tone should perhaps be a little less assertive, a little more deferential. "Oh!" Churchill replied dismissively. "That is the way we talked to her while we were wooing her; now that she is in the harem, we talk to her quite differently!") There was evidently a phone conversation that day between Washington and London during which Washington stressed the risk to the Prime Minister's life that would accompany his return journey to England when Germany's air force and U-boats, knowing of his presence in America, would make strenuous efforts to destroy him; a December 10 message from the Former Naval Person to the President said, "[W]e do not think there is any serious danger about return journey. There is, however, great danger in our not having a full discussion at the highest level. . . . I feel it would be disastrous to wait for another month before we settled common action in face of new adverse situation particularly in the Pacific. I had hoped to start tomorrow night, but will postpone my sailing till I have received rendezvous from you." The third draft of Roosevelt's reply message, the one finally sent that day, said: "Delighted to have you here at White House. . . . My one reservation is great person[al] risk to you—believe this should be given most careful consideration for the Empire needs you at the helm and we need you there too."[12]

Churchill sailed from Greenock on Scotland's river Clyde aboard the new battleship *Duke of York* on December 14. With him were Lord Beaverbrook, the supply minister; Admiral Pound, the first sea lord; Air Marshal Portal, chief of the air staff; and Field Marshal Dill, who had just been replaced by General Sir Alan Brooke as chief of the imperial general staff (Brooke was left in England to "mind the store" while familiarizing himself with his great new assignment). Also aboard were the Prime Minister's personal physician, Sir Charles Wilson (later Lord Moran), and American lend-lease expediter Averell Harriman, who in Washington was to consult with the President and Hopkins on lend-lease matters and work with Beaverbrook on the setting of war production goals for American and British industry, goals that both he and Beaverbrook were convinced must be far higher than those of the initial Victory Program. The whole of the eight-day voyage was on stormy seas under gloomy skies. This was fortunate for all aboard during the voyage's first day, for as the battleship sailed southwestward from Ireland athwart the main path of outgoing and incoming U-boats, it sailed also within four hundred miles of the German air base at Brest, and four hundred miles, as Churchill "could not help remembering," was approximately the distance the *Prince of Wales* and the *Repulse* had been from the base of the Japanese planes that sank them. Thereafter, however, the perpetual storm was not deemed fortunate by the battleship's passengers, most of whom, cooped up belowdecks, suffered greatly from seasickness. Churchill, who remained well,* worked incessantly. Radio messages poured in bearing what he called "a great deal of business," much of which it was possible to complete via radio after the ship reached the Azores. For there swift-sailing escort vessels joined her, and these during daylight hours could read Morse code signals from her and "then, dropping off a hundred miles or so, . . . transmit [by radio] . . . without revealing our position."[14]

An important part of the "business" came through London from Anthony Eden in Moscow.

In early November, when it was proposed to Stalin that British Generals Wavell and Bernard Paget† visit Moscow to discuss military collaboration, the Russian dictator had indicated that his acceptance of the proposal depended upon London's agreeing to a conference agenda that included war aims and postwar settlements, two subjects that the generals were not qualified to discuss. The tone of this reply was harsh. Churchill was angered by it. He let Soviet Ambassador Maisky know that he was. Stalin then apologized for "the manner of his last message," and Churchill responded with a proposal (November 20) that

---

*The Prime Minister insisted upon telling stories [at the dining table] about seasickness to his mostly seasick companions, Harriman would remember.[13] ". . . He particularly enjoyed telling . . . of the passenger on an ocean liner who rushed up the companionway, heading for the nearest rail. The steward protested, 'But, sir, you can't be sick here.' To which the unfortunate passenger replied, 'Oh, can't I?' "

†Paget had just been designated the British commander in chief in the Far East.

Eden, "whom you know," come to Moscow "accompanied by high military and other experts . . . to discuss every question relating to the war." Though Churchill deemed discussions of postwar settlements to be extremely premature, he added: "I notice that you wish also to discuss the post-war organization of peace. . . . The Foreign Secretary will be able to discuss the whole of this field with you." Eden had begun his arduous journey on the morning of December 7. Twenty-four hours later, at Invergordon, a phone call from Churchill told him all that England then knew of the Pearl Harbor attack—told him also that Churchill was determined to go at once to the United States. Eden expressed doubts about the timing of the Washington journey. He "was not sure that the Americans would want him [Churchill] so soon"; he was very sure that the Russians would resent a postponement of his own Russian visit and that he and Churchill ought not to be out of England at the same time. But his implied suggestion that Churchill postpone the American visit until Eden's return from Moscow was brusquely dismissed. The whole "emphasis of the war" had shifted, said Churchill. Nothing was now more important to British welfare than "the intentions of our two great allies." Hence, "We must each go [at once] to one of them."[15]

What Churchill had termed the "post-war organization of peace" was what produced, when discussed in Moscow, the most serious part of the Russian "business" he had to deal with during his westward voyage. Stalin, in his first meeting with Eden, on December 16, proposed an agreement with Britain that East Prussia become a part of Poland after the war, this in compensation for establishing, as the postwar Soviet-Polish border, the so-called Curzon Line, which was considerably farther west of the prewar border. In his second meeting next day, Stalin pressed for immediate British agreement to the inclusion in the Soviet Union of Latvia, Lithuania, and Estonia, which Russia had forcibly occupied in 1939—the inclusion also (by restoring the 1941 Russo-Finnish border) of territory totaling some sixteen thousand square miles that had been seized from Finland in the Russo-Finnish War. He wanted this agreement to be a secret protocol of a treaty between Britain and the Soviet Union, a draft of which he had had prepared. Eden protested that he could not possibly enter into any such agreement on his own authority; he would have to consult colleagues in London, and London would have to consult Roosevelt, who had specifically requested that Britain enter into no postwar frontier agreements without prior consultation with him. Churchill, informed of this aboard the *Duke of York,* "reacted violently" in a way that indicated some doubt on his part of Eden's ability to stand up to the Russian dictator. He at once (December 20) told London, for transmittal to Eden, that Stalin's demands concerning Finland and the Baltic States were "directly contrary" to the "first, second, and third articles of the Atlantic Charter, to which Stalin has subscribed. There can be no question whatever of our making such an agreement, secret or public, direct or implied, without prior agreement with the U.S. The time has not yet come to settle frontier questions, which can only be resolved at the Peace Conference when we have won the war. The mere desire to have an agreement which can be published should never lead us into making wrongful promises." Eden thoroughly agreed. But for a time it appeared that the issue would render his mission a failure. "In the absence of a settlement of the frontier question," Molotov said flatly at the conclusion of what Eden described as an "unsatisfactory two and a half hours" with him, "no sound basis would be created for relations between Great Britain and the Soviet Union." Fortunately, Stalin proved less adamant. Indeed, Eden was able to telegraph Churchill at the conference's end that "[o]ur work has ended on a friendly note. Final discussions with Stalin were the best and I am sure the visit has been worthwhile."[16]

One of the questions dealt with by Eden in Moscow was that of the Soviet Union's entrance into the war with Japan. In a December 12 message to the foreign secretary, who was then at sea en route to Murmansk, Churchill had reported the "considered views" of the British chiefs of staff on this question to be "as follows: Russian declaration of war on Japan would be greatly to our advantage,* provided, but only provided, that the Russians are confident that it would not impair their Western front either now or next spring." Stalin indicated no such confidence. Conditions had greatly improved on the Russian front. The Soviet Union had been conducting a "fighting retreat" that had worn down the Germans. "This December the German army has shown itself tired and ill-clad," said Stalin, "and just at this time new Soviet armies and formations reached the front. . . . The Germans attempted to dig themselves in but . . . [o]ur troops were able to break through and now we have the possibility of attacking; counter-attacks have gradually developed into counter-offensives. We shall try and carry this on all through the winter." But this task would absorb nearly all of Russia's resources of manpower and matériel. "[W]e are not ready" for war with Japan. "A considerable number of our troops were removed from the Far East to the Western front. New troops are being got ready but we shall require about four months before they are fully prepared." And in any case "it would be far better for the Soviet Union if Japan were to attack us. This would create a better political and psychological atmosphere amongst the Soviet people."[18]

Averell Harriman, aboard the *Duke of York,* wrote out a long list of topics he proposed to discuss with the President, Hopkins, and others in Washington. It was a document abundantly illustrative of the reason there was tension between Harriman's operation and Ambassador Winant's in London. Less than half its

---

*For one highly important thing, it would enable the bombing of Japan from air bases in Siberia. Averell Harriman stressed this in a note written aboard the *Duke of York.* We should "[i]nduce Russia to enter war vs. Japan [with] view to sap Jap strength but chiefly to bomb Japan," he wrote; we should "[s]end [American] bomb air force to Siberia to bomb Japan."[17]

items had to do with matters clearly within the province of a lend-lease "expe-diter." These dealt with the crucial shipping "bottleneck" as follows: "Action which would reduce volume of imports (example: the more concentrated foods Britain gets, the less wheat is consumed. Concentrated foods are of less volume and tonnage). Reduce wasteful forms—less canned fruits and more dried. Im-prove packaging to reduce space and weight. Reduce sharply U.S.A. civilian use to conform if need be to U.K. practices. . . . Increase shipbuilding . . . coor-dinating U.S.A. and U.K. programs." The remainder of the items (that is, most of them) showed Harriman operating as an "expediter" of overall relations be-tween Churchill and Roosevelt and as advocate of a strategic policy that was es-sentially Churchillian. "Obtain cooperation from Eire for use of bases and airfields," wrote Harriman. "Send 3 divisions to Ulster to replace 3 British divi-sions. Send additional troops to defend Eire if necessary [to obtain cooperation above mentioned]. . . . [Send] few squadrons of air to bomb Germany (particu-larly 4-engine). . . . Continue flow of aircraft and tanks to strengthen Middle East & Iran supply, and to India to develop Indian mechanized divisions. . . . Undertake strong Vichy policy with view obtaining cooperation for U.S. and British forces in North Africa. Send expeditionary force to North Africa in col-laboration with British. . . . Reinforce Singapore with air and 1 division. Merge two fleets in Pacific for joint action to regain command of Pacific. . . ."19

How this dovetailed with Churchill's thinking is revealed by a perusal of three papers, outlining his view of the present war situation and of the course to be followed into the future, whose composition absorbed the bulk of Churchill's long working hours aboard ship and which would provide the basic subject mat-ter of the Washington discussions. The first paper, headed "The Atlantic Front," began by acknowledging that "the prime fact in the war at this time" was "Hitler's failure" in Russia. Accustomed to "easily and cheaply won successes," the Nazi regime had "imagined" a swift conquest of Russia, instead of which it had "now to face the shock of a winter of slaughter and expenditure on the largest scale." But neither Great Britain nor the United States had "any part to play in this event, except to make sure that we send, without fail and punctually, the supplies we have promised. In this way alone shall we hold our influence over Stalin and be able to weave the mighty Russian effort into the general tex-ture of the war." The principal focus of what followed was upon North Africa, where the British situation had markedly improved in the months since Auchin-leck replaced Wavell as British commander of the Middle East theater. Strongly reinforced with tanks and planes, Auchinleck, after four months of preparation, was about to launch an offensive that, in Churchill's happy belief, would drive Rommel out of Cyrenaica and Libya and "should [soon] give him possession of Tripoli, and so bring his armoured vanguard to the French frontier of Tunis. . . . *We ought therefore to try hard to win over French North Africa, and now is the moment to use every inducement and form of pressure at our disposal upon the*

Government of Vichy and the French authorities in North Africa."* The French, he went on, should be promised the reestablishment of France as a great power in the postwar world, including the restoration to her of her empire, this to secure Vichy's connivance now in the British and American occupation of French North Africa. If this happened, the Germans would occupy the whole of France, but this should make little difference in the lives of the French people, Churchill thought, since living conditions in the occupied and unoccupied zones were not now widely different. Yet this threat of full occupation in conjunction with the pro-Axis proclivities of key members of the Pétain government might cause Vichy to refuse to connive with the British and Americans but, instead, to "help German troops to enter North Africa." In that case the Anglo-American move upon French North and West Africa must be delayed. But *only* delayed. *"A campaign must be fought in 1942 to gain possession of, or conquer, the whole of the North African shore, including the Atlantic ports of Morocco. Dakar and other French West African ports must be captured before the end of the year."* This would constitute "the main offensive effort" of the year's war in the West.[20]

The second paper, "The Pacific Front," had as its prime concern the deterrence of any tendency on the part of the American people to concentrate on the Pacific front in ways that gravely weakened the Atlantic one. It faced squarely the fact that the Japanese, having won naval supremacy in the Pacific, were now enabled "to transport troops to almost any desired point, possess themselves of it, and establish for it an air-naval fuelling base." The British and Americans "must expect therefore to be deprived one by one of our possessions and strongpoints in the Pacific" during the next few months. This, however, was an "interim period" during which "our duty is one of stubborn resistance at each point attacked" while we developed "a definitely superior battle fleet in the Pacific," something we should aim to accomplish by May. For Japan's resources "are a wasting factor"; the Japanese "were at their maximum strength on the day of the Pearl Harbour attack"; and therefore "[w]e need not fear that this war in the Pacific will, after the first shock is over, absorb an unduly large proportion of United States forces." What *would* greatly harm Britain and the United States alike would be the creation of *"a vast American Army of ten millions . . . which for at least two years while it was training would absorb all the available supplies and stand idle defending the American continent."*[21]

The third paper, "The Campaign of 1943," presented Churchill's conception of what might be called, to employ a chess term, the war's end game.

If the operations he had outlined in his first two papers were successful, he wrote, the United States and Britain "at the beginning of 1943 . . . would have recovered effective naval superiority in the Pacific, and all Japanese overseas

*All italicized portions are so emphasized in the original document.

commitments would be endangered both from the assailing of their communications and from British and American expeditions to recover places lost." The British Isles would "remain intact and more strongly prepared against invasion than ever before." The whole shoreline of West and North Africa "from Dakar to the Suez Canal," as well as the shoreline from Suez "to the Turkish frontier would be in Anglo-American hands." And Turkey, whether or not she were formally at war, "would be definitely incorporated in the American-British-Russian front." As for the Russians, their strength would be far greater relative to their enemy's than it now was, having been nourished by "the supplies of British and American material as promised" as well as by the partial restoration of their own "munitions-making capacity." Also, "a footing" might by then "have been established in Sicily and Italy, with reactions inside Italy which might be highly favourable." Thus the stage would be set for a direct engagement on the Continent of "the German armies" and air force whose defeat would mean Japan's doom and hence, essentially, the final Allied victory. This engagement, however, as conceived by Churchill, would not be a massively concentrated assault. He proposed "the liberation of the captive countries of Western and Southern Europe by the landing at suitable points, successively or simultaneously, of British and American armies strong enough to enable the conquered populations to revolt." Landings could be made in "Norway, Denmark, Holland, Belgium, the French Channel coasts and the French Atlantic coasts, as well as in Italy and possibly the Balkans." It would be "impossible for the Germans . . . to have sufficient troops in each of these countries . . . to cope with both the strength of the liberating forces and the fury of the revolting peoples." All this would require of Britain and America no such masses of men as had fought and fallen, maimed or dead, upon the western front during World War I, for "[i]f the incursion of the armoured formations is successful, the uprising of the local population, for whom weapons must be brought, will supply the corpus of the liberating offensive." By Churchill's estimate, forty armored divisions totaling six hundred thousand men backed by "another million men of all arms would suffice to wrest enormous territories from Hitler's domination." Of course, the "campaigns, once started," would "require nourishing on a lavish scale."[22]

(Whether Churchill thought these widely dispersed attacks would of themselves alone be finally decisive is unclear, though the weight of the evidence is that he did so think. He read this third paper aloud to a meeting of his chiefs of staff aboard ship on the day it was written. The official note of this meeting has him describing "the three phases of the war" as "[1] Closing the ring; [2] Liberating the populations; [3] Final assault on the German citadel." This would seem to indicate that he deemed the scattered assaults aimed at inciting revolts to be but a prelude to the ultimately decisive action. But in his war memoirs, wherein he is vehemently concerned to discredit the published "tales" of his "rooted aversion from large-scale operations on the Continent," he says, "I always considered that a decisive assault upon the German-occupied countries *on the largest possible scale* [present author's emphasis] was the only way in which the war could be won, and that the summer of 1943 should be chosen as the target date." And since he follows this assertion with a total quote of his third paper, as if it evinced the truth of his assertion, it would seem that forty armored divisions backed by "another million . . . of all arms," divided into perhaps half a dozen separate forces, constituted for him, as he viewed it in December 1941, "the largest possible scale" of attack.)[23]

III

WHILE the *Duke of York* pursued its circuitous route and zigzag sailing pattern through the Atlantic storm, Roosevelt in Washington was extremely busy.

His most immediate concern was to solidify the national unity that Pearl Harbor had created.

On the day of the declaration of war upon Germany and Italy, he had gratefully accepted a pledge by the chairmen of the Republican and Democratic National Committees that, for the war's duration, the two parties would suspend their normal partisanship in order to cooperate in support of the national war effort. The pledge, he had said publicly, demonstrated the "determined intent of a united people to carry . . . the struggle for human liberty to a victorious conclusion" but did not demonstrate any loss of faith in democracy as a form of government. The "people will appreciate that the political truce is for the period of the emergency" and that even during this period "the principles of our respective parties will continue to dominate our courses." When the war ended we would "still be adhering to our historic method of settling our domestic problems which has . . . shown the world that democratic freedom is a perfectly workable system of government."[24]

On that same day, acting on Sidney Hillman's suggestion, he called a conference of labor and industry leaders "to consider the problem of labor disputes during the war," the conference to begin in Washington on December 17. "We are all agreed that 'strikes as usual' can no more be tolerated than 'business as usual,' " Hillman had said. ". . . In this respect Congress is right." But most of the anti-strike legislation that had been introduced in Congress would "impair one of the nation's priceless assets," namely, the "growing consciousness among all workers of labor's stake in this nation's defense of labor's liberties against aggression." Roosevelt agreed. There was, however, no agreement at the conference between the representatives of labor (twelve of them, six from the CIO, six from the AFL) and the representatives of industry (also twelve, chosen by the U.S. Chamber of Commerce and the National Association of Manufacturers) on the basic crucial question of union security. The conferees, with William H. Davis serving as moderator, quickly agreed to a pledge of no strikes and no lockouts for the duration. They also agreed that all labor-management disputes should be settled by peaceful means and that, to assure such settlement, a new War Labor Board should be established as an independent governmental agency armed with conciliation and arbitration powers. But industry representatives balked at permitting this board to deal with disputes over the inclusion of the closed shop in collective bargaining agreements. Labor representatives insisted that simple justice demanded such board dealing, since labor, by giving up its right to strike, relinquished its sole ultimate shield against management's anti-unionism. So desperate, so agitated, did the labor representatives become over what they saw as industry's determination to use the war crisis to enfeeble organized labor that they phoned the White House, begging for presidential intervention. Roosevelt refused to intervene. There ensued four more days of fruitless wrangling, the conferees remaining deadlocked 12–12 on the crucial issue, until a despairing Moderator Davis declared the conference adjourned and went then with Secretary of Labor Perkins to the Oval Office to report what seemed to the two of them a failure.[25]

Roosevelt's response surprised them. "Oh, well, I can handle that," he said cheerfully. "We can't expect perfection." He then addressed a letter to "Gentlemen of the Conference" in which he took happy notice of the three points on which they had early and easily agreed. "I accept without reservation your covenants that there shall be no strikes or lockouts and [that] all disputes shall be settled by peaceful means," he wrote. "I shall proceed at once to act on your third point [the creation of a new board]. . . . I congratulate you—I thank you—and our people will join me in appreciation of your great contribution." He referred only by implication to the conference-deadlocking issue, saying: "Government must act in general. . . . Particular disputes must be left to the consideration of those who can study the particular differences. . . ." Two weeks later (on January 12, 1942), he by executive order established a National War Labor Board (NWLB) to replace the now moribund National Defense Mediation Board. On it were twelve special commissioners appointed by the President, four of them representing the public, four of them representing employees, and four representing employers, with the board chairman chosen by the President from among the public representatives. William H. Davis, who had chaired the National Defense Mediation Board, was again chosen. No limitation was placed in the organic order upon the board's jurisdiction; it was to make its own procedural rules, was to determine its own jurisdiction; and we may here forecast its skillfull and successful dealings with numerous cases involving union security and closed-shop issues during the years ahead. By and large, thanks in no small part to War Labor Board operations, labor's no-strike pledge and industry's no-lockout pledge would be honored—and those work stoppages that did result from dispute would be of short duration. From Pearl Harbor to the war's end the percentage of all working time so lost would amount to 11/100 of 1 percent.[26]

To determine the whys and wherefores of the palpable unreadiness of the army and navy commands at Pearl Harbor on December 7 and thereby to quiet the divisive popular agitation provoked by wild rumors of treasonable conspiracy, Roosevelt on December 18 created by executive order a commission to investigate that attack. Three days before, he had received from Knox in oral and written form a report of the observations the navy secretary had made during a flying visit to Pearl Harbor immediately following the attack. "The United States services were not on the alert against the surprise . . . ," Knox said bluntly in a December 15 press release. "This fact calls for a formal investigation. . . . We are all entitled to know (A) if there was any error of judgement which contributed to the surprise, (B) if there was any dereliction of duty prior to the attack." The appointed commission had as its chairman Associate Justice Owen J. Roberts of the U.S. Supreme Court. Under him were two retired navy admirals (William H. Standley, Joseph M. Reeves), a retired army general (Frank R. McCoy), and an active one (Joseph T. McNarney, whom Marshall had just brought to Washington to take charge of the drastic War Department reorganization that he and Stimson deemed long overdue). The Roberts Commission, as it was called, went at once to Hawaii, where both General Walter C. Short, commander of the Hawaiian Department of the Army, and Admiral Husband E. Kimmel, commander of the U.S. Pacific Fleet, had by then been relieved of their commands.* There, and later in Washington, some two thousand pages of testimony were gathered from 127 witnesses, testimony summarized in a report that Justice Roberts personally presented to the President, in the Oval Room, on Saturday, January 24. Roosevelt read it at once, very carefully, in Roberts's presence, a reading that took approximately an hour. At its end he asked the commission chairman if he, Roberts, knew of any reason why the full report should not be at once made public. Roberts knew of none: no information in it would aid our enemies; it had been cleared for publication by both Stimson and Knox. So in their Sunday papers next day, the American people read that the primary responsibility for the Pearl Harbor disaster precisely seven Sundays before rested upon the two top commanders there. Kimmel and Short had been adequately warned. They were under orders to "take joint cooperative action" in defense of the base. It was therefore "dereliction of duty on the part of each of

---

*General Douglas MacArthur, the Philippines commander, was not relieved, indeed was promoted to four-star generalship, despite the fact that he, who had been much more emphatically warned of imminent Japanese attack upon his command than Short and Kimmel had been of the attack on theirs, was as totally surprised by the Japanese as the Pearl Harbor commanders had been. The bulk of his air force, including the precious B-17s recently delivered to him, was destroyed on the ground when Japanese bombers roared in over Clark Field nine hours after the Pearl Harbor disaster. Unlike Short or Kimmel, MacArthur was protected by a shining reputation, a worshipful popular constituency that included some of the nation's most powerful conservatives, and a warm, close personal relationship with President Manuel Quezon of the Philippine Commonwealth. His removal at that point would have had a disruptive effect upon the Philippine defense and U.S.-Philippine relations and would have divided American public opinion.

them not to consult and confer with each other respecting the meaning and intent of the warnings and the appropriate means of defense required by the imminence of hostilities."

This prompt investigation by men of unquestioned ability and integrity,
and the prompt full publication of their findings, had upon American public
opinion the immediately soothing effect, muffling subversive divisive rumor,
that Roosevelt had hoped for. It also went far toward refuting later charges that
Roosevelt had deliberately provoked the attack and had made sure that the commanders on the ground were inadequately warned that it impended.[27]

For those knowledgeable few who read the report with the eyes of the mind
(Marshall, for one), it had another, wider significance: It provided evidence of
the validity of a doctrine preached by one of Marshall's great teachers and early
promoters, General Fox Conner, namely, that successful modern warfare could
not be waged upon the principle of "cooperation" and "coordination" among
equal, separate commands. "We must insist on single and individual responsibility," Conner had said over and over again, not only to Marshall, but also to a
certain Major Dwight D. Eisenhower, who had served as Conner's executive officer in the Canal Zone in the early 1920s and who, as a brand-new brigadier
general, had just been brought to Washington by Marshall to serve as assistant
chief of the army's war plans division. Both Marshall and Eisenhower were
firmly convinced that singleness of command was an absolute essential of military success, and each took note of the glaring lack of it at Pearl Harbor on
December 7, 1941.

There and then the overall command structure was as complicated and confused as a typically Rooseveltian administrative structure—so tangled and
confused that a firm, final, definite assessment of individual authorities and responsibilities was virtually impossible to achieve. Nominally, Short and Kimmel had been Hawaii's supreme commanders, Kimmel in charge of the U.S.
Pacific Fleet, Short in charge of the Hawaiian Department of the Army. Actually
the two had shared their commands in ill-defined ways with a third man, Rear
Admiral Claude C. Bloch, commandant of the Fourteenth Naval District, a district that included the physical facilities of Pearl Harbor. On paper Bloch was
subordinate to Kimmel, but he was also directly responsible to the Navy Department in Washington; his assigned duties clearly included the administration
of the naval base, which existed "solely for the support of the Fleet," but they
might also be interpreted to include some measure of responsibility for the *defense* of the physical facilities. Bloch had more seniority than Kimmel; he had
himself formerly commanded the Pacific Fleet. Neither he nor Kimmel had felt
that he was in actual fact Kimmel's subordinate, and neither had operated as if
he were. As for the working relationship between Short and Kimmel, the two
"cooperated" as the heads of sovereign states cooperate, diplomatically, in
terms of treaties, and their relationship was affected by the fact that Kimmel's

sovereign power greatly exceeded Short's. In accordance with an agreement drawn up by the services in 1935, Short's was a local defensive mission: he was responsible for the base's security, was to defend it against attack. Kimmel's was a far-flung offensive assignment: he was to seek out and engage the enemy throughout the whole wide Pacific. Obviously the success of Short's mission required air reconnaissance, whereby early warning of an enemy's approach could be obtained,* but his air arm, the army's Hawaiian air force under Major General Frederick L. Martin's command, lacked the long-range planes needed for distant air searches. Short had had to depend for reconnaissance upon the navy's long-range PBY seaplanes, which at Pearl Harbor were elements of the air command of Rear Admiral P. N. L. Bellinger. Bellinger's precise position in the chain of command was impossible to determine. As fleet air wing commander he was responsible to Kimmel, but as commander of the PBYs and the Naval Defense Air Force he was also responsible to Bloch and to the base command at San Diego. Altogether he had five different superiors to whom he was in some part responsible, but neither Short nor any other army officer was among them. And not one of his PBYs was out on patrol at the dawn of December 7, 1941. . . .[28]

The lesson was clear, and Marshall, as we shall see, had acted upon it decisively on the largest scale, and with consequences that would be world historical, by the time the Roberts Commission report was in the President's hands.

IV

THE original intention had been for the *Duke of York* to sail up Chesapeake Bay and the Potomac, with Churchill going by automobile to the White House from the point of disembarkation. But the impatient Prime Minister, begrudging the hours that this would take, insisted upon disembarking at Hampton Roads and flying from there, through a mere forty-five minutes of an early winter evening's darkness, to Washington's National Airport. So Roosevelt went that evening to the airport. He was standing (that is, with his leg braces locked, he was propped upright) against his parked automobile when, at precisely two minutes before seven o'clock on that Monday evening, Churchill's plane came to a halt on the runway. A minute later, the Prime Minister came down the wheeled stairway from the plane's opened door and, followed by Beaverbrook, Portal, Harriman, and his physician, Wilson, made his way to the outstretched hand of his broadly smiling host. He clasped that "strong hand with comfort and pleasure" while Roosevelt smiled down upon him, the President being a full head taller than he.

---

*There had been a primitive radar station at Pearl Harbor, and its screen had indeed shown the approach of the first wave of attacking planes while these were yet far out at sea, but the warning had been ignored by the officers to whom it was reported.

Fifteen minutes later the two were at the White House, where, at the porticoed entrance facing the south grounds and the now darkened mall and Washington Monument, a small crowd of reporters and press photographers awaited them, having been alerted by Steve Early. In accordance with custom, no pictures were taken during the long moment of awkwardness required for Roosevelt's assisted emergence from the car and his "walk" on the arm of his naval aide, Captain Beardall, to the mansion's doorway. But thereafter came a veritable explosion of flash bulbs and camera clicks. On the morrow, millions of newspaper readers would see that the short, stocky figure of Churchill, Roosevelt's towering over it, was clad in a knee-length double-breasted coat "buttoned high in seaman fashion," also a cape with a circled insignia on it; they would read in picture captions that this was the uniform of a British semigovernmental organization known as the Elder Brothers of Trinity House, whose concern was with lifesaving and the operation of lighthouses. They would read also that the Prime Minister's apparent mood was much more subdued, far less buoyant, than that of the President—a fact the photographs revealed. Churchill did not smile into the camera's eyes. He appeared grim and tired. He showed relief when, the brief press encounter ended, he could turn away and, clamping one of his famous huge cigars again between his teeth, enter the mansion where he was to live for more than three weeks (the other principals of his personal party were ensconced in the nearby Mayflower Hotel) save for a brief trip to Ottawa to address the Canadian Parliament and five days of highly secret vacation in Florida's sunshine.[29]

His bedroom was directly across the hall from that of Hopkins—a convenience for him since he conferred with Hopkins alone as frequently as he did with Roosevelt alone (Hopkins was also a third party at virtually every intimate session, including every lunch, that the President and Prime Minister had together). The wide hallway itself, normally one of the quietest areas of the White House, became for three weeks the summit office of the British empire, an extremely busy place, with British officers and officials and secretaries scurrying through it carrying their traditional red leather dispatch cases stuffed with official papers while typewriters clicked and phones rang. Next door to Hopkins's was the Monroe Room, where Eleanor Roosevelt normally held her press conferences; here was established Churchill's traveling war room, its walls covered with large detailed maps of every theater of the global war, maps on which colored pins traced daily and sometimes hourly the movements of troops and ships. Roosevelt and Churchill held several of their private sessions together in that room, under those maps, and Roosevelt was so taken with them that after Churchill left he established an even more elaborate war room of his own in a basement room of the White House proper, formerly a women's coatroom, which was easily accessible to the handicapped President: it was directly across the hall from the elevator. Since Churchill made little effort to adjust his long-established daily routine to that of the White House, the White House routine had to be adjusted to his; and his unique habits of work and sleep—above all, the total unpredictability of his wishes—amazed and continuously disconcerted the White House staff. His consumption of alcoholic beverage was awesome. He daily required, according to the White House butler's remembrance, a tumbler of sherry in his room before breakfast, two Scotch and sodas in his room before lunch, French Champagne and brandy in his room at bedtime. As for this bedtime, it was *very* late: in the White House, as at No. 10 Downing and Chequers, he napped for an hour or two every afternoon, then stayed up until around three o'clock in the morning. He transacted considerable portions of his daily business after dinner at night.[30]

He made few public appearances during this Washington visit, but each of these made emphatic, alliance-strengthening impressions upon the popular mind.

He was at Roosevelt's side during the latter's press conference of Tuesday, December 23—a conference in which Roosevelt announced the establishment by executive order of an Office of Defense Transportation, headed by Joseph Eastman, to "coordinate and direct" traffic through the nation's railway, automobile, inland waterway, and coastwise and intercoastal transport systems. The announcement made, Roosevelt introduced Churchill, who became thereafter the center of the reporters' attention. He fielded their most pointed questions with adroit evasiveness. Asked if Singapore wasn't "the key to the whole situation" in the Far Pacific, he replied that "the key to the whole situation" was "the resolute manner in which the British and American democracies are going to throw themselves into the conflict." Singapore was of course a "strategic point . . . of high importance." Asked how long it would take to "lick these boys," he replied: "If we manage it well it will take only half as long as if we manage it badly." Asked if, during the talks in Washington, the conferees would "take up economic, and diplomatic, and postwar problems," he said that he hoped not, or at any rate that not "too much" attention would be paid them, because "one has only so much life and strength," and "we have to concentrate on the grim emergencies" and "solve them" before going on "to deal with the future of the world." Asked about "the prospect of an anti-Axis command," he doubted its feasibility if what was meant was a single top commander of anti-Axis global forces. "I do not think there has ever been a man born . . . who could assume the functions of world commander in chief," he said. He was directly affirmatively responsive only when asked if he thought the war had been "turning in our favor in the last month or so." He replied: "I can't describe the feelings of relief with which I find Russia victorious, and the United States and Great Britain standing side by side," he said. "It is incredible to anyone who has lived through the lonely months of 1940." He had now not the slightest doubt of "ultimate victory."[31]

Churchill was again at Roosevelt's side on the following evening, 1941's Christmas Eve, when the traditional national Christmas tree was ceremonially lighted by the President. For security reasons, this year's tree was on the White House's south lawn instead of in Lafayette Park across the street from the mansion's north front, and only a few hundred invited spectators were permitted to gather around it on the mansion grounds. But fifteen thousand others were outside the steel fence when the President and the Prime Minister came together out of the mansion onto the south portico and stood there side by side, acknowledging cheers and applause with broad smiles and waved hands. The Marine Band played "Joy to the World." Roosevelt, having pressed the button whereby the dark tree became a blaze of colored lights, spoke briefly of the conjoined incongruity and necessity of celebrating the Prince of Peace in a world at war before introducing "my associate, my old and good friend," the Prime Minister of Great Britain. Churchill had prepared his brief remarks with care. Though he was physically "far from my home, far from my family" on this "anniversary and festival," he said, he did not feel that he was. "Whether it be the ties of blood on my mother's side, or the friendships I have developed here over many years of active life, or the commanding sentiment of comradeship in the common cause of great peoples who speak the same language, who kneel at the same altars, and . . . pursue the same ideals, I cannot feel myself a stranger here in the center and at the summit of the United States. I feel a sense of unity and fraternal association. . . ." He closed: "Let the children have their night of fun and laughter. Let the gifts of Father Christmas delight their play. Let us grown-ups share to the full in their unstinted pleasures before we turn again to the stern task and the formidable years that lie before us, resolved that, by our sacrifice and daring, these same children shall not be robbed of their inheritance nor denied their right to live in a free and decent world."[32]

(A small social gathering in the Red Room immediately following the tree-lighting ceremony included Eleanor Roosevelt, Sir Charles Wilson, Beaverbrook, Hopkins, and Norway's Princess Martha with her husband, Crown Prince Olav, who had come over from England at Roosevelt's invitation, and with Roosevelt's help, to spend Christmas with his wife and children. During this social moment, Eleanor, perhaps prompted by unpleasant emotions aroused in her by the princess's presence, asked her husband if he had phoned Missy, who in her wheelchair at Warm Springs doubtless waited and longed for the sound of his voice wishing her a Merry Christmas. Roosevelt, perhaps prompted by a sense that malice lurked at the root of Eleanor's question and that his relationship with Princess Martha was an object of it, replied coldly that he had *not* phoned Missy and did not intend to. To Eleanor, this manifested incredible callousness; she told her young friend Joe Lash a day or so later that she simply could not understand it. According to Lash's diary entry for January 1, 1942, she went on to say that she could not conceive of her husband's ever doing "a reckless thing for a friend because of personal attachment." She admitted that this might be an asset to him as political leader and supreme executive; it helped him to avoid mistaken exercises of the great power in his hands; but it appalled her all the same. She herself derived "refreshment and strength for her duties and work" from her "contact with people she loved." She could not have functioned without it. Her husband, however, seemed able to function in total essential isolation, utterly alone, utterly detached from the people around him. He revealed to them nothing of his innermost feeling; he "seemed to have no bond to people" at all, not even to his children.)33

"This is a strange Christmas Eve," Churchill had said—and next morning began a Christmas Day that was even more strange for the Roosevelt White House. None of the Roosevelt children or grandchildren was there: every Roosevelt son was in uniform elsewhere; daughter Anna remained with her husband and children in her Seattle home; and only two Christmas stockings, one for little Diana Hopkins, one for the President's pet Scottie dog, Fala, were hung at the fireplace where in former years a dozen or more had hung. The only Christmas tradition fully honored by the President and Prime Minister was their joint attendance at religious services that morning in the Foundry Methodist Church. "It is good for Winston to sing hymns with the Methodies," Roosevelt had said, and among those hymns was one the Prime Minister had (strangely) never heard before, "O Little Town of Bethlehem," its central stanza being pregnant with meaning in that hour:

> Yet in thy dark streets shineth
> The everlasting light;
> The hopes and fears of all the years
> Are met in thee tonight.

Afterward Churchill told Wilson, "I am glad I went. It's the first time my mind has been at rest for a long time." Otherwise, that December 25 was no holiday for him or Roosevelt. Both had a great deal of conference business to deal with—and in addition to this, Churchill had to prepare (that is, dictate every word of) what he jocularly called "impromptu remarks" to be delivered tomorrow to a joint session of Congress.34

Unaccompanied by the President, and unwontedly apprehensive, the Prime Minister went next day to the Capitol. The occasion, he had said to Wilson, was historic: "The two democracies were to be joined together and he had been chosen to give out the banns." But he could not do so in simple ritualistic fashion; he must do so uniquely, in full awareness that the occasion could be unhappy, possibly disastrous. For he knew there were in Congress, especially the Senate, a considerable number of isolationist Anglophobes, all of whom were among a much larger number whose ruling political passion was hatred of Churchill's great friend Franklin Roosevelt. He was, however, literally inspired. He felt, he would say in his memoirs, that he was "being used, however unworthy," as an instrument of a mighty higher purpose. And he scored one of the greatest of his numerous oratorical triumphs. He won his audience with his opening remark, "I cannot help reflecting that if my father had been American and my mother British, instead of the other way around, I might have got here on my own," then made an eloquently passionate plea for permanent Anglo-American unity, closing: "Twice in a single generation the catastrophe of world war has fallen upon us; twice in our lifetime has the long arm of Fate reached across the ocean to bring the United States into the forefront of the battle. If we had kept together after the last war . . . this renewal of the curse need never have fallen upon us. . . . Prodigious hammer-strokes have been needed to bring us together again, or, if you will allow me to use other language, I will say that . . . some great purpose and design is being worked out here below, of which we have the honor to be the faithful servants. It is not given us to peer into the mysteries of the future. Still, I avow my hope and faith, sure and inviolate, that in the days to come the British and American peoples will for their own safety and for the good of all walk together side by side in majesty, in justice, and in peace." His condemnation of the failure of the two nations to act together after the last war was quietly received; but as soon as he had spoken the last word of his address every congressman and senator rose to his feet, all loudly applauding and many cheering.[35]

Four days later, in Ottawa, Churchill scored a similar triumph with his address to the Canadian Parliament, part of which he delivered in French (though he spoke French badly) in deference to the representatives of French-speaking Quebec. He excoriated the French politicians who now constituted the Vichy government for their refusal to go to North Africa in 1940 and there establish themselves, with the French fleet in their hands, as the continuing government of the French empire, the continuing fighting ally of Britain in the war against Hitler. "When I warned them that Britain would fight on . . . whatever they did, their generals told their Prime Minister and his divided Cabinet, 'In three weeks England will have her neck wrung like a chicken.' " Churchill paused, then said in a voice that throbbed with sarcasm, defiance, pride: "Some chicken! Some neck!" He extolled the Free French as "Frenchmen who would not bend their knees and who under General de Gaulle have continued the fight. . . . They have been condemned to death by the men of Vichy, but their names will be held, and are being held, in increasing respect by nine out of ten Frenchmen throughout the once happy, smiling land of France." Thanks to de Gaulle and the Free French, "Hope is springing up again in the hearts of a warrior race. . . . We shall never lose confidence that France will play the role of free men again, and by hard paths will once again attain her place in the great company of freedom-bestowing and victorious nations." The address, superbly delivered, provoked in its immediate audience paroxysms of laughter, cheers, and applause.[36]

. . .

The joint press conference and the two Churchill addresses, especially his address to Congress, along with the Atlantic Charter and Roosevelt's public emphasis upon the closeness of the personal bond between him and His Majesty's first minister, had by the end of 1941 encouraged a popular belief that what was now happening at the Washington Conference, code-named Arcadia, was something more than the shaping of another international military alliance. An alliance is a linkage between sharply defined sovereign powers. The powers have space between them; their alliance is but a narrow bridge, generally a flimsy one, cast across this space for a limited time. But now in Washington, or so the more thoughtful and idealistic among the populace were encouraged to believe, a considerable portion of this separateness, this international space, was in process of being annihilated. There appeared to be occurring a limited pooling of sovereignty in a new supranational organism, an organism radically different from the failed League of Nations insofar as it was, to the extent of this pooling, not a league but a union—a making of one out of many. The end of the process, attainable, perhaps, within the lifetime of millions who now struggled on the battlefields of Europe and Asia and Africa, might be a United States of the civilized world!

This public perception was sharpened and clarified on New Year's Day 1942 when, barely twenty-four hours after Churchill's return to Washington from Ottawa, there was signed in the Oval Room of the White House a joint declaration by the twenty-six nations who were at war with Axis powers. It was headed DECLARATION BY UNITED NATIONS, and its full text appeared in the newspapers of January 2 as follows:

"A Joint Declaration by The United States of America, The United Kingdom of Great Britain and Northern Ireland, the Union of Soviet Socialist Republics, China, Australia, Belgium, Canada, Costa Rica, Cuba, Czechoslovakia, Dominican Republic, El Salvador, Greece, Guatemala, Haiti, Honduras, India, Luxembourg, Netherlands, New Zealand, Nicaragua, Norway, Panama, Poland, South Africa, Yugoslavia.

"The Governments signatory hereto,

"Having subscribed to a common program of purposes and principles embodied in the Joint Declaration of the President of the United States and the Prime Minister of the United Kingdom of Great Britain and Northern Ireland, dated August 14, 1941, known as the Atlantic Charter.

"Being convinced that complete victory over their enemies is essential to defend life, liberty, independence, and religious freedom, and to preserve human rights and justice in their own lands as well as in other lands, and that they are now engaged in a common struggle against savage and brutal forces seeking to subjugate the world, DECLARE:

"(1) Each Government pledges itself to employ its full resources, military or economic, against those members of the Tripartite Pact and its adherents with which such Government is at war.

"(2) Each Government pledges itself to cooperate with the Governments signatory hereto, and not to make a separate armistice or peace with the enemies.

"The foregoing Declaration may be adhered to by other nations which are, or which may be, rendering material assistance and contributions in the struggle for victory over Hitlerism.

"Done at Washington
January First, 1942"

Like the Atlantic Charter, this document was prepared at the instigation of Roosevelt, who proposed the enterprise to Churchill on December 23. Like the Atlantic Charter, it was in its final form a revised blend of two drafts originally prepared separately by Roosevelt and Churchill. And, even more than in the case of the charter, its preparation was marvelous for the speed with which it was accomplished. For this last, too, Roosevelt was largely responsible; he pressed for a New Year's Day publication of the document because he was anxious to offset the effect upon the public mind of the horrendous news that was pouring night and day out of the Far East. Finally, it was Roosevelt who had come up with "United Nations" as a replacement for the dull-sounding "Associated Nations" in the Declaration's heading, "Allies" being ruled out because the word had treaty implications, and a treaty had to be ratified by the U.S. Senate. (Plausible legend has it that Roosevelt was so excitedly pleased by his "United Nations" inspiration that he hurried to communicate it to Churchill, wheeling himself into the latter's quarters without knocking and finding the Prime Minister emerging stark naked from the bathtub. He began to retreat, with an embarrassed apology. "Think nothing of it," Churchill said airily. "The Prime Minister of Great Britain has nothing to conceal from the President of the United States.")[37] A number of difficulties had to be overcome. In what order, for instance, was the document to be signed? In the first joint draft, the United States signed first, the United Kingdom second, then four British Dominions and Commonwealths (Australia, Canada, New Zealand, South Africa), then the other nations in alphabetical order. India was omitted at the behest of Churchill and the British war cabinet. But this was clearly unsatisfactory. It placed the Union of Soviet Socialist Republics far down the list, though the USSR was the chief of Hitler's fighting opponents; it ignored the fact that Indian troops were a major component of the British forces now fighting the Japanese. The problem was solved by listing with the United States and Britain the other two of what Roosevelt called the "Big Four," namely, the USSR and China, and then listing the others alphabetically, India being finally included after both Halifax and Eden had vehemently protested her exclusion.

Another problem arose when Hopkins, reviewing the first joint draft, remarked the absence from it of any reference to religious freedom, a subject whose omission from the Atlantic Charter had exposed that document to much adverse criticism. Hopkins strongly recommended that "every effort" be made "to get religious freedom in this document" and that, since atheistic Communist Russia might object, Roosevelt press the point with Maxim Litvinov, who had just replaced the abrasive Oumansky as Soviet ambassador in Washington. Roosevelt did so when he lunched with the new ambassador, and with Hopkins, on December 27. Litvinov, the failed architect of a united front against Hitler in the 1930s, had lived in poverty, disgrace, and a fully justified fear for his life after his replacement by Molotov as Soviet foreign minister in 1939. He knew that Stalin suspected him of excessively pro-Western, pro-democratic sympathies; he was acutely aware that such suspicion, if he did anything to confirm it in Stalin's mind, could be fatal to him. He was consequently extremely reluctant to seek Stalin's approval of the proposed insertion in the draft document he had already cabled to Moscow. At last, fearfully, he did so. Whereupon, to quote Churchill's memoirs, Stalin accepted the insertion "as a matter of course."[38]

Litvinov's palpable fear of Stalin also worked against the inclusion of the words "and Authorities" after the word "Governments" in the first sentence of the declaration. Churchill proposed doing so in order to permit the listing of Free France as a declaration signer. Roosevelt had initially no objection to this, and the Free French would certainly have been delighted to sign. But Litvinov said that he, as an official of the Soviet Foreign Office, had no authority to approve the slightest textual change in a document that committed the whole of the Soviet government and that had already received Moscow's approval. If the word "Authorities" were inserted, he would be unable to sign the declaration unless and until Moscow had specifically authorized his doing so. And since it was impossible to obtain such permission, assuming it were forthcoming,* without delaying the ceremonial signing beyond the New Year's Day deadline, the insertion was not made. ". . . Litvinov is a mere automaton, evidently frightened out of his wits after what he has gone through," a disgusted Churchill cabled Clement Attlee, head of Britain's Labour Party and, by that token, generally regarded as Britain's Deputy Prime Minister. But, Churchill went on, "This can be covered by an exchange of letters making clear that the word 'Nations' covers authorities such as the Free French, or insurgent organizations

---

*Writes Hopkins in his note on this discussion: "Later I learned that Litvinov had cabled for approval to include the word 'authorities' and his Government had given it to him." Evidently the approval message arrived at the signing.

which may arise in Spain, in North Africa, or in Germany itself. Settlement was imperative because . . . President was . . . very keen on January 1."³⁹

V

BUT even had Litvinov dared exercise in this case such freedom of judgment as is commonly allotted an ambassador, the Free French would almost certainly have been excluded from the list of signers. By New Year's Day Roosevelt himself was opposed to their signing, his change of mind consequent upon an event that occurred on Christmas Eve 1941 on two bleak, tiny islands situated some twenty-odd miles off the southernmost tip of Newfoundland.

Saint Pierre and Miquelon, they were called; they had been French possessions since the sixteenth century; and the five thousand people who inhabited them, nearly all of whom were Free French in political sympathy, made their hard livings by fishing the frigid stormy waters around them. Three facts now conferred upon them, and upon the barren, sea-washed specks of land they occupied, a marginal importance in world affairs: *one,* the islands were governed by a detested local Vichyite administrator of tyrannical temper who operated under the authority of Admiral Georges Robert, the Vichy governor of the Antilles; *two,* Saint Pierre had upon it a powerful radio transmitter that was being used to broadcast pro-totalitarian Vichy propaganda and might be used to aid the assault of German U-boats upon Allied shipping; *three,* Vichy agents were suspected of tapping the Western Union transatlantic cables that ran through Saint Pierre and passing on to the Nazis whatever information about Allied convoys they thus obtained. These facts led de Gaulle to the conclusion that the islands should be taken away from Vichy by the Free French, something that would be easy to do now that a Vichy warship formerly stationed at the islands had been withdrawn to Martinique for repairs. To de Gaulle's assertively legalistic, assertively nationalistic mind, the matter was wholly one of internal French politics, properly to be dealt with by Free France (the *real* France, fighting France) alone. He felt obliged by his circumstances, however, if only as a matter of courtesy, to seek prior approval of the operation from his British hosts, and in an October 1941 letter to Eden he did so. The British foreign secretary expressed himself as favorable to the project and continued to favor it even after the Canadian government made the counterproposal that it seize and destroy the Saint Pierre radio transmitter; Eden feared such Canadian action would provoke damaging charges of British imperialism. But when Washington was consulted on the matter by the British and Canadians, the State Department expressed a flat, even vehement opposition not only to the Free French proposal, but also, if less adamantly, to the Canadian one. Washington remained wedded to the policy of friendship with the totalitarians of Vichy on the ground that this was necessary to assure the continued neutralization of the powerful French naval forces now anchored at Toulon, at Martinique, and in French North African ports. The policy was highly unpopular in the United States. It was viewed by a considerable portion of the general public as a dishonorable and futile attempt by State Department reactionaries to appease an utterly evil enemy at the expense of those Frenchmen who were committed to human freedom and willing to fight for it. But Roosevelt and Hull clung stubbornly to this policy even after America's full entrance into the war. Indeed, Roosevelt on December 14 addressed to Pétain through Ambassador Leahy a cordial message assuring the marshal that the warm close relationship between Washington and Vichy, along with the status quo for French possessions in the Western Hemisphere, would be maintained.[40] As regards Saint Pierre–Miquelon, the only action Washington would agree to was the application of mild economic pressure upon the islands' governor with the aim of persuading him to accept a Canadian supervision of the radio transmitter, and the Canadians were sure this wouldn't work—not, at least, within a reasonable period of time.

A rather desultory discussion of the matter was proceeding in Washington between the Canadians and the Americans when Admiral Emile Muselier, commander of Free France's meager naval forces, arrived in Ottawa from London on December 16. The admiral was under orders from his chief to proceed to Halifax and use a Free French submarine cruiser and three corvettes, anchored in the harbor there, to "liberate" Saint Pierre–Miquelon. The orders were, in de Gaulle's intention, secret; but within twenty-four hours after his arrival in the Canadian capital, Muselier, a willful man who had far outranked de Gaulle in the prewar French military establishment and now felt no personal loyalty to him, told the American minister to Canada, J. Pierrepont Moffat, what his orders were and asked if Washington approved them. Washington, of course, in response to Moffat's prompt query, expressed again a most emphatic disapproval. Muselier then explicitly promised that the operation would not be carried out. De Gaulle, too, in London, feeling forced by Muselier's report to him, explicitly promised to desist.

A day or so later, however, he learned for the first time that the Canadians proposed, with American support, to seize the island transmitter. This would be, in his view, an intolerable violation of French sovereignty. He promptly cabled Muselier, who was then preparing to return to London: "We know for certain that the Canadians intend to [destroy] radio station at St. Pierre. Therefore I order you to carry out the rallying of St. Pierre and Miquelon with your own means and without saying anything to the foreigners. I take complete responsibility for this operation. . . ."[41] And this time Muselier, his own patriotic passions aroused, did as he was told. He went to Halifax. After boarding one of the corvettes there, he sailed northward, accompanied by the submarine and the other two corvettes, to Saint Pierre, whose harbor he entered in midafternoon of December 24. No resistance was made by the handful of Vichyite officials. Not a shot was fired as he took control of the local government in the name of Free France. In a courteous and friendly interview with the local U.S. consul, Maurice Pasquet, he said that from now on the island's facilities would be freely available to the Allies but added that despite his initial opposition to the decision to proceed against the wishes of the Allied governments, he would defend the islands "to the last man" against any attempt by anyone, Canadian or American or Vichyite, to take them away from him.[42] As for the island populace, it welcomed the admiral with deliriously joyful celebration. When a formal plebiscite was held on Christmas Day, 98 percent of the male citizenry (the female citizenry was not allowed to vote) declared in favor of Free France.

Scarcely less enthusiastically approving was the general public of the United States. For weeks that public had fed upon a diet of unrelieved bad news from the far Pacific: Guam and Wake Island taken by the Japanese, also Tarawa and Makin in the Gilberts; Hong Kong conquered; airborne Japanese troops landed in the Dutch East Indies; Japanese swarming down the Malay Peninsula toward Singapore; MacArthur forced to abandon the bulk of Luzon and concentrate his forces in the narrowing twenty-five-mile-long Bataan peninsula, where in the absence of massive reinforcements, he could not hold out for long. Hard upon the tragic news of *Prince of Wales* and *Repulse* in the Far East had come one report after another of British fleet disasters in the Mediterranean: cruiser *Galatia* sunk off the Egyptian coast by a German submarine; battleships *Queen Elizabeth* and *Valiant* disabled in Alexandria harbor by so-called human torpedo teams of Italians; cruiser *Neptune* sunk by mines off Malta with a single survivor of its crew of many hundreds. In Libya there was evident stalemate, albeit an active one, with advances followed by retreats on the part of both British and Axis forces, deciding nothing. From the gigantic clash of dictatorships on the Russian front came news welcome to the West, since one of the dictatorships was our enemy: Nazi forces that had been halted before Moscow continued to be driven back by Communist forces. But nowhere for a long, long time had democracy scored a clear and solid triumph over dictatorship. Until now! And here in the Western Hemisphere! With exemplary and exhilarating audacity, a few hundred Free Frenchmen had scored a victory that, if small, was decisive; it actually liberated land and people from totalitarian power, something that had not happened before in this war. The American press and public cheered. Editorialized the *New York Post* on the evening of December 25: "Americans, Canadians, Britons and all others who are struggling to defeat the Axis have experienced great joy this Christmas Day on learning that the Free French have occupied these two French islands. . . ." Said *The New York Times* on the morning of December 26: "The bloodless investiture of these surprised islands by four little Free French warships . . . was accomplished with a display of style and manners in the best tradition of Alexander Dumas." Said the *Christian Science Monitor,* in an editorial entitled "Beau Geste": "For many Americans, seizure of the little islands of Saint Pierre and Miquelon . . . bespoke an initiative and flair that have often been lacking in Allied strategy. . . ."[43]

In stark contrast was the official reaction in Washington. Cordell Hull, having leapt to the conclusion (he had no objective evidence) that there had been secret collusion on this matter between the Canadians and the Free French, was furious at what he deemed a personal betrayal, a personal insult. He had been away from the capital for the holiday when the news came to him. He rushed back on Christmas Eve and spent most of the following day on the phone to Ottawa, attempting to persuade (force) Canadian Prime Minister Mackenzie King to act immediately, in whatever way was necessary, to evict the Free French and restore the islands to Vichy. He succeeded only in angering King. The Canadian Premier naturally resented Hull's assumption that he had deceitfully conspired with de Gaulle. Though he deplored the way de Gaulle had gone about it, he was personally not at all unhappy to see the disputed islands in friendly hands. He was to leave that night for Washington, there to join in the Arcadia Conference, and saw no reason why a decision about Saint Pierre–Miquelon could not be postponed until he arrived in the American capital. Evidently the secretary of state had lost all sense of proportion, a judgment in which King was confirmed (his anger was also increased) by a communiqué that Hull insisted upon issuing on Christmas afternoon, with Roosevelt's approval, despite pleas from Moffat that this not be done.

Our preliminary reports show that the action taken by "three so-called Free French ships" at Saint Pierre–Miquelon was "an arbitrary action contrary to the agreement of all parties concerned and certainly without the prior knowledge or consent in any sense of the U.S. government," said the State Department communiqué. "This government has inquired of the Canadian government as to the steps Canada is prepared to take to restore the status quo of the islands." This statement was, of course, welcomed by the men of Vichy, and it may have been, though probably was not, a factor in their decision to take no retaliatory action. But public opinion in the United States no less than in Canada and England was outraged. Especially offensive was the "so-called Free French" phrase. It prompted Churchill to insert in his Canadian parliamentary address that enthusiastic praise of de Gaulle and the Free French that we quoted above, and it loosed a flood of derisory commentary upon the "so-called State Department" and the "so-called Secretary of State." Editorialized the *New York Post* within hours after the Hull communiqué was issued: "The Department of State has tried cajolerie, corruption, self-delusion and stupidity in attempting to prop up Vichy against Hitler. Today it tries treason—for there is no other word to describe its sellout of the Free French at Saint Pierre and Miquelon and its attempt to restore Vichy to power there." The *Post* castigated "anonymous bureaucrats" in the department who "have been dominating American foreign policy" in a manner "more and more flagrant" and who today "outdo themselves. . . ." In an editorial entitled "A Moral Victory," the *New York Herald-Tribune* said on December 28: "The bluntness with which Washington has reprimanded the Gaullists . . . created a most unpleasant impression. . . . And naturally the moral victory rests with the cause of the Free French—which is also our own." Five days later, Walter Lippmann in his syndicated column proclaimed the "real lesson" of "this blunder, this little diplomatic Pearl Harbor" to be "that the State Department was not awake," that it "maintains its regular routine" in the face of unique and tremendous challenges. "We are right to ask if the State Department is too bureaucratic in spirit to adjust . . . to the new and immense responsibilities of war."[44]

Cordell Hull was a thin-skinned, hot-tempered man who, as a social and economic conservative, had until now suffered remarkably little personal criticism in the mass media—less of it in any year than Roosevelt or Hopkins or Ickes suffered in an average week—and he was wholly unprepared psychologically to deal with the hostility now focused upon him. Far from causing him to question the wisdom of his own action and policy, this hostility increased his fury and hardened his stubborn will. In a memorandum to Roosevelt written the day after Churchill's Ottawa speech, he quoted from the cabled report of a "conversation between [Admiral Jean] Darlan [Vichy minister of marine] and the Marshal [Pétain] with Leahy: 'Darlan then referred to the Saint Pierre–Miquelon incident and said that Germany has already used the seizure of these islands . . . as an argument for the entry of French troops into Africa in order that it may be protected against a similar invasion.' This is just the beginning of ominous and serious developments which, in my opinion, will occur. Our British friends seem to believe that the body of the entire people of France is behind de Gaulle [Churchill had asserted at Ottawa that de Gaulle and his followers 'are being held in increasing respect by nine out of ten Frenchmen throughout . . . France'] whereas according to all of my information . . . some 95 percent of the entire French people are anti-Hitler whereas more than 95 percent of the latter are not de Gaullists and would not follow him." This last, of course, failed to jibe with the results of the plebiscite at Saint Pierre–Miquelon, which was the only vote that had ever been taken by uncoerced Frenchmen on the subject. Equally at variance with evident truth was Hull's statement that "the British Government was really behind this movement." The memorandum closed with an incoherently spluttering ninety-word sentence, sarcastic in tone, seemingly doubting that Churchill "would be disposed to talk to you, or rather to let you talk to him" about the matter and then to permit an announcement "to the general public that nobody [meaning Cordell Hull primarily] is censurable. . . ." Subsequently, the secretary of state indicated he would resign his post if Roosevelt failed to do everything in his power to restore the status quo at Saint Pierre–Miquelon, a threat that caused Roosevelt to exert some pressure in this direction upon Churchill but barely enough to prevent Hull's resignation and certainly not enough to antagonize the Prime Minister or weaken in the slightest British support of de Gaulle and Free France. The chief effect of Hull's agitation was a needless prolongation and magnification of what was essentially a teapot tempest; it raged for three weeks in the public prints before subsiding. "The President . . . seemed to me to shrug his shoulders over the whole affair," says Churchill in his war memoirs. ". . . Chapters have been written about this incident . . . but it did not at all affect our main [conference] discussions."[45]

It did affect U.S. relations with Free France in ways unfortunate for the free world. Under the best of circumstances there would have been a clash of personalities between the American President and the Free French leader. We have noted that Roosevelt manifested in his personal operations hardly less than in his political ones a seemingly instinctive aversion to the simple, the straightforward, the direct—a seemingly instinctive preference for the complicated, the ambiguous, the devious. Often he evinced a kind of contempt, along with an irritation tinctured sometimes with moral unease, when dealing with men who pursued their objectives in uncompromisingly straight lines, men who disdainfully eschewed the tactics of backing-and-filling, of cajolery and concealment and misdirection, which were for Roosevelt part and parcel of the art, or game, of elective politics. If these men also manifested egotism, a love of personal power, and a willingness to achieve their ends by forceful means, he recognized them as enemies of democracy and invariably bristled with unwonted hard hostility, an animosity he made little effort to conceal. So it had been in his encounters with Robert Moses* and Huey Long and Charles Lindbergh. So it was now, and would be for as long as circumstances permitted, in his dealings with Charles de Gaulle. Saint Pierre–Miquelon personally embarrassed him, and his embarrassment helped solidify a fluid suspicion he had had that the leader of Free France was not himself committed to human freedom and would, if he had his way, establish postwar France as a dictatorship headed by Charles de Gaulle.

VI

IF Saint Pierre–Miquelon did not directly affect any of the Arcadia Conference's main discussions, as Churchill asserts, it certainly did affect the way in which an important decision initially tentatively made at the very first conference session would be carried out.

This first session was a highly informal one, held within hours after Churchill's arrival in the White House on December 22. There was a gala reception dinner hosted by Roosevelt that night at which, as it seemed to others present, the Prime Minister and the President vied with one another, alternatively, for star status. After it, at ten o'clock, the two retired from the dining room to the

---

*See pp. 791–92 of *FDR: The Beckoning of Destiny;* pp. 497–501 of *FDR: The New Deal Years.*

Oval Room for a discussion in which Hull, Welles, Hopkins, Beaverbrook, and Halifax also participated. To this group Churchill, having been relieved of his fear that Pearl Harbor might cause the Americans to shift away from the overall Europe-first strategy, presented the gist of the first of the three papers he had prepared during the Atlantic crossing, none of which Roosevelt had yet had a chance to read. "There was general agreement," wrote Churchill in a cable to the British war cabinet next day, "that if Hitler was held in Russia he must try something else" and that this "something else" would probably be a movement through Spain and Portugal "en route to North Africa." It was a probability increased by Britain's "current success in Libya," where Auchinleck's aggressive advance (alas for Churchill, it would soon bog down) presented Hitler with "the prospect of [Britain's] joining hands with French North African territory." Such "joining" would mean Allied control of the whole of North Africa and an immense strengthening of the Allied position in the Middle East. The prospect of it was likely to provoke a surprise move by Axis forces into French North Africa within the next few months, regardless of events on the Russian front. And there was "general agreement" among that night's conferees that it was "vital" to the Allies "to forestall" this move. Added to "all the other reasons" for doing so was the fact that "the two French battleships, *Jean Bart* [at Casablanca] and *Richelieu* [at Dakar] were a real prize for whoever got them. Accordingly, the discussion was not *whether,* but *how.*" As regards the forestalling action, it was suggested that efforts be made through American diplomatic connections with Vichy to persuade Pétain and/or General Weygand, commander of the French forces in North Africa, to invite the Allies into Algeria and Morocco. Was it not for just such purpose as this that the American Vichy policy had been designed? Was not this part and parcel of the end whereby morally dubious means were justified? Alas, it was now realized that "the effect" of this specific approach to Vichy "might be to extract smooth promises from Pétain and Weygand, the Germans meanwhile being advised of our intentions." Hence the conclusion that "if these approaches [to the Vichyites] were to be made, it would be desirable to have all plans made for going into North Africa *with or without invitation. . . .* The President said he was anxious [it was necessary for public morale purposes] that American land forces should give their support as quickly as possible" and thought "a plan to move into North Africa" should be prepared "for either event, i.e., with or without invitation." Had it not been for Saint Pierre–Miquelon, some consideration might have been given to the possible involvement of the Free French in the enterprise; as it was, the final agreement was simply "to remit the study of the project to Staffs. . . ."[46]

Initially code-named "Gymnast," later (when expanded) "Super-Gymnast" (it would finally become "Torch"), the project aroused no enthusiasm in Marshall and his staff, though they perforce ordered the making of plans and preparations for it. For them the commitment to "Hitler first" was, as we know, a commitment to all-out assault upon the Continent at the earliest moment such assault became feasible. Meanwhile, all that could be done to aid the Philippines and other threatened Southwest Pacific possessions *must* now be done. From this, Gymnast was a diversion. It was likely to delay the all-out European assault. It could immediately detract and distract from the Far Pacific war. And it could not, in the American staff view, achieve a result that would appreciably shorten the war. Representative of this reaction was that of the new assistant war plans chief, Brigadier General Dwight Eisenhower, whose specific mission at that time was the virtually impossible one of getting reinforcements and supplies to the American troops on Bataan. "I've been insisting that the Far East is critical—and no side-shows should be undertaken until air and ground there are in satisfactory shape," he scrawled on a memo pad on January 1, 1942. "Instead we are taking on Magnet [U.S. troops to Northern Ireland], Gymnast, etc." Three days later he wrote on his memo pad: ". . . we've got to have ships—and we need them now! Tempers are short, there are lots of amateur strategists on the job."[47]

And the suspicion is strong that Eisenhower and others of the staff were inclined by their frustration and irritation at that moment to include among the "amateurs" their commander in chief, the President of the United States. Certainly there was an explosion of wrath on the part of Marshall and Eisenhower when they learned on Christmas morning that Roosevelt on the night before, in a meeting with Churchill and some of the latter's advisers, had agreed to divert to Singapore any reinforcements intended for the Philippines that were unlikely to get through the Japanese blockade of those islands. The two generals saw this as a yielding by Roosevelt to the British willingness to sacrifice the Philippines to the defense of Singapore. They went at once in high dudgeon to Secretary Stimson. Stimson at once phoned Harry Hopkins to say that if the President persisted in this kind of decision making, he would have to find a new secretary of war. And Hopkins, shortly thereafter, when he, Churchill, and Roosevelt were alone together, told the two heads of government what Stimson had said. Roosevelt and Churchill then flatly denied that they had made any agreement on this matter,* and the episode ended with Roosevelt's emphatic assurance of his military advisers that he was firmly committed to the maximum possible supply of men and matériel to MacArthur on Bataan. Four days later he sent the following memorandum to Stimson: "I wish that War Plans would explore every possible means of relieving the Philippines. I realize great risks are involved but the

---

*Writes Forrest C. Pogue on page 266 of his *George C. Marshall: Ordeal and Hope:* "When Roosevelt later [that day] made slighting reference to incorrect statements that were going around, Stimson read him extracts from a record made by a British secretary of the informal discussions of the previous evening."

objective is important." (Subsequently, bizarre and desperate efforts were made under Eisenhower's direction to supply the doomed Americans on Bataan. In Java, Timor, New Guinea, were hired ships with crews of daring mercenaries who for huge cash payments [literally bales of money were flown to Java] attempted to run the Japanese blockade. Nearly all of them failed; at least fifteen of them were sunk or captured. Of the seven or so overage destroyers that attempted the run, none got through. Only submarines managed without loss to deliver precious supplies to Bataan, and their cargoes were severely limited by their size.)[48]

On Christmas afternoon the urgent question of how to contain the Japanese advance in the Southwest Pacific was the subject of a meeting of the British and American chiefs of staff. The assumption in London and Washington had been that the Japanese were at maximum strength when they attacked Pearl Harbor; their strength must wane as it was spent upon the easy conquests that were inevitable through the war's opening months. But now it was clear that this maximum strength had been underrated in the West, probably in part as a result of racial prejudice. Consequently the early conquests were far swifter and likely to be far more extensive than had been anticipated. Which meant that Japan's strength, far from lessening, might actually increase in coming months as it was fed by what it conquered. Singapore and the Netherlands East Indies were immediately threatened, and their conquest would threaten Australia! Burma was immediately threatened, and its conquest would threaten India! There was for the Allies a renewal, from a different angle, of the nightmare vision they had had in the weeks immediately prior to Hitler's invasion of Russia—the vision of a gigantic Axis pincers closing upon India from west and east—with the difference being that it was now by Japan and not Germany, and from the east and not the west, that the movement was launched. Hence the hasty establishment by the conferees during Arcadia's first days of a so-called ABDA theater of war in the Southwest Pacific (the initials stood for American, British, Dutch, Australian), and hence the urgency with which Marshall, on this Christmas afternoon, made a proposal for ABDA's top administration, this after a number of specific problems in that theater had been defined and some of them dealt with.

"The matters being settled here are mere details which will continuously recur unless settled in a broader way," Marshall said with some impatience, after having emphasized that what he was about to express were "my personal views," developed without consultation with either "the Navy or . . . my own War Plans Division." He felt "very strongly that the most important consideration is the question of unity of command. . . . I am convinced that there must be one man in command of the entire theater—air, ground, and ships. We cannot manage by cooperation. Human frailties are such that there would be emphatic unwillingness to place portions of troops under another service. If we make a plan for unified command now, it will solve nine-tenths of our problems." He admitted that there were "difficulties in arriving at a single command, but they are much less than the hazards that must be faced if we do not achieve this," and he himself was "willing to go to the limit to accomplish this." Of course, "[w]e must decide on a line of action here and not expect it to be done out there"—the "one man in control" in the war theater would operate "under a controlled directive from here"—but over his theater he would exercise supreme command, his authority undivided among the three services (navy, army, air) or among different nationalities. "We had to come to this in the First World War, but it was not until 1918 that it was accomplished and much valuable time, blood, and treasure had been needlessly sacrificed. If we could decide on a unified command now, it would be a great advance over what was accomplished during the World War."[49]

But ABDA was a theater vastly different from the First World War's western front. That front had consisted of a single unbroken line of battle stretching across northern France from the English Channel to the Vosges mountains. The ABDA was a sprawling collection of actual and potential land-battle sites scattered across many hundreds of miles of open sea. No war theater could be less suited, on the face of it, to a single unified command. So argued Churchill at a top-level meeting in the White House next day, after Roosevelt, rather surprisingly in view of his natural preference for diffuse administration and blurredly defined terms of reference, had announced his unqualified approval of what Marshall proposed. "The situation out there [in the Southwest Pacific]," said Churchill, according to the meeting's minutes, "is that certain particular strategic points [notably Singapore] have to be held, and the commander in each locality is quite clear as to what he should do. The difficult question is the application of resources arriving in the area. This is a matter which can only be settled by the Governments concerned." In other words, a single unified ABDA command, far from simplifying the confused situation, would add to the confusion. General Brooke in London thoroughly agreed, terming the Marshall proposal "wild and half-baked." Nor was Churchill's opposition and that of the British staff chiefs softened, as it was intended to be, when the Americans proposed that Britain's General Wavell be named the theater's supreme commander. Quite the contrary. The "honor" thus to be bestowed upon Wavell was, in the British view, worse than empty: it was a curse insofar as the command theater over which Wavell would preside was crumbling under the weight of the Japanese assault and was bound to continue to do so through the immediate future. Dill in Washington, though he favored the unified-command concept, opposed having "a British commander responsible for the disasters that are coming to the Americans as well as ourselves." So did all the British staff chiefs. They presented to Churchill a unanimous demand, concurred in by Lord Halifax, that an American, not an Englishman, be named ABDA's supreme commander. This, however, was going far too far, said Churchill—it insultingly impugned the motives of the American President and his advisers; it would do immeasurable harm to Anglo-American unity—and he rejected the demand emphatically. A few days later, in a December 29 cable to Attlee, he described the Marshall-Roosevelt idea as a "broadminded and selfless . . . proposal," of the "merits of which as a war-winner I have become convinced."[50]

Two things caused the Prime Minister to change his mind.

One was Marshall's realization, before the Christmas afternoon session had ended, that his abrupt introduction of so sweeping a proposal without having prepared the ground for it was a grave tactical error. He moved at once to correct it. At the meeting's close he ordered Eisenhower, who had sat beside him, to draft a directive for the proposed ABDA supreme commander that would clearly define the commander's mission in a way that protected the distinct and different sovereign interests in that theater of the British, the Dutch, and the Americans. According to the notes Eisenhower took that day, Marshall hoped by this means "to convince the other members of the conference that no real risk would be involved to the interests of any of the Associated Powers, while on the other hand great profits would result."[51]

The *other* thing was consequent upon a note scrawled upon a White House memo pad by Lord Beaverbrook and handed by him to Hopkins during the conference session in which the Prime Minister voiced his initial opposition to what Marshall had proposed. "You should work on Churchill," said the note. "He is being advised. He is open-minded & needs discussion." This led Hopkins to arrange a private meeting between Churchill and Marshall at which Marshall argued his case with persuasive eloquence, making it clear that he intended his ABDA proposal to be a precedent for all theater commands in the future and, indeed, as regards the principle of unity of command, for the direction of the whole Allied military effort. Marshall's mind on this matter was further sounded by Churchill when, on January 5, 1942, the general flew with him and his physician to Florida to begin that secret five-day holiday for the Prime Minister that has already been mentioned.* By then the ABDA command structure

---

*Dr. Charles Wilson insisted upon this respite from strenuous work after a worried Churchill told him, on the morning of December 27: "It was hot last night and I got up to open a window. It was very stiff. I had to use considerable force and I noticed all at once that I was short of breath. I had a dull pain over my heart. It went down my left arm. It didn't last very long, but it has never happened before. What is it?" Wilson at once applied his stethoscope to the Prime Minister's bared chest, not because he expected such examination to reveal anything definitive, but in order to gain time in which to frame his answers to Churchill's inevitable sharp questioning. Clearly, what Churchill had suffered was coronary insufficiency, for which "the textbook treatment . . . is at least six weeks in bed," to quote the doctor's diary. But this was, in the circumstances, an impossible treatment. It "would mean publishing to the world . . . that the P.M. was an invalid with a crippled heart and a doubtful future. . . . I felt that the announcement that the P.M. had had a heart attack could only be disastrous." So Wilson, though acutely aware that if Churchill had another and "fatal seizure the world would undoubtedly say that I had killed him through not insisting on rest," told his patient nothing of what he fearfully suspected. "There is nothing serious," he said in answer to Churchill's anxious question. "You needn't rest in the sense of lying up, but you mustn't do more than you can help in the way of exertion for a little while."[52]

had been finally decided and Wavell had been informed of his new assignment. ("Everyone knows how dark and difficult the situation is [in the ABDA theater]," said Churchill's December 29 message—and we may here say that the theater was destined to fall to pieces under the Japanese onslaught before Wavell's command could begin to be effectively exercised.)[53]

Thus was taken, on Marshall's initiative and largely in consequence of his single-minded persistence, a long step toward what history records as the second of Arcadia's greatest achievements, the first having been the initiation of the United Nations. This second was the establishment of a Combined Chiefs of Staff Committee, a body that was not just a means of linking the separate staffs of the British and the Americans, but an actual fusion of the two into one. Viewed in a larger context, it was another instance of progress toward that supranational government that is logically implied by scientific-technological advance but is nonetheless extremely difficult to achieve, requiring as it does the overcoming of a powerful combine of habits, customs, traditions, loyalties, and vested interests.

VII

By the time the final decision on the matter was made, the general pattern of the Allied war effort for 1942 and (more vaguely, tentatively) for 1943 had been determined. It was a pattern that was in accord, insofar as it was not identical, with that established by ABC-1 and Rainbow-5.* It was largely expressive, in other words, of British ideas put forward during the secret joint British-American staff talks of January–March 1941, again at the joint staff talks of Argentia, and yet again, with more specifics, in the first of the three papers Churchill wrote during his Atlantic crossing. Three paragraphs drafted during the Arcadia Conference summarized it:

15. In 1942 the main methods of wearing down Germany's resistance will be:
    a. Ever-increasing air bombardment by British and American Forces.
    b. Assistance to Russia's offensive by all available means.
    c. The blockade.
    d. The maintenance of the spirit of revolt in the occupied countries, and the organization of subversive movements.
16. It does not seem likely that any large scale land offensive against Germany except on the Russian front will be possible. We must, however, be ready to take advantage of any opening that may result from the wearing down process referred to in paragraph 15 to conduct limited land offensives.

*See pp. 143–44.

17. In 1943 the way may be clear for a return to the Continent, across the Mediterranean from Turkey into the Balkans, or by landings in Western Europe. Such operations will be the prelude to the final assault on Germany itself, and the scope of the victory program [that is, the material-production program] should be such as to provide means by which they can be carried out.[54]

Obviously, as regards specific items of this broad framework, there was room for disagreement between the British and the Americans. This room was fully occupied. To what extent should "ever-increasing air bombardment," which was morally outrageous and required an ever-increasing number of long-range bombers, be permitted to absorb a plane-manufacturing capacity that, if large, was not unlimited and might otherwise be devoted to the production of fighter aircraft and medium- and short-range bombers? How to measure— as against the needs of the Pacific, the Atlantic, North Africa, and that Continental "second front" that the Russians themselves were demanding—what was "available" to aid the USSR? And (especially troublesome) what precisely was meant by paragraph 17's very tentative forecast for 1943? The operations that this paragraph described in British terms as preludes "to the final assault upon Germany itself"—especially the optional "return to the Continent" across the Mediterranean or "from Turkey into the Balkans"—presented themselves to American minds as postponements of, or distractions from, the "final assault."

On each side of this disagreement there was a dim apprehension of its root cause, a cause we have already considered,* namely, that Great Britain was a waning world power, being actually and (even more) potentially weaker, economically and militarily, than greater Germany or the USSR, whereas the United States was a waxing world power, its already greatly superior productive capacity capable of further explosive growth. Britain's sense of its power deficiencies dictated a war strategy that minimized risk and maximized the conservation of resources. The British, as has been said, were psychologically prepared to fight a very long war—had been prepared for this by their history of long wars crowned with victories that maintained or restored on the Continent that balance of powers upon which their own island security and power (power derived from a fulcrum position) depended. Indeed, they seemed to their American ally willing to postpone indefinitely the hour of final decision in the present war, this in the Micawber-like hope that meanwhile "something" would "turn up" that would make the final decision more favorable to them and less costly. The Americans, on the other hand, were impatient to "get it over with." A noxious job having been forced upon them, they, conscious of their actual and po-

*See pp. 140–41.

tential strength, proposed to finish it as quickly as possible. And to such end they were willing to run large risks and to spend whatever was necessary of their material and manpower resources.

Consistent with this was a willingness on the part of the British to operate through far looser, more blurred war command arrangements than the Americans would tolerate. Thence arose the specific issue of a decentralized command in the Southwest Pacific area (an arrangement whereby local control of scattered local situations was exercised under necessarily very broad directives from London and Washington) *versus* a centralized, tightly unified command (an organizational structure in which every specific assignment contained precisely equal portions of responsibility and authority and in which the chain of command, defined with absolute clarity, extended unbroken from the highest to the lowest level). The centralized structure, insisted upon by Marshall and his American colleagues, was expressive of a distinctively "American mind," in Churchill's view—a mind that, he asserts in his war memoirs, "runs naturally to broad, sweeping, logical conclusions" on the assumption that "once the foundation has been planned on true and comprehensive lines all other stages will follow naturally and almost inevitably. The British mind," he goes on, "does not work quite in this way. We do not think that logic and clear-cut principles are necessarily the sole keys to what ought to be done in swiftly changing and indefinable situations.* In war particularly we assign a larger importance to opportunism and improvisation, seeking rather to live and conquer in accordance with the unfolding event than to aspire to dominate it often by fundamental decisions."[55] Such British way of thinking, which seemed to Churchill more sophisticated and realistic than the American way, struck George Marshall as dangerously fuzzy in that it permitted and even encouraged inconsistencies and ambiguities and instances of outright deceitfulness that, in the waging of war, could have fatal consequences. On the intellectual level, this issue was sharp enough to be widely divisive; it became sharper still and far more widely divisive as it penetrated or was infused with emotions. For on the emotional level it aroused patriotic passions—that is, the willful, prideful, mutually exclusive furies of collectivized egotism—that are the inevitable accompaniment of limitless national sovereignty. For many generations, the British had exercised a dominant role in world affairs. They were used to being deferred to—had taken for granted, as an element of the natural order of the universe, their right to govern other peoples. The present controversy over command arrangements required them to admit in practice that they were no longer number one, that they must assume from now on a secondary role, giving over first place to the Ameri-

---

*To the present author's "American mind," Churchill's use of the words "naturally," "inevitably," "necessarily," and "sole" makes this statement more revealing of his personal bias against the American administrative mind than it is of that mind's deficiencies.

cans. And such admission, such concession to bitter reality, was excruciatingly painful for them to make.

Of itself alone, the setting up of the Combined Chiefs of Staff (CCS) Committee as supreme strategy-determining body was relatively easy and painless, requiring only slightly more sacrifice of national pride by the British than by the Americans. At the outset, the American members were Marshall in his capacity as U.S. Army chief of staff; Lieutenant General Henry H. ("Hap") Arnold, commanding general of the army air forces and deputy chief of staff for air; Admiral Stark, chief of naval operations; and Admiral King, commander of the U.S. Fleet.* The British members were General Sir Alan Brooke, CIGS; Admiral Pound, first sea lord; Air Chief Marshal Portal, chief of the air staff; and the former CIGS, Field Marshal Dill, who was designated not only the ranking British member of this new supreme body, but also Churchill's personal representative upon it. Necessarily, the American members continued to operate in Washington, the British (save for Dill) in London, which meant there were physically two CCS committees, one in each capital. But the two were in constant contact with one another by telegraph, telephone, and radio; they were joined together organizationally through a Joint Staff Mission headed by Dill in Washington; and from the first they operated virtually as a single body with only a tacit recognition of the fact, humiliating to the British in its implications, that the final decisions of this single body were made and proclaimed, not in London, the former capital of the Allies, but in Washington.

Initially, the Dill designation, unbalanced as it was by a personal representative of Roosevelt on either the Washington or London branch of the CCS Committee, was deemed of questionable wisdom by the American staff chiefs. Marshall, being committed to as sharp a distinction as possible between the military and the civilian authority, and to the subordination of the military to civilian authority, most emphatically did *not* want a personal representative of the President on the CCS, but he worried lest Dill as agent of Britain's political head be forced in practice to blur the distinction between political and military authority in ways dangerously distortive of both. For instance, a former CIGS who was not only the ranking Britisher on the CCS Committee, but also the personal representative of the British head of government on that body would technically be able to protest directly to the President any CCS Committee decision with which he happened to disagree. It was at Marshall's insistence that the President and Prime Minister, in an exchange of cables after Churchill had

---

*In January 1942 there was no American equivalent of the British service-integrating Chiefs of Staff Committee whereon sat the top commanders of ground, sea, and air; but when one was established as the Joint Chiefs of Staff in March 1942, the crying need for it having been tragically demonstrated by Pearl Harbor, the two offices formerly held by Stark and King were combined under King. Stark, in what amounted to a demotion (undeserved, thought most who were most familiar with his operation), went then to London to assume command of U.S. naval forces in Europe.

returned to London, limited Dill's authority to matters that were the common responsibility of the staff chiefs. This was done by making Dill a personal representative of Churchill solely in Churchill's capacity as minister of defense, thus rendering his relationship with the Prime Minister analogous to Marshall's, through the secretary of war, with the President. By the time this happened, however, it was already becoming evident that a precise chain of command definition was in this case of no crucial importance—that Dill's appointment to this particular post, however imprecise the post's official description, was for the Allies one of the most fortunate events of the war. In good part this was because of the close personal friendship that had already been formed between Dill and George Marshall; but the friendship itself, Marshall being the kind of man he was, testifies to the Englishman's personal quality. A man of great experience and ability and iron self-control, acute of mind, selfless of disposition, absolutely trustworthy, possessed of a rare sweetness of character and warmth of personality, Dill was superbly equipped for the interpretation of British minds to American ones, and vice versa, in ways that fostered the Anglo-American unity to which he was religiously committed. Already his lubricating presence, the trust he inspired in all who dealt with him, and his shrewd assessment of what was immediately possible and necessary, had combined (they would continue to combine) to smooth into efficient operation what were initially harsh frictions, even hostile oppositions. The fact that when he died in November 1944, after a long illness, Dill would be buried among America's heroes in Arlington National Cemetery—this plus the fact that he is also seen through British eyes as a hero of the war—gives us who look back upon him some inkling of the significance of his historic role and of how very well he played it. . . .

The difficulty and pain that were mostly absent from the formal creation of the CCS Committee were abundantly vividly present in the effort, during Arcadia's last two days, to give actual substance to this form.

Specifically this effort had to do with the machinery, or the design of the machinery, for distributing war matériel among the far-flung theaters of the global war and among the Allied armed forces that fought in them.

Early in the conference, Hopkins, drawing upon his experience with lend-lease administration, had rather casually suggested the appointment of a civilian board of two, one American, the other British, to advise regarding war matériel allocations. Sympathetically received by the British, who had been long concerned over America's failure to effect a rational means of munitions assignment among those Associated (now United) Nations receiving defense aid, the suggestion stimulated a more drastic one by Beaverbrook—a suggestion that initially surprised many with its seeming contradiction of Beaverbrook's wonted egotism and passionate commitment to the British empire but reminded others that this English lord was, after all, a Canadian native who had repeatedly demonstrated, as regards material things, the expansive optimism and bold "can do" spirit that are allegedly typically American. Beaverbrook made his suggestion on December 27 in two notes, one to Roosevelt, the other to Churchill. Said the note to Roosevelt: "It is my hope that you will permit Mr. Hopkins to take charge of a committee of production with full powers and entire authority. Such a committee would not only dispose of the production requirements but would also be responsible for mobilising and distributing the necessary raw materials." Said the note to Churchill, which was attached to a copy of the Roosevelt note: "I support a Supreme Commander in supplies as well as strategy. Mr. Harry Hopkins is the proper authority and he should be asked to coordinate the production of the United States, Great Britain, and Canada, including raw materials."[56] The proposal found little favor with Churchill; he had no wish to give up to the United States any more of Britain's sovereign power than was absolutely necessary, and he saw in this case no necessity to give into an American's hands (even Hopkins's hands) full control of British production. The proposal found even less favor with Roosevelt; he continued reluctant to name an "economic czar," though he realized that the time had come when he must do something of the sort, and he was only too aware of the especially furious domestic political storm that would rage if the "czar" named were that spendthrift liberal, that power-lustful Machiavellian, that Rasputin-like White House manipulator, Harry Hopkins!

Then, in the second week of January, the British staff chiefs proposed that clear guidelines be drawn for the distribution of available weapons and ammunition, with Britain and the United States each accepting responsibility for the supply of designated "protégé" countries. The responsibility was to be exercised through parallel committees, one in London, one in Washington. Protégés of the United States would be the Latin American countries and China; protégés of Great Britain would be the British Dominions, the countries of continental Europe including France (Free France) and Turkey, and the countries of the Middle East. (The Soviet Union went unmentioned; evidently its supply was to be dealt with as a separate problem.) Obviously Britain, since it now operated at the limit of its productive capacity, yet was itself in need of American material aid, could not from its own resources serve the needs of its protégés. The United States must do so. And to this end the British chiefs proposed that the United States make bulk munitions allocations to Britain from which the London committee would supply those countries for which Britain was responsible. A Washington committee would do the same for America's protégés. From the twists and turns of the argument over this there emerged, on the next to last day of the conference, a British-proposed arrangement that seems not to have ruled out absolutely that American "committee of production" that Beaverbrook had proposed but which certainly called for the two allocation committees, in London and Washington, through which the produced goods would be distributed. The whole of the munitions production and allocation machinery would thus be exclusively under civilian control; its controlling agencies would operate independently of, and on a par with, the CCS Committee.

The proposal at once caused a division between the British and Americans, the only truly serious one in Arcadia, that was wholly strictly along nationalistic lines. Marshall, whose suspicions of Albion's natural perfidy continued high (too high, as he later admitted), saw the proposal as a deliberate devious attempt by the British to deny real substance to the already agreed concept of a Combined Chiefs of Staff organization, and to do so in a way that enabled the British to continue in ultimate control of the Allied war effort. In his view, though final decisions on overall grand strategy were properly the province of the civilian authority in a democracy, once these grand strategic decisions were made and the responsibility for their execution assigned to the subordinate military arm, the latter must have full authority to execute them untrammeled by civilian bodies operating within a political nexus. The present proposal violated this basic principle. By withholding necessary supplies, the two civilian munitions assignment agencies could make it impossible for military orders to be carried out; agreed military campaigns that had already been launched could be utterly bloodily frustrated. And was not continental Europe admittedly the crucial theater of the global war? Therefore, if the distribution of American-produced matériel throughout this theater were directed from London by the British alone, would not the net effect be an exclusively British control over the finally decisive Allied war effort? Clearly this was essentially a political proposal to be accepted or rejected at the highest political level—and Marshall insisted, in the staff chiefs' meeting on this next to last conference day, that the matter be referred to the President and Prime Minister.

At five o'clock on the following afternoon, Wednesday, January 14, 1941, just half an hour before the last plenary session of Arcadia was scheduled to begin, Marshall entered the White House Oval Room, having been summoned by the President. He was greeted warmly by Roosevelt, also by Hopkins, who was seated before the President's desk and who seemed now, after the strain of these last weeks, to be on the verge of total physical collapse. ("His lips are blanched as if he had been bleeding internally," physician Wilson had written in a recent diary entry, "his skin yellow like stretched parchment and his eyelids contracted to a slit so that you can just see his eyes moving about restlessly, as if he was in pain.")[57] Marshall, having seated himself beside his friend, hated adding to that strain; he loved and admired Hopkins as he did few others; but he felt, as he listened to Roosevelt's reading of the paper plucked from the cluttered presidential desk, that he would have to do so. For the paper, in the preparation of which Hopkins had surely had a shaping hand, proclaimed the decision reached by the Prime Minister and the President on this crucial matter of munitions allocation, a decision that Roosevelt-Hopkins seemed to regard as a compromise between the American and British positions but which was actually, in

Marshall's anguished view, an acceptance of every essential of the British position. There was to be a Munitions Assignment Board, but it was to be divided into two equal parts, one headquartered in London and directed by Beaverbrook, the other headquartered in Washington and directed by Hopkins. Each would operate independently of the Combined Chiefs of Staff Committee, Beaverbrook reporting directly to the Prime Minister, Hopkins to the President.

The reading finished, Roosevelt put down the paper and, fixing a questioning gaze upon his army chief of staff, invited Marshall's comment. Marshall minced no words. He could only reiterate, he said, the opposition he had expressed yesterday to any arrangement that wholly separated control of supply from command of the battle. The allocation of munitions, being an essential element of military strategical determinations, was an indispensable function of military command; ergo, the Munitions Assignment Board *must* be completely subordinate to the Combined Chiefs of Staff. But to this reiteration was added, uncharacteristically, a dire personal threat. In the circumstances and in his view, Marshall indicated, a final acceptance by the administration of what was now proposed would be tantamount to a vote of no confidence in George C. Marshall as army chief of staff and would be followed by his resignation of that post.

This last jarred Roosevelt badly enough to crack the facade of calm confidence and absolute self-assurance behind which he normally hid his anxieties, his insecurities. Marshall did not make idle threats or use them merely to gain tactical points; he was remarkably free of personal arrogance and lust for power; and he had at this conference firmly established himself as the dominant military figure of the Allied war command. He was in his present role indispensable. Roosevelt's manner, as he turned to Hopkins, revealed something of the dismay he felt while revealing also a hope and expectation of support from his closest friend and adviser.

Marshall, too, turned to Hopkins, his friend, not with dismay but regretfully.

Both men were surprised—Roosevelt unhappily, Marshall delightedly—by Hopkins's response.

For the scarecrow skin-and-bones figure of Harry Hopkins, theretofore slumped in his chair, was now drawn upright, as if by the surge of nervous energy that blazed out of his brown eyes, and far from defending the arrangement that Marshall assumed he had helped to shape, he voiced an absolute, unequivocal support of Marshall's position. He went further. If things were not ordered as Marshall wished, he, Hopkins, could not accept any responsibility in this matter; he would not serve as director of the proposed Washington allocations office.

Thus, when the last Arcadia session opened a few minutes later, Roosevelt knew it must be, for him, the most difficult of all the sessions. He dreaded the uncompromising stand he was now forced to take; he suffered empathetically the humiliation he must now join in inflicting upon proud men whom he liked and greatly respected; he feared the effects such humiliation might have upon his personal relations with Churchill and upon Anglo-American relations in general. Yet unless Marshall retreated, he, Roosevelt, must stand against the position he himself had occupied with Churchill earlier that day—and Marshall, of course, did not retreat. Instead, with firm support from Hopkins and Stimson, the general asserted more forcefully and vehemently than ever before that the Munitions Assignment Board *must* be a subcommittee of the Combined Chiefs of Staff. He "saw no objection . . . to having parallel Allocation Committees in Washington and London," but there must be "no duplication of the Combined Chiefs of Staff organization in Washington and London"—which meant that the London allocation committee must be a subordinate branch of the Washington one, and both must constitute a subcommittee of the CCS Committee. Hopkins again said he could head a Munitions Assignment Board only if it was a CCS subcommittee whose "recommendations" the CCS could "alter" or "throw out." Churchill, Beaverbrook, and the British staff chiefs protested, of course. They protested so heatedly, so angrily, that for a time it appeared that Arcadia would adjourn in acrimony and disarray. But in the end, in a manifestation of that instinct for justice combined with a genius for amelioration and creative compromise whereby Englishmen became the chief architects of modern Western democracy,* an Englishman made the face-saving suggestion that "the system" insisted upon by Marshall "be set up and tried for one month." A vastly relieved Roosevelt, manifesting this same instinct and genius, at once seized upon the suggestion. "We shall call it a preliminary agreement and try it out that way," he said, closing the debate.[58]

The "one month" was destined to last for the duration of the war, with the Munitions Assignment Board (Hopkins at its head) functioning far more efficiently, with far less friction, than could at the outset have been expected of an arrangement so tentatively made and so lacking in specificity.

VIII

ONE reason for this was the huge flow of supply that followed upon other decisions made at this time, since allocation problems arise only if supply is limited; their difficulty is inversely proportional to the adequacy of supply. . . .

Paralleling the military and political sessions of the Arcadia Conference were work sessions at Washington's Mayflower Hotel wherein Beaverbrook and a

---

*The thoughtful reader will see connections between this and Churchill's description of the way the English mind works—connections that indicate totalitarian dangers in the way in which, according to Churchill, the American mind works. Involved here are fundamental questions, repeatedly encountered in the course of this history, about the proper relations between freedom and organization, between the individual and the state, in a democratic society that is technologically advanced. Relevant are the views expressed in note 67 to chapter 10 of *FDR: The New Deal Years.*

staff of statisticians he had brought over with him from England joined with Averell Harriman and a select group of American production experts (with important input from the White House via Hopkins) to define war production goals that were both realistic and sufficiently high to reduce to a minimum the allocation difficulties of the future. "We had all agreed that it had taken the British too many years to get full war production," remembered Harriman in a later year, "and Hopkins had the idea, I think with Roosevelt's full approval, that this time [that is, the time in which full U.S. conversion to war production was achieved] could be shortened if we set our sights high at once." The figures that emerged from the Mayflower sessions were indeed high. They rendered puny by comparison the earlier announced Victory Program estimates. And for this, Roosevelt (it is a measure of his capacity for leadership in crisis) was, by his own contemporaneous account, far more directly responsible than Harriman seems to have realized. In the presidential press conference of January 6, devoted to the budget for the upcoming fiscal year, Roosevelt explained his method: "For example, I sent for the maritime commission, and I pointed out to them that . . . we have got to get . . . more [shipping] tonnage"; merely balancing the amount of new shipping with the amount lost through sinkings wouldn't do; "we have got to make substantial gains of building over losses. And I said to them, 'What are you making now?' 'Well, we are making over one million tons this year.' I said, 'What can you step it up to?' 'Well,' they said, 'we can step it up to five million tons.' I said, 'Not enough. Go back and sharpen your pencils.' . . . So they went back and sharpened their pencils, and they came back, and they said, 'It will hurt terribly, but we believe that if we are told to we can turn out six million tons of shipping this year.' I said, 'Now you're talking.' And I said, 'All right now, for '43 what can you do? Can you turn out four million more tons, to a total of ten million tons of shipping?' And they scratched their heads, and came back and said, 'Aye, aye, sir, we will do it.' . . . Then it came to planes, tanks, anti-aircraft guns. And I have been at them for two weeks, sometimes telling them to go back and sharpen their pencils." Even after the final high goals had been set by the conferees at the Mayflower, Roosevelt in several instances revised them upward to achieve what he called "big round figures."[59]

He did so as he worked with Hopkins and Sherwood and Rosenman in preparation of his 1942 State of the Union message to Congress, delivered later on this same January 6. The magnitude of the effort he demanded is indicated by a comparison of the original Victory Program estimates for 1942 with those announced in the message. For instance, the original program called for the production of 28,600 operational aircraft in 1942. In his speech to Congress, Roosevelt announced that "the appropriate departments" had been ordered by him to take "immediate steps . . . to increase our production of airplanes" to 60,000, of which 45,000 would be combat planes. "The rate of increase will be maintained," he continued, ". . . so that next year, 1943, we shall produce

125,000 planes, including 100,000 combat planes." The original Victory Program estimate for tanks had been to produce 20,400 of them in 1942; Roosevelt now announced a goal of 45,000 tanks in 1942 and 75,000 in 1943. Similarly with regard to antiaircraft guns: The original Victory Program estimate had been 6,300 in 1942, but Roosevelt called for 20,000 in 1942, 35,000 in 1943. As regards merchant shipping, however, Roosevelt seems actually to have revised *downward* the figure set by the Beaverbrook-Harriman group—a seeming fact that calls somewhat into question the accuracy of the story he had told his press conference but which also indicates a commitment to realism in this matter that vociferous critics would soon deny he possessed. Beaverbrook-Harriman had upped to 8 million deadweight tons the original Victory Program estimate of 6 million for 1942, but Roosevelt in his speech, as in his press conference, announced the latter figure, comparing it with the completed production of 1.1 million deadweight tons in 1941. But he added that "we shall continue that increase so that next year, 1943, we shall build 10,000,000 tons of shipping," this last being the 1943 goal set by Beaverbrook-Harriman. (Unmentioned to Congress but announced in a press release were 1942 production figures for three other weapons categories, with the lowest increase over the original Victory Program estimate being well over 100 percent. They were antitank guns, 14,900 [7,000 was the original estimate]; ground and tank machine guns, 500,000 [168,000 earlier estimated]; airplane bombs, 720,000 long tons [8½ times the 84,000 earlier estimated].) "These figures . . . will give the Japanese and the Nazis a little idea of just what they accomplished in the attack at Pearl Harbor," said the President to Congress, his voice throbbing with angry contempt—and Congress responding with a storm of applause and cheers. "Our task is hard—our task is unprecedented—and the time is short," Roosevelt went on. "We must strain every armament-producing facility to the utmost. We must convert every available plant and tool to war production. That goes all the way from the greatest plants to the smallest—from the huge automobile industry to the village machine shop."[60]

The bold expansiveness of this speech, its confident optimism, was in shining contrast with the dark news of defeat and impending doom pouring endlessly out of the Far East, and the general public welcomed it as enthusiastically as did Congress, which soon voted the huge appropriations called for. Far different was the initial response of big-business men. Those industrialists who were directly challenged by the President's words—that is, the businessmen who had been and yet remained actually in charge of American production—sensed that their profit-motivated performance up till now, their ability to estimate future possibilities accurately, their very willingness to do what must be done in the field of their presumed expertise, were by implication being held up to ridicule. They replied with ridicule of their own. Roosevelt knew perfectly well that the goals he set could not possibly be achieved, they protested (though not, significantly, through the mass media). He engaged, contemptibly, in a "numbers racket" for purely political purposes (unspoken was their dread that these purposes included the taking over of business by government); certainly some drastic change in the production program was in the offing. But by the time the final goals were set it was clear to all that reaching them required a drastic overhaul of the present complicated, ambiguously defined production-administering machinery. Industrial conversion to war production lagged now farther than ever behind necessity, because what was needed had now increased so greatly; and it was no longer possible to deny that a chief reason for this lag was the lack of a strong centralized control over the whole industrial production effort. It was to address and correct this obvious deficiency, at long last, that Roosevelt in the late afternoon of Tuesday, January 13, Hopkins at his side, summoned to the White House's Oval Room Vice President Henry Wallace, chairman of the Supply Priorities and Allocation Board (also of the Economic Defense Board), and Donald M. Nelson, SPAB's executive director.

To both men the President seemed unwontedly tired and worn as he greeted them.[61] Dark patches under his eyes accentuated the pallor of his complexion; his hands trembled slightly as he lit a cigarette. But energy seemed to return to him—seemed to be generated in him as flowing water generates electricity—by the words that thereafter poured out of him uninterruptedly (neither Wallace nor Nelson was able to speak a word) for nearly an hour. He reviewed the somber current war situation, asserted his undiminished personal faith in the resilience and flexibility and creative capabilities of free societies, spoke of the huge effort that must now be made to transform America truly into the "Arsenal of Democracy" he had proclaimed ("I wasn't just making a phrase") a year ago, and discussed the operations thus far of the agencies he'd set up for industrial mobilization, revealing as he did so a surprisingly detailed knowledge of structural deficiencies of which his critics had deemed him unaware, since he was responsible for them. Surprising also (especially to Nelson) was the frankness with which he went on to discuss the strengths and weaknesses of those to whom he had assigned administrative responsibility for production. He had words of praise for the past performance of OPM's two heads, Hillman and Knudsen, but made it clear that OPM's days as supreme production agency had come to an end, that a new and more powerful administrative organization must now be established to direct a far greater production effort, and that Bill Knudsen, in the President's judgment, was not the right man to take charge of this new huge enterprise. He, Knudsen, armed with the prestige he had earned among his fellow industrialists as a profit-making "production genius" of the automobile industry, had done some great things. For instance, he had persuaded all the major automobile manufacturers save Ford, in October 1940, to shift a significant portion of their production capacity to the manufacture of airplane parts. Probably no one but Knudsen could have done this at that time. But the very thing that had done most to render Knudsen thus effective—namely, his being and being recognized as a loyal member of the big-business community, possessed of all the basic commitments and biases of that community—had evidently militated against his overall OPM success.

The closely listening Nelson believed Knudsen to be unfairly blamed for conversion failures. He was acutely aware (most of Knudsen's severest critics were not) of the difficulties and risks industrialists faced when, in a competitive market economy, they shifted from one line of production to another. The purely economic advantage that mass production had over production by individual craftsmen, or associations of craftsmen, was obviously very great. But it was gained at the cost of flexibility.* Craftsmen and industries dominated by craftsmen could quite easily turn their skills and relatively simple tools from one kind of production to another—a woodworker from the making of tables to the making of chairs, a blacksmith from the making of plowshares to the making of swords—but a modern mass-production line, with its huge jigs and conveyor belts and complicated machine tools, was geared to the making of certain specified items to the exclusion of all others and could not be converted piecemeal to new uses. It must be converted wholly and all at once, at great expense, or not at all. The reluctance of carmakers to do this in 1940 and early 1941, despite huge government bribes in the form of tax breaks and subsidization, was as understandable as it was inevitable, given the prevailing anxiety over postwar markets, and especially so since neither the army nor the various defense agencies could then tell them definitely and authoritatively what kind of war matériel they should make or in what amounts. No, the main cause of the conversion lag had not been Knudsen's personal deficiencies, in Nelson's view; it had been, as Roosevelt now tacitly admitted, the administration's failure to set clear and definite production goals, then make clear and definite national economic plans for reaching these goals, and finally establish the administrative machinery, armed with effective government controls, to implement the plans.

But the goals were now set. The future of the free world depended upon our reaching them. And to assure our doing so, Roosevelt now proposed to establish within the Office of Emergency Management a new agency having a wider scope of economic activity and far greater authority than any he had established before. As he went on, he leaned forward to fix his gaze upon Nelson in a way that caused that worthy's heart to beat faster. The new agency would perform the functions and exercise the powers presently vested in SPAB by last August's executive order, said the President. It would have direct supervisory control of OPM. Its head, reporting directly to the chief executive and commander in chief, would exercise general direction over the whole war production and pro-

---

*Nelson might have admitted that there was also a loss of humanity to the extent that specialization transformed workers into mere adjuncts and functions of the machines they tended.

curement program. He, this head, must be a man of conciliatory temper, cooperative, sympathetic, slow to anger, capable of compromises that prevented
disasters and promoted ultimate goals. He must possess great powers of persuasion whereby to bring the strong-minded, strong-willed representatives of
naturally discordant and even hostile interests into harmonious working commitment to the national purpose, the general welfare. But he must also be tough
enough to exercise decisively, in ultimate situations, the coercive authority that
would, ex officio, be his, since the organic executive order would explicitly state
that the chairman's "decisions shall be final." Roosevelt cited, as example of the
necessary toughness, the famous presidential cabinet meeting during the Civil
War when Abraham Lincoln asked for an "aye" or "nay" vote upon a measure
he proposed to take and then, after every cabinet member had voted "nay," announced with a wry smile that "the ayes have it" since he himself voted "aye."
    There followed talk about the name to be given this superagency. Did Wal-
lace or Nelson have suggestions? Why not call it the "War Production Administration"? suggested Nelson. Roosevelt considered this for but a second or two
before shaking his head emphatically. The agency's initials would then be WPA,
and *"that,"* he said with a loud laugh, "wouldn't do at all!" He himself had considered calling it the "War Production Board," WPB. Did that seem all right to
Nelson? It did, Nelson replied.
    "I'm glad you approve," said Roosevelt, "because *you* are the chairman of
the War Production Board."
    The President asked a somewhat dazed Nelson, whose mood mingled ex-
ultation with trepidation ("the job is too big for any man I have ever heard of,
certainly including myself"), to draft the executive order that, upon the presidential signature of it three days hence (January 16), would legally establish the
new agency and define its powers, duties, responsibilities.

In future years the charge would be made that a Machiavellian Roosevelt
appointed Nelson to the second most powerful civilian post in the national
government (he was designated "arms czar" and "dictator of the economy" in
newspaper stories) with the expectation that he would fail in his job. Roosevelt
wanted him to fail, the charge goes on, because such failure would leave the
power-lustful President in full control of the national destiny. Actually, Roosevelt's motivation on this occasion was considerably less cynical or sinister
than this, if cynical or sinister at all, and considerably more complicated. He
chose Nelson for this huge new job not with the expectation or hope that Nelson
would fail, but with the expectation and hope that he would succeed, but succeed in ways that harmonized with the President's overall aims. He knew Nelson to be that rare creature, a big-business man who sympathized with the broad
socioeconomic aims of the New Deal and who had proved in his governmental
operations thus far that he subordinated personal profit making and power seek-

ing absolutely to service of the general welfare. He could therefore be trusted not to use the great power of his new position in ways that would undermine New Deal reforms or threaten in the slightest the presidential power. Moreover, Roosevelt liked him personally and got along with him easily, as Hopkins pointed out when urging Nelson's appointment. All this did mean, however, that the choice fell upon Nelson in good part because he possessed personal qualities and elements of character that, in his circumstances and in the absence of offsetting qualities, would conduce toward failure.

Nelson was now to become a major player in that historical drama whence emerged the American Leviathan of the last half of the twentieth century—an America whose whole life, economic and social and cultural (mass communications becoming primarily advertising media, education becoming primarily vocational training), was absolutely dominated by big business.[62]

There was nothing grand or heroic in his physical appearance at this beginning of the year 1942; at age fifty-three, he had the appearance of the archtypical midwestern Rotarian, big, jovial, balding, bland, and decidedly well nourished. Consistent with his appearance, and no more impressive, viewed in broad outline, was his career in business till now. Like the George F. Babbitt of Sinclar Lewis's novel, Donald M. Nelson was a midwesterner by birth [Hannibal, Missouri], an alumnus of his state's university, where he had studied "practical" courses to the virtual exclusion of the humanities. Like Babbitt, having graduated from college, he had embarked upon a career of "selling" in the marketplace, a career he had followed without interruption until he came to Washington in May 1940. In other words (Lewis's words), he in his working life had "made nothing in particular, neither butter nor shoes nor poetry," but had devoted his talents and energies instead to the merchandising of goods made by others.

His first employment, in 1912, in the great mail-order firm of Sears, Roebuck & Company, had been as a scientific tester and deviser of tests of the textiles and other products (there were many hundreds of them) sold by the company. Soon thereafter he was assigned the pioneering task of persuading the company's merchandising supervisors that they should check the accuracy of their product descriptions, in Sears's catalogs, against the test findings of the company's new laboratories—a difficult task that required much patience, resilience, and psychological acumen since it implicitly called into question the supervisors' knowledge and truthfulness and since he could exercise no power over these supervisors save that of reasonable persuasion. He had performed this task with total ultimate success, at great profit to the company. Thereafter, as he climbed steadily the Sears ladder of success, becoming vice president in charge of merchandising a dozen years ago and executive vice president and chairman of the executive committee just three years ago, Nelson had increasingly functioned not as a specialist whose work area had long been clearly defined, but as a coordinator, a synthesizer, an innovator in areas *between* specialties. Sears operated upon a very small margin of profit per item sold. It was therefore necessary for the merchandising executive to measure with accuracy the relative efficiency of firms competing for Sears contracts and, when necessary, to devise means of increasing the efficiency of contractors. Sometimes a firm having several product lines was required to convert to a single line in order to satisfy the Sears demand, and on occasion Sears's merchandising executive presided actively over such conversion. Often, too, to prevent the narrow profit margin from becoming narrower still or wiped out altogether, the merchandising executive acted as purchasing agent for the contractor, going into the commodities market to buy raw materials (steel, aluminum, rubber, lumber, wool, and so on) in greater quantity and consequently at higher discounts than any individual contractor could manage. Altogether, Nelson as Sears executive had dealt with more than five thousand manufacturing concerns, including twenty-five that were owned outright or in large part by Sears itself.

Thus, by May 1940, when at Morgenthau's bidding he came to Washington to serve as the Treasury Department's director of procurement, Donald Nelson had acquired a remarkably wide and precise knowledge of the actual workings of the American economy—the ways and means of production, packaging, transportation, and marketing. This knowledge, along with his dedication and capacity for hard work, had enabled him to become perhaps the most solidly valuable to the government of all the big-business men who had been called to the capital since World War II began. In his very first governmental assignment, that of facilitating British and French obtainment of war matériel (airplanes especially) in the desperate days of May and early June 1940, he had proved his worth. The President personally had asked him to become coordinator of national defense purchases in the newly established NDAC. And ever since—in NDAC, then as head of OPM's purchasing division and member of the priorities board, then as SPAB's executive director—he had labored with remarkable zeal and (considering his unfavorable circumstances) success to transform the American economy into a war economy and, being an affable, extroverted man, thoughtful of others and obviously concerned to be fair in all his dealings with others, had earned the respect of his peers, the admiration of his superiors, and the fierce loyalty of nearly all his subordinates in Washington. He was also personally well liked, at the time of his WPB appointment, by the dollar-a-year men with whom he had worked—was similarly initially liked by the War Department officials and army officers who had to do with procurement. But it was highly improbable that such liking would survive the first important active expression, in his new post, of Nelson's essential liberalism and exclusive commitment to the general good. He must then provoke the personal hostility and stubborn opposition of men who deemed "unrealistic," if not impossible, any action not basically motivated by self-interest. And it was with some sense of this, along with an evident fear that Nelson's affability and conciliatory temper might be a wholly inadequate substitute for the stern decisiveness called for in ultimate situations, that Roosevelt, in the interview just described, had stressed the need for toughness and cited Lincoln's exemplary handling of strong-willed, strong-minded cabinet members.

When Nelson arrived back in his office in the Social Security Building some ten minutes after the close of his momentous White House interview, on the evening of that Tuesday the thirteenth, he learned that the news of his elevation was already on the news wires, was already the lead story of the network radio evening news. He was more dismayed than gratified by this. He suspected that Knudsen, whom he personally liked and admired, had been given no warning he was being demoted (he would become subordinate to his former subordinate, Nelson). If so, Knudsen, who had certainly done his best and been led to believe as recently as a week ago that his performance greatly pleased the President, now suffered unjustified, inexcusable personal hurt and public humiliation. Nelson went at once to Knudsen's office. He found the old man sitting alone at his desk, stunned, his appearance and quavering voice testifying to the devastating shock he had suffered. He thanked Nelson for the latter's concern but refused to promise, as Nelson begged him to do, that he would stay in the government. Back in his own office, Nelson phoned Jesse Jones, who was as close a personal friend as Knudsen had in Washington, urging Jones to use his influence to prevent Knudsen's precipitous departure. Admittedly it would be almost impossible for Knudsen to operate as Nelson's subordinate, but surely another high place would be found in which Knudsen's great abilities would serve the defense effort. Jones promised to do what he could.

Not long afterward, Jones received a phone call from Hopkins, who, at dinner with the President that evening, had obtained the latter's approval of an arrangement Hopkins had worked out and cleared with Undersecretary of War Patterson. By this arrangement, Knudsen would be commissioned a lieutenant general in the army and assigned to work with Patterson on army procurement matters. Hopkins asked Jones to present this proposal to Knudsen along with assurances that the President was deeply appreciative of Knudsen's great abilities and was anxious to retain them in government service.

In the end—that is, on the following day—Knudsen said he was subject to the commander in chief's orders. He would do whatever the President told him to do. . . .[63]

IX

ON January 14, 1942, the Arcadia Conference having ended, Churchill bade good-bye to Roosevelt, who reiterated his anxiety over the Prime Minister's safety on the homeward voyage, the imminence of which was perfectly well-known to the Nazis.

The event fully justified the anxiety.

Much urgent business awaited Churchill in London, so much of it that he begrudged the time required for passage to England aboard the *Duke of York.* Having flown in what he called "an enormous Boeing flying boat," with luxurious accommodations, from Washington to Bermuda, where the great battleship with its destroyer escort awaited him and his party, he inquired of the plane's captain whether the Boeing, refueled in Bermuda, could fly on nonstop to England. It could, replied the captain. The weather reports were favorable; there would be a strong following wind to push them along; they could make the 3,500-mile flight in twenty hours. Early in the following afternoon (January 15), Churchill and his immediate party, including his personal physician, reboarded the plane. All went well until the last hours of the flight. It was then discovered that the plane had gone off course during the night and was now within six minutes or so of Brest, where it would become a target of German batteries and pursuit planes. The hurried correction then made brought the plane into England from the southeast—that is, from the direction of the enemy air base at Brest—instead of from the expected southwest, and the blip this made on radar screens caused six British Hurricane fighters to take to the air with orders to shoot down an invading plane. "However," writes Churchill with ironic laconism, "they failed in their mission."

At once upon his arrival at No. 10 Downing Street, he sent a cable to Roosevelt in which no mention was made of his close shave. Instead: "We got here with a good hop from Bermuda with a thirty mile wind."[64]

By that time, Hopkins, utterly exhausted, was again a patient in the Navy Hospital. During his two-week stay there, a stringent regimen of rest and diet was worked out for him—one that he failed to follow as strictly as his doctors ordered but which, even so, enabled him to stay alive, if often at the brink of death, through the next four years.

8

-->>X<<-

A Winter of Disasters:
A Spring of Dawning Hope

I

THE war news pouring into Washington continued dreadful all through the winter and early spring of 1942.

The three chief bastions of Western power on the South China Sea had for generations been Hong Kong, Manila, and Singapore. Each had fallen by mid-February. The British garrison at Hong Kong surrendered unconditionally to the Japanese on Christmas Day 1941 after a seventeen-day siege during which the island was heavily bombed and its water supply cut off. By that time the Philippine capital of Manila on Luzon—its air cover destroyed by the bombing of American planes parked on Clark Field, its sea defenses removed by the immobilization of Cavite (the naval force based there retreated to Australian and Javanese waters 1,500 miles to the south)—had been evacuated by the Philippine government of President Manuel Quezon, by U.S. High Commissioner to the Philippines Francis B. Sayre, and by General Douglas MacArthur, the Philippine defense force commander. All three had established headquarters on the fortress island of Corregidor at the mouth of Manila Bay. On December 26, Manila, utterly defenseless, had been declared an open city; it had nevertheless been repeatedly savagely bombed before being occupied by the Japanese on January 2, 1942. Six weeks later came climactic news: Supposedly impregnable Singapore, upon which the survival of the British empire in the Far East had been presumed to depend, and upon which certainly depended much of the defense of Burma, the Netherlands East Indies, and Australia, had become a Japanese possession!

This last conquest, in itself profoundly shocking and demoralizing to London and Washington, was rendered more so by the way of it, the evident reasons for it. It had been astonishingly swift and easy, in good part because of a British conviction, which was also a widespread conviction in the United States, that all colored peoples are inferior. This conviction nourished a smug complacency as it discouraged thought, imagination, and accurate perception and so helped prevent critical examination by the British of their assumption that the dense Malayan jungle, which extended for hundreds of miles north of Singapore island, was impenetrable by an army equipped with modern weapons. They had acted on this assumption by strongly fortifying only the island's southern, sea-facing side. There they had erected formidable barriers to any amphibious assaults; there all their heaviest guns had been concentrated, each virtually immobile and sited in such a way that its only effective fire was seaward. The northern side, facing Johore across a narrow strait, had been left virtually unprotected; and no effort had been made before the war to train British troops especially for fighting in the jungle approaches. Knowing this—as Churchill (incredibly) did not*—the Japanese had not for a moment considered a sea attack upon Singapore. Instead, with two hundred thousand toughly conditioned troops highly trained for precisely this mission, they had driven directly southward through Malaya to Johore, making frequent use of leapfrog amphibian tactics and full use of their massive air superiority and inflicting far more casualties than they suffered themselves. By the last of January, having heavily damaged Singapore's docks and military installations with bombs, they had driven the British from Johore, whence came Singapore's water supply, and were fighting on the island itself, immediately threatening Singapore town, the Kalong airfield, the water reservoirs, and the supply depots. The British situation was hopeless, or appeared so to the Singapore commander, General Sir Arthur E. Percival. Two weeks later (February 15), he surrendered unconditionally his more than sixty-four thousand British, Indian, and Australian troops.

Virtually simultaneous with the news of Singapore's fall came news from Europe only slightly less shocking, for it seemed evidence that "Britannia" was a no less inept warrior upon the "waves" she proudly claimed to "rule" than she had latterly proved to be on land. The two powerful German battle cruisers *Scharnhorst* and *Gneisenau,* along with the cruiser *Prinz Eugen,* had been for many months pent up in the harbor at Brest, presumably by fear of British naval power. But on the night of February 12, in what seemed a gesture of utter contempt for that power, they sailed from Brest directly northeastward into the English Channel; thrust through the narrow Dover Strait in broad daylight under heavy fire from the Dover batteries and continuous attacks by bombers, torpedo-bearing planes, and destroyers; pushed then through waters that had been mined from the air; and reached their home ports in Germany on the morn-

---

*Churchill first learned of it immediately upon his return to London from Washington when, in reply to direct questions from him, General Wavell told him of Singapore's vulnerability on its landed side. This reply was more staggering to him than the loss of *Repulse* and *Prince of Wales* had been. "[T]he possibility of Singapore having no landward defences [had] no more entered my mind than that of a battleship being launched without a bottom," he writes in his war memoirs. Singapore could not properly be called a "fortress" at all, he bitterly protested to General Ismay, for "a fortress is a *completely encircled* strong place."[1]

ing of February 13 apparently unscathed. The reaction to this by both the American and British publics, and especially by the British, was one of clamorous disgustful outrage.*

More serious, those high hopes for the early conquest of Libya that Churchill had brought with him to Washington and upon which he had based his plans for making all French North Africa Allied territory were dashed. At first Auchinleck's long-prepared offensive scored great early success. Besieged Tobruk was quickly relieved and Rommel's forces swept from virtually the whole of Cyrenaica. By mid-January, the crucially important port of Benghazi was retaken and Rommel driven thence southward to El Agheila, where, on a line reaching inland to Maradah, he stood on the defensive. But not for long. The recent British naval losses had so weakened Admiral Cunningham's fleet in the Mediterranean that it was unable to prevent or even reduce the flow of Axis supplies and troop reinforcements across the sea from the Continent to Tripoli, and German control of the Libyan air enabled these then to traverse without interference the hundreds of miles between Tripoli and Rommel at El Agheila. Rommel's matériel and troop losses during the long retreat were swiftly made good, and on January 21, with a reconnaissance in force that succeeded far beyond his expectations, Rommel launched a counterattack that drove more swiftly eastward than he had been forced to retreat westward. By the last of January, the Allies, whose armor had proved decidedly inferior to the Germans', had been driven back to the neighborhood of Tobruk, where for many months they would remain immobilized.

Meanwhile and thereafter, Japan's conquest of the Netherlands East Indies continued apace. Driving swiftly but methodically southward, establishing air bases on each of their conquests to assure overwhelming air support of their next, the Japanese by mid-January were firmly established in northern Borneo and on the northeast tip of Celebes. Simultaneously, east of New Guinea and so outside the ABDA area, they seized Rabaul in New Britain and Bougainville in the Solomon Islands, whence they directly threatened the vital sea line from America to Australia. By the last week of February they had occupied the capital cities of both Borneo and Celebes, had southern Sumatra in their grasp, and held both Timor and Bali, completing the isolation of Java, where, in Batavia, the Netherlands East Indies government and Wavell's ABDA headquarters were

---

*Actually, though a resounding psychological triumph for the Germans, the warships' removal from Brest was a serious strategic mistake for them (German Admiral Raeder later dubbed it an "outright retreat") in that it eliminated what had been a dangerous threat to communications between England and the Mediterranean. Sallying forth from Brest, the warships might have fatally disrupted the North African operation that was then under preparation by the Allies. In their home ports they constituted no such menace. Moreover, as the British government soon discovered but could not for security reasons reveal to the public, the German ships had *not* escaped unscathed; both *Scharnhorst* and *Gneisenau* had suffered mine damage that took many months to repair.[2]

located. On February 21 Wavell signaled Churchill his somber conclusion "that the defence of the ABDA area has broken down and . . . the defence of Java cannot last long. . . . I see little further usefulness for this H.Q. . . ."[3] Three days later the ABDA theater was officially dissolved; the yet unconquered but doomed portions of the area it had included were placed under isolated local commands. Wavell was returned to his former command in India.

Naval disasters followed immediately. The aircraft carrier USS *Langley,* bound for Java with thirty-five fighter planes aboard, was sunk in the Indian Ocean by Japanese planes on February 26. Next day, off Java itself, began a three-day naval engagement, the Battle of the Java Sea—a surface-to-surface naval combat, the first in the Pacific war and, as time would prove, the worst Allied naval defeat in the whole of the war. On the night of February 27, employing a new oxygen torpedo with the astonishing range of twenty-five miles (the best American and British torpedoes then had a range of five miles), the Japanese sank in quick succession two Dutch cruisers (*De Ruyter* and *Java*) and two destroyers (Dutch *Kortenaur* and British *Electra*). On the following day, Japanese cruisers sank by gunfire two Allied cruisers, the Australian *Perth* and the American *Houston.** On March 1, they sank by gunfire three British ships—the cruiser *Exeter* and the destroyers *Pope* and *Encounter.* By nightfall the enemy had obtained and would for many black weeks retain absolute naval dominance of the Southwest Pacific area, and at remarkably little cost; he could with impunity move troops and matériel wherever he pleased across those thousands of miles and, as it seemed (especially to the Australian government), was poised for an invasion of Australia. Indeed, he had already directly attacked Australia in an action that had contributed mightily to the total collapse of the East Indies defense. On February 19, the carrier force that under Vice Admiral Nagumo's command had dealt the devastating blow to Pearl Harbor dealt an equally devastating one to Port Darwin, the key supply base for ABDA. Some 150 planes had then bombed and strafed the defenseless harbor and town, killing and wounding hundreds of people while sinking eleven transports, a number of supply ships, and an American destroyer. . . .

But it was naturally upon the Philippines, to the defense of which American ground troops were committed, that popular attention in the United States, in these dark days, was focused most concentratedly. Luzon's defenders originally totaled something over 90,000 men—73,000 Filipino troops, including 11,000 Philippine Scouts (an elite corps), plus more than 19,000 American troops, all under General Douglas MacArthur's top command. Initially divided between a

---

*The USS *Houston* was Roosevelt's favorite naval cruise ship in the 1930s, he taking extended vacations aboard her in 1934, 1935, and 1938. It was aboard the *Houston* that the oft published photograph of him standing bareheaded, clad in his naval cape, on the windswept bridge, reviewing the Atlantic Fleet, was taken.

north Luzon Force and a south Luzon Force, they had conducted fighting withdrawals southward and northward to an assembly point at San Fernandino, just north of Manila, whence they retreated into the Bataan peninsula—all this in accordance with long-laid plans. They were deployed, as the new year opened, in a continuous battle line stretching across the twenty-mile-wide base of twenty-five-mile-long Bataan; they were commanded from headquarters established, as we have said, on Corregidor, a fortified island (a great tunneled rock) just off Bataan's southern tip. It was toward this fortress that the Japanese drove in ever stronger lunges after they opened their siege of Bataan on January 9. Luzon Force, skillfully handled, fought with remarkable bravery and stubbornness against the growing attack; it even managed to score substantial tactical victories during the first six weeks of battle; but since it could not be reinforced and every effort to supply it, each more desperate than the last, was frustrated by Japan's absolute dominance of all the sea approaches, its fate was sealed. Within days after reaching Bataan the defending troops were reduced to half rations, which within a few weeks were again halved. They supplemented their diet with the meat of dogs and mules, even of iguanas and snakes, and with roots and berries and whatever other edible jungle vegetation they could find, but they were nevertheless starved. Sickness spread among them—malaria, dengue, amoebic dysentery. And to their physical suffering was added psychological depression as they realized that the help that MacArthur had initially told them was coming, and which he continuously and urgently pleaded for in unrealistically conceived messages to Washington, was not going to be provided. They were doomed, felt they had been abandoned, and said so loudly to one another, describing themselves in bitter doggerel as the "battling bastards of Bataan" for whom "nobody gives a damn."[4] Yet somehow they found it possible to fight on, far beyond the limit of what both Washington and Tokyo had deemed possible for them, postponing the inevitable end for them as a fighting force until well into April. On April 9, the whole of what remained of Luzon Force, save for a couple of thousand who made a temporary escape onto Corregidor, surrendered unconditionally.

This, however, was by no means the end or even the worst of their ordeal. They were, of course, in very poor physical condition, half-starved, dead tired, many of them ill, on the day of their surrender. Yet six days later they were formed into columns of four for a march from the southern tip of the peninsula to the San Fernandino rail junction—a forced march of some sixty miles that, when news of it leaked out through its civilian observers and the very few Allied soldiers who escaped from it, was at once dubbed the Death March of Bataan. The captives were driven at a relentless pace through the thick humid tropic heat by Japanese guards who were not only hellfired by racial hatred, but also contemptuous of them for having surrendered (Japanese troops generally fought to the death), and who inflicted upon them the most savage cruelties.

Those who dropped out to relieve themselves at roadside (approximately 50 percent of them suffered from dysentery) were sometimes ordered to eat their excrement and slaughtered if they refused or were unable to do so. Those who dropped from exhaustion were beaten and prodded by bayonets until they staggered to their feet or, if unable to rise, were shot or bayoneted or clubbed to death. The same fate befell those who, maddened by thirst (the Japanese had confiscated their aluminum canteens), dropped out to drink from pools of foul ditch water. At one stage of the march those near the rear of the line saw scores of headless corpses lining their route, victims of Japanese swords. Of the seventy-odd thousand who began the march, only fifty-four thousand reached their final destination, Camp O'Donnell, and of those who entered the prison camp, which was woefully unprepared to handle the numbers crammed into it, 40 percent died within three months of disease, starvation, torture, or wanton murder.

Corregidor, where General Jonathan M. Wainwright had succeeded Mac-Arthur as commander of the Philippine forces, managed to hold out for nearly a month after Luzon Force's surrender. During that month, as the Japanese concentrated their forces for the island's invasion, a continuous and increasingly intense air bombardment and artillery shelling silenced two key batteries, blew up two key artillery dumps, and reduced to three thousand through death, wounds, and shell shock the four-thousand-man force that had remained under Wainwright's command on April 9. In the early hours of May 6, Japanese invasion forces made an almost unopposed landing on the north point of the island (the American troops, lacking both heavy and light artillery of their own, were pinned down by Japanese artillery fire; their communications were knocked out).

Simultaneously there arrived in Wainwright's tunnel headquarters a personal message to him from the President of the United States. "During recent weeks," wrote Franklin Roosevelt, "we have been following with growing admiration the day-by-day accounts of your heroic stand against the mounting intensity of bombardment by enemy planes and heavy siege guns. . . . The American people ask no finer example of tenacity, resourcefulness, and steadfast courage. The calm determination of your personal leadership in a desperate situation sets a standard of duty for our soldiers throughout the world. . . . You and your soldiers have become the living symbols of our war aims and the guarantee of victory." A few hours later, when Japanese advance units were within five hundred yards of the tunnel's eastern entrance and as Japanese tanks were advancing for the final assault, Wainwright broadcast a surrender message, ran up white flags, and messaged the President: "With broken heart and head bowed in sadness but not in shame I report to Your Excellency that today I must arrange terms for the surrender of the fortified islands of Manila Bay [subsequently he surrendered unconditionally all U.S. forces in the Philippines, these having been placed under his command by Washington a few weeks back]. . . . There is a limit to human endurance and that limit has long since been passed. Without prospect of relief I feel it is my duty to my country and to my gallant troops to end this useless effusion of blood. . . ." By early afternoon he and his men had become prisoners of war, entering upon a captivity only somewhat less cruel than that which had been initially suffered by those who had surrendered the month before.[5]

General MacArthur, who had lived with his wife and son in a comfortable house on Corregidor, suffering no pangs of hunger, while his men starved on the battlefield a few miles north of him, was equally exempt from the ordeal of captivity. His reputation as a brilliant general, President Quezon's friendship with him, the heroic image of him impressed by the mass media upon an American public hungry for a hero, and the political potency of this image's appeal to those Americans whose passionately exclusive nationalism had been the backbone of isolationism—all these combined rather strangely in the mind of Washington's top officialdom to render him indispensable to the Allied cause. On March 11, in obedience to direct orders from the President (MacArthur's extreme reluctance to obey was heavily stressed by him and his chief of staff in public statements), he with his wife and son had fled from Corregidor to Mindanao in a PT (motor torpedo) boat, his personal staff accompanying him in other PT boats, and had then been flown to Australia, where upon landing he announced to the world: "The President of the United States ordered me to break through the Japanese lines. . . . I came through, and I shall return." These last words, hugely publicized, impressed themselves upon the popular mind as a sacred promise, a morale-boosting prophecy, by one of the great warriors for democracy.*

To all these grievous losses to the Allies—the Philippines, Thailand (Siam), Malaya, the Netherlands East Indies, and control of the seas around them—was added, late in these black months, the loss of Burma. An area the size of Texas, its wide central expanse of fertile valley and hill bordered by jungle-covered

---

*They did not so impress the rank and file of his former command on Bataan, men upon whom his flamboyant self-glorification, his arrogant egotism, his insistence upon personal privilege as a natural right, had always grated. These now viewed his daring flight through enemy lines as a cowardly abandonment of them. In one Bataan regiment, it became standard practice for a man heeding the call of nature to say: "I am going to the latrine, but *I shall return!* Also sung with gusto to the tune of "The Battle Hymn of the Republic" were lyrics composed by some unnamed cynic:

> Dugout Doug's not timid, he's just cautious, not afraid,
> He's protecting carefully the stars that Franklin made.
> Four-star generals are as rare as good food on Bataan.
> And his troops go starving on.

> Dougout Doug is ready in his Chris-Craft for the flee
> Over bounding billows and the wildly raging sea
> For the Japs are pounding on the gates of old Bataan
> And his troops go starving on.[6]

hills and mountains, Burma, home to some seventeen million people, had major strategic importance to the Allied cause, especially after the fall of Singapore. Through it ran Chiang Kai-shek's chief overland supply route, the eight-hundred-mile Burma Road from Lashio to Kunming in China's Yunnan Province. More important, Burma barred the way to India, upon which the British grasp was in any case increasingly loose and slippery, thanks to the Indian independence movement organized through Gandhi's Congress Party. For decades, however, Burma had been badly neglected by the British. One consequence was a notable lack of love by the Burmese for their imperial masters; another was a total lack of road and rail connections of Burma with India, the development of these having been opposed by monopolistic British shipping interests that profited hugely from trade between Calcutta and Rangoon. The British now paid the price of their profiteering neglect: they must operate in Burma among a hostile population, and the lack of land communications with India made them wholly dependent upon the port of Rangoon for the adequate supply and reinforcement of their troops. Consequently, when the Japanese captured Rangoon in the first week of March, the British supply problems in Burma became insoluble. Ill equipped and untrained for jungle warfare, soon wholly deprived of air cover, the British troops were forced into steady, difficult retreat by skilled Japanese jungle fighters whose operations, launched from Thailand, had an abundance of air support and were nourished from the sea through Rangoon.[7]

Desperate efforts to help them were initiated in late March when American General Joseph W. Stilwell came down from Chungking to take command of the Fifth and Sixth Chinese Armies; the Fifth Army was in southern Burma, the Sixth held in reserve on the China-Burma border.

Stilwell, destined to play (indeed, he now begins to play) an important though tragically futile role in the development of Chinese-American relations, was a lanky, hard-bitten career officer of outstanding ability, fifty-nine years old in 1942, who had been dubbed "Vinegar Joe" because of the acerbic temper and tongue with which he implemented an absolute commitment to truth as he perceived it, and to the telling of it. Highly intelligent and an acute judge of character (his recognition of phoniness was as swift and generally accurate as his loathing of it was profound), he was a natural leader of men. During the 1940 Louisiana war games he had impressed Marshall with his strategic sense and tactical ingenuity. He also knew China as no other American general did, having served in that country for more than a decade during which he had mastered the Chinese language, learned much Chinese history, and developed a sympathetic understanding of the Chinese people along with a decidedly unsympathetic understanding of the chaotic and corrupt ways in which they had latterly been misgoverned. It was because of his China experience that, on February 2, 1942, in response to urgent requests from Chiang Kai-shek for the assistance of a high-ranking American military officer, Washington formally designated him chief of staff to the supreme commander, China theater (that is, to Chiang), and directed him to "assist in improving the combat efficiency of the Chinese Army and increase the effectiveness of U.S. assistance to the Chinese government for the prosecution of the war."[8]

The Chinese generalissimo's assignment to him of field command in Burma immediately upon his arrival in Chungking accorded with Stilwell's desire but proved to be fatally flawed. Chiang had neither a firm grasp of the basic principles of strategy nor an exclusive commitment to fighting the Japanese, being equally if not more concerned with the threat that Chinese Communists posed to his thoroughly incompetent and corrupt nationalist government. He was woefully ignorant of the actual situation in Burma; he had ludicrously mistaken notions of Burmese geography. Nevertheless, in utter disregard of supposedly firm arrangements he had made with Stilwell, he attempted to run the Chinese campaign in Burma from his headquarters in Chungking. He continuously undercut Stilwell's authority, countermanding the field commander's orders and issuing orders of his own through a direct and voluminous correspondence with Stilwell's nominal subordinates. The result was chaos and uninterrupted defeat. Chinese divisions retreated in defiance of Stilwell's orders, often without even bothering to notify him of their action (one whole division simply disappeared into the heavily jungled hill country). Finally, as Stilwell's attempt to retreat northward was blocked by the Japanese, who had outflanked him, and as his attempt to march westward to India was blocked by the lack of bridges strong enough to carry tanks, his effective command was reduced to a portion of his staff and a few dozen others, including the heroic Dr. Gordon Seagrave (known to history as the "Burma Surgeon") and Seagrave's corps of native nurses— some 114 people in all. With these he walked out of Burma, from a point fifty miles west of Indaw to Imphal in Assam, a fast-paced risky hike of some 150 miles through steep jungle-covered terrain that, under Stilwell's disciplined leadership, was accomplished in two weeks (the party arrived in Imphal just before the monsoon rains began) without a single loss. There was, alas, a considerable loss from the British and Chinese troops who then followed the route Stilwell had taken, though these arrived in sufficient strength to block for the time being any farther westward movement by the overextended Japanese.

From Imphal Stilwell went at once to Wavell's headquarters in New Delhi, where awaited him a message from Marshall conveying praise, from the President and the secretary of war, of what he had done. He reacted with a rueful, disdainful shrug: what *had* he done, save lose a crucial battle? He was sick and tired of official British communiqués that lied about what had happened and was happening—sick and tired of such public statements as those attributed to Generals Wavell and Alexander, describing the Burma debacle as a "voluntary" withdrawal and a "glorious" retreat. At a large press conference on the evening of his arrival in New Delhi he was asked to comment on what Wavell and

Alexander had reportedly said. He did so bluntly: "In the first place, no military commander in history ever made a *voluntary* withdrawal, and in the second place there's no such thing as a *glorious* retreat. All retreats are as ignominious as hell. I claim we got a hell of a licking. We got run out of Burma and it's humiliating as hell. . . ." The military censors at New Delhi tried but failed to prevent verbatim publication of these remarks, which, joined with published descriptions of his "walkout" as one of the epic marches of history, made him a famous man in Britain and the United States. . . .[9]

Simultaneous with these multiple disasters far from American shores, also more ominous for the Allied cause and more politically damaging to the Roosevelt administration, was a prolonged sea disaster just off the East Coast, some of it so near the shore that it could actually be seen and heard from there. Of more distant portions of it, horrid tangible evidence continually washed ashore, during these months, in the form of ship wreckage and, now and then, the bloated corpse of a drowned sailor. This disaster was the massacre of defenseless, unprotected merchant shipping in pursuance of a Fuehrer conference decision, in mid-December, to push Nazi submarine warfare into American home waters.

The attack began in early January in the area between Newfoundland and New York (thirty-one ships having a total of nearly two hundred thousand tons were sunk there in January) but soon moved southward to the coastal waters between New York and Florida, where oil tankers moved in steady procession between American ports and the oil ports of Venezuela and Mexico. The U.S. defense establishment, especially the navy, which had special responsibility in the matter, was woefully, inexcusably unprepared to protect this crowded and vital sea lane. The efficacy of the convoy system in reducing sinkings had been abundantly demonstrated in World War I and again during the present war, yet no effort had been made to apply this system to American coastal shipping. Neither had anything been done to develop a coastal air defense, though the efficacy of land-based aircraft as killers of submarines had also been, in this war, abundantly demonstrated. Land-based warplanes in the United States were the exclusive property of the army air corps (the navy was equipped with floatplanes and amphibian planes), and coordination between army and navy operations was, as we know, notoriously deficient. None of the corps' pilots had been trained for antisubmarine warfare. Moreover, and most inexcusable of all, no blackout had been imposed upon the coastal towns and cities, which meant that for a considerable time merchant ships operating after dark in coastal waters, though they showed no lights themselves, were silhouetted against a glowing horizon and became as perfectly targetable at night as in daylight ("Miami and its luxurious suburbs threw up six miles of neon-light glow . . . in order that the citizenry might enjoy business and pleasure as usual," writes historian Samuel Eliot Morison bitterly).[10] The result was that U-boats slaughtered with impunity. A mere handful of them, no more than a dozen to fifteen at a time, commonly operated along the whole of the eastern seaboard and in the Caribbean, yet the destruction they accomplished was prodigious; by mid-March, some sixty tankers totaling 675,000 deadweight tons had been sunk there. The whole of the Allied war economy and every major Allied operational plan was threatened. Nor did the massacre abate as spring came on. Not until late July would effective defense measures begin to reduce the rate of slaughter. . . .[11]

II

AMID this torrent of catastrophic news, rushing week after week upon the American mind, Franklin Roosevelt stood tall and straight, his withered legs steel-braced against the morale-eroding flood, his broad face (despite the smile it generally wore) set hard as flint against it. His present presidential task, as he conceived it, had similarities to that he had performed in the spring of 1933. Now as then, the tide of event flowed overwhelmingly, irresistibly as it seemed to many, toward the triumph of dictatorship. Now as then, he must by word and deed restore lost confidence and inspire new confidence in democratic government; he must impress himself upon the public as a wise, knowledgeable, supremely competent leader who was the very personification of confidence in democracy's ultimate triumph over every hostile force—for it was from his convincingly expressed confidence that millions must derive their own.

There was a difference, however, between his conscious approach to this task in 1942 and the one he had made in 1933.

In the earlier year his approach had been almost wholly that of a gambler who feels lucky, though in his case the feeling was religious, born of his faith in a benevolent God who had chosen him personally to be executor of His will. Having witnessed the dire consequences of governmental inaction in the face of deepening depression, having attributed this inaction to Hoover's personal timidity and ideologically engendered fear of positive government, he had concluded that almost any governmental action, so long as it made no radical change in the prevailing economic order (he never ceased to identify the basic tenets of the profit system with those of Christianity and democracy), was preferable in God's sight to no action at all. He had then, during the famed Hundred Days, made a swift series of almost blind bets that, despite much evidence to the contrary, capitalism remained basically sound, morally as well as practically, and that a few superficial reforms were all that was needed to put its machinery again in running order. Simultaneously, through a full exercise of his formidable role-playing talent, he had projected a public image of himself as a man possessed not only of a deep understanding of the crisis, but also of a detailed, carefully thought-out plan for dealing with it.

In early 1942 he had much less need for blind faith and false appearance; he really did know, to a far greater extent than in 1933, what it was that he was doing. The war, the overriding necessity to win it, simplified everything conceptually. It provided him with clearly perceived goals, a sharply defined set of priorities, and a pattern for action. It reduced the number and restricted the range of choices open to him, thereby lessening the pangs of indecision and lightening the burden of decision. The grand strategy for the achievement of military victory, the basic premises of which had for many months been firmly grasped by his mind, not only determined the pattern in the military field, but also guided planning and programming in other fields; and his confidence that this dark season of defeat would end in a few months, that it was but a prelude to conclusive victories, was grounded in realistic assessments of America's industrial potential and of the American character. The result was a much firmer, more clearly decisive leadership on his part than he had formerly commonly displayed. His close associates in government took grateful note of the change.

His private personal life encouraged this change in his public one. Thanks to stringent wartime security measures, it was now more private, more exclusively personal, than it had ever been before since he moved into the White House. We have noted that some of the effects of increased security upon White House routines were unwelcome. The restrictions upon access to him, and upon his access to others, occasionally irritated him intensely. But overall, by blacking out not only the White House windows, but also all news of his travels and of the visits of others to the mansion, save such as he wished to have published, the heightened security gave him decidedly welcome relief from that "life in a goldfish bowl" he had sometimes complained of to such intimates as Missy and Frances Perkins. He had now a greater freedom of movement, more repose (he could take more afternoon naps, spend more night hours in sleep), and a greater freedom for strictly personal relationships than he had had since the 1933 inaugural.

As we have seen, he had last autumn increased the frequency and length of his visits to Hyde Park. These now became more frequent and lengthy still, since he could make them without publicity and so without fear of popular censure. His first post-Pearl one was simultaneous with Churchill's secret trip to Florida during the Arcadia Conference. He boarded his train at a secluded siding in Silver Spring an hour before midnight on a bitterly cold Tuesday, January 6, and left it next morning at Highland, whence he drove to the Big House at Hyde Park, where he remained until Saturday night, January 10, arriving back in the White House Sunday morning. Delighted by the success with which the secrecy of this first trip was maintained, he made eight more of them during the next six months, staying for four days on each occasion save the last of the eight, when he remained at Hyde Park for a full nine days. These were not holidays, of course. He brought always with him key members of his personal staff, including sometimes Harry Hopkins and always Grace Tully, William Hassett, who in these war years became closest to him personally of his four official secretaries, and the indispensable White House telephone operater, Louise ("Hackie") Hackmeister, whom Roosevelt deemed unique in her ability to recognize instantly any voice after she had heard it once, to judge which calls should be put through and which shunted elsewhere, and to reach by phone in short order anyone anywhere with whom he wished to speak. Staff offices were maintained in Poughkeepsie, but, by Roosevelt's order and to his great amusement, the staff members' living quarters became the ostentatiously grand and grandly furnished Frederick W. Vanderbilt mansion* in Hyde Park village, where their comings and goings would attract less public attention than they would have in Poughkeepsie's Nelson House. He himself put in full workdays in the office he had designed for himself in the new Franklin D. Roosevelt Library. But the environment and circumstances in which he worked—the fields and meadows of his earliest memories, the trees and birds of the woods he loved, the family home he had shaped as a young man into a Georgian mansion, the fieldstone cottage he'd built on Dutchess Hill, the magnificent views from these to the distant Catskills across the great theme river of his life—these renewed vital connections with his past and dissolved in the depths of the past some of the harshness of his present ("for this, too, will pass away"). He was refreshed, physically and spiritually.

Also there could now flourish more luxuriously than before, behind security's wall of secrecy, that companionship with women, their adoration of him unbounded, that soothed and pleasured him, giving him relief from crushing pressures, as no other companionships could do. The loss to him during the last eight months of the two women who had contributed the most to him in this way—Missy LeHand by devastating illness, his mother by death—increased his dependence upon the companionship of three other women.[12] One was Crown Princess Martha of Norway; another, his favorite cousin, Laura ("Polly") Delano; the third, Margaret ("Daisy") Suckley, a very distant relative whose family had been social friends of the Roosevelts' since the mid-nineteenth century and who lived in genteel poverty in a great house in Rhinebeck called Wilderstein, her father and an elder brother of hers having managed to dissipate what had once been a large inherited fortune. Each of these three possessed a cheerful disposition, an optimistic view of the world. Each was bright, witty in her own way, and decidedly upper-class in manner and outlook. None was equipped or inclined to pass judgment upon Roosevelt's policies of government, or upon his specific dealings with public issues, yet all were convinced beyond doubt that he was unqualifiedly great as a world leader and unqualifiedly good as a man, morally and in every other way.

---

*The mansion had been given the federal government in 1940 by a niece of Frederick Vanderbilt, to avoid payment of property taxes totaling some $25,000 annually. It was and is maintained by the National Park Service as a national historic site.

In other respects the three women were very different.

Princess Martha, the youngest (at age forty) and most attractive physically of the three, and the only one of them who had ever married, was very much a mother to her three children and very much a wife to their father, Crown Prince Olav, yet was, in her relations with Roosevelt, flirtatious, though not aggressively so; her very real charm had in it some of the glamour popularly attached to a royal princess but little in it of the self-assertive.

Polly Delano, on the other hand, was a uniquely assertive and flamboyant personality whose flirtatiousness struck many as outrageous. Often described as beautiful at age fifty-two, she was certainly of striking appearance, what with her purple-dyed hair, her heavily rouged cheeks and lips, her outlandish clothes (she favored red velvet slacks), and the dazzling array of jewelry she wore— heavy necklaces, rings on every finger, and so many bracelets on each arm that a faint metallic clatter accompanied her every movement. She had rather more than her full share of the Delano ego and selfishness, was said by some of her own family to be "too selfish to marry"—though it was also said that she had once been deeply in love with a Japanese nobleman's son who had roomed with her brother at Harvard and later became a secretary in Japan's Washington embassy, that their wish to marry had been frustrated by his father's and her father's adamant opposition to racial intermarriage, and that from this disappointment she had never sufficiently recovered to permit her marrying anyone else.

No such romance attached to Daisy Suckley, who was also in her early fifties and whose many gifts to Roosevelt included his beloved Scottie dog, Fala, presented him during the election campaign of 1940. She was Polly's opposite in almost every respect. Remarkably empathic and notably unselfish, indeed dedicated to the service of others, Daisy was in many ways the archetypical middle-aged spinster, plain of face (she wore little or no makeup), quiet and retiring of manner, and old-fashioned in dress (she rarely wore a jeweled ornament of any kind). She was not merely uninterested in physical sex, she seemed to find the very idea of it repulsive in relation to her own person; the appetite for it, she seemed to believe, was strong only in the male animal. According to historian and biographer Geoffrey C. Ward, she once proposed to a young relative, as a solution to overpopulation, the sterilization of most men: "It's most efficient and I understand it does not affect . . . whatever it is they get out of it."[13]

Yet of the three women, Daisy Suckley was the closest and most important to Roosevelt, the one whose companionship was most soothing to him, most profoundly relaxing, most constant—and through its quiet music (properly so called since the relationship had a lyric quality) sounded a faint note of the erotic; it was rendered all the sweeter by the reticence that muted it. Soon after the FDR Library opened, Roosevelt had her appointed to its staff as an assistant archivist, working half-time at a salary of $1,000 a year, her assigned task the sorting, classifying, and annotating of his personal and family papers at Hyde

Park. It was a task for which she was peculiarly well fitted, and it enabled her and Roosevelt to spend long hours together, without provoking gossip, at his library office or on the second floor of the White House, poring over old letters, diaries, and business documents, and sharing personal remembrances. When apart, they corresponded in quite lengthy longhand epistles (hers to him were "always sent in specially marked envelopes and through trusted intermediaries," writes Geoffrey Ward), and it is significant that he saved most of the letters she wrote him, depositing them in the stamp box that accompanied him on all his travels. The fact would astonish and delight her when she learned of it following his death; it also aroused her concern over the effect it might have upon Eleanor and others of his surviving family. "I had no idea he had ever kept any of them [the letters]," she would write to Roosevelt's daughter Anna, "but suppose it was just easier to toss them into the stamp box rather than bother to tear them up and drop them into the waste-paper basket! . . . If there were some elsewhere & you haven't destroyed them I would love to have them— Don't worry about it one way or the other but they would fill in the spaces between his rare letters to me and everything connected with him become more & more precious! I wonder if anyone ever before was loved by so many people as your dear father—and, I might add, loved so much in a personal way." She herself never deposited these precious personal mementos in the research library that memorialized him and of whose staff she was a member; they were found in a suitcase under her bed at Wilderstein after her death in 1991 at age one hundred; and the correspondence as a whole reveals an emotional attachment considerably stronger than, and different from, ordinary friendship. Clearly, the sexual difference between them was of the essence of their overtly sexless relationship. They loved one another, she profoundly and totally, he as deeply and completely as it was possible for him to love anyone.[14]

Sometime during this period of 1941–1942, Roosevelt renewed relations with the woman who had become the great romantic love of his life a quarter century before. Lucy Mercer Rutherfurd had received and accepted secret invitations from him to all three of his inaugurals, but her first known visit with him in the White House occurred in August 1941 shortly after her husband, wealthy socialite Winthrop Rutherfurd, who was her elder by thirty years, suffered a stroke, the first of several that, during the next three years, made a helpless invalid of him. During the immediately following months she seems to have seen Roosevelt again, perhaps thrice during the first six months of 1942, always when Eleanor was out of town. Their meetings then and later were not always at the White House. More often arrangements were made by phone for him to pick her up in a presidential car at her sister's Washington home, where she stayed when in the capital, and thence take her on a long quiet drive through Rock Creek Park, or the surrounding countryside, trailed inescapably by a car full of Secret Service men. Her telephone communications with him were facilitated by standing orders from him to the White House switchboard to put her through to him whenever she called; Hackie Hackmeister always did so at once.

The intensification of these relationships with women, all of them free of illicit sexual passion on Roosevelt's part, followed an attempt by him to restore life to his ruined marriage by building upon the emotional rapport that had been momentarily reestablished between him and his wife last September when his mother and Eleanor's brother, Hall, died within three weeks of each other.* An initial move toward this end was a cruise down the Potomac that he persuaded her to take with him and a small party of her closest friends, invited by him, on her fifty-seventh birthday (October 11, 1941). During it, especially at a Champagne dinner aboard the cruise vessel that evening, he displayed before her friends great affection for her. She evinced pleasure, but it was flawed by her "not wanting anyone to mention her birthday," as Joe Lash, one of the guests, remarked in his diary. There followed no developing marital intimacy, however— and by Pearl Harbor Day Roosevelt had abandoned his attempt. Eleanor would not, could not, adequately reciprocate. She had told the four most intimate of her friends (Marion Dickerman and Nancy Cook in the 1920s, Lorena Hickok and Joe Lash later) that although she had forgiven her husband's life-threatening betrayal of her in the Lucy Mercer affair, she could not forget it. In fact, she could neither forgive nor forget. Her very survival as an individual personality had required of her a total permanent renunciation of all romantic interest in him, all emotional dependence upon him—had required also the raising against him of protective walls so thick that they could not now be reduced or even, save for flashing far-spaced moments, narrowly breached. She simply could not trust him, count upon him, in vital ways. She therefore must, and did, focus elsewhere the abnormal though typically Rooseveltian energy that was bound up with her enormous need and capacity for love.

III

ROOSEVELT, in a wholly deplorable instance of his new decisiveness, signed (February 19, 1942) an executive order, No. 9066, authorizing the secretary of war and his military subordinates to "prescribe military areas . . . from which any or all persons may be excluded" and to place such further restrictions as

---

*"That big house without his mother seems awfully big & bare," wrote Daisy Suckley in her diary on February 4, 1942, "—she gave him that personal affection which his friends and secretaries cannot do, in the same way— He was always 'my boy,' and he seemed to me often rather pathetic, and hungry for that kind of thing. His wife is a wonderful person, but she lacks the ability to give him the things his mother gave him. She is away so much, and when she is here she has so many people around—the splendid people who are trying to do good and improve the world, 'uplifters,' the P. calls them—that he can not relax and really rest. On this visit and the one before, in January, he has relaxed. . . . It has been a real rest."[15]

they deemed necessary upon "the right of any person to enter, remain in, or leave" these areas. The War Department was also authorized to "provide transportation, food, shelter, and other accommodations" for those displaced. Though it made no specific reference to Japanese Americans, the order's intent, as Roosevelt knew when he signed it, was the evacuation of all people of Japanese blood, whether Issei (born in Japan, hence ineligible for American citizenship under U.S. immigration laws) or Nisei (born in the United States, hence citizens by birth under the Constitution) from the western coastal states, all of which would be designated a "military area" for this single purpose. Those displaced were to be interned in isolated areas of what the army called the Zone of the Interior for as long as the army deemed necessary.

Eleanor Roosevelt, whose absolute commitment to civil rights was normally relentlessly active, made but a single feeble protest to her husband against what was to become, in the words of the American Civil Liberties Union, the "worst single wholesale violation of civil rights of American citizens in our history."[16] The sweeping nature of the order appalled her when she first read it. Under its terms, habeas corpus and all constitutional protections against search and seizure were suspended. The army was enabled to incarcerate American citizens—scores of thousands of them, women and children as well as men—in what Roosevelt himself would later call "concentration camps." Much of their property, left inadequately or wholly unprotected, would be at the mercy of rapacious neighbors. And why? Not because they had committed a crime, or because evidence that they conspired to do so was in hand, but simply and solely because they were of Japanese extraction. A fearful concern over the Yellow Peril had long been prevalent on the West Coast, and racial bigotry must certainly be involved in this present vicious injustice. Eleanor said so to her husband. He received her complaint coldly, dismissively. He curtly asked her not to mention the subject to him again. And she, uncharacteristically in such matters as this, complied with his request. . . .

Immediately after Pearl Harbor she had flown with La Guardia to the West Coast for an inspection tour of civil defense activities. The two had found that, though woefully little was being done about civilian defense in any city save San Diego, coastal Californians were in a state of extreme jitters over the possibility of Japanese air attacks, even of landings by Japanese troops.

Sharing these jitters—indeed, in good part responsible for them—was the intelligence branch of the U.S. Fourth Army, which, assigned the defense of the West Coast, was commanded by a sixty-one-year-old lieutenant general named John L. De Witt from headquarters at the Presidio in San Francisco. On December 8, Fourth Army intelligence falsely reported thirty Japanese planes over San Francisco, precipitating a hurried, frightened blackout and flash news reports, spread nationwide, that San Francisco was under bombing attack. On the following day, it reported thirty-four Japanese ships off the California coast between San Francisco and Los Angeles (they turned out to be fourteen trawlers from the Monterey fishing fleet fleeing homeward in response to the news from Pearl Harbor); two days later, De Witt's personal headquarters ordered a "[g]eneral alert of all units" because the "main Japanese battle fleet" was "164 miles off San Francisco." Not long afterward, during an air raid alarm, some 1,500 rounds of antiaircraft ammunition were fired at wholly imaginary Japanese aircraft in the skies above Los Angeles. Fourth Army itself contained in its officer ranks not a few who were thoroughly disgusted by what a top one of them, Major General Stilwell, called the "wild, farcical and fantastic stuff that G-2 Fourth Army pushes out!"[17] Soon to be called to Washington to serve briefly in war plans before being posted to China, Stilwell was commander of the southern sector of the Western Defense Zone; and since this defense area, extending down the California coast to the Mexican border, contained 80 percent of America's aviation industry, all of it within shelling distance of warships offshore, its commander must agitatedly actively respond on the instant to every frightened and frightening communication he received from the Presidio. He kept a diary, largely for the purpose of venting emotions that, remaining pent, might pile up to an explosive height, and in it he recorded his angry conviction that Fourth Army intelligence was staffed with scared "amateurs" and that De Witt was nervously, irrationally reactive.

Such false reports provided fertile soil in which could grow popular suspicions that a Fifth Column of Japanese Americans engaged in espionage and was prepared to sabotage on a huge scale at the most opportune time—say, at the moment of a Japanese landing. Yet when La Guardia and Eleanor toured the coast, they noted, amid the general jitteriness, a remarkably small amount of hysterical hostility toward Japanese Americans as such. Influential newspapers were then warning against the kind of vigilante terror that had victimized German Americans during World War I. Most of "the thousands of Japanese here and in other coastal cities [are] . . . good Americans, born and educated as such," said a Los Angeles Times editorial on December 8, 1941; therefore, let "there be no precipitation, no riots, no mob law." Two days later, the Times' lead editorial, headed "Let's Not Get Rattled," pooh-poohed the notion that Los Angeles was in imminent danger of a massive air attack; it pointed out that in order to carry out such an attack, the Japanese would have to assemble several aircraft carriers within air strike distance of the coast "together with a good-sized fleet of covering war vessels and fuel supply ships. Could such an aggregation of surface craft sneak up on this Coast undetected by our now aroused sky scouting forces?" Other West Coast papers published similar editorials. Encouraged thereby was a popular belief that the small Japanese minority should remain unmolested since it posed no threat to national security. Eleanor and La Guardia deplored the prevailing jitters, of course, during their West Coast visit; they welcomed, and themselves engaged, in efforts to "calm people down" (Eleanor felt that the calming effect of her presence was a chief justification of her visit); but she, at least, was at that time less concerned to promote calmness than to over-come complacency in key members of the coast's city officialdom. The mayor of Los Angeles, she wrote Joe Lash on December 11, had "to practically be beaten over the head to make him acknowledge that there was any danger" at all.[18]

Six weeks later, all this had changed.

The fears inspired by Japan's seeming invincibility as its armed forces swiftly tore thousands of square miles of empire out of Western hands; Secretary Knox's unsupported assertion, when he returned from his inspection trip to Pearl Harbor, that acts of sabotage as well as espionage had been committed by Hawaiian Japanese; the continuing repercussions of the December and early January excesses of Fourth Army G-2; the repeated publication of rumors (none of them verified) that light signals were being flashed nightly from the Califor-nia shore to Japanese submarines operating offshore, and that arrow shapes had been mowed in grass or shaped of rocks to point Japanese planes toward oil re-fineries and aviation plants; the Roberts Commission report that espionage had indeed aided the Pearl Harbor attack (though Roberts reported no evidence of sabotage); the mounting angry pressures from professionally "patriotic" organi-zations and from organizations whose members had interested reasons for want-ing to "get rid of the Japs";* the resultant change of mind by those newspapers that had earlier preached tolerance but now joined Hearst's and other reac-tionary papers in damning West Coast "Japs" as clear and present dangers to the general security—all these had combined by mid-January to produce a deafen-ingly clamorous demand by the most influential of West Coast citizens for a forcible removal of all "Japs" from the West Coast. De Witt had initially op-posed the idea. When his longtime personal friend General Allen W. Gullion, who as provost marshal general was the army's chief law enforcement official, phoned him about it from Washington on December 26 (the call was prompted by the Washington lobbyist of the Los Angeles Chamber of Commerce), De Witt said he had already threshed "the thing out" in his mind. To arrest, trans-port, and confine in remote places the 93,000 Japanese who lived in California plus the 30,000 who lived elsewhere in the coastal area—more than 120,000 people in all, 110,000 of them citizens—would be "an awful job" and would "alienate the loyal Japanese." Moreover, it wasn't necessary: De Witt was con-fident that selectivity, whereby grave injustice to myriad individuals would be avoided, was possible and feasible; the army had the capability to "weed the

---

*Leading pressuring organizations were the American Legion, the Native Sons and Daughters of the Golden West, the California Joint Immigration Committee, the Grower-Shipper Vegetable Associa-tion, the Western Growers Protective Association, the California Farm Bureau Federation, and the Los Angeles Chamber of Commerce.

disloyal out of the loyal and lock them up if necessary." A little over a week later, James H. Rowe, Jr., the thirty-two-year-old assistant to Attorney General Francis Biddle and a strong civil libertarian,* having returned to Washington from a conference with De Witt at the Presidio, reported to his superior that the general deemed mass evacuation to be "damn nonsense!"[19]

But even as Rowe made his report, De Witt was yielding to pressures, a principal one being the relentless, single-minded pursuit of the mass evacuation goal by Gullion, whose highly effective lieutenant in the matter was a Major Karl Bendetsen. Bendetsen, a business lawyer who had been counsel to the Washington State Taxpayers' Association when Gullion recruited him, was immensely able, immensely industrious, immensely desirous to "get ahead";† he was also uninhibited by great moral sensitivity or by strong commitments to truth and justice. He was playing the leading active role in the mass evacuation campaign by January 16, 1942, when California's Congressman Leland M. Ford, a Republican, addressed identical letters to Secretary of War Stimson and Attorney General Biddle, urgently recommending that "all Japanese, whether citizens or not, be placed in inland concentration camps." Ford, with the curious logic typical of those whose publicly professed concerns disguise private interests, added that any loyal Japanese American could demonstrate his loyalty "by permitting himself to be placed [without protest] in a concentration camp"— which is to say that any citizen of Japanese blood who insisted upon his constitutional rights demonstrated by doing so his disloyalty to the Constitution. Biddle, a man radically different in all respects from the notorious Attorney General A. Mitchell Palmer of World War I, and resolved to prevent a repetition during this war of Palmer's excesses, replied promptly that "unless the writ of habeas corpus is suspended, I do not know of any way in which Japanese born in this country, and therefore American citizens, could be interned." In other words, unless martial law were imposed upon the whole West Coast as it had been upon Hawaii,†† legal citizen internment was impossible—and so drastic an extension of army control over civilian life would certainly face strong popular opposition in the three coastal states. As for Stimson's reply to Ford, it was drafted, in company with Assistant Secretary McCloy, by none other than Karl Bendetsen, who designed it to inform internment advocates that since the army did not oppose and could implement their desire (the "internment of over a hun-

---

*A brilliant lawyer with a thorough knowledge of the workings of government, Rowe had come to the attorney general's office from the White House, where he had been one of the presidential assistants with a "passion for anonymity" who were appointed after executive reorganization was enacted.

†Bendetsen most emphatically *did* "get ahead" in the army bureaucracy. Having entered the army as a captain, he made full colonel in less than two years.

††Though Pearl Harbor was of crucial strategic importance and was more exposed to sabotage by a much greater Japanese presence than was any base on the American West Coast, no serious move toward mass internment was ever made in Hawaii.

dred thousand people involves many complex considerations . . . [but] the Army is prepared to provide internment facilities in the interior to the extent necessary"),[20] the Justice Department's legalistic scruples were all that stood in the way of their desire. The full heat of the pro-internmentists' ardor should therefore be focused upon that department—and it promptly was: the national press and radio began to bristle with angry denunciations of Francis Biddle and his quibbling assistants, who were portrayed as weak, timid, effeminate, devoid of the tough (manly) warrior virtues that the times demanded.

In the tug-of-war between war and justice that ensued, war pulled by far the heavier weight. In Congress, Democratic representatives from California joined Ford and the Republicans to exert direct pressure upon Justice. So did California's Governor Culbert L. Olson, California's Attorney General Earl Warren (destined for later fame as a champion of civil liberties), most of that state's district attorneys and sheriffs, dozens of officials in Washington and Oregon, and virtually every West Coast newspaper. On February 12, Walter Lippmann weighed in with a highly influential column headed "The Fifth Column on the West Coast," carried in hundreds of papers across the land. Without revealing that his sole source of authoritative "factual" information was De Witt, whom he had just interviewed during a trip to California and who had in hand a blatently racist "final recommendation" to the War Department prepared by Bendetsen,* Lippmann declared the whole of the West Coast to be a combat zone comparable to the deck of a warship, whereon "everyone should be compelled to prove that he has a good reason for being there." (Only people of Japanese extraction would be so compelled, of course, but Lippmann didn't say so.) "It is a fact that communication takes place between the enemy at sea and enemy agents on land," he said flatly, adding that the "fact that since the outbreak of the Japanese war there has been no important sabotage on the Pacific Coast" was "a sign that the blow is well-organized and that it is held back until it can be struck with maximum effect." Lippmann's views were promptly seconded by the notoriously reactionary columnist Westbrook Pegler, who cited Lippmann on his way to the conclusion that the "Japanese in California should be under armed guard to the last man and woman right now—and to hell with habeas corpus. . . ."[22]

---

*Signed by De Witt and sent to Washington on February 13, the memorandum said: "The Japanese race is an enemy race and while many second and third generation Japanese born on United States soil . . . have become Americanized, the racial strains are undiluted." Citing no evidence, Bendetsen asserted that the Japanese Americans were prepared to facilitate "[h]ostile Naval and air raids . . . by signalling from the coastline and the vicinity thereof; and by supplying and otherwise assisting enemy vessels and by sabotage. . . . The very fact that no sabotage has taken place to date is a disturbing and confirming indication that such action will be taken." Three days earlier, Stimson had noted as a "fact" in his diary that Japanese "racial characteristics are such that we cannot understand or trust even the citizen Japanese."[21]

Biddle found this outrageous. He said so in a Rowe-drafted memorandum addressed to Roosevelt on February 17. Lippmann and Pegler ("Armchair Strategists and Junior G-Men") had now "taken up the evacuation cry," he said, "on the ground that attack on the West Coast and widespread sabotage is imminent . . . when . . . military authorities and the F.B.I. have indicated this is not the case. It comes close to shouting FIRE! in a theater; and if race riots occur, these writers will bear heavy responsibility." In an angrily protesting letter to Lippmann himself two days later, Biddle quoted a wire just received from a Southern California newspaper editor: "Alien Japanese situation deteriorating rapidly. Lippmann's column and new newspaper attacks have started local citizens organizing some kind of irresponsible drive." Why, asked Biddle, hadn't the columnist consulted him before bestowing his prestigious blessing upon the unsupported assertions of hysterical Californians and power-lustful army officers?[23]

But by that time the evacuation authorization executive order awaited signature on the President's desk if, indeed, it was not already signed. From the very beginning of this controversy, Roosevelt had stood on the army's side of it. When Biddle lunched with him on February 7, he let Biddle know that the constitutional difficulties that loomed large in Biddle's mind measured small in his own against the army's declarations of military necessity: having listened closely to the Justice Department's argument against mass evacuation and taken special note of Biddle's statement that the FBI "was not staffed to perform it," he closed the discussion by stressing his awareness "of the dreadful risk of Fifth Column retaliation in case of a raid." Four days later, when Stimson in a phone conversation attempted to obtain specific authorization of the army's removal of citizens as well as aliens from restricted areas, Roosevelt warily sidestepped so direct a personal commitment but told the war secretary "to go ahead on the line I myself thought best" (so Stimson recorded in his diary) and promised to back up with an executive order any transfer of authority from Justice to War that Biddle agreed to. He closed *that* discussion by stressing the need for a swift settlement of the issues. Thus the die was cast. Within minutes after this last conversation ended, McCloy was talking on the phone to Bendetsen in California, saying "we have carte blanche to do what we want to do as far as the President's concerned." Whereupon McCloy and a jubilant Gullion drafted the crucial order for the President's signature.[24]

For Roosevelt, this decision was easy, made so by the priorities that the war imposed upon his compartmentalizing collector's mind. The army and the War Department had primary direct responsibility for the achievement of war victory, the achievement of war victory had top priority, and "victory" had for him a single simple meaning: the destruction by armed force of Nazi-fascism and of Japan's military dictatorship. This was prerequisite to all else, and between it and all else he made quite sharp distinctions, both substantively and temporally.

He was fond of proclaiming broad, vague, lofty war aims (the Four Freedoms, the Atlantic Charter) upon which there was, in the abstract, almost universal agreement, but this was in large part because doing so promoted national unity, strengthened the bonds of the Grand Alliance, and so was an integral part of war making. He had a profound aversion to colonialism; its abolition was a personal war aim; but, having once indicated as much to Churchill (with regard to India) in private conversation during Arcadia, provoking thereby a wrathful outburst from the passionately imperialist Prime Minister, he was careful not to do so again in any way that might endanger the Anglo-American alliance. He refused to further complicate his already complicated task by admitting to his mind any conception of war making that included, save very incidentally, the actual realization of stated war aims. Nor would he include such realization within his definition of "victory." First came the war effort; second, as outcome of the war effort, came victory; and only *then,* third, came the practical effort to implement and institutionalize war aims. The present decision was further eased by the fact that it involved no political risk, whereas a contrary decision would loose a storm of criticism of the administration. Nearly all the chief spokesmen of liberalism, whom one would have expected to protest internment in loud voices, were either cautiously and qualifiedly approving of it as an unfortunate necessity or else wholly silent on the matter. There was no formal discussion of the subject in cabinet meetings, where Harold Ickes, at least, might have vehemently supported Biddle's side of the argument had it been strongly presented. Finally, the decision-making process in this case required of Roosevelt no overcoming of a strong principled commitment to civil liberty. As we know, he had no such commitment. And there was at the core of him a curious icy coldness that, streaking the general warmth of his nature, enabled him to turn off or on at will, seemingly, his remarkably empathic sensitivities, enabling him to bear with equanimity, if not wholly without guilt feelings, human suffering he might have prevented—even suffering he sometimes, and sometimes quite needlessly, directly imposed.*

It is highly unlikely that a different presidential decision would have been made, though it is certain the decision would have been more difficult, had Francis Biddle stood rock firm on his side of the issue. He didn't. Aristocratically fastidious, with no taste for rough-and-tumble combat or harsh competitions of any kind, he was new to the cabinet, unsure of his standing with the White House, and fatally inhibited in this matter by an almost reverential admiration of, and consequent deference to, Henry L. Stimson. There was a widespread acceptance in Washington and in the country at large of the strong-willed

---

*W. Averell Harriman, in his book *Special Envoy to Churchill and Stalin,* p. 91, says flatly: "He [Roosevelt] always enjoyed other people's discomfort. I think it fair to say that it never bothered him very much when other people were unhappy."

Stimson's estimate of himself as a man of extraordinary integrity, selflessness, wisdom, and unwavering commitment to the highest code of honor,* and though evidence of this estimate's accuracy is by no means glaringly obvious in the plain record of Stimson's career as corporate lawyer and public servant, Biddle's acceptance of it was absolute. The limit of Biddle's resistance to the army's will in this case was, therefore, his refusal to participate in the actual act of internment. In the afternoon of February 17, with the supposedly finally decisive meeting on the matter scheduled for that evening between top War and Justice officials, he told the President by phone that he now supported Stimson's stand on the issue and would willingly permit the executive transfer from Justice to War of whatever legal authority was required for the War Department's execution of an evacuation order. He failed to tell Rowe and Edward J. Ennis, general counsel for the Immigration and Naturalization Service, what he had done. These two came to the presumably decisive meeting prepared to fight to the last ditch against evacuation and were flabbergasted to find the decision already made, concurred in by their own superior! And the wrong decision!†[25]

A month later, the House of Representatives, after a mere ten minutes of perfunctory discussion, passed by voice vote a bill drafted by McCloy providing criminal penalties for those Japanese Americans who dared defy the evacuation order or disobey subsequent military orders. In the Senate, only one senator, arch-conservative Robert Taft of Ohio, spoke against it, damning it as "probably the 'sloppiest' criminal law I have ever read or seen anywhere." No doubt it would be enforceable in wartime, but "in peacetime no man could ever be convicted under it, because the court would find that it was so indefinite and so uncertain that it could not be enforced under the Constitution."[27] The Senate then passed the bill by voice vote and sent it to the White House, where Roosevelt signed it into law on March 21. The onus of enforcing the statute fell upon Biddle and his department associates, all of whom were as convinced of its unconstitutionality as Taft was. . . .

By that time, Roosevelt had established by executive order a War Relocation Authority to exercise civilian control over the evacuation authorized by Executive Order No. 9066; he had named as agency director Milton Eisenhower, who was then a far more distinguished man than his elder brother, the general, having been director of information of the Department of Agriculture and, latterly, administrator of that department's multibureau land-use program. But by that time, too, the actual evacuation, conducted by the army, was already well under way. It was mandatory evacuation, though Eisenhower had accepted this assignment with the understanding that voluntary evacuation would rule. In

---

*This self-estimate is spelled out in terms of smug elitism and impregnable self-righteousness in Stimson's personal diary, also his *On Active Service in Peace and War* (written with McGeorge Bundy).
†Ennis, outraged, disgusted, wanted to resign in protest and was dissuaded by Rowe with difficulty.[26]

charge of it was Karl Bendetsen, selected for the task by De Witt and McCloy. He executed it with all the vigor and rigor that were to be expected of so energetic, ambitious, and racially bigoted a young man.[28] Great emphasis was placed upon speed of evacuation. Slight consideration was given to the property rights of the evacuees (when they received personal notice that they were to be forcibly removed, they were given a week within which to dispose of their property, much of which was promptly acquired by their greedy neighbors at rock-bottom prices). Equally little consideration was given their physical comfort and well-being. They were herded into assembly centers located on racetracks, fairgrounds, and parking lots, hundreds of them being jammed into white-washed former horse stables that yet stank of manure, where toilet facilities were communal and partitions thin or nonexistent. They were prisoners under armed guard behind barbed wire, their days empty of active life, their nights disturbed by watchtower searchlights that swept the grounds and flashed through windows upon their cots.

Milton Eisenhower tried for a more civilized handling of these dazed, frightened, helpless, innocent people. As he did so, he came at once hard against Bendetsen's stubborn opposition to voluntary migration and, a little later, against a flat refusal by western state government officials to permit evacuees to be integrated into the rural life of their states. Eisenhower had worked out a plan for the swift removal of the evacuees from the so-called assembly centers, the living conditions of which appalled him, and their resettlement in camps modeled after those of the New Deal's Civilian Conservation Corps (CCC enlistees had lived under the supervision and paramilitary discipline of the army, but their money-compensated workdays had been spent upon soil conservation and re-forestation projects administered by civil servants of the Agriculture Department). Some fifty to seventy-five of these camps were to be scattered across the western states, according to the plan, and their inhabitants, free to come and go from the camps as they pleased, were to be encouraged to find employment in the agricultural communities surrounding them. But when Eisenhower presented this to a Salt Lake City meeting of western governors on April 7, 1942, he was hooted down in what he remembered ever after as the most frustrating and humiliating experience of his life. No governor, no major state official, was willing to permit any "Jap" to be relocated in his state who was not under armed guard. Idaho Attorney General Bert Miller expressed an opinion evidently widely shared by the others when he said that ". . . all Japanese [should] be put in concentration camps for the remainder of the war," adding: "We want to keep this a white man's country." Eisenhower, demoralized, caved in. He scrapped his carefully wrought plan and concurred in the officials' insistence that the evacuees be kept under armed guard in the assembly centers until other arrangements, satisfactory to the officials, were worked out.[29] Two months later, totally frustrated and exhausted by job-induced insomnia, he resigned his war relocation post, having persuaded his Agriculture Department friend Dillon Myer to succeed him.

Myer, a tougher man than his predecessor, though equally fair-minded and more liberal politically, proved much more effective. He soon asserted civilian control over the actual internment, considerably mitigating the harshness of the theretofore exclusively army operation. Fifteen permanent "relocation centers" were within three months spread across five western states (California, Arizona, Utah, Colorado, and Wyoming) and Arkansas, each of them on federal land and all of them, save in Arkansas, on desert or semidesert land. They were far from being the pleasant communities that McCloy publicly claimed them to be, but they were far more habitable than the army's assembly center stations had been.* They remained prison camps, each consisting of approximately a square mile covered by rows of tar-papered barracks in which were housed approximately eight thousand men, women, and children. Barbed wire surrounded them. Soldiers guarded them. The blazing sun of summer beat down upon them mercilessly. And most of them were swept, in winter as in summer, by winds laden with dust and sand. And the lives lived within them were monotonous, empty, boring, and full of physical discomforts.

It is therefore remarkable that the evacuees accepted their fate with, in general, little protest, much less active resistance—evidence, perhaps, of the loyalty to the United States that most of them felt—though it had already been noted that the same strange-seeming passivity, due in part to an initial stunned inability to believe that what was happening to them was possible, characterized the behavior of the Jews who were herded en masse into Nazi concentration camps. Inevitably, however, there were a few defiant ones whom the Justice Department must and did prosecute, convict, and send to prison. Inevitably, these sentences were appealed. And inevitably, representative cases found their way at last, on appeal, to the U.S. Supreme Court. By the time the Court ruled on the first two of them, in late June 1943, an influential minority of the general public was persuaded that the mass evacuation, admittedly an outrageous injustice to myriad individuals, had not been necessary for national security in the first place and that all internees should be at once set free. The Court, however, following Justice Frankfurter's energetic and fervent lead,† voted unanimously (three of the nine did so reluctantly) to uphold the convictions in the cases before them, though on narrow grounds that excluded the question of constitu-

---

*McCloy asserted that the army had taken "extreme care to protect the persons and goods and even the comforts of each individual" when it herded evacuees by the thousand into the assembly centers.³⁰
†Frankfurter's conception of a supreme judge's proper role did not preclude judicial acts on his part that were motivated primarily by a desire to serve the interests of his friend the President and those of his former law student John McCloy, for whose entrance into government he was in considerable part responsible. He himself contended, and no doubt believed, that his decisions were wholly grounded in his profound commitment to "judicial restraint."

tionality. A year and a half later, in mid-December 1944, the Court in another internment case announced its 6–3 decision that, in the words of Chief Justice Stone, "[w]here . . . conditions call for the exercise of judgment and discretion for the choice of means by those branches of the Government on which the Constitution has placed the responsibility of war-making, it is not for any court to sit in review of the wisdom of their action or substitute its judgment for theirs." The three justices who dissented (Roberts, Jackson, and Murphy) did so sharply. The Court might "as well say that [in wartime] any military order will be Constitutional," Jackson wrote caustically. Murphy found it incredible that loyalty hearings could not have been held "for the mere 112,000 persons involved— or at least for the 70,000 American citizens—especially when a large part of this number represented children and elderly men and women." Moreover, and worse, wrote Murphy, the army based its action "mainly upon questionable racial and sociological grounds not ordinarily within the realm of expert military judgment. . . ." The whole of the army's procedure stank of racism in Murphy's nostrils and thus bore "a melancholy resemblance" to the Nazis' treatment of Jews.[31]

IV

Of Franklin Roosevelt's war-induced decisiveness a far more fortunate instance—fortunate, that is, for the winning of a war purportedly being fought for the perpetuation of democracy—occurred in early February 1942, only a few days before his final internment decision.

All through January, MacArthur had bombarded Washington with demands for more help in the Philippines. In messages intended for the eyes of "the highest authority," as he pointedly let Marshall know, he had protested with increasing vehemence what he deemed the deliberate writing off of the islands in pursuit of a grossly mistaken, defeatist strategy. He had condemned the establishment of an American base in Australia (recommended by Eisenhower, ordered by Marshall) as a diversion from the vital battlefield of desperately needed resources; had called for direct attacks by the U.S. Navy upon Japanese lines of communication; had (on the record) given little or no credence to Marshall's patient explanations of why, in the wake of the crippling strike at Pearl Harbor, these "strong measures" were impossible to take. The most that could be done, said Marshall, was to slow the Japanese advance, contain it within the smallest possible bounds, until Allied naval and military strength in the Far Pacific was restored. The doing of this "most," however, was a vitally necessary contribution to ultimate victory.[32]

Marshall said this in a message sent to MacArthur on February 8, 1942. On that same day, Quezon, who had just been sworn in for his second term as Philippine President, addressed to Washington from his Corregidor headquarters a message that fell as a bombshell upon the minds of Marshall and Stimson (Dwight Eisenhower, at his war plans post, explicitly dubbed it a "bombshell"). It had been composed in physical and spiritual agony. Quezon was an ardent patriot who felt the crushing of his country as a personal tragedy. Tubercular, he had suffered a dangerous flare-up of his chronic illness following his flight from Manila. And his mental and physical anguish sharpened the bitterness with which, in his message, if for the most part by implication, he accused Britain and the United States of callous indifference to his country's fate. The two great powers used the commonwealth as a sacrificial pawn. They bought with its unrelieved death agony a breathing space in which to strengthen the defenses of Far Pacific outposts in which they were genuinely interested, devoting to these defenses resources that were desperately needed in the Philippines. Yet the United States was directly responsible for the Philippines' dire predicament! The Japanese had come there only because the Americans were there![33] And if the Americans departed, the Japanese could probably be persuaded to do the same. Ergo, unless the American government was prepared to send saving aid to the commonwealth, it should at once grant full Philippine independence and withdraw all its forces. The Philippine government would then disband its army, abandon its fortifications, and ask Japan to withdraw also. Upon Japan's agreement, the Philippines would become neutral ground and so saved from further horrors. Explosive power was added to this bombshell by accompanying notes from American Commissioner Sayre, who unequivocally endorsed what Quezon proposed, and from MacArthur, who argued for its acceptance, though the fuzzy language in which he did so indicated unease of mind. "So far as the military angle is concerned, the problem presents itself as to whether the plan of President Quezon might offer the best possible solution of what is about to become a disastrous debacle," wrote MacArthur. The plan's acceptance by the U.S. government would not determine or even importantly affect the Philippines' ultimate fate, he went on; this would be decided by the outcome of the global war; but its rejection by the Japanese government "would strengthen our hold [upon the Philippines] because of their [Japan's] Prime Minister's public statement offering independence." If, on the other hand, Japan "accepts it, we lose no military advantage because we would still secure at least equal delay"— evidently meaning delay of Japanese conquest, though whether he meant Japan's conquest of the Philippines or its conquests elsewhere is impossible to know.[34]

It was with trepidation that Marshall and Stimson brought this missive, with its accompanying notes, to the White House. What Quezon proposed derived from faulty premises: If the United States had not occupied the Philippines following the Spanish-American War, an expansive Japan would almost certainly have done so by now. Evidences of its ambition to do so had become abundant over the years and had caused the linkage of an American promise of Philippine independence to a promise to defend the islands with American arms until the

Filipinos were strong enough to defend themselves. Quezon's conclusion that Japan would now "probably" agree to neutralization on the terms he proposed was therefore, on the face of it, absurd. Yet heavy political pressures argued for American acceptance of his proposal, bolstered as it was by the Sayre and MacArthur opinions: the withdrawal of American troops from Bataan would prevent their otherwise certain death or capture, whereas a refusal to do so, when knowledge of it became public (and Quezon's attitude seemed to guarantee its publicity), would expose the President to possibly devastating fire from those American millions who had been conditioned by the conservative media, aided and abetted by what amounted to "appeasement" by the administration itself, to regard MacArthur as one of the greatest captains in all history. Thus the question presented to Roosevelt for answer was "ghastly in its responsibility and significance," to quote Stimson's diary,[35] and the Roosevelt of old, in the experience of the secretary and staff chief, might well have answered it affirmatively, or as equivocally and ambiguously as possible.

Not so the Roosevelt who now sat across the desk from the two men.

"We can't do this at all!" he said flatly. He ordered the immediate preparation in the War Department, for his signature, of draft replies saying "No" to the Philippine President and American field commander. Stimson then drafted the message to Quezon, Marshall (with Eisenhower) the one to MacArthur, and Roosevelt, after making a few revisions designed to reduce harshness while retaining crystal clarity, dispatched both of them to Corregidor on February 11. The American government could not possibly agree to any effort toward "neutralization," now or later, the President told Quezon. MacArthur, he went on, was authorized to arrange the surrender of the Filipino forces under his command if such was Quezon's desire, but the American presence on the islands in the fullest possible force would continue, and "so long as the flag of the United States flies on Filipino Soil" that soil would be "defended by our own men to the death." To MacArthur, his reply was equally blunt. He indicated a sympathetic understanding of the extremity to which the general's command might soon be reduced but did so only after he had issued an explicit order: There must be no surrender of American troops "so long as there remains any possibility of resistance." By this reply, Quezon was shocked back into a sense of reality and a renewed dedication to duty. He accepted the President's decision at once as his own, saying nothing about a separate surrender of Filipino troops; no doubt he was encouraged to do so by his knowledge that preparations were being made in Washington to evacuate him from Corregidor and transport him, with his staff and family, to the American capital, where he could establish a commonwealth government-in-exile. MacArthur, too, acquiesced at once and without argument, save to claim that his first message had been "misunderstood." He had never had the slightest intention to surrender, he protested; he would stand and fight "to destruction" where he now was. . . .[36]

The episode committed Stimson to Roosevelt's leadership more solidly than ever before and removed from Marshall the last of the grave doubts he had formerly had of Roosevelt's personal quality. "I immediately discarded everything in my mind I had held to his discredit," he would tell his biographer thirteen years later. ". . . I decided he was a great man."[37]

As for Roosevelt's opinion of Marshall, it had been high when he named Marshall chief of staff and had since become higher still. Marshall attended strictly to business, had no small talk, seldom ventured an easing witticism of his own, and responded meagerly to the witticisms of others, including the President's. He continued to refuse every invitation to a social intimacy with Roosevelt—continued to insist upon cool, rather stiffly formal relations between himself and the commander in chief—for he remained wary of social situations in which he might, out of politeness or personal affection, make commitments not in accord with his best judgment. But though this prevented Roosevelt from greatly enjoying Marshall's company, it did not redound to the general's discredit in Roosevelt's mind. On the contrary, it sharpened the President's view of him as a man of absolute integrity and selflessness, totally honest, possessed of an iron self-control that very seldom permitted strong emotions to sway or flaw his judgment (actually, as Roosevelt sensed, Marshall was a man of strong emotions, by nature more hot tempered and impatient than most)—a man who could be counted on absolutely when the going was toughest. And Roosevelt had counted on him increasingly during the last two years; he had let Marshall know that he did.

Thus it had been with confidence that the President would support him that Marshall had in late January, with Stimson's blessing, launched an attack upon a problem closely akin to the one Roosevelt had found so difficult to solve (because of a recalcitrant Congress) in early 1937, namely, the problem of executive reorganization. The War Department, Marshall had complained as war came on, was the least efficient command post in the whole of the army. Not since 1904, when Elihu Root established the general staff, had there been a major departmental reorganization. Marshall had under him thirty separate major commands, the four top ones being the separate corps of infantry, cavalry, field artillery, and coast artillery, each headed by a major general, each virtually a sovereign power, each jealous of its territory and prerogatives. Altogether, some sixty-one officers had the right of direct access to the chief of staff—a fact that assured impossible demands upon his time and energy. Moreover, deadwood was abundant throughout the system: scores of officers had little or no important work to do yet possessed great powers of obstruction. To clean up the mess (so Marshall deemed it), General McNarney had been summoned to Washington immediately after Pearl Harbor, as has been said, but had been unable to begin his painful, difficult task until January 25, after he had completed his service on the Roberts Commission. He at once proved to be precisely the right man for the job—totally dedicated, indifferent to personal popularity, courageous and skilled as an infighter, and thick-skinned enough to bear without perturbation the pain he must inflict, for the sake of efficiency, upon scores of his army colleagues. Within four weeks the job was done. On February 28, Roosevelt signed an executive order, to become effective on March 9, reorganizing the army into three top commands under the chief of staff. The three were army ground forces, which General Lesley J. McNair would command; army air forces, General Arnold to command; and army services of supply (later to be renamed army service forces), Lieutenant General Brehon B. Somervell to command. Decentralization permitted the reduction of the number of officers under Marshall in Washington by six hundred; the number reporting directly to him was reduced to half a dozen; he and the general staff were freed of operational details and enabled to concentrate on grand strategy.

In the third week of February, the White House announced that on Monday night, February 23, the day following Washington's Birthday, the President would make a fireside chat to the nation on the progress of the war; since the President would be referring to strange faraway places whose locations were but vaguely known to most Americans, if known at all, it would be helpful to each listener to have at hand a map of the world on which to follow the President's words. There ensued days of record-breaking sales of world maps all across America—C. S. Hammond & Co. sold two thousand of them at their 43rd Street store in New York City on Saturday, February 21—and more suspense than had preceded any fireside chat since the first one, on the banking crisis, in 1933. More than sixty-one million Americans, nearly 80 percent of the nation's largest possible radio audience, were tuned in when, on Monday, the President began his speech at ten P.M. Washington time.

Washington's Birthday was "a most appropriate occasion for us to talk with each other about things as they are today and things as we know they shall be in the future," he began, for there were analogies between the crisis Washington had to deal with and that which Americans must deal with today. Washington and his Continental Army "were faced continually" through eight long years "with formidable odds and recurring defeats," while behind them "[t]hroughout the thirteen states there existed fifth columnists—and selfish men, jealous men, fearful men, who proclaimed that Washington's cause was hopeless, and that he should ask for a negotiated peace." Similarly today, there were spokesmen of doom and despair, advocates of defeatism and isolationism, who sought deliberately to undermine national confidence and unity with assertions that "the Government has withheld the truth about casualties" and destruction at Pearl Harbor, "that the fleet was all sunk or destroyed on December 7—that more than a thousand of our planes were destroyed on the ground . . .—that eleven or twelve thousand men were killed . . . instead of the figures as officially announced [2,340 killed, 946 wounded]. . . ." They thus gave aid and comfort to our enemies. "Almost every Axis broadcast—Berlin, Rome, Tokyo—directly quotes Americans who, by speech or in the press, make damnable misstatements such as these." The lying defeatists of Washington's day had not deterred him. He had "held to his course, as it had been charted in the Declaration of Independence" and so "provided the model for all Americans ever since—a model of moral stamina."

But we must now follow this model in "a new kind of war," new "not only in its methods and weapons but also in its geography," for it was "warfare in terms of every continent, every island, every sea, every air lane in the world." That was "why I have asked you to take out and spread before you a map of the whole earth, and to follow with me the references I shall make to the world-encircling battle lines of this war." He then lectured his listeners, with frequent references to the world map, on cause-effect relations or the lack of them among specific battle areas scattered round the world, and on the global strategy dictated by these relationships. For instance, between the fleet-damaging attack on Pearl Harbor and the "Japanese gains in the Philippines" there was no such cause-effect relationship as defeatists doomfully alleged. A glance at that portion of the map covering the Pacific Ocean west of Hawaii made it clear that even "[b]efore this war . . . started, the Philippine Islands were already surrounded on three sides by Japanese power. On the west, the China side, the Japanese were in possession of the coast of China and the coast of Indo-China, which had been yielded to them by the Vichy French. On the north are the islands of Japan themselves, reaching down almost to northern Luzon. On the east are the Mandated Islands—which Japan had occupied exclusively and had fortified in absolute violation of her written word. . . . It is that complete encirclement, with control of the air by Japanese land-based aircraft [not the fleet damage at Pearl], which has prevented us from sending substantial reinforcements . . . to the gallant defenders of the Philippines. For forty years it has always been our strategy . . . that in a full-scale attack on the Islands by Japan, we should fight a delaying action. . . . We knew that the war as a whole would have to be fought and won by a process of attrition against Japan itself. We knew all along that . . . we could outbuild Japan and ultimately overwhelm her on sea, on land, and in the air." The only wholly unexpected thing that had happened in this area during the last two months was "the defense put up by General MacArthur," which "has magnificently exceeded the previous estimates of endurance; and he and his men are gaining eternal glory therefore."

He spoke contemptuously of those Americans "who still think in terms of . . . sailing ships" and who demanded that we "pull our warships and our planes and our merchant ships into our own home waters and concentrate on last-ditch defense." If we did that, we could no longer send aid to Britain, to China, to Russia, to the Southwest Pacific. We would doom to Axis conquest, to totalitarian slavery, the hundreds of millions of people in those far areas and doom ourselves to the same ultimate fate. "Those Americans who believed we could live under the illusion of isolationism wanted the American eagle to imitate the tactics of the ostrich. Now many of these same people, afraid that we may be sticking our necks out, want our national bird to be turned into a turtle. . . . I know that I speak for the mass of the American people when I say that we reject the turtle policy and will continue to take the war to the enemy in distant lands and distant waters—as far away as possible from our own home grounds."

As for the "outbuilding" of Japan and the other Axis powers, all of them put together, it was no longer possible to doubt that this would be accomplished. It was *being* accomplished. He reminded his listeners of his January 6 speech setting "certain definite goals of production for airplanes, tanks, guns, and ships." The announced goals had been dubbed "fantastic" by "Axis propagandists" (they had also been privately ridiculed, angrily and resentfully, by most of the big-business men whom he had put in charge of converting American industry to war production, as we know and he was careful not to say). Yet "[t]onight, nearly two months later and after a careful survey of progress by Donald Nelson . . . I can tell you that these goals will be attained." Americans were united in their determination to attain them; with few exceptions, "labor, capital, and farming realize that this is no time either to make undue profits or to gain special advantages, one over the other."

He closed by quoting the famous words Tom Paine wrote "on a drumhead, by the light of a campfire" at Valley Forge about "the times that try men's souls" and about the "summer soldier and the sunshine patriot" who shrank at such times "from the service of their country." Washington and his men had persevered, and so would the Americans of today.[38]

According to Sam Rosenman, this speech "was one of the most important and effective chats the President ever delivered, not excepting the first fireside chat on the banking crisis" in March 1933. *The New York Times* called it "one of the greatest of Roosevelt's career." The boost given the national morale was so obviously immense that Roosevelt was urged, as he had often been urged before, to make radio addresses more frequently. He replied that he had so much work of vital importance to be done that he could not spare the time required for frequent radio speech preparation (each of them took "four or five days of long, overtime work")—also, if his talks were too frequent, they would "lose their effectiveness. . . . I think we must avoid too much personal leadership—my good friend Winston Churchill has suffered a little from this."[39]

v

A few days after Donald Nelson assumed his new task as chairman of the War Production Board, Bruce Catton of the WPB's information division brought to his office Walter Reuther, the dynamic red-haired thirty-five-year-old vice president of the Detroit chapter of the CIO's United Auto Workers. The two had not met before—which seems, in context, rather strange: Sidney Hillman had placed Reuther upon the manpower training committee of the NDAC in May 1940; Nelson was soon thereafter, as coordinator of defense purchases, virtually a member of the NDAC; Reuther, in August 1940, with Hillman's rather tepid support, had tried in vain to interest Knudsen in a proposal to convert Detroit's auto factories to the mass production of warplanes; and in early 1941 this carefully worked-out proposal, which should have been vastly interesting to Nelson since it had high relevance to his government job, was nationally famous as the "Reuther Plan."

The plan had resulted from Reuther's creative recognition of four facts. *One,* it took a minimum of eighteen months to construct and put into operation a new aircraft plant—a deplorably long period when measured against the crying immediate need for new warplanes. *Two,* gross inefficiency—idle machines, idle workers, especially highly skilled workers—was imposed by the private profit system upon Detroit's auto manufacturers; in purely market (profit-maximizing) terms, it made sense to each company to operate at no more than 80 to 90 percent of its productive capacity for no more than a few months a year, and to employ highly skilled labor (tool-and-die workers) for no more than half each year on the average, but the resultant waste of technological and human resources was enormous at a time when the maximum possible use of these was a national security necessity. *Three,* there was close similarity between, there was even some identity of, the tools and techniques of automobile engine manufacture and airplane engine manufacture, as well as those of auto body manufacture and air frame manufacture. *Four,* veteran machinists and tool-and-die workers, especially when their knowledge and skills were pooled and coordinated through their union, knew more about the actual making of automobiles—indeed, knew more about the actual techniques of factory production generally—than any individual manager or group of managers did, a fact that, being threatful to the power and prestige of business executives as a class, was of course vehemently denied by them. On the basis of these four facts, Reuther proposed "to transform the entire unused capacity of the auto industry into one huge plane production unit" capable of turning out "five hundred planes a day," as he announced publicly just before Christmas Day 1940, after his plan's feasibility had been attested to by an assemblage of skilled workers from a dozen Detroit factories.[40]

At that time there were already loud, if lonely, voices calling upon the federal government to order the immediate cessation of auto manufacture for the civilian market—a move that would have created months of mass unemployment in Detroit, and chaos generally, since the army hadn't yet decided what it wanted or how much. Reuther proposed instead that current auto production continue uninterrupted, but that tooling for the 1942 models be postponed for six months—a move that would enable some fifteen thousand skilled mechanics to work on the tools, dies, jigs, and fixtures with which to mass-produce all-metal fighter planes. In now idle body plants, the mass production of wings and fuselages could begin very soon while arrangements were completed for the pooling and efficient use, in a central facility, of the machine tools for engine manufacture—tools now existing in redundancy, thanks to competitive production for profit in the retail market. To administer the program, Reuther called for a presidentially appointed nine-member aviation production board consisting of three government representatives, three management representatives, and three labor representatives. This board would operate through a technical committee, a labor supply committee, and a committee to manage subcontracting, each with a balanced membership of management and labor representatives. The technical committee, made up of engineers from the auto and auto parts companies and of skilled labor representatives, was to plan and direct the conversion in ways that eliminated redundancies and distributed production assignments efficiently among the various companies. The labor supply committee would do the same for labor, transferring workers from one plant to another, assigning them in ways that made most efficient use of their skills, and upgrading them when doing so would increase production. The subcontracting committee, composed of auto company purchasing agents and parts manufacturer technicians, along with labor representatives, was to see to it that orders were distributed among parts suppliers in ways that maximized efficiency and ensured effective use of "the tens of thousands of small plants for which no provision has yet been made in the war effort."[41]

As 1941 opened, the Reuther Plan was the subject of excited commentary all across the land. Liberal journals made invidious comparisons between its innovative boldness, its factuality, its logical consistency, and the alleged timidity and mental fuzziness of "production genius" Knudsen's pronouncements. Henry Luce's far from liberal *Time* magazine did the same thing, saying that Reuther's plan was drawn "on a braver, broader scale than Mr. Knudsen's [recent] proposal." I. F. Stone, a principal contributor to the *Nation* and *PM,* saw it as a program for democratizing defense, adding that "only a democratic defense can be a total defense in a total war. This is what the monopolists do not understand, dare not understand, for though a democratic defense would protect our country it would undermine their power." To Dorothy Thompson, the plan was "the most important event" in many weeks, and Lippmann, her fellow *Herald-Tribune* columnist, agreed, despite his profound aversion to governmental economic planning; Lippmann devoted two columns to the plan and praised Reuther for "playing an active and responsible role in the battle of production." In the top echelons of the government, there was a flurry of affirmative response to the plan. Roosevelt was immediately impressed by it. On December 30, 1940, he addressed a letter to Knudsen saying, "It is well worth while to give a good deal of attention to this [Reuther] program." Assistant Secretary of War

Robert Lovett, committed to a vastly expanded airplane production and increasingly impatient with the "business as usual" attitudes of the big-business
community (to which he himself belonged), was intrigued by Reuther's notion
of pooling machine tools in a central facility. Better to have one plant fully
equipped to produce something, said Lovett to Undersecretary Robert Patterson, than a multitude of plants no one of which, because of equipment shortage,
could produce anything. Lovett even told Knudsen to supply Reuther with aircraft engine blueprints and arranged for Reuther's inspection tour, with army air
force officers, of a Pratt & Whitney engine plant in Hartford, Connecticut, and
a Glenn L. Martin plant in Baltimore—a breach of the sacred wall between
management and labor that men like Knudsen could not but deem alarming.[42]

For the proposal *was,* indeed, revolutionary—literally so in that, if accepted
as model, it would effect a profound structural change in the economy, shifting
power away from those now holding it into hands formerly subject to it—and
the hostility to it of the big-business community was immediate, adamant, and
total, especially on the part of those whom the plan would directly affect: the
auto company executives, the plane-manufacturing executives, and the army officers in charge of procurement. Unspoken by them publicly was the fact that, if
accepted, the plan was likely to reduce considerably the amount of tax money
that became business profit; nor did they publicize the fact that they deemed
Reuther's proposal a colossal effrontery. It was mostly in private that they expressed their outrage over labor's daring to suggest, even, that it join with traditional management on a basis of equality in the making of production decisions,
thereby acquiring a voice equal in volume with traditional management's in the
deliberations that shaped the war economy. "Everyone knows that Reuther is
smart, but this is none of his business," said General Motors president Charles
Wilson* privately. ". . . [A]s vice president of the union he has no right to talk
as if he were vice president of the company." "They wanted to come into the
shop as a union committee and try to design fixtures for the present machinery,"
said an appalled Knudsen soon after he had had a long-delayed meeting with
Reuther personally on the matter. "We had to stall on that one." Overtly, it was
on the ground of the plan's alleged impracticality, its technical infeasibility,†
that the big-business men in charge of defense production based their opposition. Covertly, since Reuther's proposal appeared to the general public to be
solidly grounded in selfless patriotism whereas their opposition to it did not,
they welcomed and encouraged an attack in the arena of public opinion upon
Reuther's patriotism.[43]

---

*He was destined for national fame as "Engine Charlie" Wilson, the secretary of defense in the Eisen-
hower administration who was sure that "what's good for General Motors is good for the country."
†Reuther had indeed underestimated the extent to which warplane manufacture required greater flexibility than auto manufacture did.

It was J. Edgar Hoover who had initiated this last, immediately after Reuther published his plan. He did so by sending to key individuals—among them Pa Watson, Knudsen, and some reactionary Southern senators—a lengthy summary of the file of "secret" information his FBI had gathered about Reuther, as it had about every American liberal of any prominence, including Eleanor Roosevelt.* The summary was designed to arouse suspicion that Reuther was a Soviet secret agent whose aim was to "Sovietize" American industry. Especially useful to Hoover's purposes was a letter signed by Reuther and his younger brother, Victor, who actually wrote it, in January 1934 when the two of them began what would become nearly two years of employment as highly skilled tool-and-die makers in a huge auto factory at Gorky in the Soviet Union.† They were then Norman Thomas Socialists. They youthfully, fervently advocated "industrial democracy," were consequently hostile to Stalinist communism. But they were anxious for the success of that portion of the "Soviet experiment" (the first Five-Year Plan) that would demonstrate the practical superiority of governmental economic planning over the chaotic profiteering of capitalism in an industrial society and were therefore inclined to emphasize the best and ignore the worst of what they experienced at Gorky, especially during their earliest days there. They most emphatically did so in the 1,500-word letter Hoover now spread abroad, nearly all of which had been published in the spring of 1934 in an American Socialist youth journal. The letter said: "We are actually helping to build a society that will forever end the exploitation of man by man. Let no one say that the workers of the USSR are not on the road to security, enlightenment and happiness. . . . Carry on the fight." (The FBI file summary helpfully added a clarifying phrase to this last sentence, making it read: "Carry on the fight for a Soviet America.")[44]

Not until March 1, 1941, did Reuther, with Hillman, at last have a face-to-face meeting with Knudsen and the latter's staff. By then it was evident to Reuther that the chances of his plan's being accepted by the powers that be were very slim. By meeting's end, he knew they were nil. He was in a bitter mood when, immediately after leaving Knudsen, he was surrounded by reporters. He told them that, having formerly sat on the opposite side of the table from Knudsen (in labor contract negotiations), he had "thought that on this matter of national defense we might sit on the same side." He now knew "I was mistaken."

---

*Hoover also accumulated and secreted in files to which only he had access information about important public officials that, if published, would gravely embarrass them, or worse. The knowledge or fear that he had such information gave him great persuasive power over these officials.

† When Ford decided to discontinue production of its Model A car, successor to the original Model T, it entered into a multimillion-dollar contract with the Soviets to provide them the machine tools needed for the mass production of Model As in Russia. Amtorg, the trading arm of the Soviet Union, then began actively recruiting skilled American workers who were experienced in the use of these tools. The adventurous, idealistic Reuther brothers were among those who accepted the Soviet offer.

The plan, wrote I. F. Stone in retrospect, had been killed by the "fear . . . of losing power, a fear of democracy in industry as instinctive as the fear and hatred kings felt for parliament."45

Donald Nelson, in the third week of January 1942, was "very glad of the chance to have a half hour's talk with him [Reuther]."

But the interview had no perceptible effect upon Nelson's actual decision making at this outset of his WPB career. He remained convinced that dollar-a-year men, though they devoted a not inconsiderable portion of their time and energy to the frustration of Reuther and others "smarter than they," were absolutely indispensable to the defense effort.

A precisely opposite conviction had been arrived at by the Truman Committee, which by then had become the most prestigious of all congressional committees, its pronouncements highly influential of popular opinion. Ever since the First World War, Truman personally had deemed the very idea of dollar-a-year men a vicious absurdity, outrageous alike of justice and common sense; and to both him and his fellow committee members the truth of this view seemed abundantly attested to by the factual information they had gathered since last spring through tough but scrupulously fair-minded investigations of war contract awards and fulfillments. They could cite instance after instance in which business executives in government had made decisions that served the interests of the corporations upon whose payrolls they remained but that slowed or otherwise harmed the defense effort; they had examined and publicized enough of these to define, in their view, a pattern of iniquitous conduct; and they were convinced, as a result—they had also convinced much of the informed public—that dollar-a-year men, far from being indispensable to the defense effort, were hazardous to it. They assumed that Nelson had arrived at the same conclusion and that abolition of the dollar-a-year arrangement would be almost his first act in his new job; it was something his huge grant of executive authority enabled him to do, and they didn't see how he could expect to succeed if he didn't do it. They were shocked, therefore, by his announcement that he intended no such thing, that the limit of his reform in this direction would be an order prohibiting the employment of any corporation executive "in any position in which he will make decisions directly affecting the affairs of his own company."46

The shock was fully recorded in the mass media. Nelson was obliged to explain and justify himself in a public hearing before the Truman Committee.

He did so at length.

"To win the war . . . we must have in government men who understand and can deal with" the "intricate structure and operation" of American industry, he said, and "such men must be drawn in large measure from industry itself." He conceded that, "all things being equal, these men ought to be brought in to serve on a regular government salary," and he had ordered that no WPB position be filled with a dollar-a-year man "if with reasonable effort a man equally qualified can be found and induced to come here . . . on a regular government salary basis." But the "unfortunate fact" was that "you can't get all the help you need, of the kind you need, on that basis." Congress had recognized and responded to this when in "successive acts beginning in June, 1940" it had authorized (i.e., permitted) "the employment of dollar-a-year men in times of national emergency." The reason was "a very simple and practical one." The men needed "have, in the main, been receiving larger salaries [several times larger] than those payable to government personnel and they have, in many cases, incurred through the years extensive financial obligations, commensurate with their salaries, which make it extremely difficult for them to adjust to a much lower salary basis (life insurance, mortgages, etc.)." He added defensively that "substantially over 70 percent" of the three hundred or so dollar-a-year men now in Washington were "not the heads of companies, but operating men, plant superintendents, technical engineers, research experts, division managers, and the like." As a group, these men had "rendered hard and valuable service."[47]

Truman, who had pressed hard for the creation of the WPB and for Nelson's appointment to head it, did not find this persuasive. He may have doubted Nelson's seeming premise that *only* in the ranks of big business could be found people who understood the "intricate structure and operation" of American industry; he certainly doubted the validity of Nelson's conclusion. He had received just that morning, he said, "a letter . . . from a young man who [in private life] is getting $25,000 a year. He is a Reserve officer. He is going to get $140 a month. He is satisfied to do that because he wants to win the war. . . . I am laboring, and have been, under the delusion, maybe, that if the government has the power to take these young men away from their jobs and their outlook on life for the purpose of this emergency, the dollar-a-year men could face the same situation and face it adequately and would be glad to do it. However, if that is not the case, and their morale won't stand it—and you say it won't—we want to win the war. Therefore we are not going to hamper you in that effort and in your way of handling it."

Closely linked and simultaneous with this Nelson decision was his decision to continue unchanged the current military procurement system.

To knowledgeable and disinterested observers it appeared obvious that the army's handling of procurement had contributed greatly to—indeed, had been part and parcel of—the fumbling failures thus far of the industrial mobilization program, especially of the failure to mobilize the small businesses in whose hands then yet remained the greater portion of America's total industrial capacity. Throughout the procurement program as a whole there had been a blurring, even (often) an actual erasure, of the line of demarcation between government and business—a line that must be maintained in sharpest clarity in such programs if, within a profit system, true democracy and overall efficiency are to

be served. It was becoming a common practice to commission corporation executives as army officers and assign them to procurement duty. The effect was
to render one and the same, as regards private interest and general outlook, the
men who awarded defense contracts and the men who received them.

Recognition of this pernicious effect had aroused in most informed and disinterested observers a growing doubt that military procurement was properly a
function of the military. *Of course* supply requirements were shaped by strategical and tactical decisions that, save in the case of grand strategy, only the army
and navy could make. *Of course* the army and navy must determine as swiftly
and precisely as possible what industrial products, and how much of each, were
needed for victory in the battles they prepared to fight. *Of course* the army and
navy must also indicate as precisely as possible *when* these supplies would be
needed. But did this mean that the army and navy must have direct control over
the awarding of purchasing contracts, thereby determining who (which business
firms) produced what was needed? Would not democracy and national security
be better served if the actual procurement of war goods was exclusively in the
hands of a civilian agency—an agency that would, of course, cooperate closely
with the military in the drawing up of specifications and the choice of producers
but would have, as regards the producers, the final say? The conclusion was
widespread among Washington insiders that the answer to the first of these
questions was "No" and to the other "Yes," and that Donald Nelson had made
the same answer. The executive order under which he now operated said that the
WPB chairman "shall exercise general direction over the war procurement and
production program" and "determine the policies, plans, procedures, and methods of the several Federal departments, establishments, and agencies in respect
to war procurement and production, including purchasing, contracting, specifications, and construction; and including conversion, requisitioning, plant expansion, and the financing thereof; and issue such directives in respect thereto
as he may deem necessary or appropriate." It further said that "Federal departments, establishments, and agencies shall comply with the policies, plans,
methods, and procedures in respect to war procurement and production as determined by the Chairman." This was widely interpreted to mean that Nelson's
"powers over procurement and production are absolute" and that every "Federal department, establishment and agency must take orders from him," as a
lead article in *The New York Times Magazine* put it a few days after his appointment. The taking away from the War Department (in essence, the army)
into his own hands of all defense contracting authority was therefore expected
to be the very first thing Nelson would do in his new job.[48]

His refusal to do it was more shocking and disappointing to many a close observer than was his retention of dollar-a-year men.

It was grounded in practical considerations. According to Bruce Catton, Nelson estimated that setting up a new procurement agency would take at least

three months—and he was evidently convinced that war production would be totally disrupted during this setup period, for he said that America did not have three months to spare, or even three weeks, at a time when her enemies defeated her on every sea and battleground. He was evidently apprehensive that the War Department would protest strongly the removal from it of contracting authority, provoking a great row between himself and Stimson (with Marshall at Stimson's side)—a row that Roosevelt, despite having stressed to Nelson the necessity to retain civilian control of the economy, and despite having told Nelson to "write his own ticket" as regards the powers of the WPB administrator, might settle on the War Department's side of the issue. He might feel forced to do so.*

In *not* ridding himself of dollar-a-year men and *not* taking over procurement, he gave away or, rather, refused to grasp powers he absolutely had to have if WPB was to be effective either as war mobilizer of America's full industrial production potential or as insurer and protector of justice-as-fairness in the American economy. These powers remained in the hands of men whose true character he fatally misperceived, despite his lengthy experience of them. Being men for whom, as for Calvin Coolidge, America *was* business, they identified their passion for personal wealth, prestige, and power with a passionate love of country. Consequently their operations, from first to last, gave credence to the cynical observation† that, in the United States of America, the recipe for winning a war is "cost plus 8 percent."

VI

To assess Franklin Roosevelt's role at this crucial juncture in American economic history, and judge his resultant responsibility for the outcome, one must ponder the kind of "iffy" question he himself emphatically refused to answer in his press conferences. (He refused, not only because answering them might close out options he wished to keep open, but also, and more important, because doing so might expose to the light of day motivations, ways of decision making, and information [or ignorance] he wanted to hide from others; the thick veils of secrecy he so continuously, compulsively, defensively maintained around his essential self might be rent, revealing something of what we have so arduously attempted, in this long history, to discover and portray.) Suppose Nelson had

---

*The reader is reminded of Marshall's threat to resign his post if the Munitions Assignment Board were not subordinate to the Combined Chiefs of Staff Committee. There are fundamental differences, however, between military control over the allocation of munitions and military control over the issuance of production contracts. Marshall would have been unlikely to insist adamantly upon the latter.
†The author is perhaps inconsistent in calling this a "cynical" observation since he has not described Stimson as cynical yet has noted on an earlier page Stimson's diary observation (August 26, 1940): "If you are going to try to go to war, or to prepare for war, in a capitalistic country, you have got to let business make money out of the process or business won't work. . . ."

done what most well-informed observers expected him to do at this outset of his WPB chairmanship—had boldly grasped and fully exercised the sweeping power that, according to the executive order under which he operated, was his for the taking. He himself had drafted that order. Perhaps this caused him to doubt the validity of the immense authority it conferred upon his office, despite the fact that his draft followed Roosevelt's specific instruction that the WPB chairman be given "complete and absolute control over the production of all implements of war and over all related activities."[49] Certainly, as we have indicated, Nelson acted as if afraid his official authority, should he attempt to assert it in ways that provoked powerful opposition, would prove merely nominal for lack of a sufficient infusion of presidential power: attempt to use it as a coercive rod and it might prove a hollow brittle wand; attempt to use it as a gun and it might prove empty or loaded with blanks. But was this so? In the first place, would the reaction of the War Department to his truly decisive action, in this opening moment, have been as violently negative as he evidently anticipated? And even if it were, would Roosevelt have yielded to it? Available evidence suggests that the answer to both questions is "No" and that Nelson should have known it was "No."

We know that Stimson not only welcomed the replacement of OPM with the more powerful WPB, but also approved the choice of Nelson to head the WPB. "Having tinkered with boards and commissions for two years," he later wrote, Roosevelt had "finally" given "real power" over production to one man—a man who "had a good reputation," a man whom Stimson initially personally liked, and a man he was therefore glad to see possessed of "the priceless advantage of . . . genuine authority."[50] His later overall criticism of the appointment was essentially that Nelson in a job that called for "strong and able" leadership proved weak and wavering.

As regards cause and effect, there was similarity between the impending failure of Nelson's WPB and the actual ending of Thurman Arnold's anti-trust crusade in this winter and spring of 1942. Both efforts collapsed under wartime pressures. Both failures contributed to a fatal weakening of small business, of small units and human individualism in general, as determining factors in the American economy. Both were thus part and parcel of a historic process pointed toward an America whose whole economic, social, and cultural life were determined by the market interests of big business, hence an America in which technological capability of itself alone largely determined technological application. For the business executive was himself in bondage to market forces—he dare not refuse to employ a technology from the application of which a competing business firm would gain competitive advantage—and so became increasingly a mere function of the corporate machine he nominally controlled.

But as regards the key men involved, and Roosevelt's responsibility for outcome, the cases were very different.

Thurman Arnold was a far bolder, more decisive man than Donald Nelson.

Born and raised in Wyoming, as big a man physically as Nelson, he had much of the stereotypical "Western" personality—was hearty, flamboyant, energetic, assertively individualistic, naturally irreverent, and possessed of the openness and breeziness (some of his enemies dubbed it windiness) characteristic of a land of long views, immense skies, and meager rain. He had no such aversion to combat and controversy, no such reluctance to exercise coercive power, no such indifference to personal publicity, as Nelson manifested—had, on the contrary, an excessive fondness for battle and the limelight, in the opinion of critical observers. His keen and agile lawyer's mind was more firmly principled, more wide-ranging, more widely informed, more critically insightful, and much more incisively analytical than Nelson's. He was also more politically astute, if personally far less politic. He had none of Nelson's faith that wartime patriotism divorced from self-interest would outweigh the latter in the businessman's motivation, was consequently acutely aware, as Nelson seemed not to be, of the need to build constituencies in support of actions big business was bound to oppose. He was wiser than Nelson in the ways in which power concentrates and flows into action within corporate bureaucracies, governmental bureaucracies, and the federal legislature.

Arnold had entered upon his duties as head of Justice's anti-trust division in early 1938* with few illusions about the possibilities of his new assignment. Just a few months before, when a law professor at Yale, he had published a widely read, much discussed book, *The Folklore of Capitalism,* in which he argued with wit, eloquence, and factual evidence that the Sherman Act had done more to hinder than to help the war on *pernicious* oligopoly and monopoly.† It had served, he said, as a smoke screen of popular reassurance, even as a defensive wall against effective governmental regulation, behind which corporate giants pursued untrammeled their aim of market price control. But he now persuaded himself and others that the Sherman Act's harmful influence up to the present was due to the meagerness, hence the deceiving ineffectiveness, of attempts to enforce it. There had never been an adequate enforcement organization, he argued. He promptly set about creating one. He made budget requests several times larger than any this division had theretofore received and, with firm White House support, won their approval by Congress. Within two years the number of lawyers in the division was increased from forty-eight to more than three hundred, and the staff's average level of competence was much elevated.

He made efficient use of this staff. Through a case-by-case approach and a

---

*See *FDR: Into the Storm,* pp. 221–22, 235–36.

†The adjective "pernicious" is emphasized here because Arnold, no Brandeisian, deemed corporate giantism detrimental to the general welfare *only* to the extent that it raised consumer prices and thus reduced the mass consumption required to maintain mass production and full employment. He deemed possible (if unlikely) instances of oligopoly and monopoly that not only increased efficiency, but also passed on the gain, fully and fairly, in lowered consumer prices.

flexible mix of criminal indictments with consent decrees (if this was a species of blackmail, as was often charged, it proved effective of its purpose), Arnold and his colleagues had by the spring of 1942 scored more successes than their predecessors had scored in decades.

At the outset of his crusade, Arnold justified it as essential to the restoration of mass consumption, hence to an increased mass production that would reduce an unemployment figure yet hovering (stagnating) at around nine million. Monopoly and oligopoly drastically contracted production (hence employment) in order to maintain an artificially high price level and so prolonged the Depression, he argued in concert with Robert Jackson, Leon Henderson, Ben Cohen, and Harry Hopkins. As World War II began—an event promising a vastly expanded defense production, hence a drastic reduction in unemployment—an event certain to provoke loud cries from monopolistic business that anti-trust prosecutions militated against rapid industrial mobilization—he swiftly shifted gears. Anti-trust law, properly employed, was "one of the most effective means of speeding national defense" in what was an "industrial war," he now said. Big business through international cartelization had "slowed down production of basic war materials and given Hitler his flying start,"[51] he went on, citing cartel arrangements entered into by Standard Oil and Alcoa, arrangements that strengthened Nazi Germany and weakened the United States as regards synthetic rubber and aluminum supply, yet arrangements these corporations had stubbornly persisted in after the war had begun and America's survival as a free society clearly required an Allied victory. Rigorous enforcement of anti-trust law would have prevented these. Of course, the war crisis generated special requirements, political as well as economic, and these must be taken account of by those in charge of anti-trust activity. This Arnold readily granted. In the defense production field, he said, anti-trust activity must be determined by the "rule of reason," not by legalistic abstractions, and any industrial activity that the government's war agencies deemed essential to national defense was prima facie "reasonable." In his anti-trust division he established a special unit to which any industrialist could submit for possible prior approval war production plans that might otherwise, the industrialist feared, expose him to indictment under the Sherman Act. But, thus safeguarded, argued Arnold (in radio broadcasts, magazine articles, newspaper interviews), anti-trust activity must be expanded, not curtailed. For a time he argued successfully. Indeed, as late as May 1941 he was publicly confident that he retained, had even perhaps actually increased, the popular and administration support he needed.

But by then this optimism was unjustified.

And it had been made so in good part by Arnold's own act!

He liked to present himself to the public as a hard-boiled pragmatist whose practical view of the world had a species of cynicism at its heart, but Thurman Arnold was actually, in temperament and mentality, an idealist—and half a year before, as 1940 ended and 1941 began, his commitment to truth as consistency and justice as fairness had led him into what, in his circumstances, was a disastrous political error. In an immensely controversial and publicized action, he had proclaimed that labor unions were not wholly exempt, as they had previously been assumed to be, from criminal indictment under the Sherman Act;* they could in certain instances be criminally prosecuted. The chosen instance was a bitter dispute that had recently arisen in St. Louis between the carpenters union and the machinists union of the AFL. The carpenters union was headed by political reactionary W. H. ("Big Bill") Hutcheson, who, of all craft unionists, was the most violently opposed (literally so) to industrial unionism. The carpenters and machinists had in effect bid against each other for a contract with Anheuser-Busch to dismantle certain plant machinery in that company's huge brewery—a fact that seemed to Arnold proof that they operated in this specific case not as organizations defending workers against exploitation by employers, but as competing units of the marketplace. Such conclusion was bolstered in his mind when, the disputed contract having been awarded the machinists union, Hutcheson not only ordered picketing of Anheuser-Busch, but also launched a nationwide media campaign urging Americans not to buy Anheuser-Busch beer. This secondary boycott was clearly an act in restraint of trade, and Arnold, citing an abundance of precedents for doing so, asked the U.S. Supreme Court to declare it a violation of the Sherman Act. He was stunned when the Court ruled instead that he, in filing this suit, had exceeded his authority! The majority opinion in *United States* v. *Hutcheson,* announced on February 4, 1941, was written by Frankfurter and concurred in by all five of the other Roosevelt appointees then on the Court (only Chief Justice Hughes and Owen Roberts dissented)†—a fact that gave sharpened point to its assertion that the Norris–La Guardia Act was relevant to this case and, when considered along with the Sherman Act, rendered jurisdictional strikes and secondary boycotts legal when conducted by unions acting in their own interest without alliance or connivance with a non-labor organization. ("I never dreamed that the Norris–La Guardia Act would [could] be interpreted to take away the criminal remedy," wrote a disgusted, indignant Arnold to a longtime friend.)[52]

Of the episode as a whole, the effect was an abrupt removal of the theretofore strong labor support of Arnold's anti-trust crusade. Not only the AFL portion of organized labor, but also an overwhelming majority of the CIO membership turned solidly against him. To his astonishment and dismay, he was suddenly

---

*The Clayton Anti-trust Act of 1914, enacted in part to prevent use of the Sherman Act to crush labor unions, had specifically affirmed the right of workers to organize and, by asserting that "the labor of a human being is not a commodity or article of commerce," exempted labor unions from prosecution as "combinations in restraint of trade."

†There were then only eight justices; the vacancy caused by McReynolds's resignation a month before had not yet been filled and would not be until Byrnes's appointment in the summer of 1941.

cast by his former friends in the role of implacable labor baiter.* This had a very
serious erosive effect upon his liberal and White House support. Organized
labor was a major component of the "Roosevelt Coalition," whereby three successive presidential elections had been won; Roosevelt could not but eye
askance the disaffection of so important a voting bloc; and liberals in general,
pro-union in any case, were convinced that the fate of their cause was intertwined with that of the Roosevelt administration. Nor was this grave loss offset
by any increase in the small-business support that Arnold felt he had a right to
expect. As for big-business men, far from evincing gratitude to Arnold for what
they regarded as anti-union action on his part, they welcomed the weakening of
his official position and took prompt advantage of it to stiffen their resistance to
the whole of his anti-trust program. And since they controlled the key positions
in the federal defense establishment, their resistance was highly effective, constituting an immediate pressure far greater than that of the anti-trusters upon
Roosevelt's mind.

On this matter, Roosevelt already had a wavering and doubtful mind. As
early as the summer of 1940 there had been a manifest waning of the White
House's never overwhelming enthusiasm for Arnold's crusade. After strongly
backing Arnold's budget increase requests for 1939 and 1940, Roosevelt refused to back further increases for 1941 and 1942, though the increases were
needed to capitalize through court action upon the grand jury findings of the
earlier years—a capitalization that might have effected substantial liberating
changes in the American marketplace. He could handle only one war at a time,
Roosevelt told Arnold.[53] He seemed not to hear Arnold's reply that there was in
this case only one war, really, since the battle against monopoly, when conducted as the anti-trust division now conducted it, was part and parcel of the war
for democracy and against the Axis. He *did* listen closely and responsively to
War Department protests that Arnold's crusade was diverting from war production the valuable (invaluable?) time of top corporation executives. Why, exclaimed a War Department report to the President, the executive vice president
of one corporation with large defense contracts had had to devote no fewer than
124 of his days and 23 of his evenings to preparing a defense against anti-trust
prosecution! It was therefore an uneasy Arnold who persevered with his case
against Standard Oil whence emerged, as March gave way to April 1942, star-
tling public revelations of the extent to which that corporation's top executives,
in their eagerness for corporate profits, had subordinated loyalty to their country to loyalty to Nazi Germany's I. G. Farben.[54] They were, alas, the last such
revelations on his part. The protests of the War and Navy Departments (War especially) against the "harassment" of men crucially important to defense pro-

---

*He had publicly supported the Wagner Act of 1935 and the highly controversial sit-down strikes of
1937.

duction became a demand that it cease forthwith.* And Roosevelt complied with the demand. He authorized the announcement on April 4 that in the interests of national defense, further enforcement of the anti-trust laws was being selectively suspended. Arnold was forced to make a settlement with Standard Oil (a consent decree whereby the corporation released several patents and paid a paltry $50,000 fine) so utterly unsatisfactory that it amounted to a Justice Department capitulation.

The manner of this announcement occasioned some surprise among knowledgeable observers. It was made by Stimson and Knox instead of by Donald Nelson, who, as the "czar" of war production, should surely have made it. Why? Had the immensely broad grant of authority to Nelson been withdrawn from him just three months after being made? Were the chiefs of the service departments now actually in charge of war production, with Nelson and the WPB subordinate to them? A curious reporter asked these questions of a high WPB official. He was told the announcement was so made because of a popular perception that the WPB was dominated by big-business men. But the same dominion prevailed over the War Department, protested the reporter. It did, the official admitted candidly, but the public didn't know it![56]

Arnold would cling unhappily to his office for nine more months, resigning in February 1943 to become, upon Roosevelt's appointment of him, a judge of the First Circuit Court of Appeals.

And by then—incited and impelled by "cost plus 8 percent," by various lucrative tax breaks, by huge tangible gifts from the public treasury, and shaped and directed by national economic planning—there would be well under way that "miracle of production" (an American industrial output greater than the combined output of all other nations on earth) that has ever since been cited by all conservatives and many liberals as testimony to the "dynamism of American capitalism" and the "genius" of American business. As an argument for the economic efficiency of private profit as production motive in an advanced industrial society, such testimony is of limited persuasiveness. For one thing, though it fully acknowledges the potency of selfishness, it leaves wholly out of account the productive effect, impossible to measure in quantitative terms, of value-oriented spiritual energies—idealistic passions that are little operative in the marketplace, which is an environment hostile to them, but were of great importance to America's overall productive effort during World War II (if most big-business men paid slight heed to governmental appeals for a subordination of private interest to the general good, most Americans responded affirmatively to them). What the "miracle" did attest to, loudly and clearly, is the immense pro-

---

*Arnold, in the outraged view of Henry Stimson, was a "self-seeking fanatic" whose activities "frightened business . . . making a very great deterrent effect upon our munitions production."[55]

ductive power of the technology that scientists, inventors, and engineers have created. It is a power great enough to absorb much error, much stupidity, and still provide the community with a cushion against disaster. Who knows what production "miracle" would have been achieved if the nation's full industrial capacity had been mobilized (only a fraction of it was) and devoted in rationally planned ways to the national purpose under the direction of able people who were so committed to this purpose, as millions of ordinary citizens then were, that they required no bribes for their performance of duty?

VII

ANY clear-cut decision is psychologically rewarded by a surge of relief from the ache of suspense, the pangs of indecision, and the painful effort of deciding the amount of such reward being directly proportionate to the closeness (the difficulty) of the decision made. But though Franklin Roosevelt in these months of 1942 made an unwonted number of clear-cut decisions, many of them close, he was denied much enjoyment of the rewards for them, for so many decisions yet remained to be made! New situations, often unanticipated, were constantly arising. And often the decision he made created the immediate necessity for another, or others, equally difficult.

So it was with the decision that abolished OPM and created WPB. From it sprang the necessity to establish at once new machinery to deal with the labor problems that had been Sidney Hillman's concern as (at least nominally) OPM's co-director.

No longer was there a shortage of jobs in the nation as a whole. Eight percent of the total labor force had remained unemployed in the spring of 1940; less than 2 percent were unemployed in the spring of 1942;* indeed, the great labor problem for national defense had become the adequate supply of efficient workers. Some 2 million young men who would otherwise have entered the labor market were to go, by army decision, into the armed forces during 1942; at the same time, 10.5 million additional workers would be needed by expanding war industries. Yet the importance of labor as a factor in production had measured small in the decision making of those who had charge of national defense contracting. The prevailing geographical pattern of the labor supply; the need for special job training; the housing, transportation, and other living needs of workers; the role of worker morale—these had received scant attention despite Hillman's efforts to focus attention on them. The labor factor had been seriously considered only *after* the contract was signed. The result was labor chaos. In

---

*By September 1944 virtually total employment of the workforce would be achieved, with the ranks of the employed including millions of women who had theretofore never worked outside the home. A mere 0.8 percent of the employable would at that time remain unemployed.

some areas of the country there was an acute and growing labor shortage, with attendant housing, health, and morale problems; in others there remained large numbers of idle or only partially employed workers. There was agitation for a labor conscription equivalent to military conscription, as in the English defense system—a move that labor, of course, opposed as it also opposed (because it seemed to threaten compulsory service) the creation of a new and powerful war manpower agency. Secretary of Labor Perkins opposed it, too, on the ground that it would function in needless competition with existing machinery in her department. To Hillman, however, new machinery seemed clearly necessary, and when he was designated director of WPB's labor division, he moved at once to transform this all-too-subordinate division into the needed agency. For this, however, another specific grant of executive authority to WPB was required. Hillman talked about it with Roosevelt on January 27, 1942, and was led to believe that Roosevelt intended to act on the matter very soon and wanted Hillman to head whatever labor agency was established. Immediately thereafter, a conference he had with Nelson convinced him that Nelson, too, wanted him to assume the new responsibilities.

Nevertheless, next day, as a last act before leaving for a week's rest in Florida (his heart condition necessitated it), Hillman wrote two letters designed to incite confirming words and deeds by Nelson and by the White House. ". . . I want you to know how deeply I appreciate our talk of yesterday," said his two-sentence note to Roosevelt. "You know how fully you can count on my willingness and determination to help you in this grave emergency. . . ." For Nelson he prepared a draft letter, addressed to Roosevelt, to be signed by Nelson—a letter of which Nelson indicated his approval. It cited a number of acute labor problems and asserted, as Nelson's personal conviction, arrived at from long "experience in the industrial field," that "all such labor problems relating to war production must be concentrated in one place and in one individual. . . . I respectfully suggest . . . that full responsibility and authority for determining all such labor questions . . . shall be vested in Sidney Hillman."[57] But when Hillman returned to Washington he learned that Nelson had not sent this letter to the White House. He never would. He was reluctant to request more responsibilities for WPB than WPB already had, he told a meeting of the production board—which left as the only alternative the setting up of an independent manpower agency as part of the presidential Office of Emergency Management. This complicated the decision-making process, and no decision on the matter was forthcoming for more than two and a half months.

For Hillman this was a period of increasing anguish and frustration. He tried for another face-to-face meeting with Roosevelt. He prepared for it by writing for his own guidance a memorandum in which he pointed out that, though theretofore neither his "responsibility for labor policy in the defense effort" nor his right of direct access to the White House had been questioned, "the picture" was now drastically "changed." Nelson had "properly the full power and responsibility for production"; some one man should have equivalent "power and responsibility" for labor.[58] Hillman was never granted the interview, however; he was unable even to get through to Roosevelt on the telephone. Meanwhile, he was subjected to an unprecedentedly savage media attack from business leaders—an attack not offset by support from labor leaders, who resented the compromises he had felt forced to make, especially his foot-dragging approach to the establishment of labor-management committees in defense industries. The attack was echoed and amplified in Congress, notably by a Republican House member who in a vitriolic floor speech accused him of gaining special contract awards for uniform manufacture to companies favored by the Amalgamated Clothing Workers, the union he had founded and led. (The charge, radio-broadcast and elaborated upon by Fulton Lewis, Jr., was later proved by thorough War Department investigation to be utterly false.) Rumors of his imminent dismissal from government became rife. They gained persuasiveness over his tormented mind when he was not consulted by the special labor advisory committee to which Roosevelt had assigned the drafting of the decisive executive order, and from which also the President had asked for recommendations on the staffing of the new agency. This committee's composition was not such as to encourage any Hillman hope for preference. Impartial and dedicated Sam Rosenman and William O. Douglas were on it, but so were Anna Rosenberg and budget director Harold Smith. Mrs. Rosenberg, head of the New York office of the Federal Security Agency (FSA), was known to be partial to her handsome boss, FSA administrator Paul V. McNutt—rather strangely so, since she was an effective personality with strong liberal views and he a man of conservative views who, in general, was more ornamental than effective.

When Hillman learned on April 14 what the committee had recommended and what Roosevelt had decided to do, namely, establish a War Manpower Commission (WMC) with Paul McNutt as its head, he was literally heartbroken. He had committed himself personally, heart and soul, to Franklin Roosevelt; this abrupt dismissal of him, unexplained and (to him) inexplicable, was therefore a devastating blow. He collapsed under it in the afternoon of that day, suffering a severe heart attack; he was rushed into intensive care in Washington's Doctors Hospital.

The precarious state of Hillman's health was no doubt a factor in Roosevelt's decision. But it was not the determining factor. More important, Roosevelt feared the deleterious effect on war production that could come from the hostility to Hillman on the part of those now occupying key defense establishment positions. Certainly naming Hillman to headship of the WMC would have raised a storm of opposition from conservatives in and out of Congress, whereas McNutt's appointment, unenthusiastically acceptable to labor and liberals, would encounter no conservative opposition whatever. And Roosevelt, though he gave no sign of such anxiety even to his intimates, must have wondered as spring came on if his own health could stand up under much more weight of opposition than he was already bearing. (He had reason to wonder: what he called a "bad nose" was now an only somewhat less constant complaint than it had been a year before; at Hyde Park in early February he had been briefly bedded by a viral infection during which his temperature sank below normal, necessitating a rush trip from New York City to his bedside by physician Admiral McIntire; his high blood pressure had also become an increasing concern.) His continued functioning required his choice, whenever possible, of the easiest among the ways open to him—and this in turn required a suspension of empathy, or an infusion of it with a species of sadism, since the easiest way for him was often the hardest for others. He liked and admired Hillman more than he did most people; he appreciated Hillman's having rendered him great and self-sacrificial service; but these very facts would have made unusually difficult for him a face-to-face meeting in which he told Hillman what he had decided to do and why. Instead he waited until April 18, the day the organic executive order was formally signed but four days *after* the evening papers had announced the new commission and McNutt's headship of it, to send a lengthy placating telegram to the labor leader's hospital bed. In it he said he was appointing Hillman "special assistant to the President on labor matters," adding: "This will mean that your relationship to me in the government will be very similar to that of Harry Hopkins"—a promise so palpably false that it could not have been persuasive. Hillman waited two weeks before replying, saying then in a gracious letter that he felt he could be "of greater service to you if I return to the presidency of the Amalgamated Clothing Workers of America," a post from which "I can effectively influence the direction and activities of labor" in ways beneficial to the war effort.[59] After a six-week hospital stay, he left Washington, never to return to a government job.

With his departure, which AFL and CIO leaders had done much to facilitate, organized labor lost the only direct, high-level official influence it had had upon the government's conduct of the war. The loss was permanent. No one of equal stature ever replaced him. . . .

As for Roosevelt, as almost every problem's "solution" continued to give rise to other problems demanding solution, the WMC's establishment meant no lightening of home front burdens.

ITEM: The decision to suspend anti-trust law enforcement increased the need to offset some of the effects of the cartel arrangements—by Standard Oil, Alcoa, Du Pont, and other giant corporations—which a rigorous enforcement of anti-trust would have prevented. A minor offset was effected by Roosevelt's executive order that established, in March, an Office of Alien Property Custodian. Through it, the frozen assets of enemy belligerents were defrosted for full use by the United States in its prosecution of the war. Included in these assets was real property valued at half a billion dollars, plus forty-six thousand patents and inventions and nearly five hundred thousand copyrights, plus more than $70 million in such personal holdings as stocks, bonds, trusts, bank balances, and the like. Enemy interests in over four hundred businesses were seized, of which a hundred or so were permitted to continue operating under Custodian-approved management; they would produce by war's end $600 million worth of valuable war matériel (airplane parts, scientific instruments, photographic equipment, dyestuffs, chemicals, and the like).[60]

ITEM: The series of decisions giving big business effective control over war production required now decisions offsetting some of the effects of this upon other business—decisions aimed at a) mobilizing a sufficient amount of small business's productive capacity to satisfy war requirements; and b) giving the small-business man a sufficiently large serving of the war profit pie to prevent his developing a ravenous, politically disruptive appetite for more. Writes Sam Rosenman: "Shortly after Pearl Harbor it became apparent that small businesses and subcontractors were being excluded from full participation in the war program simply because they lacked sufficient finances or credit to proceed with war production. . . . Therefore a plan was devised which authorized the War and Navy Departments, and the United States Maritime Commission—the major purchasers of war matériel—to guarantee the loans and credits which banks extended to producers of war matériel." The carrying out of this plan was authorized by an executive order issued by Roosevelt a week after his order dealing with alien property, an order promptly implemented by a Federal Reserve Board regulation governing the handling of the loan guarantees by Federal Reserve Bank. Since the regulation happened to be numbered five and the Roman numeral for five is V, the loans were promptly dubbed "V-loans" (V for Victory).* This action subtracted nothing, of course, from the power and private profiteering of the big-business defense establishment, but it did facilitate subcontracting and even some degree of direct contracting by small business—enough of this to prevent politically effective wrath over the matter. By the end of 1942, a total of 2,700 guaranteed loans of $2.7 billion would be made in accordance with the executive order. Of these, "27 percent were for amounts up to $25,000 and 59 percent were for amounts up to $100,000," writes Rosenman, indicating they went to small businesses. By the end of 1945, 8,000 loans totaling $10 billion would be guaranteed, with less than 8 percent of the borrowers being businesses having more than $5 million in total assets.[61]

ITEM: An unfortunate coalition of executive decision and failure to decide

---

*Churchill had by this time made famous the "V gesture"—two fingers of an upright hand of which the other fingers were folded. Radio broadcasts of the news were commonly opened with the two opening phrases of Beethoven's Fifth (V) Symphony, wherein the three dots and a dash that stand for "V" in the Morse code are duplicated musically.

had given Jesse Jones the power to obstruct, in deference to "sound banking practice," the stockpiling of rubber. His Rubber Reserve Company, set up as subsidiary of the RFC he headed, had accumulated a mere 630,356 tons of rubber by December 1941 in a country accustomed to using more than 700,000 tons each year for automobile tires. Simultaneously, American big-business cartel arrangements had continued to prevent the development of U.S. synthetic-rubber-making capacity. At year's end, only a single synthetic-rubber plant with an annual production rate of 2,500 tons was operating in America. Nelson, when he took over as WPB chief, apprehended a rubber shortage of several hundred thousand tons by early summer and a complete exhaustion of the rubber supply within fifteen months, unless drastic corrective action was taken.* A single bold move in the indicated direction had been taken by Leon Henderson of OPA when he, in January, asserting a power he may not then have legally possessed, ordered a rationing of tires so severe that it amounted to a freeze; abruptly, the ordinary American found it virtually impossible legally to buy a new tire—a great shock to a nation of thirty million car owners who had not been mentally prepared for it. Nelson and Henderson then pressed for a severe rationing of gasoline, to limit driving and so conserve tires, but promptly encountered a frustrating lapse in Roosevelt's war-induced decisiveness.

Roosevelt was affected by the furor that tire rationing provoked; he took insufficient heed (as his liberal critics thought) of the good humor and spirit of cooperation that was generally characteristic of the initial popular reaction.[62] He evidently believed this good humor, this cooperative spirit, to be temporary— that it would not stand up for long against the predictable efforts of administration opponents to arouse popular fury over the matter and focus it on Leon Henderson (as surrogate for Roosevelt) personally. So, while precious weeks slipped by, he cast around for ways of attacking the problem less likely than Henderson's to encourage the election, come November, of a Congress overwhelmingly hostile to the practical legacy and every continuing active impulse of the New Deal. In March, he issued an appeal to state governors for a lowering of the automobile speed limit to a maximum of forty miles per hour: "a large part of our rubber stockpile is on the wheels" of American cars, he said, and the lowered speed limit would cause not only tires but cars to "last much longer" (it would also save thousands of lives that would otherwise be lost in highway accidents). In June, he placed his faith in a much ballyhooed scrap rubber drive, supported enthusiastically by petroleum administrator Ickes. It proved the mer-

---

*The developing rubber shortage "should have frightened us at the beginning of 1940," Nelson confesses on page 39 of his *Arsenal of Democracy*, "us" meaning himself and his colleagues in the defense production establishment. He goes on: ". . . [W]e simply could not obtain a sufficient supply of rubber . . . except through the development of a synthetic rubber industry, which no one had thought feasible in the past." In this case, "feasible" evidently means "as profitable as cartel arrangements" for America's giant petroleum and rubber (tire-making) industries.

est stopgap: much of the nearly half-million tons gathered was unsuited to military needs, and if all of it had been, it would not have come close to satisfying the overall need.

Finally, in midsummer, Congress forced the issue by passing an ill-considered, ill-drafted bill to promote the making of synthetic rubber out of "alcohol produced from agricultural or forest products [that is, butyl rubber, for which Standard Oil held patents]"—a bill more expressive of the American Farm Bureau Federation's desire for agricultural war profits than of deep commitment to the national interest in time of war. In utter disregard of the intricate interconnectedness of the various elements of war matériel supply, an interconnectedness requiring a centralized determination of priorities, the bill would have established a new independent agency, a Rubber Supply Division, whose exclusive mission was to "make available at the earliest possible time" a supply of rubber sufficient, "when added to the supply of rubber being supplied by other agencies, . . . to meet the military *and civilian* [emphasis added] needs of the United States"— also to "make available at the earliest possible time an adequate supply of alcohol produced from agricultural products to meet any military or civilian need for alcohol in the United States."[63]

By this, Roosevelt's lapsed decisiveness was abruptly renewed.

In a blistering veto message, sent to Congress on August 6, he not only detailed the disruptive effects the proposed law would have had upon the war effort, but also announced his appointment of a highly prestigious three-man committee—Harvard president James Conant, MIT president Karl T. Compton, and Bernard Baruch, with Baruch as chairman—to "investigate [with the aid of such technical staff as was needed] the whole situation . . . and . . . report to me as quickly as possible . . . their recommendations." He realized that the "question of rubber for automobiles" was of great importance because it "so intimately affects the daily lives and habits of so many American citizens," but he was sure (an assertion evidently made against a continuing uncertainty) that "once they are given the full facts as to the supply of rubber and the military and essential civilian needs for rubber, and the amount of materials required for the production of an adequate supply of synthetic rubber," the American people "will be wholly willing to forgo their own convenience or pleasure."[64]

Clearly he expected the committee to recommend tough action.

And so it did (as we may here run yet further ahead of our story to say) just five weeks later.

On September 10 the committee proposed an eight-point program that included nationwide gasoline rationing, nationwide speed limit reduction (to thirty-five miles an hour), and a maximum possible reliance upon tire recapping—also the removal of all patent restrictions on the dissemination of technical information regarding synthetic rubber production; appointment by the WPB chairman of a rubber administrator having complete authority over all matters relating to rubber; concentration upon the construction of synthetic rubber plants, with un-interrupted flow of the needed materials; and a raising of the WPB's present production goal of 705,000 tons by the end of 1943 to 845,000 tons. A week later, by executive order, Roosevelt established the office of rubber director. To it, WPB chairman Nelson appointed William M. Jeffers, president of the Union Pacific Railroad—a hard-driving administrator who promptly ordered the carrying out of each and every one of the committee's recommendations. By 1945, the United States would be able to produce annually almost as much synthetic rubber as the whole world had produced of crude rubber in any year before the war. . . .[65]

But Roosevelt's predominant home front concern, all through the season of disasters for American arms abroad, was price inflation and its closely related problem of taxation.

In his January 1941 budget message, he had urged the adoption of a pay-as-you-go policy of war finance to as full an extent as possible. Raising progressive income tax rates sufficiently to achieve this would have an anti-inflationary effect, certainly. Moreover, properly applied, especially to corporate income, it would promote economic justice. He had said in his January 1942 budget message: "The privileged treatment given certain types of business in corporate income taxation should be reexamined. . . . The fact that a corporation had large profits before the defense program started is no reason to exempt them now."* But he had also said in his 1941 message that ordinary forms of taxation, however fairly and rigorously applied, might not of themselves alone suffice—that extraordinary forms of taxation might be required to curb inflation when "full [productive] capacity is approached" and increased purchasing power encountered in the marketplace a sharply decreased supply of consumer goods. Now the "time for such measures has come," he announced in his January 1942 budget message, going on to list several kinds of special taxes that might be employed. Among these were excise taxes. He had firmly opposed them during the Depression; he remained convinced "that they have no permanent place in the Federal tax system"; but he now conceded that use of them on a "temporary" basis might be indicated. He favored an increase in the payroll taxes that financed Social Security because doing so "would result in reserves of several billion dollars for postwar contingencies," would "absorb excess purchasing power," and, since the increased reserves would by law be invested in U.S. government bonds, "would assist in financing the war." But, he insisted, "the worker" whose payroll taxes were increased *must* be "given his full money's worth in increased social security"—to which end he recommended "an increase in the coverage of old-age and survivors' insurance, addition of per-

*See pp. 18–20.

manent and temporary payments beyond the present benefit programs, and li-
bralization and expansion of unemployment compensation in a uniform national system."[66]

A few weeks later, on January 30, 1942, he signed into law an Emergency
Price Control bill that had been introduced in Congress, at his instigation, in August 1941. The original bill had been heavily revised as the price of its passage
through the House, where its victory margin was only twenty-five votes, and in
consequence of this revision Roosevelt's approval of it was by no means whole-
hearted. "All in all," he said in faint praise, the new legislation was "workable."
It provided OPA with much needed additional authority. The price administrator (Henderson would be so designated officially under the act in early February
1942) would be able "to establish maximum prices and rents over a broad field,
to prohibit related speculative and manipulative practices, and to buy and sell
commodities in order to obtain the maximum production," as Roosevelt's signing statement said. He would also be armed with effective instruments of enforcement. Roosevelt had grave "doubts as to the wisdom and adequacy" of
those sections of the act dealing with farm prices. Here, again, the influence of
the agribusinessmen who dominated the national Farm Bureau and also, increasingly, the Department of Agriculture* was evident. As the bill made its tor-
tuous way through legislative halls, these men, joined by the leaders of less
powerful farm organizations, had tried hard to remove from it every portion giving the price administrator any control whatever over farm prices. Failing this,
they had managed to force through an amendment saying that no maximum
price could be fixed upon any agricultural commodity without the prior approval of the secretary of agriculture. Worse still, the amendment denied the
price administrator any power to fix a maximum price for any agricultural commodity at all until that commodity's price on the market had reached 110 percent of parity;† or that of October 1, 1941; or that of December 15, 1941; or
the average price for the period between July 1, 1919, and June 30, 1920—
whichever was highest. This complicated provision, Roosevelt told his press
conference on the day he signed the bill, was "a very definite violation" of the
principle agricultural leaders had subscribed to in 1933 and "a threat to the cost
of living."[67]

Soon thereafter he appointed a special committee, chaired by Vice President
Wallace, to study and make recommendations regarding taxes. In March 1942,
this committee recommended increases in ordinary taxes that would bring $11.6
billion into the federal Treasury, plus a $2 billion increase of Social Security
taxes that the federal government could and would borrow for war finance. The

---

*The story of why and how this had happened is told in *FDR: The New Deal Years*, pp. 269–74.
†"Parity" was defined in the original AAA legislation as the ratio of farm to industrial prices that had
prevailed in 1909–1914.

recommendations went to the Treasury Department for the information and guidance of those who were then drafting, with great difficulty and much disagreement among themselves, the administration's tax bill. On April 7, a Roosevelt executive order removed an anomaly from the bureaucratic structure, through which price control was exercised, by authorizing the WPB chairman to delegate specifically to the price administrator his powers and authority over priorities and rationing, including such enforcement powers as the issuance of subpoenas and the institution of civil proceedings against price control violators. Nelson promptly made this delegation.[68]

And now the moment had come, said Roosevelt's sense of timing, when presidential leadership against the inflation enemy must be exerted to the fullest possible extent. He began preparation of a special message to Congress, to be delivered on April 27, summarizing the administration's anti-inflationary policy and calling for legislative action upon it with forceful eloquence. This message was to be followed, on the evening of April 28, by a fireside chat wherein his economic program was restated, amid a survey of the current state of the war, in a way that enlisted popular support of this program.

VIII

ON Saturday, April 18, Roosevelt was in his tiny study at Hyde Park, working with Rosenman and Grace Tully on the first draft of the fireside chat, when an urgent phone call from Washington interrupted his labor. As he took it, a delighted smile spread across his broad face. It remained there when, having replaced the receiver, he reported what he had heard to Grace and Sam: An intercepted Japanese radio broadcast had just reported in a tone of near hysteria that American planes were bombing Tokyo!

And, added Roosevelt, the report was true!

But how was this possible? The Japanese had tight control of every sea approach to their homeland; no enemy aircraft carrier could come close enough to Tokyo to launch a navy bomber attack with any hope of receiving the attacking planes back again. The attackers, therefore, had to be long-range army bombers—and the distance between Japan and the nearest Allied air base, in China, was much greater than any bomber could cover round trip! Soon other Washington calls to Roosevelt came in: Osaka, Kobe, and Nagoya had also been bombed; the President was advised to be prepared with some kind of answer to the question of where the bombers had come from, for reporters were bound to press the question upon him.

When Roosevelt mentioned this last to his two companions during a teatime break in the afternoon's work, Rosenman made a suggestion: Why not say the planes came from Shangri-la, the wondrous Himalayan valley where, in James Hilton's *Lost Horizon,* time was greatly slowed? This would amusingly indicate that the takeoff place was secret and would remain so. Roosevelt promptly had Hackie put in a call to Steve Early: If anyone asked him where the attacking flight had come from, he told Steve, he was going to say "Shangri-la."[69]

To him, the news came not as a surprise, but as the hoped-for culmination of a project he himself had proposed only a few days after Pearl Harbor. He had then told Army Air Force General "Hap" Arnold that to counterbalance the morale effects of the Japanese surprise attack, he longed for an air raid upon Japan proper; he asked Arnold to check into the feasibility of this. Sometime later, after the rapid Japanese advance southward and westward had destroyed the possibility of her being air-attacked from a land base, Roosevelt in conversation with Admiral King wondered if long-range army bombers might fly off an aircraft carrier. King had promptly taken up the question with Arnold. Careful studies led to the conclusion that the suggested operation was possible, if barely so; that it should be mounted; and that Lieutenant Colonel (later Lieutenant General) James H. Doolittle, famed as aviator and aeronautical engineer, would command it.[70]

All was going according to plan in the Far Pacific early in the morning of April 18. Having sailed from the American West Coast with sixteen B-25s lashed to her decks (she could not accommodate the originally intended twenty), the newly completed aircraft carrier *Hornet* had rendezvoused on April 13 with Vice Admiral William F. Halsey's Task Force 16 some dozen miles north of Midway Island, which, as the westernmost island of the Hawaiian chain, is some 1,100 miles from Honolulu. The task force, which included the aircraft carrier *Enterprise,* four cruisers, and several destroyers, had then sailed uneventfully westward through heavy seas to a point 650 miles from Tokyo. There, however, the *Enterprise*'s radar screen descried Japanese picket vessels patrolling much farther out from the Japanese shore than the Americans had expected. This meant loss of the vital element of surprise and grave risk to Task Force 16 if the original plan were adhered to; Doolittle and Halsey had to decide on the instant whether to abort the mission or launch the attack hours sooner and nearly two hundred miles farther from the targets than had been contemplated. Doolittle insisted upon the launch. Weather conditions were decidedly unfavorable. A forty-knot gale splashed huge waves over the *Hornet*'s bow and rendered her flight deck slippery. Nevertheless, every one of the sixteen planes, Doolittle's in the lead, managed to get off safely. All save one of them unloaded their bombs and incendiaries upon designated targets several hours later. None of them, however, because of the early launching, was able to reach the landing field in China designated in the plan, and all had to end their flights in the darkness of night instead of, as planned, early morning light. Most of the planes' crews managed to parachute safely onto friendly Chinese soil. One plane landed near Vladivostok, where its crew was interned by the Russians. Two were forced down in Japanese territory, one of these in a crash landing in which two of its crew were drowned. (Eight members of these two crews became captives of the Japanese, who would execute three of them and place the others in prison camps, where one of them would die and the other four would remain prisoners until war's end.) Amazingly, of the eighty men who took part in this seemingly suicidal mission, seventy-one would survive.

Measured solely in tangible terms, the enterprise was a trivial incident. The physical damage done the enemy, and the effect upon enemy morale, were alike negligible; the Japanese public was easily persuaded that the episode was only a stunt, daring but of no real significance. Thanks to two of its consequences, however, the event had the importance of a major Allied victory. One of these consequences was an enormous uplifting of American hearts and minds that had been drooping under the weight of bad news from the Far Pacific. The other and more important was a major change in Japanese war strategy.

At the moment of the raid, a highly charged controversy over general war strategy was raging in Tokyo between top officers of the Japanese naval general staff and top officers of the Japanese combined fleet. The general staff wanted to concentrate upon operations to the south, as was originally planned, consolidating positions already gained and winning new ones from which attacks upon Australia and its sea communications with the United States could be launched. But the officers of the combined fleet, led by Admiral Yamamoto, asserted that, events having so far outrun the timetable set for them in the original plan (no one in Tokyo had expected the swift ease of Japan's early conquests), this plan should be drastically revised: a move should be made to force a general fleet engagement wherein the U.S. Pacific Fleet must fight at a great numerical disadvantage and the remaining American aircraft carriers would be eliminated. The Americans would then be unable to oppose effectively anything Japan wanted to do in the Far Pacific for a year or more, by which time the overall Japanese position in Southeast Asia and the South Pacific would be so solidified as to be almost impregnable. Yamamoto was convinced that Midway, the "keyhole" (as the Japanese dubbed it) in Japan's Pacific defense perimeter and a vital outpost of Hawaiian and American West Coast defenses, was a strategic point for which the U.S. Fleet would feel compelled to fight. He proposed, therefore, an all-out attack on Midway—and the Doolittle raid, which could have come only through the "keyhole," and which presaged more formidable attacks, caused the general staff to acquiesce reluctantly in the Yamamoto proposal. Japanese preparations for a major strike at Midway began immediately and, to precede this, an earlier date than had been originally planned was set for operations in the Coral Sea aimed at securing for Japan Guadalcanal in the Solomons and Port Moresby on New Guinea. . . .[71]

Roosevelt himself, correctly assessing the popular reaction to the raid, was inspired to adopt a tougher tone, both in the fireside chat he was preparing that weekend and in the congressional message that was already substantially prepared but was now revised. Tone was all that was toughened, however. The President's legislative proposals remained broad and vague.

He presented his proposals to Congress on April 27, as a seven-point "economic stabilization program." Each of the points, in his statement of it, was preceded by the phrase "to keep the cost of living from spiralling upward." They were: 1) heavy taxation to "keep personal and corporate profits at a reasonable rate, the word 'reasonable' being defined at a low level"; 2) price ceilings, including "ceilings on rents for dwellings in all areas affected by war industries"; 3) wage controls ("we must stabilize the remuneration received by individuals for their work"); 4) stabilization of "prices received by growers for the products of their lands"; 5) increased purchase of war bonds by "all citizens" to prevent their using war-increased earnings "to buy articles which are not essential"; 6) strict rationing "of all essential commodities of which there is a scarcity"; 7) discouragement of credit and installment buying joined with encouragement of "the paying off of debts, mortgages, and other obligations." Five of these points were adequately covered by existing legislation, he told Congress, but two called for prompt congressional action. One of the two (point four) required revision of the Emergency Price Control Act to prevent that portion of it dealing with agricultural commodity prices from opening the way to an intolerable rise in the cost of living, especially in the cost of food. (Actually the rate of living cost increase was already intolerable: since Pearl Harbor Day, the cost of food had risen nearly 5 percent, the cost of clothing nearly 8 percent, and labor was demanding wage increases that at least matched the price rises, generating pressures that the War Labor Board [WLB], lacking a clear and definite national wage policy and so forced to deal with the wage issue on a case-by-case basis, found often impossible to resist. The threat of runaway inflation was immediate.) The other, closely related point was the one first named, heavy taxation. The government was currently spending "solely for war purposes" approximately *$100 million a day!* By the end of the year the rate of expenditure would double this! Hence, to finance the war and discourage national income maldistribution, "[p]rofits must be taxed to the utmost limit consistent with continued production. This means all business profits—not only in the making of munitions, but in the making or selling of anything else." Congress must clearly and accurately "define undue or excess profits" and see to it that all profits so defined went "to the Government" through taxation. Moreover, the present wide gap "between low personal incomes and very high personal incomes"—a gap in which bred dangerous social discontents—must be reduced. "I . . . believe that in this time of grave national danger . . . *no American citizen ought to have a net income, after he has paid his taxes, of more than $25,000 a year.*" "It is indefensible," he continued, "that those who enjoy large incomes from State and local securities should be immune from taxation while we are at war." At the very least, "the interest on such securities should be subject . . . to surtaxes."[72]

On the following night (April 28, 1942), Roosevelt presented his seven-point program directly to the people in a fireside chat that, judging from its popular reception, would have been as uplifting of the national morale as his February chat had been if that morale had been as much in need of uplift in late April as it had been two months before. Yet its central formal theme, judged in the abstract by "practical" folk, must have seemed the very opposite of morale boosting. This theme was the need for personal sacrifice in service of the national need ("[t]he price of civilization must be paid in hard work and sorrow and blood")—though Roosevelt insisted, as he had to Congress the day before, that " 'sacrifice' is not exactly the proper word to describe this program of self-denial"; when at war's end "we shall have saved our free way of life, we shall have made no 'sacrifice.' " Admittedly, "every single person in the United States is going to be affected by" the program he had announced—and in that portion of his speech addressed specifically to businessmen and corporate stock owners, he reiterated his conviction that "in these days when every available dollar should go into the war effort," no personal income should exceed "$25,000 per year after payment of taxes."* He went on: "Ask the workers of France and Norway and the Netherlands, whipped to labor by the lash, whether the stabilization of wages is too great a 'sacrifice.' Ask the farmers of Poland and Denmark, of Czechoslovakia and France, looted of their livestock, starving while their own crops are stolen from their land, ask them whether 'parity' prices are too great a 'sacrifice.' Ask the businessmen of Europe, whose enterprises have been stolen from their owners, whether the limitation of profits and personal incomes is too great a 'sacrifice.' Ask the women and children whom Hitler is starving whether the rationing of tires and gasoline and sugar is too great a 'sacrifice.' "73

But the forcefulness with which all this was stated did not hide from politically sophisticated eyes and ears the fact that the presented program was deficient in specifics. Left wide open were doors of escape for those congressmen who, facing reelection battles a few months hence, feared the constituent wrath that could be provoked by congressional acts truly effective of inflation control. Consequently there would be dawdling on this issue on Capitol Hill until an equally forceful statement of it, but one accompanied by more precise definitions of the necessary legislative action, was made by the White House some months hence. Even then, as we shall see, the legislative action, as regards both taxation and farm price (food cost) control, would fall far short of the goals Roosevelt had set. . . .

IX

THE opening portion of Roosevelt's April 28 fireside chat was a swift survey of the current worldwide war situation, which had imbedded in it an important statement of war policy. It was aimed at Vichy France, where Pétain had just

---

*These last words, italicized in the popular mind, shocked and provoked angry outrage in many of the wealthy, though public expression of this shock and outrage was prudently muted.

dismissed the passionately anti-British Admiral Darlan as head of government, replacing him with oily, fervently pro-Nazi Pierre Laval. Laval was determined to make France an integral part of Hitler's Europe. His elevation compelled Roosevelt to admit tacitly, though he would never explicitly confess, grave doubts about his Vichy policy, a policy having as concomitant an official coldness, if not an actual hostility, toward de Gaulle and the Free French.* Laval's elevation also rendered acute certain anxieties that, since Singapore's fall, had been felt increasingly in London and Washington. They concerned Madagascar, which was a French colonial possession. The huge island, some five hundred miles off the east coast of southern Africa, was separated from India by thousands of miles of Indian Ocean yet was intimately involved in the Allied defense of the latter; for at its northern end were the town and fine harbor of Diégo-Suarez, which the Japanese, who contemplated an early descent upon Ceylon, were eager to possess. From Diégo-Suarez their surface war vessels and submarines could sally forth to wreak havoc upon Allied shipping that was vital to the reinforcement and supply of India (also of the Middle East and North Africa, for Axis control of the Mediterranean air compelled the sea supply route to these places from England to run all the way round the Cape of Good Hope). In other words, Madagascar was strategically as important in terms of Japan's designs upon India as French Indo-China had been in terms of her designs upon Malaya and the Netherlands East Indies—and Allied leaders were now vividly reminded that Vichy France, under a leadership less pro-Axis than Pierre Laval's was certain to be, had handed Indo-China over to Japan, upon the latter's demand for it, with little more than a murmured protest. Hence Roosevelt's war policy statement. "Throughout the Nazi occupation of France," he said, "we have hoped for the maintenance of a French Government which would strive to regain independence . . . and to restore the historic culture of France. . . . However, we are now greatly concerned lest those who have recently come to power may seek to force the brave French people into submission to Nazi despotism." Whereupon he bluntly warned these newly empowered that the "United Nations will take measures . . . to prevent the use of French territory in any part of the world for military purposes by the Axis powers." He was sure "the good people of France" would not only "understand that such action is essential for the United Nations to prevent assistance to the armies or navies or air forces of Germany, or Italy or Japan," but would also approve it. For the "overwhelming majority" of the French realized "that the fight of the United Nations is fundamentally their fight, that our victory means the restoration of a free and independent France. . . ."[74]

---

*A few days later, Roosevelt summoned home his Vichy ambassador, Leahy, who in Washington continued to insist that de Gaulle had no substantial following in metropolitan France or North Africa. Roosevelt, antipathetic to all he had read or heard of the de Gaulle personality, continued to accept as accurate the Leahy assessment.

Ever since Pearl Harbor, and especially after Singapore's fall, India and its defense had been a growing concern of Roosevelt's—and it was, for him, an unusually principled concern. A convinced anti-colonialist, he opposed imperialism on moral grounds. He fully shared the predominant American view that Britain had no right to rule and exploit the nearly four hundred million Indian people, whereas Gandhi and Nehru, with their National Congress Party, had every right to struggle for Indian independence. He was perhaps less admiring than many Americans of the way the saintly Gandhi waged this struggle—the way of nonviolence, of passive resistance, adopted from Thoreau's essay on civil disobedience. Certainly he was utterly opposed to Gandhi's extreme pacifism, being convinced of its practical ineffectiveness when employed against enemies who, unlike the British, lacked conscience and compassion. He was greatly alarmed by Gandhi's proposal of nonresistance to the Japanese, should they invade India, and was proportionately relieved when Nehru, on this issue, parted company with his great mentor, leader, and friend. Gandhi believed that the Japanese would not invade a free and independent India—that the incentive for such invasion would be removed with the removal of the British, provided free India declared itself a neutral nation—but was adamantly opposed to armed resistance in any case. The fervently democratic, fervently anti-totalitarian Nehru, on the other hand, while pressing for immediate Indian independence, favored armed resistance to the Japanese in any case. Roosevelt agreed with Gandhi and Nehru that British policy ought to aim at complete Indian independence at the earliest possible moment; he was convinced that a long stride toward this end should be taken *now,* as a war policy measure, since doing so, he was encouraged by Nehru's stand to believe, would assure a fuller active participation by the Indians in the Allied war effort. He had indicated as much in one of his private talks with Churchill during the Arcadia Conference, provoking a storm of Churchillian wrath. The empire-worshiping Prime Minister had made crystal clear his view that the Indian problem, which was immensely more complicated than holier-than-thou Americans realized, was none of America's business. "I reacted so strongly and at such length that he [Roosevelt] never raised it [the Indian question] verbally again," writes Churchill in his war memoirs.[75] And it was not only his emotional commitment to the British empire that sparked Churchill's angry impatience with Roosevelt on this matter: the Indian problem was indeed more complicated than the President realized.

The huge land's government was itself unusually complicated, being divided between two major administrative areas. British India, comprising 865,000 square miles with a population of nearly 300 million, was governed directly by Great Britain; the native states, comprising 716,000 square miles and over 93 million people, were governed indirectly by Britain through treaty arrangements with Indian princes. Further complications arose from the fact that the teeming millions were multilingual; they spoke (very few of them could read or write) dozens of different languages, though nearly three-fourths spoke Hindustani or Bengali or some other Indo-European language. The most serious complication, however, derived from the fact that the Indians were a profoundly religious people, far more prone to religious fervors and frenzies than most—and since they differed among themselves in their religious inspirations, and since their passionate religiosity was part and parcel of their politics, religion was in India more hostile than it commonly is to rational, humane, democratic procedures.* The most important religious difference was between Hindus and Muslims, the Hindus politically organized under the Congress Party, the Muslims under the Muslim League. The Hindus were by far the larger group: of the subcontinent's 389 million people, 255 million were Hindus. But some 92 million others were Muslims, largely concentrated in the northwest and in Bengal and Bombay, though there were scattered pockets of them elsewhere. (Of the remaining population, 18 million followed tribal faiths, 6 million were Christians, and 1 million were Buddhists.) There was a widespread American suspicion, shared in some degree by Roosevelt, that the British, having been helped by Hindu-Muslim hostility to conquer India, continued cynically to encourage it in order to justify the continuance of their ruling power. Certain it is that Indian Muslims had for generations been persuaded that only the British government stood between them and their general massacre by Hindus; they were terrified by the prospect of an independent India of which the Hindus were the ruling majority; and this terror was currently played upon and intensified by a fanatical Muslim leader named Mohammed Ali Jinnah. He and his followers passionately preferred British rule to "a Hindu all-Indian Government." If the British moved out, Jinnah insisted, there must be partition. Pakistan in the northwest and perhaps Bengal in the northeast, each an area where Muslims were in a majority, must be detached from a Congress-ruled India and made an independent state to which all other Muslims could migrate. (What would happen to the considerable Hindu minorities in these areas was none of his concern; presumably they must emigrate or die.) It was in part to appease Jinnah that the British, in a formal declaration on August 8, 1940, had promised the Muslims that, in Jinnah's words, "no constitutional change in India, interim or final, would be made without Muslim agreement."[76]

    Churchill, during the weeks following Arcadia, was scrupulous in keeping the President informed of Indian developments as they occurred, taking care, however, to present the Muslim side of the question (the "Americans were familiar [only] with the Hindu attitude") in a way supportive of his argument that granting India her independence now, or even promising to do so after the war, would have an effect precisely opposite what Roosevelt envisaged: instead of increasing Indian participation in the war effort, it would reduce and possibly

*Churchill, of course, in his correspondence with Roosevelt, expressed no such generalized value judgment as is here made.

eliminate it. Roosevelt remained unpersuaded. And if he never again raised the Indian question face-to-face with the Prime Minister, he did so twice within two months after Arcadia's close—once through an intermediary, once through a personal written message.

On February 26, he asked lend-lease administrator Averell Harriman, in London,* to inquire of the Prime Minister what His Majesty's government proposed to do immediately toward a settlement with Indian political leaders. Harriman, who would remember this "as one of the most difficult assignments he handled for Roosevelt," was warned to raise the question informally and with great delicacy, "since it isn't, strictly speaking, our business." Harriman did so that very night, endured a brutally frank expression of Churchill's resentment over being so prodded, and reported back to Roosevelt within hours thereafter: "The Prime Minister will not take any political steps which would alienate the Moslem population of over [*sic*] 100 million. About 75 percent of the Indian troops and volunteers are Moslems. Of the balance less than half, or perhaps 12 percent of the total, are in sympathy with the Congress group. The fighting people of India are from the northern provinces largely antagonistic to the Congress movement. The big populations of the low-lying provinces of the center and the south have not the vigor to fight anybody." A few days later (March 4, 1942), Churchill wrote Roosevelt, "We are earnestly considering whether a declaration of Dominion status [for India] after the war, carrying with it, if desired, the right to secede, should be made at this critical juncture." He went on to indicate his own feeling that it should not be, not only because of the Muslims and their contribution of fighting men, but also because of "our duty towards thirty to forty million Untouchables, and our treaties with the Princes' states of India, perhaps eighty millions. Naturally, we do not want to throw India into chaos on the eve of invasion."[77]

Six days later (March 10, 1942), Roosevelt addressed to the Former Naval Person a personal "suggestion" that, he said, was the fruit of "much thought" about "the problem of India." This was "a subject which of course you good people know far more about than I do," but he believed and hoped that "the injection of a new thought . . . might be of assistance to you." His "new thought" derived from the way thirteen sovereign American states, in the years immediately following the American Revolution, managed to make themselves into a federal union, a single national government. They did not do so at once, in one giant step. Instead they formed, under loose Articles of Confederation, "an obvious stop-gap government, to remain in effect only until such time as experience of trial and error would bring about a permanent union." Might not something of the same sort work in India? "It is merely a thought of mine to

---

*Ambassador Winant was en route to Washington for consultations, though Roosevelt would probably have entrusted Harriman with this diplomatic mission even if Winant had been available for it.

suggest the setting up of what might be called a temporary Government of India, headed by a small representative group, covering different castes, occupations, religions and geographies—this group to be recognized as a temporary Dominion Government. It would, of course, represent existing governments of the British Provinces and would also represent the Council of Princes. But my principal thought is that it would be charged with setting up a body to consider a more permanent government for the whole country—this consideration to be extended over a period of five or six years or at least until a year after the end of the war. I suppose this central temporary governing group, speaking for the new Dominion, would have certain executive and administrative powers over public services, such as finances, railways, telegraphs and other things. . . . Such a move is strictly in line with the world changes of the past half century and with the democratic processes of all who are fighting Nazism. I hope that whatever you do the move will be made from London and that there should be no criticism in India that it is being made grudgingly or by compulsion."[78]

To this, Churchill made, at the time, no known reply. But that his immediate reaction to it was one of mingled amazement, anger, and disgust is indicated in his war memoirs, wherein he quotes Roosevelt's message in its entirety. ("This document," he comments incoherently and confusedly, as if yet furious, ". . . illustrates the difficulties ['absurdity' was probably the word first used] of comparing situations in various centuries and scenes where almost every material fact is totally different, and the dangers of trying to apply any superficial resemblances which may be noticed to the conduct of war.")[79] By the time he received Roosevelt's message, he had concurred in a war cabinet decision not to publish at that moment any declaration of government policy regarding India but instead to send from London to Delhi an emissary who would present to Indian leaders face-to-face, and attempt to obtain their acceptance of, the policy the cabinet members had agreed upon. The essence of this agreed policy was a solemn promise to grant full independence to India after the war should such be then demanded by an Indian "Constituent Assembly." If this policy commitment were "rejected by the Indian parties, for whose benefit it has been devised," wrote Churchill to the Viceroy of India, "our sincerity will be proved to the world, and we shall stand together and fight on it, should that ever be necessary."[80]

The chosen emissary (actually he volunteered for the job) was the former British ambassador to Russia, Sir Stafford Cripps, the Socialist Labour Party leader who had long been on personally friendly terms with Gandhi and Nehru and was now, as Lord Privy Seal, a member of the war cabinet. (Despite the profound "differences" between Cripps's politics and his own, said the Prime Minister in his letter to the Tory Viceroy, "I have entire confidence in his overriding resolve to beat Hitler and Co. at all costs.") Cripps arrived in Delhi on March 22 and at once entered into negotiations, not with any such all-representative body as Roosevelt had seemed with his faulty analogy to suggest, but exclusively with the leadership of the Congress Party. And this leadership could not agree with what he proposed. It called instead for the immediate establishment of an Indian national government, which, to quote from the Congress president's letter to Cripps on April 11, "would function as a free Government whose members would act as members of a Cabinet in a constitutional Government." The Congress leaders were willing to leave control of fighting the war in the hands of the British commander in chief in India, cabled Cripps to Churchill on that same April 11, but "left functions of Defense Member unduly restricted." They saw little if any essential difference between this present proposal and earlier ones and concluded, as the Congress president's letter said, that the "whole object which we have in view—that is, to create a new psychological approach to the people to make them feel that their own national freedom had come, that they were defending their new-won freedom—would be completely frustrated when they saw this old picture again, which is such that Congress cannot fit into it." A weary Cripps interpreted this as a flat and final rejection of what he had proposed. "There is clearly no hope for agreement," he told Churchill, "and I shall start home on Sunday [April 12]."[81]

Churchill says in his war memoirs that he "was able to bear this news, which I had thought probable from the beginning, with philosophy." Actually he was immensely relieved by the outcome. He at once messaged Cripps, in words obviously meant to be read by the President of the United States: "You have done everything in human power and your tenacity, perseverance and resourcefulness have proved how great was the British desire for a settlement. You must not feel unduly discouraged or disappointed by the results. The effect throughout Britain and America has been wholly beneficial. The fact that the break comes on the broadest issues and not on tangled formulas about defense is a great advantage. I am very glad you are coming home at once. . . ." He then cabled to Roosevelt the texts of both Cripps's message to him and his reply to Cripps.[82]

They were read by Roosevelt with dismay and suspicion.

He at once drafted a cable remarkable for the bluntness of its language and the sharpness of its criticism, taking care, however, to have it hand-delivered to Churchill by Harry Hopkins, who was then in England—in fact, was spending the weekend with Churchill at Chequers—and whose role as buffering intermediary between the two heads of government was seldom more important than at that moment. "Please give immediately the following message to the Former Naval Person," said Roosevelt to Hopkins. "We must make every effort to prevent a breakdown." In the message itself he "most earnestly" hoped that Cripps's "departure from India" would be postponed "until one more final effort has been made. . . ." It was simply not true "that public opinion in the United States believes that the negotiations have failed on broad general issues. . . . The feeling is almost universally held [here] that the deadlock has been caused by the unwillingness of the British Government to concede to the Indians the right of self-government, notwithstanding the willingness of the Indians to entrust technical, military and naval defense to the competent British authorities. American public opinion cannot understand why, if the British Government is willing to permit the component parts of India to secede from the British Empire after the war, it is not willing to permit them to enjoy what is tantamount to self-government during the war. . . . I still feel . . . that if the component groups in India could now be given the opportunity to set up a nationalist government similar in essence to our own form of government under the Articles of Confederation with the understanding that upon the termination of a period of trial and error they would then be enabled to determine their own form of government and, as you have already promised them, to determine their future relationship with the British Empire, a solution could probably be found. If you made such an effort and . . . were still able to find an agreement, you would at least on that issue have public opinion in the United States satisfied that a real offer and a fair offer has been made. . . ."[83]

It was three o'clock on Sunday morning (it was yet Saturday night in Washington) when the Roosevelt message arrived at Chequers. Hopkins, though he was under strict orders from his doctors, and from the President, to seek an early bed each night, was yet engaged in animated conversation with Churchill. He broke this off to glance through the message, absorbing its contents with the swift accuracy of perception that was so great an asset to him in his work. He then handed it to the Prime Minister and braced himself against expected storm. The storm came. It lasted for two solid hours, during which Hopkins made written notes of Churchill's furious rush of words. What Roosevelt proposed was an act of madness! It would throw the whole subcontinent into utter confusion "while the Japanese invader is at its gate!" And he, Churchill, would have no part in a British government that gave serious consideration to it; he would "make no objection at all to retiring into private life" if that was necessary to appease American public opinion, but he was very sure that his doing so would not result in the reopening of "the Indian constitutional issue in this way at this juncture." Parliament and the war cabinet were bound to consider what any such nationalist government as the President favored would be likely to do. "Almost certainly" that government would demand the recall of the Indian troops now serving in the Middle East, weakening Allied forces there that at their present strength were strained to the utmost. It might agree to an armistice with the Japanese "on the basis of free transit through India to Karachi of Japanese forces and supplies," a move that would make of Pakistan a launching base for a drive westward toward a world-conquering linkup of Axis forces in the Middle East. "From their [the Indians'] point of view this [armistice] would be the easiest course, and one entirely in accord with Gandhi's non-violence doctrines. The Japanese would in return no doubt give the Hindus the military support necessary to impose their will upon the Moslems, the Native States, and the Depressed Classes [though such conduct was *not* in accord with Gandhi's doctrines, as Churchill failed to note]."[84]

Hopkins's ameliorative influence is evident in the cable Churchill addressed to Roosevelt some twelve hours later and which Roosevelt read late on that Washington Sunday morning. The cable had none of the harshness with which the Prime Minister had expressed himself to Hopkins personally. The opening third of it dealt in terms of hearty approval of (though there were hinted reservations concerning) the great undertaking that had brought Hopkins to England (we will tell of it later), then explained that "when the text of your message . . . about India came through," Cripps had already left for home, "and all explanations have [by now] been published on both sides." Churchill "could not decide such a matter [as Roosevelt proposed] without convening the Cabinet, which was not physically possible till Monday. . . . In these circumstances, Harry undertook to telephone you explaining the position, but owing to atmospherics could not get through. He is going to telephone you this afternoon and also cable you a report. You know the weight which I attach to everything you say to me. . . ." But since Roosevelt had addressed his message to the Former Naval Person, "I am keeping it purely private, and do not propose to bring it before the Cabinet officially unless you tell me you wish this done. Anything like a serious difference between you and me would break my heart and surely deeply injure both our countries at the height of this terrible struggle."[85]

And there the matter came to rest for the time being, never again to be raised to the dangerous height it had reached on that Sunday.

This exchange between Churchill and Roosevelt was completed a week before Laval became Vichy Premier and two weeks before Roosevelt delivered, in his April 28 fireside chat, his veiled warning to Laval. He knew when he delivered it that the British had, in mid-March, decided to storm and occupy Diégo-Suarez and, indeed, that the Madagascar invasion forces were at that moment at sea on their way to the island. They had embarked from the east South African port of Durban only a few hours before.

The project had been proposed to the British last fall by de Gaulle, who wanted it to be a Free French operation supported by British air and naval forces. The British had carefully and sympathetically considered this proposal before deciding—and the strong Roosevelt-Hull antipathy to de Gaulle was a factor in their decision—that they had best do the job themselves, and by themselves, with no Free French participation. But the British, too, needed outside support. It was impossible to weaken at that moment the British naval forces in the Far East. This meant that the whole of the British naval force then at Gibraltar, designated Force H, would have to be used for the descent on Madagascar. And this in turn meant that the western gate to the Mediterranean would be left "uncovered" for a fortnight or more, "which is most undesirable," as Churchill said in a message to Roosevelt in mid-March. He went on: "Would it be possible for you to send, say, two battleships, an aircraft carrier, some cruisers and destroyers from the Atlantic to take the place of Force H temporarily?" Roosevelt, wishing to dissociate the United States from the British expedition against French territory to an extent sufficient to enable his maintenance of friendly ties with Vichy, was unwilling to do this. He consulted with Admiral King, who was now chief of naval operations (CNO) as well as commander in chief of the U.S. Fleet,* then proposed an alternative deemed "satisfactory" by Churchill. He ordered the reinforcement of the British home fleet with an American task force consisting of a battleship, the carrier *Wasp,* two heavy cruisers (one of them was the *Tuscaloosa,* on which Roosevelt had cruised northern waters in the days immediately preceding the start of World War II), and a squadron of destroyers,† thus enabling British home fleet vessels to be detached for service at Gibraltar. When Churchill asked Roosevelt's permission to drop leaflets from British planes upon Madagascar at the time of the attack, leaflets giving the "impression" to the local populace that the expedition was Anglo-American, Roosevelt flatly refused it, saying doing so would jeopardize his diplomatic ties with Vichy, and "we are the only nation that can intervene diplomatically with any hope of success with Vichy."[86]

That he persisted in such "hope for success" seemed remarkable to many British, especially after the Vichyite governor-general of Madagascar, who the British had hoped would make merely nominal resistance, ordered instead the maximum possible resistance to the British capture of Diégo-Suarez. This maximum was not great. Diégo-Suarez was secured by the British within a couple of days after their landings on May 5, at a cost of four hundred casualties. Churchill then ordered that the best of the assault forces be at once sent on to India, in consequence of which the Madagascar ports of Majunga and Tamatave (the latter the island's capital), each of which had been regularly used by French submarines, remained in stubbornly resistant Vichy hands until late September. Not until November 5, 1942, would the British, through formal acceptance of their surrender terms by the governor-general, obtain uncontested control of the whole island.

---

*Stark, his professional reputation somewhat damaged by the Pearl Harbor debacle and investigation, resigned his CNO position in March and was sent to England as commander of U.S. naval forces in Europe and personal representative of the President on naval and military affairs.
†This task force on its way across the Atlantic ran through a huge storm during which the force commander, Rear Admiral John W. Wilcox, Jr., was swept overboard and lost, as Samuel Eliot Morison recounts in his *The Battle of the Atlantic,* page 168.

X

SIMULTANEOUS with the British capture of Diégo-Suarez (also with the final resistance and unconditional surrender of Wainwright's forces on Corregidor) was the Japanese drive south from Rabaul into the Coral Sea, the long-planned operation for which the date had been advanced by Tokyo strategists immediately after, and in part because of, the Doolittle raid. Its major objective was Port Moresby on the southern shore of New Guinea's Papuan peninsula. Lying little more than three hundred miles across the Coral Sea from Australia's Queensland, where were air and naval bases of crucial importance to the Allies, Moresby was the key element of Australia's outer defenses; it was also the essential base for that "return" to the Philippines that MacArthur had flamboyantly promised the world when he arrived in Australia. It was therefore a place of immense strategic importance for both sides of the Pacific struggle. A preliminary Japanese objective was the small island of Tulagi, an Allied seaplane base twenty miles north of the much larger island of Guadalcanal in the Solomons; it was taken without fighting on May 3, the small Australian garrison there having been forewarned and withdrawn three days before. On the following day began what would become known to history as the Battle of the Coral Sea. . . .

By this time, Magic, launched with the breaking of the Japanese diplomatic code, was master of the Japanese naval code as well, enabling American intelligence to read intercepted messages from Tokyo to Japanese fleet commanders, also messages passed between fleet units; and in early April, Magic had informed the American commander in chief of the Pacific area (CINCPAC), in Pearl Harbor, that the Japanese were preparing a major thrust into the Coral Sea. CINCPAC was Admiral Chester W. Nimitz, whom Roosevelt had personally chosen for this post nine days after the Pearl Harbor attack, despite Nimitz's relatively junior status (dozens of naval officers then outranked him); despite certain misgivings about him expressed by Admiral King, whom Roosevelt had named commander in chief of the U.S. Fleet (COMINCH) just the day before; and despite Nimitz's own manifest misgivings about taking command of a fleet he then believed to be, as he told his wife, "at the bottom of the sea." He was a handsome, white-haired (though only fifty-six), scholarly-appearing man, quiet, unassuming, and fortunately possessed of iron nerves and an orderly, incisive mind. He had need of such inner resources at that moment, for his outer material resources, measured against those of the enemy, were meager indeed. Forewarned as he was, however, he was able by late April to assemble in the battle zone a formidable force consisting of two large aircraft carriers, *Yorktown* and *Lexington,* five heavy cruisers, eleven destroyers, and a tanker. To the overall tactical commander of this force, Rear Admiral Frank Jack Fletcher, he issued on April 29 broad and simple orders. Fletcher was "to operate in the Coral Sea commencing 1 May"; there he was to "destroy enemy ships, shipping and aircraft at favorable opportunities in order to assist in checking further advance by the enemy in the New Guinea–Solomons area."[87] As he went about the arduous planning and ordering of all this, Nimitz's strong commitment to clarity of thought and precision of definition was offended by a change in the Allied command arrangements for the Pacific. Formerly, he had had supreme direction of American forces, military as well as naval, in all the Pacific; but by this new arrangement, announced on April 18, a Southwest Pacific area that embraced almost the whole of the Coral Sea was established, and MacArthur, now headquartered in Melbourne, was designated its Allied commander in chief (CINCSWPA). The need to establish a Southwest Pacific command was obvious to Nimitz, but he deplored the fact that within the new command area his authority vis-à-vis MacArthur's was ill defined—a dangerous lack of precision that was rendered especially so in this instance by the personal loathing of MacArthur which permeated the U.S. naval high command, from Admiral King on down.* Presumably Nimitz yet retained full control of Allied naval forces everywhere in the Pacific; but Task Force 44, an amalgam of Australian and American war vessels based in Sydney and commanded by a British admiral, was the main unit of what was at once dubbed "MacArthur's Navy," and Nimitz could not be absolutely certain he had authority over it until its British commander promptly obeyed his order that it join Fletcher's forces on May 1 at a designated point west of the New Hebrides. Nimitz did know that, alas, he had no authority over the land-based air forces in the Southwest Pacific. These were wholly MacArthur's to command. This meant that Nimitz and his tactical commanders could obtain land-based search flights in the Southwest Pacific area and land-based bomb or torpedo attacks only if MacArthur authorized them.[88]

Another consequence of the new command arrangement was that MacArthur's headquarters issued the early communiqués of the Coral Sea action, leading the American public to believe initially that MacArthur directed what was, in reality, wholly a naval air operation—the first sea battle in history in which the opposing vessels never came within sight of one another. It began on the morning of May 4 with an air strike upon Japanese shipping in Tulagi's harbor by planes (a dozen torpedo planes, twenty-eight dive bombers) from the American carrier *Yorktown*. It ended four days later when two evenly matched carrier forces, having struck at one another ferociously with their planes in the Coral Sea, inflicting serious wounds upon each other, withdrew from the battle zone, each initially convinced it had "won" the encounter.

The Japanese had lost a light carrier, *Soho,* which went down just ten minutes after being struck by bombs from *Yorktown* planes. They had lost at Tulagi a destroyer, a cargo ship, five anchored seaplanes, three minesweepers, and four

---

*The loathing was a long-standing one that had been augmented by MacArthur's dealings with Admiral Hart in Manila, dealings the navy deemed unjust and contemptuous.

landing barges, while another destroyer and a patrol craft had been damaged. And their large carriers *Zuikaku* and *Shokaku* had suffered damage so severe that they could not be repaired in time for participation in the upcoming Midway strike unless it was postponed, which Yamamoto refused to do. These losses seemed to them trivial, however, compared with those of their enemy, for they had been informed by remarkably inaccurate eyewitness reports from their excited pilots that they had sunk two large American carriers plus a heavy cruiser—losses many times greater than the sum total of the losses they themselves had suffered. True, they had not achieved their strategic objective, the capture of Port Moresby, but such achievement, they believed, was only postponed: they would now simply regroup at Rabaul and come down again against opposition so enfeebled that it could be easily overcome. Actually, as the withdrawing Americans knew, the Japanese had been emphatically denied their swift and easy capture of Moresby; they might not now be able to take it at all. For the Americans had not been enfeebled to anything like the extent that the Japanese believed them to be. One of the "carriers" reported sunk was actually the USS *Neosho,* a tanker; the "cruiser" reported sunk was the USS *Sims,* a destroyer. The two vessels were not worth what it had cost to destroy them. The Americans had suffered losses serious enough, however, in view of their slender resources. One of their carriers had indeed gone down, the venerable and beloved *Lexington*—a loss that of itself alone more than offset all the material damage done the Japanese. Moreover, the newer and far nimbler *Yorktown* had suffered damage that would, according to initial damage control estimates, take a minimum of ninety days to repair.

Nimitz at Pearl Harbor could therefore derive from the final reports of the Coral Sea action no exhilaration of triumph, but only relief, if very great relief, over escape from disaster. The most that he would have claimed at that moment was that for the first time in this war, the Japanese had not had all their own way in a major battle. They had received a definite check. Whether or not this check was permanent, defining the limit of their empire's expansion southward, depended upon the outcome of the much greater sea battle now impending.

There followed a month of acute anxiety at Pearl Harbor—the most tense and anxious weeks of the whole war for Chester Nimitz, and anxious enough for Roosevelt, who followed closely the moves of the Pacific war. Both knew from naval intelligence that the enemy was preparing a blow to be struck in the first week of June, that Midway was almost certainly its prime objective, and that if the blow was intelligently, concentratedly delivered, it would be with a force so much greater than the maximum Nimitz could employ that he was likely to be overwhelmed no matter what he did. Committed to the great enterprise were no fewer than 160 Japanese warships, including 11 battleships (one of them the fast, huge [64,000-ton] *Yamato,* which carried nine 18.1-inch guns), 22 cruisers, 65 destroyers, 21 submarines, and (the key elements) 8 carriers bearing 700 planes, the pilots of which were highly skilled and combat tested. To oppose all this in Midway's defense, Nimitz had at the beginning of the last week of May not a single battleship and could absolutely count upon just two carriers, *Enterprise* and *Hornet,* the latter with an air group that had had no combat experience whatever. Of course, Midway was itself an aircraft carrier, and Nimitz packed it with planes; but his need for *Yorktown* was so desperate that he absolutely refused to accept the repair-time estimate initially made by her damage control officers. When the battered carrier limped into Pearl on May 27, she went at once into dry dock, where, by Nimitz's order, hundreds of expert damage repair workmen, supported by other hundreds in the yard shops, gave her concentrated, tightly coordinated, night-and-day attention. They accomplished a miracle! Within less than forty-eight hours, the dock was flooded and *Yorktown* moved out into the narrow waters between Ford Island and the mainland; on the afternoon of May 29, she fueled while hundreds of repairmen continued to work on her.[89]

Next day, with her escort vessels, constituting Task Force 17 with Fletcher in command, she sailed for the battle zone carrying an air group hastily assembled from three carriers—men who had never before operated together as a unit. Already at sea was Task Force 16, commanded by Rear Admiral Raymond A. Spruance and consisting of *Hornet* and *Enterprise* with their escorts. The two task forces together (three large carriers, seven heavy cruisers, one light cruiser, fourteen destroyers, and nineteen submarines fueled by two tankers protected by two additional destroyers) were the sum total of the force with which Nimitz must counter the immense armada coming against him. According to orders issued by him on May 27, they were to "inflict maximum damage on the enemy by employing strong attrition tactics," but in doing so they were to "be governed by the principle of calculated risk, which you are to interpret to mean the avoidance of exposure of your force to attack by superior enemy forces without good prospect of inflicting, as a result of such exposure, greater damage on the enemy." Obviously the orders were so broad that their successful execution depended overwhelmingly upon the nerve, the judgment, the professional skill, and the self-control of the two tactical commanders—and even the possession of these assets in fullest measure could not stave off disaster unless there was added to them the advantage of prior information and the resultant element of surprise. Fortunately for them, thanks to Magic, aided by a Japanese carelessness of security that was remarkable in view of what had just happened in the Coral Sea, surprise was indeed added to the American armory. . . .

Nimitz's anxiety, shortly after he had issued his battle orders, was somewhat alleviated by intelligence reports that Yamamoto* was evidently *not* concen-

---

*He had elected to exercise overall command of the immense operation from the huge battleship *Yamato* instead of from headquarters on land, where swifter and more accurate communications with fleet elements would have been assured.

trating his overwhelming force but instead was scattering it piecemeal across the Central Pacific. In fact, as Nimitz would soon learn, the Japanese overall force was divided into three separate ones. One, designated the Northern Area Force, consisted of three heavy cruisers, four light cruisers, two light carriers, eleven destroyers, and six submarines; it was to initiate the action on June 3 with an air strike on Dutch Harbor on the Aleutian island of Unalaska, to be succeeded on immediately following days by landings on the western Aleutian islands of Attu and Kiska. This operation in the far northern mists, seemingly presaging a major Japanese attack upon the American mainland, was supposed to confuse the American command and render it hesitant as it dealt with the true main attack. (Wrote Roosevelt to MacArthur on June 2: "It looks, at this moment, as if the Japanese fleet is heading toward the Aleutian Islands or Midway and Hawaii, with a remote possibility it may attack Southern California or Seattle by air.")[90] The main attack was to be initiated on June 4 with a devastating air strike upon Midway, to be delivered by a designated main body consisting of the big carriers *Akagi, Kaga, Soryu,* and *Hiryu,* escorted by two battleships, two cruisers, and fourteen destroyers under the command of Vice Admiral Nagumo of Pearl Harbor "infamy." Nagumo would approach from the northwest, and his Midway action was supposed a) to enable landings by a Midway Occupation Force of twelve transports and freighters covered and supported by two battleships, eight cruisers, and nine destroyers; and b) to entice the U.S. Pacific Fleet into a general fleet engagement that, in view of Nagumo's superior strength, would be fatal to it. Poised halfway between the Aleutians and Midway, ready to hurry north or south as need arose, was a so-called Aleutian Screening Force consisting of four battleships, a light carrier, and two seaplane carriers.

On June 2, the American Task Forces 16 and 17, with Fletcher in command of both as a unit, rendezvoused at a point, two hundred miles north of Midway, shrewdly chosen for a flank attack upon a force coming down from the northwest. In the early dawn light of June 4, a PBY patrol plane from Midway sighted two of Nagumo's carriers 180 miles northwest of the island—precisely where Nimitz's intelligence officer had predicted it would be at that time. Soon thereafter, the radar screens on Midway reported scores of Japanese planes (actually 108 planes, from the flight decks of all four Japanese carriers) on their way to the island. The attack, though resisted by Midway's defenders with a vigor that surprised Nagumo, did great damage at little cost to the attackers (all but six of the scores of attacking planes returned to their carriers). Midway oil tanks and storehouses were set afire. The power station was partially crippled, the marine command post and mess hall ruined. But the bombers failed to incapacitate or even greatly damage their prime target, the airfield runways, and Nagumo was told that a second attack would be needed before the invasion force could come in. The validity of this information was emphasized for him shortly thereafter when he himself came under attack by planes from Midway. The attack did him no material damage whatever while costing the Americans dearly (fifteen of twenty-six attacking planes were shot down; of the eleven that returned to their base, six were so badly damaged that they would never fly again), but it had the evident effect of jangling his nerves and flawing his judgment at a moment of crucial decision.

He had assumed when he launched the Midway strike that no strong enemy naval force would be within effective range of his present position for days to come, yet he had prudently committed only a little more than half his air strength to this strike, keeping behind on his four carriers some ninety-three planes armed with torpedoes and bombs, ready for instant launching against any American naval force that came within striking distance. To insure against surprise by the enemy, he had also ordered a dawn search of the surrounding sea by seven floatplanes, though apparently without communicating any great sense of urgency to those who carried out his orders: only six of the searchers were promptly catapulted into predawn darkness from the cruisers that carried them; the seventh, from the cruiser *Tone,* was not airborne until a half hour after the others had departed. When Nagumo learned at 7:00 A.M. of the need for a second Midway strike, he therefore assumed that all his search planes had been out for two and a half hours and must in that time have searched the whole of the area within 250 miles of him, finding nothing. He waited another fifteen minutes, during which he had to deal with the Midway planes attacking him. The attack encouraged him to believe that the need to incapacitate Midway's air arm justified the risk, which seemed at that moment slight, of attack upon him by enemy naval forces—and so, at 7:15, he ordered the ninety-three planes now on the four carriers' flight decks to be taken below, where those now armed with torpedoes for attacks on ships were to be relieved of these and rearmed with bombs. After all, he told himself, he gambled with a mere hour of time (it took an hour of hard labor to accomplish the rearmament he had ordered), for his flight decks would have to be cleared in any case by 8:30 when recovery of the planes returning from Midway must begin. By rearming now, he would be able to launch his second Midway strike as soon as the first-strike planes were recovered instead of an hour later. At a little after 7:30, however, his estimate of the gambling odds was abruptly drastically changed: the laggard *Tone* searcher found and reported what it would have found a half hour sooner had it been launched promptly, namely, "what appears to be ten enemy surface ships" some two hundred miles to the northeast. Nagumo was startled, but he had at first no sense of imminent danger. Surely, had a carrier been among the enemy ships, the searcher would have recognized and reported it! His apprehension grew, however. At 7:45, he amended his earlier order. "Prepare to carry out attacks on enemy ships," he now signaled. "Leave torpedoes on those attack planes that have not as yet been changed to bombs." Two minutes later he ordered the *Tone* searcher to "ascertain ship types and maintain contact." Thus Nagumo was in an extremely awkward position, fully prepared for neither a strike against Midway nor one against hostile ships when, at 8:20, more than half an hour after receiving Nagumo's last order, the *Tone* search plane reported that a carrier did indeed "appear" to be among the previously reported cruisers and destroyers. Ten minutes later, Nagumo began recovery of his planes from Midway, a task that kept him occupied until 9:18. Only then could he begin bringing up to his flight decks his dive bombers and his planes armed with torpedoes.

And by that time the spearhead of an attack by 152 American planes was within minutes of attacking him. Most of them were from Spruance's Task Force 16, this having been detached from Task Force 17 by Fletcher and sent to the southeast as a virtually independent command. Fletcher himself remained behind to recover on *Yorktown* the planes of his dawn search, also because only two enemy carriers had then been sighted of the four or five that, according to intelligence, were in the area. Until at least one of these other carriers was sighted he was loath, as in common prudence he should have been, to commit any of his *Yorktown* planes to battle. He didn't do so until 8:30, when he sent aloft all of *Yorktown*'s torpedo planes, half his dive bombers, and half a dozen fighters. This was two hours after he had turned to follow Spruance and an hour and a half after the latter had ordered his strike at the Japanese to be launched. This launching was, on Spruance's part, a very closely calculated risk, for he ordered it two hours before he was close enough to the enemy to ensure the recovery of those of his torpedo planes (they had a combat range of only 175 miles) that survived the battle. By doing so he might, he hoped, catch the Japanese in the act of recovering planes, hence with their carrier flight decks in a state of confusion; and with this in mind he boldly launched his full force, keeping behind barely enough fighters (thirty-six of them) to maintain combat patrols above his ships. He refused to limit this attack force even after, having distantly seen a circling floatplane (we know it to have been the laggard *Tone* searcher), he assumed that the vital element of surprise was now lost.

The fighting action began at 9:20, initiated by three groups of American torpedo planes that had by mischance become separated from their fighter escorts but nevertheless did not hesitate to bore in directly upon three of the Japanese carriers. They were met by thick curtains of antiaircraft fire and by murderous machine-gun fire from swooping Japanese Zero fighters. Of the forty-one torpedo planes, thirty-five were shot down—and not a single one of the torpedoes they launched (many or most of them were shot down before they could launch) reached its target. But the heroic self-sacrifice of these brave young Americans was not in vain. Their attacks sucked down to within a few score feet above the sea the Zeros that would otherwise, flying high, have intercepted the incoming American dive bombers. As it was, these dive bombers came in unimpeded and at once bore down through heavy antiaircraft fire upon *Akagi, Kaga,* and *Soryu,* which were fairly close together (*Hiryu* was several miles ahead of these three) and whose decks were in precisely the confused condition Spruance had hoped

for. Within a remarkably short time all three were flaming wrecks, having suffered repeated direct hits and damaging near misses. A dazed, demoralized
Nagumo was forced to transfer his flag from the sinking *Akagi* to a light cruiser
and his tactical command to Admiral Hiroake Abe. The latter, who had been and
remained in charge of the strike force's battleship and cruiser screen, believing
there was only one American carrier in the area (only one had been reported)
and that its attack had been augmented by land-based planes, promptly ordered
Hiryu, the single surviving Japanese carrier, to attack that carrier, which was
Yorktown. The attackers suffered great losses but scored three direct hits upon
Yorktown, inflicting fatal injuries; she was abandoned by her crew in the late
afternoon and sunk a few hours later by a Japanese submarine. Hours before she
went down, however, her killer, *Hiryu,* was herself a flaming exploding wreck,
the victim of dive bombers flying off *Enterprise.*

Yamamoto, hundreds of miles away, yet saw a slight chance, as night fell, to
snatch victory from the jaws of defeat. His great battleships and cruisers had not
been engaged and, in a night action, when darkness rendered the air arm ineffective, might annihilate the U.S. Fleet if it came within range of his immensely
superior firepower. He ordered his mighty but scattered surface force to con-
verge upon an area north of Midway. But then he realized that if his order were
carried out and no night encounter occurred, his own fleet, overwhelmingly
strong only on the ocean surface, would be nakedly exposed in morning light to
American air attack. "Enough is enough," he muttered to his staff officers as, at
a little after three o'clock in the morning of June 5, he canceled the Midway operation totally, ordering a general withdrawal. It was well for him that he did so,
for Spruance, now in tactical command of the whole American operation, prudently declined to pursue in the dark the shattered Japanese strike force. Instead
he slanted down toward Midway and, as June 5 dawned, was within strike distance of the area where the Japanese forces would have been had Yamamoto's
orders of the night before been held to.*

As it was, Yamamoto, ashen faced, his eyes glittering feverishly, his stomach
churned by nervous strain and depression, was on that June 5 far more acutely
aware of the magnitude and significance of his defeat than Nimitz, Fletcher, and
Spruance were of their victory's dimensions. He sensed what only later become
clear to all—that the tide of the Pacific war had turned, that the limit of Japanese
expansion had not merely been reached, it had been passed. The fact would be

---

*Even withdrawal was a costly operation for the Japanese. In the predawn darkness of June 5, two of
the fastest and most powerful ships in the Japanese navy, the heavy cruisers *Mikuma* and *Magami,*
each carrying eight-inch guns, collided at fast speed while taking evasive action against an American
submarine attack. Both were so heavily damaged that the retiring Japanese were forced to leave them
behind. They were soon found by American planes, which sank *Mikuma,* then scored six direct hits on
Mogami, and left, assuming that ship was in a presumably sinking condition; as it turned out, she managed to make her way back to port. A year of labor was required to make her again battleworthy.

confirmed in the weeks and months immediately ahead by American action against Japanese-occupied Guadalcanal and Allied action in New Guinea, whereby Port Moresby was secured as MacArthur's base of operations toward the north. No longer was there any danger whatever of an invasion of India. Japan, her naval and air strength greatly depleted, was condemned to fight a defensive war from now on to the end, with the odds against her victory steadily increasing.

9

><><

An Alliance-Threatening Quarrel:
Spring and Summer 1942

I

WE have noted that, fortunately for the continuance of friendly personal relations between President and Prime Minister, Harry Hopkins was at Churchill's side, at Chequers, during the earliest hours of Sunday, April 12, 1942, nearly two months before the Midway battle. We have noted, too, that the opening third of the telegram in which Churchill answered Roosevelt's protest against the ending of Cripps's mission to India dealt not with the Indian problem, but with the great undertaking that had brought Hopkins for the third time to England. As for the undertaking, its nature was indicated in an April 1 telegram from Roosevelt to Churchill: "As I have completed survey of . . . the military situations facing the United Nations, I have come to certain conclusions which are so vital that I want you to know the whole picture and to ask your approval. The whole of it is so dependent on complete cooperation by the U.K. and U.S. that Harry and Marshall will leave for London in a few days to present first of all to you the salient points. It is a plan . . . which I hope Russia will greet with enthusiasm, and, on word from you after you have seen Harry and Marshall, I propose to ask Stalin to send two special representatives to me at once. . . . I would like to be able to label it the plan of the United Nations."[1]

The "conclusion" or "plan" that Roosevelt referred to was for the establishment at the earliest possible moment of that "second front" in Western Europe for which the Russians had been clamoring with a fluctuating but generally increasing fervor ever since Stalin first proposed it in a communication to Churchill in the third week of July 1941.* As desirous of it as the Russians, in part because they were anxious to prevent a Russian collapse, but mostly out of a conviction that it was the only way to achieve final victory over Hitler, were George Marshall and the man who had become the chief one among his assistants, Dwight David Eisenhower. Both were convinced that a postponement of

*See p. 233.

the final battle until the Germans were weakened by war attritions and internal dissensions—the wishfully thought (as it seemed to them) nibbling-at-the-edges strategy that the British had perforce pursued and proposed to continue—would increase the cost and reduce the odds in favor of ultimate Allied victory.

In mid-February, Brigadier General Eisenhower had succeeded Leonard Gerow as war plans chief, having already pleased Marshall greatly by actively participating in the carrying out of the plans he made—desperation plans for supplying the American forces in Bataan, for instance—and thus removing the barrier, which Marshall deemed artificial and pernicious in war, between conception and execution. When this Marshall view was expressed in administrative structure by the transformation of war plans into an operations division as part of the McNarney departmental reorganization, on April 2, 1942, Eisenhower became head of it, having been promoted to the rank of major general a few days before. (The new division was to function as coordinator of the far-flung fronts on which the U.S. Army was fighting—also as the active link between the army and the U.S. Joint Chiefs of Staff, and between the army and the Allies' Combined Chiefs of Staff.) He had helped Marshall shape the proposal that Roosevelt made to Churchill on March 9 for creating order out of the chaos in the global operational command setup resulting from the swift collapse of ABDA in the Southwest Pacific area.

This proposal was for a tripartite geographic division between Britain and the United States of the operational command authority and responsibility for the waging of global war. "The whole of the operation responsibility for the Pacific Area will rest on the United States," said the proposal. ". . . The middle area extending from Singapore to and including India and the Indian Ocean, Persian Gulf, Red Sea, Libya and the Mediterranean would fall directly under British responsibility. All operational matters in this area would be decided by you. But always with the understanding that as much assistance would be given to India or Near East by Australia and New Zealand as could be worked out with their governments." The United States "would continue to allocate to it [this middle area] all possible munitions and vessel assignments. It is understood that this presupposes the temporary shelving of Gymnast [the invasion of North Africa]." The third area was to include "the waters of the North and South Atlantic," the British Isles, and that portion of the European continent lying between the English Channel and Berlin, where, in the conviction of Marshall and Eisenhower, the finally decisive battles with Hitler in the West must be fought. Command of this area, wrote Roosevelt, "would be the joint responsibility of Britain and the United States and would include definite plans for establishment of a new front on the European Continent. . . . I am becoming more and more interested in the establishment of this new front *this summer* [emphasis added]." Of course, "all possible aid to Russia" should be continued; and of course, "the grand strategy of actual operations in the three areas" would continue to be the responsibility of "the Combined Staffs both here [in Washington] and in London, and the joint committees on shipping, on raw materials, and on munitions would continue to function as they do now . . . subject to our [the President's and the Prime Minister's] joint approval." This proposal raised many questions in the minds of the British, but its salient features were acceptable to them and were soon effected. Churchill, replying to Roosevelt on March 17, indicated this general agreement while stressing the impossibility of subjecting Allied global naval operations to any rigid division of command areas. "Nothing must prevent the United States and British Navies from working in a common strategy from Alaska to Capetown," wrote the Prime Minister. "The immense distances and practical facts require them to act in widely separated theaters, but they must operate with a single purpose, an exact timing, and upon closely coordinated plans."[2]

Though more lengthy and detailed than the message it replied to, Churchill's message of March 17 made, significantly, no response or even any reference to the "shelving" of Gymnast or to Roosevelt's expressed interest in "the establishment" of a "new front this summer." Yet it was to the establishment of a new front that Eisenhower, with Marshall's blessing, if not at his order, was paying at that moment concentrated, laborious attention. He and his planning staff were shaping out of a multitude of earlier suggestions and plans—"some of them British in origin," as Forrest Pogue remarks—a plan for a cross-Channel invasion of northern France. Necessarily it was a broad outline of a plan, at once sweeping and succinct, for the time limit imposed by circumstances upon the completion of it was severe.

And at the very outset of its making, Eisenhower concluded that the main Allied assault on the Continent could not possibly be made during the coming summer, or indeed at any later time in 1942. The Germans were known to have concentrated upon building an impregnable Western Wall for their *Festung Europa* (that they had succeeded in doing so was the opinion of many an experienced soldier and sailor on the Allied side), and any attempt to breach it having any chance of success required a quantity of shipping, landing craft, planes, munitions, and adequately trained troops that was simply not available to the Allies now. Nor could it be for another year. Moreover, the necessary buildup in the United Kingdom could not be achieved, and the necessary supply and reinforcement of the new front assured, unless the U-boat menace in the Atlantic, at that moment great, was much reduced. Therefore Eisenhower and his staff set the spring of 1943 as the earliest feasible date for the attack, proposing for that time a direct assault upon the Dunkirk-Calais-Boulogne portion of the northern French coast. The reasons for selecting this area were obvious. Only twenty miles of Channel water separates Calais from Dover, which meant that the area could be reached in force with less shipping than would be required for the reaching of any other part of the French coast; it could be covered by the short-ranged Spitfires of 1941–1942 (overwhelming air superiority in the assault area was an absolute essential of success); and, being nearer Berlin than any other landing place in France, it was an integral part of what Eisenhower with Marshall deemed the truly decisive Western battleground. Of course, there was an offset to these Allied advantages: The Germans, recognizing them, had made the area the most strongly fortified, the most heavily manned portion of their Western Wall. The scale of attack that Eisenhower proposed was therefore four or five times larger than any the British had theretofore contemplated. No fewer than forty-eight divisions, thirty of them American, the remainder British, were to be employed, and they were to be covered by 5,800 warplanes. Also proposed in broad outline by the planning group was a limited cross-Channel attack to be made in September 1942 for the purpose of gaining and then holding against German counterattack, a "bridgehead for use in the large [1943] invasion." This early autumn operation must be predominantly British; the United States could by that time transport only two and a half fully trained and equipped divisions to join in the operation.[3]

Code names were, of course, assigned to the three main parts in this vast undertaking. They were "Bolero" for the buildup (the gathering together, the transport, and the concentration in the United Kingdom of the men and material required), "Sledgehammer" for the operation in the fall of 1942, and "Roundup" for the main (1943) attack. All three names were destined soon to festoon the voluminous correspondence and fervent oratory of the only Anglo-American quarrel in the whole of the war that seriously threatened to weaken gravely, perhaps even destroy, the Anglo-American alliance.

The nature and subject of this quarrel are indicated by Eisenhower's confession to Marshall, when he submitted his planning report, that Sledgehammer was an extremely hazardous enterprise—far more so than the main attack, properly prepared, would be—and that his only "real reason" for favoring it was that it would prevent "our becoming so deeply involved elsewhere that the major cross-Channel attack would be indefinitely postponed, possibly even canceled." For instance: "Almost certainly a 1942 operation in the Mediterranean [Gymnast] would eliminate the possibility of a major cross-Channel venture in 1943." Clearly Eisenhower shared not only Marshall's opposition to British conceptions of grand strategy, but also Marshall's aversion to what both men then perceived as a general British penchant for indirection, dissemblance, and artful procrastination. Eisenhower seems to have shared, too, at that moment, Marshall's fear that Roosevelt might be persuaded by Churchill to go the British way. Marshall himself, however, did not consider Eisenhower's "real reason" a sufficient one for what the President would later dub, in conversation with a British officer of high rank, a "sacrifice landing." Sledgehammer should be permitted to proceed, thought Marshall (as would Roosevelt), only if the German summer offensives on the eastern front, very nervously anticipated by the Allies in this early spring, proved so successful that immediate relief of the pressure upon Russia was necessary to prevent her collapse. Marshall did agree "completely with [the] reasoning" in a memorandum Eisenhower handed him on March 25, according to his official biographer. Said Eisenhower: If the British refused to say flatly, unambiguously, and very soon that a major offensive against the Germans on the Continent constituted their eventual aim, and an aim to be achieved as quickly as such offensive could be mounted with a fair chance of success, "the United States should turn its back on the Atlantic area and go full out against Japan."[4]

On that same March 25, which was only two days or so after he had accepted and approved the Eisenhower planners' report and received Stimson's blessing upon it, Marshall, having summarized it in a memorandum, presented its substance orally to the President at a White House luncheon meeting attended by Stimson, Knox, King, Arnold, and Hopkins. The meeting started badly from Marshall's and Stimson's points of view. Roosevelt opened it with a lengthy review of the global war situation as he saw it, doing so in a way that seemed to presage, in Stimson's diary's words, "the wildest kind of dispersion debauch." He seemed to Marshall dangerously influenced by Churchill's dread of a bloodbath on the Continent if a direct frontal assault upon *Festung Europa* were made—seemed also still dangerously intrigued with the Mediterranean basin as a theater of major Anglo-American operations. But, having spoken his piece, he listened closely to Marshall's forceful presentation and was clearly greatly impressed by it and by the general's answers to his questions about it. As the meeting drew to a close, he declared his agreement with what Marshall had proposed (though the manner of his doing so convinced Stimson that "the concept was not yet his own") and suggested that it be submitted at once to the Combined Chiefs of Staff for consideration and recommendations. It was a suggestion to which Hopkins, prepared for it, strongly objected. The Combined Chiefs of Staff could engage in futile argument only over a matter that must be decided at the highest level, he said; instead, the proposal should be taken to London by special emissary (Marshall was indicated) and presented directly to the four men who had final decisive control over British war policy, namely, Churchill, CIGS Brooke, First Sea Lord Pound, and Chief of Air Staff Portal. Roosevelt promptly yielded the point. He closed the meeting by ordering that the plan be put ("over the weekend, if possible") into a shape presentable to this highest British authority.[5]

Six days later, Roosevelt sent Churchill the message, dated April 1, referring to "vital conclusions" he had reached about the establishment of a "second front." He followed it two days later with a personal letter to "Dear Winston" in which the strength of personal commitment that Stimson had earlier found lacking was fully expressed. "What Harry and Geo. Marshall will tell you about has my heart and *mind* in it," wrote Roosevelt. "Your people and mine demand the establishment of a second front to draw off pressure from the Russians

[who] . . . are today killing more Germans and destroying more equipment than you and I put together. Even if full success is not attained, the *big* objective [relief of the pressure on the Russians] will be." He closed: "Make Harry go to bed early, and let him obey Dr. [Commander James R.] Fulton, U.S.N., whom I'm sending with him as super-nurse with full authority."[6]

These two missives had their intended effect.

When Hopkins and Marshall went together to No. 10 Downing Street in the late afternoon of Wednesday, April 8, having arrived in London that morning, they found a Churchill who, during their two-hour session with him, listened to what Marshall proposed with a show of affirmative sympathy that surprised and greatly pleased the general. Hopkins, less surprised, was also less pleased. He assumed that the Prime Minister, always acutely aware that the survival of the British empire depended upon Anglo-American unity, would have been persuaded by Roosevelt's missives, especially the "Dear Winston" one, to bend a sympathetic ear to what the Americans were coming to say. No doubt he was prepared to accept "in principle" what was proposed—that is, to accept with reservations that could be utterly vitiating. Throughout the later negotiations, he was likely to leave to his chiefs of staff the expression of strong negatives and then, if he shared these negative views, as Hopkins suspected he might, yield with ostentatious reluctance to staff pressures upon him.

And Hopkins's sense of possibly impending sharp disagreement was encouraged a few hours later when he and Marshall were Churchill's dinner guests at No. 10. The only other guests at table were Deputy Prime Minister Clement Attlee, who as head of the Labour Party had become Deputy Prime Minister when the coalition government was formed, and General Sir Alan Brooke, though Eden joined the group after dinner. The conversation was "mainly social," said Hopkins's notes on the event. Churchill delivered lengthy monologues on the U.S. Civil War and the Great War of 1914–1918 without ever "coming to grips with our main business." But "General Brooke got into it enough to indicate that he had a great many misgivings about our proposal. "Brooke," the notes continued, "made an unfavorable impression on Marshall, who thinks that although he may be a good fighting man, he hasn't got Dill's brains."[7]

Actually, Brooke, whom Marshall now met for the first time, was a first-rate mind as well as a superb fighting man. A trim-figured, dark-visaged, aquiline-featured man who, at age fifty-eight, was yet youthful in reaction time and vividness of perception, he had a career résumé considerably more diversified and impressive than Marshall's. On the western front during World War I he had won a DSO and Bar, a Croix de Guerre, and six Mentions in Dispatches. Between the wars, he had had command experience in every branch of the army—infantry, artillery, tanks, antiaircraft—and been responsible for technical innovations in every one of them. In 1940, when he commanded the British II Corps in Belgium, his tactical genius and ability to improvise under extreme

pressure had been instrumental in saving the bulk of the British Expeditionary
Force (BEF) from certain destruction after the surprise Belgian surrender had
nakedly exposed its flank. He had made possible the "Miracle of Dunkirk." Immediately after this evacuation, he had returned to France as commander of
what was left there of the BEF (a total of 140,000 men) and, when France collapsed, had managed "with singular firmness and dexterity, under conditions of
unimaginable difficulty and confusion" (Churchill's words), to extricate it and
return it to England. His was a naturally irritable and impatient disposition. Like
Marshall, he had had to struggle hard for self-control, subordinating a swift and
flaming temper to a mind eminently practical and logical. Like Marshall, he
had no fondness for pomp or ceremony and great fondness for simple country
pleasures (Marshall re-created himself through gardening at his country place
near Leesburg; Brooke through bird-watching, for which he had a passion).
Like Marshall, he was unusually selfless, magnanimous, committed to the highest standards of personal conduct. But unlike Marshall, he was possessed of a
sharp-edged personality whose abrupt manner and often cutting speech grated
upon many people, especially since he failed, if he really tried, to hide his
impatience with those whose minds worked more slowly and less precisely
than his.[8]

On the evening of April 9, the day on which the Marshall memorandum
was formally submitted to the British chiefs of staff, Brooke wrote in his
diary: "I liked what I saw of Marshall, an easy and pleasant man to get on with,
rather over-filled with his own importance. But I should not put him down as a
great man." On April 13, after he and Marshall had dined together, he wrote,
"[T]he more I see of him the more I like him." But he formed no high opinion
of Marshall's intellect as his exposure to it increased. "He is, I should think . . .
good . . . at raising armies and at providing the necessary link between the military and political worlds, but his strategical ability does not impress me at all,"
he told his diary on April 15, a day on which he had had a lengthy tête-à-tête
with his American counterpart. Brooke learned from this talk that a principal
motive for Marshall's great proposal, as well as a chief energizer of his struggle
for it, was an anxiety to preserve the grand Allied strategy of Germany first,
Japan second, against the assaults upon it by Admiral King in Washington and
MacArthur in Australia. King, who had never personally accepted Stark's Plan
Dog, pressed for more and more land forces with which to take and hold land
bases in the Pacific. MacArthur pressed for more and more troops with which to
mount the offensive northward that would enable his promised "return" to the
Philippines. And to "counter these moves Marshall has started the European offensive plan and is going . . . all out for it. It is a clever move," Brooke conceded, in that it "fits in with present political opinion and the desire to help
Russia." But the British staff chief was appalled to discover that Marshall "had
not studied any of the strategic implications" of what he proposed. "He argued

that the main difficulty would be to achieve a landing. I granted that this would certainly present grave difficulties, but that our real troubles would start after the landing. We should be operating with forces initially weaker than the enemy and . . . his rate of reinforcement would be at least twice as fast as ours." Suppose the landing had been achieved, said Brooke. What would Marshall then do? "I found that he had not begun to consider any . . . plan of action. . . . Nor could he understand that until the Mediterranean was opened again we should always suffer from the critical shortage of sea-transport." In a later year, Brooke wrote that Marshall had "great charm and dignity . . . which could not fail to impress one; a big man and a very great gentleman who inspired trust but [even in this later year] did not impress me by the ability of his brain."[9]

Yet despite Brooke's profound misgivings, fully shared by most of his colleagues, the British on April 14 "accepted . . . [the Americans'] proposals for offensive action in Europe in 1942 [Sledgehammer] perhaps, and in 1943 [Roundup] for certain," to quote Brooke's diary.[10]

They did so at a late night meeting, at No. 10 Downing Street, of Britain's war cabinet Defence Committee, with Hopkins and Marshall in attendance. The committee members present were Attlee, Eden, Production Minister Oliver Lyttleton, First Lord of the Admiralty A. V. Alexander, War Secretary Sir James Grigg, Air Secretary Sir Archibald Sinclair, and Chiefs of Staff Brooke, Pound, Portal, and General Sir Hastings Ismay (Churchill's chief of staff), plus Lord Louis Mountbatten, who as head of combined operations (the commandos) had charge of daring, experimental, quick-hit amphibious assaults upon the enemy.

Churchill, presiding in his dual capacity as Prime Minister and minister of defense, opened the meeting with a warm personal endorsement of the "momentous proposal" that the United States had made and the British staff chiefs also approved. He mentioned, however, the "ominous possibility" of a physical linkage in the Middle East of Japanese power advancing through India and German power advancing through North Africa and southern Russia—a possibility (it seemed relatively small and remote to the Americans) upon which Brooke, in his presentation, placed heavy stress, pointing out that the Japanese, if they gained control of the Indian Ocean, would isolate Turkey and destroy the possibility of Western supply of Russia through Iran.* Russia, thus deprived, might not be able to withstand the upcoming German summer drive southward toward the oil of the Caucasus and the Middle East. Brooke's conclusion: As preparations went forward for the European offensive, to which he and his British colleagues now committed themselves, they must not be permitted to absorb so much of America's resources that nothing, or too little, remained to satisfy

---

*The reader is reminded that the Marshall-Hopkins mission to London took place simultaneously with the close of the Japanese conquest of Burma and the failure of the Cripps mission to India, told of earlier in this history.

needs elsewhere in the world. Marshall made no direct reference to British concerns over India during his initial presentation to the meeting but did refer to the growing American naval strength in the Pacific, saying that the U.S. Navy was positioning itself for a flank attack upon the Japanese when they drove again southward toward Australia, as they doubtless would. His implication was obvious: Any major setback for the Japanese in the Pacific would drastically reduce the potency of their present threat in the Indian Ocean. A little later he joined in a discussion of Indian Ocean problems with Churchill and Pound, emphasizing his conviction that the British and Americans together could do whatever needed to be done in the Indian Ocean while still going ahead at necessary speed toward both Sledgehammer (which he said might have to be mounted *before* this coming September if the German summer offensive in Russia proved too overpowering) and Roundup.[11]

Hopkins, listening closely to all this, noted a reversal of emphasis on the part of the British that was troubling in that it might signify a commitment to the cross-Channel operation on their part that was less complete and firm than they said it was. Three months ago, their great fear had been that the United States, shocked by Pearl Harbor, might concentrate on the Pacific at the expense of the Atlantic. Their expressions of this fear had had an unmistakable sincerity. Less certainly sincere were their present expressions of fear that the American concentration upon Europe would expose the Allied cause to fatal danger in the Far East. Hopkins, therefore, when his turn came to speak, emphasized that if American popular opinion were dictating grand strategy, the United States would be doing right now what the British had formerly feared she would do and seemed now, in some part, to want her to do. The American populace had certainly fervently favored an all-out effort against Japan on the marrow of Pearl Harbor, and the fervor of such sentiment had been increased by the bitter ending to the Bataan fighting. It would be further increased when Wainwright was forced to surrender Corregidor. And this division between the predominant public opinion of the country and the strategic thinking of the President and his military advisers could gravely endanger the whole Allied war effort (so Hopkins clearly implied) if nothing adequate was done to shift American popular attention and commitment to the European theater. One thing upon which the President, the American leaders, and the American public were all agreed was the necessity for truly significant battle action by American troops at the earliest possible date. *"Our men must fight!"* said Hopkins. And Western Europe was obviously the place, the only place, where truly decisive fighting by the Western Allies could be done. He said that of course the British fought in their own national interest, as did the Americans—a seeming non sequitur indicative of his suspicion that the British overly emphasized the danger to India because of British imperial interests not shared by the United States—but overall, in this war, the interests of the two nations coincided, and the two must therefore fight now as one against the Axis. They were pledged to do so in cross-Channel invasion, and all must recognize that the decision now taken was irreversible (he placed heavy emphasis on this) since Americans would from now on consider this operation to be their major war effort.

The meeting ended in a warm glow of enthusiasm and goodwill, with Churchill, in his closing statement, assuring Hopkins that the British government's commitment to this great enterprise was absolutely firm and wholehearted. So persuasive was this closing eloquence that the doubts and suspicions that till then had lingered in the mind of Hopkins were wholly erased. He and Marshall were exultant when, next morning, they cabled the good news to Roosevelt and Stimson respectively.[12]

The two arrived back in Washington four days later greatly pleased and encouraged by what their mission had accomplished. They would have been far less so had they known what both Ismay, Churchill's personal chief of staff, and Sir Charles Wilson, Churchill's personal physician, concluded from their observations of the Prime Minister's behavior. Wilson, who believed himself well acquainted with Churchill's strategical views and who was therefore "puzzled . . . by the manner in which the P.M. agreed with Marshall, almost . . . without a fight," told his diary that "the P.M.," as "an experienced and tenacious campaigner," must have "decided that the time has not come to take the field as an out-and-out opponent of a Second Front in France." For one thing, a great thing, the Prime Minister feared what Hopkins had warned against, namely, that "the President might [yet] be driven by public clamor to concentrate on the war with Japan," as Dr. Wilson later wrote. "It was no time for argument." Ismay, too, knew and shared the profound misgivings Churchill felt over the American proposals, especially Sledgehammer, and was unhappily aware, as he later wrote, that "[o]ur American friends went happily homewards under the mistaken impression that we had committed ourselves to both Roundup and Sledgehammer" when, in fact, the British commitment was firm only as regarded Roundup. ". . . [W]e should have come clean, much cleaner than we did."[13]

II

ROOSEVELT had told Churchill in the April 1, 1942, telegram that upon receipt of "word from you after you have seen Harry and Marshall," he proposed to ask Stalin "to send two special representatives to me at once." On April 11, though Churchill had not yet commented on this proposal, Roosevelt cabled Stalin: "I have in mind very important military proposal involving utilization of our armed forces in a manner to relieve your critical western front. . . . Therefore I wish you would consider sending Mr. Molotov and a general upon whom you rely to Washington in the immediate future. Time is of the essence if we are to help in any important way. . . . I do not want by such a trip to go over the head of my friend Mr. Litvinov in any way, as he will understand,* but we can gain time by the visit I propose. I suggest this procedure not only because of the secrecy, which is so essential, but because I need your advice before we determine with finality the strategic course of our common military action." Stalin welcomed the proposal, with the proviso "that Mr. Molotov's journey . . . be accompanied without any publicity whatever till the return of Mr. Molotov to Moscow, as was done when Mr. Eden visited Moscow in December last." There was, however, for various reasons, a considerable delay in Molotov's departure on this trip, and by the time he did at last depart, in the third week of May, Moscow had arranged for him to stop for some days in London and fly on from there to America instead of going directly to Washington, as Roosevelt would have much preferred him to do.[14]

There were two reasons for this. *One* was that, though the United States government had requested the Molotov visit for the purpose of discussing the making of a second front, as Stalin soon knew, the actual making of it in 1942 must be a largely British operation, as he also knew. It seemed logical to him, therefore, that his foreign minister should go first to London, then to Washington, to discuss the matter. The *other* reason was that Great Britain had been carrying the main burden of a continuing disagreement between the Soviet government and the Western Allies over the fate of the Baltic States, which Russia had occupied when Hitler and Stalin divided Poland between themselves.

It will be recalled that Russia's insistence upon retaining Latvia, Lithuania, and Estonia within the Soviet Union, her demand that a guarantee of this be a secret protocol in a formal treaty between her and Great Britain, had been the major hazard to the success of Eden's mission to Moscow in December 1941. Churchill had then vigorously opposed any such arrangement on the ground that it violated the Atlantic Charter, which Russia had signed, and would never be agreed to by the United States. In early March 1942, however, he had shifted ground. "The increasing gravity of the war had led me to feel that the principles of the Atlantic Charter ought not to be construed so as to deny Russia the frontiers she occupied when Germany attacked her," he cabled Roosevelt on March 7, 1942. "This [he now said, in contradiction of his earlier view] was the basis on which Russia acceded to the Charter. . . . I hope therefore that you will be able to give us a free hand to sign the treaty which Stalin desires as soon as possible. Everything portends an immense renewal of the German invasion of Russia . . . and there is very little we can do to help." Two days later, he cabled Stalin, saying: "I have sent a message to President Roosevelt urging him to approve our signing the agreement with you about the frontiers of Russia at the

---

*Litvinov, when he learned of this, may have understood, but his understanding did nothing to reduce the unease he felt over it. His demeanor in Molotov's presence, during the Washington visit, would be unwontedly stiff and tense.

end of the war." Roosevelt did *not* approve of this, however; he maintained his opposition to any international discussion of territorial settlements until the end of the war. His view was decisive. Churchill quickly yielded the point.[15]

So when Molotov arrived in London on May 20, he faced on this issue the solid opposition of both the British and American governments. "I must tell you that we received invaluable help from Winant during our Russian negotiations," Churchill would cable Roosevelt on June 4. "He made the Russians understand as no one else could do how injurious to good relations between us three must have been the American reaction to the old treaty [the treaty containing the territorial concessions the Russians demanded]." The impasse was broken when, on the morning of May 23, Eden, at precisely the right moment, proposed to substitute for the draft treaty Molotov had brought with him a formal, general, and public twenty-year pact for peace between the Soviet Union and Great Britain—a document, prepared in the British Foreign Office, that contained no reference whatever to frontiers. By the evening of that day, "the Russians," in Churchill's words, "showed signs of giving way." On the following day, Molotov asked for and received Stalin's permission to negotiate on the basis of Eden's proposal, and on May 26, after only minor changes in the original proposal, Molotov, on behalf of the Soviet Union, signed the pact.[16]

Molotov's military discussions in London were less conclusive—indeed, not conclusive at all.

In his formal conversation with Churchill on May 22, the Russian stressed the need for complete frankness in the discussion of "the establishment of a 'Second Front' " and, in a show of frankness, spoke of the strain his country was under and the possibility that the strain, unrelieved, might break her. Russia's great need was for the Allies to invade Western Europe within the next few months on a scale sufficient to draw forty German divisions away from the Russian front. If such a second front were opened, he said, "the doom of Hitler was sealed, if not in 1942, at any rate very soon thereafter." If it were *not* done, Russia just might be crushed under the coming German pressure. For at the present time, the "advantage in armed strength lies with the Germans. . . . It must be remembered that Hitler can call upon vast resources seized from the subjugated and enslaved people scattered over a large part of Europe." Churchill, in reply, stressed the difficulties of a seaborne attack upon a highly fortified coast. In former times, control of the sea had given the nation possessing it a wide range of choices among possible landing places on a hostile shore because "it was impossible for the enemy to be prepared at every point to meet [such] . . . invasion." The advent of airpower had changed this. Defensive enemy airpower could now be brought massively to bear in major force upon any point on Europe's Atlantic coast within hours after an invasion was attempted at that point, and the only successful answer for the invader was to gain and retain absolute control by his own planes of the air above the landing area. This meant that victorious seaborne assaults by the Western Allies could be made only on those Atlantic coastal areas that were within range of fighter planes based in England. "Our choice is, in fact, narrowed down to the Pas de Calais, the Cherbourg 'tip' and part of the Brest area," and the "problem of landing a force this year in one or more of these areas is being studied, and preparations are being made, with utmost energy" by both Great Britain and the United States. The plans were based on the assumption that "successive waves of assault forces" would compel the enemy to commit the bulk of his airpower to great air battles above the invasion area, battles that "if continued over a week or ten days" would, because the quality of Allied fighter planes was higher than that of Axis fighters, result in "the virtual destruction of the enemy's air power on the Continent." Further landings could then be made at points presently impregnable. A crucial limiting factor was the lack of a sufficient number "of the special landing craft required for effecting the initial landing on the very heavily defended enemy coastline."[17]

Molotov then asked what the British would do if Russia "failed to hold out against the maximum effort" that Hitler was now preparing. Churchill deprecated the possibility. Last year, the military experts of both the Allies and the Axis had predicted a swift Russian collapse. "In the event the Soviet forces . . . defeated Hitler and nearly brought his army to disaster." And was it not significant that the massive German offensive predicted for May had not yet been launched and, according to intelligence reports, was likely not to be until well into June? Did this not probably mean that the offensive, when it came, would not "be as strong or so menacing as that of 1941"? However, if the "worst came to the worst," the British would fight on and, with the United States, would "build up overwhelming air superiority, which, in the course of the next eighteen months or two years, would enable us to [mount] . . . a devastating . . . air attack on German cities and industries. We should, moreover, maintain the blockade and make landings on the Continent against an increasingly enfeebled opposition. Ultimately, the power of Great Britain and the United States would prevail."[18]

This opening conversation between Molotov and Churchill went as far as the Russian foreign minister was able to get, during this first London visit, toward the second front guarantee he wanted. But it was arranged that he return to London on his way back to Moscow from Washington. "We can then continue our discussions, which I hope will lead to the development of close military cooperation between our three countries," said a cable from Churchill to Stalin on May 23. "Moreover, I shall then be able to give him the latest developments in our own military plans."[19]

Five days later, after the Soviet plane carrying Molotov and his party had landed at Washington but before the President and Molotov had met, Churchill sent Roosevelt a full report of the formal conversations he had had with the Russian foreign minister. "We made great progress in intimacy and good will," he

said in his cover message, adding that with British and American officers working hard together, "all preparations [for the cross-Channel operation] are proceeding . . . on the largest scale." His following statements, however, boded ill
for the actual mounting of Sledgehammer and portended grave trouble for the
Anglo-American military alliance in general. Churchill said that Mountbatten,
who was about to depart for Washington to confer on cross-Channel plans,
would "explain to you the difficulties of 1942 when he arrives. I have also told
the Staffs to study a landing in the north of Norway [Narvik its main objective]
the occupation of which seems necessary to ensure the flow of our supplies next
year.* I have told Molotov we would have something ready for him about this
to discuss on his return here. We did not go deeply into it in any way. Personally, I set great importance upon it if a good plan can be made." He closed, ominously from Marshall's point of view: "We must never let Gymnast pass from
our minds. All other preparations would help if need be toward that."[20]

Molotov arrived for his first meeting with Roosevelt in the White House at
four o'clock in the afternoon of May 29, 1942. With the President were Hull,
Hopkins, and an American interpreter of Russian.† With Molotov were Ambassador Litvinov and a Russian interpreter of English. The meeting was primarily
a "get acquainted" session, and during it, Roosevelt was unwontedly ill at ease,
though the fact could be evident only to someone intimately acquainted with
him. There were two reasons for this unease. One was the frustration of his
natural conversational style by the long wait that the need for translation imposed between any statement and its reply. The other was the nature, the character, of this visitor from Moscow. Never in all his enormously wide experience
of men had Roosevelt encountered anyone as rigidly self-controlled, as exclusively focused upon whatever was being discussed, as devoid of spontaneity
and invulnerable to Rooseveltian "charm," as this wooden-faced (even when
nominally smiling) Russian. Compared with him, Marshall, for all his personal
aloofness, his avoidance of social intimacies and small talk, was a riotously entertaining companion. Knowing something about the way in which Stalin and
the men around him had come to power, Roosevelt as he dealt with Stalin's
envoy had a sense of mysterious reserve wherein dwelt memories of events and
personal acts that might horrify if revealed. They somehow added potency to
whatever Molotov did express. (While this conversation was under way, a
White House valet discovered that the foreign minister, who was staying that
night in the White House, had a pistol in his luggage. The valet agitatedly reported his discovery to Chief White House Usher Howell Crim, who promptly

---

*Convoys making the "Murmansk run," during the months of almost continuous Arctic sunlight, were
now virtually defenseless against attacks by Axis planes operating from northern Norwegian bases.
Their losses were huge.
†He was Samuel H. Cross, Harvard professor of Slavic languages and literature. Pavlov, Stalin's interpreter, interpreted for Molotov.

reported it by phone to the Secret Service. When he'd hung up, Crim told the valet that nothing could be done about it: "Just hope he doesn't use it on you.") Nevertheless, Roosevelt was convinced that a common ground on which to base a sympathetic understanding with this strange creature existed somewhere. He was determined to find it, was challenged to find it as he had seldom if ever been so challenged before.[21]

Yet to Hopkins, comparing Molotov's demeanor now with what it had been when Hopkins talked with him in Moscow, the Russian seemed to be trying hard for amiability, even cordiality. His capacity for truly personal relationships was limited and machinelike (all his capacities seemed machinelike), and the machinery was in this case stiffened and rusted by disuse. Yet it was *almost* as an ordinary human being that he now spoke of his ten-hour flight directly from Moscow to London—a flight not without danger, since it was made over the Russian fighting front and Nazi-occupied Denmark—and of his flight from London via Iceland and Labrador to Washington. They had been interesting experiences, he said, but not unpleasant or especially tiring. He came to Washington, he went on, with the intention of discussing fully the military situation, as he had done with the British, but he must now do so, alas, as both soldier and diplomat, for the military adviser he had brought with him to London had been forced to remain there by a broken kneecap suffered in an automobile accident. Roosevelt responded that no one now present was a military expert, but that tomorrow General Marshall and Admiral King would take part in the discussions. He added, apropos, that major action seemed to be shaping up in the Far Pacific, information having been received of heavy Japanese fleet and troop transport concentrations in the Marianas and elsewhere. They were concentrations poised to strike in any one of four directions: to the south at New Caledonia and Australia, to the east at Midway and Hawaii, to the northeast at the Aleutians, or (Roosevelt looked hard at Molotov as the translation was made) due north at Siberia's Kamchatka peninsula. Molotov replied calmly that Kamchatka could be only lightly defended. The demands made upon Russia's resources by the Nazi invasion precluded a heavier defense. And it was to be expected that Japan, as an Axis partner, would do all it could to prevent the transfer of Russian divisions from Siberia to Russia's western front. But Hitler, one must never forget, was the main enemy. To this last Roosevelt quickly asserted, saying that he had from the first insisted that "we remain on the defensive in the Pacific until the European front was cleared up" and that he believed this view was now generally accepted by the American public, if reluctantly.

There followed some discussion, initiated by Roosevelt at Hull's behest, and worse than useless in Hopkins's opinion, of Germany's treatment of its Russian war prisoners and of the possibility that Germany and the Soviet Union might sign or mutually agree to adhere to the Geneva Convention on this matter, an agreement that would permit the inspection of prisoner-of-war camps by a neutral body such as the International Red Cross. Motolov refused to consider it:

the Nazis might well make such an agreement, but they would never honor it; they would continue their appalling treatment of their Russian prisoners and use the agreement as a cover-up. He was equally dismissive of a State Department offer of its "good offices" for the settlement of what the department coyly termed "difficulties" between the Soviets and Iran, and between the Soviets and Turkey. Molotov, despite his evident wish to be amiable, expressed no gratitude whatever for this. He simply expressed, dryly, a belief that he and his Foreign Office colleagues knew a good deal more about Soviet relations with Turkey and Iran than did the American State Department. At that point, the "conference seemed to be getting nowhere rapidly," as Hopkins recorded in his notes, "and I suggested that Molotov might like to rest." The suggestion was accepted.[22]

On the following morning (May 30, 1942), there gathered in the Executive Office Molotov, King, Marshall, Roosevelt, and Hopkins—just these five, with the two interpreters. Molotov presented his case for a second front massive enough to draw forty German divisions westward from the Russian front in 1942. The prospects for success of a major cross-Channel operation this year were better than those for such an operation in 1943, he argued. Hitler's present margin of superiority over the Russians on the eastern front would be erased if he were compelled to send forty divisions, even "distinctly second-rate divisions," to France, and his final defeat next year, if not this year, would be assured. On the other hand, if no western front were opened, the impending German offensive might be too powerful for Russian arms to withstand. It was given, he went on, that the Russians would never surrender, but they might become so weakened that their front became "secondary," enabling a Hitler strengthened by "the foodstuffs and raw materials of the Ukraine and the oil wells of the Caucasus" to shift far more than forty divisions westward, rendering a 1943 cross-Channel operation impossible. Molotov, of course, realized that the brunt of major action in the West this year would have to be borne by the British and that the British, therefore, must have the final say in the matter, but he also realized that the British decision depended upon the American attitude.* That was why Churchill had postponed telling him definitely what the British would do until he, Molotov, returned to London. Hence his need for a frank straight answer to his crucial question: Was the United States prepared to establish a second front in 1942?[23]

Roosevelt turned to Marshall: Were developments sufficiently far advanced to enable us to say definitely to Mr. Stalin that we were preparing a second front? They were, said Marshall. Whereupon, precipitously, as Marshall thought, and to the general's considerable alarm, Roosevelt said that we did indeed ex-

---

*He clearly did *not* realize that his estimate of the German margin of superiority over the Russian forces was much too narrow to argue, in such logical military minds as Brooke's, for a cross-Channel invasion attempt in 1942; it indicated a risk of Russian collapse this year, or of a German victory of the magnitude Molotov described, that was far smaller than the risk of disaster for the invasion attempt.

pect to create a second front this year (the contextual implication was that it would be a front in northern France of the requested size) and that Mr. Molotov should say so to Mr. Stalin. Marshall hastened to qualify the promise. We were indeed determined to establish a second front, he said. Our aim was to create a situation on the continent that would force the Germans into an all-out air engagement, and only a massive landing of Allied ground troops could do so. The enterprise was difficult, however. We had sufficient trained troops, munitions, aviation, and armored divisions to effect a landing in force, but we did not have the necessary sea transport or landing craft and could not obtain them for many months ahead. The shipping problem was complicated by the demands made by the Russian supply shipments to Murmansk—a point that Admiral King then elaborated. As the meeting drew to a close, Roosevelt handed Molotov a schedule of lend-lease matériel to be produced during the year beginning July 1. It totaled 8 million tons, but no more than 4.1 million tons of it, said Roosevelt, could with the available shipping be delivered to the Soviet Union. And if the matériel needed for establishing a second front in 1942 were to be transported to England, even this amount, as Molotov understood from what Marshall and King had said, would have to be reduced. In other words, the supply figures just handed Molotov could not be those incorporated in the Second Protocol on lend-lease aid to the Soviet Union that was currently being negotiated (the First Protocol, negotiated by Harriman and Beaverbrook during last September's Moscow Conference, would expire on July 1); there were simply not enough ships with which to maintain the present Murmansk run, plus the present flow of supplies through the Persian Gulf, and at the same time greatly expand the English run.[24]

How great the reduction must be was decided by Roosevelt, Hopkins, Marshall, and King on the afternoon of May 31. The figure they agreed upon was 1.6 million tons—a reduction from 4.1 million tons to 2.5 million—as Roosevelt wrote in a memorandum at the meeting's close. The President insisted, however, that the whole of the reduction be made in general supplies (these were cut nearly in half, from 1.3 million tons to 700,000) and not in the 1.8 million tons of planes, tanks, and guns that the Russians desperately needed this summer and which the first draft of the Second Protocol had promised. He stressed this last when, with Hopkins at his side, he presented the figures to Molotov and Litvinov in a meeting of these four only, plus the two interpreters, on the morning of Monday, June 1. (The meeting was somewhat shortened by the fact that Roosevelt "had to entertain the Duke and Duchess of Windsor at lunch at twelve," as he announced with some acerbity to those assembled.)*

---

*The duke and duchess "are in Washington at their own invitation and about as welcome as a pair of pickpockets, a luxury both England and ourselves could dispense with in these days of blood and sweat and tears," said William Hassett in his diary entry for June 1, 1942.[25]

Nothing that the Russians could immediately use for fighting purposes was to be removed from the shipment schedule, said the President. All the cuts were in raw materials or in items whose use was for the production of weapons and munitions, material that could not be available for fighting purposes until the battles there immediately impended had ended. Molotov replied that many non-military supplies, such as railroad equipment and metals, were essential to the maintenance of a solid fighting front; he hoped the reduction in the shipment of these would not be too severe. Evidently the way in which he said this (or perhaps the way in which it was translated) seemed to Roosevelt indicative of an unrealistic, uncooperative attitude, for he responded a bit irritably. Every ship shifted from the Murmansk run to the English run brought the second front closer to realization, he repeated. "After all, ships cannot be in two places at once," nor could the Soviets "eat their cake and have it too." This caused Molotov to bristle: The success of a second front depended upon the steadfastness of the first quite as much as it did upon the abundance of its own supply, he said ("with some emphasis," according to the American interpreter's report); and what if the flow of supplies to his country were reduced, yet no second front eventuated? The aid reduction ought to be joined with an absolute assurance that a true second front would be established *this year,* and so far he had been told definitely only that a second front was being prepared and that Mr. Roosevelt *expected* it to be established in 1942.

It was a moment of challenge that Roosevelt, judging from the record of this meeting, met with characteristic and effective adroitness.

In earlier discussion, he had expressed to Molotov his conviction that after this war had ended, an international organization should not, because it could not, be counted upon of itself alone to maintain world peace. Witness the dismal failure of the League of Nations to do so. A world international organization properly conceived and set up could make many valuable contributions to a viable world peace—was no doubt even an essential of true peace-making and -keeping—but in a community of sovereign states, as in a community of individual men and women, keeping the peace required occasional forceful action against aggressors. It required the exercise of police power. Implied by the analogy was an international organization to which each member state assigned *all* of that portion of its sovereignty that was essential to war making, but such inference was neither drawn nor acceptable as a practical conclusion by Roosevelt. He proposed instead that the four most powerful nation-states in the world assume the peacekeeping responsibility, these four being the Soviet Union, the United States, Great Britain, and China. They should become the "four policemen" of the world. That the head of the most powerful of the Western states should thus propose equal status and power sharing between his state and the Soviet Union had pleased Molotov greatly and exerted a decidedly softening effect upon his attitude. He had at once forwarded the idea to Stalin and been immediately informed, as he in turn had informed Roosevelt, that the "idea [if with a certain tentativeness as regards China's inclusion] had the full approval of the Soviet Government, which would support it fully." The friendly psychological atmosphere thus engendered now helped Roosevelt to mollify the Soviet commissar without making the absolute commitment the Russian had called for. In a way that made the event seem probable *almost* to the point of certainty and that left no doubt in the Russian mind that he personally was enormously desirous that it occur, he reiterated his expectation that the front would be established this year. He fervently expressed again his profound personal admiration for the gallant struggle the Russian people were waging against Hitler's theretofore all-conquering legions. "The conversation . . . ended with decreased tension on the Russian side," says the interpreter's report. "The President bade Mr. Molotov a cordial farewell [Roosevelt was to depart that evening for Hyde Park; he would not see the commissar again], wished him a safe return home, and presented him with his photograph."[26]

(In the end, the Russians would agree to a Second Protocol that incorporated the supply reductions. They would also agree to accept the delivery to them in Alaska of American-made planes flown there from Montana, with Russian pilots flying them from Alaska to Siberia, something they had earlier been reluctant to do; ultimately, 7,308 American planes, or 56 percent of all those Russia received during the war, would be delivered this way.)[27]

A couple of days later, Molotov found unsatisfactory a draft public statement about his Washington visit that, at Roosevelt's order, had been prepared by the State Department. Combined with a British statement about his London visit, it was to be issued simultaneously in Moscow, London, and Washington on the day (it turned out to be June 11) that the Russian envoy arrived back in Moscow. Molotov wrote out a statement of his own, the key sentence of which, as published, was "In the course of the conversations full understanding was reached with regard to the urgent tasks of creating a Second Front in 1942.* Marshall, when he read this, immediately objected to it. He would continue to be in favor of Sledgehammer, but chiefly as a guarantor of Roundup, and he was becoming more and more cognizant of its hazards and of the distinct possibility that the British, who must provide by far the greater portion of the troops for it, might in the end refuse to launch it. Hence, as Marshall insisted to his friend Hopkins, all references to the dates of continental invasion operations should be removed from the communiqué announcing the Molotov visits. Hopkins quite forcefully

---

*One suspects that this published sentence was a State Department revision of what Molotov originally wrote, this having said that agreement had been reached upon the opening of a second front in 1942. Certainly the circumlocution, "full understanding . . . with regard to the urgent tasks of," has the all-too-familiar smell of State Department prose. And certainly, as Robert Sherwood says, questions about the "exact meaning of these words . . . provoked interminable and often violently acrimonious discussion for a long time thereafter."[28]

called the general's objection to Roosevelt's attention. But Roosevelt's primary concern at that moment was to bolster the Russians' morale in the face of the terrific ordeal they were about to undergo. He had told Churchill in a May missive that Molotov was obviously greatly worried "as to the next four or five months" and that he himself had "a very strong feeling that the Russian position is precarious and may grow steadily worse during the coming weeks." Since he was "inclined to think that at present all the Russians are a bit down in the mouth," he was "especially anxious" that "when Molotov leaves . . . he carry back some real results of his Mission and . . . give a favorable account to Stalin." He therefore approved publication of the challenged statement.[29]

And so did Churchill, if for somewhat different reasons, when Molotov returned to London. The Prime Minister increasingly doubted the feasibility of any major cross-Channel operation in 1942. The British staff had been and still were "actively studying this in conjunction with the American staff, and nothing but difficulties had as yet emerged," as he writes in his war memoirs. But the present benefits from "a public statement which might make the Germans apprehensive" and cause them "to hold as many of their troops in the West as possible" justified in his mind the risk of future trouble for the military alliance with the Soviet Union—a potential trouble the proportions of which he simultaneously sought to reduce. At the very meeting in the cabinet room at which the communiqué was formally approved, he personally handed to Molotov an aide-mémoire saying: "We are making preparations for a landing on the Continent in August or September, 1942. . . . Clearly however it would not further the Russian cause or that of the Allies as a whole if, for the sake of action at any price, we embarked on some operation which ended in disaster. . . . It is impossible to say in advance whether the situation will be such as to make this operation feasible when the time comes. *We can therefore give no promise in the matter* [italicized in Churchill's memoirs as well as by subsequent events], but provided that it appears sound and sensible we shall not hesitate to put our plans into effect." Strange to say, the hedge seemed not to dampen the Russian envoy's spirits as, in Churchill's words, "he sailed off into the air on his somewhat dangerous homeward flight."[30]

III

LORD Mountbatten arrived in Washington on June 3, having flown the Atlantic as one of a party that included Lieutenant General Arnold, chief of the U.S. Army Air Force; Rear Admiral John H. Towers, chief of the U.S. Navy Bureau of Aeronautics; and Major Generals Eisenhower and Mark Clark, the latter chief of staff to General McNair of the newly established U.S. Army Ground Forces. The four Americans had been in England since the third week of May— Arnold and Towers to consult on the air offensive against Germany, Eisenhower to consult on preparations for the cross-Channel operation. (Eisenhower was at this time identified in American press releases as a "tank expert" but seems to have been recognized by the British as the man who would probably soon command the American troops then pouring in ever-increasing numbers into the British Isles. How otherwise explain the fact that he, with Winant and Harriman, among others, was a weekend guest at Chequers on May 30 when the RAF made its first one-thousand-bomber attack upon a German city, in this case, Cologne?)[31] During technical discussions with the Joint Chiefs of Staff on following days—discussions of the requirements for success in amphibious operations, with heavy stress on the number and kinds of landing craft needed per unit landed, and of the role of air bombardment and naval shellfire— Mountbatten did indeed communicate to the Americans the British view of the difficulties that must be overcome if any landing in France with intent to stay were to succeed in 1942.

These discussions began on the day (June 4) of the Battle of Midway. As they continued, and the first news of American victory was confirmed and augmented by later information, the discussions were affected by the growing realization that the Midway victory was not merely tactical but also strategic, and on a global scale, in that the balance of power in the whole of the Pacific was altered by it. Tactical and even strategical initiatives of major importance could still be taken by Japan, but her overall fighting strength relative to that of her enemies must from now on steadily decline, and more and more, her battle actions would be dictated by, would be responses to, her enemies' initiatives. Yet, ironically, this longed-for event did not reduce Marshall's immediate anxieties; it increased them. In London he had argued by implication that a major victory in the Pacific war would relieve the Japanese threat to India, enabling resources that would otherwise have been needed for the defense of India to become part of the buildup for cross-Channel attack. But now that a much greater Pacific victory than anyone expected had been achieved and the threat to India was virtually eliminated, the pressure for a diversion of resources to the Pacific was greater than before! The proponents of such diversion argued that Midway made the final defeat of Japan certain in the near future provided a major portion of America's available resources was devoted to the task, whereas no such certainty attended an all-out effort, this year or next, against Hitler's Germany. The popular persuasiveness of the counterargument, namely, that the defeat of Germany assured the defeat of Japan, whereas Japan's defeat did not assure, and might well increase the difficulty of achieving, the defeat of Germany, was reduced: Tokyo having surrendered, we would still, possibly in a weakened condition, have to face a Hitler possibly stronger than he now was. King now called more forcefully than before for army ground forces to augment his marines in attacks upon Japanese-held Pacific islands—"island-hopping" toward Tokyo. MacArthur proposed a drive northward by his forces toward Rabaul and began making grandiose plans for an offensive that would have absorbed the bulk of America's available ground forces in 1943. And the shared sense that fundamental decisions about grand strategy were now in the process of being made in the White House caused both King and Marshall to worry about the meeting of Mountbatten with the President, whom they deemed far too susceptible to the blandishments of the British. Their worry became acute anxiety when they were not invited to be present (they had taken for granted that they would be) at a discussion of the war situation by the President and the Prime Minister's envoy.[32]

The crucial meeting of Roosevelt with Mountbatten was, in fact, a very private affair—a dinner and after-dinner meeting at the White House on Tuesday, June 9, with only Harry Hopkins present aside from the two principals. During it, Roosevelt stressed the absolute need, as he saw it, for battle action against the Germans by American ground forces at the earliest possible moment and expressed his strong aversion to sending a million American troops to England during the immediately coming months, when there was a distinct possibility that, owing to Russian collapse, a frontal attack upon Hitler's Germany would become impossible. Apropos of this, he asked Mountbatten to remind Churchill of "the agreement reached the last time he [the Prime Minister] was in Washington" that in the event of things going very badly for the Russians this summer, "a sacrifice landing would be carried out in France to assist them." Mountbatten promised to do so but "pointed out that no landing . . . we could carry out [this year] could draw off any [German] troops [from the Russian front], since there were some 25 German divisions already in France and landing craft shortage prevented our putting ashore" more troops than these divisions could deal with. The "sacrifice," in other words, would be in vain. This jarred the President. No doubt it determined his going on, as he did, to protest the sending of American troops to England simultaneously with the shipping of British troops *out* of England—to North Africa, the Middle East, India—and to suggest that, instead, the British "leave about six divisions in England" while the United States sent six of its divisions "straight to fight in North Africa, either round the Cape or directly into Morocco with a view to joining hands with the Army of the Nile and reopening the Mediterranean." He had been greatly impressed, he said, by the Prime Minister's statement in a recent telegram: "Do not lose sight of Gymnast." As regards the Pacific war, he and Marshall were agreed that advantage should be taken of the Midway victory to the fullest extent consistent with the continued buildup for the cross-Channel attack. "There was a general desire to take the offensive [against Japan] from Australia using existing U.S. Marine forces and combat shipping," and to support these operations, he and Marshall "were anxious" to have "two British aircraft carriers with their destroyer screen . . . join the American naval forces in Australia."[33]

Four days later, Mountbatten, having arrived back in London, reported all this to Churchill in a lengthy night interview. The Prime Minister had already (on June 11) asked for and obtained from the British war cabinet a formal agreement that no substantial landing in France would be made by the Allies unless and until they were prepared to stay there—also, that no landing whatever would be attempted in 1942 unless the Germans were so utterly demoralized by the outcome of the Russian battle that they could not effectively resist it. This last was so unlikely an event that the cabinet decision was, in Churchill's view, a final repudiation of Sledgehammer. It alarmed and dismayed him, therefore, that the President, according to Mountbatten, believed him to have committed himself absolutely, during Arcadia, to a "sacrifice landing" if things went very badly for the Russians this summer. On the following morning (June 13) he cabled Roosevelt that "in view of the impossibility of dealing by correspondence with all the many difficult points outstanding, I feel it is my duty to come see you." (He knew, for Hopkins had informed him in a personal communication, that Roosevelt was about to invite him to "make a quick trip" to Washington to decide "certain matters of high policy.") He therefore proposed boarding his plane for the transatlantic flight on "Thursday 18th," weather permitting, bringing with him General Ismay, who was his personal military chief of staff, and General Brooke, chief of the imperial general staff (Marshall's British counterpart), "whom you have not yet met." He informed Brooke of this decision a few hours later, remarking as he did so that Roosevelt seems to be "getting a little off the rails" and that, obviously, "some good talks as regards Western Front are required."[34]

There were high British officials who wondered if both the head of the British government and the head of Britain's military forces should be away from London at that moment. It was an anxious moment. From his Cairo headquarters in early May, Auchinleck had wired that owing to a shortage of tanks, he was postponing for a month the Eighth Army offensive against Rommel in Cyrenaica that had been originally scheduled to begin the middle of that month. Audacious Rommel declined to patiently await the onslaught. In mid-May, he again took the offensive—an Afrika Korps attack that by mid-June had pushed the Eighth Army back almost to the Egyptian border and was gravely threatening the vital Allied supply port of Tobruk. Should Tobruk fall, Allied control of Egypt and the Suez Canal would be threatened; should Suez be lost, the Middle East with its rich oil reserve was likely to be also. Allied supply of India across the Indian Ocean would be curtailed, possibly eliminated. Britain's weakening grip upon India, where mass unrest markedly increased after the failure of the Cripps mission, might be lost altogether. Allied supply of Russia through the Persian Gulf would probably become impossible. And the Russians' need for such supply was increasingly dire, for things had indeed begun to go very badly for them on their southern front. They had launched in May a major drive toward Nazi-held Kharkov, a drive designed to forestall the German movement eastward to the Volga, southward to the Caucasus, but their effort had failed miserably; a German counterattack, which had trapped scores of thousands of Russian troops west of the Donets River, now continued relentlessly eastward and southward. Simultaneously, the Russians had lost Kerch, their last stronghold in the Crimea save for Sevastopol—and Sevastopol, most of whose thirteen fortresses had been knocked out by the besieging Germans, was now obviously doomed (it would fall on June 22). Brought into sharper question than before in many minds was Russia's ability to hold, against Hitler's onslaught, the rich grain fields south of Rostov, the oil fields of Baku.

But both Churchill and Brooke answered this latter question affirmatively, as they did also the question of whether Tobruk would be held. Tobruk's situation appeared to them less desperate now than it had been last year when, invested and besieged, it had held out for months. And Russia's overall military situation also appeared to them less desperate than it had been last year, leading them to conclude that her military strength relative to Germany's was likely to be approximately the same in the autumn as it was now. In any case, they were both convinced that nothing was at present more important to the total war effort than successful transaction of the business that brought them to the American capital.

As for their westward journey itself, a 26½-hour-flight in a Boeing clipper from Scotland's Stranraer Loch to the Potomac River at Washington, it was for Churchill a repetition, so far as physical comfort was concerned, of his return flight from Arcadia. For Brooke, it was a pleasant surprise—indeed, a luxurious respite from anxious labor. The "huge flying boat" was, in Brooke's diary's words, "beautifully fitted up with bunks to sleep in, dining-saloon, steward's office, lavatories, etc." There was plenty of room in which those of the small party (it included, as always, Churchill's personal physician, Sir Charles Wilson) could stretch their legs; there were large windows through which to view sea, land, the ever-changing cloud formations, and the glories of sunrise and sunset; overall, there was a traveling environment far better for the human body and soul than the narrow corridors jammed with as many seats as they could hold to which the long-distance air traveler of today is condemned. Excellent meals could be leisurely consumed in the dining-saloon, though it must be added that sharing them with the Prime Minister was, for Brooke, "a little trying on the constitution," since each of them, as he later recalled, was "washed down with champagne and brandy."[35]

It was eight o'clock in the evening of June 18 (two A.M. in the morning of June 19 in London) when the great flying boat touched down upon the Potomac. The welcoming party at the river's side included Lord Halifax, who took Churchill to the British embassy for that night's stay, and Sir John Dill, in whose house Brooke was to stay for the duration of his visit and to which Dill now took him. Roosevelt was not one of the welcoming party, as he certainly would have been had he been in Washington. "I find I must be in Hyde Park nineteenth, twentieth, and twenty-first," he had cabled the Prime Minister on June 13 (*why* he must be has never been explained, but as Warren Kimball surmises, he may have wanted a private talk with Churchill before the two of them entered upon the crucial strategy discussion with the staff chiefs that were scheduled to open June 22). "If you land any time before noon Sunday the twenty-first," his June 13 message had continued, "come to Hyde Park and we can leave for Washington that night getting to the White House Monday morning."[36]

So, early in the morning of Friday, June 19, Churchill flew in a small plane to an airfield near Poughkeepsie where Roosevelt, seated at the wheel of his hand-controlled Ford, "saw us make the roughest bump landing I have ever experienced." Even more memorable for Churchill, and for the same reason (a sense of vital risk), was his tour of the Roosevelt family estate, which began an hour or so later. It was made in Roosevelt's Ford with Roosevelt at the wheel, and during it "I had some thoughtful moments," as Churchill writes in his war memoirs. "An ingenious arrangement enabled him [Roosevelt] . . . to do everything with his arms, which were amazingly strong and muscular. He invited me to feel his biceps, saying a famous prize-fighter [Jack Dempsey] had envied them. This was reassuring, but I confess that on several occasions when the car poised and backed on grass verges of the precipices over the Hudson I hoped that the mechanical devices and brakes would show no defects. All the time we talked business . . . though I was careful not to take his attention off the driving. . . ."[37]

IV

THE first item on Churchill's agenda bore, in the papers he'd brought with him, the curious label "Tube Alloys."

When the MAUD committee's final report came to No. 10 Downing Street in the summer of 1941, the Prime Minister had ordered the all-out maximum-priority effort toward an atomic bomb that MAUD had urgently recommended. To handle this work, a special division dubbed "Directory of Tube Alloys" had been established within Britain's Department of Scientific and Industrial Research. A little over a month later (October 9, 1941), and in good part owing to this same MAUD report, Roosevelt, acting upon the advice of Vannevar Bush and Henry Wallace, had authorized a crash review, by men competent to make it, of the MAUD findings, also of all research thus far aimed at producing an atomic explosive. He as commander in chief would then finally decide whether or not to authorize the indicated all-out effort. Actually, the research review Roosevelt called for was then already under way and had been for months, conducted at Bush's behest by the already mentioned special committee of the National Academy of Sciences, chaired by Arthur Compton.* The committee's

*See pp. 305–307.

specific mission was "to consider the *possibilities of an explosive fission reaction with U-235*"—and by the summer of 1941 it had arrived at substantially the conclusion that Frisch and Peierls had reached on this subject in England in early 1940. The committee's final report and recommendation, hand-delivered by Compton to Bush on November 6, 1941, closely paralleled MAUD's. *"A fission bomb of superlatively destructive power will result from bringing quickly together a sufficient mass of element U-235,"* it said. Such bombs, if a full effort were made, might be available "in significant quantity" in America "within three or four years," the report said, and might decide the outcome of the war.

Three weeks later, the report was in Roosevelt's hands along with a Bush cover note with his strong recommendation that the work be continued and expanded, and Roosevelt promptly acted upon this recommendation, arranging for the work to be financed from his secret fund. (It was not until January 19, 1942, that this decision received any of the documentation historians crave; Roosevelt that day scribbled on a sheet of White House stationery a note to Bush, attaching it to the copy of the Compton committee's final report that Bush had given him in early November. It said: "V.B. OK—returned—I think you had best keep this in your own safe. FDR.")[38]

On Saturday morning, December 6, 1941, the day before Pearl Harbor, Compton, Ernest Lawrence, and Briggs gathered in an office of the Carnegie Institute, at 1530 P Street, N.W., in Washington, to learn from Conant what the President had decided. Having told them, Conant asked the three to constitute the nucleus of a committee, chaired by Conant and dubbed Section 1 (S-1) of the Office of Scientific Research and Development, to direct all fission research toward the single goal of producing *the bomb*.

The assumption at that moment was, of course, that the bomb would be armed with separate segments of U-235 of sufficient size to form, when slammed together by some mechanism, a critical (that is, explosive) mass. But when Compton lunched with Bush and Conant immediately following the close of the committee meeting, he spoke to them for the first time of plutonium as bomb explosive—that is, of the possibility of making plutonium bombs as well as uranium ones. Plutonium was even more radioactive, hence more fissionable, than U-235. This meant that its critical mass would be smaller than that of U-235; less of it would be needed in a bomb whose explosive force was equal to that of a uranium bomb. In view of this, Compton asked his luncheon companions, should there not be launched a major effort to make a plutonium bomb?

The question was initially answered negatively by both Bush and Conant. The odds against the practical success—that is, success within a reasonable time frame—of a project involving so many unknowns seemed to Bush, at that moment, impossibly high. Conant agreed. Conant opined that many years would pass, the war would be long over, before enough plutonium to arm a bomb could become available. Compton replied that an immensely more optimistic prediction was made by Glenn Seaborg (he was the young chemist at Berkeley who, using the university's sixty-inch cyclotron, had been the first to isolate the new element [in February 1941]; who had demonstrated its fissionability with slow neutrons a month later; and who had given it its name, after Pluto, outermost planet of the solar system). Seaborg said flatly that *within six months* after the nuclear reactor had created enough plutonium to arm a bomb, he would have it ready for delivery at the bomb-making site.

Conant shook his head in disbelief. Seaborg "is a very competent young chemist," he said, "but he isn't that good."* Compton conceded that obtaining "useful quantities" of plutonium would take longer than obtaining "useful quantities" of U-235, but not a great deal longer, and this disadvantage was offset by the fact that, according to his estimate, the explosive unit of a plutonium bomb need be no more than half the size of that of a uranium bomb.

Bush and Conant remained skeptical. Before the luncheon had ended, however, both agreed with Compton that, in the fateful circumstances, common prudence required the energetic pursuit of *every* lead showing *any* promise whatever and that, therefore, *this* lead must be pursued. Had the decision been otherwise, as Compton would later write, "there might well have been no development of the nuclear reactor as a wartime project," for it was the reactor's production of plutonium, not its ultimate usefulness as an energy source, that justified in military terms Enrico Fermi's urgent striving toward a self-sustaining chain reaction.[39]

Fermi had proceeded in cautious steps with what he called his "exponential experiments" at Columbia. He began with "exponential piles" far smaller than any that could possibly generate a self-sustaining chain reaction. The first of these, employing a cubical lattice of graphite bricks into which were inserted sheet-iron cans packed with uranium oxide, had by September 1941 yielded 13 percent less release of neutrons than was needed for chain reaction. This was, for Fermi, and for Szilard, who worked with him, a disappointing but by no means dismaying result. More encouraging still was the result of an exponential experiment conducted by Samuel Allison at the University of Chicago almost simultaneously with Fermi's second experiment and in accordance with the lessons learned from Fermi's first.

Allison's experiment was conducted in a squash double court beneath the west stands of Stagg Field at the University of Chicago.† By the time it was

---

*In the event, as Compton points out in his *Atomic Quest* (page 71), enough plutonium to arm a bomb was delivered to the bomb-making site in just a little over two months after it was created in the uranium piles of the huge plant built to produce it.

†The stadium was available for such use because, shortly after young Robert Maynard Hutchins became chancellor of the University of Chicago in 1929, intercollegiate football, for which the stadium had been built, was abandoned by the university. The new administration saw football as an increasingly commercialized mass entertainment that distracted from, and had a corruptive influence upon, the university's proper role of higher education.

completed there had been concentrated at the university, in a so-called Metallurgical Laboratory, the work for which Compton had overall responsibility—research theretofore so widely distributed that its overall efficiency was reduced. The laboratory, headquartered in the university's Eckhart Hall, became the nerve center for a nationwide Metallurgical Project that would ultimately employ five thousand people, two thousand in the laboratory itself, the others in various institutions across the land. Fermi and Szilard were brought from New York to Chicago, Fermi thereafter conducting his exponential experiments in the Stagg Field squash court. Seaborg soon came from Berkeley as a key member of the laboratory staff. Traveling often between Berkeley and Chicago that spring and summer would be a tall, extremely thin, dreamy-looking man in his late thirties named J. Robert Oppenheimer, a brilliant theoretical physicist, a great teacher (his students worshiped him), who, for all his unworldly manner and appearance, proved to be solidly grounded in practical realities. Compton, having brought him "into the theoretical division of our Chicago operation," was surprised and impressed by Oppenheimer's "wisdom and firmness of policy matters involving allocation of research effort and problems of personnel" and soon invited him to administer "the division . . . responsible for the design of atomic weapons." Oppenheimer accepted the invitation. He continued, however, to headquarter that summer at Berkeley.[40]

On June 17, as he awaited Churchill's arrival in Washington, Roosevelt received another progress report, this one with a cover letter in which Bush proposed that from now on administration of the bomb project be divided between the OSRD and the U.S. Army Corps of Engineers, the OSRD continuing to direct the project's research and development, while the Army Corps of Engineers assumed responsibility for procurement and engineering. The proposal was not unexpected by the President—was, in fact, implicit in the operational decision that he, at Bush's behest, had made last October 9.*

From the first he had taken it for granted that the atomic bomb effort, if or when it advanced beyond its research phase, must come under army control. He seems also to have recognized, as Bush may not then have done, that what was now proposed was an interim, transitional arrangement. Inevitably, gradually over the next ten or twelve months, as the army officers involved become acquainted with the nature of the scientific effort and of the men engaged in it, the army would take over the whole of the project, *including* research and development. The project was, after all, an ordnance project for which absolute secrecy was a prime military necessity. As soon as he read Bush's cover letter, therefore, Roosevelt scribbled, "OK, FDR," upon it and returned it to its sender. Wheels already well greased began at once to turn. On that very day, a forewarned chief of the Army Corps of Engineers made the command assignment indicated: one

*See pp. 308–309.

Colonel James C. Marshall, experienced in the building of air bases, was ordered from Syracuse to Washington and told to organize a new district of the
Army Corps of Engineers to handle a so-called DSM (for development of substitute materials) project. It would soon be officially labeled the Manhattan Engineer District, Marshall having established his headquarters in New York
City.[41]

This, then, was the status of the U.S. atomic bomb project when Churchill on
June 19, 1942, at what he deemed a relatively hazard-free moment during his
Roosevelt-conducted tour of the Hyde Park estate, broached to his host the subject of "Tube Alloys." Roosevelt replied that although certainly a decision by
the two of them on this matter was an immediate necessity, he needed more information from his scientific advisers before joining in the making of it. He
would order it by phone as soon as they were back at the house. So it was not
until the afternoon of the following day, a Saturday, that the decisive discussion
took place, this in the dark and tiny first-floor study of the Big House, with only
Hopkins present besides the two principals.

To Churchill, fresh from the green coolness of an English June, the humid
heat of a typical Hudson River Valley summer day seemed "intense." The very
darkness of the little room had for him the palpability of a smotheringly over-
warm gas (he marveled that his "two American friends did not seem to mind
the . . . heat"). He was consequently extremely grateful for the rapid ease with
which the matter was disposed of. Churchill "strongly urged that we [the British and Americans] . . . at once pool all our information, work together on equal
terms, and share the results, if any, equally between us."

Roosevelt readily assented, if disingenuously; he was by then well aware that
the promise to work on "equal terms" and with an equivalence of control could
not be kept. Indeed, within minutes, the two leaders further agreed that the
United States would assume the whole burden of atomic bomb making (the design, the engineering, the manufacture)—this in tacit recognition of the fact that
Britain after three years of war was simply not strong enough economically to
carry a burden as massive as this one must evidently become, or even to share
that burden equally with the United States. The sharp-edged fact plunged as a
knife into Churchill's personal pride, which was very largely identified with
pride in the British empire, and the salve with which he sought to ease the smart
of the wound thus inflicted is patent in his description of this historic transaction
in his war memoirs. He says it would have been "a hard decision to spend several hundreds of millions pounds sterling, not so much of money as of competing forms of war energy, upon a project the success of which no scientist on
either side of the Atlantic could guarantee" but asserts, defensively, that "if the
Americans had not been willing to undertake the venture, we should certainly
have gone forward on our own power in Canada, or . . . in some other part of the
Empire." He admits to great relief "when the President said he thought the

United States would have to do it" but concludes, again defensively, that "it was the progress . . . we had made in Britain and the confidence of our scientists in ultimate success, imparted [by me] to the President, that led him to his grave and fateful decision."[42]

V

THE staff of the Metallurgical Laboratory learned of the army's administrative takeover (it also meant a large measure of big-business takeover) of the atomic bomb project on June 27 at a special meeting of the lab's planning board and group leaders called by Compton. Some five dozen of the best physical scientists in America were gathered that morning in a lecture room of Eckhart Hall (Szilard, Fermi, Seaborg, and Edward Teller were among them) to hear their leader deliver his message. He did so in what young Seaborg, for one, deemed a "pep talk" (unlike most first-rate scientists, of whom he was certainly one, Compton was very much a Bush-type organization man). He described the new development as, in general, a happy, hopeful one for all those present; it meant that the work in which they were all engaged had at last been fully recognized by the highest national authority as of crucial military importance. Their work was thus assured government support for the whole of the war's duration on a scale far beyond their initial dreams. A measure of the special importance attached to their project was the thickness and tightness of the security in which, by presidential order, it was wrapped: in the whole of the U.S. military establishment, only Secretary of War Stimson and half a dozen army officers of high rank were permitted to know anything about it. Compton seems to have stressed this in a rather blatant attempt to flatter his mostly youthful listeners: nearly all of them had been recently recruited from the groves of academe, many were fresh from graduate school, yet they were privy to information denied to all save a handful of the most famous and powerful, in the land![43] Colonel Marshall, the newly named commander of the atomic bomb project, had already selected the great construction engineering corporation of Stone & Webster, headquartered in Boston, to be the bomb project's principal contractor. Strong protests were immediately voiced, especially against "working for an industrial contractor." Compton seems to have answered these, first, by insisting that the scientists would be working not *for* a corporation, but *with* it; second, by citing a much worse but distinctly possible alternative, namely, their being absorbed, all of them, into the army as commissioned officers and compelled thereafter to work under army orders. This increased the vehemence of the protests. The meeting ended in unhappy turmoil.

And far from abating, the unhappiness increased that summer as Stone & Webster engineers came into the laboratory to familiarize themselves with the way in which a nuclear reaction would produce plutonium. They were highly experienced construction men. They knew how to put up buildings, dig canals, bridge streams, dam rivers. They knew nothing of nuclear physics and seemed unable to grasp mentally the emergent problems of nuclear industrial production. Yet they evidently felt nothing of the humility that comes from self-acknowledged ignorance; every now and then they imparted to the scientists, in authoritative tones, some of their developing notions (half-baked, the scientists thought) of how the work of pile design and cooling system design should be done. Consequently, an increasingly serious morale problem plagued the scientific staff of the Metallurgical Laboratory as the summer days added up to weeks, the weeks to months.[44]

More and more acutely, the scientists realized that they were being deprived of all ultimately decisive power over a project that had been born of their work and raised by them to its present stature. Until now they had felt themselves to be, and indeed they had actually been to a very considerable degree, in cooperative control of a project whose immediate purpose (the defense of civilization against Nazi-Fascist barbarism) was their own. Many of them had believed and still believed themselves competent to exercise the necessary general supervision of the activities of engineers and industrialists when their project entered its engineering and industrial phase—more competent to do this, certainly, than army officers and profit-motivated corporate officials could be to direct the scientific portion of what now became a joint scientific-industrial enterprise. Their experience of Stone & Webster engineers tended to harden this belief into conviction. Compton, who in the early days of his career had been happily employed in the research department of General Electric, disagreed. "I could not be convinced," he writes of his reaction to his fellow scientists' argument. "The engineering, the building and operating of the plants, the housing of tens of thousands of workers and technical men—these were things far beyond our experience. I agreed that we might conceivably find organizations that would do this under our direction, but this was not the kind of work for which research men should be responsible."[45]

Why not? asked other scientists.

The alternative would probably be control of the research itself, sooner or later, by people utterly incompetent for the task. The democracy that had hitherto prevailed in the project would be increasingly replaced by authoritarianism. People with first-rate intellect and uncommonly high quotients of moral sensitivity, idealism, and compassion would become subordinate to men who, though of inferior intelligence, possessed all too abundantly the "habit of command," were enamored of naked power, and took pride in a personal "toughness" indistinguishable from callousness. In many cases, such men would have an actual contempt for scientists as mere technical specialists, mere "experts," bright, conceited, narrowly focused, undisciplined, requiring for their practical utility a strict supervision by men who saw "the big picture" and knew how to organize work in a way that "got things done" in the harsh "real" world. Administrators of this sort, in the view of the scientists, would breed disaster for the project. They were hardheaded all right, as they boastfully claimed to be; their heads were so hard that few ideas could penetrate them. They were "practical" all right, which meant that their understanding of the world was a hodgepodge of piecemeal perceptions, crudely materialistic. The truth that "connectedness is the *essence* of all things," as Whitehead put it,* was beyond their grasp; hence they could not possibly see "the big picture" with any accuracy. For this reason alone they would be certain to impose an increasingly rigid compartmentalization. And, alas, this reason did not stand alone in the prevailing circumstances: it was buttressed by the military mind's passion for "security," a passion likely to overwhelm commitments to speed of bomb project execution, especially since the security would almost certainly be designed to deny vital information, not primarily to our avowed enemies, the Axis powers, but to our partner in the Grand Alliance, the Soviet Union.

It was common knowledge that in the military mind, antipathy to communism was greater by a good deal than antipathy to Nazi-fascism, and since Moscow was headquarters of a Comintern presumed to have spread round the world a remarkably efficient network of espionage and subversion, the measures deemed to keep secrets away from the Russians would no doubt be stringent in the extreme. There would be a more extensive shattering into pieces than before, with security walls around each piece, of work that could be properly done only through the cooperation of people who had a clear sense of their project's organic wholeness, who knew that no part of it could be successfully conclusively dealt with save as an element or aspect of the whole, and who had free and full access to information about each dependent upon the progress of the other two; the overall effect would be more waste of effort, more waste of material resource, more waste of time. And these could add up to months of delay in the completion of the project as a whole, months during which German science might place atomic bombs in Hitler's hands.

In September 1942, one of Stone & Webster's top engineers came to Chicago to brief the Met Lab staff on the corporation's production plans. He presented these, not as a proposal to be discussed, but as a statement of what the contractor was going to do. And since what the contractor was going to do would (by this new dispensation) determine much or most of what the scientists would have to do, they were appalled by what they heard. This engineer who presumed, in effect, to boss their future work was woefully ignorant of a subject he

*Alfred North Whitehead, *Modes of Thought* ("essence" is italicized by the present author). Whitehead writes: "A single fact in isolation is the primary myth required for finite thought, that is to say, for thought unable to embrace totality. The mythological character arises because there is no such fact. . . . Abstraction from connectedness involves the omission of an essential factor in the fact considered. No fact is merely itself."

evidently believed he had mastered. The physical plant and technology through which Stone & Webster intended to produce plutonium could not do so with any efficiency, if at all. So the unrest that had increasingly plagued the laboratory all through the summer flared into organized protest.

The leader of it was Volney Wilson, a protégé of Compton's, recognized by him as "thoughtful, idealistic, sensitive to human needs . . . impressed by the evil and futility of war . . . representative of our finest young American manhood." These very qualities prompted his organizing a protest meeting by some six dozen lab scientists (Szilard, Fermi, Seaborg, et al., again among them) on a hot, humid September evening in the commons room of Eckhart Hall. There they waited ten or more restless minutes for Compton to appear. Their specific purpose was to force the severance of all connections between the Met Lab and Stone & Webster, but they also had, many of them, the larger purpose of regaining most or all of the project control that had formerly been theirs; the sad performance of Stone & Webster seemed to them conclusive evidence that industrial corporation officials must not be permitted to exercise ultimately decisive control over large-scale plutonium production.

Compton, who was far more agitated by this unspoken larger purpose than he was by the specific spoken one, had pondered long and anxiously what he should now say to these men. He had done so religiously, in the most literal meaning of that word. Almost uniquely among first-rate scientists, he was an exceedingly pious Christian; he insisted with missionary zeal that the always tentative truths discovered through scientific research are consistent when not identical with the absolute truths asserted by Christian faith, going so far as to argue in public lectures that Werner Heisenberg's uncertainty principle evinced the existence, by God's grace, of human free will! So he humbly prayed for divine guidance as he sought a way out of his present predicament. He consulted his Bible. And he was carrying this Bible when at last he entered the Eckhart commons on that night of sultry, sullen, nerve-rasping heat. After placing it upon the lectern, he opened it to the Book of Judges and read of it to his astonished listeners the story of how Given's dedicated three hundred were chosen under God's direct supervision, from among twenty thousand Israelites, to fight the Amelikites. The moral of the story, he said, was that a "small group of united, earnest men would accomplish much more than a large group divided among themselves." He had been assigned administrative responsibility for the Metallurgical Laboratory. He had therefore "had to make" decisions concerning it "according to my best judgment." He had done so in the present case. Those among his listeners who deemed it impossible to work with industrial engineers and therefore could not cheerfully accommodate themselves to the existing order had the option of resigning from the project. "Those who wish to remain . . . with such associates will be most welcomed." He took his Bible from the lectern and seated himself. An embarrassed silence followed. He was a remarkably kind and sweet-tempered man as well as a remarkably able one, greatly liked and admired personally by his listeners. They wanted to think well of him always. They were dismayed by his performance this night, whereby an issue of personal authority (*his* authority) was made out of what they conceived to be a protest against project-threatening organizational error. The silence lengthened. It was finally broken by young Wilson, who, ignoring Compton's ultimatum, made an extended vehement attack on Stone & Webster's incompetence, citing specific instances of it. Several others then spoke along the same lines with the same vehemence. It became clear that the difficulty of working with that corporation's engineers was so great that it was practically impossible for most, if not everyone, in the room save (supposedly) Compton. Compton made no reply. The meeting ended, as the June meeting had done, in impasse.[46]

Not long afterward, Leo Szilard addressed to his Met Lab colleagues a lengthy memorandum exploring the cause and nature of the trouble they were in and defining the basic issue between them and Compton.

Szilard was a man invulnerable to the charge of ignoring or underestimating the need for security. He had been foremost among the refugee scientists who in March 1939, in the immediate aftermath of experiments confirming the possibility of a controlled chain reaction, pressed for a self-imposed censorship by free world scientists of new physics information that, published, might help Nazi-Fascist scientists toward the creation of atomic bombs.* He had composed the 1939 letter to Roosevelt, alerting the President to the possibility of Hitler's obtaining exclusive possession of atomic bombs and suggesting, to prevent this, federally funded scientific research into the possibility of creating such a bomb ourselves. He had arranged for the signing of this letter by his close friend Albert Einstein and for its delivery in person at the White House by Alexander Sachs. Thus he had evinced even before the bomb project was launched not only his concern for security, but also his realization that the best, the final, security was for the free world to gain possession of atomic bombs before Hitler had them. To hide from our enemies accurate information about our bomb making was important, of course, but only so far as it helped us win the race for the bomb. More important was a maximum possible speed of bomb development on our part. Since such speed was denied by the compartmentalization of scientific activity and information that normally prevailed in the United States (the excessive emphasis that Americans placed upon organization, administration, and administrators resulted in crampingly narrow specialties conjoined with hierarchical administrative structures), Szilard, from the moment the bomb project began, had strongly opposed compartmentalization while strongly pressing for complete democracy within it.

Hence the disgust and dismay with which he now viewed the new dispensa-

*See *FDR: Into the Storm,* pp. 482–85, 509–10.

tion, an arrangement whereby military authorities would determine on a "need to know" basis (the "need" being defined by the authorities) what information each project scientist could have about any project work outside his own immediate work area, and all the scientists would come under the control of men for whom Fermi had recently said, "If we brought the bomb to them all ready-made on a silver platter there would still be a fifty-fifty chance that they would mess it up." It need not have happened! cried Szilard. "I have often thought . . . that things would have been different if Compton's authority had actually originated in our group [as it might have been made to do, he believed, had the scientists insisted upon it at the outset] rather than the OSRD." Compton would then "have considered himself as our representative in Washington and asked for whatever was necessary to make our project successful" while refusing "to make any decision affecting our work until he had an opportunity fully to discuss the matter with us. Viewed in this light, . . . we, and we alone, are to be blamed for the frustration of our work." But Szilard would not concede that this "frustration" was final, irrevocable; he contended that he and his colleagues might yet restore, through their united action, the democracy that had been lost. Instead of passively accepting the prevailing arrangement in which "responsibility for the success of this work" was delegated in pieces of diminishing size arranged in a straight line from the White House to Bush, from Bush to Conant, from Conant to Compton, and from Compton to each of them, they could all "take the stand that those who have originated the work on this terrible weapon and those who have materially contributed to its development have, before God and the World, the duty to see to it that it should be ready to be used at the proper time and in the proper way. I believe," he concluded, "that each of us has now to decide where he feels that his responsibility lies."[47]

Actually, however, even before Szilard began writing his memorandum, the choice that he asserted to be open was in process of being wiped out; and by the time he circulated his memo, the restoration of project democracy that he called for was a practical impossibility. The only choice now open to each scientist was the "either/or" that organization man Compton had presented all of them at their protest meeting: Either "go along" and "fit in" with the administrative machinery now in place, doing one's bit toward creation of the bomb before Hitler obtained it, or resign from the project and thereby deny to it what might prove to be precisely that portion of vital energy, of idea energy, that would have enabled it to win the race. Szilard himself would choose to "go along," though he resolved as he did so to have his say, and to see to it that his fellow atomic scientists had their say, as to how or whether the bomb was actually used by the United States. The controlling decision had been made, of course, in Washington.

As August drew to a close, Vannevar Bush faced squarely the fact that the prevailing division of project authority between the OSRD and the army was not working. Colonel Marshall had made a bad mistake in establishing his headquarters on Manhattan island instead of in Washington, for it was in the capital that the vital questions of priority in the allocation of resources were decided. These questions were quite generally fighting issues among those competing for aluminum, steel, electricity, and so on, and Colonel Marshall was seriously handicapped in the resultant battles by the distance he had imposed between his headquarters and the battle site. He was also handicapped by an evident deficiency in the tactical adroitness and hard-driving commitment to strategic aims that victory in the priority battles demanded. The result was that he lost more of these battles that summer than the project could afford to lose if it were to achieve what Roosevelt as commander in chief had ordered. ". . . [N]othing should stand in the way of putting this whole affair through to conclusion . . . even if it does cause moderate interference with other war effort," insisted Bush in a memo addressed on the last day of August to Harvey Bundy, the war secretary's special assistant and closest personal associate. He implied that an immediate change in the administrative setup was necessary to assure prompt and unquestioned procurement of whatever materials the Manhattan Project, as it was now called, needed.

Simultaneously, he moved to assure the retention of an adequate measure of civilian control over the project in whatever new administrative machinery was now devised. Conferring with the dynamic, immensely capable, but also immensely power-loving Lieutenant General Brehon B. Somervell, whom George Marshall had named chief of the army services of supply last March, he suggested the creation of a nine-member military policy committee chaired by himself (Conant as his deputy) and consisting of civilian, army, and navy representatives. This committee would have overall policy control of the project; would join with the War Department in the choice of an army engineer possessed of the driving energy necessary for successful direction of the purely material portion of the enterprise (for example, procurement, construction, and production); and would then back that officer to the hilt. Direct control of the seminal scientific portion of the project would remain in OSRD hands. But Somervell had a different idea. He proposed doing *now* what Roosevelt seems to have realized was inevitable in the end, namely, place administrative control of the whole project in the hands of the Army Corps of Engineers, which was under Somervell's command. The committee Bush suggested might then (and it did in the event) serve as, in Bush's words, "a sort of board of directors" for the actual project director. The committee did *not* have a part in appointing the director, however. It had not yet even been established when Somervell, on September 17, 1942 (the day on which his proposed arrangement received Stimson-Roosevelt approval, two days before the Szilard memorandum was circulated), without bothering to consult Bush on the matter, named to the command of the Manhattan Engineer District a Colonel Leslie R. Groves.[48]

Groves had just completed a tour of duty during which, as deputy chief of construction for the whole of the U.S. Army, he had administered the building of the world's largest office structure—the thirty-five-acre five-story Pentagon Building in Arlington, Virginia, into which the War Department with its twenty-five thousand employees was to move in mid-January 1943. The new assignment was unwelcome to Groves. He had been in the process of receiving long desired orders to go overseas and was only somewhat mollified when Somervell told him that, with this new assignment, he would become a brigadier general. Groves at age forty-six had no perceptible gray in his brown hair, was both jowly of face and paunch of figure (he was an inch short of six feet in height; he weighed nearly three hundred pounds), and was notably blunt of speech, brusque of manner. In basic mind-set and character, he and Somervell had close similarities. Both were enamored of bigness—in organization, in construction, in business: the bigger the better! Each had immense self-confidence, if of a kind that differs from genuine self-reliance to the very considerable extent that it derives from its possessor's sense of place, of status, in a precisely ordered world whose basic assumptions he has never examined. Each was capable of bold initiatives, if always and only within previously prescribed limits. Each gloried in his capacity to deal with tough assignments. Each had a quick, formidable, and thoroughly authoritarian temper ("you scientists don't have any discipline . . . you don't know how to take orders and give orders," Groves would grumble to Compton), along with an awesome capacity for hard work. And Groves, like Somervell, was utterly ruthless in his pursuit of objectives, handling subordinates as mere tools or agents of assigned purposes, wearing them out with twelve- to fifteen-hour workdays, and crushing without a qualm anyone who "got in the way."

Groves at once made it known that his headquarters would be not in New York City, but in Washington, D.C. On September 18, the day after he received his orders, he expedited the purchase of 1,250 tons of extraordinarily rich uranium ore (pitchblende of which 65 percent was uranium oxide) that had been shipped to America from the Belgian Congo by a Belgian mining firm in 1940, to keep it out of the hands of the Germans, and that had since reposed in steel drums (two thousand of them) stacked in the open air at Port Richmond on Staten Island. The Belgian firm had been trying to sell it to the U.S. government for at least six months. Next day, which was the date of Szilard's memo, he forced a reluctant Donald Nelson to grant the Manhattan Engineer District a triple-A priority rating (the top priority in materials allocation), doing so by threatening to tell the White House that this project the President had ordered would have to be "abandoned because the War Production Board is unwilling to cooperate with the President's wishes." He also approved on that same day the purchase of land along the Clinch River in Tennessee, easily accessible by the aluminum and electric power produced by TVA, on which to site a gaseous diffusion isotope-separation plant—the plant that would produce the U-235 for uranium bombs (Colonel Marshall had thought it prudent to delay this purchase until a self-sustaining chain reaction had actually been achieved). Four days later, on September 23, he attended a meeting in Stimson's office of the war secretary, an admiral representing the navy secretary, Bush, Conant, Army Staff Chief Marshall, Somervell, and Brigadier General Wilhelm D. Styer, Somervell's chief of staff. The main item on the agenda was the establishment of the nine-member military policy committee that Bush had proposed, but Groves, having presented to those assembled his operation plans, and done so in impressive fashion, protested that a nine-member committee was too large to decide questions as swiftly as he wished them decided. He proposed instead a three-man committee (Bush [Conant as deputy], a qualified general, and a qualified admiral) and won his way. He then startled Stimson by asking to be excused so that he could catch a train for Tennessee, there to inspect the Clinch River site. In Tennessee a day or so later, he decided that the two thousand acres whose purchase he had approved was not nearly enough land for the necessary plant; he promptly expanded the purchase to some fifty-two thousand acres (eighty square miles), whereon would rise with remarkable speed what in postwar years would become famous as the Oak Ridge laboratory and U-235 production plant.[49]

Such whirlwind and effective activity evoked an initially reluctant admiration from Bush. Groves had in full measure, Bush concluded, the kind of practical intelligence, along with the driving "can do" energy, that the project needed at its top administrative level. This revised estimate was totally confirmed in Bush's mind when Groves made in late November the choice of thirty-eight-year-old J. Robert Oppenheimer to direct (lead) the large team of scientists who were to design, assemble, and test the ultimate products of all this labor, namely, uranium and plutonium bombs. With Oppenheimer's help, the general had selected and purchased the remote desert site, Los Alamos in New Mexico, where this extremely difficult labor was to be performed in total isolation from the outside world (it was the only major portion of the entire bomb project into which "no [private] industrial organization . . . [was] called into a responsible position," writes Compton).[50] Unique leadership qualities were required for this work's success. And Groves, acting upon the advice of Compton, became convinced that Oppenheimer had them. Others in high places did not share his conviction. Bush himself, with Conant, initially deemed this choice highly dubious: Oppenheimer was a man of great emotional sensitivity and high nervous tension who had never administered the work of any large body of men; he was a theoretical physicist whose poor eye-and-hand coordination incapacitated him for physical experiment, and Los Alamos' primary concerns would be with experiment and engineering. Army security officers (including Groves's own top one) and the FBI were strongly opposed to the appointment on security grounds: Oppenheimer's wife had once been married to an American Communist official who was killed in the Spanish Civil War and had during this brief marriage become for a year or two a Party member; Oppenheimer himself had in former years joined Communist-front organizations. But Groves insisted that Oppenheimer, whom he had sounded deeply and at length, was a profoundly patriotic American who, precisely because of his former left-wing connections, was less likely than most to be duped by subversive persons or propaganda; that he was a genius not just in his special field of science, but universally; that he was, as Compton had said, remarkably sound in his judgments of personnel and organizational needs; and that no other available man was anywhere near as well equipped for this post as he was. With stubborn persistence and adroit maneuvering, Groves won the necessary approval.

Bush's approving opinion of Groves came to be shared by most of those in the project who had direct working experience with him, including Oppenheimer. It was emphatically *not* shared by a great many, if not most, of the project scientists. They loathed and resented the general at first sight and, from first to last, deemed him to have as high a percentage of fat above his eyebrows as he had beneath his chin.

The Met Lab scientists who had been on the verge of open organized rebellion in late September, and who simmered on this verge all through October and early November, were somewhat mollified when Groves, taking cognizance of their hostility to Stone & Webster (also of a strike in November by Stone & Webster workers), persuaded E. I. du Pont de Nemours to take over the engineering and construction of plutonium-production facilities on subcontract from the Boston firm. Du Pont's engineers were far more competent for this work than Stone & Webster's.

Nevertheless, construction of the plutonium-production facility (the Hanford Engineer Works) at Richland, Washington, would have begun at least three months sooner than it actually did if Met Lab scientists and not Du Pont engineers had been in charge. In the summer of 1942, a team working under Eugene Wigner designed a safe and efficient water-cooled uranium-metal pile. Du Pont engineers raised what Wigner and his colleagues deemed foolish objections to it and postponed its use until a much more complicated and less efficient helium-cooled system could be tested. Wigner, whose fear of German progress toward the bomb was even more passionately intense than that of most of the refugee scientists, fumed in helpless anger over the wasted time. Not until February 1943 did Du Pont decide that the water-cooled system worked better than any other, and not until then could the Hanford construction begin.[51]

Citing such instances, many of the scientists remained convinced, even when they viewed the matter in lengthening retrospect after the war had ended, that the first atomic bombs would have been produced considerably sooner than they were, perhaps as much as half a year sooner, if the executive energy that Groves and his kind manifested, along with the special abilities of the industrial engineers brought into the project, had been under their ultimately decisive control. . . .

VI

AFTER the "Tube Alloys" matter had been dealt with at Hyde Park on Saturday, June 20, by Roosevelt and Churchill, the Prime Minister placed in the President's hand a note he had written about the question of strategy that had brought him and Brooke to Washington. It presented the British side of an argument that, as Roosevelt realized more acutely than Churchill did, must be carefully managed lest it grow into an alliance-threatening quarrel. His sense of this had been sharpened by a lengthy letter to him from Stimson, dated June 19, stating the American side of the argument—a letter rushed to him at Hyde Park for the purpose, obviously, of arming him against Churchillian wiles.

The British, wrote Churchill, had accepted in April and remained committed to the American proposal of a cross-Channel attack "if possible in 1942 [Sledgehammer], . . . certainly in 1943 [Roundup]." Preparations continued to be made for the "landing of six or eight divisions on the coast of Northern France early in September." But the wisdom of actually doing so, dubious from the first in the British mind, had become increasingly so. Certainly no landing conceived as a "sacrifice" on behalf of the Russians (Roosevelt had seemed so to have conceived it) should be made, since it "would not" in fact "help the Russians whatever their plight, would compromise and expose to Nazi vengeance the French population involved, and would gravely delay the main operation in 1943." In other words, there should be "no substantial landing in France this year unless we are going to stay"—and so far "no responsible British military authority has . . . been able to make a plan for September, 1942," which "has any chance of " achieving a permanent lodgment "unless the Germans become utterly demoralized, of which there is no likelihood." Perhaps the American staffs had a plan, or perhaps the American and British together could now devise one "which offers a reasonable prospect of success." If so, "His Majesty's Government will cordially welcome it, and will share to the full . . . the risks and sacrifices." But the evident probability was that no such plan could be made and that the 1942 operation must consequently be canceled, in which case a new crop of questions sprang up: "Can we afford to stand idle in the Atlantic theater during the whole of 1942? Ought we not to be preparing within the general structure of 'Bolero' some other operation by which we may gain positions of advantage and also . . . take some of the weight off Russia? It is in this setting and on this background that the French Northwest Africa operation [Gymnast] should be studied."[52]

Stimson's letter was a vehement defense of Bolero (he meant by this code word not just the buildup for cross-Channel operations, but the operations themselves)* against any and all proposals that might weaken it. Among the latter was Gymnast, in Stimson's emphatic opinion—an opinion shared, it should here be noted, by CIGS Brooke to the extent that he thought the costs and risks of Gymnast greatly outweighed its possible benefit to the Allied cause. At the time of Bolero's adoption, wrote Stimson, "the greatest threat to America's prosecution of it lay in the Pacific . . . where our then inferiority in aircraft carriers subjected us to the dangers of enemy raids [upon the West Coast] which might seriously cripple the vital airplane production upon which a prompt Bolero offensive primarily rests." This threat had been removed by the Midway battle. Meanwhile, the "psychological pressure of our preparation for Bolero" was now evident in "unmistakable signs of uneasiness in Germany as well as increasing unrest in the subject populations" of countries occupied by the Nazis. In these circumstances, no "new plan should even be whispered . . . unless it is so sure of immediate success and so manifestly helpful to Bolero that it could not possibly be taken as evidence of doubt or vacillation in the prosecution of Bolero." Gymnast wholly failed to meet these specifications. It would be a "diversion" from Bolero; it would tie up so much shipping that the United States would not be able to rush aid to Britain if, to assume "the worst," Russia collapsed in 1942 and Germany swiftly mounted an air- and sea-borne invasion of the British Isles; and it would "strain and risk . . . our [limited] aircraft carrier forces" and so "could not fail to diminish the superiority over Japan which we now precariously hold in the Pacific." He concluded with an appeal to prideful nationalism of a kind inimical, Roosevelt recognized, to harmonious Anglo-American relationships. "To my mind," said Stimson, "Bolero in inception and in its present development is an essentially American project, brought into this war as the vitalizing contribution of our fresh and unwearied leaders and forces. . . . [I]t would be a mistake to hazard it by any additional expeditionary proposal. . . ."[53]

By the time Roosevelt read the Churchill note, he had already decided to return with his British guests to Washington that night instead of on the following night, as had been originally scheduled. He had arranged for George Marshall to come to the Oval Room at eleven o'clock next morning (Sunday, June 21) and had asked Stimson, Knox, and King to be available for a White House conference that afternoon or early evening. Accordingly, shortly before eleven o'clock that night, the President and Prime Minister, accompanied by their respective

---

*This imprecision of language, surprising in a legal mind that had presumably studied carefully the strategy proposal it defended, flawed Stimson's conception of the issue between himself and Churchill. The distinction the British made between Sledgehammer, which they opposed, and Roundup, to which they were (or said they were) firmly committed in June 1942, seems not to have been perceived with any clarity by the secretary of war until FDR himself defined the code words in a mid-July memorandum.

personal staffs, boarded the presidential train at Highland and (though the hour was early for the Prime Minister) went at once to bed.

While they slept their way through the peaceful American dark, there occurred in the violent blaze of an African sun an event that would shorten and exert a shaping influence upon the upcoming strategy conference. On June 16, in Libya, after a pause of only two days, Rommel had renewed the offensive against the British Eighth Army that he had begun a month before. In a swift series of blows, taking full advantage of his overwhelming superiority in the air (his earlier successes had caused the British to withdraw their planes to distant airfields), he had within twenty-four hours captured Acroma, some fifteen miles west of Tobruk; El Adem, about the same distance south of Tobruk; and Belhamed, barely twenty miles southeast of Tobruk. Immediately thereafter, he knocked out virtually the whole of the British armor in the vicinity of Sidi Rezegh, reducing to twenty tanks the strength of Britain's Fourth Armoured Brigade. By the time Churchill's plane landed in Washington, Tobruk was wholly isolated and closely invested. Nevertheless, the Prime Minister, when he went to bed shortly before midnight on June 20, remained confident that Tobruk was strongly enough garrisoned and well enough provisioned to hold out until a relieving counterattack was launched, as it had done last year. Presumably he went at once to sleep, for he, like Roosevelt, was generally able to do so even at moments of intense crisis; certainly his sleep was undisturbed by any extra-sensory perception of what had happened at Tobruk less than two hours later. By then Rommel, having directly assaulted the Tobruk fortress, had occupied much of it after exceptionally bloody fighting whereby the commander of the British there, one General Klopper, became convinced that his situation was hopeless. In the dark hours of the morning of June 21, the general informed Eighth Army headquarters that he was compelled to "do the worst" (in other words, capitulate), and he did so at 7:45 A.M., Libyan time, surrendering nearly thirty-five thousand troops, sufficient rations, and other supplies to maintain them for three months, and, according to Rommel's chief of staff, "more than 10,000 cubic meters of petrol." ("Without this booty adequate rations and clothing for the armored divisions would not have been possible in the coming months," writes the staff chief. "Stores arriving by sea had only one occasion—in April, 1942—been enough to supply the army for one whole month.")[54]

Churchill learned of this immediately after lunch in the White House on Sunday, June 21. He and Brooke were standing beside the Oval Room desk at which Roosevelt was seated, the three of them talking animatedly, when Marshall entered bearing a telegram reporting tersely the fall of Tobruk and the capture of its garrison, with the latter underestimated at twenty-five thousand. Marshall handed this to Roosevelt, who, having read it at a glance, handed it without a word to Churchill. "This was one of the heaviest blows I can recall during the war," says Churchill in his war memoirs. It was "a staggering blow," remembered Brooke a dozen years later, for neither "Winston nor I had contemplated such an eventuality." Both felt not only dreadful anxiety over what might now happen in North Africa and the Middle East, but also shame and embarrassment over the performance of British arms. "At Singapore 85,000 men had surrendered to inferior numbers of Japanese," writes Churchill. "Now in Tobruk a garrison of 25,000 (actually 33,000) seasoned soldiers had laid down their arms to perhaps half their number. . . . I did not attempt to hide from the President the shock I had received. It was a bitter moment. Defeat is one thing; disgrace is another."55

But this bitter moment was also a defining one, and what it defined was an increase of personal affection and sympathetic understanding among the men then gathered in the Oval Room—an increase that may have made the difference between the survival and the death or permanent enfeeblement of an Anglo-American alliance gravely threatened at that time by the developing quarrel over grand strategy.

Roosevelt spoke no judgmental word. He evinced no emotion save profound sympathy and concern for friends in trouble. He simply asked, "What can we do to help?" Churchill, pulling himself together, replied: "Give us as many Sherman tanks as you can spare and ship them to the Middle East as quickly as possible." Roosevelt turned to Marshall. He, too, was all sympathy and concern. The Sherman, a medium tank (eighteen tons), designed as an answer to the twenty-ton German tank that had played a key role in the crushing of France in 1940, was just coming into production in June of 1942. Only a few hundred of them had been delivered to American armored divisions during the last few days. Marshall remarked with feeling that it was "a terrible thing to take the weapons out of a soldier's hands" but quickly added that "the British . . . must have them" if their "need is so great." He at once set about making the necessary arrangements. By the end of that day three hundred tanks and a hundred self-propelled 105-millimeter guns were earmarked for shipment by fast convoy to North Africa. (Some days later, when one of the six ships of the convoy was sunk off Bermuda by a U-boat, with the loss of seventy tanks, Marshall immediately ordered another seventy onto another fast ship that managed to overtake the convoy.) " 'A friend in need is a friend indeed,' " quotes a grateful Churchill in his war memoirs. Said Brooke after the war: "I always feel that the Tobruk episode in the President's study did a great deal toward laying the foundations of friendship and understanding built up during the war between the President and Marshall on the one hand and Churchill and myself on the other."56

The gratitude that Churchill felt did not, however, mitigate in the slightest the forceful eloquence with which he, during the strategy conferences of that afternoon and evening, inveighed against any "premature" attempt upon the coast of France. Nor did the human sympathy that Marshall felt for Churchill and

Brooke in their hour of need prevent a rise of angry outrage in him as he listened, in the afternoon, to Churchill's words. Measured by their intent, they were ill-chosen words. Churchill's great capacity as a leader of men did not include much psychological acumen. He was notably deficient in the intuitive understanding of other people, the acute sensitivity to their thoughts and feelings (especially the latter), that Franklin Roosevelt so notably possessed. And his species of egotism, a self-centeredness that blunted his perception of other people and wholly prevented his awareness of subtle psychic vibrations, made it possible for him, in argument, to mingle logic with attempts at subterfuge so clumsy, so transparent, that his logic was vitiated by them. So it was that day. He insisted that Gymnast should be viewed, not as a diversion from Bolero, but as an integral part of it (Brooke, at a Combined Chiefs of Staff meeting the day before, had agreed with Marshall that Gymnast *would* be a diversion), then dwelt at length upon the alleged advantages, if not the actual necessity, of Gymnast as a prelude to Roundup. Think of the immense benefit that would accrue to the Russians if the Nazi-Fascists were driven from North Africa! cried Churchill. The collapse of Mussolini's Italy would almost certainly soon follow. This would open the Mediterranean to Allied shipping, a supply route to Russia that was ice-free the year around and was not only shorter but also easier to defend against enemy submarine and air attack than any now available. The event would be the equivalent of capture by the Soviets of millions of tons of matériel! Think, too, of the advantages Roundup would gain from what might be accurately viewed as a dress rehearsal for it! Raw green troops would go into North Africa; battle-hardened veterans in efficient tactical formations would come out, ready for the supreme test in France. Moreover, North Africa would be a testing ground for American general officers, providing a sound basis for determining which among them should command the forces invading France. Finally, Churchill pointed to the immediate dire situation of the British in North Africa. Did it not argue persuasively, even imperatively, for Gymnast?[57]

All this revived in full force in Marshall's mind the doubts about the British that had been temporarily laid to rest during his London visit last April—dark suspicions that in argument they were deceitful and manipulative, hiding their actual purposes, their real motives, behind a wall of carefully calculated weasel words. Was not Churchill's bland assertion that Gymnast fit logically into the Bolero framework palpably dishonest? Was not his enthusiastic description of Gymnast's advantages essentially an argument by implication that Roundup need not be, hence ought not to be, launched at all? Revealing to Marshall was the Prime Minister's statement that the Allied conquest of North Africa was "likely" to be followed soon by the fall of Mussolini's Italy. That would happen, and Churchill must know that it would happen, *only* if Italy were invaded by the Allies. And what would be Hitler's response to such invasion? Would it not be the same as the response he had made when Italian troops faltered in Greece and in North Africa? Would he not feel compelled to send troops of his own into Italy to fight beside Mussolini's, or in place of them, against any Allied drive northward? Gymnast, then, was designed to be a prelude, not to Roundup, but to a series of indecisive operations against Europe's southern flank, whereby, for lack of the necessary buildup of men and matériel, Roundup would be postponed indefinitely and ultimately scuttled. The effect of the Prime Minister's words upon Marshall was therefore precisely opposite the effect intended. The American chief of staff had at the outset agreed with his war plans chief that Sledgehammer was a very risky operation. He had committed himself to it primarily because it guaranteed Roundup. He had been psychologically prepared to give it up in the face of British opposition to it *provided* he was absolutely assured by the British that Roundup would be launched in 1943. But now, by his reaction to Churchill's words, Sledgehammer became so solidly welded to Roundup in his mind that the two operations became virtually one to him. Moreover, his commitment to the Sledgehammer portion of it was hardened (which is to say his fear of Gymnast was increased) by his realization that if no American troops were committed to action in the Atlantic theater in 1942, the pressure for a shift of American emphasis from the Atlantic to the Pacific, as desired by King and MacArthur, would increase, and this was a fundamental shift of strategy to which he remained at that moment *almost* as strongly opposed as were Churchill, Brooke, and Roosevelt. Hence the vehemence with which he, following Churchill's presentation, made what Stimson called in his diary "a very powerful argument for Bolero [meaning Sledgehammer, in this case], disposing of all the clouds that had been woven about it by the Mountbatten incident."[58]

Thus a welter of incongruous ideas, purposes, motives, misunderstandings, and imponderables ruled this June 21 meeting—a welter fortunately permeated by the goodwill generated by the Roosevelt-Marshall response to the Tobruk disaster. In such circumstances it was inevitable that the conclusions arrived at were of the "both/and" rather than "either/or" kind, hence essentially *in*conclusive.

They were summarized in a note evidently dictated by Churchill (certainly the language and point of view were Churchillian) late in the night of that long hot Sunday. There was general agreement, said the note, that preparations for a major cross-Channel in 1943 would be "pushed forward with all speed and energy." There was also general agreement that operations "in France or the Low Countries in 1942 [Sledgehammer] would, if successful, yield greater political and strategic gains than operations in any other theater" and that therefore planning and preparation for these, too, were "to be pressed . . . with all possible speed, energy, and ingenuity." Every effort was to be made "to overcome the obvious dangers and difficulties of the enterprise." If they were overcome in the planning stage, the assault would be launched. "If, on the other hand, detailed examination shows that" the success of a 1942 attempt "is improbable, we must be ready with an alternative," for it "is essential that the United States . . . act offensively in 1942." The preferred alternative was Gymnast, for which "plans will be completed in all details as soon as possible" and for which the forces would consist mainly of "Bolero units which have not yet left the United States." (The note added that among the alternatives that were to be "carefully considered" by the Combined Chiefs of Staff were operations on the Iberian Peninsula and in Norway, but this seems to have been stubborn wishful thinking on Churchill's part. He had proposed the Norwegian adventure, coded "Jupiter," on May 1, to the considerable discomfort of Brooke, who saw no merit in it whatever.)

The American understanding of the conclusions reached differed subtly but significantly from the British. Stimson's diary said that "towards the end [of the meeting] it was agreed that we should go ahead full blast on Bolero *until the first of September* [emphasis added by the importance Marshall attached to this date]. At that time the Prime Minister wanted to have a résumé of the situation to see whether a real attack could be made [in 1942] without the danger of disaster. If not, why then we should reconsider the rest of the field." It should be noted that in Churchill's summary no mention is made of the time (September 1) at which the final Sledgehammer decision was to be made, and Stimson himself was evidently unsure whether the British had actually pledged themselves to "full blast" pursuit of this operation through July and August, for he closed his diary entry with lame words: "At any rate that seems to have been the substance so far." Marshall, clearly, had a different view. For him, hence for Stimson in the end, the September 1 date and the promise to study and prepare for Sledgehammer *until* then were sacrosanct.[59]*

The military discussions of the following days, though they dealt with stepped-up defensive measures against U-boats in the Atlantic, convoys to Malta, and convoys to Russia, were dominated by specific problems arising out of Tobruk's fall. Meanwhile, that event's political repercussions in Britain dominated the press and radio of the United States. On June 22, while Churchill lunched with Hopkins and Roosevelt in the Oval Room, Elmer Davis was ushered into his presence. Davis was a greatly respected newspaperman and radio news commentator who had been appointed director of the Office of War Information (OWI), an agency officially established only the week before by Roo-

---

*"It had been a trying day," writes Forrest C. Pogue (on p. 334 of his *Ordeal and Hope*) of George Marshall's experience of that June 21. "Near midnight, at the conclusion of the fourth meeting with the British since morning, the President asked the Chief of Staff to stay after the others had left. To Marshall's consternation, Roosevelt suggested sending a large American force to the Middle East to control the area between Teheran and Alexandria. 'Terribly taken aback' by this new and unwelcome proposal, the General almost lost control of his temper. But he held his tongue. Not daring to trust himself, he declined to discuss the subject that evening. After a moment he turned and left the room."

sevelt to handle and augment war information and propaganda functions formerly dealt with by Archibald MacLeish's Office of Facts and Figures. Davis had with him clippings of news stories from London, printed in New York City newspapers. They were ominous stories, saying under the boldest and blackest of headlines that Churchill faced "his supreme political crisis since becoming Prime Minister," that the House of Commons demanded his immediate return to London to answer charges of catastrophic bungling, and that in a vote on a proposed resolution of censure, in Parliament, his government was in danger of falling. In view of all this, Davis questioned the political wisdom of the Prime Minister's adherence to plans Marshall had made for the Prime Minister's and Brooke's review on June 24 of a massive training exercise by American infantry, armored units, and parachute troops at Fort Jackson, South Carolina. Churchill dismissed the question brusquely. He had already decided to cut short his Washington visit, but he was determined to view in person something of the almost miraculous process by which the United States, virtually unarmed on land in 1939, was now creating, equipping, and training massive armies in a uniquely short period of time. If he must pay for this with the loss of twenty or so votes in the Commons, he was perfectly willing to do so; he doubted that much more than twenty votes would go against his National Coalition government in any case on an issue of confidence.

So on the evening of June 23, having dined with Roosevelt, who (writes Brooke) "was in very good form," Churchill and Brooke, with Ismay, boarded the special train ("air-conditioned and beautifully cool," writes Brooke, who, like Churchill, suffered much from Washington's "oppressive heat") that carried them, with Marshall and Stimson as their hosts, to the review site. There Marshall was handed a telegram from the White House saying, "You and Sir Charles Wilson are in command stop enough said stop Roosevelt." This was a follow-up of words the President had spoken to the Prime Minister's physician at dinner the night before: "You, Sir Charles, do not know the South Carolina sun in June. Be careful of the Prime Minister tomorrow." So the physician, who himself found the heat hard to bear, kept an anxious eye on Churchill as they all spent hours in a broiling sun watching a battalion parachute drop (four of the six hundred men who came down broke their legs when they landed) and a field exercise using live ammunition—an elaborate show intended by Marshall to persuade the British of U.S. readiness for continental invasion in the months immediately ahead. It failed to do so. Churchill was truly amazed by this demonstration of Marshall's ability to mass-produce in so short a time divisions capable of such acts as he had witnessed. He was fulsome in his praise of the achievement. But these troops, he was privately convinced, could not possibly be ready to face the Germans successfully in Europe in either 1942 *or* 1943. He reiterated to his British colleagues what he had often said to the Americans, that it takes at least two years to make a good soldier out of a civilian. Brooke and

Ismay were of the same mind. The CIGS found "the American system of individual and elementary training" to be "excellent" but doubted "that their higher training is good enough, or that they have yet realized the standard of training required." Ismay, asked by Churchill for an opinion, said flatly that "it would be murder to pit . . . [these troops] against continental soldiery." Churchill agreed this was true at that moment but added that these young Americans were "wonderful material" and would "learn very quickly."[60]

On the evening of the following day, June 25, having returned to Washington, Churchill and his party motored to Baltimore, boarded the flying boat that had brought them to America, and took off on the flight home. The first news that greeted them when they arrived at Stanraer Loch was of the outcome of a by-election at Maldon in which the government's candidate had gone down to overwhelming defeat, winning only 6,226 votes out of nearly 20,000. This dismayed to the extent that it seemed significant of the general reaction of Britain's citizenry to Tobruk's fall. It jarred the confidence in his political strength that Churchill had expressed to Elmer Davis. He brooded over the implications as he rode his train southward toward London through the dark morning hours of June 27 ("This seemed to me a bad time," he writes in his memoirs)—and his mood was not lightened by the harsh criticisms of his conduct of the war to which he was compelled to listen in following days.

It was with trepidation that he prepared and delivered the defense with which, on July 2, he closed the debate. He began: "This long debate has now reached its final stage. What a remarkable example it has been of the unbridled freedom of our Parliamentary institutions in time of war! Everything that could be thought of or raked up has been used to weaken confidence in the Government, has been used to prove that the Ministers are incompetent and to weaken their confidence in themselves, to make the Army distrust the backing it is getting from the civil power, to make the workmen lose confidence in the weapons they are striving so hard to make, to represent the Government as a set of nonentities over whom the Prime Minister towers, and then to undermine him in his own heart, and, if possible, before the eyes of the nation. All this is poured out by cable and radio to all parts of the world, to the distress of our friends and to the delight of all our foes! I am in favour of this freedom, which no other country would use, or dare to use, in times of mortal peril such as those through which we are passing. But this story must not end there, and I now make my appeal to the House of Commons to make sure it does not end there." He followed with a lengthy and detailed rebuttal of the criticisms that had been made, making the most of some glaring inconsistencies in his opponents' arguments. He closed: "Do not, I beg of you, . . . underrate the gravity of what has been done. . . . All over the world . . . all our friends are waiting to know whether there is a strong, solid Government in Britain. . . . If those who have assailed us are reduced to contemptible proportions and their Vote of Censure on the National Govern-

ment is converted to a vote of censure upon its authors, make no mistake, a
cheer will go up from every friend of Britain and every faithful servant of our
cause, and the knell of disappointment will ring in the ears of the tyrants we are
striving to overthrow."[61]

The House then divided and, as Churchill had said he expected it to do, but
also to his immense relief, rejected the censure motion 475–25.

In America, too, there was great relief.

"Good for you," read a message from Roosevelt (he was at Hyde Park that
day) received by the Prime Minister within an hour after the vote total was announced. Cabled Hopkins (also at Hyde Park, of course): "Action of Commons
today delighted me. These have been some of the bad days. No doubt there will
be others. . . . Your strength, tenacity, and everlasting courage will see Britain
through, and the President, you know, does not quit." Churchill's reply to Hopkins was somewhat rueful. "I hope one day I shall have something more solid
to report," he said.[62]

And certainly the facts of the case justified a streak of rue in the relief, the
cautious optimism, with which Churchill faced the immediate future. A letter
from Sir Stafford Cripps had told him that the popular "feeling" generated by
the Tobruk disaster was not "in any sense a personal one against the Prime Minister," but "a general feeling . . . that something is wrong and should be put right
without delay." What was deemed "wrong," however, according to Cripps—
poor generalship at the top, an insufficient coordination of the air and ground
arms, inferiority of tanks and antitank guns, inadequate organization and use of
the nation's scientific and technological genius (Britain seemed to be losing to
Germany the "race for efficient equipment")—clearly called into question the
quality of the Prime Minister's leadership. Churchill realized, as Roosevelt and
Hopkins realized, that his political position was now the weakest it had been
since his ministry began and that it was likely to be further eroded if the flood of
bad news pouring in from the fighting fronts continued unchecked.[63]

VII

AND it did so continue as July wore on. . . .

The powerful German drive into the Caucasus following Sevastopol's fall,
joined with the simultaneous eighty-mile retreat of the British Eighth Army to a
thinly held thirty-five-mile front between El Alamein and the impassable salt
flat known as the Qattara Depression, barely seventy-five miles west of Alexandria, raised yet again, more ominously than ever before, the specter of a giant
Nazi pincer movement, one prong rising up from Egypt, the other closing down
through Turkey, whereby the whole of the oil-rich Middle East would be
snatched into Hitler's hands. If the Soviet Union had not by then collapsed, it
must surely do so immediately thereafter for lack of the desperately needed sup-

plies that now came to her via the Persian Gulf. In the Atlantic, thanks in good part to events in what Churchill called "the U-boat paradise" along the American coast, the rate of Allied merchant ship losses climbed higher and higher. The May sinking of 120 ships with a total of nearly 602,000 tons was surpassed in June when more than 627,000 tons went down, and the rate continued to rise in July, reaching a peak when *in a single week,* the second of the month, 400,000 tons were sunk—"a rate unexampled in this war or the last," as Churchill cabled Roosevelt grimly on July 14.[64] It was a rate two and a half times that at which new ships would be built even if Roosevelt's production quotas were met, quotas then deemed absurdly high by most big-business men, though they were surpassed in the event, as we have said. Obviously, if such losses continued for long, the Allied cause was doomed (in the event, as we have also said, U.S. Navy defense of America's Atlantic coastal waters began to be effective in late July).

Only in the Pacific did beams of light relieve the prevailing gloom. There the Japanese, advantaged by interior lines of communication, yet had a sufficient superiority over the Allies in troops and matériel to concentrate their forces in one area without exposing themselves to overwhelming American strength in another. They yet held, to this extent, the strategic initiative and could be expected to exercise it in a resumption as soon as possible of the drive southward from Rabaul, which from their point of view had been only temporarily interrupted by the Battle of the Coral Sea. But they were deprived for the time being of the tactical initiative. The Battle of Midway had not only drastically reduced their superiority in aircraft carrier numbers while demonstrating once and for all that the carrier was the decisive weapon of modern-day naval warfare, it had also disorganized and scattered the forces that would otherwise have been now concentrated for this drive down from Rabaul. Moreover (so the evidence indicated), Midway had severely damaged the morale of the Japanese high command, introducing into that command's councils debilitating doubts and hesitations formerly absent from them. All this presented to MacArthur and Nimitz, and through them, if most emphatically through MacArthur, to the Joint Chiefs of Staff in Washington, a chance to initiate offensive action in the Southwest Pacific that would forestall the enemy's expected next major move, strengthen the defense of Australia and the Allies' transpacific lifeline, and be itself a first step toward the MacArthur-proclaimed "return to the Philippines." The opportunity must be seized at once, however. It could not long remain open. And the seizure of it required the acceptance of formidable risks and costs. Allied strength in the Pacific as a whole did not permit the mounting of decisive offensive action in the southwest part of it without weakening, perhaps dangerously, American forces in the Mid- and North Pacific—*unless* (and here came the severest rub) strength were withdrawn from Bolero and/or reductions were made in U.S. commitments to the British in North Africa and the Middle East. (Already, the balance of U.S. Army strength between the Atlantic and the Pacific, agreed and planned for immediately after Pearl Harbor, had been tipped somewhat toward the Pacific by the unexpectedly swift success of the Japanese offensive: the War Department had undertaken to have 237,000 army troops in the Pacific by the end of 1942, but 252,000 were actually there or en route with the year only half-gone.)

Hence the Joint Chiefs of Staff had to weigh carefully, on the scales of grand strategy, this new project's possible gains against its possible losses. They did so during late June discussions, whence emerged, with a swiftness and ease remarkable in the circumstances, the decision to conduct major offensive operations in the area of New Ireland, New Britain, and New Guinea in three successive phases, or "tasks." Task One was to take the Santa Cruz Islands, Tulagi, and adjacent positions in the lower Solomons, one of which was Guadalcanal, where the initial assault would be made by marines. Task Two was to take Lae, Salamaua, and the northeast coast of New Guinea. Task Three was to take Rabaul and adjacent positions in the area of New Ireland–New Britain. But then came difficulty: There arose a disagreement between Marshall (army) and King (navy) over who (which service) was to have supreme command of the operation. Was it to be Admiral Nimitz or General MacArthur?

We have mentioned* the Southwest Pacific command arrangement that was made after MacArthur arrived in Australia from the Philippines. It was dictated in part by Australian political pressures, in part by Washington's felt need to accommodate the general's immense ego and politically potent prestige among nationalistic American conservatives, this in order to make full use of his undoubted military abilities; and it badly blurred the line separating the army's authority and responsibility from the navy's in the officially designated Southwest Pacific Area. It thus provided abundant opportunities for interservice quarrel. These were not likely to be neglected by such men as MacArthur and King, each of whom was intensely jealous of his own and his service's prerogatives, and each of whom loathed the other personally. The effect on the present discussions was to prolong them, complicate them, and heat them well beyond a point easily endured amid the hot, humid weather of a Washington June. Marshall argued that MacArthur should command the whole of the operation since it lay "almost entirely in the Southwest Pacific area" and was "designed to add to the security of that area." King argued that Nimitz must have control of the commitment and withdrawal of naval forces throughout the Pacific since the navy in the whole of the Pacific was his assigned command concern; most certainly he should be in charge of any operation that was primarily naval and amphibious. The matter was finally settled, as it could only be, in a compromise: Nimitz was assigned command of Task One and MacArthur of the other two. The directive for all this

*See pp. 473–74.

was issued on July 2, the day of the censure vote in Parliament. It set a target date of August 1 for Task One's launching and of July 20 at the latest for the completion of arrangements for Tasks Two and Three.

MacArthur, of course, at once complained to Marshall that assuming command between phases of an ongoing operation would be difficult. Marshall was not disposed to listen. He replied on the day he received the complaint: "I feel that a workable plan has been set up and a unity of command [over land, sea, and air forces] established without previous precedent for an offensive operation. I wish you to make every conceivable effort to promote a complete accord throughout this affair. There will be difficulties and irritations inevitably but the end in view demands a determination to suppress these manifestations."[65]

Of "difficulties," "irritations," and acute anxieties, Marshall himself had had more than enough these last weeks. They had worn thin his hard-won patience and self-control. And he could see no end to them. For instance, three days before (on June 30), Roosevelt and Hopkins had wired him from Hyde Park a series of questions about "the situation in the Middle East." What was Marshall's personal estimate of it? If the Nile delta were evacuated by the British, could the Suez Canal be effectively blocked? If so, for how long? What was Rommel's or Germany's next move in this area likely to be? "Are there any moves that we can make immediately that might favorably affect the situation . . . ?" Answering all this promptly and adequately was no easy chore, but Marshall, conferring with his top intelligence and operations staff officers, and with Sir John Dill, had managed to do so. The British were prepared to block the Suez Canal so effectively that the Germans would be unable to use it for at least six months, he informed the anxious pair at Hyde Park, but this might be the limit of their ability to frustrate the German will. "Army G-2 estimates Rommel may reach Cairo in one week; Army Operations say two weeks and another week to re-fit before further movement, which will probably be directed towards destruction of the remaining British forces." This last was Rommel's primary objective, following which he might move upon both Cyprus and Syria on the way toward seizure of oil-rich Mosul and the Iranian port of Basra on the Persian Gulf, vital to the supply of Russia. An effort would probably also be made to cut the American air ferry route across Africa and the Middle East to Russia. To the question of what the United States could do immediately to "favorably affect" the battle for Egypt, the answer was, alas, "Nothing" beyond perhaps adding a little to the amount of material aid already pledged, and to the speed of its delivery. Nor was there anything we could do effectively to counter the moves the Germans would subsequently make if they did indeed conquer the Upper Nile Valley. An "expansion far beyond our capacity" would be required for the defense of Syria and the neutralization of Turkey, and "a major effort in" the Mosul-Basra area "would bleed us white." However, the dark predictions of G-2 and Operations just might be mistaken. "I feel that we need 48 hours more to judge the capacity of Auchinleck to meet the situation. . . .* Rommel is greatly extended and if checked by the destruction of his supply bases and interruption of his supply lines, he would be in a difficult position." But Rommel's most pressing supply problems had apparently been solved for him for the time being by his capture of Tobruk with its immense booty, and the new Eighth Army command did not perceptibly improve the situation during Marshall's forty-eight-hour suspension of judgment. On July 2, in the same hour in which he replied to MacArthur's complaint, the army staff chief communicated to Hopkins at Hyde Park his sense of the need to brace the American public against the dire consequences of the imminent German conquest of Egypt. The United Nations must "present to the world a solid front," he said. "To this end it is suggested that the President make public comment so as to indicate that the United Nations stand together in adversity as they ultimately will in victory."[67]

Hopkins no doubt told the President what Marshall had said, but he knew that the man he served had little need, ever, for this kind of advice. Certainly Roosevelt did not need it at that moment. He was as harried by untoward event as Marshall was, but his remarkable sense of public mood and of the proper timing of his public speech and acts was unimpaired, and he yet retained (with who knows what health-eroding, deeply inward effort?) his emotional and intellectual balance along with a firm grasp of basic strategical principles. In the eyes of the world, he remained perfectly poised, serenely confident, imperturbably good-humored, in absolute control of himself and his office. And out of the sight of the great world, in the privacy that wartime security measures bestowed upon that office, he now made, calmly and coolly, a number of close decisions that, wrongly made, could gravely injure the Grand Alliance.

Two of them concerned American war matériel that happened at that time to be passing through the Middle East en route to the Soviet Union and to China. On July 4, Churchill told Roosevelt of the "great work" that "the Boston Bomber [the A-20]" was "doing . . . in Egypt" but pointed out that only ten additional ones were scheduled "to reach us in the Middle East during July," while forty of them "ready to fly," and desperately needed by Auchinleck, were in Iraq on their way to Russia. "Would you consider allowing us to have these forty Bostons at once: and if so, would you approach Stalin and tell him that you will make them up to him as quickly as possible? With Russia in the thick of the battle, this is a hard request and I shall quite understand if you do not feel able to do as I ask." Roosevelt, having conferred with Marshall, at once sent Stalin a

---

*Auchinleck, who in Cairo had exercised and yet retained British command responsibility for the whole of the Middle East, took direct operational command of the Eighth Army on June 25, a long month after Churchill had urged him to do so. Before that date, the army had been commanded by Auchinleck's former chief of staff, General Ritchie—a bad arrangement, in Churchill's view, since "the personal association between Auchinleck and Ritchie did not give Ritchie a chance of those independent conceptions on which the command of violent events depends."[66]

cable telling of Churchill's request and pointing out that the critical situation in Egypt gravely threatened the Middle Eastern supply line to Russia. Immediate use of the forty Bostons by the British might provide the margin of survival for them in Egypt, he implied. But he also said that he lacked sufficient knowledge of the situation on the Russian front to form a judgment on the relative needs of the two great battles and asked Stalin to answer Churchill's question "with the interests of our total war effort in mind." Stalin replied promptly that he had no objection to the diversion of the Bostons to the British, whereupon Roosevelt ordered this, informed Churchill of the fact, and, in a thank-you note, told Stalin that 115 medium tanks, with ammunition and spare parts for them, were being added to the shipments now leaving America for the Soviet Union.[68]

Roosevelt's dealing was more cavalier with the other shipment of lend-lease matériel then moving through the Middle East—a contingent of heavy bombers destined for the Tenth Air Force operating in China. Without informing Chiang Kai-shek, he ordered these planes diverted to the British while the British yet remained in Libya. In Chungking, Chiang and his formidable wife, when they learned what had been done, called Stilwell to them and poured out upon him a scalding flood of wrath. Stilwell, who in this case was inclined by his own need to sympathize with them, immediately communicated to the President directly their bitter, threatful protest. Chiang "had assurances that Tenth Air Force was to operate in China and expected notification before any part of it was taken away," cabled Stilwell. "Now it appears that the Allies have no interest in the China theater and he wants an answer yes or no to the question 'Do the Allies want the China Theater maintained?' " Stilwell's own opinion was that "the matter has reached a very serious stage," and he was sending by air to Washington one of his own staff, General W. R. Gruber, to consult with Marshall about it. Roosevelt, again with Marshall's assistance, wrote immediately to Chiang: "The rapid advance of the Axis forces in the Middle East suddenly confronted the United Nations with a most critical situation. This movement, if not stopped, will result in the severance of the air routes to India and China, and seriously interfere if not interrupt our sea lanes to India." Hence the order. The heavy bombers would be returned to the Tenth Air Force as soon as possible. "In the meantime the medium bombardment and pursuit echelon of the Tenth Air Force will continue in the support of your forces. I reassure you that the United States and our Allies do regard China as a vital part of our common war effort and depend upon the maintenance of the China theater as an urgent necessity for the defeat of our enemies."[69]

And it is distinctly possible that these two Rooseveltian decisions provided the narrow margin whereby the Eighth Army managed to save Egypt. For it was Auchinleck's superior airpower, his ability to commit all he had of it to the battle, knowing that his plane losses would be replaced, that enabled him to hold against Rommel. Far from being in Cairo in mid-July, Rommel, having fought off with difficulty Eighth Army counterattacks launched by Auchinleck during the first two weeks of the month, was attempting at midmonth a new offensive and finding himself too weak, especially in air cover, to succeed in it. July would end with the Afrika Korps and the Eighth Army facing each other in stalemate on the Alamein line. . . .

During the days between the fifth and the seventh of the month, there was no easing of pressures upon a harried Marshall. He was a practical man, a logical man, a clear and definite man. He loathed and feared the ambiguous, the paradoxical. Yet he was compelled by the present war situation to find his way, or try to, through a country that was ruled by ambiguity and paradox; a fluid, fog-shrouded landscape in which things continuously and swiftly became something else and there were very few solid certainties by which he could orient himself. Among these few, however, was the grand strategical agreement with the British that had been arrived at last April and reaffirmed with modification during Churchill's June visit. No doubt his inward need, joined with a pride of authorship (the memorandum in which the cross-Channel operations were initially proposed was called the "Marshall Memorandum"), inclined him to endow this modified agreement with greater certainty and solidity than it appeared to have in other, less interested eyes—inclined him, indeed, to deem the outcome of the June 21 conference a kind of quid pro quo whereby the special American aid given the British after Tobruk's fall was paid for by a strict adherence on their part to every element of the conclusions then reached. In any case, the agreement had become for him the one sure guide and basis for purposeful activity in the eastern Atlantic.

Then, abruptly, this guidepost, this solid ground for thought, ceased to exist.

On July 8, Marshall was officially informed that in a war cabinet meeting in London, the British had definitely decided *not* to go ahead "full blast" with Bolero-Sledgehammer until September 1, as they had pledged themselves to do, in his conception, barely three weeks before! They were not going to mount Sledgehammer at all! They hoped that the United States would agree to an invasion of North Africa.

Reasons were given. Sledgehammer's mounting would tie up 250,000 tons of shipping and all the landing craft in the British Isles (this would prevent any large-scale raids by Mountbatten's forces). It would force the suspension of amphibious training for any troops not committed to Sledgehammer. It would delay preparations for the major cross-Channel assault in 1943. It could be justified, therefore, only if Sledgehammer's launching were absolutely assured, and this was most emphatically not the case. Indeed, the likelihood of that event was so small as to be almost imperceptible, its having been agreed by all parties that the operation would not go forward unless the Germans were demoralized by reverses on the eastern front, where, in actual fact, the Germans had just inflicted two major defeats upon the Russians and now drove triumphantly to the east and south.

It was Field Marshal Sir John Dill who brought this news to the U.S. Army chief of staff and had then to witness the rare and awesome spectacle of George Catlett Marshall in full wrathful eruption. He, Marshall, was sick and tired of arrangements made with the British only to be unmade by them shortly thereafter; it had happened over and over again. He was sick and tired of their proposals of risky, costly operations that, even if successful, could have no important effect upon the outcome of the war. He was most emphatically sick and tired of the slipperiness, the evident phoniness, of their "commitment" to the only operations against the Germans that could possibly be truly decisive. Take, for example, their present statement of the agreed circumstances in which Sledgehammer would be launched. The actual agreement, as Marshall understood it, had been that Sledgehammer was an "emergency" operation that would go forward in the autumn not just if the Germans were then demoralized by defeats on the Russian front, as the British now said, but also if the Russians were then mortally endangered by German victories on that front, as the British very carefully did *not* now say. In terms of the actual agreement, fairly stated, the present situation in Russia argued more strongly *for* than *against* Sledgehammer. For was not the inability of the Russians to halt the present German offensive creating a dangerous emergency? Would not the German advance through the Don basin, if continued at its present rate, render "negligible in magnitude" Russia's future participation in the war and enable a German concentration in the West that would make a full-scale cross-Channel invasion impossible next spring? Fortunately, Gymnast was not the only alternative to Sledgehammer that was available to the Americans: an offensive operation was now being mounted in the Southwest Pacific that, though currently severely limited in scope by the resources available to it, could have decisive effect upon global war if it were greatly expanded—and it could be greatly expanded by reductions in America's military commitments to its just established European theater. . . .[70]

This last sent a chill through the British field marshal. He left Marshall's office agitatedly, apprehensively. And as he made his way back to his own office he thanked God that Admiral King, who of course would eagerly welcome the threatened reversal of grand strategy, was out of town that day and would be tomorrow. Not until July 10 could the Joint Chiefs of Staff again meet in decisive session. And by then, Dill devoutly hoped, Marshall's rage would be spent, his eminently practical logical mind again in control, and his commitment to "Europe first" consequently restored.

Alas (so Dill deeply felt), this didn't happen.

For of Marshall's wrath, initially lavalike and red hot, only the heat had been spent and only the form had been changed when the JCS came together on Friday afternoon. The wrath, though now frozen and shaped by passion-distorted logic into a solid block of cold fury, was quantitatively unchanged. And it yet ruled the army chief of staff. The extent to which it did so, overwhelming his normally stern commitment to fairness and strict truth telling, is revealed by the fact that when he opened the JCS meeting by reading aloud from the British war cabinet dispatch (he read in unwontedly vibrant tones), he confined himself to the portions announcing the abandonment of Sledgehammer and proposing the North African invasion in its stead. He deliberately ignored the extended portion in which the British gave their strong reasons for deciding as they had. He then presented two questions for discussion. His first: Should the United States agree to the North African invasion? His second: Did the British really want (intend) to invade the Continent in 1943? His own answer to both was an emphatic "No." Gymnast would be "expensive and ineffectual," as he had often said, and the very fact that the British again pressed for it meant that they had never really intended Bolero-Sledgehammer and did not now intend Bolero-Roundup. For it was obvious that Gymnast, far from fitting logically into Bolero, as Churchill argued, would render impossible the launching of a major cross-Channel operation in the spring of 1943. Equally obvious was the fact that neither Sledgehammer nor Roundup could succeed "without full aggressive British support."

What, then, should the United States do?

If the British stubbornly maintained their present position, rendering decisive action against Germany impossible in the foreseeable future, the United States should "turn to the Pacific for decisive action against Japan," said Marshall. Admittedly this was a drastic and momentous change in grand strategy, but "it would be highly popular throughout the U.S., particularly on the West Coast"; it would be joyfully welcomed by "the Pacific War Council, the Chinese, and the personnel of the Pacific Fleet . . . ; and . . . it would [second only to Bolero-Roundup] be the operation which would "do the most towards relieving the pressure on Russia."[*71]

All this was promptly seconded by King, who was convinced that the British in general "had never been in whole-hearted accord" with the American cross-Channel proposal; by Deputy Staff Chief McNarney, who was sure that the Royal Air Force had never been; and by Admiral Towers, chief of the navy's air arm, who declared that the transfer of U.S. aircraft carriers from the Pacific to the Atlantic, required by Gymnast, would produce a "most unfavorable" distribution of U.S. forces. No dissent from this was voiced by the others present. They all then agreed that the President should be presented with a memorandum that Marshall had already prepared, that Stimson had already "cordially endorsed," and that would be signed by all three of the Joint Chiefs of Staff (Marshall, King, Arnold)—a memo succinctly presenting the argument Marshall had made (he would point out in it that Sledgehammer's cancellation voided the "commitment to Russia" that Roosevelt personally had made in his talk with

---

*It will be remembered that Eisenhower had proposed this strategy shift, for precisely the present contingency, in his March 25, 1942, memorandum to Marshall. See pp. 485–86.

Molotov) and proposing that the British be given a last chance to commit themselves absolutely and irrevocably to a "concentrated effort against Germany." If they refused to do so, the United States would "turn to the Pacific and strike decisively against Japan; in other words assume a defensive attitude against Germany, except for air operations; and use all available means in the Pacific. Such action would not only be . . . decisive against one of our principal enemies, but would bring concrete aid to the Russians in case Japan attacks them."[72]

This memo was delivered to Roosevelt on the morning of Saturday, July 11, at Hyde Park, where he had arrived from Washington twenty-four hours earlier for an open-ended stay of several days. The memo was accompanied by an informal cover message from Marshall making it clear that, though his (and Stimson's) "object" was "to force the British into an acceptance of a concentrated effort against Germany" and "at once," the means he had chosen was no mere bluff. It was an ultimatum. If the British persisted in their present decision, the United States really would, if Marshall had his way, "turn immediately" full force against Japan.

The effect of this upon Roosevelt was electric. No high American army officer had been a more fervent supporter of "Europe first" against King's claims for the Pacific than George C. Marshall. None had laid a heavier stress upon Anglo-American unity as a necessity for victory. It was consequently a profoundly disturbed President who, early in the morning of the following day, phoned to Washington a request that Marshall and King send him by plane that afternoon "a detailed comprehensive outline" of their plan for what he called "your Pacific alternative." He wanted to know what effect the proposed strategic shift would have on the overall disposition of forces and shipping and on the defense of the Soviet Union and the Middle East.[73]

The reply he received to this, not that afternoon but on the following day (Sunday, July 12), was far from satisfactory. No "detailed comprehensive outline" of the plan for the Pacific could be sent because, as Roosevelt had suspected, no such plan had yet been made; the planning staffs were at work on one. Upon naval strength in the Atlantic, the effect of the strategic shift would be negligible, but upon ground and air force deployment it would be huge: the ground troops moved across the North Atlantic in the coming months would be reduced from many hundreds of thousands to only two divisions for Great Britain plus fifteen thousand troops for Iceland (this in fulfillment of Arcadia commitments); and instead of the fifty-two air force groups that had been scheduled for Bolero, only eighteen would now go to the British Isles. Moreover, as the great bulk of U.S. Army strength was assigned to the Pacific, the rate of overseas deployment was bound to be far slower than it now was. There were three reasons: The battle sites across the Pacific action were much farther from U.S. shores than those across the North Atlantic; there were at present few developed U.S. bases from which Far Pacific operations could be launched; and little if any of the British shipping now operating in the Atlantic would be available for Pacific transport. Instead of one hundred thousand troops going overseas each month, as presently scheduled, only forty thousand would go. As to the overall effect upon the eastern front, it, frankly, would be unfavorable—though the Soviet Union could benefit to the extent that Japan's attack upon Siberia was prevented or, if launched, weakened. Upon Middle Eastern defense, the effect would be slight (Roosevelt, as concerned with the possible as with the actual, almost certainly questioned this assertion), but possibly favorable insofar as Japan's attention was distracted from India and from any attempt at a Middle Eastern linkage of Japanese and German forces.[74]

VIII

OF all those with whom Roosevelt associated during these Hyde Park days, and he associated in effortful ways with more different people than he usually did when "relaxing" on his private estate, only Harry Hopkins knew of his primary concern and how deeply he was disturbed by it. . . .

To bookish ex-newspaperman William Hassett, whose official relationship to him was destined never to be clearly defined but who since January 1942 had functioned actually as his confidential secretary, he seemed as at ease and high-spirited as he normally was when at his one real home. On Saturday morning, July 11, he evinced to Hassett only two relatively minor concerns, plus some disgust with MacArthur's "constant playing to the grandstand" (the general "seems to have forgotten," said Roosevelt, that the command laxity that permitted the destruction of MacArthur's air force *on the ground* at Clark Field, despite abundant warning that a Japanese attack impended, was every bit as reprehensible as the Pearl Harbor command failures for which Kimmel and Short faced court-martial). One concern was an interview with Wendell Willkie, who was coming up from New York City to talk about "state and congressional politics" (so Roosevelt told Hassett, who noted that the two men had "in common" a loathing of "Ham Fish and Tom Dewey"); the other was an imminent weekend visit by Queen Wilhelmina of the Netherlands. The first of these he looked forward to; he personally liked Willkie. The second he "rather dreaded," as Hassett had noted in his diary the night before, for unpleasant stories of Wilhelmina's "arbitrary ways" and implacable Puritanism had preceded her. For instance, she, a teetotaler, was said to have "left the room" on one social occasion "when drinks were brought in!"

Yet when the Queen arrived at precisely the scheduled time, 12:30 noon on Saturday, accompanied by Crown Princess Juliana and two other princesses, also by her private secretary and her lady-in-waiting, she turned out to be pleasant enough, at least in her dealings with those she must accept as equals. These included not only Eleanor Roosevelt, who had come up to hostess the royal personage and would remain at Hyde Park until that personage departed, but also Willkie, whom the Roosevelts welcomed at the Big House shortly before the Queen arrived and who was one of that day's luncheon party. Princess Juliana seemed to enjoy not only the luncheon but also, astonishingly, the typically exuberant and emphatically democratic Rooseveltian picnic supper in Eleanor's Val Kill Cottage that rainy Saturday evening; there and then she solved "one perplexing problem by sipping sherry," noted Hassett in his diary. She manifested great interest in the new presidential library and in Roosevelt's hilltop house when he showed her these. All the same, she remained too unbending, too formal and formidable a personage, to be really enjoyable as company, and her departure on Monday morning was "not unwelcome" to her host, as Hassett noted.[75]

Immediately following the Saturday lunch, Willkie and Roosevelt were closeted for an hour or so in the Big House study. Some mention of politics there may have been, and Fish and Dewey may have figured in it, but Willkie had not come to "talk politics," as Hassett had been led to believe. He had come to discuss an overseas trip he proposed to make in the late summer and early fall if the President approved it. Some two months before, he had received a cablegram from three American newspaper correspondents stationed in Kuibishev, where the Soviet Union capital had been temporarily located (they were Eddy Gilmore of the Associated Press, Maurice Hindus representing the *New York Herald-Tribune,* and Ben Robertson representing *PM*), urging him to make a goodwill visit to Russia. The idea thus planted in his fertile mind had grown as he thought about it. Why limit his trip to Russia? Why not visit the countries of the Middle East on the way to Moscow? Indeed, why not continue on from Moscow to India and China and so on around the world, and do it in a way that served the cause of freedom for which the United States fought? He could do that if he traveled not only as a private citizen who happened to be titular head of the Republican Party, but also as the designated special representative of the President who had defeated him in the last, hard-fought presidential election. As private citizen and head of the administration's political opposition, he would pay all his food and lodging expenses; as presidential representative, he would ride in a U.S. Army plane flown by a U.S. Army Air Force crew; and this unique anomaly would of itself alone demonstrate the unanimity with which Americans, regardless of their political differences, supported the war effort. It would also demonstrate dramatically the absolute control that the Allies had of the strategic air routes of the globe. Finally, since Willkie was a recognized leader of American business and industry and would travel with abundant statistical information in his briefcase (also possibly with professional communicators assigned to his mission by Elmer Davis of the OWI), he could convincingly spread round the world accurate news, heartening to our allies, frightening to our foes, of the unprecedentedly vast quantities of war matériel (planes, tanks, ships, guns, ammunition, and travel and communications facilities) that were beginning to come out of America's expanded and expanding industrial plant. Almost at once, Roosevelt approved the project with enthusiasm. He would have to make delicate decisions about the guidelines Willkie should follow—what Willkie in his capacity as presidential representative could properly say and do in his contacts with foreign governments and the press—but he was sure that the guidelines settled upon would give Willkie ample freedom of speech and action and would therefore be acceptable by him.[76]

As for Hopkins, though he alone among those at Hyde Park shared Roosevelt's immediate primary concern during those crowded days, he did not do so with the empathic completeness that was usual for him. His remarkable capacity to become as one with the man he served, thinking his thoughts, feeling his emotions, was diminished by a primary concern of his own. At age fifty-two, he had fallen passionately in love!

The object of his passion was a Mrs. Louise Macy, a woman considerably younger than he, who had graduated from the exclusive Madeira School in Washington, had gone to Smith College, had married and divorced a wealthy lawyer, and had been the Paris editor of *Harper's Bazaar* for a couple of years. She had entered Hopkins's life via a letter of introduction from a mutual friend, a "society" friend, sent him while he was hospitalized in late January of that year. The letter had described her as "conscientious," a "hard worker" with a "grand personality . . . good-looking, smart," and "as healthy and strong as ten horses." She wanted "to work for her country," preferably in England, but could not "afford to work for nothing." Could Hopkins "possibly spare a moment to see her some time"? He had met her in person ("at the home of Averell and Marie Harriman," according to Doris Kearns Goodwin) shortly after his release from the hospital, and she had turned out to be much more glamorous than the letter description of her could have led him to expect—was slender of figure and graceful of motion, with dark hair worn in a long bob that framed a decidedly pretty face. She was vivacious, full of joie de vivre, glowing with good health and good humor. Hopkins was immediately charmed by her and, as spring came on, spent as much of his severely limited free time with her as he possibly could, feeding his meager but intense vital energy from her abundant supply of it. He was suddenly happier in his personal life than he had been since the death of his beloved Barbara. It was probably as much for this reason as for the beneficial effects of the medicines and severe regimen now imposed upon him by his physicians that his health improved markedly during these months (he gained ten pounds, a fact deemed noteworthy by Eleanor and Hassett). On June 25, when he accompanied Churchill from Washington to Baltimore, where waited the seaplane that was to take the Prime Minister's party back to London, he told his great friend that he was engaged to be married, quickly adding that his marriage would *not* affect his personal and working relationship with the President. He would continue in his present role as Roosevelt's right-hand man. Churchill, who had not been told by Roosevelt of this great change in their mutual friend's life (the personal ties between Hopkins and Churchill were closer than those between Churchill and Roosevelt), was surprised and delighted. He said so with great warmth.[77]

Roosevelt, too, was delighted.

By early July, however, he was aware that a difference in his relationship with his top assistant had already been made and that, measured wholly in terms of his personal interest, it might not prove an altogether happy one. Hopkins was less immediately available for consultation, for relaxed talk, for fun—was less exclusively *his*—than formerly he had been. His fiancée had become a frequent overnight guest at the White House and Hyde Park, and always, during these visits, she was the main focus of his attention. She had come up from New York City to Hyde Park on the morning of Friday, July 3, when rumors that he was engaged first appeared in the press, and Harry had then devoted most of the day to her. She had been one of the presidential party that boarded the special train to Washington that night and spent the following day, Saturday, July 4, in the White House. (It was in the afternoon of that day, in a White House press conference presided over by Eleanor and attended by Harry and Louise, that the couple's engagement was publicly announced; the wedding ceremony would be in the White House on July 30, it was said, and the newlyweds then would live in the White House, so that the groom would "be close to his job.") Louise was again at Hyde Park during this time of Wilhelmina's visit there, arriving from New York City on the morning of Sunday, July 12, "to the happiness of H.H., who languishes with love," noted Hassett; she returned to New York the following evening "leaving H.H. very desolate," noted Hassett.[78]

Hence Roosevelt's momentous decision making during that long mid-July weekend was a somewhat lonelier emotional experience than his decision making normally was, though Hopkins was, of course, involved in it. To this extent, the problem situation he faced was abnormal in its circumstances.

In its nature, it was unprecedented.

Unlike Churchill, Roosevelt had no supreme confidence in himself as military strategist. Unlike Churchill, therefore, he did not ordinarily involve himself directly in the making of strategy decisions. He left this to military professionals whose judgment, especially Marshall's, he had come to respect greatly. Not that he was a mere figurehead commander in chief. He chose with care the men who filled the top army and navy command posts, as we have seen. He permitted no truly major strategic proposal to be enacted that had not been reviewed by him and tested for consistency with the basic strategy agreed upon by the army and navy commands years before America's active entry into the war. And thus far, each major proposal, having passed this test, had received his approval. But he was now faced with a strategy proposal to which Marshall was deeply emotionally committed, which was fervently concurred in by every other top officer in the nation's armed forces, and which had the support (evidently) of every top civilian in the War and Navy Departments, yet which was, in Roosevelt's conviction, profoundly mistaken. Carried into action, it would certainly prolong the war and might well lead to Hitler's victory! As for the use Marshall-Stimson wanted to make of it, in an ultimatum to the British, the very idea was outrageous, especially in this dark time of troubles for them! Mingled with this wholly negative reaction, however, was a deeply felt need on Roosevelt's part to assuage the outraged feelings and stiffen the evidently sadly sagging morale of both Marshall and Stimson. It would be horrible if this dangerous quarrel among friends cost the nation the services of either man, especially the services of Marshall! The situation was ticklish, to say the least. Its successful handling required absolute firmness as regards ends, flexible ingenuity as regards means, and overall, great delicacy of perception and act.

For two days, during the brief periods when he was solitary, and also when alone with Hopkins, Roosevelt pondered what he should do. Then, on the morning of Tuesday, July 14, he telegraphed Marshall, saying: "I have definitely decided to send you, King, and Harry to London immediately." By "immediately" he meant their departure on Thursday, July 16, if at all possible. He himself would be back in the White House on Wednesday morning, he said, and his first order of business there would be to confer with Stimson and Marshall. He closed: "I want you to know that I do not approve the Pacific proposal."[79]

He gave his reasons why to the secretary of war and army chief of staff next morning. Truly decisive action against Japan could not be taken until the U.S. Navy was greatly strengthened, and to concentrate resources in the Pacific during this waiting period would be to risk "complete German domination of Europe and Africa" within the next few months. We must continue to bear in mind, for it continued to be true, that Japan's defeat would not of itself alone assure a victorious end to the global war, for upon Japan's surrender, we would still face a possibly greatly strengthened Germany; but Germany's defeat would assure the defeat of a by then weakened Japan very soon thereafter, perhaps "without firing a shot." He was at great pains to express his sympathetic understanding of Marshall and Stimson's exasperation with the British. He even shared it, being himself "absolutely sound on Bolero" and wanting it to be pressed unremittingly (he thus responded to a somewhat accusatory Stimson question). But he was dead set against using the Pacific alternative as a threat, "to force the British" to do what we wanted them to do. If an empty threat, a bluff, as an uneasy Stimson had begun to hint it might be, it was "something of a red herring." If serious, it was like "taking up your dishes and going away," by which he meant that there was a childish petulance in it. And such petulance would have disastrous effects. The most immediate of them would be the personal humiliation and further political weakening of a Prime Minister who was already under severe domestic pressures and whose continuance in full power was of vital importance to the United States.

Indeed, it was Roosevelt's conviction that ultimatums should not be presented by one ally to another at any time on any question whatever in this war. There were bound to be disagreements from time to time. Some of them would be wide and deep and acrimonious. But every disagreement *must* be negotiated into a workable compromise, for Allied victory was absolutely dependent upon Allied unity. It was to negotiate, therefore, and not to command or demand, that he was sending Marshall and King to London—and he was sending Hopkins to assure the negotiating team of wide plenary powers. Their mission was to meet with Churchill and the British chiefs of staff and shape with them a truly definite decision regarding operations in the eastern Atlantic—one that, this time, would stay made. They were authorized to strive with all their might for a reinstatement of Sledgehammer. He expressed a strong hope that it would be. But if they failed to overcome British opposition to it (in his secret heart, he was almost sure they would fail), they must be prepared to consider and reach agreement upon an alternative that would bring "U.S. ground troops . . . into action in 1942." This last was "of the highest importance."[80]

In lengthy private talk with Hopkins after dinner that night, Roosevelt gave more specific instructions. A shift of our major objective from Germany to Japan was not to be considered. If Sledgehammer could not be reinstated, "we should press forward vigorously for the 1943 enterprise [Roundup]" but must not "wait until 1943 to strike at Germany." He wanted "a determination . . . as to a specific . . . theater" for 1942 operations by American ground and sea forces against the Germans. The "theaters to be considered are North Africa and the Middle East," and his evident preference was North Africa. Gymnast had "the great advantage of being a purely American enterprise," would "secure Western Africa," and would lead toward "ultimate control of the Mediterranean . . . the shortest route" for supplies to Russia. He realized that major operations in either theater would "require a substantial reduction in Bolero for the next three months." He was "prepared to accept this." But he was *not* prepared to abandon Bolero-Roundup, which remained "essential." All this was spelled out in detail next day in a formal three-page directive to Hopkins, Marshall, and King, signed by the President as commander in chief. It closed: "Please remember three cardinal principles—speed of decision on plans, unity of plans, attack combined with defense but not defense alone. This affects the immediate objective of U.S. ground forces fighting against Germans in 1942. I hope for total agreement within one week of your arrival."[81]

This last was a hope fully shared by Hopkins, who was anxious to avoid postponement of his wedding.

And in the event, Roosevelt's stated aims were substantially achieved.

Landing at Prestwick, Scotland, in the early hours of Saturday, July 18, in weather that would not permit their flying south, the three Americans and their companions found a special train, sent by Churchill, waiting for them, along with Churchill's personal assistant, Commander Charles Thompson of the Royal Navy. Thompson was instructed to bring them to Chequers for the weekend. Instead, at Marshall's insistence, they rode the special train nonstop to London. A European Theater of Operations for the U.S. Army (ETOUSA) had been established in mid-June, Dwight D. Eisenhower had been appointed its commander by the staff chief, and Marshall was anxious to consult with his appointee and the latter's staff, then to meet informally with their British counterparts, before the formal conference was opened by Churchill on Monday morning. This infuriated Churchill. He promptly phoned Hopkins at Claridge's hotel and poured his fury into Hopkins's unwilling ear. The American chief of staff, he cried, acted as if he were the American commander in chief and as if the British chiefs of staff operated independently of and on the same level as the Prime Minister. He emphasized that he was both Prime Minister and minister of defense, that the British chiefs were subject to his orders, and that to meet with them before meeting with him in defiance of his expressed desire was therefore as subversive of constituted authority as it was personally insulting. Hopkins, finding it impossible to pacify his irate friend over the phone, and concerned over the effect this friend's anger might have upon upcoming negotiations, went to Chequers on the following (Sunday) morning. There, again, the "Prime Minister threw the British Constitution at me with some vehemence," Hopkins reported to Roosevelt, adding that he had suffered no injury, however, since that constitution "is an unwritten document." And by Sunday night his mollifying efforts had succeeded—"Winston was his old self and full of battle"—in some part, perhaps, because Hopkins reminded him that the President personally was more inclined than not to agree with the Prime Minister's views regarding Gymnast.[82]

There followed five days of incessant and sometimes angry argument during which the clarifying, concentrating, and ameliorating influence of Harry Hopkins was of vital importance. The discussions took place at No. 10 Downing Street, where Churchill opened the Combined Chiefs of Staff discussions on Monday morning; at Claridge's, where sixteen rooms on the fourth floor were temporarily converted into a closely guarded U.S. military headquarters; at No. 20 Grosvenor Square, a former apartment building now become ETOUSA headquarters; and in the British War Office in Whitehall. They ended on Friday, July 24, with an agreement by the Combined Chiefs of Staff upon Allied landings in the fall on both the Atlantic and the Mediterranean coasts of northwestern North Africa. And, strange to say, the instrument of this agreement was a memorandum prepared and presented, not by those British who had always supported Gymnast, but by the chief American who had always opposed it!

The story of this irony is instructive in the ways of committee politics.

On Tuesday night, having fought stubbornly through Monday and Tuesday for Sledgehammer's reinstatement, Marshall and King were forced to concede defeat. (When Hopkins reported this to Roosevelt, the latter promptly replied that he was not surprised, then reiterated that some other operation involving American ground troops must be promptly agreed upon, his own preferences being either "an offensive with Algeria and/or French Morocco as targets" or the original proposal for North Africa [Gymnast], the first stages of the latter to be carried out *exclusively* by American troops because Vichy France would be less likely to resist an American than a British invasion of French colonies.) Marshall refused, however, to give up his side of the fundamental issue between him and the British. His prime conference objective was a truly firm, irrevocable commitment by the British to 1943 Roundup, and he now devised a tactical maneuver that might, in his opinion, achieve it. Throughout the first two days of discussions, whenever the Gymnast alternative to Sledgehammer came up, Brooke and British Air Marshal Portal supported the Prime Minister's position that a North African operation was no contradiction of Bolero-Roundup, that both could be carried out, and that therefore there was no necessity to choose between the two. But Marshall was convinced that Brooke, at least, did not really believe this. After all, Brooke had "admitted" as much in talk with Marshall in Washington just a few weeks ago! And wasn't it probable that Churchill was so insistent upon the alleged consistency of Gymnast with Roundup precisely because he knew, or at least feared, that a flat choice between the two would favor Roundup? Here, then, was a vulnerable point in the British position, and Marshall's maneuver was designed to attack it.

With King, he submitted to the CCS on that decisive Friday a formal tripartite proposal. Part One: Planning and preparation would continue for a large-scale cross-Channel operation to be executed by July 1, 1943. Part Two: "[A] combined operation against the North and Northwest coasts of Africa" would be launched in 1942, but with the explicit understanding that commitment to this operation "renders Roundup, in all probability, impracticable in 1943 and therefore that we have definitely accepted a defensive, encircling line for the Continental European Theater, except as to air operation." If the British balked at this proviso, as Brooke might feel compelled to do by his loyal subordination to the Prime Minister, they must prove with hard facts (about the availability of troops, ships, planes, landing craft, and so on) that both offensives were possible within the stated time period, and Marshall was convinced they couldn't do it. They would be forced to choose between North Africa and continental invasion, and since there were disagreements among themselves on these matters, there seemed a better than fifty-fifty chance that their choice would be Roundup. This was especially so if the making of the final decision on North Africa were postponed for as long as possible. Hence Part Three of the memo, which proposed that the decision to abandon Roundup and accept the strategic defensive be put off until September 15, which meant, in Marshall's conception, that the final decision on North Africa was also delayed until September 15, since (as per Part Two) North Africa was contingent upon the acceptance of the strategic defensive in Europe.[83]

But, alas for such calculated subtlety on the part of a man with remarkably little talent for it, the British chose to regard Marshall's document as (in Brooke's words) "a paper containing almost everything we had asked them [the Americans] to agree to at the start." It was, in their view, simply a proposal to substitute Gymnast for Sledgehammer; and, far from balking at the stated "probability" that North Africa 1942 precluded Roundup 1943, they were more relieved than not to accept it. Admiral of the Fleet Sir Dudley Pound went so far as to say that in his opinion, Gymnast and Roundup were every bit as contradictory as the Americans had always claimed they were. Brooke, with Portal, refused to admit this explicitly, but he did so in effect. As his official historian says, he had always "doubted" that the cross-Channel assault "would be possible in 1943" and therefore "made no attempt to challenge . . . [the American] view." He and the other British did insist upon adding to the memo language indicating that a decision to go into North Africa constituted no such sharp break in the continuity of Allied strategy as Marshall, in his original draft, had intentionally implied: "blockade" was added to "air operations" as an exception to the agreed "defensive" strategy for Europe in the first half of 1943; and a clause was added saying "that the organization, planning, and training for eventual entry in the Continent should continue so that this operation can be staged should a marked deterioration in German military strength become apparent, and the resources of the United Nations, available after meeting other requirements, so permit."[84]

Thus the memorandum formally adopted by the Combined Chiefs of Staff as CCS 94, on July 24, served Marshall's tactical purpose only insofar as it retained his postponement of final decision until September 15. And this item was promptly rendered null and void by Roosevelt's blithe ignoring of it!

On Saturday, July 25, a few hours before the CCS (for security reasons) substituted "Torch" for Gymnast as the code name for a now expanded North African operation, and agreed that the commander of the operation should be an American (Eisenhower was indicated), Hopkins dispatched a personal message to the White House in which he deplored the element of tentativeness in the documented CCS commitment to North Africa. "What I fear . . . is that if we do not make [now, instead of September 15] a firm decision on Gymnast and fix a reasonably early date there may be procrastinations and delay," he said. "Although I believe the intention here is to mount the operation aggressively, unless the written language of the orders is precise there may be difficulty when it comes to carrying out the orders by the secondary personnel." Roosevelt thoroughly agreed. He sent word that the North African landings should be no later than October 30, which was the target date Hopkins had suggested, and asked Hopkins to tell the Prime Minister he was "delighted" with this *final* decision, and that the orders now were "full speed ahead." He then called into his office Stimson and Admiral Leahy, along with Generals Arnold and McNarney, and read to them the message he had sent. There was "no discussion," McNarney at once notified Marshall, though the President did say that "he desired action and . . . *could see no reason why the withdrawal of a few troops in 1942 would prevent Bolero in 1943.*"* On July 27, Churchill replied to what Roosevelt had said to him through Hopkins: "I was sure you would be as pleased as I am, indeed as we all are here, at the results of this strenuous week. Besides reaching agreement on action, relations of cordial intimacy and comradeship have been cemented between our high officers. I doubt that success would have been achieved without Harry's invaluable aid." On the evening (in Washington) of that same day, Roosevelt cabled Churchill: "The three musketeers [Hopkins, King, Marshall] arrived safely this afternoon and the wedding is still scheduled. . . . I cannot help feeling that the past week represented a turning point of the whole war and that we are now on our way shoulder to shoulder."[85]

(Three days later, during the noon hour of Thursday, July 30, Harry Hopkins and Louise Macy were married in a ceremony performed in the President's study [the Oval Room]—the first wedding in the White House since Woodrow Wilson's marriage to Edith Bolling Galt in December 1915. "And a very nice affair it was, too," writes William Hassett. "The mantel to the left as one went in was banked with palms and white flowers. . . . From the gold frame above the doorway giving into the President's bedroom, Grandma Roosevelt looked down—majestic, benign." The President in white linen suit with matching shoes was Hopkins's best man; Eleanor Roosevelt was there with Hopkins's daughter, Diana; all three of Hopkins's sons were there; a few of the close relatives of the bride were there. "Harry trembled like an aspen leaf throughout the service," continues Hassett; "but managed to fish the wedding ring out of his pants pocket at the proper time, albeit with trembling fingers. The "Wedding March" from *Lohengrin* was played by an orchestra stationed outside in the long hall. It was all over in about ten minutes.")[86]

Even now, however, Marshall refused to give up. He continued to insist that the final decision had not yet been made. He did so, for instance, in a letter to Eisenhower,† written on Hopkins's wedding day. He did so again on that same July 30 in a meeting of the Washington branch of the CCS, the first to be held

---

*Italicized by present author.

†Eisenhower had been informed by Marshall, before the latter left London, that he was to command Torch if the operation were carried through and that he was immediately in charge of the planning and preparation for it. The formal official proposal of this was not made by the CCS until August 6 and was approved by Roosevelt the same day.

after his return from London and the first ever to be presided over by Admiral Leahy. Leahy, whose ambassadorship to Vichy France had effectively ended with Pierre Laval's return to power there, had just (July 21) been named chief of staff to the President as commander in chief, an unprecedented position the duties of which were very vaguely described by Roosevelt to his press conference, but one of which included chairing the meetings of the JCS and the Washington CCS. He opened this July 30 meeting with a statement of his "impression that both the President and the Prime Minister now firmly believe that the decision to undertake Torch has . . . been reached and that all . . . arrangements [for it] are proceeding as rapidly as possible in order that the operation may be undertaken at the earliest possible date." Sir John Dill concurred in this. But Marshall did not. He insisted, as per CCS 94, that the decision to mount Torch had as necessary corollary the abandonment of Roundup and that until the President and Prime Minister explicitly acknowledged that fact—that is, until they said definitely that Roundup was canceled—no final decision had been made. King agreed, saying it was "his impression that the President and Prime Minister had not yet reached an agreement to abandon Roundup in favor of Torch," adding that before they did so, they must carefully consider the effect the reduction of Bolero would have upon the security of the British Isles against invasion. Marshall no longer maintained, however, that this final decision could wait until September 15. "Logistical considerations" required a decision "almost immediately," though it might well be put off for a week, by which time "a staff study . . . of all the implications of Torch" would be completed. Leahy then closed the meeting, saying that (to quote the official minutes) "he would now tell the President that a definite decision was yet to be made" and should not be until a staff study now under way was completed next week. The decision then must be "definite, with the date of landing set," concluded Leahy.[87]

Roosevelt would have none of this.

On that very evening, within three hours or so after he'd received Leahy's report, he summoned the admiral to the Oval Room along with "Hap" Arnold and Brigadier General Walter Bedell Smith, who, destined to become Eisenhower's highly talented chief of staff, was at that time serving as secretary of both the JCS and the Washington CCS. It was he who reported to the two staff organizations, in writing, the President's words. They were hard, unequivocal words. Roosevelt as commander in chief had "definitely" decided that Torch would be undertaken at the earliest possible date. He considered this operation to be now our "principal objective." Assembling the means to carry it out must therefore take precedence over the preparations for any other operation, *including* Bolero-Roundup. Since this decision of his canceled the CCS 94 provision putting off the making of the final decision till September 15, he wondered aloud if he should send a message immediately to Churchill asking for his written agreement with it, just to clear the record.[88]

Yet still Marshall refused to concede total defeat!

He perforce pressed concentrated planning and preparation for the operation, but in conduct the most questionable in the whole of his great service to the nation—conduct the most contradictory of his code of honor, conduct the most nearly subversive of Section 2 of Article II of the Constitution—he continued well into August his opposition to the operation's launching. He resorted to covert hairsplitting tactics, saying in a memo to his operations (planning) division that the "decision to mount the operation has been made, but it [the operation] is still subject to the vicissitudes of war" and adding: "Whether or not we should discuss this phase of the matter with General Eisenhower I do not know." By August's second week, his planners' knowledge of his negative attitude was having a dangerously vitiating effect upon their work, in the opinion of Dill, who, in a personal letter on August 9, gently but strongly rebuked his friend. "I am just a little concerned about Torch," he wrote, meaning (as Marshall knew) that he was greatly concerned. "For good or ill it has been accepted and therefore . . . we should go at it with all possible enthusiasm and give it absolute priority. . . . All I aim at is to ensure that we all think alike—and enthusiastically." A stung Marshall immediately replied that the officers charged with executing Torch must of course give it their "complete support" and "most energetic cooperation," but that among the planners "absolute candor" was far more important than thinking "alike—and enthusiastically." Indeed, he implied, thinking alike in the absence of candor could lead to disaster. He added: "You may be sure that U.S. Planners will enthusiastically and effectively support decisions made by the Commander-in-Chief," thus evincing his continued stubborn insistence that, since the highest authorities had not yet explicitly acknowledged that going into North Africa meant a basic change in grand strategy, no truly final decision could be said to have been made.[89]

Inevitably, rumors of Marshall's and his colleagues' disaffection reached the ears of news reporters. Inevitably, this prompted charges in some of the most reactionary papers and radio commentaries that a bullheaded egotistical dictatorial President, possessed of little military competence, ignored the advice of highly competent military advisers. These charges Roosevelt hotly denied in a cabinet meeting on August 6 at which, evidently, Marshall was present. He said that the views of all his advisers had been carefully considered as he made his decision—and he said this in a way that boded ill for any officer caught "leaking" contrary information to a hostile press. Marshall seems to have been jarred by this toward the channels of behavior that he normally followed—channels determined by his rigid honor code conjoined with a conviction that, in America, the top military authority not only is but *ought* to be subordinate to the top civilian authority. His behavior changed abruptly, and quite drastically. During preceding weeks, he had eagerly seized upon every perceptible possible hazard and difficulty in the North African venture and had so stressed their magnitude in talks with Stimson that the latter became convinced the operation was utterly hopeless, absolutely doomed. In consequence, the cabinet meeting had an effect upon the secretary very different from that it had on Marshall. Appalled by what he saw as Roosevelt's arrogant disregard of truth, his wishful-thinking blindness to unwelcome realities, Stimson was moved to address to the White House yet another of his lecturing epistles, this one stressing not the moral responsibility of the President to exercise leadership, but his moral responsibility to heed accurately informed advice. The secretary showed it to Marshall as soon as he had completed it; he was surprised by Marshall's immediate flat opposition to the sending of it. Stimson protested: a self-deceived Roosevelt didn't know what he was doing; if he was not set right great harm would be done the Allied cause! Marshall replied ("sternly," according to his biographer) that the President at the cabinet meeting had known exactly what he was doing and was acting deliberately. Stimson finally reluctantly agreed to leave his letter unsent, but not until he had exacted from Marshall a solemn promise that the general and his staff "would not permit Gymnast [so Stimson still called it] to become effective if it seemed clearly headed to a disaster."[90]

IX

PREVIOUSLY we have spoken of the Christian fatalism that was the base and root of Roosevelt's optimistic courage and of his attitude toward power and its exercise. In this, and in his consequent sense of his own historical role, we once compared him to General Kutuzov as perceived by Tolstoy in *War and Peace:* he believed that his personal will, even when fully implemented by the executive powers of his high office (often it could not be), was far too weak a force to influence significantly, of itself alone, the immense stream of world event.* He believed also that he was under no obligation to attempt to do so. His assigned task, like Tolstoy's Kutuzov's, was not "to bring in any plan of his own" to impose upon history's flow, but simply to recognize the significance bestowed upon events by their places in the mainstream of event (also by such signs and cues concerning them as came to him from On High)† and then to encourage the happening of "anything useful" while discouraging the happening of "anything harmful." Thus his decision making on many, if not most, occasions was, as we have often noted, simply a measurement as precise as possible of the strength of the external pressures immediately focused upon him, followed by a yielding to those that were, by this measurement, the strongest. It was "outer" rather than "inner directed."

This was most emphatically not so, however, in the episode just recounted.

---

*See pp. 38–39, *FDR: The New Deal Years.*
†See pp. 34–35 for analysis of the forms of prayer through which Roosevelt sought divine guidance.

Far from yielding to the heaviest of the immediate pressures focused upon him—in this case, to the united and vehement urgings of virtually the whole of the American military establishment—he stood rock firm against it upon ground defined by his own thought, his own conviction, his own sense of what ought to be. And by doing so at a crucial pivotal moment, he did exert a profound influence upon the course of world history.

For consider what might have happened had he permitted the fundamental shift in American global strategy pressed for by the Joint Chiefs of Staff. . . .

Russia's survival of the German onslaught in the summer and fall of 1942 was by a narrow margin. A goodly portion of this margin consisted of the material aid Russia received from the West. And the amount of this aid might well have been sufficiently reduced by America's shift of strategy, involving as it did a massive diversion of shipping from the Atlantic to the Pacific, to ensure Russia's collapse in early 1943, if not late 1942. That event would have been encouraged also by the fall of Churchill's coalition government, which might well have occurred soon after what amounted to a repudiation of it (a vote of no confidence in it) by the Americans. The British government that succeeded might well have been less adamantly hostile to Nazi-fascism and more fearfully hostile to Russian communism than Churchill's had been, more prone therefore to accept the peace offer (or ultimatum) that Hitler would almost certainly have made in the aftermath of his Russian conquest. Or this successor government, if it refused the peace offer, was likely to be less resolute and skillful in its resistance of Hitlerian invasion than Churchill's would have been; and this invasion would have been launched while the Americans were heavily engaged with the Japanese and so unable to come to Britain's aid with the strength and rapidity that would otherwise have been possible. Indeed, the American government might by then have lacked the will to commit to Britain's aid even the full strength it did have available for that purpose.

For would not such events as are described above have had immediate and strong repercussions within American politics? And would not these have created grave dissensions between and within the nation's executive and legislative branches? The covert but powerful reactionary forces that Roosevelt had recognized as a grave threat to the American democracy during the 1940 presidential campaign—forces that would have welcomed and been strengthened by the shift in strategic emphasis but were rendered relatively impotent, in the actual event, by Allied victories across the Atlantic—would have become much stronger, feeding as reaction always does feed upon selfish passions gone out of rational control. In the present instance, the passions would have been jarred out of control and augmented in force by mass perceptions of Hitler's invincibility and hence inevitable ultimate triumph. Thus fed, they might have grown strong enough to force a negotiated peace between the United States and the European portion of the Axis. "This would have meant the death of democratic society and the establishment of a totalitarian government in the United States," the present author once wrote. "The spirit of scientific humanism which had animated Western civilization would have been greatly enfeebled if not wholly destroyed and the death of the body of that civilization would probably soon have followed."*

There is, of course, an alternative possibility—a somewhat less distinct possibility, in this author's judgment—that the direst consequences described above would have been avoided. Russia, despite the reduction in her aid, might have survived the loss of the Caucasus and remained in the war, if less effectively so. Allied defensive efforts might have succeeded in preventing Hitler's conquest of North Africa and the Middle East. Japan might have been crushed by the beginning of 1944, enabling the United States to concentrate exclusively upon her European enemy. But this enemy would then have been stronger than the one the Allies actually faced in late 1944. Not only would Italy have remained in the war, but Hitler, with his involvement in Russia probably reduced in proportion to the reduction in American aid to Russia and with his material resources increased by those of the Caucasus, would have had more time free of serious Allied harassment in which to consolidate his European conquests and strengthen greatly the Atlantic Wall of his Fortress Europe. In these circumstances, the ultimate decision would have been made by Allied use in Europe, not the Far East, of the dread weapon the development of which we have described, a development far advanced by the close of 1942. The targets of the first atomic bombs would have been the key cities of Germany, possibly of Italy, possibly even of other parts of conquered Europe. What effect would this have had upon a Western civilization and culture already wounded near to death by barbarians armed with the scientific technology that civilized men have created? What effect would it have had upon the postwar relations between the Western Allies and the Soviet Union, or between Western civilization and the teeming millions of Africa and the Orient?

*Davis, *Experience of War* (New York, 1965), p. 264.

BOOK FOUR

❧❊❧

The Turning of the Tide

IO

The Difficult Lighting of Torch

I

IN early June at the close of their face-to-face meetings with Molotov, Roosevelt and Churchill gave a large hostage to fortune when they approved for issuance simultaneously in Washington, London, and Moscow a communiqué saying "full understanding was reached" during the talks regarding "a second front in 1942." The communiqué, by encouraging Moscow's belief in an Anglo-American cross-Channel invasion to be launched in the coming fall on a scale sufficient to draw enemy divisions away from the eastern front, had served Washington's and London's primary concern at that moment, which was to boost Russia's morale on the eve of a renewed terrific Nazi onslaught. But now, as July gave way to August, the strength of the belief thus encouraged measured the danger that its disillusionment posed to the Russo-Western alliance.

Roosevelt more than Churchill, it must be said, was responsible for the hazard's magnitude; he in conversation with Molotov had much more emphatically "expected" the making of a 1942 second front of the kind Molotov called for than Churchill had done. Indeed, Churchill, the reader is reminded, had prudently handed the Soviet envoy an aide-mémoire saying no flat promise of a 1942 "second front" could at that moment be made because no one could calculate accurately, thus far in advance of the event, what chance a major cross-Channel operation had of success. And this difference between the two men's dealings with Molotov in June instanced the basic difference between their personal approaches to the problems of Soviet relations. The Prime Minister—never forgetful of either the Nazi-Soviet pact or the utter evil (as he saw it) of Communist totalitarianism, and believing that the Russian dictator was utterly ruthless, utterly disregardful of all else, in his pursuit of his own or his country's exclusive interests—"took an unabashedly British viewpoint" in all his dealings with him, as Warren Kimball has said. He cared little, if at all, how Stalin felt about him personally. Very different in this regard was the President of the United States. Roosevelt operated on the premise that "Uncle Joe," though extremely "difficult," was a human being possessed of human feelings that could and should be cultivated in the interests of the Grand Alliance and the postwar world order. He put himself out to gain the maximum possible of Stalin's personal trust and affection, was supremely confident of his ability to do so, and was unhampered in this effort by any such passionate aversion to communism on moral and ideological grounds as trammeled the Prime Minister.

But President and Prime Minister were as one in their anxiety to preserve the East-West military alliance in full force, and both were acutely aware that the difficulty of doing so was increased by the fact that the news of Sledgehammer's cancellation must now come to Moscow hard upon the heels of news that the Western Allies were discontinuing, for the time being, at least, all effort to get supplies to Russia by convoys around Norway's North Cape.

On July 14, the day Roosevelt told Stimson and Marshall that he disapproved their "Pacific proposal," he received a "personal and secret" message from Churchill telling of the dire fate of the last convoy (designated PQ seventeen) to attempt the supply run from Britain to the White Sea port of Archangel. Only four of the thirty-three ships in the convoy had got through, "with four or five more precariously in the ice off Nova Zembla . . . ," wrote Churchill. "If half had got through we should have persevered, but with only a quarter arriving the operation is not good enough. For instance, out of nearly six hundred tanks in PQ seventeen little over one hundred have arrived. . . . We therefore advise against running [convoy] PQ eighteen which must start on [July] eighteen at the latest. If it were composed [exclusively] of our merchant ships we would certainly not send them, but no fewer than twenty-two [of that convoy] are . . . American ships. We should therefore like to know how you feel about it." There was not much prospect, either, the Prime Minister went on, that this northern supply could be resumed on anything like its former scale as winter came on. Murmansk was "largely burnt out" by German air attack and could no longer function adequately as a supply port, and Archangel on the White Sea would be icebound by the time the lengthening northern nights made ship passage through the Barents Sea generally feasible. There might be some offsetting increase of Russian supply through the southern supply route from Basra over the Persian railroad to the Caspian Sea. This was "being pressed." But the increase could not "amount to much," for the Persian railroad, though only recently completed by a British firm ("a remarkable engineering achievement" with its "390 major bridges . . . through the mountain gorges," as Churchill writes in his memoirs), was already being used to very near its full capacity. A message "explaining" to Stalin the convoy discontinuance had been prepared, said the Prime Minister in conclusion, and a copy of it would come to Roosevelt "later today" for his review before its dispatch to Moscow.[1]

The message copy, which arrived at the White House a few hours later, was lengthy, eloquent, and absolutely firm as regards the decision reached. Roosevelt perused it with great care. And on the following day, having consulted Admiral King, he cabled Churchill his "reluctant" approval of both the northern convoy cancellation and "your message to Stalin," which, he said, was "a good one." He "assumed" it would be sent at once.* But he clearly indicated his disinclination to accept Churchill's judgment that nothing could be done to increase significantly the supply flow from Basra to the Caspian Sea. ". . . [W]e must omit nothing that will increase the traffic through Persia," he said. "A suggestion has been made that American railway men take over the operation of the railroad. . . . They are first-class at this sort of thing." He knew that, in saying this, he risked giving offense, the railroad being currently under British management, so there was diffidence in his question: "Have you any opinion about this?"[2]

Both men then waited, with an anxiety somewhat greater (or at any rate qualitatively different) in the White House than at No. 10 Downing Street, for Stalin's reply to the Churchill message. It was received in London on July 28, just four days after the London strategy conference's final decision to abandon Sledgehammer in favor of Torch. Stalin's tone was rough and surly. He brusquely, even contemptuously, dismissed as "untenable" Churchill's argument for discontinuing the northern supply. He indicated, ominously, as if apropos this discontinuance, his suspicions regarding the conclusions reached at the London Conference, which he knew had just ended. "[T]he Soviet Union," he said flatly, "cannot tolerate the second front in Europe being postponed till 1943." The implication was that in his belief, a general pattern of betrayal of the Soviet Union was unfolding in action, a pattern the wily Churchill sought to dissemble—and if Churchill didn't actually bristle inwardly at this implication, he reacted to what Stalin said without sympathy, or even due allowance, for the anguish of its sayer. "I do not propose to embark on an argument," he cabled Roosevelt, to whom a copy of the Stalin message was delivered on July 29 via the British embassy in Washington, "but since Stalin will no doubt expect some account of our recent conversations here on the second front . . . I propose to refer [him] to the *aide-mémoire* . . . handed Molotov here just before he left . . . and to say that it still represents our general position, but that we have agreed with you on certain action, although at present stage nothing can be said about time and place. We might also say that we hope to resume convoys in September, if Russians can provide necessary air force to deny German surface ships use of Barents Sea. . . ." He manifested not the slightest concern over Stalin's "feelings."[3]

But Roosevelt did.

"I agree with you that your reply to Stalin must be handled with great care,"

---

*Actually, it was not sent until three days later. Revisions to emphasize further the fatal hazards of northern convoying had by then been made in it.

he cabled Churchill (who had actually said no such thing) within an hour or two after he'd digested the information Churchill had sent him, then went on to say in a somewhat chiding tone: "We have got always to bear in mind the personality of our ally and the very difficult and dangerous situation that confronts him. No one can be expected to approach the war from a world point of view whose country has been invaded. I think we should try to put ourselves in his place." He further thought Stalin "should be told . . . quite specifically that we have determined upon a course of action in 1942" and that, "without advising him of the precise nature of our proposed operations the fact that they are going to be made should be told him without any qualification." As regards the northern convoy in September, "I think you should not raise any false hopes," but "I agree with you that we should run one if there is any possibility of success. . . ."4

Gnawing at Washington's mind and provoking much anxiety at this point was the question of how Moscow was to be informed of the decision just taken in London. The question was a delicate one: The way in which the news was conveyed might of itself greatly affect Moscow's response to it, and the nature of this response would in turn affect, happily or detrimentally, the health of the Grand Alliance. But in fact, unbeknownst to Washington, the question had by then been substantially answered. On the evening of the day the crucial London decision was definitely, finally made (Friday, July 24), Churchill had gone from London to Chartwell, his private country home, where he had had as his sole dinner guest Averell Harriman, and to Harriman he had disclosed his decision to go himself to Russia to deliver the news to Stalin in person. He had been convinced for some time that he must go very soon to Cairo, accompanied by CIGS Brooke, to make on the spot in his capacity as minister of defense whatever changes were needed in the British high command of the Middle East (that the needed changes were drastic seemed indicated by the fact that some ninety thousand highly trained, well-equipped British troops had been repeatedly humiliatingly defeated by Rommel with barely half as many troops); and from Cairo he could go on to Russia, there to meet Stalin in Moscow or wherever else was agreeable to the dictator. He could then speak "the plain truth," answering as fully and frankly as possible whatever challenging questions the Russians asked. Admittedly, such a task would be difficult and unpleasant; it "was like carrying a large lump of ice to the North Pole," he later said. He would have to steel himself against the dictator's predictable wrath in order to bear it without losing his own self-control or yielding an inch of the ground of necessity on which he stood. But he felt this "was the only way . . . to put the suspicions of the recent past behind us and establish a solid . . . relationship of trust."5

Four nights later (July 28), during a dinner meeting of the British war cabinet in No. 10 Downing Street where the King was a guest, Churchill received formal official approval of these proposals. The telegram he sent Stalin on July 30 began: "We are making preliminary arrangements . . . to run a large convoy through to Archangel in the first week of September." It went on: "I am willing, if you invite me, to come myself to meet you. . . . We could then survey the war together and take decisions hand-in-hand. I could . . . tell you plans we have made with President Roosevelt for offensive action in 1942." He at once sent a copy of this to Roosevelt with a cover note saying he hoped "you will authorize me to tell him what we have settled. I am sure I can state the case in all its bearings." On the following day, he received from Stalin an official invitation to come to Moscow, bringing with him whomever he chose to bring and arriving whenever was convenient to him: "You may be sure beforehand that any date would suit me. Let me express my gratitude for your consent to send the next convoy . . . at the beginning of September."*6

Meanwhile, Harriman worried with increasing intensity over a hazard to the success of Churchill's Russian enterprise that neither the Prime Minister nor Foreign Secretary Eden seemed to recognize, or to which, at any rate, they paid insufficient attention. Molotov upon his return to London from Washington in June had said to Harriman that there was a division of opinion between the Americans and the British regarding the feasibility of a second front in 1942: Roosevelt and Marshall were much more optimistic about it, more committed to it, than were Churchill, Brooke, and the other British chiefs of staff. Stalin would certainly have been told the same thing by his commissar for foreign affairs. If, therefore, no fully authorized representative of the American President were a member of Churchill's mission to Moscow, Stalin was unlikely to "believe a word of what Churchill was telling him" about Anglo-American solidarity but "would think that the British alone had blocked the Second Front," as Harriman later put it. The Churchill mission, instead of allaying the Russian's suspicions, would increase them, with who knew what dire effect upon the conduct of the war. So on the morning of Tuesday, August 4, two days after Churchill had departed for Cairo with a party that included Sir Alexander Cadogan of the British Foreign Office as well as Brooke and (as always) Dr. Wilson, Harriman spoke his fears to Eden. The foreign secretary at once recognized the validity of Harriman's concern, apologized for not having seen the hazard himself, and asked who the American presidential representative should be. "Hopkins would be best," was Harriman's reply, "but if he is not available I am ready to go." To this, Eden at once agreed. Harriman promptly cabled this information to Roosevelt, whose initial response was negative, despite Eden's approval of what Harriman proposed. He feared that for him to suggest to the Prime Minister that a presidential representative become a member of the mission would cause the Prime Minister to suspect that the Americans didn't trust him to handle things properly. ". . . I do not want anyone [either Churchill or Stalin] to

---

*This convoy (PQ eighteen) did sail as promised in early September. A new defense scheme was devised for it, consisting of a close escort of sixteen destroyers plus an escort carrier bearing a dozen fighter planes. These planes, heroically and skillfully piloted, destroyed in fierce air battle twenty-four of nearly one hundred enemy planes. Ten merchant ships were sunk by U-boat and bomber attack, but twenty-seven arrived in Archangel with cargoes intact.

have the slightest suspicion that you are acting as an observer," replied Roosevelt to Harriman's message. ". . . I know you would be useful but I think it wiser not to run any risks of misconception." Simultaneously, however, Eden had communicated Harriman's and his own concern to Churchill, who had just arrived (that is, on the morning of August 4) in Cairo, and Churchill at once cabled Roosevelt: "I should greatly like to have your aid and countenance in my talks with Joe. Would you be able to let Averell come with me? I feel that things would be easier if we all seemed to be together. I have a somewhat raw job." Roosevelt then cabled Harriman: "Have wire from Former Naval Person saying he thinks you would be helpful. . . . I am sending the following wire to Stalin: 'I am asking Harriman to proceed to Moscow to be at the disposal of yourself and your visitor to help in any way possible.' "[7]

Harriman departed at once, going not to Moscow but to Cairo, there to become one of the Prime Minister's party. He flew from Cornwall in a converted bomber* whose principal other passenger was Charles de Gaulle. Because of the narrowness of the aisle separating the facing benches on which these two tall men sat during their twenty hours in the air, they were forced into a physical intimacy, their knees interlocking, that was decidedly unmatched by any meeting of minds. The Frenchman, always stiff, aloof, touchy, and humorless, had surmised from a London conversation with Marshall that the 1942 invasion of northern France had been canceled. He suspected that a landing in French North Africa, in which the Free French would not be permitted by pro-Vichy Americans to have any part, might be substituted for it. And his suspicion was confirmed in his mind, according to his memoirs, by the reticence of "this ordinarily frank and fluent diplomat." Harriman seemed to de Gaulle "to be nursing some weighty secret," and "these symptoms assured me that a major operation would soon be underway without us in the Mediterranean."[9]

II

THE Cairo business occupied Churchill and Brooke until August 10.

Both men were quite sure before they boarded their plane in England that Auchinleck must be relieved of his present command. They agreed he was a man of splendid personal qualities, a first-class soldier, possessed of great strength of character. But in Churchill's view he lacked a sense of proportion and was consequently woefully mistaken in his assessments of priorities; he continually permitted what were in fact relatively minor problems in Palestine,

---

*Churchill and his party had also flown to Cairo in an unheated converted bomber, though not a crowded one—"a very different kind of travel from the comforts of the Boeing flying-boats," as Churchill remarks in his memoirs, and "a rather feckless way of sending . . . [the Prime Minister] over the world when he is approaching his seventieth year," in the words of Sir Charles Wilson. But, as it happened, Churchill slept soundly through the one night they were in the air "and when we got to Gibraltar" in the morning "was ready for anything."[8]

Syria, and Iraq to distract him from the absolutely essential task of beating Rommel. He had repeatedly gone on the defensive at moments most propitious, as Churchill saw it, for a continued or renewed offensive against the Afrika Korps. As for Brooke, he, as he stressed in conversation with Charles Wilson, deplored Auchinleck's evident inability to pick the right subordinates: "Those he appointed had so dispersed our forces in the desert that Rommel, with his more effective tanks and guns, had little difficulty in defeating the scattered fragments piecemeal," as Wilson recorded. These denigrating judgments were abundantly confirmed by what the Prime Minister and the CIGS saw and heard during swift concentrated field tours of the ground and air forces. Churchill, for instance, was dismayed by the fact that the yeomanry division, an elite fighting unit in which he took special interest, had for two years been kept in the Levant, mostly in Palestine, and though it had now been for some time in Africa, "had never yet effectively engaged the enemy." Moreover, there was evident ill feeling between air and ground forces—ill feeling of a kind that would not have occurred had the two been properly coordinated in battle action.

All this had confirmed the Prime Minister in his long-held conviction that the war theater currently designated as "Middle East" was far too large and various in its problems (political, military) to be effectively administered in a single command. He had always deplored as inaccurate the labeling that made Iraq and Persia as well as Egypt and the Levant parts of the Middle East. According to geographers, Egypt, Palestine, Syria, and Turkey constituted the Near East; Iraq and Persia were the Middle East; India, Burma, and Malaya were the East; China and Japan were the Far East. It was therefore in accord with what he deemed geographic accuracy that on August 6, Churchill, with the concurrence of Brooke and Field Marshal Jan Christian Smuts (Churchill, who deemed Smuts one of the great wise men of the world, had summoned him from South Africa, of which he was Premier, to help in the decision making), proposed to split in two the presently designated "Middle East Command." The new arrangement was for a "Near East Command" encompassing Egypt, Palestine, and Syria, headquartered in Cairo, and a "Middle East Command" comprising Iraq and Persia, headquartered in Baghdad. General Auchinleck was to be relieved as commander in Cairo and offered the command of the Middle East theater as newly defined. In Cairo, he would be replaced by General Sir Harold R. L. G. Alexander, whose theater of command was designated the Near East. Since Alexander was currently in London as commander of the British First Army, which was the British component of operation Torch, a replacement for him in that post must be found at once. The obvious choice, immediately made, was General Bernard Law Montgomery. Replacing Auchinleck meant replacing his former chief of staff, Ritchie, as commander of the Eighth Army, and for this post was chosen General W. H. E. ("Straffer") Gott, who had distinguished himself as brigade and then corps commander during the desert fighting and was immensely popular with the troops.

The war cabinet members at once approved these personnel changes. They balked, however, at splitting the Middle East command. This seemed to them a retreat from the principle of unified command that had been adopted during the Arcadia Conference and to which they were all now firmly committed. Moreover, much popular confusion would arise from the fact that, by this new theater nomenclature, Auchinleck, though shifted to Baghdad, would retain the same title he now held, that of commander in chief, Middle East. And Churchill, after a single strong protest ("We are all convinced that the arrangement . . . proposed is sound on geographical, strategic, and administrative grounds"), yielded the point, being encouraged to do so by Auchinleck's unwillingness to accept the Baghdad post.*[10]

But now a tragic event supervened: On the very day of Gott's official elevation to Eighth Army command, the plane in which he was flying to Cairo from the airfield serving Britain's El Alamein position, and in very nearly the same airspace that Churchill had traversed two days before, was shot down by an enemy fighter. Gott died instantly.

For a long moment, consternation, mingled with grief, reigned in the ruling circles of Cairo and London. But only for a moment. The Eighth Army post must be filled at once, and though Brooke and Churchill had no doubt that the right man to fill it now was Montgomery, and that Montgomery's just assigned post at First Army could well go to General Kenneth Anderson, an officer of high reputation, they were concerned over how Torch's supreme commander might respond to the repeated top personnel changes being forced upon him. The new appointments were, however, made promptly. By midafternoon of August 8, Montgomery was winging his way to Cairo and Anderson was being introduced to Eisenhower as First Army's new commander.

As for Eisenhower, he did indeed find these top command changes highly vexatious. He was heavily burdened by the anxieties and complexities of planning and mounting what was to be the largest amphibian operation ever attempted till then, an operation he with most other military men deemed extremely hazardous and one whose success depended upon a number of factors (mostly political) over which he had little or no control. He had welcomed and been greatly relieved by the assistance of Alexander, with whom he at once established cordial and efficient working relations.† Then, abruptly, Alexander

---

*Auchinleck eventually returned to the post he had held before going to Cairo, that of commander in chief of British forces in India.

†Eisenhower had been concerned over how he would be accepted as commanding officer by Alexander. The latter outranked him, had directed the Dunkirk evacuation, had also commanded in Burma, whereas he, Eisenhower, had never commanded troops in battle. He had been greatly relieved by Alexander's warm approval of the way the American had started upon the difficult task of creating an unprecedentedly tight unity of Allied command while simultaneously directing the planning and preparation of the operation to be commanded.[11]

had been snatched away. Eisenhower's sharp regret of this had been only somewhat offset by Ismay's glowing description of the man who would take Alexander's place, followed immediately by Ismay's introduction to him of this man personally. Montgomery had presented himself (this would later seem strange to the Americans and British who must work with him) as a willing, loyal subordinate, affable, cooperative, and easy to get along with. But on the very next morning, Eisenhower was again confronted by Churchill's chief of staff as a bearer of evil tidings: Montgomery, too, was being snatched away. Small wonder that the American general, having listened to glowing accounts, presented in close succession by Ismay, of Alexander's brilliant qualities, then of Montgomery's, and now of Anderson's, remarked with feeling ("rather sadly," according to Ismay's remembrance; with sarcasm, obviously) that the British seemed to have "a lot of Wellingtons" in their army. "Tell me, frankly," he demanded, "are the British serious about Torch?"[12]

III

LATE at night on August 10, Churchill began his flight from Cairo to Moscow with a party now so enlarged that two planes were required to carry it. Included in it were not only Brooke, Cadogan, and Dr. Wilson, but also Air Marshal Arthur Tedder, who was in top command of British airpower in the Middle East, and General Wavell, who had been summoned from India to help in the making of the Cairo command decisions and whose going on to Moscow was determined in large part by the fact that he spoke Russian. By nine o'clock the following morning, this party was in Teheran.

It was met there by Harriman, who had come on from Cairo twenty-four hours earlier in order to review, as an experienced railroad man, the Persian railroad situation.* This became the subject of a lengthy conference that afternoon in the garden of the summer headquarters of the British legation, which was a huge luxurious tent set up in a spot of great beauty some ten miles from, some seven hundred feet higher, and much cooler than the sweltering capital city. In these pleasant surroundings, Harriman reported on what he had learned the day before during consultations with the current railroad management and with three U.S. Army officers stationed in Persia, one of them a former Santa Fe railroad engineer. Only four or five trains a day were running over the newly completed railroad—and the days were seldom when 3,300 tons of freight, which was the British daily goal, were delivered at the Caspian Sea terminal. Deficiencies in the railroad's management, also in its equipment, were obvious. If these were properly supplied, said Harriman, the rail line could double (that is,

*Harriman, it will be remembered, was the son of railroad empire builder E. H. Harriman; he had himself been president of the Union Pacific before entering the U.S. government.

increase to 6,000 tons daily) its delivery of freight from Basra to the Caspian; but this was likely to happen quickly only if the railroad were placed in hands long experienced, as the British were not, in continental railroading. Harriman therefore proposed that the railroad's control be transferred immediately from Great Britain to the United States. He did so as diplomatically as possible, he had a natural talent for diplomacy, but the proposal was of itself alone an aspersion of British competence, bound to be resented by any Englishman whose patriotism had personal pride as a major component. It *was* resented by both Churchill and Brooke, Brooke especially. Out of their resentment, which was well hidden, rose up objections. Of these, a chief one was that British troops now in Persia were dependent on the railroad for their supply, and to do what was now proposed would place these troops wholly at the mercy of a foreign power, albeit a friendly one. The two patriots hated to do this. So the conference ended inconclusively, a final decision of the matter being deferred until after the upcoming Moscow Conference.[13]

At six-thirty on the following morning, Churchill and his party took off for Moscow in two Liberator bombers. The one bearing Brooke, Wavell, and Cadogan, among others, was soon forced by engine trouble to turn back to Teheran, and these men were not again airborne until the following morning, this time in a Russian plane with a Russian pilot. The other plane, carrying Churchill and Harriman, flew a circuitous route by way of Kuibyishev to avoid German planes ranging out from a battle front that was advancing relentlessly, furiously eastward toward Stalingrad. (Wednesday, August 12, was a bad day for Soviet arms. Five days before, on August 7, the German Sixth Army under General Friedrich Paulus had encircled forward elements of two Russian armies west of the Don at Kalach, where the river makes a sharp bend southward in its flow toward the Sea of Azov. On the day of Churchill's Moscow flight, fifty thousand Russian survivors of the bloody fighting that ensued became German prisoners of war. Battered but relatively [locally] more powerful than before, the enemy at his front having been more weakened than he, Paulus was now positioned for a final thrust across the Don toward Stalingrad, just thirty-five miles away.) Churchill and Harriman landed in Moscow a little after five o'clock that afternoon and were welcomed at the airfield, with ceremony, by Molotov, the whole of Moscow's diplomatic corps, assorted Soviet generals, and a faultlessly drilled honor guard.

Two hours later, the two visitors met Stalin in the large plain room of the Kremlin with which Harriman had become familiar in early October 1941—a room furnished only with a long table, accompanying chairs, and a large globe, its walls bare save for a portrait photograph of Lenin (Brooke, when he entered the room next day, was reminded "of a [railway] station waiting room"). Stalin was clad precisely as he had been when Harriman last saw him—knee-high highly polished boots into which trouser legs were tucked, plain light-colored tunic bearing not a single decoration—and his mustached pockmarked face, though showing in repose the strain he labored under (it was a little grayer and tireder than it had been last October), gave the same impression of hardness, crafty shrewdness, and immense controlled energy. The only others present were Molotov, Soviet Marshal K. M. Voroshilov, British Ambassador Archibald Clark Kerr, and two interpreters whose translations were almost wholly of words spoken by Churchill and Stalin. None other contributed to the conversation save Harriman, who pitched in only when this seemed necessary to convince Stalin that the American President was at one with the British Prime Minister in a decision or stand to which Stalin objected.

The conference lasted nearly four hours. The first two were as "bleak and somber" as Churchill had feared the whole of his contacts with the Soviet dictator might be. At the outset, he announced flatly, unequivocally, that there could be no such second front in 1942 as Stalin had been demanding ("the only way to swallow a bitter mixture . . . is to take it in a single gulp," he later explained to colleagues). He then presented the reasons why, every one of which Stalin immediately contested "with bluntness, almost to the point of insult," as Harriman put it in a report marked "Personal for the President Only" that he sent the White House next day. "You can't win wars if you aren't willing to take risks," said Stalin to Churchill. "You must not be so afraid of the Germans." Churchill, who as a young soldier in India and Egypt, and as a war correspondent during the Boer War, had repeatedly demonstrated reckless physical courage, and whose presence here today testified to his moral courage, bore these taunts with admirable dignity and self-control, refusing to reply in kind, but also refusing to permit patently false assertions to go unchallenged. Thus, when Stalin said that there was not a single German division in France that was any good, Churchill at once replied that of the twenty-five German divisions in France, nine "were of the first line." He wondered aloud if Stalin "had ever asked himself why Hitler did not come to England in 1940 when he was at the height of his power and we had only 20,000 trained troops, 200 guns, and 50 tanks." Clearly, Hitler did not come, as Napoleon had not, "because he was afraid of the operation. It is not so easy to cross the Channel." To which Stalin replied that Churchill resorted to false analogy. The English people would have resisted en masse Hitler's invasion forces, but the French people would welcome en masse the invasion forces of the Allies. This might be so, replied Churchill, but the English people's resistance would have been futile, since they had nothing to fight with, and the French people would be even more defenseless against Hitler's retaliatory wrath if, having openly aided the Allied invasion forces, these forces were annihilated or forced to withdraw. Stalin then expressed doubt that Roundup, for which Churchill said full preparations continued to be made, would in fact be launched in 1943—a doubt encouraged by a passing remark of Churchill's (it caused Stalin to frown ferociously) that by the spring of 1943 the Germans might well be stronger in France than they now were. Certainly, "grave difficulties" of the same kind as now scuttled Sledgehammer would confront a cross-Channel operation next spring, said Stalin, who, according to Harriman's report to the President, "showed [consequently?] little interest" in Roundup. Finally, Stalin stated ("abruptly, but with dignity," writes Harriman) that he had neither the right nor the power to dictate Allied strategy but was bound to say he disagreed wholly with the argument Churchill had made.

"So far [in the conference] there had been no agreement and the atmosphere was tense," wrote Harriman to Roosevelt next day.

But the atmosphere changed perceptibly as Churchill went on to discuss the growing bombing attack upon Germany, the weight and fury of which would multiply as the Americans increasingly participated in it. "Here came the first agreement between the two men," reported Harriman; when Stalin "said that [workers'] homes as well as factories should be destroyed" and the "Prime Minister agreed that destroying civilian morale was a military objective . . . [t]he tension began to ease and a certain understanding of common purpose began to grow. Between the two of them, they soon had destroyed most of the important industrial cities of Germany." Whereupon, Churchill abruptly reverted to the subject of a "second front." Was northern France, he asked, the only possible theater for major land action by the Western Allies against the Axis? Of course it wasn't. Leaning forward, he swiftly sketched on a sheet of paper the outline of a crocodile, handed it to Stalin, and said that striking this animal's "soft underbelly," analogous in this case to Europe's Mediterranean coastline, might be more effective, as it was certainly less dangerous at that moment, than striking its snout. The Allies proposed to do both, he hastened to add. But the snout attack must come later. Right now, the Western Allies could engage Axis forces in a major way only in the Mediterranean area. And this only viable option had at once been seized upon by the British and Americans when they were compelled to abandon the 1942 cross-Channel operation. They had decided upon an Anglo-American landing in French North Africa, and he, Churchill, had been "authorized by the American President" to tell Stalin all about it, though in the greatest secrecy ("I emphasized the vital need of secrecy"; Stalin, smiling, "said he hoped nothing about it would appear in the British press"). He then outlined in considerable detail the plans for Torch. Stalin's interest quickened. When was this operation to be launched? he asked. Not later than October 30, replied Churchill, but he and the President were pressing for a D-day of October 7—information received "with great relief " by "the three Russians." By the time of launching, according to Churchill's optimistic scenario, Rommel would have been defeated on the Alamein line (the offensive to accomplish this was being prepared in Cairo) and would be retreating westward across the Libyan sands, driven relentlessly by the British Eighth Army. Feints and raids upon

Europe's western coast would keep Hitler's forces tied down there. The initial landings in Morocco and Algeria would be by American troops, with British support, and Churchill believed they would encounter little or no French resistance.

Stalin had doubts about this last. Indeed, the probing questions he now asked indicated that although the proposed operation seemed to him militarily sound, grave political difficulties beset it, in his opinion. What about Franco's Spain? he asked. Churchill was confident Franco would not enter the war. Was de Gaulle involved in the operation? De Gaulle was not, replied Churchill; he had not even been told of it, in good part for security reasons. "The plain fact," Harriman chimed in, "is that de Gaulle talks too much." Stalin shook his head, figuratively, at least. If de Gaulle were in charge of the operation, he said, the North African French would support him, but they were likely to be antagonized by an Anglo-American invasion, or even an exclusively American one, seeing it as an annexation of northwest Africa. Harriman disagreed. The President, he said, was well informed on the North African political situation, thanks to the Vichy contacts of Admiral Leahy and to American agents in North Africa, the agents reporting that an overwhelming majority of North African Frenchmen would welcome an American landing, whereas many of them were suspicious of de Gaulle's political aspirations. Besides, great pains would be taken at the outset of the operation, said Churchill, to assure the French that the Allies came not as conquerors but as liberators and that the freeing of North Africa was the first step toward restoration of the French empire. Whereupon—abruptly, astonishingly—Stalin seemed to reverse himself, becoming all at once an enthusiastic advocate of Torch. He listed four advantages of the operation. *First,* it would threaten the Afrika Korps from the rear. *Second,* it would lead to combat between Frenchmen and Germans, loosening whatever grasp the Vichy collaborationists had upon the French people. *Third,* it would force Italy out of the war. *Fourth,* it would so intimidate Franco as to assure the continued neutralization of Spain. "May God prosper this undertaking!" prayed this seminary-educated ruler of a godless state. (Writes Churchill: "I was deeply impressed with this remarkable statement. It showed the Russian dictator's swift and complete mastery of a problem hitherto novel to him. Very few people alive could have comprehended in so few minutes the reasons which we had all been so busily wrestling with for months.") A little later, as the three men were gathered round the great globe, Harriman added to Stalin's listing a *fifth* great advantage of Torch: It would open the Mediterranean to Allied shipping, enabling supplies for Russia to come from the West through the Suez Canal instead of around the Cape of Good Hope.[14]

The meeting ended shortly before midnight in a show of friendship and sympathetic understanding on the part of Stalin that elated Churchill and Harriman. In the detailed account of what had transpired, dictated by the Prime Minister before going to bed in the early morning of August 13,* he told his war cabinet (a copy of his dispatch going to Roosevelt) that he expected to "establish a solid and sincere relationship with this man [Stalin]. . . . I told Stalin I should hold myself at his disposition should he wish to see me again. He replied that the Russian custom was that the visitor should state his wishes and that he was ready at any time. Accordingly, I am going to propose another talk this evening. . . . He knows the worst, and we parted in an atmosphere of great good will."[15]

This euphoria was short-lived. It was dissipated at the very outset of Churchill and Harriman's second meeting with Stalin, in the Kremlin on the night of August 13. Cadogan, Brooke, Tedder, and Wavell, whose Russian plane had landed them in Moscow two and a half hours before, were also in attendance. As soon as Stalin, with Molotov, entered the room, he handed Churchill and Harriman a memorandum purporting to be a summary of the discussion of the night before. It was in fact a reiteration of the bitter protest Stalin had then made against Great Britain's "refusal to create a second front in 1942," as became clear to Churchill and Harriman during the interpreter's oral translation of it. This "refusal," which broke a solemn Allied promise to the Soviet Union (so Stalin more than implied), inflicted "a mortal blow to the whole of Soviet public opinion," since that opinion had been led to count absolutely upon this "second front" in the fall. The Red Army had also counted upon this "front" as it made its strategic decisions. The "most favorable conditions exist in 1942" for cross-Channel attack because "almost all of the forces of the German Army, and the best forces . . . , have been withdrawn to the Eastern front," a circumstance that might not prevail in 1943. Concluded Stalin: "I was . . . unfortunately unsuccessful in convincing Mr. Prime Minister hereof, while Mr. Harriman, the representative of the President of the U.S.A., fully supported Mr. Prime Minister. . . ." As soon as the translation was completed, Churchill, in an effort to avoid a profitless rehash of yesterday's opening discussion, promised a written reply to it at the earliest opportunity, saying of it now only that he agreed with its last sentence: the United States and Great Britain were indeed as one in the decision Stalin opposed. To the truth of this, Harriman promptly testified. The President was also determined, said Harriman, "to use all available resources as early as possible in the most effective way for the United Nations, including the Soviet Union, and was ready for any sacrifice that promised a reasonable prospect of success." This oblique reference to Torch was at once pounced upon by Stalin. No doubt Torch was a "correct operation," but it was no substitute for

---

*At least Churchill explicitly says, on page 483 of *Hinge of Fate*, that he dictated the telegram before going to bed. According to his personal physician (*Churchill, taken from the Diaries of Lord Moran*, page 62), he dined heartily, having had no food since lunch, then, "plainly very weary," decided that "the telegrams must wait till the morning" and went to bed, happily convinced that Stalin, at meeting's end, had been "enthusiastic—in a glow."

cross-Channel attack, it did not directly concern the Soviet Union, and, compared with the Russian front, it was of decidedly "secondary importance."[16]

There followed two long hours of what Churchill in his report to the President called "argument" ("wrangling" would have been a more accurate label), during which Stalin repeated and enlarged upon the insulting remarks he'd made during the first two hours of the meeting the night before, adding to his charges of British cowardice a bitter complaint about the failure of the Western Allies to deliver to the Soviet Union on schedule the supplies that had been promised. He again dismissed contemptuously Churchill's explanation, backed now by Harriman, that an attempt to continue the Arctic convoys during the season of perpetual sunlight would have benefited only the enemy. The truth was, said Stalin, that the Western powers underrated (deliberately?) the importance of the Russian front, where ten thousand Russian troops a day were being sacrificed, and gave the Soviet Union only "leftovers" from the supply of their own forces, their own relatively minor projects. Churchill "repulsed all his contentions squarely but without taunts of any kind," as he wrote Roosevelt next day. ". . . . At one point I said: 'I pardon that remark only on account of the bravery of the Russian troops.' " Actually, this last statement, made after the Prime Minister had angrily "crashed his fist down upon the table," was the opening of "a wonderful spontaneous oration" (so Brooke later described it) that thereafter "poured forth" as a flood of impassioned eloquence so high and swift that the interpreter, overwhelmed, soon put down his pencil helplessly.* "It was one of the most brilliant statements I ever heard from Churchill," remembered Harriman, ". . . a magnificent performance" during which, evincing a self-control remarkable in so pugnacious and impulsive a man, Churchill "did not once reproach Stalin for his infamous treaty with Hitler" (Churchill did pointedly remark that he could sympathize with what Russia now went through because England had stood alone against Hitler for a long frightful year). Stalin, too, was impressed—not by Churchill's words, but by the manner of their delivery. At last the dictator stood up, took from between broadly smiling lips the large bent pipe he habitually smoked, and, interrupting the orator with a raised hand, said through his own interpreter: "Your words are of no importance. What is important is your spirit."

This eased the tension. It also shifted toward Churchill the balance of force between the two antagonists (for this is what they had become), as came clear when, a little later, Stalin flatly accused Britain of breaking a solemn promise given Russia less than three months before. "I repudiate that statement, every promise has been kept," replied a glowering Churchill; and he quoted, from the aide-mémoire he'd given Molotov in London, the sentence specifically saying

---

*The hapless interpreter, one Dunlop, thus became also an object of Churchillian wrath. Churchill did not use him again.

that "no promise" of a second front could at that time be made. Whereupon, as Harriman later said, "Stalin made a kind of apology, saying there was no mistrust between the Allies, only a difference of view." He then abruptly invited Churchill and the others to dine with him, Molotov, and other high Soviet officials at eight o'clock the following night, August 14. Churchill, caught by surprise, accepted the invitation, but with no show of enthusiasm; he would, he added, be leaving Moscow at dawn on the fifteenth. So soon? asked an obviously jarred Stalin. Could not the Prime Minister stay longer? Churchill replied he could, certainly, if any good could come of his doing so, and finally he agreed to postpone his departure until the morning of the sixteenth.[17]

It was after midnight when Churchill, with Harriman and the others, left the Kremlin. Churchill was profoundly depressed. His mission, he said, had failed. Harriman, who with Cadogan rode with him to the luxurious dacha some miles outside Moscow where he was housed (it was State Villa Number Seven; Harriman stayed in the American embassy), and whom Churchill kept with him, talking, until three-thirty in the morning, tried to cheer up the Prime Minister by referring to the experience of Stalin that he and Beaverbrook had had nearly a year ago, an experience paralleled by that Eden had had when he journeyed to Moscow last December. On both occasions, Stalin had alternated warmth with coldness, amiability with belligerency, but had closed out the meeting on a note of friendly cooperation, if not actual cordiality. Why was this? Churchill and Harriman asked themselves. Was it because Stalin had less ruling power, and the Politburo more, than the West had assumed? If so, Harriman suggested, Stalin's harshly worded aide-mémoire and display of hostility during this last meeting had been less an expression of his actual feeling toward the Western Allies than a gesture designed to persuade or reassure the Politburo that he had done all he could, all any man could, to force a 1942 second front. "I'm positive that things will be quite cordial when you get together with Stalin again," said Harriman. But Churchill remained, as he later put it to Charles Wilson, "downhearted and dispirited"—so much so that Cadogan proposed to tell Stalin "in confidence" that the Prime Minister was having second thoughts about his acceptance of the dinner invitation. This brought Churchill up short. "No," he said after a pause, "that would be going too far." Stalin *might* make amends during the dinner. But Churchill's expectation of this was too slight to reduce his depression, his resentment of insult; he carried these with him when, at last, near dawn, he went to bed.

Nor was his mood brighter when he awoke. Harriman wired Roosevelt in the late morning of August 14: "The technique used by Stalin last night resembled closely that used with Beaverbrook and myself in our second meeting last year. I cannot believe there is cause for concern and I confidently expect a clear-cut understanding before the Prime Minister leaves." Churchill's simultaneous message to the President, a highly diffuse account of what had happened, expressed no such confidence. "I make great allowances for the stresses through which they are passing," he wrote, adding as evidence of his broad-mindedness that when Stalin "held out his hand to me on leaving . . . I took it. In the public interest I shall go to the dinner tonight." He conveyed no feeling that his going was anything but the performance of an unpleasant duty—an ordeal from which nothing worthwhile would emerge.[18]

And in the event nothing did.

Indeed, if its intent was to restore harmony between Churchill and Stalin, the dinner was a disaster.

Held in the ornate state rooms of the palace built in the Kremlin by Catherine the Great, it was attended by nearly a hundred people, including most of the members of the Politburo and all the highest-ranking officers of the Russian army who happened to be then in Moscow. It was a distinctively Russian affair, characterized by what to Western tastes was gross Oriental excessiveness. There was too much of everything: too many courses (nineteen of them), too much food in each of them, too many toasts, too much 105-proof vodka flowing freely between toasts, and too much coarse camaraderie of a kind that seemed to the Westerners often streaked with malice. It dragged on for far too long a time (almost four hours were spent at table). Brooke, who was bored, restless, and almost nauseated by the sight and smell of food long before the feast ended, took great pains to limit his intake of alcohol. So did every other member of the Churchill mission with the possible exception of Churchill himself, who had a seemingly limitless capacity to drink without becoming inebriated, or even seemingly affected at all, and whose mood was certainly not changed by what he consumed that night. Most of the Russians, however, drank heavily, and not a few of them showed the effects: Commissar for Defense Voroshilov and Commissar of Foreign Trade Mikoyan were among those who were staggeringly drunk (they had to lean on colleagues to get themselves safely out of the room) when the festivities were at last closed down.

It was Churchill who closed them down. He said he was too fatigued to view the film that his hosts had planned to show him. He must seek his bed. Stalin, who seemed to a closely watching Charles Wilson to have been trying all night to establish friendly relations with his principal guest, insisted that Churchill not leave until a photograph had been taken of the two of them together with Molotov and Harriman. Churchill consented. He even managed a faint smile in return for the broad ones bestowed upon him by the two Russians (Harriman, seated between him and them, had a delighted smile on his face) when the camera clicked. He also, after the picture taking, permitted Molotov to lead him and Harriman over to a table, where, seated, he perused a document handed him by the Soviet foreign minister (it was probably the Russian draft of the official communiqué to be issued at the conference's end; certainly, the next day, in conference with Cadogan, he railed against the Russian draft as a "disaster"—a charge that Cadogan, who deemed such communiqués to be generally "bosh," regarded as a ridiculous exaggeration). Then Stalin came over and took a chair beside Churchill, at which point "something went wrong," writes Dr. Wilson, who observed all this from a distance too great to permit his hearing what was said. Stalin spoke to Churchill and seemed to be trying to open a conversation with him. The Prime Minister, continuing to read the document, made no reply. Then, abruptly, he laid the document upon the table, rose to his feet, spoke a curt good-bye, and strode from the room, his face "set and resolute," according to Wilson. Stalin seemed momentarily stunned, but he quickly started after Churchill, almost trotting to catch up with him (". . . I thought of the importunity of a small boy who is asking for a cigarette card and will not take 'No' for an answer," writes Wilson), and insisted on accompanying him all the way down the seemingly endless corridors and stairways that led at last to the great building's front door. There again Churchill said "good-bye" and, summoning Cadogan to come with him, entered his waiting car.[19]

In the car he vented a fury that surprised Cadogan with its "violence and depth," as the latter told Wilson a little later. ". . . I don't know what would have happened at the Kremlin if the party had continued much longer. Nor was I able to discover the exact cause of the P.M.'s mood. . . . He declared that he really did not know what he was supposed to be doing here. He would return to London without seeing Stalin again." He reiterated this in talk with his physician after Cadogan had left the villa. He had deliberately said "good-bye" to the dictator, not "good night," he stressed as he rose to go to bed (it was nearly four o'clock in the morning of August 15); he wouldn't go near Stalin again.

And after he arose shortly before noon of that Saturday, he persisted in this intransigence, his attitude encouraged by the fact that there was no real meeting of minds, no meaningful exchange of information, between the British officers (Brooke, Tedder, and Wavell) and the Russian officers (Voroshilov and Russian Chief of Staff Shaposhnikov) when they conferred, twice, that day.* The Russian generals stubbornly refused to accept the fact that the 1942 cross-Channel invasion proposal was dead. They also refused at first to answer Brooke's questions about their capacity to defend the Caucasus, saying they had no permission to do so; later, having sought and received the necessary permission from the highest authority, they gave information Brooke believed to be false. For instance, Voroshilov spoke of the strong fixed defenses "with anti-tank ditches and concrete pill-boxes for anti-tank guns and machine-guns" that guarded the main approach route between the Caucasus and the Caspian Sea; but Brooke, who had flown at low altitude over the whole of this route on the way to

---

*American General R. L. Maxwell was also present at these meetings, but solely as U.S. observer. General Marshall in Washington, granting Harriman's request that Maxwell come with him to Moscow, had stipulated that Maxwell not be empowered to discuss strategic matters there.

Moscow just two days before, knew from direct observation that the fixed defenses there "consisted of only one half-completed anti-tank ditch, badly revetted and without any covering defences." The Russians also said they had twenty-five divisions with corresponding tank and air forces with which to hold the Caucasus—a gross overestimate, Brooke had reason to believe, of the actually available Russian strength. When the gist of all this was reported by Brooke to the Prime Minister, it deepened his depression and fueled his anger; only with great difficulty was he thereafter, in midafternoon of that day, persuaded by a nearly distraught Ambassador Kerr, among others, to request a final meeting with Stalin. And by the time he did so, having finally and somewhat shame-facedly confessed to Kerr that the quarrel was to some extent "my fault," he was seemingly rebuffed by a Russian dictator who had become miffed in his turn. At any rate, two anxious hours passed before Stalin sent word that he would receive the Prime Minister at seven o'clock that evening.[20]

Meanwhile, Harriman continued optimistic. Stalin had swallowed with no more anguish than was to be expected the bitter medicine Churchill had served him. He seemed to accept Torch as a substitute, albeit an inadequate one, for Sledgehammer. He had expressed absolute confidence in Russia's ability to withstand the current Hitler onslaught (Churchill, in a message to Roosevelt, had estimated at fifty-fifty the Soviet chances of holding the Caucasus; Brooke's estimate was lower than that). And in dinner conversation with Harriman, he had expressed an eagerness to talk with Roosevelt face-to-face, after Harriman said the President wished for such a meeting. "It is of great importance," said Stalin, who suggested for it a date in the winter, when war pressures upon him were not so great. He also indicated a surprising flexibility as to the meeting place, saying it might be in Western Europe, or the Far East, or "Iceland in December." When Harriman protested that Iceland would mean a long and dangerous flight for Stalin, the latter brushed aside the protest; Russia had good airplanes, he said. All this portended a happy conclusion to this Moscow mission, in Harriman's view. He confidently expected good, if not cordial, relations to be established between Stalin and Churchill when the two met alone, as scheduled, that evening.[21]

And his confidence was justified in the event.

When Churchill left the villa to keep his appointment, he told his doctor that although he would "make one final effort to break down the wall of misunderstanding," he expected his conversation with Stalin to last no more than an hour. He would be back at the villa by eight-thirty. He ordered his dinner to be served at that time. Actually, it was not until three-thirty in the morning of August 16 that he returned—and those who awaited him could then immediately tell from his facial expression and jaunty manner as he "broke in" (his doctor's words) that the meeting had gone well.

It had not started well.

During the first of the more than seven hours the two men were together, Stalin, though seemingly frankly responsive to Churchill's questions about the defense of the Caucasus ("we shall stop them [the Germans]; they will not cross the mountains"), had made no response in kind to Churchill's determined efforts to establish a personally friendly relationship. It was only when the Prime Minister rose to say good-bye that his host's demeanor changed. The dictator seemed then "suddenly embarrassed." Did Churchill still intend to leave Moscow at dawn? he asked. Churchill said he did indeed. Was he "preoccupied" (that is, did he have another engagement) for the remainder of the evening? Churchill said no. Well, then, said Stalin, somewhat diffidently, "why should we not go to my house and have some drinks?" Churchill promptly replied that he "was in principle always in favor" of a drink; and the two, with their interpreters (Pavlov for Stalin, Major A. H. Birse for Churchill)* then walked some hundred yards or more through many passageways and rooms and along a Kremlin roadway to the modest apartment in which the widowed dictator lived with his daughter and an aged housekeeper.

There Stalin became wholly the smiling, hospitable, warmly friendly host. He showed Churchill the four plainly furnished, moderate-size rooms—bedroom, workroom, dining room, bathroom—that constituted his personal quarters. When they returned to the apartment's main room and an attractive red-haired teenage girl came shyly into it, dutifully kissing the dictator's rough cheek, he introduced his daughter, Svetlana, "with a twinkle in his eye" that seemed to Churchill to say: "You see, even we Bolsheviks have a family life." She began to set the dining table. He began to uncork bottles from the impressive array of them on a sideboard. And as he did so, he remarked that Molotov was "worrying about" the official conference communiqué (thanks to Churchill's fervent objections to the initial Russian draft, Cadogan had been unable to work out a final draft with the Russian foreign minister) and suggested that Molotov be asked to join them for dinner (only then did Churchill realize he was to stay for dinner). This communiqué matter could then be promptly "settled." Churchill agreed to this and had his interpreter phone Cadogan, asking him to come and to bring with him the British draft communiqué that he had been struggling vainly to revise in a way satisfactory not only to the Prime Minister, but also to the Russians. Molotov arrived almost at once, as if he had been awaiting the summons, displaying an unwontedly affable mood, whereby both Stalin and Churchill were encouraged to chaff him unmercifully. This warmed the atmosphere and helped "make things go." Food arrived upon the table, delivered there by the ancient housekeeper not all at once, but in "a succession of choice dishes" accompanied by "a variety of excellent wines"—and the conver-

---

*Described by Churchill in his *Hinge of Fate* (p. 496) as an "excellent interpreter" (in marked contrast with poor Dunlop), Birse "had lived twenty years in Moscow and got on very well with the Marshal."

sation flowed as freely as the wine, so much so that Churchill at one point dared ask his host to compare the stresses of this war with those he had suffered when the collectivized-farm policy was carried out. The latter were immensely greater, said Stalin. "I thought you would have found it bad," said Churchill, "because you were not dealing with a few score thousands of aristocrats, but with millions of small men." "Ten millions," replied Stalin. "Ten millions died." It was a four-year crisis, a period of horrible unmitigated strain, Stalin went on; but it was absolutely necessary for the good of the nation. The private farmers had refused to use properly the tractors supplied them, had resisted all the government's efforts toward scientific agriculture, and Soviet food-and-fiber production simply *had* to be greatly increased, its quality improved. Collectivization made this happen. Churchill prudently refrained from comment upon this "end justifies the means" argument. But he commented promptly when mention was made by Stalin, sometime during the night, of the possible meeting between him and Roosevelt in the near future that Harriman had suggested the night before; he said he hoped that he, too, could be present. Of course he should be, Stalin as promptly replied; they were three men with an overwhelmingly important common interest (and "no antagonistic interests," interjected Churchill) who must work closely together.[22]

It was well after one o'clock when Cadogan at last arrived with the draft communiqué. At two A.M., when Stalin went into the next room to receive reports from the war fronts, as he always did at that hour, Cadogan, Molotov, and Churchill set to work on the communiqué revision. By the time Stalin returned to the room, twenty minutes later, the communiqué language had been agreed upon. It said: "A number of decisions were reached covering the field of the war against Hitlerite Germany and her associates in Europe. . . . The discussions, which were carried on in an atmosphere of cordiality and complete sincerity, provided an opportunity of reaffirming the existence of the close friendships and understanding between the Soviet Union, Great Britain, and the United States of America, in entire accordance with the Allied relationships existing between them." This wording Stalin at once approved. He then, departing from his usual extreme reticence regarding Russian military affairs, volunteered comment on the news he'd just received from the fighting fronts. It was not good news that day, he said: the Germans had established bridgeheads across the Don, had made further advances into the northern Caucasus. But it was by no means as bad news as it might seem, or have been. Certainly it was far from disastrous. The Germans had not achieved the objectives planned for this date, and they were in for a great and doomful surprise in the not distant future. A great Russian counteroffensive was in preparation, using fresh troops now held in reserve behind the central front; it would be launched when the Germans were most fully extended, hence most vulnerable. (Stalin imparted this to Churchill under a seal of total secrecy.) All in all, Stalin expressed that night an optimism regarding Russia's military situation so markedly in contrast with the dark picture he had painted of it two days before as to suggest to Churchill that this picture had been less a portrait of perceived reality than a propagandistic effort to influence Western Allied strategy.[23]

Shortly thereafter, at nearly three o'clock in the morning of Sunday, August 16, Churchill took his leave. Two hours later, he and his party were at the airport, where Molotov, who was obviously as dead tired as Churchill was, saw them off as ceremoniously as he had welcomed them five days before.

In the plane, Churchill went at once to sleep and did not awaken until he was over the Elburz Mountains, approaching Teheran. From the airport there, he went directly to the British summer legation, where the quiet and coolness of a summer day in the English countryside prevailed and where he dictated a "thank you" telegram to Stalin and a report to his war cabinet, with a copy to the President, of his farewell meeting with the Russian dictator. "The greatest good will prevailed and for the first time we got on easy and friendly terms," he said. "I feel that I have established a personal relationship which will be helpful. . . . On the whole, I am definitely encouraged by my visit to Moscow. I am sure that the disappointing news I brought could not have been imparted except by me personally without leading to really serious drifting apart. . . . Now they know the worst, and having made their protest, are entirely friendly. . . ."[24]

IV

EVER since the failure of the Cripps mission to India in April 1942,* the agitation for India's immediate independence of British rule had increased relentlessly, and while Churchill was away from London on his journey to Cairo and Moscow, there were signs of its becoming actual revolution. There was scattered mob violence in the streets of Indian cities, there were isolated riots in the countryside, there were acts of railroad sabotage—contradictions of Gandhi's truth that were perfectly expressive of a growing popular rebelliousness.

It was in anticipation of this, and in fear of the effect it would have upon the outcome of the Far Eastern war, that Chiang Kai-shek addressed to Roosevelt on July 29 a long message on "the Indian situation"—a message characterized by prayerful earnestness but also by an incoherence and vagueness of expression that rendered difficult Roosevelt's understanding of what, precisely, the Chinese leader wanted him to do. The generalissimo referred to a visit he had made to India shortly after Singapore's fall, a visit during which, he now said, he had urged upon the Indian people "their primary duty to join the anti-aggression front in a common struggle for mankind." He went on to say that these people, though "of a passive disposition," were "apt to go to extremes";

*See pp. 468–69.

that "in launching its freedom movement today when Axis aggression is a pressing reality, the Indian Congress must have felt in their hearts a certain amount of anguish"; that the "only way to make them reconsider their course of action is for the United Nations, and especially the United States . . . to come forward as third parties and to offer them sympathy and consolation"; that if this should *not* be done, "the Indian people will have the same feeling toward other members of the United Nations as towards Britain"; and that "when this comes to pass it will be the world's greatest tragedy. . . ." As for Britain, her "wisest and most enlightened policy . . . would be to restore to India her complete freedom. . . . Therefore I earnestly hope that the United States would advise both Britain and India . . . to seek a reasonable and satisfactory solution. . . ." Meanwhile, he himself would "persevere" in his "efforts" (to do what?). In closing, he stressed that "this dispatch is strictly confidential. It is only for Your Excellency's personal reference."[25]

Whereupon, Roosevelt, his overwhelming concern at that tense moment being the maintenance of the Anglo-U.S.-Soviet alliance in full strength, sent a "strictly confidential" message to "the Former Naval Person" in which he enclosed the whole of the text the generalissimo had sent him. He would "have to reply . . . in the near future," he said to the Prime Minister, and would be "grateful if you will let me have as soon as possible . . . any suggestions you may wish to offer with regard to the nature of the reply I should make. . . ."[26]

Churchill, then in the midst of hectic preparations for his journey to Cairo, answered immediately, brusquely, succinctly: "We do not agree with Chiang Kai-shek's estimate of the Indian situation. The Congress Party in no way represents India and is strongly opposed by over ninety million Mohammedans, forty million untouchables, and the Indian States comprising some ninety million, to whom we are bound by treaty. Congress represents mainly the intelligentzia [*sic*] of non fighting Hindu elements and can neither defend India nor raise revolt. The military classes on whom everything depends are thoroughly loyal. . . . The Government of India [headed by His Majesty's Viceroy] have no doubt of their ability . . . to carry on government with efficiency and secure India's maximum contribution to the war effort whatever Congress may say or even do, provided of course that their authority is not undermined. . . . I earnestly hope therefore, Mister President, that you will do your best to dissuade Chiang Kai-shek from his completely misinformed activities, and will lend no countenance to putting pressure upon His Majesty's Government."[27]

Roosevelt, however, being convinced Churchill's Indian policy was wrong, could not bring himself to do quite what the Prime Minister asked. He delayed replying to Chiang for a week and a half and then, on August 9, dispatched to Chungking a carefully phrased message that was by no means as strongly dissuasive of the Chinese leader's activities as Churchill desired. He sent no copy of it to the Prime Minister. Instead, he summarized it in a "Personal and Most

Secret" message addressed to the Former Naval Person in Cairo. He had told the generalissimo, he said, that it was not in his opinion "wise or expedient for the time being to take any of the steps which" Chiang had suggested. "I . . . emphasized . . . that we would of course not wish to pursue any course which would undermine the authority of the Indian Government at this time." But he had also "told him I would be glad to have him keep in close touch with regard to this and any other questions which affect the vital interests of the United Nations. . . ." He had done so, he explained, "because of my belief that it is wiser to have him feel that his suggestions sent to me receive friendly consideration." Otherwise, Chiang "would be more inclined to take action on his own initiative which I know you will agree with me might be very dangerous at this moment."[28]

But by that time, the Indian Viceroy's council, a twelve-man executive body of whom only one was European, had unanimously resolved to outlaw the Congress Party and arrest and imprison its principal leaders. Within two days thereafter, the arrests had been made, Churchill had wired the Viceroy his hearty support of what had been done, and Roosevelt had received (August 11) from Chiang Kai-shek a second message dealing with the Indian situation. "I feel certain that you are as concerned as I am at the news of the arrest of the working committee of the Indian Congress, including Gandhi and Nehru," it began. The British action was "a great setback to the Allied cause in the Far East" and would certainly "have a disastrous effect on the entire war situation" insofar as it contradicted the "avowed object of the Allies in waging the war," undermined faith in the "professed principles of the United Nations," and strengthened "the influence of the Axis powers" throughout the world. "I earnestly appeal to you as the inspired author of the Atlantic Charter to take . . . measures . . . to solve the pressing problem . . . so that normalcy will return and unimpeded [Indian?] war effort may continue to hasten our common effort. Your policy will serve as a guide to all of us who have resisted for so long and so bitterly the brute force of the aggressors." He asked for the "favor" of an "early reply."[29]

On that same day, perhaps within the same hour, Roosevelt received a cable from Winant. His ambassador to Britain was as dismayed as Chiang by what had happened. The Congress Party leaders had been preparing formal appeals to the United States and the Soviet Union, Winant explained, and it was to prevent this that the British had taken this unwise and possibly disastrous step. He said he had discussed the Indian crisis with Soviet Ambassador Maisky, who had repeated to him a suggestion the Russian had earlier made to Cripps. It was that an Indian council representing all the Indian political parties and armed with governing authority be substituted for the present Viceroy's council. Winant saw merit in this Maisky idea and offered to pursue it if Roosevelt agreed. He admitted, however, that the British were likely to reject the suggestion totally; even if they agreed to a representative council, they would almost certainly insist that the Viceroy have veto power over that council's decisions.[30]

Roosevelt's immediate response was to cable the full text of Chiang's message to Churchill, then in Moscow, and to ask, "What do you think?"

Churchill made an exasperated reply on August 14—the day of his profound depression over the way his second meeting with Stalin had gone. "I take it amiss Chiang should seek to make difficulties between us," he wrote, "and should interfere in matters about which he has proved himself most ill-informed [and] which affect our sovereign rights." The decision that Chiang protested had been taken by Indians who "are as good Indian patriots and as able men as any of the congress leaders. They have shown great courage and it is essential not to weaken their authority." As for "Chiang's talk of congress leaders wishing us to quit in order that they may help the Allies," it was simply "eye wash." The only thing that concerned those leaders was "congress supremacy." Roosevelt might "remind Chiang that Gandhi was prepared to negotiate" with the Japanese "a free passage of Japanese troops through India" with a view to their "joining hands with Hitler" in the Middle East. "Personally I have no doubts that in addition there would have been an understanding that the congress would have the use of sufficient Japanese troops to keep down the composite majority of ninety million Moslems, forty million Untouchables and ninety million in the princes states." He more than hinted his suspicion that the actual writer of the message had been Madame Chiang Kai-shek (the message's "style prompts me to say *Cherchez la femme*"), whose strong mind and will were co-equal with her husband's as a ruling force in China and to whose feminine charms Americans (including the American President) seemed to Churchill unduly susceptible.[31]

Soon thereafter, Roosevelt made another bland, cordially phrased reply to Chungking in which he committed himself to no action whatever regarding the Indian situation.

V

THE closing words of Churchill's message from Teheran to Roosevelt, reporting the final outcome of the Moscow talks, were: ". . . Stalin is entirely convinced of the great advantages of 'Torch,' and I do trust that it is being driven forward with superhuman energy on both sides of the ocean."[32]

And certainly Torch *was* being addressed with great energy at that time, both in London and in Washington. This energy was not, however, "superhuman." It was all too normally human insofar as a large part of it was diffusively emotional—a mingling of the anger, dismay, resentment, mortification, and foreboding engendered by a disagreement (it came close to being a quarrel) between the British and the Americans over the shape that Torch should have and over the precise manner in which the torch should be lit.

Marshall and the American Joint Chiefs of Staff, who had been more than willing to run huge risks with the predominantly British forces that would have manned Sledgehammer,* became cautious in the extreme, as it seemed to the British, in their planning of an operation employing predominantly American forces. When the North African venture was first proposed, during the Arcadia Conference, Marshall had stressed that it "might result in the first contact between American and German troops" and that a "failure in this first venture" would have a disastrous "effect upon the morale of the American people."³³ The fear of this was reinforced by a continued, if suppressed, doubt that the operation was worth doing at all. How ghastly it would be if an enterprise whose success was so little likely to contribute greatly to ultimate victory became a costly, morale-blasting failure! The risks, therefore, must be kept at a minimum; the dubious bet must be hedged to the maximum! Such was the emphatic view of the U.S. Joint Chiefs of Staff. In a draft memo to the President prepared by the Operations Division in late July, the dangers of hastily improvised expeditions were stressed, allusion being made to the "disasters" suffered "by the British in Norway, France, the Balkans, and Greece." The War Department was determined to prevent Torch's being "like the battles of Norway and Bull Run," this same memo said.³⁴ The Joint Chiefs therefore demanded at least one set of master amphibious exercises for the troops that were to make possibly opposed landings on the North African shore, despite the fact such exercise would postpone the landings until the first week of November at the earliest. Stressing the vulnerability of overextended lines of communication, they flatly opposed any substantial initial landing farther inside the Mediterranean than Algiers; even Algiers seemed to them dangerously far east. They also refused to commit the whole of the invasion force inside the Mediterranean: they insisted that one major landing be made in the Casablanca area of French Morocco's Atlantic coast, this to assure reinforcement and supply (admittedly over severely limited transportation facilities) to troops that would otherwise be doomed if Franco Spain closed the Strait of Gibraltar. They took account of the high surf common on Morocco's Atlantic coast in the autumn; they recognized it as a serious hazard to the success of an opposed landing there. But they measured this hazard smaller by far than that of a closed Gibraltar Strait despite the fact that a dangerously high surf at Casablanca in October or November was a virtual cer-

---

*The nature and extent of these risks were tragically demonstrated in a raid by British commandos and five thousand troops of the Canadian Second Division upon the French coastal resort town of Dieppe on August 19, 1942. Of the four thousand Canadians who stormed ashore (a thousand were never landed), one-fourth were dead and two-thirds, including many wounded, captured by four o'clock that afternoon. Valuable lessons were learned about landing-craft types, the use of naval guns upon coastal fortifications, and amphibious tactics—lessons that would reduce casualties when the full-force invasion of northern France was launched ("Honour to the brave who fell," writes Churchill in his war memoirs. "Their sacrifice was not in vain")—but military historians are generally agreed that the cost of this teaching was far greater than it need have been, thanks to bungling at its command level.

tainty, whereas the likelihood of Franco's being provoked into the war was, as the British stressed, relatively small.

Indeed, little of this American conception made much sense to the British chiefs of staff. It seemed to them a mistaken attempt to deal in a static, logically coherent way with what was in reality a flowing stream of contingent events, a stream whose volume and direction could be determined, or even influenced, *only* through what the Americans condemned as "hasty improvisations." A major purpose of the North African expedition, in the British chiefs' own conception, was relief of the intense Axis pressure on Malta, the holding of which was essential to the defense of Egypt and the reopening of the Mediterranean to Allied shipping. The strategic island had long suffered grievously from the enemy's dominance of the air over the Malta Channel, through which supply convoys from Gibraltar must pass; British control of the island had become increasingly precarious. This was a major reason why the British were anxious to launch the North African operation at the earliest possible date. But they were also convinced that time and surprise (the two elements were fused) were of the essence of the operation's success: the earlier the landings, the greater the surprise and the longer the time period in which Tunisia, where the Nazi counterattack must be mounted and launched, would remain in its present weakly defended state. There could be no doubt that Hitler would respond with a maximum possible swiftness to this threat to his Mediterranean flank, and thanks to the dense land-based air cover that the Axis had spread over the Tunisian sea approaches, there could be little effective Allied interference with a Tunisian buildup. After winter slowed operations on the Russian front, the buildup with Axis troops from that front could be massive. The early Allied occupation of Tunisia was therefore of major importance to the success of the North African expedition. "We must have occupied the key points of Tunisia within twenty-six days of passing Gibraltar and preferably within fourteen days," said a so-called brief appreciation of Torch prepared by the planning staff of the British staff chiefs (a copy of it went from Eisenhower to Marshall, with an Eisenhower letter, on August 9).[35] To this end, the British were willing to run greater initial risks than the Americans would countenance. For instance, they were willing to employ smaller forces in the initial landings than the Americans thought necessary, and they wanted to land the whole of the expeditionary force inside the Mediterranean, with one part of it landing as far east as Bône, which was but a few miles west of the Tunisian border. They also wanted the operation launched in early October, though this gave barely enough time for the combat training of ten transports and no time at all for amphibious rehearsals as a climax to the training of assault troops. They recognized the danger that Franco Spain might yield to Nazi pressure and enter the war as an Axis partner. But they said that this danger would become negligible if a swift conquest of the strategic area presented Franco with a North Africa substantially in the hands of the Allies.

Only if the landings, despite their American complexion, were strongly and effectively opposed by the North African French, who might then in their folly go so far as to bomb Gibraltar (they had done so, ineffectively, when the British attacked Dakar in 1940)—only then would Franco be likely to cast his lot irrevocably with that of Hitler and Mussolini. But did not this *also* argue for the expeditionary force's concentration inside the Mediterranean? The greater the concentration, the more swift and certain the overcoming of whatever French resistance occurred.

Conditioning this international disagreement and complicating its resolution were the demands that U.S. operations in the Southwest Pacific were making at this time upon overall Allied resources.

On August 7, one week after the target date set for the launching of Task One,* U.S. Marines landed on Florida Island (a designation inclusive of Tulagi) and on Guadalcanal in the Solomons, achieving complete tactical surprise in both cases. On Guadalcanal they easily captured on the first day their prime objective, which was the airstrip they promptly named Henderson Field.† But their time of good fortune lasted barely forty-eight hours. It was terminated on the night of August 9 by a naval battle off the small island of Savo, just north of Guadalcanal, in which the U.S. Navy suffered one of the worst defeats in all its history. During the darkest hours of that night, Japanese warships, their images blotted off radar by mountains behind them, slipped undetected between the American vessels and the island shore. They sent up from there star shells that exploded behind the American ships, silhouetting these as perfect targets. Within minutes thereafter, three U.S. cruisers and an Australian cruiser had been sunk by torpedoes and gunfire. The Japanese remained virtually undamaged. Next day, defenseless against air attack, all naval support for the marines on Guadalcanal was withdrawn, including the cargo ships that had been unloading ammunition, food, and equipment on the island shore. This meant that for the time being, the Japanese could build up and adequately supply their troops on Guadalcanal with little or no interference, whereas the capacity of the Americans to do so was nil. Abruptly, the marines on the island were forced to operate on severely reduced rations, their situation dangerous in the extreme.

The effect of all this upon the North African operation was to limit its scope and increase the anxious difficulty of planning it. The British assigned every warship they could spare from other duties to the escort of North African convoys and the protection of their landings; they reduced India's naval defense in order to strengthen that of the North African invasion; but there remained a

---

*The date was set in the July 2, 1942, directive from the U.S. Joint Chiefs of Staff to Nimitz and MacArthur. See p. 533.

† Named after Major Lofton R. Henderson, commander of the marine aviation squadron based on Midway on June 4, 1942. He was killed that day when he dove his plane into the stack of a Japanese warship.

shortage of escort vessels that the U.S. Navy could not make up, despite the new vessels now coming down the ways of American shipyards in record and increasing numbers. Especially serious was the shortage of aircraft carriers, for until airfields in North Africa were obtained, the only land-based air cover for the invading Allies must fly off the single small field at Gibraltar. This field was itself vulnerable to air attack by the Germans and Italians, and to land attack should Franco enter the war; some Spanish machine guns were set up barely twenty feet from the field's edge.

Dwight David Eisenhower, under whose operational command Torch was being mounted and would be launched, was, of course, at the very center of the decision-making process whereby Torch's final shape was being determined. His mind, temperament, and personality thus became for the first time importantly influential of history.

He was fifty-two years old in 1942 (his birthday came on October 14), stood nearly six feet tall, and was proportionately broad of shoulder, though his weight of some 190 pounds was so evenly and compactly distributed over a trim figure that he did not impress others as being of more than average size. He moved with the quick energy of smaller men and with the easy, well-coordinated grace of an athlete (he had been touted as a potential all-American halfback on the army football team until a knee injury cut short his West Point sports career in the fall of 1912). Though almost completely bald, his head was so shaped that its baldness somehow suited it and was not at all unattractive. His countenance was pleasant and open, with wide-spaced eyes and a wide mouth, its features remarkable for neither handsomeness nor homeliness, but for a highly expressive mobility; and what they most commonly expressed was an inwardly secure, outwardly focused personality, a sunny disposition, and an intelligence quick in its perceptions and swift in its reactions. Like Marshall and Brooke, he had been born with an unusually quick and fiery temper that he had with difficulty learned to control but that, controlled, enhanced the respect others had for him and the confidence they reposed in him. He was personally immensely likable, more so than Marshall, far more so than Brooke, an integral part of his likability being a wide, lopsided grin that came easy and often to his face, a grin that somehow harmonized perfectly with his nickname, "Ike."

There was a peculiar aptness in his being placed, in this opening hour of his world fame, upon a middle ground, in a literally compromising position, where he was challenged to reconcile and mediate widely divergent views in ways that resulted in a single-minded unity of action. It was as if a special destiny had formed him for precisely this role. A curious mingling of opposing cultural forces had played upon him all through his formative years, encouraging a seemingly innate urge and capacity to ameliorate, encouraging also the development of what might be called a "psychology of middleness" or "togetherness," whence came, no doubt, that preference for "broad front" strategy that he displayed when, later on, he was presented with flat choices between this and a strategy of concentrated "narrow front" attack.

Born in Texas, he had been but six months in the world when his parents brought him to the small town of Abilene, Kansas, in the spring of 1891. He had grown to young manhood in that town, just a few score miles from both the geographic center of the contiguous United States and the geodetic datum of North America.* Nor was it only geographically that the Kansas of his boyhood and youth was a meeting ground of East and West, North and South, in approximate equivalence. Historically and culturally, too, during the pre–Civil War "Bleeding Kansas" days and for a couple of decades thereafter, the cavalier tradition of the American South and the democratic tradition of the American North had met here in ways conflicting, mingling, and lasting. So had the strict law-and-order Puritanism of New England and the lawless individualism of the Wild West. They had done so, if in special ways, within the bosom of the Eisenhower family. Even by the standards prevailing in that town at that time, the economic circumstances in which Dwight was raised were modest. His father was a mechanic employed as a "stationary engineer" in a large local creamery at a wage never high enough to support adequately a family of, ultimately, six sons. All the Eisenhower brothers had as boys and youths to contribute through wage-paying jobs to the family's sustenance, and all save the youngest, Milton, became acutely aware that they were "looked down upon" by children of the prosperous who lived on the north side (the Eisenhowers lived on the south side) of the Santa Fe railroad tracks that bisected the town. They resented the unfairness, but, influenced by a religious training that stressed both industrious self-reliance and egalitarian individualism, they did so in a way that increased their motivation to "succeed." Religion was important in their lives. In a town of generally pious citizenry, no citizens were more pious, more pacifistic by religious conviction, or more addicted to family prayer and Bible reading than the Eisenhower parents, both of whom came of Mennonite stock (the father from Pennsylvania's Lancaster County, the mother from Virginia's Shenandoah Valley) and both of whom ultimately joined the extreme fundamentalist pacifistic cult now known as Jehovah's Witnesses. The effect upon Dwight was not at all what his parents hoped and prayed for. The excessive and excessively boring Bible reading and sermonizing to which he was forcibly subjected as a child developed in him a profound lifelong antipathy to insistent religiosity, and with this religiosity he lumped, and thus utterly rejected, the pacifist doctrine his parents embraced and preached.

He was far more susceptible, he reacted far more positively, to the opposing

---

*That is, the central point from which the mapping of the whole continent proceeds through radiating lines.

environmental force operative in that town—the force arising from the fact that Abilene, a sedate town of many churches in the late 1890s and early 1900s, had thirty years before been the wildest, roughest cow town on the western border, the place where Wild Bill Hickok won national notoriety as a gun-fighting, man-killing town marshal. The Wild West tradition, with its cult of combative toughness, its emphasis upon the concrete and physical to the virtual exclusion of the abstract and spiritual, had a profound shaping influence upon the generation of Abilene boys to which Dwight belonged. "Cowboys and Indians" was a young boys' game universally favored: all the Eisenhower boys engaged in it hours on end during their early childhood. Fistfights between Abilene boys were of uncommon frequency and savagery: Dwight was a principal in the longest and most savage of all those fought during his grade and high school years. Athletic prowess garnered even more peer prestige among Abilene boys than it did among boys in other towns: Dwight starred in football and baseball when in high school. And all this combined into the environmental force that, in opposition to the family religion, determined Dwight's seeking a "service school" appointment and accepting one to West Point in 1910, a move his parents did not actively oppose (their pacifistic piety and commitment to personal freedom permitted no coercive interference with any son's career decision) but that, nevertheless, dismayed his father and nearly broke his mother's heart.

Yet the prolonged baths he had been forced to take in spiritual waters, the seemingly endless hours of reading and listening to admonitions to be "good" and "kind" and to abhor as Devil-born the sin of pride—these had influenced his development profoundly, if subtly. He became a soldier who had no love of war or personal power (he would in fact prove reluctant in the extreme to exercise the supreme power thrust into his hands in years to come); a soldier invincibly democratic in basic attitude (he regarded with mingled loathing and amusement the arrogant posturings of Douglas MacArthur); a soldier who in seeming incongruity was temperamentally disinclined toward violent confrontations and strongly inclined toward coalitions, amalgamations, homogenizations on the basis of perceived common denominators among diverse people and things and forces—a soldier, in sum, who was peculiarly fitted for the kind of top command, closely analogous to the board chairmanship of a large corporation, rendered necessary by scientific technology's impact on warfare. He had a "civilian mind," like George C. Marshall's, as some newspapers were already saying of him in the summer of 1942.

Certainly Marshall himself had recognized in Eisenhower a remarkably sympathetic mind and personality when the two came into a close working relationship immediately before, during, and after the Arcadia Conference. The two had been psychologically prepared for such a relationship by their common experience of Major General Fox Conner, who was probably the most brilliant mind among the general officers of the U.S. Army during the 1920s. The general had become a fervent admirer of Marshall's in 1918 when the then colonel, as G-3 (Operations) of the AEF's First Army, accomplished what the general recognized as "a masterpiece of logistics," transferring half a million men and 2,700 guns from the Saint-Mihiel sector of the western front to the Argonne with such swift efficiency that the Germans had no inkling of it until the Argonne offensive began. When Major Eisenhower served as Conner's executive officer in Panama in the early 1920s, he found his superior's highest praise to be "Eisenhower, you handled that just the way Marshall would have done," and the major was consequently immensely pleased when the general told him that "you and Marshall are a lot alike; I've noticed time and again that you attack problems in the same way." To Marshall himself, Conner had later been fulsome in his praise of Eisenhower, who by then had graduated first, in a class of 275, from the notoriously tough Command and General Staff School at Fort Leavenworth, Kansas (Conner had been instrumental in securing Eisenhower's appointment to the school), and whose name was consequently high on the General Staff Corps eligibility list. Both Marshall and Eisenhower had been profoundly influenced by Conner's command doctrine, especially by his insistence upon the necessity of a totally unified command in the successful conduct of modern warfare.*

The creation of such a command for Torch had been the initial task to which Eisenhower addressed himself when told by Marshall that he was to command the operation. He must fuse at the command level the heretofore separate services of land, sea, and air; he must make into a single instrument of command a group of strong personalities of different national backgrounds and loyalties. He managed to accomplish the latter, not by denying the existence of national personal differences (he in fact stressed his own Americanisms), but by overwhelmingly asserting the dominance over these of devotion to a transcendent cause. By early August, there was emerging a command structure unprecedented in alliance warfare (Foch, operating under the Beauvais Agreement in the closing year of the Great War, could not come close to achieving it)—a structure in which, to quote Major H. A. DeWeerd, "Americans and Britons in alternating layers" were "fused together like a plywood board."[36]

His first attempt to reconcile the divergent British and American views in an operational plan for Torch was a tentative outline proposal submitted to the American Joint Chiefs of Staff in Washington and the British Joint Chiefs of Staff in London on August 9. It called for three major simultaneous landings to be made in early November at Oran, Algiers, and Casablanca. The last was to be made, if Atlantic coastal surf conditions did not render it too risky, by American troops brought directly from the States across the Atlantic (their commander was to be General George S. Patton). If the surf was too dangerously

*See p. 364.

high, this force was to proceed through Gibraltar Strait and land inside the Mediterranean. Thus the plan went much further toward satisfying American than it did British strategical concepts, but this tilt of the balance between the two was offset by Eisenhower's cover message, in which he said that he personally was inclined to agree with British criticisms of it. These were that, since the prime objective was the seizure of Tunisia before Hitler could build up there, the operation should be launched in early October, preferably by October 7, even though the assault forces must then be much smaller and less well trained than they would be a month later; that a major landing should be made at Bône; and that the proposed Casablanca landing, being "unfeasible and irrelevant," should be canceled. Roosevelt was even more strongly inclined than Eisenhower to agree with the British as regards the timing of the operation. He promptly (August 12), in a directive to Marshall and King, ordered a restudy of Torch with a view to launching it on October 7—a move supported on the very next day by an Eisenhower message saying that he and his staff were now convinced the British were right and that a new plan was being made in which the Casablanca landing was canceled, a landing in force at Bône was added, and the target date was advanced into October. Eisenhower's stated "conviction" was of no rocklike firmness, however. When Marshall gave it as Washington's opinion that an operation planned as Eisenhower now proposed had a less than fifty-fifty chance of success, Eisenhower promptly (August 15) concurred in it. Nevertheless, he and his staff continued to plan along the lines favored by the British, completing the outline on August 21.

In the new version, the landings were to be made on October 15 at Oran, Algiers, and Bône. The troops brought by convoy directly from the United States were to make the Oran landing; they were designated the Western Force. The troops brought from the United Kingdom in a single convoy, which was to divide inside the Mediterranean to effect the Algiers and Bône landings, were designated the Eastern Force. Thus, this second plan reversed the emphasis of the first one, going much further toward satisfying the British than the Americans. But, again, there was an Eisenhower offset. He sent the new plan to the British and American staff chiefs with a cover message in which he not only anticipated the criticisms the American Joint Chiefs would make of it, but also indicated his personal inclination to agree with these. The October 15 date was probably too early, he said, to permit landings of sufficient size to discourage or cope with the determined French resistance that was distinctly possible; and as the drive toward Tunis was made, the expedition's right flank and rear would, in this new plan, be dangerously exposed. He wished that simultaneous landings *could* be made outside as well as inside the Mediterranean—in other words, that the British and American governments could "find a way to cut their commitments elsewhere so as to provide the [needed] additional naval cover."[37] The British staff chiefs, operating in this period without Brooke's presence, he having gone with Churchill to Cairo and Moscow, responded to this second plan in a spirit of compromise. They at once conceded the main point of difference in it between themselves and their American counterparts, saying they were now willing to postpone the assault until early November. This would permit the amphibious training exercise that the Americans insisted was necessary to prevent disaster if the North African landings were strongly opposed.

VI

SUCH was the state of affairs as regards Torch when Churchill and Brooke, flying from Cairo, arrived back in London in the evening of August 24.

On the following day, Churchill had Eisenhower and Eisenhower's deputy, the American General Mark Clark, to dine with him at No. 10 Downing Street, where, as Churchill put it in his memoirs, they discussed "the state of the [Torch] operation." The Prime Minister was less inclined than his staff chiefs were to postpone the landings until November, and he believed, was led by Eisenhower to believe, that Torch's operational commander was of the same mind as he. He was also inclined strongly to believe that Torch affairs had become so tangled by staff chief differences that only he and the President could now straighten them out. So on the following day (August 26) he cabled Roosevelt: "It seems to me from talks I have had with Eisenhower and Clark and our own people here that the best and indeed the only way to put this job through is to fix a date for the party and make everything conform to that, rather than saying it will start when everything is ready. It would be an immense help if you and I were to give Eisenhower a directive something like this:—'You will start Torch on October 14, attacking with such troops as are available and at such places as you deem fit.' " This, he went on, would give Eisenhower the power he should have as the Allied commander in chief. "As I see it this operation is primarily political in its foundations [a fact that argued for quick and final decision at the highest political level]. The first victory we have to win is to avoid a battle. The second, if we cannot avoid it, to win it. In order to give the best chances of winning the first victory we must (a) present the maximum appearance of overwhelming strength at the moment of first attack, and (b) attack at as many places as possible." Time was of the essence. "Risks and difficulties will be doubled by delay. . . . Careful planning in every detail, safety first in every calculation . . . however admirable in theory, will ruin the enterprise in fact. Anything later than the date I have mentioned enormously increases the danger of leakage and forestallment."[38]

But within hours after this message was sent, and before the President could have read it, he had reviewed a memorandum (dated August 25), promptly cabled to London, in which the American Joint Chiefs of Staff rejected Eisenhower's second draft plan, refused also to satisfy Roosevelt's wish for an early

October launch date, and outlined a plan of their own—a plan so totally at odds with British views that the possibility of achieving any working agreement between the two Allies appeared more remote than ever.* For Marshall and his colleagues now proposed to eliminate not only the landing at Bône, but also the one at Algiers! Their drastically reduced objective, to be achieved in November, was "the early and complete military domination of Northwest Africa from Rio de Oro [Spanish Sahara], exclusive, to Oran, inclusive."[39]

Upon the British, this missive fell as a "bombshell," to quote Churchill's memoirs. The Prime Minister immediately (on August 27) wired Roosevelt: "We are all profoundly disconcerted. . . . It seems to me that the whole pith of the operation will be lost if we do not take Algiers as well as Oran on the first day," with "landings at Philippeville and Bône for day three," as Eisenhower was "in fact planning" with "our cordial support." With Oran "making good the communications, we could fight the Germans for Tunis, even if they got there [before the Allies did]. But not to go east of Oran is making the enemy the present not only of Tunis but of Algiers," whereas the taking of Algiers followed by swift movement toward Tunis and Bizerte "is an indispensable part of the attack upon Italy which is the best chance of enlisting French cooperation and one of the main objects of our future campaign." If the Americans insisted upon the Casablanca landing "on a large scale with all its risks," they must certainly also "continue to be directed on Oran as now planned," for the British were not strong enough to do both Oran and Algiers. But Algiers simply had to be done, and all that the British now asked of the Americans with regard to it was "a small contact team to show the [American] flag." Finally, pointedly, Churchill reminded Roosevelt of the way in which information about Torch had just been used in Moscow to bolster the Grand Alliance. "I hope, Mr. President," he wrote, "you will bear in mind the language I have held to Stalin supported by Harriman with your full approval. If Torch collapses or is cut down as is now proposed, I should feel my position painfully affected. For all these reasons I most earnestly beg that the memorandum may be reconsidered. . . ."[40]

Roosevelt had now to deal not only with the differences between his and Churchill's views, but also with those between himself and the American Joint Chiefs of Staff.

He at once called Marshall to his office, where the two men, with Harry Hopkins, lunched together on Friday, August 28. He impressed upon the general his sense of the importance of a) the earliest possible initiation of the action; and

---

*The tide of Marshall's near rebellion against civilian authority, described in chapter 9 (see pp. 548–52), was ebbing as August drew toward a close, but he continued to believe that the North African operation was badly mistaken and continued to hope against hope that the operation would, after all, be canceled. This secret hope, which King certainly shared, undoubtedly influenced the shaping of the August 25 plan; indeed, the plan may actually have been designed in part—perhaps not wholly consciously, perhaps quite deliberately—to *force* the operation's cancellation.

b) initial landings by American troops only. Then he listened without interruption to Marshall's argument in defense of the memorandum that had so dismayed the British. If the initial landings were to be by American troops only (the general was as convinced as the President that they should be), they could not possibly be made until November, for not until then would enough Americans have sufficient training to give them a reasonable chance for success against the strong opposition that was possible—a possibility that made absolutely necessary at least one full-scale amphibious exercise as a major element of the troops' training. Even in November, because of the demands made by Southwest Pacific operations upon available naval resources, no more than two all-American landings would be possible. And one of these two *must* be outside the Mediterranean, in the Casablanca area. As regards this last, the general was adamant. His position was firmly supported by King and Arnold when, immediately following the luncheon, the conference was expanded to include the admiral and the air corps chief, along with War Production Board chairman Donald Nelson.

Immediately after the conclusion of this conference, Roosevelt with a party of five (Hopkins, Sherwood, Hassett, Grace Tully, and Grace's stenographic assistant, Dorothy Brady) entered two cars on the south grounds of the White House, whence they were driven by a circuitous route to a country retreat newly developed for him on Catoctin Mountain in northern Maryland; its location being "secret," though easily ascertainable by enemy agents, Roosevelt had dubbed it "Shangri-la."* The party arrived there a little after six in the evening. And there it was that, next day, he with Hopkins read the draft reply to Churchill's message prepared by Marshall at his request. Evidently, Roosevelt's response to the Marshall argument the day before had been so sympathetically understanding that Marshall deemed it an unqualified approval of what he, the general, had said. For what now came to Roosevelt for presidential signature was in essence a flat endorsement, uncompromisingly phrased, of the JCS operational plan to which Churchill and his colleagues so vehemently objected. "We are not, in my opinion, justified in assuming the risks involved in a single line of communication through the Straits of Gibraltar," it said. "The continuous attrition of naval vessels and other shipping which will undoubtedly result from maintaining supply through the Straits subsequent to the landings cannot be accepted in view of our present limited resources and already overextended lines of communications. . . . I do not agree that landings at Oran and Casablanca [only] will certainly result in the Germans seizing Tunisia and possibly Algiers. Accordingly it is my opinion that the initial landings should be

---

*The reader will recall that he had first used this name, taken from James Hilton's *Lost Horizon,* when telling the press of the Doolittle air attack of Japan. Doolittle's planes, he had then said, took off from an airfield at Shangri-la.

made at Oran and on the Northwest coast of Africa. . . . This matter has been most carefully considered by me and by my naval and military advisors. I feel strongly that my conception of the operation as outlined herein must be accepted and that such a solution promises the greatest chance for success in this particular theater."[41]

Roosevelt at once found this draft (dated August 29) to be unsatisfactory, not only in what was said, but also, and especially, in the way of its saying. He and Hopkins did a complete redraft,* which, after being reviewed with Marshall and King, was sent to Churchill on August 30. "The operation should be undertaken on the assumption that the French will offer less resistance to us than they will to the British," this redraft said. "I would even go so far as to say I am reasonably sure a simultaneous landing by British and Americans would result in full resistance by all French in Africa whereas an initial American landing without British ground forces offers a real chance that there would be no French resistance or only a token resistance. . . . As to the place of the landings it seems to me that we must have a sure and permanent base on the Northwest coast of Africa because a single line of communication through the Straits is far too hazardous. . . ." This meant there could be only two initial landings, for there were "not enough cover and combat loadings" for more than two exclusively American ones, with one of them in the Casablanca area ("I want to emphasize . . . that under any circumstances one of our landings must be on the Atlantic") and the other at Oran. He took a step, however, and quite a long one, toward the British position, saying: "I need a week . . . after we land to consolidate the position for both of us. . . . Then your force can come in to the eastward. I realize full well that your landing must be made before the enemy can get there," but "[i]t is our belief that German air and parachute troops cannot get to Algiers or Tunis in any large force for at least two weeks after the initial attack. Meanwhile your troops would be ashore we hope without opposition and would be moving eastward." As regards the time of the initial attack, Roosevelt continued to press for an earlier date than Marshall deemed practicable. "The date should be consistent with the preparations necessary for an operation with a fair chance of success and accordingly it should be determined by the Commander-in-Chief [Eisenhower]," he conceded, but it should "in no event" be "later than October 30," and "I still would hope for October 14th."[42]

This hope was vain, Churchill indicated in his September 1 reply, which Roosevelt, having returned to Washington on the evening of Sunday, August 30, read in the White House. The "sudden abandonment [by the American JCS] of the plan on which we have been working" meant inevitably "grievous delay,"

---

*The bulk of the original redraft, in the FDR Library, is in Hopkins's handwriting, but there are numerous strikeouts and insertions, most of these quite extensive, that are in Roosevelt's distinctive hand.

wrote Churchill. "General Eisenhower says that October thirtieth will be the very earliest date. I myself think it may well mean the middle of November." And "the substitution of November for October" opened up "a whole new set of dangers far greater than those which must anyhow be faced. Finally, in spite of the difficulties it seems to us vital that Algiers be occupied *simultaneously* [emphasis added] with Casablanca and Oran. To give up Algiers for the sake of . . . Casablanca" could lead "to the Germans forestalling us not only in Tunis but in Algeria" with "results . . . lamentable throughout the Mediterranean." He closed with what was, in effect, a concession of his own: "Mr. President, . . . Torch like Gymnast before it has always been viewed as primarily a United States enterprise. We have accepted an American command and your leadership and will do our utmost to make a success of any plan on which you decide." However, "I am sure that if we both strip ourselves to the bone as you say, we could find sufficient naval cover and combat loadings for simultaneous landings at Casablanca, Oran, and Algiers."[43]

Roosevelt's reply to this on the following day (September 2) finally conceded the truly essential point of difference between the American and British staff chiefs and in so doing, since Marshall was, of course, consulted in its drafting, signalized the absolute end, at long last, of Marshall's attempt to subvert Torch and the beginning of his truly wholehearted and highly effective effort to make Torch a success. "In view of your urgent desire that Algiers should be occupied simultaneously with Casablanca and Oran," said Roosevelt's message, "we offer the following solution: (1) Simultaneous landings at Casablanca, Oran and Algiers with assault and immediate follow up troops generally as follows: (A) Casablanca (U.S. troops): 34,000 in the assault and 24,000 in the immediate follow up to land at a port, (B) Oran (U.S. troops): 25,000 in the assault and 20,000 in the immediate follow up to land at a port, (C) Algiers (U.S. and British troops): in the beach landing 10,000 U.S. troops followed within the hour by British troops to make the landing secure. . . . I am willing to risk explanation of British troops in Algiers by telling the French that they are not intended to remain in French territory but that their object is primarily to march into Axis held Tripoli from the rear." Three days later (on September 5), following an exchange of messages regarding the allocation of resources for the three landings, Churchill wrote Roosevelt: "We agree to the military layout as you propose it. We have plenty of troops highly trained for landing. If convenient, they can wear your uniform. They will be proud to do so. . . . It is imperative now to drive straight ahead and save every hour."

Roosevelt's reply on that same day consisted of a single word: "Hurrah!"

Churchill promptly responded with a succinct Americanism: "Okay full blast."[44]

11

->->>X<<-

The Home Front:
Late Summer and Fall 1942

I

WE must constantly remind ourselves, as we view and judge Roosevelt's performance on history's stage during these years of war, that he was compelled to play simultaneously three quite different roles. He was *soldier,* commander in chief of his nation's armed forces, committed to achieving as swift and complete a military victory as possible over barbarous foes. He was *statesman,* concerned to preserve against reactionary wartime pressures the social gains of the New Deal and to keep alive, ready for renewed active expression when peace returned, the principles of government from which social reform had sprung—this while also, in cooperation with other national governments, laying foundations for a peacemaking, peacekeeping world organization. He was *politician,* concerned with national and state party organization and with the winning of elections. The demands these different roles made upon him at any given moment were seldom perfectly harmonious; often, they were harshly dissonant; on occasion, they were, in the forms of their initial presentation to him, flatly contradictory.*

For instance, in mid-August, when soldier Roosevelt was deeply involved in the planning of Torch and statesman Roosevelt was equally involved in efforts to preserve and strengthen the Western alliance with Soviet Russia, politician Roosevelt was forced to deal with a developing quarrel within the New York

---

*When this last happened, he had to make difficult choices between politics and statesmanship (*not* between military victory and the other two; military victory was the constant in this tripartite relativity)—either that or so change the terms of their original presentation that they could be harmonized and then fused, in some kind of "higher synthesis," with victorious war making. Lincoln as President was responding to this kind of challenge when he politicked on the slavery issue, patiently, cautiously, artfully, in ways that kept the border states in the Union and only then, having thus strengthened the Union's body, fused emancipation with war conduct in ways that immensely increased the moral strength of his administration and of the Union cause. The synthesis is epitomized in the first two sentences of the Gettysburg Address; the moral triumph sings through the address's closing sentence.

Democratic Party, a relatively petty matter in itself, but one having national implications.

Herbert Lehman, despite White House pressure, had refused to run for reelection to the state governorship. This had opened a way through which Jim Farley, alienated from FDR in 1940 and now (again) chairman of the New York Democratic Party, could effectively thwart Roosevelt's will. Liberal James M. Mead, who in 1938, with White House support, had won the U.S. Senate seat vacated by Royal Copeland's death, was the logical White House choice for the Democratic gubernatorial candidacy in 1942. Farley therefore set out to secure the nomination for New York State Attorney General John J. Bennett, who had less political potency than Mead but whose election would assure conservative Farley's control of the New York delegation to the Democratic National Convention in 1944. In July, Farley had informed Berle in New York City and then Roosevelt in the White House of his intention, saying he already had the votes to nominate his candidate. Whereupon Roosevelt, on July 17, had covertly given his secretary McIntyre permission to promote, with the help of Berle and Senator Mead himself, a petition drive culminating in Mead's announcement of *his* candidacy. There had ensued a clash between Mead supporters and Bennett supporters, the bitterness of which increased as the date of the state Democratic nominating convention approached.

The national significance of all this derived not only from the effect that a Farley-dominated New York delegation might have upon the Democratic National Convention in 1944, but also, and more so, from the fact that the Republican gubernatorial candidate was Thomas E. Dewey, who, though covertly opposed by Willkie as a "straddler" of the isolationism vs. internationalism issue, was likely to win the Republican presidential nomination in 1944 if he became governor of New York (on the evidence, politician Roosevelt had already discounted to virtual nullity Willkie's chance of capturing the hearts and alleged minds of the dominant powers in the Republican Party). A Governor Dewey would be a formidable opponent for any Democrat, including Roosevelt himself. Roosevelt took no action on the matter, however, beyond reiterating publicly his preference for Mead, until the evening of August 18, with the state Democratic convention due to open in Brooklyn on the following morning. At Hyde Park, he then hand-wrote (Grace Tully had gone to Baltimore to dedicate a ship) a "confidential" letter to the convention leaders saying he had no quarrel "with my old friend Jim Farley" or with "my old friend Jack Bennett" but was "convinced" that Bennett "would not be a strong enough candidate against Dewey" and that his "nomination would cause serious defections in the normal Democratic vote this fall," whereas Mead's nomination "would guarantee an overwhelming victory in the fall." If neither Mead nor Bennett could be nominated "except by a bitter convention fight, I would prefer, rather than to see the party split up, any good compromise candidate that you gentlemen agree on."

His letter had no perceptible effect upon the convention, which, after a final bitter battle between Mead and Bennett supporters, gave Bennett the nomination.[1]

A week and a half later, during the weekend at Shangri-la when Roosevelt (with Hopkins) drastically revised Marshall's draft reply to Churchill's message of August 27, the pressures generated by his three roles were especially intensely focused and discordant. The revision itself reveals a clash between military and political concerns, especially in the closing sentence saying that the date of Torch's launching "should be determined by the [operation's] Commander in Chief " but *must* "in no event be later than October 30." The latter assertion was dictated, not by the military strategic considerations that prompted Britain's original insistence upon an early October date, but by politician Roosevelt's worry over the upcoming midterm elections: a successful, predominantly American invasion of North Africa weeks or even days before the election (November 3) would greatly improve the chances of victory at the polls for congressional and gubernatorial candidates supportive of the administration. Which is to say that the insistence upon an October date was not an order, but an emphatically expressed wish that, despite its great strength, Roosevelt was psychologically prepared to sacrifice, as in the event he did, without protest, to Eisenhower and Marshall's conclusion that an October landing was militarily unfeasible.[2]

Yet he was surely justified in pressing to the limit his desire for an October landing. He thereby forced his military subordinates not only to justify absolutely their refusal of his desire, but also to launch the invasion at the earliest possible later date.

And he had good reason for anxiety about the upcoming election.

Two factors pointed toward a considerably greater loss of congressional seats and governorships by administration candidates in this year 1942 than was normally to be expected at midterm by the party occupying the White House; and about neither of these factors, absent a launching of Torch before election day, was Roosevelt able to do much. *One* of the two was the impact upon the public mind of the bulk of the news that had poured in from the fighting fronts since Pearl Harbor. This news, per se and overall, had not been of a kind to inspire public confidence in the administration's conduct of the war. Pearl Harbor itself had testified to gross negligence and incompetence in the highest ranks of the nation's armed forces. So had the Clark Field disaster, which made certain the swift loss of the Philippines, though skillful public relations manipulations had kept knowledge of this from becoming widespread. So, most emphatically, had the U-boat slaughter of shipping in American coastal waters. Much of this had been offset, of course, by the enormous strategic victory achieved through the Coral Sea and Midway battles, but even this had imbedded in it the Japanese landing in the Aleutian Islands, the first invasion of U.S. North American territory by a foreign power since 1812 and one whose seriousness had been hugely exaggerated by opinion makers in the mass media, arousing intense anxiety all down the West Coast from Nome to Tiajuana. Moreover, there had just been added to the long list of Pacific defeats the Savo island naval disaster and the consequent dire straits in which the U.S. Marines now found themselves upon Guadalcanal, though censorship had thus far kept the general public in ignorance of the extent of the Savo naval losses. There was a distinct possibility that by November 3, the Japanese would have won the battle now raging on Guadalcanal.

The *other*, more important factor pointing toward a conservative, anti-administration victory at the polls was a predicted voter turnout abnormally low even for a midterm election: a low vote invariably favored conservatives in any contest where conservatism vs. liberalism was an issue; the lower the vote, the greater the conservative advantage. One reason for the expected low vote was the war-induced manpower dislocation of the last two years; another was widespread voter apathy—a tendency of average citizens to regard partisan campaigning and the act of voting itself as distractions from, if not contradictions of, the nation's main business of winning the war. The electorate's mood was akin to that prevailing in 1918, when the last preceding midterm election in an America at war had been held. Roosevelt vividly remembered how Woodrow Wilson had then gravely injured himself, his presidency, and the cause of post-war international organization with his issuance of a personal partisan appeal to an electorate that was allergic to "politics as usual" when America's sons, those of Republican equally with those of Democratic parentage, were fighting and dying in France. It was the kind of mistake that Roosevelt was determined to avoid absolutely.

For instance, in early February, Ed Flynn, the Democratic National Party chairman, had asserted in public speech that the Republican voting record on defense issues in Congress had served, and the current incessant Republican attacks upon the administration's handling of the war effort now served, only the malign interests of Berlin, Rome, and Tokyo; he had then gone on to assert flatly that the election of a Republican majority to the House of Representatives in the coming autumn would be a national disaster tantamount to a major battle-field defeat. The degree to which this impugning of their patriotism stung the Republican leadership was measured by the angry outrage with which they charged Flynn with impugning their patriotism. Asked about this in his press conference of February 6, Roosevelt had made careful reply, saying, "[W]hen a country is at war we want congressmen, regardless of party—get that—to back up the Government of the United States in an emergency. . . ." The latter part of the statement might have been interpreted as supportive of Flynn's conclusion, but as a whole and in context the statement had been seen as a rebuff of Flynn, a repudiation of what he had said. It had been intended to be so perceived.

Such avoidance of partisanship, however, if necessary to preserve his public image as the personification of national unity, meant a rejection of the only means by which he might have injected drama into the campaign, overcoming voter apathy to some degree. What he *could* and had already decided to do, substituting pageantry for drama as a way of encouraging voter support of the administration, was make a "secret" inspection tour of major war plants and shipyards and training camps all across the country, showing himself to multitudes but permitting no publicity of the fact until he returned to Washington, when he would publicize it to the maximum. ("Mike, I want to see everything I can, from coast to coast," he had said a few days ago to Michael Reilly, chief of the White House Secret Service detail. "Here are the places I'd like to visit, and you get together with the Army and fix it up. I'd like to leave in the middle of September.")[3]

As for manpower dislocation—though it was at least as great a vote reducer as apathy was and would have been considerably smaller than it now was if a different set of basic White House decisions had been made in 1939 and 1940—there was nothing Roosevelt could do about it at this late date. It would have been great in any case, of course, as myriad men of voting age entered the armed forces and many others, women as well as men, moved into new war-inspired jobs; it had been rendered massive by the way industrial mobilization and war goods procurement had been (and were being) handled. We have noted that the big-business men who in government office made war contract decisions in cahoots with like-minded procurement officers in the army had generally done so in terms of an immediate "efficiency" that just happened to prosper the great corporations of which they were also officials and on whose payrolls most of them remained. They had rejected out of hand every proposal whereby a greater efficiency might have been achieved by direct governmental contracting with small businesses through cooperative organizations of these.* They had placed as little emphasis as their circumstances permitted upon the interests, personal desires, and welfare of workers. This meant that for more millions of people than need have been, the act of voting had been made difficult: to vote, they would have to reregister or use absentee ballots because they had moved to a different city in, often, a different state. And it was the labor vote, which for a decade had been overwhelmingly supportive of the administration, that was thus most affected. The farm vote, normally more conservative than the labor vote, was almost wholly unaffected, agricultural production for war being the same per se as agricultural production for peace and requiring no relocation.

---

*Admittedly, this last was not initially the "easy way," requiring as it did a solid commitment to a clearly defined general good implemented by hard, clear, analytical, and constructive thought. As we have seen, it was much easier for those in charge to follow the route they chose, a route that did *not* lead toward full war economic mobilization but *did* lead, as they may or may not have wished to do, toward a complete dominance by big business of postwar America's economic, social, and cultural life.

Moreover, to the further disadvantage of administration-supporting candidates, more of the farm vote than of the urban vote was being alienated from the administration by Leon Henderson's efforts to control prices.

We have told of the strong objections Roosevelt had made to the Emergency Price Control bill's farm price provisions when he signed it into law last January 30. These provisions denied to the price administrator the power to establish any farm price ceiling below 110 percent of parity or below whichever was highest of the following: the price on October 1, 1941, the price on December 1, 1941, or the average price between July 1, 1919, and June 30, 1920—these last being stipulations that could permit some farm prices to rise far above 110 percent of parity. All this was "a very definite violation" of the theretofore agreed national agricultural price policy, Roosevelt had told his press conference, and constituted a serious flaw in an otherwise "workable" law; it would significantly increase the average family's cost of living, foodstuffs being a major item in every such family's budget, which in turn would cause irresistible demands for wage increases matching the cost-of-living rise, exerting upward pressure on industrial prices.

Chiefly responsible for the flaw was the Farm Bureau, the organization through which, thanks in good part to the AAA's organic linkage with it during the early New Deal, large-scale farmers and agribusinessmen had come to dominate the Department of Agriculture and exert, through senators and representatives from the leading farm states, a decisive influence upon Congress. Public opinion polls had indicated that most American farmers were willing to accept parity as the price standard. In November 1941, for instance, a survey showed 52 percent of the farmers to be content with prevailing price levels. By June 1942, despite a massive propaganda campaign designed to foment farmer discontent with crop prices, the percentage of farmers content with these had risen to 58, according to a Gallup poll. "The American Farm Bureau Federation, however," says the 1946 U.S. Bureau of the Budget publication *The United States at War,* "was adamant on the 110-percent-of-parity limitation."4 And not only had the bureau created this inflationary loophole, it had further contracted the power of the price administrator by writing into the act a provision requiring the concurrence of the secretary of agriculture, over whom it had large influence, in any agricultural price set by the OPM.

Inflation control was Roosevelt's greatest concern during this highly pressurized weekend at Shangri-la: it made demands upon him as politician and statesman that were heavier and more difficult to respond to correctly than were the demands Torch made upon him as soldier—also more urgently important since the war effort as a whole could survive a catastrophic failure of Torch but could not survive the runaway inflation now immediately threatening. Two options were open to him. He could renew his request for immediate congressional action along the necessary lines, doing so with a threatful force tantamount to a command, or he could stabilize prices and wages by executive decree as his presidential war powers enabled him to do. Urging Congress to act would postpone action for at least several dangerous weeks; an executive decree could be done at once. Which to choose? Rosenman and Sherwood, among others of his entourage, were sure he should issue an executive decree, bypassing Congress and publicizing to the maximum his reasons for doing so. The current price rise was so rapid and steep, they said, that further delay of action was intolerable. Moreover, not a few members of Congress itself, as Roosevelt knew, including those accustomed to berating him for alleged dictatorial tendencies, would be glad to have him pursue this course; it relieved them of the necessity to risk grave political injury in a political minefield. And Roosevelt, by the time he drove up from Washington for this weekend at Shangri-la, had decided to do it. His plan then was to proclaim the executive order on Labor Day in a message to Congress, giving the reasons for it, following this up that evening with a fireside chat broadcast to the general public from Hyde Park, where he would be for that long weekend. A draft of the message and another of much of the fireside chat had already been prepared—and when Rosenman arrived by car at Shangri-la at five o'clock on Saturday afternoon, August 29, he had with him a draft of the executive order itself, prepared by him, in consultation with others, through weeks of concentrated, highly difficult labor.

There was much tentativeness, however, in this Rooseveltian decision. The very reason why so many congressmen and senators covertly favored the Executive's assumption of what was normally constitutionally a legislative function was a reason for politician Roosevelt to be extremely reluctant to do it. *For one thing,* he could be sure that if he did what they secretly longed for him to do, the conservatives among them, and nearly all of them were conservative (liberals were pressing for a strong price control act), would promptly, fervently, and publicly damn him for doing it—could be sure, indeed, that a part of what they secretly longed for was another opportunity to attack him as a would-be American Hitler or Mussolini. *For another and more important thing,* as viewed by statesman Roosevelt, his doing what they wished him to do would actually *be* a totalitarian victory to the extent that it confessed to the world at large that in crises requiring swift and total subordination of private selfish interests to national good or need, democratic process did not work, could not work, in the United States of America.

Hence the sympathetic ear with which Roosevelt listened to the advice of Hopkins, who was sure that the worse of the two options open to the President was being chosen. Hopkins may have reminded him that his April 27 message and public speech, though a forceful statement of the general problem and of the need for its speedy solution, had been woefully lacking in solution specifics and had not been followed up aggressively by the White House. Surely, under the Constitution, even in such times as these, the Executive should not assume legislative functions without having proved absolutely to himself, to the public, and to Congress itself, that the Legislature would not, for whatever reason, perform them. Instead of announcing an executive order in his upcoming congressional message, therefore, Roosevelt should issue an ultimatum to Congress: If the necessary legislative action were not taken by a given date (say, October 1, at the latest), he would use his war emergency powers to the full extent necessary to prevent economic disaster. This advice gained persuasive power over Roosevelt from the fact that it proposed something unexpected, hence attention grasping—its coercive potency would be augmented, perhaps, by the shock of surprise it would occasion—for press and public and members of Congress were now almost unanimously of the opinion that the route of the executive order was the one the President had decided to take. The advice gained yet more persuasive power from the fact that it was emphatically concurred in by price administrator Henderson himself, the man who bore the brunt of the battle against inflation and was now, in consequence, the target of such massive, virulent, public abuse as few other national government officials in all American history had had to endure.*

Hence, though the work done that weekend on special message and fireside chat continued along the lines Rosenman and Sherwood favored, its amount and the pressure relief derived from the doing of it were severely limited by the tentativeness of the decision on which the work was based. More conclusive was the work done on two other speeches the President must deliver in the coming week. One was a fairly routine performance at the dedication of a Naval Medical Center in Bethesda, Maryland. The other, far more important, was a radio broadcast from the White House to the youth of the world, the occasion being an International Student Service Assembly made up of delegates from all twenty-nine of the United Nations, meeting in Washington. The event was enthusiastically sponsored by Eleanor Roosevelt, and its international importance was attested to by the pains the Axis governments were taking to prevent accurate news of it from reaching the people under their control. "Our listening stations have picked up an increasing volume of Axis broadcasts, including controlled stations in France, Hungary, The Netherlands, and elsewhere, referring to this meeting . . . in terms . . . of growing hate and, of course, complete falsehood," Roosevelt would say at noon on Thursday, September 3, seated be-

---

*Hopkins was among these few; and it must be said that in both his case and Henderson's some of this abuse was invited by its target's seeming contempt for and defiance of his abusers. Henderson was as flamboyant and loudly assertive a personality as he was a fearless, dedicated, intellectually brilliant, immensely able public servant. He had what Sherwood describes as an "unfortunate flair" for off-putting personal publicity—"was often photographed dancing the rhumba and wearing funny hats and that made him all the more unpopular with the conservative elements which as always were strongest in the rural areas."5 Many who admired his courage and abilities, and shared his liberal principles (Ickes, for one), found him personally obnoxious.

fore clustered microphones in the White House's diplomatic cloakroom. "Our listening stations . . . expect that at this moment the air on all Axis-dominated nations will be thoroughly jammed—blacked out—in order that no sound of what I am saying, either in English or in translation, will be heard by any restless young people who are under Hitler's heel." But what he said "here in Washington" *was* being heard "by several million American soldiers, sailors, and marines, not only within the continental limits of the United States, but in far distant points" around the world "and on all the seas of the world." (He would go on to stress the necessity, and his government's determination, to avoid the mistakes made after the First World War. This time, there must be no "false prosperity" followed by profound economic depression, no such cause for the disillusionment, bitterness, cynicism, and despair that, after World War I, had opened the ears of many of the young to "siren voices that offered glib answers to all the questions they asked," that proclaimed "democracy" to be "dead," that promised "to teach . . . efficiency" and enable "you" [the youth of Germany, Italy, Japan] to conquer the world—all this merely for the giving up of a "freedom" that had proved but a burden of painful and futile decision making. "Victory is essential; but victory is not enough. We must be sure that when you [America's youth in the armed forces] have won victory, you will not have to tell your children that you fought in vain. . . ." Economic security, schools in which "only the living truth will be taught," churches in which "there may be preached without fear a faith in which men may deeply believe," these must be guaranteed. But the "better world for which you fight, and for which some of you give your lives, will not come merely because we shall have won the war. . . . It will be made possible only by bold vision, intelligent planning, and hard work" under the aegis and through the processes of democratic government. "This Government has accepted the responsibility for seeing to it that . . . work has been provided for those who were willing and able, but could not find work," he would say. "That responsibility will continue after the war. And when you come home, we do not propose to involve you, as last time, in a domestic mess" born of "political cynicism and timidity and incompetence.")[6]

Also dealt with that weekend was the transfer of the Trans-Persian Railroad from British to American hands. Averell Harriman, having flown with Churchill from Moscow to Teheran at the conclusion of the Moscow visit, had stayed on in Iran for a couple of days to talk with the newly installed Shah and make a concentrated personal inspection of the railroad. This last he had done from a low-flying airplane, gathering through his railroad-experienced eyes much information about grades, curves, roundhouses, repair shops ("the worst mess I have ever seen," said his notes), tunnels, and the harbor shipping whereby tonnage was transferred from freighters to port railheads. He also had renewed interviews with the present top operating officials of the railroad. From all this he derived a conviction, carried with him as he flew via Basra and Baghdad to

Cairo, that the supply tonnage moved by railroad through Persia to Russia could be increased even more than he had originally thought. To Churchill in Cairo, he had presented in a one-page memorandum his fact-supported argument for the transfer and had won, over General Brooke's continued objections, the Prime Minister's final approval of it.* Churchill then, on August 22, wired from Cairo to Washington his long delayed response to the proposal Roosevelt had so diffidently made on July 16. "I . . . welcome and accept your most helpful proposal . . . that the railroad should be taken over, developed and operated by the United States Army," he wrote the President. "With the railway should be included the [Iranian] ports of Khorranshahr and Bandarshahpur. . . . Averell is cabling you detailed suggestions." The "suggestions" had as major ingredient the replacement of steam locomotives with diesels. "Diesels were bound to be more efficient than coal-fired locomotives in the extreme heat of the desert and the excessively long tunnels through the mountains," Harriman explains in his memoirs. "They also made fewer demands on scarce water along the right of way."[8]

A few days later, having returned to London, Harriman flew from there to Washington, whence, on the afternoon of August 29, he came at the President's invitation to Shangri-la in the same automobile that carried Rosenman. There the railroad matter, to the extent that Roosevelt was actively concerned with it, was quickly and easily disposed of; he simply authorized Harriman to work with Marshall and Somervell along the lines Harriman had suggested and told Marshall that the U.S. Army was from now on to run the Persian railroad. (Harriman would concentrate on this during his two-week stay in the United States. Consulting repeatedly with W. M. Jeffers, his successor as president of the Union Pacific, and obtaining cooperation from the executives of other lines and of locomotive manufacturers, he would facilitate the acquisition of enough diesels to begin diesel service within a few weeks and to dieselize the road completely within a few months. Scores of experienced American railroad men would be recruited. An army engineer, Major General Donald H. Connolly, carefully chosen by Marshall, would take charge of the operation in Persia and do so with exceptional energy and skill. By May 1943, the supply tonnage being moved daily by railroad from the Persian Gulf to Russia would be two and a half times what it had been nine months before.)[9]

But the railroad matter was incidental to Roosevelt's main purpose in summoning Harriman to his mountain retreat: His main interest was to obtain Harriman's personal view of what had happened during Churchill's mission to

---

*The reader will recall that the pro-German reigning Shah in 1941, when British and Russian troops occupied Persia, had abdicated his throne in favor of his son, twenty-two-year-old Mohammad Reza Pahlavi, who evinced sympathy for the Allied cause. As regards the railroad, the arrangement would leave the British in Iran wholly dependent upon the United States for their supply, Brooke had again protested. "In whose hands could we be better dependent?" Churchill had replied.[7]

Moscow, Harriman's judgment of Churchill's firmness in support of the Russian war effort, Harriman's assessment of the state of mind of the Soviet leadership, and Harriman's view of Russia's chances to hold at Stalingrad and the Caucasus Mountains. All this Harriman imparted fully and freely during talks the two men had together, in the Roosevelt cottage at Shangri-la and, at greater length, in the car that carried the two back to Washington in the early evening of Sunday, August 30. As regards Stalingrad and the Caucasus, Harriman believed strongly that the Russians would hold both. His admiration of their determination, their fighting courage, their staying power, their energy and organizational ingenuity, was immense; he stressed, as example, the wholesale transfer of Soviet munitions factories out of the way of the advancing Germans to new locations behind the Urals, where, even there, "each piece of machinery was tagged and numbered, fastened to the concrete floor by bolts and ready to be moved at a moment's notice." When he told of "Churchill's discomfiture in those long, reproach-filled sessions at the Kremlin," Roosevelt frankly enjoyed the story immensely (he seemed at that moment a bit miffed with the Prime Minister, "touchy about the possibility that Churchill might upset arrangements" for Torch), but he was gratified and relieved to learn that this unpleasantness had not caused, in Harriman's opinion, any change in the Prime Minister's "utterly realistic" Soviet policy. The opinion accorded perfectly with what Churchill himself had expressed in his cabled reports to the White House. The Prime Minister, however, said Harriman, was considerably less hopeful than Roosevelt that the wartime partnership of the Soviet Union and the Western Allies "could be extended into long-term understandings" solid enough, strong enough, to guarantee peace in the postwar world.

This last triggered an extended restatement by Roosevelt, as the automobile approached Washington's suburbs in the lengthening shadows of a late summer evening, of a thesis he had earlier expounded to Donald Nelson, Sumner Welles, Hopkins, and Harriman himself, among others of his inner circle, namely, that historic forces now at work within both the Soviet Union and the United States were inexorably narrowing the gap, originally wide and filled with acrimony, between the Russian and American "systems." The narrowing would make increasingly possible and even likely the development of solid peaceful understandings between the two countries, he felt. "Being a religious man himself," Harriman would later write, "he felt that the atheistic Communist system would not be able to suppress permanently the deeply religious tradition of the Russian people. In time, he felt, greater freedom was bound to evolve in the Soviet system." Retained there, no doubt, would be much national economic planning and control by government, much direct participation by government in the production and distribution of goods, but this government would itself become increasingly decentralized; there would be a gradual shifting of decisive power from the Communist hierarchy to the Russian people and, in international affairs, a gradual replacement of "the ideological drive to promote world Communism with more traditional aspects of Russian imperialism." Simultaneously there would continue in the United States what the New Deal had begun—the transformation of what had once been simon-pure laissez-faire capitalism, the government functioning merely as referee and alleged guarantor of allegedly "fair" market competition, into a mixed economy in which democratic government actively participated to make sure that the material abundance that our advanced technology enabled us to produce was indeed produced and was distributed in such a way as to bolster with "freedom from want" the human spiritual freedoms of speech, press, religious worship, and general choice. In sum, Russian society would become more democratic, the American economy more socialistic, each in ways that encouraged what was truly virtuous in their originally widely disparate systems, while reducing or eliminating that which was evil.* "Above all, he [Roosevelt] believed that the intimacies the war had forced upon us could, and should, be used to establish the basis for postwar collaboration," Harriman later recalled. "He recognized that the appalling devastation of vast areas of Russia would call for an enormous effort at reconstruction—and he was disposed to offer generous American help. He had seen Russia rebuffed and isolated by the Western powers before the war, in the League of Nations and outside it. [He] . . . felt that this must not be allowed to happen again. He was determined, by establishing a close personal relationship with Stalin in wartime, to build confidence among the Kremlin leaders that Russia . . . could trust the West."[10]

With that portion of all this that was determinative of America's Russian policy through the years just ahead, Harriman found himself basically in agreement, but he says he "was far less optimistic" than Roosevelt regarding "the time it would take" to dissolve essential conflict-engendering differences between the two states. "I also believed that it would be far more difficult than Roosevelt imagined to develop a real basis of mutual confidence with Stalin. However, I fully agreed with Roosevelt's basic objective of using the wartime relationship to attempt to develop postwar agreements."[11]

A mere two-hour ride in an automobile traveling at thirty-five miles per hour, which was the national speed limit recently imposed as a rubber-saving mea-

---

*The suggested end of an evolutionary process driven by the relentless advance of scientific technology was a form of democratic socialism in each country, though it is highly unlikely that Roosevelt ever permitted such conclusion to enter, thus starkly, his essentially conservative traditionalist mind. He, the self-proclaimed savior of the profit system, was inclined to view democracy-capitalism as a single entity, neither element of which could function apart from the other—a view strongly held by Hoover and the Communist Party. (Communists commonly loathed and feared social democrats more than they did capitalists. Witness their undermining of the Weimar Republic in Germany when Nazism was the alternative.)

sure, sufficed to bring Roosevelt to Shangri-la. From now on to the end of Roosevelt's life, Shangri-la would exert almost as important an environmental influence upon him and, through him, upon the course of great events as the very different environments of Hyde Park and Warm Springs (they were as different from each other as they were from Shangri-la) had long done. Here as there, and as nowhere else save aboard ship on blue water, he could relax and be re-created in his own natural image.

At Shangri-la, Roosevelt wove the absorbent blanket he wrapped round his innermost self to relieve tensions, soothe anxieties, cushion pressures, hide insecurities, smother impatience, and soak away the ache of indecision and the sharp pain that often accompanied decision itself. Thus it was, and also through his strong, simple religious faith and the various and peculiar forms of prayer by which he implemented it—seeking guidance from On High, gaining confidence in the rightness of his decisions when these won (as he surmised from signs and cues) approval from On High, and then shifting from himself to On High the responsibility for the consequences of these decisions—he was enabled to bear as few others could have begun to do, and for far longer than he himself could otherwise have done, the crushing weight of the world. . . .

II

DURING the days immediately following his return to the White House on the evening of August 30, Roosevelt's ache of indecision over price controls, and over whether or not to bypass Congress with an executive order on the matter, became for him and his personal staff (especially speechwriters Rosenman, Hopkins, and Sherwood) a throbbing anguish. For three days he held to the executive order route he had decided to follow while at Shangri-la, but several factors operated further to reduce the firmness with which he so held. The arguments against using an executive order continued to be strongly pressed by Hopkins and Henderson, both of whom feared the effect it might have upon the upcoming elections. The draft executive order Rosenman had brought with him to Shangri-la failed to pass muster with these two or with Donald Nelson, with Treasury officials, and with the Bureau of the Budget, nor did subsequent draft revisions prove more satisfactory. In consequence, the strength of that acid of doubt that was already working in Roosevelt's mind at Shangri-la was increased, and it worked with such erosive effect upon his original decision that on Thursday morning, September 3, both the final decision as to procedure and several final decisions on substantive details remained yet unmade. This meant that final drafts of both the special message to Congress and the fireside chat remained unwritten. And both were scheduled for delivery just four days hence!

He held two conferences in succession in the Executive Office that morning. One was with Secretary of Agriculture Claude R. Wickard, American Farm Bureau Federation president Ed O'Neal, and the respective heads of the National Council of Farm Cooperatives, the Farmer's Union, and the National Grange. The other was with William Green of the American Federation of Labor and Philip Murray of the Congress of Industrial Organizations. The counsel he received in each of them, especially in the one dealing with agricultural matters, was so vehement in tone and self-contradictory in substance that by noon, when he gave his radio address to the youth of the world, he had despaired of his ability to weigh and decide at once, as he was being challenged to do, between the opposing opinions and judgments. Hand in hand with this despair came rebellious resentment. After all (so he reiterated in his troubled mind), decision making of the kind being forced upon him was a legislative function, not an executive one, under the Constitution of the United States; it was Congress's refusal to do its plain duty that had put him in a false position that was also a politically dangerous one. For whatever effective executive order he now issued was bound to expose him to the firestorm of controversy and criticism that now swirled so furiously round Leon Henderson, controversy that would lower his stature as the personification and administrator of national unity in war. By ten-thirty that night, when he boarded his special train at Arlington Cantonment for the journey to Hyde Park, where he would spend the long Labor Day weekend, he had finally definitely decided against the executive order route to which he had earlier committed himself; instead, he would follow the road urged upon him by Hopkins and Henderson.

Three days of anxious and highly concentrated labor then faced him and his three-man speechwriting team. Three extra stenographers came with him to Hyde Park* to help Grace Tully with the typing, under intense time pressure, of the numerous draft messages and speeches out of which the final documents would be fashioned. An extra telegraph operator also came, to help the regular one if both the message and the radio speech had to be wired to Washington to meet congressional and press deadlines. As late as Sunday morning, when Roosevelt with his writers were working over the sixth draft of the chat, the need for more statistical information about the increase and rate of increase in average family income, also in cost of living, caused Isador Lubin, commissioner of the Bureau of Labor Statistics, to be summoned from Washington (he flew up) to supply it. And not until that evening was the seventh draft of the fireside chat given a final approving review by a weary President, who announced with emphasis that he didn't want to see it again, was sick of the sight of it, then wheeled himself to a table in a corner of the Big House library, where he called for a pack of cards and laid out a hand of solitaire. In an opposite corner of the room, his equally weary speechwriters, joined by Hopkins's wife, Louise, relieved their tensions with a game of bridge.

*One of them, Toinette Bacheler, was a former patient at Warm Springs, where she had become acquainted with Roosevelt.

No such rest and relaxation were the lot of Grace Tully and Bill Hassett. Even with the extra stenographic help, a clean copy of the seventh draft of the chat could not be made in Hyde Park and got to Washington in time to be processed into handouts to the press by noon, when the congressional message was to be delivered. So Hassett and Tully took the marked-up seventh draft and carbon copies of the sixth draft into the dining room, where they carefully entered upon three of the carbons, in longhand, the corrections and revisions that had been made of the final rough draft. Not until midnight was the job completed. The material was then rushed by special messenger, via automobile and railroad, to the capital, where in the early morning hours of Monday, hectic labor by stenographers and mimeograph operators ensued. The deadline was met. Meanwhile, in Hyde Park, Roosevelt anticipated with pleasure the discomfiture of the political commentators of press and radio who had so confidently predicted what he would do in this matter ("Good morning, suckers," was his wired Monday morning greeting to the White House press corps). But he remained more than annoyed, he was greatly angered, by the virtual unanimity with which the savants of the press had told the public, on Saturday and Sunday, not only that an executive order would be issued, but also what its salient provisions would be. Obviously there had been outrageous leaks by "blabbermouth" government officials of senior rank—they were of the Budget Bureau and the War Production Board, according to Rosenman, who named one of them—and Hassett predicted in his diary entry for Sunday, September 6, that "some tall heads" were likely "to fall into the basket" in consequence. "The Boss is mad."[12]

For Roosevelt, Monday was a restful day, much of it spent in a solitude not often permitted him as President for any long period. He was unwontedly withdrawn and grave. The reason came clear to his associates when, immediately after lunch, he had flowers placed in his Ford as he left the Big House for a drive: His associates were reminded (he had made no mention of the fact to them) that this day, September 7, 1942, was the first anniversary of the death of his mother—and it was to the grave of his mother, who lay beside his father (dead now for nearly forty years) in Hyde Park's St. James Church cemetery, that he now went, alone, save for the omnipresent Secret Service agent. . . .

The opening words of the fireside chat were spoken at nine-thirty that night into a forest of microphones in his office in the new FDR Library at Hyde Park (for security reasons, no reference was made to his location; the public believed him to be in the White House). What followed them was, in substance, a reiteration of the message delivered to Congress at noon that day—a message reminding the legislators of the seven-point economic stabilization program he had presented them last April 27 and of the two special and crucially important pieces of legislation, needed to implement effectively two of the points, for whose swift passage he had called.

One of these two was a program of heavy taxation that would not only greatly increase federal revenues, but also reduce that market demand for scarce consumer goods that pushed up prices. "The Federal Treasury is losing millions of dollars each and every day because the bill has not yet been passed," and the need for more money was great. "The Nation must have more money to run the war. . . . For this is a global war, and it will cost our Nation nearly $100 billion in 1943." Today, he had "told the Congress once more that all net incomes, after payment of all taxes, should be limited effectively by further taxation to a maximum income of $25,000 a year. And it is equally important that corporate profits should not exceed a reasonable amount in any case." The other urgently needed legislation was for the correction of the imbalance between agricultural and industrial prices resulting from those provisions of the Emergency Price Control Act of last January that left many farm prices uncontrolled, permitted none of them to be lowered below 110 percent of parity, and permitted others to rise even higher than 110 percent of parity. Some of them had already done so, and others were doing so. "The average possible ceiling is now about 116 percent of parity for agricultural products as a whole. This act of favoritism for one particular group . . . increased the cost of food to everybody—not only to the workers in the city or in the munitions plant, and their families, but also to the families of the farmers themselves." It constituted the single major gap, a yawning gap, in the price ceiling that since last May had been firmly placed "on nearly all commodities, rents, and services." Through this gap, the cost of food was rising higher and higher into stormy skies, menacing that stabilization of wages that had been achieved "in certain key industries"; for "it is obvious that if the cost of food continues to go up, the wage earner . . . will have a right to a wage increase." Thus, under present conditions, there impended a "vicious spiral of inflation" that would cause "the whole economic system" to "stagger. Prices and wages will go up so rapidly that the entire production program will be threatened." And this despite the clear lesson taught by our "experience . . . during the last few months," namely, that "the rising cost of living can be controlled, providing that all elements making up the cost of living are controlled at the same time."

Hence his call upon Congress for legislation "specifically" authorizing him as President to regulate "the price of all farm commodities," enabling him "to hold farm prices at parity, or at levels of a recent date, whichever is higher," and thereby establish and maintain a just balance between those prices and wage levels. Moreover, he had demanded that this be done "by the first of October. . . . I have told the Congress that inaction on their part by that date will leave me with the inescapable responsibility" to do through executive order whatever was necessary to remove "the threat" to the war effort posed by "economic chaos." He as President had the power, "under the Constitution and under Congressional Acts, to take" the "measures necessary," and he had "given the most careful and thoughtful consideration" to urgent advice that he exercise these powers now "without further reference to the Congress." But he had "decided that the course of conduct which I am following in this case is consistent with my sense of responsibility as President in time of war, and with my deep and unalterable devotion to the process of democracy." Surely the American farmers, whom "I know . . . are as wholehearted in their patriotism as any other group," should be more anxious for economic stability than any other major economic group, having had an especially bitter experience of a wartime inflation of farm prices followed by "postwar deflationary panic." Of course, such stability required, and farmers had a right to insist upon, guarantees that postwar farm prices did not fall below parity; he therefore was asking Congress to provide not only a ceiling on farm prices, but also "a definite floor under those prices now, continuing through the war, and for as long as necessary a period after the war." Such "collapse of farm prices" as "happened after the last war" must not be permitted to happen again.

He concluded: "Battles are not won by soldiers or sailors who think first of their own personal safety. And wars are not won by people who are concerned primarily with their own comfort, their own convenience, their own pocketbooks. . . . All of us here at home are being tested—for our fortitude, for our selfless devotion to our country and to our cause. This is the toughest war of all time. We need not leave it to the historians of the future to answer the question whether we are tough enough to meet this unprecedented challenge. We can give the answer now. The answer is 'yes.' "[13]

III

A week and a half later, at precisely 10:15 P.M. of what had been a day of thick humid summer heat in Washington (it was Thursday, September 17, 1942), the President's special train pulled out of the siding on which it had been parked in Silver Spring, Maryland, to begin his "secret" cross-continental inspection tour of war plants and military installations. The people he had invited to accompany him were all intimates of his personal life: his wife, Eleanor, and her personal secretary (Malvina "Tommy" Thompson), who were to leave the party after two days but return to it for the closing part of the trip; lawyer Harry Hooker; Laura Delano; and Daisy Suckley, who had in her care during the trip the beloved Scottie dog, Fala, which she had given Roosevelt and which, every time she walked it outside the train, advertised the President's presence—a fact of which she was acutely aware. Also of the party, in their professional capacities, were Ross McIntire, his doctor; U.S. Navy Captain John R. McCrae, his naval aide; Steve Early, his press secretary; and the three wire service reporters assigned to cover the President full-time: Merriman Smith of United Press, Douglas Cornell of the Associated Press, and J. William Theiss of the International News Service.

The three journalists had not theretofore been permitted to accompany the

President on any of his out-of-town trips since Pearl Harbor, though his visits to Hyde Park and, since early July, Shangri-la had become increasingly frequent and lengthy and had twice resulted in embarrassing "scoops" of the White House reporters when trip information "leaked" accidentally. Nor were they allowed on this trip to function as spot-news reporters. They might write stories covering the President as fully and closely as they did in the White House, they were told, but could not file a word of them with their home offices until their return to Washington. Moreover, Roosevelt insisted upon personally reviewing, while he and they were yet on the train, everything they wrote—an insistence that encouraged the production of more copy about the trip than might otherwise have been produced and was perhaps intended to do so. If the reporters did not suspect as much (they had learned to suspect ulterior motives for a great deal of what he did and said), they knew that the elaborate "secrecy" that frustrated them was dictated less by security needs than by Roosevelt's peculiar sense of "fun" conjoined with a calculated use of dramatic surprise as a political tool. The surprise in this case would suddenly release upon the public mind a huge flood of publicity favorable to the administration just eight weeks before the midterm election.

The first stop was Detroit, where, at ten-thirty in the morning of September 18, Roosevelt and his party left the train, which was backed up to the gate of a Chrysler tank plant, and boarded waiting automobiles. These then bore them at a walker's pace (one reporter made the tour on foot, walking at the rear of the President's car) through the plant's long corridors, where they viewed in succession every stage, from material assemblage to final assembly, of the process by which thirty M-4 (General Lee) tanks were made each day. Meanwhile the visitors were themselves viewed with initial astonishment followed by immense excitement by thousands of workers—a "reaction of surprise" with which Roosevelt was "openly pleased" and upon which he "commented . . . all through the tour," according to Merriman Smith.[14]

From this plant, they went by train some thirty miles west of Detroit to what had become and would remain the most publicized of all American war plants, the Ford Motor Company's giant facility for the manufacture of B-24 bombers at Willow Run. Proclaimed in current periodicals as a triumph of American industry, destined for enshrinement in World War II folklore as a major contributor to the American "miracle of production" and hence to Allied victory, Willow Run was originally conceived by the highly able production chief of the Ford Motor Company, Charles E. Sorenson. Soon after the October 1940 meeting of Knudsen with automobile executives, of which we have earlier told, Sorenson visited several West Coast aircraft plants; noted in them what seemed to him great and needless confusion, much duplication of effort, adding up to gross overall inefficiency; and then, in his hotel room one night, sketched the design for a single huge self-contained production unit in which big bombers would be mass-produced in the same assembly-line way as Ford made automobiles. The project plan then focused upon machinery and machine process to the virtual exclusion of the human element of production. Its makers were obviously more concerned to assure Ford a maximum of immediate profit and ultimate market advantage than they were to assure a maximum production of planes in a minimum possible time—indeed, to the extent that they deemed this project to be a business enterprise (and they were businessmen), they deemed the production of bombers to be incidental to, a means to the end of, Ford Motor Company profit—and what they proposed was swiftly and evidently uncritically endorsed by the big-business men who staffed OPM. Neither they nor the War Department's procurement officers gave any decisive weight to Ford's dismal labor relations record and notoriously stubborn defiance of federal labor law. The huge contract was entered into with evident enthusiasm by both parties to it.

What resulted was of awe-inspiring physical dimensions. On what had been an open country of fields and woods ten miles from the nearest town (the college town of Ypsilanti, population twelve thousand), there was erected an enormous L-shaped building whose single room, the biggest room in the world, was a mile in length and a quarter mile in width, covered sixty-seven acres, and ultimately housed more than 1,600 pieces of heavy machinery and 7,500 jigs. The adjacent airfield from which test pilots flew the assembly line's product covered 1,434 acres and had six concrete runways, of which one was a mile and three-quarters in length. Some of the plant's initial glowing publicity predicted that when in full operation, it would employ one hundred thousand workers and produce up to one thousand B-24 bombers *a day*![15]

When Roosevelt saw it, however, some fifteen months after the ground-breaking for it, the plant "was not yet in production," as he would tell his press conference immediately after his return to Washington—a conference during which he betrayed no such enthusiasm for the project as its initial grandiose publicity was intended to inspire. Indeed, there is evidence that he viewed what he saw at Willow Run with a jaundiced eye. He was accompanied on the short train ride from Detroit, as he had been (along with Chrysler's president) in the automobile that drove through the tank plant, by Murray D. VanWaggoner, Michigan's governor, a Democrat who would be defeated by Republican Harry Kelly in the upcoming election; and as they rode westward, the governor poured into the presidential ear some information about Willow Run that may not have been wholly new to Roosevelt but was certainly not going to be given him by eighty-year-old Henry Ford or his son Edsel, both of whom met the President at the plant entrance and personally conducted his plant tour. Roosevelt used some of this information to self-gratifying effect when his automobile reached the point where the L-wing joined the main portion of the huge plant. Theretofore, during the tour, he had displayed toward his principal host what Eleanor knew to be a spuriously affectionate admiration, "patting him on the knee etc.," as

Daisy Suckley recorded in her diary; Eleanor would make upon this a teasing comment not untinged with disapproval at the dinner table that night; but now, turning to Henry Ford, he remarked smilingly but pointedly, "And so *this* is the city line!" Ford was obviously taken aback.[16] Clearly, Roosevelt knew why the immense building was shaped as it was and so probably knew other things about the project that ill accorded with national patriotism or concern for the general welfare. Ford had insisted that the plant be outside Wayne County, in which Detroit was located. He wanted this because organized labor was strong in Detroit, and the city dominated the county. Yet the plant must be within commuting distance of Detroit, where the needed skilled labor resided. Hence the placing of the plant barely outside Wayne, or barely inside adjacent Washtenaw County— and hence the L-shape: the corner formed by the joining of the two wings of the L was only twenty-five feet from the county line. There were tax and other governmental advantages, for Ford now dominated Washtenaw's government as it did Washtenaw's economy.[17]

Consequences sad for the war effort had already begun to flow at Willow Run and would soon flow in flood from Ford's passionate hostility to labor unions, his resultant choice of plant site, his lack of concern for the personal welfare of his workers—this in an enterprise wholly financed by government but also wholly unsupervised or even adequately overseen by government. The thirty-mile distance from Detroit became an impracticably long commute after the rubber shortage forced the imposition of both strict gasoline rationing and a thirty-five-mile speed limit. Nevertheless, since there was an acute housing shortage at Willow Run, more than half the plant's workers must spend two hours a day driving from and to Detroit, or else ride a bus whose fare used up a substantial portion of their daily wages. This also discouraged labor union enrollment or activity among Willow Run's workers, however, so the Ford company adamantly opposed efforts to establish permanent housing near the plant and were supported in this by local real estate interests. When the Federal Public Housing Authority sought to implement what *Architectural Forum* described as a model plan for a six-thousand-unit federal housing project near the plant, the thugs with whom Ford's security department was staffed, commanded by the notorious Harry Bennett, "went so far as to rip up government surveying stakes," says author Richard R. Lingeman. "The . . . Authority finally backed down on its plans, saying they would require too many critical materials. Finally about 10,000 units of temporary housing were built, including 5,000 dormitory units for single persons, 2,500 temporary family units, and 2,000 trailers." This added up to far less than was needed. Small wonder that both absenteeism and labor turnover at Willow Run were horrendously high, absenteeism ranging from 8 to 17 percent a day, labor turnover amounting to 10 percent a month. During the three and a half years of its operation, Ford hired "a total of 114,000 workers to maintain an average strength of 27,400," writes historian Edward L. McNeill, adding: "No one calculated what this churning meant in terms of lost production, but it must have amounted to hundreds, if not thousands, of aircraft." Charles Lindbergh went to work for Ford in April 1942 after having been rejected by the armed services and refused employment in his field of expertise by the government and several private corporations, this because of a Nazi-serving isolationist leadership prior to Pearl Harbor that recommended him to anti-Semitic Roosevelt-hating Henry Ford. Soon thereafter, Lindbergh concluded in the diary he kept during these years that Ford should not be making planes at all since its executives were technically incompetent to direct such activity and too arrogantly egotistical to follow or even listen to expert advice. For all these reasons, Willow Run never came close to achieving the production figures originally predicted for it. By the end of the summer of 1944, the giant plant—having been scaled down from a complete plane-making operation to an assembly one, and having rescinded its ban against the employment of women (40 percent of the plant's jobs became filled by women)—was producing 500 Liberator bombers a month. Ultimately, it produced 8,564.[18]

From Detroit, the Roosevelt party rode overnight to the Great Lakes Naval Training Station on Lake Michigan, in a northern Chicago suburb, where they made a thirty-five-mile tour of this largest of all America's naval training facilities. Sixty-eight thousand men were currently undergoing training there; eighty-three thousand at a time soon would be, when the station's expansion now under way was completed. Again, thousands saw the President. Again, thousands cheered him. Then, without Eleanor and Tommy, who left the train to return to the capital, the Roosevelt party went northward to Milwaukee, where they toured the Allis-Chalmers plant, of whose bitter labor troubles in early 1941 we have told. "That's a case of an old plant with I think only one new building in it which . . . has been turned almost exclusively into Government work [it made turbines for the navy and various items, including large munitions, for the army], and is now getting on very well," Roosevelt would tell his press conference upon his return to Washington. That night, arriving at eleven P.M., they toured a plant located between Minneapolis and St. Paul (the Federal Cartridge Corporation) that was turning out thirty- and fifty-caliber cartridges at a high rate, though it was not yet at its full productive capacity. ". . . [T]he thing that struck all of us most [during these first days of inspection] was the large number of women that were employed in machine work," Roosevelt said at his press conference, "and that means not merely running the small, what might be— what shall I say?—the sewing-machine type of machine, but also some of the largest and heaviest machines, which require great skill and great accuracy, and at the same time do not require heavy manual labor."[19]

The initially novel sight of women performing "men's jobs" became commonplace for the tourists in the following days, when, having visited a yet-building naval training station on Pend Oreille Lake in northern Idaho on their way to the West Coast, they toured defense establishments from Seattle to San Diego. Women made up a higher proportion (47 percent) of the Boeing airplane factory's workforce in Seattle than they did of Willow Run's, they were over 20 percent of the workforce in some Seattle shipyards, and this work was not limited to pushbutton machine tending; it comprised such relatively heavy and certainly physically tiring labor as welding and riveting ("Rosie the Riveter" and "Sadie the Welder" became stereotypical images of women at work in defense plants). Moreover, despite the prevailing popular disapproval of the employment of housewives and mothers, half or more of the working women were married, were thirty-five or more years of age, and had children, though few of these last were younger than fourteen.

There were women among the more than five thousand shipworkers at the navy's Bremerton (Washington) Yard whom Roosevelt addressed briefly through a hand microphone from his open car. With an evident delight that had as one of its ingredients the equally evident irritation of the three wire service newsmen who observed him from a few feet away, he said, "I am not really here, because I am taking this trip under navy orders and that means that my cruise is not published in the papers, so just remember . . . for about ten days that you haven't seen me." The crowd roared with laughter. A little later, he shared his "secret" with virtually all Seattle ("an entire city off-the-record," records newsman Smith) when, word of his visit to Boeing having spread by telephone, he drove with Daisy Suckley and Laura Delano from the plant through streets lined by cheering thousands to the Mercer Island home of his daughter Anna and her husband, John Boetigger. This home was an old farmhouse that had been added to and made into a rambling structure—very "natural and homelike," writes Daisy—with a wide back lawn sloping down to the shore of Lake Washington, and Roosevelt was enormously pleased with it, saying it was "such a peaceful place," he wished he could "spend a week or two there for a real rest."[20]

Next day, in Portland, his daughter beside him, he toured the shipyard of the Oregon Shipbuilding Corporation, one of the largest of the eight such yards established by Henry J. Kaiser along the West Coast for the making of Liberty ships. He watched there the launching of one of the yard's products, the ten-thousand-ton *Teal,* of which the keel had been laid just ten days before* and across whose bow a laughing Anna Boetigger now broke, upon her third try, a christening bottle of Champagne with such force that she was "showered to the skin," as Daisy Suckley recorded. This ceremony was very much on the record (news cameras snapped pictures that were on newsprint a few hours later) save

---

*"Of course . . . when you read about launching a ship in ten days," Roosevelt said later, "it does not mean that the whole ship has been built in ten days." It meant that parts prefabricated in an adjacent plant were "taken to the ways" and there "put together" in ten days.[21]

for the fact that the President of the United States watched the proceedings from a high platform atop the ramp up which his car had been driven and addressed from there a crowd of more than twenty thousand. "You know, I am not supposed to be here today," he said, smiling broadly and again provoking not only crowd laughter, but also angry disgust in the newsmen of his party. "You are the possessor of a secret which even the newspapers don't know. I am under military and naval orders, and like the ship we have just seen go down the ways my movements are secret."[22]

Seated in the backseat of the President's car as these words were spoken, a broad smile on his broad face, was Kaiser himself, a bald, bespectacled man of burly build and torrential energy—"a dynamo," said Roosevelt to Daisy. He had already become and was destined to remain the most famous of American war industrialists, his only close rival for this distinction being a fellow seacraft builder, Andrew Jackson Higgins, whose New Orleans yards Roosevelt would visit on his way back to Washington across southern United States. Both men had gained their fame through a bold, imaginative entrepreneurship that, though it hardly testified to the productive power of "free enterprise" or a "free market" system (it was government funded; its private profitability was guaranteed by "cost-plus"), did evince an authentic individual genius for getting nationally important things done on a huge scale in a minimum of time. Kaiser, like Higgins, had engaged in much corner cutting of dubious legality—had been practically forced to do so if he were to function successfully amid the bureaucratic chaos resulting from Roosevelt's aversion to clear-cut definitions of authority and of the power relations between them. He had acquired scarce materials and labor in frequent defiance of priority and manpower recruitment regulations. His cost accounting revealed extravagances that appalled government comptrollers. But his performance as a whole, like Higgins's, argued as plausibly in favor of the administration's industrial mobilization policy* as Ford's Willow Run operation argued strongly and flatly against it: by the time Kaiser rode with Roosevelt through the Portland shipyard, his personal enterprise was the major single reason why the "impossibly high" goal of eight million tons of new shipping set by the President for 1942 would in fact be reached. In 1943, he and the Six Companies would produce 30 percent of all the new shipping the administration called for that year, an amount much greater than the goal for 1942. By war's end, his yards would have produced almost a third of all America's new wartime shipping—1,490 vessels in all. Among these would be fifty small

---

*That is, the policy whereby the government set production goals, financed with tax money (much of it a free gift) the needed new and expanded plant, let cost-plus contracts to private industry for the goals' achievement, and then exercised a minimal supervision or even oversight of what the contractors did thereafter.

[eighteen-thousand-ton] aircraft carriers, escort carriers carrying up to thirty planes each, which the navy insisted could not possibly be built by Kaiser's methods, but the building of which Roosevelt authorized, overruling Admiral King, after a personal interview with the industrialist. These "baby flattops" would play an important role in the Allied victory over the Axis in the Atlantic.

Kaiser's response to the war production challenge he faced differed radically from Ford's at Willow Run. He was experienced in the execution of huge, federally funded projects, hence in the walking of lines between governmental and private business bureaucracy that tend to be rendered dim and wavering, when not erased altogether, by the profit motive's operations upon a technologically advanced society. Originally a sand-and-gravel company in Washington State, his had become a chief one of the Six Companies consortium that, under federal contracts, built the Boulder, Bonneville, and Grand Coulee dams—huge engineering projects that had been triumphantly completed when, in 1940, Kaiser acquired with consortium money a West Coast shipyard, then moved with characteristic energy and ingenuity to obtain federal contracts for the construction of, to begin with, Liberty ships exclusively.* Acutely aware that he knew nothing about the building of ships, he had initially approached his (to him) novel task with more humility and open-mindedness than Ford and his key executives ever displayed. Sorenson's initial assumption seems to have been that established plane manufacturers did their work wastefully, with much duplication of effort, simply and solely because they lacked the wit and will to employ line-production methods. Kaiser made no such assumption about established shipbuilders. He studied their enterprise; he did not find it to be, as means to its purposed end, grossly inefficient. He recognized that the imposition of mass-production techniques upon the making of ships must be partial (much would have to be done as it had formerly been) and must involve sacrifices of quality. But he also recognized that in a time when shipping was being sunk in the Atlantic faster than it could be replaced, quality was far less vitally important than quantity of shipping—and if ever a ship was suited to assembly line–production methods it was the squat, graceless, slow (ten knots or so) Liberty ship, a vessel in the very design of which quality had been deliberately sacrificed to quantity. By the spring of 1942, Kaiser's yards were completing ships in 50 days or so instead of the 105 originally projected (one of his ships was later launched just 4 days after its keel was laid). And his enterprise was not limited to the yards themselves. When Bethlehem and U.S. Steel, for whatever reason (certainly they resented the loss of their former market control of West Coast shipbuild-

---

*His principal Washington lobbyist was Thomas G. Corcoran, the disillusioned and embittered ex–New Dealer who, having established his own law firm, became, lucratively, one of the capital's leading "influence peddlers." Through Corcoran, Kaiser had made useful personal contacts with RFC head Jesse Jones, William Knudsen as co-chairman of OPM, and presidential assistant Lauchlin Currie.

ing), refused to supply him the steel he needed, he created his own supply: he went with Tommy Corcoran to Jesse Jones and, playing upon that Texan's bias against Eastern financiers, obtained the RFC loan he needed to build, at Fontana, the first complete steel mill in California. "On this occasion," writes political economist Eliot Janeway, "Jesse Jones moved swiftly."[23]

Neither Kaiser nor Higgins ignored or minimized, as Ford did at Willow Run, the human factor in industrial production. They stressed it. Both were less discriminatory than most industrialists in their hiring policies: Kaiser engaged in a massive recruitment of untrained, unskilled labor on the assumption that since so many of his production techniques were uniquely his, most of his workers would have to be trained on the job in any case; Higgins defied the prevailing racial bigotry among Southern whites by employing a considerable number of blacks and was one of the first to employ women on a large scale. Both men paid the top wage in the localities where they operated and used "cost-plus" to assure their workers adequate housing, recreational and shopping facilities, schools and day care centers, and medical services, Kaiser establishing for this last purpose a pioneering health maintenance organization that would still be functioning as a model of its kind half a century later. Both men encouraged high worker morale through plant newspapers, the public recognition of outstanding individual worker achievements, and the ceremonial celebration of their companies' production records; neither was actively hostile to labor organization (Higgins, especially, got on well with unions); and in consequence of all this, neither man had at any time the debilitating absentee problem that plagued Ford's Willow Run all the time until the last months of that plant's existence.

It was on September 29 that Roosevelt's train was backed into one of the Higgins yards in New Orleans.

He and his party had begun their long train ride eastward four days before, on the evening of September 25, having by then toured the California coast from the Oakland area, where they inspected the Mare Island Navy Yard north of Oakland and the naval supply base in Oakland itself, to San Diego, where they inspected the Consolidated plane plant, a naval hospital the beds of which were occupied by wounded from the Pacific war, and U.S. Marine Corps installations. In between, they'd visited in Los Angeles the Douglas aircraft plant (what most impressed Daisy Suckley here was the plant's "blue lighting," which had "a horrible effect on the looks of the workers" ["skin looks green, brown hair looks purple"] and, she was convinced, lowered worker morale; Douglas's employees, especially the women, seemed to her as "apathetic" as she herself "would [be] if I had to work in such light").[24] From San Diego, the train had moved across the vast open reaches of the Southwest through El Paso into western Texas, where its first stop, on a hot Sunday morning, was the small, dusty, remote town of Uvalde.

In a sign beside the tracks, Uvalde proclaimed itself "the Honey Capital of the World"; but it was known abroad, where known at all, as the home of John Nance Garner. More than two years had passed since he, in a mood openly and bitterly hostile to Franklin Roosevelt, had come back here from Washington; almost two years had passed since his much publicized refusal to vote in 1940's presidential election because, as he told the world, he was a Democrat and no true Democrat was on the presidential ticket that year. He and the President had not met since. Hence the high interest with which all, and the anxiety with which some of Roosevelt's party, anticipated this out-of-the-way and obviously political "courtesy call." Roosevelt himself had wondered aloud if there would be "crowds at the station." Actually, no one was there when the train came to a stop. Minutes passed before the former Vice President drove up alone in a battered 1929 roadster, dismounted from it, and, having ducked under the hanging "honey" sign, almost trotted down the track to Roosevelt's car at the rear of the train. Entering the presidential compartment, he shouted: "Well, God bless you, sir, I'm glad to see you!" Roosevelt made equally cordial reply, saying, "Gosh, you look well," as they shook hands. The two then chatted animatedly for six minutes, during which Garner lighted a cigar—two old friends too long separated, joshing one another, each inquiring about the other's "missus"—while a navy photographer snapped pictures. (". . . I asked him in passing," Roosevelt would say to his press conference, "what he thought about farm parity and the prevention of inflation, and he agreed with every other person that I had talked to all the way out and down the coast that the people were . . . jittery in regard to an increase in the cost of living and [would welcome] anything we could do to check [it]. . . .") As he stepped off the train, Garner spied Ross McIntire standing by the depot; he paused to say to the physician, "Keep that man in good health and all the rest will take care of itself."[25]

There had followed stops in San Antonio, with visits to Kelly and Randolph Fields; at Fort Sam Houston, where Roosevelt "had the pleasure of seeing . . . the old Second Division, which I saw on the other side in the summer of 1918" when it contained "two regiments of marines," this last having been his "excuse" for an official visit as assistant secretary of the navy; and at Fort Worth, where the train arrived early on the morning of Tuesday, September 28, enabling him to visit that morning his daughter-in-law Ruth Googins Roosevelt, wife of Elliott (he was in dangerous service as a U.S. Army Air Corps reconnaissance pilot in the North Atlantic) at the 1,500-acre ranch they owned some miles outside the city.[26]

On the following morning, at a Higgins Industries yard, Roosevelt met for the first time Andrew Jackson Higgins, the great boat maker who, while sharing with Kaiser a genius for converting energy into mass in practical ways, differed from him in other respects as widely as the stereotypical Southerner does from the stereotypical Westerner. *Fortune* magazine once described Higgins as part Huey Long, part Henry Ford. Actually, he resembled Ford only in his mastery of mass-production techniques and in his strong aversion to the finance capitalists of the East along with the Washington bureaucrats, whom he regarded, not without reason, as finance capital's agents. He resembled Long only in certain of his personal tastes (for "loud" clothes, for colorful invective) and in his aggressive contentiousness: his disagreements, which were many, tended to be extremely disagreeable. "His trouble is that he is too blunt & fights with everybody," Daisy Suckley wrote of him, obviously expressing the President's views, "so that the maritime commission hates him & won't play ball with him. . . . The P. says this is one of his present problems—to get the right people to let Higgins go ahead. . . ." For Higgins's "going ahead" was of obviously immense value to the war effort, especially at that moment when a shortage of landing craft was gravely inhibiting the mounting of both Torch and the "island-hopping" operations across the Pacific to which King, with Roosevelt's approval, had committed the navy. Unlike the maritime commission, the navy had long had good relations with Higgins. A decade before Pearl Harbor, he had produced small boats that, in part because of their unprecedentedly shallow draft, broke Mississippi River speed records. Two years before Pearl Harbor, his design of a landing craft had been adopted as the navy's own when it proved superior to the design of the navy's bureau of ships. The yard Roosevelt visited was making torpedo boats as well as landing craft, each having as a principal material a plywood as strong and impervious as a plate of steel, the thin wood sheets being bound together by a glue of Higgins's own invention. Ultimately, Higgins Industries would produce, with a speed that was a match for Kaiser's, a considerable majority of all the small craft used in the American war effort, over twenty thousand in all, and of widely various nature, the most famous of them the "Higgins boat," or LCVP (landing craft for both vehicles and personnel)—a flat, remarkably light, extremely shallow-draft, uncovered craft of Higgins's own design. Its prow could be easily, quickly converted into a ramp down which troops could pour, or tanks and trucks and jeeps could drive, onto hostile shores. (Higgins was, of course, well paid for an entrepreneurial service to the government that was immeasurable in monetary terms: his company's total sales were $400,000 in 1935; they were $120 million in 1943; and his profit margin in the latter year, if much narrower than in the earlier one, remained substantial.)[27]

Next day, at Columbia, South Carolina, the President inspected an infantry division in training at Fort Jackson. At dinner that evening, the party's last aboard a train on which they had slept every night for two weeks, Roosevelt said to Laura and Daisy and Harry Hooker that this trip had been "the most restful & satisfactory he had ever taken," as Daisy proudly recorded. "It was a "great compliment to us for not having controversial talk etc. . . . So I think he has had a complete mental rest & is now ready to go back & 'talk turkey' to a good many people— He can talk from what he has seen with his own eyes."[28]

On the following morning, Thursday, October 1, Roosevelt was back in the White House.

And within a few hours thereafter, he was giving a specially summoned press conference his impressions of the state of the nation at war, along with conclusions drawn from these. His was, by and large, a predictably glowing report. Thanks to the fact "that both labor and management are going along magnificently with the whole objective of output . . . production is . . . nearly up to its goals." The people were united in their commitment to victory. "Everywhere I went the spirit was excellent." It was a cooperative community spirit in the agricultural areas he had passed through. "The number of stories that I heard," he exclaimed, "about how they are getting the crops in, with half the hired hands gone!" Town and country worked together, the town setting aside "three or four days" during which "the banker, and the editor of the paper, and the drugstore fellow, and the garage man, and the children . . . give up what they are doing and go into the fields . . . and—by gosh!—get the crops in." He emphasized the non-political nature of this trip, anticipating the interpretation bound to be made of it once news of it was released. The only people he'd seen on the trip who were "connected with politics . . . were the eleven governors of the eleven states that we passed through," and with none of these had he discussed "politics at any moment." He had seen "[n]obody running for Congress, or the Senate, or for local or State office. No chairman, no committee member. Nobody at all but the eleven governors, all of whom we saw at the plants and said goodbye to at the plants."[29]

His hearers sensed a renewed spirit in him.

And indeed, his two weeks of direct physical and psychological contact with a great democratic people hard at work along lines he himself had done much to determine, his vivid personal experience of an America whose immense energies were unprecedentedly (if far from perfectly) focused in nationally planned ways upon the achievement of a single great common objective—this had excited, inspired, and exhilarated him. The trip, so crowded with physical activity and novel sense experiences, had also been for him a rest, a relaxation, refreshing and re-creative of mind and spirit—this in good part because of his chosen companionship. ("We all get along peacefully, & of course we all just think of him, to make it nice for him," writes Daisy.) Thus, it was with a resurgence of his old zestful personal energy that he went again to work in what he told the reporters was "the one place in the country" where the nature and necessities of the war effort were the least well understood, the commitment to it the least wholehearted, namely, Washington, D.C.[30]

IV

ON the following day, October 2, only forty-eight hours after the deadline Roosevelt had set in his Labor Day message, Congress passed the Economic Stabilization Act of 1942. It substantially met the requirements he had stated. He signed it next day, saying in his signature statement: "The Congress has done its part in helping . . . to stabilize the cost of living. The new legislation removes the exemption of certain foods, agricultural commodities, and related products from the price controls of the Emergency Price Control Act with the result that I have today taken action to stabilize 90 percent of the country's food bill [he did so by directing the price administrator, in consultation with the secretary of agriculture, to set ceiling prices on eggs, chickens, butter, cheese, potatoes, and flour]. It leaves the parity principle unimpaired, it reaffirms the powers of the Executive over wages and salaries. It establishes a floor for wages and for farm prices." It also enabled the President to establish an Office of Economic Stabilization (OES), of which the stated function would be "to control so far as possible the inflationary tendencies and the vast dislocations attendant thereon which threaten our military effort and our domestic economic structure." Roosevelt did so by Executive Order No. 9250 at the same time as he signed the enabling bill into law. He also named the man who would head this office.[31]

He had been substantially prepared to take this action by the time he began his inspection trip. . . .

Among those whose advice he had sought and largely followed regarding his political handling of the developing inflation crisis was James F. Byrnes, who, upon becoming a Supreme Court justice, had not severed his personal ties with senators and congressmen or ceased to act as one of Roosevelt's most valued political consultants. Neither had he ceased to advance, to the extent of his capacity to do so, the views of his great friend, mentor, and patron, Bernard Baruch, especially as to the need for a single wartime "economic czar" in whom were combined and augmented the decisive powers now divided between the respective "czars" (so the press had dubbed Henderson and Nelson) of price control and war production. He had specifically recommended to Roosevelt, in an early September phone call, the creation under the requested legislation of an "economic stabilization" officer competent to operate upon economic concerns with the authority, the decisiveness, of the President himself. And Roosevelt knew, when he accepted this phone call, that the man who made it was finding life in the "marble mausoleum" (so Byrnes called the Supreme Court Building) sadly deficient in excitements; knew that Byrnes greatly missed the hurly-burly of the political arena; knew that if Byrnes were asked by the President to give up his prestigious lifetime post in order to render a war emergency service having even greater prestige, and one that might lead him who rendered it toward the highest political office, he almost certainly would do it.[32]

Hence Roosevelt's suggestion that Byrnes consider becoming himself head of the recommended new agency, a suggestion that soon became a request that he do so. Promises were made. Byrnes would have the official title of economic stabilization director and, as such, would "advise and consult" with an Economic Stabilization Board composed of four cabinet members (the secretaries of the Treasury and the Departments of Agriculture, Commerce, and Labor); the

chairman of the Federal Reserve and the WPB; and two representatives each of
labor, management, and agriculture, appointed by the President. But he would
be chairman of this board, the role of which would be *wholly* advisory. All decisions within the economic realm defined by the organic order would be his
alone to make. And this realm of decision would be wide indeed, extending to
the very limit set by the Constitution upon a President's ability, even in wartime, to delegate authority to an appointee. Subject only to a presidential approval that was bound, in the circumstances, to be virtually automatic, Byrnes
(to quote Executive Order No. 9250) was to "formulate and develop a national
economic policy relating to the control of civilian purchasing power, prices,
rents, wages, salaries, profits, subsidies, and all related matters. . . ." He would
"have power to issue directives on policy to the Federal departments and agencies concerned" and, though "the administration of activities related to the national economic policy" was to "remain with the departments and agencies now
responsible" for them, "such administration shall conform to the directives . . .
issued by the Director." In other words, Byrnes would be fully authorized to
umpire, mediate, and ultimately decide the issue of all interagency disputes on
economic matters and, as Roosevelt had told him, "[Y]our decision is my decision and . . . there is no appeal. For all practical purposes you will be assistant
President."33

Byrnes accepted the appointment. He resigned from the Supreme Court on
October 3 and formally assumed his new duties on October 15, being by then
ensconced in the new East Wing of the White House. His office, next door to
Leahy's, was only a few score feet east of the Executive Office; and along the
corridor connecting the two, Byrnes daily walked to see the President, often two
or three times. His staff, aside from his personal secretary, consisted only of his
general counsel, who was the brilliant Ben Cohen, and Cohen's two assistants,
one of whom was Samuel Lubbell, later nationally known as a political analyst.
("The position calls primarily for judicial consideration," the President had explained in his announcement of Byrnes's appointment. "The organization will
be small because the administrative action will be carried out by existing agencies.") Even so, Byrnes's quarters were so cramped that the indispensable wire
service news ticker had to be placed in the men's room.34

The announcement of the new agency's creation and of Byrnes's appointment
fell upon Donald Nelson as a bolt of lightning out of cloudless skies. Typically,
the President had not consulted the WPB administrator regarding impending
changes in the government's economic organization machinery that directly affected that administrator's job. He had not so much as hinted to Nelson that
changes were being contemplated. So when Nelson learned of the new arrangement in the same way as Knudsen had learned of the creation of WPB—that is,
from news reports to the world at large—his initial assumption was that WPB
was being superseded by this new office, as OPM had been by WPB, and that he

himself was being cast aside as carelessly as Knudsen had been. He was not reassured by the fact (if, indeed, in his agitated state, he noticed) that, according to the presidential announcement, the WPB chairman was ex officio a member of the new Economic Stabilization Board. It was not until he had lived through twenty-four hours of personal anguish that a phone conversation with the President made clear to him the difference between what was happening now and what had happened last December: WPB was *not* being superseded as OPM had been; it would continue to function under White House policy directives as it had from the first, the only difference being that these directives would now be issued through an economic stabilization director who functioned as an arm of the President's mind and will. The sole purpose of the new arrangement was to lighten Roosevelt's crushing workload, enabling him to concentrate more fully on crucial military and diplomatic matters that only the President as commander in chief could handle. There was no White House dissatisfaction with Nelson's performance of his assigned role. Far from it. That performance had been "grand," and Roosevelt wanted it continued.

Nelson, vastly relieved, returned to work.

All the same, the event had a lowering effect upon the WPB chairman's power and prestige—a fact that Nelson's astute public relations officer, Bruce Catton, sensed at once. Catton was sure that since actual war production was increasing at a fairly satisfactory rate despite a very partial industrial mobilization, this new arrangement would not have been made if the top production administrative machinery in Washington had been working as the President had hoped it would. Nelson by the summer of 1942 was beginning to suffer the consequences of the two crucial decisions he had made at the outset of his WPB administration, and of which we have already told,* namely, his decision to retain the dollar-a-year method of top WPB staff recruitment and his decision to permit war matériel procurement to remain an army and navy function instead of taking it into his own hands, as his blanket authority permitted him to do. He had thus made it certain that a jurisdictional war between the WPB and the armed services would break out, with himself at a distinct disadvantage in it, and that dissension between himself and some of his own staff members would be created, if and when he moved strongly to exert that civilian control of the national economy that Roosevelt said he intended WPB to maintain. Nelson had begun so to move during the summer. His move had been at once disputed by the formidable War Department team of Undersecretary Patterson and General Somervell. The dispute had become more and more acrimonious and, as autumn came on, began to spill over into front-page newspaper stories, often through calculated leaks (mostly by the War Department) of information that was always partial, generally misleading, and sometimes wholly false. Simultane-

*See pp. 440–44.

ously, Nelson's authority over his own staff was eroded by the tendency of its
dollar-a-year members to side with Patterson-Somervell, whose procurement
policy favored the market interests of great corporations. All this was disappointing to an overburdened President who had counted on Nelson to assume a
significant portion of his burden without challenging his authority but who also,
from the first, as we have seen, had had some doubt that Nelson would prove
tough enough to do so. "The inevitable result," writes Catton, "was that Nelson
presently ceased to be one of the true inner circle of White House favorites." He
was in effect demoted. For by the new arrangement, power no longer flowed in
full measure directly to him from the President; it flowed through a highly ambitious, highly able, shrewdly manipulative man who absorbed a decisive segment of it insofar as it was he, not the President himself, who umpired the power
struggle between (chiefly) the army and the WPB.[35]

As for Byrnes's personal commitment to full civilian control of the national
war economy (that is, his personal opposition to military–big business control),
its strength was as yet unknown. Equally unknown, though known to be great,
was the extent of Byrnes's personal ambition, and both Hopkins and Morgenthau sought to measure this at the outset of the new arrangement, and to determine its nature, in face-to-face talk with the new director. Hopkins, who as
Roosevelt's right-hand man had had to deal with many of the matters Byrnes
would now handle, and who as relief director had sometimes clashed with
conservative Senator Byrnes during the New Deal years, stopped by the new director's office, immediately after Byrnes moved into it, to ask if there were anything he might do to ease Byrnes's way into the new job. He was told: "There's
just one suggestion I want to make to you, Harry, and that is to keep the hell
out of my business." Byrnes "smiled very pleasantly when he said it," reported
Hopkins afterward to his friend Sherwood, "but by God he meant it, and I'm
going to keep the hell out." ("It is improbable that Hopkins was entirely faithful in living up to this resolve," was Sherwood's wry comment five years
later.)[36]

Morgenthau, though far less jarred initially by Byrnes's appointment than
Nelson was, worried greatly that the former senator's lust for power, implemented by superior abilities, would seriously interfere with Treasury's performance of its constitutional role as shaper of fiscal and monetary policy. The
worry became acute as October gave way to November 1942, for this was the
time when preparation of the administration's revenue bill of 1943 (for fiscal
1944) must begin. By whom and through what procedure was the bill to be prepared for the President? Specifically, did Byrnes consider taxes (tax policy) to
be among his new responsibilities? Morgenthau came to the new director's office to find out and was not at all reassured by Byrnes's reply to the question.
The director said that "anybody who holds this [my] position . . . has to include
taxes" among his chief concerns because taxes, their amount and kind, were a

principal means of price control, a major weapon in the war against inflation. The secretary reminded Byrnes that taxes were not once mentioned in the executive order under which the director operated; indeed, he continued, an earlier draft of that order had "explicitly exempted" monetary and fiscal policy from the list of the director's responsibilities.* Moreover, the President, in his announcement to key government officials of the new office's creation, had "orally confirmed" this "exemption." Byrnes said he had not been present at the night meeting where this announcement was made and "had never [before] heard of it." He then smilingly but bluntly asked a question of his own: "You don't claim that you are over me, do you?" Replied an unsmiling Morgenthau, "No, and you don't claim you are over me?" Of course not, said Byrnes, who then emphatically agreed when Morgenthau went on to say that both of them were "here to lick inflation," to "save the President a headache," and could and should work together to this end. The conversation ended, if inconclusively, on an amicable note. "Byrnes will have to be watched, that is all," Morgenthau reported to his staff.

But when he talked to Roosevelt immediately thereafter, he took the precaution of asking whether or not the President expected Treasury "to prepare the tax bill [for fiscal 1944] as we have in the past and present it as we have in the past." Roosevelt replied, "Absolutely." Morgenthau asked the question, he explained, because he "didn't know whether Byrnes was thinking of something and I wanted to find out whether you said anything to him or to leaders on the Hill." Roosevelt said he had not. "This proves to me," a relieved Morgenthau told his diary, "that Byrnes is groping for power and hasn't gotten any direction from the President. It also proves I am right in thinking that one should not be scared by anyone like Byrnes. The only thing to do is go directly to the President and find out where you stand."37

By mid-October, two weeks after the October 1 deadline the President had set in his Labor Day message (though it was not clear that the ultimatum had applied to the tax bill as it did to emergency price control), the revenue bill of 1942 to finance the government through fiscal 1943 was in the final stage of enactment. The House version had gone to the Senate on July 10, the Senate passed its version on October 10, and the considerable differences between the two were being ironed out, more swiftly than usual, in conference committee. The final bill passed both houses on October 20 and was signed into law by the President on the following day.

For Morgenthau, the history of this legislation was one of long and bitter political warfare, the outcome of which, though by no means wholly happy, was

---

*This exemption was consequent upon Treasury's strenuous objection to the wording in Title I of the initial draft order that Rosenman brought with him to Shangri-la, in the car with Harriman, on August 29. (See pp. 600 and 607.)

far less unhappy than he had feared in midsummer that it would be. His department's proposal of steep increases in surtaxes on individual income, on estates,
and on gifts; his efforts to close tax loopholes; every proposal for eliminating
or drastically reducing excess corporate profits; every effort on behalf of the
President's proposal to permit no annual individual income to rise higher than
$25,000 after taxes (that is, to impose a confiscatory tax on every individual in-
come above $25,000)—all these had been summarily dismissed by the House
Ways and Means Committee. Morgenthau's adamant opposition to a sales tax,
preferred by conservatives to income tax increases precisely because it was regressive, lightening the tax burden of the affluent by increasing that of the less
affluent, may have been a factor in the committee's failure to include it, despite
a sales tax's obvious effectiveness as a reducer of inflationary pressures, in the
bill it voted onto the House floor. Otherwise, the bill that passed the whole
House in July was, in Treasury's view, a nauseating mess. It would have contributed inadequately to the battle against inflation and raised but 67 percent of
the minimum $8.7 billion of additional revenue that, in Treasury's estimation,
was needed by the nation at war.

Improving changes were made in the Senate Finance Committee. But Morgenthau failed in his effort to increase corporate and high personal income taxes
sufficiently to prevent a lowering of personal exemptions. This last was done on
a scale that constituted a revolutionary change in the federal tax structure: the
bill finally enacted lowered personal exemptions from $750 to $500 for single
persons, from $1,500 to $1,200 for married persons, and from $400 to $350 for
dependents; it increased the number of Americans who must file income tax returns from seven million for 1941 to forty-two million for 1942. In addition,
nearly all of these taxpayers—that is, everyone with an annual income in excess
of $624—would pay a flat so-called Victory Tax of 5 percent on any wage or
salary in excess of $12 a week. The bulk of this Victory Tax would be collected
at its source through withholdings from paychecks by employers—an innova-
tion destined for extension to income taxes in general in 1943. Those who received income from other than wages or salaries were themselves responsible
for Victory Tax payments from that income. There would be a postwar refund
of a portion of this tax, however—a refund that would militate against a postwar
collapse of markets: single persons would be eligible for refunds of 25 percent
of the Victory Tax and married persons for refunds of 40 percent plus 2 percent
for each dependent, with the stipulation that no single person receive a refund of
more than $500 and no married person a refund of more than $1,000. The new
act did increase taxes on profits a good deal more than had seemed likely last
spring; it was, on the whole, far less unfair in its apportionment of the total tax
burden than had then been fearfully expected by knowledgeable observers; and
it would increase federal revenues by an estimated $8 billion, an increase that
came close to what Treasury had originally claimed was necessary.[38]

Morgenthau's bitterest disappointment in all this was the flat rejection, with no serious legislative consideration, of a remarkably ingenious Treasury proposal that, he was convinced, would have greatly increased revenues in a way that was fair and that held down inflation more effectively than any system of governmental price regulation could possibly do. It was the brainchild of Randolph Paul, the liberal New York City tax lawyer who had come into the Treasury Department as head of its tax division just before Pearl Harbor (he had become the department's general counsel in July 1942), and of Paul's close associate, Raymond Blough. Morgenthau, thoroughly briefed on it by Blough and Paul during the weekend of August 22–23, an unusually hot and humid weekend, was excitedly enthusiastic about it—and so were his principal subordinates when they learned of it from its authors at a staff meeting in Morgenthau's office on Monday morning, August 24. Its central feature was a graduated "spendings tax" that, as a supplement to the income tax, would be imposed on the whole of the amount spent during the year by a family or individual, excepting that amount spent on necessities, with "necessities" carefully defined in the law. Such a tax, its authors argued, would be progressive, not regressive, as was a sales tax. It would be less difficult to administer than rationing and no more difficult than a sales tax. Conjoined with rationing and steeply graduated, it would go far toward nullifying the inflationary pressures currently exerted by consumers who had more money in their pockets than many of them had ever had before. And since unspent income was exempt, the new tax, along with the massive voluntary war bond purchases for which Treasury campaigned vigorously, would insure savings in an amount that could fill much of the gap that must open in market demand when war emergency government spending ceased; it could be made to fill yet more of the gap, while also insuring greater fairness to people of low income, if a portion of it were designated a compulsory loan, to be repaid after the war. Finally, this spendings tax would produce an estimated *$5 billion more in federal revenue* than anyone had so far asked for!

When Blough, acting on Morgenthau's orders, explained the proposal to Henderson and the other top people of OPA, to Nelson and his top staff of the WPB, to budget director Harold Smith, and to Eccles and members of his Federal Reserve Board, they all agreed that it was sound in principle and, or so Morgenthau reported to Roosevelt, "a healthy step in the right direction." Roosevelt himself found the idea intensely interesting. He agreed with the secretary that it was well worth urging upon Congress "even at this late stage in the progress of the tax bill," as Morgenthau put it. Whereupon, with the President's permission, Morgenthau outlined the proposal to Senator George, the Georgia conservative who now chaired the Senate Finance Committee.* George, though he expressed doubt of the scheme's political viability, raised no objection to Treasury's pre-

---

*Walter George, it will be remembered, was a chief target of Roosevelt's failed effort to "purge" anti-administration Democrats from Congress in 1938's primary elections. See *FDR: Into the Storm*, pp. 277–79.

senting it to the full committee. Morgenthau did so in hastily but carefully prepared testimony on the morning of September 3. He received a barely respectful hearing, then was immediately rebuffed. "Not a man on the committee is for
it," Pennsylvania's Senator Guffy told the press next day. Democratic Senator
Harry Byrd of Virginia joined with Republican Senator Robert Taft of Ohio to
damn it as "the most complicated and unworkable [tax plan] that has been submitted . . . in nine years." (Taft himself was arguing vehemently for a 10 percent
retail sales tax on all except food purchases.) Both *The Wall Street Journal* and
The Washington Post ridiculed it editorially. And when the finance committee
voted on it, after very brief and perfunctory discussion, it was unanimously formally rejected.

Personally publicly humiliated, Morgenthau then asked for support from the
President, who, after all, had encouraged him out onto a fragile limb while remaining himself wrapped in silence at the tree's main trunk. He wanted the
President to say, at the very least, that the "hare-brained scheme" that Morgenthau was alleged to have proposed "on his own" was actually one the President
recommended to Congress. Roosevelt refused. "I never make any recommendation to Congress when a bill is pending before them," he said flatly, an assertion of such obvious utter falsity that, as Morgenthau told his diary, "it took my
breath away." Roosevelt himself, taking note of his friend's aghast countenance
and fully conscious of the injustice of his friend's painful embarrassment,
backed off at once. "Well, you know, Henry," he said with an apologetic laugh,
"I always have to have a couple of whipping boys." And Morgenthau, re-
signedly, ruefully, at once accepted the tacit apology, saying with a tight and
joyless smile, "Yes, I realize that I am one of them, and right now I am getting
plenty of whippings." (His whippings, at any rate, he might have consoled himself, were less numerous and severe than those being suffered by the other of
Roosevelt's "couple" at that time, Leon Henderson.)[39]

A day or so later, Senator George proposed, as a scheme of his own, the flat 5
percent Victory Tax. It was harder to administer than the spendings tax would
have been, bore more unjustly on low-income families, produced but half as
much revenue as the rejected scheme would have done, and was a much less effective check upon inflation.

V

BY the spring of 1942, Henry Agard Wallace, Vice President of the United
States and chairman of the Board of Economic Warfare, was becoming the most
frequent, most fervent, and most widely influential public spokesman for what
remained of liberalism in the top decisive ranks of Roosevelt's war administration. His central concern in public speech was with the world-historical significance of the conflict; his central purpose, to define this significance in ways

influential of U.S. postwar policy. For he was convinced that this policy must be determined while the fighting was going on—that its making, and the actual laying of the foundations of postwar world organization, could not be postponed till victory was assured, as Churchill had once explicitly said should be done* and as Roosevelt was now doing; they were properly an integral part of the war effort itself. Wallace pursued this end with the homely eloquence characteristic of him on May 8, 1942, in an address entitled "The Price of Free World Victory," delivered to the Free World Association in New York City. What he then said, though enthusiastically received by its immediate audience, was little noticed in the press next day. But soon thereafter, it was reprinted in full (twice) in Ralph Ingersoll's liberal New York daily *PM*, which in those years was one of the most influential papers in the country. Then it appeared in full in *The Washington Post* and *Women's Wear Daily*, space for it having been bought at advertising rates by the president of the International Latex Corporation. Then Archibald MacLeish's Office of Facts and Figures began distributing copies of it by the hundred thousand nationwide. Whereupon it provoked and became the focus of a national debate between liberal proponents and conservative opponents of the views it expressed, a debate that continued through the rest of the war and into the first few of the years that followed.

Wallace's opening words likened the present-day world to America at the time of the Civil War. Owing to technological advances, especially in communications and transportation (though he did not explicitly say this), the whole of the present-day world was effectively as small, its parts as tightly interconnected, as the United States had been eighty years ago. "This is a fight between a slave world and a free world," said he. "Just as the United States in 1862 could not remain half slave and half free, so in 1942 the world must make its decision for a complete victory one way or the other." But though the present struggle might thus be viewed as a world civil war, Wallace preferred to view it, and he described it in his speech, as part of "a long-drawn-out people's revolution," having as earlier episodes "the American Revolution of 1775, the French Revolution of 1792, the Latin American revolutions of the Bolivian era, the German Revolution of 1848, and the Russian Revolution of 1917." Each of these had been a stage in the "march of freedom" of the "common man"; each had resulted in a wider, more inclusive extension of "freedom of religion, freedom of expression, and freedom from the fear of secret police."† But, he went on, "when we begin to think about the significance of freedom from want [the third

---

*On August 9, 1941, Churchill had told the Commons he opposed the formulation of war or peace aims "when the end . . . is not in sight, when conflict sways to and fro with alternating fortunes and when conditions and associations at the end of the war are unforeseeable."

†That this last was true of the Russian Revolution was a wishful thought quite often implied though never directly stated in the public speech of American governmental office-holders during a war in which Russia was our military ally and bore the brunt of the battle against Nazi Germany.

of Roosevelt's Four Freedoms] for the average man, then we know that this revolution cannot stop until freedom from want has actually been attained" not only in the United States and Britain and the other members of the United Nations, including the presently underdeveloped ones, "but also in Germany and Italy and Japan." The practical means to do this were at hand; it was now "technologically possible" for everyone in the world to "get enough to eat," to be decently clothed and housed, to be freed of backbreaking, life-shortening manual labor. And to assure the realization of this possibility, "a better standard of living for the common man," everywhere in the world, was a central "object of this war." Publisher Henry Luce had recently proclaimed in his *Life* magazine that out of the war would come, for the whole of the world, an "American Century." Wallace deemed this a false interpretation of what was now actually happening, a falsity rendered vicious by its imperialistic motivation. Instead: "I say that the century which we are entering—the century which will come out of this war— can and must be the century of the common man. Everywhere the common man must learn to build his own industries with his own hands. . . . Everywhere the common man must . . . increase his productivity. . . . Modern science, when devoted wholeheartedly to the general welfare, has in it productivity of which we do not yet dream. And modern science must be released from German slavery. International cartels that serve American greed and the German will to power must go. Cartels in the peace to come must be subjected to international control for the common man, as well as being under adequate control by the respective home governments. . . . Yes, and when the time of peace comes, the citizen will again have a duty, the supreme duty of sacrificing the lesser interest for the greater interest of the general welfare. Those who write the peace must think of the whole world."[40]

Among those temperamentally and mentally most susceptible to the Wallace message, having himself arrived at some of the same conclusions, was, incongruously, the 1940 Republican candidate for President of the United States. Indeed, Wallace's speech may well have been a major inspiration of Wendell Willkie's decision to fly round the world at war and then spread abroad as widely as possible his vision of that world, his sense of the historical significance of what was happening in it. At any rate, the published Willkie vision itself, the interpretations Willkie made of what he saw and heard during his trip, coincided at several essential points with what Wallace said in what became known as his "Century of the Common Man" address.

The flight began on August 26 when Willkie took off from New York's Mitchel Field in a converted Consolidated bomber (C-87), christened the *Gulliver*, operated by a U.S. Army Air Force crew. His chosen companions were upper-echelon officials of the Office of War Information who were also personal friends of his: Joseph Barnes, former foreign editor of the *New York Herald-Tribune*, who knew the Russian language well; and Gardner ("Mike") Cowles,

Jr., of the family that published newspapers in Des Moines and the Twin Cities, also the picture magazine *Look,* which, published in New York, rivaled Luce's *Life* in that year. When the flight ended in Minneapolis in mid-October, it had covered thirty-one thousand miles in forty-nine days—days in which the absence of the national titular head of the Republican Party from a midterm election campaign that mounted to its height while he was gone was glaringly conspicuous (several Republican officeholders who had risked their political lives to support him during his campaign for the 1940 nomination were up for reelection). Thirty of these days he spent on the ground of thirteen different countries, each a day of novel excitements and incessant activity followed, often, by a night of limited and restless sleep. When he returned to American soil, there were fifteen pounds less of flesh (admittedly, there had been somewhat too much before) upon his tall, burly frame, and he was dead tired.

His *Gulliver*'s travels dramatically demonstrated the Allies' control of the strategic air routes of the world. No Axis plane could in that year have come anywhere near matching the wide-ranging freedom with which this one, with nary a hitch in a carefully planned travel schedule, circled the globe: from New York to Puerto Rico; from Puerto Rico to Belém and Natal in Brazil; from Natal across the South Atlantic to the British Gold Coast port of Accra, then to what Joe Barnes called a "fantastic walled city in the middle of Nigeria" named Kano; from Kano to Khartoum at the juncture of the White Nile and the Blue in the Anglo-Egyptian Sudan; from Khartoum to Cairo and then to the British air base at Lydda and a visit to Beirut; thence to Baghdad and Teheran; from Iran, then, into Russia, landing at Moscow and Kuibishev; from Kuibishev to Tashkent and thence through the back door of China at Tihwa in the Far Western Chinese province of Sinkiang; from Tihwa to Lanchow and on down to Chengtu and Chungking; then north again to Siberia, to Chita and then much farther north to Yakutsk, capital of the Siberian Republic of Yakutsk, which was the last major stop on the journey. From Yakutsk the *Gulliver* flew to Fairbanks, Alaska, and from there via Edmonton, Canada, to the Willkie party's final landing in Minnesota on October 14.

The trip was well reported in the American and British press while it was going on. It became major headline news in the British and American press on two occasions.

The first of these was on September 26, when Willkie was in Moscow.

He was convinced by what he saw and heard in Russia that the Soviet Union was an "effective society," that "it works," that it consequently had "survival value," and that the Russians, a continental people with a continental outlook, were similar to Americans in many ways of mind and temperament. They were so in their consciousness of wide spaces around them that, richly endowed with undeveloped natural resources, were realms of immense possibility—in their sense that almost anything was possible and would become reality if the will to make it so, devoting organized energies on whatever scale was necessary for the doing of it, was present. The two peoples could therefore "work together for the economic welfare and peace of the world" after the war ended, despite the great economic and political differences between them; they *must* do so, for "there can be no enduring peace, no economic stability," in the world without such collaboration. Nor had he any fear that this "working together" with Communists would corrupt or subvert the American spirit, the American way of life; his "faith in the fundamental rightness of our free economic and political institutions" was too deep, too strong, for that.* Far more subversive would be collaboration's alternative, namely, the stresses and strains of an all-out armaments race and the increasing threat of a third world war.

This collaboration, however, must be firmly grounded in mutual respect and understanding while the war was going on. *Now* was the time to do it, while the unifying force of a common enemy was operating—precisely now, in this very hour when Russian troops waged a bloody hand-to-hand, building-by-building defensive battle against the enemy in ruined Stalingrad, a battle the Russians were in grave danger of losing. Their need for relief from our common enemy's pressure had never been greater than now, was in fact nothing less than desperate according to Stalin, with whom Willkie had just had what he deemed a remarkably frank as well as lengthy personal interview. So Willkie dictated a statement, issued from Moscow to the world press, calling for a "second front" in Europe "at the earliest possible moment our military men will approve." Some of these military men might "need some public prodding" to make sure they acted soon enough, he added provocatively; next summer might be "too late." He had insisted, when the terms under which he traveled were being decided, that insofar as he traveled as a private American citizen who paid his own way, his freedom of public speech would be untrammeled. Roosevelt had agreed. But Willkie's Moscow statement at once called down upon his tousled head a sufficient official wrath, in both Washington and London, to remind him forcefully of the personal responsibility that necessarily accompanies every exercise of personal freedom.† Roosevelt told his press conference on October 6

---

*All the same, Willkie was shaken, and provoked into defensive overstatement, on one occasion, when a young Soviet factory superintendent attacked capitalism on moral grounds, arguing that the profit-motivated marketplace rewarded selfishness, penalized generosity, and encouraged callousness, sensuality, and childish triviality. Willkie countered that, selfish or not, the desire for a personal profit measurable in monetary terms was the prime motivation of *all* human endeavor—a defense that embarrassed the *Gulliver*'s army pilot who, listening to this debate, feared the young Russian was being led to wrong conclusions about Americans and their values. The pilot spoke up to say that while he himself was, of course, pleased with the pay raise that accompanied his promotion from captain to major, the money meant nothing to him compared to the Distinguished Flying Cross awarded him at the same time.

†Wallace had stressed in his "Century of the Common Man" speech that "every freedom has . . . its corresponding duty without which it cannot be enjoyed."

that dispatches quoting Willkie on matters of military strategy were not worth reading because they were purely speculative. Almost simultaneously, Churchill told the House of Commons, in reference to the Willkie statement, that speculation "as to the time and place of future Allied offensive operations" was highly undesirable.[41]

Willkie's "speculation," it must be added, aroused in the minds of high British officials, not for the first or last time, grave questions about Roosevelt's own sense of responsibility. The British found it incredible that the President would permit this very important and highly influential American to travel abroad, on what everyone knew to be a quasi-official mission, during which he would talk face-to-face with heads of governments as, in some degree, the President's personal representative, without having briefed him thoroughly on administration foreign policy, on agreed Allied military strategy, and on an immediately impending military operation bound to influence at least somewhat the balance of international power. Yet that is what the President had evidently done: Willkie obviously knew nothing of the upcoming invasion of North Africa when he talked with Stalin, who had been fully informed of it, as we know. Equally obvious was the fact that Willkie's ignorance of this matter must lower his effectiveness with Stalin. The Russian dictator would, of course, not give his visitor information with which that visitor's own government had not entrusted him, nor could he attach much practical importance to any opinion this visitor voiced. He *would* be encouraged to use his visitor as an influential spokesman of Soviet views. . . .[42]

The second occasion on which Willkie made major front-page news was on October 7 in Chungking, China.

He had landed at the Chungking airport on October 1 and been at once engulfed in a lavish hospitality carefully organized along precise lines of purpose by Generalissimo and Madame Chiang Kai-shek. In the eyes of the Chinese government, he was the American of "highest rank" to visit China since ex-President Grant did so in 1879; he just might become President of the United States in 1945; and the generalissimo and his wife were at the greatest pains to enlist his support of themselves and, at that moment, of a radically new Chinese war strategy, proposed by American Brigadier General Clair Lee Chennault, which if adopted would cancel out Stilwell's recently approved plan to retake northern Burma and, indeed, remove Stilwell himself from the top American military command in China. "He [Willkie] is to be smothered [by hospitality]," was Stilwell's diary comment upon the Chinese arrangements for Willkie's visit. The visitor would see and hear what his hosts wanted him to see and hear, and, as far as possible, nothing else—certainly nothing contradictory of the impression the Kuomintang leaders wished to make. He would be housed, not in the U.S. embassy, but in a Chinese guest house, where he would be "well insulated from pollution by Americans," to continue Stilwell's comment. Two carefully selected Chinese escorts would accompany him everywhere he went. As far as possible, evidences of the miserably low living standard of the bulk of the Chinese citizenry were to be hidden from his sight (Chungking police destroyed the most miserable of the hovels in the areas Willkie would visit; those who had lived in them, along with the more wretched of the multitudinous beggars, were driven out of town for the time being). Great popular demonstrations of the Chinese people's affection for America and this particular American were being governmentally organized. "The idea is to get him [Willkie] so exhausted and so torpid with food and drink that his faculties will be dulled and he'll be stuffed with the right doctrines."[43]

Certainly, Willkie seemed dead tired, his perceptions dulled, his weary mind closed against "doctrines" contradictory to those the Kuomintang preached, on the two occasions when Stilwell attempted serious talk with him. That he was by then wholly convinced of Chiang's abilities and probity is evidenced by his later published opinion that the trim-figured, ascetic-countenanced generalissimo had the manners and appearance of a "scholar" and was, as a historic figure, "even bigger than his legendary reputation." As for Madame Chiang, whose lovely figure, closely clasped by silken gowns with slitted skirts that permitted titillative glimpses of shapely legs clad in the sheerest of hose, she had "brains, persuasiveness and moral force," along with "wit and charm, a generous and understanding heart . . . and a burning conviction." Thus immunized against Stilwell's personal opinions of the same subjects, Willkie was rendered highly susceptible to the strong views, wholly contrary to Stilwell's, that were expressed by Chennault. Willkie heard these last in a private interview that was held, and could only be held, with Stilwell's permission, since Chennault was under Stilwell's command—an interview that Stilwell, having told Chennault to say whatever he pleased to the visitor, actually facilitated. He accompanied Willkie to the airfield, just outside Chungking, where Chennault was headquartered, introduced Chennault to him, then left the two alone together for a two-hour tête-à-tête that was of some historical importance insofar as the chain of events it initiated helped determine the sad future of Chinese-American relations.[44]

Chennault, fifty-two years old in 1942, was a fighter pilot by training and temperament, hard-bitten, assertive, supremely self-confident, a fervent advocate of the extremist views expounded in Alexander Seversky's recently published best-selling book, *Victory Through Air Power.* He was also an authentic hero of the air war over China. Retired as a major from the U.S. Army Air Corps in 1936 because of defective hearing, he in the following year had become Chiang's air adviser and, in 1941, the organizer of an American Volunteer Group of pilots rigorously trained by him in tactics that stressed the strengths and minimized the weaknesses of the American P-40 when measured in combat against the Japanese Zero. The group soon became world famous as the Flying Tigers. Between Pearl Harbor Day and July 1942, though always greatly outnumbered by the enemy, it established total dominance of the air over the areas its planes could cover. It shot down, by official count, 297 Japanese planes for certain and probably 300 more; killed altogether 1,500 Japanese at the cost of only 10 of its own pilots' lives in combat (9 more were killed in accidents); and brought to a total halt the bombing attacks that during the three preceding years had killed hundreds of Chungking civilians and ruined much of the city. At the time of Willkie's visit, Chennault, who had been recalled to active duty in the U.S. Army last April as commander of the newly created Fourteenth Air Force, had just completed a lengthy letter that he wanted delivered to the President of the United States without going through official channels. It outlined a plan calling for a massive shift of logistical support from ground to air forces in China. Many new airfields were to be built; Chennault was to be provided with more planes, more gasoline, more needed supplies of all kinds; and Japan, overwhelmed in air combat, was then to be bombed into submission by planes flying from Chinese air bases. His way having been so well prepared by the generalissimo and (especially) the lovely Madame Chiang, Chennault had little difficulty persuading the distinguished visitor to accept the missive for hand delivery at the White House.[45]

It was, this letter, "one of the extraordinary documents of the war," as historian Barbara Tuchman says, literally breathtaking in its egoistic audacity.* Chennault said that if he were given 105 modern fighters plus 30 medium and a dozen heavy bombers, and supplied with the replacements needed to maintain this force level, he could by himself "accomplish the downfall of Japan . . . probably within six months, within one year at the outside." The Japanese had too limited a plane-manufacturing capacity to replace the losses they would sustain if compelled "to fight me in a position of my own selection," he asserted, and his air offensive would absorb so much of their air strength that the American Southwest Pacific drive northward could proceed "at will." Nor was his self-confidence limited to the purely military sphere; it extended at full strength into the diplomatic one. ". . . I can not only bring about the downfall of Japan but I can make the Chinese lasting friends of the United States," creating "such good will that China will be a great and friendly trade market for generations." These wonderful things had as prerequisite, of course, the vesting in him, Chennault, of "full authority as the American military commander in China." He would then be free to build up and defend the needed supply route from India, though not in the ways currently planned for the doing of it, ways that showed "a complete lack of conception of the true use of air power or even of basic military strategy."[46]

Marshall's reaction to what Chennault said and to his use of Willkie for direct

---

*Chennault's audacity persisted even after the strategy proposed in his letter had been rendered obviously ridiculous by events: his autobiographical *Way of a Fighter* (New York, 1949), pp. 212–15, is Tuchman's source for the quotes here reprinted.

access to the White House was predictable. Infuriated by this undercutting of Stilwell and bypassing of both the chief of staff and the secretary of war, unswerving in his conviction that a flexibly balanced combine of ground-air-sea power was absolutely essential to the successful waging of this global war, he damned the Chennault proposal, when he belatedly learned of it via the White House, as "nonsense; not bad strategy, just nonsense." What Roosevelt thought of it is unrecorded, though he could have wished, perhaps even hoped, that Chennault could do what he said he could. We do know that the President, when he read this letter, was already inclined to recall Stilwell, being under strong pressure to do so by Hopkins and presidential assistant Lauchlin Currie, then in China as lend-lease administrator, as well as by Generalissimo and Madame Chiang. Only Marshall's and Stimson's adamant opposition to it prevented the recall at this time. (The disagreement over Stilwell, on this and later occasions, was the only serious one between Marshall and Hopkins in the whole of the war.) As for Stilwell, he, too, when he learned of it, deemed Chennault's proposal utterly nonsensical. A drastic increase in the logistical support of the air, in view of the limited supply capability, meant a drastic reduction in the support of Chinese ground forces, yet it was these ground forces that must defend the new advanced airfields from which Chennault's planes were to take off. They could not possibly do so against the determined Japanese assaults that the building of these bases was bound to incite. Not in their present sorry state. Not in the foreseeable future, given Chiang's stubborn resistance to every Stilwell proposal for radical army reform.[47]

Willkie, of course, received no inkling from his hosts of the ground forces' unfitness. He was instead treated to a military review, on a wide parade ground, employing Chinese troops especially trained for such exhibitions. He was also taken by train, with what he thought was the reluctant permission of Chiang, to what Stilwell and all knowledgeable others knew to be one of the several "show" fronts to which influential visitors were exposed. This one was on a bend in the Yellow River. The visit to it was proposed by a Chinese general at a cocktail reception in the Chinese War Ministry, a party having both the generalissimo and Stilwell among its guests. ("Of course Mr. Willkie must go," said Stilwell to a fellow American, though loudly enough to be heard by several ranking Chinese officers. "He mustn't miss it. It's the biggest market in China. It's where the Japanese and Chinese meet to trade all the goods they need from each.") The "front" consisted of the Yellow River itself, which was nearly three-quarters of a mile wide at that point, and Willkie, who had anticipated the thrill of battle, found it disappointingly quiet. He was able to see Japanese artillery across the river, however, and was given a number of Japanese cavalry swords and served fine wines, just captured, he was told, in night raids across the river.[48]

It was in a press conference on October 7 (the Chennault letter was dated October 8) that Willkie vented to reporters the resentful anger provoked in him by the comments that Churchill and Roosevelt had just made on his Moscow statement. He was especially angered by Roosevelt's, which he regarded as personally insulting. He had been commissioned by the President to do certain things of a very general nature, he told the reporters. As regards those things, he was the President's personal envoy and must speak and act in accord with administration policy. He had done so to the best of his ability. "But when I speak for myself I am Wendell Willkie and I say what I damned please!" Whereupon he proceeded to do just that. He issued a strong prepared statement of personal views that he knew would outrage the Churchill government and the American State Department but that were held, he was convinced, by a majority of the American people.

He said he had visited on this trip a dozen countries having a bewildering variety of races, religions, customs, forms of government, and ways of life, but who, he had found, were alike in one thing: The great mass of "ordinary people" in every one of them desired a United Nations victory in this war and hoped with increasing fervor that they themselves would be able to live after the war "in liberty and independence." The passion for freedom was a rising force everywhere around the globe where freedom was denied. But it was accompanied, alas, by doubts about the willingness of the two leading democracies of the world "to stand up and be [themselves] counted for freedom for others after the war is over"—doubts that limited what would otherwise be full "enthusiastic participation on our side" by countless millions in Africa and Asia. Urgently needed from the Western democracies, therefore, was a "clear and simple statement of where we stand." The Atlantic Charter was no such statement because it was far from certain that its terms applied outside America and Western Europe. (Before Willkie began his trip, Churchill had issued two interpretive statements about the charter. One of them said that the document's authors, when they drafted it, had "had in mind primarily the restoration of the sovereignty, self-government, and national life of the nations of Europe now under the Nazi yoke." The other said that the charter's provisions must not be so construed as to "qualify in any way the various statements of policy which have been made from time to time about the developments of constitutional government in India, Burma, or other parts of the British Empire.") "Some of the plans to which . . . [the needed statement] would lead are already clear, I deeply believe, to most Americans," said Willkie, going on boldly to declare: "We [Americans] believe that this war must mean an end to the empire of nations over other nations. No foot of Chinese soil, for example, should be or can be ruled from now on except by the people who live on it. And we must say so *now,* not after the war. . . . We believe it is the world's job to find some system for helping colonial peoples who join the United Nations' cause after the war. . . . We believe it is the world's job to find some system for helping colonial peoples who join the United Nations' cause to become free and independent nations. We must set up *firm timetables* [italicized because no high official of the democracies had yet made this proposal] under which they can work out and train governments of their own choosing, and we must establish ironclad guarantees, administered by all the United Nations jointly, that they shall not slip back into colonial status."⁴⁹

The high wind raised by Willkie's Moscow statement was but a gentle breeze compared with the hurricane-force winds provoked by his Chungking one.

It was by no means wholly a wind of wrath.

Wrathful indeed were the reactions of those British who had vested interests in India and Hong Kong, of the native ruling cliques of the colonial peoples whom Willkie proposed to liberate, and of officials of the State Department. These last damned the Willkie statement as almost treasonable in that it endangered the Anglo-American alliance. Churchill was furious, of course. Yet of almost equal height in the United Kingdom, and of much greater height in the United States, was the wind of approval of what Willkie had said—an approval in which Roosevelt the anti-colonialist joined.

On the night of October 26, twelve days after the *Gulliver*'s landing in Minneapolis, eight days before the midterm elections, Willkie delivered over network radio a report to the nation of his trip. He said: "Men and women all over the world are on the march, physically, intellectually, and spiritually. After centuries of ignorant and dull compliance hundreds of millions of people in Eastern Europe and Asia have opened the books. Old fears no longer frighten them. They are no longer willing to be Eastern slaves for Western profits. They are beginning to know that men's welfare throughout the world is interdependent. They are resolved, as we must be, that there is no more place for imperialism within their own society than in the society of nations." Next morning, Roosevelt was asked in his press conference whether he had listened to his radio "from ten-thirty to eleven last night." "I did," he replied. "Several people dining—we listened to it." What did he think of it? "I guess the easiest thing to say is to paraphrase an old cigarette advertisement: there isn't a controversy in a carload of speeches."* Interpreting this to mean that the President endorsed what Willkie had said, the reporters tried to obtain his specific endorsement of specific Willkie statements. They wholly failed, until one of them asked him whether the Atlantic Charter applied only to the Atlantic community of democracies, as its title suggested and as, according to Willkie, myriad millions around the world feared. "If you'll look back in the record you will find that I, twice last spring, and Mr. Hull on one or two occasions, have already made it perfectly clear that we believed that the Atlantic Charter applied to all humanity," Roosevelt replied. His remark, in its context, added greatly to the persuasive force

---

*A dozen years before, a major tobacco company's ad campaign asserting, with typical commercial mendacity, that its cigarettes did not irritate the throat, had dinned inextricably into the public mind the phrase "Not a Cough in a Carload."

of Willkie's speech, especially in England—and there Churchill, some two weeks later, was provoked by it, along with the expressed Willkie views, into one of the most famous of his wartime pronouncements. In a November 10 statement acclaiming the landing of British and American troops in North Africa, the Prime Minister stressed that the British had no acquisitive designs upon North Africa or any other part of the world but added in his most belligerent tone: "Let me make one thing clear, in case there should be any mistake about it in any quarter. We mean to hold our own. I have not become the King's First Minister in order to preside over the liquidation of the British Empire."[50]

This had a shocking effect on American public opinion and was almost universally deplored in the United Kingdom, even by those who shared the Prime Minister's imperialistic commitments. One of the latter, in a letter to the *Times,* claimed that Churchill's words had been misinterpreted, that the Prime Minister's real "meaning was precisely what His Majesty's Government, and I think Mr. Roosevelt also, have declared—namely that as trustees for the dependent peoples they would never surrender that trust to anyone else, e.g., to an international body, well knowing that no body of supermen could in practice carry on the administration of some scores of colonies, and perform the work which at present occupies the large expert staff of the various colonial ministries." Others among the British expressed their agreement with Willkie that the age of imperialism was over but stressed the need for a carefully planned, wholly benevolent transition period from dependency to self-government for the presently colonial peoples. Antipathy to British imperialism was natural for a people whose sovereign independence had been won through armed rebellion against it, said one influential writer in the *Times,* but the "holier than thou" attitude toward Britain that Americans now commonly expressed was hardly justified by the history of their own westward expansion across a continent: "In this expansion the rights and interests of the Red Indians were considered as little as those of the Australian aborigines. Force, bloodshed and insurrection marked the subjection of the Filipinos as it did that of the Maori and Metabole."[51]

VI

On October 21, precisely one week after Willkie and his party arrived back in the United States, Eleanor Roosevelt with an official party that consisted solely of Malvina ("Tommy") Thompson,* left Washington by plane for England. She had been longing and occasionally pressing her husband for permission to make

---

*Accompanying this "official" party, at Eleanor's request, was Major Oveta Culp Hobby, director of the Women's Army Auxiliary Corps (WAAC), which had been created by act of Congress last May, would become the Women's Army Corps (WAC) in the spring of 1943 (with Mrs. Hobby elevated to colonel), and would ultimately have in it one hundred thousand women, six thousand of them officers. Eleanor wanted Mrs. Hobby's company as she toured women's military establishments in England.

this trip ever since his return from the Argentia Conference in late August 1941. Her eagerness for it had increased in proportion to her sense of futility after her forced resignation from the Office of Civil Defense in February 1942. And, latterly, reports of difficulties between British troops and American GIs stationed in Britain (the Americans had "snappier" uniforms, were better fed, received higher pay than their British counterparts), of racial tensions between American Negro and white troops in Britain (especially Southern whites), and of the British citizenry's resentment of the American public's incomprehension of what this citizenry had and still suffered in this war, had convinced her that a visit by her to the yet beleaguered island would indeed serve a useful war purpose. Her husband, too, was convinced, and in mid-September the visit had been arranged, with her acceptance of an invitation from the Queen of England to visit the United Kingdom and spend her first two nights there with the royal couple in Buckingham Palace. She then wrote an Allenswood classmate with whom she had kept in touch that she wanted to help the British and American people to know "more about each other" and especially wanted those American women who complained of wartime hardships to know "what the average household in England is going through."[52]

Her twenty-four-hour transatlantic flight was uneventful, but she was prevented by bad weather from flying on to England from Foynes, Ireland, where the flying boat had come down. A long night and day passed before she could again fly, this time in a special plane sent by Churchill, to Bristol, where Ambassador Winant greeted her and rode with her in the special train, also sent by Churchill, that took her and Tommy to London. She arrived at Paddington Station in the late afternoon of Friday, October 23, receiving there a literally royal welcome. The King and Queen headed a small welcoming party that included Foreign Secretary Anthony Eden and General Eisenhower. With the latter were his staff chief, General Walter Bedell ("Beetle") Smith, and Admiral Harold ("Betty") Stark, who had come with him from an important conference on air force plans to defend against possible U-boat attacks on the Allied convoys that were about to sail for North Africa. From Paddington, Eleanor rode with the King and Queen in the royal automobile, a Daimler, to Buckingham Palace. There, she and Tommy shared an enormous suite; it had "four bedrooms" and was luxuriously furnished but, according to Morgenthau, who was then on a two-week official visit to England,* was very gloomy when he called upon her,

---

*Morgenthau had come to London to confer with the British Treasury on monetary matters regarding which the British and the Americans were in fundamental disagreement. The U.S. Treasury secretary had embraced the monetary nationalism, or imperialism, of Assistant Secretary Harry White. White insisted that although an International Monetary Fund must be established to assure international monetary stability in the postwar world (he labored tirelessly and effectively toward this end), the dollar must become the dominant currency of that world. Hence, the expansion of Britain's dollar balances by lend-lease operations should be kept at the minimum necessary to maintain a viable British

as evening shadows fell, because, not having an electric torch, "she could not find any light switches." He gave her the hooded torch he'd been using to find his way through London's blacked-out streets. A little later, in a letter to Lorena Hickok, she wrote, "We [Tommy and she] are lost in space but we have a nice sitting room with a coal fire," this last worth mentioning because, due to the fuel shortage, a room comfortably warm by American standards was at a premium in the cool and cold months, and even in the so-called warm ones, of wartime England. A small dinner party in her honor was hosted by the King and Queen in the palace on that same night, the eleven guests including the Prime Minister and Mrs. Churchill, Lord and Lady Mountbatten, Ambassador Winant, Field Marshal Smuts, and, to Eleanor's great joy, Lieutenant Colonel Elliott Roosevelt, whose photo reconnaissance unit was now based near Cambridge and with whom, after dinner and a viewing of Noël Coward's film *In Which We Serve,* she stayed up talking until two o'clock Saturday morning.[53]

By then, she had placed in Churchill's hand a letter her husband had asked her to give him. Dated October 19, it began: "I confide my Missus to take care of you and Mrs. Churchill.† I know our better halves will hit it off beautifully." Roosevelt also confided in this missive something of the anxiety he felt over the precarious situation of American troops on Guadalcanal, saying that "though we are killing [every day] a number of Jap ships and planes, . . . there is no use blinking the fact that we are greatly outnumbered." Churchill replied at once: "I am delighted to report that Mrs. Roosevelt has arrived safely. . . . Thank you indeed for the letter she brought me from you." He added, apropos Roosevelt's indicated anxiety, "I am convinced that better days are coming in."[54]

It is notable that Winant was invited to the dinner in the palace on Friday, while Harriman, who was much more influential of relations between the Roosevelt and Churchill governments, was not. This was in accord with Eleanor's wishes. She had been on friendly social terms with Averell Harriman ever since his teenage years at Groton, where he had been a classmate of her brother, Hall; she had been gratified by his switch from the Republican to the Democratic Party in 1928; and she greatly respected his demonstrated abilities as public administrator and policy adviser. But she also greatly respected the abilities of Winant, to whose moral character she was much more closely attuned, and her sense of fairness had been outraged by the written terms under which her hus-

wartime economy—and the British thought the Morgenthau-White estimate of this minimum much too low. The British also felt that the year and a half of anguish and fatal danger that they had endured as the sole fighting champions of freedom's cause, a dark period during which they were bled white economically, justified the buildup of their dollar balances to a height sufficient to enable the recovery of their prewar great power status. Consequently, Morgenthau's conversations with his British counterparts were often difficult, but he felt that during his English visit they went well.

†The "take" in this sentence is evidently a mistake made by Roosevelt in his dictation and uncorrected in the typing. He must have meant to say: "I confide my missus to the care. . . ."

band had dispatched Harriman to London as lend-lease administrator, terms that undercut Winant's authority and reduced his ambassadorial influence. She had held Hopkins to blame, in large part, for this unfairness, and her blame had become furious when, as she prepared for her trip, Hopkins advised her "not to bother with Winant but . . . deal [only] with . . . Harriman" while in England. She had then determined to do (and she now did) the precise opposite; she paid no attention to Harriman but dealt constantly with Winant, during the whole of her English visit.[55]

Saturday, October 24, her first full day in London, was, like all that followed, crowded with activity. In the morning, she faced an intimidatingly large press conference in the American embassy and handled it, by all accounts, superbly. At lunch in the palace, hosted by the King and Queen, she met and conversed with a dozen heads of various British women's organizations. After lunch, the King and Queen took her on a tour of the greatly bomb-damaged city of London and of the East End, where, as the Queen remarked, the Luftwaffe had done a ruthlessly thorough job of slum clearance, leveling whole blocks of substandard dwellings that, the Queen went on, could now be replaced by decent housing (nevertheless, wrote Eleanor in her diary, "they were the homes of people," and the destruction of every one of them "speaks of a personal tragedy"). That evening, the invited dinner guests were Minister of Labour Ernest Bevin and several leaders of the Labour Party, with whom she found the dinner conversation much easier than it had been with the Churchills.

As a matter of fact, she came close to quarreling with the Prime Minister when she, on Tuesday evening, was one of a small dinner party at No. 10 Downing Street. . . .

She had spent Sunday with the Churchills at Chequers, had then moved on Sunday evening from Buckingham Palace into a suite assigned her in the American embassy by Winant, and on Monday morning had visited the Red Cross Washington Club, where she learned from the woman in charge of the dispensary that GIs by the thousand were suffering blistered feet and head colds because the cotton socks issued them were too thin; they all should have heavier woolen socks, the dispensary head said. Immediately thereafter, Eleanor told the hundreds of soldiers who had gathered at the club to see and hear her that she intended to do something about this but that they shouldn't "expect this change too soon," because "you know the Army hates to change," a remark greeted by the soldiers with loud cheers and thunderous applause. She took the matter up with Eisenhower himself that evening. Eisenhower promptly had a check made by his supply officers and was informed, as he wrote the First Lady, that "all normal issues" of woolen socks had been made and that "we have at the minute two and one-half million pairs" of them in English warehouses. "Naturally I cannot guarantee that every individual soldier has his full allotment, since it is entirely possible that some have been lost and replacement not yet made."

Nevertheless, he evidently feared that slipups in the supply distribution might have occurred, for he said in his closing sentence that he had "already started the various commanders on a check-up to see that no man needs to march without proper footgear."[56]

Eleanor's escort to the Downing Street dinner was Henry Morgenthau. The only other guests were Minister of Information Brendan Bracken and Lady Limerick of the British Red Cross. As the last course was being consumed, Churchill asked Morgenthau if the United States was sending food to Spain in sufficient quantity to assure Franco's continued neutrality. When Morgenthau answered affirmatively, Eleanor said (impulsively or deliberately?) that it was a pity Great Britain and the United States had not been similarly concerned with the welfare of Loyalist Spain; had they been, there would now be no need to bribe a Fascist dictator to remain neutral in a world war that a Loyalist victory might conceivably have prevented. Churchill, unaccustomed to women who boldly intervened in "men's talk," seemed startled. After a somewhat embarrassing pause, he reminded his guest of honor, mildly, that he himself had been pro-Franco during the Civil War—strongly pro-Franco, until Germany and Italy became active participants on Franco's side. When Eleanor repeated that the Loyalists should have been helped, Churchill told her that under such a regime as the Loyalist one, he, her husband, and she herself would be the first to lose their heads. She brushed this aside as irrelevant to the question of principled policy. Churchill said that she might not mind losing her head, but he didn't want her to do so, or to lose his—at which point, Mrs. Churchill rather surprisingly remarked: "I think perhaps Mrs. Roosevelt is right." She may have meant this as oil poured on troubled waters; it had the effect of oil poured on smoldering embers. Her husband bristled ominously. "I have held certain beliefs for sixty years," he said belligerently, "and I am not going to change now." Whereupon Clementine Churchill abruptly rose to her feet and moved away from the table, signaling the dinner's end.[57]

There followed for Eleanor two and a half weeks of whirlwind public activity, ceaseless between dawn and late night of every day, during which she exhausted all who accompanied her and amazed all who merely observed. Yet she managed simultaneously to meet her daily newspaper column deadlines, write many letters, and keep a full diary of her trip that would serve as her report of it to her husband. "Hustle? you say," wrote a *London Daily Mail* reporter who covered the seven-day tour she made of the Midlands, Ulster, and Scotland; she "walked me off my feet," covering on foot an estimated "fifty miles through factories, clubs and hospitals," at the end of which she was still going strong, though the journalists who reported her were "glassy-eyed and sagging at the knees." Clementine Churchill, accompanying her one day, found it impossible to keep up; when they came to a building housing the Women's Voluntary Services, which handled clothing sent from America for distribution to those whose wardrobes had been destroyed by bombs, she told Eleanor, who was about to climb four flights of stairs in order to visit the volunteer workers, that she'd wait for her at the foot of the stairway, where she promptly sat down upon a lower step. Eleanor herself contracted "a vile cold in the head" as her tour approached its end, yet she refused to reduce in the slightest her hectic schedule. She knew by then that her visit had been in all respects, and especially as regards public relations, a triumph surpassing even that scored by Wendell Willkie in early 1941. As a reporter on the London staff of America's *Newsweek* magazine put it: "The First Lady is receiving the greatest ovation ever paid any American touring Britain. Groups loiter about the American Embassy all day long hoping to catch a glimpse of her. There are outbursts of cheers and clapping at stations when she unexpectedly appears."[58]

Churchill's brief set-to with her over Loyalist Spain did not dim his admiration of her performance and of her personally (he was not a man who held grudges; magnanimity was one of his outstanding characteristics). He wrote Roosevelt on November 1: "Mrs. Roosevelt has been winning golden opinions from all here for her kindness and her unfailing interest in everything we are doing. I think she has been impressed herself, and we are most grateful for her visit and for all the encouragement it is giving our women workers. I did my best to advise a reduction of her programme and also interspersing it with blank dates, but I have not met with success, and Mrs. Roosevelt proceeds indefatigably." Indeed, the last day of her tour was the most strenuous. It was spent in Scotland inspecting shipyards along the river Clyde. For nearly two morning hours she stood in the prow of a steamer taking her down the river, waving cheerfully and continuously to the thousands of workers on the shore. She was tormented cruelly by a bitterly cold wind, against which her clothing gave inadequate protection ("I was so cold that my hands became congealed," she wrote in her trip diary), yet showed no sign of her discomfort as she gave a short speech to the workers of a shipyard that had just completed an aircraft carrier. After a luncheon in her honor, she drove to Edinburgh, arguing on the way "with the awesome Lord Rosebery about Russia's future," according to Joseph P. Lash. From Edinburgh, where she was presented by the lord provost at a huge reception, she took the night train to London.

The plane in which she flew home was no such roomy and luxurious plane as the flying boat in which she had come; it was an army transport in which her and Tommy's companions were dozens of ferry pilots returning from U.S. plane deliveries.

She was surprised and delighted to find her husband waiting for her at Washington's airport and to learn from him that he had read the newspaper columns she'd written while abroad.[59]

VII

THE weather at Hyde Park in the early morning of election day, Tuesday, November 3, 1942, was as dismal as the outlook that morning for administration success at the polls.

Franklin Roosevelt, in his bedroom in the Big House of his Hyde Park estate, where he had been since Saturday morning, opened his day as he usually did, perusing morning papers in his bed, and though greatly pleased by what he read in them of the triumph his wife was scoring in Britain, he derived no pleasure from what he read of the electorate's prevailing mood, of the continued Republican attacks upon his administration (they had been more than normally vituperative in recent weeks), and of the progress of the Pacific war. Still reverberating through the press was the news, released Sunday evening, of the loss of the fourth of the seven aircraft carriers with which the United States had entered the war, this in a Guadalcanal-related action off Santa Cruz Island on October 26;* Admiral King, typically, had tried to suppress entirely this news, which Elmer Davis, typically, wanted to release in full on the basis of the American people's "right to know"; and Roosevelt, to prevent later charges that he suppressed the news because of its probable adverse effect on the administration's election chances, had, typically, split the difference, ordering release of the fact that another carrier had been lost but not of the name of the ship (it was, in fact, the *Hornet*). The papers were also still recording the shock of Leon Henderson's announcement just three days ago that because of the shipping shortage, coffee rationing would become so severe three weeks from now that a single cup per day was all of the brew that would be allotted any American (three cups was the average daily individual consumption of the nation's eighty-five million coffee drinkers)—news that must further increase the popular mind's tendency to credence charges of incompetence, injustice, and even corruption in the government's rationing program.

Depressing news, overall.

Nor could whatever lowering effect this news had upon Roosevelt's spirits have been in any part alleviated by what he saw when, having laid aside the papers and, with help, arisen from his bed, he looked out his bedroom window. From a dreary sky a chill rain fell steadily, monotonously, as if it would never cease to fall; the carpet of fallen leaves that lay beneath the naked boughs of the great elms and the now thin-leaved boughs of the oaks in the lawn, a carpet that had been of a pale yellow color intermingled with light brown when he had last looked upon it, was now a black sodden mass, and the grass across which it spread was almost as dark.

---

*The *Lexington* was lost in the Coral Sea action and the *Yorktown* in the Battle of Midway, it will be remembered. The *Wasp* had been sunk while patrolling south and east of the Solomons on October 15.

He wheeled himself into his bathroom. He shaved. And in the midst of his shaving, having heard Bill Hassett enter the bedroom, he called this good friend and secretary to him, motioning him to a seat upon the only sitting accommodation available, which was the closed lid of the toilet bowl.

He made but brief comment upon the election, confining his remarks to the New York gubernatorial race and the contest for the congressional seat in his own home district, the state's twenty-sixth. In neither race did the Democrats have any chance of success: colorless John Bennett, having proved an even weaker candidate than Roosevelt had predicted he would be, was obviously about to be overwhelmed at the polls by the smooth and glamorous young "crime buster" Tom Dewey; Ham Fish, whom Willkie had joined Roosevelt in denouncing, was headed for a victory less overwhelming, but still considerable, over the amiable mediocrity (one Ferdinand Hoyt) whom the local Democrats had chosen to run against him (Hoyt was also the candidate of the American Labor Party, but that party's strength in such Republican strongholds as Dutchess County was negligible). Roosevelt then told Hassett to inform the State Department that Thursday, November 19, was the preferred date of several suggested for a visit to the White House by the President of Ecuador, one of the succession of heads of state whom he felt compelled to receive, for wartime diplomacy purposes, at that time. "And find out when the presidents of Cuba, Poland, Chile, and the other one are due," he added somewhat wearily. He frankly confessed to Hassett that there were "too many" of these "visiting firemen," that language differences made conversation with them difficult, and that most of them simply bored him. But in general, he seemed to Hassett remarkably cheerful in the face of what both men knew would be a disastrous day for them at the polls.

If this outward cheerfulness required inward effort for its maintenance, the day's weather seemed to be cooperating with that effort when he left the house at eleven-thirty for the short drive to Hyde Park's Town Hall, there to cast his vote. Rain no longer fell. The sky was clearing. And this brightening of his physical world, as he rode toward the village, may have driven nearly all melancholy from his spirit save a sense of loneliness. Two years before and, indeed, in every earlier election since 1920, he had been accompanied to the polls by his mother, his wife, and Missy LeHand. This year—his mother dead, Missy isolated in her Massachusetts home by her debilitating stroke, Eleanor thousands of miles away—he came alone. Nor was any crowd gathered, as always before, in the street before the Town Hall when his car entered it. Mike Reilly had ordered the block cleared of all "strangers" for the few minutes the President would be in the area; he was using Roosevelt's longtime friend and farmer, Moses Smith, to determine whether or not any given individual was "strange"; and it was Smith, notable for strong opinions and profane language, who greeted Roosevelt with loud exuberance at the hall's entrance. The President, smiling broadly, must have responded with a deliberately provocative question, perhaps: "Has the Honorable Hamilton Fish voted yet?" For Smith was heard to say: "That son of a bitch! Pardon me, Mr. President, but why doesn't that son of a bitch die?" Smith explained to those around him, after Roosevelt had entered the building, that the question he'd asked was not merely rhetorical but indicated a very real possibility: the recent unexpected death of a prominent local Republican had been attributed to his passionate hatred of Roosevelt, said Smith, and no one hated Roosevelt more passionately than that son of a bitch Ham Fish.

Inside the hall, the President of the United States became the 175th Hyde Park citizen to vote that day. He commented upon the lowness of this number to the election board chairman, J. W. Finch.

"Yes," replied Finch, "it's a little slow so far."[60]

And it remained slow in Hyde Park, and more than a little slow over the whole of the nation, for the whole of that day. The vote total proved smaller even than the meager one that had been forecast. Too effective among that major portion of the electorate who normally supported Roosevelt, it would seem, and not effective at all among that portion who opposed him, had been his repeated post–Pearl Harbor calls for an adjournment of "partisan politics" for the duration of the war, while the reverse of this seemed true of his nationally proclaimed election eve "hope" that "all citizens of the United States" would go to the polls—though he might well wonder if the employing class, normally hostile to him, had fully heeded his plea that they "so arrange the work day" as to permit "all their employees" to vote with "no reduction in pay for [the] reasonable time necessarily taken." For, as statistics would later show, the turnout of registered Republican voters was very close to its average in an off-year election, while the turnout of registered Democrats was far less than its off-year average. Early in the evening, Hassett in the local Democratic headquarters in Poughkeepsie's Nelson House and Roosevelt in the library living room of the Big House learned that Dewey would indeed be the next governor of New York, that the ineffable, insufferable Ham Fish would remain a congressman, and that the tide of defeat for liberal Democrats rose higher and higher as it swept westward across prairie and plain. Roosevelt soon had his fill of this news; he went to bed before eleven o'clock.[61]

And awoke to no better news next morning.

Even greater than the most pessimistic liberals had feared it would be was the conservative triumph. In the Seventy-eighth Congress, as in the preceding five, Democrats would hold a majority of the seats. In the Senate would be 57 Democrats, 38 Republicans, and 1 Progressive—a net gain of 10 for the Republicans. In the House would be 222 Democrats, 209 Republicans, 2 Progressives, and 1 Farmer-Laborite—a net gain of 47 for the Republicans. And within the Democratic Party itself, the shift was rightward. The ranks of conservative (mostly

Southern) Democrats were not reduced by this election, but those of Northern liberal Democrats were decimated, and the few candidates who were essentially liberal independents of either major party were virtually wiped out. Of the latter, the great George Norris of Nebraska was one. His defeat by a Republican named Kenneth Wherry was crushingly incomprehensible by Norris. ("I can't understand it," he told friends. "I went down to defeat for reasons my own enemies can't understand.") It was also a slap in the face for Franklin Roosevelt. Aside from John Bennett in New York, Norris was the only man in that national election race whose candidacy the President had personally explicitly endorsed, and he had done so in the most glowing terms, repeating his 1936 statement that Norris was "one of the major prophets of America" whose candidacy "transcends state and party lines."*62

Nor was the outcome of the gubernatorial races any happier, from Roosevelt's point of view. The Republicans had a net gain of nine governorships, and the states that would have Republican governors in 1943 held 325 of the 531 votes in the electoral college, which pointed toward the election of a Republican President in 1944. Who was it most likely to be? the newspapers were already speculating. Dewey? Taft? John W. Bricker, who had won a third successive term as Ohio governor with a majority of nearly 400,000 and who was, if anything, more conservative than Taft? Few of the political pundits of the press seemed to believe it would be Willkie, and Roosevelt was now absolutely sure it would not be: the election had greatly strengthened the grip that old guard Republicans had had upon the national GOP even in 1940 (Roosevelt was more convinced than ever that in the last stage of that campaign, Willkie had revealed that he was but a pawn of these reactionaries and would have remained one, helpless against them, had he won the White House); they had been outraged by every salient Willkie act, every major Willkie public statement, these last two years, and they would see to it that he was drummed out of the party, to all intents and purposes, by 1944.†

Yet on Wednesday morning, Hassett "[f]ound the President in high spirits,

---

*Running as an independent in a three-way race, Norris lost to Wherry by a vote of 186,207–108,899; he would have defeated the Republican by 5,398 votes had he won the 83,763 cast for the Democratic candidate, one Foster May. Another senator from Nebraska, Roman Hruska, is remembered in history for his championship of mediocrity. Responding to a Republican President's nomination to the Supreme Court of a man loudly condemned by the legal community and virtually every other knowledgeable citizen as wholly unfitted by his utter mediocrity for so august and decisively important a post, Hruska defended the nomination with the argument that a mediocrity *should* be on the Court to represent that very large proportion of the American citizenry that is mediocre.

†He would thus join the considerable list of those who, in the twentieth century, had been driven out of the party or rendered impotent within it by the Republican leadership's allergic reactions to intelligence, generosity of mind and spirit, and any expressed willingness to subordinate to the general welfare the special interests of the business community. The list includes Robert La Follette, Theodore Roosevelt, George Norris, Bronson Cutting, Harold Ickes, and William Allen White.

not a trace of the postelection gloom which should encircle him this morning." Added to yesterday's determined cheerfulness was an obviously great relief that the election was over. Of course, he had for weeks been discounting the expected bad news, telling his close associates that this election, which the *New Republic* had asserted to be the most important since the Civil War (he had called this "perfectly silly"), was in reality of no profound significance whatever; its admittedly probable outcome would measure no seismic shift of public opinion away from liberalism toward conservatism, but simply the causal effectiveness of several war-related factors (we have earlier reviewed them) that would become inoperative when peace returned. He might have admitted, if challenged, that the conservative victory would have deplorable effects—government of the people, by the people, for the people, is inevitably diminished when the levers of ultimate governing power are grasped by the morally callused hands of property's worshipers—but these effects could be erased, he comforted himself, by a renewed concentration of the forces of social progress and reform that were now scattered and thus rendered impotent by the necessities of the war. He had every intention of presiding actively over a resurgence of liberalism two years hence, when a final war victory should be in sight, if it were not by then actually achieved—and in his as yet vague plans for doing so, he included Wendell Willkie as an increasingly important factor.[63]

This optimistic view rested upon an unrecognized assumption that time is a series of static segments, or compartments, among which a political leader may pick and choose, putting "first things first" in accordance with his own sense of relative importance. But, alas for such optimism, time actually is a flowing river of merging events wherein the past does not die in the present but moves through it, continuously modified, into a future of which it will be a substantial part. Hence, to the extent that Roosevelt's optimism was not a mere whistling in the dark, or a deliberate morale-boosting design upon the sagging spirits of his liberal support—to the extent, in other words, that he really believed this election had little real significance—he misperceived what was happening in American political history. Not *all* of the margin of the 1942 Republican victory was due to low voter turnout. Some small but highly significant part of it was due to an actual shift away from liberalism toward conservatism among the electorate at large. Which is to say that even if the voter turnout had been of normal midterm proportions, the administration's congressional support would have been reduced.

This shift of voter sentiment from left to right had begun when Roosevelt made his disingenuous proposal for court reform in 1937. The increase of conservatism's relative political strength that came of the bitter political battle thus incited, a battle that split and reduced Roosevelt's liberal support while unifying and solidifying his conservative opposition, had been continuous, if at a various pace, ever since. It had been accelerated by the sharp economic recession of

1937, then slowed by the resumption of government spending; it had manifested itself in the outcome of 1938's midterm elections, which effectively ended the New Deal; it had been speeded up again as world war came on, encouraged by every administration concession to big business as the price of its "cooperation" in the war effort, by the installation of a big-business man in virtually every key defense post in government, and by Roosevelt's cautious shying away from every liberal effort to make social reform a part of the war effort even where the lack of it (for instance, in America's health care delivery system) clearly reduced the country's fighting strength.*

Big business was thus able to trumpet to the world, through *Reader's Digest,* the *Saturday Evening Post,* and the daily press it so largely controlled, the uncontested claim that it was individual enterprise within a profit-driven marketplace that, despite "government interference," had made possible the current "miracle of production." Many an uneducated but skilled worker, whose skill may have been acquired through a government training program, proved all too susceptible to the economic individualism that the businessman preached; he found it pleasant to believe that the fat paychecks he now received (often or generally accompanied by those paid his wife)—perhaps the first he'd ever received, certainly the first since the Depression had cast him into the ranks of the unemployed—was the proper reward of his own virtue, resulting from the exercise of his individual abilities in a business and industrial world at last freed by war necessities from crippling governmental restrictions. Though honestly and profoundly patriotic, willing to sacrifice whatever of his own was necessary to achieve victory over his nation's horrid foes, he and his wife were irritated by the war rationing that drastically limited their enjoyment of their unwonted prosperity, especially since they suspected (they were loudly told by the businessman's propaganda) that the rationing program was designed and administered by a bunch of arrogant Washington left-wingers who were incompetent, if not also subversive of "true Americanism," as well as personally corrupt. They remained averse to, or at least highly suspicious of, the Republican Party, which they yet believed had been responsible somehow for the Great Depression. But they were also dubious of the Democrats. They couldn't understand, for instance, why Roosevelt was giving to the Russians arms and munitions that American troops on Guadalcanal needed for use against the Japanese. Hence, it was by no means a foregone conclusion that had they taken the trouble to reregister, as they must do in order to vote (they had moved from another state

---

*Different from the Roosevelt administration in this respect was the Churchill ministry, wherein the Conservative and Labour Parties participated on almost equal terms. In Britain, the government-sponsored Beveridge Report calling for a dramatic expansion of Britain's social security program, including government "cradle to grave" health care for every citizen and explicitly stating "freedom from want as a practicable post-war aim," was at that moment in the final stages of preparation. It would be announced with great fanfare a few months hence.

to their present location since they last voted), they would have registered as Democrats. They might have registered as independents. Conceivably, swayed by the flood of partisan propaganda from the Right that went unanswered by an administration that eschewed "partisan politics," they might even have cast their votes then for a personable plausible Republican candidate for the House in their district, perhaps also for the Republican running for the Senate, if an upper house seat were being contested in that state in that year.[64]

In the light of the election's outcome, Roosevelt, insofar as he was deeply committed to the liberal cause—and to the extent that he permitted his attention to be diverted from what he deemed the supreme object of all national effort at that time, namely, military victory in this war—must have felt at least *some* doubt of the wisdom of the "hands off" campaign strategy he had followed. Questions must have arisen in his mind whose disturbing effect required for its stifling and hiding from the world an inward effort. Had he been wholly wise in his public response to Ed Flynn's furor-provoking speech of last February—a response that had established the pattern he had publicly followed ever since in his dealings with election year politics? For what had been the consequences? As Kenneth Crawford pointed out in *PM* on October 5, 1942 (and as paraphrased by James MacGregor Burns decades later), "Wilson had called for a Democratic Congress in 1918 and lost seats in the House and Senate; Roosevelt had not called for anything and lost twice as many."

David Lawrence's *U.S. News* gleefully reported that there was now evident the emergence of "an unofficial coalition . . . between anti–New Deal Democrats and Republicans to pluck all budding social reforms from future war legislation." Nor were "budding" reforms the only ones at fatal risk. Clearly in the line of fire from the conservative coalition, and rendered virtually defenseless against it by the need for congressional appropriations, were the National Youth Administration (NYA), the Farm Security Administration (FSA), and the Natural Resources Planning Board (NRPB), three agencies that on the evidence had clearly served the general welfare at some slight tax expense and a more considerable risk, potentially, to the special interests of individualistic property. In the event, none of the three would survive the first session of the Seventy-eighth Congress, despite Roosevelt's efforts (strenuous on behalf of the NYA and the NRPB) to save them.[65]

⇢⇥⇤⇠

12

The Torch Flames but Lights
the Way to What End?

I

BUT, on the evidence, the election did *not* absorb enough of Roosevelt's overall attention to make its outcome a serious depressant of his spirits. Most of his attention remained focused upon the war, where great events were occurring and yet greater ones were in the final phase of their preparation. Bright news came to him from the fighting fronts in the Far Pacific, in Russia, in Egypt; bright hopes mingled with intense anxieties colored the prospect of events immediately impending; and these concerns left but small room in his mind, at that moment, for those of domestic politics.

For it was precisely during the four days that constituted Roosevelt's long election day weekend at Hyde Park that the tide of battle fortune for the Grand Alliance, its ebb having been slowed to a near halt in the Pacific by the Battle of Midway, ceased altogether to ebb and became poised on the verge of flood in every grand theater of this global war save, perhaps, that of China-Burma-India—and even in CBI there was at least a cessation of defeat, there was the establishment of counterpoise. The great fact could be clearly seen only in retrospect, of course; the immediate perception of it, lacking the definition that could come only in the context of events that had not yet occurred, was blurred, tentative, doubtful. But both Roosevelt and Churchill, viewing it from that summit of world power where they spent their days and nights—viewing it, that is, from a height that gave them a considerable historical perspective—felt quite sure at the time that it was indeed a fact.

The Battle of Santa Cruz Island, wherein the only two operating U.S. aircraft carriers in the Southwest Pacific were eliminated from the nation's naval strength, the *Hornet* permanently by sinking, the *Enterprise* temporarily by severe damage—wherein also seventy-four U.S. planes had been destroyed, twenty by the enemy, fifty-four by other misfortunes—was in reality an Allied victory, if a costly one, and was seen as such within days after the battle ended. Three Japanese aircraft carriers, plus two destroyers, had been seriously damaged; one hundred Japanese planes had been destroyed; the number of skilled and scarce Japanese pilots had been reduced; and not only had the Japanese effort to prevent the supply and reinforcement of American forces on Guadalcanal been frustrated, but also the difficulty and hazards for the Japanese of supporting their own Guadalcanal forces had been greatly increased. On the strategic island itself, for many agonizing weeks following the Savo island naval disaster, some sixteen thousand U.S. Marines (the 1st Marine Division), their supplies dwindling, their reinforcement impossible, had clung desperately to a narrow strip of jungle, seven miles long, four miles wide, along the northeastern shore. Within that strip was Henderson Field. But in those dark days, Henderson was an airfield without airplanes. The marines had been wholly without air cover as they fought off attacks by Japanese who were well supplied and constantly reinforced and whose offensive efforts were aided by the bombs and strafing fire of carrier-based planes to the extent that bombs and bullets could be effectively delivered from the air in a thickly forested terrain. Now all was changed. It was the Japanese on the island who lacked air support, all Japanese carriers having been withdrawn from the area, while twenty-nine operational aircraft were on Henderson Field by the last week of October, with more on the way. Between October 23 and October 28, the marines, themselves increasingly well supplied, inflicted heavy casualties upon the enemy at relatively little cost to themselves as they beat off and forced the cessation of his all-out effort to envelop them (an estimated six hundred Japanese were killed and at least eight of their tanks knocked out at a cost of only thirty-nine marine casualties—twenty-five dead, fourteen wounded). Then, on November 1, the marines went on the offensive. Strengthened by a regiment sent from Tulagi, they launched a drive westward that gained ground steadily. By election day, it was evident that from now on it would be the Japanese who fought defensively on the island, and with diminishing strength; soon, army troops would be able to take over the island combat, replacing the marines as active supreme command of the battle was shifted from Nimitz to MacArthur. Much hard Guadalcanal fighting remained to be done (not until February 9, 1943, would all organized Japanese resistance on the island cease), but by election day there was no doubt in Roosevelt's mind of an American victory there. The whole of the southward drive of the Japanese was definitely, permanently, halted.

In Russia, by November 1, the German offensive aimed at the oilfields of Baku was halted north of Grozny—indeed, was stalled all along the Caucasus Mountains line, where every pass continued to be held by the Russians. The Germans had taken or were about to take Maikop but were obviously running out of driving force there and could not go much, if any, farther into the mountains bordering the Black Sea. They were yet so far from their objectives of Baku and Tiflis, in fact, that almost certainly they would never reach them—and the German war machine badly needed the Caucasus oil. Without it, the machine might actually run out of gasoline in a few months, according to some "expert" observers, whose assertions, however, Roosevelt and his military advisers dared not admit to their counsels as they made their strategic plans. It was also quite clear by America's election day that the Germans would *not* drive the Russians out of Stalingrad. The combat there was a bloody stalemate in which the antagonists were locked in such close embrace that the normally great advantage that the Germans had over the Russians in tactical skill (mobility, maneuverability), and in the use of aircraft in close support of ground troops, was nullified. Moreover, the long flanks of the German spearhead, guarded by unreliable German allies (mostly Romanian), were dangerously exposed to the massive Russian counterattack that Roosevelt knew was being prepared, Churchill having told him what Stalin had said in Moscow. If German General Paulus were not permitted to withdraw his Sixth Army from the ruined city—and Hitler notoriously refused ever to permit a major strategic withdrawal—he was in grave danger of encirclement and annihilation in the weeks ahead.

On October 23, Roosevelt had been informed by the Former Naval Person that the long-prepared British offensive at El Alamein would begin that night "at 8 P.M. London time"; that the "whole force of the [Eighth] Army [under Montgomery]" would be engaged; and that all "the Shermans and self-propelled guns which you gave me on that dark Tobruk morning will play their part."[1] The top command of the German-Italian force, whose key unit consisted of the two panzer divisions of the Afrika Korps, was at that moment in disarray. Rommel had gone to Germany on sick leave in late September. His place in Egypt had been taken by General Georg von Stumme, with General Ritter von Thoma as his subordinate in command of the Afrika Korps. Neither of these officers was experienced in desert warfare, both having been recently transferred from the Russian front. And within twenty-four hours after the British attack began, Stumme was dead of a heart attack. Rommel, responding to a telephoned request (or order) from Hitler, at once checked out of the hospital and hurried to Egypt, arriving late in the night of October 25—but his active presence had no such triumphant importance as it had theretofore had in the desert war. The Alamein battlefield was of a kind that severely limited the exercise of tactical skill and daring. There were no flanks to be turned: the fighting line stretched continuously from the Mediterranean in the north to the impassable Qattara Depression in the south: and in the head-on collision thus determined, the British held great advantages. Indeed, it would appear to some people, in retrospect, that the Germans might have retreated from El Alamein very soon even had there been no great frontal pressure upon them,[2] for the British dominated the air over that part of North Africa, their navy was supreme in the Mediterranean, and German communications were gravely impaired and in danger of total disruption by incessant British air and naval attacks. Nevertheless, the defense that Rommel conducted was skillful, stubborn, and bloody alike for him and his attackers. It was also, for him, hopeless. On the opening day of the battle, the Afrika Korps killed four British tanks for every one lost of its own but had at day's end only ninety tanks left, whereas the British Eighth Army had some eight hundred. This huge disparity was increased after Montgomery launched his exhaustively planned and prepared breakthrough operation, code-named "Supercharge," at noon on November 1. In a fierce tank battle next day, the leading British armored brigade lost three-fourths of its tanks and the brigades that followed some two hundred more but scored a victory all the same (of the kind Grant won in Virginia), since the British still had some six hundred tanks at day's end, whereas the Germans had only thirty operational and the Italians none at all.

On Wednesday, November 4, Roosevelt at Hyde Park received from Churchill a copy of General Alexander's report from Cairo: "After twelve days of heavy fighting Eighth Army has inflicted a severe defeat on the enemy's German and Italian forces under Rommel's command in Egypt. The enemy's front has broken and British armored formations in strength have passed through and are now operating in the enemy's rear areas. Such portions of the enemy's forces as can get away are in full retreat and are being harassed by our armored and mobile forces and by our air forces. Other enemy divisions are still in position endeavoring to stave off defeat and these are likely to be surrounded and cut off. The RAF [then and there under Tedder's command] has throughout given superb support to the battle and are bombing the enemy's retreating columns incessantly."[3]

There now loomed a shining opportunity to cut off and destroy the whole of Rommel's army. All that was necessary for this was a swift, bold exploitation of the victory gained, and certainly the British had the material means to do so. But Montgomery was a general very like McClellan of the American Civil War—a superb organizer and trainer of troops who planned his battles in detail, seemed temperamentally incapable of making any major move that had not been carefully planned (though he was notably flexible tactically), and had prepared no sufficient plan (sufficient by his standards) for the great opportunity now opened to him. It was, in this magnitude, unexpected. To procure the ultimate triumph, he must take a chance, acting in some part blindly and without hesitation. Instead, he acted with a reluctance, a cautiousness, that enabled the swift-moving, risk-taking, desperate Rommel to get away with a significant remnant of his troops; he retreated all the way to Mersa Brega, a strong defensive position well inside Cyrenaica.

(We may here forecast that Montgomery did not reach Mersa Brega until November 26, long after Rommel was as well established there as his limited means permitted and where, soon after, the most pressing of his material needs were supplied and he was reinforced with an Italian armored division and three Italian infantry divisions. It was not until the second week of December

that Montgomery felt himself well enough prepared to carry out an elaborate plan "to annihilate the enemy in his defenses" at Mersa Brega through
a frontal assault accompanied by a wide-swinging flanking movement that
cut off Rommel's line of retreat. Rommel, alas, refused to accommodate him.
Alerted by large-scale preliminary British raids on his front on the night of December 11–12, raids designed to distract his attention from the flank movement
that was simultaneously begun, Rommel simply slipped away during the night
of December 12–13, just hours before the "annihilating" frontal assault was
scheduled to begin; he retreated at maximum possible speed all the way to a position near Buerat some 250 miles west of Mersa Brega and a full five hundred
miles from Benghazi, where Montgomery had by then established the British
Eighth Army's advanced base. Rommel would still be in the Buerat position at
year's end, because "this time there was a month's pause, for a move-up and
build-up, before Montgomery was ready to resume his drive," as Basil Liddle
Hart writes.)[4]

All the same, the El Alamein battle was indeed a famous British victory. At a
cost of some 13,500 casualties, the British had inflicted 15,000 (killed, wounded,
and missing) upon the Axis forces; taken 30,000 prisoners, one-third of them
of the elite Afrika Korps, including their commander, General von Thoma; and
forced a virtually disarmed Rommel to abandon huge supply dumps.* When
the wily Desert Fox fled from Egypt into Cyrenaica, he was far too weak to fight
any real battle. His fighting strength was reduced to just 5,000 Germans and
2,500 Italians (the bulk of the 15,000 Germans and almost all of the Italians
who escaped did so without any of their fighting equipment), twenty-one tanks
(eleven German, ten Italian), and only thirty-five German antitank guns and
sixty-five German field guns, plus a few Italian guns.

Abundantly justified was the satisfaction that Churchill conveyed to Roosevelt in typically British understatement as he transmitted Alexander's battle
report to the White House. "I feel sure you will regard this as a good prelude to
Torch," said the Prime Minister to the President.

II

IT was, of course, upon Torch that Roosevelt's most concentrated attention was
fixed: it was only with regard to Torch, of all the operations now under way in
the global war, that he could then take important decisive action.

The operation was unprecedentedly complicated, perhaps the most complicated major military-naval operation in all history. Certainly it was more so,
though of course far smaller, than the Normandy invasion would be. In both

---

*The quantity of captured matériel increases one's doubt that the Axis force would have soon retreated
even if no major attack upon it had been made.

cases, the achievement of tactical surprise was an essential of success. But such achievement was rendered more difficult in Torch's case than in that of "Overlord," as the Normandy invasion would be code-named, by the much greater distances between the ports from which the ships bearing the separate segments of the attacking armies and their logistical support must sail (altogether, some 350 transport and cargo vessels and 500 warships were involved); by the wider stretches of submarine-infested ocean that these ships must then traverse without being detected by the enemy or their purpose and destination surmised if they *were* detected; and by the immensely greater distances that separated the initial objectives of the three task forces. The distances involved made extremely difficult the swift concentration of force that was needed if the ultimate Torch objective, the occupation of Tunisia before the Axis forces could build up there, was to be achieved. Veritable miracles of timing, of coordination, must be performed, and pure good luck must bless the whole of the enterprise, especially at Casablanca, where, it seemed, success required a temporary calming of the waters that normally raged against the Moroccan shore at that time of year.

To these military-naval hazards were added those of a political nature. These were consequences of the Spanish policy that Britain had followed, and in which the United States had concurred, during the Spanish Civil War—also of the pro-Vichy, anti-Gaullist policy initiated by the Roosevelt government after the fall of France and stubbornly maintained in the face of mounting evidence that it failed to serve its avowed purpose, complicated Anglo-American relations, and provoked popular outrage in both the United States and Britain.

We have seen how greatly Franco's cause in the Spanish war was aided by the hypocritical "neutrality" that the British and American governments maintained while Hitler and Mussolini actively, strongly, decisively intervened on Franco's side. We have seen how Franco's triumph, in good part consequent upon this phony "neutrality," adversely affected the planning of Torch, arousing what to the British seemed an excessive fear by the American military that Franco's response to the Torch landings might be the closing of Gibraltar Strait. Franco's supremacy in Spain also greatly complicated the naval portion of the Torch launching operation, requiring the separate convoys of troop transports and cargo vessels assembled off U.K. shores to sail at different times and different speeds, their movements thereafter carefully, precisely planned to assure their simultaneous arrival at Gibraltar, and passage through the strait, on November 5, thereafter to divide into the convoy headed for Oran and one headed for Algiers. The movement of these separate convoys must then be carefully regulated so that they arrived simultaneously on November 8 at their respective immediate objectives.

Even more serious in its adverse effect upon Torch was the President's and State Department's French policy of friendliness toward Vichy and hostility toward de Gaulle. . . .

As October gave way to November, Roosevelt sent to Churchill a copy of the personal message he proposed to flash to Marshal Pétain at the instant the initial landings were made in Morocco, Oran, and Algiers. It had evidently been composed in August or early September, when he yet believed that the Torch landings would be made in mid-October, for the original draft, signed in his characteristically bold and heavy hand, as if he meant it to be the actual document that Pétain received, was dated October 15. Its opening was effusive. "My dear old friend," it began, "I am sending this message to you not only as Chef d'État of the United States to the Chef d'État of the Republic of France but also as one of your friends and comrades of the great days of 1918. May we both live to see France victorious again against the ancient enemy." Its third sentence absolved the Pétain government of all blame for the French surrender of 1940, saying "your government concluded, of necessity, the Armistice Convention" at a time when "it was impossible for any of us to foresee the program of systematic plunder which the German Reich would inflict upon the French people." There followed a carefully worded argument for the action the United States now took (it was portrayed as a preemptive strike on behalf of France, since Germany and Italy were preparing "to invade French North Africa" and the "powerful American armed forces" now landing were "to cooperate with the governing agencies of Algeria, Tunisia, and Morocco in repelling" the Axis aggression); but effusiveness again entered at the message's close. Pétain, "the venerated hero of Verdun," was asked to accept "warm regards" from "your friend."[5]

Churchill's immediate response to this gave muted expression to the outrage and anxiety it provoked in him (in his war memoirs, he makes acid comment upon Roosevelt's attempt to "revive" the "somewhat outdated glories of Verdun"). Even so, his message of November 2 had the tone of a rebuke: "Will you allow me to say that your proposed message to Pétain seems to me too kind? . . . He has used his reputation to do our cause injuries no lesser man could have done. I beg you to think of the effect on the De Gaullists, to whom we have serious obligations and who have now to go through the great trial of being kept outside. I am advised that unfavourable reactions would be produced in other quarters." He conceded that the Roosevelt missive should be a "friendly" one. "But will you consider toning it down a bit?" Two days later, Roosevelt replied, saying he agreed the message should be "toned down" and had "rewritten it so that I am sure it will not offend the friends of France." (His "rewriting" consisted of substituting "Marshall Pétain" for "My dear old friend" in the salutation, striking out of the missive's first sentence that portion referring to "comradeship" during "the great days of 1918," eliminating the third sentence altogether, striking "of necessity" from the sentence about the surrender of 1940, and eliminating all reference to Verdun along with the subscriptive "your friend.")[6]

Wholly different was the situation as regards de Gaulle. Here Churchill's concern was with an excess of antipathy, not of amiability.

From the very first of the Torch planning, Roosevelt had insisted that de Gaulle and the Free French must be wholly excluded from the operation. Further: "I . . . consider it essential that de Gaulle . . . be permitted to have no repeat no information whatever [about Torch] regardless of how irritated or irritating he may become," he had wired the Prime Minister on September 16. And in this, Churchill had initially concurred ("I did not contest these resolves," is the way he puts it in his war memoirs), largely for security reasons; he vividly remembered that a cooperative attempt by the British and de Gaulle's Free French to seize Dakar in the fall of 1940 had been fatally compromised by the leakage of prior information about it to the Vichy French, allegedly by loose-tongued Gaullists of whom de Gaulle himself may have been one. But Churchill's concurrence was reluctant. He felt that Roosevelt's insistence was determined in considerable part by "prejudices against General de Gaulle," as he puts it in his war memoirs. He agreed that open participation of the Free French in Torch would make certain a maximum resistance by the Vichyites, who controlled French North Africa's military forces—de Gaulle had damned them as betrayers of France; they had formally condemned him (in absentia) to death for treason—and that therefore there should be no such participation. But he doubted that the French military would be persuaded by American policy to offer no resistance to an American invasion even if initially convinced, as they could hardly be in the circumstances, that it truly *was* an exclusively American operation. He worried, too, that thanks to the Roosevelt-Hull "prejudices," American Fifth Column activities in North Africa, upon whose garnered information Roosevelt and the military staff chiefs heavily relied, were ignoring or wholly failing to cultivate precisely those elements of the general populace that were most passionately anti-Vichy and pro-Ally; indeed, they were bound to do so, since these elements were certain to be strongly inclined toward the Free French movement, if not actually partisans of it. And underlying and permeating all these concerns was an acute consciousness "of our British relationship with de Gaulle and the gravity of the affront which he would have to suffer by being deliberately excluded from all share in the design."[7]

On November 5, the day on which the convoys bound for Oran and Algiers converged for passage that night through the Strait of Gibraltar, the Former Naval Person wired Roosevelt: "It will be necessary for me to explain Torch to De Gaulle sometime during D minus one when it is certain the weather is right. You will remember that I have exchanged letters with him of a solemn kind in 1940 recognizing him as the Leader of Free Frenchmen. I am confident his military honour can be trusted. . . . I shall explain to him that the reason I have not mentioned Torch to him is that it is a United States enterprise and a United States secret and that the reason he and his friends are not in on it is not any want of goodwill on our joint part toward him and his movement, but because of the local complications in the Torch area and the need to have as little fighting as possible." He went on to say that "as consolation prize" and "proof we do not think of throwing over the Free French," he planned to permit de Gaulle's announcement on that same D minus one (Friday, November 7) that the governor-general of Madagascar would be one General Paul Legentilhomme, whom de Gaulle had urgently recommended for the post.[8]

He was jarred by Roosevelt's immediate response to this—more jarred, no doubt, than Roosevelt had been by the Churchillian response to the proposed letter to Pétain, since Churchill's objection was grounded in facts that Roosevelt recognized as facts, whereas Roosevelt's present reaction had, in Churchill's view, no factual justification whatever.

Within minutes after reading what Churchill had written, the President talked with Admiral Leahy about it. Within an hour or so thereafter, he wired the Prime Minister that he was "very apprehensive in regard to the adverse effect . . . any introduction of de Gaulle into the Torch operation [as if this were what Churchill had proposed] would have upon our promising efforts to attach a large part of the French African forces to our expedition. Therefore I consider it inadvisable for you to give de Gaulle any information in regard to Torch until subsequent to a successful landing." Churchill might then "inform him that the American Command of an American expedition with my approval insisted upon complete secrecy as a safety precaution." He manifested no concern whatever for de Gaulle's "feelings." The Free French leader's "announcement on Friday of a Governor-General of Madagascar," he said, ". . . should be sufficient at the present time to maintain his prestige with his followers."

Next day, the Prime Minister perforce agreed to do what the President wished. He did so regretfully. "We are ready to accept your view," he wrote, but "I am . . . sorry about De Gaulle," who actually posed no security risk since "[o]f course we control all his telegrams outward."[9]

III

ON that same eventful November 5, in a fully armed Flying Fortress dubbed the *Red Gremlin,* accompanied by five other B-17s, Eisenhower flew to Gibraltar, where an advance command post had been prepared for him. It was a hazardous flight. In England and all the way south, the weather was fouled by rain, fog, and a ceiling near zero—so fouled that the pilot of the general's plane* had strongly recommended another postponement of a takeoff already

---

*This pilot was Major Paul W. Tibbets, Jr., destined to be remembered in history as the Colonel Tibbets who piloted the B-29 *Enola Gay* that, on August 6, 1945, dropped a U-235 bomb on Hiroshima, Japan.

twice postponed. "No," Eisenhower had said, "we have to go." Most of the way down, they rode the dark air barely a hundred feet above the dark waves, and in order to reach the landing pattern over Gibraltar's airfield, they had to climb steeply into clouds where, it was rumored, a German plane might be lurking. Eisenhower frankly confessed to great relief when, at last safe on the ground at four-thirty in the afternoon, he shook hands with Lieutenant General Sir F. N. Mason-MacFarlane, Gibraltar's governor.[10]

The office in which he was to work, and to which he was introduced early in the following morning, was one of a series of fourteen chambers carved deep into the bowels of the fabled Rock (the largest of them, which had a thirty-foot ceiling and a huge operations map of North Africa on one of its walls, served as the supreme command's war room). To reach it, he had to walk—though actually, after the first morning, he always trotted—through half a mile of chilly, dripping, ill-lit tunnel, and the room he then entered, though well lighted, was a cheerless place, also a crowded one, since, though of very modest size, it was shared by him with his deputy, Mark Clark. In the dank, heavy, perpetually chilly atmosphere of these headquarters, one somehow *felt* the weight of the 1,400 feet of limestone that towered above it, and God knows Eisenhower needed not even the slightest environmental addition to the spiritual burden he already carried! Heavy enough was the responsibility he bore for great military events, now under way, over which he no longer had any decisive control. Active management of the operation had passed wholly, for the time being, into the hands of the tactical commanders; all the supreme commander could now do with regard to them was await the outcome of what had been ordered; and he must do so in full consciousness of how very much there was in this hugely complicated enterprise that could go disastrously wrong!

The American troops sailing from England were inadequately trained for any strongly opposed landing, a fact that had been glaringly demonstrated in the single set of master exercises it had been possible to hold in the limited time available. Ghastly errors were made upon Scottish shores that, if repeated on African shores, could spell catastrophe, *unless* complete tactical surprise were achieved. And the possibility of this last might no longer exist. The German top command, forewarned by reports of unprecedentedly massive Allied movements toward northwestern Africa, might at this very moment be concentrating U-boat wolf-packs in Mediterranean waters and Luftwaffe power on Mediterranean airfields. Soon, submarines might penetrate the screen of escort vessels and torpedo troop transports, slaughtering Allied soldiers and sailors by the thousands and disrupting the operation before the convoys were within fifty miles of their objectives. Simultaneously, the air over these objectives, which Allied land-based aircraft could reach only from the single (though now greatly enlarged) airfield at Gibraltar, might be dominated by Axis planes, enabling perhaps the capture by Nazi paratroops of Algerian airstrips essential to the exploitation of any initial success. And what if the powerful French fleet came out of Toulon to join the Italian? What if Franco, giving the lie to all "expert" assurances that he would not do so, attacked Gibraltar's airfield and opened his northern border to German troops sweeping down through Vichy France? What if the meteorological forecasts for the French Moroccan coast proved inaccurate and an Atlantic storm piled a raging surf so high upon the beaches that every landing attempt was frustrated by it?

Eisenhower did not, of course, dwell upon these anxieties. On the contrary, though compelled to remain constantly aware of their root causes, since these would be factors in any ultimate decision between aborting Torch and going on with it, he raised a thick wall of will against the anxieties themselves. "Don't worry about things you can do nothing about," he had often counseled his wife, Mamie. "Worry only about those you can."

But alas, at Gibraltar, he was at once required to "do something," hence to worry, about crucially important political matters for the handling of which he was woefully unprepared by experience or education or natural interest and concerning which, as he would soon suspect, he had been badly misinformed, or at best very partially informed, by his chief political adviser on North African affairs.

This adviser was Robert Daniel Murphy.

Eisenhower had first heard of him soon after assuming command of Torch, a Washington communication having then told him that this man, a veteran of twenty-odd years of service in the U.S. State Department's diplomatic corps, had been designated head of Torch's civil affairs section. Subsequently, the general had learned something of Murphy's professional career. The diplomat, fluent in both the German and French languages, had headed the U.S. consular office in Munich in 1921–1925, the years during which Hitler's National Socialist Party, headquartered in Munich, made its first important appearance upon the German political scene (the abortive Munich Beer Hall Putsch was in 1923). He had served ten consecutive years, 1930–1940, in the U.S. embassy in Paris, under three ambassadors, becoming under the third of these, William Bullitt, the embassy counselor and second in command; had remained in Paris with Bullitt after the French government had fled to Bordeaux and the Germans occupied the city; had then gone to Vichy as chargé d'affaires and acting head of the U.S. embassy after Bullitt returned to Washington and before Leahy arrived in Vichy. He was not at all the "striped pants" son of privilege deemed typical of the State Department's diplomatic corps. His childhood background was every bit as humble as Eisenhower's own. His Irish Catholic father, a Milwaukee native, had been a ne'er-do-well whose formal education ended with the fourth grade and whose widely various employments (they included saloon keeping and work as a railroad section hand) had been interspersed with long periods of unemployment. The boy Robert had grown up accustomed to economic insecurity

and hard work—had had to work his way through high school and college, relying heavily upon the typing and shorthand skills he had acquired in a Milwaukee business college—had had to exercise to the full his natural ability and
industriousness to obtain a law degree from George Washington University and
win admission to the District of Columbia Bar Association. He had begun his
foreign service career in 1920, after passing the examinations required for becoming a career consular. He believed that he identified himself emotionally
with the underprivileged, but if he actually did, it was not in ways that hindered
his "upward mobility": strongly attracted by the wealthy and powerful, he fully
exercised in his contacts with them an ingratiating Irish charm. He was, by nature, a remarkably likable man. Eisenhower would judge him intelligent, widely
informed, and genuinely modest (his humor inclined toward self-deprecation),
but also self-secure, self-respective, and self-confident—a man who called himself and sincerely believed himself to be "a liberal" and whose personal experience of the Nazis in Munich had made him anti-Nazi years before most
Americans were aware of Hitler's existence.[11]

His intimate concern with French North African affairs was initiated in September 1940 when he was abruptly, mysteriously summoned to Washington
from Vichy. Not until he arrived in the capital had he learned that the President
himself had summoned him for what proved a lengthy off-the-record tête-à-tête
in the Oval Office. By the end of it, Murphy was committed to the covert gathering of information about the political situation in Tunisia, Algeria, and French
Morocco and also to the recruitment and organization of pro-Allies support
among the North African French. The belief that such activity could be fruitful had been encouraged in Roosevelt's mind by the fact that French General
Maxime Weygand had just been named delegate general of French North
Africa, with command of all land and air forces in those colonies. Rumor had it
(a rumor possibly originated and spread by Gaullists) that Weygand intended to
reorganize and rearm a formidable North African army of 120,000, with some
200,000 reserves, for anti-Axis action, and Roosevelt thought there might be
truth in this. Surely the elderly (seventy-two) but still vigorous former supreme
commander of France's land forces, whose devotion to the honor of French
arms was notoriously passionate, could not condone for long an abject subservience to the Germans. Murphy therefore should make the establishment of
cooperative relations with the general his first order of business, said the President, who authorized the diplomat to promise and expedite covert American aid
of whatever pro-Allies movement developed. But what about de Gaulle, in this
context? The question occurred to Murphy, but it is significant of his mind-set
and way of operating that he did not voice it at that time. Less than three months
had passed since the exiled general "broadcast from London his historic denunciation of the French-German armistice"—the armistice Weygand had forced
upon Reynaud, who wanted to continue the war—yet the President, while dis-

cussing "every pertinent topic [every topic he deemed pertinent] with me during our unhurried conversation," made but a single reference to the Free French leader, saying then "that the ill-fated attempt to capture Dakar confirmed his poor opinion of de Gaulle's judgment." Clearly, he had "already decided" that the Free French leader was not to be considered "a major factor in French affairs." He closed the interview with an offhand remark: "If you learn any-thing . . . of special interest, send it to me. Don't bother going through State De-partment channels."[12]

This last had startled Murphy. He puzzled over it while crossing the street to the State Department and, as soon as he could do so, asked Acting Secretary Welles if the President "really meant for me to communicate directly with the White House." He was assured that Roosevelt did. "This is the way he often operates," said Welles, his tone and expression showing no such resentment of this procedure as Hull would probably have shown. This meant in practice that Murphy was to be the President's personal representative, his secret agent, in Africa.[13]

He began his North African operation with a whirlwind three-week tour of Algeria and French Morocco, during which, as per Roosevelt's instructions, he established friendly relations with Weygand and initiated a French-American economic agreement. This became, after months of confusion and many vicis-situdes, an official document known to history as the Murphy-Weygand Accord. By its terms, A) French officials were permitted to use French funds that had been frozen in U.S. banks to purchase specified quantities of nonstrategic American goods for use in North Africa; and B) the United States arranged with the British, after lengthy and difficult negotiations, the passage of the cargo thus purchased through the stringent economic blockade that the British had im-posed upon France in July 1940. Of almost equal importance was a secret un-derstanding, embodied in a marginal note (initialed by Murphy and Weygand) on the official document, extending to the U.S. consular staffs in North Africa a privilege normally limited to the diplomatic corps—that of using secret codes and couriers with locked pouches for communication with Washington. Since these consular staffs now included twelve newly installed "vice consuls" who were actually intelligence agents working under Murphy's direction, the privi-lege "became the basis of one of the most effective intelligence operations of the war," writes Murphy, "for it provided that Americans not only could watch what transpired in North Africa, but also could get out uncensored confidential reports to our government."[14]

The secret intelligence these reports contained, however, was, as Churchill feared, limited in extent, deformed in shape, and flawed in substance by the Washington policy that ruled its gathering. As coming events would abundantly demonstrate, there *was* in the French colonies, as in metropolitan France, an or-ganized resistance movement of growing effectiveness. But since it was wholly Gaullist, Murphy and his minions shunned contact with it. They dealt instead with a various collection of non- or anti-Gaullists of whom a significant number were dubious characters possessed of pasts highly unsavory to all who were truly committed to democracy. Several of them were wealthy businessmen, highly conservative or blackly reactionary in their politico-economic views, who had contributed actively to the corruption and downfall of the Third Republic and who, after that event, had easily accommodated themselves to an authoritarian pro-Axis regime in unoccupied France. In consequence of this, they were acutely aware that their fortunes and even their lives would be at risk if ever the Gaullists gained ruling power. They had begun to worry, as England continued to refuse to "have her neck wrung like a chicken" (Weygand's words) and the United States came increasingly to her aid, that the Axis just might lose the war after all. Their fear would become acute anxiety after Hitler invaded Russia and Russia stubbornly refused to collapse. They were at great pains to hedge their bets.

Representative of these men, and a chief one among them, was Jacques Lemaigre-Dubreuil.

He was soon to be presented to the Anglo-American public by Murphy and the State Department as "a leader of the French underground." Actually, and not only according to the Free French, he was among the most notorious of the French collaborators with the Nazis. He was executive head of Huiles Lesieur, the largest vegetable oil company in the French empire, an immensely lucrative enterprise in a time when fats were in extremely short supply. In the 1930s, he had organized, financed, and headed the Taxpayers' League, a reactionary pressure group that bitterly, actively opposed democratic institutions and procedures in France. He had been a moving force behind the Fascist march upon the Chamber of Deputies in early February 1934 (addressing a mass rally on the eve of this event, he cried: ". . . [I]f necessary we will use whips and sticks to sweep out this chamber of incompetents").[15] He was widely believed to have financed from his ample resources the Cougaulard attempt to overthrow the Republic in 1937. After the fall of France, he had suffered no such reduction of fortune or freedom of movement as was the bitter lot of most of the French citizenry. He received special treatment from the Nazi conquerors of his country. He was permitted, indeed encouraged, to reopen his company's great Dunkirk plant, in occupied France—was permitted to retain the regency of the Bank of France, which had been his for years before the war, a post in which, according to the Free French, he operated as an agent of the Banque Worms, through which the French economy was enslaved by the Third Reich—was permitted by Vichy to travel freely through occupied France and France's African colonies, whence came the peanuts that supplied the bulk of the oil his company marketed. In conversation with fellow big-business men, he emphatically agreed with Laval, he even asserted, that a German victory was essential to the welfare of France, since the alternative to it would be the Bolshevization of Europe.

But this last, he explained to Murphy during their first private talks, in Algiers in December 1940, was camouflage. His real commitment was to the Allied cause, his expressed pro-Nazism a mere and false appearance. He "would do anything he could to bring about the defeat of Germany." He went so far as to claim he had fabricated a "police record of himself which indicated that he had been a pro-Nazi collaborator long before the war" and "had placed this record in files available to the Germans." Murphy, by his own account, found this "melodramatic tale . . . pretty hard to believe but . . . passed it on to Washington, sprinkling my report liberally with salt." Lemaigre-Dubreuil was, however, a highly polished gentleman—*too* highly polished, said those who deemed him as slippery as the oil that enriched him—whose luxurious abode in Algiers became a place of refreshing relaxation for the overworked, overwrought American diplomat. His manners were impeccable, his conversation agreeable. And as he "continued to bring me information about relations between French industrialists and the Germans which proved correct," writes Murphy, "my confidence in him grew." Also, one may be sure, the information he brought accorded well with the policy directive under which the American worked in that it downplayed or excluded any evidence of strength in the Gaullist movement in Africa.[16]

In the end, Murphy's confidence in Lemaigre-Dubreuil was absolute. It was to him Murphy turned after Torch had been decided upon and the quest for a pro-Ally general whom the North African French would follow became increasingly urgent.

Weygand was by that time out of the picture, as he should have been from the first. He had shown his true colors when, in the fall of 1940, he promptly forwarded to Pétain a confidential message from Churchill to him promising full British support if he would sever his ties with Vichy and head a North African government of his own. And when Pétain, at German insistence, recalled him in November 1941, he obeyed the order at once and without demur, retiring with evident relief to private life. The man who replaced him as delegate general, Admiral Raymond Fenard, was assigned no military command authority and in any case declared himself unavailable for any such service as the Americans proposed.

Who, then?

Lemaigre-Dubreuil proposed General Henri Honoré Giraud, who during World War I and the suppression of the Riff rebellion in French Morocco had become one of the greatest of French national heroes; whose heroic standing was now at its highest as a result of his recent daring escape from the German fortress of Königstein, where he had been a Nazi prisoner since his capture in the summer of 1940; and whose hatred of Germans was notorious. Admittedly, he was no politician, was indeed famously antipathetical to politics and politicians (he was equally famously antipathetical to Charles de Gaulle, as Lemaigre-Dubreuil no doubt mentioned, having bitterly clashed with him in the years between the wars over the proper employment of tanks in battle), but he had great leadership capacity, said the French industrialist. The North African French would be certain to rally round him enthusiastically if he asked them to do so. And though he was now in hiding, in his sister's house near Lyons, there would be no difficulty in establishing swift and secure confidential communications with him, for Lemaigre-Dubreuil was on intimate, friendly terms with him. Murphy acted promptly upon this suggestion. Lemaigre-Dubreuil was authorized to sound out the French general. He learned that Giraud was waiting and planning for the day when American troops would land in France but doubted that the Americans could land in sufficient strength upon North African shores to be successful in the fall of 1942. Only after several clandestine visits by Lemaigre-Dubreuil were the general's doubts overcome and a promise secured from him to participate in the planned operation. His promise was conditional, however. He demanded two things: one, the landing force must be exclusively American; two, either he or another French general must have overall command of all the troops, American as well as French, who fought on French soil.[17]

Giraud had not yet firmly committed himself to the North African operation, though it seemed highly probable that he would soon do so, at the time of the only face-to-face meeting with Murphy that Eisenhower had had prior to his flight to Gibraltar.

This was on September 14. The diplomat had then come secretly to England in a bomber flown by Ferry Command from Washington, where he had been summoned from North Africa for final pre-Torch consultations with Roosevelt, the Joint Chiefs of Staff, and State Department officials. He came in U.S. Army uniform under the nom de guerre of "Colonel McGowan"—a highly imperfect disguise, as it seemed to General Walter ("Beetle") Smith, Eisenhower's chief of staff, who greeted him at Hendon airfield and took him by car to Telegraph Cottage, Eisenhower's secret retreat in the English countryside some forty minutes from the general's office at 20 Grosvenor Square. Smith was a stickler for military discipline and decorum, and in his eyes the uniform the visitor wore failed to hide, it rather emphasized, a physical posture and facial demeanor that were unmistakably civilian. Though Murphy was tall and broad shouldered, his shoulders were constantly slightly stooped, and the expression on his initially smiling countenance became, when his smile faded, both tense and tired. He, who normally appeared to most people youthful for his years, looked at that moment older than his actual age of forty-seven (he would be forty-eight on October 28). He had been under intense pressure for many months and knew he was now to be critically examined by men who must decide how much trust should be placed in the information he gave them and how far he himself should be entrusted with information about the time and force strength of the upcoming operation—information he had to have if he were to obtain a maximum effective cooperation from the pro-Ally French with whom he had been conspiring.

But after a couple of hours of concentrated talk with Eisenhower and Smith, the three of them seated in the shade of a pine tree on the cottage lawn, he was enabled to relax somewhat. He felt he had passed the initial test with flying colors. Nor was he given reason to fear that this judgment of him was reversed or negatively revised by the eight or so other VIPs (they included Mark Clark, Ambassador Winant, Averell Harriman, and British foreign officer W. H. B. Mack) who met and talked with him in the living room of the cottage that evening. "If all that he [Murphy] anticipates in the way of French cooperation comes to pass, many of our worries will have been needless," Eisenhower's naval aide, Harry Butcher, recorded in the diary he kept for the supreme commander. But concern was, of course, expressed over Giraud's insistence upon a French general's top command of all forces fighting on French soil, and Eisenhower was at pains to disabuse Murphy of any notion that such an arrangement was possible. He said "that the question of command . . . could not be settled at once," according to the Butcher diary, yet he made it emphatically clear that an Allied force of half a million Americans and British, which is the size it would soon have in North Africa, could not possibly "be placed under a French general." Murphy was told he might promise Giraud "that the *French* troops would remain under the command of a French general," provided that, and *only* if, they pledged to the Allied commander in chief "the fullest and most whole-hearted cooperation. . . ."[18]

Murphy stayed the night at Telegraph and, after the others had left, had a couple of hours of relaxed conversation with Eisenhower alone, during which he was given considerably more of the information he needed, though with stringent restrictions upon its use in his dealings with the Algerian French. Also, the two then developed a personal rapport that was soon to become a needed protection, in Eisenhower's mind, against what might otherwise have become a furious resentment of the difficulties now rising for the general out of the diplomat's conspiratorial arrangements.

After his day with the Torch commander, Murphy returned by plane to Washington. From there, a month later, he flew to Algiers, arriving on October 16 to find that the arrangement with Giraud was indeed becoming firm; for within an hour or so after he arrived in his office, he was informed by General Charles Emmanuel Mast, commander of the French XIX Army Corps, stationed in Algeria, that he, Mast, had been named by Giraud as his personal representative in Algiers. More surprising was Admiral Fenard's presentation of himself to Murphy on that same day as the designated representative of Admiral Jean-François Darlan. The latter had evidently "sensed that some kind of decision must have been made [by the Allies] about North Africa," to quote Murphy, and now signaled a wish for involvement in it. The move was not wholly unexpected: Darlan had made "overtures" to Murphy in the spring and summer of 1942, the first of them immediately after Laval's return to power in April, and though the diplomat's reports of them to Washington had received no reply, they had been "discussed by Eisenhower's Anglo-American staff during my visit to London in September," as Murphy writes.[19]

Though a dubious character indeed, Darlan was also (or appeared to be) a man of formidable power. He had replaced Laval as Vichy's head of government and foreign minister after Laval's downfall in December 1940 and had then also taken over the Ministries of Defense and the Interior.* In February 1942, he had by legal act been designated Pétain's successor as head of state. He had perforce given up his cabinet posts upon Laval's return to power (it was then that he first signaled his possible willingness to cooperate with the Allies), but he yet remained Pétain's legal successor and, having been returned to active duty as admiral, was now also the commander in chief of *all* of Vichy's armed forces. He therefore seemed in a position to influence Pétain to do as Roosevelt was asking Pétain to do, in the personal appeal to be dispatched on D-day. And just possibly, even if Pétain refused to do this, Darlan might somehow persuade the Vichyite French military in North Africa to welcome the troops of Torch as liberators, instead of resisting them as invaders. Hence, there was not the slightest doubt in Murphy's mind that the admiral must be dealt with, and it was with a natural excitement that he on October 17 sent "several messages" to Roosevelt and Eisenhower, the only people to whom he now reported, describing the "encouraging overtures" that had been made to him. Equal to the excitement of the sender of these messages was that aroused by them in their readers at 20 Grosvenor Square and the White House. In both places, it was immediately assumed that "Darlan wants to play ball." To Roosevelt, this meant that his highly unpopular Vichy policy might be about to be abundantly justified by events, winning for the Allies not only the French North African colonies along with a sizable French army, but also the dazzling prize that the policy had been originally designed to achieve, namely, the mighty French fleet now immobilized at Toulon. He at once, on that same October 17, sent through Leahy a cablegram to Murphy, authorizing the diplomat to initiate any arrangement with Darlan that in his judgment might assist the military operations. To Eisenhower, the news meant that the threat of any great or prolonged struggle with French troops was significantly lessened, perhaps eliminated. He, on that same October 17, "devised a formula," quickly unofficially approved in both London and Washington, whereby Giraud and Darlan would "work together as a team, dividing the top French command [in North Africa] between them." As for the attitude at No. 10 Downing Street, Churchill in his farewell talk with Eisenhower when

---

*In the latter capacity, he administered the brutal anti-Semitic activities in which Vichy willingly cooperated with the Nazis. He was also responsible, directly and indirectly, for the imprisonment, torture, and death of a number of brave Frenchmen, a few of them Jews, most of them Gaullists, who dared resist Vichy's pro-Nazi rule.

Eisenhower left for Gibraltar two and a half weeks later included the "earnest" remark "If I could meet Darlan, much as I hate him, I would cheerfully crawl on my hands and knees for a mile if by doing so I could get him to bring that fleet of his into the circle of Allied forces."[20]

In Algiers, the conspiratorial activity in which Murphy was involved now became a frenzied comedy of errors whence issued more of evil than of good for the Allied cause.

Far from welcoming the appearance of Darlan upon the African scene, Mast and his associates viewed it with alarm, believing it likely to shift ruling power away from their hero Giraud to a man whom Mast described as an unprincipled opportunist, wholly untrustworthy—an estimate of Darlan that agreed with the one Leahy had given Murphy in a March 1941 conversation. It was perhaps in part because of the Darlan overture that Mast, despite the fact that he and his colleagues believed they had months in which to prepare for an event actually only three weeks away, now insisted upon the immediate holding of staff talks between the French and Americans. Murphy at once set about arranging them, he being convinced that a refusal to do so would, in the circumstances, raise debilitating and perhaps totally disruptive suspicions in the Frenchmen's minds. The upshot was a highly secret meeting on October 22 in an isolated farmhouse near the small seacoast town of Cherchell, some twenty miles west of Algiers. Its principal participants (there were a number of others) were short, stocky Mast and tall, lanky Mark Clark, whom Churchill had dubbed the "American Eagle" because of his hawkish appearance and who, coming by plane from London to Gibraltar, arrived via submarine at the secret rendezvous. Murphy was the presiding presence. And though Eisenhower's deputy left for London in the darkness of the night of October 22–23 convinced that the meeting had been a success, he having obtained from it valuable information about the location and strengths of French North African troop units, and about the storage places and quantities of such vital supplies as gasoline and ammunition, the affair was, overall, a fiasco.

Clark, like Murphy, was under the strictest orders not to impart to the Frenchmen any precise information about the times and locations of the landings. The two Americans were unable, therefore, to correct the Frenchmen's dangerously mistaken assumption that they yet had many weeks of time in which to prepare for the operation (indeed, the meeting did more to strengthen than weaken this belief). Neither could the Americans say anything that would "clarify the status of French commanders either in military or political affairs," as Murphy later put it. When Mast demanded positive assurances that Giraud would become commander of all the Allied forces once they had landed, Clark, than whom few men could have been less suited to the role he was now required to play, made a deliberately ambiguous, hence essentially mendacious, reply, saying that of course there could be no shift of command during the actual landings but that

Giraud would be given the top command "as soon as possible." When Clark then proposed Eisenhower's formula for a division of authority between Giraud and Darlan, he encountered furious opposition from Mast. The sneaky, devious Darlan was a "political" admiral, not a fighting one, said Mast, and his belated attempt to climb onto the Allied bandwagon, if permitted to succeed, could only needlessly complicate further an already overly complex situation: the French African army and air force would follow Giraud, in any case, and the French navy would go where the army went. It was on this note of disagreement that the conference ended, late that night, with the French conspirators more widely misled and profoundly confused than before, with nothing accomplished that could importantly help Torch, but with a good deal done to ensure grave victory-threatening political troubles in the immediate future. Chief among this last was a hardening and deepening, by what Mast and his colleagues had so passionately asserted, of Murphy's conviction that Giraud's top-level association with Torch was absolutely essential to the operation's success.[21]

Next day, the diplomat sent Lemaigre-Dubreuil by plane to the south of France to report the conference results to Giraud. Four days later, the "irreplaceable intermediary" (Murphy's labeling) returned to Algiers with a letter from Giraud demanding assurances in writing that he would be assigned the "Interallied Command" *within forty-eight hours* after the landings and that the African operation would be quickly followed by an Allied landing in the south of France! Murphy says in his memoirs that he found this "disturbing." He immediately desperately begged Eisenhower for permission to inform Mast, at long last, that the expeditionary force would arrive "in early November" and, receiving it, gave the information to Mast next day (October 28, Murphy's birthday). He hoped thus to inject realistic sanity into a situation that had become for him a fantastic nightmare. Instead, he provoked in Mast a storm of protest and recrimination so violent, he feared it might result in a fatal breach of operational security. The French corps commander bitterly resented the American lack of confidence in him and his colleagues, who were risking their lives in support of this enterprise. The fullest exercise of Murphy's diplomatic skills was required to calm the general down sufficiently to enable the new information to be sent through him to Giraud. And Giraud's reaction to it was every bit as furiously negative as Mast's had been. In a November 1 missive, he told Murphy flatly that early November was impossibly soon; he was involved in the creation of a network of pro-Allied support in France, he said, and could not possibly leave until November 20 at the earliest.[22]

Murphy was now frantic. On that same Saturday, November 1, he dashed off a cable to Roosevelt, with a copy to Eisenhower, urgently recommending that the Torch landings be delayed for two weeks to enable Giraud "to perfect his metropolitan organization." Said Murphy: "I am convinced that the invasion of North Africa without favorable French High Command will be a catastrophe.

The delay of two weeks, *unpleasant as it may be* ... is insignificant compared with the result involving serious opposition of the French Army to our landing."[23]

Because of the time difference between London and the American East Coast, Eisenhower read this hours before Roosevelt did so at Hyde Park, where he arrived from Washington that Saturday morning. The harassed Torch commander's confidence in Murphy was, for the moment, overwhelmed by mingled astonishment, anger, and disgust. "It is inconceivable that Murphy can recommend such a delay with his intimate knowledge of the operation and the present location of troops and convoys afloat," he at once cabled Marshall. "It is likewise inconceivable to me that our mere failure to concede such demands as have been made would result in having the French North African Army meet us with serious opposition. Recommend the President advise Murphy immediately that his suggested action is utterly impossible in view of the advanced state of the operation and that we will proceed to execute this operation with more determination than ever." Roosevelt, who must in any case have promptly rejected the Murphy recommendation, was perhaps encouraged by the Eisenhower-Marshall advice to do so more brusquely than he might otherwise have done. To Murphy went a cable on Sunday morning, November 2, signed by Leahy: "The decision of the President is that the operation will be carried out as now planned and that you will do your utmost to secure the understanding and cooperation of the French officials with whom you are now in contact." (In the afternoon of that day, Roosevelt told Churchill, "I had to make a quick decision of great importance this morning but it was so obviously right and called for such immediate action that I did not even refer it to you. Please ask the American Eagle about it.")*[24]

A red-faced Murphy removed some of the sting of humiliating rebuke by promptly interpreting the White House order to mean that "it was up to me to deal with our French allies in whatever ways I thought best"—and what he thought best was the compounding of Clark's fumbling Cherchell mendacity. Late on that Sunday, he sent Lemaigre-Dubreuil back to France with a written message that certainly *seemed* definitely to promise the general the supreme command of the operation, not after the landings were consolidated, but as soon as he was physically present on the scene. This at least achieved its immediate intended purpose: Giraud was persuaded to abandon his obviously futile insistence upon an operational postponement and come at once out of France. Doing so was for him a life-risking enterprise. First, he must and did slip away from

---

*He wrote this at the close of his answer to the Churchill message about Eleanor Roosevelt's triumph in England, quoted on page 646. "I am delighted that my wife's visit seems to be going so successfully, thanks in large part to what you and Mrs. Churchill are doing for her," was his message's opening sentence.

his hiding place, undetected by Germans or Vichyites, to a designated point on the seacoast and there, with only three companions (aides and staff officers), ride a rowboat with muffled oars in the darkness of night out to a submarine a thousand yards offshore. He, a passionate Anglophobe, had insisted that the submarine be an American one, but since not a single American submarine was then in the Mediterranean, an American navy captain was made the nominal commander of the British vessel that Giraud boarded. The British crew of this submarine then made, many hours later, difficult contact at sea, at a stipulated place, with an Allied flying boat to which Giraud transferred and in which he was flown, not to Algiers, where Murphy had made elaborate plans for his arrival in the afternoon of November 7, or early evening at the latest, but to Gibraltar. He arrived there shortly after four o'clock in the afternoon and was at once conducted through the chilly, dim-lighted, dripping tunnel through the Rock to the dank "dungeon" (so Eisenhower called it) that was the supreme commander's office.

"General Giraud has arrived," announced General Giraud. "General Giraud is ready to assume command of the operation."

Eisenhower had been told by the two political advisers who had accompanied him to Gibraltar (H. Freeman Matthews of the State Department, Mack of the British Foreign Office) that Giraud, whose alleged ability to rally the North African French military to the Allied cause they continually stressed to the supreme commander, had some seriously mistaken notions of what his role in the enterprise was to be. It was they who had at the last minute, without notifying Murphy, suggested that Giraud be brought first to Gibraltar, so that he would (could be made to) understand the actual command situation when he arrived in Algiers. Eisenhower was therefore prepared to deal correctively, patiently, with the French general's misconceptions. But he was not prepared to deal, amid the already abundant anxieties of this D minus one, with the inflexibility, the personal arrogance, the stubborn refusal to face facts or listen to reason, that the Frenchman now manifested. Rigidity was Giraud's predominant characteristic. He came clad in a rumpled and stained civilian suit, having fallen into the sea during his risky transfer from rowboat to submarine the night before, yet "looked very much a soldier," as Eisenhower would record in his war memoirs. Though obviously tired, as well he might be after what he (at age sixty-three) had gone through during the last twenty-four hours, he held his more than six feet of height ramrod stiff as he and Eisenhower shook hands. And he thereafter made it immediately clear that the rigidity of his physical posture was matched by that of his mind, his basic attitudes, his oversize ego, his sense of national and personal honor. His impenetrable, insoluble hardness pressed harshly upon the American commander's overburdened spirit as the talk ground on, hour after hour, with Giraud speaking only French, Eisenhower only English (when the professional interpreter was worn out, Mark Clark, whose French was imperfect, replaced him), and with the same words, the same stated positions, repeated over and over again. Eisenhower laboriously explained, several times, why it was impossible for a Frenchman to be placed in command of forces that contained not a single French soldier and that, indeed, if they were forced to fight initially in the areas they approached, they would do so because Frenchmen chose to be our enemies. To prevent their making this choice was the great and only service that Giraud could at this moment render the Allies and his own country; he could and should proceed at once to North Africa and there rally his fellow countrymen to him, persuading them to turn their weapons, not against their American friends, but against their German enemies. Thus spoke Eisenhower.

The French general's reply, repeated in one form or another ad nauseam, was: "General Giraud must be given command of this operation. General Giraud has been promised this command [he produced Murphy's last letter to him in proof of what he said] and cannot accept less. His countrymen would not understand his doing so and his soldier's honor would be tarnished."

Eisenhower grew stern: If this were Giraud's final word, his chance to play a great role in history would be lost; the operation would proceed as though Giraud had never been consulted.

During the dinnertime break in the talks, Matthews and Mack proposed that Eisenhower end the impasse by giving Giraud nominal command of the operation while reserving to himself the actual command—a subterfuge that Eisenhower flatly, promptly rejected. There had already been far too much subterfuge in this matter, too many calculated ambiguities and false promises: out of them had grown the bitter fruit he now tasted. After dinner, therefore, the futile talk ground on until nearly midnight, by which time, with Giraud's cold good-night ("General Giraud will be a spectator in this affair") grating on his ears, Eisenhower had nearly exhausted his remarkably large store of patience and self-control. What kept them from becoming wholly so was his sympathetic understanding of the disillusionment and profound personal humiliation that this proud Frenchman now suffered in consequence of having been misled, if not actually lied to—this coupled with admiration of the way in which Giraud managed, through it all, to maintain a large measure of personal dignity. Obviously, the French general was brave, strong, and, for all his evident mental limitations, an honorable man.

He also became a more reasonable one, fortunately, during the hours of deep, desperately needed sleep that separated his brusque good-night from his far more genial good-morning to Eisenhower in the governor-general's house next day (by that time, the initial Torch landings were under way). He had changed his mind, he said; he would "participate in the action on the basis we desired," as Eisenhower writes in his memoirs. In return, Eisenhower, vastly relieved, promised that if Giraud succeeded in winning French support, "I would deal

with him as the administrator of that region, pending eventual opportunity for
civil authorities to determine the will of the population."[25]

IV

As always, and in sharp contrast with the average White House meal, the dinner
prepared and served by the Filipino staff at Shangri-la on that evening of Saturday, November 7, was delicious. Its main dish was unique, being musk-ox steak
from one of the vast herd of these supposedly nearly extinct animals that Elliott
Roosevelt had recently discovered as he flew low over Greenland's mile-deep
icecap. There was much talk of this among the President and his small group of
dinner guests, all save one of whom were of his inner circle of personal intimates: Hopkins, his bride, Louise, Grace Tully, Daisy Suckley, and two of the
latter's young nieces (the eighth at table was a personable young navy commander from the White House war room). This talk, however, was among preoccupied minds and did nothing to relieve the nervous tension that brooded over
that table. Roosevelt was its source: he was obviously "on edge," as Grace Tully
writes, and those of his guests who were ignorant of what impended (Grace
Tully was not, nor were Hopkins and the navy officer from the war room) were
nonetheless sure his edginess had a sufficient cause. This created suspense.
When inviting Daisy for this Shangri-la weekend, he had told her that an "egg"
was about to be either "laid" or "hatched" and that, if it were "laid," they might
have to hurry back to Washington—and all that Saturday he kept receiving
phone calls from Washington in a succession that became closer as evening
came on, he replying briefly to each of them in words that revealed nothing to
those who overheard them save that what he listened to was *not* the "important
message" he now frankly said he awaited.[26]

It, the important message, did not come until shortly after dinner—a call from
the War Department, said Grace Tully to him, handing him the phone. She noted
the shaking of his hand (its normal tremor was greatly increased) as he took the
phone and lifted the receiver to his ear. For a long moment, he listened intently,
saying nothing. But his face gradually relaxed into a broad smile, until, finally,
he burst out: "Thank God! Thank God! That sounds grand. Congratulations. Casualties are comparatively light—much below your predictions. Thank God!" It
was not an egg that had been laid, it was an egg that had been hatched; and the
hatchling was prospering! Dropping the phone into its cradle, he turned to the
others, saying: "We have landed in North Africa. Casualties are below expectations. We are striking back."

The tone in which he spoke was one of relief, the intensity of which measured
that of the anxiety, an almost unique postdecision anxiety, that had plagued him
increasingly through the last three months. Despite repeated reassurances by
George Marshall, he had been unable to down a growing fear that catastrophe

would be born of his stubborn insistence upon an operation initially urgently opposed by Marshall, by King, by every other of his key military advisers. He
could not erase from his mind the possibility that he had, after all, wholly mis-
read a key sign, wholly misinterpreted a key clue. And the felt weight of his
consequent *personal* responsibility for an impending slaughter of countless
thousands of young Americans had latterly become crushing, making it very
hard for him to maintain, as he had done, the appearance of serene self-security,
of utter self-confidence, he had presented to the world. But now, in abrupt reversal, he could feel personally responsible for a shining, remarkably bloodless
triumph—feel the discharge of his responsibility, therefore, as an uplifting force
rather than a crushing weight upon his spirit. He was suddenly gloriously happy.
At his request, a portable radio was brought into the room (the large expensive
one was, "as usual," not "working well," writes Daisy), and through it came at
nine o'clock, and in bits and pieces thereafter till midnight, when the Shangri-la
party went to bed, the news that all three of the task forces had made successful
landings and were moving rapidly, with increasing strength, upon their objectives.[27]

Next morning, Sunday, Roosevelt awoke to North African news that confirmed the success of the day before, news also that his personal appeal to the
French people, spoken in French by him and prerecorded for BBC broadcast to
metropolitan and colonial France, had been delivered. ("My friends, who suffer
day and night under the crushing yoke of the Nazis, I speak to you as one who
was with your Army and Navy in France in 1918," it began. "I have held all my
life the deepest friendship for the French people—for the entire French people.
I retain and cherish the friendship of hundreds of French people. . . . I know
your farms, your villages, and your cities. I know your soldiers, professors, and
workmen. . . . I salute again and reiterate my faith in Liberty, Equality, and Fra-
ternity. No two nations exist which are more united by historic and mutually
friendly ties than the people of France and the United States. . . . We come
among you [now] to repulse the cruel invaders who would remove forever your
rights of self-government, your rights to religious freedom and your rights to
live your own lives in peace and security. We come among you solely to defeat
and rout your enemies. Have faith in our words. . . . We assure you that once the
menace of Germany and Italy is removed from you, we shall quit your territory
at once. . . . Do not obstruct, I beg of you, this great purpose. Help us where you
are able, my friends, and we shall see again the glorious day when liberty and
peace shall reign again on earth. *Vive la France éternelle!*")[28] As yet, there was
no reply from Pétain to the personal appeal that Roosevelt had made to him.

As soon as lunch was over, he left Shangri-la and, with Daisy and her nieces
in his car, rode back to Washington. He was still tired. "He paid us the great
compliment of going to sleep," writes Daisy without irony, for she took great
pride in the fact that the President could completely relax and be his "natural"

self in her company. "I had to wake him as we approached the city," because it "wouldn't look well" if people along Washington's streets saw their wartime President "with his eyes closed and his head nodding" on a day of great event.[29]

And in the White House he received an hour or so later the Pétain reply.

"It was with stupor and sadness that I learned . . . of the aggression of your troops against North Africa," wrote the Vichy French chief of state to the President of the United States. "I have read your message. You invoke pretexts which nothing justifies. . . . I have always declared that we would defend our Empire if it were attacked. . . . You should know that I would keep my word. In our misfortune I had, when requesting the armistice, protected our Empire and it is you who acting in the name of a country to which so many memories and ties bind us have taken such a cruel initiative. France and her honor are at stake. We are attacked; we shall defend ourselves; this is the order I am giving."[30]

Though not unexpected, the reply was a disappointment, if not a great enough one to curtail significantly the glowing satisfaction he derived from what was happening, thus far, in North Africa.

Amazing, in view of the vastness and complexity of Torch, was the achievement by the Allies of total strategic as well as tactical surprise. The Germans, the Italians, the Franco Spaniards, and the Vichy French had been persuaded that the Allied convoys entering the Mediterranean through Gibraltar Strait on the night of November 5 were headed for Malta, which was in desperate need of major reinforcement and resupply. They had evidently no certain knowledge whatever of the great armada of 102 ships, 29 of them transports, commanded by U.S. Rear Admiral H. Kent Hewitt, which carried twenty-four thousand American troops under the command of General George Patton, with their supply, from the U.S. East Coast to French Morocco. Hence the ease, despite some horrendous foul-ups due to inexperience, of each of the initial landings.

Even more amazing was the way in which the weather cooperated in the Western Task Force's operation. Great anxiety had been aroused in that force's naval commander and in Washington, by reports on November 6 that, after a remarkably smooth Atlantic crossing, the armada was about to sail into a storm then raging off the Moroccan shore. According to the official weather forecast, the surf would be so high on November 8 that no landing would be possible at any of the designated Moroccan sites. However, this forecast had been contradicted by the special weather expert who advised Hewitt and who predicted that the storm would die down on November 7 and on November 8 there would be only a moderate ground swell washing the Moroccan shore. The special expert's prediction proved accurate. The surf, normally far higher in November than in October, was on D-day morning the lowest it had been since the first week in October.

At the landing site of Safi, 150 miles southwest of Casablanca, everything went quite miraculously according to plan; the Americans got ashore on schedule with no fighting whatever and began at once their northeastward move. At Port Lyautey, some sixty-odd miles northeast of Casablanca, there was fierce resistance, but it was brief; the immediate objective was soon secured. At Fedala, the central and main landing site, just ten miles northwest of Casablanca, the initial assault troops got well ashore before there was any response at all. They ran into strong opposition as they advanced toward Casablanca next day, however—an opposition that would have been far more dangerous to the whole enterprise had not a victorious battle fought by Hewitt's escorting warships the day before, after French Moroccan commander General Auguste Nogues realized what was happening, saved the as yet unloaded transports and cargo vessels offshore from a determined Vichy navy attempt to destroy them. In this attempt, the *Jean Bart* with its four 15-inch guns, though it was yet unfinished and so unable to move from its mooring in the Casablanca harbor, had an active part, but by the attempt's end she was, in Churchill's words, "gutted by fire and beached." On the morning of the third day, November 10, Eisenhower messaged Patton, saying: "Only tough nut is in your hands. Crack it open quickly." At that moment, the American advance from Fedala was halted altogether by fierce French resistance, raising by afternoon doubts among the assault troops themselves that the "nut" could be "cracked" at all. No such doubt was entertained for an instant by Patton. He spent the afternoon organizing an attack upon Casablanca to be launched in overwhelming force at dawn on November 11, his way to be prepared by a devastating shelling and air bombardment of the city by Hewitt's warships and carrier planes. Nogues, fully aware of the impending attack and of his inability to repel it, nevertheless waited until shortly before seven o'clock in the morning of November 11 to surrender. Naval guns were about to begin shelling the city; carrier bombers were actually in the air over it.[31]

Things were easier at Oran, where three landings had bracketed the city by two o'clock in the morning of November 8, and much more closely than did those at Casablanca. The landing troops, commanded by American Major General Lloyd R. Fredenhall and spearheaded by the highly trained U.S. First Infantry Division under Major General Terry Allen, encountered no opposition whatever on the beaches. So complete was the surprise that the French coastal defense batteries covering the thirteen miles of shore between the easternmost and westernmost landing sites were totally silent until after sunrise, when their fire was rendered ineffective by the British naval support of the American landings, a support that included the skillful use of smoke screens. (Unprecedented in war among forces of different nationalities, testifying to the effectiveness of the Marshall-Eisenhower insistence upon a truly unified command, was the virtually perfect coordination of British naval operations with American infantry operations at both Oran and Algiers.) There was only one serious reverse: Two hours after the first landing, when the Oran French were fully alerted, two British cutters with four hundred American troops aboard, accompanied by two motor launches, rashly attempted to take Oran harbor by direct assault. Though they displayed large American flags, they became immediately the targets of a withering shore fire that in a few minutes crippled both small ships, killed half their crews and the troops aboard, and ended with the capture of the survivors, most of them wounded. Next day, French resistance to the invading troops stiffened, but the invaders made steady progress; and at noon of the third day, November 10 (hours before the surrender of Casablanca), the Oran French gave up. Only four hundred casualties had been suffered by the Americans on land and a yet fewer number by the French.

The best news of all came from Algiers. There the Allied landing force was mostly British (there were twenty-three thousand British, only ten thousand American troops), but to maintain the myth that Torch was exclusively an American operation, the overall command was vested, not in the British general present, Kenneth A. N. Anderson, but in American Major General Charles W. Ryder. The landings met with no resistance whatever and, in the city itself, by H-hour of D-day, the pro-Allied French with whom Murphy had been conspiring were in control of the central and branch police stations, the radio station, and the main post office, where telephone and telegraph facilities were located. Also, pro-Allied French were in control of both of Algiers's desperately needed airfields, Maison Blanche east of Algiers and Blida west of it. The first Allied ground troops entered Algiers against virtually no opposition at ten o'clock on D-day morning. By evening, with the city securely in Allied hands, an armistice had been signed.

v

MEANWHILE, in this Algerian capital, political events of the gravest import for the whole of the North African enterprise were taking place—events destined to render dubious, for many weeks, the value of the military triumph and to threaten, during those same weeks, an abrupt termination of Eisenhower's career as top Allied commander. . . .

Shortly before midnight of November 7, after Murphy had set in motion the clandestine operations planned with his French conspirators—a risky move, since he was by no means fully assured that the landings would be made on schedule, and precise timing was essential to the success of his plans—he went to the Algiers suburb of el-Biar, where lived, in the grand Villa des Oliviers, the Vichy-designated commander in chief of all the French land forces in North Africa, General Alphonse Juin. Murphy regarded Juin as a personal friend. In talks between the two over many months, the French commander had repeatedly evinced pro-American attitudes and expressed his hatred of Nazi-Fascists,

his passionate dedication to the liberation of France, doing so with such conviction that Murphy had actually seriously considered him for the role Giraud was
now chosen to play. He had abandoned the idea because the general, when (like
Giraud) he became a Nazi prisoner of war in 1940, had (unlike Giraud) obtained
his release by signing a solemn pledge not to fight the Germans again—and
even if the general deemed this 1940 pledge meaningless since made under
duress (Murphy was inclined to believe he did so view it), he might feel obliged
under the terms of his present appointment "to inform Vichy of anything we told
him." That Juin, personally, would welcome the present coming of the American expeditionary force, Murphy had no doubt whatever.

Yet the diplomat approached this meeting with trepidation, his normal self-
security reduced by puzzlements and dreads whose intensity was increased by
physical weariness (not for a week had he had a good night's sleep). So many
things were now going mysteriously wrong! For instance, Roosevelt personally ·
had told him during his last trip to Washington that five thousand troops would
land in Tunisia in the first wave of the invasion, stating this as a fact that Murphy in his activities should take account of, and Murphy had therefore conveyed this information (though of course without specifying the time or size
of the landing) not only to the resistance leaders in Tunis with whom he was
in contact, but also, evidently, to Admiral Jean Esteva, the governor-general of
Tunisia.[32] But only an hour or so ago, Murphy had learned that the Torch command had canceled a Tunisian landing weeks ago, if it had ever firmly committed itself to one, without bothering to inform him. God knows what might now
happen to those Tunisian leaders who acted on the false tip they had been given!
As for Esteva, he was certain to feel betrayed by the Americans and likely to be
inclined by that fact to resist the coming of the Allies into Tunisia, especially
when he learned that most of the eastward-driving Allied troops were not
American at all, but British. And why had Giraud not come directly from France
to Algiers in accordance with carefully laid plans? Murphy had counted upon
having Giraud at his side on this visit to Juin.

Small wonder that the diplomat, as he went from his street-parked car to the
mansion door, felt as if he walked in night fog upon a quaking bog, the fragile
crust of which might give way beneath him at any instant. Compelling him was
one of the few certainties that still obtained for him on his frantic night, namely,
that Juin must be told of the landings *before* they were actually under way, because he was in a position to prevent or greatly reduce resistance to them.

But now, abruptly, even this single certainty evaporated.

From the bed in which he had been sound asleep, General Juin came clad in
pink-striped pajamas into the mansion's drawing room, where Murphy awaited
him and where he listened with astonishment to the American's announcement
that an American expeditionary force of half a million men (the British role was
deliberately unmentioned, the number of Americans deliberately inflated) was
about to land all along the coasts of French North Africa. "I wish to tell you this

in advance because I am convinced you desire above all else the liberation of France, and this can be achieved only through cooperation with the United States." The troops came by invitation, he said. By whose invitation? Juin asked sharply. General Giraud's, replied Murphy. Was Giraud, then, in Algiers? No, his arrival had been delayed, else he would be now in this room; but he was expected momentarily. An agitated, floor-pacing Juin took some time to digest this information. Finally, he said, according to Murphy, that "if the matter were entirely in my hands, I would be with you"; but the decisive power was *not* in his hands. Darlan was in Algiers. The admiral had come to visit his beloved son, Alain, who lay stricken with infantile paralysis in an Algiers hospital; and the admiral was now the ranking French official in all North Africa, able to countermand any order Juin gave.

"Then we must go to Darlan," said Murphy.[33]

Juin, agreeing, at once phoned the residence of Admiral Fenard, where Darlan was staying, had Darlan roused from his bed, then told him that Murphy had a message of the most urgent importance that could not be given over the phone and wished to come to impart it in person. Juin would accompany him. Whereupon Darlan said he preferred to come himself to the Villa des Oliviers. He arrived there, with Fenard, twenty minutes later—a plump, bald little man (he stood but little over five feet tall) who had, in Mark Clark's later description, "watery blue eyes . . . petulant lips," and a manner that struck many as furtive, almost cowering, even when there was no danger.[34]

But there was nothing furtive or cowering in his reaction to Murphy's "message." It was explosive. He turned purple with rage. He had always known the British were stupid, he spluttered, but had believed the Americans "more intelligent." Obviously, he had been mistaken: the Americans had "the same genius as the British for making massive blunders." He began to pace the room. Murphy paced with him (the tall diplomat had to shorten his stride drastically to match that of the diminutive admiral), talking incessantly, reminding him of the overtures he had made through Fenard weeks ago and stressing that now, *now* was the time to act decisively in accordance with what had seemed those overtures' intent. The admiral should at once issue the orders needed to prevent French resistance to the landings about to take place, a needless bloodshed, and to assure instead French cooperation in this great venture whose aim was the prevention of Axis domination of French African soil. The argument, reiterated in various forms for fifteen or twenty minutes, had no persuasive effect. Darlan's reply was that he had sworn allegiance to Marshal Pétain, had "preserved" it for two years, and could not revoke it now. Moreover, he had as yet seen no clear evidence that landings were actually being made; he doubted the truth of what Murphy had said of them. He did agree to send a message to Pétain, outlining the situation as he saw it and asking for a free hand in dealing with it. By that time, some forty armed young Frenchmen, members of the underground Murphy had organized, had surrounded the Juin residence without Murphy's knowing it and refused to permit anyone in the house, including Murphy, to leave it, though they permitted one of Murphy's vice consuls, Kenneth Pendar, who was waiting in Murphy's parked car, to take the Darlan message to the French naval headquarters in Algiers for dispatch. Shortly thereafter, when Murphy had gone into the mansion's garden for a breath of fresh air, he was seized by French state police, the Gardes Mobiles, a detachment of which had driven off the anti-Vichy French and surrounded the mansion in their turn. The diplomat was placed under house arrest in the mansion. He remained under arrest until midafternoon of November 8.35

By then (actually, at seven-thirty in the morning), Darlan had sent a situation report to Pétain, supplementing the message Pendar had managed to have dispatched;* in it, he said that "landings have been effected by surprise and with success," that "massive landings" were "reported to be in preparation," and that "the defenses will soon be overwhelmed." Four hours later, he had told Pétain that "Algiers will probably be taken this evening." To none of these three messages was there a recorded reply; there need not be, since Pétain at nine o'clock that morning had handed to the American chargé d'affaires in Vichy, Pinckney Tuck, his harshly negative reply to Roosevelt's personal appeal to him, and this reply had been quickly broadcast to the world. Also, "records show," according to Robert Sherwood, that Darlan late in the morning "telephoned Nogues in Morocco and ordered him to cease resistance—*and it is most important to note that Nogues refused to obey this order* [italicized by present author]." Finally, at five o'clock that afternoon, two hours after Murphy's release from the Villa des Oliviers, Darlan wired Pétain that since American troops had "entered into the city [in force; the first troops had entered that morning] in spite of our delaying action," he had "authorized General Juin, the commander-in-chief, to negotiate the surrender of . . . Algiers only." The surrender document was formally effective at seven P.M. and "[f]rom that moment," writes Churchill, "Admiral Darlan was in American power. . . ."37

On the morning of November 9, Eisenhower at Gibraltar, in overly enthusiastic relief over Giraud's agreement to do as the Americans wanted him to do, told the world through radio broadcast that Giraud, a French national hero around whom the North African French were rallying, would with the full support of the American government be the dominant military and political figure in French North African affairs. Shortly thereafter, Giraud himself informed the North African French by radio that he was assuming (to quote Eisenhower) "the leadership of French North Africa" and, in that capacity, ordered "French forces to cease fighting against the Allies." His words, to his own and Eisenhower's surprise and dismay, had no effect whatever—and when, later that morning, unaccompanied by any American, he arrived at the Blida airfield forty miles from

---

*The French naval officer who handled this message "became suspicious, *checked with Darlan on the telephone,* and then took Pendar into custody for several hours."36

Algiers, he personally was received more coldly than his radio broadcast had been. As a matter of fact, he had to go into hiding for a time to avoid arrest as a traitor by the Vichyites, who yet controlled the Algerian government. This was "a terrific blow to our expectations," writes Eisenhower. But not long thereafter, in the late afternoon, its pain was assuaged by the news that Darlan, who had already signaled his willingness to "play ball" with the Americans, was in Algiers! The Algiers armistice terms, Eisenhower noted when these arrived on his Gibraltar desk, had been "approved" by Darlan as commander in chief of all the Vichy French armed forces. Darlan's presence was a problem, of course, what to do with him (the "simple and easy answer would have been to jail him," writes Eisenhower), but he also presented a glorious opportunity. With Darlan's cooperation, thought Eisenhower, we might gain not only an end to the current resistance by the French, but also their active assistance in securing Tunisia before Axis troops could get there (the Germans already had bombers based on the Tunisian airfields). More important still, the French fleet at Toulon might obey a Darlan order to join the Allied naval forces, especially if the Germans, as they were expected soon to do, occupied the whole of France![38]

The plan had been for Clark to fly to Algiers shortly after Giraud did, to evince the American support of Giraud's authority. But immediately after Giraud's plane took off, bad weather closed down the Gibraltar airfield for many hours. It was after five in the afternoon when, at the Blida airfield, Clark climbed into a Bren-gun carrier and headed for Algiers, arriving there just as the port was undergoing its first air attack, from Tunisian-based Junkers 88s. He narrowly escaped death when one of these bombers, struck by antiaircraft fire, plummeted directly toward the vehicle in which he rode, exploding when within a thousand feet of the ground and showering lethal debris all around him. The experience may have further shortened the American Eagle's normally short temper. At any rate, having arrived at the Allied force headquarters in Algiers's St. George Hotel and been there told by Murphy that the arrangements so arduously made with Giraud were already rendered obsolete by the negotiations with Juin and Darlan now under way, negotiations that Eisenhower's deputy must now continue, Clark exploded with a fury almost matching Darlan's of the night before. This "really messes things up," he cried. The Torch high command had just publicly committed itself, and the American government, to the full enthusiastic support of Giraud; both Eisenhower and Washington would "look ridiculous" if Giraud did not now receive the (or at least a) top post in the French African administration; and he, Clark, personally bitterly resented his forced involvement in French politics, about which he knew nothing and cared less. This was not a soldier's business.[39]

His resentful impatience was abundantly evident when, at ten o'clock next morning, with Murphy (a curiously passive Murphy) at his right hand, he opened a conference with Darlan, who had at his left hand Juin and Fenard—a meeting to which Giraud, now ensconced in the home of Lemaigre-Dubreuil, was not invited.[40] Fixing a fierce eagle gaze upon Darlan, whom he disliked on sight, Clark abruptly demanded that the admiral at once order the French military's acceptance of an armistice for *all* French North Africa. Darlan shook his head sadly: Pétain had as yet made no reply to the messages sent him the day before, he would not now do so until after a meeting of the council of ministers in Vichy that afternoon, and unless the marshal's reply then authorized the action, he, Darlan, was powerless to do what Clark requested. He was sorry. But, Clark said heatedly, the present negotiations were not being conducted with Vichy, all ties between Washington and Vichy having been broken by Pétain's resistance order of the day before; the negotiations were being conducted with the North African French, whose representatives were now at this table. To which Darlan's bland reply was that *his* ties with Vichy had not been severed; hence, though personally he wished an end to the North African fighting, he could not effectively order it. He lacked the authority. Clark brought his fist down with a crash upon the table (he was a great table pounder, was the American Eagle; this was deplored by Murphy and, on the evidence, heavily discounted by Darlan as bluff and bluster), saying that if the admiral did not issue the order within thirty minutes, he, Clark, would "end this conference," take the admiral into "protective custody," and "go to General Giraud," who would "sign the terms and issue the necessary orders." Darlan smiled regretfully: Giraud might do as Clark said, but Giraud would not be obeyed by French officers in North Africa, every one of whom had sworn personal allegiance to the marshal; there would simply be more time lost, more fighting. This seems to have given Clark pause, for instead of ending the conference, arresting Darlan, and turning to Giraud, he resumed his table-pounding insistence upon an immediate all–North African cease-fire. As the hands of the conference room clock came together at high noon, Darlan asked for "five minutes with my staff for discussion," a request granted by Clark with the proviso that "no one is to leave here or communicate with anyone outside." When the French returned to the conference somewhat more than five minutes later, Darlan laid before Clark, not a draft order, but a draft message to Pétain saying that further fighting was futile and that if it were continued, France would probably lose North Africa. Would this do? asked Darlan, all innocence, provoking in Clark an explosion of rage so towering that the wily opportunistic admiral, who was certainly acutely aware of how little real power was his and how great was the general's,* finally abandoned the tactic of total

---

*News correspondent John McVane, who was in Algiers at the time, writes in his *Journey into War* (New York, 1943, p. 78) that "whomever the Americans and British wanted to name as boss of North Africa would have [had] the support of the majority of North Africans—whether he were De Gaulle or an insignificant member of the Blida town council." The same conclusion was reached by almost every other correspondent who was on the scene, though some of them also pointed out that what was true of the North African majority was not necessarily true of professional soldiers, whose primary concern was with the maintenance of their rank, pay, and pension rights.

evasiveness he had theretofore employed. He drew toward him a sheet of paper. He began to write, slowly, carefully, asking questions as he did so. He then placed in the general's hands, at long last, a cease-fire order for all French North Africa with specifications that would continue unchanged the current Vichy laws and administrative machinery. Clark, having made in consultation with a passive Murphy a couple of minor changes, approved this for immediate issuance, but with the understanding that the stipulations accompanying the cease-fire might be revised by Eisenhower after he had reviewed them. Darlan issued it "in the name of the Marshal" shortly before midafternoon of that Tuesday, November 10.

Since it is the organic document of what in a few days became known to a shocked free world as the "Darlan Deal," this order handwritten by Darlan is worth close examination, It had four main provisions: 1) "Engagements having been fulfilled and bloody battle becoming useless, the order is given to all the land, sea, and air forces in North Africa to cease the fight against the forces of America and her allies [the last three words were inserted, over Anglophobic Darlan's protest, by Clark] as upon receipt of this order and to return to their barracks and observe strictest neutrality"; 2) the French commanders were ordered to "put themselves in liaison with local American commanders on the subject of terms for the suspension of hostilities"; 3) it was announced that Darlan had assumed authority over French North Africa "in the name of the Marshal" and that "the present senior officers retain their commands, and the political and administrative organizations remain in force" unless or until (this reservation was made at Clark's insistence) a "fresh order" on the matter came from Algiers; 4) all prisoners were to be exchanged.

Point three was, of course, the crux of the "deal" and, when published to the world, would raise a storm of popular angry outrage in both the United Kingdom and the United States (especially the United Kingdom), which surprised those Americans who had initially agreed to it and the depth and nature of which, judging from their published words, they never fully comprehended. Point three meant that the Frenchmen who had most actively and effectively aided the Allies in North Africa must remain in disgrace and actual danger of their lives *because* they had done so. Indeed, as soon as Clark had approved the Darlan order as written, and before that order was actually issued, the admiral insisted that the "senior officers" who were to "retain their commands" must *not* include Mast or any others of rank who had actively sought, at risk to themselves, to aid the Allied landings. "It is to your interest to agree that I cannot tolerate these men not obeying my orders," he said with implicit threat, and one of his colleagues added: "You'd better put them in a safe place, they are bitterly resented." For instance, General Bethouart, a French divisional commander at Casablanca with whom Murphy had conspired and who had sought to prevent Nogues's resistance to the landings, had been imprisoned by Nogues and faced a court-martial for treason; under the terms of Darlan's order, he would remain in prison until executed, as he almost certainly would be unless the Americans intervened (they ultimately, belatedly, did so). Point three also meant the perpetuation in North Africa of all existent Vichy institutions and the active enforcement of Vichy laws denying human rights to Jews, suppressing freedom of speech and the press, and preventing popular assembly and free movement by ordinary citizens. Among the institutions to be preserved were concentration camps on the Nazi model, where brave and honorable men, actively committed to human freedom, were confined, continuously humiliated, often tortured, and sometimes killed. Most of Morocco's political prisoners, men who had taken action in support of loudly professed Allied principles, would remain in concentration camps under horrible conditions as late as February 1943.

Nor did Clark's capitulation to Darlan (it amounted to that) buy him even a moment of freedom from political concerns. When the order was issued, Algiers had been in Allied hands for nearly forty-eight hours. In Oran, the French commanders had accepted hours ago a provisional armistice and issued a cease-fire order; if they had not yet formally surrendered the city, they were in the process of doing so. Only in Morocco, where Patton was preparing his all-out assault on Casablanca, did active resistance continue. And before there was any sign that Nogues would be any more obedient of this second Darlan order than he had been of the first (telephoned) one, Pétain had announced by radio the removal of Darlan as head of the French armed forces and his replacement by none other than Auguste Nogues. "In view of this I shall have to revoke my order," said Darlan to Clark. To prevent this, Clark, prompted to do so by the admiral himself, placed Darlan under arrest and ordered a platoon of Americans to surround the Fenard villa, where Darlan was staying, to prevent any communication between him and the outside. (What prevented Clark's keeping Darlan incommunicado from then on and issuing whatever orders he pleased in the admiral's name? Nothing, it would seem to some, save his blindness to obvious realities of power, his incapacity to perceive glaring contradictions in the information upon which he acted, and above all, his flaming impatience with "distractions" from his "main job.") He resumed his absurd tactics of forceful feebleness, or feeble forcefulness. Giraud came forward with the demand that he be named, as promised, commander in chief of all French forces in North Africa. "I now have two Kingpins," cabled Clark plaintively to Eisenhower, "but hope to wiggle out of it somehow. I deemed it of the utmost importance to do anything to secure an order that would be obeyed to cease hostilities." He then attempted with no success to bring about a working agreement between Giraud and Darlan, as per Eisenhower's mid-October proposal.[41]

That night, German troops began to move into theretofore unoccupied France, a movement that would continue in increasing force, unresisted, all next day. The not unexpected news, reaching Clark as he breakfasted in the St.

George on the morning of November 11, galvanized him: the Germans marched toward the Mediterranean; they would be soon in Toulon! He rushed to Fenard's villa, where he told Darlan that since the Vichy government was rapidly ceasing to exist and Pétain must have been virtually a Nazi prisoner when he signed yesterday's order for Darlan's removal from command, the admiral could ignore that order, could himself order the fleet at Toulon to sail for North Africa, and could also order Esteva in Tunisia to resist the German military buildup there. He must do these things immediately. Darlan initially refused to do them at all (he assumed that Vichy under Nazi-puppet Laval, with Pétain as symbolic figurehead, would continue to function pretty much as it had since 1940). Again Clark was provoked into a towering rage; he stormed from the house, uttering dire threats. And again Darlan perforce shifted ground. Immediately after lunch, the admiral sought further conference with Clark, during which he agreed to do what the general wished. He did not precisely do it, however. What he sent to Toulon was not an order, which the fanatically anti-British commander of the French high seas fleet would not have obeyed in any case, but a most urgent "invitation" to come to North Africa; and it was only under direct pressure from Clark, with passive Murphy standing by, that he phoned Esteva an unequivocal order to resist the German invasion of Tunisia. Clark then, without waiting for any sign that the "invitation" to the Toulon commander was being accepted or that the orders to Nogues and Esteva were being obeyed, removed the guard from around Fenard's villa and restored to Darlan his freedom of movement and communication.[42]

And during the night of November 11–12, slippery Darlan, joined by Murphy's allegedly pro-Allied friend Juin, used his restored freedom to revoke his order to Esteva. Clark, roused from the bed in which he had been sound asleep (literally, figuratively), learned of this treachery at five in the morning of the twelfth. In another of his fits of fury, he summoned the French admiral and general to his presence and threatened them with a firing squad if they did not immediately reinstate the order they had revoked. They of course did so. Equally of course, the reinstated order had no effect in Tunisia. Shortly thereafter, Nogues arrived from Casablanca, intending to assume the office assigned him by Pétain's order of the day before. He was immediately informed that Pétain's order was rendered meaningless by the German troop movement southward in France; and when he then requested private conference with Clark prior to a general meeting that had been called for that afternoon for the purpose of "finalizing" the North African political situation, Clark refused the request.

It was a yet boiling mad Clark who, after lunch, opened the general meeting. He did so by reading aloud a message received from Eisenhower the day before in response to a Clark report outlining the Algerian political turmoil, a message drafted (with the help of Mack and Matthews) for precisely such presentation and appealing, therefore, to that passion for "honor" and "glory" deemed endemic to the Gallic temperament. It said in part: "What do these men want? Are they not content with leadership in a great movement to raise France from bondage or do they desire to disappear into disgraceful obscurity by allowing France to suffer without lifting a hand to save her? . . . They have an opportunity to achieve immortality in the hearts of their countrymen by uniting with the common aim of fighting for their country's liberation. They must not abandon France in her moment of despair by engaging in selfish fighting. . . ." Clark then presented, as Eisenhower had recommended, an ultimatum: If by meeting's end no working agreement acceptable by him had been reached, each and every one of the Frenchmen now before him would be locked up on a warship in the harbor. He went on to "suggest" that Darlan assume the top political office for the time being; that the present governors-general of Morocco (Nogues), Algeria (Yves Chatel), and Tunisia (Esteva) be continued in office; and that Giraud be appointed to raise a volunteer army to fight the Axis—an army that would be equipped by the United States. There followed an hour of fruitless wrangling, at the end of which Clark insisted that Giraud, whom the French had excluded from the meeting, be called in, and that Darlan and Nogues shake hands with him. This was done (one may be sure that neither Nogues nor Darlan shared Clark's faith in the efficacy of a handshake), following which the American general left them to "battle it out among themselves." When he returned an hour or so later, he found them inclined to accept his suggestion (how could they not be?)—but they asked for a postponement of the final decision until tomorrow. Clark granted the request, then cabled Eisenhower that Darlan was evidently the only Frenchman who could effect cooperation between the Allied forces and the North African French.[43]

By then, Eisenhower in Gibraltar had made a bold command decision. Despite political uncertainties out of which might emerge dangerous threats to the bases and communications of the operation, he had launched the drive into Tunisia called for in the final Torch plan. As per that plan, British General Anderson had taken over from American General Ryder command of the Allied forces constituting the Eastern Task Force (the British First Army constituted the bulk of it) as soon as the Algiers landings were firmly established, and upon Eisenhower's order, he drove eastward on November 11 at maximum speed, supported in the Mediterranean by Admiral Cunningham's naval forces. At the same time, the American troops at Oran were ordered eastward to join the Tunisian drive, despite uncertainty about the attitude of Franco, who might yet (conceivably) open Spain and Spanish Morocco to German air and land forces, and despite the fact that, because of miserably poor communications with Casablanca, the military situation in French Morocco remained obscure to him. By the night of November 12, the main ports (Bougie and Bône) in eastern Algeria and the main airfields (notably Souk-el-Arba, badly needed to give air cover to the advance) were in Allied hands, as were the western Tunisian towns of Constantine and Sétif.

On the following morning, that of Friday, November 13, Eisenhower, accompanied by Admiral Cunningham, flew from Gibraltar to Algiers. At the Maison Blanche airport, he was met by Clark and Murphy. Murphy gave him what he later termed "an exhaustive review of the whole situation," concluding: "The whole matter has become a military one. You will have to give the answer."[44]

But of course the answer was not, in the circumstances, truly *his* to give—or at any rate, to become truly his, would have required his breaking a long, strong chain (or the reversal of a huge floodtide) of events over which he had had little or no control; this would have required in turn the full exercise of a mind, a will, and a value system radically different from those that had led Eisenhower to his present position. As it was: a) Roosevelt's and Hull's attitude toward de Gaulle and the Fighting French was, of course, known to, and influential of, him; b) the State Department had strongly advised him (he claims in his war memoirs he was under "written orders") "to cooperate with any French government we should find existing at the moment of our entry into North Africa";* c) the Vichy French regime, with its anti-Semitic decrees, was popular with the Muslim Arabs, who were a large majority of the French North African population and whom the Nazis were actively attempting to stir into revolt against their French rulers; d) it was simply impossible for the Americans themselves to take over the government of North Africa, sustaining it with armed force, while conducting offensive operations against the Axis forces now pouring into Tunisia; e) the troops already driving eastward did so with a nakedly exposed right flank and could avoid disaster and achieve the crucial strategic objective only if their bases and communications were secure; f) Murphy during his "Colonel McGowan" visit to Telegraph Cottage, and again in his message a month later, had alerted him to the possibility of Darlan's "playing ball," and he was now persuaded that, in sharp contrast with the contempt with which Giraud and his call for a cease-fire had been received, Darlan's cease-fire order had been promptly obeyed; g) Clark and Murphy both stressed that French army and navy officers, and French civilian officials, adamantly demanded as a prerequisite of their cooperation a "legitimate succession of authority" whereby their rank, their pay, and their pensions would be guaranteed; h) this succession, said Clark-Murphy, required a top French official who could plausibly claim to have derived his authority from Pétain; i) Nogues was now willing publicly to relinquish to Darlan the power the marshal had "temporarily" bestowed upon him during the period

---

*What Eisenhower called "written orders" were not orders in the military sense of the word. They were parts of a State Department paper prepared as a guide to policy. As such, they did not deny Eisenhower freedom to make, in *whatever* circumstances he encountered in North Africa, such political arrangements as seemed to him necessary or helpful to his military operations. As guide, they were fatally flawed in that what they were to guide *toward* remained ill defined, if defined at all. They thereby encouraged the Torch commander to deem military victory in the present campaign an end in itself, not a means to the end, the ultimate purpose, for which, professedly, this global war was being fought.

of Darlan's "confinement"; j) the final agreement that the French must now arrive at would be along lines Eisenhower himself had laid down.

The commander in chief remained deliberately aloof from the discussions that led to the agreement. He entered the conference room only after Clark told him everything was settled, shortly after the lunch hour that day. He then shook hands with everybody, permitted photographs to be taken of him with Darlan and the others, and approved the proclamation prepared by Darlan for issuance later that day. He then flew back to Gibraltar, taking Murphy with him to help him draft, for immediate transmittal to Marshall, a full explanation of the situation he had faced and a justification of the action he had taken with regard to it.[45]

Meanwhile, back in Algiers, Yves Chatel, governor-general of Algeria, astonished the knowledgeable portion of the free world with his Algiers radio announcement of the Darlan appointment. He read Darlan's proclamation: "Inhabitants of North Africa! The Marshal appointed General Nogues as his delegate in North Africa on November 10, 1942, before the entry of German troops into the unoccupied zone of France. He did this believing that I was deprived of my liberty. General Nogues arrived yesterday, on November 12, in Algiers. In full possession of my liberty, and in full agreement with him, I resumed the responsibility for French interests in North Africa. I have the approval of the American authorities, with whom I intend to guarantee the defense of North Africa. Every governor and resident has to remain in his place, and is to take care of the administration of his territory according to the laws in force, as in the past. Frenchmen and Muslims, I rely on your complete discipline. Everybody at his post. Long live the Marshal! Long live France!"[46]

Simultaneously or immediately after this Yves Chatel broadcast, Clark presented the background and reasons for it, from his point of view, to an assembly of the press and radio correspondents then in Algiers. His manner was confident but his words apologetic—the latter in response to the shock, the bewilderment, and the skepticism mingled with actual outrage that was registered on the faces before him. "We are being realistic," he said, as men of power always say when they defend shortsighted and, at the moment, relatively easy decisions (easy because they are essentially mere yieldings to immediate pressures) that have no moral base, are at odds with known contextual facts, and flatly contradict the *ultimate* purpose for which they are professedly taken. "We cannot afford to risk our bases and lines of communication over a political squabble. . . . All of you must understand that Admiral Darlan was the one man of power here who controlled the [French] land, sea, and air forces. . . . Whatever you may think of him, he was the only man who could issue the proper orders to bring all factions together. He was the only man the armed forces would obey, and I had to play along with him." The more astute among the correspondents, and there was a remarkable number of unusually astute correspondents in Algiers at that time, at once recognized that Clark contradicted himself. For if Darlan actually had the power Clark claimed he had, how dare Clark speak of him publicly as a mere tool to be used temporarily, then discarded? Did this not risk Darlan's exercise of his allegedly great power in ways inimical to Allied interests? And what evidence was there that he was truly useful even temporarily in the ways Clark described him as being? Certainly his order to Esteva was not being obeyed; there was no sign that it would be. Nor was there any sign that the French fleet would sail from Toulon to French African ports.* Neither was there the slightest solid evidence that Darlan's cease-fire order had really had any effect at all in French Morocco, which was the only place where fighting continued at the time of the order's issuance.

(Three months later, Nogues, interviewed by highly esteemed correspondent William Stoneman of the *Chicago Daily News,* would tell how his decision to surrender Casablanca was made: "On Monday [November 9] I called Wuldeth, the German representative, and asked him whether in his opinion we had any possibility of resisting. He replied that we had fought well but that our position was hopeless. 'Now you see.' I told him, 'what you have done by taking our weapons away. It is entirely your fault.' " From which it would appear that Darlan's order had nothing to do with Nogues's action, this having been determined by the military situation and a Nazi official's opinion some thirty-six hours before the order was received. It would seem that Nogues was a man very like Darlan, a wily, ruthless, self-serving opportunist who continued the hopeless fighting as Darlan would have done until the last possible moment, sacrificing some hundreds of Allied and French lives, in order to maintain himself in a "safe" position if the Germans did at last manage to win the war.)[47]

The most critically minded of the correspondents agreed that a great majority of the French professional soldiers, in that moment of vast confusion, had as a primary concern the maintenance of their pay and pension rights. They were therefore anxious for a bridge of "legitimate authority" between Vichy and whatever French government might succeed it. But how could Darlan be deemed such a bridge? What "legitimacy" did *he* have, who had been explicitly repudiated by Pétain and whom the Allied command could jail at any time? The single real choice open to North African French soldiers after the success of the Allied landings was between joining the Allied forces and refusing to do so. If they joined the Allied forces, their pay would continue, guaranteed by the Allies; if they refused to join, their pay would stop and they risked being locked up in prisoner-of-war stockades.

---

*It never did. The French delayed Toulon's capture by establishing in its immediate approaches a free zone manned by French marines. But on November 18, the Germans demanded the withdrawal of all French forces from the zone and four days later occupied Toulon. The Toulon commander responded by executing long-laid plans for destroying the fleet: sixty-one ships totaling 225,000 tons were destroyed, including three battleships, ten cruisers, twenty-eight destroyers, and fourteen submarines. "A barren sacrifice," mourned de Gaulle.

Taking all these things into consideration, many a correspondent concluded, as many a well-informed observer outside North Africa would soon conclude, that Darlan had precisely as much political power as the Allied command chose to bestow upon him—no more, no less.

VI

IT has seemed to the author that the story of the making of the Darlan Deal should be told in experiential detail, because in such detail, and only there, lies convincing contradiction of the conclusion published in virtually every standard history of World War II and of Roosevelt's handling of foreign affairs. This conclusion, a simple repetition of the justification of the deal made at the time by those responsible for it, is that (to quote Robert Dallek) "the arrangement with Darlan brought a quick halt to French resistance, saved lives, and put Dakar under Allied control."*[48]

But we must return now to the pinnacle of power in Washington and London, where the direction of the historical forces leading to this "arrangement" had been determined and from which has come the interpretation of it now enshrined, or embalmed, in establishment histories. . . .

To Churchill in London fell the highly difficult and unpleasant task of dealing face-to-face with de Gaulle in this late autumn and early winter of 1942. The difficulty and unpleasantness were increased by the Prime Minister's conviction that the Americans treated the Free French leader in ways not only mistaken in terms of longtime Allied interests, but also needlessly hurtful, insulting, and humiliating to the man personally.

Admittedly, de Gaulle was "difficult," especially for people accustomed to deference and inclined to regard deference as their due. He tacitly demanded that he be looked up to, standing as he did, straight and tall, upon lofty principles as unyielding as himself—and this backward tilt of the neck, in a gesture of respect tinged with awe, was painful when not impossible for stiff-necked men

---

*Dakar has not been mentioned in our story thus far because it lay outside the territorial limits of Eisenhower's theater of command during the time we've been covering. It was not until the last week of November 1942 that Pierre Boisson, Vichy-appointed governor of French West Africa, harried by popular unrest encouraged by Gaullists (they were strong in the area he governed), "announced himself ready to take military orders from me," writes Eisenhower, "through Admiral Darlan, but [from] no one else [other than I, he means]." This information Eisenhower at once transmitted to Marshall, who then ordered him "to proceed toward securing the West African region precisely as I had the North African." The document putting Dakar in Allied hands was signed at Algiers on December 4, 1942. Boisson had come to Eisenhower's headquarters from Dakar to engage in what proved to be heated and unproductive conferences with British as well as American government representatives (he wanted the British to force de Gaulle to stop agitation that, he claimed, undermined his authority)— conferences in which Darlan and Murphy participated. By Eisenhower's own account, he himself in private talk with Boisson finally persuaded the Frenchman to affix his signature to the decisive document.[49]

of pride. Seldom did he smile, and then only slightly, unwillingly, to judge from the scores of published photographs of him in situations where a broad smile would not have been out of order. Never did he laugh a hearty, full-throated laugh—at least not in the recorded experiences of those closely associated with him. Certainly, he never laughed at himself. To have done so would have been, in his evident feeling, a flagrantly unpatriotic gesture, akin to a desecration of the French flag, since he was the personification of France, a national destiny, with the Cross of Lorraine his personal sign.[50] In a widely prevailing but far from majority view, shared and encouraged by Roosevelt, who reacted instinctively to de Gaulle as to a personal rebuke, the Free French leader was an odious compendium of massive egotism and insufferable self-righteousness, having as its animating force an ambition for personal power that was inimical to every form and usage of democracy. So viewed, he was a threat that grew more serious with every increase of his popular persuasiveness, and many who viewed him in this way tried to shoot him down with arrows of ridicule. He was a tempting target for ridicule. Churchill famously proclaimed, in a moment of exasperation, that of all the crosses he had to bear, the heaviest by far was the Cross of Lorraine; Roosevelt grew fond of saying that de Gaulle must finally decide whether he was Joan of Arc or Clemenceau, because he couldn't continue to alternate between the two.[51] But such arrows tended to break harmlessly against the hard integrity of their target; when they did penetrate, the venom with which they were tipped tended somehow, as they pierced their target, to be transformed into humor without malice. And the laughter they provoked was never wholly contemptuous, was always a little uneasy, made so by a suspicion on the part of him who laughed that in doing so, he measured himself small against the object of his laughter.

Churchill, indeed, for all the constant irritation and occasional fury aroused in him by the difficulties placed in his path (especially in his relations with Roosevelt) by de Gaulle's stubborn insistence upon being himself a sovereign power, had a sincere respect, admiration, and sympathy for de Gaulle the man. This Frenchman of no high rank (he was but a brigadier general in the French army) had come "naked and alone" into exile[52] in the summer of 1940, had then refused to yield a fraction of an inch of his great stature (he stood physically six and a half feet tall) to an apparently irresistibly crushing fate, and seemed now to be actually re-creating a nation, bit by bit, cohering it around himself as nucleus by sheer force of personal will and example. Moreover, de Gaulle's grandly, heroically romantic view of history, and of his personal role in it, had close similarities to Churchill's own. There was an important difference between the two, however, as both men acutely realized. History was for de Gaulle a moral drama. For him, therefore, the politics of true realism, as distinct from the "realism" of such as Clark, was rooted in conscience and guided by it, conscience being a divine implant in the individual human soul, its voice the voice of God. Not so for Churchill—at least not for Churchill in the throes of reaction against de Gaulle's maddeningly self-righteous hubris. A quarrel arose between them regarding the government of Syria-Lebanon (a French mandate under the Versailles Treaty), which had been saved from Nazi control by joint action of British and Free French military forces in the summer of 1941. It became the main subject of conversation between Churchill and de Gaulle when the two lunched together in Cairo on August 7, 1942. Churchill on this occasion frankly confessed his "concern" over his immediately upcoming face-to-face meeting with Stalin, wherein the breaking of the promise the Western Allies (Roosevelt principally) had made of a western front in 1942 must be explained and justified to the Soviet dictator, and over the Syrian dispute, wherein the British violated an agreement Churchill had made to de Gaulle, or so the latter charged. "I can understand your apprehensions," said the Frenchman at this luncheon, "but you will easily surmount them the moment your conscience has nothing to reproach you with." Replied Churchill ("growled," according to de Gaulle): "My conscience is a good girl. I can always come to terms with her."53 To the Frenchman, this was a cynicism outrageous in a national leader; and Churchill, for all his deficiency in empathic capacity, may have sensed at that moment a reaction on de Gaulle's part both deeper and sharper than the one he had intended to provoke, or wanted to provoke, and have felt, despite himself, a slight twinge of shame.

He was frankly uncomfortable when, Eden beside him, he welcomed de Gaulle to No. 10 Downing Street at midday on November 8.

De Gaulle knew, of course, why he had been summoned there: the whole world knew by then of the Allied landings in North Africa that morning, and the event had come as no surprise to de Gaulle, he having more than suspected since early August, as we know, that this operation was being mounted and that he and his Free French were to be denied any part in it (on August 27, he had flatly declared to his closest colleagues that the United States had "decided to land troops in North Africa" in an operation "launched in conjunction with a . . . British offensive in Egypt"). He also knew that "the Prime Minister had made for himself a rule to do nothing important except in agreement with Roosevelt," for though Churchill found "hard to bear the condition of subordination in which United States aid placed the British Empire" and "bitterly resented the tone of supremacy which the President adopted toward him," he bowed "to the imperious necessity [for Britain's very survival] of the American alliance."54 The French leader was therefore thoroughly prepared psychologically to see, as he now saw, an embarrassed smile upon the Prime Minister's face and to hear the apologetic words the Prime Minister now spoke. What was now happening in North Africa, said Churchill, was primarily an American "show," and it was the Americans who had insisted, unfortunately, that the Free French be totally excluded from it. "We [the British] have been obliged to go along with them in this," Churchill went on. "Rest assured, however, that we are not revoking any of our agreements with you. You are the one [Frenchman] to whom we have, since June 1940, promised our support." At which point, vivid memories of those dark days evidently rose to the surface of his mind, releasing a sudden tide of emotion, for there was a throb in his voice as he went on: "You have been with us during the war's worst moments. We shall not abandon you now that the horizon shows signs of brightening."[55] He was frankly immensely relieved by de Gaulle's reaction to this, and immensely grateful. The proud, touchy Free French leader, rising well above the occasion, betrayed none of the angry resentment of personal insult he was surely justified in feeling. He manifested a sympathetic understanding of Churchill's difficult position. When told that Giraud had been chosen to command the French forces in North Africa, he applauded the choice. Giraud was a brave man, a fine soldier, an implacable foe of the Germans; he, de Gaulle, wished him all success and would urge his own followers to support him as military commander. (He did so later that day, broadcasting an eloquent appeal "to the leaders, soldiers, sailors, airmen, officials and French *colons* of North Africa" to "rise up, help our allies, join them without reservations" and without worrying "about names or formulas.") Achieving unity among all the French who opposed the Axis was "all that mattered," de Gaulle concluded.[56]

But when Churchill surprised him with the news of Darlan's unexpected presence in Algiers, doing so in a way that suggested the possibility of a working agreement between Darlan and the Allies, de Gaulle made it emphatically clear that the needed unity could not be achieved unless "the Vichy regime and its supporters" were removed from all positions of governing power. The resistance movement and its supporters could not possibly work with these criminal traitors to France, these nauseous collaborators with Hitler.[57]

On the following day, November 9, distressed by news of the French resistance to the landings, de Gaulle told American Admiral Stark, the President's personal representative in London, of his wish to send "a mission to Algiers" and asked for facilitation of this by the American government. Stark promised to forward the request to Washington at once. De Gaulle also asked Churchill to enlist Roosevelt's support of this request, prompting a November 11 message from the Prime Minister to the President, urging the "importance" of unifying "all Frenchmen who regard Germany as the foe" and describing the German "invasion of unoccupied France" as an "opportunity to do this." Churchill reminded Roosevelt again that "His Majesty's Government are under . . . definite and solemn obligations to De Gaulle and his movement" and that therefore "we must see they have a fair deal. It seems to me," he went on, "you and I ought to avoid at all costs the creation of rival French Emigré Governments each favored by one of us." It might "take some time and nothing must prejudice the military operations, but we ought to make it clear to all parties" that "what we want and . . . are going to work for" was a fusion of all anti-German French. Roosevelt replied to this message in the evening of the day he received it, saying: "In regard to De Gaulle, I have hitherto enjoyed a quiet satisfaction in leaving him in your hands—apparently I have now acquired a similar problem in brother Giraud. I wholly agree that we must prevent rivalry between the French Emigré factions and I have no objection to a De Gaulle emissary visiting KINGPIN [Giraud] in Algiers. We must remember that there is now also a catfight in progress between KINGPIN and Darlan, each claiming full military command of French forces. . . . The principal thought to be driven home to all three of these prima donnas is that the situation is today solely in the military field and that any decision by any one of them, or all of them, is subject to review and approval by Eisenhower."[58]

Of Roosevelt's "three prima donnas," the one to whom he was most averse let him know on the following day, and also let Churchill know formally, that "there was not the slightest chance of an agreement between the Fighting French and the North African 'High Commissioner' " if that official was to be Darlan. De Gaulle transmitted this information to the White House via Admiral Stark, and it was published to the world in a communiqué from the French National Committee in London.[59] This had its effect on public opinion in Britain and the United States—a greater effect than Roosevelt recognized, or would admit he recognized, and one that was, for him, uncomfortable. It had an effect, too, directly or indirectly, upon Eisenhower's drafting of his message to Marshall explaining and defending the political arrangement he had approved the day before in Algiers; for the general found upon his Gibraltar "dungeon" desk, when he returned to it on the morning of November 14, urgent messages reflective of the confusion, the anxiety aroused, in the highest governing circles in London and Washington by news reports of Darlan's elevation and of the French National Committee communiqué and by the popular reaction to these. Eisenhower was made to realize how very hot was the spot on which he had been placed and that upon the persuasiveness of his defense of the action taken might well depend his own future, his own place in history.

"Completely understand the bewilderment in London and Washington because of the turn that negotiations with French North Africans have taken," he began. "Existing French sentiment in North Africa does not even remotely resemble prior calculations* and it is of the utmost importance that no precipitate action be taken which will upset such equilibrium as we have been able to establish." He went on to reiterate in detail the argument of "military necessity" and "expediency," based on false assumptions, with which we are already fa-

---

*This devastating commentary upon the intelligence supplied by Murphy's Fifth Column activity adds point to de Gaulle's remark that Murphy, "long familiar with the best society," was "inclined to believe that France consisted of the people he dined with in town."[60]

miliar. "Admiral Cunningham and General Clark, together with my full staff, have assisted me in making what we consider to be the only possible workable arrangement designed to secure advantages and avoid disadvantages," he concluded. ". . . In the event the British and U.S. Government, after analysis of this radio, are still dissatisfied with the nature of the agreement made, I suggest that a mission of selected U.S. and British representatives (including the Free French if deemed desirable) be dispatched immediately to Algiers where they can be convinced in short order of the soundness of the moves which have been made."[61]

When Eisenhower radioed this, Roosevelt was again in Hyde Park. He had left Washington on the night of Friday, November 13, after signing a just passed amendment to the Selective Service Act (Congress had put off the amendment's passage till after the election) lowering the draft age to eighteen. With him on his special train were Harry Hopkins and wife Louise, Crown Princess Martha, and Bill Hassett, but not Grace Tully or any of the stenographic staff: save for a brief and routine radio address occasioned by the seventh anniversary of the Philippines Commonwealth government, broadcast from the President's office in the FDR Library on Sunday, November 15, this was for him a weekend of total rest and relaxation.

So it was not until Monday, November 16, that, back in the White House, he read Eisenhower's cable to Marshall of the day before. He was so impressed by the force and clarity of the general's document, and by its author's manful shouldering of full responsibility for what had been done, that he read it aloud to Hopkins, doing so "with the same superb emphasis that he used in his public speeches" and thus sounding "as if he were making an eloquent plea for Eisenhower before the bar of history," as Sherwood later wrote. Far less enthusiastic was Churchill's response, in a message to the President dated November 15 that was also on the President's desk that Monday morning. The fact that Eisenhower's defense of what he had done was "so ably expressed," wrote Churchill, and that the arrangement itself was "endorsed by our officers on the spot," left His Majesty's government "no choice but to accept" the arrangement, but "our doubts and anxieties" were not assuaged, and he could not regard the present "solution" as "permanent or healthy. . . . We feel sure you will consult us on the long-term steps pursuing always the aim of uniting all Frenchmen who will fight Hitler."[62]

Actually, the British cabinet's "doubts and anxieties" about the Darlan Deal were increasing at that moment, for by then the initial reaction to it by the Allied citizenry was giving way in both Britain and the United States to something more serious, more ominous, for Allied political leaders. The initial action had itself been one of utter shock and total puzzlement, coupled with a willingness on the part of many to suspend final judgment until more information was available. In London, according to Raymond Daniell's report in the *New York Times,* the first popular response had been one of "disgust." The highly reputed French journalist whose *New York Times* column was signed "Pertinax" felt the Americans must be intending to employ Darlan as a "temporary makeshift" but added that "even on that assumption, the present state of affairs is truly bewildering." He made it clear that he regarded any Allied dealings at all with such a man to be mistaken. Darlan, he warned, is a "supreme intriguer" who "does not want to be a makeshift."[63] In the immediately following days, what had been shock and bewilderment became a rising tide of angry outrage. Darlan, next to Laval, was the most notorious, the most widely and justifiably hated, of all the Nazi collaborators in Vichy. How could our placing such a man in control of the government of French North Africa, there enforcing Fascist laws and sustaining brutal Fascist institutions with (ultimately) Allied arms—how could this be justified on the grounds that it "ended fighting" and "saved lives"? A military commander could always "end fighting" and "save lives" simply by yielding to the desires of the enemy (surrendering, in other words)—and surely Darlan's foul record placed him in the very front rank of our enemies. At the German border, would we, on grounds of "military necessity," strike a deal with Goering? Or one with Matsuoka, when we were about to land in Japan?* Why, then, had we gone to war in the first place? What were we fighting for?

Roosevelt was himself acutely aware of "doubts and anxieties" all around him as he, with Hopkins, drafted on November 16 replies to both the Eisenhower and the Churchill messages. To Churchill, he wrote that "the Darlan business . . . naturally disturbed me as much as it did you" (the evidence suggests that his "disturbance" was largely consequent upon Churchill's, upon that of a liberal public normally supportive of him, and upon that of several of his closest advisers). He was sure, however, that Eisenhower's "judgment on the ground is better than ours and that we must support him." He was enclosing, he said, a copy of the message he was sending Eisenhower. It said: "I am . . . not disposed to in any way question the action you have taken. Indeed you may be sure of my complete support for this and any other action you are required to take in carrying out your duties. You are on the ground. . . . However, I think you should know and have in mind the following policies of this government: 1. That we do not trust Darlan. 2. That it is impossible to keep a collaborator of Hitler and one whom we believe to be a Fascist in civil power any longer than is absolutely necessary. 3. His movements should be watched carefully and his communications supervised." But having dictated these messages, he decided

---

*When on November 23, 1942, de Gaulle representatives André Philip and Adrien Tixier (the latter an abrasive personality who managed to antagonize virtually every American he met) vehemently protested what was happening in North Africa during an interview in the Oval Office, Roosevelt's self-control gave way for a moment—something that very rarely happened. He shouted: "Of course I'm dealing with Darlan, because Darlan's giving me Algiers! Tomorrow I'd deal with Laval if Laval were to offer me Paris!"[64]

for some reason not to send them (Sherwood says they were written "to make clear on the permanent record just how Roosevelt viewed this malodorous situation"). Instead he communicated to Eisenhower, through Marshall, his three reservations regarding Darlan; he made no written reply, specifically, to the Churchill missive.[65]

On that same day (November 16), in London, de Gaulle went by invitation to No. 10 Downing Street to discuss with Churchill and Eden the proclamation by Darlan of his assumption of power in North Africa "in the name of the Marshal." He was shown the telegrams the Prime Minister and the President had exchanged on this matter. "England gave her consent to this move only on condition that it be merely an expedient," said the Prime Minister. Replied de Gaulle: "You invoke strategic reasons, but it is a strategic error to place oneself in a situation contradictory of the moral nature of this war." He then showed Churchill and Eden messages received from France revelatory of the "stupefaction" with which the French masses (whose hatred of Darlan was justifiably massive) responded to news of the admiral's elevation by the Allies. He urged them to consider "the consequences you risk incurring. If France one day discovers that because of the British and the Americans her liberation consists of Darlan, you can perhaps win the war from a military point of view but you will lose it morally, and ultimately there will be only one victor: Stalin."[66]

Next day, Churchill wrote Roosevelt: "I ought to let you know that very deep currents of feeling are stirred by the arrangement with Darlan. The more I reflect upon it the more convinced I become that it can only be a temporary expedient justified solely by the stress of battle. We must not overlook the serious political injury which may be done our cause, not only in France but throughout Europe, by the feeling that we are ready to make terms with the local quislings. Darlan has an odious record. . . ." Roosevelt received this almost simultaneously with information that Wendell Willkie had planned to close an address to a *New York Herald-Tribune* current affairs forum, nationally broadcast last night, with a ringing denunciation of the Darlan agreement as an outrageous betrayal of the cause for which the Allies were allegedly fighting, and that Secretary Stimson, somehow getting wind of this, had managed with great difficulty to persuade him to delete from his speech all reference to Darlan, this in a phone call made only forty-five minutes before Willkie's opening words were to be spoken. ("I told him flatly," Stimson would later recall, "that, if he criticized . . . at this juncture, he would run the risk of jeopardizing the success of the United States Army in North Africa." Unless changed, the speech, asserted Stimson, might cost sixty thousand American lives—a figure he seems to have snatched from the air. "I can't believe that," Willkie had replied, "but I guess I can't risk it either.")[67] Roosevelt knew also that Marshall had taken the (for him) unprecedented step of imploring editors and broadcasters, in an unofficial communication, to consider deferring criticism of North African political arrangements until "the immediate defeat of Axis forces now in the area at a minimum cost of American lives" had been achieved—a tactic that may have kept the wave of current press criticism from being even higher than it was. "I too have encountered the deep currents of feeling about Darlan," began Roosevelt's reply to Churchill, dispatched in the early evening of November 17. "I felt I should act fast so I have just given out a statement at my press conference which I hope you will like. . . . It follows . . . [in a separate message]."[68]

He had for the last two days been urged repeatedly by close associates to make such a statement. Fortunately for him, much of the fury of the rising storm was focused upon Cordell Hull and the State Department, thanks in good part to a rash public proclamation by the secretary that the success of the initial North African landings was a triumphant vindication of the much attacked Vichy policy. But there was more than enough storm left over to damage the White House seriously, and the damage to the administration increased with every hour of presidential silence on this matter. So insisted Hopkins, Rosenman, and Sherwood as they gave into Roosevelt's hand a draft presidential statement produced by OWI's Elmer Davis in collaboration with Archibald MacLeish (according to Warren F. Kimball, the final draft statement was written by Milton Eisenhower, the general's youngest brother, who was then OWI's associate director). In this draft, Roosevelt made what Sherwood calls "substantial revisions, all of them calculated to make the language tougher and more uncompromising."[69]

As released, it said in part: "I have accepted General Eisenhower's political arrangements made for the time being in Northern and Western Africa. I thoroughly understand and approve the feeling in the United States and Great Britain and among all the other United Nations that . . . no permanent arrangement should be made with Admiral Darlan. People in the United Nations likewise would never understand the recognition of a reconstituting of the Vichy Government in France or in any French territory. . . . The future French Government will be established, not by any individual in metropolitan France or overseas, but by the French people themselves after they have been set free by the victory of the United Nations forces. The present . . . arrangement in North and West Africa is only a temporary expedient, justified solely by the stress of battle [the reader will recognize Roosevelt's borrowing from the Churchill message he had received earlier that day]. . . ." It was so justified, the statement went on to say, because it had saved and was saving time and lives. He closed: "I have requested the liberation of all persons in Northern Africa who had been imprisoned because they opposed the efforts of the Nazis to dominate the world, and I have asked for the abrogation of all laws and decrees inspired by Nazi Governments or Nazi ideologists. Reports indicate that the French in North Africa are subordinating all political questions to the formation of a common front against the common enemy."[70]

VII

THE Roosevelt statement may have prevented for the time being a further rise in the storm of criticism; it did nothing to abate that storm. For there came from North Africa no sign that the ruling French authorities there were granting Roosevelt's "request" for either the liberation of political prisoners or the "abrogation" of Vichy-Nazi "laws and decrees." Quite the contrary. News reports were that anti-Semitic decrees remained in force, with officials justifying their continuance on the ground that their immediate repeal might enable German propagandists to incite Arab unrest "detrimental to the . . . military campaign" (so Murphy explained in mid-November to a delegation representing Jewish-American soldiers). Concentration camps continued to hold more than nine thousand political prisoners as November gave way to December, and December advanced, because, French officials told a sympathetic Murphy, most of these thousands were "destitute and had no place to go" (as the diplomat later wrote), and among them were "dangerous fanatics and . . . common criminals."[71] There may have been, but if so, they were outnumbered by soldiers and civilians whose only "crime" was that of aiding the Allies, in violation of Vichy orders, before and during the initial Torch landings, and this fact was reported in the American and British press. There was no perceptible increase of civil liberties for the general populace: freedom of speech, press, assembly, and movement remained severely restricted. Moreover, there was a strong tendency among top American commanders—notably Fredenhall in Oran and Patton in Casablanca—to collaborate with the Vichyites in their refusal of any real political reform, because reform meant disorder, as the Vichyites insisted, and disorder would be disastrous to military operations. In Casablanca, Patton, who was himself an emphatically authoritarian personality, actually became a warm personal friend and admirer of Governor-General Nogues of Morocco, where, as we've already noted, Bethouart remained imprisoned and where the general repression was most severe. When Eisenhower expressed his dislike and distrust of Nogues, and his determination to remove him from office at the earliest possible moment, Patton protested bitterly and at length, claiming that Nogues's regime was popular with the Arabs and that his removal, and the repeal of anti-Semitic decrees, would provoke Arab unrest so serious that sixty thousand fully equipped American troops would be required in Morocco to keep order.*

As for Eisenhower himself, after he transferred his headquarters from Gibraltar to Algiers on November 23, he was forced to realize that his effort to take Tunis swiftly and cheaply could not succeed: yet green British and U.S. troops, operating at the end of long, inadequate, and threatened lines of communica-

---

*Perhaps it was this estimate that suggested to Stimson the claim that sixty thousand American lives might be lost if Willkie attacked the Darlan Deal.

tions, managed to reach on November 28 a point only fifteen miles from Tunis, but there they came hard against first-class German troops whose communications were short, voluminous, and secure; they had to retreat, with heavy losses. Clearly, a full-scale Allied attack employing all available force would be necessary, an operation whose buildup and direction required the commander in chief's concentrated attention. Yet he was continually harassed by political concerns. By mid-December, the harsh, unremitting pressures had worn his patience so thin that it gave way, and he made what he himself soon recognized as an error: he imposed a rigorous censorship upon all political news emanating from his theater of command, maintaining it for several weeks in violation of his own conviction that "the only justifiable excuse for [news] censorship [by a commanding general] is the necessity to withhold valuable information that the enemy could not otherwise obtain." He gives his reasons in his war memoirs: "The local antagonism in the French Army and in all echelons of the government against De Gaulle was intense, but he enjoyed a distinct popularity with the civilians and this sentiment progressively increased. . . . Through every possible outlet open to them the De Gaulle forces in London and central Africa were fiercely attacking every French military and civil official in Africa, and the latter wanted to reply, publicly, in terms no less harsh. I believed that to permit the growth of such a public name-calling contest would create conditions which would make future reconciliation impossible. . . ." And reconciliation of the opposing French factions was, he claims, his policy aim at that time: "The plan of my political advisers and myself was to promote an eventual union between the local French administration and the De Gaulle forces in London."[72]

But if this was *his* policy aim at that time, and there is some evidence that it was, it was certainly not that of the chief of his political advisers, Robert Murphy—and if it was truly his own aim, he contradicted it in practice by continuing to approve the North African political arrangements that Murphy initiated or supported. At the very moment of the censorship order, the Darlan regime, with Murphy's full support, was doing everything it could to prevent any participation whatever in North African affairs by de Gaulle, his followers, or any other anti-Vichyites—and only a couple of weeks later, on the occasion of the assigning to Giraud of high political as well as military command powers, Murphy assured the French general that "outside elements," clearly a reference to the Gaullists, would never be permitted to enter North Africa. Yet Eisenhower's personal as well as official support of Murphy increased in strength and solidity during this period: it was by his order that the Distinguished Service Medal, an army decoration seldom given a civilian, was awarded the diplomat (December 16), the general personally pinning it on the diplomat's jacket following the reading of a citation, prepared by the general himself, saying that "Robert D. Murphy . . . while serving in a position of great responsibility with the Army of the United States . . . displayed exceptionally outstanding qualities of leadership, courage, and sound judgment, often under extremely hazardous circumstances."[73] A few days later, Murphy decisively concurred in (he obtained Eisenhower's approval of) the appointment by Darlan of one Marcel B. Peyrouton to succeed Yves Chatel as governor-general of Algeria.* Peyrouton had a record fully as odious as the admiral's, if not more so. He had been Vichy's interior minister in 1940 when the first Vichy anti-Semitic decrees, which he himself helped shape (he was a fervent anti-Semite), went into effect; he was the author of other severely repressive measures; and it was under his personal supervision that the Vichy police had enforced with great cruelty the brutal Vichy laws. No man was more hated by the Gaullists than he.

As for the censorship, Eisenhower later thought that, though a mistake, it "had some of the desired effect"—and indeed it may have had insofar as his "desired effect" was truly the promotion of ultimate French unity. For crucial weeks it prevented direct participation by the Vichy-appointed local French officials in public quarrel with the Gaullists of London and central Africa who, untrammeled by censorship and thoroughly incensed, mounted a massive publicity campaign that converted to their cause millions who had therefore maintained a cautious neutrality, or a misinformed preference for the Darlan side, in the great quarrel. (Strange to say, Eisenhower had imposed the censorship without consulting Murphy, who, in his memoirs, calls the censorship a serious error because it added "to the already numerous complaints about alleged reactionary . policies of Allied Force Headquarters"[74]—because, in other words, it worked against the maintenance of those policies.) The Fighting French leader's popular support throughout the free world now grew by leaps and bounds.

In the United States, de Gaulle and his cause were championed during these weeks by the nation's two most powerfully persuasive unofficial commentators on public affairs, Wendell Willkie and Walter Lippmann. Willkie, infuriated by what he deemed a cowardly and mendacious censorship by the administration (it amounted to that) of his *Tribune* forum speech, refused to have his voice muffled again by Stimson or Marshall or anyone else, and his public denunciations of the American policy in North Africa were vehement, cogent, and highly influential. Still more cogent and almost equally and (for him) uniquely vehement were the published opinions of Lippman in his syndicated "Today and Tomorrow" column. On November 17, the columnist had addressed a lengthy memorandum to Cordell Hull and George Marshall, a copy of which was

*This appointment would not be announced publicly until January 19, 1943. Like Darlan, Peyrouton was one of Laval's bitterest political foes, an antagonism grounded in personal animosities and political rivalries rather than ideological differences. Unlike Darlan, however, he had not sufficient political potency to remain safely in France after Laval returned to power; he had fled to Buenos Aires, resuming the ambassadorship to Argentina from which he had been recalled by Reynaud in the last weeks of the Third Republic. It was from Buenos Aires that he was brought to Algiers in U.S. government transport.

promptly upon the President's desk, we may be sure. In it, he expressed a willingness to accept as true the claim that an arrangement with Darlan was a "military necessity" but bitterly deplored the grant to Darlan of political power. Was Vichy, crushed in France by the German occupation, to be perpetuated in North Africa with American support? Was it our considered policy to support "quisling governments" in the lands we "liberated" from Axis rule? Or was this present fiasco, as he deemed it, an accident, an aberration consequent upon a ghastly "miscalculation [by Murphy, obviously and chiefly, though Murphy's name was unmentioned] in the political preparations" for North Africa? Clearly, as regards "the critical points of intelligence and collaboration in North Africa, General de Gaulle's intelligence was more accurate than our own, and it will be a grievous error to continue to ignore it."

The substance of this had been repeated a couple of days later in a Lippmann column calling for an Allied sponsorship of a provisional North African government composed of the various French resistance groups and claiming that the chief obstacle to the union of these groups was "the unreasoning prejudice against General de Gaulle on the part of certain of our officials"—an obvious gibe against Roosevelt and, especially, Hull. By both the memorandum and, even more, the column, thin-skinned Hull was infuriated; he fired off a letter to Lippmann accusing him of near treason. Lippmann responded with columns attacking the State Department's "propaganda campaign" against anyone who had the temerity to criticize our North African policy and naming the State Department's Robert Murphy as the individual chiefly responsible for the hazardous "muddle" in that strategic area. In later columns, he found it "astonishing that so much reliance has been placed upon his [Murphy's] judgment." The diplomat was a "most agreeable and ingratiating man whose warm heart causes him to form passionate personal and partisan attachments rather than cool and detached judgments" and who "took his political color from those he associated with." Consequently, when placed in historically decisive positions, he made one disastrous mistake after another. In evidence of this, Lippmann cited Murphy's siding, while counselor of the American embassy in Paris in the spring of 1940, with appeasement-minded Daladier against Paul Reynaud; his "staunch" advocacy of Pétain after he went from Paris to Vichy; the misinformation garnered by his well-organized two-year intelligence operation in North Africa; and now, climactically, the deal with Darlan.[75]

There is in history, as in the physical world, a natural balance (call it justice) that works relentlessly, unceasingly, against all that would deny it. If the denial is integral to a human organization, it is a structural weakness operating as an infection (to shift metaphors in midstream), a disease that tends to spread throughout the organizational body to fatality. If, having once been established, the balance is upset (we shift back to the mechanical metaphor), it will insist with the force

of gravity upon restoring itself. The restoration may be long delayed. For decades, for centuries, the imbalance may be maintained. But its maintenance requires human force, and the amount of human energy-as-force that is needed
increases over time because the implementing apparatus erodes, gradually
wearing out, as it comes hard against the sense of justice, the need for balance,
that is inherent and tends to grow in the breast of every normal human being. A
natural balance *will* be restored, ultimately, though it cost the life of individuals,
institutions, organizations, nations, even whole civilizations that persist in the
effort to prevent it.

And sometimes the processes of erosion and restoration work very rapidly.

In the present instance, tiny when measured on the scale of universal history,
they worked swiftly indeed and, very soon after they began their work, destroyed Admiral Darlan. . . .

Compassion for the numberless victims of the admiral's ruthless opportunism
need not preclude some slight measure of compassion for Darlan himself in
these last days, as they proved to be, of his life. Darlan was a man of ability who
strove more than most to think well of himself (he *had* so to strive more than
most, for the obstacles to his doing so were great and numerous)—a prideful
man who wished to be thought well of by others but knew his wish to be
doomed to frustration (the same obstacles that stood in the way of his self-
respect prevented his respect by others)—a man highly sensitive to slights and
slurs, yet so placed that he could neither prevent nor openly resent them—and a
loving father whose anxiety over the fate of his polio-stricken son was for him
a throbbing anguish through every one of his now severely numbered days. He
well knew from the first, as has been indicated, that his actual power over North
African affairs consisted for the most part of American illusions and would
probably end soon in American disillusionment. He had to have sensed that the
contempt and distrust of him quite openly displayed by Clark was shared behind
a screen of circumspection by Eisenhower (the latter writes in his war memoirs
that Darlan's "mannerisms and personality did not inspire confidence and in
view of his reputation we were always uneasy in dealing with him").[76] He felt
acutely his growing isolation and vulnerability after Roosevelt's November 17
press announcement. This last hurt him deeply, since he was disposed by Roosevelt's expressed (and practically implemented)* concern over Alain Darlan's
polio to regard the American President as a personal friend.

Hurt feelings are evident in the "rather pathetic letter," as Butcher calls it, that
he wrote to Eisenhower on November 20. "Information coming to me from
various sources tends to give credit to the opinion that 'I am but a lemon which
the Americans will drop after it is crushed,' " he began, going on to assert that
he had taken "the line of conduct" he now followed not "through pride, nor am-

---

*See note 33 for this chapter.

bition, nor intrigue, but because the place I held in my country made it my duty to act." He pointed out that official American statements describing him as a "temporary expedient" dangerously undermined his authority—a remark revelatory of the self-contradictory nature of America's North African policy (that the Americans supported him because he had an authority over the French that itself consisted of American support of him). His personal resentment was patent, and so, to a discerning eye, was his realization that, a ruined man, he now came very near the end of his "line."[77]

Yet—pridefully, defiantly, stubbornly—he pursued that line to its, and his, bitter end. Witness his Eisenhower-approved summoning of Peyrouton to Algiers late in December. Witness, too, his dealings with the representative of de Gaulle, who arrived in Algiers from London at that same time.

Evidence that Eisenhower really did aim for a unity of the Gaullist forces with the local French administrators in North Africa is the fact that in mid-December, simultaneously with his imposition of political censorship, he consented to the sending of a special Gaullist mission from London to Algiers—the mission to which Roosevelt had told Churchill a month ago he had "no objection"* but which he now, with Leahy, strongly disapproved. He warned the commander in Algiers, through Leahy, that de Gaulle's purpose was to stir up trouble for Darlan—and indeed it was, insofar as no real move toward the desired French unity was possible as long as Darlan remained high commissioner. The chosen missionary was General François d'Astier de La Vigerie, one of whose brothers was a top leader of the resistance movement in France, another a leader of the Gaullist movement in Algiers. He arrived in Algiers on December 20. No one met him at the airport, a discourtesy Murphy should have prevented; d'Astier, deeming it a deliberate slight, was angered, and his anger became fury when he was ordered arrested by Darlan immediately upon his arrival in the city. This order was promptly canceled by Eisenhower, who then had great difficulty in persuading the two men even to meet each other. He had virtually to compel them to meet, and when they did, the meeting was as profitless as it was stormy. For Darlan, it was a humiliation. The admiral, with Giraud at his side, had to endure a fiery, profoundly insulting denunciation of him by d'Astier, who closed with the blunt statement that Darlan in his present position was an insurmountable obstacle to French unity and must now, at once, get out of the way. That evening, Darlan demanded of Eisenhower the immediate return of d'Astier to London, and this time Eisenhower obliged him. The de Gaulle emissary, mission accomplished after a fashion, left Algiers on December 24 "convinced that Darlan, feeling the ground give way beneath him, would shortly abandon his position."[78]

The admiral did not live to do so.

*See pp. 697–98.

On the afternoon of that day of d'Astier's departure (Christmas Eve 1942), Darlan, returning to his office in the Palais d'Été after an abnormally prolonged luncheon, was met on the stairway by an intense, pale, burning-eyed youth named Fernard Bonnier de la Chapelle—by occupation a student at the University of Lyons, by political persuasion a Gaullist-Royalist (such strange alliances were quite common in the chaotic politics of war-broken France)—who drew from his jacket pocket a twenty-two-caliber revolver, which he fired point-blank, twice, into the admiral's face. Darlan toppled forward, mortally wounded; he died on a hospital operating table forty-five minutes later.

He was not long survived by his assassin.

Chapelle was immediately arrested and roughly interrogated, was tried and condemned to death by a military tribunal on Christmas Day, was executed by a firing squad on the following morning. And only the bare facts of this suspiciously hasty procedure were permitted by an intensified Allied military censorship to be publicly known; even the assassin's name was, for a time, denied the public. All interrogation and trial records were sealed by order of Giraud, who immediately succeeded to the post of high commissioner; they remain sealed to this day if, indeed, they were not soon destroyed. Why? Did the executing authorities have something to hide that they feared the youth (he was barely twenty) might reveal? De Gaulle in his memoirs more than hints that, in his opinion, this was the case—that those who had placed Darlan in power and now found him an increasingly dangerous embarrassment had duped young Chapelle into the performance of this act, which Mark Clark, in *his* memoirs, frankly calls an "act of providence" and the "lancing of a troublesome boil."[79] Writes de Gaulle: "This young man, this child overwhelmed by the spectacle of odious events, thought his action would be a service to his lacerated country, would remove from the road to French reconciliation an obstacle shameful in his eyes. He believed, moreover, as he repeatedly said to the moment of his execution, that an intervention would be made in his behalf by some outside source so high and powerful that the North African authorities could not refuse to obey it. That is why the strange, brutal and summary way the investigation was conducted in Algiers . . . led to the suspicion that someone wanted to conceal at any price the origin of his [the assassin's] decision. . . ."[80]

Others spread abroad the story that de Gaulle himself, through his agent Henri d'Astier in Algiers, was implicated: it was said that the assassin, during his interrogation, had revealed a close connection with d'Astier. And Roosevelt and Leahy may have found it convenient to accept as true this version of the event. At any rate, Roosevelt, who during his meeting with de Gaulle's representatives on November 23 had asked them to tell the general how "desirable" an early visit by him to Washington would be, prompting de Gaulle to prepare to leave London for Washington on December 27, now abruptly asked the general (on December 26) to postpone his visit indefinitely.

13

The End of 1942:
Brightening Horizons, East and West

I

ROOSEVELT learned of Darlan's assassination, via a White House news ticker, shortly after the noon hour of December 24. By nightfall, when he went out on the south porch of the White House to deliver his Christmas Eve message to the crowd shivering on the lawn (the Washington weather had been abnormally bitterly cold for the last ten days), he had prepared a public statement denouncing young Chapelle's act as utterly evil and "cowardly"—and though the latter adjective may seem contradictory of what it purports to modify, it evidently indicates accurately what Roosevelt felt at that moment. He felt outrage. He seems to have truly believed that the conversations of d'Astier, Giraud, Darlan, and Eisenhower in Algiers during the preceding week had prepared the way for a reconstituted French National Committee inclusive of both de Gaulle and Giraud, but not dominated by de Gaulle, that this committee would soon peacefully replace the Darlan administration of French North Africa, and that Darlan's assassination was a disruption of his hopeful process that might prove fatal to it.

But by the brute fact of Darlan's removal from the African scene, he could hardly have been distressed. The devious admiral, writes blunt Mark Clark, had "served his purpose"; his "death solved . . . a very difficult problem of what to do with him."[1] And certainly Roosevelt was sick and tired of the opprobrium that had been focused upon him through the last six weeks by the Darlan Deal. It was much harder to bear than the opprobrium of the business community, and of the affluent in general. This he could deem a shoddy product of mere selfishness, an assertion of materialistic self-interest to be expected and shrugged off by any public official whose primary commitment is to the general good. The present opprobrium was very different, having as its constituents the disinterested opinions of people whom he respected and from whom he was accustomed to receiving approval and political support. Moreover, it was of a kind that provoked guilt feelings. His capacity for self-analysis, being of a piece with his overall capacity for logical analysis, was severely limited and, such as it was, seldom exercised: he shied away from any deep exploration of his own motives (it would inhibit action) and was helped to do so by a religious faith that largely absolved him of personal responsibility for the consequences of his public acts. Nevertheless, in this present case, it required a painful inward effort for him to deny as he did, even to himself, that the whole of the North African political imbroglio was rooted in and shaped by his French policy, itself determined in good part by a personal antipathy to the man Charles de Gaulle that would have been hard for him to justify on purely rational grounds. Psychologically revealing is the fact that, according to Sam Rosenman, he "showed more resentment and more impatience with his critics throughout this period than at any other time I know about. He so sincerely detested Fascism and Nazism that the charges of undue and unnecessary collaboration with the former Fascists in North Africa were painfully distressing." And Ickes writes in his diary of Roosevelt's "fuming" to his cabinet in late November that he was no partisan of Darlan's, "that so far as he [personally] was concerned, Darlan stank; he was a skunk."[2]

The elimination of this "skunk" to whose widow and desperately ill son he was extending condolences and concrete aid on this Christmas Eve, would not, however, eliminate the opprobrium focused upon Roosevelt by the Darlan Deal. By nightfall of that day, Roosevelt had also told Marshall that he wanted "no announcement . . . made reference Darlan's successor without reference here," to quote Marshall's message to Eisenhower that night.[3] The North African commander would find it on his desk when he arrived back in Algiers on Christmas Day after a miserable and dangerous all-night jeep ride from the Tunisian front. He was a tired and dispirited commander who would read the Marshall message: in Tunisia, he had been forced to cancel the final all-out drive toward Bizerte and Tunis, so arduously prepared and on the verge of its launching, because successive days of heavy rain had immobilized his troops in a sea of mud. He would, of course, obey the President's order as regards any public announcement, but the fact to be announced was already determined. Giraud was already in place as Darlan's successor, he being the only man save Nogues who could possibly be there—and Nogues knew himself to be placed out of the running by Eisenhower's dislike and distrust of him. Giraud's appointment would be confirmed on December 27 by a so-called Imperial Council, which, created by Darlan, consisted wholly of the admiral's Vichyite appointees. Of it, Nogues would be the dominant figure. Hence, the new arrangement was not really new, but a continuation of the one that had bred grave political trouble; and it would continue to breed, without surcease, the same kind of trouble well into the new year 1943.

The shivering crowd that stood before the President, as he and his wife came out onto the White House's south porch to greet it, did so in winter night darkness. This year, for the first time during Roosevelt's presidency, there would be no ceremonial lighting of the National Community Christmas Tree. The Office of Civilian Defense had asked that all outside lighting be dispensed with, to conserve war-needed energy. Not until next morning would the colored ornaments of the tall, stately spruce be clearly visible.

But there was light and warmth in the words that Roosevelt now spoke, specially in those words that echoed ones he had used when he delivered an address to the *New York Herald-Tribune* forum on November 17, the day he announced his approval of Eisenhower's political arrangements in North Africa and just one week after Willkie had delivered his truncated address to this same forum.

The President had then prefaced his hopeful words with statements revelatory of a mind that distinguished military from political concerns, the making of war from the making of peace, with a sharpness that seemed to many an observer to misperceive realities and contradict objective truths. ". . . [I]n time of war," he had said, "the American people know that the one all-important job before them is fighting and working to win. Therefore, of necessity, while long-range social and economic problems are by no means forgotten, they are a little like books which for the moment we have laid aside in order that we might get out the old atlas to learn the geography of the battle areas. . . . I think you will realize that I have made a constant effort as Commander in Chief to keep politics out of the fighting of this war." He had gone on to stress the need in wartime for censorship, self-censorship as well as governmental censorship, in order to protect military secrets and avoid giving aid and comfort to the enemy. Only after he had done this had he come to the one portion of the speech that deeply impressed the public. "During the last two weeks we have had a great deal of good news and it would seem that the turning point of this war is no time for exultation. There is no time now for anything but fighting and working to win." (Eight days earlier, Churchill, in the speech proclaiming his determination to maintain the British empire, had said apropos the North African invasion, "Now this is not the end. It is not even the beginning of the end. But it is, perhaps, the end of the beginning.") Roosevelt's cautious use of "seem" had had no effect upon the interpretation at once placed upon what he had said by radio commentators and newspaper headline writers. The papers proclaimed in front-page banners the next morning: TURNING POINT OF THE WAR REACHED SAYS F.D.R. On this Christmas Eve, speaking extemporaneously, he said: "I give you a message of good cheer. I cannot say 'Merry Christmas'—for I think constantly of those thousands of soldiers and sailors who are in actual combat throughout the world—but I can express to you my thought that this is a happier Christmas than last year in the sense that the forces of darkness stand against us with less confidence in the success of their evil ways." He closed: "It is significant that tomorrow—Christmas Day—our plants and factories will be stilled. This is not true of the other holidays we have long been accustomed to celebrate. On all other holidays the work goes on—gladly—for the winning of the war. So

Christmas becomes the only holiday in all the year. I like to think that this is so because Christmas is [truly] a holy day. May all it stands for live and grow throughout the years."4

He acknowledged with a smile and hand wave the audience applause, then returned with Eleanor to the second-floor family quarters of the White House, where, in the dining room, the Roosevelt family Christmas Eve dinner was served. Since every Roosevelt son was in uniform abroad, and personal travel in the United States was restricted, the family gathering this year was the smallest of the nine Roosevelt Christmas celebrations that had been held since Roosevelt's first presidential inauguration. It consisted only of the President and First Lady; Mrs. Franklin D. Roosevelt, Jr., the former Ethel du Pont, with her two children, Franklin D. III and Christopher; Mrs. J. R. Roosevelt, widow of FDR's half-brother, Rosy; lawyer Harry Hooker; and Harry Hopkins and his new wife, Louise, and daughter Diana. After dinner, this group seated itself beside the small family Christmas tree in the second floor's West Hall to hear Roosevelt's traditional reading aloud, with an actor's gestures and intonations, of an abridged version of Dickens's *A Christmas Carol.* Nor was there any departure from family tradition on Christmas Day, though thanks to the absence of numerous Roosevelt grandchildren, the holiday festivities were far less noisy than usual. In the morning, the President and Eleanor, accompanied by Ethel du Pont Roosevelt and the Hopkinses, including Diana, attended religious services conducted under the auspices of the Washington Federation of Churches in the poinsettia-decorated Church of the Epiphany, where they heard a traditional Christmas sermon delivered by the Reverend Howard Stone Anderson, pastor of Washington's First Congregational Church, the church in which Calvin Coolidge had worshiped. Back in the White House, the family gathered in the afternoon around the Christmas tree for the traditional distribution of gifts, and that evening they were served a traditional Christmas dinner consisting, as the interested world was told through the newspapers, of oyster cocktail, clear soup with sherry, roast turkey with chestnut dressing, cranberry jelly, deerfoot sausage, beans, cauliflower au gratin, casserole sweet potatoes with orange, grapefruit and avocado salad, plum pudding with hard sauce, and coffee.5 Roosevelt carved the turkey with his usual (actually unusual) skill and exuberant, cheer-spreading talk.

II

THERE were periods of restful solitude during that day when he may have, and probably did, cast his mind back over the year now ending. It had been a year of awful hazards—hazards that the country, at the year's beginning, had been physically woefully ill prepared to face. During the first half of it, an unbroken succession of disastrous defeats for Allied arms seemed at times to have reduced to paper thinness what had already been at the year's outset a dangerously narrow margin of survival for the Western democracies. Yet there had been not merely survival, but a widening of its margin into what had now become a margin of victory, and Roosevelt need have not the slightest doubt that this margin would widen greatly during the year ahead. Nor need he doubt that, for this happy event, he himself deserved much credit. This was conceded, with more or less reluctance, by many of the most severe of his critics.

Among them, and perhaps the most intelligently critical of all those who wrote for the public prints, was the liberal political commentator I. F. Stone.

Ten or twelve days ago, someone had called to Roosevelt's attention one of Stone's weekly contributions to *The Nation,* a journal the President did not regularly read. "Looking back across the year since Pearl Harbor, the President has much with which to be pleased," Stone had begun. ". . . Examined closely, by the myopic eye of the perfectionist, Mr. Roosevelt's performance in every sphere has been faulty. Regarded in the perspective of his limited freedom of choice and the temper of the country, which has never been really warlike, the year's achievements have been extraordinary. The curtailment and conversion of civilian industry for war, the peaceful resolution of capital-labor difficulties, the preservation to a remarkable extent of both social gains and civil liberties, the great expansion of arms output, the successful launching of our first major offensive represent stupendous and back-breaking tasks. The President is only a man, with twenty-four hours a day at his disposal, and amid the clamor of criticism, much of it justified, it will not hurt to pause a moment in gratitude for his work in the service of our country." Of course, "Mr. Roosevelt achieved what he did by taking the easiest route," Stone had gone on to say. ". . . He let big business mobilize our economy for war pretty much on its own terms, and established what is in effect a government of coalition with the right." But for this development, deplorable from Stone's point of view, "we must also in fairness criticize ourselves." Progressives could and should have made "the easiest route" far more difficult for the President to follow than it had been. "Just as King John had to sign [the Magna Carta] on the dotted line for the barons before they would fight, so the President had to come to terms with the quasi-independent corporate sovereignties that control so much of our productive resources. . . .* Had labor and the middle-class progressives been better organized, politically more astute, less divided, more competently led, they would have exerted more pressure in the national tug-of-war. The last congressional

---

*But did Roosevelt really *have* to reimpose upon the national economy the Wilson administration's industrial mobilization program of 1917–1918, without revision, in the spring of 1940? Had he had then no alternative? As for liberalism's disarray, had it not come about in good part because Roosevelt, in crucial situations where leadership was not only possible but loudly demanded, had refused to lead the progressive forces he presumably represented? These questions Stone himself had answered with two *no*'s and a *yes* in earlier articles; they were raised in many a mind by this present one.

elections were an adequate, if rough, test of just how much influence the labor and liberal elements have [at present] in national and local politics." We now had a Congress dominated by right-wingers, with reactionary Southern Democrats in the driver's seat. Upon these last, the White House was dependent for the passage of administration legislation. In consequence, the immediate future for liberalism, for American progressivism, was dark—which is to say that the prospect for a postwar world organized to secure peace and freedom for all humankind was dimming. "In a sense we are already losing the peace more rapidly than we are winning the war, for the shape of our society is being determined by the monopolistic and undemocratic fashion in which it has been mobilized for war production." But all was not forever lost, concluded Stone. "The pendulum now swinging away from social reform will swing back." The businessman's endeavor to destroy all government save that part that profited him personally was bound to be blocked when it threatened Social Security, for instance. Meanwhile, Stone found comforting the realization that, though the "immediate outlook" for liberalism was dark, it was "nowhere near as bleak as Hitler's."[6]

Roosevelt had read all this with more pleasure than pain. He *knew* that without his insistence upon setting industrial production goals far higher than the industrialists themselves wanted, or deemed possible, and his insistence upon a strenuous pursuit of those goals, the American industrial production now everywhere described as a "miracle" and the "wonder of the world" would not have been achieved. He *knew* that the battle against inflation was being fought as it had never been during the Great War, was succeeding as it had never then done, and that this was due in part to his own forceful dealings with Congress, his persuasive appeals to the general public, on this crucial matter. He *knew* that on every occasion when he had exercised his power as commander in chief to override the strong and emphatically expressed opinions of his top military subordinates, he, taking account of factors outside their purview, had been proved right. As he so often said to associates who railed against his failure to act with what they deemed the necessary dispatch, a sense of timing, based upon sensitivity to shifts of popular mood and attuned to the rhythms of history, was of paramount importance to successful political leadership—a fact that many or most of his critics failed to realize or, at any rate, failed to weigh accurately; he remained convinced that he had moved as swiftly and strongly as his circumstances permitted, taking advantage of every perceived breach or weakening in the wall of opposition, to preserve New Deal social advances and hold the ground, intact and fertile, out of which future reform could grow. For the "pendulum" was indeed bound to swing back, as Stone said, and more rapidly, in Roosevelt's opinion, than Stone seemed to believe it would. Stone had written that "1944 may see a right-wing Republican election" President. Roosevelt was less despondent. He had vaguely in mind a project involving cooperation between himself and Willkie whereby a fundamental realignment of America's two major political parties might be achieved: those Southern Democrats who held Republican views might be compelled to become frankly Republican, while those rank-and-file Republicans who accepted Willkie as their leader (there were still more of these, Roosevelt believed, than the old guard in control of the Republican Party machinery would ever admit) might follow him into a Democratic Party that could then be accurately labeled (and might actually be renamed) the Progressive Party. The American electorate would then have, for the first time since the era of Jefferson and Hamilton, a clear choice between two fundamentally different political philosophies. And Roosevelt, feeling that this just *might* begin to happen by the summer of 1944, when Willkie's bid for the Republican presidential nomination would certainly be defeated by the Republican old guard's machinations, believed he had done and was doing all he could to encourage this development.

Far from stifling or softening liberalism's voice, he had encouraged it to speak up, even at the occasional cost of considerable discomfort to himself. Speech after speech, magazine article after magazine article, and news interview after news interview vehemently arguing the liberal view of the war and the making of peace had been published with his permission, if not always his approval, by Eleanor Roosevelt, by Harold Ickes, by Henry Wallace, by Francis Biddle, and by several others whose public speech he might have controlled through exercise of the war power now assigned the presidency. Nor had he used these powers to impose censorship upon the Right, even when its voices spoke blatant falsehoods or published loudly to the world (as the *Chicago Tribune* had done) sensitive information that the government strove to keep secret and whose disclosure gave aid and comfort to the enemy. It was not his fault that liberal voices were not permitted to speak with anything like their full force, when permitted to speak at all, through the print media (the magazines, the syndicated columns, the individual and chain newspapers) from which a majority of the population derived its information on public affairs—this while the voices of allegedly individualistic and certainly utterly materialistic "private" enterprise spoke thunderously and incessantly through these same media. It was not his fault, in other words, that idealistic liberalism was gravely disadvantaged in an allegedly free "market of ideas" that was in reality sufficiently managed by the business interest to tilt it, for the great mass of Americans, quite steeply to the right. The consequences of this rightward tilt had been commented upon by Stone in that December 12 article that approved Roosevelt's role in preserving, to a degree remarkable in wartime, free speech on public affairs. Stone had referred to an address Attorney General Biddle had presented at the University of Virginia on Friday, December 4. "Is the sentiment of the public really moved by the vision of a better world or is it merely disturbed by anxiety about increased taxation and the threat of unemployment after the war?"

Biddle had asked. "Do the people of our land fight only to win the war and have it over—or to use the war for great and democratic ends?" Big business's answer to this question had been given two days before Biddle asked it, Stone went on to say, by the president of the National Association of Manufacturers (NAM) in a speech to the annual convention of that organization. In contemptuous dismissal of Wallace's "Century of the Common Man" and Wendell Willkie's "globaloney," as Mrs. Henry Luce would label it, the NAM president had said: "I am not fighting for a quart of milk for every Hottentot or for a TVA on the Danube." (What *was* he "fighting" for, who did so without danger or physical discomfort? Clearly, he "fought" for his own profit and power.)[7]

But if Roosevelt, in his mellow mood on that climactic day of the season of charity and goodwill toward all humankind (the Axis leaders were excluded from such charity on the ground they were inhuman), could thus look back over his year's performance with satisfaction, even pride, his retrospection, if at all detailed, must have been punctuated by a few instants of unease, perhaps even a few twinges of actual pain. There had been a number of regrettable casualties among administration personnel since Pearl Harbor. Had he done all he could to prevent them or to reduce the suffering that attended them?

In what he permitted himself to recall of his personal role in the termination of Sidney Hillman's governmental service, for instance, he must have felt something sharper than unease and been grateful for the fact that Hillman harbored no ill will toward him personally and was now, in the wake of the midterm election, and despite ill health, strenuously engaged in the organization of a CIO political action committee (a new departure in American politics) that, as long as it was unmatched by right-wing political action committees, might do much to even the odds in the contest between liberal and conservative. Thus, what Hillman had said in his letter refusing Roosevelt's offer to make him a special presidential assistant, namely, that he could serve the President's cause far better by resuming his leadership of union labor than by accepting a White House appointment, was being proved a statement of fact.

No such personal service to the administration was likely to be rendered by Leon Henderson, now that he had, just a few days ago, resigned his office as OPA director, ending a long and remarkably brave and creative governmental career—and though Roosevelt need feel no such shame over this ending as, despite himself, may have attended his remembrance of Hillman's, he could not but feel some personal responsibility for it. Had he not quite ruthlessly used Henderson as his "whipping boy," subjecting him to anguish that would have been reduced by timely public presidential support of him? And had not this contributed much to the erosion of both Henderson's effectiveness in office and his physical health? His health had suffered especially from the pressures to which he had been subjected during the period when he had had to rely wholly upon threats, fait accompli tactics, and persuasion to reach his ends; his eyesight was now dimming, and he suffered severe stress-induced lower-back pain. Moreover, though he had not asked for the OPA director's resignation, as several of his advisers had urged him to do, he had let OES director Jimmy Byrnes know that, in his opinion, Henderson's departure was probably made inevitable by a conservative midterm election victory for which, or for the proportions of which, many Democrats in Congress, also in state offices across the country, bitterly blamed Henderson's handling of his job—and Henderson had, of course, consulted Byrnes before writing his letter of resignation.

Not that Byrnes's words to him had been determinative of Henderson's decision; they had been merely confirmative. For the OPA director's eyesight, though failing, was not so dim that he could not read handwriting as large as it was on the wall now facing him. A powerful segment of what, come January, would be the new Congress was threatening to reduce drastically OPA funding if Henderson were not replaced—and of defenders, Henderson had almost none who were very effective with either the general public or the federal legislature. In his frighteningly exposed position, he had been unable to do the job that had to be done, while at the same time developing a potent personal constituency. Inflation control had required his stepping, even tromping now and then, on everybody's toes (he had, alas, given the impression to many that he rather enjoyed doing so). The farm bloc headed by the Farm Bureau hated him because he stood in the way of their war profiteering. Rank-and-file labor could develop no enthusiasm for a man who denied them the wage increases they wished they could have and which they believed were no more than fairly proportionate to business's rising war profits. He was the target of the most vicious attacks that the business interest, with its hired men in Congress and the mass media, could mount against him, because price control *did* limit business profiteering. And— perhaps out of a fear that his liberal bias might prevent his being fair to those who did not share his views, perhaps because it seemed the easiest way to bear his enormous burdens—he had allowed much of the actual price control machinery and personnel selection to be determined by state political machines, many or most of which, even when Democratic (several were Republican), were strongly inclined toward conservatism. As for the ordinary citizenry, though they were more than willing to submit to whatever rationing of food, coffee, gasoline, tires, and so on was truly necessary for war victory, they were vulnerable to interestedly narrow right-wing definitions of this necessity and were outraged to the extent that they believed what the conservative mass media so loudly told them, namely, that much of the deprivation, inconvenience, and discomfort imposed by rationing resulted from the arrogant power lust, the gross incompetence, of Leon Henderson. Finally, Henderson's flamboyant personality antagonized not only the pious conservatives of the Bible Belt, but also many a liberal who thoroughly approved his policy decisions. All in all, he had become a more costly embarrassment to the administration than Admiral

Darlan. A new man could continue Henderson's remarkably successful anti-inflation war while incurring a greatly reduced wrathful opposition, if he were the right choice*—now that this war's opening battles had been won, if narrowly, and the ground prepared for future victories. Each of these facts, including the unfortunate effect of his personality, was recognized by Henderson himself. "I have determined to cut my connection with the government completely," he had written, not without bitterness, in his December 15 letter to the President. "Different times require different types of men. I hope I have been suited to the battling formative period. I am decidedly not adjustable to the requirements of the future as it now begins to disclose its outline."[9]

(Thus Leon Henderson passes out of our history into an obscure private life that can never be fully satisfactory to him. For the "future" whose "outline" he discerned is destined to become, in the years ahead, a full reality dominated by men and forces he will not have the slightest desire to accommodate—which is to say that his great passion for public service will from now on be frustrated.)

III

UNHAPPY prospect mingled with a generally happy retrospect in Roosevelt's mind if his retrospection included, on this Christmas Day 1942, a review of the bitter, months-long quarrel between Vice President Henry Wallace and Secretary of Commerce Jesse Jones, who had as tacit ally Secretary of State Hull. The prospect was unhappy because this quarrel, though its latest flare-up had just been damped down in a way discomfiting to Jones, yet continued and was bound to continue, provoking one headline-producing flare-up after another, as long as the basic issue between its two sides remained unresolved—and such resolution required presidential decision of the basic kind from which Roosevelt always shied away. . . .

Wallace was chairman of the Board of Economic Warfare (BEW), which had been established by executive order on December 17, 1941 (ten days after Pearl Harbor), as a replacement with expanded powers of the Economic Defense Board, which Wallace had also chaired. The board members named by the organic order were (in addition to the Vice President) the secretaries of the Departments of State, Treasury, Justice, War, Navy, Agriculture, and Commerce, plus the heads of the WPB (Nelson), lend-lease administration (Stettinius), and inter-American affairs (Nelson Rockefeller). The board held fortnightly meetings, at most of which, of course, the nominal members were represented by designated delegates and in which the chairman's decisions outweighed those

---

*The initial choice would be Prentiss M. Brown, a Michigan Democrat who in November had lost his Senate seat, in part because he had been a stalwart supporter of the administration's anti-inflation programs.[8]

of all the other members, which is to say that the board per se functioned exclusively as an advisory oversight committee. BEW as an operating agency had as its executive director Wallace's close friend and longtime associate, Milo Perkins. A hardheaded, skillful, and energetic administrator, shrewd in his choice of staff personnel, Perkins had constantly in view long-range as well as immediate goals. He fully shared not only Wallace's conviction that war- and peace-making were inseparable parts of a single enterprise, but also Wallace's conception of the kind of peace that should be made. He strove therefore to have BEW's work contribute not only to military victory, but also, through solid foundation laying, to the world peace and order envisaged in Wallace's "Century of the Common Man"; and the agency's work toward these ends he divided among three sections, or offices. The most important was an Office of Imports, which had as its primary responsibilities the acquisition from foreign countries of strategic materials needed by the American war effort and the denial to Axis powers, through what was called "preclusive buying," of materials they were known to need. The other agency sections were an Office of Exports, which was expected to use its assigned licensing authority to prevent shipments of goods to Axis nations; and an Office of Warfare Analysis, which was to select important economic targets for strategic bombing. The work of each of these divisions was clearly implied by the organic executive order, whereby the responsibilities assigned BEW were of huge dimension.

But as was generally true of Roosevelt's administrative arrangements, these responsibilities were not accompanied by a commensurate assignment of authority, or power. The power was divided among BEW; the State Department, which claimed total constitutional control of *all* American negotiations with foreign governments; and the Commerce Department, which under Jesse Jones was in charge of the agencies from which BEW must obtain the money to pay for its purchases. The divided authority, given the very different natures and philosophies of the agencies and men among which it was divided, provided fertile ground for quarrel. Wallace complained of this in a remarkably frank accusatory letter to Roosevelt on April 8, 1942, saying that the "specific clause" in the executive order "indicating that where necessary my decision shall be final" was "worthless to me unless the other affected departments know that you are wholeheartedly behind me. The present situation on foreign raw materials is in a terrible mess because no one has power commensurate with his responsibilities, and because no one feels that he can do what ought to be done with the certainty that you are backing him up."[10]

On May 20, 1942, the President issued a statement that "defined the relations" between State and BEW in a way that left the final decisive power in his own hands. "In the making of decisions," said the statement, "the board and its officers will continue to recognize the primary responsibility ... under the President, of the Secretary of State in the formulation and conduct of our foreign policy and our joint relations with other nations. In matters of business judgment concerned with providing for the production and procurement of materials to be imported into this country for the war effort, including civilian supply, the Department will recognize the primary position and responsibility of the Board. In many cases a decision may involve matters of both foreign policy and business judgment in varying degrees. No clear-cut separation is here possible. Accordingly, if occasions arise in which the proposed action of the Board or its officers is thought by officials of the State Department to be variance with essential considerations of foreign policy, the Secretary of State and Chairman of the Board will discuss such matters and reach a joint decision, in matters of sufficient importance receiving direction from the President."[11]

The chief focus of BEW's quarrel with both State and Commerce was in Latin America. This was the most important theater of BEW operations because Central and South America were not only richly productive of tin, copper, rubber, fiber, quinine, and other badly needed materials, but, unlike similarly productive areas elsewhere on the globe, were also under no direct military threat by Germany or Japan. Their productivity *was* threatened, however, and gravely, by the failure of their governments to enforce the advanced labor and social legislation that had long been on most of their statute books. The consequent lack of decent pay, decent housing, and adequate health care for workers meant a lack of anything like full production of needed products. BEW therefore was writing into its purchasing contracts clauses requiring the contractor to obey all labor and social laws—clauses that the State Department perforce overtly agreed to while simultaneously complaining, covertly, that BEW's activity along these lines constituted U.S. governmental interference in the internal affairs of other countries, thereby violating principles of international relations to which the State Department was utterly committed. In actual practice, historically, the State Department had itself continuously violated this taboo in Latin America and done so in ways that gave it a considerable responsibility for the conditions BEW now strove to change. All through the decades of "dollar diplomacy," it had conceived its role to be that of serving the American corporations that, always prominent and often dominant in Latin American national economies, sought to keep labor costs as low as possible.

In addition to this BEW–State Department quarrel focused in Latin America was one focused in North Africa. BEW personnel in Algeria had discovered that since the signing of the Murphy-Weygand Accord in February 1941, shipments of oil from America to Vichy-governed North Africa, made under the terms of that agreement, had been used to replace oil sent from French North Africa to Libya to fuel Axis forces there. There was at least one case in which thousands of tons of American motor oil, aviation gasoline, and lubricating oil delivered to the Vichy governors of Algeria had then gone directly to Rommel in Libya. BEW's Office of Exports had then declined to authorize certain specified shipments to North Africa out of fear the shipped materials would end up in Nazi hands—a decision that was now resulting in the deaths of American soldiers, according to an angry but unsubstantiated charge made by Assistant Secretary Adolf Berle in a State Department meeting at which BEW members were present. (When inquiries were made of the military authorities in North Africa, these authorities denied that BEW's activity there had endangered any soldier's life; they said the agency's work had helped military operations.)[12]

These, then, were the grounds for the tacit alliance, in opposition to Wallace, between Hull and Jones. Jones, whose arrogant temper was short fused and whose appetite for raw power was enormous (far greater than his general intelligence),* reacted with virulent fury, instinctively, against Wallace's "Century of the Common Man," hence against BEW's labor and social contract clauses—indeed, against BEW's very existence. The agency was redundant, he wrathfully charged, in that it did nothing useful that Jones's RFC and other lending agencies weren't already doing better; it was worse than redundant insofar as whatever it did that *hadn't* been better done before violated every principle of sound business, sound government, and sound international relations. It was a vast worldwide liberal "boondoggle" that aimed at the establishment of an "international WPA" (so said Ohio's Republican Senator Taft, speaking Jones's views, in a Senate floor speech)[13] and wasted taxpayers' money at an appalling rate. The persuasiveness of banker Jones's fuming, however, was severely limited in the winter, spring, and summer of 1942 by the shocking public revelation of abysmal failures in the strategic materials stockpiling program for which he had primary responsibility, failures obviously due to his far greater concern for thrifty business practice than for the actual acquisition of essential materials. In two years, he had spent on actual acquisition less than 1 percent of the half-billion-dollar revolving fund assigned him by Congress for that purpose, with the result that there loomed darkly on a near horizon a catastrophic rubber shortage. Even Republicans accustomed to cheering Jesse on as the greatest champion of right principle in whole of the administration—even they, with the upcoming midterm elections weighing heavily on their minds, had last spring been publicly critical of their hero. It was at that time that Roosevelt had transferred primary responsibility for the acquisition of raw materials abroad from Jones's loan agencies to BEW, doing so in an executive order (on April 13) that responded to the already quoted Wallace letter of April 8. The transfer was not made in the clear-cut, wholly unequivocal fashion that Wallace and Perkins would have preferred, of course, but it authorized BEW to "coordinate the policies and actions of the several departments and agencies" and "develop inte-

---

*This is commonly the case. Truly intelligent people operating from decent instincts want no more power over others than is necessary to reach clearly defined, rationally justified, widely agreed goals, and they strive to make the power they wield as completely persuasive, as little coercive, as possible.

grated defense plans and programs" with respect to all international economic activities. Among these activities were "the acquisition and distribution of materials . . . from foreign countries, including preclusive buying."[14] BEW was to negotiate the contracts, then direct Jones's RFC to make the actual purchases and pay transportation and warehousing costs—to write the checks, in other words, on what was presumably, though by no means absolutely clearly, BEW's own bank account. This lack of clarity meant a continued, if reduced, mismatch in BEW of responsibility and effective power: a significant portion of the power needed to fulfill BEW's assigned responsibility (the power of the purse) remained in Jones's stingy, manipulative hands. He and his staff of experienced, business-minded bureaucrats could frustrate and obstruct BEW operations by taking their own sweet time about making the payments they were directed to make. Nevertheless, both Perkins and Wallace, assuming they now had firm backing from the White House, were for the time being satisfied with the arrangement—and during the immediately following months, RFC had generally performed pretty much as it was required, on paper, to do.

But the conservative triumph in the midterm elections had restored Jones to his rightful place as the champion of right (right-wing) principles. Voices that two months ago had been silent concerning him, when not actually (mutely) critical, were again loud in their praise of him. And within a week or so after the election, emboldened Senate Republicans had joined with Southern Democrats in an effort to restore to him the final authority over raw material purchases that had last spring been taken away. Their device for doing so was a so-called Danaher Amendment—a party measure reluctantly introduced on the Senate floor by Senator John A. Danaher* of Connecticut at the behest of Oregon's Charles McNary, the Senate minority leader. But Jones himself ensured the defeat of this effort on his behalf when he presented arrogantly assertive, sloppily prepared, and thoroughly mendacious testimony to the Senate Banking and Currency Committee in early December 1942. He charged that Perkins ran BEW dictatorially without any supervision whatever, that BEW's expenditures were unaudited, and that there was no precedent for the power given that agency to order RFC to spend specified sums of money. He apparently had no fear of contradiction as he left the hearing room, and there might have been none (his had been a private hearing) if the committee chairman, Senator Wagner, had not insisted that the BEW side of this argument be heard. Both Wallace and Perkins had come before the committee on December 8 and had easily demonstrated the falsity of all three of Jones's major contentions. They pointed out that it was RFC, not BEW, that paid for the materials BEW ordered from abroad, and if there was one thing that Jones's agency could be counted upon to do thoroughly,

---

*The amendment episode would contribute to Danaher's loss of his Senate seat, in 1944, to liberal Democrat Brian McMahon.

it was keep track of its own expenditures (the RFC audits were not publicized, however). They made it abundantly clear that Perkins as BEW's executive director was far more closely supervised than were Jones and his RFC; the board under which Perkins operated, of which Jones was himself a member, met at least once every two weeks, and if Jones wasn't present at these meetings, his proxy was. As for the "unprecedented" portion of the executive order enabling BEW to direct RFC to make specified expenditures of money, it was word for word the same as a clause in the order under which Nelson operated as head of WPB. Without such authority, no war emergency agency could function with any independence whatever of power-lustful Jesse Jones.[15]

The Danaher Amendment had then died in committee.

But still very much alive and active were the motives and means of the quarrel from which the amendment had sprung; and Roosevelt, in whatever prospect was imbedded in his retrospection on that Christmas Day, must have anticipated the letter he would actually receive from Wallace a few days hence. In it, the Vice President would ask, as he had asked before, for the granting to BEW of a borrowing authority that would enable the agency to become self-financing and thus wholly protected against Jones's interference with its work. Roosevelt need not ponder what his response would be; it was predetermined by an administrative technique so deeply rooted in his psyche that he probably would not have given the why of it, much less have justified it against criticism in open rational argument. Wallace's request would again be refused—and there would be increasingly bitter and (to the war effort) dangerous conflict between Wallace and Jones in the months ahead.

IV

ALMOST certainly excluded from whatever retrospect and prospect moved through Roosevelt's mind that day was any review of the response he had made and intended to make to information that had long been coming to him in bits and pieces but was now cohered into undeniable horrible fact, about what was not happening to the Jews of Europe. . . .

V

"IF the international Jewish financiers . . . again succeed in plunging the nations into a world war the result will be . . . the annihilation of the Jewish race throughout Europe," Hitler had shouted in a speech to the Reichstag on January 30, 1939. He had said (screamed) the same thing in precisely the same words five times during the immediately following months, in public speech to German crowds who cheered his words. After he himself had "succeeded" in "plunging the nations" in world war and his arms had brought virtually the whole of continental Western Europe under his control, including all of western Russia, destroying in the process (so he believed) Russia's industrial and fighting capacity, he had concluded that, his war being substantially won, the time had come to launch full-scale what he called, in oral communications with his top officials, the "final solution" of the "Jewish question."[16]

By then, since the war began, scores of thousands of European Jews had already died of organized Nazi brutality. Immediately after Poland's fall, Reich Marshal Hermann Goering in a secret meeting of Nazi officials had designated "the first step of the final solution [his words]" to be the gathering of all Jews into city ghettos, where they could be closely confined until the organization and material means of their ultimate disposal were in place. Hundreds of thousands had then been jammed into, for one, the Warsaw ghetto (it could decently accommodate no more than a fourth the number), where they soon began dying by the thousands of disease and starvation and outright murder. When the Low Countries and France became Nazi provinces in the summer of 1940, the mortality rate among the Jews living there increased dramatically. But the carefully planned, systematic mass murder of Jews had not begun until the Einsatzgruppen began their butchery immediately behind the eastward-moving front in Russia, in June 1941. Shortly thereafter, on July 31, forty days after the Russian invasion began, Goering directed Reinhard Heydrich, head of the security arm of the SS, "to carry out all preparations with regard to . . . a total solution of the Jewish question in those territories of Europe which are under German influence. . . . [Also] to submit to me as soon as possible a draft showing the . . . measures already taken for the intended final solution of the Jewish question."[17] This assignment was fulfilled with enthusiastic efficiency by ambitious, conscienceless Heydrich—and on January 20, 1942, his plans and preparations having been approved, he presided over a meeting in the Berlin suburb of Wannsee at which the final solution operation was officially launched in full force. It was a small meeting: only fifteen Nazi officials who were to play decisive roles in this enterprise (they included representatives of the Ministries of Justice and the Interior, the Foreign Office, the Gestapo, and the Nazi governor-general of Poland) were in attendance. Heydrich told them that every single one of the estimated eleven million Jews in Europe (man, woman, child, babe in arms) was to be "involved." Those not already in the East, which had the largest Jewish populations, were to be brought there and placed in "big labor gangs, with separation of sexes . . . and employed in road building, in which task undoubtedly a great part will fall [their treatment on the job would be of a kind that ensured this happening]. . . . The remnant . . . able to survive all this—since this is the part with the strongest resistance—must be treated accordingly [in other words, killed outright] since these people, representing a natural selection, are to be regarded as the germ cell of a new Jewish development."[18]

Some dissatisfaction was expressed at this meeting over the work-to-death formula. It was felt to be too slow and inefficient a killing process. For instance, the Polish governor-general's representative, State Secretary Josef Buehler, complained to Heydrich that the nearly two and a half million Jews in Poland constituted a great immediate danger; they were "bearers of disease"; they were "black-market operators"; and since most of them were unfit to work in any case, and all of them were already in the East, hence need not be transported there, surely a faster way of disposing of them should be followed. "I have but one request, that the Jewish problem in my territory be solved as quickly as possible," said Buehler at the conclusion of his plea.[19] His impatience was shared and soon thereafter decisively manifested at the very pinnacle of Nazi officialdom. There was at that moment no labor shortage in the Nazi empire, which is to say that there was no apparent need, early in that year,* to add large numbers of Jewish vermin to the workforce even temporarily. So within a week or two, orders came from Hitler through SS chief Heinrich Himmler for a drastic revision of the plan Heydrich had announced. Facilities for the mass extermination of Jews were already at hand. Five large concentration camps designed to gas people to death in batches had been established in Poland at Auschwitz, Treblinka, Chelmno, Belzec, and Sobibor. Five smaller extermination camps, which did their killing (far less efficiently) with guns, operated in Latvia, Lithuania, and White Russia. It was ordered that the Jews be transported directly to these lethal institutions, each of which now had its workload, already heavy, greatly increased. There began a systematic rounding up of the Jews of Western Europe, in specific numbers determined by the killing rates of the death camps to which they were dispatched in trainloads—and not infrequently, the trains that transported them were so overcrowded and devoid of creature necessities that a high percentage of their passengers died en route.

Of all the camps, Auschwitz was the largest and most efficient, its superior efficiency due in good part to its first commander, an ex-convict (murderer) and early Nazi named Rudolf Hoess. He would depose during the Nuremberg Trials years later that he "was ordered to establish extermination facilities" at Auschwitz "in June 1941" and that in preparation for his assigned task, he visited the already established camp at Treblinka to see how the work was being done there. Treblinka killed with carbon monoxide, as did most, if not all, of the others then in operation. (An account of monoxide's use at Chelmno came to Washington in May 1942 as part of a report, funneled through the Polish government-in-exile by what remained of Poland's Jewish Labor Bund, that seven hundred thousand Polish Jews had been killed up to that time and that the killing continued apace. The method employed at Chelmno was ingenious: A sealed chamber into which ninety people could be crowded was placed upon a

---

*It was not until 1942 drew near its end that a serious German labor shortage developed, at which time the work phase of the original final solution formula was partially reinstated.

diesel truck's frame; these people were then killed by monoxide gas hosed into the chamber from the motor exhaust as the truck drove toward the site at which their corpses would be buried en masse. On the average, one thousand people were gassed every day at Chelmno, said the report.)[20] At Treblinka, ten gas chambers had been established, each able to kill two hundred people at a time, and the Treblinka commander told Hoess with pride that he "had liquidated 80,000 in the course of half a year." Hoess was unimpressed. "I did not think his methods were very efficient," he deposed. "So when I set up the extermination building at Auschwitz, I used Zyklon B, . . . a crystallized prussic acid [it evaporated at a certain temperature into cyanide gas], which we dropped from a small opening. It took from three to fifteen minutes to kill the people. . . . We knew when [all] the people were dead because their screaming stopped. . . . Another improvement we made over Treblinka was that we built our gas chambers [there were four of them, with crematoria attached] to accommodate 2,000 people at one time." (At the height of Auschwitz's operation, between 10,000 and 12,000 Hungarian Jews a day would arrive there to be promptly disposed of; between 400,000 and 435,000 were killed during a single forty-six-day period—and on one occasion during that period, Hoess rushed to Budapest to complain in person to his superiors that his personnel and facilities were being overworked, especially those of his crematoria.)[21]

The whole of this huge criminal enterprise, unprecedented in its viciousness, in its size, and in its cold-blooded efficiency, was shrouded by its perpetrators in as thick a blanket of secrecy as possible. All who attended the initiating meetings, and all the many thousands later employed in it directly or indirectly, were sworn to silence on the matter. Nothing about it was put by them in plain speech or plain writing; euphemisms and code words were employed in whatever communications on the subject became necessary. But of course, it was impossible to keep secret from the world for very long so massive and shocking an endeavor, and news of it began to arrive in Washington well before its culminating phase was officially launched. As early as October 7, 1941, more than three months before the Wannsee Conference, Ray Atherton of the State Department's European Division passed on to Colonel Donovan* a sixty-page document headed "Poland Under German Occupation." It had come from a highly respected Pole to a former official of the U.S. embassy in Berlin who vouched for his correspondent's reportorial accuracy; it told of what had been happening in Poland between its fall and the Nazi invasion of Russia. The German authorities there had embarked, he said flatly, upon a program to "ruthlessly and entirely exterminate the Jewish element from the life of Aryan communities,"

---

*"Wild Bill" Donovan's official title then was coordinator of information. Actually, he headed the intelligence and espionage agency that, stripped of all its original propaganda functions, would become the Office of Strategic Services, forerunner of the CIA.

and such words as "liquidation," "elimination," and "extermination" were frequent in what followed this opening assertion. Among the very first to publicize what was happening was the great German novelist Thomas Mann, now self-exiled from his native land, who told the world in a series of BBC broadcasts in December 1941–January 1942 that the Nazis were engaged in mass killings; he presented specifics that were discounted, however, by State Department officials (they were eager to do so) because the specifics were unconfirmed by other sources. Thereafter, reports came to Washington in increasing number of the mysterious disappearance of Jews, sometimes of all the Jews, from communities in which they had been numerous. One lengthy message, dated July 20, 1942, which came from Lisbon to Washington (it was found in OSS files after the war), began: "Germany no longer persecutes the Jews, it is systematically exterminating them. . . . These facts . . . have been corroborated by many returning citizens of European origin now here [in Lisbon]."[22]

How much of this early information reached FDR it is impossible to say, but it is wholly impossible to believe that none of it did—and one can be certain that it initially failed to overcome in him, as it failed to overcome in others, a will, almost a vital necessity, to disbelieve it. It was so horrifying, so utterly incredible, so literally insane! For one thing, it meant, if true, that the Nazi leadership, out of pure hatred, was deliberately, systematically subtracting from the supply of the fighting fronts, and on a large scale, resources badly needed there—was, indeed, deliberately destroying a substantial potential labor force during what Washington believed to be already a serious German labor shortage and one that was bound to become more so. This was something especially difficult for a mind like Roosevelt's to comprehend, much less to believe true. (Indeed, there was virtually no possibility of common understanding on any subject between the President and Der Fuehrer. The mental processes of no two men could have been more widely different. We have often remarked that Roosevelt's was a mind quite rigidly compartmentalized; it was also a mind walled away from, or defensively against, his feeling self over which it had, by his assignment at least, a crushing authority. Hitler, on the other hand, was a creature of surging emotion undefined [or undefiled, as he might have put it] by intellect and to which such intellect as he had was wholly subordinate. He could not "put first things first" in the mutually exclusive way that Roosevelt did because in his passionately conceived totalitarian world there were no such sharply distinct, completely separate "things" as Roosevelt perceived, or thought he perceived— "things" that could be numbered and prioritized. For Hitler, everything flowed into everything else to make a seething universe perceptible only and wholly through the feeling self—a universe that was to be not understood, but mastered through sheer, assertive, dominating willpower. The elimination of the Jewish "race," therefore, was not for him a war aim distinguishable from the war itself, it was a [if not *the*] purposeful essential of *"mein Kampf."* Which is to say that the resources devoted to it were not diversions from, but direct contributions to, his war effort.) As the summer of 1942 advanced, Roosevelt continued to insist to himself and others, against rapidly mounting evidence to the contrary, that the Jews whose deportation en masse he could no longer deny were being transported to the East to work on fortifications and such. He would say so as late as mid-September 1942, in efforts to soothe the expressed anxieties of Felix Frankfurter, who came to him at the frantic behest of the head of the American Jewish Congress, Rabbi Stephen S. Wise, with whom Roosevelt was and would remain on warmly friendly terms.[23]

But in this last saying, at so late a date, Roosevelt was deliberately untruthful. He knew better, or worse.

He had clearly indicated as much in an August 21 public statement warning the Axis perpetrators of "barbaric crimes" against civilians in the countries they occupied, crimes about which "[o]ur Government is constantly receiving additional information from dependable sources," would, after the United Nations had won their inevitable victory, be tried in courts of law in the countries they now occupied. Evidence of the guilt of specified individuals, now being gathered, would be used against these individuals. In a politician's deference to the anti-Semitism then affecting (in widely variant ways and degrees) some 40 percent of the American citizenry, he refrained from saying that in the European countries dominated by the Nazis or their collaborators, Jews were the chief victims of these crimes. He *did* say that a recently received "communication signed by the Ambassador of The Netherlands and the Ministers of Yugoslavia and Luxembourg on behalf of the Governments of Belgium, Greece, Luxembourg, Norway, Netherlands, Poland, Czechoslovakia, Yugoslavia, and the French National Committee in London" stated "that . . . acts of oppression and terror have [now] taken proportions and forms giving rise to the fear that as the defeat of the enemy countries approaches, the barbaric and unrelenting character of the occupational regime will become more marked and may even lead to the extermination of *certain populations*."*[24]

By then he had read a report of the Nazis' Jewish extermination program that had been received by the State Department's Foreign Affairs Division ten days before his statement was issued—a report, from what seemed an unimpeachably reliable source, so initially convincing per se (it told of the Wannsee Conference and of Hoess's decision to use Zyklon B at Auschwitz) as well as so perfectly consistent with the fragmentary information already in hand and with the information that continued to come to Washington from elsewhere, that it soon overwhelmed most of the stubborn wills to disbelieve. These wills were especially concentrated in the State Department, where Catholics tainted with anti-Semitism constituted a significant proportion of the middle-rank officials;

*Italics added.

where the most decisive voice on this matter was that of Roosevelt's good long-time friend Assistant Secretary Breckinridge Long, whose strong anti-Semitism was evident even in his published, carefully edited war diary; and where, when the willful wall of disbelief was breached, every proposal for doing anything truly helpful about it came hard against an iron determination to maintain intact the barriers the United States had raised against immigration. These were necessary barriers against an influx of foreign secret agents and other subversives, claimed Long, who deemed the Jewishness of Jews to be of itself alone subversive of true Americanism.

The report came from Gerard Riegner, the thirty-year-old representative in Geneva of the World Jewish Congress—a man of sober mind, sober mien, and judicial temperament whose teachers in the German law school he attended in the early 1930s (he fled the country when Hitler came to power in 1933) had predicted for him an early judgeship. The information his report contained had been given him orally on August 1 by a prominent German industrialist who loathed Nazi barbarism but occupied a position of sufficient importance in the German war economy to give him access to the highest circles of Nazidom.* Riegner was skeptical about what he heard that day, though (or perhaps because) his emotions were deeply stirred by it. He spent more than a week inquiring into the reliability of his informant and checking this new information against the information already in hand (the Germans themselves had announced by radio on July 16 that eighteen thousand Jews had just been deported eastward from Paris; since then, Riegner had received reports of mass deportations of Jews from Vienna, Prague, and Holland). He learned that information earlier given by the industrialist had proved to be of a remarkably detailed accuracy. It had predicted an impending drastic change in the Nazi high command long before British and American intelligence had any inkling of dissension among the Nazis; it also included a prediction, five weeks in advance of the event, that the invasion of Russia would be launched in the morning of June 22, 1941. Thus it was with his initial skepticism overcome, and an agonizing sense that time was of the essence of any effort to rescue the imperiled Jews or reduce the rate of their slaughter, that Riegner came on August 8 to the U.S. consulate in Geneva with a written report of what he had learned. He gave it to Vice Con-

---

*His identity was disclosed at the time to a very few, all of whom promised him they would never reveal it publicly. According to Arthur D. Morse, whose *While Six Million Died* was published in 1968, he was a top executive of a German firm that produced war goods and had thirty thousand German employees; he had ready access to Hitler's headquarters, and it was there, he said, that he had learned of the final solution order. Walter Laqueur, who made a prolonged effortful search for the industrialist's identity, writes in a footnote on page 100 of his *The Terrible Secret*, published in 1980, that he may have been Eduard Schulte, general manager of the Georg von Giesche mining company in Breslau. "Schulte frequently visited Switzerland during the war and eventually became a defector," writes Laqueur. "He . . . seems to have brought important information out of Germany." In November 1983, three historians announced that Schulte was indeed Riegner's informant.[25]

sul Harold Elting, Jr. (Consul Paul Chapin Squire, with whom Riegner was on personally friendly terms, was away on vacation) with the request that it be delivered to Rabbi Wise in New York and that its contents be disclosed to the Allied governments by the U.S. State Department. In his cover letter to Washington, Elting stressed that Riegner "is a serious and balanced individual."[26]

But the bureaucrats of State's European Affairs Division, over whom Breckinridge Long had large influence, quickly decided that Riegner's message should *not* be delivered to Wise. Its contents were of a "fantastical nature," said one division member, and even if they were true, there was no possibility "of our being of any assistance" to the alleged victims. So on August 17, the U.S. minister to Switzerland, Leland Harrison, was told by a telegram from State that because "of the apparently unsubstantiated nature of the information" it contained, Riegner's message had not been delivered to Wise and would not be; to deliver it would be to stir up needless trouble for the department.

All the same, Wise did receive the report intended for him. On the same day Riegner gave it to the U.S. consulate, he gave a copy to the British consulate in Geneva with a request that it go to Samuel Sydney Silverman in London, a member of Parliament who chaired the British section of the World Jewish Congress. To it, he appended a note of his own: "Please inform and consult New York." The Foreign Office, in the absence of confirming evidence that the report was true, was reluctant to pass so sensational a message on to Silverman but did so after a week's hesitation—and on August 28, Silverman cabled it directly to Wise. The cable cleared both War and State Department censorship, failed for some reason to be noticed by State's European Affairs Division, and so reached its intended recipient after only a few days' delay. Wise did not know, of course, that Riegner's report, addressed to him, had been received and suppressed by the State Department weeks before he himself knew of it, and on September 2, he sent a copy to Undersecretary Sumner Welles, asking in an agitated cover letter that the information be passed on to Roosevelt.

By then, Welles had received an eight-page single-spaced memorandum prepared by a member of the Czechoslovak State Council, Ernest Frischer, and forwarded to the State Department on August 26 by Anthony J. Drexel Biddle, Jr., U.S. ambassador to the governments-in-exile in London. Biddle deemed it so important that he simultaneously sent a copy to the President, a personal friend of his. It corroborated, in considerable detail, what Riegner had reported, concluding: "There is no precedent for such *organized wholesale dying* [his italics] in all Jewish history, nor indeed in the whole history of mankind."[27] Yet when Welles phoned Wise on the day (September 3) he received Wise's communication, he strove to soothe the distraught rabbi with the assertion that the Jews were being deported eastward, according to authoritative reports received by the State Department, to labor on roads, fortifications, and the like. He also (the chief purpose of his call) asked Wise not to release the report to the press until the State Department had had time to test its accuracy against information from other sources. Wise promised to comply with this request.

He did so with great reluctance, a reluctance infused with maddening anxiety after he received, on the morrow of the Welles phone call, a message from Europe that was not only confirmative of what Riegner had said, but even more sensational in nature. It came to Wise from Jacob Rosenheim, president of an Orthodox Jewish body called the Agudath Israel World Organization, headquartered in New York, who had it from his organization's representative in Switzerland, Isaac Sternbuch. After detailing the Nazi mass murder of Jews in Czechoslovakia and other Central European countries, Sternbuch wrote: "These mass murders are continuing. The corpses of the murdered victims are used for the manufacture of soap and artificial fertilizers. Similar fate is awaiting the Jews deported to Poland from other occupied territories. Suppose only energetical steps from America may halt these persecutions. Do whatever you can to cause an American reaction to halt these persecutions."[28] Wise questioned the claim that human corpses were being used in the manufacture of soap (lying propaganda issued by Allied governments during World War I had contained this assertion), but otherwise Sternbuch's report, following hard upon Riegner's, was only too convincing—and, indeed, every claim Sternbuch made save that of soap was later authenticated.

The effect upon the rabbi was devastating. He was almost "demented," he wrote to the Protestant Reverend John Haynes Holmes, by the horror of what was happening to his European brethren, hour by hour, day by day—by this, conjoined with the State Department's flat refusal to consider what was happening to be an emergency demanding swift response, also by his own inability to discern even the vague outline of a practical large-scale rescue program. At the very least, there should be, he was convinced, an immediate world-headline-making expression by the U.S. government of moral outrage, accompanied by mass meetings voicing the loudest possible protest against the horror, also by concentrated and well-publicized governmental and private efforts to devise and implement a practical large-scale rescue program. For there would continue to be a general skepticism about reports of atrocities against Jews as long as Jews and Jewish organizations remained the sole acknowledged source of them. Moreover, a powerful manifestation of concern by the American government and people must have some deterrent effect, if not upon Nazi officials, then upon their collaborators, active or passive, actually or potentially, in this most appalling of all crimes. Distraught as he was, Wise found it difficult to believe that his great hero and personal friend, Franklin Roosevelt, whose compassionate concern for the exploited, the downtrodden, was a salient feature of his public as of (Wise was convinced) his private character, and in whose administration an unprecedented number of Jews were importantly involved, had been fully and accurately informed on this matter. Surely, if he had been, he would have made some overt response to what he had learned! ("To be silent in this hour when thousands of unarmed, innocent Jewish human beings are murdered each day is not only a betrayal of elementary human solidarity," wrote Pierre Van Paasen in a letter to *The New York Times* in early December 1942, "it is tantamount to giving the bloodthirsty Gestapo carte blanche to . . . speed its ghastly program of extermination.")²⁹ It was to make certain the President *was* truly informed that Wise incited the Frankfurter visit to Roosevelt of which we have already spoken.

The State Department's efforts to determine the validity of Riegner's report were driven by no sense of urgency. Wise waited through September, October, nearly all November, with ever more desperate anxiety, for delivery of the fruits of the inquiry. He kept his promise not to publicize Riegner's report. He engaged in no public agitation. But he was by no means inactive. He formed a temporary committee of Jewish leaders who headed organizations normally at odds with one another (the so-called Jewish community of the United States was as badly splintered as the U.S. political Left) to shape a design for European Jewish rescue—a design that turned out to be a vague outline, not of a practical rescue program, but of a way of possibly arriving at such a program. He conferred with the President's Advisory Committee on Political Refugees, which Roosevelt had ignored almost from the moment it was established in 1938 and of which James G. McDonald was chairman. He conferred with a highly sympathetic Harold Ickes on the possible use of the Virgin Islands (these U.S. territories were administered by the Department of the Interior) as at least a way station for Jews escaping from Nazi Europe (Ickes's immediate proposal of such use to Roosevelt was, in effect, turned down). Finally, early in the morning of November 24, Welles by telegram summoned Wise to Washington, where the rabbi arrived from New York in the late afternoon. Welles at once handed him several documents, saying as he did so: "I regret to tell you, Doctor Wise, that these confirm and justify your deepest fears. There is no exaggeration. These documents are evidently correct." The public should be informed of their contents, he went on, and though he himself could not release them to the press, "for reasons you will understand [what reasons? why would Wise have no trouble understanding them?], there is no reason why you should not."³⁰

Wise held a press conference that very evening, announcing the State Department's confirmation of the fact that a program of total Jewish extermination in Europe had been launched by the Nazis, that two million Jews had already been murdered, and that mass deportations from all over Europe to slaughter facilities in Poland continued apace. On the afternoon of the following day, in New York, the rabbi held another press conference in which he spoke as the voice of most of the principal American Jewish organizations; he repeated the information he'd given out in Washington and added that its validity had been further confirmed in a communication from Roosevelt's special ambassador to the Vatican, Myron Taylor. The press reportage of these conferences was, for Wise and those he spoke for, remarkably, shockingly meager, given the sensational character of the news imparted. Only five of nineteen major newspapers across the country carried the Washington press conference story on their front pages, on no front page was the story given a topmost position, and two of the nineteen papers didn't carry the story at all. Even more disappointing was the coverage of Wise's New York press conference—no doubt because the information then given out was repetitive, in large part, of that released the day before. Only ten of the sample nineteen papers printed the news, none of them as a major front-page story, most of them inconspicuously on an inside page.

More successful in publicizing the ongoing genocidal horror was the Temporary Committee's sponsorship of a Day of Mourning and Prayer, observed on December 2 throughout the United States and in twenty-nine other countries. The major, most publicized observance of this was in New York City, with its large Jewish population. Mayor La Guardia, in whom Jewish and "pure" Italian blood mingled on equal terms, summoned his city to prayer; half a million workers, Jewish and non-Jewish, stopped work at a prescribed time for ten minutes of prayer (they added the ten minutes to their next workday, as was announced, to avoid a charge of interference with the war effort), a number of radio stations silenced themselves for two minutes, and there was a radio network mourning service during the noon hour. But this was by no means enough. Wise and his committee could only conclude, from the press coverage given their public announcements of November 24–25, that the horrendous information would never penetrate the American consciousness in full force as long as it came to the public solely through Jewish leaders and organizations. Desperately needed was a forceful public expression of concern by the President of the United States, a statement making it clear that the "certain populations" that, he had said in his August 21 press conference, might be targeted for "extermination" were in fact being exterminated and consisted wholly of Jews. It was therefore decided, during a hastily summoned Temporary Committee meeting on November 25, that Wise attempt to arrange an interview with the President.[31]

On the Day of Mourning and Prayer, Wise wrote Roosevelt, addressing him as "Dear Boss" and saying: "I do not wish to add an atom to the awful burden which you are bearing with magic and, as I believe, heaven-inspired strength at this time. But you do know that the most overwhelming disaster of Jewish history has befallen Jews in the form of the Hitler mass-massacres." He asked that Roosevelt meet as soon as possible with him and others representing the leading American Jewish organizations; he supported his request with an implied argument that doing this would serve the President's political interests, whereas not doing it would gravely injure these; for now that the fact of the Jewish extermination program had been certified by the State Department and made known to the electorate, "it would be gravely misunderstood [that is, an important part of the electorate would accurately perceive the subordination of humanitarian concerns to political ones on Roosevelt's part] if, despite your overwhelming preoccupation, you did not make it possible to receive our delegation and utter what I am sure will be your heartening and consoling reply." These last words expressed a confidence in the soothing efficacy of Roosevelt's "charm," even in a situation as seething with passionate emotion as this one, which bolstered Roosevelt's own great confidence in it. He promptly granted Wise's request, jamming into his crowded schedule for December 8 a thirty-minute session with Wise and others of Wise's committee. It was to be the only meeting that Roosevelt ever held with Jewish leaders concerning what became known in history as the Holocaust.[32]

At noon that day, Wise and four others, representing B'nai B'rith, the Union of Orthodox Rabbis, the American Jewish Committee, and the Jewish Labor Committee, were ushered into the Oval Office, where they were cordially welcomed by the President. Roosevelt opened the meeting with what one of his listeners—Adolph Held of the Jewish Labor Committee, whose notes are the only written record of the conference—described as a rather lengthy "semi-humorous" story about his plans for postwar Germany. Wise then read aloud a two-page statement prepared by the Temporary Committee stressing the need for "immediate action," else "the Jews of Hitler Europe are doomed," but that did not say what such action might be, beyond warning the Nazis they would "be held strictly accountable for their crimes" and forming a commission to collect and report to the world facts about Nazi barbarism against civilians. His message reading completed, Wise placed in Roosevelt's hand a twenty-page document summarizing the extermination information already gathered, then begged him to do all in his power to focus the world's attention on the enormous crime in progress and on ways to stop it. Roosevelt replied that the U.S. government was already well-informed of the facts Wise and his colleagues now presented to him ("Unfortunately we have received confirmation from many sources"); promised to endorse any statement of his response to these that was prepared for immediate release by those present ("I am sure that you will put the words into it that express my thoughts [he knew he could count on hero-worshipful Wise to do it in a way favorable to him])"; then asked for any recommendations for action they might have. Alas, they had none of a concrete practical nature. Roosevelt expressed a sympathetic understanding of why they didn't. "We are dealing with an insane man," he said. "Hitler and the group around him represent . . . a national psychopathic case. We cannot act toward them by normal means. That is why the problem is very difficult." He then launched upon a monologue on matters that, though unrelated to this meeting's purpose, were of sufficient importance to make his listeners feel privileged and honored by his frank exposure to them of the presidential mind. The monologue continued until an aide entered to indicate that the allotted half hour was at an

end. Roosevelt had talked 80 percent of the allotted time.* As his visitors rose
to leave, he reiterated his promise to approve whatever public statement they
prepared and vowed that "we" of the government "shall do all in our power to
be of service to your people in this tragic moment."[33]

But by this arrangement, it was Wise, not Roosevelt himself, who announced
the presidential response to what Jewish leaders had had to say. Wise met with
White House reporters within a few minutes after the interview. He had been authorized to say, he told them, that the President "was profoundly shocked to
learn that two million Jews had perished as a result of Nazi rule and crimes" and
that "the American people will hold the perpetrators of these crimes to strict accountability in a day of reckoning which will surely come." Wise then released
to the reporters copies of the twenty-page summary of extermination data he
had given Roosevelt. Again, press coverage was shockingly meager when measured against the world-historical importance of the subject reported, the desperate purpose and hope of Wise and his colleagues, or even the news emphasis
normally given a presidential statement on any subject having any importance
whatever. Few newspapers, even among those most respected for the fullness
and accuracy of their reporting, gave the story much space or printed it on the
front page. *The New York Times,* which prided itself upon being the "newspaper
of [historical] record" and was owned and published by Jews, was the only one
that gave the story space proportionate to its importance; indeed, its account of
the White House meeting and the information there released was full and accurate; but the account was printed on page 20. Those other papers that covered
the story at all, including the highly respected *Washington Post,* did so in much
less space far inside the paper.[34]

Yet the meeting may have accomplished something more along the lines of its
purpose than Wise and the others could be aware of. . . .

In June 1942, during Churchill's Washington visit, Roosevelt had handed the
Prime Minister a memorandum prepared by Hopkins recommending the establishment of a United Nations commission to deal with Nazi atrocities against
civilians. Churchill presented the memo to the British cabinet, which was already under growing public pressure to respond actively to increasingly horrifying atrocity reports, and the cabinet at once set up a committee to discuss "the
judicial framework" (that is, a framework of international law) within which a
War Crimes Commission might effectively work—also to make specific recommendations regarding the work itself. U.S. Ambassador Winant was invited to
participate in this discussion. He, a compassionate man passionately committed
to civil rights, did so with dedicated effectiveness. Conclusions and recommendations for action were soon worked out, and Winant, on August 6, sent the
committee memorandum embodying them directly to Roosevelt by air courier,

---

*According to Held's notes.

saying in his cover letter (dated August 5) that he had conferred with Hopkins on the treatment of war criminals during the latter's July visit to London, that he had just talked the matter over with Churchill, and that the recommendations were forwarded to the President at the Prime Minister's request for whatever comments and recommendations of his own the President might wish to make. Winant added that the governments-in-exile in London were clamoring for "some action that might act as a deterrent against further atrocities by the enemy" and that announcement of the establishment of the recommended commission might be considered an action of this sort.[35]

There ensued, for the ambassador, a period of growing puzzlement, anxiety, and frustration. No reply to his communication, not even an acknowledgment of its receipt, came to him from either White House or State Department as days added up to weeks and weeks passed. At the end of the third of them, a Labour Party delegation called upon both Winant and Eden to talk with fervent outrage about fresh reports of what was happening to the Jews in Eastern Europe and to demand a governmental response, prompting Winant to write Hopkins on that same day, saying he had received no reply to his August 6 communication and that the British were "eager" for a U.S. answer. To this, he received no reply. A month later, on September 20, he wrote Hopkins again, saying that during the long silence from Washington following his August message, he had received over two hundred petitions from British organizations calling for action on this matter and that the British were anxious for answers to three questions: Were the British suggestions for setting up a War Crimes Commission satisfactory? What proposals should be made to other Allied governments? Did the United States agree that there should be an armistice clause requiring the enemy, at war's end, to surrender war criminals? This time, Hopkins replied at once. Winant's message had been "mislaid," he explained. As a consequence, it had only now been referred to the State Department, from which, Hopkins "hoped," Winant would soon receive advice.

This referral was disappointing to the ambassador, who had hoped for a direct presidential reply and whose past experience of State Department bureaucracy inspired no confidence in its ability to act either swiftly or wisely. He promptly, on the day he received the Hopkins reply (September 22), cabled Hull, pointing out that for nearly two months, he had been unable to give the British the U.S. answers to their urgent questions and that Foreign Secretary Eden was pressing him to provide these answers. He begged the secretary to give the matter his personal attention. A few days later, he again cabled Hull to say that Eden, accompanied by the Lord Chancellor, had just come to his office to apply more pressure for a U.S. response, because the matter had been before both houses of Parliament for many weeks now and the Churchill government had already been forced to request two postponements of parliamentary debate of it. Finally, on October 4, Winant sent Hull and Welles a cable quoting a just received personal letter to him from Eden saying that the parliamentary debate of this matter was scheduled for October 7 and that the government could not possibly request another postponement of it; the foreign minister urged the ambassador to try to obtain, within the three days remaining before Commons debate opened, American answers to the questions that had been asked. Otherwise, it was clearly implied, the Churchill government would be compelled to make the proposed announcement unilaterally.[36] The imminence of this alliance-damaging embarrassment forced, at long last, decisive State Department action.

On October 5, Welles wired Winant that the text of the British cabinet committee document Winant had sent in early August was "acceptable to us and may be announced as having the joint support of United States and Great Britain." Two requests were made, namely, that the word "Atrocities" be stricken from the new agency's title and that public announcement of the War Crimes Commission include a reassuring statement that the United States and Britain intended only "the ringleaders of Germany" (a number "obviously . . . very small in relation to the total population of Germany") to be tried and punished as war criminals. This last, the British were told, was Roosevelt's personal wish. Obviously, the President's concern here was to prevent the announcement's stiffening a will to fight to the bitter end on the part of the German masses, and it *may* have effectively served this purpose. But if it did, it was at the cost of limiting the War Crimes Commission's future investigative activities and, as Henry L. Feingold writes, established grounds for the argument in the postwar court trials of "men like [arch-criminal] Eichmann, who had actually operated the killing apparatus, . . . that they were bound to obey the orders of their superiors," hence could not be held personally responsible for the horrors they had perpetrated. Winant, however—a remarkably selfless and magnanimous man—was not inclined in that moment of immense relief to find flaws in that which so greatly relieved him. He at once wired Welles his thanks and that of the British, adding that the Allied governments-in-exile headquartered in London "warmly welcomed" the announcement and wished to be associated with what it proposed.[37] All the same, he must have remarked an irony tinged with bitterness in the way in which the news of the new international commission was presented on the front pages of America's newspapers on October 7, 1942, for the Washington-datelined stories more than implied that the War Crimes Commission resulted from an American initiative and had been brought to practical fruition through the efforts of the American government!

And this irony must have been highlighted in Winant's mind by the State Department's reaction a little less than two months later (that is, immediately following the international Day of Mourning and Prayer) to a British proposal prompted by the steadily increasing popular pressure throughout the United Kingdom, and concentratedly in the House of Commons, for an unequivocal top-level governmental pronouncement making it clear that men, women, and children were being slaughtered en masse by the German government, as a matter of policy, solely because they were Jews. The proposed statement, to be concurred in by the three principal Allies, had as its opening words: "The attention of His Majesty's Government in the United Kingdom, of the Soviet Union, and of the United States Government has been drawn to reports from Europe which leave no room for doubt that the German authorities, not content with denying to persons of Jewish origin in all the territories over which their barbarous rule has been extended the most elementary human rights, are now carrying into effect Hitler's oft-repeated intention to exterminate the Jewish people in Europe." It went on to tell of the mass deportations of people who "are never heard of again" and condemned "in the strongest possible terms this bestial policy of cold-blooded extermination," then pledged that "the necessary practical measures" would be taken by the three governments to punish the perpetrators of this monstrous crime.[38]

In the State Department, this document went initially, for his recommendations concerning it, to one Robert Borden Reams, an ambitious thirty-eight-year-old member of the foreign service who had his full share of that service's "sophisticated" or "realistic" indifference to moral considerations and who was acutely aware that the path to "success" for him ran through the mind, the fervent convictions, of Assistant Secretary Breckinridge Long. Reams had come into the European Affairs Division only a few months before, after consular service in South Africa and four European countries, and had somehow become responsible (it is unclear how or why he had become thus responsible) for the division's dealings with "Jewish questions." He evidently personally agreed with—he certainly conceived his official role to be the execution of—Long's policy of opposition to any and all special efforts to aid Europe's mortally threatened Jews, this on the ground that such efforts would "divert" time and energy from the "war effort." Moreover, Reams seems to have been convinced that on this matter, Long spoke not only his own mind, but also the mind of the President of the United States, Long's great longtime friend. Predictable, therefore, was Reams's immediate reaction to the British proposal. "I have grave doubts in regard to the desirability of issuing a statement of this nature," he wrote his superiors. "In the first place, these reports are unconfirmed and emanate to a great extent from the Riegner letter to Rabbi Wise. The statement . . . will support Rabbi Wise's contention of official confirmation from State Department sources.* The way will then be open for further pressure from interested groups for action that might affect the war effort."[40]

On the following day, the first secretary of the British embassy in Washing-

---

*A few days earlier, Reams had suggested to his superiors that Wise be advised "to call off, or at least tone down, the present world-wide publicity campaign concerning 'mass murders' and particularly . . . to avoid any implications that the State Department furnished him with official documentary proof of these stories." Evidently, he by early December had not received the confirming evidence Welles had given Wise on November 24—a communication failure difficult to understand. How, in these circumstances, could Reams even execute established policy efficiently, much less make new policy wisely? And were not his memoranda on this matter policy-making efforts?[39]

ton called upon Reams to tell him that, though the Foreign Office believed the proposed declaration was per se innocuous (it would do neither good nor harm), His Majesty's government "were" anxious to have it promptly released because of the extreme pressures coming from many directions, including that of the House of Commons. But Reams objected that the proposed statement was "extremely strong and definite [the State Department bureaucracy recoiled instinctively from any statement on any subject whatever that was clear, strong, and definite]" and that its "issuance would be accepted by the Jewish communities of the world as complete proof of the stories that are now being spread about. . . . In addition the various Governments of the United Nations would expose themselves to increased pressure from all sides to do something more specific in order to aid these people." To his European Affairs Division superiors, Reams then recommended that if the declaration *must* be issued, the phrase "reports from Europe which leave no room for doubt" be removed from it and replaced by "numerous and trustworthy reports from Europe."[41]

It was at this point that the Wise delegation's December 8 interview with Roosevelt may have effected some of its purpose. For it seems highly probable that at this point, perhaps in the afternoon following the delegation's visit with him, Roosevelt let Welles and Hull know that he believed the proposed statement should be issued, wanted it to be as strongly worded as possible without committing the United States to any specific action, and wanted the governments-in-exile to be associated with it as a UN document. At any rate, the State Department approved what the British had proposed more swiftly, with fewer weakening revisions, than its earlier handling or the proposal indicated it would do. The department's top echelon did, however, weaken even more than Reams had recommended the crucial phrase about the authenticity of the Jewish extermination reports; the opening sentence of the final version of the declaration, broadcast to the world on December 17, merely said that the Allied governments had received "numerous reports from Europe" that Hitler's intention "to exterminate the Jewish people" was being carried into effect. Signed by the three major Allied governments and concurred in by eight governments-in-exile, the statement received more publicity in the United States than any of the earlier developments in the Jewish extermination story had received. Most American newspapers reported the statement, many on the front page. But there followed no national outburst of popular outrage, no massive demand by the American citizenry for a large-scale rescue effort. Doubts of the authenticity of the extermination reports continued to be deliberately encouraged by several State Department officials and were further encouraged by the failure of the President of the United States to make any direct strong personal statement of his own on the subject, something he would surely have done, it was felt, had he been absolutely convinced the reports were true. Not until after the war's end would the average American become aware that six million Jewish men, women, and children had been deliberately, cold-bloodedly slaughtered by the Germans during the war in ways that denied to their deaths any individual dignity whatever.[42]

Small wonder that Nazi propaganda minister Josef Goebbels could write with conviction in his diary entry for December 13, 1942, that the "question of Jewish persecution in Europe" was being given "top news priority by the English and the Americans [actually, it was not]. . . . At bottom, however, I believe both the English and the Americans are happy that we are exterminating the Jewish riff-raff."[43]

VI

HISTORIANS who are convinced, as is the author of this book, that Franklin Delano Roosevelt was the greatest American president of the twentieth century and one of the three or four greatest in all American history; biographers of him who long to see and portray their subject in the most favorable possible light, as does the hero-needful author of this book, but without compromising a primary commitment to telling the truth about him to the fullest extent that the truth of so multilayered, devious, and secretive a role-player can be discovered—such historians and such biographers come to the most painfully difficult and hazardous portion of their immensely difficult and hazardous task when they are forced to deal with their subject's response to the Holocaust. The first undeniably true reports, in the late summer of 1942, that the German government was actually carrying out Hitler's final solution brought Roosevelt face-to-face with a great moral challenge, the greatest such of his public life, in the opinion of this author. He was called upon to subordinate political considerations wholly to those of moral right and wrong, making politics the servant of morality—in short, to exercise moral leadership. And he didn't do it. Indeed, he refused to recognize that he was so called upon. He asserted in practice that what the Holocaust presented his presidency was just another political problem, to be dealt with in his usual ways, through a careful measurement of opposing pressures and a cautious tipping of balances, at fulcrum points, toward whatever best served the national interest overall—and he conceived the supreme national interest, overriding all else, to be at that moment military victory in the war.

Was it possible for him, in his circumstances, to have responded otherwise to any practical effect? Could he have done anything to reduce the Holocaust? The present author says "Yes." But some of the finest American historians, among whose devoted admirers the present author numbers himself, answer "No" emphatically. They say there was *nothing* other than Roosevelt actually did, either then or later, that could have saved any of the lives Hitler was determined to destroy. These lives, they point out, were utterly, helplessly in Hitler's brutal hands. He could do what he would with them. Their only salvation, therefore, was the destruction of Hitler—that is, the winning of the war against him—in the shortest possible time. Anything that interfered with this, including Jewish rescue efforts, would prolong the massacre of Jews and so cost more Jewish lives than the rescue efforts themselves could possibly save. This is what responsible officials of the Roosevelt administration said at the time, of course, insofar as they publicly commented at all upon the ongoing horror. It is also, when made by historians, more nearly a naked assertion than it is a conclusion arrived at by logical inference from available evidence. Indeed, instead of being derived from the evidence, the assertion (as it seems to this author after his study of the most extended [book-length] presentation of it) has itself determined the selection of evidence. All that seemingly supports it is cited in its behalf; all that does not is either ignored or "disproved," the latter (again) rather more by assertion than by objective analysis, especially analysis of the arguments made by army and government officials, after the war's end, in defense of their harshly criticized response, or failure to respond, to the Holocaust while the Holocaust was under way. Moreover, the assertion is made with a vehemence that seems more expressive of the historians' wish (need?) to defend Roosevelt, or their published portrayals of him, against reputation-damaging fact than it is of their normally scrupulous regard for objective truth. As for the argument that winning the war in the shortest possible time was the *only* way to save Jews, it was rendered obviously phony, even at the time it was originally made, by the fact that at the current rate of Jewish slaughter, virtually no European Jews would still be alive at the end of this "shortest possible time."

What, then, could Roosevelt have done?

He could have made it absolutely certain, as it was fully within his power to do, that everyone (*everyone!*) in the whole of the free world knew what the Germans were doing to thousands upon thousands of utterly helpless and wholly innocent human beings every single day. He could have spread this news in a way that stressed a furious outrage of his own (an outrage he seems not, in fact, to have felt; his emotional reaction to the event was much cooler, milder, easily controllable) over what was happening, a way that stressed the urgency of the need for action, thus capitalizing upon the immense moral authority that was his by virtue of his position as the foremost leader of the free world and, among these leaders, the recognized champion of democracy, the downtrodden, the exploited. He could have done so in a way that integrated with the war effort on the level of morale by increasing that hatred of the enemy prerequisite to passionately determined efforts to destroy him, also that faith in the righteousness of the Allied cause prerequisite to the shaping of a peace in which Nazi-fascism could never again occur. He could have done so in a way that expressed and inspired an iron-hard determination to seek, to find, and to realize every possibility of saving the maximum possible number of Jews, finding safe havens for them, and doing this *now,* while millions of the doomed were yet alive. He could, moreover, have taken immediate steps to implement this determination.

If he did not already know how the "Jewish question" was being handled by the State Department (if he didn't know, it was because he had chosen not to), he could have ordered an inquiry that quickly gave him this information, then acted upon it by taking out of such hands as Breckinridge Long's and Robert Borden Reams's all dealings with the war refugee problem, transferring these to people who were wholly free of anti-Semitism, who were wholly dedicated to saving from Nazi barbarism the maximum possible number of human lives, and who operated under a specific grant of presidential authority to do so. In other words, he could have done in late 1942 what in the event he did not do until January 1944, after a majority of Europe's Jews had already perished in Nazi murder camps, namely, establish a special governmental agency, a War Refugee Board, to handle the war refugee problem. (Roosevelt would do so in 1944 only under extreme pressure.)

Admittedly, the obstacles to swift, determined rescue action were formidable in the autumn of 1942. The barrier raised by U.S. immigration law, itself re-inforced in this case by a widely prevailing American anti-Semitism—raised also by Britain's determination to maintain British imperial interests in the Middle East and the consequent British opposition to the establishment of a Jewish state in Palestine—was high and strong. How high and strong had just been un-happily demonstrated to Roosevelt by the fate of a war powers bill (it would have become the Third War Powers Act) he had requested of Congress in early November. The bill would have enabled the President to suspend laws hamper-ing "the free movement of persons, property and information into and out of the United States"; its purpose was to ease the use in the military effort of foreign military, scientific, and industrial consultants. But the broad wording of the bill would, if it became law, enable the President to admit Jewish war refugees. The United States might become a safe haven for hundreds of thousands of other-wise doomed men, women, and children (but *Jewish* men, women, and chil-dren)! The possibility was viewed with horror by the conservative coalition of Republicans and Southern Democrats whose power in Congress was now greatly augmented by the outcome of the midterm elections. It was viewed with equal horror by many a mass-media mouthpiece of American conservatism. How were the immigrants to be handled here? Were they to be lodged and fed at the taxpayers' expense? Were they to be permitted to become American citi-zens who deprived native-born citizens of jobs in the postwar depression that was at that time greatly feared? Loud, bitter, and persuasive of a large segment of the electorate was the voiced opposition to these possibilities. The conserva-tives easily, swiftly killed the bill in committee.

At least one important conservative periodical, while it did not advocate any drastic change in U.S. immigration law, saw and deplored what this event re-vealed of the American psyche. "The ugly truth is that anti-Semitism was a defi-nite factor in the bitter opposition to the President's request," said *Newsweek*.[44]

And the magazine's use of "ugly" here is revealing. Anti-Semitism, its essential bestiality, the essence of all racial and religious bigotry, when nakedly exposed by its practical consequences in Nazi Europe, *was* repulsively ugly in the sight of a vast majority of Americans, including most of those who practiced it by discriminating against the Jewish purchase of homes in their neighborhoods and by excluding Jews from their social clubs and from hotels of which they were valued clientele. These were generally sufficiently ashamed of themselves, or sufficiently fearfully respectful of American public opinion, to avoid all publicity of what they did. Indeed, they were generally at pains to hide their actual motivation behind walls of obfuscation and subterfuge. This, of course, provided warriors against such bigotry in America, as in other free societies, with an effective strategy: To gain a great advantage over their opposition, they had only to compel their opponents to speak aloud, to expose fully to the light of day, that which motivated them. . . .

In other words, though the obstacles to the mounting of an effective Jewish rescue effort were indeed formidable in 1942, so were the moral energies, then scattered and rendered impotent by their diffusion, that might have been mobilized, organized, and focused for this effort by a leader of Roosevelt's stature. So powerfully persuasive was the image Roosevelt had projected of himself as a liberal humanitarian, especially during his election campaigns—so eager for an opportunity to define itself again sharply against conservatism's coldly selfish materialism was the liberalism yet preponderate among the electorate (liberal attitudes, selfless idealism, were of the essence of the kind of patriotism this war had fanned into flame throughout the nation)—that he could have done this in large part simply by forcefully expressing his personal will that it be done, provided he did so in a way that exposed anti-Semitism as a major element of the opposition.

The political force Roosevelt would thus have created would have been great enough and (above all) intelligent enough to overcome all the obstacles to the achievement of a world-historic, world-changing triumph of the democratic mind and spirit and have speeded rather than retarded the achievement of military victory. Certainly, the requisite moral energy was latent, awaiting an opportunity for expression, in the bosoms of most American citizens, raised as they had been in the democratic tradition, their minds and spirits imbued with the emotion, the principles, expressed in the Declaration of Independence, the Bill of Rights, the Gettysburg Address. The opportunity was there for the taking by the President of the United States. Roosevelt not only did not take it, he actually deliberately employed his unique circumstances, his persuasive talents, his personal charm (a significant part of it was the impression of personal decency and moral goodness he made upon those who talked with him face-to-face), to *prevent* any forceful coalescence of the scattered moral energies. The pattern he would follow was evident in his joining with the State Department to deny, to disturbed visitors about it, the authenticity of information they had received about Jewish mass murder, this after he and the top department officials knew the information to be true—also in his joining with State in calculated efforts to soften as much as possible the impact of this news upon the public mind when the news was at last released. It was clearly evident in his dealings with Rabbi Wise in that fall and early winter. A widely circulated saying was that Roosevelt could "charm the balls off a man," and on the evidence, that is precisely what he did to Wise. Having had numerous personal contacts with Roosevelt and been persuaded thereby that he best served his constituency by defending the President against all criticism, the rabbi had become and now remained one of the most effective of all Roosevelt apologists. "I don't know whether I'm getting to be the J of Jude," he said to Frankfurter (a fellow Jew, a fellow Roosevelt apologist) in mid-September 1942, when he was maintaining silence about the Riegner report at the request of the administration and begging Frankfurter to talk with Roosevelt about it, "but I find that a good part of my work is to explain to my fellow Jews why our government cannot do all the things asked or expected of it."45

One can easily see how Roosevelt's mind worked as he faced this immense challenge. Personal anti-Semitism had absolutely no part in his motivation. No one was less prone to that kind of bigotry than he. No national leader had publicly condemned it more often or strongly than he. No other President, as we've said, had placed as many Jews in high governmental posts, administrative and advisory. But though no anti-Semite himself, he was acutely aware that other Americans were and that their shared prejudice, which aroused in him no such profound angry disgust as it did in many, constituted a factor that he, as a politician occupying the supreme political office, must weigh, and respect in proportion to its weight, as he made his decisions on this matter. We know he was a highly skilled politician who took pride in that fact and richly enjoyed (excessively enjoyed, some thought) the exercise of his skills. But we also know that he was an extremely cautious politician whose commitment to civil liberties and human rights was not so great as to permit his running of grave political risks on their behalf. He was in general inclined to measure larger rather than smaller than they actually were the obstacles to his doing what he knew and sometimes admitted to his intimates were things that ought to be done.

This had been manifest in his adoption of what was actually a pro-Franco policy during the Spanish Civil War, out of a probably excessive fearful respect for pro-Franco Catholicism as a political force. It had been manifest in his refusal to endorse the Wagner-Costigan anti-lynching bill, either when it first came to the floor of the Senate in 1937 or when his doing so would have forced cloture on Senate debate of it in early 1938, thus ending a Southern Democratic filibuster and ensuring the bill's passage: he had then acted upon a sense of absolute dependence, for success in Congress, upon the support of racially bigoted Southern Democrats and made no effort to assess the gain in political strength that could have come to him from the then disenfranchised Negroes of the South, and from liberals now alienated from him or only weakly supportive of him, had he coupled his endorsement of this legislation with an expressed determination to enforce the Fourteenth Amendment. The same fearful caution had been manifest in his handling of the Evian Conference in 1938, an operation quite obviously designed by him to diffuse political energies that otherwise would have focused upon a lowering of barriers to Jewish immigration and so have "caused trouble." It was manifest in his avoidance of head-on, issue-defining collisions with isolationism during the prewar years; in his lagging behind rather than leading public opinion toward a recognition of the necessity for U.S. entrance into the war, during the period between September 1939 and December 1941; and in his endorsement of the War Department's proposal, strongly opposed by the Justice Department, to send American citizens to concentration camps simply because they were of Japanese extraction.

We see this cautiousness again now. As politician, he was fully aware of the possible coalescence of emotional moral energies into a potent force for Jewish rescue, but he perceived this possibility, not as an opportunity to save human lives, but as a dangerous threat to the national unity he deemed an absolute essential of military victory. There would be, he was convinced, a violently disruptive national quarrel over any serious effort to mount a really effective Jewish rescue attempt. Hence the response or lack of it made by him to the challenge presented by the swiftly, indisputably authenticated Riegner report.

There is another major factor to be considered in any fair-minded effort to understand and assess in moral terms Roosevelt's presidential performance. He was, as I. F. Stone put it, "only a man." A mortal man. And aged beyond his numbered years. During the last two of these years, though he was at pains to hide this from others and (evidently) himself, he had had unmistakable intimations of his mortality. To add to the burdens he was already carrying, at this end of anxiety-ridden 1942, the risks and anxieties of a massive Jewish rescue effort, a burden that perhaps weighed heavier in his imagination than it would actually have been for him personally, must have seemed to him utterly impossible. He may well have felt, deep down, that to do so would be fatal to him. Certainly, the burdens he now bore would have been crushing to a strong young man in perfect health. The bearing of them required his full employment of every single one of the techniques or strategies for survival perfected by him over the years. One of these was a deliberate suspension or severe limitation of his remarkable sensitivity, his really quite amazing empathic capacity. He seems to have been able to turn empathy on or off at will, as if it were water in a faucet,* and to have turned it off in this case as he had in several of those men-

---

*But was not the effectiveness of this, as a survival technique, severely limited? One suspects he was unable to turn off completely the flow of empathic energy and that the drip that continued, after he had shut all of it that he could, became a corrosive acid of guilt feeling that ate ever more deeply into the very core of him.

tioned above, and in the case of Missy LeHand's personal tragedy, to which his reaction, or at least the one evident in his outward demeanor, shocked Ickes and profoundly shocked his wife. Like a physician who must daily operate in life-and-death situations, he simply could not afford to let himself feel too acutely the pain of those who suffered; doing so would impair his professional performance. . . .

At any rate, because of all this, we can never know with any certainty, or even guess with any assurance of accuracy, how many Jewish lives might have been saved had a determined effort to save them been launched by the Roosevelt administration in 1942. All we can know for sure is that the effort was never made.

VII

WE may be absolutely certain of the inclusion in whatever retrospecting and prospecting Roosevelt engaged in that Christmas Day, of a world-historical development that occurred, in extreme secrecy, simultaneously with the arrival in Washington of the first thoroughly authenticated reports of the final solution.

We can be certain of this because the historical development, of which the world would know nothing until thirty-one months had passed, provided the President with substantial relief from the anxiety that had necessarily attended the fateful decision he had made on October 9, 1941—the decision to commit whatever was needed of America's scientific, material, and manpower resources, resources that would otherwise be devoted to the development of weaponry of proven effectiveness, to an effort to make an atomic bomb, though the success of such an effort was admitted to be not certain, but only highly probable, by the very scientists who urgently recommended that the effort be made. The decisive factor here, for him, had been the possibility that if we did not fully exploit every chance that the superbomb could be made, it might come into Hitler's exclusive possession.

Physicists in England and the United States reached their conclusion that a bomb of theretofore unimaginable destructive power, using the rare uranium isotope U-235 as explosive, could probably be made before the present war ended. We have told of Italian immigrant Enrico Fermi's "exponential experiments" designed to prove the possibility, and develop the means of achieving, a controlled self-sustaining nuclear chain reaction in natural uranium.

What Fermi did* was embed pellets of natural uranium in holes bored into bricks of superpure graphite; he then built, one after another, larger and differently designed "piles" of these bars, the earlier of them rectangular, the last a

---

*Leo Szilard was Fermi's associate in the original experiments; his contributions to the creation of controlled atomic energy were as great as, if not greater than, those of any other scientist, a fact not generally recognized.

sphere squashed into an oval within a carefully carpentered wooden framework. To control the reaction, Fermi used wooden rods coated with cadmium, which is highly absorptive of neutrons. When the self-sustaining chain reaction occurred, it could be slowed down or speeded up by pushing in or pulling out the cadmium rods. There seemed an extremely slight risk that the reaction would go out of control.

Nevertheless, the proportions of the catastrophe that would occur if it did go out of control in an area crowded with people had caused everyone knowledgeable about the project to conclude that the experiment that finally achieved the self-sustaining reaction could not be performed in the midst of a great city. But when Fermi told Compton in early November 1942 that his next experiment would be the critical one and that he could carry it out within the next five or six weeks provided he did it at Stagg Field, he also stated his conviction that he could do it there without risk of life. A time-consuming removal of it to some isolated spot in the country was unnecessary. Compton's confidence in Fermi's judgment in such matters was immense. Compton told Fermi to go ahead full speed. He did not, however, inform university president Robert Hutchins of what impended, because he was sure Hutchins would then feel compelled to forbid the experiment's performance on his campus.[46]

The critical experiment was conducted next day, December 2, 1942, which was not only the International Day of Mourning and Prayer for Europe's Jews, but also the second day of national gasoline rationing. The weather was bitterly cold. The temperature was below zero on Chicago's windswept streets, where automobile traffic was but a fraction of what it usually was; it was little above that in the squash doubles court at Stagg Field when at nine o'clock Fermi and his colleagues began their last-minute preparations for the critical experiment.

There was a comfortable warmth, however, in the conference room at Eckhart Hall where Compton met at that same time with a four-man committee appointed by General Groves to review the present state of the entire atomic bomb program and make a "feasibility report" concerning it. At midmorning, Compton received a phone call from Volney Wilson, who told him that Fermi was about to begin the crucial experiment and that, though space in the squash court was severely limited, there was room on the spectators' balcony for one more person besides Compton. Compton quickly decided that his companion should be the youngest of the review committee's members, forty-year-old Crawford Greenewalt (he was destined to become Du Pont's president half a dozen years later), because, according to actuarial tables, Greenewalt was likely to remember longer than any of the others what Compton was sure would be an event of permanent world-historical importance.

And so it proved to be.

There was no obvious drama in the way the experiment was conducted. Fermi, slide rule in hand, stood on the balcony where Compton and nineteen others also stood, most of them operating measuring and monitoring instruments. Calmly, he called his orders down to a young scientist named George Weil, who had worked with him on the early Columbia University exponential experiments and who now hand-operated the single cadmium rod that remained inserted in the pile; all the others had been withdrawn after Fermi had determined that the measurements of radioactivity made the night before by his chief assistant were identical with those he himself now made. Pull it "halfway out," was Fermi's first instruction. Weill did so. At once the scalers or counters measuring the intensity of radioactivity began to clatter faster and faster before leveling off as, after the release of the delayed neutrons, they were supposed to do. Fermi with his slide rule calculated the rate of intensity increase, recording it on the back of the slide rule and checking it against what he had predicted for it at that point of control rod withdrawal. Pull it out "another six inches," he called down. Again the scaler clicking increased briefly, then leveled off. Again Fermi made his calculation, checking it against his prediction and finding that the two matched almost perfectly. A further six-inch rod withdrawal was ordered, a further calculation made. And so the tedious inch-by-inch approach continued until, at 11:30 A.M., an automatic safety rod that the physicists had labeled "ZIP" suddenly, unexpectedly shot through its groove into the pile with a loud crash that startled everybody. It failed to ruffle Fermi's calm: he immediately surmised that the level of intensity of ionization at which release of the safety rod would be triggered had been set too low. "I'm hungry," he said. "Let's go to lunch." At two o'clock, the preliminary testing was resumed, with test readings that continued to match those predicted. After an hour and a half of this, Fermi ordered a precautionary reinsertion of ZIP into the pile, then the withdrawal of the manually controlled rod a full foot beyond the seven at which it had been set before lunch. ZIP was then cautiously withdrawn. "This is going to do it," said Fermi to Compton. The trace recording of the level of nuclear fissioning "will climb and continue to climb," he went on. "It will not level off."[47]

And that is what happened.

With the withdrawal of ZIP, the clicking of the neutron counters increased in rapidity until, within seconds, the clicks blurred into a steady roar while the trace on the chart recorder climbed steadily. At 3:49 P.M., December 2, 1942, there had been "achieved . . . the first self-sustaining chain reaction . . . [which] initiated the controlled release of nuclear energy," as a plaque later placed on the Stagg Stadium wall puts it. "The pile has gone critical," Fermi announced, as if anyone present needed to be told. A minute passed, then another, then another— increasingly long minutes for the people on the balcony. Their anxiety mounted as the instruments began to record a dangerously high radiation. Why on earth didn't Fermi turn this monster off? Not until four and a half minutes had passed after the self-sustaining reaction began did he do so, calling down in a calm voice: "ZIP in." He added, "Lock the control rods in the safety position and come back tomorrow. Then we'll start the new series of experiments."[48]

. . .

In his memory of that moment, Compton writes, "Three faces . . . stand sharply before me." Fermi's swarthy one "showed no signs of elation. The experiment had worked precisely as expected. The theoretical calculations were confirmed, and that was that." Young Volney Wilson's face "was troubled." He had resigned from the project early on because he wanted no part in the making of a weapon of such horrifying destructiveness and had rejoined it only to help prevent Hitler from grasping such world-destroying power into his exclusive possession, but he had continued to hope against hope that "even at the last moment, something would happen which would make it impossible to effect the chain reaction." The "most clearly" seen, however, of the three faces in Compton's memory (the fact is suggestive of Compton's own priorities) was that of "dark, tall, slender" Greenewalt, whose "eyes were aglow . . . with ideas of how atomic energy could mean great things in the practical lives of men and women," ideas he excitedly voiced as he walked back with Compton through the cold dark December air to Eckhart Hall.[49]

At the squash court, Eugene Wigner presented to Fermi a bottle of Chianti he had managed, with difficulty because of the war embargo, to obtain. The Italian (he had filed for American citizenship but had not yet obtained it) accepted the gift with thanks, opened it, and poured out paper-cup portions of it for each of the colleagues now gathered around him. Their prevailing mood was self-congratulatory, but far from ecstatically joyous. "For some time we had known we were about to unlock a giant," Wigner would remember; "still we could not escape an eerie feeling when we knew we had actually done it. We felt as, I presume, everyone feels who has done something that he knows will have very far-reaching consequences which he cannot foresee." Leo Szilard, who as a very young man had dreamed of the use of atomic energy to power space exploration and render obsolete coal and oil as energy sources but who was appalled by the present necessity (he admitted it to be a necessity) to make military application of it, felt much as Volney Wilson did. After the others had left, he and Fermi stood briefly alone together. They shook hands, but Szilard said as he did so that in his opinion, "this day will go down as a black day in the history of mankind."[50]

Back in his office, Compton phoned Conant in Washington. "Jim," he said, "you'll be interested to know that the Italian navigator has just landed in the new world. The earth was not as large as he had estimated, and he arrived at the new world sooner than he had expected."

"Is that so!" said Conant, excitement in his voice. "Were the natives friendly?"

"Everyone landed safe and happy."[51]

On the following day, Vannevar Bush went to the White House to convey the news orally to Roosevelt.

VIII

FOR Roosevelt, this news further lighted the already brightened view of the world's situation, and of his own, that by early December had almost wholly replaced the darkly shadowed one he had been compelled theretofore, since the very beginning of the war, to take. For him, it meant simply a great increase in the likelihood that the United States would win the race (if there *was* a race; no one in Washington knew what the Nazis were doing in this regard) for a super-weapon of such awesome power that it might of itself alone win the war for whichever side first possessed it. This in turn augmented the optimism bred in him by news that had latterly come to him from every theater of the global war—news indicating that fortune, which had frowned upon the Allied cause on most of the war's battlefields through most of 1942, now blessed that cause with a smile that broadened, at least a little bit, almost every day.

On November 19–20, eleven days after the successful Allied landings in French North Africa, Russian forces in the Stalingrad area had launched the long-planned, carefully prepared counterattack of which Stalin had spoken to Churchill last August. The long and inadequately manned northern and southern flanks of the German advance to the Volga, the spearhead of which (Paulus's Nazi Sixth Army) was now stuck in the heart of ruined Stalingrad, virtually invited flank attack. The Germans had long assumed that this would sooner or later be attempted. Nevertheless, the Axis troops on the flanks were totally surprised by both the timing and the strength of the attack when it came. The northern flank, manned almost exclusively by Romanian, Hungarian, and Italian troops, with Romanians preponderant, was pierced by midafternoon of the first day and soon completely shattered. Its scattered remnants fled westward in panic. On the southern flank, the German Fourth Panzer Army fought more bravely and with greater skill but nevertheless suffered disaster. It was split in two. Its own southern portion managed to retreat to the west in fairly good order, but its northern portion was forced into the Stalingrad pocket, where, along with Paulus's casualty-shrunk forces in the environs of Stalingrad and in the ruined city itself, it was doomed to engage in hopeless close-quarter, no-quarter, often hand-to-hand fighting among heaps of rubble and collapsing walls. Within a week, during which German air forces were grounded by the onset of the white mists and lowering clouds of early winter, the jaws of the trap were snapped shut. Completely surrounded, in an area that stretched twenty-five miles east and west and twelve miles north and south along the Volga, were twenty German and two Romanian divisions, along with scattered units of engineer and other specialized forces, including Luftwaffe ground staffs—some 250,000 to 300,000 men in all.

They might have escaped had they tried to do so as soon as the trap's jaws came together. These jaws were not then so tightly clamped shut that they might not have been pried open by a determined Sixth Army attack westward—and Paulus begged for permission to make the attempt. Hitler flatly refused it. By the dictator's passion-distorted mind, the Stalingrad pocket was seen not as the trap it so obviously was, but as a besieged fortress that could be adequately supplied by air until relieved. Goering assured his master that it could be: he promised that the Luftwaffe would deliver to the pocket 600 tons of supplies a day (Paulus had radioed his need for a minimum of 750 tons a day). In the event, thanks to Germany's shortage of transport planes, to Russian winter weather that often grounded what planes there were, and to the dominance of the sky over the crucial area by Russian fighters, it was seldom that as many as 200 tons were delivered within any twenty-four hours. Hitler did at once order the mounting of a relief attempt to be made as soon as possible. On November 20, he created a new army group, Army Group Don, and ordered to its command Field Marshal Fritz Erich von Manstein, perhaps the most skillful of his field commanders, who had been commanding an army of Army Group Center, fronting Moscow. The new group was a hastily snatched together body of troops who were far smaller in number than an army group normally was and who possessed far too little armor (tanks, armored gun carriers) for success in the task assigned them. This task was to hold a bridgehead at the confluence of the Don River and the Chir, a bridgehead that would protect a drive he was then to launch from Kolnikovo northwest into Stalingrad, opening the way for ground supply of the Sixth Army. Manstein did his best toward this end, and far better than Hitler had a right to expect. But it was not enough. He was unable to begin his drive toward Stalingrad until December 12, and though he made considerable progress during the next four days, he was then stalled some thirty-five miles from the pocket. He urged upon Hitler the necessity for a simultaneous attempt by Paulus to break out of the pocket in a drive to the southwest, its objective being linkage with the Manstein force—but again Hitler flatly refused to permit it: Paulus must remain in Stalingrad and fight if necessary to the last man. . . .

By Christmas Day, news of the failure of the Manstein relief effort had reached Washington, making it clear to Roosevelt that the tide of war had now turned most emphatically in Russia and would from now on flow there in increasing strength against the Axis. He sensed what history would prove to be true: The event, conjoined with the Allied victories at Midway, the Solomon Islands, and North Africa, marked the turning point of the whole war.*

True, the joy brought him by the Stalingrad news was somewhat offset by the disappointment he felt over the bogging down of Eisenhower's drive into Tunisia. . . .

---

*The price the Russians paid in casualties for their Stalingrad victory was immense. They "lost more men at Stalingrad than the United States lost in combat in all theaters of the entire war," writes Louis Snyder.[52]

In a conference on November 25 with Leahy, Hopkins, King, Arnold, and Marshall, the army staff chief had estimated that "the occupation of Tunisia could be accomplished" within two or three weeks, provided Eisenhower found two divisions sufficient for the task; it would take somewhat longer if he found four divisions necessary, this "because of the delay involved in assembling this many troops." Roosevelt had been encouraged by this to cable Stalin on that same day: "We are going to drive the Germans out of Africa soon I hope, and then we will give Mussolini's Fascists a taste of some real bombing. I feel quite sure they will never stand up under that kind of pressure." He went on to speak of American success in the Solomon Islands. "We have probably broken the power of their fleet," he said, for though they "still have too many aircraft carriers to suit me . . . we may well sink some more of them," and he was sure that the Japanese were now losing planes and ships faster than they could build them. He concluded with "my warmest congratulations on the . . . encouraging news . . . we are receiving from the Stalingrad area." Also on that same day, he cabled Churchill his belief "that as soon as we have knocked the Germans out of Tunisia we should proceed with a military strategical conference between Great Britain, Russia, and the United States" to be held within the next month or six weeks. The Anglo-American Combined Chiefs of Staff would no doubt have a recommendation as to "the next steps" within a few days, "but I feel very strongly that we have got to sit down to the table with the Russians." What he had in mind was a conference in either Cairo or Moscow at which "each of us [that is, Churchill, Roosevelt, and Stalin] would be represented by a small group, meeting very secretly." Marshall would probably "head up" the U.S. group, "but I presume that all services should be represented."[53]

Churchill's immediate response to this (on November 26) had been negative. He agreed "that there should be conference with the Russians" but had no belief that a meeting of military representatives of the three heads of government "would be of much value. Certainly if a Russian delegation went to Cairo, which I deem unlikely, they . . . would have to refer every point of substance back to Stalin at Moscow. If the conference were held in Moscow there would be less delay, but I trust that before the British and United States Missions went to Moscow they would have a joint and agreed view, to serve at least as a basis for discussion." It would be far better, the Prime Minister went on, to press for a meeting in person of the three heads of government themselves. "Stalin talked to me in Moscow in the sense of being willing to come to meet you and me somewhere this winter," he went on, "and he mentioned Iceland." Though Iceland in midwinter seemed an unlikely conference site, it had, "apart from the climate," a good deal to recommend it: "Our ships might lie together at Halfjord and we could place a suitable ship at Stalin's disposal wearing the Soviet flag pro tem. . . . What about proposing it for January? By that time Africa should be cleared and the great battle in South Russia decided."[54]

Roosevelt welcomed, with evident eagerness, the idea of a meeting of the Big

Three. On December 2, he informed Churchill that he had "today" sent Stalin a message "urging him to meet you and me. I believe he will accept." He had been "giving a good deal of thought" to the nature and timing of the conference and had concluded that "each of us" should "be accompanied by a very small staff made up of our top Army, Air, and Naval Chiefs of Staff. I should bring Harry and Averell, but no State Department representative. . . . I should like the conference to be held about January 15, or soon thereafter. Tunis and Bizerte should have been cleared up and Rommel's army liquidated before the conference." As for the place of meeting, "Iceland and Alaska [the latter as meeting place had been earlier suggested to Stalin] are impossible for me at this time of year and I believe also for Stalin [though it was Stalin who had suggested Iceland in winter]. I should prefer a secure place south of Algiers or in or near Khartoum. I don't like mosquitoes. I think the conference should be very secret and that the press should be excluded." He doubted the wisdom of a meeting between American and British "military people" or between Churchill and himself prior to the meeting with Stalin "because I do not want to give [him] . . . the impression that we are settling everything between ourselves before we meet him." Also, "I think you and I understand each other so well that prior conferences between us are unnecessary." He concluded with a jocular reference to the 1807 meeting on a raft in the Neman River at which the Treaty of Tilsit was drawn up and signed by Napoleon I of France and Alexander I of Russia. "I prefer a comfortable oasis to the raft at Tilsit," wrote Roosevelt.[55]

Stalin, however, did *not* accept this invitation. On December 6, he sent identical messages to Roosevelt and Churchill saying that though he welcomed the idea of a meeting, he to his "great regret" would be unable to leave the Soviet Union at the suggested time "for even a day." At that very moment, "important military operations of our winter campaign are developing," and these would "not be relaxed in January, probably the contrary." Nor did subsequent telegrams to him from both Churchill and Roosevelt, asking if a postponement of the conference until early March would enable him to come, elicit a different reply. Stalin on December 17 telegraphed his reply to Roosevelt, who promptly communicated the information to Churchill. It would be impossible for him to leave the Soviet Union even in March. "Front business absolutely" demanded "my constant presence near our troops." But he also hinted at another reason for his refusal. "So far I do not know exactly what are the problems which you, Mr. President, and Mr. Churchill intend to discuss at our joint conference," he wrote. "I wonder whether it would not be possible to discuss these problems by way of correspondence between us. . . ." He presumed there would be "no disagreement between us" since he was confident that the promise of "the opening of a second front given by you, Mr. President, and by Mr. Churchill in regard to 1942, and in any case in regard to the spring of 1943, will be fulfilled and that a second front in Europe will actually be opened by the joint forces of Great Britain and the United States of America in the spring of the next year."[56]

Three days before this Stalin missive was received in Washington, Roosevelt (on December 14) sent Churchill by courier what the Prime Minister in his war memoirs calls "a very genial letter," a personal letter, its salutation "Dear Winston." He had as yet received no answer to his "second invitation to our Uncle Joe," he said, but "on the assumption that he will again decline I think that in spite of it you and I should get together as there are things which can be definitely determined only by you and me in conference with our Staff people." He did not suggest that Churchill come again to Washington or that he himself go to London. It "would do me personally an enormous amount of good to get out of the political atmosphere of Washington for a couple of weeks," he said, but "England must be out for me for political reasons." He reiterated that Iceland was impossible because of the danger that iced wings would force down the planes they must ride to get there and because of the "vile climate" they would find when or if they did get there. ". . . [O]n condition that I can get away in absolute secrecy and have my trip kept secret until I get back, I have just about made up my mind to go along with the African idea." American public opinion would no doubt "gasp, but be satisfied when they hear about it after it is over." A "mitigating circumstance" for the public would be the "knowledge that I had seen our military leaders in West and North Africa." For that reason, "I think it would be best if we could meet somewhere in that neighborhood" instead of Khartoum, as earlier suggested. "My thought is, therefore, that . . . we meet back of Algiers or back of Casablanca about January 15. . . . In view of Stalin's absence, I think you and I need no foreign affairs people with us—for our work will be essentially military. Perhaps your three top men and my three top men could meet at the same place four or five days in advance of our arrival and have plans in fairly good shape by the time we get there. . . . One of our dictionaries says 'an oasis is never wholly dry.' Good old dictionary." Churchill agreed to this arrangement promptly and enthusiastically. "I am greatly relieved," he wired on December 21. "It is the only thing to do. . . . Suggested code-name [it was accepted] 'Symbol.' "[57]

While these important arrangements were being completed, battlefield events in Tunisia belied Marshall's hopeful November 25 prediction of an Allied conquest of Tunisia by Christmas Day. We have told how Eisenhower, in a command decision rendered exceedingly bold by French political uncertainties that could spell disaster for the operation, had on November 10 ordered the British First Army under General Anderson to drive full speed eastward, its objective the seizure of the whole of Tunisia before the Germans could build up sufficient strength there to hold the country. The gamble had *almost* paid off, as we've said. The slender brittle spearhead of Anderson's force (the spearhead consisted of little more than three infantry brigades and a brigade of obsolescent tanks) had driven through Souk-el-Khemis and Beja to the very outskirts of Tunis before being stopped by German troops whose buildup had been remarkable in size and rapidity. British First Army and the driblets of American troops that

Eisenhower and Clark had been able to feed into it had then been forced into precipitous and costly retreat. Roosevelt, disappointed and unwontedly impatient over this delay, believing as he did that the conquest of Tunisia was a necessary prerequisite to any fruitful face-to-face discussion of strategy with Stalin, had then placed a somewhat desperate hope in the new, much larger offensive that Eisenhower scheduled for launching on Christmas Eve. When he learned on Christmas Day of Eisenhower's weather-compelled postponement indefinitely of this offensive, the pain of his great disappointment was considerably less than it would have been if the meeting with Stalin had also been postponed indefinitely.

In the following days, the last week of 1942, Roosevelt's preponderant concerns were with the writing of his State of the Union address to the new Congress, to be delivered on January 7, 1943, and with preparations for the conference. As regards the address, many observers had predicted, and liberals in general had hoped, that the President would take a firm stand in defense of New Deal social gains and in support of the kind of postwar world envisaged by Wallace and Willkie against the active hostility of the conservatives who would control the Seventy-eighth Congress. Roosevelt himself had told David Lilienthal in mid-December that he was "really going to *tell* this next Congress," challenging the conservatives with a laid-out program of government for *people:* "These boys on Guadalcanal and in Africa—does this Congress propose to tell them that they are going to come back to fear about jobs, fear about things a man can't prevent, like accidents, disease, and so on? Well, they will have a chance to go on record about it, to divide on that *political* issue." He went on for some minutes along that line, to Lilienthal's delight, mingled with a growing nervousness since Leahy and Marshall were waiting impatiently in the anteroom. But this outburst of liberal sentiment would prove a brief interruption of the President's overriding commitment to unity. In the end, he with his speechwriters would produce what Sherwood later described as "perhaps the most amiable and conciliatory speech he ever made to the Congress, at any rate, since the end of the New Deal honeymoon."[58]

Meanwhile, conference preparations proceeded full speed. Eisenhower had by Christmas been told by Marshall of the meeting's imminence and been asked to find a suitable location for it in French Morocco. Churchill then sent one of his personal secretaries to Algiers (he arrived there on December 27) to help in this. Two days later, Eisenhower reported to Marshall that this secretary and a representative of Eisenhower's chief of staff, Bedell Smith, had "found a very suitable site for operation 'Symbol.' It consists of a hotel surrounded by a group of excellent villas," he went on, "situated five miles south of Casablanca and one mile inland. Area is detached and lends itself to segregation and can be guarded easily. Airfield is two miles distant which is satisfactory for B-24's except in very rainy weather. If protracted spell of bad weather precedes Symbol, landing field at Marrakech, 120 miles distant, can be used and onward air carriage can be arranged."[59]

Evening, December 31, 1942 . . .

There was more unalloyed good cheer in the White House this year, as Franklin and Eleanor Roosevelt seated themselves with their guests at eight o'clock for New Year's Eve dinner, than there had been on such year-end occasions for a number of years.[60] All the guests were White House familiars: Harry and Louise Hopkins, Henry and Elinor Morgenthau, Sam and Dorothy Rosenman, Bob and Madeline Sherwood, Prince Olav and Princess Martha of Norway. After dinner, they moved to the room that had become the White House motion picture theater, where they viewed a film that, when released for public showing a few days hence, would become an instant box office hit and was destined to become a movie classic that would thrill scores of millions, again and again, through all the remaining decades of the twentieth century. A bittersweet story of love amid war, of individual lives overwhelmed by history and enabled to become significant of good or evil only through their willed responses to it, the film was soaked through and through with the selfless idealism and spirit of personal sacrifice to a transcendent cause (that of a postwar world democracy) that was a dominant theme of the prevailing public mood in the 1940s. Even people who deemed themselves hardheaded realists and objected to the sentimental as a perversion of honest emotion were often deeply moved by this picture story. Perhaps Franklin Roosevelt was moved by it to add to his customary midnight toast "To the United States of America" the words "and to United Nations' victory."

The name of the film, which starred Humphrey Bogart and Ingrid Bergman, was *Casablanca*.

Notes

1. Overture: Themes, Issues, Recapitulations

1. *New York Times,* November 6, 1940.
2. See David E. Lilienthal, *The Journals of . . . : The TVA Years, 1939–1945* (including "The Early Journals, 1917–1939") (New York, 1964), pp. 61–62, 66, 69–70.
3. Robert E. Sherwood, *Roosevelt and Hopkins* (New York, 1948), p. 9.
4. Dean Acheson, *Morning and Noon* (Boston, 1965), p. 165.
5. See Walter Lippmann's letter to Edward Sheldon, quoted in Ronald Steel, *Walter Lippmann and the American Century* (Boston, 1980), p. 316; Marriner Eccles, *Beckoning Frontiers* (New York, 1951), p. 341; John Maynard Keynes's comments to Frances Perkins after a lengthy conversation with FDR, in Perkins's *The Roosevelt I Knew* (New York, 1946), pp. 225–26; George Kennan, in his introduction to Orville H. Bullitt, ed., *For the President: Personal and Secret* (Boston, 1972), pp. xiv–xv.
6. Bullitt, ed., *op. cit.,* p. xiv.
7. *New York Times,* July 5, 1929. Ms., typescript interspersed with handwritten script, in FDR Group 9, Franklin D. Roosevelt Library (hereafter FDRL); Daniel R. Fusfeld, *The Economic Thought and the Origins of the New Deal* (New York, 1956), pp. 49–51; *Public Papers and Addresses of Franklin D. Roosevelt 1940* (hereafter *PPA 1940*) (New York, 1969), pp. 1–5; *Public Papers and Addresses of Franklin D. Roosevelt 1937* (New York, 1950), pp. 1–6.
8. Henry L. Stimson and McGeorge Bundy, *On Active Service in Peace and War* (New York, 1948), p. 348, quoting Stimson diary entry of October 29, 1940; *New York Times,* November 7, 1940.
9. *New York Times,* November 6, 1940.
10. *Ibid.*
11. *PPA 1940,* pp. 230–40.
12. *Ibid.,* pp. 236–38; *Newsweek,* May 27, 1940; Quoted by Geoffrey Perrett, *Days of Sadness, Years of Triumph: The American People, 1939–1945* (Penguin [softbound], 1974), pp. 72–73.
13. *PPA 1940,* p. 276.
14. Stimson and Bundy, *op. cit.,* p. 353.
15. John Morton Blum, *Roosevelt and Morgenthau* (Boston, 1970), p. 379.

16. Joseph P. Lash, *Eleanor and Franklin* (New York, 1971), p. 626.

17. Blum, *Roosevelt and Morgenthau,* pp. 378–79.

18. *Ibid.,* p. 380.

19. Matthew Josephson, *Sidney Hillman: Statesman of Labor* (Garden City, N.Y., 1952), p. 516, citing Herbert J. Emmerich, "The War Contribution of Sidney Hillman," ms. in FDRL.

20. *New York Times,* September 1, 1940; Josephson, *op. cit.,* quoting National Defense Advisory Commission Minutes, September 6, 1940 p. 520.

21. *New York Times,* October 2, 1940; Josephson, *op. cit.,* p. 521.

22. Josephson, *op. cit.,* p. 522.

23. *New York Times,* October 9, 1940.

24. *PPA 1940,* p. 517.

25. *New York Times,* November 6, 1940.

26. *Ibid.*

27. John Morton Blum, ed., *The Price of Vision: The Diary of Henry A. Wallace* (Boston, 1973), footnote quoting Wallace's Columbia Oral History Collection (hereafter COHC), transcript, pp. 358–60.

28. *New York Times,* November 6, 1940; Winston S. Churchill, *Their Finest Hour* (Boston, 1949), pp. 595–97.

29. *PPA 1940,* p. 466.

30. Herbert Feis, *The Road to Pearl Harbor* (Princeton, N.J., 1950), p. 116, footnote 17.

31. *Ibid.,* pp. 119–20.

32. *Ibid.,* p. 122, note 2.

33. Charles A. Lindbergh, "Aviation, Geography, and Race," *Reader's Digest,* November 1939; "What Substitute for War?," *Atlantic Monthly,* March 1940.

34. Feis, *op. cit.,* p. 122; *New York Times,* September 28, 1940.

35. Warren F. Kimball, ed., *Churchill and Roosevelt: The Complete Correspondence,* vol. 1. "Alliance Emerging" (Princeton, N.J., 1984), pp. 74–75.

36. Joseph C. Grew, *Turbulent Era* (Boston, 1952), pp. 1224–29, presents the "green light" message in toto.

37. Writes Grace Tully, *F.D.R. My Boss* (New York, 1949), p. 22: "The Boss was superstitious, particularly about the number thirteen and the practice of lighting three cigarettes on a single match. On several occasions I received last-minute summonses to attend a lunch or dinner party because a belated default or a late addition had brought the guest list to thirteen. My first invitation to a Cuff Links Club dinner, held annually on the President's birthday, came about in 1932 when withdrawal of one of the guests left a party of thirteen." Famous became Roosevelt's addiction to "luck objects"— especially to old brown felt hats. Back in 1910, as he once explained to a reporter, he missed his grip as he tried to board a Lexington Avenue streetcar in New York City and fell backward. The battered brown felt hat he was wearing cushioned the blow to his skull, preventing what would otherwise have been serious injury. Ever since, "I have had a feeling that old brown felt hats bring me luck." See *New York Times,* November 5, 1928.

38. "Mother was a very jealous person," daughter Anna Roosevelt wrote a friend after Eleanor's death. "She was jealous of Missy, of Betsey [Betsey Cushing Roosevelt, wife of James], of Louise [Harry Hopkins's second wife], even of me." Writes Lash: "Eleanor's most complex relationship was with Missy. There was affection and motherly solicitude—and also resentment." Lash tells of two occasions in which the editor

of *Liberty* magazine, Fulton Oursler, with his wife, were made aware of "a murkier side of the relationship between Franklin and Eleanor with regard to Missy." After the second occasion, Oursler, whose close friendship was with Missy, noted in his journal: "We feel we are part of a much darker quarrel which we can only guess about." See Lash, *op. cit.,* pp. 507–9.

39. Author interview with Anna Roosevelt Halsted in summer of 1973.
40. Eleanor Roosevelt, *This Is My Story* (New York, 1937), p. 253.
41. Frank Freidel, *Franklin D. Roosevelt: The Ordeal* (Boston, 1954), p. 100, based on personal interview with Frances Perkins.
42. Lash, *op. cit.,* pp. 531–32; *New York Times,* November 10, 1940.
43. Constance Drexel, "Unpublished Letter of F.D.R. to His French Governess," *Parents* magazine, September 1951, p. 30.
44. *New York Times,* November 7, 1940.

2. Of Conflagration, Fire Hose, and Hydrant

1. *New York Times,* November 8, 1940.
2. One of these "routine" letters was to Roosevelt and Eleanor's close longtime friend, Mary W. (Molly) Dewson of Castine, Maine, who since World War I had been a powerful battler for women's rights and a chief organizer, with Eleanor, of political support among women for Franklin Roosevelt in every political campaign he'd waged since 1928. On one of the closing days of the 1940 campaign she had addressed to the President through the regular mail, instead of through Eleanor as she usually did, a protest against Selective Service regulations, just adopted, which excluded women from boards of appeal from conscription—a protest that had been shunted, either by Roosevelt or by one of his assistants, to the War Department for a draft reply. The resultant letter gave three reasons why women were unfit to serve on the indicated boards: 1) it might be "necessary to check upon registrants for physical defects" and women should not "be subjected to this duty"; 2) "in general, outstanding men of a community would be better fitted by reason of their knowledge of economic and business conditions to pass upon the problems arising in connection with occupational deferments"; and 3) "it is believed that at times the work of the members of the local boards may become quite strenuous and that it would be inadvisable to impose such obligations upon women." Signing this, obviously without having read it, Roosevelt appended a handwritten comment: "Molly—don't you like the formality of this?" The formality did not disturb her, but the letter's absurd contents did—and shortly thereafter, dining at the White House one evening, she let Roosevelt know how she felt. At table, she was seated at the President's right, the director of the women's division of the Democratic National Committee at his left, his mother opposite him, and along the table's sides were foreign correspondent Martha Gellhorn, humorist Robert Benchley, and Harry Hopkins, who completed the party. All these roared with laughter when Molly, having mentioned her receipt of "the most amusing letter I've read in a long, long time," proceeded to state its three points. Harry Hopkins then led the guests in a mock serious discussion of the President's "stand" on this matter. Roosevelt, though he joined in the laughter, was unable to hide his embarrassment. "It was the only time I ever saw the President blush," wrote Molly to the editors of Roosevelt's published personal letters. See *F.D.R., His Personal Letters, 1928–1945* (hereafter *PL*), edited by Elliott Roosevelt, assisted by Joseph P. Lash (New York, 1950), pp. 1075–76.

3. Warren F. Kimball, ed., *Churchill and Roosevelt: The Complete Correspondence* (Princeton, N.J., 1984), vol. 1, pp. 80–81. Churchill, *Their Finest Hour,* p. 553.

4. William L. Langer and S. Everett Gleason, *The Challenge to Isolationism* (New York, 1952), pp. 521–22.

5. William L. Langer and S. Everett Gleason, *The Undeclared War* (New York, 1953), p. 216; *PPA 1940,* p. 564.

6. Langer and Gleason, *Undeclared War,* pp. 216–17; *PPA 1940,* pp. 563–64. Langer and Gleason were commissioned by the Council on Foreign Relations to write this book; they had the full cooperation of the State Department and other Roosevelt administration officials, and the resultant work can be considered as (with minor qualifications) a primary source.

7. Warren R. Kimball, *The Most Unsordid Act, Lend-Lease, 1939–1941* (Baltimore, 1969), p. 87, quoting Morgenthau Diary, October 5, 1940.

8. Langer and Gleason, *Undeclared War,* p. 217.

9. Harold L. Ickes, *Secret Diary of . . . The Lowering Clouds, 1939–1941* (New York, 1955), p. 367.

10. Langer and Gleason, *Undeclared War,* pp. 218–19, citing Stimson's Diary (ms.) entries for November 12, 13, 1940; *New York Times,* December 5, 6, 1940.

11. Richard J. Purcell, *Labor Policies of the National Defense Advisory Commission and the Office of Production Management,* Special Study No. 23 [in typewritten script] of Historical Reports of War Administration: War Production Board (Washington, D.C., October 31, 1946), pp. 51–52.

12. *Ibid.,* pp. 54–55.

13. Josephson, *op. cit.,* p. 526.

14. Bullitt, ed. *op. cit.,* pp. 504–6; *PL,* pp. 1080–81.

15. *PL,* pp. 1079–80.

16. Bullitt, ed., *op. cit.,* pp. 504–6.

17. The quotation, and the discussion that follows of the evolution of global strategy, derives from "Germany First: The Basic Concept of Allied Strategy in World War II," by Louis Morton, which is chapter 1 of *Command Decisions* (Washington, D.C., 1959). See also Kenneth S. Davis, *Experience of War* (New York, 1965), pp. 130–32; and Langer and Gleason, *Undeclared War,* pp. 176–80.

18. "In my view Admiral Stark is right and Plan D[og] is strategically sound, and also most highly adapted to our interests," Churchill minuted the first lord of the admiralty and first sea lord, with General Ismay to see, on November 22, 1940. "We should therefore, so far as opportunity serves, in every way cooperate to strengthen the policy of Admiral Stark, and should not use arguments inconsistent with it." See Churchill, *Their Finest Hour,* pp. 690–92.

19. James Roosevelt, *My Parents* (Chicago, 1976), pp. 208–9; Michael R. Beschloss, *Kennedy and Roosevelt: The Uneasy Alliance* (New York, 1980), pp. 152–53.

20. Beschloss, *op. cit.,* p. 221.

21. *Ibid.,* pp. 222–28. The Louis Lyons *Globe* story on Kennedy is reprinted in full in Max Freedman, ed., *Roosevelt and Frankfurter: Their Correspondence, 1928–1945* (Boston, 1967), pp. 553–60. In a note attached to a clipping of the story sent Roosevelt by Frankfurter, November 11, 1940, Frankfurter wrote that "what is printed watered down some of the things Joe said. They were so raw the *Globe* did not want to print them."

22. Ickes, *The Lowering Clouds,* p. 386.

23. Beschloss, *op. cit.,* p. 229; Joseph P. Lash, *Eleanor: The Years Alone* (New York, 1972), p. 287.

24. Beschloss, *op. cit.,* p. 230.

25. FDR to King George VI, November 22, 1940, President's Secretary's File (PSF), Franklin D. Roosevelt Library (FDRL).

26. Kimball, ed., *Churchill and Roosevelt,* p. 83; Churchill, *Their Finest Hour,* p. 558; Kimball, *Unsordid Act,* p. 96. The quoted biographer is J. R. M. Butler.

27. Kimball, *Unsordid Act,* p. 100; *PPA 1940,* p. 581; Joseph P. Lash, *Roosevelt and Churchill, 1939–1941* (New York, 1976), p. 261.

28. John Morton Blum, *From the Morgenthau Diaries: Years of Urgency, 1938–1941* (Boston, 1965), pp. 190–200.

29. Lash, *Roosevelt and Churchill,* p. 261; Kimball, *Unsordid Act,* pp. 97–98.

30. Langer and Gleason, *Undeclared War,* p. 228.

31. *Ibid.,* p. 227; Kimball, *Unsordid Act,* pp. 101, 103–4; Blum, *Years of Urgency,* p. 199.

32. Langer and Gleason, *Undeclared War,* p. 227.

33. *Ibid.,* p. 228.

34. Kimball, *Unsordid Act,* p. 108; Langer and Gleason, *Undeclared War,* pp. 229–30.

35. Ickes, *The Lowering Clouds,* p. 376. For details of the *Tuscaloosa* I am indebted to Mr. Harold Duffy of Holden, Massachusetts, who as an ensign graduate of the Naval Academy was assigned to the admiral's cabin on this ship (all other quarters were filled) in early January 1943.

36. Sherwood, *op. cit.,* p. 223.

37. Kimball, ed., *Churchill and Roosevelt,* pp. 102–9.

38. Kimball, *Unsordid Act,* p. 115.

39. Sherwood, *op. cit.,* p. 224; Kimball, ed., *Churchill and Roosevelt,* p. 112.

40. The materials of which Roosevelt made up his mind on this occasion are obvious in the available evidence. See *PPA 1940,* p. 605; Lash, *Roosevelt and Churchill,* footnote on p. 260, citing Ickes letter to FDR, August 2, 1940; *Churchill: Taken from the Diaries of Lord Moran, 1940–1965* (Boston, 1966), p. 202; Churchill, *Their Finest Hour,* pp. 567–68; Sherwood, *op. cit.,* p. 224; Kimball, *Unsordid Act,* pp. 119–20. (Kimball thinks that Hopkins played a larger role in this particular decision making than he ever admitted: "Although there is no concrete evidence that Hopkins tried to play down his influence at this time, it seems implausible to accept his story fully." I myself do not find the Hopkins account implausible.)

41. *New York Times,* December 13, 1940; Langer and Gleason, *Undeclared War,* p. 235.

42. *New York Times,* December 16, 1940.

43. Blum, *Years of Urgency,* p. 209.

44. *PPA 1940,* pp. 604–9; *New York Times,* December 18, 1940.

45. *PPA 1940,* pp. 609–15; *New York Times,* December 18, 1940.

46. Among the secrets was the cavity magnetron, an electron tube, developed in the laboratory of Mark Oliphant in Birmingham, that could generate intense microwave radiation and was a key element of ground and air radar development, also of the proximity fuse, which was of immense value to Allied arms in the last stages of the war. C. P. Snow calls it, in his *Science and Government* (Cambridge, Mass., 1961), "probably the most valuable single device in the Hitler war." See Snow, *op. cit.,* pp. 44–45; Richard Rhodes, *The Making of the Atomic Bomb* (New York, 1986), p. 351; Churchill, *Their Finest Hour,* pp. 381, 396.

47. "Report of the United States–British Staff Conversations," March 27, 1941 ("Pearl

Harbor Attack," XV, pp. 1485–1550), quoted by Langer and Gleason, *Undeclared War,* p. 285.

48. Quoted from Stimson's manuscript diary, presumably the entry for December 17, 1940, by Langer and Gleason, *Undeclared War,* p. 242.

49. *Ibid.,* p. 243; *New York Times,* December 20, 1940; *PPA 1940,* pp. 684–87.

50. *New York Times,* December 22, 1940.

51. Kimball, ed., *Churchill and Roosevelt,* pp. 114, 116.

52. *PPA 1940,* pp. 631–33.

53. Sherwood, *op. cit.,* p. 227.

54. James MacGregor Burns, *Roosevelt: The Soldier of Freedom* (New York, 1970), p. 27.

55. *PPA 1940,* pp. 633–44. According to Sherwood, *op. cit.,* p. 226, "Hopkins provided (during the speech drafting) the key phrase which had already been used in some newspaper editorial: 'We must become the great arsenal of democracy.' I have been told that the phrase was originated by William S. Knudsen and also by Jean Monnet."

56. Kimball, *Unsordid Act,* p. 129.

57. *Ibid.,* p. 131. Kimball explains that France's Jean Monnet, who after the fall of France had been asked by Churchill to serve as adviser to the British Purchasing Commission, had developed the balance sheet technique as "a highly simplified means of presenting Allied requirements to American officials in a way that produced maximum understanding and shock while avoiding the confusion of comprehensive statistics. The sheet was divided into three columns: the estimate of requirements; the estimate of production; and the deficient that had to be filled by the United States."

58. *Ibid.,* p. 134, citing Morgenthau diary, January 3, 1940.

59. *New York Times,* December 31. 1940.

60. Three years later, in his *U.S. Foreign Policy: Shield of the Republic* (Boston, 1943), Walter Lippmann wrote (p. 50) that Americans "must examine our national prejudices, and we may begin by asking ourselves whether peace, as many say, is the supreme end of foreign policy. Merely to ask the question would have sounded shocking a short while ago [say, in early 1940]. At the moment [Lippmann was writing in 1942], it is obvious that the survival of the nation in its independence and security is a greater end than peace. For we can see now that a surrender to Germany and Japan would give us peace, and the more absolute the surrender, the more absolute the peace." Yet such surrender, as Lippmann did not need to say, was in that year unthinkable.

61. Walter Johnson, *William Allen White's America* (New York, 1947), pp. 536–37.

62. Walter Johnson, *The Battle Against Isolation* (Chicago, 1944), p. 170ff.; Johnson, *White's America,* pp. 542–43; Langer and Gleason, *Undeclared War,* p. 224. The committee's statement also called for an embargo on the shipment of war material to Japan and for an explicit naval understanding with Great Britain whereby British and U.S. naval forces could be so disposed as to check the spread of war in the Pacific.

63. Johnson, *White's America,* pp. 544–46.

64. Wayne S. Cole, *America First: The Battle Against Intervention, 1940–1941* (Madison, Wisc., 1953), p. 43; Kimball, *Unsordid Act,* p. 129.

65. Harold Ickes is quoted using "the Bible" term in *New York Times,* April 14, 1941, p. 19; Wayne S. Cole, *Roosevelt and the Isolationists, 1932–1945* (Lincoln, Nebr., 1983), p. 461.

66. Kenneth S. Davis, *A Prophet in His Own Country: The Triumphs and Defeats of Adlai E. Stevenson* (New York, 1957), p. 218.

67. *Ibid.,* p. 221.

68. *Ibid.,* p. 228.

3. The Birth of the Grand Alliance

1. The Lend-Lease Act is Appendix I to Edward R. Stettinius, Jr., *Lend-Lease: Weapon for Victory* (New York, 1944); Kimball, *Unsordid Act,* pp. 132–40, citing Morgenthau diary, which, as Kimball says, enables an hour-by-hour account of this bill drafting.

2. Kimball, *Unsordid Act,* pp. 144–47; Langer and Gleason, *Undeclared War,* pp. 254–62; Stettinius, Jr., *op. cit.,* pp. 70–71.

3. *PPA 1940,* pp. 651–62.

4. *Ibid.,* pp. 645–49.

5. *Ibid.,* pp. 663–72.

6. According to Kimball, *Unsordid Act,* pp. 151–52, the numbering of the bill was the deliberate act of Lewis Deschler, parliamentarian of the House. Majority Leader McCormack feared that his introduction of it would cause it to be popularly identified as the "McCormack Bill" with harmful effects to him politically, since a significant and highly vocal portion of Massachusetts's Twelfth Congressional District, which he represented, was composed of Anglophobic Irish Catholics. It was an easy thing to arrange, Deschler told Kimball in October 1966, because the bill numbering for that session was already well into the 1770s. The stratagem "worked." No news account identified the bill with McCormack; all made a point of its number 1776.

7. *New York Times,* January 13, 1941.

8. *Ibid.,* January 12, 1941; Cole, *Roosevelt and the Isolationists,* p. 414.

9. *PPA 1940,* pp. 711–12.

10. Cole, *Roosevelt and the Isolationists,* p. 415; Burns, *op. cit.,* p. 45.

11. Ellsworth Bernard, *Wendell Willkie: Fighter for Freedom* (Marquette, Mich., 1966), pp. 275–76; Joseph Barnes, *Willkie* (New York, 1952), pp. 244–45; *New York Times,* January 13, 19, 1941.

12. Kimball, ed. *Churchill and Roosevelt,* p. 129.

13. Sherwood, *op. cit.,* pp. 233–34; Barnes, *op. cit.,* p. 245.

14. Sherwood, *op. cit.,* pp. 2–3.

15. Kimball, ed., *Churchill and Roosevelt,* p. 131. Barnes, *op. cit.,* pp. 245–46. Barnes says Carl Sandburg "wrote a poem about this incident, called 'Mr. Longfellow and His Boy' "—apropos of which the following, from pp. 312–13 of volume 2 of Sandburg's *Abraham Lincoln: The War Years* (New York, 1939), is interesting: "Early in the war a newspaper clipping of a speech delivered in New York came into Lincoln's hands, and at its close his eye caught stanzas from Longfellow's 'The Building of the Ship,' beginning:

> Thou, too, sail on, O Ship of State!
> Sail on, O Union, strong and great!

Nicolay was surprised at the way these lines hit the President. He seemed to be reading them for the first time. And as Brooks had memorized the piece at school he recited it to Lincoln to the last lines:

> Our hearts, our hopes, our prayers, our tears,
> Our faith triumphant o'er our fears.

They stirred something deep in Lincoln. 'His eyes filled with tears, and his cheeks were wet,' wrote Brooks. 'He did not speak for some time, but finally said with simplicity: "It is a wonderful gift to be able to stir men like that." ' "

16. Kimball, ed., *Churchill and Roosevelt,* pp. 130–31, 133.

17. Burns, *op. cit.,* p. 35.

18. *PPA 1941* (New York, 1950), pp. 3–6.

19. *Ibid.,* p. 7.

20. Kimball, *Unsordid Act,* pp. 156–57; Langer and Gleason, *Undeclared War,* p. 262. Kimball evidently developed during his research an overwhelming dislike for Hull, which he frankly displays, describing Hull's reaction to Foley's request as "that of a petulant little boy" and Hull's arguments on the matter, some of which had weight, as "whining complaints." In his bibliographical notes he describes Hull's *Memoirs,* which are indeed full of factual errors, as a "virtually useless source consisting largely of a long-winded defense of his and the Administration's policies." A careful historian must take Kimball's anti-Hull bias into account when using his valuable, carefully researched lend-lease history.

21. *Hearings Before the Committee on Foreign Affairs, House of Representatives, Seventy-seventh Congress,* Second Session on H.R. 1776 (Washington: Government Printing Office, 1941), p. 2ff.

22. Blum, *Years of Urgency,* pp. 217–18; *PL 1938–1945,* pp. 1103–5; Kimball, *Unsordid Act,* pp. 143–44; Kimball, ed., *Churchill and Roosevelt,* pp. 123–24.

23. Langer and Gleason, *Undeclared War,* p. 264, citing *House Hearings* (Morgenthau Testimony), pp. 51ff.

24. Langer and Gleason, *Undeclared War,* p. 264; Kimball, *Unsordid Act,* p. 171.

25. Kimball, *Unsordid Act,* p. 178.

26. Langer and Gleason, *Undeclared War,* pp. 266–67.

27. *Ibid.,* p. 267.

28. *Ibid.,* p. 270; *House Hearings,* pp. 636, 678ff.

29. David E. Koskoff, *Joseph P. Kennedy: A Life and Times* (Englewood Cliffs, N.J., 1974), pp. 307–8.

30. Ibid., p. 308; Langer and Gleason, *Undeclared War,* p. 268.

31. Langer and Gleason, *Undeclared War,* p. 268.

32. *Ibid.,* pp. 268–69; Kenneth S. Davis, *The Hero* (New York, 1959), p. 398.

33. Langer and Gleason, *Undeclared War,* pp. 269–71; Kimball, *Unsordid Act,* pp. 161–66, 177–78.

34. Langer and Gleason, *Undeclared War,* p. 269.

35. *Ibid.,* p. 273.

36. *Ibid.,* pp. 277–79; Davis, *The Hero,* p. 398.

37. *PPA 1941,* p. 11.

38. Nina Davis Howland, *Ambassador John Gilbert Winant: Friend of Embattled Britain, 1941–1946* (authorized facsimile of Ph.D. dissertation, University of Maryland, 1983), p. 11.

39. *PPA 1941,* pp. 11–12.

40. Lash, *Roosevelt and Churchill,* p. 280; Fred L. Israel, ed., *The War Diary of Breckinridge Long* (Lincoln, Nebr., 1966), p. 181.

41. Barnes, *op. cit.,* p. 249.

42. *New York Times,* February 10, 1941.

43. Langer and Gleason, *Undeclared War,* pp. 279–80; Barnes, *op. cit.,* p. 252.

44. Barnes, *op. cit.,* p. 254; *New York Times,* February 12, 1941.

45. Quoted by Sherwood, *op. cit.,* p. 233.

46. Sherwood, *op. cit.,* pp. 234–35.

47. *Ibid.,* pp. 235–36.

48. *Ibid.,* pp. 236–37.

49. *Ibid.;* James Leutze, ed., *The London Journal of General Raymond E. Lee, 1940–1941* (Boston, 1971), pp. 201, 216–17.

50. Sherwood, *op. cit.,* p. 236; Winston S. Churchill, *The Grand Alliance* (Boston, 1950), p. 23.

51. Sherwood, *op. cit.,* p. 237; John Colville, *The Fringes of Power: Downing Street Diaries, 1939–1955* (New York, 1985), p. 331.

52. Sherwood, *op. cit.,* p. 238–39; Churchill, *Grand Alliance,* p. 23.

53. Leutze, ed., *op. cit.,* pp. 218–19.

54. *Ibid.,* p. 220; Lash, *Roosevelt and Churchill,* p. 282.

55. Colville, *op. cit.,* pp. 333–34, gives a circumstantial eyewitness account of this after-dinner conversation. The quotation of Lyttelton and the direct quotation of Churchill's words are from Oliver Lyttelton, *The Memoirs of Lord Chandos* (London, 1962), pp. 165–66. The "unsigned memorandum" is told of by Lash, *Roosevelt and Churchill,* pp. 277–78. There is an interesting discrepancy between the Colville-Lyttelton accounts here cited and what Hopkins told Eleanor Roosevelt in response to her eager questioning of him about Churchill's war aims, as reported by Lash on p. 286 of *Roosevelt and Churchill.* According to Lash, Hopkins told Eleanor that "Churchill's approach [was] that this was not the time to discuss them [war aims]."

56. Colville, *op. cit.,* pp. 215–16, 333–34; Lash, *Roosevelt and Churchill,* pp. 277–78.

57. Churchill, *Grand Alliance,* p. 673.

58. Hopkins said the same thing to someone who came to him, as relief administrator, with plans for a work relief project that would take a long time to prepare but was bound "to work out in the long run." See Sherwood. *op. cit.,* p. 52.

59. Leutze, ed., *op. cit.,* pp. 224–25.

60. Sherwood, *op. cit.,* p. 243.

61. *Ibid.,* pp. 247–50.

62. *Ibid.,* pp. 257–58, 259–60.

63. Lash, *Roosevelt and Churchill,* p. 285.

64. Kimball, ed., *Churchill and Roosevelt,* pp. 129, 133–34.

65. Churchill, *Grand Alliance,* pp. 23–24.

66. Langer and Gleason, *Undeclared War,* p. 281.

67. Sherwood, *op. cit.,* p. 257.

68. Kimball, *Unsordid Act,* pp. 223–24, citing memo from Herbert Feis to Hull and Welles, February 6, 1941, and a *Financial News* quote sent through Hull to Treasury on February 3, 1941, by Herschel Johnson of the U.S. embassy in London; Lash, *Roosevelt and Churchill,* pp. 287–88; A. J. P. Taylor, *Beaverbrook* (London, 1972), p. 440; Langer and Gleason, *Undeclared War,* p. 281, footnote 69.

69. *New York Times,* February 26, 1941; Langer and Gleason, *Undeclared War,* pp. 281–82.

70. Blum, *Years of Urgency,* p. 277; Langer and Gleason, *Undeclared War,* pp. 282–83; Kimball, *Unsordid Act,* pp. 212–13; Edward R. Stettinius, *Lend-Lease: Weapon of Victory* (Harmondsworth, Middlesex, England, 1944), Appendix I, pp. 272–73.

71. Sherwood, *op. cit.,* p. 265; Kimball, ed., *Churchill and Roosevelt,* p. 143; Churchill, *Their Finest Hour,* p. 569.

72. Langer and Gleason, *Undeclared War,* p. 284.

73. Sherwood, *op. cit.,* pp. 265–66. Sherwood's further quote of Hopkins on this occasion is famous and revealing of the hold Roosevelt had, the powerful if differing impressions he made, on people as diverse in personality as Rex Tugwell, Missy LeHand,

Sam Rosenman, Adolf Berle, Ray Moley, and Harold Ickes. Said Hopkins to Sherwood: "You and I are for Roosevelt because he's a great spiritual leader, because he's an idealist, like Wilson, and he's got the guts to drive through against any opposition to realize those ideals. Oh—he sometimes tries to appear tough and cynical and flippant, but that's an act he puts on, especially at press conferences. He wants to make the boys think he's hard-boiled. Maybe he fools some of them, now and then—but don't ever let him fool you, or you won't be any use to him. You can see the real Roosevelt when he comes out with something like the Four Freedoms. And don't get the idea that these are any catch phrases. *He believes them!* He believes they can be practically attained. That's what you and I have got to remember in everything we may be able to do for him. Oh—there are a lot of people in this town who are constantly trying to cut him down to their size, and sometimes they have some influence. But it's your job and mine—as long as we're around here—to keep reminding him that he's unlimited, and that's the way he's got to talk because that's the way he's going to act. Maybe we'll make ourselves unpopular now and then—but not in the long run, because he knows what he really is, even if he doesn't like to admit to you or me or anybody."

74. *PPA 1941*, pp. 63–64, 66.
75. Sherwood, *op. cit.*, p. 267; Halifax telegram to foreign office, March 18, 1941; T. North Whitehead commentary, March 20, 1941, quoted by Lash, *Roosevelt and Churchill*, pp. 289–90.
76. Though arrangements had been made to hoist him in his wheelchair aboard *King George V,* and despite his eagerness to inspect the battleship, he prudently remained on the *Potomac* and saw only as much of the battleship as could be seen from his yacht's deck.
77. Winston S. Churchill, *The World Crisis,* one-volume abridgment of four volumes (New York, 1931), p. 300.
78. *Ibid.,* p. 552. The quote is from a chapter entitled "The Blood Test," which is in effect and sum a scathing indictment of Allied commanders in 1914–1918 on a charge of criminal stupidity and callousness.
79. For figures on world manufacturing production, see the League of Nations *World Economic Survey* (Geneva, 1945), table III, p. 154. For figures on national shares of world manufacturing output, see Paul Kennedy, *The Rise and Fall of the Great Powers* (New York, 1987), pp. 330, 331, citing a table on p. 439 of A. J. Toynbee and F. T. Ashton-Gwatkin, ed., *The World in March 1939* (London, 1952).
80. Kennedy, *op. cit.,* p. 331.
81. Maurice Matloff and Edwin L. Snell, *Strategic Planning for Coalition Warfare, 1941–1942* (Department of the Army, Washington, D.C., 1953), p. 46, citing a memorandum of General Watson's oral statement as he returned the unapproved documents to the army chief of staff. A footnote on pp. 46–47 says, "On 5 July 1941 Under Secretary Welles [of State Department] informed President Roosevelt that Lord Halifax wished the President to know that the British Government had in fact approved the ABC-1 report." In other words, Roosevelt's stated reason for *not* approving was invalid. He continued to withhold his approval, however.
82. *Ibid.,* p. 47; Kenneth S. Davis, *Experience of War* (New York, 1965), pp. 132–33. The British-American disagreement over the reinforcement of Singapore is discussed in detail on pp. 393–400 of Mark Skinner Watson, *Chief of Staff: Prewar Plans and Preparations* (Department of the Army, Washington, D.C., 1950).

4. Black Spring 1941

1. In response to a request from Churchill, Roosevelt permitted the *Illustrious* to be repaired (though with no public announcement of the fact) in Norfolk, Virginia. That she was there did not become public knowledge until Lord Louis Mountbatten, having been named to command the ship, came to America to do so in August 1941.

2. Raoul de Roussy de Sales, ed., *My New Order: Adolf Hitler's Speeches, 1918–1941* (New York, 1941), p. 563. Winston S. Churchill, *The Gathering Storm* (Boston, 1948), p. 287; Shirer, *The Rise and Fall of the Third Reich* (New York, 1960), p. 365.

3. Minutes of OKW (German high army command), in *Nuremberg Documents,* quoted by Churchill, *Grand Alliance,* p. 163, and Shirer, *Rise and Fall,* p. 824.

4. Shirer, *Rise and Fall,* p. 826.

5. Langer and Gleason, *Undeclared War,* pp. 421–22.

6. Martin Gilbert, *Winston S. Churchill,* vol. VI, *Finest Hour, 1939–1941* (London, 1983), p. 996, quoting John Colville's diary.

7. Sherwood, *op. cit.,* p. 293.

8. Robert H. Ferrell, *Ill Advised: Presidential Health and Public Trust* (Columbia, Mo., 1992), pp. 28–29.

9. *PPA 1941,* pp. 21–22, 24; W. Averell Harriman and Elie Abel, *Special Envoy to Churchill and Stalin* (New York, 1975), pp. 3–5.

10. *Ibid.,* p. 17.

11. Lash, *Roosevelt and Churchill,* p. 302; George McJimsey, *Harry Hopkins* (Cambridge, Mass., 1987), p. 153.

12. McJimsey, *Harry Hopkins,* p. 159, quoting letter from John Maynard Keynes to Sir Horace Wilson.

13. Blum, *Roosevelt and Morgenthau,* p. 357.

14. Blum, *Roosevelt and Morgenthau,* pp. 357–58; Ickes, *The Lowering Clouds,* p. 459.

15. Ickes, *The Lowering Clouds,* pp. 459, 442.

16. *Ibid.,* pp. 466–67.

17. *Ibid.,* p. 468; McJimsey, *Harry Hopkins,* p. 154.

18. *PPA 1941,* pp. 82–83.

19. Sherwood, *op. cit.,* pp. 267–68.

20. McJimsey, *Harry Hopkins,* p. 156.

21. Sherwood, *op. cit.,* p. 280.

22. *Ibid.,* p. 280.

23. In writing of this strike, I referred to *New York Times* of appropriate dates; Perrett, *Days of Sadness,* p. 178; William L. O'Neill, *Democracy at War* (New York, 1993), pp. 203–4; Josephson, *op. cit.,* pp. 544–46; Burns, *op. cit.,* p. 117.

24. S. S. Huebner, "The Security and Money Markets," in *American Year Book* 1941, p. 361.

25. *Newsweek,* May 27, 1940.

26. The quote is from an FDR letter to Felix Frankfurter, February 9, 1937, reprinted on pp. 381–82 of Max Freedman, ed., *op. cit.*

27. Stimson and Bundy, *op. cit.,* p. 369.

28. Cole, *Roosevelt and the Isolationists,* p. 464.

29. *New York Times,* April 14, 1941; Cole, *Roosevelt and the Isolationists,* p. 461.

30. *Vital Speeches,* vol. 7, pp. 425–26, "We Cannot Win This War for England."

31. *New York Times,* April 26, 1941. Davis, *The Hero,* pp. 402–4. The supposedly ver-

batim report of this press conference in *PPA 1941* was carefully edited by Samuel
Rosenman: Lindbergh's name and every reference to him was removed.

32. A typescript of Swing's article is in Box 5, President's Personal Papers: Speech Materials, FDRL. Attached to it is a memo from Hopkins to Grace Tully, asking her to put it
with material for Roosevelt's next speech, which was then scheduled for Pan-American
Day, May 14, 1941.

33. Shirer, *Rise and Fall*, p. 829.

34. Kimball, ed., *Churchill and Roosevelt*, p. 176.

35. Churchill, *Grand Alliance*, pp. 420–22.

36. *Ibid.*, pp. 422–23.

37. Kimball, ed., *Churchill and Roosevelt*, pp. 177, 179–80.

38. *Ibid.*, p. 177, for Churchill's minute to Eden. Martin Gilbert's massively detailed, multivolumed biography of Churchill, wherein is chronicled Churchill's activity on a daily
and even hour-and-minute basis, is replete with instances of Churchill's "black dog."
Jerrold M. Post, M.D., and Robert S. Robins discuss Churchill's depression as illness
in their *When Illness Strikes the Leader: The Dilemma of the Captive King* (New
Haven, 1993). In his message to the President, Winant reported that Churchill had just
returned from bomb-ravaged Plymouth when he read Roosevelt's letter and that he
seemed "sad and deeply discouraged."

39. *PPA 1941*, pp. 132–34. This is the same press conference in which Roosevelt, at its
end, castigated Lindbergh as a "Vallandigham." During it, Roosevelt made a sharp distinction between the meanings of "patrol" and "convoy," claiming the difference was
as great as that between "cow" and "horse." He was asked: "Mr. President, if this patrol should discover some apparently aggressive ship headed toward the Western
Hemisphere, what would it do about it?" Replied Roosevelt: "Let me know," provoking loud laughter. He was asked: ". . . has this Government any idea of escorting convoys?" He replied: "No, no. . . ."

40. Churchill, *Grand Alliance*, pp. 236–37.

41. Kimball, ed., *Churchill and Roosevelt*, pp. 181–82.

42. At a meeting to discuss Churchill's draft message to Roosevelt and "tone it down,"
held in Eden's office on May 3, 1941, and attended by Deputy Prime Minister Clement
Attlee, among others, a minute by T. North Whitehead was read. It proved persuasive.
"The President has always shown great skill in making it appear that his public was
leading him rather than the reverse; he has not always shown an equal facility for coming out in the open and leading them at a crisis. We appear to be at such a crisis now,
and if the Prime Minister would put it into the mind of the President to take a bold step
forward Americans would probably accept his lead with positive relief." Which is precisely what Stimson was thinking and saying at that time. See Lash, *Roosevelt and
Churchill*, pp. 309–10.

43. Kimball, ed., *Churchill and Roosevelt*, pp. 184–85.

44. Churchill, *Grand Alliance*, p. 51.

45. *Ibid.*, p. 50; Kimball, ed., *Churchill and Roosevelt*, pp. 187–88.

46. Kimball, ed., *Churchill and Roosevelt*, p. 197. Details of the action are in Churchill,
Grand Alliance, pp. 309–19.

47. Churchill, *Grand Alliance*, p. 295, quoting message from Freyberg to Wavell.

48. *Documents on American Foreign Policy*, vol. III, pp. 291ff, gives full text of pact;
Churchill, *Grand Alliance*, p. 192.

49. Kimball, ed., *Churchill and Roosevelt*, pp. 196–97.

50. Letter, Stimson to Roosevelt, with enclosure, Box 25, President's Personal File, Speech Material, FDRL.

51. Adolf Berle, *Navigating the Rapids* (New York, 1973), pp. 369–70; Sherwood, *op. cit.,* pp. 296–97. There is a considerable difference between Berle's and Sherwood's accounts of the drafting of this speech, and I have, as regards chronology, accepted Berle's account as correct since it is recorded in his diary entries at the time (those of May 26 and May 29, 1941). Berle's contribution to the drafting process was far greater than Sherwood recorded.

52. Sherwood, *op. cit.,* pp. 297–98, gives circumstantial account of the speech's delivery.

53. *PPA 1941,* pp. 181–84, 187–90, 193–94.

54. Sherwood, *op. cit.,* p. 298.

55. *Ibid.*

56. *New York Times,* May 28, 29, 1941; Kimball, ed., *Churchill and Roosevelt,* p. 198.

57. *New York Times,* May 29, 1941. It is significant that no portion of the transcript of this press conference, and no mention of it, appears in *PPA 1941,* which includes transcripts of conferences considerably less important. One suspects that Roosevelt was not proud of his performance on this occasion, may even have been ashamed of it, and that Sam Rosenman respected what he knew would have been his beloved chief's wishes when he made his selections for the 1941 volume, published five years after Roosevelt's death.

58. Sherwood, *op. cit.,* p. 299.

59. Kimball, *Churchill and Roosevelt,* p. 208.

60. *Ibid.,* pp. 208–10; Sherwood, *op. cit.,* pp. 290–91.

61. Sherwood, *op. cit.,* p. 299.

62. *PPA 1941,* pp. 227–30.

63. Churchill, *Grand Alliance,* p. 142; Langer and Gleason, *op. cit.,* p. 517.

64. Lash, *Eleanor and Franklin,* p. 617. Lash was evidently personally present at this conversation. In his note for it he cites his diary entry for June 3, 1940.

65. Eleanor Roosevelt, *This I Remember* (New York, 1949), p. 239; Lash, *Eleanor and Franklin,* p. 639. Eleanor said in 1949 of Hopkins's "feeling": "He was probably right, but I could never entirely agree with him." Which, to those who accurately discount the gentility of Eleanor's authorial style, means that she most emphatically disagreed.

66. *PPA 1941,* p. 156.

67. Lash, *Eleanor and Franklin,* p. 639.

68. *Ibid.,* pp. 637–40; Ickes, *The Lowering Clouds,* pp. 407–8.

69. *PPA 1941,* p. 44.

70. *Ibid.,* p. 162.

71. Columbia Oral History Collection (hereafter COHC), "The Reminiscences of Will Winton Alexander"; Jervis Anderson, *A. Philip Randolph* (New York, 1973), p. 242.

72. Lash, *Eleanor and Franklin,* pp. 528–29.

73. Anderson, *op. cit.,* pp. 8–10.

74. *Ibid.,* pp. 243–44.

75. *Ibid.,* p. 244; Geoffrey Hodgson, *The Colonel: The Life and Wars of Henry Stimson* (New York, 1990), p. 250, quoting Stimson's diary entry for January 24, 1941 (Hodgson in a footnote mistakenly dates it 1942).

76. *New York Times,* October 10, 12, 1940; Walter White, *A Man Called White* (New York, 1948), pp. 186–88; Anderson, *op. cit.,* pp. 244–46; letter from Roosevelt to

White, Randolph, and Hill, October 25, 1940, is in President's Official Correspondence, FDRL.

77. *New York Times,* October 26, 1940; Anderson, *op. cit.,* pp. 248–49.

78. *Ibid.,* Anderson.

79. Herbert Garfinkle, *When Negroes March* (Glencoe, Ill., 1959), p. 56.

80. Lash, *Eleanor and Franklin,* p. 534.

81. Anderson, *op. cit.,* pp. 256–58, gives a highly circumstantial account of this meeting, deriving his information from a number of accounts given by Randolph, the first of them immediately after the meeting. Randolph's absolute commitment to truth telling was notorious, and I have here followed his account. See also Lerone Bennett, Jr., *Confrontation: Black and White* (Chicago, 1965), pp. 176–79. According to Lash, *Eleanor and Franklin,* p. 535, the final draft of the order sat for some days on the President's desk. "Finally, according to [Aubrey] Williams, spurred on by Eleanor, Anna Rosenberg bought a new hat, marched into the president's office, fished out the order, and cajoled him: 'Sign it, Mr. President—sign it.' "

82. *PPA 1941,* pp. 233–35.

83. David Robertson, *Sly and Able: A Political Biography of James F. Byrnes* (New York, 1944), p. 299. Quoting telegram, Walter White to FDR, March 16, 1941.

84. Leutze, ed. *op. cit.,* pp. 302–3.

85. Harriman and Abel, *op. cit.,* p. 63.

86. Tully, *op. cit.,* p. 246; Doris Kearns Goodwin, *No Ordinary Time: Franklin and Eleanor Roosevelt: The Home Front in World War II* (New York, 1994), pp. 242–45.

87. Goodwin, *op. cit.,* pp. 117–18. She says flatly that Missy's anxiety over threatened changes in her relationship with FDR caused her nervous collapses; I have always thought it only probable that they did so. Goodwin, deriving her information from personal interviews with people who lived through the time of which she writes (James Roosevelt, former Secret Service agent Milton Lipson, former *Chicago Tribune* reporter Walter Trohan [a cynically dishonest reporter, in my opinion], Missy's friends Barbara Mueller Curtis and Egbert Curtis), is also my source for a good deal of the Princess Martha story I tell.

88. Fulton Oursler, *Behold the Dreamer* (New York, 1964), pp. 424–25.

89. Lash, *Eleanor and Franklin,* p. 715.

5. The Grand Alliance Is Enlarged and Strengthened

1. Sherwood, *op. cit.,* p. 303.

2. Adam B. Ulam, *Stalin: The Man and His Era* (New York, 1973), pp. 538–40.

3. Cordell Hull, *Memoirs* (New York, 1948), pp. 967–73; Langer and Gleason, *Undeclared War,* pp. 336–37; Shirer, *Rise and Fall,* pp. 810, 842–43.

4. Hull, *op. cit.,* p. 968; Sumner Welles, *The Time for Decision* (New York, 1944), pp. 170–71.

5. Churchill, *Grand Alliance,* pp. 356–61.

6. Langer and Gleason, *Undeclared War,* p. 342, quoting Soviet embassy, *Information Bulletin,* December 15, 1941.

7. Shirer, *Rise and Fall,* pp. 849–51. The letter is in *Nazi-Soviet Relations,* from the files of the German Foreign Office, pp. 349–53.

8. Ulam, *op. cit.,* pp. 541–42, quoting Ivan Maisky writing in *New World,* published in Moscow, December 1964, p. 165.

9. Langer and Gleason, *Undeclared War,* pp. 535–36.

10. Colville, *op. cit.,* pp. 404; Kimball, ed., *Churchill and Roosevelt,* p. 208.

11. Colville, *op. cit.,* p. 404.

12. Churchill, *Grand Alliance,* pp. 371–73. It is the present author's opinion that this speech, promptly announcing with passionate eloquence a policy whose making and effective implementation were by no means foregone conclusions, was one of the major decisive acts of the war. Historians are rather blindly following the lead given them by Churchill himself, it seems to me, when they write of this decision as *of course* the only one that could have been made, and so announced, in the circumstances. In fact, a much more tentative policy, announced in much more temperate language—the kind of policy and announcement that Roosevelt now made on this subject—was much more likely in the circumstances for a Prime Minister of Churchill's background and published opinions. Had Churchill followed this more likely route, it would, I think, have led to a resurgence in England, and in England's ruling class, of that view of Nazi-fascism as bulwark against communism that had determined Chamberlain's appeasement policy. This view yet persisted among English Tories and required but little time and slight encouragement to become effectively expressed politically.

13. Langer and Gleason, *Undeclared War,* pp. 541–42; Welles, *The Time for Decision,* p. 171.

14. Langer and Gleason, *Undeclared War,* p. 541.

15. Sherwood, *op. cit.,* pp. 303–5.

16. See, for instance, Sumner Welles, *Where Are We Heading?* (New York, 1946), pp. 37–38.

17. Joseph E. Davies, *Mission to Moscow* (New York, 1941), pp. 33–34; George F. Kennan, *Memoirs, 1925–1950* (New York, 1967), p. 279; FDR to "Dear Joe," facsimile in Davies, *op. cit.,* facing p. 488.

18. Davies, *op. cit.,* pp. 475, 488; Sherwood, *op. cit.,* pp. 306–8, quotes the Davies memo to Hopkins in full; the edited version of it in Davies *op. cit.,* pp. 493–97, has removed from it all that the Kremlin might deem critical of it.

19. Davies, *op. cit.,* p. 489; Sherwood, *op. cit.,* pp. 307–8.

20. Langer and Gleason, *Undeclared War,* p. 546.

21. Shirer, *Rise and Fall,* p. 855, quoting Nuremberg documents and Halder's diary. Halder's claim that the Germans had identified 360 Soviet divisions by August 11 is at variance with Stalin's statement to Hopkins in Moscow on the evening of July 31, 1941, that he could mobilize in toto 350 divisions and would have that many under arms by May 1942. See Sherwood, *op. cit.,* pp. 333–34.

22. Stimson diary, June 30, 1941; *PPA, 1941,* pp. 248, 250.

23. Sherwood, *op. cit.,* pp. 314–15.

24. Sherwood, *op. cit.,* pp. 308–10.

25. General Raymond E. Lee, the military attaché at the embassy, liked Harriman personally but resented the Harriman mission as an outrageous undercutting of Ambassador Winant's authority and effectiveness. "Never did any Ambassador undertake such a new appointment with such a handicap as another man, bearing a wide-open letter from the President which describes him as his personal representative and authorizes him to interfere in anything and everything," wrote Lee in his diary on July 30, 1941. "Winant has been entirely too patient." Leutze, ed., *op. cit.,* p. 359.

26. Bruce Catton, *The War Lords of Washington* (New York, 1948), p. 32.

27. Elliott Roosevelt, *As He Saw It* (New York, 1946), p. 27.

28. Leutze, *op. cit.,* pp. 341–42, 353.

29. Harriman and Abel, *op. cit.,* p. 71.

30. Churchill, *Grand Alliance,* p. 427. Churchill's account, studiedly casual, is at variance, as regards tone, with other accounts. Kimball, ed., *Churchill and Roosevelt,* p. 223.

31. Lash, *Roosevelt and Churchill,* p. 381.

32. Ivan Maisky, *Memoirs of a Soviet Ambassador: The War, 1939–43* (London, 1967), p. 177; Henry H. Adams, *Harry Hopkins* (New York, 1977), p. 232.

33. Churchill, *Grand Alliance,* p. 385.

34. Lash, *Roosevelt and Churchill,* p. 385; Maisky, *op. cit.,* p. 180; Adams, *op. cit.,* pp. 231–32. There has been some disagreement among historians regarding the original idea for Hopkins's Moscow trip, some claiming that it was Hopkins's alone, others that Roosevelt had broached the subject with Hopkins before the latter's departure for London, but I am persuaded by contextual information that Maisky's account is substantially accurate.

35. Kimball, ed., *Churchill and Roosevelt,* p. 233.

36. Sherwood, *op. cit.,* pp. 317–18.

37. Quoted by Adams, *op. cit.,* p. 235, from reel 19 of Hopkins's papers on microfilm in FDRL.

38. Sherwood, *op. cit.,* p. 318.

39. *Ibid.,* pp. 321–22.

40. *Ibid.,* p. 323–26, quoting Flight Lieutenant McKinley's report of the trip; Harry L. Hopkins, "The Inside Story of My Meeting with Stalin," *American* magazine, December 1941.

41. Margaret Bourke-White, *Shooting the Russian War* (New York, 1942), pp. 207–8. Cited by McJimsey, *op. cit.,* p. 185, who also reprints the photograph referred to in my following paragraph.

42. Hopkins, *American* magazine; Sherwood, *op. cit.,* pp. 327–30, quoting extensively Hopkins's report to the President.

43. Sherwood, *Ibid.* On p. 330 are quoted the official minutes of the meeting with Yakovlev, whose first name is not given either in the text or in the index of Sherwood's book. I must assume that Hopkins's designation of the general as an artilleryman is accurate, but I'm rendered uneasy about this by the fact that the only Yakovlev I've read of elsewhere as operating in the Kremlin, in such works as Adam Ulam's *Stalin: The Man and His Era,* for instance, is Alexander Yakovlev, the Soviet Union's leading aircraft designer, who in the summer of 1941 was an assistant minister in the Kremlin and may conceivably have been a general. As if it were apropos of the Hopkins-Yakovlev interview, Sherwood, in the first sentence following his quotation of the official minutes, writes that Hopkins was greatly impressed by the Moscow blackout against air raids, a blackout even more impenetrable than London's. One knows that the Lenin-Stalin regimes did indeed have a genius for blackouts.

44. Most of this July 2, 1941, "Outline of the Policy of the Imperial [Japanese] Government in View of Present Developments," is printed on pp. 215–16 of Herbert Feis, *op. cit.;* Sherwood, *op. cit.,* p. 331.

45. The whole of Hopkins's report to the President of this conversation is printed on pp. 333–43 of Sherwood, *op. cit.,* and all my account of what was said derives from this.

46. Sherwood, *op. cit.,* p. 345. "Before my three days in Moscow ended, the difference between democracy and dictatorship was clearer to me than any words of a philosopher, historian, or journalist could make it," Hopkins later wrote. Hopkins "could never rec-

oncile himself to a system which . . . concentrated such absolute power in one mortal man," writes Sherwood.

47. Hopkins, *American* magazine, pp. 14–15.
48. Sherwood, *op. cit.,* p. 352.
49. *Ibid.,* p. 348.
50. Adams, *op. cit.,* p. 241.
51. Kimball, ed., *Churchill and Roosevelt,* p. 226.
52. *New York Times,* August 5, 1941; Ross McIntire, *White House Physician* (New York, 1946), p. 130; Goodwin, *op. cit.,* p. 263.
53. H. H. Arnold, *Global Mission* (New York, 1949), p. 247.
54. *PPA 1941,* pp. 275–76.
55. Langer and Gleason, *Undeclared War,* p. 573.
56. *Ibid.,* pp. 560–61; Ickes, *The Lowering Clouds,* pp. 592–93; Goodwin, *op. cit.,* p. 261.
57. *PPA 1941,* pp. 284–88.
58. *Ibid.,* p. 290.
59. *Ibid.,* pp. 306, 313.
60. Geoffrey C. Ward, ed., *Closest Companion: The Unknown Story of the Intimate Relationship Between Franklin Roosevelt and Margaret Suckley* (Boston, 1995), p. 140.
61. *Ibid.;* Theodore A. Wilson, *The First Summit: Roosevelt and Churchill at Placentia Bay 1941* (Boston, 1969), p. 69.
62. Ward, ed., *op. cit.,* p. 141.
63. Sherwood, *op. cit.,* p. 353; Wilson, *op. cit.,* p. 83; Elliott Roosevelt, *As He Saw It* (New York, 1946), p. 20.
64. Ward, *op. cit.,* p. 141; Wilson, *op. cit.,* p. 84.
65. Arnold, *op. cit.,* p. 252; Wilson, *op. cit.,* pp. 102–6.
66. Churchill, *Grand Alliance,* pp. 431–32.
67. Feis, *op. cit.,* pp. 236–38, quoting Radio Bulletin No. 176, issued by White House on July 25, 1941.
68. Feis, *op. cit.,* quoting Welles memo in *Foreign Relations: Japan II,* p. 527, *et. seq.*
69. Kimball, ed., *Churchill and Roosevelt,* p. 225.
70. Feis, *op. cit.,* p. 249; *Foreign Relations: Japan II,* p. 549 *et. seq.*
71. Sherwood, *op. cit.,* pp. 354–55; Langer and Gleason, *Undeclared War,* pp. 674–75.
72. Prime Minister to foreign secretary, August 11, 1941, printed in its entirety in Churchill, *Grand Alliance,* pp. 439–40.
73. Feis, *op. cit.,* p. 258; Winston S. Churchill, *The End of the Beginning* (Boston, 1943), p. 33.
74. Sherwood, *op. cit.,* pp. 356–57; Feis, *op. cit.,* pp. 256–57; Langer and Gleason, *Undeclared War,* p. 695.
75. Feis, *op. cit.,* p. 260, footnote citing memorandum of talk between Roosevelt and Nomura, printed in *Foreign Relations: Japan II,* pp. 572–73.
76. Churchill, *Grand Alliance,* pp. 444–45, prints full joint message to Stalin.
77. Forrest C. Pogue, *Marshall: Ordeal and Hope* (New York, 1966), p. 16.
78. Wilson, *op. cit.,* quoting "Review of General Strategy by the British Chiefs of Staff," dated July 31, 1941, p. 139.
79. *New York Times,* July 4, 8, 1941; Langer and Gleason, *Undeclared War,* p. 571.
80. Wilson, *op. cit.,* p. 131.
81. Churchill, *Grand Alliance,* p. 446.
82. *Ibid.,* pp. 433–34.

83. *Ibid.,* p. 437; See also Welles, *Where Are We Heading?,* and Forrest Davis and Ernest K. Lindley, *How War Came* (New York, 1942), pp. 268–70, for the story of the shaping of this point in the Atlantic Charter.

84. The original typewritten draft of the Atlantic Charter with Churchill's handwritten "corrections" upon it is reproduced in facsimile as p. 435 of his *Grand Alliance.*

85. Kenneth Young, *Churchill and Beaverbrook* (London, 1966), p. 201, and Sherwood, *op. cit.,* p. 359, have Beaverbrook arriving on the morning of August 11 instead of, as he did, on the morning of August 12, (see Wilson, *op. cit.,* pp. 171, 207–8), and Young has him participating in major decisions that had actually been made before he arrived. Beaverbrook's own memo of the final drafting of point 4 claims that *he* inserted the qualifying clause. This seems, on the evidence, a deliberate falsification.

86. Wilson, *op. cit.,* p. 210.

87. *New York Times,* August 13, 1941; Langer and Gleason, *Undeclared War,* p. 574. There seems little doubt that a more emphatic early leadership on this matter by the White House would have considerably widened the margin of victory for the administration.

88. Ward, ed., *op. cit.,* p. 142.

89. Gilbert, *Winston S. Churchill,* vol. VI, *Finest Hour,* p. 1168, quoting minutes of war cabinet (No. 84 of 1941), August 19, 1941.

90. *PPA 1941,* pp. 322–23.

91. *Ibid.,* p. 327.

92. Kenneth S. Davis, *The Politics of Honor,* a biography of Adlai E. Stevenson (New York, 1967), pp. 144–45.

6. Toward Culmination: The Day of Infamy

1. Langer and Gleason, *Undeclared War,* pp. 743–44; Samuel Eliot Morison, *The Battle of the Atlantic* (Boston, 1964), pp. 79ff; James MacGregor Burns, *Roosevelt: The Soldier of Freedom* (New York, 1970), p. 139, bases his authoritative account on Gerard E. Hasselwander, "Der US-Zerstorer 'Greer' und U 652, am 4, September 1941," *Marine-Rundschau,* Heft 3, 1962, pp. 140–60.

2. Kimball, ed., *Churchill and Roosevelt,* pp. 235–36, 237.

3. Geoffrey C. Ward, *A First-Class Temperament* (New York, 1989), p. 2; Goodwin, *op. cit.,* pp. 270–71; *New York Times,* September 9, 1941.

4. Ward, *op. cit.,* pp. 5–6; Goodwin, *op. cit.,* pp. 271–72.

5. Michael F. Reilly, as told to William J. Slocum, *Reilly of the White House* (New York, 1947), p. 84.

6. Sherwood, *op. cit.,* p. 371.

7. *New York Times,* September 9, 1941; Reilly, *op. cit.,* pp. 84–85.

8. *New York Times,* September 11, 1941; Ward, *op. cit.,* p. 8; Goodwin, *op. cit.,* p. 273.

9. Tully, *op. cit.,* p. 105.

10. Joseph P. Lash, *Love, Eleanor* (Garden City, N.Y., 1982), p. 356; James Roosevelt, *My Parents: A Differing View* (Chicago, 1976), p. 113.

11. Lash, *Love, Eleanor,* p. 357; Eleanor Roosevelt, *This I Remember* (New York, 1949), pp. 229–30; James Roosevelt, *op. cit.,* p. 113.

12. Sherwood, *op. cit.,* pp. 371–72; Langer and Gleason, *Undeclared War,* p. 744.

13. *PPA 1941,* pp. 384–86, 389–92.

14. Morison, *The Battle of the Atlantic,* p. 79; Langer and Gleason, *Undeclared War,* p. 746.

15. Langer and Gleason, *Undeclared War,* p. 747, citing *Chicago Tribune,* September 24, 1941, and *New York Journal-American,* September 25, 1941.

16. Wayne S. Cole, *America First: The Battle Against Intervention, 1940–41* (Madison, Wisc., 1953), p. 144; Davis, *The Hero,* p. 412.

17. Davis, *The Hero,* p. 413; *New York Times,* September 25, 1941.

18. Anthony Martienssen, *Hitler and His Admirals* (New York, 1949), p. 118.

19. *PPA 1941,* p. 350.

20. *Ibid.,* p. 359.

21. Harriman and Abel, *op. cit.,* p. 86.

22. *Ibid.,* pp. 83, 85–90.

23. Donald. M. Nelson, *Arsenal of Democracy* (New York, 1946), p. 134; Lester V. Chandler, Donald H. Wallace, eds., *Economic Mobilization and Stabilization, Selected Materials on the Economics of War and Defense* (New York, 1951); paper entitled "Determination War Production Objective for 1941 and 1943" is excerpted from John R. Brigante, *The Feasibility Dispute* (Washington, D.C., 1950), pp. 14–41; Langer and Gleason, *Undeclared War,* pp. 436–37.

24. Chandler and Wallace, eds., *op. cit.,* p. 70; Langer and Gleason, *Undeclared War,* pp. 738–39.

25. Langer and Gleason, *Undeclared War,* pp. 738–39.

26. *Ibid.,* 739–40; Sherwood, *op. cit.,* pp. 410–18, gives extensive quotes from "Joint Board Estimate of United States Over-all Production Requirements."

27. Chandler and Wallace, eds., *op. cit.,* pp. 71–74; Bruce Catton, *The War Lords of Washington* (New York, 1948), pp. 42–43.

28. Catton, *op. cit.,* pp. 34–35, tells Beaver County story.

29. Eliot Janeway, *The Struggle for Survival* (New York, 1951), p. 199.

30. Catton, *op. cit.,* pp. 34–35.

31. Immediately after the interview, Truman wrote Lou Holland: "I don't know whether I made any impression . . . because the President is always courteous and cordial when anyone calls on him, and when you come out you [may] think you are getting what you wanted when nine times out of ten you are just getting the cordial treatment." Quoted by Richard Lawrence Miller, *Truman: The Rise to Power* (New York, 1986), p. 352.

32. Truman's friend Lewis Schwellenbach of Washington State wrote him on March 3, 1941: "The idea of expecting anyone to do a job as important as this for that sum [$15,000] is just silly. Between ourselves, I would spend it all as quickly as possible and then go back and ask for more. With the $15,000 you can work out plans for committee work of such an important nature that they won't dare turn you down on it." Miller, *op. cit.,* p. 353, quoting this letter.

33. *Ibid.,* p. 353; *American Year Book, 1941* (New York, 1942), p. 10.

34. Catton, *op. cit.,* pp. 34–35.

35. *New York Times,* October 22, 1941; Catton, *op. cit.,* pp. 36–37.

36. Nelson, *op. cit.,* pp. 175–77; Catton, *op. cit.,* p. 37.

37. Margaret Gowing, *Britain and Atomic Energy, 1939–1945* (New York, 1964), pp. 394–436, prints the MAUD report in full. Quoted by James G. Hershberg, *James B. Conant* (New York, 1993), p. 149. See also Richard Rhodes, *op. cit.,* p. 369.

38. M. L. E. (Mark) Oliphant, "The Beginning: Chadwick and the Neutron," *Bulletin of Atomic Scientists,* December 1962. Quoted by Rhodes, *op. cit.,* p. 372.

39. James Bryant Conant, *My Several Lives* (New York, 1970), p. 279.

40. Arthur Holly Compton, *Atomic Quest* (New York, 1956), pp. 6–8, tells of the fireplace conversation that in Compton's belief (see p. 53 of his book) was "the start of the wartime atomic race."

41. Hershberg, *op. cit.,* p. 149.

42. Rhodes, *op. cit.,* pp. 378–79.

43. *Ibid.,* p. 378.

44. Vannevar Bush, *Pieces of the Action* (New York, 1970), pp. 60–61, indicates that the function and purpose of this Top Policy Committee was as I've described it. For instance, he had no discussions with committee member General Marshall regarding "atomic energy or any other aspect of new weapons." Marshall was "just too busy" with other matters. ". . . Mr. Stimson usually told me I could assume General Marshall's approval. . . ."

45. Feis, *op. cit.,* pp. 268–69.

46. *Ibid.,* p. 291, quotes Nomura telegrams of October 20 and 22 to Japanese Foreign Minister Shigenori Togo; Langer and Gleason, *Undeclared War,* p. 849; Hull, *Memoirs,* pp. 1056–62.

47. Kimball, ed., *Churchill and Roosevelt,* p. 266.

48. Langer and Gleason, *Undeclared War,* p. 849; Hull, *Memoirs,* pp. 1056–62.

49. Langer and Gleason, *Undeclared War,* quotes the memorandum in full on pp. 845–46.

50. Feis, *op. cit.,* p. 300.

51. Feis, *op. cit.,* pp. 295–96. Feis points out in a footnote that the first sentence of the Combined Fleet Secret Operations Order No. 1 drawn up on the battleship *Nagoto* on November 1, 1941, is differently translated as "The Japanese Empire will declare war on the United States, Great Britain, and The Netherlands."

52. Stimson's diary entry for November 7, 1941; Langer and Gleason, pp. 858–59, quoting *Foreign Relations of the United States: Japan* II, p. 708, and *Tokyo War Crimes Documents,* Defense Document No. 1401-F-2. I have broken what was a single sentence in the FRUS document into two sentences. Robert Dallek, *Franklin D. Roosevelt and American Foreign Policy, 1932–1945* (New York, 1979), pp. 305–6.

53. Langer and Gleason, *Undeclared War,* p. 866.

54. The penciled note in State Department files has attached to it a note saying it was written "shortly after November 20, 1941," but Langer and Gleason are convinced this is erroneous, that it was written days earlier. See *Undeclared War,* p. 872. Feis, *op. cit.,* in a footnote on p. 312 says the note "may have been written earlier."

55. Feis, *op. cit.,* p. 309, and Langer and Gleason, *Undeclared War,* pp. 867–68, prints Plan B in full.

56. Feis, *op. cit.,* pp. 305–6, quoting telegrams Nomura to Togo, November 14, 1941, and Togo to Nomura, November 16, 1941.

57. Kimball, ed., *Churchill and Roosevelt,* pp. 277–78.

58. Gordon W. Prange, *At Dawn We Slept* (New York, 1981), pp. 369, 387; Feis, *op. cit.,* p. 313.

59. *PPA 1941,* pp. 408–11.

60. *Ibid.,* pp. 414–17.

61. *Ibid.,* pp. 438, 440–41, 444.

62. Sherwood, *op. cit.,* p. 382.

63. *Ibid.,* p. 383.

64. *PPA 1941,* p. 481.

65. Perrett, *op. cit.,* p. 184.

66. Royal R. Montgomery, *Organized Labor* (New York, 1945), p. 695; Burns, *Roosevelt: The Soldier of Freedom*, p. 194.

67. *PPA 1941*, pp. 490–92, 494–95.

68. *Ibid.*, p. 494.

69. *Ibid.*, p. 495.

70. *Ibid.*, pp. 433, 464, 509.

71. Freedman, ed., *op. cit.*, pp. 577–78.

72. Bullitt, ed., *op. cit.*, pp. 512–14; Richard Gid Powers, *Secrecy and Power: The Life of J. Edgar Hoover* (New York, 1987), p. 264; Irwin F. Gellman, *Secret Affairs: Franklin Roosevelt, Cordell Hull, and Sumner Welles* (Baltimore, 1995). Bullitt's vehement adamance in this matter seems excessive (he doth protest too much) and, coupled with the abnormally frequent mention in his dispatches of kissing and being kissed by European statesmen, makes one wonder about his own basic sexual orientation.

73. Bullitt, ed., *op. cit.*, p. 514.

74. Langer and Gleason, *Undeclared War*, p. 892, quoting Stimson diary entry for November 26, 1941, and the text of the document printed in *Foreign Relations of the United States: Japan* II, pp. 766–70; Hull, *Memoirs*, pp. 766–70. A cartoon by Rollin Kirby, published in the *New York Post*, December 2, 1941, has Uncle Sam presenting a paper labeled "ultimatum" to a bespectacled figure labeled "Japan" who holds behind his back a paper labeled "Axis reverses in Russia" as he pleads: "Please, Mister, let's keep talking." On the eastern front a Russian counterattack had retaken Rostov.

75. Langer and Gleason, *Undeclared War*, p. 898, quoting Stimson diary entry for November 27, 1941, and p. 899, quoting *Pearl Harbor Attack*, XIV, p. 1406.

76. *New York Times*, November 30, 1941.

77. *PPA 1941*, pp. 508–10.

78. Ickes, *The Lowering Clouds*, p. 659.

79. *PPA 1941*, pp. 512–13.

80. The circumstantial account that follows derives from Commander Schulz's testimony before the Joint Committee on the Investigation of Pearl Harbor, key portions of which are quoted by Sherwood, *op. cit.*, pp. 426–27. That Hopkins and Roosevelt had been discussing the political repercussions of the *Chicago Tribune* episode before Schulz entered is confidently made by Stanley Weintraub in his *Long Day's Journey into War* (New York, 1991), p. 99. He cites no source and lists no bibliography, but numerous other statements of alleged fact made by him without source citation are accurate, I know, and I therefore assume this one is. Certainly the *Tribune* outrage was very much on Roosevelt's and Hopkins's minds at that time.

81. Langer and Gleason, *Undeclared War*, pp. 933–34. Part fourteen is, of course, quoted in numerous other works, including Walter Millis's *This Is Pearl!* (New York, 1947), which I wish especially to mention because I think it remains the best-written succinct account of the Pearl Harbor attack and the events leading up to it.

82. The memorandum of the conversation, quoted in many books, is in *Foreign Relations of the United States: Japan* II, pp. 786–87.

83. Kimball, ed., *Churchill and Roosevelt*, pp. 281–82.

84. The transcript of the congressional meeting is in *Pearl Harbor Attack*, part 11, pp. 3503–7; Burns, *Roosevelt: The Soldier of Freedom*, p. 164.

85. Weintraub, *op. cit.*, pp. 328, 460; Burns, *Roosevelt: The Soldier of Freedom*, p. 165.

86. *PPA 1941*, pp. 514–15.

7. Arcadia: The Birth of the United Nations

1. Doris Kearns Goodwin, *op. cit.,* pp. 289–90; James Roosevelt, *My Parents: A Differing View* (Chicago, 1976), p. 266.
2. COHC, Frances Perkins Transcript. Quoted by Goodwin, *op. cit.,* p. 294.
3. Sherwood, *op. cit.,* p. 383.
4. Richard R. Lingeman, *Don't You Know There's a War On? The American Home Front, 1941–1945* (New York, 1970), p. 29.
5. *New York Times,* December 9, 1941. The congressional leaders who called at the White House on December 7, 1941, would have been the ranking party members of the key defense committees of the two houses if Hamilton Fish of Dutchess County had not been the ranking Republican member of the House Military Affairs Committee. Fish had once made unforgivable remarks about Roosevelt's mother, and Roosevelt refused to permit his entrance into the White House. See Burns, *op. cit.,* pp. 37, 164; Sherwood, *op. cit.,* p. 432.
6. *PPA 1941,* pp. 523–31.
7. Churchill, *Grand Alliance,* p. 620.
8. William L. Shirer, *Rise and Fall,* pp. 897–900; Kennan, *op. cit.,* pp. 135–36.
9. *PPA 1941,* pp. 532–33.
10. William Seale, *The President's House* (Washington, D.C., 1986), vol. II, pp. 975–77.
11. Kimball, ed., *op. cit.,* pp. 283–84.
12. *Ibid.,* pp. 284–86; Forrest C. Pogue, *George C. Marshall: Ordeal and Hope, 1939–1942* (New York, 1966), pp. 264.
13. Harriman and Abel, *op. cit.,* p. 114.
14. Churchill, *Grand Alliance,* p. 627.
15. Anthony Eden, *Memoirs: The Reckoning* (Boston, 1965), pp. 327, 330–31.
16. *Ibid.,* pp. 335–37, 347–51; Churchill, *Grand Alliance,* pp. 628–31.
17. Harriman and Abel, *op. cit.,* p. 115.
18. Eden, *op. cit.,* pp. 341, 349; Churchill, *Grand Alliance,* p. 627.
19. Harriman and Abel, *op. cit.,* pp. 114–16.
20. Churchill, *Grand Alliance,* pp. 646–51.
21. *Ibid.,* pp. 652, 654–55.
22. *Ibid.,* pp. 655–58.
23. *Ibid.,* p. 659.
24. *PPA 1941,* p. 531.
25. Josephson, *op. cit.,* pp. 567–69; Frances Perkins, *op. cit.,* pp. 369–70.
26. Perkins, *op. cit.,* p. 369; *PPA 1942,* pp. 42–48.
27. *PPA 1941,* pp. 563–65; Gordon W. Prange, *At Dawn We Slept* (New York, 1981), pp. 588–89, 599–600.
28. Dwight D. Eisenhower, *Crusade in Europe* (New York, 1948), p. 18; Davis, *Experience of War,* p. 111; Walter Millis, *op. cit.,* pp. 61–64; Husband E. Kimmel, *Admiral Kimmel's Story* (Chicago, 1955), pp. 13–15.
29. Lord Moran, *Churchill: Taken from the Diaries of Lord Moran* (Boston, 1966), p. 11; *New York Times,* December 23, 1941.
30. Moran, *op. cit.,* p. 11; Churchill, *Grand Alliance,* pp. 662–63; J. B. West (with Mary Lynn Kotz), *Upstairs at the White House* (New York, 1974), p. 41; Goodwin, *op. cit.,* p. 302; Seale, *op. cit.,* pp. 973–74.
31. *PPA 1941,* pp. 585–91.

32. *Ibid.,* pp. 593–95; Churchill, *Grand Alliance,* pp. 669–70; Seale, *op. cit.,* pp. 974–75.

33. Goodwin, *op. cit.,* p. 306, citing Lash diary. I have not been able to ascertain whether or not Roosevelt phoned Missy on Christmas Day. It seems to me distinctly possible that he did, though this was a very crowded day for him.

34. *New York Times,* December 16, 1941; Sherwood, *op. cit.,* p. 443; Churchill, *Grand Alliance,* pp. 670; Moran, *op. cit.,* p. 14.

35. Churchill, *Grand Alliance,* pp. 671–72; Sherwood, *op. cit.,* pp. 443–44; *New York Times,* December 27, 1941; Moran, *op. cit.,* pp. 15–16.

36. *New York Times,* December 31, 1941; Raoul Aglion, *Roosevelt and de Gaulle* (New York, 1988), pp. 67–68; Churchill, *Grand Alliance,* p. 678.

37. Hopkins often told this story. To Sherwood, years later, Churchill asserted he had never received the President without at least a bath towel wrapped around him and that he "could not possibly have made" the statement attributed to him. "The President himself would have known that it was not strictly true." See Sherwood, *op. cit.,* pp. 442–43.

38. Sherwood, *op. cit.,* p. 449; Churchill, *Grand Alliance,* p. 683.

39. Churchill, *Grand Alliance,* pp. 685–86.

40. Aglion, *op. cit.,* p. 60.

41. Sherwood, *op. cit.,* p. 480; Charles de Gaulle, *The Complete War Memoirs of Charles de Gaulle* (New York, 1998), pp. 214–15.

42. Milton Viorst, *Hostile Allies: FDR and de Gaulle* (New York, 1965), p. 79.

43. Quoted by Aglion, *op. cit.,* p. 65.

44. *Ibid.,* p. 63; Hull, *op. cit.,* p. 1,130.

45. William L. Langer, *Our Vichy Gamble* (Hamden, Conn., 1965), pp. 217–18. This book is a defense of U.S. Vichy policy and was prepared with the encouragement and cooperation of the State Department. Sherwood, *op. cit.,* pp. 484–85; Churchill, *Grand Alliance,* p. 667.

46. Churchill, *Grand Alliance,* pp. 664–65.

47. Dwight D. Eisenhower, *Crusade in Europe* (New York, 1948), p. 22.

48. Forrest C. Pogue, *Marshall: Ordeal and Hope,* pp. 265–66. Stimson diary, December 25, 1941; Kenneth S. Davis, *Soldier of Democracy* (New York, 1945), p. 287.

49. Marshall's words are quoted from the official minutes by Sherwood, *op. cit.,* pp. 455, 457; Pogue, *Marshall: Ordeal and Hope,* p. 276.

50. Churchill, *Grand Alliance,* p. 676. Pogue, *Marshall: Ordeal and Hope,* pp. 276–78, 281.

51. Pogue, *Marshall: Ordeal and Hope,* p. 277, quoting "Notes taken at Jt. Conference of Chiefs of Staff on afternoon of 25 Dec 41," in War Plans Division files.

52. Moran, *op. cit.,* pp. 17–18. In his *Grand Alliance,* p. 691, Churchill says he flew to Florida on January 6, 1942, and that "the night before I started . . . I strained my heart slightly" in the way I've described. But Churchill's World War II memoirs are in general poorly organized and sloppily written; he dictated them under, for the most part, holiday conditions, paying slight heed to chronology and making no effort actually to incorporate in a flow of narrative the substance of quoted documents. Moran's diary entry for December 27, 1941, tells of Churchill's worrisome experience "last night," and his entry for January 5, 1942, lists Florida as his and the Prime Minister's location that day.

53. Churchill, *Grand Alliance,* p. 677; Sherwood, *op. cit.,* p. 457.

54. Sherwood, *op. cit.,* p. 459, from official conference document.

55. Churchill, *Grand Alliance,* p. 673.
56. The notes are quoted by Sherwood, *op. cit.,* p. 470.
57. Moran, *op. cit.,* p. 13.
58. Sherwood, *op. cit.,* p. 472, quoting Hopkins's Arcadia notes.
59. Harriman and Abel, *op. cit.,* pp. 120–21; *PPA 1942,* pp. 23, 24; Sherwood, *op. cit.,* pp. 473–74.
60. *PPA 1942,* p. 37.
61. The lengthy circumstantial account of the January 13, 1942, White House interview derives from Donald M. Nelson, *Arsenal of Democracy* (New York, 1946), pp. 22–23; and Davis, *Experience of War,* pp. 170–72.
62. The following biographical portrait of Nelson derives chiefly from the opening portions of his *op. cit.*
63. Sherwood, *op. cit.,* pp. 475–77; Jesse Jones, *Fifty Billion Dollars* (New York, 1951), pp. 272–73.
64. Churchill, *Grand Alliance,* pp. 710–11.

8. A Winter of Disasters: A Spring of Dawning Hope

1. Churchill, *Hinge of Fate* (Boston, 1950), p. 49.
2. *Ibid.,* pp. 115–16; Kimball, ed., *op. cit.,* pp. 362–63. In a February 18, 1942, message to Churchill (see Kimball, ed., *op. cit.,* p. 363), Roosevelt said: "When I speak on the radio next Monday evening [he was to make a fireside chat on the progress of the war on February 23] I shall say a word or two about those people who treat the episode in the Channel as a defeat. I am more and more convinced that the location of all the German ships in Germany makes our North Atlantic naval problem more simple." In a February 22 message to Churchill (see Kimball, ed., *op. cit.,* p. 369), Roosevelt said: "In Monday night's speech I am leaving out proposed reference to German ships running the Channel because over here the first bad comments have died down. All agree it is best not to stir up the controversy again. I hope you concur."
3. Churchill, *Hinge of Fate,* p. 144.
4. The full verse from which the quoted words are taken runs as follows:

> We're the battling bastards of Bataan:
> No momma, no poppa, no Uncle Sam.
> No aunts, no uncles, no nephews, no nieces,
> No rifles, no guns or artillery pieces,
> And nobody gives a damn.

The verse is printed in Jonathan M. Wainwright (Robert Considine, ed.), *General Wainwright's Story* (Westport, Conn., 1946), p. 54.
5. Wainwright, *op. cit.,* pp. 118, 122–23.
6. Quoted by John Toland, *But Not in Shame: The Six Months after Pearl Harbor* (New York, 1961), p. 301.
7. Louis L. Snyder, *The War: A Concise History, 1939–1945* (New York, 1960), p. 223.
8. Mary H. Williams, compiler, *Chronology, 1941–1945,* a special study issued by the Office of Military History, Department of the Army (Washington, D.C., 1960), p. 21.
9. Barbara Tuchman, *Stilwell and the American Experience in China* (New York, 1971), pp. 337–85 of Bantam paperback edition (1972); Eric Larrabee, *Commander in*

Chief: Franklin D. Roosevelt, His Lieutenants and Their War (New York, 1987), pp. 523–38.

10. Samuel Eliot Morison, *The Battle of the Atlantic,* p. 130.

11. Churchill, *Hinge of Fate,* devotes a chapter, pp. 108–31, to the merchant-shipping slaughter, giving the official statistics concerning it.

12. For much of my description of these three women I am indebted to Doris Kearns Goodwin, *op. cit.,* and Geoffrey C. Ward, editor and annotator of *Closest Companion* (Boston, 1995), the latter a treasure trove of intimate information about FDR and his entourage contained in a diary kept by Ms. Suckley, letters she wrote to FDR, letters he wrote to her.

13. Ward, ed., *Closest Companion,* p. xiii.

14. *Ibid.,* pp. xix–xx.

15. *Ibid.,* p. 148.

16. Quoted by (among many others) Francis Biddle, *In Brief Authority* (New York, 1962), p. 213. At the time that this "worst violation . . . in history" was going on, however, the response to it by Roger Baldwin and the ACLU he had founded and at that time headed was, as Dwight MacDonald charged, "feeble and confused." Baldwin later confessed that he was "ashamed of it now," saying it was due to bad advice he had accepted from those upon whom he depended for policy guidance. See Peter Irons, *Justice at War* (New York, 1983), p. 360. A chief one of these advisers, I have learned to my consternation and dismay, was Alexander Meiklejohn, my great teacher and friend, to whom one of the volumes of this FDR history is dedicated and who was certainly one of the greatest of the civil libertarians of American history. (His little book, *Free Speech,* in which he rejects the "natural right" argument for such speech and describes it instead as "a necessity of self-government," is classic; his personal expression of unpopular ideas and his unequivocating defense of such expression by others were in good part responsible for his dismissal [after twelve years] from the presidency of Amherst College and for the wrecking [after four years or so] of the Experimental College he had started and headed at the University of Wisconsin—career blows that deeply wounded him personally.) Yet in mid-March 1942, Meiklejohn, who was then heading an institute affiliated with the University of California at Berkeley, wrote Baldwin in defense of the evacuation, saying: "The Japanese citizens, as a group, are dangerous both to themselves and to their fellow citizens. And that being true, discriminatory action is justified." In the late summer of 1942, he went to Washington as a Baldwin emissary in an effort to persuade the War Department to permit the evacuees to leave the assembly centers in the coastal states and find jobs inland. He dined and spent a long cordial evening with Assistant Secretary of War John J. McCloy, whose personal charm is almost universally attested to and who had been one of Meiklejohn's "favorite Amherst boys [*cum laude,* 1916] whom I used to lick at tennis," as Meiklejohn explained to an ACLU official. He reported that McCloy had listened sympathetically to the ACLU recommendation and indicated an open mind on the subject. See Kai Bird, *The Chairman: The Making of the American Establishment* (New York, 1992), p. 165.

17. Stilwell made the remark on December 19, 1941, in Los Angeles, according to Richard N. Current, *Secretary Stimson: A Study in Statecraft* (New Brunswick, N.J., 1954), p. 193. On February 8, 1942, in Washington, Stimson questioned Stilwell about the "Jap situation on the coast" and was fully briefed about it in ways that might well have caused Stimson to caution De Witt and Fourth Army G-2 against the spread of wild ru-

mors arousing false fears in the California public. According to Stilwell's diary, Stimson himself remarked "that the Fourth Army was always exaggerating things." But Stimson was undeterred from his pursuit (following Gullion's lead) of the Japanese evacuation order.

18. Irons, *op. cit.,* pp. 6–7; Lash, *Eleanor and Franklin,* p. 648.

19. Irons, *op. cit.,* pp. 29–30, 37.

20. *Ibid.,* pp. 38–39.

21. Quoted by Irons, *Ibid.,* pp. 58–59.

22. Steel, *op. cit.,* p. 394; Irons, *op. cit.,* pp. 60–61; Biddle, *op. cit.,* pp. 217–18.

23. Steel, *op. cit.,* p. 394; Irons, *op. cit.,* p. 61.

24. Irons, *op. cit.,* pp. 53, 57–58.

25. *Ibid.,* pp. 61–62; Harriman and Abel, *op. cit.,* p. 91.

26. *Ibid.,* p. 62.

27. *Ibid.,* p. 68.

28. Biddle, *op. cit.,* p. 213, notes that Bendetsen, in his *Who's Who* entry for the 1948–1949 edition, credited himself with having "conceived the method, formulated the details, and directed the evacuation of 125,000 persons of Japanese ancestry from military areas." In the next *Who's Who* edition, issued after the evacuation had become widely recognized as a gross injustice, a disgrace to the American democracy, Bendetsen made no reference to it in his entry.

29. In the mid- and late 1940s, when Milton Eisenhower was president of what was then Kansas State College of Agriculture and Applied Science (it is now Kansas State University, in some part due to his presidential efforts), he and I were close associates and friends. My description of his WRA experience derives from remembered conversations with him as well as from Irons, *op. cit.,* pp. 70–72, and Kai Bird, *op. cit.,* pp. 160–63.

30. Bird, *op. cit.,* p. 163.

31. Irons, *op. cit.,* pp. 332, 336.

32. Louis Morton, *Strategy and Command: The First Two Years* (of the war in the Pacific), a volume of the Department of the Army's official history of the U.S. Army in World War II (Washington, D.C., 1962), p. 189.

33. The bill granting Philippine independence in 1946 was passed over Hoover's veto during the interregnum of 1933. The Filipinos, though they had agitated for independence, some of them initially fighting for it, ever since the American seizure of the islands, were by 1933 fearful of an expanding Japan and for this reason refused to accept the proffered sovereign status (effective in 1946) until the United States in 1934 took steps to guarantee the Philippines against foreign aggression during the interim of 1934–1946. The islands were designated a commonwealth during this interim period. In other words, the Filipinos themselves had demanded the U.S. military presence that Quezon now claimed was the incitement of the Japanese invasion.

34. Morton, *op. cit.,* p. 190. Stimson and Bundy, *op. cit.,* p. 398. Larrabee, in *op. cit.,* p. 315, writes of the "incredible but thoroughly documented" discovery, published in 1979 by Rutgers doctoral candidate Carol M. Petrillo, "that Quezon, on January 3, 1942, one month into the war, had given MacArthur personally a half-million dollars out of the Philippine treasury. . . . MacArthur was at that time receiving an $18,000 salary and $15,000 in allowances from the Philippine Commonwealth in addition to his suite in the Manila Hotel and his pension as a U.S. major general. The transfer was arranged by the Chase Bank with the assurance that the President of the United States and the

secretary of war had been informed. The whole affair was conducted with the utmost discretion. . . . Army regulations then as now state that 'every member of the Military Establishment, when subject to military law, is bound to refrain from [acceptance] of a substantial loan or gift or any emolument from a person or firm with whom it is the officer's duty as an agent of the government to carry on negotiations.' What can have possessed them all, President and secretary of war included? The entire transaction was appallingly improper; if it had come to light, the impact upon all concerned must have been enormous. The unanswered questions fall all over themselves in the asking: Did MacArthur actually believe that there was no impropriety? Would he have answered, if asked, that he had acted as a Philippine and not an American officer? Why did Roosevelt and Stimson allow it? Did they feel that they had an angry and unruly general on their hands who needed pacifying? How much effect was there on MacArthur's subsequent favoring of Quezon's departure to Australia? What was the role of Manuel Roxas, who countersigned the order as Philippine treasurer and later received much needed support from MacArthur in his campaign to become Quezon's successor?" The late Eric Larrabee seems not to have known of Quezon's "neutralization" proposal and MacArthur's support of it when he wrote his book, for he makes no mention of these. Had he done so, he would surely have asked: Was there a connection between MacArthur's acceptance of Quezon's money gift and his support of Quezon's proposal just one month later?

35. Quoted by Pogue, *Ordeal and Hope,* p. 247.
36. *Ibid.,* pp. 247–48; Stimson and Bundy, *op. cit.,* pp. 400–03, printing in full Roosevelt's message to MacArthur; Morton, *op. cit.,* p. 190.
37. Pogue, *Ordeal and Hope,* pp. 247–48, quoting from author interview of Marshall.
38. *PPA 1942,* pp. 105–16.
39. *Ibid.,* p. 116, quoting editorial note; *New York Times,* February 2, 1942; *PL 1928–1945,* pp. 1,298–99.
40. Goodwin, *op. cit.,* p. 196, quoting Walter Reuther, "A Program for the Utilization of the Auto Industry for Mass Production of Defense Plants," submitted to the President with cover letter by CIO head Philip Murray, December 20, 1940. The incredibly diligent and accurate reporter I. F. Stone, whose record of "scoops" on events of public importance has never been matched, broke the story of the plan in *The Nation* on December 21, 1940, which means he must have obtained a copy of the Reuther memorandum several days before the President did.
41. Nelson Lichtenstein, *The Most Dangerous Man in Detroit: Walter Reuther and the Fate of American Labor* (New York, 1995), p. 162; Catton, *op. cit,* pp. 92–93.
42. Lichtenstein, *op. cit.,* pp. 165–66.
43. *Ibid.,* p. 166.
44. *Ibid.,* p. 167; Powers, *op. cit.,* p. 238, quotes the FBI's version of the Victor Reuther letter, with "for a Soviet America" added to the last sentence.
45. Goodwin, *op. cit.,* p. 197; I. F. Stone, *Business as Usual: The First Year of Defense* (New York, 1941), p. 235.
46. Richard Lawrence Miller, *op. cit.,* pp. 369–70; Catton, *op. cit.,* p. 116; Nelson, *op. cit.,* p. 334.
47. Nelson, *op. cit.,* pp. 333–35.
48. *PPA 1942,* pp. 54–56; W. H. Lawrence, "Too Much, Too Soon," *New York Times Magazine,* January 25, 1942.
49. *Ibid.,* p. 19.

50. Stimson and Bundy, *op. cit.,* pp. 492, 494.

51. Arnold, "How Monopolies Have Hobbled Defense," *Reader's Digest,* July 1941.

52. Gressley, *op. cit.,* p. 51.

53. Gressley writes in his *op. cit.,* p. 49, about the bitterness that Arnold continued to feel over "being forsaken by the president," going on to quote an Arnold contribution to the *Harvard Business Review* for January 1948, "Must 1929 Repeat Itself?": "F.D.R. recognizing that he could have only one war at a time was content to declare a truce in the fight against monopoly. He was to have his foreign war; monopoly was to give him patriotic support—on its own terms. And so more than 90 percent of all war contracts went to a handful of giant empires, many of them formerly linked by strong ties with the corporations of the Reich. The big fellows got the contracts, the little fellows were dependent upon subcontracts with the big boys."

54. William Hassett, *Off the Record with F.D.R., 1942–1945* (New Brunswick, N.J., 1958), p. 26, tells of a "delightful hour with the President" during breakfast at Hyde Park on March 28, 1942: "I nominated Sir Basil Zaharoff as my candidate for the most evil man within living memory. The President agreed that Sir Basil's operations were forerunners of Standard Oil's dealings with the Nazis and attempted dealings in occupied France as well as plans for postwar dealing with Japan—all disclosed by Thurman Arnold in Washington this week. I wonder if the President is the man who will face the scoundrels at the peace conference . . . and break the backs of these international usurers and others who have been doing this thing for so long. Will he make the Four Freedoms a fact in the life of man?"

55. Quoted by John Morton Blum, *V Was for Victory* (New York, 1976), p. 133.

56. I. F. Stone, *The War Years, 1939–1945* (Boston, 1988), an anthology of Stone's contributions to *The Nation,* writes on p. 118: "One of the sources of this new policy [the suspension of the anti-trust laws in April 1942] is a General Walter N. Pyron in Under Secretary of War Patterson's office. Pyron is liaison man between the War Department and the oil industry. He sits in on meetings of the Petroleum War Industrial Council, a private, not a government, body. Suspension of the antitrust laws for the duration was one of the main objectives of the council's meeting on March 3 and 4 [1942], and General Pyron carried the council's wishes to Patterson. The General was until recently vice-president of the Mellon Gulf Oil Company."

57. Quoted by Josephson, *op. cit.,* pp. 574–75.

58. *Ibid.,* p. 576.

59. *Ibid.,* pp. 583–84, 586. In his diary entry for April 18, 1942, William D. Hassett writes (Hassett, *op. cit.,* p. 38): "When the President came down to his study, he signed the Manpower Order and sent a soothing telegram to Sidney Hillman explaining why McNutt gets the chairmanship and signifying the Boss's purpose to make Sidney a special assistant on labor matters. Hillman is in Doctor's Hospital and reports say it's heart trouble. The brush-off will hardly help him."

60. *PPA 1942,* p. 154.

61. *Ibid.,* pp. 189–90.

62. Expressive of the popular reaction was a *New Yorker* cartoon by Garret Price depicting a seated man with bandaged head, one arm in a sling, and a heavily bandaged foot resting on a footstool, and a woman, obviously his wife, standing behind his chair, conversing with a visitor. Says she: "The most marvelous thing—the tires came through without a scratch."

63. *PPA 1942,* pp. 312–15, quoting the bill.

64. *Ibid.*, p. 317.

65. *Ibid.*, pp. 320–21.

66. *Ibid.*, pp. 15, 16–17.

67. *Ibid.*, pp. 68, 76.

68. *Ibid.*, p. 191.

69. *Ibid.*, pp. 214–16.

70. Letter to Rosenman from General H. H. Arnold, dated April 25, 1949, reprinted in *PPA 1942*, pp. 214–15.

71. Among the most authoritative of the many accounts of the Doolittle Raid and its historic effects is that of Ronald H. Spector in his *Eagle Against the Sun* (New York, 1985), pp. 154–55. Writes Sherwood in *op. cit.*, p. 542: "The men who risked and sacrificed their lives on this raid helped accomplish as much as the winning of a great battle would have done. . . . It was a classic demonstration of the inestimable morale element in war which can turn fear of defeat into assurance of victory."

72. *PPA 1942*, pp. 216–24.

73. *Ibid.*, pp. 231–33.

74. *PPA 1942*, p. 228.

75. Churchill, *Hinge of Fate*, p. 209.

76. *Ibid.*, p. 210; Kimball, ed., *op. cit.*, p. 376.

77. Harriman and Abel, *op. cit.*, p. 130; Kimball, ed., *op. cit.*, pp. 374–76; Churchill, *Hinge of Fate*, p. 209.

78. Kimball, ed., *op. cit.*, pp. 401–04; Churchill, *Hinge of Fate*, pp. 212–14. Churchill dates this March 11, 1942, which was the time of its arrival in London.

79. Churchill, *Hinge of Fate*, p. 214.

80. *Ibid.*, p. 215.

81. *Ibid.*, pp. 215–16.

82. *Ibid.*, p. 217.

83. Kimball, ed., *op. cit.*, pp. 446–47.

84. Sherwood, *op. cit.*, pp. 530–31; Kimball, ed., *op. cit.*, pp. 447, 449.

85. Kimball, ed., *op. cit.*, p. 449.

86. Churchill, *Hinge of Fate*, pp. 226, 229–30.

87. Nimitz had become personally known to Roosevelt through his work as chief of the navy's bureau of navigation (later renamed the bureau of personnel), to which he was appointed in 1939 and in which a major concern of his was the assignment and promotion of top naval officers. This was an operation in which navy man Roosevelt was greatly interested and in which he as commander in chief played an actively decisive part. "Between the two men there developed a curious bond," writes E. B. Potter, *Nimitz* (New York, 1976), p. 3, though quoted comments of the admiral indicate that he did not share Roosevelt's political views insofar as these were liberal and, in Eric Larrabee's words, "thought Roosevelt not quite natural, more than a little the actor. . . ." See Eric Larrabee, *Commander in Chief* (New York, 1987), pp. 354–55; Kenneth S. Davis, *Experience of War* (New York, 1965), p. 192.

88. The danger inherent in the command division between MacArthur (army) and Nimitz (navy) was demonstrated late in the Coral Sea battle when three B-26's of the U.S. Army Air Force flying from Australia attacked by mistake the USS *Saratoga*, a destroyer in Task Force 44 (key unit of "MacArthur's Navy"). The *Saratoga* narrowly escaped the B-26 bombs, and the incident was reported to MacArthur's headquarters with furious indignation by the destroyer's crew and by the task force's commander,

British Rear Admiral J. G. Crace. The truth of the report was proved when the photographs automatically taken of their target by the attacking planes were developed at Townsend, Australia, where the B-26's were based. But MacArthur's headquarters not only refused to admit that the incident had occurred, they also refused to accept the plans to improve army pilots' recognition of naval vessels when these were later submitted by the American commander of "MacArthur's Navy," Vice Admiral Herbert F. Leary. Instead, all further discussion of the matter was prohibited. See Samuel Eliot Morison, *Coral Sea, Midway and Submarine Actions, May 1942–August 1942,* a volume of Morison's *History of United States Naval Operations in World War II* (Boston, 1967), pp. 38–39.

89. Used as sources for the description of the Midway battle were Morison, *op. cit.;* E. B. Potter and Chester W. Nimitz, eds., *The Great Sea War* (New York, 1960); Walter Karig and Eric Purden, *Battle Report: Pacific War, Middle Phase* (New York, 1947); Edward P. Stafford, *The Big E: The Story of the USS* Enterprise (New York, 1962); Thaddeus V. Tuleja, *Climax at Midway* (New York, 1960); Mitsui Fuchida and Masatake Okumiya, *Midway: The Battle That Doomed Japan* (U.S. Naval Institute, 1955); and Ronald Spector, *op. cit.*

90. Burns, *op. cit.,* p. 226.

9. An Alliance-Threatening Quarrel: Spring and Summer 1942

1. Kimball, ed. *op. cit.,* p. 437.
2. *Ibid.,* pp. 398–99, 411; Sherwood, *op. cit.,* pp. 509–10.
3. Dwight D. Eisenhower, *Crusade in Europe* (New York, 1948), p. 70; Pogue, *Ordeal and Hope,* pp. 305–6; Arthur Bryant, *The Turn of the Tide: A History of the War Years Based on the Diaries of Field-Marshal Lord Allenbrooke* (New York, 1957), p. 285.
4. Pogue, *Ordeal and Hope,* p. 306.
5. Stimson and Bundy, *op. cit.,* pp. 416–17.
6. Kimball, ed., *op. cit.,* pp. 437, 441.
7. Sherwood, *op. cit.,* p. 523.
8. Bryant, *op. cit.,* pp. 6–7.
9. *Ibid.,* pp. 285–90.
10. *Ibid.,* p. 286.
11. Sherwood, *op. cit.,* pp. 535–36.
12. *Ibid.,* pp. 536–38.
13. Moran, *op. cit.,* pp. 38–39; Pogue, *Ordeal and Hope,* pp. 319–20, quoting Pogue's interview with Ismay, October 18, 1960.
14. Kimball, ed., *op. cit.,* p. 437; Sherwood, *op. cit.,* pp. 527–28.
15. Churchill, *Hinge of Fate,* pp. 327–28.
16. Kimball, ed., *op. cit.,* p. 505; Churchill, *Hinge of Fate,* pp. 335–36.
17. Churchill, *Hinge of Fate,* pp. 332–33.
18. *Ibid.,* pp. 334–35.
19. *Ibid.,* p. 338.
20. Kimball, ed, *op. cit.,* p. 494.
21. Sherwood, *op. cit.,* p. 561; West, *Upstairs at the White House,* pp. 46–47.
22. Sherwood, *op. cit.,* pp. 557–58.
23. *Ibid.,* pp. 562–63.
24. *Ibid.,* pp. 563–64; 568.

25. Hassett, *op. cit.,* p. 54.

26. Sherwood, *op. cit.,* pp. 571, 574–75 (consists of the interpreter Cross's report of the conversation).

27. Figures on plane deliveries to Siberia are from Otis Hays, Jr., *The Alaska-Siberia Connection* (College Station, TX, 1966).

28. Sherwood, *op. cit.,* p. 577.

29. Kimball, ed., *op. cit.,* pp. 503–04.

30. Churchill, *Hinge of Fate,* pp. 341–42.

31. According to Churchill's *Hinge of Fate,* p. 384, Eisenhower along with Clark was introduced to the Prime Minister by Harry Hopkins on June 21, 1942, during Churchill's second wartime visit to Washington; but Hopkins himself reports (Sherwood, *op. cit.,* p. 582) that Churchill phoned him on May 30 from Chequers, where he was "entertaining Winant, Harriman, Arnold, Somervell, and Eisenhower for the weekend." I accept Hopkins's account, made at the time, as accurate.

32. Kimball, ed., *op. cit.,* pp. 509–10; Pogue, *Ordeal and Hope,* p. 327.

33. Sherwood, *op. cit.,* pp. 582–83, where is printed in full a summary by Mountbatten of his conversation with the President.

34. Kimball, ed., *op. cit.,* p. 510; Sherwood, *op. cit.,* p. 581; Bryant, *op. cit.,* p. 320.

35. Bryant, *op. cit.,* p. 322.

36. Kimball, ed., *op. cit.,* p. 511.

37. Churchill, *Hinge of Fate,* pp. 376–77.

38. Kimball, ed., *op. cit.,* p. 249; Compton, *op. cit.,* pp. 58–59; James Phinney Baxter III, *Scientists Against Time* (Boston, 1946), p. 428; Rhodes, *op. cit.,* p. 388.

39. Enrico Fermi, *Collected Papers, Vol. II: United States 1939–45* (Chicago, 1965).

40. Compton, *op. cit.,* p. 127. Compton, on this page and the next of his book, tells of a July weekend in 1942 when Oppenheimer rushed all the way from Berkeley to a vacation cottage in northern Michigan where Compton and his wife were vacationing for a few days, to discuss with Compton a danger the Berkeley team had discovered, namely, that the heat of an atomic bomb explosion might be great enough to induce nuclear fusion (the union of hydrogen nucleii to form helium nucleii) and thereby somehow explode the oceans of the world. And if hydrogen, why not also the nitrogen in the atmosphere, which "is also unstable, though in less degree"? What Oppenheimer's group had discovered was the principle of the atomic bomb—and the lay reader finds an eerie nightmarish quality in this portrait of two men discussing whether or not to continue their work on the atom bomb if it might, it just might, result in the blowing up of the world! "We agreed there would be only one answer," writes Compton. "Oppenheimer's team must go ahead with their calculations. Unless they came up with a firm and reliable conclusion that our atomic bomb would not explode the air or the sea, these bombs must never be made." As if there were need for "agreement" on such a matter by any two mortal men! Of course, the further studies proved these July-night fears to have been unfounded, while also pointing the way toward hydrogen bomb making—an enterprise that Teller zealously pursued to a "successful" conclusion and which Oppenheimer vehemently opposed, at great cost to himself, in postwar years.

41. Rhodes, *op. cit.,* p. 412.

42. Churchill, *Hinge of Fate,* pp. 380–81.

43. Eyewitness account by Glenn T. Seaborg, *History of Met Lab Section C-1, April 1942 to April 1943* (Lawrence Berkeley Laboratory, 1977), pp. 86 ff. Quoted by Rhodes, *op. cit.,* p. 412.

44. Rhodes, *op. cit.,* pp. 413, 422.

45. Compton, *op. cit.,* p. 109.

46. Rhodes, *op. cit.,* pp. 422–23; Compton, *op. cit.,* pp. 42, 109–10. As Rhodes points out, Compton in his book confuses the September rebellion with the June meeting of the laboratory scientists as described on p. 511.

47. Spencer R. Weart and Gertrud Weiss Szilard, eds., *Leo Szilard: His Version of the Facts* (Cambridge, Mass., 1978), pp. 153 ff., and Szilard memo of September 19, 1942, both cited by Rhodes, *op. cit.,* pp. 423–24.

48. Rhodes, *op. cit.,* p. 424; Bush, *op. cit.,* pp. 61–62.

49. Leslie R. Groves, *Now It Can Be Told: The Story of the Manhattan Project* (New York, 1962), pp. 22–26; Rhodes, *op. cit.,* pp. 427–28; Compton, *op. cit.,* p. 156.

50. Compton, *op. cit.,* p. 153. "These bombs could not be produced in mass," Compton explains. "Each was a unique device that was really a complex instrument. It was research scientists rather than industrial men who were most familiar with the construction and use of such devices." It might be added that no industrial corporation would have been eager, if willing at all, to take over this portion of the project as corporations did of the isotope-separation and plutonium-production portions: the likelihood of future monetary profit from it was small.

51. Rhodes, *op. cit.,* p. 498; Compton, *op. cit.,* pp. 167, 168.

52. Churchill, *Hinge of Fate,* pp. 381–82.

53. Stimson and Bundy, *op. cit.,* pp. 420–23, print the entire letter. Revelatory of Roosevelt's reaction to the letter is the fact that he promptly showed it to Churchill—a fact disconcerting to the letter's author. "I had not expected that because I said some very plain things in it about the British," commented Stimson in his diary, quoted in *op. cit.,* p. 424.

54. Churchill, *Hinge of Fate,* pp. 418–19.

55. Bryant, *op. cit.,* p. 329; Churchill, *Hinge of Fate,* p. 383.

56. Churchill, *Hinge of Fate,* p. 383; Pogue, *Ordeal and Hope,* p. 333; Bryant, *op. cit.,* p. 329. Writes Pogue: "In explaining his action to his advisers, Marshall found it advisable to avoid basing his assistance on grounds of generosity. Instead, he accepted the explanation proposed by an aide that the tanks and guns were given to hold the British to their promise to mount Roundup."

57. Kenneth S. Davis, *Experience of War,* p. 247.

58. Stimson and Bundy, *op. cit.,* p. 424.

59. Churchill, *Hinge of Fate,* pp. 383–84. (Churchill writes of the summary note on the June 21, 1942, conference that "General Ismay has preserved a note of the military conclusions" but, as I've said, the stylistic evidence is that Churchill was the note's author); Stimson and Bundy, *op. cit.,* p. 424.

60. Churchill, *Hinge of Fate,* pp. 386–87; Sherwood, *op. cit.,* pp. 592–93; Bryant, *op. cit.,* pp. 331–33; Moran, *op. cit.,* pp. 42–43.

61. Churchill, *Hinge of Fate,* pp. 390, 401–08 (quoting at length the Churchill defense).

62. Kimball, ed., *op. cit.,* p. 517; Sherwood, *op. cit.,* p. 602; Churchill, *Hinge of Fate,* p. 408.

63. The Stafford Cripps letter is printed in full on pp. 395–96 of Churchill, *Hinge of Fate.* Sherwood, *op. cit.,* p. 602, stresses Roosevelt's concern for Churchill's "emotional endurance . . . after six months of mortification" as a "highly important consideration in the negotiations [on military strategy] of far-reaching consequences which followed."

64. Kimball, ed., *op. cit.,* p. 528.

65. Maurice Matloff and Edwin M. Snell, *Strategic Planning for Coalition Warfare,*

1941–1942 (Washington, D.C., 1953), a volume of the War Department's *History of the U.S. Army in World War II,* pp. 261–63.

66. Churchill, *Hinge of Fate,* p. 420.

67. Sherwood, *op. cit.,* pp. 595–98, gives full text of FDR's June 30, 1942, telegram to Marshall and extended excerpts of Marshall's reply to it. Sherwood also (p. 598) quotes Marshall's July 2, 1942, message to Roosevelt.

68. Kimball, ed., pp. 518–19; Sherwood, *op. cit.,* p. 599.

69. Sherwood, *op. cit.,* pp. 598–99.

70. Matloff and Snell, *op. cit.,* pp. 266–67; Stimson and Bundy, pp. 424–25; George A. Harrison, *Cross-Channel Attack* (Washington, D.C., 1951), a volume in the War Department's *History of the U.S. Army in World War II,* p. 27; Davis, *Experience of War,* p. 256.

71. Matloff and Snell, *op. cit.,* pp. 267–69; Pogue, *Ordeal and Hope,* pp. 340–41.

72. The staff chiefs' memorandum to the President is extensively quoted on pp. 268–69 of Matloff and Snell, *op. cit.*

73. *Ibid.,* p. 270.

74. *Ibid.,* pp. 270–71.

75. Walter D. Hassett, *op. cit.,* pp. 87–88, 91, 93.

76. Joseph Barnes, *Willkie* (New York, 1952), pp. 289, 293.

77. Henry H. Adams, *Harry Hopkins* (New York, 1977), p. 270, prints in full the letter to hospitalized Hopkins about Louise Macy; Goodwin, *op. cit.,* pp. 349–50; Sherwood, *op. cit.,* p. 593.

78. Hassett, *op. cit.,* pp. 91, 92; *New York Times,* July 5, 1942.

79. Harriman and Abel, *op. cit.,* pp. 27–28; Matloff and Snell, *op. cit.,* p. 272; Ernest J. King and Walter Muir Whitehill, *Fleet Admiral King* (New York, 1952), cover the whole of this controversy on pp. 390–408.

80. Matloff and Snell, *op. cit.,* pp. 272–73; Sherwood, *op. cit.,* p. 605; Stimson and Bundy, *op. cit.,* p. 425.

81. Matloff and Snell, *op. cit.,* pp. 273–78; Sherwood, *op. cit.,* pp. 603–05, prints the whole of Roosevelt's memo or instructions.

82. Sherwood, *op. cit.,* pp. 607–08; Adams, *op. cit.,* p. 285; Pogue, *Ordeal and Hope,* pp. 343–44; Harry S. Butcher, *My Three Years with Eisenhower* (New York, 1945), pp. 24–25.

83. Matloff and Snell, *op. cit.,* pp. 279–80; Bryant, *op. cit.,* p. 347; Davis, *Experience of War,* p. 260; Sherwood, *op. cit.,* p. 610.

84. Marloff and Snell, *op. cit.,* p. 281; Bryant, *op. cit.,* pp. 345, 347.

85. Sherwood, *op. cit.,* pp. 611–12; Matloff and Snell, *op. cit.,* p. 282; Kimball, ed., *op. cit.,* pp. 541, 543–44.

86. Hassett, *op. cit.,* pp. 95–96.

87. Matloff and Snell, *op. cit.,* pp. 282–83.

88. *Ibid.,* p. 283.

89. *Ibid.,* p. 295.

90. Stimson diary, August 6, 1942; Pogue, *Ordeal and Hope,* pp. 348–49.

10. The Difficult Lighting of Torch

1. Kimball, ed., *op. cit.,* p. 528.

2. *Ibid.,* pp. 528, 529–33. Insufficient attention has been paid by the U.S. government, the U.S. press, and historians to the role played by the merchant marine in World War II.

The press and radio that extolled the heroism of members of the armed forces had little to say about the heroism of merchant sailors, who made, and often died while making, the inadequately protected Murmansk run and the almost wholly unprotected tanker run through American coastal waters. These men were ineligible for the governmental pensions, medical services, and other benefits accorded those who served in the army or navy.

3. *Ibid.,* pp. 544–45.

4. *Ibid.,* p. 545.

5. Harriman and Abel, *op. cit.,* p. 146.

6. Kimball, ed., *op. cit.,* p. 551; Churchill, *Hinge of Fate,* pp. 453–54.

7. Harriman and Abel, *op. cit.,* pp. 146–47; Kimball, ed., *op. cit.,* p. 553; Churchill, *Hinge of Fate,* p. 473.

8. Lord Moran, *op. cit.,* p. 54.

9. Harriman and Abel, *op. cit.,* pp. 149–50; Charles de Gaulle, *op. cit.,* pp. 318–19.

10. Churchill, *Hinge of Fate,* pp. 460–62; Lord Moran, *op. cit.,* p. 58.

11. Harry C. Butcher, *My Three Years with Eisenhower* (New York, 1946), p. 43.

12. Churchill, *Hinge of Fate,* pp. 464–65; General Lord Ismay, *Memoirs of General Lord Ismay* (New York, 1960), pp. 263–64.

13. Harriman and Abel, *op. cit.,* p. 151.

14. Churchill, *Hinge of Fate,* pp. 477–83; Harriman and Abel, *op. cit.,* pp. 152–55.

15. Kimball, ed., *op. cit.,* pp. 560–62.

16. Churchill, *Hinge of Fate,* p. 486; Harriman and Abel, *op. cit.,* pp. 155–56.

17. Bryant, *op. cit.,* pp. 373–74; Harriman and Abel, *op. cit.,* pp. 157–59; Kimball, ed., *op. cit.,* p. 565.

18. Churchill, *Hinge of Fate,* p. 489; Harriman and Abel, *op. cit.,* p. 159; Lord Moran, *op. cit.,* pp. 63–64. This last work, by Churchill's personal physician, is uniquely valuable to the historian in its view of the Prime Minister from a closer distance (there was an intimate personal friendship between these two as well as the intimacy common to prolonged doctor-patient relationships) than existed with any other of Churchill's associates who published their views of him. The doctor was an acute psychologist as well as medical physiologist, and his published analyses of Churchill's temperament, mind, and overall personality are the most persuasive of any such I have read. Very different in tone and significance from that of Churchill is Moran's account of the Stalin-Churchill quarrel during this Moscow Conference, and Moran's account has been heavily leaned upon in my upcoming portrayal of this quarrel. Moran himself remarks the discrepancy between what he knows to have happened between the two heads of government and what Churchill's memoirs say happened. "As one reads [in Churchill's memoirs] of those now-distant days," writes Moran on p. 71 of his book, "they seem to have been smoothed out, and as it were edited; the terrifically alive pugnacious, impatient and impulsive Winston Churchill has been dressed up as a sagacious, tolerant elder statesman. . . . He himself once said he was not designed by nature for that particular role."

19. Bryant, *op. cit.,* pp. 376–78; Churchill, *Hinge of Fate,* pp. 492–93; Harriman and Abel, *op. cit.,* pp. 160–61; Lord Moran, *op. cit.,* pp. 64–66. There is discrepancy between Churchill and Brooke regarding the number of guests at the dinner. Churchill says about forty, Brooke nearly one hundred. If all the top officials, generals, and Politburo members were present, plus Churchill's sizable party, the Brooke figure is the more realistic of the two.

20. Lord Moran, *op. cit.,* pp. 66–69.
21. Harriman and Abel, *op. cit.,* p. 160.
22. Lord Moran, *op. cit.,* p. 69; Churchill, *Hinge of Fate,* pp. 495–99.
23. *Ibid.,* p. 499; Lord Moran, *op. cit.,* pp. 69–70.
24. Churchill, *Hinge of Fate,* pp. 500–502.
25. Kimball, ed., *op. cit.,* pp. 546–49.
26. *Ibid.,* pp. 549–50.
27. *Ibid.,* p. 550.
28. *Ibid.,* p. 556.
29. *Ibid.,* p. 558.
30. Nina Davis Howland, *Ambassador John Gilbert Winant: Friend of Embattled Britain, 1941–46* (University of Maryland doctoral diss., University Microfilm International reprint, 1984), p. 198.
31. Kimball, ed., *op. cit.,* p. 563.
32. *Ibid.,* p. 572.
33. Minutes of Chiefs of Staff Conference, December 27, 1941. Quoted by Maurice M. Matloff and Edwin M. Snell, *Strategic Planning for Coalition Warfare, 1941–1942* (Washington, D.C., 1953), p. 112.
34. *Ibid.,* p. 285.
35. *Ibid.,* p. 287.
36. H. A. De Weerd, *Great Soldiers of World War II* (New York, 1944), p. 270.
37. Matloff and Snell, *op. cit.,* p. 289.
38. Churchill, *Hinge of Fate,* pp. 526–28.
39. Matloff and Snell, *op. cit.,* p. 291.
40. Kimball, ed., *op. cit.,* pp. 577–79.
41. *Ibid.,* pp. 581–82.
42. *Ibid.,* pp. 583–84.
43. *Ibid.,* p. 586.
44. *Ibid.,* pp. 587, 589, 591–92.

11. The Home Front: Late Summer and Fall 1942

1. Hassett, *op. cit.,* pp. 105–06.
2. Said Marshall to his official biographer, Forrest C. Pogue, in an October 5, 1956, interview: "When I went to see Roosevelt and told him about Torch he held up his hands in an attitude of prayer and said, 'Please make it before Election Day.' However, when I found we had to have more time . . . he never said a word. . . . Steve Early . . . who was told only an hour before the attack, blew up because it came after the election." See Pogue, *Ordeal and Hope,* p. 402.
3. *PPA 1942,* p. 80; Reilly, *op. cit.,* p. 128.
4. Chandler and Wallace, eds., *op. cit.,* p. 282.
5. Sherwood, *op. cit.,* p. 631.
6. *PPA 1942,* pp. 347–48, 350–53.
7. Harriman and Abel, *op. cit.,* p. 166.
8. *Ibid.,* p. 166; Kimball, ed., *op. cit.,* p. 574.
9. Harriman and Abel, *op. cit.,* pp. 166, 169.
10. *Ibid.,* pp. 169–70.
11. *Ibid.,* p. 170.

12. Hassett, *op. cit.,* p. 122.

13. *PPA 1942,* pp. 368–77.

14. A. Merriman Smith, *Thank You, Mr. President* (New York, 1946), p. 51.

15. O'Neill, *op. cit.,* pp. 218–19; *PPA 1942,* p. 384.

16. Ward, ed., *Closest Companion,* p. 175. Roosevelt's jaundiced view of Ford's operation was revealed in his cabinet meeting of October 2, 1942. Wrote Henry Wallace in his diary entry for that day: ". . . [T]he President was in the very highest spirits. He told about his trip in some detail. He said Henry Ford still was not producing any bombers at Willow Run but he probably would in three or four weeks. He felt that Ford had not done an especially good job. He thought that on the whole the best job was being done on the Pacific Coast." See John Morton Blum, ed., *The Price of Vision: The Diary of Henry A. Wallace, 1942–1946* (Boston, 1973), p. 116.

17. Richard R. Lingeman, *Don't You Know There's a War On?: The American Home Front, 1941–1945* (New York, 1970), p. 109; *The Wartime Journals of Charles A. Lindbergh* (New York, 1970), p. 645. In the fall of 1943, Lindbergh left Ford to become technical consultant at the Connecticut plant of the United Aircraft Corporation, which produced Corsair fighters and fighter-bombers for the navy and its marine corps. In the spring of 1944, he went to the Pacific to study the performance in combat of the planes United Aircraft produced. Designated a "technical representative" of the corporation, he deemed "study" to mean actually flying the planes in combat. He did so, with the connivance of air corps officers, in defiance of military regulations and international law, and of the normal age limit for combat flying, he being a forty-two-year-old civilian (thirty was deemed old for a fighter pilot). Had he fallen into enemy hands, he could have been shot as a spy. On two of his fifty missions, flying a P-38 Lightning (manufactured by United Aircraft), he shot down Japanese Zeros. His single greatest contribution to the American Pacific war was his addition of some five hundred miles to the Lightning's flying range by setting the propeller's RPM lower and its air bite higher while cruising than his fellow combat pilots did—habits of fuel economy he had acquired when such economy was essential to his survival of long-distance flights in the *Spirit of St. Louis*. It had been assumed that doing as he did would damage the P-38 engine, but careful tests of the engines he flew proved this not so. The doing of it enabled, for instance, an attack of Palau island by planes based on Biak, off New Guinea, completely surprising the Japanese, who had been convinced that a flight of this distance was impossible for P-38's. "Lindbergh, in effect, gave us a new, much better airplane," said Colonel Charles H. MacDonald, who led the Palau attack. (See Davis, *The Hero,* pp. 422–23.)

18. Lingeman, *op. cit.,* pp. 107–10. William L. O'Neill, *A Democracy at War* (New York, 1993), pp. 219–20.

19. *PPA 1942,* pp. 385, 391.

20. Smith, *op. cit.,* p. 53; Ward, ed., *op. cit.,* p. 178.

21. *PPA 1942,* p. 387.

22. Ward, ed., *op. cit.,* p. 179; Smith, *op. cit.,* p. 54.

23. Blum, *V Was for Victory, op. cit.,* pp. 112–14; Lingeman, *op. cit.,* p. 131; Eliot Janeway, *The Struggle for Survival* (New York, 1951), p. 194.

24. Ward, ed., *op. cit.,* p. 180.

25. Smith, *op. cit.,* pp. 54–55; Ward, ed., *op. cit.,* pp. 181–82.

26. *PPA 1942,* p. 389; Ward, ed., *op. cit.,* p. 182.

27. Ward, ed., *op. cit.,* pp. 182–83; Blum, *V Was for Victory,* p. 111.

28. Ward, ed., *op. cit.,* p. 183.
29. *PPA 1942,* pp. 391, 395.
30. *Ibid.,* p. 393; Ward, ed., *op. cit.,* p. 183.
31. *New York Times,* October 4, 1942.
32. Robertson, *op. cit.,* p. 318.
33. *Ibid.,* p. 320; James F. Byrnes, *All in One Lifetime* (New York, 1958), p. 161; Bernard M. Baruch, *Baruch: The Public Years* (London, 1960), pp. 284–85, tells how an allegedly surprised Byrnes first learned that he was in line for appointment to the OES post. Harry Hopkins had come to Baruch's Carleton Hotel apartment to ask the great financier and presidential adviser whom he recommended for this (Baruch himself had earlier declined to be considered for it, citing as his reason his advanced age and uncertain health). "As always when an important and difficult job was to be done, I suggested James F. Byrnes," writes Baruch. Barely had he done so than who should enter the apartment but Byrnes himself. The justice had just "happened" to be passing by the Carleton and, on the spur of the moment, decided to call upon his great friend and benefactor. "I can still see him [as he entered the room and found Hopkins there], his head cocked birdlike on one side in a characteristic Byrnes attitude," writes Baruch. The justice listened carefully, thoughtfully, as Hopkins and Baruch explained the situation; he remained thoughtfully silent for a long moment, then said: "If the commander in chief asks me, I'll accept." Robertson, repeating this story in his *op. cit,* p. 319, pooh-poohs "the episode" as a " 'Children's Hour,' in FDR's phrase," though FDR's phrase referred to the ritual White House cocktail hour, as we know, and not the "political intrigue . . . in which Franklin Roosevelt always seemed to delight," as Robertson has it.
34. Byrnes, *op. cit.,* p. 161.
35. Bruce Catton, *The War Lords of Washington* (New York, 1948), p. 203.
36. Sherwood, *op. cit.,* p. 634.
37. Blum, *Roosevelt and Morgenthau,* p. 440.
38. *Ibid.,* pp. 437–38.
39. *Ibid.,* p. 438.
40. The speech is printed in full in Blum, ed., *Price of Vision,* pp. 635–40, as the first of three appendices. It is revealing of that visionary religious mysticism, literally nonsensical, that sadly flawed Wallace's genius mentality and, in my opinion, prevented his making what might otherwise have been a huge contribution to the general welfare of America, indeed of the world. It incapacitated him for top political leadership in a world and time that required for creative leadership a close accuracy of objective perception; a capacity for, a commitment to, logical thought grounded in moral feeling (he certainly had the capacity, he lacked the commitment); and a rigorous avoidance of that "wishful thinking" that is so often the very essence of religious faith. He asserts, for instance, in the second paragraph of this "Century of the Common Man" address that "the idea of freedom is derived from the Bible," that the Old Testament prophets "were the first to preach social justice," and that "[d]emocracy is the . . . political expression of Christianity"—his seeming implication being that democracy and Christianity are inseparable, though in reality, organized Christianity has been through much of Western history, and today remains among passionately religious fundamentalists an implacable foe of freedom of thought and speech and of the science born of these. He makes no mention of ancient Greek definitions of human freedom, political freedom, which certainly influenced writers of the New Testament. Religious exaltation of the

most deplorable kind dictated the conclusion of this speech: "The people's revolution is on the march, and the devil and all his angels cannot prevail against it. They cannot prevail for on the side of the people is the Lord. He giveth power to the weak; to them who have no might. He increaseth strength. . . . They that wait upon the Lord shall mount up with wings as eagles; they shall run and not be weary; they shall walk and not be faint. Strong in the strength of the Lord, we who fight the people's fight will never stop until that cause is won."

41. Wendell Willkie, *One World* (softbound, New York, 1943), p. 23; Barnes, *op. cit.,* pp. 299–300; Sherwood, *op. cit.,* p. 635.

42. Sherwood, *op. cit.,* p. 635.

43. Barbara Tuchman, *Stilwell and the American Experience in China 1911–45* (New York, 1971; softbound edition, 1972), p. 425 (of softbound edition).

44. Tuchman, *op. cit.,* pp. 428, 430–31; Willkie, *op. cit.,* pp. 54–59.

45. Tuchman, *op. cit.,* p. 431.

46. *Ibid.,* pp. 431–32.

47. *Ibid.,* p. 432. For Marshall's reaction, Tuchman cites unpublished notes of an interview with Marshall on July 6, 1949, by Charles Romanus and Riley Sunderland, authors of three volumes of the Department of the Army's multivolumed *History of the U.S. Army in World War II: Stilwell's Mission to China, Stilwell's Command Problems,* and *Time Runs Out in CBI.* The notes are, or were, in the Office of the Chief of Military History, Department of the Army, Washington, D.C.

48. *Ibid.,* pp. 426–27. Tuchman's source for the quote of Stilwell at the cocktail party is a letter to her from Joseph Barnes, who was a guest at this party and to whom the quoted remark may well have been directed.

49. *Wendell L. Willkie's Report to the People* (New York, 1942); *Vital Speeches* magazine (1942), IX, pp. 34–39.

50. *PPA 1942,* pp. 436–37. William Roger Louis, *Imperialism at Bay: The United States and the Decolonization of the British Empire, 1941–1945* (New York, 1978), p. 199. Professor Louis's work is a remarkably valuable combine of meticulous original scholarship and good writing.

51. Louis, *op. cit.,* pp. 200–01. The quoted imperialist interpreter of Churchill's meaning was Lord Lugard, who from 1923 to 1938 was the British representative on the Permanent Mandates Commission of the League of Nations and who might have denied that he was imperialistic in the literal common meaning of that term. In a 1922 book, *The Dual Mandate,* he defined this "mandate" as "the dual responsibility of controlling powers in the tropics viz as trustees of civilization for the adequate development of their resources and as trustees for the welfare of native races." He claimed that the dual purpose of British rule in Africa was a) to promote British prosperity; and b) to facilitate the progress of the "native races" to a "higher plane." The quoted "influential writer" to *The Times* was Margery Perham of Oxford, a leading academic authority on British colonialism who, though herself an anti-imperialist, was a frequent critic of American criticism of the British empire.

52. Lash, *Eleanor and Franklin,* pp. 656–57.

53. Butcher, *op. cit.,* p. 151; Lash, *Eleanor and Franklin,* pp. 659–61; Blum, *Roosevelt and Morgenthau,* p. 483, quoting Morgenthau diaries.

54. Kimball, ed., *op. cit.,* pp. 633, 636.

55. Lash, *Eleanor and Franklin,* p. 659.

56. *Ibid.,* pp. 661–62; Goodwin, *op. cit.,* p. 380.

57. Lash, *Eleanor and Franklin,* p. 664.

58. *Newsweek,* November 9, 1942; Goodwin, *op. cit.,* p. 383.

59. Kimball, ed., *op. cit.,* p. 655; Lash, *Eleanor and Franklin,* p. 668.

60. Circumstantial detail of Roosevelt's election day morning is from Hassett, *op. cit.,* pp. 132–34.

61. Hassett, *op. cit.,* p. 134.

62. *PPA 1942,* pp. 432–34.

63. Hassett, *op. cit.,* p. 135 (for quotation on Roosevelt's "high spirits").

64. My analysis of the political evolution of "an uneducated but skilled worker" derives much from John Morton Blum's excellent *V Was for Victory,* pp. 230–31, wherein he explores the political mind of "a typical Italian-American machinist of Hartford, Connecticut."

65. *PPA 1942,* p. 80; Burns, *Soldier of Freedom,* p. 281.

12. The Torch Flames but Lights the Way to What End?

1. Kimball, ed., *op. cit.,* p. 636; *Ibid.,* pp. 646–47, has Churchill reporting to Roosevelt, on October 31, 1942, "great satisfaction [at Alamein] with Shermans. Position of gun has enabled maximum concealment in Hull-Down positions with good observation by commander. Have definite information that enemy tanks including Mark IV special being destroyed at ranges up to 2,000 yards using good American M sixty-one ammunition. 105 MM S P guns have done well. . . . They have not yet been used in a very mobile role but consider they have possibilities against enemy guns which we hope to exploit soon."

2. Tedder made this claim in a conversation the present author had with him in London in the summer of 1944.

3. Kimball, ed., *op. cit.,* p. 660.

4. B. H. Lidell Hart, *History of the Second World War* (New York, 1970), p. 308.

5. Sherwood, *op. cit.,* p. 645.

6. Kimball, ed., *op. cit.,* pp. 656–57, 659; Sherwood, *op. cit.,* has facsimile of the original (October 14, 1942) message as revised by him following Churchill's criticism, pp. 646–47.

7. Kimball, ed., *op. cit.,* p. 599; Churchill, *Hinge of Fate,* pp. 604–05.

8. Churchill, *Hinge of Fate,* pp. 605–06.

9. Kimball, ed., *op. cit.,* pp. 661–62.

10. Butcher, *op. cit.,* p. 162.

11. Eisenhower gave me his personal assessment of Murphy, stressing his conviction that Murphy was "a liberal," during a lengthy conversation at his tent-camp forward headquarters in Normandy (code-named "Shellburst") in August 1944. The assessment was part of his defense of, or apology for, the Darlan Deal.

12. Robert D. Murphy, *Diplomat among Warriors* (New York, 1964), pp. 69–70; Harold Macmillan, *The Blast of War* (New York, 1968), p. 189. Macmillan would come to Algiers in January 1942 as Churchill's personal representative in Eisenhower's headquarters—as Murphy's British counterpart, in other words. His title was minister resident at Allied headquarters in North Africa.

13. Murphy, *op. cit.,* p. 70.

14. *Ibid.,* p. 90.

15. William L. Shirer, *The Collapse of the Third Republic* (New York, 1969), p. 200.

16. Murphy, *op. cit.,* pp. 116–17.

17. *Ibid.,* p. 117. Not known to the Americans when they made their arrangement with Giraud was the fact that upon reaching Vichy after his escape, he had pledged in writing
his loyalty to Pétain. He had written to the marshal: "Following our recent talks, and
to remove all doubt on my attitude, I want to express my sentiments of perfect loyalty
to you. You have been good enough to explain to me, together with the head of government [Laval], the policy you intend to follow towards Germany. I am fully in agreement with you. I give you my word as an officer that I shall do nothing which might
embarrass in any way your relations with the German government or impede the task
with which you have charged Admiral Darlan and Prime Minister Pierre Laval to carry
out under your high authority. My past is the guarantee of my loyalty. I ask you, *Mon-
sieur le Maréchal,* to accept the assurance of my absolute devotion." The broadcast of
this by Vichy following announcement of the Darlan Deal was acutely embarrassing to
Giraud and the Americans. See Brian Crozier, *De Gaulle* (New York, 1973), p. 197.

18. Butcher, *op. cit.,* pp. 106, 108–09. During Murphy's American visit (that is, on September 4, 1942), Roosevelt, with Hopkins at his side, received the diplomat in the library
office at Hyde Park and there gave him a prolonged briefing on North African policy.
(It was a hot afternoon; both the President and Hopkins were in their shirtsleeves, and
soon Murphy was, too.) "During our conversation," writes Murphy, "the President repeated what he had told me . . . two years before. . . . He declared that his wartime
policy vis-à-vis the French was to refrain from the recognition of any one person or
group as the Government of France until a liberated French population could freely
choose their own government. To me, he said, very solemnly and firmly, 'You will
restrict your dealings to French officials at the local level, prefects, and the military. I
will not help anyone impose a Government on the French people.' This . . . governed
my relations with the French before and after the Allied landings [the reader can
judge whether or not it was so]. Of course this was in direct conflict with General de
Gaulle's . . . passionate conviction [was it?]." Murphy, *op. cit.,* pp. 101–02.

19. Murphy, *op. cit.,* p. 115.

20. Eisenhower, *op. cit.,* p. 105.

21. Murphy, *op. cit.,* p. 119; Mark W. Clark, *Calculated Risk* (New York, 1950), pp. 80–81.

22. Murphy, *op. cit.,* p. 120.

23. *Ibid.,* pp. 120–21. Murphy's quotation of Eisenhower's message to Marshall, and of
his own preceding message to the President, testifies to an essential honesty not often
manifest in personal memoirs. The episode could not but have been excruciatingly embarrassing to Murphy, and he might have been far more reticent concerning it.

24. Kimball, ed., *op. cit.,* p. 656.

25. Eisenhower, *op. cit.,* pp. 99–101.

26. Ward, ed., *op. cit.,* p. 184.

27. *Ibid.,* pp. 184–86; Tully, *op. cit.,* pp. 263–64.

28. *PPA 1942,* pp. 451–52.

29. Ward, ed., *op. cit.,* p. 186.

30. *PPA 1942,* p. 457. Laval drafted the message.

31. George F. Howe, *Northwest Africa: Seizing the Initiative in the West,* a volume in the
United States Army in World War II series (Washington, D.C., 1957), has been deemed
authoritative for all details of the Torch operation and has been used extensively; Kenneth S. Davis, *Soldier of Democracy* (Garden City, N.Y., 1945), p. 365.

32. Writes Murphy on p. 141 of his memoirs: "On the long-distance telephone I listened

[at some time unspecified, soon after the initial Torch landings] to Darlan urge Admiral Jean Esteva . . . to resist the imminent invasion of German troops. Darlan asked: 'Esteva, are you willing to become an American?' He was referring to our pre-landing assurances that the American troops would disembark in Tunisia on the first day of the invasion, as had been originally planned."

33. Murphy here seems at some pains to gloss over the fact that Darlan's presence in Algiers on Torch D-day was no surprise either to him or to Franklin Roosevelt, that he knew of it when he came to Juin's residence in the late evening of November 7. He does have Juin say, "As you know, Darlan is in Algiers," but the impression left with the reader (deliberately?) is that he really had not known, else his approach to Juin would have been made in different fashion, using different words. In his following chapter, on p. 142, he writes that he had "informed Leahy by cablegram two days before the landings that Darlan had arrived in Algiers because of his son's [infantile] paralysis," and Leahy "had promptly informed Roosevelt." Leahy himself writes in his *I Was There*, p. 132: "The first thing that impressed Roosevelt was the nature of the boy's illness. Roosevelt remembered his own illness and proposed that we send a letter to Darlan [would he have proposed a letter to de Gaulle if de Gaulle's son had been stricken?]. I replied I thought it would be a nice thing to do." In early December, Roosevelt sent Darlan's son to Warm Springs and kept him there for a considerable time. That this typically Rooseveltian kindness had mixed up in it a typically Rooseveltian ulterior motive is suggested by Leahy's following words: "Darlan was most grateful, and it is my belief that this thoughtfulness on the part of the President helped us in the critical situation that was then developing."

34. Clark, *op. cit.*, p. 106.
35. Murphy, *op. cit.*, p. 129.
36. *Ibid.*, p. 130.
37. Churchill, *Hinge of Fate*, pp. 614–15; Sherwood, *op. cit.*, p. 649.
38. Eisenhower, *op. cit.*, pp. 104–05.
39. Clark, *op. cit.*, pp. 103–05.
40. *Ibid.*, p. 106.
41. *Ibid.*, pp. 108–13.
42. *Ibid.*, pp. 117–18.
43. *Ibid.*
44. Eisenhower, *op. cit.*, p. 107.
45. *Ibid.*, p. 109; Howe, *op. cit.*, pp. 265–66. The latter has photographs of Eisenhower and other principals at Algiers on November 13, 1942.
46. Numerous books print the Darlan proclamation, including Davis, *Soldier of Democracy*, p. 379.
47. *Chicago Daily News*, February 9, 1943; Quoted by Waverly Root, *The Secret History of the War*, vol. 2 (New York, 1945), pp. 464–65.
48. Dallek, *op. cit.*, p. 365.
49. Eisenhower, *op. cit.*, pp. 112–13.
50. "All my life I have thought of France in a certain way," writes de Gaulle in the opening sentence of *The Call to Honour, 1940–1942* (London, 1955), the first volume of his war memoirs. ". . . The emotional side of me tends to imagine France . . . as dedicated to an exalted and exceptional destiny. Instinctively I have the feeling that Providence has created her either for complete successes or exemplary misfortunes. If, in spite of this, mediocrity shows in her acts and deeds, it strikes me as an absurd anomaly, to be

imputed to the faults of Frenchmen, not the genius of the land. . . . In short, to my mind, France cannot be France without greatness." Since nothing approaching greatness could be imputed to Laval and the other men of Vichy, he himself must fill the gap in France's essential history that had been created by their cowardly traitorous conduct. It was the historical duty of the leader of the Free French, "the French who fight," to lift up from the dust of defeat (I employ de Gaulle's natural style of expression) the banner that had been dropped by palsied hands and bear it again, streaming aloft, into righteous battle.

51. Churchill later denied ever having made the "Cross of Lorraine" statement, but his denial is unconvincing. The description of de Gaulle as a combine of Clemenceau and Joan of Arc, though much repeated by Roosevelt, who did not care if de Gaulle learned of it, did not originate with him but was appropriated from a lengthy message from Churchill to him on July 21, 1943. Arguing the necessity of including de Gaulle on a French National Committee to be recognized by the Allies as the legitimate government of France, Churchill wrote: ". . . I have always taken the view that De Gaulle should be made to settle down to honest team work. I am no more enamored of him than you are, but I would rather have him on the Committee than strutting about as a combination of Joan of Arc and Clemenceau." See Warren F. Kimball, ed., vol. II of *Churchill and Roosevelt: The Complete Correspondence,* entitled *Alliance Forged,* p. 335.

52. Refrain used by Thomas Wolfe in his novel *Look Homeward, Angel* (New York, 1930), which was at the high tide of its popularity and reputation in the early 1940s.

53. De Gaulle, *op. cit.,* p. 321.

54. *Ibid.,* pp. 232–33, 330.

55. *Ibid.,* pp. 349–50.

56. *Ibid.,* p. 351.

57. *Ibid.*

58. Kimball, ed., *op. cit.,* vol. 1, pp. 667, 669.

59. De Gaulle, *Complete War Memoirs,* p. 360.

60. *Ibid.,* p. 314.

61. The Eisenhower message is published in full, though paraphrased to protect codes, in Eisenhower, *op. cit.,* pp. 109–10; and in full, save for the first sentence, in Sherwood, *op. cit.,* p. 652. That any Free French representative would have approved the Darlan arrangement once he "understood" the "situation" was, of course, a wholly mistaken assumption on Eisenhower's part; the Free Frenchmen, operating under precise and firm instructions from Charles de Gaulle, would have arrived in Algiers possessed of a far better understanding of North African political realities than Eisenhower would ever have.

62. Kimball, ed., *op. cit.,* vol. 2, p. 4.

63. *New York Times,* November 14, 1942.

64. De Gaulle, *Complete War Memoirs,* p. 357.

65. Kimball, ed., *op. cit.,* vol. 2, p. 5; Sherwood, *op. cit.,* pp. 654–55.

66. De Gaulle, *Complete War Memoirs,* p. 361.

67. Kimball, ed., *op. cit.,* vol. 2, p. 7; Stimson and Bundy, *op. cit.,* p. 543; Barnes, *op. cit.,* pp. 311–12.

68. Kimball, ed., *op. cit.,* vol. 2, p. 8.

69. *Ibid.,* p. 8; Sherwood, *op. cit.,* p. 653.

70. Kimball, ed., *op. cit.,* vol. 2, pp. 8–9.

71. Murphy, *op. cit.,* p. 150.
72. Eisenhower, *op. cit.,* p. 131. What Eisenhower claims was the policy aim of his advisers was certainly that of one of them, Henry Mack of the British Foreign Office. Mack was more astute than Murphy but also less influential of the general. On December 7, 1942, he minuted the British cabinet: "Darlan is Vichy, and Vichy is representative of those selfish interests which led to the downfall of France. There may be civil war if Darlan remains." See Robin Edmonds, *The Big Three: Churchill, Roosevelt, and Stalin in Peace and War* (New York, 1991), p. 312. Mack's assessment of the North African situation prompted a Churchill message to Roosevelt on December 9, 1942, saying: "I am disturbed by reports received during the last few days . . . about conditions in French Morocco and Algeria. These reports . . . all paint the same picture of the results that follow from our inability in existing circumstances to exercise a proper control over local French authorities in internal administrative matters. . . . These reports show that [Fascist organizations] . . . continue their activities and victimize our former French sympathizers. . . . Well-known German sympathizers who had been ousted have been reinstated. Not only have our enemies been thus encouraged but our friends have been correspondingly confused and cast down. There have been cases of French soldiers being punished for desertion because they tried to support the Allied forces during the landing. There is an almost complete lack of control on the Franco-Spanish frontier. The result of this is that undesirables of all sorts, including Axis agents, cross the frontier in both directions carrying information to the enemy and preparing trouble for us throughout North Africa. . . . Veiled and positive enemy propaganda increases daily. . . . All this reinforces the need for immediate political and administrative support for Eisenhower." Roosevelt sent the substance of the reports that Churchill summarized to Eisenhower, without saying they came to him through the Prime Minister, and communicated to Churchill on December 16 a paraphrase of Eisenhower's reply, which was also dated December 16. The general said that he, too, had had many reports of the kind Roosevelt had received and was dealing with them as they arose. He claimed that all those imprisoned for aiding the Allies had been released [this was not true], that the Allies were in control of postal and telegraphic communications "to the outside world," and that the reports of "hidden Axis propaganda" in North African press and radio were false. In his cover letter to Churchill, Roosevelt said that there "can be no doubt" that Eisenhower's "handling of political and civic affairs in North Africa has been a tremendous aid to his military operations" and that therefore he "should be allowed to continue to handle such matters" until "the military situation has been stabilized." See Kimball, ed., *op. cit.,* vol. 2, pp. 68–70, 75–77.
73. Murphy, *op. cit.,* p. 155.
74. *Ibid.,* p. 146.
75. Ronald Steel, *Walter Lippmann and the American Century* (Boston, 1980), pp. 400–02.
76. Eisenhower, *op. cit.,* p. 130.
77. Butcher, *op. cit.,* pp. 206–07, prints the Darlan letter in full.
78. Milton Viorst, *Hostile Allies: FDR and Charles de Gaulle* (New York, 1965), pp. 130–31.
79. Mark Clark, *op. cit.,* p. 130.
80. De Gaulle, *Complete War Memoirs,* p. 379.

13. The End of 1942: Brightening Horizons, East and West

1. Mark Clark, *op. cit.,* p. 131.
2. Frank Freidel, *Franklin D. Roosevelt: A Rendezvous with Destiny* (Boston, 1990), p. 457, quoting Ickes diary, November 22, 1942 (the Ickes diaries are in the Library of Congress).
3. Peter Tompkins, *The Murder of Admiral Darlan* (New York, 1965), p. 187. (Incidentally, Marshall's Christmas gift to Roosevelt in 1942 was a huge global map [the globe's diameter was approximately four feet], which the President placed in the Executive Office, where he consulted it almost every day. A photograph of Roosevelt contemplating it on one of 1942's last days is on p. 308 of Thomas Parrish, *Roosevelt and Marshall* [New York, 1989].)
4. *PPA 1942,* pp. 483, 485, 532–33.
5. *New York Times,* December 13, 22, 1942.
6. I. F. Stone, *The War Years, 1939–1945* (Boston, 1988), pp. 134–36.
7. *Ibid.,* p. 136.
8. Brown would resign this post in October 1943 and be succeeded by Chester Bowles, a Connecticut citizen who had made a fortune during the depressed 1930s as a partner of the New York City advertising firm of Benton and Bowles but was, as was his partner, William Benton, a fighting liberal. Benton, as U.S. senator from Connecticut in the early 1950s, would be instrumental in the downfall of Senator Joseph McCarthy of Wisconsin, the lying demagogue whom the Republican Party found useful to its twin purposes of a) portraying the Democrats as a party of treason; and b) distracting popular attention from real issues that, if fairly presented to the electorate, would greatly disadvantage Republican candidates for office.
9. *New York Times,* December 17, 1942.
10. John Morton Blum, *The Price of Vision: The Diary of Henry A. Wallace, 1942–1946* (Boston, 1973), pp. 65–66.
11. *PPA 1942,* pp. 243–44.
12. Jordan Schwartz, *Liberal: Adolf A. Berle and the Vision of an American Era* (New York, 1987), pp. 202, 209–10; Stone, *op. cit.,* pp. 140–41.
13. *New York Times,* December 17, 1942.
14. Blum, ed., *op. cit.,* p. 66 footnote.
15. Stone, *op. cit.,* p. 138; *New York Times,* December 16, 1942.
16. Shirer, *Rise and Fall,* p. 964.
17. *Ibid.,* quoting vol. III, pp. 525–26, of *Nazi Conspiracy and Aggression,* which is one of the Nuremberg documents.
18. *Ibid.,* pp. 965–66.
19. *Ibid.*
20. Arthur D. Morse, *While Six Million Died* (New York, 1968) p. 5; Walter Laqueur, *The Terrible Secret* (Boston, 1980), pp. 127–28; David S. Wyman, *The Abandonment of the Jews* (New York, 1984), p. 40.
21. Shirer, *Rise and Fall,* pp. 967–68, quoting Nuremberg Trial documents; Henry F. Feingold, *The Politics of Rescue* (New Brunswick, N.J., 1970), p. 255.
22. Feingold, *op. cit.,* p. 169; Laqueur, *op. cit.,* p. 94.
23. Feingold. *op. cit.,* p. 170. In the Max Freedman–edited Roosevelt-Frankfurter correspondence, *op. cit.,* there is no mention whatever of the massacre of Jews or of war refugee rescue. Indeed, the words "Jew" and "Jewish" do not occur in the index of this massive tome. Nor do they occur in the index of Sherwood, *op. cit.* Not until the pub-

lication of Morse's book in 1968 did references to the Jewish tragedy begin to creep into Roosevelt administration histories and Roosevelt biographies—an indication of how very little attention was paid to the tragedy by the administration while the tragedy was in process and how low a priority was given to rescue attempts.

24. *PPA 1942*, pp. 329–30.
25. Morse, *op. cit.,* p. 4; Laqueur, *op. cit.,* p. 100.
26. Morse, *op. cit.,* p. 9.
27. Morse, *op. cit.,* pp. 10–11; Laqueur, *op. cit.,* p. 81; Feingold, *op. cit.,* p. 171.
28. Wyman, *op. cit.,* pp. 45–46.
29. Morse, *op. cit.,* pp. 35–36.
30. Wyman, *op. cit.,* p. 51; Morse, *op. cit.,* p. 24; Feingold, *op. cit.,* pp. 170–71.
31. Wyman, *op. cit.,* pp. 61 (footnotes), 70.
32. *Ibid.,* pp. 72–73. (All other above sourcebooks tell of this.)
33. *Ibid.,* pp. 72–73.
34. *Ibid.,* p. 73.
35. Nina Davis Howland, *Ambassador John Gilbert Winant* (doctoral diss. earlier cited), pp. 229–30.
36. *Ibid.,* pp. 230–32; Feingold, *op. cit.,* pp. 172–73; Morse, *op. cit.,* pp. 25–27.
37. Howland, *op. cit.,* pp. 232–33; Feingold, *op. cit.,* p. 173.
38. Wyman, *op. cit.,* pp. 74–75; Howland, *op. cit.,* p. 235.
39. Wyman, *op. cit.,* pp. 73–74.
40. *Ibid.,* p. 74.
41. *Ibid.,* pp. 74–75.
42. Laqueur, *op. cit.,* pp. 223–28.
43. Louis P. Lochner. ed. and trans., *The Goebbels Diaries* (Westport, Conn., 1970), p. 241. Entry for December 13, 1942.
44. *Newsweek,* November 30, 1942; quoted by Wyman, *op. cit.,* p. 57, and by Goodwin, *op. cit.,* p. 397.
45. Feingold, *op. cit.,* p. 172. Note: The book-length assertion of the impossibility of Jewish rescue, referred to on p. 742 is *The Myth of Rescue,* by William D. Rubenstein (London and New York, 1997).
46. Compton, *op. cit.,* pp. 137–38.
47. Rhodes, *op. cit.,* p. 439.
48. Compton, *op. cit.,* p. 143.
49. *Ibid.,* pp. 143–44.
50. Weart and Szilard, eds., *op. cit.,* p. 146.
51. Compton, *op. cit.,* p. 144.
52. Louis L. Snyder, *The War: A Concise History, 1939–1945* (New York, 1960), p. 307.
53. Sherwood, *op. cit.,* pp. 658, 659; Kimball, ed., vol. 2 of *Churchill and Roosevelt,* pp. 41–42.
54. Kimball, ed., *op. cit.,* pp. 42–43.
55. *Ibid.,* pp. 54–55.
56. *Ibid.,* pp. 63, 80–81. The courier who delivered this December 14 missive was unconscionably slow in doing so, evidently delayed by transportation difficulties over which he had no control, with the result that delivery was not made until December 23. Churchill felt helpless to make plans for the immediate future until he knew what this delayed letter said, so Roosevelt cabled him the concise substance of it on December 21. It was in reply to this last that Churchill cabled the here quoted words to Roosevelt.
57. *Ibid.,* pp. 73–74, 86.

58. Sherwood, *op. cit.*, p. 667.
59. *Ibid.*, p. 664.
60. Very different from the festive mood in the White House on that New Year's Eve was the one in the house in Somerville, Massachusetts, where stroke-crippled Missy LeHand lived with her sister, Ann Rochon. Ann Rochon wrote the President on New Year's Day: "She [Missy] started crying New Year's Eve about 11:30 and we couldn't stop her. And then she had a heart spell and kept calling 'F.D., come, Please come. Oh F.D.' It really was the saddest thing I ever hope to see, we were all crying, she was very depressed all through the Holidays and that was the climax. She was expecting you to call Christmas Day and when we sat down to dinner her eyes filled with tears and she said 'A toast to the President's health' and there again in the middle of dinner—another toast to you. She loves your gift and kept saying sweet, lovely, beautiful, I love it. She watches for the postman every trip. . . . She worries about you all the time." (Quoted by Goodwin, *op. cit.*, p. 400.)

ABOUT THE TYPE

This book was set in Times Roman, designed by Stanley Morison specifically for *The Times* of London. The typeface was introduced in the newspaper in 1932. Times Roman has had its greatest success in the United States as a book and commercial typeface, rather than one used in newspapers.

ABOUT THE AUTHOR

A biographer of Eisenhower, Lindbergh, and Adlai Stevenson as well as a novelist, KENNETH S. DAVIS was awarded the prestigious Francis Parkman Prize for *FDR: The Beckoning of Destiny,* which was also a nominee for the National Book Award. In addition, his next two volumes on FDR were both chosen as among the ten best books of the year by *The New York Times.*

A graduate of Kansas State University, with a master of science degree from the University of Wisconsin and an honorary doctorate of letters from Assumption College, Davis was a journalism instructor at New York University, a war correspondent attached to General Eisenhower's headquarters, special assistant to Milton Eisenhower, the president of Kansas State University, a member of the State Department's UNESCO relations staff, editor of *The Newberry Library Bulletin* in Chicago, adjunct professor of English at Clark University, and an adjunct professor of history at both Kansas University and Kansas State University. Kenneth S. Davis died in June 1999.